PROFESSIONAL C# 6 AND .NET CORE 1.0

P9-DGF-780

Continues

PROFESSIONAL

C# 6 and .NET Core 1.0

PROFESSIONAL

C# 6 and .NET Core 1.0

Christian Nagel

wrox

A Wiley Brand

Professional C# 6 and .NET Core 1.0

Published by
John Wiley & Sons, Inc.
10475 Crosspoint Boulevard
Indianapolis, IN 46256
www.wiley.com

Copyright © 2016 by John Wiley & Sons, Inc., Indianapolis, Indiana

Published simultaneously in Canada

ISBN: 978-1-119-09660-3

ISBN: 978-1-119-09671-9 (ebk)

ISBN: 978-1-119-09663-4 (ebk)

Manufactured in the United States of America

10 9 8 7 6 5 4 3 2 1

For general information on our other products and services please contact our Customer Care Department within the United States at (877) 762-2974, outside the United States at (317) 572-3993 or fax (317) 572-4002.

Wiley publishes in a variety of print and electronic formats and by print-on-demand. Some material included with standard print versions of this book may not be included in e-books or in print-on-demand. If this book refers to media such as a CD or DVD that is not included in the version you purchased, you may download this material at http://booksupport.wiley.com. For more information about Wiley products, visit www.wiley.com.

Library of Congress Control Number: 2016932153

This book is dedicated to my family—Angela, Stephanie, and Matthias—I love you all!

ABOUT THE AUTHOR

 **CHRISTIAN NAGEL** is Microsoft MVP for Visual Studio and Development Technologies, and has been Microsoft Regional Director for more than 15 years. Christian is an associate of thinktecture and founder of CN innovation, where he offers training and consulting on how to develop solutions using the Microsoft platform. He draws on more than 25 years of software development experience.

Christian started his computing career with PDP 11 and VAX/VMS systems at Digital Equipment Corporation, covering a variety of languages and platforms. Since 2000, when .NET was just a technology preview, he has been working with various technologies to build .NET solutions. Currently, he mainly coaches people on development of Universal Windows Platform apps and ASP.NET MVC, using several Microsoft Azure service offerings.

Even after many years in software development, Christian still loves learning and using new technologies and teaching others how to use the new technologies in various forms. Using his profound knowledge of Microsoft technologies, he has written numerous books, and is certified as Microsoft Certified Trainer and Certified Solution Developer. Christian speaks at international conferences such as TechEd, BASTA!, and TechDays. He founded INETA Europe to support .NET user groups. You can contact Christian via his website www.cninnovation.com and follow his tweets at @christiannagel.

ABOUT THE TECHNICAL EDITOR

 **ISTVÁN NOVÁK** is an associate and the chief technology consultant with SoftwArt, a small Hungarian IT consulting company. He works as a software architect and community evangelist. In the last 25 years, he has participated in more than 50 enterprise software development projects. In 2002, he coauthored the first Hungarian book about .NET development. In 2007, he was awarded the Microsoft Most Valuable Professional (MVP) title, and in 2011 he became a Microsoft Regional Director. István coauthored *Visual Studio 2010 and .NET 4 Six-in-One* (Wiley, 2010) and *Beginning Windows 8 Application Development* (Wiley, 2012), and he authored *Beginning Visual Studio LightSwitch Development* (Wiley, 2011). István holds master's degree from the Technical University of Budapest, Hungary and also has a doctoral degree in software technology. He lives in Dunakeszi, Hungary, with his wife and two daughters. He is a passionate scuba diver. You may have a good chance of meeting him underwater in the Red Sea, any season of the year.

CREDITS

SENIOR ACQUISITIONS EDITOR
Ken Brown

PROJECT EDITOR
Charlotte Kughen

TECHNICAL EDITOR
István Novák

PRODUCTION EDITOR
Dassi Zeidel

MANAGER OF CONTENT DEVELOPMENT & ASSEMBLY
Mary Beth Wakefield

PRODUCTION MANAGER
Kathleen Wisor

MARKETING DIRECTOR
David Mayhew

MARKETING MANAGER
Carrie Sherrill

PROFESSIONAL TECHNOLOGY & STRATEGY DIRECTOR
Barry Pruett

BUSINESS MANAGER
Amy Knies

ASSOCIATE PUBLISHER
Jim Minatel

PROJECT COORDINATOR, COVER
Patrick Redmond

PROOFREADER
Amy J. Schneider

INDEXER
John Sleeva

COVER DESIGNER
Wiley

COVER IMAGE
© Digital Storn/Shutterstock

ACKNOWLEDGMENTS

I WANT TO THANK Charlotte Kughen, who made my text so much more readable. Often I was working late at night writing while .NET Core was continuously evolving. Charlotte was of enormous help to change my ideas into great readable text. I'm almost sure that Charlotte now knows a lot more about programming than she would like to. Special thanks also goes to István Novák, who has authored several great books. Despite all the issues we had with the fast-evolving .NET Core and the interim builds I was using while working on the book, István challenged me to enhance the code samples that allow you—the reader—to better follow the flow. Thank you, Charlotte and István—you've been of great help for the quality of this book.

I also would like to thank Kenyon Brown and Jim Minatel and everyone else at Wiley who helped to get edition 10 of this great book to be published. I also want to thank my wife and children for supporting my writing. You understood and helped with the time I was working on the book, including evenings, nights, and weekends. Angela, Stephanie, and Matthias—you are my loved ones. This would not have been possible without you.

CONTENTS

PART II: .NET CORE AND WINDOWS RUNTIME

CHAPTER 17: VISUAL STUDIO 2015   455

INTRODUCTION

IF YOU WERE TO DESCRIBE THE C# LANGUAGE and .NET as the most significant technology for developers available, you would not be exaggerating. .NET is designed to provide an environment within which you can develop almost any application to run on Windows. Runs on *Windows*—wait, I would have said that with previous versions of the .NET Framework. The new version, .NET Core 1.0 not only runs on Windows, but it also runs on Linux and Mac systems. The C# programming language is designed specifically to work with .NET. By using C#, you can, for example, write a web page, a Windows Presentation Foundation (WPF) application, a REST web service, a component of a distributed application, a database access component, a classic Windows desktop application, or even a Universal Windows Platform (UWP) app that enables online and offline capabilities. This book covers .NET Core 1.0 and also the full .NET Framework stack, .NET Framework 4.6. If you code using any of the prior versions, there may be sections of the book that will not work for you.

Where possible, samples of this book make use of .NET Core 1.0. The book code is built on a Windows system, but you can run the samples on other platforms as well; small changes might be needed to run them on Linux. Read Chapter 1, ".NET Application Architectures," to see how to build the applications for the Linux platform. What's not possible to run on Linux? WPF applications still need the full .NET Framework and run only on Windows. UWP apps are using .NET Core, but also require the Windows Runtime. These apps require Windows as well. These UI technologies are covered in Part III of the book, "Core Apps."

So what's the big deal about .NET and C#?

THE SIGNIFICANCE OF .NET CORE

To understand the significance of .NET Core, you must consider the long-lived .NET Framework. The .NET Framework 1.0 was released in the year 2002. Since then about every two years a new major release has been made available. With Visual Studio 2013 we had C# 5 and .NET 4.5. The .NET Framework 4.5 is huge, with more than 20,000 classes.

> **NOTE** *Get into more details of the releases of the .NET Framework and C# in Chapter 1.*

What are the problems with this huge framework? How is this solved with .NET Core?

For new developers, getting into this huge framework is not easy. Many things exist that are important for legacy applications, but they're not really important for new applications. For experienced developers it's not that easy to *decide between these technologies* to select the best one. You have to decide between ASP.NET Web Forms and ASP.NET MVC for web applications, decide between Windows Forms and WPF or the Universal Windows Platform for client applications, decide between the Entity Framework and LINQ to SQL for data access, decide between `ArrayList` and `List<T>` for storing collections. . . . For some experienced developers the choice is obvious; for most it's not that easy. It's even more difficult for developers just starting with .NET.

.NET Core is based on smaller units, small NuGet packages. The `Console` class is only needed with console applications. With the .NET Framework, the `Console` class is available with `mscorlib`, an assembly that's referenced by every .NET application. Using .NET Core, you have to explicitly decide to use the `System.Console` NuGet package. Otherwise, the `Console` class is not available.

Smaller packages also allow you to get rid of parts of the framework more easily. In case you need older collection classes for legacy applications, they are available with the NuGet package `System.Collections.NonGeneric`. With new applications you can define a list of packages that can be used, and `System.Collections.NonGeneric` can be excluded from this list.

Nowadays, development is going a lot faster. With many products, customers receive ongoing updates of products instead of receiving new versions every 2 years. Even Windows, with Windows 10, is on this fast pace. Customers receive smaller features with each update, but they receive them at a faster pace. Having 2-year release cycles with the .NET Framework nowadays is not fast enough. Some technologies, like the Entity Framework, already circumvented the problem by offering new features via NuGet packages that can be released independently of the .NET Framework.

Updating smaller pieces allows for faster innovation. .NET Core, which is based on many small NuGet packages, can be changed more easily. .NET Core and ASP.NET are now open source. You can find the source code for .NET Core at `http://www.github.com/dotnet` and for ASP.NET at `http://www.github.com/aspnet`.

When .NET was released, Windows had a big market share both on the client and on the server. Now the world is more fragmented. Companies decided against running server-side code with ASP.NET because it didn't run on Linux. ASP.NET Core 1.0 with .NET Core can run on Linux.

.NET Core is platform-independent and supports Windows, Linux, and Mac systems. For client applications, you can use .NET with Xamarin on iPhone and Android.

The .NET Framework required having the same version of the .NET runtime that was used during development to be installed on the target system. Many application developments have been restricted by the version of the .NET Framework to use based on client needs. This is not only an issue for client-based application development but also for the server. I had to switch back to older .NET runtime versions because my provider didn't support the newest one. With .NET Core, the runtime is delivered with the application.

When ASP.NET was built, compatibility with the predecessor technology Active Server Pages (ASP) that was built with JavaScript or VBScript code running on the server was an important aspect. Nowadays this is not needed anymore. ASP.NET Web Forms was built with the idea that the developer doesn't need to know anything about JavaScript and HTML, and everything could be done with server-side code. Now, because of the huge number of JavaScript frameworks and enhancements in HTML, more control on JavaScript and HTML is needed.

With the new version of ASP.NET, performance has a big role in the framework architecture. You only have performance impacts for the things you really need. In case you don't have static files with your web application, you have to explicitly decide on using it, otherwise you don't pay a performance impact for this. With fine-grained control you can decide what features you need.

To get an even bigger performance improvement, .NET Core can be built to native code. This is possible not only on Windows but also on Linux and Mac systems. With this you can get performance improvement especially on program startup, and you use less memory.

Now there's an issue with *legacy applications*. Most applications can't switch that easily to .NET Core. The full .NET Framework—running just on Windows—is evolving as well. It's not evolving in such big steps as .NET Core, but it is a mature framework. At the time of this writing, .NET 4.6.1 is released, with small updates compared to the previous versions. Applications that have been written with Windows Forms or ASP.NET Web Forms still need to use the full framework, but they can take advantage of the enhancements of .NET 4.6.1. Using .NET 4.6.1, you can also use NuGet packages built for .NET Core. Many new NuGet packages are built in a portable manner. With ASP.NET MVC 5 web applications you can also decide to change to ASP.NET

MVC 6 running on ASP.NET Core 1.0. ASP.NET Core 1.0 allows using either .NET Core or .NET 4.6. This can make the switch easier. However, for running ASP.NET MVC on Linux, you need to migrate the ASP.NET MVC application to use .NET Core, but running on Linux wasn't available previously as well.

Here's a summary of some of the features of .NET Core:

➤ .NET Core is open source.

➤ Smaller NuGet packages allow for faster innovation.

➤ .NET Core supports multiple platforms.

➤ .NET Core can compile to native code.

➤ ASP.NET can run on Windows and Linux.

➤ Existing applications still run and can evolve into the future.

As you can see with the features of .NET Core, this technology made the biggest change for .NET in the history since the first version of .NET. This is a new start. From here we can continue our journey on new developments in a fast pace.

THE SIGNIFICANCE OF C#

When C# was released in the year 2002, it was a language developed for the .NET Framework. C# was designed with ideas from C++, Java, and Pascal. Anders Hejlsberg had come to Microsoft from Borland and brought experience with language development of Delphi. At Microsoft, Hejlsberg worked on Microsoft's version of Java, named J++, before creating C#.

C# started not only as an object-oriented general purpose programming language but was a component-based programming language that supported properties, events, attributes (annotations), and building assemblies (binaries including metadata).

Over time, C# was enhanced with generics, Language Integrated Query (LINQ), lambda expressions, dynamic features, and easier asynchronous programming. C# is not an easy programming language because of the many features it offers, but it's continuously evolving with features that are practical to use. With this, C# is more than an object-oriented or component-based language; it also includes ideas of functional programming—things that are of practical use for a general-purpose language developing all kind of applications.

WHAT'S NEW IN C# 6

With C# 6 a new C# compiler is available. It's not only that a source code cleanup was done; the features of the compiler pipeline can now be used from custom programs, and are used by many features of Visual Studio.

This new compiler platform made it possible to enhance C# with many new features. Although there's not a feature with such an impact as LINQ or the `async` keyword, the many enhancements increase developer productivity. What are the changes of C# 6?

static using

The static `using` declaration allows invoking static methods without the class name:

In C# 5

```
using System;
// etc.
Console.WriteLine("Hello, World!");
```

In C# 6

```
using static System.Console;
// etc.
WriteLine("Hello, World");
```

The `using static` keyword is covered in Chapter 2, "Core C#."

Expression-Bodied Methods

With expression-bodied methods, a method that includes just one statement can be written with the lambda syntax:

In C# 5

```
public bool IsSquare(Rectangle rect)
{
  return rect.Height == rect.Width;
}
```

In C# 6

```
public bool IsSquare(Rectangle rect) => rect.Height == rect.Width;
```

Expression-bodied methods are covered in Chapter 3, "Objects and Types."

Expression-Bodied Properties

Similar to expression-bodied methods, one-line properties with only a `get` accessor can be written with the lambda syntax:

In C# 5

```
public string FullName
{
  get
  {
    return FirstName + " " + LastName;
  }
}
```

In C# 6

```
public string FullName => FirstName + " " + LastName;
```

Expression-bodied properties are covered in Chapter 3.

Auto-Implemented Property Intializers

Auto-implemented properties can be initialized with a property initializer:

In C# 5

```
public class Person
{
  public Person()
  {
    Age = 24;
  }
  public int Age {get; set;}
}
```

In C# 6

```
public class Person
{
    public int Age {get; set;} = 42;
}
```

Auto-implemented property initializers are covered in Chapter 3.

Read-Only Auto Properties

To implement read-only properties, C# 5 requires the full property syntax. With C# 6, you can do this using auto-implemented properties:

In C# 5

```
private readonly int _bookId;

public BookId
{
    get
    {
        return _bookId;
    }
}
```

In C# 6

```
public BookId {get;}
```

Read-only auto properties are covered in Chapter 3.

nameof Operator

With the new `nameof` operator, names of fields, properties, methods, or types can be accessed. With this, name changes are not missed with refactoring:

In C# 5

```
public void Method(object o)
{
    if (o == null) throw new ArgumentNullException("o");
```

In C# 6

```
public void Method(object o)
{
    if (o == null) throw new ArgumentNullException(nameof(o));
```

The `nameof` operator is covered in Chapter 8, "Operators and Casts."

Null Propagation Operator

The null propagation operator simplifies null checks:

In C# 5

```
int? age = p == null ? null : p.Age;
```

In C# 6

```
int? age = p?.Age;
```

The new syntax also has an advantage for firing events:

In C# 5

```
var handler = Event;
if (handler != null)
{
   handler(source, e);
}
```

In C# 6

```
handler?.Invoke(source, e);
```

The null propagation operator is covered in Chapter 8.

String Interpolation

The string interpolation removes calls to string.Format. Instead of using numbered format placeholders in the string, the placeholders can include expressions:

In C# 5

```
public override ToString()
{
   return string.Format("{0}, {1}", Title, Publisher);
}
```

In C# 6

```
public override ToString() => $"{Title} {Publisher}";
```

The C# 6 sample is reduced that much compared to the C# 5 syntax because it uses not only string interpolation but also an expression-bodied method.

String interpolation can also use string formats and get special features on assigning it to a FormattableString. String interpolation is covered in Chapter 10, "Strings and Regular Expressions."

Dictionary Initializers

Dictionaries can now be initialized with a dictionary initializer—similar to the collection initializer.

In C# 5

```
var dict = new Dictionary<int, string>();
dict.Add(3, "three");
dict.Add(7, "seven");
```

In C# 6

```
var dict = new Dictionary<int, string>()
{
   [3] = "three",
   [7] = "seven"
};
```

Dictionary initializers are covered in Chapter 11, "Collections."

Exception Filters

Exception filters allow you to filter exceptions before catching them.

In C# 5

```
try
{
  //etc.
}
catch (MyException ex)
{
  if (ex.ErrorCode != 405) throw;
  // etc.
}
```

In C# 6

```
try
{
  //etc.
}
catch (MyException ex) when (ex.ErrorCode == 405)
{
  // etc.
}
```

A big advantage of the new syntax is not only that it reduces the code length but also that the stack trace is not changed—which happens with the C# 5 variant. Exception filters are covered in Chapter 14, "Errors and Exceptions."

Await in Catch

`await` can now be used in the `catch` clause. C# 5 required a workaround.

In C# 5

```
bool hasError = false;
string errorMessage = null;
try
{
  //etc.
}
catch (MyException ex)
{
  hasError = true;
  errorMessage = ex.Message;
}
if (hasError)
{
  await new MessageDialog().ShowAsync(errorMessage);
}
```

In C# 6

```
try
{
  //etc.
}
catch (MyException ex)
{
  await new MessageDialog().ShowAsync(ex.Message);
}
```

This feature doesn't need an enhancement of the C# syntax; it's functionality that's working now. This enhancement required a lot of investment from Microsoft to make it work, but that really doesn't matter to you using this platform. For you, it means less code is needed—just compare the two versions.

> **NOTE** *The new C# 6 language features are covered in the mentioned chapters, and in all chapters of this book the new C# syntax is used.*

WHAT'S NEW WITH THE UNIVERSAL WINDOWS PLATFORM

Windows 8 introduced a new programming API, the Windows Runtime. Applications using the Windows Runtime could be made available via the Microsoft Store and were known with many different names. It started with Metro apps or Metro style apps, and they are also known as Modern apps, Windows Store apps (although they can also be installed with PowerShell scripts without using the store), and Universal apps. Probably there are some names I missed. Nowadays, these are just Windows apps, running on the Universal Windows Platform (UWP).

The idea of these apps was to allow end users to find them easily via the Microsoft store and to offer a touch-friendly environment, a modern user interface that looks nice and smooth and allows fluid interactions, and apps that can be trusted. More than that, the users who already know the Windows user interfaces should be attracted to using the new environment.

The first version of the design guidelines was very restrictive and had some flaws. How can I search for stuff in the app? Many users didn't find the charms bar on the right side, and found out it allowed searching in many apps. Windows 8.1 moved the search to a search box directly on the desktop. Also, users often didn't find the app bar located at the top or bottom if they didn't perform a touch gesture from top to bottom or bottom to top.

Windows 10 made the design much more open. You can use the things that are useful for your apps and can decide on the user interface as it best matches your users and apps. Of course, it's still best to create a nice looking, smooth, and fluid design. It's better for having users happily interacting with the app, and they should not have a hard time finding out how things can be done.

The new Windows Runtime, Windows Runtime 3.0, steps on the predecessor versions to define an XAML user interface, implements an application lifecycle, and allows background functionality, sharing of data between applications, and more. Indeed, the new version of the runtime offers more features in all the areas.

Windows apps now make use of .NET Core. You can use the same .NET libraries available via NuGet packages with Windows apps. Finally, native code gets compiled for a faster app startup and less memory consumption.

What might be even more important than the additional features offered is the universality that's now available. The first update of Visual Studio 2013 included a new project type for Windows 8 apps: Universal apps. Here, Universal apps have been done with three projects: one project for the Windows app, one project for the Windows phone app, and a shared code project. It was possible to even share XAML code between these platforms. The new Universal project template consists of one project. You can use the same binary not only for Windows and Windows Phone, but also for the Xbox, Internet of Things (IoT) devices, the HoloLens, and more. Of course, these different platforms offer features that are not available everywhere, but using this differing feature you can still create one binary image that runs on every Windows 10 device.

WHAT YOU NEED TO WRITE AND RUN C# CODE

.NET Core runs on Windows, Linux, and Mac operating systems. You can create and build your programs on any of these operating systems using Visual Studio Code (https://code.visualstudio.com). The best developer tool to use, and the tool used with this book, is Visual Studio 2015. You can use Visual Studio Community 2015 edition (https://www.visualstudio.com), but some features shown are available only with the Enterprise edition of Visual Studio. It will be mentioned where the Enterprise edition is needed. Visual Studio 2015 requires the Windows operating system. Windows 8.1 or later is required.

To build and run WPF applications shown in this book, you need a Windows platform. Running WPF applications is still supported on Windows 7.

For building Universal Windows apps, you can use Windows 8.1 with Visual Studio, but for testing and running these apps, you need a Windows 10 device.

WHAT THIS BOOK COVERS

This book starts by reviewing the overall architecture of .NET in Chapter 1 to give you the background you need to write managed code. You'll get an overview about the different application types and learn how to compile with the new development environment CLI. After that, the book is divided into a number of sections that cover both the C# language and its application in a variety of areas.

Part I: The C# Language

This section gives a good grounding in the C# language. This section doesn't presume knowledge of any particular language, although it does assume you are an experienced programmer. You start by looking at C#'s basic syntax and data types and then explore the object-oriented features of C# before looking at more advanced C# programming topics like delegates, lambda expressions, Language Integrated Query (LINQ), reflection, and asynchronous programming.

Part II: .NET Core and Windows Runtime

This section starts with tools, and it looks at the main integrated development environment (IDE) utilized by C# developers worldwide: Visual Studio 2015. You'll learn about the tools available with the Enterprise edition of Visual Studio in Chapter 17, "Visual Studio 2015."

You also learn what's behind the C# compiler and how you can use the .NET Compiler Platform to change your code programmatically in Chapter 18, ".NET Compiler Platform."

When you're creating functionality with C# code, don't skip the step of creating unit tests. It takes more time in the beginning, but over time you'll see advantages when you add functionality and maintain code. Chapter 19, "Testing," covers creating unit tests, web tests, and coded UI tests.

Chapters 20 to 28 cover topics from .NET Core and the Windows Runtime that are independent of application types. In Chapter 20, "Diagnostics and Application Insights," you'll learn writing diagnostic information from the application that can also be used in the production environment. Chapters 21, "Tasks and Parallel Programming," and 22, "Task Synchronization," cover parallel programming using the Task Parallel Library (TPL) as well as various objects for synchronization. In Chapter 23, "Files and Streams," you'll read about accessing the file system and reading files and directories. Using streams, you'll learn using both streams from the System.IO namespace and streams from the Windows Runtime for programming Windows apps. Chapter 24, "Security," makes use of streams when you learn about security and how to encrypt data and allow for secure conversion. You'll also learn the core foundation of networking using sockets, as well as using higher-level abstractions like the `HttpClient` (Chapter 25, "Networking"). Chapter 26, "Composition," covers Microsoft Composition that allows creating independence between containers and parts. In Chapter 27, "XML and JSON," you learn about serializing objects into XML and JSON, as well as different techniques for reading and writing XML. Finally, in Chapter 28, "Localization," you learn to localize applications using techniques for localizations that are important both for Windows and web applications.

Part III: Windows Apps

This section is about building applications with XAML—both Universal Windows apps and WPF. You'll learn about the foundation of XAML in Chapter 29, "Core XAML," with the XAML syntax, dependency properties, and also markup extensions where you can create your own XAML syntax. In Chapter 30, "XAML Styles and Resources," you learn about styling your XAML-based apps. A big focus on the MVVM (model-view-view model) pattern is in Chapter 31, "Patterns with XAML Apps." Here you learn to take advantage of the data-binding features of XAML-based applications, which allow sharing a lot of code between UWP apps and WPF applications. You can also share a lot of code for developing for the iPhone and Android platforms using Xamarin. However, developing with Xamarin is not covered in this book. After the introductory chapters covering both UWP apps and WPF applications, two chapters cover the specific features of UWP apps, and two chapters cover WPF applications. In Chapters 32, "Windows Apps: User Interfaces," and 33, "Advanced Windows Apps," you learn about specific XAML controls with UWP apps such as the `RelativePanel` and `AdaptiveTrigger`, the new compiled binding, and the application life cycle, sharing data, and creating background tasks. Chapters 34, "Windows Desktop Applications with WPF," and 35, "Creating Documents with WPF," go into WPF-specific features such as the Ribbon control, `TreeView` to show hierarchical data, WPF-specific data binding features, creating flow and fixed documents, and creating XML Paper Specification (XPS) files.

This section is concluded with deployment in Chapter 36 to deploy WPF applications using ClickOnce, and information to get UWP apps in the store.

Part IV: Web Applications and Services

In this section you look at web applications and services. You'll find two chapters about ADO.NET in this section as well. Although you can use ADO.NET (Chapter 37, "ADO.NET") and the Entity Framework (Chapter 38, "Entity Framework Core") from client applications as well, typically these technologies are used on the server, and you invoke services from the client.

In Chapter 39, "Windows Services," you can read how to create your own Windows services that run when the operating system is started.

The new version of ASP.NET, ASP.NET Core 1.0, is covered in Chapter 40. Here you can read the foundation of ASP.NET and get ideas on how ASP.NET MVC 6 is built using these foundations. The features of ASP.NET MVC 6 are covered in Chapter 41.

> **NOTE** *ASP.NET Web Forms are not covered in this book, although ASP.NET 4.6 offers new features for ASP.NET Web Forms. This book fully concentrates on the new version of ASP.NET technologies using ASP.NET Core 1.0. For information about ASP.NET Web Forms and ASP.NET MVC 5 you should read* Professional C# 5 and .NET 4.5.1.

Chapter 42 covers the REST service features of ASP.NET MVC 6: ASP.NET Web API. Publish and subscribe technologies for web applications, in the form of using the ASP.NET technologies WebHooks and

SignalR, are covered in Chapter 43. Chapter 44 discusses an older technology for communication with services using SOAP and WCF.

Again, like the previous section, this section concludes with deployment—deployment of websites running on Internet Information Server (IIS) or using Microsoft Azure to host websites.

CONVENTIONS

To help you get the most from the text and keep track of what's happening, a number of conventions are used throughout the book.

> **WARNINGS** *Warnings hold important, not-to-be-forgotten information that is directly relevant to the surrounding text.*

> **NOTE** *Notes indicate notes, tips, hints, tricks, and/or asides to the current discussion.*

As for styles in the text:

➤ We *highlight* new terms and important words when we introduce them.

➤ We show keyboard strokes like this: Ctrl+A.

➤ We show filenames, URLs, and code within the text like so: `persistence.properties`.

We present code in two different ways:

```
We use a monofont type with no highlighting for most code examples.
We use bold to emphasize code that's particularly important in the present context or to show
changes from a previous code snippet.
```

SOURCE CODE

As you work through the examples in this book, you may choose either to type in all the code manually or to use the source code files that accompany the book. All the source code used in this book is available for download at `www.wrox.com/go/professionalcsharp6`. When at the site, simply locate the book's title (either by using the Search box or by using one of the title lists) and click the Download Code link on the book's detail page to obtain all the source code for the book.

> **NOTE** *Because many books have similar titles, you may find it easiest to search by ISBN; this book's ISBN is 978-1-119-09660-3.*

After you download the code, just decompress it with your favorite compression tool. Alternatively, you can go to the main Wrox code download page at `http://www.wrox.com/dynamic/books/download.aspx` to see the code available for this book and all other Wrox books.

With the fast pace of updates with .NET Core, the source code of the book is also available at `http://www.github.com/ProfessionalCSharp`. Be aware that the source code on GitHub offers living source files that will be updated with minor update versions of Visual Studio, as well as new experimental C# features. For updates to the source code and additional samples done after the release of the book, check the GitHub site. The stable version of the source code that corresponds to the content of the printed book is available from the Wrox site.

ERRATA

We make every effort to ensure that there are no errors in the text or in the code. However, no one is perfect, and mistakes do occur. If you find an error in one of our books, like a spelling mistake or faulty piece of code, we would be grateful for your feedback. By sending in errata you may save another reader hours of frustration, and at the same time you can help provide even higher-quality information.

To find the errata page for this book, go to http://www.wrox.com and locate the title using the Search box or one of the title lists. Then, on the book details page, click the Book Errata link. On this page you can view all errata that have been submitted for this book and posted by Wrox editors. A complete book list including links to each book's errata is also available at www.wrox.com/misc-pages/booklist.shtml.

If you don't spot "your" error on the Book Errata page, go to www.wrox.com/contact/techsupport.shtml and complete the form there to send us the error you have found. We'll check the information and, if appropriate, post a message to the book's errata page and fix the problem in subsequent editions of the book.

P2P.WROX.COM

For author and peer discussion, join the P2P forums at p2p.wrox.com. The forums are a web-based system for you to post messages relating to Wrox books and related technologies and interact with other readers and technology users. The forums offer a subscription feature to e-mail you topics of interest of your choosing when new posts are made to the forums. Wrox authors, editors, other industry experts, and your fellow readers are present on these forums.

At http://p2p.wrox.com you can find a number of different forums to help you not only as you read this book, but also as you develop your own applications. To join the forums, just follow these steps:

1. Go to p2p.wrox.com and click the Register link.
2. Read the terms of use and click Agree.
3. Complete the required information to join and any optional information you want to provide, and click Submit.
4. You will receive an e-mail with information describing how to verify your account and complete the joining process.

> **NOTE** *You can read messages in the forums without joining P2P but to post your own messages, you must join.*

After you join, you can post new messages and respond to messages other users post. You can read messages at any time on the web. If you want to have new messages from a particular forum e-mailed to you, click the Subscribe to this Forum icon by the forum name in the forum listing.

For more information about how to use the Wrox P2P, read the P2P FAQs for answers to questions about how the forum software works as well as many common questions specific to P2P and Wrox books. To read the FAQs, click the FAQ link on any P2P page.

PROFESSIONAL

C# 6 and .NET Core 1.0

PART I
The C# Language

.NET Application Architectures

WHAT'S IN THIS CHAPTER?

➤ Reviewing the history of .NET

➤ Understanding differences between .NET Framework 4.6 and .NET Core 1.0

➤ Assemblies and NuGet Packages

➤ The Common Language Runtime

➤ Features of the Windows Runtime

➤ Programming Hello, World!

➤ Universal Windows Platform

➤ Technologies for creating Windows Apps

➤ Technologies for creating Web Apps

WROX.COM CODE DOWNLOADS FOR THIS CHAPTER

The wrox.com code downloads for this chapter are found at www.wrox.com/go/professionalcsharp6 on the Download Code tab. The code for this chapter is divided into the following major examples:

➤ DotnetHelloWorld

➤ HelloWorldApp (.NET Core)

CHOOSING YOUR TECHNOLOGIES

In recent years, .NET has become a huge ecosystem for creating any kind of applications on the Windows platform. With .NET you can create Windows apps, web services, web applications, and apps for the Microsoft Phone.

The newest release of .NET is a big change from the last version—maybe the biggest change to .NET since its invention. Much of the .NET code has become open-source code, and you can create applications for other platforms as well. The new version of .NET (.NET Core) and NuGet packages allow Microsoft to provide faster update cycles for delivering new features. It's not easy to decide what technology should be used for creating applications. This chapter helps you with that. It gives you information about the different technologies available for creating Windows and web applications and services, offers guidance on what to choose for database access, and highlights the differences between .NET and .NET Core.

REVIEWING .NET HISTORY

To better understand what is available with .NET and C#, it is best to know something about its history. The following table shows the version of .NET in relation to the Common Language Runtime (CLR), the version of C#, and the Visual Studio edition that gives some idea about the year when the corresponding versions have been released. Besides knowing what technology to use, it's also good to know what technology is not recommended because there's a replacement.

.NET	CLR	C#	VISUAL STUDIO
1.0	1.0	1.0	2002
1.1	1.1	1.2	2003
2.0	2.0	2.0	2005
3.0	2.0	2.0	2005 + Extensions
3.5	2.0	3.0	2008
4.0	4.0	4.0	2010
4.5	4.0	5.0	2012
4.5.1	4.0	5.0	2013
4.6	4.0	6	2015
.NET Core 1.0	CoreCLR	6	2015 + Extensions

The following sections cover the details of this table and the progress of C# and .NET.

C# 1.0—A New Language

C# 1.0 was a completely new programming language designed for the .NET Framework. At the time it was developed, the .NET Framework consisted of about 3,000 classes and the CLR.

After Microsoft was not allowed by a court order (filed by Sun, the company that created Java) to make changes to the Java code, Anders Hejlsberg designed C#. Before working for Microsoft, Hejlsberg had his roots at Borland where he designed the Delphi programming language (an Object Pascal dialect). At Microsoft he was responsible for J++ (Microsoft's version of the Java programming language). Given Hejlsberg's background, the C# programming language was mainly influenced by C++, Java, and Pascal.

Because C# was created later than Java and C++, Microsoft analyzed typical programming errors that happened with the other languages, and did some things differently to avoid these errors. Some differences include the following:

➤ With `if` statements, Boolean expressions are required (C++ allows an integer value here as well).

➤ It's permissible to create value and reference types using the `struct` and `class` keywords (Java only allows creating custom reference types; with C++ the distinction between `struct` and `class` is only the default for the access modifier).

➤ Virtual and non-virtual methods are allowed (this is similar to C++; Java always creates virtual methods).

Of course there are a lot more changes as you'll see reading this book.

At this time, C# was a pure object-oriented programming language with features for inheritance, encapsulation, and polymorphism. C# also offered component-based programming enhancements such as delegates and events.

Before the existence of .NET with the CLR, every programming language had its own runtime. With C++, the C++ Runtime is linked with every C++ program. Visual Basic 6 had its own runtime with VBRun. The runtime of Java is the Java Virtual Machine—which can be compared to the CLR. The CLR is a runtime that is used by every .NET programming language. At the time the CLR appeared on the scene, Microsoft offered JScript.NET, Visual Basic .NET, and Managed C++ in addition to C#. JScript.NET was Microsoft's JavaScript compiler that was to be used with the CLR and .NET classes. Visual Basic.NET was the name for

Visual Basic that offered .NET support. Nowadays it's just called Visual Basic again. Managed C++ was the name for a language that mixed native C++ code with Managed .NET Code. The newer C++ language used today with .NET is C++/CLR.

A compiler for a .NET programming language generates *Intermediate Language* (IL) code. The IL code looks like object-oriented machine code and can be checked by using the tool ildasm.exe to open DLL or EXE files that contain .NET code. The CLR contains a just-in-time (JIT) compiler that generates native code out of the IL code when the program starts to run.

> **NOTE** *IL code is also known as* managed code.

Other parts of the CLR are a garbage collector (GC), which is responsible for cleaning up managed memory that is no longer referenced; a security mechanism that uses code access security to verify what code is allowed to do; an extension for the debugger to allow a debug session between different programming languages (for example, starting a debug session with Visual Basic and continuing to debug within a C# library); and a threading facility that is responsible for creating threads on the underlying platform.

The .NET Framework was already huge with version 1. The classes are organized within namespaces to help facilitate navigating the 3,000 available classes. Namespaces are used to group classes and to solve conflicts by allowing the same class name in different namespaces. Version 1 of the .NET Framework allowed creating Windows desktop applications using Windows Forms (namespace System.Windows. Forms), creating web applications with ASP.NET Web Forms (System.Web), communicating with applications and web services using ASP.NET Web Services, communicating more quickly between .NET applications using .NET Remoting, and creating COM+ components for running in an application server using Enterprise Services.

ASP.NET Web Forms was the technology for creating web applications with the goal for the developer to not need to know something about HTML and JavaScript. Server-side controls that worked similarly to Windows Forms itself created HTML and JavaScript.

C# 1.2 and .NET 1.1 was mainly a bug fix release with minor enhancements.

> **NOTE** *Inheritance is discussed in Chapter 4, "Inheritance"; delegates and events are covered in Chapter 9, "Delegates, Lambdas, and Events."*

> **NOTE** *Every new release of .NET has been accompanied by a new version of the book* Professional C#. *With .NET 1.0, the book was already in the second edition as the first edition had been published with Beta 2 of .NET 1.0. You're holding the 10th edition of this book in your hands.*

C# 2 and .NET 2 with Generics

C# 2 and .NET 2 was a huge update. With this version, a change to both the C# programming language and the IL code had been made; that's why a new CLR was needed to support the IL code additions. One big change was *generics*. Generics make it possible to create types without needing to know what inner types are used. The inner types used are defined at instantiation time, when an instance is created.

This advance in the C# programming language also resulted in many new types in the Framework—for example, new generic collection classes found in the namespace `System.Collections.Generic`. With this, the older collection classes defined with 1.0 are rarely used with newer applications. Of course, the older classes still work nowadays, even with the new .NET Core version.

> **NOTE** *Generics are used all through the book, but they're explained in detail in Chapter 6, "Generics." Chapter 11, "Collections," covers generic collection classes.*

.NET 3—Windows Presentation Foundation

With the release of .NET 3.0 no new version of C# was needed. 3.0 was only a release offering new libraries, but it was a huge release with many new types and namespaces. Windows Presentation Foundation (WPF) was probably the biggest part of the new Framework for creating Windows desktop applications. Windows Forms wrapped the native Windows controls and was based on pixels, whereas WPF was based on DirectX to draw every control on its own. The vector graphics in WPF allow seamless resizing of every form. The templates in WPF also allow for complete custom looks. For example, an application for the Zurich airport can include a button that looks like a plane. As a result, applications can look very different from the traditional Windows applications that had been developed up to that time. Everything below the namespace `System.Windows` belongs to WPF, with the exception of `System.Windows.Forms`. With WPF the user interface can be designed using an XML syntax: XML for Applications Markup Language (XAML).

Before .NET 3, ASP.NET Web Services and .NET Remoting were used for communicating between applications. Message Queuing was another option for communicating. The various technologies had different advantages and disadvantages, and all had different APIs for programming. A typical enterprise application had to use more than one communication API, and thus it was necessary to learn several of them. This was solved with Windows Communication Foundation (WCF). WCF combined all the options of the other APIs into the one API. However, to support all of the features WCF has to offer, you need to configure WCF.

The third big part of the .NET 3.0 release was Windows Workflow Foundation (WF) with the namespace `System.Workflow`. Instead of creating custom workflow engines for several different applications (and Microsoft itself created several workflow engines for different products), a workflow engine was available as part of .NET.

With .NET 3.0, the class count of the Framework increased from 8,000 types in .NET 2.0 to about 12,000 types.

> **NOTE** *In this book, WPF is covered in Chapters 29, 30, 31, 34, 35, and 36. You can read information about WCF in Chapter 44, "Windows Communication Foundation."*

C# 3 and .NET 3.5—LINQ

.NET 3.5 came together with a new release of C# 3. The major enhancement was a query syntax defined with C# that allows using the same syntax to filter and sort object lists, XML files, and the database. The language enhancements didn't require any change to the IL code as the C# features used here are just syntax sugar. All of the enhancements could have been done with the older syntax as well, just a lot more code would be necessary. The C# language makes it really easy to do these queries. With LINQ and lambda expressions, it's possible to use the same query syntax and access object collections, databases, and XML files.

For accessing the database and creating LINQ queries, LINQ to SQL was released as part of .NET 3.5. With the first update to .NET 3.5, the first version of Entity Framework was released. Both LINQ to SQL and Entity Framework offered mapping of hierarchies to the relations of a database and a LINQ provider. Entity Framework was more powerful, but LINQ to SQL was simpler. Over time, features of LINQ to SQL have been implemented in Entity Framework, and now this one is here to stay. (Nowadays it looks very different from the first version released.)

Another technology introduced as part of .NET 3.5 was the System.AddIn namespace, which offers an add-in model. This model offers powerful features that run add-ins even out of process, but it is also complex to use.

> **NOTE** *LINQ is covered in detail in Chapter 13, "Language Integrated Query." The newest version of the Entity Framework is very different from the .NET 3.5 release; it's described in Chapter 38, "Entity Framework Core."*

C# 4 and .NET 4—Dynamic and TPL

The theme of C# 4 was dynamic—integrating scripting languages and making it easier to use COM integration. C# syntax has been extended with the dynamic keyword, named and optional parameters, and enhancements to co- and contra-variance with generics.

Other enhancements have been made within the .NET Framework. With multi-core CPUs, parallel programming had become more and more important. The Task Parallel Library (TPL), with abstractions of threads using Task and Parallel classes, make it easier to create parallel running code.

Because the workflow engine created with .NET 3.0 didn't fulfill its promises, a completely new Windows Workflow Foundation was part of .NET 4.0. To avoid conflicts with the older workflow engine, the newer one is defined in the System.Activity namespace.

The enhancements of C# 4 also required a new version of the runtime. The runtime skipped from version 2 to 4.

With the release of Visual Studio 2010, a new technology shipped for creating web applications: ASP.NET MVC 2.0. Unlike ASP.NET Web Forms, this technology required programming HTML and JavaScript, and it used C# and .NET with server-side functionality. As this technology was very new as well as being out of band (OOB) to Visual Studio and .NET, ASP.NET MVC was updated regularly.

> **NOTE** *The dynamic keyword of C# 4 is covered in Chapter 16, "Reflection, Metadata, and Dynamic Programming." The Task Parallel Library is covered in Chapter 21, "Tasks and Parallel Programming."*
>
> *Version 5 of ASP.NET and Version 6 of ASP.NET MVC are covered in Chapter 40, "ASP.NET Core," and Chapter 41, "ASP.NET MVC."*

C# 5 and Asynchronous Programming

C# 5 had only two new keywords: async and await. However, they made programming of asynchronous methods a lot easier. As touch became more significant with Windows 8, it also became a lot more important to not block the UI thread. Using the mouse, users are accustomed to scrolling taking some time. However, using fingers on a touch interface that is not responsive is really annoying.

Windows 8 also introduced a new programming interface for Windows Store apps (also known as Modern apps, Metro apps, Universal Windows apps, and, more recently, Windows apps): the Windows Runtime. This is a native runtime that looks like .NET by using language projections. Many of the WPF controls have been redone for the new runtime, and a subset of the .NET Framework can be used with such apps.

As the `System.AddIn` framework was much too complex and slow, a new composition framework was created with .NET 4.5: Managed Extensibility Framework with the namespace `System.Composition`.

A new version of platform-independent communication is offered by the ASP.NET Web API. Unlike WCF, which offers stateful and stateless services as well as many different network protocols, the ASP.NET Web API is a lot simpler and based on the Representational State Transfer (REST) software architecture style.

> **NOTE** *The* `async` *and* `await` *keywords of C# 5 are discussed in detail in Chapter 15, "Asynchronous Programming." This chapter also shows the different asynchronous patterns that have been used over time with .NET.*
>
> *Managed Extensibility Framework (MEF) is covered in Chapter 26, "Composition." Windows apps are covered in Chapters 29 to 33, and the ASP.NET Web API is covered in Chapter 42, "ASP.NET Web API."*

C# 6 and .NET Core

C# 6 doesn't involve the huge improvements that were made by generics, LINQ, and async, but there are a lot of small and practical enhancements in the language that can reduce the code length in several places. The many improvements have been made possible by a new compiler engine code named Roslyn.

> **NOTE** *Roslyn is covered in Chapter 18, ".NET Compiler Platform."*

The full .NET Framework is not the only .NET Framework that was in use in recent years. Some scenarios required smaller frameworks. In 2007, the first version of Microsoft Silverlight was released (code named WPF/E, WPF Everywhere). Silverlight was a web browser plug-in that allowed dynamic content. The first version of Silverlight supported programming only via JavaScript. The second version included a subset of the .NET Framework. Of course, server-side libraries were not needed because Silverlight was always running on the client, but the Framework shipped with Silverlight also removed classes and methods from the core features to make it lightweight and portable to other platforms. The last version of Silverlight for the desktop (version 5) was released in December 2011. Silverlight had also been used for programming for the Windows Phone. Silverlight 8.1 made it into Windows Phone 8.1, but this version of Silverlight is also different from the version on the desktop.

On the Windows desktop, where there is such a huge framework with .NET and the need for faster and faster development cadences, big changes were also required. In a world of DevOps where developers and operations work together or are even the same people to bring applications and new features continuously to the user, there's a need to have new features available in a fast way. Creating new features or making bug fixes is a not-so-easy task with a huge framework and many dependencies.

With several smaller .NET Frameworks available (e.g. Silverlight, Silverlight for the Windows Phone), it became important to share code between the desktop version of .NET and a smaller version. A technology to share code between different .NET versions is the portable library. Over time, with many different .NET Frameworks and versions, the management of the portable library has become a nightmare.

With all these issues, a new version of .NET is a necessity. (Yes, it's really a requirement to solve these issues.) The new version of the Framework is invented with the name *.NET Core*. .NET Core is smaller with modular NuGet packages, has a runtime that's distributed with every application, is open source, and is available not only for the desktop version of Windows but also for many different Windows devices, as well as for Linux and OS X.

For creating web applications, ASP.NET Core 1.0 is a complete rewrite of ASP.NET. This release is not completely backward compatible to older versions and requires some changes to existing ASP.NET MVC code (with ASP.NET MVC 6). However, it also has a lot of advantages when compared with the older versions, such as a lower overhead with every network request—which results in better performance—and it can also run on Linux. ASP.NET Web Forms is not part of this release because ASP.NET Web Forms was not designed for best performance; it was designed for developer friendliness based on patterns known by Windows Forms application developers.

Of course, not all applications can be changed easily to make use of .NET Core. That's why the huge framework received improvements as well—even if those improvements are not completed in as fast a pace as .NET Core. The new version of the full .NET Framework is 4.6. Small updates for ASP.NET Web Forms are available on the full .NET stack.

> **NOTE** *Roslyn is covered in Chapter 18. The changes to the C# language are covered in all the language chapters in Part I—for example, read-only properties are in Chapter 3, "Objects and Types"; the* nameof *operator and null propagation are in Chapter 8, "Operators and Casts"; string interpolation is in Chapter 10, "Strings and Regular Expressions"; and exception filters are in Chapter 14, "Errors and Exceptions."*
>
> *Where possible, .NET Core is used in this book. You can read more information about .NET Core and NuGet packages later in this chapter.*

Choosing Technologies and Going Forward

When you know the reason for competing technologies within the Framework, it's easier to select a technology to use for programming applications. For example, if you're creating new Windows applications it's not a good idea to bet on Windows Forms. Instead, you should use an XAML-based technology, such as Windows apps or Windows desktop applications using WPF.

If you're creating web applications, a safe bet is to use ASP.NET Core with ASP.NET MVC 6. Making this choice rules out using ASP.NET Web Forms. If you're accessing a database, you should use Entity Framework rather than LINQ to SQL, and you should opt for the Managed Extensibility Framework instead of System.AddIn.

Legacy applications still use Windows Forms and ASP.NET Web Forms and some other older technologies. It doesn't make sense to change existing applications just to use new technologies. There must be a huge advantage to making the change—for example, when maintenance of the code is already a nightmare and a lot of refactoring is needed to change to faster release cycles that are being demanded by customers, or when using a new technology allows for reducing the coding time for updates. Depending on the type of legacy application, it might not be worthwhile to switch to a new technology. You can allow the application to still be based on older technologies because Windows Forms and ASP.NET Web Forms will still be supported for many years to come.

The content of this book is based on the newer technologies to show what's best for creating new applications. In case you still need to maintain legacy applications, you can refer to older editions of this book, which cover ASP.NET Web Forms, Windows Forms, System.AddIn, and other legacy technologies that are still part of and available with the .NET Framework.

.NET 2015

.NET 2015 is an umbrella term for all the .NET technologies. Figure 1-1 gives an overall picture of these technologies. The left side represents the .NET Framework 4.6 technologies such as WPF and ASP.NET 4. ASP.NET Core 1.0 can run on .NET Framework 4.6 as well, as you can see in this figure. The right side represents the new .NET Core technologies. Both ASP.NET Core 1.0 and the Universal Windows Platform (UWP) run on .NET Core. You can also create console applications that run on .NET Core.

A part of .NET Core is a new runtime: the CoreCLR. This runtime is used from ASP.NET Core 1.0. Instead of using the CoreCLR runtime, .NET can also be compiled to native code. The UWP automatically makes use of this feature; these .NET applications are compiled to native code before being offered from the Windows Store. You can also compile other .NET Core applications—and the applications running on Linux—to native code.

In the lower part of Figure 1-1, you can see there's also some sharing going on between .NET Framework 4.6 and .NET Core. *Runtime components,* such as the code for the garbage collector and the RyuJIT (this is a new JIT compiler to compile IL code to native code) are shared. The garbage collector is used by CLR, CoreCLR, and .NET Native. The RyuJIT just-in-time compiler is used by CLR and CoreCLR. Libraries can be shared between applications based on the .NET Framework 4.6 and .NET Core 1.0. The concept of NuGet packages helps put these libraries in a common package that is available on all .NET platforms. And, of course, the new .NET compiler platform is used by all these technologies.

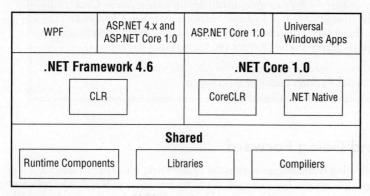

FIGURE 1-1

.NET Framework 4.6

NET Framework 4.6 is the .NET Framework that has been continuously enhanced in the past 10 years. Many of the technologies that have been discussed in the history section are based on this framework. This framework is used for creating Windows Forms and WPF applications. Also, although ASP.NET 5 can run on .NET Core, it can also run on .NET Framework 4.6.

If you want to continue working with ASP.NET Web Forms, ASP.NET 4.6 with .NET Framework 4.6 is the way to go. ASP.NET 4.6 also has new features compared to version 4.5, such as support for HTTP2 (a new version of the HTTP protocol that is discussed in Chapter 25, "Networking"), compilation on the fly with the Roslyn compiler, and asynchronous model binding. However, you can't switch to .NET Core with ASP. NET Web Forms.

You can find the libraries of the framework as well as the CLR in the directory `%windows%\Microsoft .NET\Framework\v4.0.30319`.

The classes available with the .NET Framework are organized in namespaces starting with the name `System`. The following table describes a few of the namespaces to give you an idea about the hierarchy.

NAMESPACE	DESCRIPTION
System.Collections	This is the root namespace for collections. Collections are also found within sub-namespaces such as System.Collections.Concurrent and System.Collections.Generic.
System.Data	This is the namespace for accessing databases. System.Data.SqlClient contains classes to access the SQL Server,
System.Diagnostics	This is the root namespace for diagnostics information, such as event logging and tracing (in the namespace System.Diagnostics.Tracing).
System.Globalization	This is the namespace that contains classes for globalization and localization of applications.
System.IO	This is the namespace for File IO, which are classes to access files and directories. Readers, writers, and streams are here.
System.Net	This is the namespace for core networking, such as accessing DNS servers and creating sockets with System.Net.Sockets.
System.Threading	This is the root namespace for threads and tasks. Tasks are defined within System.Threading.Tasks.
System.Web	This is the root namespace for ASP.NET. Below this namespace, many sub-namespaces are defined, such as System.Web.UI, System.Web.UI.WebControls, and System.Web.Hosting.
System.Windows	This is the root namespace for Windows desktop applications with WPF. Example subnamespaces are System.Windows.Shapes, System.Windows.Data, and System.Windows.Documents.

> **NOTE** *Some of the new .NET classes use namespaces that start with the name* Microsoft *instead of* System, *like* Microsoft.Data.Entity *for the Entity Framework and* Microsoft.Extensions.DependencyInjection *for the new dependency injection framework.*

.NET Core 1.0

.NET Core 1.0 is the new .NET that is used by all new technologies and has a big focus in this book. This framework is *open source*—you can find it at http://www.github.com/dotnet. The runtime is the *CoreCLR* repository; the framework containing collection classes, file system access, console, XML, and a lot more is in the *CoreFX* repository.

Unlike the .NET Framework, where the specific version you needed for the application had to be installed on the system, with .NET Core 1.0 the framework, including the runtime, is delivered with the application. Previously there were times when you might have had problems deploying an ASP.NET web application to a shared server because the provider had older versions of .NET installed; those times are gone. Now you can deliver the runtime with the application and are not dependent on the version installed on the server.

.NET Core 1.0 is designed in a modular approach. The framework splits up into a large list of NuGet packages. With the application you decide what packages you need. The .NET Framework was growing larger and larger when new functionality was added. It was not possible to remove old functionality that's no longer needed, such as the old collection classes that are unnecessary because of the generic collection classes that were added, .NET Remoting that has been replaced by the new communication technology, or LINQ to SQL that has been updated to Entity Framework. Applications can break when something is removed. This does not apply to .NET Core, as the application distributes the parts of the framework that it needs.

The framework of .NET Core is currently as huge as .NET Framework 4.6 is. However, this can change, and it can grow even bigger, but because of the modularity that growth potential is not an issue. .NET Core is already so huge that we can't cover every type in this book. Just have a look at http://www.github.com/dotnet/corefx to see all the sources. For example, old nongeneric collection classes are already covered with .NET Core to make it easier to bring legacy code to the new platform.

.NET Core can be updated at a fast pace. Even updating the runtime doesn't influence existing applications because the runtime is installed with the applications. Now Microsoft can improve .NET Core, including the runtime, with faster release cycles.

> **NOTE** *For developing apps using .NET Core, Microsoft created new command-line utilities named .NET Core Command line (CLI). These tools are introduced later in this chapter through a "Hello, World!" application in the section "Compiling with CLI."*

Assemblies

Libraries and executables of .NET programs are known by the term *assembly*. An assembly is the logical unit that contains compiled IL code targeted at the .NET Framework.

An assembly is completely self-describing and is a logical rather than a physical unit, which means that it can be stored across more than one file. (Indeed, dynamic assemblies are stored in memory, not on file.) If an assembly is stored in more than one file, there will be one main file that contains the entry point and describes the other files in the assembly.

The same assembly structure is used for both executable code and library code. The only difference is that an executable assembly contains a main program entry point, whereas a library assembly does not.

An important characteristic of assemblies is that they contain metadata that describes the types and methods defined in the corresponding code. An assembly, however, also contains assembly metadata that describes the assembly. This assembly metadata, contained in an area known as the *manifest*, enables checks to be made on the version of the assembly and on its integrity.

Because an assembly contains program metadata, applications or other assemblies that call up code in a given assembly do not need to refer to the registry, or to any other data source, to find out how to use that assembly.

With the .NET Framework 4.6, assemblies come in two types: *private* and *shared* assemblies. Shared assemblies don't apply to the Universal Windows Platform because all the code is compiled to one native image.

Private Assemblies

Private assemblies normally ship with software and are intended to be used only with that software. The usual scenario in which you ship private assemblies is when you supply an application in the form of an executable and a number of libraries, where the libraries contain code that should be used only with that application.

The system guarantees that private assemblies will not be used by other software because an application may load only private assemblies located in the same folder that the main executable is loaded in, or in a subfolder of it.

Because you would normally expect that commercial software would always be installed in its own directory, there is no risk of one software package overwriting, modifying, or accidentally loading private assemblies intended for another package. And, because private assemblies can be used only by the software package that they are intended for, you have much more control over what software uses them. There is, therefore, less need to take security precautions because there is no risk, for example, of some other commercial software overwriting one of your assemblies with some new version of it (apart from software designed specifically to perform malicious damage). There are also no problems with name collisions. If classes in your private assembly happen to have the same name as classes in someone else's private assembly, that does not matter because any given application can see only the one set of private assemblies.

Because a private assembly is entirely self-contained, the process to deploy it is simple. You simply place the appropriate file(s) in the appropriate folder in the file system. (No registry entries need to be made.) This process is known as *zero impact (xcopy) installation*.

Shared Assemblies

Shared assemblies are intended to be common libraries that any other application can use. Because any other software can access a shared assembly, more precautions need to be taken against the following risks:

➤ Name collisions, where another company's shared assembly implements types that have the same names as those in your shared assembly. Because client code can theoretically have access to both assemblies simultaneously, this could be a serious problem.

➤ The risk of an assembly being overwritten by a different version of the same assembly; the new version is incompatible with some existing client code.

The solution to these problems is placing shared assemblies in a special directory subtree in the file system, known as the *global assembly cache (GAC)*. With private assemblies, this can be done by simply copying the assembly into the appropriate folder, but with shared assemblies it must be specifically installed into the cache. This process can be performed by a number of .NET utilities and requires certain checks on the assembly, as well as setting up of a small folder hierarchy within the assembly cache used to ensure assembly integrity.

To prevent name collisions, shared assemblies are given a name based on private key cryptography. (Private assemblies are simply given the same name as their main filename.) This name is known as a *strong name*; it is guaranteed to be unique and must be quoted by applications that reference a shared assembly.

Problems associated with the risk of overwriting an assembly are addressed by specifying version information in the assembly manifest and by allowing side-by-side installations.

NuGet Packages

In the early days, assemblies were reusable units with applications. That use is still possible (and necessary with some assemblies) when you're adding a reference to an assembly for using the public types and methods from your own code. However, using libraries can mean a lot more than just adding a reference and using it. Using libraries can also mean some configuration changes, or scripts that can be used to take advantage of some features. This is one of the reasons to package assemblies within NuGet packages.

A NuGet package is a zip file that contains the assembly (or multiple assemblies) as well as configuration information and PowerShell scripts.

Another reason for using NuGet packages is that they can be found easily; they're available not only from Microsoft but also from third parties. NuGet packages are easily accessible on the NuGet server at http://www.nuget.org.

From the references within a Visual Studio project, you can open the NuGet Package Manager (see Figure 1-2). There you can search for packages and add them to the application. This tool enables you to search for packages that are not yet released (include prerelease option) and define the NuGet server where the packages should be searched.

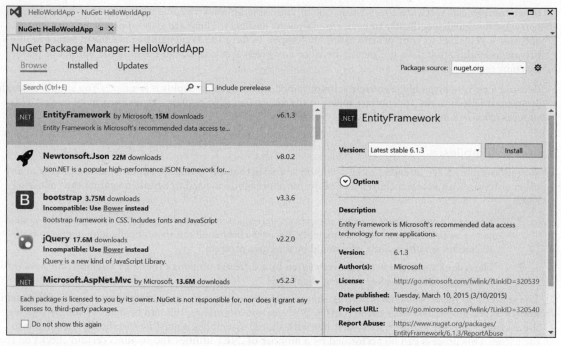

FIGURE 1-2

> **NOTE** *When you use third-party packages from the NuGet server, you're always at risk if a package is available at a later time. You also need to check about the support availability of the package. Always check for project links with information about the package before using it. With the package source, you can select Microsoft and .NET to only get packages supported by Microsoft. Third-party packages are also included in the Microsoft and .NET section, but they are third-party packages that are supported by Microsoft.*
>
> *You can also use your own NuGet server with your development team. You can define to only allow packages from your own server to be used by the development team.*

Because .NET Core is so modular, all applications—other than the simplest ones—need additional NuGet packages. To make it easier for you to find the package, with every sample application that's built with .NET Core this book shows a table that lists packages and namespaces that need to be added.

> **NOTE** *More information about the NuGet Package Manager is covered in Chapter 17, "Visual Studio 2015."*

Common Language Runtime

The Universal Windows Platform makes use of Native .NET to compile IL to native code. With all other scenarios, with both applications using the .NET Framework 4.6 and applications using .NET Core 1.0, a *Common Language Runtime* (CLR) is needed. However, .NET Core uses the CoreCLR whereas the .NET Framework uses the CLR. So, what's done by a CLR?

Before an application can be executed by the CLR, any source code that you develop (in C# or some other language) needs to be compiled. Compilation occurs in two steps in .NET:

1. Compilation of source code to Microsoft Intermediate Language (IL)
2. Compilation of IL to platform-specific native code by the CLR

The IL code is available within a .NET assembly. During runtime, a Just-In-Time (JIT) compiler compiles IL code and creates the platform-specific native code.

The new CLR and the CoreCLR include a new JIT compiler named *RyuJIT*. The new JIT compiler is not only faster than the previous one; it also has better support for the Edit & Continue feature while debugging with Visual Studio. The Edit & Continue feature enables you to edit the code while debugging, and you can continue the debug session without the need to stop and restart the process.

The runtime also includes a type system with a type loader that is responsible for loading types from assemblies. Security infrastructure with the type system verifies whether certain type system structures are permitted—for example, with inheritance.

After creating instances of types, the instances also need to be destroyed and memory needs to be recycled. Another feature of the runtime is the garbage collector. The garbage collector cleans up memory from the managed heap that isn't referenced anymore. Chapter 5, "Managed and Unmanaged Resources," explains how this is done and when it happens.

The runtime is also responsible for threading. Creating a managed thread from C# is not necessarily a thread from the underlying operating system. Threads are virtualized and managed by the runtime.

> **NOTE** *How threads can be created and managed from C# is covered in Chapter 21, "Tasks and Parallel Programming," and in Chapter 22, "Task Synchronization."*

.NET Native

A new feature of .NET 2015 is to compile a managed program to native code, *.NET Native*. With Windows apps this generates optimized code that can have a startup time that's up to 60 percent faster and uses 15 to 20 percent less memory.

.NET Native started with compiling UWP apps to native code for apps deployed to the Windows Store. Now, .NET Native is also available with other .NET Core applications. You can compile .NET Core applications running on both Windows and Linux to native code. Of course, you need different native images on each of these platforms. Behind the scenes, .NET Native shares the C++ optimizer for generating the native code.

Windows Runtime

Starting with Windows 8, the Windows operating system offers another framework: the Windows Runtime. This runtime is used by the Windows Universal Platform and was version 1 with Windows 8, version 2 with Windows 8.1, and version 3 with Windows 10.

Unlike the .NET Framework, this framework was created using native code. When it's used with .NET applications, the types and methods contained just look like .NET. With the help of language projection, the Windows Runtime can be used with the JavaScript, C++, and .NET languages, and it looks like it's native to the programming environment. Methods are not only behaving differently in regard to case sensitivity; the methods and types can also have different names depending on where they are used.

The Windows Runtime offers an object hierarchy organized in namespaces that start with `Windows`. Looking at these classes, there's not a lot with duplicate functionality to the .NET Framework; instead, extra functionality is offered that is available for apps running on the Universal Windows Platform.

NAMESPACE	DESCRIPTION
`Windows.ApplicationModel`	This namespace and its subnamespaces, such as `Windows.ApplicationModel.Contracts`, define classes to manage the app lifecycle and communication with other apps.
`Windows.Data`	`Windows.Data` defines subnamespaces to work with Text, JSON, PDF, and XML data.
`Windows.Devices`	Geolocation, smartcards, point of service devices, printers, scanners, and other devices can be accessed with subnamespaces of `Windows.Devices`.
`Windows.Foundation`	`Windows.Foundation` defines core functionality. Interfaces for collections are defined with the namespace `Windows.Foundation.Collections`. You will not find concrete collection classes here. Instead, interfaces of .NET collection types map to the Windows Runtime types.
`Windows.Media`	`Windows.Media` is the root namespace for playing and capturing video and audio, accessing playlists, and doing speech output.
`Windows.Networking`	This is the root namespace for socket programming, background transfer of data, and push notifications.
`Windows.Security`	Classes from `Windows.Security.Credentials` offer a safe store for passwords; `Windows.Security.Credentials.UI` offers a picker to get credentials from the user.
`Windows.Services.Maps`	This namespace contains classes for location services and routing.
`Windows.Storage`	With `Windows.Storage` and its subnamespaces, it is possible to access files and directories as well as use streams and compression.
`Windows.System`	The `Windows.System` namespace and its subnamespaces give information about the system and the user, but they also offer a `Launcher` to launch other apps.
`Windows.UI.Xaml`	In this namespace, you can find a ton of types for the user interface.

HELLO, WORLD

Let's get into coding and create a *Hello, World* application. Since the 1970s, when Brian Kernighan and Dennis Ritchie wrote the book *The C Programming Language*, it's been a tradition to start learning programming languages using a Hello, World application. Interestingly, the syntax for Hello, World changed with C# 6; it's the first time this simple program has looked different since the invention of C#.

The first samples will be created without the help of Visual Studio so you can see what happens behind the scenes by creating the application with command-line tools and a simple text editor (such as Notepad). Later, you'll switch to using Visual Studio because it makes programming life easier.

Type the following source code into a text editor, and save it with a `.cs` extension (for example, `HelloWorld.cs`). The `Main` method is the entry point for a .NET application. The CLR invokes a static `Main` method on startup. The `Main` method needs to be put into a class. Here, the class is named `Program`, but you could call it by any name. `WriteLine` is a `static` method of the `Console` class. All the static members of the `Console` class are opened with the using declaration in the first line. `using static System.Console` opens the static members of the `Console` class with the result that you don't need to type the class name calling the method `WriteLine` (code file Dotnet/HelloWorld.cs):

```
using static System.Console;

class Program
{
  static void Main()
  {
```

```
      WriteLine("Hello, World!");
    }
  }
```

As previously mentioned, the syntax of Hello, World changed slightly with C# 6. Previous to C# 6, `using` `static` was not available, and only a namespace could be opened with the `using` declaration. Of course, the following code still works with C# 6 (code file `Dotnet/HelloWorld2.cs`):

```
using System;

class Program
{
  static void Main()
  {
    Console.WriteLine("Hello, World!");
  }
}
```

The `using` declaration is there to reduce the code with opening a namespace. Another way to write the Hello, World program is to remove the `using` declaration and add the `System` namespace to the `Console` class with the invocation of the `WriteLine` method (code file `Dotnet/HelloWorld3.cs`):

```
class Program
{
  static void Main()
  {
    System.Console.WriteLine("Hello, World!");
  }
}
```

After writing the source code, you need to compile the code to run it.

COMPILING WITH .NET 4.6

You can compile this program by simply running the C# command-line compiler (`csc.exe`) against the source file, like this:

```
csc HelloWorld.cs
```

If you want to compile code from the command line using the `csc` command, you should be aware that the .NET command-line tools, including `csc`, are available only if certain environment variables have been set up. Depending on how you installed .NET (and Visual Studio), this may or may not be the case on your machine.

> **NOTE** *If you do not have the environment variables set up, you have three options: The first is to add the path to the call of the* `csc` *executable. It is located at* `%Program Files%\MsBuild\14.0\Bin\csc.exe` *With the dotnet tools installed, you can also find the* `csc` *at* `%ProgramFiles%\dot.net\bin\csc.exe`*. The second option is to run the batch file* `%Microsoft Visual Studio 2015%\Common7\Tools\vsvars32.bat` *from the command prompt before running* `csc`*, where* `%Microsoft Visual Studio 2015%` *is the folder to which Visual Studio 2015 has been installed. The third, and easiest, way is to use the Visual Studio 2015 command prompt instead of the Windows command prompt. To find the Visual Studio 2015 command prompt from the Start menu, select Programs ⇨ Microsoft Visual Studio 2015 ⇨ Visual Studio Tools. The Visual Studio 2015 command prompt is simply a command prompt window that automatically runs* `vsvars32.bat` *when it opens.*

Compiling the code produces an executable file named `HelloWorld.exe`, which you can run from the command line. You can also run it from Windows Explorer as you would run any other executable. Give it a try:

```
> csc HelloWorld.cs
Microsoft (R) Visual C# Compiler version 1.1.0.51109
Copyright (C) Microsoft Corporation. All rights reserved.
> HelloWorld
Hello World!
```

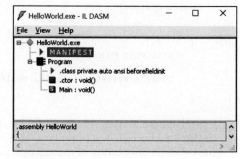

Compiling an executable this way produces an assembly that contains Intermediate Language (IL) code. The assembly can be read using the Intermediate Language Disassembler (IL DASM) tool. If you run `ildasm.exe` and open `HelloWorld.exe`, you see that the assembly contains a `Program` type and a `Main` method as shown in Figure 1-3.

Double-click the MANIFEST node in the tree view to reveal metadata information about the assembly (see Figure 1-4). This assembly makes use of the `mscorlib` assembly (because the `Console` class is located there), and some configuration and version of the HelloWorld assembly.

FIGURE 1-3

```
// Metadata version: v4.0.30319
.assembly extern mscorlib
{
  .publickeytoken = (B7 7A 5C 56 19 34 E0 89 )       // .
  .ver 4:0:0:0
}
.assembly HelloWorld
{
  .custom instance void [mscorlib]System.Runtime.CompilerServices.Compilati
  .custom instance void [mscorlib]System.Runtime.CompilerServices.RuntimeCo


  // --- The following custom attribute is added automatically, do not unco
  //   .custom instance void [mscorlib]System.Diagnostics.DebuggableAttribut

  .hash algorithm 0x00008004
  .ver 0:0:0:0
}
.module HelloWorld.exe
// MVID: {7E6EA73C-6BB6-41C4-8F22-1F655979E41E}
.imagebase 0x00400000
```

FIGURE 1-4

Double-click the `Main` method to reveal the IL code of this method (see Figure 1-5). No matter what version of the Hello, World code you compiled, the result is the same. The string `Hello, World!` is loaded before calling the method `System.Console.WriteLine` that is defined within the `mscorlib` assembly passing the string. One feature of the CLR is the JIT compiler. The JIT compiler compiles IL code to native code when running the application.

```
.method private hidebysig static void  Main() cil managed
{
  .entrypoint
  // Code size       13 (0xd)
  .maxstack  8
  IL_0000:  nop
  IL_0001:  ldstr      "Hello, World!"
  IL_0006:  call       void [mscorlib]System.Console::WriteLine(string)
  IL_000b:  nop
  IL_000c:  ret
} // end of method Program::Main
```

FIGURE 1-5

COMPILING WITH .NET CORE CLI

very confusing

Using the new .NET Core Command line (CLI), some preparations need to be done to compile the application without the help of Visual Studio. Let's have a look at the new tools next to compile the Hello, World sample application.

Setting Up the Environment

In case you have Visual Studio 2015 with the latest updates installed, you can immediately start with the CLI tools. Otherwise, you need to install .NET Core and the CLI tools. You can find instructions for the download at http://dotnet.github.io for Windows, Linux, and OS X.

With Windows, different versions of .NET Core runtimes as well as NuGet packages are installed in the user profile. As you work with .NET, this folder increases in size. Over time as you create multiple projects, NuGet packages are no longer stored in the project itself; they're stored in this user-specific folder. This has the advantage that you do not need to download NuGet packages for every different project. After you have this NuGet package downloaded, it's on your system. Just as different versions of the NuGet packages as well as the runtime are available, all the different versions are stored in this folder. From time to time it might be interesting to check this folder and delete old versions you no longer need.

Installing .NET Core CLI tools, you have the dotnet tools as an entry point to start all these tools. Just start

```
> dotnet
```

to see all the different options of the dotnet tools available.

The repl (read, eval, print, loop') command is good to learn and test simple features of C# without the need to create a program. Start repl with the dotnet tool:

```
> dotnet repl
```

This starts an interactive repl session. You can enter the following statements for a Hello, World using a variable:

```
> using static System.Console;
> var hello = "Hello, World!";
> WriteLine(hello);
```

The output you'll see as you enter the last statement is the Hello, World! string.

Building the Application

The dotnet tools offer an easy way to create a Hello, World application. You create a new directory HelloWorldApp, and change to this directory with the command prompt. Then enter this command:

```
> dotnet new
```

This command creates a Program.cs file that includes the code for the Hello, World program, a NuGet.config file that defines the NuGet server where NuGet packages should be loaded, and project.json, the new project configuration file.

> **NOTE** *With* dotnet new *you can also create the initial files needed for libraries and ASP.NET web applications (with the option* --type*). You can also select other programming languages, such as F# and Visual Basic (with the option* --lang*).*

The created project configuration file is named project.json. This file is in JavaScript Object Notation (JSON) format and defines the framework application information such as version, description, authors, tags, dependencies to libraries, and the frameworks that are supported by the application. The generated project configuration file is shown in the following code snippet (code file `HelloWorldApp/project.json`):

```
{
    "version": "1.0.0-*",
    "compilationOptions": {
        "emitEntryPoint": true
    },

    "dependencies": {
        "NETStandard.Library": "1.0.0-*"
    },

    "frameworks" : {
        "netstandardapp1.5": {
            "imports": "dnxcore50"
        }
    },
    "runtimes" : {
        "ubuntu.14.04-x64": { },
        "win7-x64": { },
        "win10-x64": { },
        "osx.10.10-x64": { },
        "osx.10.11-x64": { }
    }
}
```

With the `compilationOptions` settings, the `emitEntryPoint` is set. This is necessary if you create a `Main` method as a program entry point. This `Main` method is invoked when you run the application. This setting is not needed with libraries.

With the dependencies section, you can add all dependencies of the program, such as additional NuGet packages needed to compile the program. By default, `NetStandard.Library` is added as a dependency. `NetStandard.Library` is a reference NuGet package—a package that references other NuGet packages. With this you can avoid adding a lot of other packages, such as `System.Console` for the `Console` class, `System.Collections` for generic collection classes, and many more. `NetStandard.Library` 1.0 is a standard that defines a list of assemblies that all .NET platforms must support. At the website `https://github.com/dotnet/corefx/blob/master/Documentation/project-docs/standard-platform.md` you can find a long list of assemblies and their version numbers that are part of 1.0 and the assemblies that are added with 1.1, 1.2, 1.3, and 1.4 of the .NET standard.

Having a dependency on `NetStandard.Library` 1.0, you can support the .NET Framework 4.5.2 and up (support for .NET 4, 4.5, 4.5.1 ended in January 2016), .NET Core 1.0, the UWP 10.0, and other .NET Frameworks such as Windows Phone Silverlight 8.0, Mono, and Mono/Xamarin. Changing to version 1.3 restricts the support to .NET 4.6, .NET Core 1.0, UWP 10.0, and Mono/Xamarin platforms. Version 1.4 restricts support to .NET 4.6.1, .NET Core 1.0, and Mono/Xamarin platforms, but you get newer versions and a larger list of assemblies available.

The `frameworks` section in `project.json` lists the .NET Frameworks that are supported by your application. By default, the application is only built for .NET Core 1.0 as specified by the `netstandardapp1.5` moniker. `netstandardapp1.5` is used with applications built for .NET Core. With libraries, you can use the moniker `netstandard1.0`. This allows using the library both from .NET Core applications and applications using the .NET Framework. The `imports` section within `netstandardapp1.5` references the older name `dnxcore50`, which maps the old moniker to the new one. This allows packages that still use the old name to be used.

.NET Core is the new open source version of the framework that is available on Windows, Linux, and OS X. The runtime that should be supported needs to be added to the runtimes section. The previous code snippet shows support for the Ubuntu Linux distribution, Windows 7 (which also allows running the app on Windows 8), Windows 10, and OS X.

Adding the string net46, the program is built for the .NET Framework, version 4.6, as well:

```
"frameworks" : {
   "netstandardapp1.5" : { }
   "net46" : { }
}
```

Adding net46 to the frameworks section also results in no more support for non-Windows runtimes, and thus you need to remove these runtimes.

You can also add additional metadata, such as a description, author information, tags, project, and license URL:

```
"version": "1.0.0-*",
"description": "HelloWorld Sample App for Professional C#",
"authors": [ "Christian Nagel" ],
"tags": [ "Sample", "Hello", "Wrox"  ],
"projectUrl": "http://github.com/professionalCSharp/",
"licenseUrl": "",
```

As you add multiple frameworks to the project.json file, you can specify dependencies that are specific to every framework in a dependencies section below the framework. The dependencies specified in the dependencies section that is at the same hierarchical level as the frameworks section specify the dependencies common to all frameworks.

After having the project structure in place, you can download all dependencies of the application using the command

```
> dotnet restore
```

while your command prompt is positioned in the same directory where the project.json file resides. This command downloads all dependencies needed for the application, as defined in the project.json file. Specifying the version 1.0.0-* gets version 1.0.0 and the latest available version for the *. In the file project.lock.json you can see what NuGet packages with which version were retrieved, including dependencies of dependencies. Remember, the packages are stored in a user-specific folder.

To compile the application, start the command dotnet build and you can see output like this—compiling for .NET Core 1.0 and .NET Framework 4.6:

```
> dotnet build
Compiling HelloWorldApp for .NETStandardApp, Version=1.5"
Compilation succeeded.
    0 Warning(s)
    0 Error(s)
Time elapsed 00:00:02.6911660

Compiling HelloWorldApp for .NETFramework,Version=v4.6
Compilation succeeded.
    0 Warning(s)
    0 Error(s)
Time elapsed 00:00:03.3735370
```

As a result of the compilation process, you find the assembly containing the IL code of the Program class within the bin/debug/[netstandardapp1.5|net46] folder. If you compare the build of .NET Core with .NET 4.6, you will find a DLL containing the IL code with .NET Core, and an EXE containing the IL code with .NET 4.6. The assembly generated for .NET Core has a dependency to the System.Console assembly, whereas the .NET 4.6 assembly finds the Console class in the mscorlib assembly.

You can also compile the program to native code using this command line:

```
> dotnet build --native
```

Compiling to native code results in a faster startup of the application as well as less memory consumption. The native compilation process compiles the IL code of the application as well as all dependencies to a single native image. Don't expect that all functionality of .NET Core will be available to compile to native code, but as time continues and development from Microsoft proceeds, more and more applications can be compiled to native code.

To run the application, you can use the `dotnet` command

```
> dotnet run
```

To start the application using a specific version of the framework, you can use the option `-framework`. This framework must be configured with the `project.json` file:

```
> dotnet run --framework net46
```

You can also run the application starting the executable that you can find in the `bin/debug` directory.

> **NOTE** As you've seen building and running the Hello, World app on Windows, the dotnet tools work the same on Linux and OS X. You can use the same dotnet commands on either platform. Before using the dotnet commands, you just need to prepare the infrastructure using the sudo utility for Ubuntu Linux and install a PKG package on OS X as described at `http://dotnet.github.io`. After installing the .NET Core CLI, you can use the dotnet tools in the same way as you've seen in this section—with the exception that the .NET Framework 4.6 is not available. Other than that, you can restore NuGet packages and compile and run the application with `dotnet restore`, `dotnet compile`, and `dotnet run`.
>
> The focus of this book is on Windows, as Visual Studio 2015 offers a more powerful development platform than is available on the other platforms, but many code samples from this book are based on .NET Core, and you will be able to run them on other platforms as well. You can also use Visual Studio Code, a free development environment, to develop applications directly on Linux and OS X. See the section "Developer Tools" later in this chapter for more information about different editions of Visual Studio.

Packaging and Publishing the Application

With the dotnet tool you can also create a NuGet package and publish the application for deployment.

The command `dotnet pack` creates a NuGet package that you can put on a NuGet server. Developers can now reference the package using this command:

```
> dotnet pack
```

Running this command with the `HelloWorldApp` creates the file `HelloWorldApp.1.0.0.nupkg` that contains the assemblies for all supported frameworks. A NuGet package is a ZIP file. If you rename this file with a `.zip` extension, you can easily look into it to see the content. With the sample app, two folders are created named `dnxcore500` and `net46` that contain the respective assemblies. The file `HelloWorldApp.nuspec` is an XML file that describes the NuGet package, lists the content for supported frameworks, and lists assembly dependencies that are required before the NuGet package can be installed.

To publish the application, on the target system the runtime is needed as well. The files that are needed for publishing can be created with the `dotnet publish` command:

```
> dotnet publish
```

Using optional arguments, you can specify only a specific runtime to publish for (option `-r`) or a different output directory (option `-o`). After running this command on a Windows system you can find a `win7-x64` folder with all the files needed on the target system. Be aware that with .NET Core the runtime is included; thus it doesn't matter what runtime version is installed.

APPLICATION TYPES AND TECHNOLOGIES

You can use C# to create console applications; with most samples in the first chapters of this book you'll do that exact thing. For real programs, console applications are not used that often. You can use C# to create applications that use many of the technologies associated with .NET. This section gives you an overview of the different types of applications that you can write in C#.

Data Access

Before having a look at the application types themselves, let's look at technologies that are used by all application types: access to data.

Files and directories can be accessed by using simple API calls; however, the simple API calls are not flexible enough for some scenarios. With the stream API you have a lot of flexibility, and the streams offer many more features such as encryption or compression. Readers and writers make using streams easier. All of the different options available here are covered in Chapter 23, "Files and Streams." It's also possible to serialize complete objects in XML or JSON format. Chapter 27, "XML and JSON," discusses these options.

To read and write to databases, you can use ADO.NET directly (see Chapter 37, "ADO.NET"), or you can use an abstraction layer, the ADO.NET Entity Framework (Chapter 38, "Entity Framework Core"). Entity Framework offers a mapping of object hierarchies to the relations of a database.

The ADO.NET Entity Framework made it through several iterations. The different versions of the Entity Framework are worth discussing; this gives you good information about why NuGet packages are a good idea. You'll also learn what parts of the Entity Framework shouldn't be used going forward.

The following table describes the different versions of the Entity Framework and each version's new features.

ENTITY FRAMEWORK	DESCRIPTION
1.0	Available with .NET 3.5 SP1. This version offered a mapping through an XML file to map tables to objects.
4.0	With .NET 4, Entity Framework made a jump from version 1 to 4.
4.1	Code First Support.
4.2	Bug fixes.
4.3	Migrations added.
5.0	Released together with .NET 4.5 and offering performance improvements, supporting new SQL Server features.
6.0	Moved to a NuGet package.
7.0	A complete rewrite, also supporting NoSQL, running on Windows apps as well.

Let's get into some details. Entity Framework was originally released as part of the .NET Framework classes that come preinstalled with the .NET Framework. Entity Framework 1 was part of the first service pack of .NET 3.5, which was a feature update: .NET 3.5 Update 1.

The second version had so many new features that the decision was made to move to version 4 together with .NET 4. After that, Entity Framework was released at a faster cadence than the .NET Framework. To get a newer version of Entity Framework, a NuGet package had to be added to the application (versions 4.1, 4.2, 4.3). There was a problem with this approach. Classes that have already been delivered with the .NET

Framework had to be used as is. Just additional features, such as Code First, have been added with NuGet packages.

With .NET 4.5, Entity Framework 5.0 was released. Again some of the classes come with the preinstalled .NET Framework, and additional features are part of NuGet packages. The NuGet package also made it possible to allow installing the NuGet package for Entity Framework 5.0 with .NET 4.0 applications. However, in reality the package decided (via a script) in a case when Entity Framework 5.0 is added to a .NET 4.0 project that the result would be Entity Framework 4.4 because some of the types required belong to .NET 4.5 and are not part of .NET 4.

The next version of Entity Framework solved this problem by moving all the Entity Framework types to a NuGet package; the types that come with the Framework itself are ignored. This allows using version 6.0 with older versions of the Framework; you aren't restricted to 4.5. To not conflict with classes of the Framework, some types moved to a different namespace. Some features of ASP.NET Web Forms had an issue with that because original classes of the Entity Framework have been used, and these do not map that easily to the new classes.

During the different releases, Entity Framework gives different options for mapping the database tables to classes. The first two options were Database First and Model First. With both of these options, the mapping was done via XML files. The XML file is presented via a graphical designer, and it's possible to drag entities from the toolbox to the designer for doing the mapping.

With version 4.1, mapping via code was added: Code First. Code First doesn't mean that the database can't exist beforehand. Both are possible: A database can be created dynamically, but also the database can exist before you write the code. Using Code First, you don't do the mapping via XML files. Instead, attributes or a fluent API can define the mapping programmatically.

Entity Framework Core 1.0 is a complete redesign of Entity Framework, as is reflected with the new name. Code needs to be changed to migrate applications from older versions of Entity Framework to the new version. Older mapping variants, such as Database First and Model First, have been dropped, as Code First is a better alternative. The complete redesign was also done to support not only relational databases but also NoSQL. Azure Table Storage is one of the options where Entity Framework can now be used.

Windows Desktop Applications

For creating Windows desktop applications, two technologies are available: Windows Forms and Windows Presentation Foundation. *Windows Forms* consists of classes that wrap native Windows controls; it's based on pixel graphics. *Windows Presentation Foundation (WPF)* is the newer technology and is based on vector graphics.

WPF makes use of XAML in building applications. XAML stands for eXtensible Application Markup Language. This way to create applications within a Microsoft environment was introduced in 2006 and is part of the .NET Framework 3.0. .NET 4.5 introduced new features to WPF, such as ribbon controls and live shaping.

XAML is the XML declaration used to create a form that represents all the visual aspects and behaviors of the WPF application. Though you can work with a WPF application programmatically, WPF is a step in the direction of declarative programming, which the industry is moving to. *Declarative programming* means that instead of creating objects through programming in a compiled language such as C#, Visual Basic, or Java, you declare everything through XML-type programming. Chapter 29, "Core XAML," introduces XAML (which is also used with XML Paper Specification, Windows Workflow Foundation, and Windows Communication Foundation). Chapter 30 covers XAML styles and resources. Chapter 34, "Windows Desktop Applications with WPF," gives details on controls, layout, and data binding. Printing and creating documents is another important aspect of WPF that's covered in Chapter 35, "Creating Documents with WPF."

What's the future of WPF? Isn't the UWP the UI platform to use for new applications going forward? UWP has advantages in supporting mobile devices as well. As long as some of your users have not upgraded to

Windows 10, you need to support older operating systems such as Windows 7. UWP apps don't run on Windows 7 or Windows 8. You can use WPF. In case you also would like to support mobile devices, it's best to do as much code sharing as possible. You can create apps with both WPF and UWP by using as much common code as possible by supporting the MVVM pattern. This pattern is covered in Chapter 31, "Patterns with XAML Apps."

Universal Windows Platform

The Universal Windows Platform (UWP) is a strategic platform from Microsoft. When you use the UWP to create Windows apps, you're limited to Windows 10 and newer versions of Windows. But you're not bound to the desktop version of Windows. With Windows 10 you have a lot of different options, such as Phone, Xbox, Surface Hub, HoloLens, and IoT. There's one API that works on all these devices!

One API for all these devices? Yes! Each device family can add its own Software Development Kit (SDK) to add features that are not part of the API that's available for all devices. Adding these SDKs does not break the application, but you need to programmatically check whether an API from such an SDK is available on the platform the app is running. Depending on how many API calls you need to differentiate, the code might grow into a mess; dependency injection might be a better option.

> **NOTE** *Dependency injection is discussed in Chapter 31, along with other patterns useful with XAML-based applications.*

You can decide what device families to support with your applications. Not all device families will be useful for every app.

Will there be newer versions of Windows after Windows 10? Windows 11 is not planned. With Windows apps (which are also known as Metro apps, Windows Store apps, Modern apps, and Universal Windows apps) you've targeted either Windows 8 or Windows 8.1. Windows 8 apps typically were also running on Windows 8.1, but not the other way around. Now this is very different. When you create an app for the Universal Windows Platform, you target a version such as 10.0.10130.0 and define what minimum version is available and what latest version was tested, and the assumption is that it runs on future versions as well. Depending on the features you can use for your app and what version you're expecting the user to have, you can decide what minimum version to support. Personal users will typically automatically update to newer versions; Enterprise users might stick to older versions.

Windows Apps running on the Universal Windows Platform make use of the Windows Runtime and .NET Core. The most important chapters for these app types are Chapter 32, "Windows Apps: User Interfaces," and Chapter 33, "Advanced Windows Apps." These apps are also covered in many other chapters, such as Chapter 23 and Chapters 29 through 31.

SOAP Services with WCF

Windows Communication Foundation (WCF) is a feature-rich technology that was meant to replace all communication technologies that were available before WCF by offering SOAP-based communication with all the features used by standards-based web services such as security, transactions, duplex and one-way communication, routing, discovery, and so on. WCF provides you with the ability to build your service one time and then expose this service in many ways (even under different protocols) by making changes within a configuration file. WCF is a powerful but complex way to connect disparate systems. Chapter 44, "Windows Communication Foundation," covers this in detail.

Web Services with the ASP.NET Web API

An option that is a lot easier for communication and fulfills more than 90 percent of requirements by distributed applications is the ASP.NET Web API. This technology is based on REST (Representational State Transfer), which defines guidelines and best practices for stateless and scalable web services.

The client can receive JSON or XML data. JSON and XML can also be formatted in a way to make use of the Open Data specification (OData).

The features of this new API make it easy to consume from web clients using JavaScript and also by using the Universal Windows Platform.

The ASP.NET Web API is a good approach for creating microservices. The approach to build microservices defines smaller services that can run and be deployed independently, having their own control of a data store.

With ASP.NET 5, the older version of ASP.NET Web API that was separated from ASP.NET MVC now merged with ASP.NET MVC 6 and uses the same types and features.

> **NOTE** *The ASP.NET Web API and more information on microservices are covered in Chapter 42.*

WebHooks and SignalR

For real-time web functionality and bidirectional communication between the client and the server, WebHooks and SignalR are ASP.NET technology that can be used.

SignalR allows pushing information to connected clients as soon as information is available. SignalR makes use of the WebSocket technology, and it has a fallback to a pull-based mechanism of communication in case WebSockets are not available.

WebHooks allows you to integrate with public services, and these services can call into your public ASP.NET Web API service. WebHooks is a technology to receive push notification from services such as GitHub or Dropbox and many other services.

The foundation of SignalR connection management, grouping of connections, and authorization and integration of WebHooks are discussed in Chapter 43, "WebHooks and SignalR."

Windows Services

A web service, whether it's done with WCF or ASP.NET Web Services, needs a host to run. Internet Information Server is usually a good option because of all the services it offers, but it can also be a custom program. With the custom option, creating a background process that runs with the startup of Windows is a Windows Service. This is a program designed to run in the background in Windows NT kernel–based operating systems. Services are useful when you want a program to run continuously and be ready to respond to events without having been explicitly started by the user. A good example is the World Wide Web Service on web servers, which listens for web requests from clients.

It is easy to write services in C#. .NET Framework base classes are available in the System. ServiceProcess namespace that handles many of the boilerplate tasks associated with services. In addition, Visual Studio .NET enables you to create a C# Windows Service project, which uses C# source code for a basic Windows Service. Chapter 39, "Windows Services," explores how to write C# Windows Services.

Web Applications

The original introduction of ASP.NET 1 fundamentally changed the web programming model. ASP.NET 5 is the new major release, which allows the use of .NET Core for high performance and scalability. This new release can also run on Linux systems, which was a high demand.

With ASP.NET 5, ASP.NET Web Forms is no longer covered (this can still be used and is updated with .NET 4.6), so this book has a focus on the modern technology ASP.NET MVC 6, which is part of ASP.NET 5.

ASP.NET MVC is based on the well-known Model View Controller (MVC) pattern for easier unit testing. It also allows a clear separation for writing user interface code with HTML, CSS, and JavaScript, and it only uses C# on the backend.

> **NOTE** *Chapter 41, "ASP.NET MVC," covers ASP.NET MVC 6.*

Microsoft Azure

Nowadays you can't ignore the cloud when considering the development picture. Although there's not a dedicated chapter on cloud technologies, Microsoft Azure is referenced in several chapters in this book.

Microsoft Azure offers Software as a Service (SaaS), Infrastructure as a Service (IaaS), and Platform as a Service (PaaS), and sometimes offerings are in between these categories. Let's have a look at some Microsoft Azure offerings.

Software as a Service

SaaS offers complete software; you don't have to deal with management of servers, updates, and so on. Office 365 is one of the SaaS offerings for using e-mail and other services via a cloud offering. A SaaS offering that's relevant for developers is *Visual Studio Online*, which is not Visual Studio running in the browser. Visual Studio Online is the Team Foundation Server in the cloud that can be used as a private code repository, for tracking bugs and work items, and for build and testing services.

Infrastructure as a Service

Another service offering is IaaS. Virtual machines are offered by this service offering. You are responsible for managing the operating system and maintaining updates. When you create virtual machines, you can decide between different hardware offerings starting with shared Cores up to 32 cores (at the time of this writing, but things change quickly). 32 cores, 448 GB RAM, and 6,144 GB local SSD belong to the "G-Series" of machines, which is named after Godzilla.

With preinstalled operating systems you can decide between Windows, Windows Server, Linux, and operating systems that come preinstalled with SQL Server, BizTalk Server, SharePoint, and Oracle.

I use virtual machines often for environments that I need only for several hours a week, as the virtual machines are paid on an hourly basis. In case you want to try compiling and running .NET Core programs on Linux but don't have a Linux machine, installing such an environment on Microsoft Azure is an easy task.

Platform as a Service

For developers, the most relevant part of Microsoft Azure is PaaS. You can access services for storing and reading data, use computing and networking capabilities of app services, and integrate developer services within the application.

For storing data in the cloud, you can use a relational data store SQL Database. SQL Database is nearly the same as the on-premise version of SQL Server. There are also some NoSQL solutions such as DocumentDB that stores JSON data, and Storage that stores blobs (for example, for images or videos) and tabular data (which is really fast and offers huge amounts of data).

Web apps can be used to host your ASP.NET MVC solution, and API Apps can be used to host your ASP. NET Web API services.

Visual Studio Online is part of the Developer Services offerings. Here you also can find Visual Studio Application Insights. With faster release cycles, it's becoming more and more important to get information about how the user uses the app. What menus are never used because the users probably don't find them? What paths in the app is the user is taking to fulfill his or her tasks? With Visual Studio Application Insights, you can get good anonymous user information to find out the issues users have with the application, and with DevOps in place you can do quick fixes.

> **NOTE** *In Chapter 20, "Diagnostics and Application Insights," you can read about tracing features and also how to use the Visual Studio Application Insights offering of Microsoft Azure. Chapter 45, "Deployment of Websites and Services," not only shows deployment to the local Internet Information Server (IIS) but also describes deployment to Microsoft Azure Web Apps.*

DEVELOPER TOOLS

This final part of the chapter, before we switch to a lot of C# code in the next chapter, covers developer tools and editions of Visual Studio 2015.

Visual Studio Community

This edition of Visual Studio is a free edition with features that the Professional edition previously had. There's a license restriction for when it can be used. It's free for open-source projects and training, and also free to academic and small professional teams. Unlike the Express editions of Visual Studio that previously have been the free editions, this product allows using add-ins with Visual Studio.

Visual Studio Professional with MSDN

This edition includes more features than the Community edition, such as the CodeLens and Team Foundation Server for source code management and team collaboration. With this edition, you also get an MSDN subscription that includes several server products from Microsoft for development and testing.

Visual Studio Enterprise with MSDN

Visual Studio 2013 had Premium and Ultimate editions. Visual Studio 2015 instead has the Enterprise edition. This edition offers Ultimate features with a Premium price model. Like the Professional edition, this edition contains a lot of tools for testing, such as Web Load & Performance Testing, Unit Test Isolation with Microsoft Fakes, and Coded UI Testing. (Unit testing is part of all Visual Studio editions.) With Code Clone you can find code clones in your solution. Visual Studio Enterprise also contains architecture and modeling tools to analyze and validate the solution architecture.

> **NOTE** *Be aware that with an MSDN subscription you're entitled to free use of Microsoft Azure up to a specific monthly amount that is contingent on the type of the MSDN subscription you have.*

> **NOTE** *Chapter 17, "Visual Studio 2015," includes details on using several features of Visual Studio 2015. Chapter 19, "Testing," gets into details of unit testing, web testing, and creating Coded UI tests.*

> **NOTE** *For some of the features in the book—for example, the Coded UI Tests —you need Visual Studio Enterprise. You can work through most parts of the book with the Visual Studio Community edition.*

Visual Studio Code

Visual Studio Code is a completely different development tool compared to the other Visual Studio editions. While Visual Studio 2015 offers project-based features with a rich set of templates and tools, Visual Studio is a code editor with little project management support. However, Visual Studio Code runs not only on Windows, but also on Linux and OS X.

With many chapters of this book, you can use Visual Studio Code as your development editor. What you can't do is create WPF, UWP, or WCF applications, and you also don't have access to the features covered in Chapter 17, "Visual Studio 2015." You can use Visual Studio Code for .NET Core console applications, and ASP.NET Core 1.0 web applications using .NET Core.

You can download Visual Studio Code from `http://code.visualstudio.com`.

SUMMARY

This chapter covered a lot of ground to review important technologies and changes with technologies. Knowing about the history of some technologies helps you decide which technology should be used with new applications and what you should do with existing applications.

You read about the differences between .NET Framework 4.6 and .NET Core 1.0, and you saw how to create and run a Hello, World application with all these environments without using Visual Studio.

You've seen the functions of the Common Language Runtime (CLR) and looked at technologies for accessing the database and creating Windows apps. You also reviewed the advantages of ASP.NET Core 1.0.

Chapter 2 steps into using Visual Studio to create the Hello, World application and goes on to discuss the syntax of C#.

2

Core C#

WHAT'S IN THIS CHAPTER?

➤ Creating Hello, World! with Visual Studio
➤ Declaring variables
➤ Initialization and scope of variables
➤ Predefined C# data types
➤ Dictating execution flow within a C# program
➤ Enumerations
➤ Namespaces
➤ The Main method
➤ Using internal comments and documentation features
➤ Preprocessor directives
➤ Guidelines and conventions for good programming in C#

WROX.COM CODE DOWNLOADS FOR THIS CHAPTER

The wrox.com code downloads for this chapter are found at www.wrox.com/go/
professionalcsharp6 on the Download Code tab. The code for this chapter is divided into the following major examples:

➤ HelloWorldApp
➤ VariablesSample
➤ VariableScopeSample
➤ IfStatement
➤ ForLoop
➤ EnumerationsSample
➤ NamespacesSample
➤ ArgumentsSample
➤ StringSample

FUNDAMENTALS OF C#

Now that you understand more about what C# can do, you need to know how to use it. This chapter gives you a good start in that direction by providing a basic understanding of the fundamentals of C# programming, which is built on in subsequent chapters. By the end of this chapter, you will know enough C# to write simple programs (though without using inheritance or other object-oriented features, which are covered in later chapters).

CREATING HELLO, WORLD! WITH VISUAL STUDIO

Chapter 1, ".NET Application Architectures," explains how to write a "Hello, World!" C# program using the `csc` Compiler for .NET 4.6 and using dotnet tools for .NET Core 1.0. You can also create it with Visual Studio 2015, which is done in this chapter.

> **NOTE** *In the first chapters of this book, Visual Studio is used as a code editor and compiler without employing all the other features of Visual Studio. Chapter 17, "Visual Studio 2015," covers more about all the other options and features offered by Visual Studio.*

Creating a Solution

First, create a solution file within Visual Studio. A solution enables you to group multiple projects and to open all the projects of a solution together.

You can create an empty solution by selecting File ➪ New Project and then selecting Installed ➪ Templates ➪ Other Project Types ➪ Visual Studio Solutions. Select the Blank Solution template (see Figure 2-1). With the New Project dialog, you can define the name of the solution as well as the directory where the solution should be stored. You can also define whether the solution should be added to a Git repository for source control management.

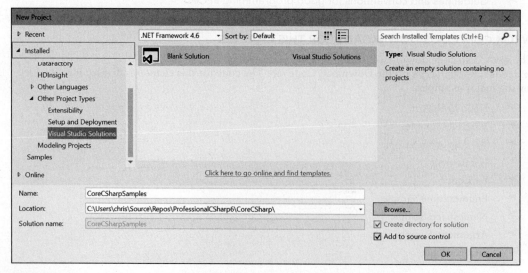

FIGURE 2-1

After creating the solution, you see the content of the solution within the Solution Explorer (see Figure 2-2). Currently, there's only a solution file without any content.

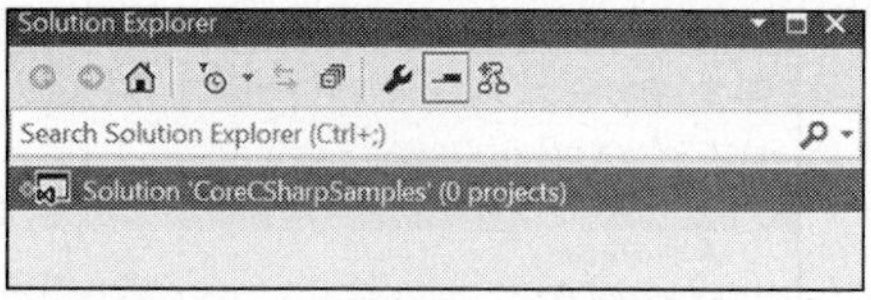

Creating a New Project

Now add a new project to create the Hello, World! app. Right-click the solution in Solution Explorer, or use the Menu button on the keyboard to open the context menu (refer to Figure 2-2), and open the application context menu and select Add ⇨ New Project to open the Add New Project dialog. Alternatively, you can select File ⇨ Add ⇨ New Project. In the Add New Project dialog, select the Console Application (Package) template to create a console application targeting .NET Core. You can find this project type in the tree within Installed ⇨ Templates ⇨ Visual C# ⇨ Web (see Figure 2-3). Set the name of the application to `HelloWorldApp`.

FIGURE 2-2

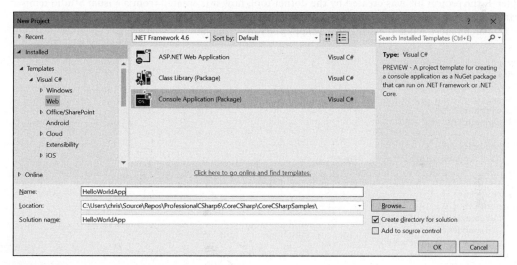

FIGURE 2-3

> **NOTE** *To open the context menu of an application, you have different options: right-click while selecting the item where the context menu should be opened (or left-click if you are left-handed), or select the item and press the menu key on the keyboard (usually located between the Alt and Ctrl keys on the right side). If your keyboard doesn't have a menu key, press Shift + F10. Lastly, if you have a touch pad, you can make a two-finger touch.*

The Solution Explorer is no longer empty. It now shows the project and all the files belonging to the project (see Figure 2-4).

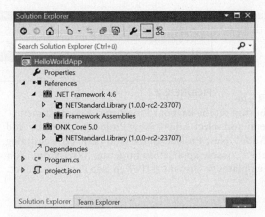

FIGURE 2-4

In Chapter 1, the project file was created by the dotnet tool, now it is created from a Visual Studio template. Two Frameworks—.NET 4.6 and .NET Core 1.0 are specified. With both frameworks, the NetStandard. Library 1.0 is referenced (code file `HelloWorldApp/project.json`):

```
{
  "version": "1.0.0-*",
  "description": "",
  "authors": [ "" ],
  "tags": [ "" ],
  "projectUrl": "",
  "licenseUrl": "",

  "dependencies": {
    "NETStandard.Library": "1.0.0-*"
  },

  "frameworks": {
    "net46": { },
    "netstandardapp1.5": {
      "dependencies": { },
      "imports": "dnxcore50"
    }
  },
  "runtimes": {
    "win7-x64": { },
    "win10-x64": { }
  }
}
```

The generated C# source file `Program.cs` contains a `Main` method within the `Program` class that itself is defined within the namespace `HelloWorldApp` (code file `HelloWorldApp/Program.cs`):

```
using System;
using System.Collections.Generic;
using System.Linq;
using System.Threading.Tasks;

namespace HelloWorldApp
{
  class Program
  {
    static void Main(string[] args)
    {
    }
  }
}
```

Change this to the Hello, World! app. You need to open the namespace for using the `WriteLine` method of the `Console` class, and you need to invoke the `WriteLine` method. You also change the namespace for the `Program` class. The `Program` class is now defined within the namespace `Wrox.HelloWorldApp` (code file `HelloWorldApp/Program.cs`):

```
using static System.Console;

namespace Wrox.HelloWorldApp
{
  class Program
  {
    static void Main()
    {
      WriteLine("Hello, World!");
    }
  }
}
```

Select the project in Solution Explorer and use the context menu to open Properties (or View ⇨ Property Pages) to open the project configuration (see Figure 2-5). On the Application tab, you can select the name of the application, the default namespace (this is only used for new items added), and the version of the .NET Core version that should be used for the solution. In case you select a version that is different from your default selection, a global.json file is created that contains this configuration setting.

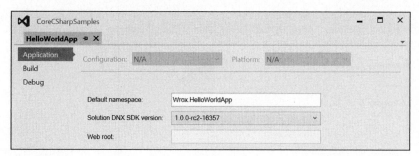

FIGURE 2-5

Compiling and Running the Program

The Build menu offers different options for building the program. You can either use Build ⇨ Build Solution to build all projects of the solution, or you can build a single project with Build ⇨ Build HelloWorldApp. Also have a look at the other options available with the Build menu.

To generate persistent files, you can check the Produce Outputs on Build option on the Build tab in the project properties (see Figure 2-6).

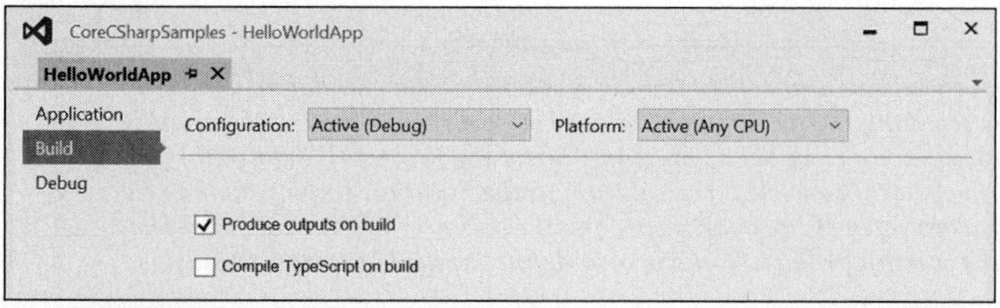

FIGURE 2-6

After building the program with the Produce Outputs on Build option selected, you can see in File Explorer the directory `artifacts` that contains subdirectories for all the supported .NET Framework versions listed with the binaries.

You can run the application from within Visual Studio by using Debug ⇨ Start Without Debugging. This starts the app as shown in Figure 2-7.

FIGURE 2-7

> **NOTE** *Be sure to not start the app with Debug ⇨ Start Debugging; if you do you will not see the output of the app because the console window immediately closes after the app completes. You can use this method to run the app either with setting breakpoints and debugging into the app, or by adding a* ReadLine *method before the end of the* Main *method.*

You can use the Debug tab in the project properties to configure the runtime version that should be used while running the app (see Figure 2-8).

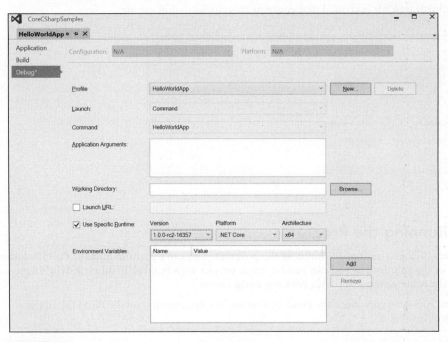

FIGURE 2-8

> **TIP** *When you have multiple projects in the same solution, you can define what project should run by selecting the project in Solution Explorer and opening the context menu. In the context menu click Set as Startup Project (or Project ⇨ Set as Startup Project). Alternatively, you can select the solution in the Solution Explorer, and select Set Startup Projects to open the property page for the solution where you can select what should be the startup project. You can also define multiple projects to start.*

Taking a Closer Look at the Code

Now let's concentrate on the C# source code. First, I have a few general comments about C# syntax. In C#, as in other C-style languages, statements end in a semicolon (;) and can continue over multiple lines without needing a continuation character. Statements can be joined into blocks using curly braces ({}). Single-line comments begin with two forward slash characters (//), and multiline comments begin with a slash and an asterisk (/*) and end with the same combination reversed (*/). In these aspects, C# is identical to C++ and Java but different from Visual Basic. It is the semicolons and curly braces that give C# code such a different visual appearance from Visual Basic code. If your background is predominantly Visual Basic, take extra care to remember the semicolon at the end of every statement. Omitting this is usually the biggest single cause of compilation errors among developers who are new to C-style languages. Another thing to remember is that C# is case sensitive. That means the variables named myVar and MyVar are two different variables.

The first few lines in the previous code example are related to *namespaces* (mentioned later in this chapter), which is a way to group associated classes. The namespace keyword declares the namespace with which your class should be associated. All code within the braces that follow it is regarded as being within that namespace. The using declaration specifies a namespace that the compiler should look at to find any classes that are referenced in your code but aren't defined in the current namespace. This serves the same purpose as the import statement in Java and the using namespace statement in C++.

```
using static System.Console;

namespace Wrox
{
```

The reason for the presence of the using static declaration in the Program.cs file is that you are going to use a library class: System.Console. The using static System.Console declaration enables you to refer to the static members of this class and omit the namespace and class names. Just declaring using System; instead, you need to add the class name for calling the WriteLine method:

```
using System;

// etc.
Console.WriteLine("Hello World!");
```

Omitting the complete using declaration, you need to add the namespace name invoking the WriteLine method:

```
System.Console.WriteLine("Hello World!");
```

The standard System namespace is where the most commonly used .NET types reside. It is important to realize that everything you do in C# depends on .NET base classes. In this case, you are using the Console class within the System namespace to write to the console window. C# has no built-in keywords of its own for input or output; it is completely reliant on the .NET classes.

> **NOTE** *Because almost every sample in this and the next chapters makes use of static members of the* Console *class, we will assume that a* using static System. Console; *statement is present in the file for all code snippets.*

Within the source code, a class called Program is declared. However, because it has been placed in a namespace called Wrox.HelloWorldApp, the fully qualified name of this class is Wrox.HelloWorldApp.Program:

```
namespace Wrox.HelloWorldApp
{
  class Program
  {
```

All C# code must be contained within a class. The class declaration consists of the `class` keyword, followed by the class name and a pair of curly braces. All code associated with the class should be placed between these braces.

The class `Program` contains a method called `Main`. Every C# executable (such as console applications, Windows applications, Windows services, and web applications) must have an entry point—the `Main` method (note the capital `M`).

```
static void Main()
{
```

The method is called when the program is started. This method must return either nothing (`void`) or an integer (`int`). Note the format of method definitions in C#:

```
[modifiers] return_type MethodName([parameters])
{
    // Method body. NB. This code block is pseudo-code.
}
```

Here, the first square brackets represent certain optional keywords. Modifiers are used to specify certain features of the method you are defining, such as from where the method can be called. In this case the `Main` method doesn't have a public access modifier applied. You can do this in case you need a unit test for the `Main` method. The runtime doesn't need the public access modifier applied, and it still can invoke the method. The `static` modifier is required as the runtime invokes the method without creating an instance of the class. The return type is set to `void`, and in the example parameters are not included.

Finally, we come to the code statement themselves:

```
WriteLine("Hello World!");
```

In this case, you simply call the `WriteLine` method of the `System.Console` class to write a line of text to the console window. `WriteLine` is a `static` method, so you don't need to instantiate a `Console` object before calling it.

Now that you have had a taste of basic C# syntax, you are ready for more detail. Because it is virtually impossible to write any nontrivial program without *variables*, we start by looking at variables in C#.

WORKING WITH VARIABLES

You declare variables in C# using the following syntax:

```
datatype identifier;
```

For example:

```
int i;
```

This statement declares an `int` named `i`. The compiler won't actually let you use this variable in an expression until you have initialized it with a value.

After it has been declared, you can assign a value to the variable using the assignment operator, `=`:

```
i = 10;
```

You can also declare the variable and initialize its value at the same time:

```
int i = 10;
```

If you declare and initialize more than one variable in a single statement, all the variables will be of the same data type:

```
int x = 10, y =20; // x and y are both ints
```

To declare variables of different types, you need to use separate statements. You cannot assign different data types within a multiple-variable declaration:

```
int x = 10;
bool y = true;              // Creates a variable that stores true or false
int x = 10, bool y = true; // This won't compile!
```

Notice the `//` and the text after it in the preceding examples. These are comments. The `//` character sequence tells the compiler to ignore the text that follows on this line because it is included for a human to better understand the program; it's not part of the program itself. Comments are explained further later in this chapter in the "Using Comments" section.

Initializing Variables

Variable initialization demonstrates an example of C#'s emphasis on safety. Briefly, the C# compiler requires that any variable be initialized with some starting value before you refer to that variable in an operation. Most modern compilers will flag violations of this as a warning, but the ever-vigilant C# compiler treats such violations as errors. This prevents you from unintentionally retrieving junk values from memory left over from other programs.

C# has two methods for ensuring that variables are initialized before use:

➤ Variables that are fields in a class or struct, if not initialized explicitly, are by default zeroed out when they are created (classes and structs are discussed later).

➤ Variables that are local to a method must be explicitly initialized in your code prior to any statements in which their values are used. In this case, the initialization doesn't have to happen when the variable is declared, but the compiler checks all possible paths through the method and flags an error if it detects any possibility of the value of a local variable being used before it is initialized.

For example, you can't do the following in C#:

```
static int Main()
{
    int d;
    WriteLine(d); // Can't do this! Need to initialize d before use
    return 0;
}
```

Notice that this code snippet demonstrates defining `Main` so that it returns an `int` instead of `void`.

If you attempt to compile the preceding lines, you receive this error message:

```
Use of unassigned local variable 'd'
```

Consider the following statement:

```
Something objSomething;
```

In C#, this line of code would create only a *reference* for a `Something` object, but this reference would not yet actually refer to any object. Any attempt to call a method or property against this variable would result in an error.

To instantiate a reference object in C#, you must use the `new` keyword. You create a reference as shown in the previous example and then point the reference at an object allocated on the heap using the `new` keyword:

```
objSomething = new Something();   // This creates a Something on the heap
```

Using Type Inference

Type inference makes use of the `var` keyword. The syntax for declaring the variable changes by using the `var` keyword instead of the real type. The compiler "infers" what the type of the variable is by what the variable is initialized to. For example:

```
var someNumber = 0;
```

becomes:

```
int someNumber = 0;
```

Even though `someNumber` is never declared as being an `int`, the compiler figures this out and `someNumber` is an `int` for as long as it is in scope. Once compiled, the two preceding statements are equal.

Here is a short program to demonstrate (code file `VariablesSample/Program.cs`):

```
using static System.Console;

namespace Wrox
{
  class Program
  {
    static void Main()
    {
      var name = "Bugs Bunny";
      var age = 25;
      var isRabbit = true;
      Type nameType = name.GetType();
      Type ageType = age.GetType();
      Type isRabbitType = isRabbit.GetType();
      WriteLine($"name is type {nameType}");
      WriteLine($"age is type {ageType}");
      WriteLine($"isRabbit is type {isRabbitType}");
    }
  }
}
```

The output from this program is as follows:

```
name is type System.String
age is type System.Int32
isRabbit is type System.Bool
```

There are a few rules that you need to follow:

➤   The variable must be initialized. Otherwise, the compiler doesn't have anything from which to infer the type.

➤   The initializer cannot be null.

➤   The initializer must be an expression.

➤   You can't set the initializer to an object unless you create a new object in the initializer.

Chapter 3, "Objects and Types," examines these rules more closely in the discussion of anonymous types.

After the variable has been declared and the type inferred, the variable's type cannot be changed. When established, the variable's type strong typing rules that any assignment to this variable must follow the inferred type.

Understanding Variable Scope

The *scope* of a variable is the region of code from which the variable can be accessed. In general, the scope is determined by the following rules:

➤   A *field* (also known as a member variable) of a class is in scope for as long as its containing class is in scope.

➤   A *local variable* is in scope until a closing brace indicates the end of the block statement or method in which it was declared.

➤   A local variable that is declared in a `for`, `while`, or similar statement is in scope in the body of that loop.

Scope Clashes for Local Variables

It's common in a large program to use the same variable name for different variables in different parts of the program. This is fine as long as the variables are scoped to completely different parts of the program so that there is no possibility for ambiguity. However, bear in mind that local variables with the same name can't be declared twice in the same scope. For example, you can't do this:

```
int x = 20;
// some more code
int x = 30;
```

Consider the following code sample (code file `VariableScopeSample/Program.cs`):

```
using static System.Console;

namespace VariableScopeSample
{
  class Program
  {
    static int Main()
    {
      for (int i = 0; i < 10; i++)
      {
        WriteLine(i);
      }  // i goes out of scope here
      // We can declare a variable named i again, because
      // there's no other variable with that name in scope
      for (int i = 9; i >= 0; i-)
      {
        WriteLine(i);
      }  // i goes out of scope here.
      return 0;
    }
  }
}
```

This code simply prints out the numbers from 0 to 9, and then back again from 9 to 0, using two `for` loops. The important thing to note is that you declare the variable `i` twice in this code, within the same method. You can do this because `i` is declared in two separate loops, so each `i` variable is local to its own loop.

Here's another example (code file `VariableScopeSample2/Program.cs`):

```
static int Main()
{
  int j = 20;
  for (int i = 0; i < 10; i++)
  {
    int j = 30; // Can't do this - j is still in scope
    WriteLine(j + i);
  }
  return 0;
}
```

If you try to compile this, you'll get an error like the following:

```
error CS0136: A local variable named 'j' cannot be declared in
this scope because that name is used in an enclosing local scope
to define a local or parameter
```

This occurs because the variable `j`, which is defined before the start of the `for` loop, is still in scope within the `for` loop and won't go out of scope until the `Main` method has finished executing. Although the second `j` (the illegal one) is in the loop's scope, that scope is nested within the `Main` method's scope. The compiler has no way to distinguish between these two variables, so it won't allow the second one to be declared.

Scope Clashes for Fields and Local Variables

In certain circumstances, however, you can distinguish between two identifiers with the same name (although not the same fully qualified name) and the same scope, and in this case the compiler allows you to declare the second variable. That's because C# makes a fundamental distinction between variables that are declared at the type level (fields) and variables that are declared within methods (local variables).

Consider the following code snippet (code file `VariableScopeSample3/Program.cs`):

```
using static System.Console;

namespace Wrox
{
  class Program
  {
    static int j = 20;
    static void Main()
    {
      int j = 30;
      WriteLine(j);
      return;
    }
  }
}
```

This code will compile even though you have two variables named `j` in scope within the `Main` method: the `j` that was defined at the class level and doesn't go out of scope until the class `Program` is destroyed (when the `Main` method terminates and the program ends), and the `j` defined within `Main`. In this case, the new variable named `j` that you declare in the `Main` method *hides* the class-level variable with the same name, so when you run this code, the number `30` is displayed.

What if you want to refer to the class-level variable? You can actually refer to fields of a class or struct from outside the object, using the syntax `object.fieldname`. In the previous example, you are accessing a static field (you find out what this means in the next section) from a static method, so you can't use an instance of the class; you just use the name of the class itself:

```
// etc.
static void Main()
{
  int j = 30;
  WriteLine(j);
  WriteLine(Program.j);
}
// etc.
```

If you are accessing an instance field (a field that belongs to a specific instance of the class), you need to use the `this` keyword instead.

Working with Constants

As the name implies, a constant is a variable whose value cannot be changed throughout its lifetime. Prefixing a variable with the `const` keyword when it is declared and initialized designates that variable as a constant:

```
const int a = 100; // This value cannot be changed.
```

Constants have the following characteristics:

➤ They must be initialized when they are declared. After a value has been assigned, it can never be overwritten.

➤ The value of a constant must be computable at compile time. Therefore, you can't initialize a constant with a value taken from a variable. If you need to do this, you must use a read-only field (this is explained in Chapter 3).

➤ Constants are always implicitly static. However, notice that you don't have to (and, in fact, are not permitted to) include the static modifier in the constant declaration.

At least three advantages exist for using constants in your programs:

➤ Constants make your programs easier to read by replacing magic numbers and strings with readable names whose values are easy to understand.

➤ Constants make your programs easier to modify. For example, assume that you have a SalesTax constant in one of your C# programs, and that constant is assigned a value of 6 percent. If the sales tax rate changes later, you can modify the behavior of all tax calculations simply by assigning a new value to the constant; you don't have to hunt through your code for the value .06 and change each one, hoping you will find all of them.

➤ Constants help prevent mistakes in your programs. If you attempt to assign another value to a constant somewhere in your program other than at the point where the constant is declared, the compiler flags the error.

USING PREDEFINED DATA TYPES

Now that you have seen how to declare variables and constants, let's take a closer look at the data types available in C#. As you will see, C# is much stricter about the types available and their definitions than some other languages.

Value Types and Reference Types

Before examining the data types in C#, it is important to understand that C# distinguishes between two categories of data type:

➤ Value types

➤ Reference types

The next few sections look in detail at the syntax for value and reference types. Conceptually, the difference is that a *value type* stores its value directly, whereas a *reference type* stores a reference to the value.

These types are stored in different places in memory; value types are stored in an area known as the *stack*, and reference types are stored in an area known as the *managed heap*. It is important to be aware of whether a type is a value type or a reference type because of the different effect each assignment has. For example, int is a value type, which means that the following statement results in two locations in memory storing the value 20:

```
// i and j are both of type int
i = 20;
j = i;
```

However, consider the following example. For this code, assume you have defined a class called Vector and that Vector is a reference type and has an int member variable called Value:

```
Vector x, y;
x = new Vector();
x.Value = 30; // Value is a field defined in Vector class
y = x;
WriteLine(y.Value);
y.Value = 50;
WriteLine(x.Value);
```

The crucial point to understand is that after executing this code, there is only one Vector object: x and y both point to the memory location that contains this object. Because x and y are variables of a reference type, declaring each variable simply reserves a reference—it doesn't instantiate an object of the given type. In neither case is an object actually created. To create an object, you have to use the new keyword, as shown. Because x and y refer to the same object, changes made to x will affect y and vice versa. Hence, the code will display 30 and then 50.

If a variable is a reference, it is possible to indicate that it does not refer to any object by setting its value to null:

```
y = null;
```

If a reference is set to null, then clearly it is not possible to call any nonstatic member functions or fields against it; doing so would cause an exception to be thrown at runtime.

In C#, basic data types such as bool and long are value types. This means that if you declare a bool variable and assign it the value of another bool variable, you will have two separate bool values in memory. Later, if you change the value of the original bool variable, the value of the second bool variable does not change. These types are copied by value.

In contrast, most of the more complex C# data types, including classes that you yourself declare, are reference types. They are allocated upon the heap, have lifetimes that can span multiple function calls, and can be accessed through one or several aliases. The CLR implements an elaborate algorithm to track which reference variables are still reachable and which have been orphaned. Periodically, the CLR destroys orphaned objects and returns the memory that they once occupied back to the operating system. This is done by the garbage collector.

C# has been designed this way because high performance is best served by keeping primitive types (such as int and bool) as value types, and larger types that contain many fields (as is usually the case with classes) as reference types. If you want to define your own type as a value type, you should declare it as a struct.

.NET Types

The C# keywords for data types—such as int, short, and string—are mapped from the compiler to .NET data types. For example, when you declare an int in C#, you are actually declaring an instance of a .NET struct: System.Int32. This might sound like a small point, but it has a profound significance: It means that you can treat all the primitive data types syntactically, as if they are classes that support certain methods. For example, to convert an int i to a string, you can write the following:

```
string s = i.ToString();
```

It should be emphasized that behind this syntactical convenience, the types really are stored as primitive types, so absolutely no performance cost is associated with the idea that the primitive types are notionally represented by .NET structs.

The following sections review the types that are recognized as built-in types in C#. Each type is listed, along with its definition and the name of the corresponding .NET type. C# has 15 predefined types, 13 value types, and 2 (string and object) reference types.

Predefined Value Types

The built-in .NET value types represent primitives, such as integer and floating-point numbers, character, and Boolean types.

Integer Types

C# supports eight predefined integer types, shown in the following table.

NAME	.NET TYPE	DESCRIPTION	RANGE (MIN:MAX)
sbyte	System.SByte	8-bit signed integer	-128:127 ($-2^7:2^7-1$)
short	System.Int16	16-bit signed integer	-32,768:32,767 ($-2^{15}:2^{15}-1$)
int	System.Int32	32-bit signed integer	-2,147,483,648:2,147,483,647 ($-2^{31}:2^{31}-1$)
long	System.Int64	64-bit signed integer	-9,223,372,036,854,775,808: 9,223,372,036,854,775,807 ($-2^{63}:2^{63}-1$)
byte	System.Byte	8-bit unsigned integer	0:255 ($0:2^8-1$)
ushort	System.UInt16	16-bit unsigned integer	0:65,535 ($0:2^{16}-1$)
uint	System.UInt32	32-bit unsigned integer	0:4,294,967,295 ($0:2^{32}-1$)
ulong	System.UInt64	64-bit unsigned integer	0:18,446,744,073,709,551,615 ($0:2^{64}-1$)

Some C# types have the same names as C++ and Java types but have different definitions. For example, in C# an int is always a 32-bit signed integer. In C++ an int is a signed integer, but the number of bits is platform-dependent (32 bits on Windows). In C#, all data types have been defined in a platform-independent manner to allow for the possible future porting of C# and .NET to other platforms.

A byte is the standard 8-bit type for values in the range 0 to 255 inclusive. Be aware that, in keeping with its emphasis on type safety, C# regards the byte type and the char type as completely distinct types, and any programmatic conversions between the two must be explicitly requested. Also be aware that unlike the other types in the integer family, a byte type is by default unsigned. Its signed version bears the special name sbyte.

With .NET, a short is no longer quite so short; it is now 16 bits long. The int type is 32 bits long. The long type reserves 64 bits for values. All integer-type variables can be assigned values in decimal or hex notation. The latter requires the 0x prefix:

```
long x = 0x12ab;
```

If there is any ambiguity about whether an integer is int, uint, long, or ulong, it defaults to an int. To specify which of the other integer types the value should take, you can append one of the following characters to the number:

```
uint ui = 1234U;
long l = 1234L;
ulong ul = 1234UL;
```

You can also use lowercase u and l, although the latter could be confused with the integer 1 (one).

Floating-Point Types

Although C# provides a plethora of integer data types, it supports floating-point types as well.

NAME	.NET TYPE	DESCRIPTION	SIGNIFICANT FIGURES	RANGE (APPROXIMATE)
float	System.Single	32-bit, single-precision floating point	7	$\pm1.5 \times 10^{245}$ to $\pm3.4 \times 10^{38}$
double	System.Double	64-bit, double-precision floating point	15/16	$\pm5.0 \times 10^{2324}$ to $\pm1.7 \times 10^{308}$

The float data type is for smaller floating-point values, for which less precision is required. The double data type is bulkier than the float data type but offers twice the precision (15 digits).

If you hard-code a non-integer number (such as 12.3), the compiler will normally assume that you want the number interpreted as a `double`. To specify that the value is a `float`, append the character F (or f) to it:

```
float f = 12.3F;
```

The Decimal Type

The `decimal` type represents higher-precision floating-point numbers, as shown in the following table.

NAME	.NET TYPE	DESCRIPTION	SIGNIFICANT FIGURES	RANGE (APPROXIMATE)
decimal	System.Decimal	128-bit, high-precision decimal notation	28	$\pm1.0 \times 10^{228}$ to $\pm7.9 \times 10^{28}$

One of the great things about the .NET and C# data types is the provision of a dedicated `decimal` type for financial calculations. How you use the 28 digits that the decimal type provides is up to you. In other words, you can track smaller dollar amounts with greater accuracy for cents or larger dollar amounts with more rounding in the fractional portion. Bear in mind, however, that `decimal` is not implemented under the hood as a primitive type, so using `decimal` has a performance effect on your calculations.

To specify that your number is a `decimal` type rather than a `double`, a `float`, or an integer, you can append the M (or m) character to the value, as shown here:

```
decimal d = 12.30M;
```

The Boolean Type

The C# `bool` type is used to contain Boolean values of either `true` or `false`.

NAME	.NET TYPE	DESCRIPTION	SIGNIFICANT FIGURES	RANGE
bool	System.Boolean	Represents true or false	NA	true or false

You cannot implicitly convert `bool` values to and from integer values. If a variable (or a function return type) is declared as a `bool`, you can only use values of `true` and `false`. You get an error if you try to use zero for `false` and a nonzero value for `true`.

The Character Type

For storing the value of a single character, C# supports the `char` data type.

NAME	.NET TYPE	VALUES
char	System.Char	Represents a single 16-bit (Unicode) character

Literals of type `char` are signified by being enclosed in single quotation marks—for example, `'A'`. If you try to enclose a character in double quotation marks, the compiler treats the character as a string and throws an error.

As well as representing `chars` as character literals, you can represent them with four-digit hex Unicode values (for example, `'\u0041'`), as integer values with a cast (for example, `(char)65`), or as hexadecimal values (for example, `'\x0041'`). You can also represent them with an escape sequence, as shown in the following table.

ESCAPE SEQUENCE	CHARACTER
\'	Single quotation mark
\"	Double quotation mark
\\	Backslash
\0	Null
\a	Alert
\b	Backspace
\f	Form feed
\n	Newline
\r	Carriage return
\t	Tab character
\v	Vertical tab

Predefined Reference Types

C# supports two predefined reference types, `object` and `string`, described in the following table.

NAME	.NET TYPE	DESCRIPTION
object	System.Object	The root type. All other types (including value types) are derived from `object`.
string	System.String	Unicode character string

The object Type

Many programming languages and class hierarchies provide a root type, from which all other objects in the hierarchy are derived. C# and .NET are no exception. In C#, the `object` type is the ultimate parent type from which all other intrinsic and user-defined types are derived. This means that you can use the `object` type for two purposes:

➤ You can use an `object` reference to bind to an object of any particular subtype. For example, in Chapter 8, "Operators and Casts," you see how you can use the `object` type to box a value object on the stack to move it to the heap; `object` references are also useful in reflection, when code must manipulate objects whose specific types are unknown.

➤ The `object` type implements a number of basic, general-purpose methods, which include `Equals`, `GetHashCode`, `GetType`, and `ToString`. Responsible user-defined classes might need to provide replacement implementations of some of these methods using an object-oriented technique known as *overriding*, which is discussed in Chapter 4, "Inheritance." When you override `ToString`, for example, you equip your class with a method for intelligently providing a string representation of itself. If you don't provide your own implementations for these methods in your classes, the compiler picks up the implementations in `object`, which might or might not be correct or sensible in the context of your classes.

You examine the `object` type in more detail in subsequent chapters.

The string Type

C# recognizes the `string` keyword, which under the hood is translated to the .NET class, `System.String`. With it, operations like string concatenation and string copying are a snap:

```
string str1 = "Hello ";
string str2 = "World";
string str3 = str1 + str2; // string concatenation
```

Despite this style of assignment, `string` is a reference type. Behind the scenes, a `string` object is allocated on the heap, not the stack; and when you assign one string variable to another string, you get two references to the same string in memory. However, `string` differs from the usual behavior for reference types. For example, strings are immutable. Making changes to one of these strings creates an entirely new `string` object, leaving the other string unchanged. Consider the following code (code file `StringSample/Program.cs`):

```
using static System.Console;

class Program
{
  static void Main()
  {
    string s1 = "a string";
    string s2 = s1;
    WriteLine("s1 is " + s1);
    WriteLine("s2 is " + s2);
    s1 = "another string";
    WriteLine("s1 is now " + s1);
    WriteLine("s2 is now " + s2);
  }
}
```

The output from this is as follows:

```
s1 is a string
s2 is a string
s1 is now another string
s2 is now a string
```

Changing the value of `s1` has no effect on `s2`, contrary to what you'd expect with a reference type! What's happening here is that when `s1` is initialized with the value `a string`, a new string object is allocated on the heap. When `s2` is initialized, the reference points to this same object, so `s2` also has the value `a string`. However, when you now change the value of `s1`, instead of replacing the original value, a new object is allocated on the heap for the new value. The `s2` variable still points to the original object, so its value is unchanged. Under the hood, this happens as a result of operator overloading, a topic that is explored in Chapter 8. In general, the `string` class has been implemented so that its semantics follow what you would normally intuitively expect for a string.

String literals are enclosed in double quotation marks (`". "`); if you attempt to enclose a string in single quotation marks, the compiler takes the value as a `char` and throws an error. C# strings can contain the same Unicode and hexadecimal escape sequences as `chars`. Because these escape sequences start with a backslash, you can't use this character unescaped in a string. Instead, you need to escape it with two backslashes (`\\`):

```
string filepath = "C:\\ProCSharp\\First.cs";
```

Even if you are confident that you can remember to do this all the time, typing all those double backslashes can prove annoying. Fortunately, C# gives you an alternative. You can prefix a string literal with the at character (@) and all the characters after it are treated at face value; they aren't interpreted as escape sequences:

```
string filepath = @"C:\ProCSharp\First.cs";
```

This even enables you to include line breaks in your string literals:

```
string jabberwocky = @"'Twas brillig and the slithy toves
Did gyre and gimble in the wabe.";
```

In this case, the value of `jabberwocky` would be this:

```
'Twas brillig and the slithy toves
Did gyre and gimble in the wabe.
```

C# 6 defines a new string interpolation format that is marked by using the $ prefix. You've previously seen this prefix in the section "Working with Variables." You can change the earlier code snippet that demonstrated string concatenation to use the string interpolation format. Prefixing a string with $ enables you to put curly braces into the string that contains a variable—or even a code expression. The result of the variable or code expression is put into the string at the position of the curly braces:

```
public static void Main()
{
  string s1 = "a string";
  string s2 = s1;
  WriteLine($"s1 is {s1}");
  WriteLine($"s2 is {s2}");
  s1 = "another string";
  WriteLine($"s1 is now {s1}");
  WriteLine($"s2 is now {s2}");
}
```

> **NOTE** *Strings and the features of string interpolation are covered in detail in Chapter 10, "Strings and Regular Expressions."*

CONTROLLING PROGRAM FLOW

This section looks at the real nuts and bolts of the language: the statements that allow you to control the *flow* of your program rather than execute every line of code in the order it appears in the program.

Conditional Statements

Conditional statements enable you to branch your code depending on whether certain conditions are met or what the value of an expression is. C# has two constructs for branching code: the `if` statement, which tests whether a specific condition is met, and the `switch` statement, which compares an expression with several different values.

The if Statement

For conditional branching, C# inherits the C and C++ `if.else` construct. The syntax should be fairly intuitive for anyone who has done any programming with a procedural language:

```
if (condition)
  statement(s)
else
  statement(s)
```

If more than one statement is to be executed as part of either condition, these statements need to be joined into a block using curly braces ({ . }). (This also applies to other C# constructs where statements can be joined into a block, such as the `for` and `while` loops):

```
bool isZero;
if (i == 0)
{
  isZero = true;
  WriteLine("i is Zero");
}
else
{
  isZero = false;
  WriteLine("i is Non-zero");
}
```

If you want to, you can use an if statement without a final else statement. You can also combine else if clauses to test for multiple conditions (code file IfStatement/Program.cs):

```
using static System.Console;

namespace Wrox
{
  class Program
  {
    static void Main()
    {
      WriteLine("Type in a string");
      string input;
      input = ReadLine();
      if (input == "")
      {
        WriteLine("You typed in an empty string.");
      }
      else if (input.Length < 5)
      {
        WriteLine("The string had less than 5 characters.");
      }
      else if (input.Length < 10)
      {
        WriteLine("The string had at least 5 but less than 10 Characters.");
      }
      WriteLine("The string was " + input);
    }
  }
}
```

There is no limit to how many else ifs you can add to an if clause.

Note that the previous example declares a string variable called input, gets the user to enter text at the command line, feeds this into input, and then tests the length of this string variable. The code also shows how easy string manipulation can be in C#. To find the length of input, for example, use input.Length.

Another point to note about the if statement is that you don't need to use the braces when there's only one statement in the conditional branch:

```
if (i == 0)
    WriteLine("i is Zero");       // This will only execute if i == 0
WriteLine("i can be anything");  // Will execute whatever the
                                 // value of i
```

However, for consistency, many programmers prefer to use curly braces whenever they use an if statement.

> **TIP** *Not using curly braces with if statements can lead to errors in maintaining the code. It happens too often that a second statement is added to the if statement that runs no matter whether the if returns true or false. Using curly braces every time avoids this coding error.*
>
> *A good guideline in regard to the if statement is to allow programmers to not use curly braces only when the statement is written in the same line as the if statement. With this guideline, programmers are less likely to add a second statement without adding curly braces.*

The if statements presented also illustrate some of the C# operators that compare values. Note in particular that C# uses == to compare variables for equality. Do not use = for this purpose. A single = is used to assign values.

In C#, the expression in the if clause must evaluate to a Boolean. It is not possible to test an integer directly (returned from a function, for example). You have to convert the integer that is returned to a Boolean true or false, for example, by comparing the value with zero or null:

```
if (DoSomething() != 0)
{
    // Non-zero value returned
}
else
{
    // Returned zero
}
```

The switch Statement

The switch / case statement is good for selecting one branch of execution from a set of mutually exclusive ones. It takes the form of a switch argument followed by a series of case clauses. When the expression in the switch argument evaluates to one of the values beside a case clause, the code immediately following the case clause executes. This is one example for which you don't need to use curly braces to join statements into blocks; instead, you mark the end of the code for each case using the break statement. You can also include a default case in the switch statement, which executes if the expression doesn't evaluate to any of the other cases. The following switch statement tests the value of the integerA variable:

```
switch (integerA)
{
  case 1:
    WriteLine("integerA = 1");
    break;
  case 2:
    WriteLine("integerA = 2");
    break;
  case 3:
    WriteLine("integerA = 3");
    break;
  default:
    WriteLine("integerA is not 1, 2, or 3");
    break;
}
```

Note that the case values must be constant expressions; variables are not permitted.

Though the switch.case statement should be familiar to C and C++ programmers, C#'s switch.case is a bit safer than its C++ equivalent. Specifically, it prohibits fall-through conditions in almost all cases. This means that if a case clause is fired early on in the block, later clauses cannot be fired unless you use a goto statement to indicate that you want them fired, too. The compiler enforces this restriction by flagging every case clause that is not equipped with a break statement as an error:

```
Control cannot fall through from one case label ('case 2:') to another
```

Although it is true that fall-through behavior is desirable in a limited number of situations, in the vast majority of cases it is unintended and results in a logical error that's hard to spot. Isn't it better to code for the norm rather than for the exception?

By getting creative with goto statements, you can duplicate fall-through functionality in your switch. cases. However, if you find yourself really wanting to, you probably should reconsider your approach.

The following code illustrates both how to use `goto` to simulate fall-through, and how messy the resultant code can be:

```
// assume country and language are of type string
switch(country)
{
  case "America":
    CallAmericanOnlyMethod();
    goto case "Britain";
  case "France":
    language = "French";
    break;
  case "Britain":
    language = "English";
    break;
}
```

There is one exception to the no-fall-through rule, however, in that you can fall through from one case to the next if that case is empty. This allows you to treat two or more cases in an identical way (without the need for `goto` statements):

```
switch(country)
{
  case "au":
  case "uk":
  case "us":
    language = "English";
    break;
  case "at":
  case "de":
    language = "German";
    break;
}
```

One intriguing point about the `switch` statement in C# is that the order of the cases doesn't matter—you can even put the `default` case first! As a result, no two cases can be the same. This includes different constants that have the same value, so you can't, for example, do this:

```
// assume country is of type string
const string england = "uk";
const string britain = "uk";
switch(country)
{
  case england:
  case britain:      // This will cause a compilation error.
    language = "English";
    break;
}
```

The previous code also shows another way in which the `switch` statement is different in C# compared to C++: In C#, you are allowed to use a string as the variable being tested.

Loops

C# provides four different loops (`for`, `while`, `do. . .while`, and `foreach`) that enable you to execute a block of code repeatedly until a certain condition is met.

The for Loop

C# `for` loops provide a mechanism for iterating through a loop whereby you test whether a particular condition holds true before you perform another iteration. The syntax is

```
for (initializer; condition; iterator):
    statement(s)
```

where:

➤ The *initializer* is the expression evaluated before the first loop is executed (usually initializing a local variable as a loop counter).

➤ The *condition* is the expression checked before each new iteration of the loop (this must evaluate to true for another iteration to be performed).

➤ The *iterator* is an expression evaluated after each iteration (usually incrementing the loop counter).

The iterations end when the condition evaluates to false.

The for loop is a so-called pretest loop because the loop condition is evaluated before the loop statements are executed; therefore, the contents of the loop won't be executed at all if the loop condition is false.

The for loop is excellent for repeating a statement or a block of statements for a predetermined number of times. The following example demonstrates typical usage of a for loop. It writes out all the integers from 0 to 99:

```
for (int i = 0; i < 100; i = i + 1)
{
   WriteLine(i);
}
```

Here, you declare an int called i and initialize it to zero. This is used as the loop counter. You then immediately test whether it is less than 100. Because this condition evaluates to true, you execute the code in the loop, displaying the value 0. You then increment the counter by one, and walk through the process again. Looping ends when i reaches 100.

Actually, the way the preceding loop is written isn't quite how you would normally write it. C# has a shorthand for adding 1 to a variable, so instead of i = i + 1, you can simply write i++:

```
for (int i = 0; i < 100; i++)
{
   // etc.
}
```

You can also make use of type inference for the iteration variable i in the preceding example. Using type inference, the loop construct would be as follows:

```
for (var i = 0; i < 100; i++)
{
   // etc.
}
```

It's not unusual to nest for loops so that an inner loop executes once completely for each iteration of an outer loop. This approach is typically employed to loop through every element in a rectangular multidimensional array. The outermost loop loops through every row, and the inner loop loops through every column in a particular row. The following code displays rows of numbers. It also uses another Console method, Console.Write, which does the same thing as Console.WriteLine but doesn't send a carriage return to the output (code file ForLoop/Program.cs):

```
using static System.Console;

namespace Wrox
{
  class Program
  {
    static void Main()
    {
      // This loop iterates through rows
      for (int i = 0; i < 100; i+=10)
```

```
        {
            // This loop iterates through columns
            for (int j = i; j < i + 10; j++)
            {
                Write($"  {j}");
            }
            WriteLine();
        }
    }
}
```

Although j is an integer, it is automatically converted to a string so that the concatenation can take place.

The preceding sample results in this output:

```
 0  1  2  3  4  5  6  7  8  9
10 11 12 13 14 15 16 17 18 19
20 21 22 23 24 25 26 27 28 29
30 31 32 33 34 35 36 37 38 39
40 41 42 43 44 45 46 47 48 49
50 51 52 53 54 55 56 57 58 59
60 61 62 63 64 65 66 67 68 69
70 71 72 73 74 75 76 77 78 79
80 81 82 83 84 85 86 87 88 89
90 91 92 93 94 95 96 97 98 99
```

It is technically possible to evaluate something other than a counter variable in a for loop's test condition, but it is certainly not typical. It is also possible to omit one (or even all) of the expressions in the for loop. In such situations, however, you should consider using the while loop.

The while Loop

Like the for loop, while is a pretest loop. The syntax is similar, but while loops take only one expression:

```
while(condition)
    statement(s);
```

Unlike the for loop, the while loop is most often used to repeat a statement or a block of statements for a number of times that is not known before the loop begins. Usually, a statement inside the while loop's body will set a Boolean flag to false on a certain iteration, triggering the end of the loop, as in the following example:

```
bool condition = false;
while (!condition)
{
    // This loop spins until the condition is true.
    DoSomeWork();
    condition = CheckCondition();   // assume CheckCondition() returns a bool
}
```

The do. . .while Loop

The do. . .while loop is the post-test version of the while loop. This means that the loop's test condition is evaluated after the body of the loop has been executed. Consequently, do. . .while loops are useful for situations in which a block of statements must be executed at least one time, as in this example:

```
bool condition;
do
{
    // This loop will at least execute once, even if Condition is false.
    MustBeCalledAtLeastOnce();
    condition = CheckCondition();
} while (condition);
```

The foreach Loop

The `foreach` loop enables you to iterate through each item in a collection. For now, don't worry about exactly what a collection is (it is explained fully in Chapter 11, "Collections"); just understand that it is an object that represents a list of objects. Technically, for an object to count as a collection, it must support an interface called `IEnumerable`. Examples of collections include C# arrays, the collection classes in the `System.Collections` namespaces, and user-defined collection classes. You can get an idea of the syntax of `foreach` from the following code, if you assume that `arrayOfInts` is (unsurprisingly) an array of ints:

```
foreach (int temp in arrayOfInts)
{
   WriteLine(temp);
}
```

Here, `foreach` steps through the array one element at a time. With each element, it places the value of the element in the `int` variable called `temp` and then performs an iteration of the loop.

Here is another situation where you can use type inference. The `foreach` loop would become the following:

```
foreach (var temp in arrayOfInts)
{
   // etc.
}
```

`temp` would be inferred to `int` because that is what the collection item type is.

An important point to note with `foreach` is that you can't change the value of the item in the collection (`temp` in the preceding code), so code such as the following will not compile:

```
foreach (int temp in arrayOfInts)
{
   temp++;
   WriteLine(temp);
}
```

If you need to iterate through the items in a collection and change their values, you must use a `for` loop instead.

Jump Statements

C# provides a number of statements that enable you to jump immediately to another line in the program. The first of these is, of course, the notorious `goto` statement.

The goto Statement

The `goto` statement enables you to jump directly to another specified line in the program, indicated by a *label* (this is just an identifier followed by a colon):

```
goto Label1;
   WriteLine("This won't be executed");
Label1:
   WriteLine("Continuing execution from here");
```

A couple of restrictions are involved with `goto`. You can't jump into a block of code such as a `for` loop, you can't jump out of a class, and you can't exit a `finally` block after `try...catch` blocks (Chapter 14, "Errors and Exceptions," looks at exception handling with `try.catch.finally`).

The reputation of the `goto` statement probably precedes it, and in most circumstances, its use is sternly frowned upon. In general, it certainly doesn't conform to good object-oriented programming practices.

The break Statement

You have already met the break statement briefly—when you used it to exit from a case in a switch statement. In fact, break can also be used to exit from for, foreach, while, or do...while loops. Control switches to the statement immediately after the end of the loop.

If the statement occurs in a nested loop, control switches to the end of the innermost loop. If the break occurs outside a switch statement or a loop, a compile-time error occurs.

The continue Statement

The continue statement is similar to break, and you must use it within a for, foreach, while, or do...while loop. However, it exits only from the current iteration of the loop, meaning that execution restarts at the beginning of the next iteration of the loop rather than restarting outside the loop altogether.

The return Statement

The return statement is used to exit a method of a class, returning control to the caller of the method. If the method has a return type, return must return a value of this type; otherwise, if the method returns void, you should use return without an expression.

WORKING WITH ENUMERATIONS

An *enumeration* is a user-defined integer type. When you declare an enumeration, you specify a set of acceptable values that instances of that enumeration can contain. Not only that, but you can also give the values user-friendly names. If, somewhere in your code, you attempt to assign a value that is not in the acceptable set of values to an instance of that enumeration, the compiler flags an error.

Creating an enumeration can save you a lot of time and headaches in the long run. At least three benefits exist to using enumerations instead of plain integers:

➤ As mentioned, enumerations make your code easier to maintain by helping to ensure that your variables are assigned only legitimate, anticipated values.

➤ Enumerations make your code clearer by allowing you to refer to integer values by descriptive names rather than by obscure "magic" numbers.

➤ Enumerations make your code easier to type. When you begin to assign a value to an instance of an enumerated type, Visual Studio 2015 uses IntelliSense to pop up a list box of acceptable values to save you some keystrokes and remind you of the possible options.

You can define an enumeration as follows:

```
public enum TimeOfDay
{
  Morning = 0,
  Afternoon = 1,
  Evening = 2
}
```

In this case, you use an integer value to represent each period of the day in the enumeration. You can now access these values as members of the enumeration. For example, TimeOfDay.Morning returns the value 0. You will typically use this enumeration to pass an appropriate value into a method and iterate through the possible values in a switch statement (code file EnumerationSample/Program.cs):

```
class Program
{
  static void Main()
  {
    WriteGreeting(TimeOfDay.Morning);
```

```
            }

            static void WriteGreeting(TimeOfDay timeOfDay)
            {
                switch(timeOfDay)
                {
                    case TimeOfDay.Morning:
                        WriteLine("Good morning!");
                        break;
                    case TimeOfDay.Afternoon:
                        WriteLine("Good afternoon!");
                        break;
                    case TimeOfDay.Evening:
                        WriteLine("Good evening!");
                        break;
                    default:
                        WriteLine("Hello!");
                        break;
                }
            }
        }
```

The real power of enums in C# is that behind the scenes they are instantiated as structs derived from the base class—System.Enum. This means it is possible to call methods against them to perform some useful tasks. Note that because of the way the .NET Framework is implemented, no performance loss is associated with treating the enums syntactically as structs. In practice, after your code is compiled, enums exist as primitive types, just like int and float.

You can retrieve the string representation of an enum, as in the following example, using the earlier TimeOfDay enum:

```
TimeOfDay time = TimeOfDay.Afternoon;
WriteLine(time.ToString());
```

This returns the string Afternoon.

Alternatively, you can obtain an enum value from a string:

```
TimeOfDay time2 = (TimeOfDay) Enum.Parse(typeof(TimeOfDay), "afternoon", true);
WriteLine((int)time2);
```

The preceding code snippet illustrates both obtaining an enum value from a string and converting to an integer. To convert from a string, you need to use the static Enum.Parse method, which, as shown, takes three parameters. The first is the type of enum you want to consider. The syntax is the keyword typeof followed by the name of the enum class in brackets. (Chapter 8 explores the typeof operator in more detail.) The second parameter is the string to be converted, and the third parameter is a bool indicating whether case should be ignored while the conversion is done. Finally, note that Enum.Parse actually returns an object reference—you need to explicitly convert this to the required enum type (this is an example of an unboxing operation). For the preceding code, this returns the value 1 as an object, corresponding to the enum value of TimeOfDay.Afternoon. Converting explicitly to an int, this produces the value 1 again.

Other methods on System.Enum do things such as return the number of values in an enum definition or list the names of the values. Full details are in the MSDN documentation.

GETTING ORGANIZED WITH NAMESPACES

As discussed earlier in this chapter, namespaces provide a way to organize related classes and other types. Unlike a file or a component, a namespace is a logical, rather than a physical, grouping. When you define a class in a C# file, you can include it within a namespace definition. Later, when you define another class that performs related work in another file, you can include it within the same namespace, creating a logical grouping that indicates to other developers using the classes how they are related and used:

```
using System;

namespace CustomerPhoneBookApp
{
  public struct Subscriber
  {
    // Code for struct here..
  }
}
```

Placing a type in a namespace effectively gives that type a long name, consisting of the type's namespace as a series of names separated with periods (.), terminating with the name of the class. In the preceding example, the full name of the Subscriber struct is CustomerPhoneBookApp.Subscriber. This enables distinct classes with the same short name to be used within the same program without ambiguity. This full name is often called the *fully qualified name*.

You can also nest namespaces within other namespaces, creating a hierarchical structure for your types:

```
namespace Wrox
{
  namespace ProCSharp
  {
    namespace Basics
    {
      class NamespaceExample
      {
        // Code for the class here..
      }
    }
  }
}
```

Each namespace name is composed of the names of the namespaces it resides within, separated with periods, starting with the outermost namespace and ending with its own short name. Therefore, the full name for the ProCSharp namespace is Wrox.ProCSharp, and the full name of the NamespaceExample class is Wrox.ProCSharp.Basics.NamespaceExample.

You can use this syntax to organize the namespaces in your namespace definitions too, so the previous code could also be written as follows:

```
namespace Wrox.ProCSharp.Basics
{
  class NamespaceExample
  {
    // Code for the class here..
  }
}
```

Note that you are not permitted to declare a multipart namespace nested within another namespace.

Namespaces are not related to assemblies. It is perfectly acceptable to have different namespaces in the same assembly or to define types in the same namespace in different assemblies.

You should define the namespace hierarchy prior to starting a project. Generally the accepted format is CompanyName.ProjectName.SystemSection. In the previous example, Wrox is the company name, ProCSharp is the project, and in the case of this chapter, Basics is the section.

The using Directive

Obviously, namespaces can grow rather long and tiresome to type, and the capability to indicate a particular class with such specificity may not always be necessary. Fortunately, as noted earlier in this chapter, C#

allows you to abbreviate a class's full name. To do this, list the class's namespace at the top of the file, prefixed with the `using` keyword. Throughout the rest of the file, you can refer to the types in the namespace simply by their type names:

```
using System;
using Wrox.ProCSharp;
```

As mentioned earlier, many C# files have the statement `using System;` simply because so many useful classes supplied by Microsoft are contained in the `System` namespace.

If two namespaces referenced by `using` statements contain a type of the same name, you need to use the full (or at least a longer) form of the name to ensure that the compiler knows which type to access. For example, suppose classes called `NamespaceExample` exist in both the `Wrox.ProCSharp.Basics` and `Wrox.ProCSharp.OOP` namespaces. If you then create a class called `Test` in the `Wrox.ProCSharp` namespace, and instantiate one of the `NamespaceExample` classes in this class, you need to specify which of these two classes you're talking about:

```
using Wrox.ProCSharp.OOP;
using Wrox.ProCSharp.Basics;

namespace Wrox.ProCSharp
{
  class Test
  {
    static void Main()
    {
      Basics.NamespaceExample nSEx = new Basics.NamespaceExample();
      // do something with the nSEx variable.
    }
  }
}
```

Your organization will probably want to spend some time developing a namespace convention so that its developers can quickly locate functionality that they need and so that the names of the organization's home-grown classes won't conflict with those in off-the-shelf class libraries. Guidelines on establishing your own namespace convention, along with other naming recommendations, are discussed later in this chapter.

Namespace Aliases

Another use of the `using` keyword is to assign aliases to classes and namespaces. If you need to refer to a very long namespace name several times in your code but don't want to include it in a simple `using` statement (for example, to avoid type name conflicts), you can assign an alias to the namespace. The syntax for this is as follows:

```
using alias = NamespaceName;
```

The following example (a modified version of the previous example) assigns the alias `Introduction` to the `Wrox.ProCSharp.Basics` namespace and uses this to instantiate a `NamespaceExample` object, which is defined in this namespace. Notice the use of the namespace alias qualifier (`::`). This forces the search to start with the `Introduction` namespace alias. If a class called `Introduction` had been introduced in the same scope, a conflict would occur. The `::` operator enables the alias to be referenced even if the conflict exists. The `NamespaceExample` class has one method, `GetNamespace`, which uses the `GetType` method exposed by every class to access a `Type` object representing the class's type. You use this object to return a name of the class's namespace (code file `NamespaceSample/Program.cs`):

```
using Introduction = Wrox.ProCSharp.Basics;
using static System.Console;

class Program
{
  static void Main()
  {
```

```
      Introduction::NamespaceExample NSEx =
         new Introduction::NamespaceExample();
      WriteLine(NSEx.GetNamespace());
   }
}

namespace Wrox.ProCSharp.Basics
{
   class NamespaceExample
   {
      public string GetNamespace()
      {
         return this.GetType().Namespace;
      }
   }
}
```

UNDERSTANDING THE MAIN METHOD

As described at the beginning of this chapter, C# programs start execution at a method named Main. Depending on the execution environment there are different requirements.

➤ Have a static modifier applied

➤ Be in a class with any name

➤ Return a type of int or void

Although it is common to specify the public modifier explicitly—because by definition the method must be called from outside the program—it doesn't actually matter what accessibility level you assign to the entry-point method; it will run even if you mark the method as private.

The examples so far have shown only the Main method without any parameters. However, when the program is invoked, you can get the CLR to pass any command-line arguments to the program by including a parameter. This parameter is a string array, traditionally called args (although C# accepts any name). The program can use this array to access any options passed through the command line when the program is started.

The following example loops through the string array passed in to the Main method and writes the value of each option to the console window (code file ArgumentsSample/Program.cs):

```
using System;
using static System.Console;

namespace Wrox
{
   class Program
   {
      static void Main(string[] args)
      {
         for (int i = 0; i < args.Length; i++)
         {
            WriteLine(args[i]);
         }
      }
   }
}
```

For passing arguments to the program when running the application from Visual Studio 2015, you can define the arguments in the Debug section of the project properties as shown in Figure 2-9. Running the application reveals the result to show all argument values to the console.

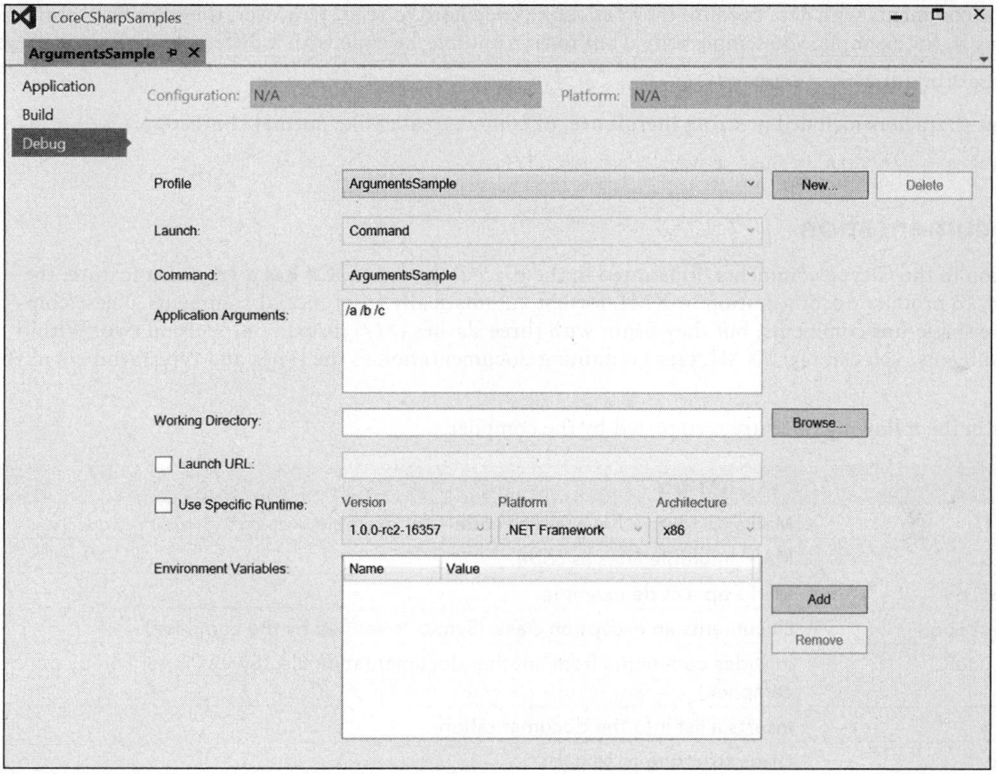

FIGURE 2-9

USING COMMENTS

The next topic—adding comments to your code—looks very simple on the surface, but it can be complex. Comments can be beneficial to other developers who may look at your code. Also, as you will see, you can use comments to generate documentation of your code for other developers to use.

Internal Comments Within the Source Files

As noted earlier in this chapter, C# uses the traditional C-type single-line (`//..`) and multiline (`/* .. */`) comments:

```
// This is a single-line comment
/* This comment
   spans multiple lines. */
```

Everything in a single-line comment, from the `//` to the end of the line, is ignored by the compiler, and everything from an opening `/*` to the next `*/` in a multiline comment combination is ignored. Obviously, you can't include the combination `*/` in any multiline comments, because this will be treated as the end of the comment.

It is possible to put multiline comments within a line of code:

```
WriteLine(/* Here's a comment! */ "This will compile.");
```

Use inline comments with care because they can make code hard to read. However, they can be useful when debugging if, for example, you temporarily want to try running the code with a different value somewhere:

```
DoSomething(Width, /*Height*/ 100);
```

Comment characters included in string literals are, of course, treated like normal characters:

```
string s = "/* This is just a normal string .*/";
```

XML Documentation

In addition to the C-type comments, illustrated in the preceding section, C# has a very neat feature: the capability to produce documentation in XML format automatically from special comments. These comments are single-line comments, but they begin with three slashes (///) instead of the usual two. Within these comments, you can place XML tags containing documentation of the types and type members in your code.

The tags in the following table are recognized by the compiler.

TAG	DESCRIPTION
`<c>`	Marks up text within a line as code—for example, `<c>int i = 10;</c>`.
`<code>`	Marks multiple lines as code.
`<example>`	Marks up a code example.
`<exception>`	Documents an exception class. (Syntax is verified by the compiler.)
`<include>`	Includes comments from another documentation file. (Syntax is verified by the compiler.)
`<list>`	Inserts a list into the documentation.
`<para>`	Gives structure to text.
`<param>`	Marks up a method parameter. (Syntax is verified by the compiler.)
`<paramref>`	Indicates that a word is a method parameter. (Syntax is verified by the compiler.)
`<permission>`	Documents access to a member. (Syntax is verified by the compiler.)
`<remarks>`	Adds a description for a member.
`<returns>`	Documents the return value for a method.
`<see>`	Provides a cross-reference to another parameter. (Syntax is verified by the compiler.)
`<seealso>`	Provides a "see also" section in a description. (Syntax is verified by the compiler.)
`<summary>`	Provides a short summary of a type or member.
`<typeparam>`	Describes a type parameter in the comment of a generic type.
`<typeparamref>`	Provides the name of the type parameter.
`<value>`	Describes a property.

Add some XML comments to the `Calculator.cs` file from the previous section. You add a `<summary>` element for the class and for its `Add` method, and a `<returns>` element and two `<param>` elements for the `Add` method:

```
// MathLib.cs
namespace Wrox.MathLib
{
  ///<summary>
  ///   Wrox.MathLib.Calculator class.
  ///   Provides a method to add two doublies.
  ///</summary>
  public class Calculator
```

```
        {
            ///<summary>
            ///    The Add method allows us to add two doubles.
            ///</summary>
            ///<returns>Result of the addition (double)</returns>
            ///<param name="x">First number to add</param>
            ///<param name="y">Second number to add</param>
            public static double Add(double x, double y) => x + y;
        }
    }
```

UNDERSTANDING C# PREPROCESSOR DIRECTIVES

Besides the usual keywords, most of which you have now encountered, C# also includes a number of commands that are known as *preprocessor directives*. These commands are never actually translated to any commands in your executable code, but they affect aspects of the compilation process. For example, you can use preprocessor directives to prevent the compiler from compiling certain portions of your code. You might do this if you are planning to release two versions of it—a basic version and an enterprise version that will have more features. You could use preprocessor directives to prevent the compiler from compiling code related to the additional features when you are compiling the basic version of the software. In another scenario, you might have written bits of code that are intended to provide you with debugging information. You probably don't want those portions of code compiled when you actually ship the software.

The preprocessor directives are all distinguished by beginning with the # symbol.

> **NOTE** C++ *developers will recognize the preprocessor directives as something that plays an important part in C and C++. However, there aren't as many preprocessor directives in C#, and they are not used as often. C# provides other mechanisms, such as custom attributes, that achieve some of the same effects as C++ directives. Also, note that C# doesn't actually have a separate preprocessor in the way that C++ does. The so-called preprocessor directives are actually handled by the compiler. Nevertheless, C# retains the name preprocessor directive because these commands give the impression of a preprocessor.*

The following sections briefly cover the purposes of the preprocessor directives.

#define and #undef

#define is used like this:

```
#define DEBUG
```

This tells the compiler that a symbol with the given name (in this case DEBUG) exists. It is a little bit like declaring a variable, except that this variable doesn't really have a value—it just exists. Also, this symbol isn't part of your actual code; it exists only for the benefit of the compiler, while the compiler is compiling the code, and has no meaning within the C# code itself.

#undef does the opposite, and removes the definition of a symbol:

```
#undef DEBUG
```

If the symbol doesn't exist in the first place, then #undef has no effect. Similarly, #define has no effect if a symbol already exists.

You need to place any #define and #undef directives at the beginning of the C# source file, before any code that declares any objects to be compiled.

#define isn't much use on its own, but when combined with other preprocessor directives, especially #if, it becomes very powerful.

> **NOTE** *Incidentally, you might notice some changes from the usual C# syntax. Preprocessor directives are not terminated by semicolons and they normally constitute the only command on a line. That's because for the preprocessor directives, C# abandons its usual practice of requiring commands to be separated by semicolons. If the compiler sees a preprocessor directive, it assumes that the next command is on the next line.*

#if, #elif, #else, and #endif

These directives inform the compiler whether to compile a block of code. Consider this method:

```
int DoSomeWork(double x)
{
  // do something
  #if DEBUG
    WriteLine($"x is {x}");
  #endif
}
```

This code compiles as normal except for the Console.WriteLine method call contained inside the #if clause. This line is executed only if the symbol DEBUG has been defined by a previous #define directive. When the compiler finds the #if directive, it checks to see whether the symbol concerned exists, and compiles the code inside the #if clause only if the symbol does exist. Otherwise, the compiler simply ignores all the code until it reaches the matching #endif directive. Typical practice is to define the symbol DEBUG while you are debugging and have various bits of debugging-related code inside #if clauses. Then, when you are close to shipping, you simply comment out the #define directive, and all the debugging code miraculously disappears, the size of the executable file gets smaller, and your end users don't get confused by seeing debugging information. (Obviously, you would do more testing to ensure that your code still works without DEBUG defined.) This technique is very common in C and C++ programming and is known as *conditional compilation*.

The #elif (=else if) and #else directives can be used in #if blocks and have intuitively obvious meanings. It is also possible to nest #if blocks:

```
#define ENTERPRISE
#define W10
// further on in the file
#if ENTERPRISE
    // do something
    #if W10
        // some code that is only relevant to enterprise
        // edition running on W10
    #endif
#elif PROFESSIONAL
    // do something else
#else
    // code for the leaner version
#endif
```

#if and #elif support a limited range of logical operators too, using the operators !, ==, !=, and ||. A symbol is considered to be true if it exists and false if it doesn't. For example:

```
#if W10 && (ENTERPRISE==false) // if W10 is defined but ENTERPRISE isn't
```

#warning and #error

Two other very useful preprocessor directives are #warning and #error. These will respectively cause a warning or an error to be raised when the compiler encounters them. If the compiler sees a #warning directive, it displays whatever text appears after the #warning to the user, after which compilation continues. If it encounters a #error directive, it displays the subsequent text to the user as if it is a compilation error message and then immediately abandons the compilation, so no IL code is generated.

You can use these directives as checks that you haven't done anything silly with your #define statements; you can also use the #warning statements to remind yourself to do something:

```
#if DEBUG && RELEASE
   #error "You've defined DEBUG and RELEASE simultaneously!"
#endif
#warning "Don't forget to remove this line before the boss tests the code!"
   WriteLine("*I hate this job.*");
```

#region and #endregion

The #region and #endregion directives are used to indicate that a certain block of code is to be treated as a single block with a given name, like this:

```
#region Member Field Declarations
   int x;
   double d;
   Currency balance;
#endregion
```

This doesn't look that useful by itself; it doesn't affect the compilation process in any way. However, the real advantage is that these directives are recognized by some editors, including the Visual Studio editor. These editors can use the directives to lay out your code better on the screen. You find out how this works in Chapter 17.

#line

The #line directive can be used to alter the filename and line number information that is output by the compiler in warnings and error messages. You probably won't want to use this directive very often. It's most useful when you are coding in conjunction with another package that alters the code you are typing before sending it to the compiler. In this situation, line numbers, or perhaps the filenames reported by the compiler, don't match up to the line numbers in the files or the filenames you are editing. The #line directive can be used to restore the match. You can also use the syntax #line default to restore the line to the default line numbering:

```
#line 164 "Core.cs"    // We happen to know this is line 164 in the file
                       // Core.cs, before the intermediate
                       // package mangles it.
// later on
#line default          // restores default line numbering
```

#pragma

The #pragma directive can either suppress or restore specific compiler warnings. Unlike command-line options, the #pragma directive can be implemented on the class or method level, enabling fine-grained control over what warnings are suppressed and when. The following example disables the "field not used" warning and then restores it after the `MyClass` class compiles:

```
#pragma warning disable 169
public class MyClass
{
   int neverUsedField;
}
#pragma warning restore 169
```

C# PROGRAMMING GUIDELINES

This final section of the chapter supplies the guidelines you need to bear in mind when writing C# programs. These are guidelines that most C# developers use. When you use these guidelines, other developers will feel comfortable working with your code.

Rules for Identifiers

This section examines the rules governing what names you can use for variables, classes, methods, and so on. Note that the rules presented in this section are not merely guidelines: they are enforced by the C# compiler.

Identifiers are the names you give to variables, to user-defined types such as classes and structs, and to members of these types. Identifiers are case sensitive, so, for example, variables named `interestRate` and `InterestRate` would be recognized as different variables. Following are a few rules determining what identifiers you can use in C#:

➤   They must begin with a letter or underscore, although they can contain numeric characters.

➤   You can't use C# keywords as identifiers.

The following table lists the C# reserved keywords.

abstract	event	new	struct
as	explicit	null	switch
base	extern	object	this
bool	false	operator	throw
break	finally	out	true
byte	fixed	override	try
case	float	params	typeof
catch	for	private	uint
char	foreach	protected	ulong
checked	goto	public	unchecked
class	if	readonly	unsafe
const	implicit	ref	ushort
continue	in	return	using
decimal	int	sbyte	virtual
default	interface	sealed	void
delegate	internal	short	volatile
do	is	sizeof	while
double	lock	stackalloc	
else	long	static	
enum	namespace	string	

If you need to use one of these words as an identifier (for example, if you are accessing a class written in a different language), you can prefix the identifier with the @ symbol to indicate to the compiler that what follows should be treated as an identifier, not as a C# keyword (so abstract is not a valid identifier, but @abstract is).

Finally, identifiers can also contain Unicode characters, specified using the syntax \u*XXXX*, where *XXXX* is the four-digit hex code for the Unicode character. The following are some examples of valid identifiers:

➤ Name

➤ Überfluß

➤ _Identifier

➤ \u005fIdentifier

The last two items in this list are identical and interchangeable (because 005f is the Unicode code for the underscore character), so obviously these identifiers couldn't both be declared in the same scope. Note that although syntactically you are allowed to use the underscore character in identifiers, this isn't recommended in most situations. That's because it doesn't follow the guidelines for naming variables that Microsoft has written to ensure that developers use the same conventions, making it easier to read one another's code.

> **NOTE** *You might wonder why some newer keywords added with the recent versions of C# are not in the list of reserved keywords. The reason is that if they had been added to the list of reserved keywords, it would have broken existing code that already made use of the new C# keywords. The solution was to enhance the syntax by defining these keywords as contextual keywords; they can be used only in some specific code places. For example, the* async *keyword can be used only with a method declaration, and it is okay to use it as a variable name. The compiler doesn't have a conflict with that.*

Usage Conventions

In any development language, certain traditional programming styles usually arise. The styles are not part of the language itself but rather are conventions—for example, how variables are named or how certain classes, methods, or functions are used. If most developers using that language follow the same conventions, it makes it easier for different developers to understand each other's code—which in turn generally helps program maintainability. Conventions do, however, depend on the language and the environment. For example, C++ developers programming on the Windows platform have traditionally used the prefixes psz or lpsz to indicate strings—char *pszResult; char *lpszMessage;—but on Unix machines it's more common not to use any such prefixes: char *Result; char *Message;.

Notice from the sample code in this book that the convention in C# is to name variables without prefixes: string Result; string Message;.

> **NOTE** *The convention by which variable names are prefixed with letters that represent the data type is known as Hungarian notation. It means that other developers reading the code can immediately tell from the variable name what data type the variable represents. Hungarian notation is widely regarded as redundant in these days of smart editors and IntelliSense.*

Whereas many languages' usage conventions simply evolved as the language was used, for C# and the whole of the .NET Framework, Microsoft has written very comprehensive usage guidelines, which are detailed in the .NET/C# MSDN documentation. This means that, right from the start, .NET programs have a high degree of interoperability in terms of developers being able to understand code. The guidelines have also been developed with the benefit of some 20 years' hindsight in object-oriented programming. Judging by the relevant newsgroups, the guidelines have been carefully thought out and are well received in the developer community. Hence, the guidelines are well worth following.

Note, however, that the guidelines are not the same as language specifications. You should try to follow the guidelines when you can. Nevertheless, you won't run into problems if you have a good reason for not doing so—for example, you won't get a compilation error because you don't follow these guidelines. The general rule is that if you don't follow the usage guidelines, you must have a convincing reason. When you depart from the guidelines you should be making a conscious decision rather than simply not bothering. Also, if you compare the guidelines with the samples in the remainder of this book, you'll notice that in numerous examples I have chosen not to follow the conventions. That's usually because the conventions are designed for much larger programs than the samples; although the guidelines are great if you are writing a complete software package, they are not really suitable for small 20-line standalone programs. In many cases, following the conventions would have made the samples harder, rather than easier, to follow.

The full guidelines for good programming style are quite extensive. This section is confined to describing some of the more important guidelines, as well as those most likely to surprise you. To be absolutely certain that your code follows the usage guidelines completely, you need to refer to the MSDN documentation.

Naming Conventions

One important aspect of making your programs understandable is how you choose to name your items—and that includes naming variables, methods, classes, enumerations, and namespaces.

It is intuitively obvious that your names should reflect the purpose of the item and should not clash with other names. The general philosophy in the .NET Framework is also that the name of a variable should reflect the purpose of that variable instance and not the data type. For example, `height` is a good name for a variable, whereas `integerValue` isn't. However, you are likely to find that principle is an ideal that is hard to achieve. Particularly when you are dealing with controls, in most cases you'll probably be happier sticking with variable names such as `confirmationDialog` and `chooseEmployeeListBox`, which do indicate the data type in the name.

The following sections look at some of the things you need to think about when choosing names.

Casing of Names

In many cases you should use *Pascal casing* for names. With Pascal casing, the first letter of each word in a name is capitalized: `EmployeeSalary`, `ConfirmationDialog`, `PlainTextEncoding`. Notice that nearly all the names of namespaces, classes, and members in the base classes follow Pascal casing. In particular, the convention of joining words using the underscore character is discouraged. Therefore, try not to use names such as `employee_salary`. It has also been common in other languages to use all capitals for names of constants. This is not advised in C# because such names are harder to read—the convention is to use Pascal casing throughout:

```
const int MaximumLength;
```

The only other casing convention that you are advised to use is *camel casing*. Camel casing is similar to Pascal casing, except that the first letter of the first word in the name is not capitalized: `employeeSalary`, `confirmationDialog`, `plainTextEncoding`. Following are three situations in which you are advised to use camel casing:

➤   For names of all private member fields in types:

```
private int subscriberId;
```

Note, however, that often it is conventional to prefix names of member fields with an underscore:

```
private int _subscriberId;
```

➤ For names of all parameters passed to methods:

```
public void RecordSale(string salesmanName, int quantity);
```

➤ To distinguish items that would otherwise have the same name. A common example is when a property wraps around a field:

```
private string employeeName;
public string EmployeeName
{
    get
    {
        return employeeName;
    }
}
```

If you are wrapping a property around a field, you should always use camel casing for the private member and Pascal casing for the public or protected member, so that other classes that use your code see only names in Pascal case (except for parameter names).

You should also be wary about case sensitivity. C# is case sensitive, so it is syntactically correct for names in C# to differ only by the case, as in the previous examples. However, bear in mind that your assemblies might at some point be called from Visual Basic applications—and *Visual Basic is not case sensitive*. Hence, if you do use names that differ only by case, it is important to do so only in situations in which both names will never be seen outside your assembly. (The previous example qualifies as okay because camel case is used with the name that is attached to a `private` variable.) Otherwise, you may prevent other code written in Visual Basic from being able to use your assembly correctly.

Name Styles

Be consistent about your style of names. For example, if one of the methods in a class is called `ShowConfirmationDialog`, then you should not give another method a name such as `ShowDialogWarning` or `WarningDialogShow`. The other method should be called `ShowWarningDialog`.

Namespace Names

It is particularly important to choose Namespace names carefully to avoid the risk of ending up with the same name for one of your namespaces as someone else uses. Remember, namespace names are the *only* way that .NET distinguishes names of objects in shared assemblies. Therefore, if you use the same namespace name for your software package as another package, and both packages are used by the same program, problems will occur. Because of this, it's almost always a good idea to create a top-level namespace with the name of your company and then nest successive namespaces that narrow down the technology, group, or department you are working in or the name of the package for which your classes are intended. Microsoft recommends namespace names that begin with `<CompanyName>.<TechnologyName>`, as in these two examples:

```
WeaponsOfDestructionCorp.RayGunControllers
WeaponsOfDestructionCorp.Viruses
```

Names and Keywords

It is important that the names do not clash with any keywords. In fact, if you attempt to name an item in your code with a word that happens to be a C# keyword, you'll almost certainly get a syntax error because the compiler will assume that the name refers to a statement. However, because of the possibility that your classes will be accessed by code written in other languages, it is also important that you don't use names that are keywords in other .NET languages. Generally speaking, C++ keywords are similar to C# keywords, so confusion with C++ is unlikely, and those commonly encountered keywords that are unique to Visual

C++ tend to start with two underscore characters. As with C#, C++ keywords are spelled in lowercase, so if you hold to the convention of naming your public classes and members with Pascal-style names, they will always have at least one uppercase letter in their names, and there will be no risk of clashes with C++ keywords. However, you are more likely to have problems with Visual Basic, which has many more keywords than C# does, and being non-case-sensitive means that you cannot rely on Pascal-style names for your classes and methods.

Check the MSDN documentation at `http://msdn.microsoft.com/library`. In Development Tools and Languages, C# reference, you find a long list of C# keywords that you shouldn't use with classes and members. Also check the list of Visual Basic keywords if Visual Basic could be used as a language accessing your classes.

Use of Properties and Methods

One area that can cause confusion regarding a class is whether a particular quantity should be represented by a property or a method. The rules are not hard and fast, but in general you should use a property if something should look and behave like a variable. (If you're not sure what a property is, see Chapter 3.) This means, among other things, that

➤ Client code should be able to read its value. Write-only properties are not recommended, so, for example, use a `SetPassword` method, not a write-only `Password` property.

➤ Reading the value should not take too long. The fact that something is a property usually suggests that reading it will be relatively quick.

➤ Reading the value should not have any observable and unexpected side effect. Furthermore, setting the value of a property should not have any side effect that is not directly related to the property. Setting the width of a dialog has the obvious effect of changing the appearance of the dialog on the screen. That's fine, because that's obviously related to the property in question.

➤ It should be possible to set properties in any order. In particular, it is not good practice when setting a property to throw an exception because another related property has not yet been set. For example, to use a class that accesses a database, you need to set `ConnectionString`, `UserName`, and `Password`, and then the author of the class should ensure that the class is implemented such that users can set them in any order.

➤ Successive reads of a property should give the same result. If the value of a property is likely to change unpredictably, you should code it as a method instead. `Speed`, in a class that monitors the motion of an automobile, is not a good candidate for a property. Use a `GetSpeed` method here; but `Weight` and `EngineSize` are good candidates for properties because they will not change for a given object.

If the item you are coding satisfies all the preceding criteria, it is probably a good candidate for a property. Otherwise, you should use a method.

Use of Fields

The guidelines are pretty simple here. Fields should almost always be private, although in some cases it may be acceptable for constant or read-only fields to be public. Making a field public may hinder your ability to extend or modify the class in the future.

The previous guidelines should give you a foundation of good practices, and you should use them in conjunction with a good object-oriented programming style.

A final helpful note to keep in mind is that Microsoft has been relatively careful about being consistent and has followed its own guidelines when writing the .NET base classes, so a very good way to get an intuitive feel for the conventions to follow when writing .NET code is to simply look at the base classes—see how classes, members, and namespaces are named, and how the class hierarchy works. Consistency between the base classes and your classes will facilitate readability and maintainability.

SUMMARY

This chapter examined some of the basic syntax of C#, covering the areas needed to write simple C# programs. We covered a lot of ground, but much of it will be instantly recognizable to developers who are familiar with any C-style language (or even JavaScript).

You have seen that although C# syntax is similar to C++ and Java syntax, there are many minor differences. You have also seen that in many areas this syntax is combined with facilities to write code very quickly—for example, high-quality string handling facilities. C# also has a strongly defined type system, based on a distinction between value and reference types. Chapters 3 and 4 cover the C# object-oriented programming features.

3

Objects and Types

WHAT'S IN THIS CHAPTER?

- ➤ The differences between classes and structs
- ➤ Class members
- ➤ Expression-bodied members
- ➤ Passing values by value and by reference
- ➤ Method overloading
- ➤ Constructors and static constructors
- ➤ Read-only fields
- ➤ Enumerations
- ➤ Partial classes
- ➤ Static classes
- ➤ The Object class, from which all other types are derived

WROX.COM CODE DOWNLOADS FOR THIS CHAPTER

The wrox.com code downloads for this chapter are found at www.wrox.com/go/professionalcsharp6 on the Download Code tab. The code for this chapter is divided into the following major examples:

- ➤ MathSample
- ➤ MethodSample
- ➤ StaticConstructorSample
- ➤ StructsSample
- ➤ PassingByValueAndByReference
- ➤ OutKeywordSample
- ➤ EnumSample
- ➤ ExtensionMethods

CREATING AND USING CLASSES

So far, you've been introduced to some of the building blocks of the C# language, including variables, data types, and program flow statements, and you have seen a few very short complete programs containing little more than the Main method. What you haven't seen yet is how to put all these elements together to form a longer, complete program. The key to this lies in working with classes—the subject of this chapter. Note Chapter 4, "Inheritance," covers inheritance and features related to inheritance.

> **NOTE** *This chapter introduces the basic syntax associated with classes. However, we assume that you are already familiar with the underlying principles of using classes— for example, that you know what a constructor or a property is. This chapter is largely confined to applying those principles in C# code.*

CLASSES AND STRUCTS

Classes and structs are essentially templates from which you can create objects. Each object contains data and has methods to manipulate and access that data. The class defines what data and behavior each particular object (called an *instance*) of that class can contain. For example, if you have a class that represents a customer, it might define fields such as CustomerID, FirstName, LastName, and Address, which are used to hold information about a particular customer. It might also define functionality that acts upon the data stored in these fields. You can then instantiate an object of this class to represent one specific customer, set the field values for that instance, and use its functionality:

```
class PhoneCustomer
{
  public const string DayOfSendingBill = "Monday";
  public int CustomerID;
  public string FirstName;
  public string LastName;
}
```

Structs differ from classes because they do not need to be allocated on the heap (classes are reference types and are always allocated on the heap). Structs are value types and are usually stored on the stack. Also, structs cannot derive from a base struct.

You typically use structs for smaller data types for performance reasons. In terms of syntax, however, structs look very similar to classes; the main difference is that you use the keyword struct instead of class to declare them. For example, if you wanted all PhoneCustomer instances to be allocated on the stack instead of the managed heap, you could write the following:

```
struct PhoneCustomerStruct
{
  public const string DayOfSendingBill = "Monday";
  public int CustomerID;
  public string FirstName;
  public string LastName;
}
```

For both classes and structs, you use the keyword new to declare an instance. This keyword creates the object and initializes it; in the following example, the default behavior is to zero out its fields:

```
var myCustomer = new PhoneCustomer();        // works for a class
var myCustomer2 = new PhoneCustomerStruct();// works for a struct
```

In most cases, you use classes much more often than structs. Therefore, this chapter covers classes first and then the differences between classes and structs and the specific reasons why you might choose to use a struct instead of a class. Unless otherwise stated, however, you can assume that code presented for a class works equally well for a struct.

> **NOTE** *An important difference between classes and structs is that objects of type of class are passed by reference, and objects of type of a struct are passed by value. This is explained later in this chapter in the section "Passing Parameters by Value and by Reference."*

CLASSES

A class contains members, which can be static or instance members. A static member belongs to the class; an instance member belongs to the object. With static fields, the value of the field is the same for every object. With instance fields, every object can have a different value. Static members have the static modifier attached.

The kind of members are explained in the following table.

MEMBER	DESCRIPTION
Fields	A field is a data member of a class. It is a variable of a type that is a member of a class.
Constants	Constants are associated with the class (although they do not have the static modifier). The compiler replaces constants everywhere they are used with the real value.
Methods	Methods are functions associated with a particular class.
Properties	Properties are sets of functions that can be accessed from the client in a similar way to the public fields of the class. C# provides a specific syntax for implementing read and write properties on your classes, so you don't have to use method names that are prefixed with the words Get or Set. Because there's a dedicated syntax for properties that is distinct from that for normal functions, the illusion of objects as actual things is strengthened for client code.
Constructors	Constructors are special functions that are called automatically when an object is instantiated. They must have the same name as the class to which they belong and cannot have a return type. Constructors are useful for initialization.
Indexers	Indexers allow your object to be accessed the same way as arrays. Indexers are explained in Chapter 8, "Operators and Casts."
Operators	Operators, at their simplest, are actions such as + or –. When you add two integers, you are, strictly speaking, using the + operator for integers. C# also allows you to specify how existing operators will work with your own classes (operator overloading). Chapter 8 looks at operators in detail.
Events	Events are class members that allow an object to notify a subscriber whenever something noteworthy happens, such as a field or property of the class changing, or some form of user interaction occurring. The client can have code, known as an event handler, that reacts to the event. Chapter 9, "Delegates, Lambdas, and Events," looks at events in detail.
Destructors	The syntax of destructors or finalizers is similar to the syntax for constructors, but they are called when the CLR detects that an object is no longer needed. They have the same name as the class, preceded by a tilde (~). It is impossible to predict precisely when a finalizer will be called. Finalizers are discussed in Chapter 5, "Managed and Unmanaged Resources."
Types	Classes can contain inner classes. This is interesting if the inner type is only used in conjunction with the outer type.

Let's get into the details of class members.

Fields

Fields are any variables associated with the class. You have already seen fields in use in the PhoneCustomer class in the previous example.

After you have instantiated a PhoneCustomer object, you can then access these fields using the object.FieldName syntax, as shown in this example:

```
var customer1 = new PhoneCustomer();
customer1.FirstName = "Simon";
```

Constants can be associated with classes in the same way as variables. You declare a constant using the const keyword. If it is declared as public, then it is accessible from outside the class:

```
class PhoneCustomer
{
    public const string DayOfSendingBill = "Monday";
    public int CustomerID;
    public string FirstName;
    public string LastName;
}
```

It's a good idea *not* to declare fields public. If you change a public member of a class, every caller that's using this public member needs to be changed as well. For example, in case you want to introduce a check for the maximum string length with the next version, the public field needs to be changed to a property. Existing code that makes use of the public field must be recompiled for using this property (although the syntax from the caller side looks the same with properties). If instead you just change the check within an existing property, the caller doesn't need to be recompiled for using the new version.

It's good practice to declare fields private and use properties to access the field, as described in the next section.

Properties

The idea of a *property* is that it is a method or a pair of methods dressed to look like a field. Let's change the field for the first name from the previous example to a private field with the variable name _firstName. The property named FirstName contains a get and set accessor to retrieve and set the value of the backing field:

```
class PhoneCustomer
{
    private string _firstName;
    public string FirstName
    {
        get { return _firstName; }
        set { firstName = value; }
    }
    // etc.
}
```

The get accessor takes no parameters and must return the same type as the declared property. You should not specify any explicit parameters for the set accessor either, but the compiler assumes it takes one parameter, which is of the same type again, and which is referred to as value.

Let's get into another example with a different naming convention. The following code contains a property called Age, which sets a field called age. In this example, age is referred to as the backing variable for the property Age:

```
private int age;
public int Age
```

```
{
    get { return age; }
    set { age = value; }
}
```

Note the naming convention used here. You take advantage of C#'s case sensitivity by using the same name—Pascal-case for the public property, and camel-case for the equivalent private field if there is one. In earlier .NET versions, this naming convention was preferred by Microsoft's C# team. Recently they switched to the naming convention to prefix field names by an underscore. This provides an extremely convenient way to identify fields in contrast to local variables.

> **NOTE** *Microsoft teams use either one or the other naming convention. For using private members of types, .NET doesn't have strict naming conventions. However, within a team the same convention should be used. The .NET Core team switched to using an underscore to prefix fields, which is the convention used in this book in most places (see* `https://github.com/dotnet/corefx/blob/master/Documentation/coding-guidelines/coding-style.md`*).*

Auto-Implemented Properties

If there isn't going to be any logic in the properties `set` and `get`, then auto-implemented properties can be used. Auto-implemented properties implement the backing member variable automatically. The code for the earlier `Age` example would look like this:

```
public int Age { get; set; }
```

The declaration of a private field is not needed. The compiler creates this automatically. With auto-implemented properties, you cannot access the field directly as you don't know the name the compiler generates.

By using auto-implemented properties, validation of the property cannot be done at the property set. Therefore, with the `Age` property you could not have checked to see if an invalid age is set.

Auto-implemented properties can be initialized using a *property initializer*:

```
public int Age { get; set; } = 42;
```

Access Modifiers for Properties

C# allows the `set` and `get` accessors to have differing access modifiers. This would allow a property to have a public `get` and a private or protected `set`. This can help control how or when a property can be set. In the following code example, notice that the `set` has a private access modifier but the `get` does not. In this case, the `get` takes the access level of the property. One of the accessors must follow the access level of the property. A compile error is generated if the `get` accessor has the `protected` access level associated with it because that would make both accessors have a different access level from the property.

```
public string Name
{
    get
    {
        return _name;
    }
    private set
    {
        _name = value;
    }
}
```

Different access levels can also be set with auto-implemented properties:

```
public int Age { get; private set; }
```

> **NOTE** *You can also define properties that only have a* get *or* set *accessor. Before creating a property with only a* set *accessor, it's a good practice to create a method instead. You can use properties with only a* get *accessor for read-only access. Auto-implemented properties with only* get *accessors are new with C# 6 and discussed in the section "Readonly Members."*

> **NOTE** *Some developers may be concerned that the previous sections have presented a number of situations in which standard C# coding practices have led to very small functions—for example, accessing a field via a property instead of directly. Will this hurt performance because of the overhead of the extra function call? The answer is no. There's no need to worry about performance loss from these kinds of program-ming methodologies in C#. Recall that C# code is compiled to IL, then JIT compiled at runtime to native executable code. The JIT compiler is designed to generate highly optimized code and will ruthlessly inline code as appropriate (in other words, it replaces function calls with inline code). A method or property whose implementation simply calls another method or returns a field will almost certainly be inlined.*
>
> *Usually you do not need to change the inlining behavior, but you have some control to inform the compiler about inlining. Using the attribute* MethodImpl*, you can define that a method should not be inlined (*MethodImplOptions.NoInlining*), or inlining should be done aggressively by the compiler (*MethodImplOptions. AggressiveInlining*). With properties, you need to apply this attribute directly to the* get *and* set *accessors. Attributes are explained in detail in Chapter 16, "Reflection, Metadata, and Dynamic Programming."*

Methods

Note that official C# terminology makes a distinction between functions and methods. In C# terminology, the term "function member" includes not only methods, but also other nondata members of a class or struct. This includes indexers, operators, constructors, destructors, and—perhaps somewhat surprisingly—properties. These are contrasted with data members: fields, constants, and events.

Declaring Methods

In C#, the definition of a method consists of any method modifiers (such as the method's accessibility), fol-lowed by the type of the return value, followed by the name of the method, followed by a list of input argu-ments enclosed in parentheses, followed by the body of the method enclosed in curly braces:

```
[modifiers] return_type MethodName([parameters])
{
  // Method body
}
```

Each parameter consists of the name of the type of the parameter, and the name by which it can be refer-enced in the body of the method. Also, if the method returns a value, a return statement must be used with the return value to indicate each exit point, as shown in this example:

```
public bool IsSquare(Rectangle rect)
{
  return (rect.Height == rect.Width);
}
```

If the method doesn't return anything, specify a return type of void because you can't omit the return type altogether; and if it takes no arguments, you still need to include an empty set of parentheses after the method name. In this case, including a return statement is optional—the method returns automatically when the closing curly brace is reached.

Expression-Bodied Methods

If the implementation of a method consists just of one statement, C# 6 gives a simplified syntax to method definitions: *expression-bodied methods*. You don't need to write curly brackets and the return keyword with the new syntax. The operator => (the lambda operator) is used to distinguish the declaration of the left side of this operator to the implementation that is on the right side.

The following example is the same method as before, IsSquare, implemented using the expression-bodied method syntax. The right side of the lambda operator defines the implementation of the method. Curly brackets and a return statement are not needed. What's returned is the result of the statement, and the result needs to be of the same type as the method declared on the left side, which is a bool in this code snippet:

```
public bool IsSquare(Rectangle rect) => rect.Height == rect.Width;
```

Invoking Methods

The following example illustrates the syntax for definition and instantiation of classes, and definition and invocation of methods. The class Math defines instance and static members (code file MathSample/Math.cs):

```
public class Math
{
  public int Value { get; set; }

  public int GetSquare() => Value * Value;

  public static int GetSquareOf(int x) => x * x;

  public static double GetPi() => 3.14159;

}
```

The Program class makes use of the Math class, calls static methods, and instantiates an object to invoke instance members (code file MathSample/Program.cs);

```
using static System.Console;

namespace MathSample
{
  class Program
  {
    static void Main()
    {
      // Try calling some static functions.
      WriteLine($"Pi is {Math.GetPi()}");
      int x = Math.GetSquareOf(5);
      WriteLine($"Square of 5 is {x}");

      // Instantiate a Math object
      var math = new Math();   // instantiate a reference type

      // Call instance members
      math.Value = 30;
      WriteLine($"Value field of math variable contains {math.Value}");
      WriteLine($"Square of 30 is {math.GetSquare()}");
    }
  }
}
```

Running the `MathSample` example produces the following results:

```
Pi is 3.14159
Square of 5 is 25
Value field of math variable contains 30
Square of 30 is 900
```

As you can see from the code, the `Math` class contains a property that contains a number, as well as a method to find the square of this number. It also contains two static methods: one to return the value of pi and one to find the square of the number passed in as a parameter.

Some features of this class are not really good examples of C# program design. For example, `GetPi` would usually be implemented as a `const` field, but following good design would mean using some concepts that have not yet been introduced.

Method Overloading

C# supports method overloading—several versions of the method that have different signatures (that is, the same name but a different number of parameters and/or different parameter data types). To overload methods, simply declare the methods with the same name but different numbers of parameter types:

```
class ResultDisplayer
{
  public void DisplayResult(string result)
  {
    // implementation
  }

  public void DisplayResult(int result)
  {
    // implementation
  }
}
```

It's not just the parameter types that can differ; the number of parameters can differ too, as shown in the next example. One overloaded method can invoke another:

```
class MyClass
{
  public int DoSomething(int x)
  {
    return DoSomething(x, 10); // invoke DoSomething with two parameters
  }

  public int DoSomething(int x, int y)
  {
    // implementation
  }
}
```

> **NOTE** *With method overloading, it is not sufficient to only differ overloads by the return type. It's also not sufficient to differ by parameter names. The number of parameters and/or types needs to difffer.*

Named Arguments

Invoking methods, the variable name need not be added to the invocation. However, if you have a method signature like the following to move a rectangle

```
public void MoveAndResize(int x, int y, int width, int height)
```

and you invoke it with the following code snippet, it's not clear from the invocation what numbers are used for what:

```
r.MoveAndResize(30, 40, 20, 40);
```

You can change the invocation to make it immediately clear what the numbers mean:

```
r.MoveAndResize(x: 30, y: 40, width: 20, height: 40);
```

Any method can be invoked using named arguments. You just need to write the name of the variable followed by a colon and the value passed. The compiler gets rid of the name and creates an invocation of the method just like the variable name would not be there—so there's no difference within the compiled code.

You can also change the order of variables this way, and the compiler rearranges it to the correct order. The real advantage to this is shown in the next section with optional arguments.

Optional Arguments

Parameters can also be optional. You must supply a default value for optional parameters, which must be the last ones defined:

```
public void TestMethod(int notOptionalNumber, int optionalNumber = 42)
{
    WriteLine(optionalNumber + notOptionalNumber);
}
```

This method can now be invoked using one or two parameters. Passing one parameter, the compiler changes the method call to pass 42 with the second parameter.

```
TestMethod(11);
TestMethod(11, 22);
```

> **NOTE** *Because the compiler changes methods with optional parameters to pass the default value, the default value should never change with newer versions of the assembly. With a change of the default value in a newer version, if the caller is in a different assembly that is not recompiled, it would have the older default value. That's why you should have optional parameters only with values that never change. In case the calling method is always recompiled when the default value changes, this is not an issue.*

You can define multiple optional parameters, as shown here:

```
public void TestMethod(int n, int opt1 = 11, int opt2 = 22, int opt3 = 33)
{
    WriteLine(n + opt1 + opt2 + opt3);
}
```

This way, the method can be called using 1, 2, 3, or 4 parameters. The first line of the following code leaves the optional parameters with the values 11, 22, and 33. The second line passes the first three parameters, and the last one has a value of 33:

```
TestMethod(1);
TestMethod(1, 2, 3);
```

With multiple optional parameters, the feature of named arguments shines. Using named arguments you can pass any of the optional parameters—for example, this example passes just the last one:

```
TestMethod(1, opt3: 4);
```

> **NOTE** *Pay attention to versioning issues when using optional arguments. One issue is to change default values in newer versions; another issue is to change the number of arguments. It might look tempting to add another optional parameter as it is optional anyway. However, the compiler changes the calling code to fill in all the parameters, and that's the reason earlier compiled callers fail if another parameter is added later on.*

Variable Number of Arguments

Using optional arguments, you can define a variable number of arguments. However, there's also a different syntax that allows passing a variable number of arguments—and this syntax doesn't have versioning issues.

Declaring the parameter of type array—the sample code uses an int array—and adding the params keyword, the method can be invoked using any number of int parameters.

```
public void AnyNumberOfArguments(params int[] data)
{
  foreach (var x in data)
  {
    WriteLine(x);
  }
}
```

> **NOTE** *Arrays are explained in detail in Chapter 7, "Arrays and Tuples."*

As the parameter of the method AnyNumberOfArguments is of type int[], you can pass an int array, or because of the params keyword, you can pass one or any number of int values:

```
AnyNumberOfArguments(1);
AnyNumberOfArguments(1, 3, 5, 7, 11, 13);
```

If arguments of different types should be passed to methods, you can use an object array:

```
public void AnyNumberOfArguments(params object[] data)
{
  // etc.
```

Now it is possible to use any type calling this method:

```
AnyNumberOfArguments("text", 42);
```

If the params keyword is used with multiple parameters that are defined with the method signature, params can be used only once, and it must be the last parameter:

```
WriteLine(string format, params object[] arg);
```

Now that you've looked at the many aspects of methods, let's get into constructors, which are a special kind of methods.

Constructors

The syntax for declaring basic constructors is a method that has the same name as the containing class and that does not have any return type:

```
public class MyClass
{
  public MyClass()
```

```
    {
    }
    // rest of class definition
```

It's not necessary to provide a constructor for your class. We haven't supplied one for any of the examples so far in this book. In general, if you don't supply any constructor, the compiler generates a default one behind the scenes. It will be a very basic constructor that initializes all the member fields by zeroing them out (null reference for reference types, zero for numeric data types, and false for bools). Often, that is adequate; if not, you need to write your own constructor.

Constructors follow the same rules for overloading as other methods—that is, you can provide as many overloads to the constructor as you want, provided they are clearly different in signature:

```
public MyClass()    // zeroparameter constructor
{
  // construction code
}

public MyClass(int number)    // another overload
{
  // construction code
}
```

However, if you supply any constructors that take parameters, the compiler does not automatically supply a default one. This is done only if you have not defined any constructors at all. In the following example, because a one-parameter constructor is defined, the compiler assumes that this is the only constructor you want to be available, so it does not implicitly supply any others:

```
public class MyNumber
{
  private int _number;
  public MyNumber(int number)
  {
    _number = number;
  }
}
```

If you now try instantiating a MyNumber object using a no-parameter constructor, you get a compilation error:

```
var numb = new MyNumber();    // causes compilation error
```

Note that it is possible to define constructors as private or protected, so that they are invisible to code in unrelated classes too:

```
public class MyNumber
{
  private int _number;
  private MyNumber(int number)    // another overload
  {
    _number = number;
  }
}
```

This example hasn't actually defined any public, or even any protected, constructors for MyNumber. This would actually make it impossible for MyNumber to be instantiated by outside code using the new operator (though you might write a public static property or method in MyNumber that can instantiate the class). This is useful in two situations:

➤ If your class serves only as a container for some static members or properties, and therefore should never be instantiated. With this scenario, you can declare the class with the modifier static. With this modifier the class can contain only static members and cannot be instantiated.

➤ If you want the class to only ever be instantiated by calling a static member function (this is the so-called factory pattern approach to object instantiation). An implementation of the Singleton pattern is shown in the following code snippet.

```
public class Singleton
{
    private static Singleton s_instance;

    private int _state;
    private Singleton(int state)
    {
        _state = state;
    }

    public static Singleton Instance
    {
        get { return s_instance ?? (s_instance = new MySingleton(42); }
    }
}
```

The `Singleton` class contains a private constructor, so you can instantiate it only within the class itself. To instantiate it, the static property `Instance` returns the field `s_instance`. If this field is not yet initialized (`null`), a new instance is created by calling the instance constructor. For the null check, the coalescing operator is used. If the left side of this operator is null, the right side of this operator is processed and the instance constructor invoked.

> **NOTE** *The coalescing operator is explained in detail in Chapter 8.*

Calling Constructors from Other Constructors

You might sometimes find yourself in the situation where you have several constructors in a class, perhaps to accommodate some optional parameters for which the constructors have some code in common. For example, consider the following:

```
class Car
{
    private string _description;
    private uint _nWheels;

    public Car(string description, uint nWheels)
    {
        _description = description;
        _nWheels = nWheels;
    }

    public Car(string description)
    {
        _description = description;
        _nWheels = 4;
    }
    // etc.
```

Both constructors initialize the same fields. It would clearly be neater to place all the code in one location. C# has a special syntax known as a *constructor initializer* to enable this:

```
class Car
{
    private string _description;
    private uint _nWheels;
```

```
public Car(string description, uint nWheels)
{
  _description = description;
  _nWheels = nWheels;
}

public Car(string description) : this(description, 4)
{
}
// etc
```

In this context, the this keyword simply causes the constructor with the nearest matching parameters to be called. Note that any constructor initializer is executed before the body of the constructor. Suppose that the following code is run:

```
var myCar = new Car("Proton Persona");
```

In this example, the two-parameter constructor executes before any code in the body of the one-parameter constructor (though in this particular case, because there is no code in the body of the one-parameter constructor, it makes no difference).

A C# constructor initializer may contain either one call to another constructor in the same class (using the syntax just presented) or one call to a constructor in the immediate base class (using the same syntax, but using the keyword base instead of this). It is not possible to put more than one call in the initializer.

Static Constructors

One feature of C# is that it is also possible to write a static no-parameter constructor for a class. Such a constructor is executed only once, unlike the constructors written so far, which are instance constructors that are executed whenever an object of that class is created:

```
class MyClass
{
  static MyClass()
  {
    // initialization code
  }
  // rest of class definition
}
```

One reason for writing a static constructor is if your class has some static fields or properties that need to be initialized from an external source before the class is first used.

The .NET runtime makes no guarantees about when a static constructor will be executed, so you should not place any code in it that relies on it being executed at a particular time (for example, when an assembly is loaded). Nor is it possible to predict in what order static constructors of different classes will execute. However, what is guaranteed is that the static constructor will run at most once, and that it will be invoked before your code makes any reference to the class. In C#, the static constructor is usually executed immediately before the first call to any member of the class.

Note that the static constructor does not have any access modifiers. It's never called explicitly by any other C# code, but always by the .NET runtime when the class is loaded, so any access modifier such as public or private would be meaningless. For this same reason, the static constructor can never take any parameters, and there can be only one static constructor for a class. It should also be obvious that a static constructor can access only static members, not instance members, of the class.

It is possible to have a static constructor and a zero-parameter instance constructor defined in the same class. Although the parameter lists are identical, there is no conflict because the static constructor is executed when the class is loaded, but the instance constructor is executed whenever an instance is created. Therefore, there is no confusion about which constructor is executed or when.

If you have more than one class that has a static constructor, the static constructor that is executed first is undefined. Therefore, you should not put any code in a static constructor that depends on other static constructors having been or not having been executed. However, if any static fields have been given default values, these are allocated before the static constructor is called.

The next example illustrates the use of a static constructor. It is based on the idea of a program that has user preferences (which are presumably stored in some configuration file). To keep things simple, assume just one user preference—a quantity called `BackColor` that might represent the background color to be used in an application. Because we don't want to get into the details of writing code to read data from an external source here, assume also that the preference is to have a background color of red on weekdays and green on weekends. All the program does is display the preference in a console window, but that is enough to see a static constructor at work.

The class `UserPreferences` is declared with the `static` modifier; thus it cannot be instantiated and can only contain static members. The static constructor initializes the `BackColor` property depending on the day of the week (code file `StaticConstructorSample/UserPreferences.cs`):

```
public static class UserPreferences
{
  public static Color BackColor { get; }

  static UserPreferences()
  {
    DateTime now = DateTime.Now;
    if (now.DayOfWeek == DayOfWeek.Saturday
        || now.DayOfWeek == DayOfWeek.Sunday)
    {
      BackColor = Color.Green;
    }
    else
    {
      BackColor = Color.Red;
    }
  }
}
```

This code makes use of the `System.DateTime` struct that is supplied with the .NET Framework. `DateTime` implements a static property `Now` that returns the current time. `DayOfWeek` is an instance property of `DateTime` that returns an enum value of type `DayOfWeek`.

`Color` is defined as an enum type and contains a few colors. The enum types are explained in detail later in the section Enums (code file `StaticConstructorSample/Enum.cs`):

```
public enum Color
{
    White,
    Red,
    Green,
    Blue,
    Black
}
```

The `Main` method just invokes the `WriteLine` method and writes the user preferences back color to the console (code file `StaticConstructorSample/Program.cs`):

```
class Program
{
  static void Main()
  {
    WriteLine(
      $"User-preferences: BackColor is: {UserPreferences.BackColor}");
  }
}
```

Compiling and running the preceding code results in the following output:

```
User-preferences: BackColor is: Color Red
```

Of course, if the code is executed during the weekend, your color preference would be Green.

Readonly Members

If you do not want to change a data member after initialization, the readonly keyword can be used. Let's get into the details of readonly fields and readonly properties.

Readonly Fields

To guarantee that fields of an object cannot be changed, fields can be declared with the readonly modifier. Fields with the readonly modifier can be assigned only values from constructors. This is different from the const modifier. With the const modifier, the compiler replaces the variable by its value everywhere it is used. The compiler already knows the value of the constant. Read-only fields are assigned during runtime from a constructor. Contrary to const fields, read-only fields can be instance members. For using a read-only field as a class member, the static modifier needs to be assigned to the field.

Suppose that you have a program that edits documents, and for licensing reasons you want to restrict the number of documents that can be opened simultaneously. Assume also that you are selling different versions of the software, and it's possible for customers to upgrade their licenses to open more documents simultaneously. Clearly, this means you can't hard-code the maximum number in the source code. You would probably need a field to represent this maximum number. This field has to be read in—perhaps from a registry key or some other file storage—each time the program is launched. Therefore, your code might look something like this:

```
public class DocumentEditor
{
  private static readonly uint s_maxDocuments;

  static DocumentEditor()
  {
    s_maxDocuments = DoSomethingToFindOutMaxNumber();
  }
}
```

In this case, the field is static because the maximum number of documents needs to be stored only once per running instance of the program. This is why it is initialized in the static constructor. If you had an instance readonly field, you would initialize it in the instance constructor(s). For example, presumably each document you edit has a creation date, which you wouldn't want to allow the user to change (because that would be rewriting the past!).

As noted earlier, date is represented by the class System.DateTime. The following code initializes the _creationTime field in the constructor using the DateTime struct. After initialization of the Document class, the creation time cannot be changed anymore:

```
public class Document
{
    private readonly DateTime _creationTime;
    public Document()
    {
        _creationTime = DateTime.Now;
    }
}
```

CreationDate and MaxDocuments in the previous code snippet are treated like any other field, except that because they are read-only they cannot be assigned outside the constructors:

```
void SomeMethod()
{
    s_maxDocuments = 10; // compilation error here. MaxDocuments is readonly
}
```

It's also worth noting that you don't have to assign a value to a `readonly` field in a constructor. If you don't do so, it is left with the default value for its particular data type or whatever value you initialized it to at its declaration. That applies to both static and instance `readonly` fields.

Readonly Properties

It is possible to create a read-only property by simply omitting the `set` accessor from the property definition. Thus, to make `Name` a read-only property, you would do the following:

```
private readonly string _name;

public string Name
{
  get
  {
    return _name;
  }
}
```

Declaring the field with the `readonly` modifier only allows initializing the value of the property in the constructor.

It is similarly possible to create a write-only property by omitting the `get` accessor. However, this is regarded as poor programming practice because it could be confusing to authors of client code. In general, it is recommended that if you are tempted to do this, you should use a method instead.

Auto-implemented Readonly Properties

C# 6 offers a simple syntax with auto-implemented properties to create read-only properties accessing read-only fields. These properties can be initialized using property initializers.

```
public string Id { get; } = Guid.NewGuid().ToString();
```

Behind the scenes, the compiler creates a read-only field and a property with a `get` accessor to this field. The code from the initializer moves to the implementation of the constructor and is invoked before the constructor body is called.

Of course, read-only properties can also be initialized from the constructor as shown with this code snippet:

```
public class Person
{
  public Person(string name)
  {
    Name = name;
  }
  public string Name { get; }
}
```

Expression-Bodied Properties

Another extension with C# 6 in regard to properties are expression-bodied properties. Similar to expression-bodied methods, expression-bodied properties don't need curly brackets and return statements. Expression-bodied properties are properties with the `get` accessor, but you don't need to write the `get` keyword. Just the implementation of the `get` accessor follows the lambda operator. With the `Person` class, the `FullName` property is implemented using an expression-bodied property and returns with this property the values of the `FirstName` and `LastName` properties combined:

```
public class Person
{
  public Person(string firstName, string lastName)
  {
    FirstName = firstName;
```

```
      LastName = lastName;
    }
    public string FirstName { get; }
    public string LastName { get; }
    public string FullName => $"{FirstName} {LastName}";
}
```

Immutable Types

If a type contains members that can be changed, it is a *mutable* type. With the `readonly` modifier, the compiler complains if the state is changed. The state can only be initialized in the constructor. If an object doesn't have any members that can be changed—only `readonly` members—it is an immutable type. The content can only be set on initialization time. This is extremely useful with multithreading, as multiple threads can access the same object with the information it can never change. Because the content cannot change, synchronization is not necessary.

An example of an immutable type is the `String` class. This class does not define any member that is allowed to change its content. Methods such as `ToUpper` (which changes the string to uppercase) always return a new string, but the original string passed to the constructor remains unchanged.

ANONYMOUS TYPES

Chapter 2, "Core C#," discusses the `var` keyword in reference to implicitly typed variables. When used with the `new` keyword, anonymous types can be created. An anonymous type is simply a nameless class that inherits from `object`. The definition of the class is inferred from the initializer, just as with implicitly typed variables.

For example, if you needed an object containing a person's first, middle, and last name, the declaration would look like this:

```
var captain = new
{
  FirstName = "James",
  MiddleName = "T",
  LastName = "Kirk"
};
```

This would produce an object with `FirstName`, `MiddleName`, and `LastName` properties. If you were to create another object that looked like this:

```
var doctor = new
{
  FirstName = "Leonard",
  MiddleName = string.Empty,
  LastName = "McCoy"
};
```

then the types of `captain` and `doctor` are the same. You could set `captain = doctor`, for example. This is only possible if all the properties match.

If the values that are being set come from another object, then the initializer can be abbreviated. If you already have a class that contains the properties `FirstName`, `MiddleName`, and `LastName` and you have an instance of that class with the instance name `person`, then the `captain` object could be initialized like this:

```
var captain = new
{
  person.FirstName,
  person.MiddleName,
  person.LastName
};
```

The property names from the person object would be projected to the new object named captain, so the object named captain would have the FirstName, MiddleName, and LastName properties.

The actual type name of these new objects is unknown. The compiler "makes up" a name for the type, but only the compiler is ever able to make use of it. Therefore, you can't and shouldn't plan on using any type reflection on the new objects because you will not get consistent results.

STRUCTS

So far, you have seen how classes offer a great way to encapsulate objects in your program. You have also seen how they are stored on the heap in a way that gives you much more flexibility in data lifetime but with a slight cost in performance. This performance cost is small thanks to the optimizations of managed heaps. However, in some situations all you really need is a small data structure. In those cases, a class provides more functionality than you need, and for best performance you probably want to use a struct. Consider the following example:

```
public class Dimensions
{
  public double Length { get; set; }
  public double Width { get; set; }
}
```

This code defines a class called Dimensions, which simply stores the length and width of an item. Suppose you're writing a furniture-arranging program that enables users to experiment with rearranging their furniture on the computer, and you want to store the dimensions of each item of furniture. It might seem as though you're breaking the rules of good program design by making the fields public, but the point is that you don't really need all the facilities of a class for this. All you have is two numbers, which you'll find convenient to treat as a pair rather than individually. There is no need for a lot of methods, or for you to be able to inherit from the class, and you certainly don't want to have the .NET runtime go to the trouble of bringing in the heap, with all the performance implications, just to store two doubles.

As mentioned earlier in this chapter, the only thing you need to change in the code to define a type as a struct instead of a class is to replace the keyword class with struct:

```
public struct Dimensions
{
  public double Length { get; set; }
  public double Width { get; set; }
}
```

Defining functions for structs is also exactly the same as defining them for classes. The following code demonstrates a constructor and a property for a struct (code file StructsSample/Dimension.cs):

```
public struct Dimensions
{
  public double Length { get; set; }
  public double Width { get; set; }

  public Dimensions(double length, double width)
  {
    Length = length;
    Width = width;
  }

  public double Diagonal => Math.Sqrt(Length * Length + Width * Width);
}
```

Structs are value types, not reference types. This means they are stored either in the stack or inline (if they are part of another object that is stored on the heap) and have the same lifetime restrictions as the simple data types:

➤ Structs do not support inheritance.

➤ There are some differences in the way constructors work for structs. If you do not supply a default constructor, the compiler automatically creates one and initializes the members to its default values.

➤ With a struct, you can specify how the fields are to be laid out in memory (this is examined in Chapter 16, which covers attributes).

Because structs are really intended to group data items together, you'll sometimes find that most or all of their fields are declared as public. Strictly speaking, this is contrary to the guidelines for writing .NET code—according to Microsoft, fields (other than const fields) should always be private and wrapped by public properties. However, for simple structs, many developers consider public fields to be acceptable programming practice.

The following sections look at some of these differences between structs and classes in more detail.

Structs Are Value Types

Although structs are value types, you can often treat them syntactically in the same way as classes. For example, with the definition of the Dimensions class in the previous section, you could write this:

```
var point = new Dimensions();
point.Length = 3;
point.Width = 6;
```

Note that because structs are value types, the new operator does not work in the same way as it does for classes and other reference types. Instead of allocating memory on the heap, the new operator simply calls the appropriate constructor, according to the parameters passed to it, initializing all fields. Indeed, for structs it is perfectly legal to write this:

```
Dimensions point;
point.Length = 3;
point.Width = 6;
```

If Dimensions were a class, this would produce a compilation error, because point would contain an uninitialized reference—an address that points nowhere, so you could not start setting values to its fields. For a struct, however, the variable declaration actually allocates space on the stack for the entire struct, so it's ready to assign values to. The following code, however, would cause a compilation error, with the compiler complaining that you are using an uninitialized variable:

```
Dimensions point;
double D = point.Length;
```

Structs follow the same rule as any other data type: Everything must be initialized before use. A struct is considered fully initialized either when the new operator has been called against it or when values have been individually assigned to all its fields. Also, of course, a struct defined as a member field of a class is initialized by being zeroed out automatically when the containing object is initialized.

The fact that structs are value types affects performance, though depending on how you use your struct, this can be good or bad. On the positive side, allocating memory for structs is very fast because this takes place inline or on the stack. The same is true when they go out of scope. Structs are cleaned up quickly and don't need to wait on garbage collection. On the negative side, whenever you pass a struct as a parameter or assign a struct to another struct (as in A = B, where A and B are structs), the full contents of the struct are copied, whereas for a class only the reference is copied. This results in a performance loss that varies according to the size of the struct, emphasizing the fact that structs are really intended for small data structures.

Note, however, that when passing a struct as a parameter to a method, you can avoid this performance loss by passing it as a ref parameter—in this case, only the address in memory of the struct will be passed in, which is just as fast as passing in a class. If you do this, though, be aware that it means the called method can, in principle, change the value of the struct. This is shown later in this chapter in the section "Passing Parameters by Value and by Reference."

Structs and Inheritance

Structs are not designed for inheritance. This means it is not possible to inherit from a struct. The only exception to this is that structs, in common with every other type in C#, derive ultimately from the class `System.Object`. Hence, structs also have access to the methods of `System.Object`, and it is even possible to override them in structs; an obvious example would be overriding the `ToString` method. The actual inheritance chain for structs is that each struct derives from the class, `System.ValueType`, which in turn derives from `System.Object`. `ValueType` does not add any new members to `Object` but provides override implementations of some members of the base class that are more suitable for structs. Note that you cannot supply a different base class for a struct: Every struct is derived from `ValueType`.

Constructors for Structs

You can define constructors for structs in exactly the same way that you can for classes.

That said, the default constructor, which initializes all fields to zero values, is always present implicitly, even if you supply other constructors that take parameters.

With C# 6 it's also possible to implement a default constructor and supplying initial values for fields (this wasn't possible in earlier C# versions). You just need to initialize every data member:

```
public Dimensions()
{
  Length = 0;
  Width = 1;
}
public Dimensions(double length, double width)
{
  Length = length;
  Width = width;
}
```

Incidentally, you can supply a `Close` or `Dispose` method for a struct in the same way you do for a class. The `Dispose` method is discussed in detail in Chapter 5.

PASSING PARAMETERS BY VALUE AND BY REFERENCE

Let's assume you have a type named A with a property of type int named X. The method `ChangeA` receives a parameter of type A and changes the value of X to 2 (code file `PassingByValueAndByReference/Program.cs`):

```
public static void ChangeA(A a)
{
    a.X = 2;
}
```

The Main method creates an instance of type A, initializes X to 1, and invokes the `ChangeA` method:

```
static void Main()
{
  A a1 = new A { X = 1 };
  ChangeA(a1);
  WriteLine($"a1.X: {a1.X}");
}
```

What would you guess is the output? 1 or 2?

The answer is . . . it depends. You need to know if A is a class or a struct. Let's start with A as a struct:

```
public struct A
{
   public int X { get; set; }
}
```

Structs are passed by value; with that the variable a from the ChangeA method gets a copy from the variable a1 that is put on the stack. Only the copy is changed and destroyed at the end of the method ChangeA. The content of a1 never changes and stays 1.

This is completely different with A as a class:

```
public class A
{
    public int X { get; set; }
}
```

Classes are passed by reference. This way, a is a variable that references the same object on the heap as the variable a1. When ChangeA changes the value of the X property of a, the change makes it a1.X because it is the same object. Here, the result is 2.

ref Parameters

You can also pass structs by reference. Changing the declaration of the ChangeA method by adding the ref modifier, the variable is passed by reference—also if A is of type struct:

```
public static void ChangeA(ref A a)
{
    a.X = 2;
}
```

It's good to know this from the caller side as well, so with method parameters that have the ref modifier applied, this needs to be added on calling the method as well:

```
static void Main()
{
    A a1 = new A { X = 1 };
    ChangeA(ref a1);
    WriteLine($"a1.X: {a1.X}");
}
```

Now the struct is passed by reference likewise the class type, so the result is 2.

What about using the ref modifier with a class type? Let's change the implementation of the ChangeA method to this:

```
public static void ChangeA(A a)
{
    a.X = 2;
    a = new A { X = 3 };
}
```

Using A of type class, what result can be expected now? Of course, the result from the Main method will not be 1 because a pass by reference is done by class types. Setting a.X to 2, the original object a1 gets changed. However, the next line a = new A { X = 3 } now creates a new object on the heap, and a references the new object. The variable a1 used within the Main method still references the old object with the value 2. After the end of the ChangeA method, the new object on the heap is not referenced and can be garbage collected. So here the result is 2.

Using the ref modifier with A as a class type, a reference to a reference (or in C++ jargon, a pointer to a pointer) is passed, which allows allocating a new object, and the Main method shows the result 3:

```
public static void ChangeA(ref A a)
{
    a.X = 2;
    a = new A { X = 3 };
}
```

Finally, it is important to understand that C# continues to apply initialization requirements to parameters passed to methods. Any variable must be initialized before it is passed into a method, whether it is passed in by value or by reference.

out Parameters

If a method returns one value, the method usually declares a return type and returns the result. What about returning multiple values from a method, maybe with different types? There are different options to do this. One option is to declare a class and struct and define all the information that should be returned as members of this type. Another option is to use a tuple type. Tuples are explained in Chapter 7. The third option is to use the out keyword.

Let's get into an example by using the Parse method that is defined with the Int32 type. The ReadLine method gets a string from user input. Assuming the user enters a number, the int.Parse method converts the string and returns the number (code file OutKeywordSample/Program.cs):

```
string input1 = ReadLine();
int n = int.Parse(input1);
WriteLine($"n: {n}");
```

However, users do not always enter the data you would like them to enter. In case the user does not enter a number, an exception is thrown. Of course, it is possible to catch the exception and work with the user accordingly, but this is not a good idea to do for a "normal" case. Maybe it can be assumed to be the "normal" case that the user enters wrong data. Dealing with exceptions is covered in Chapter 14, "Errors and Exceptions."

A better way to deal with the wrong type of data is to use a different method of the Int32 type: TryParse. TryParse is declared to return a bool type whether the parsing is successful or not. The result of the parsing (if it was successful) is returned with a parameter using the out modifier:

```
public static bool TryParse(string s, out int result);
```

Invoking this method, the result variable needs to be defined before calling this method. With out parameters, the variable does not need to be initialized beforehand; the variable is initialized within the method. Similar to the ref keyword, the out keyword needs to be supplied on calling the method and not only with the method declaration:

```
string input2 = ReadLine();
int result;
if (int.TryParse(input2, out result))
{
  WriteLine($"n: {n}");
}
else
{
  WriteLine("not a number");
}
```

NULLABLE TYPES

Variables of reference types (classes) can be null while variables of value types (structs) cannot. This can be a problem with some scenarios, such as mapping C# types to database or XML types. A database or XML number can be null, whereas an int or double cannot be null.

One way to deal with this conflict is to use classes that map to database number types (which is done by Java). Using reference types that map to database numbers to allow the null value has an important disadvantage: It creates extra overhead. With reference types, the garbage collector is needed to clean up. Value types do not need to be cleaned up by the garbage collector; they are removed from memory when the variable goes out of scope.

C# has a solution for this: nullable types. A nullable type is a value type that can be null. You just have to put the ? after the type (which needs to be a struct). The only overhead a value type has compared to the underlying struct is a Boolean member that tells whether it is null.

With the following code snippet, x1 is a normal int, and x2 is a nullable int. Because x2 is a nullable int, null can be assigned to x2:

```
int x1 = 1;
int? x2 = null;
```

Because an int cannot have a value that cannot be assigned to int?, passing a variable of int to int? always succeeds and is accepted from the compiler:

```
int? x3 = x1;
```

The reverse is not true. int? cannot be directly assigned to int. This can fail, and thus a cast is required:

```
int x4 = (int)x3;
```

Of course, the cast generates an exception in a case where x3 is null. A better way to deal with that is to use the HasValue and Value properties of nullable types. HasValue returns true or false, depending on whether the nullable type has a value, and Value returns the underlying value. Using the conditional operator, x5 gets filled without possible exceptions. In a case where x3 is null, HasValue returns false, and here -1 is supplied to the variable x5:

```
int x5 = x3.HasValue ? x3.Value : -1;
```

Using the coalescing operator, there's a shorter syntax possible with nullable types. In a case where x3 is null, -1 is set with the variable x6; otherwise you take the value of x3:

```
int x6 = x3 ?? -1;
```

> **NOTE** *With nullable types, you can use all operators that are available with the underlying types—for example, +, -, *, / and more with int?. You can use nullable types with every struct type, not only with predefined C# types. You can read more about nullable types and what's behind the scenes in Chapter 6, "Generics."*

ENUMERATIONS

An enumeration is a value type that contains a list of named constants, such as the Color type shown here. The enumeration type is defined by using the enum keyword (code file EnumSample/Color.cs):

```
public enum Color
{
  Red,
  Green,
  Blue
}
```

You can declare variables of enum types, such as the variable c1, and assign a value from the enumeration by setting one of the named constants prefixed with the name of the enum type (code file EnumSample/Program.cs):

```
Color c1 = Color.Red;
WriteLine(c1);
```

Running the program, the console output shows Red, which is the constant value of the enumeration.

By default, the type behind the enum type is an `int`. The underlying type can be changed to other integral types (byte, short, int, long with signed and unsigned variants). The values of the named constants are incremental values starting with 0, but they can be changed to other values:

```
public enum Color : short
{
  Red = 1,
  Green = 2,
  Blue = 3
}
```

You can change a number to an enumeration value and back using casts.

```
Color c2 = (Color)2;
short number = (short)c2;
```

You can also use an enum type to assign multiple options to a variable and not just one of the enum constants. To do this, the values assigned to the constants must be different bits, and the `Flags` attribute needs to be set with the enum.

The enum type `DaysOfWeek` defines different values for every day. Setting different bits can be done easily using hexadecimal values that are assigned using the `0x` prefix. The `Flags` attribute is information for the compiler for creating a different string representation of the values—for example, setting the value 3 to a variable of `DaysOfWeek` results in `Monday, Tuesday` when the `Flags` attribute is used (code file `EnumSample/DaysOfWeek.cs`):

```
[Flags]
public enum DaysOfWeek
{
  Monday = 0x1,
  Tuesday = 0x2,
  Wednesday = 0x4,
  Thursday = 0x8,
  Friday = 0x10,
  Saturday = 0x20,
  Sunday = 0x40
}
```

With such an enum declaration, you can assign a variable multiple values using the logical OR operator (code file `EnumSample/Program.cs`):

```
DaysOfWeek mondayAndWednesday = DaysOfWeek.Monday | DaysOfWeek.Wednesday;
WriteLine(mondayAndWednesday);
```

Running the program, the output is a string representation of the days:

```
Monday, Tuesday
```

Setting different bits, it is also possible to combine single bits to cover multiple values, such as `Weekend` with a value of `0x60` by that combines `Saturday` and `Sunday` with the logical OR operator, `Workday` to combine all the days from `Monday` to `Friday`, and `AllWeek` to combine `Workday` and `Weekend` with the logical OR operator (code file `EnumSample/DaysOfWeek.cs`):

```
[Flags]
public enum DaysOfWeek
{
  Monday = 0x1,
  Tuesday = 0x2,
  Wednesday = 0x4,
  Thursday = 0x8,
  Friday = 0x10,
  Saturday = 0x20,
  Sunday = 0x40,
  Weekend = Saturday | Sunday
```

```
    Workday = 0x1f,
    AllWeek = Workday | Weekend
}
```

With this in place, it's possible to assign DaysOfWeek.Weekend directly to a variable, but also assigning the separate values DaysOfWeek.Saturday and DaysOfWeek.Sunday combined with the logical OR operator results in the same. The output shown is the string representation of Weekend.

```
DaysOfWeek weekend = DaysOfWeek.Saturday | DaysOfWeek.Sunday;
WriteLine(weekend);
```

Working with enumerations, the class Enum is sometimes a big help for dynamically getting some information about enum types. Enum offers methods to parse strings to get the corresponding enumeration constant, and to get all the names and values of an enum type.

The following code snippet uses a string to get the corresponding Color value using Enum.TryParse (code file EnumSample/Program.cs):

```
Color red;
if (Enum.TryParse<Color>("Red", out red))
{
    WriteLine($"successfully parsed {red}");
}
```

> **NOTE** Enum.TryParse<T>() *is a generic method where* T *is a generic parameter type. This parameter type needs to be defined with the method invocation. Generic methods are explained in detail in Chapter 6.*

The Enum.GetNames method returns a string array of all the names of the enumeration:

```
foreach (var day in Enum.GetNames(typeof(Color)))
{
    WriteLine(day);
}
```

When you run the application, this is the output:

```
Red
Green
Blue
```

To get all the values of the enumeration, you can use the method Enum.GetValues. Enum.GetValues returns an Array of the enum values. To get the integral value, it needs to be cast to the underlying type of the enumeration, which is done by the foreach statement:

```
foreach (short val in Enum.GetValues(typeof(Color)))
{
    WriteLine(val);
}
```

PARTIAL CLASSES

The partial keyword allows the class, struct, method, or interface to span multiple files. Typically, a code generator of some type is generating part of a class, having the class in multiple files can be beneficial. Let's assume you want to make some additions to the class that is automatically generated from a tool. If the tool reruns then your changes are lost. The partial keyword is helpful for splitting the class in two files and making your changes to the file that is not defined by the code generator.

To use the `partial` keyword, simply place `partial` before `class`, `struct`, or `interface`. In the following example, the class `SampleClass` resides in two separate source files, `SampleClassAutogenerated.cs` and `SampleClass.cs`:

```
//SampleClassAutogenerated.cs
partial class SampleClass
{
   public void MethodOne() { }
}

//SampleClass.cs
partial class SampleClass
{
   public void MethodTwo() { }
}
```

When the project that these two source files are part of is compiled, a single type called `SampleClass` will be created with two methods: `MethodOne` and `MethodTwo`.

If any of the following keywords are used in describing the class, the same must apply to all partials of the same type:

➤ `public`

➤ `private`

➤ `protected`

➤ `internal`

➤ `abstract`

➤ `sealed`

➤ `new`

➤ generic constraints

Nested partials are allowed as long as the `partial` keyword precedes the `class` keyword in the nested type. Attributes, XML comments, interfaces, generic-type parameter attributes, and members are combined when the partial types are compiled into the type. Given these two source files:

```
// SampleClassAutogenerated.cs
[CustomAttribute]
partial class SampleClass: SampleBaseClass, ISampleClass
{
   public void MethodOne() { }
}

// SampleClass.cs
[AnotherAttribute]
partial class SampleClass: IOtherSampleClass
{
   public void MethodTwo() { }
}
```

the equivalent source file would be as follows after the compile:

```
[CustomAttribute]
[AnotherAttribute]
partial class SampleClass: SampleBaseClass, ISampleClass, IOtherSampleClass
{
   public void MethodOne() { }

   public void MethodTwo() { }
}
```

Partial classes can contain *partial methods*. This is extremely useful if generated code should invoke methods that might not exist at all. The programmer extending the partial class can decide to create a custom implementation of the partial method, or do nothing. The following code snippet contains a partial class with the method MethodOne that invokes the method APartialMethod. The method APartialMethod is declared with the partial keyword; thus it does not need any implementation. If there's not an implementation, the compiler removes the invocation of this method:

```
//SampleClassAutogenerated.cs
partial class SampleClass
{
  public void MethodOne()
  {
    APartialMethod();
  }

  public partial void APartialMethod();
}
```

An implementation of the partial method can be done within any other part of the partial class, as shown in the following code snippet. With this method in place, the compiler creates code within MethodOne to invoke this APartialMethod declared here:

```
// SampleClass.cs
partial class SampleClass: IOtherSampleClass
{
  public void APartialMethod()
  {
    // implementation of APartialMethod
  }
}
```

A partial method needs to be of type void. Otherwise the compiler cannot remove the invocation in case no implementation exists.

EXTENSION METHODS

There are many ways to extend a class. Inheritance, which is covered in Chapter 4, is a great way to add functionality to your objects. Extension methods are another option that can also be used to add functionality to classes. This option is also possible when inheritance cannot be used (for example, the class is sealed).

Extension methods are static methods that can look like part of a class without actually being in the source code for the class.

Let's say you want the `string` type to be extended with a method to count the number of words within a string. The method `GetWordCount` makes use of the `String.Split` method to split up a string in a string array, and counts the number of elements within the array using the `Length` property (code file `ExtensionMethods/Program.cs`):

```
public static class StringExtension
{
  public static int GetWordCount(this string s) =>
    s.Split().Length;
}
```

The `string` is extended by using the `this` keyword with the first parameter. This keyword defines the type that is extended.

Even though the extension method is static, you use standard method syntax. Notice that you call `GetWordCount` using the `fox` variable and not using the type name:

```
string fox = "the quick brown fox jumped over the lazy dogs down " +
    "9876543210 times";
int wordCount = fox.GetWordCount();
WriteLine($"{wordCount} words");
```

Behind the scenes, the compiler changes this to invoke the static method instead:

```
int wordCount = StringExtension.GetWordCount(fox);
```

Using the instance method syntax instead of calling a static method from your code directly results in a much nicer syntax. This syntax also has the advantage that the implementation of this method can be replaced by a different class without the need to change the code—just a new compiler run is needed.

How does the compiler find an extension method for a specific type? The `this` keyword is needed to match an extension method for a type, but also the namespace of the static class that defines the extension method needs to be opened. If you put the `StringExtensions` class within the namespace `Wrox.Extensions`, the compiler finds the `GetWordCount` method only if `Wrox.Extensions` is opened with the using directive. In case the type also defines an instance method with the same name, the extension method is never used. Any instance method already in the class takes precedence. When you have multiple extension methods with the same name to extend the same type, and when all the namespaces of these types are opened, the compiler results in an error that the call is ambiguous and it cannot decide between multiple implementations. If, however, the calling code is in one of these namespaces, this namespace takes precedence.

> **NOTE** *Language Integrated Query (LINQ) makes use of many extension methods. LINQ is discussed in Chapter 13, "Language Integrated Query."*

THE OBJECT CLASS

As indicated earlier, all .NET classes are ultimately derived from `System.Object`. In fact, if you don't specify a base class when you define a class, the compiler automatically assumes that it derives from `Object`. Because inheritance has not been used in this chapter, every class you have seen here is actually derived from `System.Object`. (As noted earlier, for structs this derivation is indirect—a struct is always derived from `System.ValueType`, which in turn derives from `System.Object`.)

The practical significance of this is that—besides the methods, properties, and so on that you define—you also have access to a number of public and protected member methods that have been defined for the `Object` class. These methods are available in all other classes that you define.

For the time being, the following list summarizes the purpose of each method:

➤ ToString—A fairly basic, quick-and-easy string representation. Use it when you want a quick idea of the contents of an object, perhaps for debugging purposes. It provides very little choice regarding how to format the data. For example, dates can, in principle, be expressed in a huge variety of formats, but DateTime.ToString does not offer you any choice in this regard. If you need a more sophisticated string representation—for example, one that takes into account your formatting preferences or the culture (the locale)—then you should implement the IFormattable interface (see Chapter 10, "Strings and Regular Expressions").

➤ GetHashCode—If objects are placed in a data structure known as a map (also known as a hash table or dictionary), it is used by classes that manipulate these structures to determine where to place an object in the structure. If you intend your class to be used as a key for a dictionary, you need to override GetHashCode. Some fairly strict requirements exist for how you implement your overload, which you learn about when you examine dictionaries in Chapter 11, "Collections."

➤ Equals (both versions) and ReferenceEquals—As you'll note by the existence of three different methods aimed at comparing the equality of objects, the .NET Framework has quite a sophisticated scheme for measuring equality. Subtle differences exist between how these three methods, along with the comparison operator, ==, are intended to be used. In addition, restrictions exist on how you should override the virtual, one-parameter version of Equals if you choose to do so, because certain base classes in the System.Collections namespace call the method and expect it to behave in certain ways. You explore the use of these methods in Chapter 8 when you examine operators.

➤ Finalize—Covered in Chapter 5, this method is intended as the nearest that C# has to C++-style destructors. It is called when a reference object is garbage collected to clean up resources. The Object implementation of Finalize doesn't actually do anything and is ignored by the garbage collector. You normally override Finalize if an object owns references to unmanaged resources that need to be removed when the object is deleted. The garbage collector cannot do this directly because it only knows about managed resources, so it relies on any finalizers that you supply.

➤ GetType—This object returns an instance of a class derived from System.Type, so it can provide an extensive range of information about the class of which your object is a member, including base type, methods, properties, and so on. System.Type also provides the entry point into .NET's reflection technology. Chapter 16 examines this topic.

➤ MemberwiseClone—The only member of System.Object that isn't examined in detail anywhere in the book. That's because it is fairly simple in concept. It just makes a copy of the object and returns a reference (or in the case of a value type, a boxed reference) to the copy. Note that the copy made is a shallow copy, meaning it copies all the value types in the class. If the class contains any embedded references, then only the references are copied, not the objects referred to. This method is protected and cannot be called to copy external objects. Nor is it virtual, so you cannot override its implementation.

SUMMARY

This chapter examined C# syntax for declaring and manipulating objects. You have seen how to declare static and instance fields, properties, methods, and constructors. You have also seen new features that have been added with C# 6, such as expression-bodied methods and properties, auto-implemented read-only properties, and default constructors with structs.

You have also seen how all types in C# derive ultimately from the type System.Object, which means that all types start with a basic set of useful methods, including ToString.

Inheritance comes up a few times throughout this chapter, and you examine implementation and interface inheritance in C# in Chapter 4.

Inheritance

WHAT'S IN THIS CHAPTER?

- ➤ Types of inheritance
- ➤ Implementing inheritance
- ➤ Access modifiers
- ➤ Interfaces
- ➤ is and as Operators

WROX.COM CODE DOWNLOADS FOR THIS CHAPTER

The wrox.com code downloads for this chapter are found at www.wrox.com/go/professionalcsharp6 on the Download Code tab. The code for this chapter is divided into the following major examples:

- ➤ VirtualMethods
- ➤ InheritanceWithConstructors
- ➤ UsingInterfaces

INHERITANCE

The three most important concepts of object-orientation are *inheritance*, *encapsulation*, and *polymorphism*. Chapter 3, "Objects and Types," talks about creating individual classes to arrange properties, methods, and fields. When members of a type are declared `private`, they cannot be accessed from the outside. They are *encapsulated* within the type. This chapter's focus is on inheritance and polymorphism.

The previous chapter explains that all classes ultimately derive from the class `System.Object`. This chapter covers how to create a hierarchy of classes and how polymorphism works with C#. It also describes all the C# keywords related to inheritance.

TYPES OF INHERITANCE

Let's start by reviewing some object-oriented (OO) terms and look at what C# does and does not support as far as inheritance is concerned.

> ➤ **Single inheritance**—With single inheritance, one class can derive from one base class. This is a possible scenario with C#.

> ➤ **Multiple inheritance**—Multiple inheritance allows deriving from multiple base classes. C# does not support multiple inheritance with classes, but it allows multiple inheritance with interfaces.

> ➤ **Multilevel inheritance**—Multilevel inheritance allows inheritance across a bigger hierarchy. Class B derives from class A, and class C derives from class B. Here, class B is also known as intermediate base class. This is supported and often used with C#.

> ➤ **Interface inheritance**—Interface inheritance defines inheritance with interfaces. Here, multiple inheritance is possible. Interfaces and interface inheritance is explained later in this chapter in the "Interfaces" section.

Let's discuss some specific issues with inheritance and C#.

Multiple Inheritance

Some languages such as C++ support what is known as *multiple inheritance,* in which a class derives from more than one other class. With implementation inheritance, multiple inheritance adds complexity and also overhead to the generated code even in cases where multiple inheritance is not used. Because of this, the designers of C# decided not to support multiple inheritance with classes because support for multiple inheritance increases complexity and adds overhead even in cases when multiple inheritance is not used.

C# does allow types to be derived from multiple interfaces. One type can *implement multiple interfaces.* This means that a C# class can be derived from one other class, and any number of interfaces. Indeed, we can be more precise: Thanks to the presence of System.Object as a common base type, every C# class (except for Object) has exactly one base class, and every C# class may additionally have any number of base interfaces.

Structs and Classes

Chapter 3 distinguishes between structs (value types) and classes (reference types). One restriction of using structs is that they do not support inheritance, beyond the fact that every struct is automatically derived from System.ValueType. Although it's true that you cannot code a type hierarchy of structs, it is possible for structs to implement interfaces. In other words, structs don't really support implementation inheritance, but they do support interface inheritance. The following summarizes the situation for any types that you define:

> ➤ *Structs* are always derived from System.ValueType. They can also be derived from any number of interfaces.

> ➤ *Classes* are always derived from either System.Object or a class that you choose. They can also be derived from any number of interfaces.

IMPLEMENTATION INHERITANCE

If you want to declare that a class derives from another class, use the following syntax:

```
class MyDerivedClass: MyBaseClass
{
  // members
}
```

If a class (or a struct) also derives from interfaces, the list of base class and interfaces is separated by commas:

```
public class MyDerivedClass: MyBaseClass, IInterface1, IInterface2
{
  // members
}
```

> **NOTE** *In case a class and interfaces are used to derive from, the class always must come first—before interfaces.*

For a struct, the syntax is as follows (it can only use interface inheritance):

```
public struct MyDerivedStruct: IInterface1, IInterface2
{
  // members
}
```

If you do not specify a base class in a class definition, the C# compiler assumes that System.Object is the base class. Hence, deriving from the Object class (or using the object keyword) is the same as not defining a base class.

```
class MyClass // implicitly derives from System.Object
{
  // members
}
```

Let's get into an example to define a base class Shape. Something that's common with shapes—no matter whether they are rectangles or ellipses—is that they have position and size. For position and size, corresponding classes are defined that are contained within the Shape class. The Shape class defines read-only properties Position and Shape that are initialized using auto property initializers (code file VirtualMethods/Shape.cs):

```
public class Position
{
  public int X { get; set; }
  public int Y { get; set; }
}

public class Size
{
  public int Width { get; set; }
  public int Height { get; set; }
}

public class Shape
{
  public Position Position { get; } = new Position();
  public Size Size { get; } = new Size();
}
```

Virtual Methods

By declaring a base class method as virtual, you allow the method to be overridden in any derived classes:

```
public class Shape
{
  public virtual void Draw()
  {
    WriteLine($"Shape with {Position} and {Size}");
  }
}
```

In case the implementation is a one-liner, with C# 6, expression bodied methods (using the lambda operator) can also be used with the virtual keyword. This syntax can be used independent of the modifiers applied:

```
public class Shape
{
```

```
    public virtual void Draw() => WriteLine($"Shape with {Position} and {Size}");
}
```

It is also permitted to declare a property as `virtual`. For a virtual or overridden property, the syntax is the same as for a non-virtual property, with the exception of the keyword `virtual`, which is added to the definition. The syntax looks like this:

```
public virtual Size Size { get; set; }
```

Of course, it is also possible to use the full property syntax for virtual properties:

```
private Size _size;
public virtual Size Size
{
  get
  {
    return _size;
  }
  set
  {
    _size = value;
  }
}
```

For simplicity, the following discussion focuses mainly on methods, but it applies equally well to properties.

The concepts behind virtual functions in C# are identical to standard OOP concepts. You can override a virtual function in a derived class; when the method is called, the appropriate method for the type of object is invoked. In C#, functions are not virtual by default but (aside from constructors) can be explicitly declared as `virtual`. This follows the C++ methodology: For performance reasons, functions are not virtual unless indicated. In Java, by contrast, all functions are virtual. C# differs from C++ syntax, though, because it requires you to declare when a derived class's function overrides another function, using the `override` keyword (code file `VirtualMethods/ConcreteShapes.cs`):

```
public class Rectangle : Shape
{
  public override void Draw() =>
      WriteLine($"Rectangle with {Position} and {Size}");
}
```

This syntax for method overriding removes potential runtime bugs that can easily occur in C++, when a method signature in a derived class unintentionally differs slightly from the base version, resulting in the method failing to override the base version. In C#, this is picked up as a compile-time error because the compiler would see a function marked as `override` but would not see a base method for it to override.

The `Size` and `Position` types override the `ToString` method. This method is declared as `virtual` in the base class `Object`:

```
public class Position
{
  public int X { get; set; }
  public int Y { get; set; }
  public override string ToString() => $"X: {X}, Y: {Y}";
}

public class Size
{
  public int Width { get; set; }
  public int Height { get; set; }
  public override string ToString() => $"Width: {Width}, Height: {Height}";
}
```

> **NOTE** *The members of the base class* Object *are explained in Chapter 3.*

> **NOTE** *When overriding methods of the base class, the signature (all parameter types and the method name) and the return type must match exactly. If this is not the case then you can create a new member that does not override the base member.*

Within the Main method, a rectangle named r is instantiated, its properties initialized, and the method Draw invoked (code file VirtualMethods/Program.cs):

```
var r = new Rectangle();
r.Position.X = 33;
r.Position.Y = 22;
r.Size.Width = 200;
r.Size.Height = 100;
r.Draw();
```

Run the program to see the output of the Draw method:

```
Rectangle with X: 33, y: 22 and Width: 200, Height: 100
```

Neither member fields nor static functions can be declared as virtual. The concept simply wouldn't make sense for any class member other than an instance function member.

Polymorphism

With polymorphism, the method that is invoked is defined dynamically and not during compile time. The compiler creates a virtual method table (vtable) that lists the methods that can be invoked during runtime, and it invokes the method based on the type at runtime.

Let's have a look at one example. The method DrawShape receives a Shape parameter and invokes the Draw method of the Shape class (code file VirtualMethods/Program.cs):

```
public static void DrawShape(Shape shape)
{
    shape.Draw();
}
```

Use the rectangle created before to invoke the method. Although the method is declared to receive a Shape object, any type that derives from Shape (including the Rectangle) can be passed to this method:

```
DrawShape(r);
```

Run the program to see the output of the Rectangle.Draw method instead of the Shape.Draw method. The output line starts with Rectangle. If the method of the base class wouldn't be virtual or the method from the derived class not overridden, the Draw method of the type of the declared object (the Shape) would be used, and thus the output would start with Shape:

```
Rectangle with X: 33, y: 22 and Width: 200, Height: 100
```

Hiding Methods

If a method with the same signature is declared in both base and derived classes but the methods are not declared with the modifiers virtual and override, respectively, then the derived class version is said to *hide* the base class version.

In most cases, you would want to override methods rather than hide them. By hiding them you risk calling the wrong method for a given class instance. However, as shown in the following example, C# syntax is designed to ensure that the developer is warned at compile time about this potential problem, thus making it safer to hide methods if that is your intention. This also has versioning benefits for developers of class libraries.

Suppose that you have a class called Shape in a class library:

```
public class Shape
{
    // various members
}
```

At some point in the future, you write a derived class Ellipse that adds some functionality to the Shape base class. In particular, you add a method called MoveBy, which is not present in the base class:

```
public class Ellipse: Shape
{
    public void MoveBy(int x, int y)
    {
        Position.X += x;
        Position.Y += y;
    }
}
```

At some later time, the developer of the base class decides to extend the functionality of the base class and, by coincidence, adds a method that is also called MoveBy and that has the same name and signature as yours; however, it probably doesn't do the same thing. This new method might be declared virtual or not.

If you recompile the derived class you get a compiler warning because of a potential method clash. However, it can also happen easily that the new base class is used without compiling the derived class; it just replaces the base class assembly. The base class assembly could be installed in the global assembly cache (which is done by many Framework assemblies).

Now let's assume the MoveBy method of the base class is declared virtual and the base class itself invokes the MoveBy method. What method will be called? The method of the base class or the MoveBy method of the derived class that was defined earlier? Because the MoveBy method of the derived class is not defined with the override keyword (this was not possible because the base class MoveBy method didn't exist earlier), the compiler assumes the MoveBy method from the derived class is a completely different method that doesn't have any relation to the method of the base class; it just has the same name. This method is treated the same way as if it had a different name.

Compiling the Ellipse class generates a compilation warning that reminds you to use the new keyword to hide a method. In practice, not using the new keyword has the same compilation result, but you avoid the compiler warning:

```
public class Ellipse: Shape
{
    new public void Move(Position newPosition)
    {
        Position.X = newPosition.X;
        Position.Y = newPosition.Y;
    }
    //. . . other members
}
```

Instead of using the new keyword, you can also rename the method or override the method of the base class if it is declared virtual and serves the same purpose. However, in case other methods already invoke this method, a simple rename can lead to breaking other code.

> **NOTE** *The* new *method modifier shouldn't be used deliberately to hide members of the base class. The main purpose of this modifier is to deal with version conflicts and react to changes on base classes after the derived class was done.*

Calling Base Versions of Methods

C# has a special syntax for calling base versions of a method from a derived class: base.<MethodName>. For example, you have the Move method declared in the base class Shape and want to invoke it in the derived class Rectangle to use the implementation from the base class. To add functionality from the derived class, you can invoke it using base (code file VirtualMethods/Shape.cs):

```
public class Shape
{
  public virtual void Move(Position newPosition)
  {
    Position.X = newPosition.X;
    Position.Y = newPosition.Y;
    WriteLine($"moves to {Position}");
  }
  //. . . other members
}
```

The Move method is overridden in the Rectangle class to add the term Rectangle to the console. After this text is written, the method of the base class is invoked using the base keyword (code file VirtualMethods/ConcreteShapes.cs):

```
public class Rectangle: Shape
{
  public override void Move(Position newPosition)
  {
    Write("Rectangle ");
    base.Move(newPosition);
  }
  //. . . other members
}
```

Now move the rectangle to a new position (code file VirtualMethods/Program.cs):

```
r.Move(new Position { X = 120, Y = 40 });
```

Run the application to see output that is a result of the Move method in the Rectangle and the Shape classes:

```
Rectangle moves to X: 120, Y: 40
```

> **NOTE** *Using the* base *keyword you can invoke any method of the base class—not just the method that is overridden.*

Abstract Classes and Methods

C# allows both classes and methods to be declared as abstract. An abstract class cannot be instantiated, whereas an abstract method does not have an implementation and must be overridden in any nonabstract derived class. Obviously, an abstract method is *automatically* virtual (although you don't need to supply the virtual keyword, and doing so results in a syntax error). If any class contains any abstract methods, that class is also abstract and must be declared as such.

Let's change the Shape class to be abstract. With this it is necessary to derive from this class. The new method Resize is declared abstract, and thus it can't have any implementation in the Shape class (code file VirtualMethods/Shape.cs):

```
public abstract class Shape
{
    public abstract void Resize(int width, int height);    // abstract method
}
```

When deriving a type from the abstract base class, it is necessary to implement all abstract members. Otherwise, the compiler complains:

```
public class Ellipse : Shape
{
    public override void Resize(int width, int height)
    {
        Size.Width = width;
        Size.Height = height;
    }
}
```

Of course, the implementation could also look like the following example. Throwing an exception of type NotImplementationException is also an implementation, just not the implementation that was meant to be and usually just a temporary implementation during development:

```
public override void Resize(int width, int height)
{
    throw new NotImplementedException();
}
```

> **NOTE** *Exceptions are explained in detail in Chapter 14, "Errors and Exceptions."*

Using the abstract Shape class and the derived Ellipse class, you can declare a variable of a Shape. You cannot instantiate it, but you can instantiate an Ellipse and assign it to the Shape variable (code file VirtualMethods/Program.cs):

```
Shape s1 = new Ellipse();
DrawShape(s1);
```

Sealed Classes and Methods

In case it shouldn't be allowed to create a class that derives from your class, your class should be sealed. Adding the sealed modifier to a class doesn't allow you to create a subclass of it. Sealing a method means it's not possible to override this method.

```
sealed class FinalClass
{
    // etc
}

class DerivedClass: FinalClass        // wrong. Cannot derive from sealed class.
{
    // etc
}
```

The most likely situation in which you'll mark a class or method as `sealed` is if the class or method is internal to the operation of the library, class, or other classes that you are writing, to ensure that any attempt to override some of its functionality might lead to instability in the code. For example, maybe you haven't tested inheritance and made the investment in design decisions for inheritance. If this is the case, it's better to mark your class `sealed`.

There's another reason to seal classes. With a sealed class, the compiler knows that derived classes are not possible, and thus the virtual table used for virtual methods can be reduced or eliminated, which can increase performance. The string class is sealed. As I haven't seen a single application not using strings, it's best to have this type as performant as possible. Making the class sealed is a good hint for the compiler.

Declaring a method as `sealed` serves a purpose similar to that for a class. The method can be an overridden method from a base class, but in the following example the compiler knows another class cannot extend the virtual table for this method; it ends here.

```
class MyClass: MyBaseClass
{
  public sealed override void FinalMethod()
  {
    // implementation
  }
}

class DerivedClass: MyClass
{
  public override void FinalMethod()  // wrong. Will give compilation error
  {
  }
}
```

In order to use the `sealed` keyword on a method or property, it must have first been overridden from a base class. If you do not want a method or property in a base class overridden, then don't mark it as virtual.

Constructors of Derived Classes

Chapter 3 discusses how constructors can be applied to individual classes. An interesting question arises as to what happens when you start defining your own constructors for classes that are part of a hierarchy, inherited from other classes that may also have custom constructors.

Assume that you have not defined any explicit constructors for any of your classes. This means that the compiler supplies default zeroing-out constructors for all your classes. There is actually quite a lot going on under the hood when that happens, but the compiler is able to arrange it so that things work out nicely throughout the class hierarchy, and every field in every class is initialized to whatever its default value is. When you add a constructor of your own, however, you are effectively taking control of construction. This has implications right down through the hierarchy of derived classes, so you have to ensure that you don't inadvertently do anything to prevent construction through the hierarchy from taking place smoothly.

You might be wondering why there is any special problem with derived classes. The reason is that when you create an instance of a derived class, more than one constructor is at work. The constructor of the class you instantiate isn't by itself sufficient to initialize the class; the constructors of the base classes must also be called. That's why we've been talking about construction through the hierarchy.

With the earlier sample of the `Shape` type, properties have been initialized using the auto property initializer:

```
public class Shape
{
  public Position Position { get; } = new Position();
  public Size Size { get; } = new Size();
}
```

Behind the scenes, the compiler creates a default constructor for the class and moves the property initializer within this constructor:

```
public class Shape
{
    public Shape()
    {
        Position = new Position();
        Size = new Size();
    }
    public Position Position { get; };
    public Size Size { get; };
}
```

Of course, instantiating a Rectangle type that derives from the Shape class, the Rectangle needs Position and Size, and thus the constructor from the base class is invoked on constructing the derived object.

In case you don't initialize members within the default constructor, the compiler automatically initializes reference types to null and value types to 0. Boolean types are initialized to false. The Boolean type is a value type, and false is the same as 0, so it's the same rule that applies to the Boolean type.

With the Ellipse class, it's not necessary to create a default constructor if the base class defines a default constructor and you're okay with initializing all members to their defaults. Of course, you still can supply a constructor and call the base constructor using a *constructor initializer*:

```
public class Ellipse : Shape
{
    public Ellipse()
        : base()
    {
    }
}
```

The constructors are always called in the order of the hierarchy. The constructor of the class System. Object is first, and then progress continues down the hierarchy until the compiler reaches the class being instantiated. For instantiating the Ellipse type, the Shape constructor follows the Object constructor, and then the Ellipse constructor comes. Each of these constructors handles the initialization of the fields in its own class.

Now, make a change to the constructor of the Shape class. Instead of doing a default initialization with Size and Position properties, assign values within the constructor (code file InheritanceWithConstructors/Shape.cs):

```
public abstract class Shape
{
    public Shape(int width, int height, int x, int y)
    {
        Size = new Size { Width = width, Height = height };
        Position = new Position { X = x, Y = y };
    }

    public Position Position { get; }
    public Size Size { get; }
}
```

When removing the default constructor and recompiling the program, the Ellipse and Rectangle classes can't compile because the compiler doesn't know what values should be passed to the only nondefault constructor of the base class. Here you need to create a constructor in the derived class and initialize the base class constructor with the *constructor initializer* (code file InheritanceWithConstructors/ConcreteShapes.cs):

```
public Rectangle(int width, int height, int x, int y)
    : base(width, height, x, y)
{
}
```

Putting the initialization inside the constructor block is too late because the constructor of the base class is invoked before the constructor of the derived class is called. That's why there's a constructor initializer that is declared before the constructor block.

In case you want to allow creating `Rectangle` objects by using a default constructor, you can still do this. You can also do it if the constructor of the base class doesn't have a default constructor. You just need to assign the values for the base class constructor in the constructor initializer as shown. In the following snippet, named arguments are used because otherwise it would be hard to distinguish between `width`, `height`, `x`, and `y` values passed.

```
public Rectangle()
    : base(width: 0, height: 0, x: 0, y: 0)
{
}
```

> **NOTE** *Named arguments are discussed in Chapter 3.*

As you can see, this is a very neat and well-designed process. Each constructor handles initialization of the variables that are obviously its responsibility; and, in the process, your class is correctly instantiated and prepared for use. If you follow the same principles when you write your own constructors for your classes, even the most complex classes should be initialized smoothly and without any problems.

MODIFIERS

You have already encountered quite a number of so-called modifiers—keywords that can be applied to a type or a member. Modifiers can indicate the visibility of a method, such as `public` or `private`, or the nature of an item, such as whether a method is `virtual` or `abstract`. C# has a number of modifiers, and at this point it's worth taking a minute to provide the complete list.

Access Modifiers

Access modifiers indicate which other code items can view an item.

MODIFIER	APPLIES TO	DESCRIPTION
public	Any types or members	The item is visible to any other code.
protected	Any member of a type, and any nested type	The item is visible only to any derived type.
internal	Any types or members	The item is visible only within its containing assembly.
private	Any member of a type, and any nested type	The item is visible only inside the type to which it belongs.
protected internal	Any member of a type, and any nested type	The item is visible to any code within its containing assembly and to any code inside a derived type.

> **NOTE** public, protected, *and* private *are logical access modifiers.* internal *is a physical access modifier whose boundary is an assembly.*

Note that type definitions can be internal or public, depending on whether you want the type to be visible outside its containing assembly:

```
public class MyClass
{
    // etc.
```

You cannot define types as protected, private, or protected internal because these visibility levels would be meaningless for a type contained in a namespace. Hence, these visibilities can be applied only to members. However, you can define nested types (that is, types contained within other types) with these visibilities because in this case the type also has the status of a member. Hence, the following code is correct:

```
public class OuterClass
{
    protected class InnerClass
    {
        // etc.
    }
    // etc.
}
```

If you have a nested type, the inner type is always able to see all members of the outer type. Therefore, with the preceding code, any code inside InnerClass always has access to all members of OuterClass, even where those members are private.

Other Modifiers

The modifiers in the following table can be applied to members of types and have various uses. A few of these modifiers also make sense when applied to types.

MODIFIER	APPLIES TO	DESCRIPTION
new	Function members	The member hides an inherited member with the same signature.
static	All members	The member does not operate on a specific instance of the class. This is also known as *class member* instead of instance member.
virtual	Function members only	The member can be overridden by a derived class.
abstract	Function members only	A virtual member that defines the signature of the member but doesn't provide an implementation.
override	Function members only	The member overrides an inherited virtual or abstract member.
sealed	Classes, methods, and properties	For classes, the class cannot be inherited from. For properties and methods, the member overrides an inherited virtual member but cannot be overridden by any members in any derived classes. Must be used in conjunction with override.
extern	Static [DllImport] methods only	The member is implemented externally, in a different language. The use of this keyword is explained in Chapter 5, "Managed and Unmanaged Resources."

INTERFACES

As mentioned earlier, by deriving from an interface, a class is declaring that it implements certain functions. Because not all object-oriented languages support interfaces, this section examines C#'s implementation of interfaces in detail. It illustrates interfaces by presenting the complete definition of one of the interfaces that has been predefined by Microsoft: `System.IDisposable`. `IDisposable` contains one method, `Dispose`, which is intended to be implemented by classes to clean up code:

```
public interface IDisposable
{
  void Dispose();
}
```

This code shows that declaring an interface works syntactically in much the same way as declaring an abstract class. Be aware, however, that it is not permitted to supply implementations of any of the members of an interface. In general, an interface can contain only declarations of methods, properties, indexers, and events.

Compare interfaces to abstract classes: An abstract class can have implementations or abstract members without implementation. However, an interface can never have any implementation; it is purely abstract. Because the members of an interface are always abstract, the `abstract` keyword is not needed with interfaces.

Similarly to abstract classes, you can never instantiate an interface; it contains only the signatures of its members. In addition, you can declare variables of a type of an interface.

An interface has neither constructors (how can you construct something that you can't instantiate?) nor fields (because that would imply some internal implementation). An interface is also not allowed to contain operator overloads—although this possibility is always discussed with the language design and might change at some time in the future.

It's also not permitted to declare modifiers on the members in an interface definition. Interface members are always implicitly `public`, and they cannot be declared as `virtual`. That's up to implementing classes to decide. Therefore, it is fine for implementing classes to declare access modifiers, as demonstrated in the example in this section.

For example, consider `IDisposable`. If a class wants to declare publicly that it implements the `Dispose` method, it must implement `IDisposable`, which in C# terms means that the class derives from `IDisposable`:

```
class SomeClass: IDisposable
{
  // This class MUST contain an implementation of the
  // IDisposable.Dispose() method, otherwise
  // you get a compilation error.
  public void Dispose()
  {
    // implementation of Dispose() method
  }
  // rest of class
}
```

In this example, if `SomeClass` derives from `IDisposable` but doesn't contain a `Dispose` implementation with the exact same signature as defined in `IDisposable`, you get a compilation error because the class is breaking its agreed-on contract to implement `IDisposable`. Of course, it's no problem for the compiler if a class has a `Dispose` method but doesn't derive from `IDisposable`. The problem is that other code would have no way of recognizing that `SomeClass` has agreed to support the `IDisposable` features.

> **NOTE** `IDisposable` *is a relatively simple interface because it defines only one method. Most interfaces contain more members. The correct implementation of* `IDisposable` *is not really that simple; it's covered in Chapter 5.*

Defining and Implementing Interfaces

This section illustrates how to define and use interfaces by developing a short program that follows the interface inheritance paradigm. The example is based on bank accounts. Assume that you are writing code that will ultimately allow computerized transfers between bank accounts. Assume also for this example that there are many companies that implement bank accounts, but they have all mutually agreed that any classes representing bank accounts will implement an interface, IBankAccount, which exposes methods to deposit or withdraw money, and a property to return the balance. It is this interface that enables outside code to recognize the various bank account classes implemented by different bank accounts. Although the aim is to enable the bank accounts to communicate with each other to allow transfers of funds between accounts, that feature isn't introduced just yet.

To keep things simple, you keep all the code for the example in the same source file. Of course, if something like the example were used in real life, you could surmise that the different bank account classes would not only be compiled to different assemblies, but also be hosted on different machines owned by the different banks. That's all much too complicated for the purposes of this example. However, to maintain some realism, you define different namespaces for the different companies.

To begin, you need to define the IBankAccount interface (code file UsingInterfaces/IBankAccount.cs):

```
namespace Wrox.ProCSharp
{
  public interface IBankAccount
  {
    void PayIn(decimal amount);
    bool Withdraw(decimal amount);
    decimal Balance { get; }
  }
}
```

Notice the name of the interface, IBankAccount. It's a best-practice convention to begin an interface name with the letter I, to indicate it's an interface.

> **NOTE** *Chapter 2, "Core C#," points out that in most cases, .NET usage guidelines discourage the so-called Hungarian notation in which names are preceded by a letter that indicates the type of object being defined. Interfaces are one of the few exceptions for which Hungarian notation is recommended.*

The idea is that you can now write classes that represent bank accounts. These classes don't have to be related to each other in any way; they can be completely different classes. They will all, however, declare that they represent bank accounts by the mere fact that they implement the IBankAccount interface.

Let's start off with the first class, a saver account run by the Royal Bank of Venus (code file UsingInterfaces/VenusBank.cs):

```
namespace Wrox.ProCSharp.VenusBank
{
  public class SaverAccount: IBankAccount
  {
    private decimal _balance;

    public void PayIn(decimal amount) => _balance += amount;

    public bool Withdraw(decimal amount)
    {
      if (_balance >= amount)
      {
```

```
            _balance -= amount;
            return true;
        }
        WriteLine("Withdrawal attempt failed.");
        return false;
    }

    public decimal Balance => _balance;

    public override string ToString() =>
        $"Venus Bank Saver: Balance = {_balance,6:C}";
    }
}
```

It should be obvious what the implementation of this class does. You maintain a private field, `balance`, and adjust this amount when money is deposited or withdrawn. You display an error message if an attempt to withdraw money fails because of insufficient funds. Notice also that because we are keeping the code as simple as possible, we are not implementing extra properties, such as the account holder's name! In real life that would be essential information, of course, but for this example it's unnecessarily complicated.

The only really interesting line in this code is the class declaration:

```
public class SaverAccount: IBankAccount
```

You've declared that `SaverAccount` is derived from one interface, `IBankAccount`, and you have not explicitly indicated any other base classes (which means that `SaverAccount` is derived directly from `System.Object`). By the way, derivation from interfaces acts completely independently from derivation from classes.

Being derived from `IBankAccount` means that `SaverAccount` gets all the members of `IBankAccount`; but because an interface doesn't actually implement any of its methods, `SaverAccount` must provide its own implementations of all of them. If any implementations are missing, you can rest assured that the compiler will complain. Recall also that the interface just indicates the presence of its members. It's up to the class to determine whether it wants any of them to be `virtual` or `abstract` (though `abstract` functions are only allowed if the class itself is `abstract`). For this particular example, you don't have any reason to make any of the interface functions virtual.

To illustrate how different classes can implement the same interface, assume that the Planetary Bank of Jupiter also implements a class to represent one of its bank accounts—a Gold Account (code file `UsingInterfaces/JupiterBank.cs`):

```
namespace Wrox.ProCSharp.JupiterBank
{
    public class GoldAccount: IBankAccount
    {
        // etc
    }
}
```

The details of the `GoldAccount` class aren't presented here; in the sample code, it's basically identical to the implementation of `SaverAccount`. We stress that `GoldAccount` has no connection with `SaverAccount`, other than they both happen to implement the same interface.

Now that you have your classes, you can test them. You first need a few `using` statements:

```
using Wrox.ProCSharp;
using Wrox.ProCSharp.VenusBank;
using Wrox.ProCSharp.JupiterBank;
using static System.Console;
```

Now you need a `Main` method (code file `UsingInterfaces/Program.cs`):

```
namespace Wrox.ProCSharp
{
```

```
class Program
{
  static void Main()
  {
      IBankAccount venusAccount = new SaverAccount();
      IBankAccount jupiterAccount = new GoldAccount();

      venusAccount.PayIn(200);
      venusAccount.Withdraw(100);
      WriteLine(venusAccount.ToString());

      jupiterAccount.PayIn(500);
      jupiterAccount.Withdraw(600);
      jupiterAccount.Withdraw(100);
      WriteLine(jupiterAccount.ToString());
  }
}
```

This code produces the following output:

```
> BankAccounts
Venus Bank Saver: Balance = $100.00
Withdrawal attempt failed.
Jupiter Bank Saver: Balance = $400.00
```

The main point to notice about this code is the way that you have declared both your reference variables as `IBankAccount` references. This means that they can point to any instance of any class that implements this interface. However, it also means that you can call only methods that are part of this interface through these references—if you want to call any methods implemented by a class that are not part of the interface, you need to cast the reference to the appropriate type. In the example code, you were able to call `ToString` (not implemented by `IBankAccount`) without any explicit cast, purely because `ToString` is a `System.Object` method, so the C# compiler knows that it will be supported by any class (put differently, the cast from any interface to `System.Object` is implicit). Chapter 8, "Operators and Casts," covers the syntax for performing casts.

Interface references can in all respects be treated as class references—but the power of an interface reference is that it can refer to any class that implements that interface. For example, this allows you to form arrays of interfaces, whereby each element of the array is a different class:

```
IBankAccount[] accounts = new IBankAccount[2];
accounts[0] = new SaverAccount();
accounts[1] = new GoldAccount();
```

Note, however, that you would get a compiler error if you tried something like this:

```
accounts[1] = new SomeOtherClass();     // SomeOtherClass does NOT implement
                                        // IBankAccount: WRONG!!
```

The preceding causes a compilation error similar to this:

```
Cannot implicitly convert type 'Wrox.ProCSharp. SomeOtherClass' to
 'Wrox.ProCSharp.IBankAccount'
```

Interface Inheritance

It's possible for interfaces to inherit from each other in the same way that classes do. This concept is illustrated by defining a new interface, `ITransferBankAccount`, which has the same features as `IBankAccount` but also defines a method to transfer money directly to a different account (code file `UsingInterfaces/ ITransferBankAccount`):

```
namespace Wrox.ProCSharp
{
```

```
      public interface ITransferBankAccount: IBankAccount
      {
        bool TransferTo(IBankAccount destination, decimal amount);
      }
  }
```

Because `ITransferBankAccount` is derived from `IBankAccount`, it gets all the members of `IBankAccount` as well as its own. That means that any class that implements (derives from) `ITransferBankAccount` must implement all the methods of `IBankAccount`, as well as the new `TransferTo` method defined in `ITransferBankAccount`. Failure to implement all these methods results in a compilation error.

Note that the `TransferTo` method uses an `IBankAccount` interface reference for the destination account. This illustrates the usefulness of interfaces: When implementing and then invoking this method, you don't need to know anything about what type of object you are transferring money to—all you need to know is that this object implements `IBankAccount`.

To illustrate `ITransferBankAccount`, assume that the Planetary Bank of Jupiter also offers a current account. Most of the implementation of the `CurrentAccount` class is identical to implementations of `SaverAccount` and `GoldAccount` (again, this is just to keep this example simple—that won't normally be the case), so in the following code only the differences are highlighted (code file `UsingInterfaces/JupiterBank.cs`):

```
  public class CurrentAccount: ITransferBankAccount
  {
    private decimal _balance;

    public void PayIn(decimal amount) => _balance += amount;

    public bool Withdraw(decimal amount)
    {
      if (_balance >= amount)
      {
        _balance -= amount;
        return true;
      }
      WriteLine("Withdrawal attempt failed.");
      return false;
    }

    public decimal Balance => _balance;

    public bool TransferTo(IBankAccount destination, decimal amount)
    {
      bool result = Withdraw(amount);
      if (result)
      {
        destination.PayIn(amount);
      }
      return result;
    }

    public override string ToString() =>
      $"Jupiter Bank Current Account: Balance = {_balance,6:C}";

  }
```

The class can be demonstrated with this code:

```
  static void Main()
  {
    IBankAccount venusAccount = new SaverAccount();
    ITransferBankAccount jupiterAccount = new CurrentAccount();
```

```
venusAccount.PayIn(200);
jupiterAccount.PayIn(500);
jupiterAccount.TransferTo(venusAccount, 100);
WriteLine(venusAccount.ToString());
WriteLine(jupiterAccount.ToString());
}
```

The preceding code produces the following output, which, as you can verify, shows that the correct amounts have been transferred:

```
> CurrentAccount
Venus Bank Saver: Balance = $300.00
Jupiter Bank Current Account: Balance = $400.00
```

IS AND AS OPERATORS

Before concluding inheritance with interfaces and classes, we need to have a look at two important operators related to inheritance: the is and as operators.

You've already seen that you can directly assign objects of a specific type to a base class or an interface—if the type has a direct relation in the hierarchy. For example, the SaverAccount created earlier can be directly assigned to an IBankAccount because the SaverAccount type implements the interface IBankAccount:

```
IBankAccount venusAccount = new SaverAccount();
```

What if you have a method accepting an object type, and you want to get access to the IBankAccount members? The object type doesn't have the members of the IBankAccount interface. You can do a cast. Cast the object (you can also use any parameter of type of any interface and cast it to the type you need) to an IBankAccount and work with that:

```
public void WorkWithManyDifferentObjects(object o)
{
  IBankAccount account = (IBankAccount)o;
  // work with the account
}
```

This works as long as you always supply an object of type IBankAccount to this method. Of course, if an object of type object is accepted, there will be the case when invalid objects are passed. This is when you get an InvalidCastException. It's never a good idea to accept exceptions in normal cases. You can read more about this in Chapter 14. This is where the is and as operators come into play.

Instead of doing the cast directly, it's a good idea to check whether the parameter implements the interface IBankAccount. The as operator works similar to the cast operator within the class hierarchy—it returns a reference to the object. However, it never throws an InvalidCastException. Instead, this operator returns null in case the object is not of the type asked for. Here, it is a good idea to verify for null before using the reference; otherwise a NullReferenceException will be thrown later using the following reference:

```
public void WorkWithManyDifferentObjects(object o)
{
  IBankAccount account = o as IBankAccount;
  if (account != null)
  {
    // work with the account
  }
}
```

Instead of using the as operator, you can use the is operator. The is operator returns true or false, depending on whether the condition is fulfilled and the object is of the specified type. After verifying whether the condition is true, a cast can be done because now this cast always succeeds:

```
public void WorkWithManyDifferentObjects(object o)
{
```

```
    if (o is IBankAccount)
    {
      IBankAccount account = (IBankAccount)o;
      // work with the account
    }
  }
}
```

Instead of having bad surprises by exceptions based on casts, conversions within the class hierarchy work well with the `is` and `as` operators.

SUMMARY

This chapter described how to code inheritance in C#. The chapter described how C# offers rich support for both multiple interface and single implementation inheritance and explained that C# provides a number of useful syntactical constructs designed to assist in making code more robust. These include the `override` keyword, which indicates when a function should override a base function; the `new` keyword, which indicates when a function hides a base function; and rigid rules for constructor initializers that are designed to ensure that constructors are designed to interoperate in a robust manner.

The next chapter shows the details of the interface `IDisposable` and explains managing resources allocated from native code.

5

Managed and Unmanaged Resources

WHAT'S IN THIS CHAPTER?

➤ Allocating space on the stack and heap at runtime
➤ Garbage collection
➤ Releasing unmanaged resources using destructors and the `System.IDisposable` interface
➤ The syntax for using pointers in C#
➤ Using pointers to implement high-performance stack-based arrays
➤ Platform Invoke to access native APIs

WROX.COM CODE DOWNLOADS FOR THIS CHAPTER

The wrox.com code downloads for this chapter are found at www.wrox.com/go/professionalcsharp6 on the Download Code tab. The code for this chapter is divided into the following major examples:

➤ PointerPlayground
➤ PointerPlayground2
➤ QuickArray
➤ PlatformInvokeSample

RESOURCES

Resources is an overloaded term. One use of the term resources you can find with localization. With localization, resources are used to translate text and images. Based on the user's culture, the correct resource is loaded. (This is discussed in Chapter 28, "Localization.") Another use of the term resources you can read in this chapter. Here, resources are used with a different topic: using managed and unmanaged resources—objects that are stored on the managed or the native heap. Although the garbage collector frees up managed objects that are stored in the managed heap, it isn't responsible for the objects in the native heap. You have to free them on your own.

When you use a managed environment, you can easily be misled to not pay attention to memory management because the *garbage collector* (GC) deals with that anyway. A lot of work is done by the GC; it's very practical to know how it works, what the small and the large object heap are, and what data types are stored within the stack. Also, while the garbage collector deals with managed resources, what about unmanaged ones? You have to free them on your own. Probably your programs are fully managed programs, but what about the types of the Framework? For example, file types (discussed in Chapter 23, "Files and Streams"), wrap a native file handle. This file handle needs to be released. To release this handle early, it's good to know the `IDisposable` interface and the `using` statement that's explained in this chapter.

This chapter starts with various aspects of memory management and memory access. A good understanding of memory management and knowledge of the pointer capabilities provided by C# will better enable you to integrate C# code with legacy code and perform efficient memory manipulation in performance-critical systems.

MEMORY MANAGEMENT UNDER THE HOOD

One of the advantages of C# programming is that the programmer does not need to worry about detailed memory management; the garbage collector deals with the problem of memory cleanup on your behalf. As a result, you get something that approximates the efficiency of languages such as C++ without the complexity of having to handle memory management yourself as you do in C++. However, although you do not have to manage memory manually, it still pays to understand what is going on behind the scenes. Understanding how your program manages memory under the covers will help you increase the speed and performance of your applications. This section looks at what happens in the computer's memory when you allocate variables.

> **NOTE** *The precise details of many of the topics of this section are not presented here. This section serves as an abbreviated guide to the general processes rather than as a statement of exact implementation.*

Value Data Types

Windows uses a system known as *virtual addressing*, in which the mapping from the memory address seen by your program to the actual location in hardware memory is entirely managed by Windows. As a result, each process of a 32-bit application sees 4GB of available memory, regardless of how much hardware memory you actually have in your computer (with 64-bit applications on 64-bit processors this number is greater). This memory contains everything that is part of the program, including the executable code, any DLLs loaded by the code, and the contents of all variables used when the program runs. This 4GB of memory is known as the *virtual address* space or *virtual memory*. For convenience, this chapter uses the shorthand *memory*.

> **NOTE** *With .NET Core applications you specify whether to debug 32- or 64-bit applications by selecting the architecture in the Visual Studio Project Properties, Debug settings (see Figure 5-1). When you select x86, you debug a 32-bit application that runs on 32- and 64-bit systems; when you select x64, you debug a 64-bit application that runs on 64-bit systems. In case you don't see different options here, you have to install the specific runtimes as explained in Chapter 1, ".NET Application Architectures."*

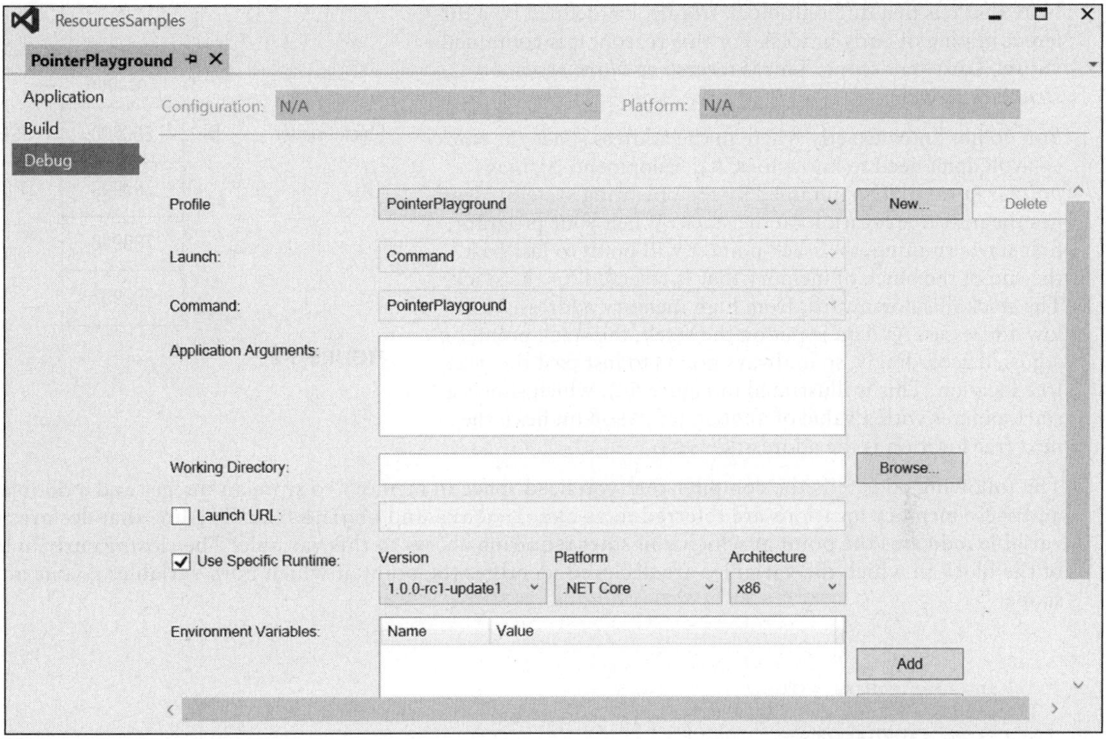

FIGURE 5-1

Each memory location in the available 4GB is numbered starting from zero. To access a value stored at a particular location in memory, you need to supply the number that represents that memory location. In any compiled high-level language, the compiler converts human-readable variable names into memory addresses that the processor understands.

Somewhere inside a processor's virtual memory is an area known as the *stack*. The *stack* stores value data types that are not members of objects. In addition, when you call a method, the stack is used to hold a copy of any parameters passed to the method. To understand how the stack works, you need to understand the importance of variable *scope* in C#. If variable a goes into scope before variable b, then b will always go out of scope first. Consider the following code:

```
{
  int a;
  // do something
  {
    int b;
    // do something else
  }
}
```

First, the variable a is declared. Then, inside the inner code block, b is declared. Then the inner code block terminates and b goes out of scope, then a goes out of scope. Therefore, the lifetime of b is entirely contained within the lifetime of a. The idea that you always de-allocate variables in the reverse order of how you allocate them is crucial to the way the stack works.

Note that b is in a different block from code (defined by a different nesting of curly braces). For this reason, it is contained within a different scope. This is termed as *block scope* or *structure scope*.

You do not know exactly where in the address space the stack is—you don't need to know for C# development. A *stack pointer* (a variable maintained by the operating system) identifies the next free location on the stack. When your program first starts running, the stack pointer will point to just past the end of the block of memory that is reserved for the stack. The stack fills downward, from high memory addresses to low addresses. As data is put on the stack, the stack pointer is adjusted accordingly, so it always points to just past the next free location. This is illustrated in Figure 5-2, which shows a stack pointer with a value of 800000 (0xC3500 (in hex); the next free location is the address 799999.

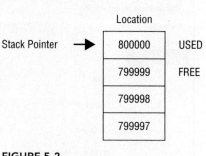

FIGURE 5-2

The following code tells the compiler that you need space in memory to store an integer and a double, and these memory locations are referred to as nRacingCars and engineSize. The line that declares each variable indicates the point at which you start requiring access to this variable. The closing curly brace of the block in which the variables are declared identifies the point at which both variables go out of scope:

```
{
    int nRacingCars = 10;
    double engineSize = 3000.0;
    // do calculations;
}
```

Assuming that you use the stack shown in Figure 5-2, when the variable nRacingCars comes into scope and is assigned the value 10, the value 10 is placed in locations 799996 through 799999, the 4 bytes just below the location pointed to by the stack pointer (4 bytes because that's how much memory is needed to store an int). To accommodate this, 4 is subtracted from the value of the stack pointer, so it now points to the location 799996, just after the new first free location (799995).

The next line of code declares the variable engineSize (a double) and initializes it to the value 3000.0. A double occupies eight bytes, so the value 3000.0 is placed in locations 799988 through 799995 on the stack, and the stack pointer is decremented by eight, so that it again points to the location just after the next free location on the stack.

When engineSize goes out of scope, the runtime knows that it is no longer needed. Because of the way variable lifetimes are always nested, you can guarantee that whatever happened while engineSize was in scope, the stack pointer is now pointing to the location where engineSize is stored. To remove engineSize from the stack, the stack pointer is incremented by eight and it now points to the location immediately after the end of engineSize. At this point in the code, you are at the closing curly brace, so nRacingCars also goes out of scope. The stack pointer is incremented by 4. When another variable comes into scope after engineSize and nRacingCars have been removed from the stack, it overwrites the memory descending from location 799999, where nRacingCars was stored.

If the compiler hits a line such as int i, j, then the order of variables coming into scope looks indeterminate. Both variables are declared at the same time and go out of scope at the same time. In this situation, it does not matter in what order the two variables are removed from memory. The compiler internally always ensures that the one that was put in memory first is removed last, thus preserving the rule that prohibits crossover of variable lifetimes.

Reference Data Types

Although the stack provides very high performance, it is not flexible enough to be used for all variables. The requirement that the lifetime of a variable must be nested is too restrictive for many purposes. Often, you need to use a method to allocate memory for storing data and keeping that data available long after that method has exited. This possibility exists whenever storage space is requested with the new operator—as is the case for all reference types. That is where the *managed heap* comes in.

If you have done any C++ coding that required low-level memory management, you are familiar with the heap. The managed heap is not quite the same as the native heap C++ uses, however; the managed heap works under the control of the garbage collector and provides significant benefits compared to traditional heaps.

The managed heap (or heap for short) is just another area of memory from the processor's available memory. The following code demonstrates how the heap works and how memory is allocated for reference data types:

```
void DoWork()
{
  Customer arabel;
  arabel = new Customer();
  Customer otherCustomer2 = new EnhancedCustomer();
}
```

This code assumes the existence of two classes, Customer and EnhancedCustomer. The EnhancedCustomer class extends the Customer class.

First, you declare a Customer reference called arabel. The space for this is allocated on the stack, but remember that this is only a reference, not an actual Customer object. The arabel reference occupies 4 bytes, enough space to hold the address at which a Customer object will be stored. (You need 4 bytes to represent a memory address as an integer value between 0 and 4GB.)

The next line,

```
arabel = new Customer();
```

does several things. First, it allocates memory on the heap to store a Customer object (a real object, not just an address). Then it sets the value of the variable arabel to the address of the memory it has allocated to the new Customer object. (It also calls the appropriate Customer constructor to initialize the fields in the class instance, but you don't need to worry about that here.)

The Customer instance is not placed on the stack—it is placed on the heap. In this example, you don't know precisely how many bytes a Customer object occupies, but assume for the sake of argument that it is 32. These 32 bytes contain the instance fields of Customer as well as some information that .NET uses to identify and manage its class instances.

To find a storage location on the heap for the new Customer object, the .NET runtime looks through the heap and grabs the first adjacent, unused block of 32 bytes. Again for the sake of argument, assume that this happens to be at address 200000, and that the arabel reference occupied locations 799996 through 799999 on the stack. This means that before instantiating the arabel object, the memory content looks similar to Figure 5-3.

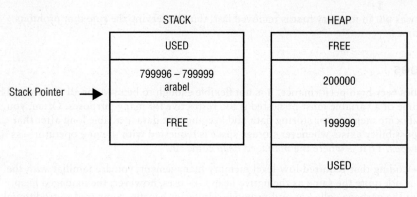

STACK

HEAP

USED	FREE
799996 – 799999 arabel	200000
FREE	199999
	USED

Stack Pointer →

FIGURE 5-3

After allocating the new Customer object, the content of memory looks like Figure 5-4. Note that unlike the stack, memory in the heap is allocated upward, so the free space is above the used space.

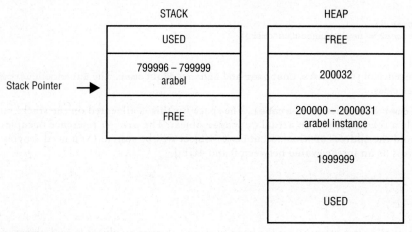

STACK

HEAP

USED	FREE
799996 – 799999 arabel	200032
FREE	200000 – 2000031 arabel instance
	1999999
	USED

Stack Pointer →

FIGURE 5-4

The next line of code both declares a Customer reference and instantiates a Customer object. In this instance, space on the stack for the otherCustomer2 reference is allocated and space for the mrJones object is allocated on the heap in a single line of code:

```
Customer otherCustomer2 = new EnhancedCustomer();
```

This line allocates 4 bytes on the stack to hold the otherCustomer2 reference, stored at locations 799992 through 799995. The otherCustomer2 object is allocated space on the heap starting at location 200032.

It is clear from the example that the process of setting up a reference variable is more complex than that for setting up a value variable, and there is performance overhead. In fact, the process is somewhat oversimplified here, because the .NET runtime needs to maintain information about the state of the heap, and this information needs to be updated whenever new data is added to the heap. Despite this overhead, you now have a mechanism for allocating variables that is not constrained by the limitations of the stack. By assigning the value of one reference variable to another of the same type, you have two variables that reference the same object in memory. When a reference variable goes out of scope, it is removed from the stack as described in the previous section, but the data for a referenced object is still sitting on the heap. The data remains on the heap until either the program terminates or the garbage collector removes it, which happens only when it is no longer referenced by any variables.

That is the power of reference data types, and you will see this feature used extensively in C# code. It means that you have a high degree of control over the lifetime of your data, because it is guaranteed to exist in the heap as long as you are maintaining some reference to it.

Garbage Collection

The previous discussion and diagrams show the managed heap working very much like the stack, to the extent that successive objects are placed next to each other in memory. This means that you can determine where to place the next object by using a heap pointer that indicates the next free memory location, which is adjusted as you add more objects to the heap. However, things are complicated by the fact that the lives of the heap-based objects are not coupled with the scope of the individual stack-based variables that reference them.

When the garbage collector runs, it removes all those objects from the heap that are no longer referenced. The GC finds all referenced objects from a root table of references and continues to the tree of referenced objects. Immediately after, the heap has objects scattered on it, which are mixed up with memory that has just been freed (see Figure 5-5).

If the managed heap stayed like this, allocating space for new objects would be an awkward process, with the runtime having to search through the heap for a block of memory big enough to store each new object. However, the garbage collector does not leave the heap in this state. As soon as the garbage collector has freed all the objects it can, it compacts the heap by moving all the remaining objects to form one continuous block of memory. This means that the heap can continue working just like the stack, as far as locating where to store new objects. Of course, when the objects are moved about, all the references to those objects need to be updated with the correct new addresses, but the garbage collector handles that, too.

FIGURE 5-5

This action of compacting by the garbage collector is where the managed heap works very differently from unmanaged heaps. With the managed heap, it is just a question of reading the value of the heap pointer, rather than iterating through a linked list of addresses to find somewhere to put the new data.

> **NOTE** *Generally, the garbage collector runs when the .NET runtime determines that garbage collection is required. You can force the garbage collector to run at a certain point in your code by calling* `System.GC.Collect`. *The* `System.GC` *class is a .NET class that represents the garbage collector, and the* `Collect` *method initiates a garbage collection. The* `GC` *class is intended for rare situations in which you know that it's a good time to call the garbage collector; for example, if you have just de-referenced a large number of objects in your code. However, the logic of the garbage collector does not guarantee that all unreferenced objects will be removed from the heap in a single garbage collection pass.*

> **NOTE** *It is useful to run* `GC.Collect` *during testing. With this you can see memory leaks where objects that should have been garbage collected are still alive. Because the garbage collector does a good job, it's not a good idea to collect memory programmatically in your production code. If you invoke* `Collect` *programmatically, objects move faster to the next generation, as shown next. This causes more time for the GC to run.*

When objects are created, they are placed within the managed heap. The first section of the heap is called the generation 0 section, or gen 0. As your new objects are created, they are moved into this section of the heap. Therefore, this is where the youngest objects reside.

Your objects remain there until the first collection of objects occurs through the garbage collection process. The objects that remain alive after this cleansing are compacted and then moved to the next section or generational part of the heap—the generation 1, or gen 1, section.

At this point, the generation 0 section is empty, and all new objects are again placed in this section. Older objects that survived the GC (garbage collection) process are further down in the generation 1 section. This movement of aged items actually occurs one more time. The next collection process that occurs is then repeated. This means that the items that survived the GC process from the generation 1 section are moved to the generation 2 section, and the gen 0 items go to gen 1, again leaving gen 0 open for new objects.

> **NOTE** *A garbage collection occurs when you allocate an item that exceeds the capacity of the generation 0 section or when a* `GC.Collect` *is called.*

This process greatly improves the performance of your application. Typically, your youngest objects are the ones that can be collected, and a large number of younger-related objects might be reclaimed as well. If these objects reside next to each other in the heap, then the garbage collection is faster. In addition, because related objects are residing next to each other, program execution is faster all around.

Another performance-related aspect of garbage collection in .NET is how the framework deals with larger objects that are added to the heap. Under the covers of .NET, larger objects have their own managed heap, referred to as the large object heap. When objects greater than 85,000 bytes are utilized, they go to this special heap rather than the main heap. Your .NET application doesn't know the difference, as this is all managed for you. Because compressing large items in the heap is expensive, it isn't done for the objects residing in the large object heap.

In an effort to improve GC even more, collections on the generation 2 section and from the large object heap are now done on a background thread. This means that application threads are only blocked for generation 0 and generation 1 collections, which reduces the overall pause time, especially for large-scale server apps. This feature is on by default for both servers and workstations.

Another optimization to help in application performance is GC balancing. This is specific to server GC. Typically a server will have a pool of threads doing roughly the same thing. The memory allocation will be similar across all the threads. For servers there is one GC heap per logical server. So when one of the heaps runs out of memory and triggers a GC, all of the other heaps most likely will benefit from the GC as well. If a thread happens to use a lot more memory than other threads and it causes a GC, the other threads may not be close to requiring the GC so it's not efficient. The GC will balance the heaps—both the small object heap and also the large object heap. By doing this balancing process, you can reduce unnecessary collection.

To take advantage of hardware with lots of memory, the GC has added the `GCSettings.LatencyMode` property. Setting the property to one of the values in the `GCLatencyMode` enumeration gives a little control to how the GC performs collections. The following table shows the possible values for the `GCLatencyMode` that can be used.

MEMBER	DESCRIPTION
Batch	Disables the concurrency settings and sets the GC for maximum through-put with the expense of responsiveness. This overrides the configuration setting.
Interactive	The default behavior on a workstation. This uses garbage collection concurrency and balances throughput and responsiveness.
LowLatency	Conservative GC. Full collections only occur when there is memory pressure on the system. This setting should only be used for short periods of time to perform specific operations.
SustainedLowLatency	Does full blocking collections only when there is system memory pressure.
NoGCRegion	New with .NET 4.6. With GCSettings, this is a read-only property. You can set it within a code block calling GC.TryStartNoGCRegion and EndNoGCRegion. Invoking TryStartNoGCRegion you define the size of the memory that needs to be available, which the GC tries to reach. After a successful call to TryStartNoGCRegion you define that the garbage collector should not run—until calling EndNoGCRegion.

The amount of time that the LowLatency or NoGCRegion settings are used should be kept to a minimum. The amount of memory being allocated should be as small as possible. An out-of-memory error could occur if you're not careful.

STRONG AND WEAK REFERENCES

The garbage collector cannot reclaim memory of an object that still has a reference—that is a strong reference. It can reclaim managed memory that is not referenced from the root table directly or indirectly. However, sometimes it can be missed to release references.

> **NOTE** *In case you have objects that reference each other but are not referenced from the root table—for example Object A references B, B references C, and C references A—the GC can destroy all these objects.*

When the class or struct is instantiated in the application code, it has a strong reference as long as there is any other code that references it. For example, if you have a class called MyClass and you create a reference to objects based on that class and call the variable myClassVariable as follows, as long as myClassVariable is in scope there is a strong reference to the MyClass object:

```
var myClassVariable = new MyClass();
```

This means that the garbage collector cannot clean up the memory used by the MyClass object. Generally this is a good thing because you might need to access the MyClass object. You might create a cache object that has references to several other objects, like this:

```
var myCache = new MyCache();
myCache.Add(myClassVariable);
```

Now you're finished using the `myClassVariable`. It can go out of scope, or you assign `null`:

```
myClassVariable = null;
```

In case the garbage collector runs now, it can't release the memory that was referenced by the `myClassVariable`, because the object is still referenced from the cache object. Such references can easily be missed, and you can avoid this using the `WeakReference`.

> **NOTE** *With events, it's easy to miss cleaning up of references. Here, you can use weak references as well. Events and weak references with events are covered in Chapter 9, "Delegates, Lambdas, and Events."*

A weak reference allows the object to be created and used, but if the garbage collector happens to run, it collects the object and frees up the memory. This is not something you would typically want to do because of potential bugs and performance issues, but there are certainly situations in which it makes sense. Weak references also don't make sense with small objects, as weak references have an overhead on their own, and that might be bigger than the small object.

Weak references are created using the `WeakReference` class. With the constructor, you can pass a strong reference. The sample code creates a `DataObject` and passes the reference returned from the constructor. On using `WeakReference`, you can check the `IsAlive` property. For using the object again, the `Target` property of `WeakReference` returns a strong reference. In case the value of the property returned is not null, you can use the strong reference. Because the object could be collected at any time, it's important that the existence of the object is valid before trying to reference it. After retrieving the strong reference successfully, you can use it in a normal way, and now it can't be garbage collected because you have a strong reference again:

```
// Instantiate a weak reference to MathTest object
var myWeakReference = new WeakReference(new DataObject());

if (myWeakReference.IsAlive)
{
  DataObject strongReference = myWeakReference.Target as DataObject;
  if (strongReference != null)
  {
    // use the strongReference
  }
}
else
{
  // reference not available
}
```

WORKING WITH UNMANAGED RESOURCES

The presence of the garbage collector means that you usually do not need to worry about objects you no longer need; you simply allow all references to those objects to go out of scope and let the garbage collector free memory as required. However, the garbage collector does not know how to free unmanaged resources (such as file handles, network connections, and database connections). When managed classes encapsulate direct or indirect references to unmanaged resources, you need to make special provisions to ensure that the unmanaged resources are released when an instance of the class is garbage collected.

When defining a class, you can use two mechanisms to automate the freeing of unmanaged resources. These mechanisms are often implemented together because each provides a slightly different approach:

➤ Declare a *destructor* (or finalizer) as a member of your class.

➤ Implement the System.IDisposable interface in your class.

The following sections discuss each of these mechanisms in turn and then look at how to implement the mechanisms together for best results.

Destructors or Finalizers

You have seen that constructors enable you to specify actions that must take place whenever an instance of a class is created. Conversely, destructors are called before an object is destroyed by the garbage collector. Given this behavior, a destructor would initially seem like a great place to put code to free unmanaged resources and perform a general cleanup. Unfortunately, things are not so straightforward.

> **NOTE** *Although we talk about destructors in C#, in the underlying .NET architecture these are known as finalizers. When you define a destructor in C#, what is emitted into the assembly by the compiler is actually a* Finalize *method. It doesn't affect any of your source code, but you need to be aware of it when examining generated Intermediate Language (IL) code.*

The syntax for a destructor will be familiar to C++ developers. It looks like a method, with the same name as the containing class, but prefixed with a tilde (~). It has no return type, and takes no parameters or access modifiers. Here is an example:

```
class MyClass
{
  ~MyClass()
  {
    // Finalizer implementation
  }
}
```

When the C# compiler compiles a destructor, it implicitly translates the destructor code to the equivalent of an override of the Finalize method, which ensures that the Finalize method of the parent class is executed. The following example shows the C# code equivalent to the Intermediate Language (IL) that the compiler would generate for the ~MyClass destructor:

```
protected override void Finalize()
{
  try
  {
    // Finalizer implementation
  }
  finally
  {
    base.Finalize();
  }
}
```

As shown, the code implemented in the ~MyClass destructor is wrapped in a try block contained in the Finalize method. A call to the parent's Finalize method is ensured by placing the call in a finally block. You can read about try and finally blocks in Chapter 14, "Errors and Exceptions."

Experienced C++ developers make extensive use of destructors, sometimes not only to clean up resources but also to provide debugging information or perform other tasks. C# destructors are used far less than their C++ equivalents. The problem with C# destructors as compared to their C++ counterparts is that they are nondeterministic. When a C++ object is destroyed, its destructor runs immediately. However, because of the way the garbage collector works when using C#, there is no way to know when an object's destructor will actually execute. Hence, you cannot place any code in the destructor that relies on being run at a certain time, and you should not rely on the destructor being called for different class instances in any particular order. When your object is holding scarce and critical resources that need to be freed as soon as possible, you do not want to wait for garbage collection.

Another problem with C# destructors is that the implementation of a destructor delays the final removal of an object from memory. Objects that do not have a destructor are removed from memory in one pass of the garbage collector, but objects that have destructors require two passes to be destroyed: The first pass calls the destructor without removing the object, and the second pass actually deletes the object. In addition, the runtime uses a single thread to execute the Finalize methods of all objects. If you use destructors frequently, and use them to execute lengthy cleanup tasks, the impact on performance can be noticeable.

The IDisposable Interface

In C#, the recommended alternative to using a destructor is using the System.IDisposable interface. The IDisposable interface defines a pattern (with language-level support) that provides a deterministic mechanism for freeing unmanaged resources and avoids the garbage collector–related problems inherent with destructors. The IDisposable interface declares a single method named Dispose, which takes no parameters and returns void. Here is an implementation for MyClass:

```
class MyClass: IDisposable
{
  public void Dispose()
  {
    // implementation
  }
}
```

The implementation of Dispose should explicitly free all unmanaged resources used directly by an object and call Dispose on any encapsulated objects that also implement the IDisposable interface. In this way, the Dispose method provides precise control over when unmanaged resources are freed.

Suppose that you have a class named ResourceGobbler, which relies on the use of some external resource and implements IDisposable. If you want to instantiate an instance of this class, use it, and then dispose of it, you could do so like this:

```
var theInstance = new ResourceGobbler();

// do your processing

theInstance.Dispose();
```

Unfortunately, this code fails to free the resources consumed by theInstance if an exception occurs during processing, so you should write the code as follows using a try block (as covered in detail in Chapter 14):

```
ResourceGobbler theInstance = null;
try
{
  theInstance = new ResourceGobbler();
  // do your processing
}
finally
{
  theInstance?.Dispose();
}
```

The using Statement

Using `try`/`finally` ensures that `Dispose` is always called on `theInstance` and that any resources consumed by it are always freed, even if an exception occurs during processing. However, if you always had to repeat such a construct, it would result in confusing code. C# offers a syntax that you can use to guarantee that `Dispose` is automatically called against an object that implements `IDisposable` when its reference goes out of scope. The syntax to do this involves the `using` keyword—though now in a very different context, which has nothing to do with namespaces. The following code generates IL code equivalent to the `try` block just shown:

```
using (var theInstance = new ResourceGobbler())
{
  // do your processing
}
```

The `using` statement, followed in brackets by a reference variable declaration and instantiation, causes that variable to be scoped to the accompanying statement block. In addition, when that variable goes out of scope, its `Dispose` method is called automatically, even if an exception occurs.

> **NOTE** *The* using *keyword has multiple uses with C#. The* using *declaration is used to import namespaces. The* using *statement works with objects implementing* IDisposable *and invokes the* Dispose *method with the end of the using scope.*

> **NOTE** *With several classes of the .NET Framework both a* Close *and a* Dispose *method exists. If it is common to close a resource (such as a file and a database), both* Close *and* Dispose *have been implemented. Here, the* Close *method simply calls* Dispose. *This approach provides clarity in the use of these classes and supports the* using *statement. Newer classes only implement the* Dispose *method as we're already used to it.*

Implementing IDisposable and a Destructor

The previous sections discussed two alternatives for freeing unmanaged resources used by the classes you create:

➤ The execution of a destructor is enforced by the runtime but is nondeterministic and places an unacceptable overhead on the runtime because of the way garbage collection works.

➤ The IDisposable interface provides a mechanism that enables users of a class to control when resources are freed but requires discipline to ensure that Dispose is called.

If you are creating a finalizer, you should also implement the IDisposable interface. You implement IDisposable on the assumption that most programmers will call Dispose correctly, but implement a destructor as a safety mechanism in case Dispose is not called. Here is an example of a dual implementation:

```
using System;

public class ResourceHolder: IDisposable
{
    private bool _isDisposed = false;

    public void Dispose()
    {
        Dispose(true);
        GC.SuppressFinalize(this);
    }

    protected virtual void Dispose(bool disposing)
    {
        if (!_isDisposed)
        {
            if (disposing)
            {
                // Cleanup managed objects by calling their
                // Dispose() methods.
            }
            // Cleanup unmanaged objects
        }
        _isDisposed = true;
    }

    ~ResourceHolder()
    {
        Dispose(false);
    }

    public void SomeMethod()
    {
        // Ensure object not already disposed before execution of any method
        if(_isDisposed)
        {
            throw new ObjectDisposedException("ResourceHolder");
        }

        // method implementation...
    }
}
```

You can see from this code that there is a second protected overload of Dispose that takes one bool parameter—and this is the method that does all the cleaning up. Dispose(bool) is called by both the destructor and by IDisposable.Dispose. The point of this approach is to ensure that all cleanup code is in one place.

The parameter passed to Dispose(bool) indicates whether Dispose(bool) has been invoked by the destructor or by IDisposable.Dispose—Dispose(bool) should not be invoked from anywhere else in your code. The idea is this:

➤ If a consumer calls `IDisposable.Dispose`, that consumer is indicating that all managed and unmanaged resources associated with that object should be cleaned up.

➤ If a destructor has been invoked, all resources still need to be cleaned up. However, in this case, you know that the destructor must have been called by the garbage collector and you should not attempt to access other managed objects because you can no longer be certain of their state. In this situation, the best you can do is clean up the known unmanaged resources and hope that any referenced managed objects also have destructors that will perform their own cleaning up.

The `_isDisposed` member variable indicates whether the object has already been disposed of and ensures that you do not try to dispose of member variables more than once. It also enables you to test whether an object has been disposed of before executing any instance methods, as shown in `SomeMethod`. This simplistic approach is not thread-safe and depends on the caller ensuring that only one thread is calling the method concurrently. Requiring a consumer to enforce synchronization is a reasonable assumption and one that is used repeatedly throughout the .NET class libraries (in the `Collection` classes, for example). Threading and synchronization are discussed in Chapter 21, "Tasks and Parallel Programming," and Chapter 22, "Task Synchronization."

Finally, `IDisposable.Dispose` contains a call to the method `System.GC.SuppressFinalize`. GC is the class that represents the garbage collector, and the `SuppressFinalize` method tells the garbage collector that a class no longer needs to have its destructor called. Because your implementation of `Dispose` has already done all the cleanup required, there's nothing left for the destructor to do. Calling `SuppressFinalize` means that the garbage collector will treat that object as if it doesn't have a destructor at all.

IDisposable and Finalizer Rules

Learning about finalizers and the `IDisposable` interface you already learned the Dispose pattern and some rules on using these constructs. Because releasing resources is such an important aspect with managed code, the rules are summarized in this list:

➤ If your class defines a member that implements `IDisposable`, the class should also implement `IDisposable`.

➤ Implementing `IDisposable` does not mean that you should also implement a finalizer. Finalizers create additional overhead with both creating an object and releasing the memory of the object as an additional pass from the GC is needed. You should implement a finalizer only if needed—for example, to release native resources. To release native resources, a finalizer is really needed.

➤ If a finalizer is implemented, you should also implement the interface `IDisposable`. This way the native resource can be released earlier, not only when the GC is finding out about the occupied resource.

➤ Within the finalization code implementation, don't access objects that might have been finalized already. The order of finalizers is not guaranteed.

➤ If an object you use implements the `IDisposable` interface, call the `Dispose` method when the object is no longer needed. In case you're using this object within a method, the using statement comes handy. In case the object is a member of the class, make the class implement `IDisposable` as well.

UNSAFE CODE

As you have just seen, C# is very good at hiding much of the basic memory management from the developer, thanks to the garbage collector and the use of references. However, sometimes you will want direct access to memory. For example, you might want to access a function in an external (non-.NET) DLL that requires a pointer to be passed as a parameter (as many Windows API functions do), or possibly for performance reasons. This section examines the C# facilities that provide direct access to the content of memory.

Accessing Memory Directly with Pointers

Although I am introducing *pointers* as if they are a new topic, in reality pointers are not new at all. You have been using references freely in your code, and a reference is simply a type-safe pointer. You have already seen how variables that represent objects and arrays actually store the memory address of where the corresponding data (the *referent*) is stored. A pointer is simply a variable that stores the address of something else in the same way as a reference. The *difference* is that C# does not allow you direct access to the address contained in a reference variable. With a reference, the variable is treated syntactically as if it stores the actual content of the referent.

C# references are designed to make the language simpler to use and to prevent you from inadvertently doing something that corrupts the contents of memory. With a pointer, however, the actual memory address is available to you. This gives you a lot of power to perform new kinds of operations. For example, you can add 4 bytes to the address in order to examine or even modify whatever data happens to be stored 4 bytes further in memory.

There are two main reasons for using pointers:

➤ Backward compatibility—Despite all the facilities provided by the .NET runtime, it is still possible to call native Windows API functions, and for some operations this may be the only way to accomplish your task. These API functions are generally written in C++ or C# and often require pointers as parameters. However, in many cases it is possible to write the `DllImport` declaration in a way that avoids use of pointers—for example, by using the `System.IntPtr` class.

➤ Performance—On those occasions when speed is of the utmost importance, pointers can provide a route to optimized performance. If you know what you are doing, you can ensure that data is accessed or manipulated in the most efficient way. However, be aware that more often than not, there are other areas of your code where you can likely make the necessary performance improvements without resorting to using pointers. Try using a code profiler to look for the bottlenecks in your code; Visual Studio includes a code profiler.

Low-level memory access has a price. The syntax for using pointers is more complex than that for reference types, and pointers are unquestionably more difficult to use correctly. You need good programming skills and an excellent ability to think carefully and logically about what your code is doing to use pointers successfully. Otherwise, it is very easy to introduce subtle, difficult-to-find bugs into your program when using pointers. For example, it is easy to overwrite other variables, cause stack overflows, access areas of memory that don't store any variables, or even overwrite information about your code that is needed by the .NET runtime, thereby crashing your program.

In addition, if you use pointers your code must be granted a high level of trust by the runtime's code access security mechanism or it will not be allowed to execute. Under the default code access security policy, this is only possible if your code is running on the local machine. If your code must be run from a remote location, such as the Internet, users must grant your code additional permissions for it to work. Unless the users trust you and your code, they are unlikely to grant these permissions. Code access security is discussed in more detail in Chapter 24, "Security."

Despite these issues, pointers remain a very powerful and flexible tool in the writing of efficient code.

> **WARNING** *I strongly advise against using pointers unnecessarily because your code will not only be harder to write and debug, but it will also fail the memory type safety checks imposed by the CLR.*

Writing Unsafe Code with the unsafe Keyword

As a result of the risks associated with pointers, C# allows the use of pointers only in blocks of code that you have specifically marked for this purpose. The keyword to do this is unsafe. You can mark an individual method as being unsafe like this:

```
unsafe int GetSomeNumber()
{
    // code that can use pointers
}
```

Any method can be marked as unsafe, regardless of what other modifiers have been applied to it (for example, static methods or virtual methods). In the case of methods, the unsafe modifier applies to the method's parameters, allowing you to use pointers as parameters. You can also mark an entire class or struct as unsafe, which means that all its members are assumed unsafe:

```
unsafe class MyClass
{
    // any method in this class can now use pointers
}
```

Similarly, you can mark a member as unsafe:

```
class MyClass
{
    unsafe int* pX; // declaration of a pointer field in a class
}
```

Or you can mark a block of code within a method as unsafe:

```
void MyMethod()
{
    // code that doesn't use pointers
    unsafe
    {
        // unsafe code that uses pointers here
    }
    // more 'safe' code that doesn't use pointers
}
```

Note, however, that you cannot mark a local variable by itself as unsafe:

```
int MyMethod()
{
    unsafe int *pX; // WRONG
}
```

If you want to use an unsafe local variable, you need to declare and use it inside a method or block that is unsafe. There is one more step before you can use pointers. The C# compiler rejects unsafe code unless you tell it that your code includes unsafe blocks. Using DNX, you can set allowUnsafe to true with the compilationOptions in the project.json file (code file PointerPlayground/project.json):

```
"compilationOptions": {"allowUnsafe": true},
```

With the traditional csc compiler, you can set the /unsafe option, or set the Build configuration in the Project setting to Allow Unsafe Code with Visual Studio 2015:

```
csc /unsafe MySource.cs
```

Pointer Syntax

After you have marked a block of code as unsafe, you can declare a pointer using the following syntax:

```
int* pWidth, pHeight;
double* pResult;
byte*[] pFlags;
```

This code declares four variables: pWidth and pHeight are pointers to integers, pResult is a pointer to a double, and pFlags is an array of pointers to bytes. It is common practice to use the prefix p in front of names of pointer variables to indicate that they are pointers. When used in a variable declaration, the symbol * indicates that you are declaring a pointer (that is, something that stores the address of a variable of the specified type).

When you have declared variables of pointer types, you can use them in the same way as normal variables, but first you need to learn two more operators:

➤ & means take the address of, and converts a value data type to a pointer—for example, int to *int. This operator is known as the address operator.

➤ * means get the content of this address, and converts a pointer to a value data type—for example, *float to float. This operator is known as the indirection operator (or the de-reference operator).

You can see from these definitions that & and * have opposite effects.

> **NOTE** *You might be wondering how it is possible to use the symbols & and * in this manner because these symbols also refer to the operators of bitwise AND (&) and multiplication (*). Actually, it is always possible for both you and the compiler to know what is meant in each case because with the pointer meanings, these symbols always appear as unary operators—they act on only one variable and appear in front of that variable in your code. By contrast, bitwise AND and multiplication are binary operators—they require two operands.*

The following code shows examples of how to use these operators:

```
int x = 10;
int* pX, pY;
pX = &x;
pY = pX;
*pY = 20;
```

You start by declaring an integer, x, with the value 10 followed by two pointers to integers, pX and pY. You then set pX to point to x (that is, you set the content of pX to the address of x). Then you assign the value of pX to pY, so that pY also points to x. Finally, in the statement *pY = 20, you assign the value 20 as the contents of the location pointed to by pY—in effect changing x to 20 because pY happens to point to x. Note that there is no particular connection between the variables pY and x. It is just that at the present time, pY happens to point to the memory location at which x is held.

To get a better understanding of what is going on, consider that the integer x is stored at memory locations 0x12F8C4 through 0x12F8C7 (1243332 to 1243335 in decimal) on the stack (there are four locations because an int occupies 4 bytes). Because the stack allocates memory downward, this means that the variables pX will be stored at locations 0x12F8C0 to 0x12F8C3, and pY will end up at locations 0x12F8BC to 0x12F8BF. Note that pX and pY also occupy 4 bytes each. That is not because an int occupies 4 bytes, but because on a 32-bit application you need 4 bytes to store an address. With these addresses, after executing the previous code, the stack will look like Figure 5-6.

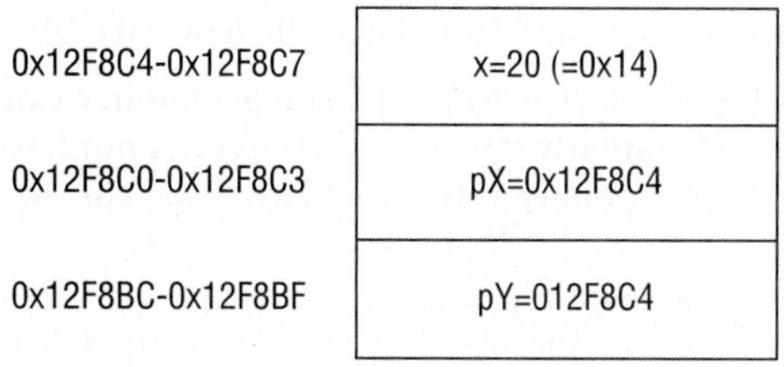

0x12F8C4-0x12F8C7	x=20 (=0x14)
0x12F8C0-0x12F8C3	pX=0x12F8C4
0x12F8BC-0x12F8BF	pY=012F8C4

FIGURE 5-6

NOTE *Although this process is illustrated with integers, which are stored consecutively on the stack on a 32-bit processor, this does not happen for all data types. The reason is that 32-bit processors work best when retrieving data from memory in 4-byte chunks. Memory on such machines tends to be divided into 4-byte blocks, and each block is sometimes known under Windows as a DWORD because this was the name of a 32-bit unsigned* int *in pre-.NET days. It is most efficient to grab DWORDs from memory—storing data across DWORD boundaries normally results in a hardware performance hit. For this reason, the .NET runtime normally pads out data types so that the memory they occupy is a multiple of 4. For example, a short occupies 2 bytes, but if a short is placed on the stack, the stack pointer will still be decremented by 4, not 2, so the next variable to go on the stack will still start at a DWORD boundary.*

You can declare a pointer to any value type (that is, any of the predefined types uint, int, byte, and so on, or to a struct). However, it is not possible to declare a pointer to a class or an array; this is because doing so could cause problems for the garbage collector. To work properly, the garbage collector needs to know exactly what class instances have been created on the heap, and where they are; but if your code started manipulating classes using pointers, you could very easily corrupt the information on the heap concerning classes that the .NET runtime maintains for the garbage collector. In this context, any data type that the garbage collector can access is known as a *managed type*. Pointers can only be declared as *unmanaged* types because the garbage collector cannot deal with them.

Casting Pointers to Integer Types

Because a pointer really stores an integer that represents an address, you won't be surprised to know that the address in any pointer can be converted to or from any integer type. Pointer-to-integer-type conversions must be explicit. Implicit conversions are not available for such conversions. For example, it is perfectly legitimate to write the following:

```
int x = 10;
int* pX, pY;
pX = &x;
pY = pX;
*pY = 20;
ulong y = (ulong)pX;
int* pD = (int*)y;
```

The address held in the pointer pX is cast to a `uint` and stored in the variable y. You have then cast y back to an `int*` and stored it in the new variable pD. Hence, now pD also points to the value of x.

The primary reason for casting a pointer value to an integer type is to display it. The interpolation string (and similarly `Console.Write`) does not have any overloads that can take pointers, but they do accept and display pointer values that have been cast to integer types:

```
WriteLine($"Address is {pX}"); // wrong -- will give a compilation error
WriteLine($"Address is {(ulong)pX}"); // OK
```

You can cast a pointer to any of the integer types. However, because an address occupies 4 bytes on 32-bit systems, casting a pointer to anything other than a `uint`, `long`, or `ulong` is almost certain to lead to over-flow errors. (An `int` causes problems because its range is from roughly –2 billion to 2 billion, whereas an address runs from zero to about 4 billion.) If you are creating a 64-bit application, you need to cast the pointer to `ulong`.

It is also important to be aware that the `checked` keyword does not apply to conversions involving pointers. For such conversions, exceptions are not raised when overflows occur, even in a `checked` context. The .NET runtime assumes that if you are using pointers, you know what you are doing and are not worried about possible overflows.

Casting Between Pointer Types

You can also explicitly convert between pointers pointing to different types. For example, the following is perfectly legal code:

```
byte aByte = 8;
byte* pByte= &aByte;
double* pDouble = (double*)pByte;
```

However, if you try something like this, be careful. In this example, if you look at the `double` value pointed to by pDouble, you are actually looking up some memory that contains a `byte` (aByte), combined with some other memory, and treating it as if this area of memory contained a `double`, which does not give you a meaningful value. However, you might want to convert between types to implement the equivalent of a C union, or you might want to cast pointers from other types into pointers to `sbyte` to examine individual bytes of memory.

void Pointers

If you want to maintain a pointer but not specify to what type of data it points, you can declare it as a pointer to a void:

```
int* pointerToInt;
void* pointerToVoid;
pointerToVoid = (void*)pointerToInt;
```

The main use of this is if you need to call an API function that requires `void*` parameters. Within the C# language, there isn't a great deal that you can do using `void` pointers. In particular, the compiler flags an error if you attempt to de-reference a `void` pointer using the `*` operator.

Pointer Arithmetic

It is possible to add or subtract integers to and from pointers. However, the compiler is quite clever about how it arranges this. For example, suppose that you have a pointer to an int and you try to add 1 to its value. The compiler assumes that you actually mean you want to look at the memory location following the

int, and hence it increases the value by 4 bytes—the size of an int. If it is a pointer to a double, adding 1 actually increases the value of the pointer by 8 bytes, the size of a double. Only if the pointer points to a byte or sbyte (1 byte each) does adding 1 to the value of
the pointer actually change its value by 1.

You can use the operators +, -, +=, -=, ++, and -- with pointers, with the variable on the right side of these operators being a long or ulong.

> **NOTE** *It is not permitted to carry out arithmetic operations on void pointers.*

For example, assume the following definitions:

```
uint u = 3;
byte b = 8;
double d = 10.0;
uint* pUint= &u;        // size of a uint is 4
byte* pByte = &b;       // size of a byte is 1
double* pDouble = &d;   // size of a double is 8
```

Next, assume the addresses to which these pointers point are as follows:

➤   pUint: 1243332

➤   pByte: 1243328

➤   pDouble: 1243320

Then execute this code:

```
++pUint;                       // adds (1*4) = 4 bytes to pUint
pByte -= 3;                    // subtracts (3*1) = 3 bytes from pByte
double* pDouble2 = pDouble + 4; // pDouble2 = pDouble + 32 bytes (4*8 bytes)
```

The pointers now contain this:

➤   pUint: 1243336

➤   pByte: 1243325

➤   pDouble2: 1243352

> **NOTE** *The general rule is that adding a number X to a pointer to type T with value P gives the result P + X*(sizeof(T)). If successive values of a given type are stored in successive memory locations, pointer addition works very well, allowing you to move pointers between memory locations. If you are dealing with types such as* byte *or* char, *though, with sizes not in multiples of 4, successive values will not, by default, be stored in successive memory locations.*

You can also subtract one pointer from another pointer, if both pointers point to the same data type. In this case, the result is a long whose value is given by the difference between the pointer values divided by the size of the type that they represent:

```
double* pD1 = (double*)1243324; // note that it is perfectly valid to
                                // initialize a pointer like this.
```

```
double* pD2 = (double*)1243300;
long L = pD1-pD2;              // gives the result 3 (=24/sizeof(double))
```

The sizeof Operator

This section has been referring to the size of various data types. If you need to use the size of a type in your code, you can use the `sizeof` operator, which takes the name of a data type as a parameter and returns the number of bytes occupied by that type, as shown in this example:

```
int x = sizeof(double);
```

This sets x to the value 8.

The advantage of using `sizeof` is that you don't have to hard-code data type sizes in your code, making your code more portable. For the predefined data types, `sizeof` returns the following values:

```
sizeof(sbyte) = 1;  sizeof(byte) = 1;
sizeof(short) = 2;  sizeof(ushort) = 2;
sizeof(int) = 4;    sizeof(uint) = 4;
sizeof(long) = 8;   sizeof(ulong) = 8;
sizeof(char) = 2;   sizeof(float) = 4;
sizeof(double) = 8; sizeof(bool) = 1;
```

You can also use `sizeof` for structs that you define yourself, although, in that case, the result depends on what fields are in the struct. You cannot use `sizeof` for classes.

Pointers to Structs: The Pointer Member Access Operator

Pointers to structs work in exactly the same way as pointers to the predefined value types. There is, however, one condition: The struct must not contain any reference types. This is due to the restriction mentioned earlier that pointers cannot point to any reference types. To avoid this, the compiler flags an error if you create a pointer to any struct that contains any reference types.

Suppose that you had a struct defined like this:

```
struct MyStruct
{
   public long X;
   public float F;
}
```

You could define a pointer to it as follows:

```
MyStruct* pStruct;
```

Then you could initialize it like this:

```
var myStruct = new MyStruct();
pStruct = &myStruct;
```

It is also possible to access member values of a struct through the pointer:

```
(*pStruct).X = 4;
(*pStruct).F = 3.4f;
```

However, this syntax is a bit complex. For this reason, C# defines another operator that enables you to access members of structs through pointers using a simpler syntax. It is known as the *pointer member access operator*, and the symbol is a dash followed by a greater-than sign, so it looks like an arrow: ->.

> **NOTE** *C++ developers will recognize the pointer member access operator because C++ uses the same symbol for the same purpose.*

Using the pointer member access operator, the previous code can be rewritten like this:

```
pStruct->X = 4;
pStruct->F = 3.4f;
```

You can also directly set up pointers of the appropriate type to point to fields within a struct,

```
long* pL = &(Struct.X);
float* pF = &(Struct.F);
```

or,

```
long* pL = &(pStruct->X);
float* pF = &(pStruct->F);
```

Pointers to Class Members

As indicated earlier, it is not possible to create pointers to classes. That is because the garbage collector does not maintain any information about pointers—only about references—so creating pointers to classes could cause garbage collection to not work properly.

However, most classes do contain value type members, and you might want to create pointers to them. This is possible, but it requires a special syntax. For example, suppose that you rewrite the struct from the previous example as a class:

```
class MyClass
{
  public long X;
  public float F;
}
```

Then you might want to create pointers to its fields, X and F, in the same way as you did earlier. Unfortunately, doing so produces a compilation error:

```
var myObject = new MyClass();
long* pL = &(myObject.X);   // wrong -- compilation error
float* pF = &(myObject.F);  // wrong -- compilation error
```

Although X and F are unmanaged types, they are embedded in an object, which sits on the heap. During garbage collection, the garbage collector might move MyObject to a new location, which would leave pL and pF pointing to the wrong memory addresses. Because of this, the compiler does not let you assign addresses of members of managed types to pointers in this manner.

The solution is to use the `fixed` keyword, which tells the garbage collector that there may be pointers referencing members of certain objects, so those objects must not be moved. The syntax for using `fixed` looks like this when you want to declare only one pointer:

```
var myObject = new MyClass();
fixed (long* pObject = &(myObject.X))
{
  // do something
}
```

You define and initialize the pointer variable in the brackets following the keyword `fixed`. This pointer variable (`pObject` in the example) is scoped to the `fixed` block identified by the curly braces. As a result, the garbage collector knows not to move the `myObject` object while the code inside the `fixed` block is executing.

If you want to declare more than one pointer, you can place multiple `fixed` statements before the same code block:

```
var myObject = new MyClass();
fixed (long* pX = &(myObject.X))
fixed (float* pF = &(myObject.F))
{
  // do something
}
```

You can nest entire `fixed` blocks if you want to fix several pointers for different periods:

```
var myObject = new MyClass();
fixed (long* pX = &(myObject.X))
{
  // do something with pX
  fixed (float* pF = &(myObject.F))
  {
    // do something else with pF
  }
}
```

You can also initialize several variables within the same `fixed` block, if they are of the same type:

```
var myObject = new MyClass();
var myObject2 = new MyClass();
fixed (long* pX = &(myObject.X), pX2 = &(myObject2.X))
{
  // etc.
}
```

In all these cases, it is immaterial whether the various pointers you are declaring point to fields in the same or different objects or to static fields not associated with any class instance.

Pointer Example: PointerPlayground

For understanding pointers, it's best to write a program using pointers and to use the debugger. The following code snippet is from an example named `PointerPlayground`. It does some simple pointer manipulation and displays the results, enabling you to see what is happening in memory and where variables are stored (code file `PointerPlayground/Program.cs`):

```
using System;
using static System.Console;

namespace PointerPlayground
{
  public class Program
  {
    unsafe public static void Main()
    {
      int x=10;
      short y = -1;
      byte y2 = 4;
      double z = 1.5;
      int* pX = &x;
      short* pY = &y;
      double* pZ = &z;

      WriteLine($"Address of x is 0x{(ulong)&x:X}, " +
          $"size is {sizeof(int)}, value is {x}");
      WriteLine($"Address of y is 0x{(ulong)&y2:X}, " +
          $"size is {sizeof(short)}, value is {y}");
      WriteLine($"Address of y2 is 0x{(ulong)&y2:X}, " +
          $"size is {sizeof(byte)}, value is {y2}");
      WriteLine($"Address of z is 0x{(ulong)&z:X}, " +
          $"size is {sizeof(double)}, value is {z}");
      WriteLine($"Address of pX=&x is 0x{(ulong)&pX:X}, " +
          $"size is {sizeof(int*)}, value is 0x{(ulong)pX:X}");
      WriteLine($"Address of pY=&y is 0x{(ulong)&pY:X}, " +
          $"size is {sizeof(short*)}, value is 0x{(ulong)pY:X}");
      WriteLine($"Address of pZ=&z is 0x{(ulong)&pZ:X}, " +
          $"size is {sizeof(double*)}, value is 0x{(ulong)pZ:X}");

      *pX = 20;
      WriteLine($"After setting *pX, x = {x}");
      WriteLine($"*pX = {*pX}");

      pZ = (double*)pX;
      WriteLine($"x treated as a double = {*pZ}");

      ReadLine();
    }
  }
}
```

This code declares four value variables:

➤   An int x

➤   A short y

➤   A byte y2

➤   A double z

It also declares pointers to three of these values: pX, pY, and pZ.

Next, you display the value of these variables as well as their size and address. Note that in taking the address of pX, pY, and pZ, you are effectively looking at a pointer *to* a pointer—an address of an address of a value. Also, in accordance with the usual practice when displaying addresses, you have used the {0:X} format specifier in the WriteLine commands to ensure that memory addresses are displayed in hexadecimal format.

Finally, you use the pointer pX to change the value of x to 20 and do some pointer casting to see what happens if you try to treat the content of x as if it were a double.

Compiling and running this code results in the following output:

```
Address of x is 0x376943D5A8, size is 4, value is 10
Address of y is 0x376943D5A0, size is 2, value is -1
Address of y2 is 0x376943D598, size is 1, value is 4
Address of z is 0x376943D590, size is 8, value is 1.5
Address of pX=&x is 0x376943D588, size is 8, value is 0x376943D5A8
Address of pY=&y is 0x376943D580, size is 8, value is 0x376943D5A0
Address of pZ=&z is 0x376943D578, size is 8, value is 0x376943D590
After setting *pX, x = 20
*pX = 20
x treated as a double = 9.88131291682493E-323
```

> **NOTE** *When you run the application with the CoreCLR, different addresses are shown every time you run the application.*

Checking through these results confirms the description of how the stack operates presented in the "Memory Management Under the Hood" section earlier in this chapter. It allocates successive variables moving downward in memory. Notice how it also confirms that blocks of memory on the stack are always allocated in multiples of 4 bytes. For example, y is a short (of size 2) and has the (hex) address 0xD4E710, indicating that the memory locations reserved for it are locations 0xD4E710 through 0xD4E713. If the .NET runtime had been strictly packing up variables next to each other, Y would have occupied just two locations, 0xD4E712 and 0xD4713.

The next example illustrates pointer arithmetic, as well as pointers to structs and class members. This example is named PointerPlayground2. To start, you define a struct named CurrencyStruct, which represents a currency value as dollars and cents. You also define an equivalent class named CurrencyClass (code file PointerPlayground2/Currency.cs):

```
internal struct CurrencyStruct
{
  public long Dollars;
  public byte Cents;

  public override string ToString() => $"$ {Dollars}.{Cents}";
}

internal class CurrencyClass
{
  public long Dollars = 0;
  public byte Cents = 0;

  public override string ToString() => $"$ {Dollars}.{Cents}";
}
```

Now that you have your struct and class defined, you can apply some pointers to them. Following is the code for the new example. Because the code is fairly long, I'm going through it in detail. You start by displaying the size of CurrencyStruct, creating a couple of CurrencyStruct instances and creating some CurrencyStruct pointers. You use the pAmount pointer to initialize the members of the amount1 CurrencyStruct and then display the addresses of your variables (code file PointerPlayground2/Program.cs):

```
unsafe public static void Main()
```

```
  {
    WriteLine($"Size of CurrencyStruct struct is {sizeof(CurrencyStruct)}");
    CurrencyStruct amount1, amount2;
    CurrencyStruct* pAmount = &amount1;
    long* pDollars = &(pAmount->Dollars);
    byte* pCents = &(pAmount->Cents);

    WriteLine("Address of amount1 is 0x{(ulong)&amount1:X}");
    WriteLine("Address of amount2 is 0x{(ulong)&amount2:X}");
    WriteLine("Address of pAmount is 0x{(ulong)&pAmount:X}");
    WriteLine("Address of pDollars is 0x{(ulong)&pDollars:X}");
    WriteLine("Address of pCents is 0x{(ulong)&pCents:X}");
    pAmount->Dollars = 20;
    *pCents = 50;
    WriteLine($"amount1 contains {amount1}");
```

Now you do some pointer manipulation that relies on your knowledge of how the stack works. Due to the order in which the variables were declared, you know that amount2 will be stored at an address immediately below amount1. The sizeof(CurrencyStruct) operator returns 16 (as demonstrated in the screen output coming up), so CurrencyStruct occupies a multiple of 4 bytes. Therefore, after you decrement your currency pointer, it points to amount2:

```
    --pAmount;    // this should get it to point to amount2
    WriteLine($"amount2 has address 0x{(ulong)pAmount:X} " +
        $"and contains {*pAmount}");
```

Notice that when you call WriteLine, you display the contents of amount2, but you haven't yet initialized it. What is displayed is random garbage—whatever happened to be stored at that location in memory before execution of the example. There is an important point here: Normally, the C# compiler would prevent you from using an uninitialized variable, but when you start using pointers, it is very easy to circumvent many of the usual compilation checks. In this case, you have done so because the compiler has no way of knowing that you are actually displaying the contents of amount2. Only you know that, because your knowledge of the stack means that you can tell what the effect of decrementing pAmount will be. After you start doing pointer arithmetic, you will find that you can access all sorts of variables and memory locations that the compiler would usually stop you from accessing, hence the description of pointer arithmetic as unsafe.

Next, you do some pointer arithmetic on your pCents pointer. pCents currently points to amount1.Cents, but the aim here is to get it to point to amount2.Cents, again using pointer operations instead of directly telling the compiler that's what you want to do. To do this, you need to decrement the address pCents contains by sizeof(Currency):

```
    // do some clever casting to get pCents to point to cents
    // inside amount2
    CurrencyStruct* pTempCurrency = (CurrencyStruct*)pCents;
    pCents = (byte*) ( -pTempCurrency );
    WriteLine("Address of pCents is now 0x{0:X}", (ulong)&pCents);
```

Finally, you use the fixed keyword to create some pointers that point to the fields in a class instance and use these pointers to set the value of this instance. Notice that this is also the first time that you have been able to look at the address of an item stored on the heap, rather than the stack:

```
    WriteLine("\nNow with classes");
    // now try it out with classes
    var amount3 = new CurrencyClass();

    fixed(long* pDollars2 = &(amount3.Dollars))
```

```
fixed(byte* pCents2 = &(amount3.Cents))
{
    WriteLine($"amount3.Dollars has address 0x{(ulong)pDollars2:X}");
    WriteLine($"amount3.Cents has address 0x{(ulong)pCents2:X}");
    *pDollars2 = -100;
    WriteLine($"amount3 contains {amount3}");
}
```

Compiling and running this code gives output similar to this:

```
Size of CurrencyStruct struct is 16
Address of amount1 is 0xD290DCD7C0
Address of amount2 is 0xD290DCD7B0
Address of pAmount is 0xD290DCD7A8
Address of pDollars is 0xD290DCD7A0
Address of pCents is 0xD290DCD798
amount1 contains $ 20.50
amount2 has address 0xD290DCD7B0 and contains $ 0.0
Address of pCents is now 0xD290DCD798

Now with classes
amount3.Dollars has address 0xD292C91A70
amount3.Cents has address 0xD292C91A78
amount3 contains $ -100.0
```

Notice in this output the uninitialized value of amount2 that is displayed, and notice that the size of the CurrencyStruct struct is 16—somewhat larger than you would expect given the size of its fields (a long and a byte should total 9 bytes).

Using Pointers to Optimize Performance

Until now, all the examples have been designed to demonstrate the various things that you can do with pointers. You have played around with memory in a way that is probably interesting only to people who like to know what's happening under the hood, but that doesn't really help you write better code. Now you're going to apply your understanding of pointers and see an example of how judicious use of pointers has a significant performance benefit.

Creating Stack-based Arrays

This section explores one of the main areas in which pointers can be useful: creating high-performance, low-overhead arrays on the stack. As discussed in Chapter 2, "Core C#," C# includes rich support for handling arrays. Chapter 7, "Arrays and Tuples," give more details on arrays. Although C# makes it very easy to use both one-dimensional and rectangular or jagged multidimensional arrays, it suffers from the disadvantage that these arrays are actually objects; they are instances of System.Array. This means that the arrays are stored on the heap, with all the overhead that this involves. There may be occasions when you need to create a short-lived, high-performance array and don't want the overhead of reference objects. You can do this by using pointers, although this is easy only for one-dimensional arrays.

To create a high-performance array, you need to use a new keyword: stackalloc. The stackalloc command instructs the .NET runtime to allocate an amount of memory on the stack. When you call stackalloc, you need to supply it with two pieces of information:

➤ The type of data you want to store
➤ The number of these data items you need to store

For example, to allocate enough memory to store 10 decimal data items, you can write the following:

```
decimal* pDecimals = stackalloc decimal[10];
```

This command simply allocates the stack memory; it does not attempt to initialize the memory to any default value. This is fine for the purpose of this example because you are creating a high-performance array, and initializing values unnecessarily would hurt performance.

Similarly, to store 20 double data items, you write this:

```
double* pDoubles = stackalloc double[20];
```

Although this line of code specifies the number of variables to store as a constant, this can equally be a quantity evaluated at runtime. Therefore, you can write the previous example like this:

```
int size;
size = 20; // or some other value calculated at runtime
double* pDoubles = stackalloc double[size];
```

You can see from these code snippets that the syntax of stackalloc is slightly unusual. It is followed immediately by the name of the data type you want to store (which must be a value type) and then by the number of items you need space for, in square brackets. The number of bytes allocated is this number multiplied by sizeof(data type). The use of square brackets in the preceding code sample suggests an array, which is not too surprising. If you have allocated space for 20 doubles, then what you have is an array of 20 doubles. The simplest type of array that you can have is a block of memory that stores one element after another (see Figure 5-7).

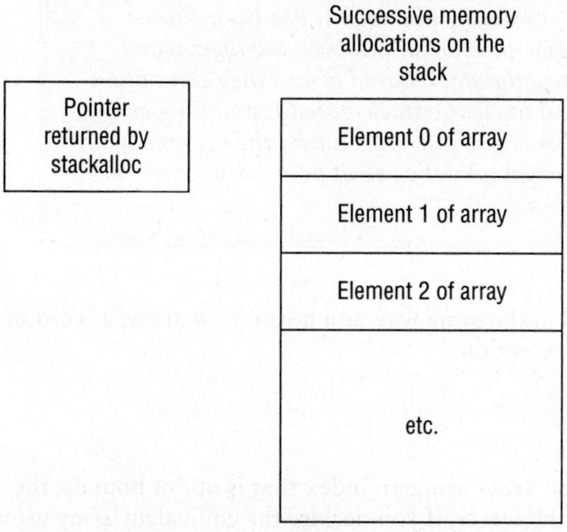

FIGURE 5-7

This diagram also shows the pointer returned by stackalloc, which is always a pointer to the allocated data type that points to the top of the newly allocated memory block. To use the memory block, you simply de-reference the returned pointer. For example, to allocate space for 20 doubles and then set the first element (element 0 of the array) to the value 3.0, write this:

```
double* pDoubles = stackalloc double[20];
*pDoubles = 3.0;
```

To access the next element of the array, you use pointer arithmetic. As described earlier, if you add 1 to a pointer, its value will be increased by the size of whatever data type it points to. In this case, that's just enough to take you to the next free memory location in the block that you have allocated. Therefore, you can set the second element of the array (element number 1) to the value 8.4:

```
double* pDoubles = stackalloc double[20];
*pDoubles = 3.0;
*(pDoubles + 1) = 8.4;
```

By the same reasoning, you can access the element with index X of the array with the expression *(pDoubles + X).

Effectively, you have a means by which you can access elements of your array, but for general-purpose use, this syntax is too complex. Fortunately, C# defines an alternative syntax using square brackets. C# gives a very precise meaning to square brackets when they are applied to pointers; if the variable p is any pointer type and X is an integer, then the expression p[X] is always interpreted by the compiler as meaning *(p+X). This is true for all pointers, not only those initialized using stackalloc. With this shorthand notation, you now have a very convenient syntax for accessing your array. In fact, it means that you have exactly the same syntax for accessing one-dimensional, stack-based arrays as you do for accessing heap-based arrays that are represented by the System.Array class:

```
double* pDoubles = stackalloc double [20];
pDoubles[0] = 3.0; // pDoubles[0] is the same as *pDoubles
pDoubles[1] = 8.4; // pDoubles[1] is the same as *(pDoubles+1)
```

> **NOTE** *This idea of applying array syntax to pointers is not new. It has been a fundamental part of both the C and the C++ languages ever since those languages were invented. Indeed, C++ developers will recognize the stack-based arrays they can obtain using* stackalloc *as being essentially identical to classic stack-based C and C++ arrays. This syntax and the way it links pointers and arrays is one reason why the C language became popular in the 1970s, and the main reason why the use of pointers became such a popular programming technique in C and C++.*

Although your high-performance array can be accessed in the same way as a normal C# array, a word of caution is in order. The following code in C# raises an exception:

```
double[] myDoubleArray = new double [20];
myDoubleArray[50] = 3.0;
```

The exception occurs because you are trying to access an array using an index that is out of bounds; the index is 50, whereas the maximum allowed value is 19. However, if you declare the equivalent array using stackalloc, there is no object wrapped around the array that can perform bounds checking. Hence, the following code does *not* raise an exception:

```
double* pDoubles = stackalloc double [20];
pDoubles[50] = 3.0;
```

In this code, you allocate enough memory to hold 20 doubles. Then you set sizeof(double) memory locations, starting at the location given by the start of this memory + 50*sizeof(double) to hold the double value 3.0. Unfortunately, that memory location is way outside the area of memory that you have allocated for the doubles. There is no knowing what data might be stored at that address. At best, you might have used some currently unused memory, but it is equally possible that you might have just overwritten some locations in the stack that were being used to store other variables or even the return address from the method currently being executed. Again, you see that the high performance to be gained from pointers comes at a cost; you need to be certain you know what you are doing, or you will get some very strange run-time bugs.

QuickArray Example

The discussion of pointers ends with a `stackalloc` example called `QuickArray`. In this example, the program simply asks users how many elements they want to be allocated for an array. The code then uses `stackalloc` to allocate an array of `long`s that size. The elements of this array are populated with the squares of the integers starting with `0`, and the results are displayed on the console (code file `QuickArray/Program.cs`):

```
using static System.Console;

namespace QuickArray
{
  public class Program
  {
    unsafe public static void Main()
    {
      Write("How big an array do you want? \n> ");
      string userInput = ReadLine();
      uint size = uint.Parse(userInput);

      long* pArray = stackalloc long[(int) size];
      for (int i = 0; i < size; i++)
      {
        pArray[i] = i*i;
      }

      for (int i = 0; i < size; i++)
      {
        WriteLine($"Element {i} = {*(pArray + i)}");
      }

      ReadLine();
    }
  }
}
```

Here is the output from the `QuickArray` example:

```
How big an array do you want?
> 15
Element 0 = 0
Element 1 = 1
Element 2 = 4
Element 3 = 9
Element 4 = 16
Element 5 = 25
Element 6 = 36
Element 7 = 49
Element 8 = 64
Element 9 = 81
Element 10 = 100
Element 11 = 121
```

```
Element 12 = 144
Element 13 = 169
Element 14 = 196
```
—

PLATFORM INVOKE

Not all the features of Windows API calls are available from the .NET Framework. This is true not only for old Windows API calls but also for very new features from Windows 10 or Windows Server 2016. Maybe you've written some DLLs that export unmanaged methods and you would like to use them from C# as well.

To reuse an unmanaged library that doesn't contain COM objects—it contains only exported functions—you can use Platform Invoke (P/Invoke). With P/Invoke, the CLR loads the DLL that includes the function that should be called and marshals the parameters.

To use the unmanaged function, first you have to determine the name of the function as it is exported. You can do this by using the `dumpbin` tool with the `/exports` option.

For example, the command

```
dumpbin /exports c:\windows\system32\kernel32.dll | more
```

lists all exported functions from the DLL `kernel32.dll`. In the example, you use the `CreateHardLink` Windows API function to create a hard link to an existing file. With this API call, you can have several filenames that reference the same file as long as the filenames are on one hard disk only. This API call is not available from .NET Framework 4.5.1, so you must use platform invoke.

To call a native function, you have to define a C# external method with the same number of arguments, and the argument types that are defined with the unmanaged method must have mapped types with managed code.

The Windows API call `CreateHardLink` has this definition in C++:

```
BOOL CreateHardLink(
    LPCTSTR lpFileName,
    LPCTSTR lpExistingFileName,
    LPSECURITY_ATTRIBUTES lpSecurityAttributes);
```

This definition must be mapped to .NET data types. The return type is a `BOOL` with unmanaged code; this simply maps to the `bool` data type. `LPCTSTR` defines a `long` pointer to a `const` string. The Windows API uses the Hungarian naming convention for the data type. `LP` is a `long` pointer, `C` is a const, and `STR` is a null-terminated string. The `T` marks the type as a generic type, and the type is resolved to either `LPCSTR` (an ANSI string) or `LPWSTR` (a wide Unicode string), depending on the compiler's settings to 32 or 64 bit. C strings map to the .NET type `String`. `LPSECURITY_ATTRIBUTES`, which is a long pointer to a struct of type `SECURITY_ATTRIBUTES`. Because you can pass `NULL` to this argument, mapping this type to `IntPtr` is okay. The C# declaration of this method must be marked with the `extern` modifier because there's no implementation of this method within the C# code. Instead, the method implementation is in the DLL `kernel32.dll`, which is referenced with the attribute `[DllImport]`. The return type of the .NET declaration `CreateHardLink` is of type `bool`, and the native method `CreateHardLink` returns a `BOOL`, so some additional clarification is useful. Because there are different Boolean data types with C++ (for example, the native `bool` and the Windows-defined `BOOL`, which have different values), the attribute `[MarshalAs]` specifies to what native type the .NET type `bool` should map:

```
[DllImport("kernel32.dll", SetLastError="true",
        EntryPoint="CreateHardLink", CharSet=CharSet.Unicode)]
[return: MarshalAs(UnmanagedType.Bool)]
```

```
public static extern bool CreateHardLink(string newFileName,
                                         string existingFilename,
                                         IntPtr securityAttributes);
```

> **NOTE** *The website* http://www.pinvoke.net *is very helpful with the conversion from native to managed code.*

The settings that you can specify with the attribute [DllImport] are listed in the following table.

DLLIMPORT PROPERTY OR FIELD	DESCRIPTION
EntryPoint	You can give the C# declaration of the function a different name than the one it has with the unmanaged library. The name of the method in the unmanaged library is defined in the field EntryPoint.
CallingConvention	Depending on the compiler or compiler settings that were used to compile the unmanaged function, you can use different calling conventions. The calling convention defines how the parameters are handled and where to put them on the stack. You can define the calling convention by setting an enumerable value. The Windows API usually uses the StdCall calling convention on the Windows operating system, and it uses the Cdecl calling convention on Windows CE. Setting the value to CallingConvention. Winapi works for the Windows API in both the Windows and the Windows CE environments.
CharSet	String parameters can be either ANSI or Unicode. With the CharSet setting, you can define how strings are managed. Possible values that are defined with the CharSet enumeration are Ansi, Unicode, and Auto. CharSet. Auto uses Unicode on the Windows NT platform, and ANSI on Microsoft's older operating systems.
SetLastError	If the unmanaged function sets an error by using the Windows API SetLastError, you can set the SetLastError field to true. This way, you can read the error number afterward by using Marshal. GetLastWin32Error.

To make the CreateHardLink method easier to use from a .NET environment, you should follow these guidelines:

➤ Create an internal class named NativeMethods that wraps the platform invoke method calls.

➤ Create a public class to offer the native method functionality to .NET applications.

➤ Use security attributes to mark the required security.

In the following example, the public method CreateHardLink in the class FileUtility is the method that can be used by .NET applications. This method has the filename arguments reversed compared to the native Windows API method CreateHardLink. The first argument is the name of the existing file, and the second argument is the new file. This is similar to other classes in the framework, such as File.Copy. Because the third argument used to pass the security attributes for the new filename is not used with this implementation, the public method has just two parameters. The return type is changed as well. Instead of returning an error by returning the value `false`, an exception is thrown. In case of an error, the unmanaged method `CreateHardLink` sets the error number with the unmanaged API `SetLastError`. To read this value from .NET, the `[DllImport]` field `SetLastError` is set to `true`. Within the managed method `CreateHardLink`, the error number is read by calling `Marshal.GetLastWin32Error`. To create an error message from this number, the `Win32Exception` class from the namespace `System.ComponentModel` is used. This class accepts an error number with the constructor, and returns a localized error message. In case of an error, an exception of type `IOException` is thrown, which has an inner exception of type `Win32Exception`. The public method `CreateHardLink` has the `FileIOPermission` attribute applied to check whether the caller has the necessary permission. You can read more about .NET security in Chapter 24 (code file `PInvokeSample/NativeMethods.cs`).

```csharp
using System;
using System.ComponentModel;
using System.IO;
using System.Runtime.InteropServices;
using System.Security;
using System.Security.Permissions;

namespace Wrox.ProCSharp.Interop
{
  [SecurityCritical]
  internal static class NativeMethods
  {
    [DllImport("kernel32.dll", SetLastError = true,
      EntryPoint = "CreateHardLinkW", CharSet = CharSet.Unicode)]
    [return: MarshalAs(UnmanagedType.Bool)]
    private static extern bool CreateHardLink(
      [In, MarshalAs(UnmanagedType.LPWStr)] string newFileName,
      [In, MarshalAs(UnmanagedType.LPWStr)] string existingFileName,
      IntPtr securityAttributes);


    internal static void CreateHardLink(string oldFileName,
                                        string newFileName)
    {
      if (!CreateHardLink(newFileName, oldFileName, IntPtr.Zero))
      {
        var ex = new Win32Exception(Marshal.GetLastWin32Error());
        throw new IOException(ex.Message, ex);
      }
    }
  }

  public static class FileUtility
  {
    [FileIOPermission(SecurityAction.LinkDemand, Unrestricted = true)]
    public static void CreateHardLink(string oldFileName,
                                      string newFileName)
    {
      NativeMethods.CreateHardLink(oldFileName, newFileName);
    }
  }
}
```

You can now use this class to easily create hard links . If the file passed with the first argument of the program does not exist, you get an exception with the message: The system cannot find the file specified. If the file exists, you get a new filename referencing the original file. You can easily verify this by changing text in one file; it shows up in the other file as well (code file PInvokeSample/Program.cs):

```csharp
using PInvokeSampleLib;
using System.IO;
using static System.Console;

namespace PInvokeSample
{
  public class Program
  {
    public static void Main(string[] args)
    {
      if (args.Length != 2)
      {
        WriteLine("usage: PInvokeSample " +
          "existingfilename newfilename");
        return;
      }
      try
      {
        FileUtility.CreateHardLink(args[0], args[1]);
      }
      catch (IOException ex)
      {
        WriteLine(ex.Message);
      }
    }
  }
}
```

With native method calls, often you have to use Windows handles. A Window handle is a 32- or 64-bit value for which, depending on the handle types, some values are not allowed. With .NET 1.0 for handles, usually the IntPtr structure was used because you can set every possible 32-bit value with this structure. However, with some handle types, this led to security problems and possible threading race conditions and leaked handles with the finalization phase. That's why .NET 2.0 introduced the SafeHandle class. The class SafeHandle is an abstract base class for every Windows handle. Derived classes inside the Microsoft.Win32.SafeHandles namespace are SafeHandleZeroOrMinusOneIsInvalid and SafeHandleMinusOneIsInvalid. As the name indicates, these classes do not accept invalid 0 or –1 values. Further derived handle types are SafeFileHandle, SafeWaitHandle, SafeNCryptHandle, and SafePipeHandle, which can be used by the specific Windows API calls.

For example, to map the Windows API CreateFile, you can use the following declaration to return a SafeFileHandle. Of course, usually you could use the .NET classes File and FileInfo instead.

```csharp
[DllImport("Kernel32.dll", SetLastError = true,
        CharSet = CharSet.Unicode)]
internal static extern SafeFileHandle CreateFile(
  string fileName,
  [MarshalAs(UnmanagedType.U4)] FileAccess fileAccess,
  [MarshalAs(UnmanagedType.U4)] FileShare fileShare,
  IntPtr securityAttributes,
  [MarshalAs(UnmanagedType.U4)] FileMode creationDisposition,
  int flags,
  SafeFileHandle template);
```

SUMMARY

Remember that in order to become a truly proficient C# programmer, you must have a solid understanding of how memory allocation and garbage collection work. This chapter described how the CLR manages and allocates memory on the heap and the stack. It also illustrated how to write classes that free unmanaged resources correctly, and how to use pointers in C#. These are both advanced topics that are poorly understood and often implemented incorrectly by novice programmers. At a minimum, this chapter should have helped you understand how to release resources using the IDisposable interface and the using statement.

The next chapter continues with an important C# language construct that also affects the generation of the IL code: generics.

Generics

WHAT'S IN THIS CHAPTER?

➤ An overview of generics
➤ Creating generic classes
➤ Features of generic classes
➤ Generic interfaces
➤ Generic structs
➤ Generic methods

WROX.COM CODE DOWNLOADS FOR THIS CHAPTER

The wrox.com code downloads for this chapter are found at www.wrox.com/go/
professionalcsharp6 on the Download Code tab. The code for this chapter is divided into the following major examples:

➤ Linked List Objects
➤ Linked List Sample
➤ Document Manager
➤ Variance
➤ Generic Methods
➤ Specialization

GENERICS OVERVIEW

Generics are an important concept of not only C# but also .NET. Generics are more than a part of the
C# programming language; they are deeply integrated with the IL (Intermediate Language) code in
the assemblies. With generics, you can create classes and methods that are independent of contained
types. Instead of writing a number of methods or classes with the same functionality for different
types, you can create just one method or class.

Another option to reduce the amount of code is using the `Object` class. However, passing using types derived from the `Object` class is not type safe. Generic classes make use of generic types that are replaced with specific types as needed. This allows for type safety: The compiler complains if a specific type is not supported with the generic class.

Generics are not limited to classes; in this chapter, you also see generics with interfaces and methods. You can find generics with delegates in Chapter 9, "Delegates, Lambdas, and Events."

Generics are not specific only to C#; similar concepts exist with other languages. For example, C++ templates have some similarity to generics. However, there's a big difference between C++ templates and .NET generics. With C++ templates, the source code of the template is required when a template is instantiated with a specific type. The C++ compiler generates separate binary code for each type that is an instance of a specific template. Unlike C++ templates, generics are not only a construct of the C# language but are defined with the Common Language Runtime (CLR). This makes it possible to instantiate generics with a specific type in Visual Basic even though the generic class was defined with C#.

The following sections explore the advantages and disadvantages of generics, particularly in regard to the following:

➤ Performance
➤ Type safety
➤ Binary code reuse
➤ Code bloat
➤ Naming guidelines

Performance

One of the big advantages of generics is performance. In Chapter 11, "Collections," you see non-generic and generic collection classes from the namespaces `System.Collections` and `System.Collections.Generic`. Using value types with non-generic collection classes results in boxing and unboxing when the value type is converted to a reference type, and vice versa.

> **NOTE** *Boxing and unboxing are discussed in Chapter 8, "Operators and Casts." Here is just a short refresher about these terms.*

Value types are stored on the stack, whereas reference types are stored on the heap. C# classes are reference types; structs are value types. .NET makes it easy to convert value types to reference types, so you can use a value type everywhere an object (which is a reference type) is needed. For example, an `int` can be assigned to an object. The conversion from a value type to a reference type is known as *boxing*. Boxing occurs automatically if a method requires an object as a parameter, and a value type is passed. In the other direction, a boxed value type can be converted to a value type by using unboxing. With unboxing, the cast operator is required.

The following example shows that the `ArrayList` class from the namespace `System.Collections` stores objects; the `Add` method is defined to require an object as a parameter, so an integer type is boxed. When the values from an `ArrayList` are read, unboxing occurs when the object is converted to an integer type. This may be obvious with the cast operator that is used to assign the first element of the `ArrayList` collection to the variable `i1`, but it also happens inside the `foreach` statement where the variable `i2` of type `int` is accessed:

```
var list = new ArrayList();
```

```
list.Add(44);    // boxing - convert a value type to a reference type

int i1 = (int)list[0];    // unboxing - convert a reference type to
                          // a value type

foreach (int i2 in list)
{
  WriteLine(i2);    // unboxing
}
```

Boxing and unboxing are easy to use but have a big performance impact, especially when iterating through many items.

Instead of using objects, the `List<T>` class from the namespace `System.Collections.Generic` enables you to define the type when it is used. In the example here, the generic type of the `List<T>` class is defined as `int`, so the `int` type is used inside the class that is generated dynamically from the Just-In-Time (JIT) compiler. Boxing and unboxing no longer happen:

```
var list = new List<int>();
list.Add(44);  // no boxing - value types are stored in the List<int>

int i1 = list[0];  // no unboxing, no cast needed

foreach (int i2 in list)
{
  WriteLine(i2);
}
```

Type Safety

Another feature of generics is type safety. As with the `ArrayList` class, if objects are used, any type can be added to this collection. The following example shows adding an integer, a string, and an object of type `MyClass` to the collection of type `ArrayList`:

```
var list = new ArrayList();
list.Add(44);
list.Add("mystring");
list.Add(new MyClass());
```

If this collection is iterated using the following `foreach` statement, which iterates using integer elements, the compiler accepts this code. However, because not all elements in the collection can be cast to an `int`, a run-time exception will occur:

```
foreach (int i in list)
{
  WriteLine(i);
}
```

Errors should be detected as early as possible. With the generic class `List<T>`, the generic type `T` defines what types are allowed. With a definition of `List<int>`, only integer types can be added to the collection. The compiler doesn't compile this code because the `Add` method has invalid arguments:

```
var list = new List<int>();
list.Add(44);
list.Add("mystring");   // compile time error
list.Add(new MyClass());   // compile time error
```

Binary Code Reuse

Generics enable better binary code reuse. A generic class can be defined once and can be instantiated with many different types. Unlike C++ templates, it is not necessary to access the source code.

For example, here the `List<T>` class from the namespace `System.Collections.Generic` is instantiated with an int, a string, and a MyClass type:

```
var list = new List<int>();
list.Add(44);

var stringList = new List<string>();
stringList.Add("mystring");

var myClassList = new List<MyClass>();
myClassList.Add(new MyClass());
```

Generic types can be defined in one language and used from any other .NET language.

Code Bloat

You might be wondering how much code is created with generics when instantiating them with different specific types. Because a generic class definition goes into the assembly, instantiating generic classes with specific types doesn't duplicate these classes in the IL code. However, when the generic classes are compiled by the JIT compiler to native code, a new class for every specific value type is created. Reference types share all the same implementation of the same native class. This is because with reference types, only a 4-byte memory address (with 32-bit systems) is needed within the generic instantiated class to reference a reference type. Value types are contained within the memory of the generic instantiated class; and because every value type can have different memory requirements, a new class for every value type is instantiated.

Naming Guidelines

If generics are used in the program, it helps when generic types can be distinguished from non-generic types. Here are naming guidelines for generic types:

➤ Prefix generic type names with the letter T.

➤ If the generic type can be replaced by any class because there's no special requirement, and only one generic type is used, the character T is good as a generic type name:

```
public class List<T> { }

public class LinkedList<T> { }
```

➤ If there's a special requirement for a generic type (for example, it must implement an interface or derive from a base class), or if two or more generic types are used, use descriptive names for the type names:

```
public delegate void EventHandler<TEventArgs>(object sender,
  TEventArgs e);

public delegate TOutput Converter<TInput, TOutput>(TInput from);

public class SortedList<TKey, TValue> { }
```

CREATING GENERIC CLASSES

The example in this section starts with a normal, non-generic simplified linked list class that can contain objects of any kind, and then converts this class to a generic class.

With a linked list, one element references the next one. Therefore, you must create a class that wraps the object inside the linked list and references the next object. The class `LinkedListNode` contains a property named `Value` that is initialized with the constructor. In addition to that, the `LinkedListNode` class contains references to the next and previous elements in the list that can be accessed from properties (code file `LinkedListObjects/LinkedListNode.cs`):

```
public class LinkedListNode
{
  public LinkedListNode(object value)
  {
    Value = value;
  }

  public object Value { get; private set; }

  public LinkedListNode Next { get; internal set; }
  public LinkedListNode Prev { get; internal set; }
}
```

The `LinkedList` class includes `First` and `Last` properties of type `LinkedListNode` that mark the beginning and end of the list. The method `AddLast` adds a new element to the end of the list. First, an object of type `LinkedListNode` is created. If the list is empty, then the `First` and `Last` properties are set to the new element; otherwise, the new element is added as the last element to the list. By implementing the `GetEnumerator` method, it is possible to iterate through the list with the `foreach` statement. The `GetEnumerator` method makes use of the `yield` statement for creating an enumerator type:

```
public class LinkedList: IEnumerable
{
  public LinkedListNode First { get; private set; }
  public LinkedListNode Last { get; private set; }

  public LinkedListNode AddLast(object node)
  {
    var newNode = new LinkedListNode(node);
    if (First == null)
    {
      First = newNode;
      Last = First;
    }
    else
    {
      LinkedListNode previous = Last;
      Last.Next = newNode;
      Last = newNode;
      Last.Prev = previous;
    }
    return newNode;
  }

  public IEnumerator GetEnumerator()
  {
    LinkedListNode current = First;
    while (current != null)
    {
      yield return current.Value;
      current = current.Next;
    }
  }
}
```

> **NOTE** *The* yield *statement creates a state machine for an enumerator. This statement is explained in Chapter 7, "Arrays and Tuples."*

Now you can use the LinkedList class with any type. The following code segment instantiates a new LinkedList object and adds two integer types and one string type. As the integer types are converted to an object, boxing occurs as explained earlier in this chapter. With the foreach statement, unboxing happens. In the foreach statement, the elements from the list are cast to an integer, so a runtime exception occurs with the third element in the list because casting to an int fails (code file LinkedListObjects/Program.cs):

```
var list1 = new LinkedList();
list1.AddLast(2);
list1.AddLast(4);
list1.AddLast("6");

foreach (int i in list1)
{
  WriteLine(i);
}
```

Now make a generic version of the linked list. A generic class is defined similarly to a normal class with the generic type declaration. You can then use the generic type within the class as a field member or with parameter types of methods. The class LinkedListNode is declared with a generic type T. The property Value is now type T instead of object; the constructor is changed as well to accept an object of type T. A generic type can also be returned and set, so the properties Next and Prev are now of type LinkedListNode<T> (code file LinkedListSample/LinkedListNode.cs):

```
public class LinkedListNode<T>
{
  public LinkedListNode(T value)
  {
    Value = value;
  }

  public T Value { get; private set; }
  public LinkedListNode<T> Next { get; internal set; }
  public LinkedListNode<T> Prev { get; internal set; }
}
```

In the following code, the class LinkedList is changed to a generic class as well. LinkedList<T> contains LinkedListNode<T> elements. The type T from the LinkedList defines the type T of the properties First and Last. The method AddLast now accepts a parameter of type T and instantiates an object of type LinkedListNode<T>.

Besides the interface IEnumerable, a generic version is also available: IEnumerable<T>. IEnumerable<T> derives from IEnumerable and adds the GetEnumerator method, which returns IEnumerator<T>. LinkedList<T> implements the generic interface IEnumerable<T> (code file LinkedListSample/ LinkedList.cs):

> **NOTE** *Enumerators and the interfaces* IEnumerable *and* IEnumerator *are discussed in Chapter 7.*

```csharp
public class LinkedList<T>: IEnumerable<T>
{
  public LinkedListNode<T> First { get; private set; }
  public LinkedListNode<T> Last { get; private set; }

  public LinkedListNode<T> AddLast(T node)
  {
    var newNode = new LinkedListNode<T>(node);
    if (First == null)
    {
      First = newNode;
      Last = First;
    }
    else
    {
      LinkedListNode<T> previous = Last;
      Last.Next = newNode;
      Last = newNode;
      Last.Prev = previous;
    }
    return newNode;
  }

  public IEnumerator<T> GetEnumerator()
  {
    LinkedListNode<T> current = First;

    while (current != null)
    {
      yield return current.Value;
      current = current.Next;
    }
  }

  IEnumerator IEnumerable.GetEnumerator() => GetEnumerator();
}
```

Using the generic `LinkedList<T>`, you can instantiate it with an `int` type, and there's no boxing. Also, you get a compiler error if you don't pass an `int` with the method `AddLast`. Using the generic `IEnumerable<T>`, the `foreach` statement is also type safe, and you get a compiler error if that variable in the `foreach` statement is not an `int` (code file `LinkedListSample/Program.cs`):

```csharp
var list2 = new LinkedList<int>();
list2.AddLast(1);
list2.AddLast(3);
list2.AddLast(5);

foreach (int i in list2)
{
  WriteLine(i);
}
```

Similarly, you can use the generic `LinkedList<T>` with a `string` type and pass strings to the `AddLast` method:

```csharp
var list3 = new LinkedList<string>();
list3.AddLast("2");
list3.AddLast("four");
```

```
list3.AddLast("foo");

foreach (string s in list3)
{
  WriteLine(s);
}
```

> **NOTE** *Every class that deals with the object type is a possible candidate for a generic implementation. Also, if classes make use of hierarchies, generics can be very helpful in making casting unnecessary.*

GENERICS FEATURES

When creating generic classes, you might need some additional C# keywords. For example, it is not possible to assign `null` to a generic type. In this case, the keyword `default` can be used, as demonstrated in the next section. If the generic type does not require the features of the `Object` class but you need to invoke some specific methods in the generic class, you can define constraints.

This section discusses the following topics:

➤ Default values

➤ Constraints

➤ Inheritance

➤ Static members

This example begins with a generic document manager, which is used to read and write documents from and to a queue. Start by creating a new Console project named `DocumentManager` and add the class `DocumentManager<T>`. The method `AddDocument` adds a document to the queue. The read-only property `IsDocumentAvailable` returns true if the queue is not empty (code file `DocumentManager/DocumentManager.cs`):

> **NOTE** *With .NET Core, this sample needs a reference to the NuGet package* `System.Collections`.

```
using System;
using System.Collections.Generic;

namespace Wrox.ProCSharp.Generics
{
  public class DocumentManager<T>
  {
    private readonly Queue<T> documentQueue = new Queue<T>();

    public void AddDocument(T doc)
    {
      lock (this)
      {
        documentQueue.Enqueue(doc);
      }
```

```
    }

    public bool IsDocumentAvailable => documentQueue.Count > 0;
  }
}
```

Threading and the lock statement are discussed in Chapter 21, "Tasks and Parallel Programming," and Chapter 22, "Task Synchronization."

Default Values

Now you add a `GetDocument` method to the `DocumentManager<T>` class. Inside this method the type `T` should be assigned to `null`. However, it is not possible to assign `null` to generic types. That's because a generic type can also be instantiated as a value type, and `null` is allowed only with reference types. To circumvent this problem, you can use the `default` keyword. With the `default` keyword, `null` is assigned to reference types and `0` is assigned to value types:

```
public T GetDocument()
{
  T doc = default(T);
  lock (this)
  {
    doc = documentQueue.Dequeue();
  }
  return doc;
}
```

> **NOTE** *The* `default` *keyword has multiple meanings depending on its context. The* `switch` *statement uses a* `default` *for defining the default case, and with generics* `default` *is used to initialize generic types either to* `null` *or to* `0`, *depending on whether it is a reference or value type.*

Constraints

If the generic class needs to invoke some methods from the generic type, you have to add constraints.

With `DocumentManager<T>`, all the document titles should be displayed in the `DisplayAllDocuments` method. The `Document` class implements the interface `IDocument` with the properties `Title` and `Content` (code file `DocumentManager/Document.cs`):

```
public interface IDocument
{
  string Title { get; set; }
  string Content { get; set; }
}

public class Document: IDocument
{
  public Document()
  {
  }

  public Document(string title, string content)
```

```
    {
      Title = title;
      Content = content;
    }

    public string Title { get; set; }
    public string Content { get; set; }
}
```

To display the documents with the `DocumentManager<T>` class, you can cast the type `T` to the interface `IDocument` to display the title (code file `DocumentManager/DocumentManager.cs`):

```
public void DisplayAllDocuments()
{
  foreach (T doc in documentQueue)
  {
    WriteLine(((IDocument)doc).Title);
  }
}
```

The problem here is that doing a cast results in a runtime exception if type `T` does not implement the interface `IDocument`. Instead, it would be better to define a constraint with the `DocumentManager<TDocument>` class specifying that the type `TDocument` must implement the interface `IDocument`. To clarify the requirement in the name of the generic type, `T` is changed to `TDocument`. The `where` clause defines the requirement to implement the interface `IDocument`:

```
public class DocumentManager<TDocument>
    where TDocument: IDocument
{
```

> **NOTE** *When adding a constraint to a generic type, it's a good idea to have some information with the generic parameter name. The sample code is now using `TDocument` instead of `T` for the generic parameter. For the compiler, the parameter name doesn't matter, but it is more readable.*

This way you can write the `foreach` statement in such a way that the type `TDocument` contains the property `Title`. You get support from Visual Studio IntelliSense and the compiler:

```
public void DisplayAllDocuments()
{
  foreach (TDocument doc in documentQueue)
  {
    WriteLine(doc.Title);
  }
}
```

In the `Main` method, the `DocumentManager<TDocument>` class is instantiated with the type `Document` that implements the required interface `IDocument`. Then new documents are added and displayed, and one of the documents is retrieved (code file `DocumentManager/Program.cs`):

```
public static void Main()
{
  var dm = new DocumentManager<Document>();
```

```
        dm.AddDocument(new Document("Title A", "Sample A"));
        dm.AddDocument(new Document("Title B", "Sample B"));

        dm.DisplayAllDocuments();

        if (dm.IsDocumentAvailable)
        {
            Document d = dm.GetDocument();
            WriteLine(d.Content);
        }
    }
```

The `DocumentManager` now works with any class that implements the interface `IDocument`.

In the sample application, you've seen an interface constraint. Generics support several constraint types, indicated in the following table.

CONSTRAINT	DESCRIPTION
where T: struct	With a struct constraint, type T must be a value type.
where T: class	The class constraint indicates that type T must be a reference type.
where T: IFoo	Specifies that type T is required to implement interface IFoo.
where T: Foo	Specifies that type T is required to derive from base class Foo.
where T: new()	A constructor constraint; specifies that type T must have a default constructor.
where T1: T2	With constraints it is also possible to specify that type T1 derives from a generic type T2.

> **NOTE** *Constructor constraints can be defined only for the default constructor. It is not possible to define a constructor constraint for other constructors.*

With a generic type, you can also combine multiple constraints. The constraint `where T: IFoo, new()` with the `MyClass<T>` declaration specifies that type T implements the interface `IFoo` and has a default constructor:

```
public class MyClass<T>
    where T: IFoo, new()
{
    //...
```

> **NOTE** *One important restriction of the* where *clause with C# is that it's not possible to define operators that must be implemented by the generic type. Operators cannot be defined in interfaces. With the* where *clause, it is only possible to define base classes, interfaces, and the default constructor.*

Inheritance

The `LinkedList<T>` class created earlier implements the interface `IEnumerable<T>`:

```
public class LinkedList<T>: IEnumerable<T>
{
  //...
```

A generic type can implement a generic interface. The same is possible by deriving from a class. A generic class can be derived from a generic base class:

```
public class Base<T>
{
}

public class Derived<T>: Base<T>
{
}
```

The requirement is that the generic types of the interface must be repeated, or the type of the base class must be specified, as in this case:

```
public class Base<T>
{
}

public class Derived<T>: Base<string>
{
}
```

This way, the derived class can be a generic or non-generic class. For example, you can define an abstract generic base class that is implemented with a concrete type in the derived class. This enables you to write *generic specialization* for specific types:

```
public abstract class Calc<T>
{
  public abstract T Add(T x, T y);
  public abstract T Sub(T x, T y);
}

public class IntCalc: Calc<int>
{
  public override int Add(int x, int y) => x + y;

  public override int Sub(int x, int y) => x - y;
}
```

You can also create a partial specialization, such as deriving the `StringQuery` class from `Query` and defining only one of the generic parameters, for example, a `string` for `TResult`. For instantiating the `StringQuery`, you need only to supply the type for `TRequest`:

```
public class Query<TRequest, TResult>
{
}

public StringQuery<TRequest> : Query<TRequest, string>
{
}
```

Static Members

Static members of generic classes are shared with only one instantiation of the class, and they require special attention. Consider the following example, where the class `StaticDemo<T>` contains the static field x:

```
public class StaticDemo<T>
{
  public static int x;
}
```

Because the class `StaticDemo<T>` is used with both a `string` type and an `int` type, two sets of static fields exist:

```
StaticDemo<string>.x = 4;
StaticDemo<int>.x = 5;
WriteLine(StaticDemo<string>.x);    // writes 4
```

GENERIC INTERFACES

Using generics, you can define interfaces that define methods with generic parameters. In the linked list sample, you've already implemented the interface `IEnumerable<out T>`, which defines a `GetEnumerator` method to return `IEnumerator<out T>`. .NET offers a lot of generic interfaces for different scenarios; examples include `IComparable<T>`, `ICollection<T>`, and `IExtensibleObject<T>`. Often older, non-generic versions of the same interface exist; for example, .NET 1.0 had an `IComparable` interface that was based on objects. `IComparable<in T>` is based on a generic type:

```
public interface IComparable<in T>
{
  int CompareTo(T other);
}
```

> **NOTE** *Don't be confused by the* in *and* out *keywords used with the generic parameter. They are explained soon in the "Covariance and contra-variance" section.*

The older, non-generic `IComparable` interface requires an object with the `CompareTo` method. This requires a cast to specific types, such as to the `Person` class for using the `LastName` property:

```
public class Person: IComparable
{
  public int CompareTo(object obj)
  {
    Person other = obj as Person;
    return this.lastname.CompareTo(other.LastName);
  }
  //
```

When implementing the generic version, it is no longer necessary to cast the `object` to a `Person`:

```
public class Person: IComparable<Person>
{
  public int CompareTo(Person other) => LastName.CompareTo(other.LastName);
  //...
```

Covariance and Contra-variance

Prior to .NET 4, generic interfaces were invariant. .NET 4 added important changes for generic interfaces and generic delegates: covariance and contra-variance. Covariance and contra-variance are used for the conversion of types with arguments and return types. For example, can you pass a `Rectangle` to a method that requests a `Shape`? Let's get into examples to see the advantages of these extensions.

With .NET, parameter types are covariant. Assume you have the classes `Shape` and `Rectangle`, and `Rectangle` derives from the `Shape` base class. The `Display` method is declared to accept an object of the `Shape` type as its parameter:

```
public void Display(Shape o) { }
```

Now you can pass any object that derives from the `Shape` base class. Because `Rectangle` derives from `Shape`, a `Rectangle` fulfills all the requirements of a `Shape` and the compiler accepts this method call:

```
var r = new Rectangle { Width= 5, Height=2.5 };
Display(r);
```

Return types of methods are contra-variant. When a method returns a `Shape` it is not possible to assign it to a `Rectangle` because a `Shape` is not necessarily always a `Rectangle`; but the opposite is possible. If a method returns a `Rectangle` as the `GetRectangle` method,

```
public Rectangle GetRectangle();
```

the result can be assigned to a `Shape`:

```
Shape s = GetRectangle();
```

Before version 4 of the .NET Framework, this behavior was not possible with generics. Since C# 4, the language is extended to support covariance and contra-variance with generic interfaces and generic delegates. Let's start by defining a `Shape` base class and a `Rectangle` class (code files `Variance/Shape.cs` and `Rectangle.cs`):

```
public class Shape
{
  public double Width { get; set; }
  public double Height { get; set; }

  public override string ToString() => $"Width: {Width}, Height: {Height}";
}

public class Rectangle: Shape
{
}
```

Covariance with Generic Interfaces

A generic interface is covariant if the generic type is annotated with the `out` keyword. This also means that type `T` is allowed only with return types. The interface `IIndex` is covariant with type `T` and returns this type from a read-only indexer (code file `Variance/IIndex.cs`):

```
public interface IIndex<out T>
{
```

```
      T this[int index] { get; }
      int Count { get; }
}
```

The `IIndex<T>` interface is implemented with the `RectangleCollection` class. `RectangleCollection` defines `Rectangle` for generic type `T`:

```
public class RectangleCollection: IIndex<Rectangle>
{
  private Rectangle[] data = new Rectangle[3]
  {
    new Rectangle { Height=2, Width=5 },
    new Rectangle { Height=3, Width=7 },
    new Rectangle { Height=4.5, Width=2.9 }
  };

  private static RectangleCollection _coll;
  public static RectangleCollection GetRectangles() =>
    _coll ?? (coll = new RectangleCollection());

  public Rectangle this[int index]
  {
    get
    {
      if (index < 0 || index > data.Length)
        throw new ArgumentOutOfRangeException("index");
      return data[index];
    }
  }

  public int Count => data.Length;
}
```

The `RectangleCollection.GetRectangles` method returns a `RectangleCollection` that implements the `IIndex<Rectangle>` interface, so you can assign the return value to a variable `rectangle` of the `IIndex<Rectangle>` type. Because the interface is covariant, it is also possible to assign the returned value to a variable of `IIndex<Shape>`. `Shape` does not need anything more than a `Rectangle` has to offer. Using the shapes variable, the indexer from the interface and the `Count` property are used within the `for` loop (code file `Variance/Program.cs`):

```
public static void Main()
{
```

```
IIndex<Rectangle> rectangles = RectangleCollection.GetRectangles();
IIndex<Shape> shapes = rectangles;

for (int i = 0; i < shapes.Count; i++)
{
  WriteLine(shapes[i]);
}
}
```

Contra-Variance with Generic Interfaces

A generic interface is contra-variant if the generic type is annotated with the in keyword. This way, the interface is only allowed to use generic type T as input to its methods (code file Variance/IDisplay.cs):

```
public interface IDisplay<in T>
{
  void Show(T item);
}
```

The ShapeDisplay class implements IDisplay<Shape> and uses a Shape object as an input parameter (code file Variance/ShapeDisplay.cs):

```
public class ShapeDisplay: IDisplay<Shape>
{
  public void Show(Shape s) =>
    WriteLine($"{s.GetType().Name} Width: {s.Width}, Height: {s.Height}");
}
```

Creating a new instance of ShapeDisplay returns IDisplay<Shape>, which is assigned to the shapeDisplay variable. Because IDisplay<T> is contra-variant, it is possible to assign the result to IDisplay<Rectangle>, where Rectangle derives from Shape. This time the methods of the interface define only the generic type as input, and Rectangle fulfills all the requirements of a Shape (code file Variance/Program.cs):

```
public static void Main()
{
  //...
  IDisplay<Shape> shapeDisplay = new ShapeDisplay();
  IDisplay<Rectangle> rectangleDisplay = shapeDisplay;
  rectangleDisplay.Show(rectangles[0]);
}
```

GENERIC STRUCTS

Similar to classes, structs can be generic as well. They are very similar to generic classes with the exception of inheritance features. In this section you look at the generic struct Nullable<T>, which is defined by the .NET Framework.

An example of a generic struct in the .NET Framework is Nullable<T>. A number in a database and a number in a programming language have an important difference: A number in the database can be null, whereas a number in C# cannot be null. Int32 is a struct, and because structs are implemented as value types, they cannot be null. This difference often causes headaches and a lot of additional work to map the data. The problem exists not only with databases but also with mapping XML data to .NET types.

One solution is to map numbers from databases and XML files to reference types, because reference types can have a null value. However, this also means additional overhead during runtime.

With the structure Nullable<T>, this can be easily resolved. The following code segment shows a simplified version of how Nullable<T> is defined. The structure Nullable<T> defines a constraint specifying that the generic type T needs to be a struct. With classes as generic types, the advantage of low overhead is eliminated; and because objects of classes can be null anyway, there's no point in using a class with the Nullable<T> type. The only overhead in addition to the T type defined by Nullable<T> is the hasValue Boolean field that defines whether the value is set or null. Other than that, the generic struct defines the read-only properties HasValue and Value and some operator overloads. The operator overload to cast the Nullable<T> type to T is defined as explicit because it can throw an exception in case hasValue is false. The operator overload to cast to Nullable<T> is defined as implicit because it always succeeds:

```csharp
public struct Nullable<T>
    where T: struct
{
  public Nullable(T value)
  {
    _hasValue = true;
    _value = value;
  }
  private bool _hasValue;
  public bool HasValue => _hasValue;

  private T _value;
  public T Value
  {
    get
    {
      if (!_hasValue)
      {
        throw new InvalidOperationException("no value");
      }
      return _value;
    }
  }

  public static explicit operator T(Nullable<T> value) => _value.Value;

  public static implicit operator Nullable<T>(T value) => new Nullable<T>(value);

  public override string ToString() => !HasValue ? string.Empty : _value.ToString();
}
```

In this example, Nullable<T> is instantiated with Nullable<int>. The variable x can now be used as an int, assigning values and using operators to do some calculation. This behavior is made possible by casting operators of the Nullable<T> type. However, x can also be null. The Nullable<T> properties HasValue and Value can check whether there is a value, and the value can be accessed:

```csharp
Nullable<int> x;
x = 4;
x += 3;
if (x.HasValue)
{
  int y = x.Value;
}
x = null;
```

Because nullable types are used often, C# has a special syntax for defining variables of this type. Instead of using syntax with the generic structure, the ? operator can be used. In the following example, the variables x1 and x2 are both instances of a nullable int type:

```
Nullable<int> x1;
int? x2;
```

A nullable type can be compared with null and numbers, as shown. Here, the value of x is compared with null, and if it is not null it is compared with a value less than 0:

```
int? x = GetNullableType();
if (x == null)
{
  WriteLine("x is null");
}
else if (x < 0)
{
  WriteLine("x is smaller than 0");
}
```

Now that you know how Nullable<T> is defined, let's get into using nullable types. Nullable types can also be used with arithmetic operators. The variable x3 is the sum of the variables x1 and x2. If any of the nullable types have a null value, the result is null:

```
int? x1 = GetNullableType();
int? x2 = GetNullableType();
int? x3 = x1 + x2;
```

> **NOTE** *The* GetNullableType *method, which is called here, is just a placeholder for any method that returns a nullable* int. *For testing you can implement it to simply return* null *or to return any integer value.*

Non-nullable types can be converted to nullable types. With the conversion from a non-nullable type to a nullable type, an implicit conversion is possible where casting is not required. This type of conversion always succeeds:

```
int y1 = 4;
int? x1 = y1;
```

In the reverse situation, a conversion from a nullable type to a non-nullable type can fail. If the nullable type has a null value and the null value is assigned to a non-nullable type, then an exception of type InvalidOperationException is thrown. That's why the cast operator is required to do an explicit conversion:

```
int? x1 = GetNullableType();
int y1 = (int)x1;
```

Instead of doing an explicit cast, it is also possible to convert a nullable type to a non-nullable type with the coalescing operator. The coalescing operator uses the syntax ?? to define a default value for the conversion in case the nullable type has a value of null. Here, y1 gets a 0 value if x1 is null:

```
int? x1 = GetNullableType();
int y1 = x1 ?? 0;
```

GENERIC METHODS

In addition to defining generic classes, it is also possible to define generic methods. With a generic method, the generic type is defined with the method declaration. Generic methods can be defined within non-generic classes.

The method Swap<T> defines T as a generic type that is used for two arguments and a variable temp:

```
void Swap<T>(ref T x, ref T y)
{
    T temp;
    temp = x;
    x = y;
    y = temp;
}
```

A generic method can be invoked by assigning the generic type with the method call:

```
int i = 4;
int j = 5;
Swap<int>(ref i, ref j);
```

However, because the C# compiler can get the type of the parameters by calling the Swap method, it is not necessary to assign the generic type with the method call. The generic method can be invoked as simply as non-generic methods:

```
int i = 4;
int j = 5;
Swap(ref i, ref j);
```

Generic Methods Example

This example uses a generic method to accumulate all the elements of a collection. To show the features of generic methods, the following Account class, which contains Name and Balance properties, is used (code file GenericMethods/Account.cs):

> **NOTE** *With .NET Core, this sample needs a reference to the NuGet package* System.
> Collections.

```
public class Account
{
    public string Name { get; }
    public decimal Balance { get; private set; }

    public Account(string name, Decimal balance)
    {
        Name = name;
        Balance = balance;
    }
}
```

All the accounts in which the balance should be accumulated are added to an accounts list of type List<Account> (code file GenericMethods/Program.cs):

```
var accounts = new List<Account>()
```

```
{
  new Account("Christian", 1500),
  new Account("Stephanie", 2200),
  new Account("Angela", 1800),
  new Account("Matthias", 2400)
};
```

A traditional way to accumulate all `Account` objects is by looping through them with a `foreach` statement, as shown here. Because the `foreach` statement uses the `IEnumerable` interface to iterate the elements of a collection, the argument of the `AccumulateSimple` method is of type `IEnumerable`. The `foreach` statement works with every object implementing `IEnumerable`. This way, the `AccumulateSimple` method can be used with all collection classes that implement the interface `IEnumerable<Account>`. In the implementation of this method, the property `Balance` of the `Account` object is directly accessed (code file `GenericMethods/ Algorithms.cs`):

```
public static class Algorithms
{
  public static decimal AccumulateSimple(IEnumerable<Account> source)
  {
    decimal sum = 0;
    foreach (Account a in source)
    {
      sum += a.Balance;
    }
    return sum;
  }
}
```

The `AccumulateSimple` method is invoked like this:

```
decimal amount = Algorithms.AccumulateSimple(accounts);
```

Generic Methods with Constraints

The problem with the first implementation is that it works only with `Account` objects. This can be avoided by using a generic method.

The second version of the `Accumulate` method accepts any type that implements the interface `IAccount`. As you saw earlier with generic classes, you can restrict generic types with the `where` clause. You can use the same clause with generic methods that you use with generic classes. The parameter of the `Accumulate` method is changed to `IEnumerable<T>`, a generic interface that is implemented by generic collection classes (code file `GenericMethods/Algorithms.cs`):

```
public static decimal Accumulate<TAccount>(IEnumerable<TAccount> source)
    where TAccount: IAccount
{
  decimal sum = 0;

  foreach (TAccount a in source)
  {
    sum += a.Balance;
  }
  return sum;
}
```

The Account class is now refactored to implement the interface IAccount (code file GenericMethods/Account.cs):

```
public class Account: IAccount
{
    //...
```

The IAccount interface defines the read-only properties Balance and Name (code file GenericMethods/IAccount.cs):

```
public interface IAccount
{
    decimal Balance { get; }
    string Name { get; }
}
```

The new Accumulate method can be invoked by defining the Account type as a generic type parameter (code file GenericMethods/Program.cs):

```
decimal amount = Algorithm.Accumulate<Account>(accounts);
```

Because the generic type parameter can be automatically inferred by the compiler from the parameter type of the method, it is valid to invoke the Accumulate method this way:

```
decimal amount = Algorithm.Accumulate(accounts);
```

Generic Methods with Delegates

The requirement for the generic types to implement the interface IAccount may be too restrictive. The following example hints at how the Accumulate method can be changed by passing a generic delegate. Chapter 9 provides all the details about how to work with generic delegates, and how to use lambda expressions.

This Accumulate method uses two generic parameters: T1 and T2. T1 is used for the collection-implementing IEnumerable<T1> parameter, which is the first one of the methods. The second parameter uses the generic delegate Func<T1, T2, TResult>. Here, the second and third generic parameters are of the same T2 type. A method needs to be passed that has two input parameters (T1 and T2) and a return type of T2 (code file GenericMethods/Algorithms.cs).

```
public static T2 Accumulate<T1, T2>(IEnumerable<T1> source,
                                    Func<T1, T2, T2> action)
{
    T2 sum = default(T2);
    foreach (T1 item in source)
    {
        sum = action(item, sum);
    }
    return sum;
}
```

In calling this method, it is necessary to specify the generic parameter types because the compiler cannot infer this automatically. With the first parameter of the method, the accounts collection that is assigned is of type IEnumerable<Account>. With the second parameter, a lambda expression is used that defines two parameters of type Account and decimal, and returns a decimal. This lambda expression is invoked for every item by the Accumulate method (code file GenericMethods/Program.cs):

```
decimal amount = Algorithm.Accumulate<Account, decimal>(
                    accounts, (item, sum) => sum += item.Balance);
```

Don't scratch your head over this syntax yet. The sample should give you a glimpse of the possible ways to extend the Accumulate method. Chapter 9 covers lambda expressions in detail.

Generic Methods Specialization

You can overload generic methods to define specializations for specific types. This is true for methods with generic parameters as well. The Foo method is defined in four versions. The first accepts a generic parameter; the second one is a specialized version for the int parameter. The third Foo method accepts two generic parameters, and the fourth one is a specialized version of the third one with the first parameter of type int. During compile time, the best match is taken. If an int is passed, then the method with the int parameter is selected. With any other parameter type, the compiler chooses the generic version of the method (code file Specialization/Program.cs):

```
public class MethodOverloads
{
  public void Foo<T>(T obj)
  {
    WriteLine($"Foo<T>(T obj), obj type: {obj.GetType().Name}");
  }

  public void Foo(int x)
  {
    WriteLine("Foo(int x)");
  }

  public void Foo<T1, T2>(T1 obj1, T2 obj2)
  {
    WriteLine($"Foo<T1, T2>(T1 obj1, T2 obj2); {obj1.GetType().Name} " +
      $"{obj2.GetType().Name}");
  }

  public void Foo<T>(int obj1, T obj2)
  {
    WriteLine($"Foo<T>(int obj1, T obj2); {obj2.GetType().Name}");
  }

  public void Bar<T>(T obj)
  {
    Foo(obj);
  }
}
```

The Foo method can now be invoked with any parameter type. The sample code passes int and string values to invoke all four Foo methods:

```
static void Main()
{
  var test = new MethodOverloads();
  test.Foo(33);
  test.Foo("abc");
```

```
      test.Foo("abc", 42);
      test.Foo(33, "abc");
  }
```

Running the program, you can see by the output that the method with the best match is taken:

```
Foo(int x)
Foo<T>(T obj), obj type: String
Foo<T1, T2>(T1 obj1, T2 obj2); String Int32
Foo<T>(int obj1, T obj2); String
```

Be aware that the method invoked is defined during compile time and not runtime. This can be easily demonstrated by adding a generic `Bar` method that invokes the `Foo` method, passing the generic parameter value along:

```
public class MethodOverloads
{
  // ...
  public void Bar<T>(T obj)
  {
    Foo(obj);
  }
}
```

The `Main` method is now changed to invoke the `Bar` method passing an `int` value:

```
static void Main()
{
  var test = new MethodOverloads();
  test.Bar(44);
}
```

From the output on the console you can see that the generic `Foo` method was selected by the `Bar` method and not the overload with the `int` parameter. That's because the compiler selects the method that is invoked by the `Bar` method during compile time. Because the `Bar` method defines a generic parameter, and because there's a `Foo` method that matches this type, the generic `Foo` method is called. This is not changed during runtime when an `int` value is passed to the `Bar` method:

```
Foo<T>(T obj), obj type: Int32
```

SUMMARY

This chapter introduced a very important feature of the CLR: generics. With generic classes you can create type-independent classes, and generic methods allow type-independent methods. Interfaces, structs, and delegates can be created in a generic way as well. Generics make new programming styles possible. You've seen how algorithms, particularly actions and predicates, can be implemented to be used with different classes—and all are type safe. Generic delegates make it possible to decouple algorithms from collections.

You will see more features and uses of generics throughout this book. Chapter 9 introduces delegates that are often implemented as generics; Chapter 11 provides information about generic collection classes; and Chapter 13, "Language Integrated Query," discusses generic extension methods. The next chapter demonstrates the use of some generic methods with arrays.

7

Arrays and Tuples

WHAT'S IN THIS CHAPTER?

➤ Simple arrays

➤ Multidimensional arrays

➤ Jagged arrays

➤ The `Array` class

➤ Arrays as parameters

➤ Enumerations

➤ Tuples

➤ Structural comparison

WROX.COM CODE DOWNLOADS FOR THIS CHAPTER

The wrox.com code downloads for this chapter are found at www.wrox.com/go/
professionalcsharp6 on the Download Code tab. The code for this chapter is divided into the following major examples:

➤ SimpleArrays

➤ SortingSample

➤ ArraySegment

➤ YieldSample

➤ TuplesSample

➤ StructuralComparison

MULTIPLE OBJECTS OF THE SAME AND DIFFERENT TYPES

If you need to work with multiple objects of the same type, you can use collections (see Chapter 11, "Collections") and arrays. C# has a special notation to declare, initialize, and use arrays. Behind the scenes, the `Array` class comes into play, which offers several methods to sort and filter the elements inside the array. Using an enumerator, you can iterate through all the elements of the array.

To use multiple objects of different types, the type `Tuple` can be used. See the "Tuples" section later in this chapter for details about this type.

SIMPLE ARRAYS

If you need to use multiple objects of the same type, you can use an array. An *array* is a data structure that contains a number of elements of the same type.

Array Declaration

An array is declared by defining the type of elements inside the array, followed by empty brackets and a variable name. For example, an array containing integer elements is declared like this:

```
int[] myArray;
```

Array Initialization

After declaring an array, memory must be allocated to hold all the elements of the array. An array is a reference type, so memory on the heap must be allocated. You do this by initializing the variable of the array using the new operator, with the type and the number of elements inside the array. Here, you specify the size of the array:

```
myArray = new int[4];
```

> **NOTE** *Value types and reference types are covered in Chapter 3, "Objects and Types."*

With this declaration and initialization, the variable `myArray` references four integer values that are allocated on the managed heap (see Figure 7-1).

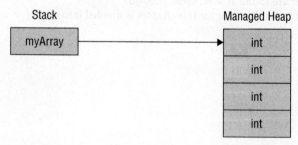

FIGURE 7-1

> **NOTE** *An array cannot be resized after its size is specified without copying all the elements. If you don't know how many elements should be in the array in advance, you can use a collection (see Chapter 11).*

Instead of using a separate line to declare and initialize an array, you can use a single line:

```
int[] myArray = new int[4];
```

You can also assign values to every array element using an array initializer. You can use array initializers only while declaring an array variable, not after the array is declared:

```
int[] myArray = new int[4] {4, 7, 11, 2};
```

If you initialize the array using curly brackets, you can also omit the size of the array because the compiler can count the number of elements:

```
int[] myArray = new int[] {4, 7, 11, 2};
```

There's even a shorter form using the C# compiler. Using curly brackets you can write the array declaration and initialization. The code generated from the compiler is the same as the previous result:

```
int[] myArray = {4, 7, 11, 2};
```

Accessing Array Elements

After an array is declared and initialized, you can access the array elements using an indexer. Arrays support only indexers that have integer parameters.

With the indexer, you pass the element number to access the array. The indexer always starts with a value of 0 for the first element. Therefore, the highest number you can pass to the indexer is the number of elements minus one, because the index starts at zero. In the following example, the array `myArray` is declared and initialized with four integer values. The elements can be accessed with indexer values 0, 1, 2, and 3.

```
int[] myArray = new int[] {4, 7, 11, 2};
int v1 = myArray[0];   // read first element
int v2 = myArray[1];   // read second element
myArray[3] = 44;       // change fourth element
```

> **NOTE** *If you use a wrong indexer value that is bigger than the length of the array, an exception of type* `IndexOutOfRangeException` *is thrown.*

If you don't know the number of elements in the array, you can use the `Length` property, as shown in this `for` statement:

```
for (int i = 0; i < myArray.Length; i++)
{
   WriteLine(myArray[i]);
}
```

Instead of using a `for` statement to iterate through all the elements of the array, you can also use the `foreach` statement:

```
foreach (var val in myArray)
{
   WriteLine(val);
}
```

> **NOTE** *The* `foreach` *statement makes use of the* `IEnumerable` *and* `IEnumerator` *interfaces and traverses through the array from the first index to the last. This is discussed in detail later in this chapter.*

Using Reference Types

In addition to being able to declare arrays of predefined types, you can also declare arrays of custom types. Let's start with the following `Person` class, the properties `FirstName` and `LastName` using auto-implemented properties, and an override of the `ToString` method from the `Object` class (code file `SimpleArrays/Person.cs`):

```
public class Person
{
  public string FirstName { get; set; }
  public string LastName { get; set; }

  public override string ToString() => $"{FirstName} {LastName}";
}
```

Declaring an array of two `Person` elements is similar to declaring an array of `int`:

```
Person[] myPersons = new Person[2];
```

However, be aware that if the elements in the array are reference types, memory must be allocated for every array element. If you use an item in the array for which no memory was allocated, a `NullReferenceException` is thrown.

> **NOTE** *For information about errors and exceptions, see Chapter 14, "Errors and Exceptions."*

You can allocate every element of the array by using an indexer starting from 0:

```
myPersons[0] = new Person { FirstName="Ayrton", LastName="Senna" };
myPersons[1] = new Person { FirstName="Michael", LastName="Schumacher" };
```

Figure 7-2 shows the objects in the managed heap with the `Person` array. `myPersons` is a variable that is stored on the stack. This variable references an array of `Person` elements that is stored on the managed heap. This array has enough space for two references. Every item in the array references a `Person` object that is also stored in the managed heap.

Similar to the `int` type, you can also use an array initializer with custom types:

```
Person[] myPersons2 =
{
  new Person { FirstName="Ayrton", LastName="Senna"},
  new Person { FirstName="Michael", LastName="Schumacher"}
};
```

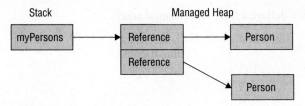

FIGURE 7-2

MULTIDIMENSIONAL ARRAYS

Ordinary arrays (also known as one-dimensional arrays) are indexed by a single integer. A multidimensional array is indexed by two or more integers.

$$a = \begin{bmatrix} 1, 2, 3 \\ 4, 5, 6 \\ 7, 8, 9 \end{bmatrix}$$

FIGURE 7-3

Figure 7-3 shows the mathematical notation for a two-dimensional array that has three rows and three columns. The first row has the values 1, 2, and 3, and the third row has the values 7, 8, and 9.

To declare this two-dimensional array with C#, you put a comma inside the brackets. The array is initialized by specifying the size of every dimension (also known as rank). Then the array elements can be accessed by using two integers with the indexer:

```
int[,] twodim = new int[3, 3];
twodim[0, 0] = 1;
twodim[0, 1] = 2;
twodim[0, 2] = 3;
twodim[1, 0] = 4;
twodim[1, 1] = 5;
twodim[1, 2] = 6;
twodim[2, 0] = 7;
twodim[2, 1] = 8;
twodim[2, 2] = 9;
```

> **NOTE** *After declaring an array, you cannot change the rank.*

You can also initialize the two-dimensional array by using an array indexer if you know the values for the elements in advance. To initialize the array, one outer curly bracket is used, and every row is initialized by using curly brackets inside the outer curly brackets:

```
int[,] twodim = {
                  {1, 2, 3},
                  {4, 5, 6},
                  {7, 8, 9}
                };
```

> **NOTE** *When using an array initializer, you must initialize every element of the array. It is not possible to defer the initialization of some values until later.*

By using two commas inside the brackets, you can declare a three-dimensional array:

```
int[,,] threedim = {
            { { 1, 2 }, { 3, 4 } },
            { { 5, 6 }, { 7, 8 } },
            { { 9, 10 }, { 11, 12 } }
            };

WriteLine(threedim[0, 1, 1]);
```

JAGGED ARRAYS

A two-dimensional array has a rectangular size (for example, 3 × 3 elements). A jagged array provides more flexibility in sizing the array. With a jagged array every row can have a different size.

Figure 7-4 contrasts a two-dimensional array that has 3 × 3 elements with a jagged array. The jagged array shown contains three rows, with the first row containing two elements, the second row containing six elements, and the third row containing three elements.

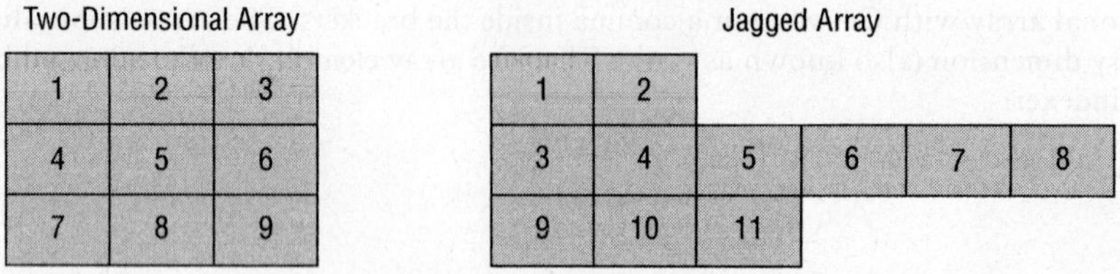

FIGURE 7-4

A jagged array is declared by placing one pair of opening and closing brackets after another. To initialize the jagged array, only the size that defines the number of rows in the first pair of brackets is set. The second brackets that define the number of elements inside the row are kept empty because every row has a different number of elements. Next, the element number of the rows can be set for every row:

```
int[][] jagged = new int[3][];
jagged[0] = new int[2] { 1, 2 };
jagged[1] = new int[6] { 3, 4, 5, 6, 7, 8 };
jagged[2] = new int[3] { 9, 10, 11 };
```

You can iterate through all the elements of a jagged array with nested `for` loops. In the outer `for` loop every row is iterated, and the inner `for` loop iterates through every element inside a row:

```
for (int row = 0; row < jagged.Length; row++)
{
  for (int element = 0; element < jagged[row].Length; element++)
  {
    WriteLine($"row: {row}, element: {element}, value: {jagged[row][element]}");
  }
}
```

The output of the iteration displays the rows and every element within the rows:

```
row: 0, element: 0, value: 1
row: 0, element: 1, value: 2
row: 1, element: 0, value: 3
```

```
row: 1, element: 1, value: 4
row: 1, element: 2, value: 5
row: 1, element: 3, value: 6
row: 1, element: 4, value: 7
row: 1, element: 5, value: 8
row: 2, element: 0, value: 9
row: 2, element: 1, value: 10
row: 2, element: 2, value: 11
```

ARRAY CLASS

Declaring an array with brackets is a C# notation using the Array class. Using the C# syntax behind the scenes creates a new class that derives from the abstract base class Array. This makes it possible to use methods and properties that are defined with the Array class with every C# array. For example, you've already used the Length property or iterated through the array by using the foreach statement. By doing this, you are using the GetEnumerator method of the Array class.

Other properties implemented by the Array class are LongLength, for arrays in which the number of items doesn't fit within an integer, and Rank, to get the number of dimensions.

Let's have a look at other members of the Array class by getting into various features.

Creating Arrays

The Array class is abstract, so you cannot create an array by using a constructor. However, instead of using the C# syntax to create array instances, it is also possible to create arrays by using the static CreateInstance method. This is extremely useful if you don't know the type of elements in advance, because the type can be passed to the CreateInstance method as a Type object.

The following example shows how to create an array of type int with a size of 5. The first argument of the CreateInstance method requires the type of the elements, and the second argument defines the size. You can set values with the SetValue method, and read values with the GetValue method (code file SimpleArrays/Program.cs):

```
Array intArray1 = Array.CreateInstance(typeof(int), 5);
for (int i = 0; i < 5; i++)
{
  intArray1.SetValue(33, i);
}

for (int i = 0; i < 5; i++)
{
  WriteLine(intArray1.GetValue(i));
}
```

You can also cast the created array to an array declared as int []:

```
int[] intArray2 = (int[])intArray1;
```

The CreateInstance method has many overloads to create multidimensional arrays and to create arrays that are not 0 based. The following example creates a two-dimensional array with 2 x 3 elements. The first dimension is 1 based; the second dimension is 10 based:

```
int[] lengths = { 2, 3 };
int[] lowerBounds = { 1, 10 };
Array racers = Array.CreateInstance(typeof(Person), lengths, lowerBounds);
```

Setting the elements of the array, the `SetValue` method accepts indices for every dimension:

```
racers.SetValue(new Person
{
  FirstName = "Alain",
  LastName = "Prost"
}, 1, 10);
racers.SetValue(new Person
{
  FirstName = "Emerson",
  LastName = "Fittipaldi"
}, 1, 11);
racers.SetValue(new Person
{
  FirstName = "Ayrton",
  LastName = "Senna"
}, 1, 12);
racers.SetValue(new Person
{
  FirstName = "Michael",
  LastName = "Schumacher"
}, 2, 10);
racers.SetValue(new Person
{
  FirstName = "Fernando",
  LastName = "Alonso"
}, 2, 11);
racers.SetValue(new Person
{
  FirstName = "Jenson",
  LastName = "Button"
}, 2, 12);
```

Although the array is not 0 based, you can assign it to a variable with the normal C# notation. You just have to take care not to cross the boundaries:

```
Person[,] racers2 = (Person[,])racers;
Person first = racers2[1, 10];
Person last = racers2[2, 12];
```

Copying Arrays

Because arrays are reference types, assigning an array variable to another one just gives you two variables referencing the same array. For copying arrays, the array implements the interface `ICloneable`. The `Clone` method that is defined with this interface creates a shallow copy of the array.

If the elements of the array are value types, as in the following code segment, all values are copied (see Figure 7-5):

```
int[] intArray1 = {1, 2};
int[] intArray2 = (int[])intArray1.Clone();
```

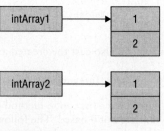

FIGURE 7-5

If the array contains reference types, only the references are copied, not the elements. Figure 7-6 shows the variables `beatles` and `beatlesClone`, where `beatlesClone` is created by calling the `Clone` method from `beatles`. The `Person` objects that are referenced are the same for `beatles` and `beatlesClone`. If you change a property of an element of beatlesClone, you change the same object of beatles (code file SimpleArray/Program.cs):

```
Person[] beatles = {
                new Person { FirstName="John", LastName="Lennon" },
                new Person { FirstName="Paul", LastName="McCartney" }
            };
Person[] beatlesClone = (Person[])beatles.Clone();
```

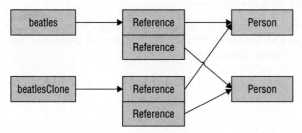

FIGURE 7-6

Instead of using the Clone method, you can use the Array.Copy method, which also creates a shallow copy. However, there's one important difference with Clone and Copy: Clone creates a new array; with Copy you have to pass an existing array with the same rank and enough elements.

> **NOTE** *If you need a deep copy of an array containing reference types, you have to iterate the array and create new objects.*

Sorting

The Array class uses the Quicksort algorithm to sort the elements in the array. The Sort method requires the interface IComparable to be implemented by the elements in the array. Simple types such as System. String and System.Int32 implement IComparable, so you can sort elements containing these types.

With the sample program, the array name contains elements of type string, and this array can be sorted (code file SortingSample/Program.cs):

```
string[] names = {
        "Christina Aguilera",
        "Shakira",
        "Beyonce",
        "Lady Gaga"
    };

Array.Sort(names);

foreach (var name in names)
{
  WriteLine(name);
}
```

The output of the application shows the sorted result of the array:

```
Beyonce
Christina Aguilera
Lady Gaga
Shakira
```

If you are using custom classes with the array, you must implement the interface IComparable. This interface defines just one method, CompareTo, which must return 0 if the objects to compare are equal; a value smaller than 0 if the instance should go before the object from the parameter; and a value larger than 0 if the instance should go after the object from the parameter.

Change the Person class to implement the interface IComparable<Person>. The comparison is first done on the value of the LastName by using the Compare method of the String class. If the LastName has the same value, the FirstName is compared (code file SortingSample/Person.cs):

```
public class Person: IComparable<Person>
{
  public int CompareTo(Person other)
  {
    if (other == null) return 1;

    int result = string.Compare(this.LastName, other.LastName);
    if (result == 0)
    {
      result = string.Compare(this.FirstName, other.FirstName);
    }
    return result;
  }
  //...
```

Now it is possible to sort an array of Person objects by the last name (code file SortingSample/Program.cs):

```
Person[] persons = {
       new Person { FirstName="Damon", LastName="Hill" },
       new Person { FirstName="Niki", LastName="Lauda" },
       new Person { FirstName="Ayrton", LastName="Senna" },
       new Person { FirstName="Graham", LastName="Hill" }
     };

Array.Sort(persons);
foreach (var p in persons)
{
   WriteLine(p);
}
```

Using the sort of the Person class, the output returns the names sorted by last name:

```
Damon Hill
Graham Hill
Niki Lauda
Ayrton Senna
```

If the Person object should be sorted differently, or if you don't have the option to change the class that is used as an element in the array, you can implement the interface IComparer or IComparer<T>. These interfaces define the method Compare. One of these interfaces must be implemented by the class that should be compared. The `IComparer` interface is independent of the class to compare. That's why the `Compare` method defines two arguments that should be compared. The return value is similar to the `CompareTo` method of the `IComparable` interface.

The class `PersonComparer` implements the `IComparer<Person>` interface to sort `Person` objects either by `firstName` or by `lastName`. The enumeration `PersonCompareType` defines the different sorting options that are available with `PersonComparer`: `FirstName` and `LastName`. How the compare should be done is defined with the constructor of the class `PersonComparer`, where a `PersonCompareType` value is set. The `Compare` method is implemented with a `switch` statement to compare either by `LastName` or by `FirstName` (code file `SortingSample/PersonComparer.cs`):

```
public enum PersonCompareType
{
  FirstName,
  LastName
}

public class PersonComparer: IComparer<Person>
{
  private PersonCompareType _compareType;

  public PersonComparer(PersonCompareType compareType)
  {
    _compareType = compareType;
  }

  public int Compare(Person x, Person y)
  {
    if (x == null && y == null) return 0;
    if (x == null) return 1;
    if (y == null) return -1;

    switch (_compareType)
    {
      case PersonCompareType.FirstName:
        return string.Compare(x.FirstName, y.FirstName);
      case PersonCompareType.LastName:
        return string.Compare(x.LastName, y.LastName);
      default:
        throw new ArgumentException("unexpected compare type");
    }
  }
}
```

Now you can pass a `PersonComparer` object to the second argument of the `Array.Sort` method. Here, the people are sorted by first name (code file `SortingSample/Program.cs`):

```
Array.Sort(persons, new PersonComparer(PersonCompareType.FirstName));
foreach (var p in persons)
{
  WriteLine(p);
}
```

The persons array is now sorted by first name:

```
Ayrton Senna
Damon Hill
Graham Hill
Niki Lauda
```

> **NOTE** *The* `Array` *class also offers* `Sort` *methods that require a delegate as an argument. With this argument you can pass a method to do the comparison of two objects rather than relying on the* `IComparable` *or* `IComparer` *interfaces. Chapter 9, "Delegates, Lambdas, and Events," discusses how to use delegates.*

ARRAYS AS PARAMETERS

Arrays can be passed as parameters to methods, and returned from methods. Returning an array, you just have to declare the array as the return type, as shown with the following method `GetPersons`:

```
static Person[] GetPersons()
{
  return new Person[] {
      new Person { FirstName="Damon", LastName="Hill" },
      new Person { FirstName="Niki", LastName="Lauda" },
      new Person { FirstName="Ayrton", LastName="Senna" },
      new Person { FirstName="Graham", LastName="Hill" }
  };
}
```

Passing arrays to a method, the array is declared with the parameter, as shown with the method `DisplayPersons`:

```
static void DisplayPersons(Person[] persons)
{
  //...
}
```

Array Covariance

With arrays, covariance is supported. This means that an array can be declared as a base type and elements of derived types can be assigned to the elements.

For example, you can declare a parameter of type `object[]` as shown and pass a `Person[]` to it:

```
static void DisplayArray(object[] data)
{
  //...
}
```

> **NOTE** *Array covariance is only possible with reference types, not with value types. In addition, array covariance has an issue that can only be resolved with runtime exceptions. If you assign a* `Person` *array to an object array, the object array can then be used with anything that derives from the object. The compiler accepts, for example, passing a string to array elements. However, because a* `Person` *array is referenced by the object array, a runtime exception,* `ArrayTypeMismatchException`, *occurs.*

ArraySegment<T>

The struct `ArraySegment<T>` represents a segment of an array. If you are working with a large array, and different methods work on parts of the array, you could copy the array part to the different methods. Instead of creating multiple arrays, it is more efficient to use one array and pass the complete array to the methods. The methods should only use a part of the array. For this, you can pass the offset into the array and the count of elements that the method should use in addition to the array. This way, at least three parameters are needed. When using an array segment, just a single parameter is needed. The `ArraySegment<T>` structure contains information about the segment (the offset and count).

The method `SumOfSegments` takes an array of `ArraySegment<int>` elements to calculate the sum of all the integers that are defined with the segments and returns the sum (code file `ArraySegmentSample/ Program.cs`):

```
static int SumOfSegments(ArraySegment<int>[] segments)
{
  int sum = 0;
  foreach (var segment in segments)
  {
    for (int i = segment.Offset; i < segment.Offset + segment.Count; i++)
    {
      sum += segment.Array[i];
    }
  }
  return sum;
}
```

This method is used by passing an array of segments. The first array element references three elements of `ar1` starting with the first element; the second array element references three elements of `ar2` starting with the fourth element:

```
int[] ar1 = { 1, 4, 5, 11, 13, 18 };
int[] ar2 = { 3, 4, 5, 18, 21, 27, 33 };

var segments = new ArraySegment<int>[2]
{
  new ArraySegment<int>(ar1, 0, 3),
  new ArraySegment<int>(ar2, 3, 3)
};
var sum = SumOfSegments(segments);
```

> **NOTE** *Array segments don't copy the elements of the originating array. Instead, the originating array can be accessed through `ArraySegment<T>`. If elements of the array segment are changed, the changes can be seen in the original array.*

ENUMERATORS

By using the `foreach` statement you can iterate elements of a collection (see Chapter 11) without needing to know the number of elements inside the collection. The `foreach` statement uses an enumerator. Figure 7-7 shows the relationship between the client invoking the `foreach` method and the collection. The array or collection implements the `IEnumerable` interface with the `GetEnumerator` method. The `GetEnumerator` method returns an enumerator implementing the `IEnumerator` interface. The interface `IEnumerator` is then used by the `foreach` statement to iterate through the collection.

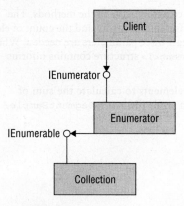

FIGURE 7-7

> **NOTE** *The* GetEnumerator *method is defined with the interface* IEnumerable. *The* foreach *statement doesn't really need this interface implemented in the collection class. It's enough to have a method with the name* GetEnumerator *that returns an object implementing the* IEnumerator *interface.*

IEnumerator Interface

The foreach statement uses the methods and properties of the IEnumerator interface to iterate all elements in a collection. For this, IEnumerator defines the property Current to return the element where the cursor is positioned, and the method MoveNext to move to the next element of the collection. MoveNext returns true if there's an element, and false if no more elements are available.

The generic version of this interface IEnumerator<T> derives from the interface IDisposable and thus defines a Dispose method to clean up resources allocated by the enumerator.

> **NOTE** *The* IEnumerator *interface also defines the* Reset *method for COM interoperability. Many .NET enumerators implement this by throwing an exception of type* NotSupportedException.

foreach Statement

The C# foreach statement is not resolved to a foreach statement in the IL code. Instead, the C# compiler converts the foreach statement to methods and properties of the IEnumerator interface. Here's a simple foreach statement to iterate all elements in the persons array and display them person by person:

```
foreach (var p in persons)
{
    WriteLine(p);
}
```

The foreach statement is resolved to the following code segment. First, the GetEnumerator method is invoked to get an enumerator for the array. Inside a while loop, as long as MoveNext returns true, the elements of the array are accessed using the Current property:

```
IEnumerator<Person> enumerator = persons.GetEnumerator();
while (enumerator.MoveNext())
{
  Person p = enumerator.Current;
  WriteLine(p);
}
```

yield Statement

Since the first release of C#, it has been easy to iterate through collections by using the foreach statement. With C# 1.0, it was still a lot of work to create an enumerator. C# 2.0 added the yield statement for creating enumerators easily. The yield return statement returns one element of a collection and moves the position to the next element, and yield break stops the iteration.

The next example shows the implementation of a simple collection using the yield return statement. The class HelloCollection contains the method GetEnumerator. The implementation of the GetEnumerator method contains two yield return statements where the strings Hello and World are returned (code file YieldSample/Program.cs):

```
using System;
using System.Collections;

namespace Wrox.ProCSharp.Arrays
{
  public class HelloCollection
  {
    public IEnumerator<string> GetEnumerator()
    {
      yield return "Hello";
      yield return "World";
    }
  }
}
```

> **NOTE** *A method or property that contains yield statements is also known as an iterator block. An iterator block must be declared to return an* IEnumerator *or* IEnumerable *interface, or the generic versions of these interfaces. This block may contain multiple* yield return *or* yield break *statements; a* return *statement is not allowed.*

Now it is possible to iterate through the collection using a foreach statement:

```
public void HelloWorld()
{
  var helloCollection = new HelloCollection();
  foreach (var s in helloCollection)
  {
    WriteLine(s);
  }
}
```

With an iterator block, the compiler generates a yield type, including a state machine, as shown in the following code segment. The yield type implements the properties and methods of the interfaces IEnumerator and IDisposable. In the example, you can see the yield type as the inner class Enumerator.

The GetEnumerator method of the outer class instantiates and returns a new yield type. Within the yield type, the variable state defines the current position of the iteration and is changed every time the method MoveNext is invoked. MoveNext encapsulates the code of the iterator block and sets the value of the current variable so that the Current property returns an object depending on the position:

```
public class HelloCollection
{
  public IEnumerator GetEnumerator() => new Enumerator(0);

  public class Enumerator: IEnumerator<string>, IEnumerator, IDisposable
  {
    private int _state;
    private string _current;

    public Enumerator(int state)
    {
      _state = state;
    }

    bool System.Collections.IEnumerator.MoveNext()
    {
      switch (state)
      {
        case 0:
          _current = "Hello";
          _state = 1;
          return true;
        case 1:
          _current = "World";
          _state = 2;
          return true;
        case 2:
          break;
      }

      return false;
    }

    void System.Collections.IEnumerator.Reset()
    {
      throw new NotSupportedException();
    }

    string System.Collections.Generic.IEnumerator<string>.Current => current;

    object System.Collections.IEnumerator.Current => current;

    void IDisposable.Dispose()
    {
    }
  }
}
```

> **NOTE** *Remember that the* yield *statement produces an enumerator, and not just a list filled with items. This enumerator is invoked by the* foreach *statement. As each item is accessed from the* foreach, *the enumerator is accessed. This makes it possible to iterate through huge amounts of data without reading all the data into memory in one turn.*

Different Ways to Iterate Through Collections

In a slightly larger and more realistic way than the Hello World example, you can use the `yield return` statement to iterate through a collection in different ways. The class `MusicTitles` enables iterating the titles in a default way with the `GetEnumerator` method, in reverse order with the `Reverse` method, and through a subset with the `Subset` method (code file `YieldSample/MusicTitles.cs`):

```
public class MusicTitles
{
  string[] names = { "Tubular Bells", "Hergest Ridge", "Ommadawn", "Platinum" };

  public IEnumerator<string> GetEnumerator()
  {
    for (int i = 0; i < 4; i++)
    {
      yield return names[i];
    }
  }

  public IEnumerable<string> Reverse()
  {
    for (int i = 3; i >= 0; i--)
    {
      yield return names[i];
    }
  }

  public IEnumerable<string> Subset(int index, int length)
  {
    for (int i = index; i < index + length; i++)
    {
      yield return names[i];
    }
  }
}
```

> **NOTE** *The default iteration supported by a class is the* `GetEnumerator` *method, which is defined to return* `IEnumerator`. *Named iterations return* `IEnumerable`.

The client code to iterate through the string array first uses the `GetEnumerator` method, which you don't have to write in your code because it is used by default with the implementation of the `foreach` statement. Then the titles are iterated in reverse, and finally a subset is iterated by passing the index and number of items to iterate to the `Subset` method (code file `YieldSample/Program.cs`):

```
var titles = new MusicTitles();
foreach (var title in titles)
{
  WriteLine(title);
}
WriteLine();

WriteLine("reverse");
foreach (var title in titles.Reverse())
{
  WriteLine(title);
}
```

```
  WriteLine();

  WriteLine("subset");
  foreach (var title in titles.Subset(2, 2))
  {
    WriteLine(title);
  }
```

Returning Enumerators with Yield Return

With the `yield` statement you can also do more complex things, such as return an enumerator from `yield return`. Using the following Tic-Tac-Toe game as an example, players alternate putting a cross or a circle in one of nine fields. These moves are simulated by the `GameMoves` class. The methods `Cross` and `Circle` are the iterator blocks for creating iterator types. The variables `cross` and `circle` are set to `Cross` and `Circle` inside the constructor of the `GameMoves` class. By setting these fields, the methods are not invoked, but they are set to the iterator types that are defined with the iterator blocks. Within the `Cross` iterator block, information about the move is written to the console and the move number is incremented. If the move number is higher than 8, the iteration ends with `yield break`; otherwise, the enumerator object of the circle yield type is returned with each iteration. The `Circle` iterator block is very similar to the `Cross` iterator block; it just returns the cross iterator type with each iteration (code file `YieldSample/GameMoves.cs`):

```
public class GameMoves
{
  private IEnumerator _cross;
  private IEnumerator _circle;

  public GameMoves()
  {
    _cross = Cross();
    _circle = Circle();
  }

  private int _move = 0;
  const int MaxMoves = 9;

  public IEnumerator Cross()
  {
    while (true)
    {
      WriteLine($"Cross, move {_move}");
      if (++_move >= MaxMoves)
      {
        yield break;
      }
      yield return _circle;
    }
  }

  public IEnumerator Circle()
  {
    while (true)
    {
      WriteLine($"Circle, move {move}");
      if (++_move >= MaxMoves)
      {
        yield break;
      }
      yield return _cross;
    }
  }
```

```
    }
  }
```

From the client program, you can use the class GameMoves as follows. The first move is set by setting enumerator to the enumerator type returned by game.Cross. In a while loop, enumerator.MoveNext is called. The first time this is invoked, the Cross method is called, which returns the other enumerator with a yield statement. The returned value can be accessed with the Current property and is set to the enumerator variable for the next loop:

```
var game = new GameMoves();
IEnumerator enumerator = game.Cross();
while (enumerator.MoveNext())
{
  enumerator = enumerator.Current as IEnumerator;
}
```

The output of this program shows alternating moves until the last move:

```
Cross, move 0
Circle, move 1
Cross, move 2
Circle, move 3
Cross, move 4
Circle, move 5
Cross, move 6
Circle, move 7
Cross, move 8
```

TUPLES

Whereas arrays combine objects of the same type, tuples can combine objects of different types. Tuples have their origin in functional programming languages such as F#, where they are used often. With the .NET Framework, tuples are available for all .NET languages.

The .NET Framework defines eight generic Tuple classes and one static Tuple class that act as a factory of tuples. The different generic Tuple classes support a different number of elements—for example, Tuple<T1> contains one element, Tuple<T1, T2> contains two elements, and so on.

The method Divide demonstrates returning a tuple with two members: Tuple<int, int>. The parameters of the generic class define the types of the members, which are both integers. The tuple is created with the static Create method of the static Tuple class. Again, the generic parameters of the Create method define the type of tuple that is instantiated. The newly created tuple is initialized with the result and remainder variables to return the result of the division (code file TupleSample/Program.cs):

```
public static Tuple<int, int> Divide(int dividend, int divisor)
{
  int result = dividend / divisor;
  int remainder = dividend % divisor;

  return Tuple.Create(result, remainder);
}
```

The following example demonstrates invoking the Divide method. The items of the tuple can be accessed with the properties Item1 and Item2:

```
var result = Divide(5, 2);
WriteLine($"result of division: {result.Item1}, remainder: {result.Item2}");
```

If you have more than eight items that should be included in a tuple, you can use the Tuple class definition with eight parameters. The last template parameter is named TRest to indicate that you must pass a tuple itself. That way you can create tuples with any number of parameters.

The following example demonstrates this functionality:

```
public class Tuple<T1, T2, T3, T4, T5, T6, T7, TRest>
```

Here, the last template parameter is a tuple type itself, so you can create a tuple with any number of items:

```
var tuple = Tuple.Create<string, string, string, int, int, int, double,
    Tuple<int, int>>("Stephanie", "Alina", "Nagel", 2009, 6, 2, 1.37,
        Tuple.Create<int, int>(52, 3490));
```

STRUCTURAL COMPARISON

Both arrays and tuples implement the interfaces IStructuralEquatable and IStructuralComparable. These interfaces compare not only references but also the content. This interface is implemented explicitly, so it is necessary to cast the arrays and tuples to this interface on use. IStructuralEquatable is used to compare whether two tuples or arrays have the same content; IStructuralComparable is used to sort tuples or arrays.

With the sample demonstrating IStructuralEquatable, the Person class implementing the interface IEquatable is used. IEquatable defines a strongly typed Equals method where the values of the FirstName and LastName properties are compared (code file StructuralComparison/Person.cs):

```
public class Person: IEquatable<Person>
{
  public int Id { get; private set; }
  public string FirstName { get; set; }
  public string LastName { get; set; }

  public override string ToString() => $"{Id}, {FirstName} {LastName}";

  public override bool Equals(object obj)
  {
    if (obj == null)
    {
      return base.Equals(obj);
    }
    return Equals(obj as Person);
  }

  public override int GetHashCode() => Id.GetHashCode();

  public bool Equals(Person other)
  {
    if (other == null)
      return base.Equals(other);

    return Id == other.Id && FirstName == other.FirstName &&
        LastName == other.LastName;
  }
}
```

Now two arrays containing Person items are created. Both arrays contain the same Person object with the variable name janet, and two different Person objects that have the same content. The comparison operator != returns true because there are indeed two different arrays referenced from two variable names, persons1 and persons2. Because the Equals method with one parameter is not overridden by the Array class, the same happens as with the == operator to compare the references, and they are not the same (code file StructuralComparison/Program.cs):

```
var janet = new Person { FirstName = "Janet", LastName = "Jackson" };
Person[] persons1 = {
  new Person
  {
    FirstName = "Michael",
    LastName = "Jackson"
  },
  janet
};

Person[] persons2 = {
  new Person
  {
    FirstName = "Michael",
    LastName = "Jackson"
  },
  janet
};

if (persons1 != persons2)
{
  WriteLine("not the same reference");
}
```

Invoking the Equals method defined by the IStructuralEquatable interface—that is, the method with the first parameter of type object and the second parameter of type IEqualityComparer—you can define how the comparison should be done by passing an object that implements IEqualityComparer<T>. A default implementation of the IEqualityComparer is done by the EqualityComparer<T> class. This implementation checks whether the type implements the interface IEquatable, and invokes the IEquatable.Equals method. If the type does not implement IEquatable, the Equals method from the base class Object is invoked to do the comparison.

Person implements IEquatable<Person>, where the content of the objects is compared, and the arrays indeed contain the same content:

```
if ((persons1 as IStructuralEquatable).Equals(persons2,
    EqualityComparer<Person>.Default))
{
  WriteLine("the same content");
}
```

Next, you'll see how the same thing can be done with tuples. Here, two tuple instances are created that have the same content. Of course, because the references t1 and t2 reference two different objects, the comparison operator != returns true:

```
var t1 = Tuple.Create(1, "Stephanie");
var t2 = Tuple.Create(1, "Stephanie");
if (t1 != t2)
{
  WriteLine("not the same reference to the tuple");
}
```

The Tuple<> class offers two Equals methods: one that is overridden from the Object base class with an object as parameter, and the second that is defined by the IStructuralEqualityComparer interface with object and IEqualityComparer as parameters. Another tuple can be passed to the first method as shown. This method uses EqualityComparer<object>.Default to get an ObjectEqualityComparer<object> for the comparison. This way, every item of the tuple is compared by invoking the Object.Equals method. If every item returns true, the result of the Equals method is true, which is the case here with the same int and string values:

```
if (t1.Equals(t2))
{
  WriteLine("the same content");
}
```

You can also create a custom IEqualityComparer, as shown in the following example, with the class TupleComparer. This class implements the two methods Equals and GetHashCode of the IEqualityComparer interface:

```
class TupleComparer: IEqualityComparer
{
  public new bool Equals(object x, object y) => x.Equals(y);

  public int GetHashCode(object obj) => obj.GetHashCode();
}
```

> **NOTE** *Implementation of the* Equals *method of the* IEqualityComparer *interface requires the* new *modifier or an implicit interface implementation because the base class* Object *defines a static* Equals *method with two parameters as well.*

The TupleComparer is used, passing a new instance to the Equals method of the Tuple<T1, T2> class. The Equals method of the Tuple class invokes the Equals method of the TupleComparer for every item to be compared. Therefore, with the Tuple<T1, T2> class, the TupleComparer is invoked two times to check whether all items are equal:

```
if (t1.Equals(t2, new TupleComparer()))
{
  WriteLine("equals using TupleComparer");
}
```

SUMMARY

In this chapter, you've seen the C# notation to create and use simple, multidimensional, and jagged arrays. The Array class is used behind the scenes of C# arrays, enabling you to invoke properties and methods of this class with array variables.

You've seen how to sort elements in the array by using the IComparable and IComparer interfaces; and you've learned how to create and use enumerators, the interfaces IEnumerable and IEnumerator, and the yield statement.

Finally, you have seen how to unite objects of the same type to an array, and objects of different types to a tuple.

The next chapter focuses on operators and casts.

Operators and Casts

WHAT'S IN THIS CHAPTER?

➤ Operators in C#

➤ Using new C# 6 Operators nameof and null propagation

➤ Implicit and explicit Conversions

➤ Converting value types to reference types using boxing

➤ Comparing value types and reference types

➤ Overloading the standard operators for custom types

➤ Implementing the Index Operator

➤ Converting between reference types by casting

WROX.COM CODE DOWNLOADS FOR THIS CHAPTER

The wrox.com code downloads for this chapter are found at www.wrox.com/go/
professionalcsharp6 on the Download Code tab. The code for this chapter is divided into the
following major examples:

➤ OperatorOverloadingSample

➤ OperatorOverloadingSample2

➤ OverloadingComparisonSample

➤ CustomIndexerSample

➤ CastingSample

OPERATORS AND CASTS

The preceding chapters have covered most of what you need to start writing useful programs using
C#. This chapter completes the discussion of the essential language elements and illustrates some
powerful aspects of C# that enable you to extend its capabilities.

OPERATORS

C# operators are very similar to C++ and Java operators; however, there are differences.

C# supports the operators listed in the following table:

CATEGORY	OPERATOR
Arithmetic	`+ - * / %`
Logical	`& | ^ ~ && || !`
String concatenation	`+`
Increment and decrement	`++ --`
Bit shifting	`<< >>`
Comparison	`== != < > <= >=`
Assignment	`= += -= *= /= %= &=` `|= ^= <<= >>=`
Member access (for objects and structs)	`.`
Indexing (for arrays and indexers)	`[]`
Cast	`()`
Conditional (the ternary operator)	`?:`
Delegate concatenation and removal (discussed in Chapter 9, "Delegates, Lambdas, and Events")	`+ -`
Object creation	`new`
Type information	`sizeof is typeof as`
Overflow exception control	`checked unchecked`
Indirection and address	`[]`
Namespace alias qualifier (discussed in Chapter 2, "Core C#")	`::`
Null coalescing operator	`??`
Null propagation operator	`?. ?[]`
Name of an identifier	`nameof()`

> **NOTE** Note that four specific operators (`sizeof`, `*`, `->`, and `&`) are available only in unsafe code (code that bypasses C#'s type-safety checking), which is discussed in Chapter 5, "Managed and Unmanaged Resources."

One of the biggest pitfalls to watch out for when using C# operators is that, as with other C-style languages, C# uses different operators for assignment (=) and comparison (==). For instance, the following statement means "let x equal three":

```
x = 3;
```

If you now want to compare x to a value, you need to use the double equals sign ==:

```
if (x == 3)
{
}
```

Fortunately, C#'s strict type-safety rules prevent the very common C error whereby assignment is performed instead of comparison in logical statements. This means that in C# the following statement will generate a compiler error:

```
if (x = 3)
{
}
```

Visual Basic programmers who are accustomed to using the ampersand (&) character to concatenate strings will have to make an adjustment. In C#, the plus sign (+) is used instead for concatenation, whereas the & symbol denotes a logical AND between two different integer values. The pipe symbol, |, enables you to perform a logical OR between two integers. Visual Basic programmers also might not recognize the modulus (%) arithmetic operator. This returns the remainder after division, so, for example, x % 5 returns 2 if x is equal to 7.

You will use few pointers in C#, and therefore few indirection operators. More specifically, the only place you will use them is within blocks of unsafe code, because that is the only place in C# where pointers are allowed. Pointers and unsafe code are discussed in Chapter 5.

Operator Shortcuts

The following table shows the full list of shortcut assignment operators available in C#:

SHORTCUT OPERATOR	EQUIVALENT TO
x++, ++x	x = x + 1
x--, --x	x = x - 1
x += y	x = x + y
x -= y	x = x-y
x *= y	x = x * y
x /= y	x = x / y
x %= y	x = x % y
x >>= y	x = x >> y
x <<= y	x = x << y
x &= y	x = x & y
x |= y	x = x	y

You may be wondering why there are two examples each for the ++ increment and the – – decrement operators. Placing the operator *before* the expression is known as a prefix; placing the operator *after* the expression is known as a postfix. Note that there is a difference in the way they behave.

The increment and decrement operators can act both as entire expressions and within expressions. When used by themselves, the effect of both the prefix and postfix versions is identical and corresponds to the statement x = x + 1. When used within larger expressions, the prefix operator increments the value of x *before* the expression is evaluated; in other words, x is incremented and the new value is used in the expression. Conversely, the postfix operator increments the value of x *after* the expression is evaluated—the expression is evaluated using the original value of x. The following example uses the increment operator (++) as an example to demonstrate the difference between the prefix and postfix behavior:

```
int x = 5;

if (++x == 6) // true - x is incremented to 6 before the evaluation
{
    WriteLine("This will execute");
}

if (x++ == 7) // false - x is incremented to 7 after the evaluation
{
    WriteLine("This won't");
}
```

The first if condition evaluates to true because x is incremented from 5 to 6 *before* the expression is evaluated. The condition in the second if statement is false, however, because x is incremented to 7 only after the entire expression has been evaluated (while x == 6).

The prefix and postfix operators – –x and x– – behave in the same way, but decrement rather than increment the operand.

The other shortcut operators, such as += and -=, require two operands, and are used to modify the value of the first operand by performing an arithmetic or logical operation on it. For example, the next two lines are equivalent:

```
x += 5;
x = x + 5;
```

The following sections look at some of the primary and cast operators that you will frequently use within your C# code.

The Conditional Operator (?:)

The conditional operator (? :), also known as the ternary operator, is a shorthand form of the if...else construction. It gets its name from the fact that it involves three operands. It allows you to evaluate a condition, returning one value if that condition is true, or another value if it is false. The syntax is as follows:

```
condition ? true_value: false_value
```

Here, condition is the Boolean expression to be evaluated, true_value is the value that is returned if condition is true, and false_value is the value that is returned otherwise.

When used sparingly, the conditional operator can add a dash of terseness to your programs. It is especially handy for providing one of a couple of arguments to a function that is being invoked. You can use it to quickly convert a Boolean value to a string value of true or false. It is also handy for displaying the correct singular or plural form of a word:

```
int x = 1;
string s = x + " ";
```

```
s += (x == 1 ? "man": "men");
WriteLine(s);
```

This code displays 1 man if x is equal to one but displays the correct plural form for any other number. Note, however, that if your output needs to be localized to different languages, you have to write more sophisticated routines to take into account the different grammatical rules of different languages.

The checked and unchecked Operators

Consider the following code:

```
byte b = byte.MaxValue;
b++;
WriteLine(b);
```

The byte data type can hold values only in the range 0 to 255. Assigning byte.MaxValue to a byte results in 255. With 255, all bits of the 8 available bits in the bytes are set: 11111111. Incrementing this value by one causes an overflow and results in 0.

How the CLR handles this depends on a number of issues, including compiler options; so whenever there's a risk of an unintentional overflow, you need some way to ensure that you get the result you want.

To do this, C# provides the checked and unchecked operators. If you mark a block of code as checked, the CLR enforces overflow checking, throwing an OverflowException if an overflow occurs. The following changes the preceding code to include the checked operator:

```
byte b = 255;
checked
{
    b++;
}
WriteLine(b);
```

When you try to run this code, you get an error message like this:

```
System.OverflowException: Arithmetic operation resulted in an overflow.
```

> **NOTE** *You can enforce overflow checking for all unmarked code in your program by specifying the* /checked *compiler option.*

If you want to suppress overflow checking, you can mark the code as unchecked:

```
byte b = 255;
unchecked
{
    b++;
}
WriteLine(b);
```

In this case, no exception is raised, but you lose data because the byte type cannot hold a value of 256, the overflowing bits are discarded, and your b variable holds a value of zero (0).

Note that unchecked is the default behavior. The only time you are likely to need to explicitly use the unchecked keyword is when you need a few unchecked lines of code inside a larger block that you have explicitly marked as checked.

> **NOTE** *The default compilation setting is* /unchecked *because enforcing checks has a performance impact. When you use* /checked, *the result of every arithmetic operation needs to be verified whether the value is out of bounds. Arithmetic operations are also done with* for *loops using* i++. *For not having this performance impact it's better to keep the default* /unchecked *compiler setting and use the* checked *operator where needed.*

The is Operator

The is operator allows you to check whether an object is compatible with a specific type. The phrase "is compatible" means that an object either is of that type or is derived from that type. For example, to check whether a variable is compatible with the object type, you could use the following bit of code:

```
int i = 10;
if (i is object)
{
    WriteLine("i is an object");
}
```

int, like all C# data types, inherits from object; therefore, the expression i is object evaluates to true in this case, and the appropriate message will be displayed.

The as Operator

The as operator is used to perform explicit type conversions of reference types. If the type being converted is compatible with the specified type, conversion is performed successfully. However, if the types are incompatible, the as operator returns the value null. As shown in the following code, attempting to convert an object reference to a string returns null if the object reference does not actually refer to a string instance:

```
object o1 = "Some String";
object o2 = 5;

string s1 = o1 as string; // s1 = "Some String"
string s2 = o2 as string; // s2 = null
```

The as operator allows you to perform a safe type conversion in a single step without the need to first test the type using the is operator and then perform the conversion.

> **NOTE** *The* is *and* as *operators are shown with inheritance in Chapter 4, "Inheritance."*

The sizeof Operator

You can determine the size (in bytes) required on the stack by a value type using the sizeof operator:

```
WriteLine(sizeof(int));
```

This displays the number 4 because an int is 4 bytes long.

If you are using the `sizeof` operator with complex types (and not primitive types), you need to block the code within an `unsafe` block as illustrated here:

```
unsafe
{
  WriteLine(sizeof(Customer));
}
```

Chapter 5 looks at unsafe code in more detail.

The typeof Operator

The `typeof` operator returns a `System.Type` object representing a specified type. For example, `typeof(string)` returns a `Type` object representing the `System.String` type. This is useful when you want to use reflection to find information about an object dynamically. For more information, see Chapter 16, "Reflection, Metadata, and Dynamic Programming."

The nameof Operator

The `nameof` operator is new with C# 6. This operator accepts a symbol, property, or method and returns the name.

How can this be used? One example is when the name of a variable is needed, as in checking a parameter for null:

```
public void Method(object o)
{
  if (o == null) throw new ArgumentNullException(nameof(o));
```

Of course, it would be similar to throw the exception by passing a string instead of using the `nameof` operator. However, passing a string doesn't give a compiler error if you misspell the name. Also, when you change the name of the parameter, you can easily miss changing the string passed to the `ArgumentNullException` constructor.

```
  if (o == null) throw new ArgumentNullException("o");
```

Using the `nameof` operator for the name of a variable is just one use case. You can also use it to get the name of a property—for example, for firing a change event (using the interface `INotifyPropertyChanged`) in a property set accessor and passing the name of a property.

```
public string FirstName
{
  get { return _firstName; }
  set
  {
    _firstName = value;
    OnPropertyChanged(nameof(FirstName));
  }
}
```

The `nameof` operator can also be used to get the name of a method. This also works if the method is overloaded because all overloads result in the same value: the name of the method.

```
public void Method()
{
  Log($"{nameof(Method)} called");
```

The index Operator

You've already used the index operator (brackets) accessing arrays in Chapter 7, "Arrays and Tuples." Here, the index operator is used to access the third element of the array named `arr1` by passing the number 2:

```
int[] arr1 = {1, 2, 3, 4};
int x = arr1[2]; // x == 3
```

Similar to accessing elements of an array, the index operator is implemented with collection classes (discussed in Chapter 11, "Collections").

The index operator doesn't require an integer within the brackets. Index operators can be defined with any type. The following code snippet creates a generic dictionary where the key is a `string`, and the value an `int`. With dictionaries, the key can be used with the indexer. In the following sample, the string `first` is passed to the index operator to set this element in the dictionary and then the same string is passed to the indexer to retrieve this element:

```
var dict = new Dictionary<string, int>();
dict["first"] = 1;
int x = dict["first"];
```

> **NOTE** *Later in this chapter in the "Implementing Custom Index Operators" section, you can read how to create index operators in your own classes.*

Nullable Types and Operators

An important difference between value types and reference types is that reference types can be `null`. A value type, such as `int`, cannot be `null`. This is a special issue on mapping C# types to database types. A database number can be `null`. In earlier C# versions, a solution was to use a reference type for mapping a nullable database number. However, this method affects performance because the garbage collector needs to deal with reference types. Now you can use a nullable `int` instead of a normal `int`. The overhead for this is just an additional Boolean that is used to check or set the `null` value. A nullable type still is a value type.

With the following code snippet, the variable `i1` is an `int` that gets 1 assigned to it. `i2` is a nullable `int` that has `i1` assigned. The nullability is defined by using the `?` with the type. `int?` can have an integer value assigned similar to the assignment of `i1`. The variable `i3` demonstrates that assigning `null` is also possible with nullable types.

```
int i1 = 1;
int? i2 = 2;
int? i3 = null;
```

Every struct can be defined as a nullable type as shown with `long?` and `DateTime?`:

```
long? l1 = null;
DateTime? d1 = null;
```

If you use nullable types in your programs, you must always consider the effect a `null` value can have when used in conjunction with the various operators. Usually, when using a unary or binary operator with nullable types, the result will be `null` if one or both of the operands is `null`. For example:

```
int? a = null;

int? b = a + 4;      // b = null
int? c = a * 5;      // c = null
```

When comparing nullable types, if only one of the operands is `null`, the comparison always equates to `false`. This means that you cannot assume a condition is `true` just because its opposite is `false`, as often happens in programs using non-nullable types. For example, in the following example if a is null, the `else` clause is always invoked no matter whether b has a value of +5 or -5.

```
int? a = null;
int? b = -5;

if (a >= b)
{
    WriteLine("a >= b");
}
else
{
    WriteLine("a < b");
}
```

> **NOTE** *The possibility of a* `null` *value means that you cannot freely combine nullable and non-nullable types in an expression. This is discussed in the section "Type Conversions" later in this chapter.*

> **NOTE** *When you use the C# keyword* ? *with the type declaration—for example,* `int?`*— the compiler resolves this to use the generic type* `Nullable<int>`*. The C# compiler converts the shorthand notation to the generic type to reduce typing needs.*

The Null Coalescing Operator

The null coalescing operator (`??`) provides a shorthand mechanism to cater to the possibility of `null` values when working with nullable and reference types. The operator is placed between two operands—the first operand must be a nullable type or reference type, and the second operand must be of the same type as the first or of a type that is implicitly convertible to the type of the first operand. The null coalescing operator evaluates as follows:

➤   If the first operand is not `null`, then the overall expression has the value of the first operand.

➤   If the first operand is `null`, then the overall expression has the value of the second operand.

For example:

```
int? a = null;
int b;

b = a ?? 10;      // b has the value 10
a = 3;
b = a ?? 10;      // b has the value 3
```

If the second operand cannot be implicitly converted to the type of the first operand, a compile-time error is generated.

The null coalescing operator is not only important with nullable types but also with reference types. In the following code snippet, the property `Val` returns the value of the `_val` variable only if it is not null. In case it is null, a new instance of `MyClass` is created, assigned to the `_val` variable, and finally returned from the property. This second part of the expression within the get accessor only happens when the variable _val is null.

```
private MyClass _val;
public MyClass Val
{
  get { return _val ?? (_val = new MyClass()); }
}
```

The Null Propagation Operator

A great new feature of C# 6 is the null propagation operator. A great number of code lines in production code verifies null conditions. Before accessing members of a variable that is passed as a method parameter, it needs to be checked to determine whether the variable has a value of null. Otherwise a NullReferenceException would be thrown. A .NET design guideline specifies that code should never throw exceptions of these types and should always check for null conditions. However, such checks could be missed easily. This code snippet verifies whether the passed parameter p is not null. In case it is null, the method just returns without continuing:

```
public void ShowPerson(Person p)
{
  if (p == null) return;
  string firstName = p.FirstName;
  //...
}
```

Using the null propagation operator to access the FirstName property (p?.FirstName), when p is null, only null is returned without continuing to the right side of the expression.

```
public void ShowPerson(Person p)
{
  string firstName = p?.FirstName;
  //...
}
```

When a property of an int type is accessed using the null propagation operator, the result cannot be directly assigned to an int type because the result can be null. One option to resolve this is to assign the result to a nullable int:

```
int? age = p?.Age;
```

Of course, you can also solve this issue by using the null coalescing operator and defining another result (for example, 0) in case the result of the left side is null:

```
int age = p?.Age ?? 0;
```

Multiple null propagation operators can also be combined. Here the Address property of a Person object is accessed, and this property in turn defines a City property. Null checks need to be done for the Person object, and if it is not null, also for the result of the Address property:

```
Person p = GetPerson();
string city = null;
if (p != null && p.Address != null)
{
  city = p.Address.City;
}
```

When you use the null propagation operator, the code becomes much simpler:

```
string city = p?.Address?.City;
```

You can also use the null propagation operator with arrays. With the following code snippet, a `NullReferenceException` is thrown using the index operator to access an element of an array variable that is `null`:

```
int[] arr = null;
int x1 = arr[0];
```

Of course, traditional null checks could be done to avoid this exceptional condition. A simpler version uses `?[0]` to access the first element of the array. In case the result is `null`, the null coalescing operator returns the value for the `x1` variable:

```
int x1 = arr?[0] ?? 0;
```

Operator Precedence and Associativity

The following table shows the order of precedence of the C# operators. The operators at the top of the table are those with the highest precedence (that is, the ones evaluated first in an expression containing multiple operators).

GROUP	OPERATORS
Primary	`. ?. () [] ?[] x++ x-- new typeof sizeof checked unchecked`
Unary	`+ -! ~ ++x --x and casts`
Multiplication/division	`* / %`
Addition/subtraction	`+ -`
Shift operators	`<< >>`
Relational	`< ><= >= is as`
Comparison	`== !=`
Logical AND	`&`
Logical XOR	`^`
Logical OR	`|`
Conditional AND	`&&`
Conditional OR	`||`
Null coalescing	`??`
Conditional operator	`?:`
Assignment and Lambda	`= += -= *= /= %= &= |= ^= <<= >>= >>>= =>`

Besides operator precedence, with binary operators you need to be aware of operator evaluations from left to right or right to left. With a few exceptions, all binary operators are left associative.

For example,

```
x + y + z
```

is evaluated as

```
(x + y) + z
```

You need to pay attention to the operator precedence before the associativity. With the following expression, first y and z are multiplied before the result of this multiplication is assigned to x, because multiplication has a higher precedency than addition:

```
x + y * z
```

The important exceptions with associativity are the assignment operators; these are right associative. The following expression is evaluated from right to left:

```
x = y = z
```

Because of the right associativity, all variables x, y, and z have the value 3 because it is evaluated from right to left. This wouldn't be the case if this operator would be evaluated from left to right:

```
int z = 3;
int y = 2;
int x = 1;
x = y = z;
```

An important right associative operator that might be misleading is the conditional operator. The expression

```
a ? b: c ? d: e
```
is evaluated as

```
a = b: (c ? d: e)
```
because it is right-associative.

> **NOTE** *In complex expressions, avoid relying on operator precedence to produce the correct result. Using parentheses to specify the order in which you want operators applied clarifies your code and prevents potential confusion.*

TYPE SAFETY

Chapter 1, ".NET Application Architectures," noted that the Intermediate Language (IL) enforces strong type safety upon its code. Strong typing enables many of the services provided by .NET, including security and language interoperability. As you would expect from a language compiled into IL, C# is also strongly typed. Among other things, this means that data types are not always seamlessly interchangeable. This section looks at conversions between primitive types.

> **NOTE** *C# also supports conversions between different reference types and allows you to define how data types that you create behave when converted to and from other types. Both of these topics are discussed later in this chapter.*
>
> *Generics, however, enable you to avoid some of the most common situations in which you would need to perform type conversions. See Chapter 6, "Generics," and Chapter 11, "Collections," for details.*

Type Conversions

Often, you need to convert data from one type to another. Consider the following code:

```
byte value1 = 10;
byte value2 = 23;
byte total;
total = value1 + value2;
WriteLine(total);
```

When you attempt to compile these lines, you get the following error message:

```
Cannot implicitly convert type 'int' to 'byte'
```

The problem here is that when you add 2 bytes together, the result is returned as an `int`, not another `byte`. This is because a `byte` can contain only 8 bits of data, so adding 2 bytes together could very easily result in a value that cannot be stored in a single `byte`. If you want to store this result in a `byte` variable, you have to convert it back to a `byte`. The following sections discuss two conversion mechanisms supported by C#—*implicit* and *explicit*.

Implicit Conversions

Conversion between types can normally be achieved automatically (implicitly) only if you can guarantee that the value is not changed in any way. This is why the previous code failed; by attempting a conversion from an `int` to a `byte`, you were potentially losing 3 bytes of data. The compiler won't let you do that unless you explicitly specify that's what you want to do. If you store the result in a `long` instead of a `byte`, however, you will have no problems:

```
byte value1 = 10;
byte value2 = 23;
long total;                // this will compile fine
total = value1 + value2;
WriteLine(total);
```

Your program has compiled with no errors at this point because a `long` holds more bytes of data than a `byte`, so there is no risk of data being lost. In these circumstances, the compiler is happy to make the conversion for you, without your needing to ask for it explicitly.

The following table shows the implicit type conversions supported in C#:

FROM	TO
sbyte	short, int, long, float, double, decimal, BigInteger
byte	short, ushort, int, uint, long, ulong, float, double, decimal, BigInteger
short	int, long, float, double, decimal, BigInteger
ushort	int, uint, long, ulong, float, double, decimal, BigInteger
int	long, float, double, decimal, BigInteger
uint	long, ulong, float, double, decimal, BigInteger
long, ulong	float, double, decimal, BigInteger
float	double, BigInteger
char	ushort, int, uint, long, ulong, float, double, decimal, BigInteger

As you would expect, you can perform implicit conversions only from a smaller integer type to a larger one, not from larger to smaller. You can also convert between integers and floating-point values; however, the rules are slightly different here. Though you can convert between types of the same size, such as int/uint to float and long/ulong to double, you can also convert from long/ulong back to float. You might lose 4 bytes of data doing this, but it only means that the value of the float you receive will be less precise than if you had used a double; the compiler regards this as an acceptable possible error because the magnitude of the value is not affected. You can also assign an unsigned variable to a signed variable as long as the value limits of the unsigned type fit between the limits of the signed variable.

Nullable types introduce additional considerations when implicitly converting value types:

➤ Nullable types implicitly convert to other nullable types following the conversion rules described for non-nullable types in the previous table; that is, int? implicitly converts to long?, float?, double?, and decimal?.

➤ Non-nullable types implicitly convert to nullable types according to the conversion rules described in the preceding table; that is, int implicitly converts to long?, float?, double?, and decimal?.

➤ Nullable types *do not* implicitly convert to non-nullable types; you must perform an explicit conversion as described in the next section. That's because there is a chance that a nullable type will have the value null, which cannot be represented by a non-nullable type.

Explicit Conversions

Many conversions cannot be implicitly made between types, and the compiler returns an error if any are attempted. The following are some of the conversions that cannot be made implicitly:

➤ int to short—Data loss is possible.

➤ int to uint—Data loss is possible.

➤ uint to int—Data loss is possible.

➤ float to int—Everything is lost after the decimal point.

➤ Any numeric type to char—Data loss is possible.

➤ decimal to any numeric type—The decimal type is internally structured differently from both integers and floating-point numbers.

➤ int? to int—The nullable type may have the value null.

However, you can explicitly carry out such conversions using *casts*. When you cast one type to another, you deliberately force the compiler to make the conversion. A cast looks like this:

```
long val = 30000;
int i = (int)val;   // A valid cast. The maximum int is 2147483647
```

You indicate the type to which you are casting by placing its name in parentheses before the value to be converted. If you are familiar with C, this is the typical syntax for casts. If you are familiar with the C++ special cast keywords such as static_cast, note that these do not exist in C#; you have to use the older C-type syntax.

Casting can be a dangerous operation to undertake. Even a simple cast from a long to an int can cause problems if the value of the original long is greater than the maximum value of an int:

```
long val = 3000000000;
int i = (int)val;        // An invalid cast. The maximum int is 2147483647
```

In this case, you get neither an error nor the result you expect. If you run this code and output the value stored in i, this is what you get:

```
-1294967296
```

It is good practice to assume that an explicit cast does not return the results you expect. As shown earlier, C# provides a checked operator that you can use to test whether an operation causes an arithmetic overflow. You can use the checked operator to confirm that a cast is safe and to force the runtime to throw an overflow exception if it is not:

```
long val = 3000000000;
int i = checked((int)val);
```

Bearing in mind that all explicit casts are potentially unsafe, take care to include code in your application to deal with possible failures of the casts. Chapter 14, "Errors and Exceptions," introduces structured exception handling using the try and catch statements.

Using casts, you can convert most primitive data types from one type to another; for example, in the following code, the value 0.5 is added to price, and the total is cast to an int:

```
double price = 25.30;
int approximatePrice = (int)(price + 0.5);
```

This gives the price rounded to the nearest dollar. However, in this conversion, data is lost—namely, everything after the decimal point. Therefore, such a conversion should never be used if you want to continue to do more calculations using this modified price value. However, it is useful if you want to output the approximate value of a completed or partially completed calculation—if you don't want to bother the user with a lot of figures after the decimal point.

This example shows what happens if you convert an unsigned integer into a char:

```
ushort c = 43;
char symbol = (char)c;
WriteLine(symbol);
```

The output is the character that has an ASCII number of 43: the + sign. You can try any kind of conversion you want between the numeric types (including char) and it will work, such as converting a decimal into a char, or vice versa.

Converting between value types is not restricted to isolated variables, as you have seen. You can convert an array element of type double to a struct member variable of type int:

```
struct ItemDetails
{
  public string Description;
  public int ApproxPrice;
}

//..

double[] Prices = { 25.30, 26.20, 27.40, 30.00 };

ItemDetails id;
id.Description = "Hello there.";
id.ApproxPrice = (int)(Prices[0] + 0.5);
```

To convert a nullable type to a non-nullable type or another nullable type where data loss may occur, you must use an explicit cast. This is true even when converting between elements with the same basic underlying type—for example, int? to int or float? to float. This is because the nullable type may have the value null, which cannot be represented by the non-nullable type. As long as an explicit cast between two equivalent non-nullable types is possible, so is the explicit cast between nullable types. However, when casting from a nullable type to a non-nullable type and the variable has the value null, an InvalidOperationException is thrown. For example:

```
int? a = null;
int b = (int)a;     // Will throw exception
```

Using explicit casts and a bit of care and attention, you can convert any instance of a simple value type to almost any other. However, there are limitations on what you can do with explicit type conversions— as far as value types are concerned, you can only convert to and from the numeric and char types and enum types. You cannot directly cast Booleans to any other type or vice versa.

If you need to convert between numeric and string, you can use methods provided in the .NET class library. The Object class implements a ToString method, which has been overridden in all the .NET predefined types and which returns a string representation of the object:

```
int i = 10;
string s = i.ToString();
```

Similarly, if you need to parse a string to retrieve a numeric or Boolean value, you can use the Parse method supported by all the predefined value types:

```
string s = "100";
int i = int.Parse(s);
WriteLine(i + 50);   // Add 50 to prove it is really an int
```

Note that Parse registers an error by throwing an exception if it is unable to convert the string (for example, if you try to convert the string Hello to an integer). Again, exceptions are covered in Chapter 14.

Boxing and Unboxing

In Chapter 2 you learned that all types—both the simple predefined types, such as int and char, and the complex types, such as classes and structs—derive from the object type. This means you can treat even literal values as though they are objects:

```
string s = 10.ToString();
```

However, you also saw that C# data types are divided into value types, which are allocated on the stack, and reference types, which are allocated on the managed heap. How does this square with the capability to call methods on an int, if the int is nothing more than a 4-byte value on the stack?

C# achieves this through a bit of magic called *boxing*. Boxing and its counterpart, *unboxing*, enable you to convert value types to reference types and then back to value types. We include this in the section on casting because this is essentially what you are doing—you are casting your value to the object type. Boxing is the term used to describe the transformation of a value type to a reference type. Basically, the runtime creates a temporary reference-type box for the object on the heap.

This conversion can occur implicitly, as in the preceding example, but you can also perform it explicitly:

```
int myIntNumber = 20;
object myObject = myIntNumber;
```

Unboxing is the term used to describe the reverse process, whereby the value of a previously boxed value type is cast back to a value type. Here we use the term *cast* because this has to be done explicitly. The syntax is similar to explicit type conversions already described:

```
int myIntNumber = 20;
object myObject = myIntNumber;        // Box the int
int mySecondNumber = (int)myObject;   // Unbox it back into an int
```

A variable can be unboxed only if it has been boxed. If you execute the last line when myObject is not a boxed int, you get a runtime exception thrown at runtime.

One word of warning: When unboxing, you have to be careful that the receiving value variable has enough room to store all the bytes in the value being unboxed. C#'s ints, for example, are only 32 bits long, so unboxing a `long` value (64 bits) into an `int`, as shown here, results in an `InvalidCastException`:

```
long myLongNumber = 333333423;
object myObject = (object)myLongNumber;
int myIntNumber = (int)myObject;
```

COMPARING OBJECTS FOR EQUALITY

After discussing operators and briefly touching on the equality operator, it is worth considering for a moment what equality means when dealing with instances of classes and structs. Understanding the mechanics of object equality is essential for programming logical expressions and is important when implementing operator overloads and casts, the topic of the rest of this chapter.

The mechanisms of object equality vary depending on whether you are comparing reference types (instances of classes) or value types (the primitive data types, instances of structs, or enums). The following sections present the equality of reference types and value types independently.

Comparing Reference Types for Equality

You might be surprised to learn that `System.Object` defines three different methods for comparing objects for equality: `ReferenceEquals` and two versions of `Equals`. Add to this the comparison operator (`==`) and you actually have four ways to compare for equality. Some subtle differences exist between the different methods, which are examined next.

The ReferenceEquals Method

`ReferenceEquals` is a `static` method that tests whether two references refer to the same instance of a class, specifically whether the two references contain the same address in memory. As a `static` method, it cannot be overridden, so the `System.Object` implementation is what you always have. `ReferenceEquals` always returns `true` if supplied with two references that refer to the same object instance, and `false` otherwise. It does, however, consider `null` to be equal to `null`:

```
SomeClass x, y;
x = new SomeClass();
y = new SomeClass();
bool B1 = ReferenceEquals(null, null);   // returns true
bool B2 = ReferenceEquals(null,x);       // returns false
bool B3 = ReferenceEquals(x, y);         // returns false because x and y
                                         // point to different objects
```

The Virtual Equals Method

The `System.Object` implementation of the virtual version of `Equals` also works by comparing references. However, because this method is virtual, you can override it in your own classes to compare objects by value. In particular, if you intend instances of your class to be used as keys in a dictionary, you need to override this method to compare values. Otherwise, depending on how you override `Object.GetHashCode`, the dictionary class that contains your objects either will not work at all or will work very inefficiently. Note that when overriding `Equals`, your override should never throw exceptions. Again, that's because doing so can cause problems for dictionary classes and possibly some other .NET base classes that internally call this method.

The Static Equals Method

The static version of `Equals` actually does the same thing as the virtual instance version. The difference is that the static version takes two parameters and compares them for equality. This method is able to cope when either of the objects is `null`; therefore, it provides an extra safeguard against throwing exceptions if there is a risk that an object might be `null`. The static overload first checks whether the references it has been passed are `null`. If they are both `null`, it returns `true` (because `null` is considered to be equal to `null`). If just one of them is `null`, it returns `false`. If both references actually refer to something, it calls the virtual instance version of `Equals`. This means that when you override the instance version of `Equals`, the effect is the same as if you were overriding the static version as well.

Comparison Operator (==)

It is best to think of the comparison operator as an intermediate option between strict value comparison and strict reference comparison. In most cases, writing the following means that you are comparing references:

```
bool b = (x == y);   // x, y object references
```

However, it is accepted that there are some classes whose meanings are more intuitive if they are treated as values. In those cases, it is better to override the comparison operator to perform a value comparison. Overriding operators is discussed next, but the obvious example of this is the `System.String` class for which Microsoft has overridden this operator to compare the contents of the strings rather than their references.

Comparing Value Types for Equality

When comparing value types for equality, the same principles hold as for reference types: `ReferenceEquals` is used to compare references, `Equals` is intended for value comparisons, and the comparison operator is viewed as an intermediate case. However, the big difference is that value types need to be boxed to be converted to references so that methods can be executed on them. In addition, Microsoft has already overloaded the instance `Equals` method in the `System.ValueType` class to test equality appropriate to value types. If you call `sA.Equals(sB)` where `sA` and `sB` are instances of some struct, the return value is `true` or `false`, according to whether `sA` and `sB` contain the same values in all their fields. On the other hand, no overload of `==` is available by default for your own structs. Writing (`sA == sB`) in any expression results in a compilation error unless you have provided an overload of `==` in your code for the struct in question.

Another point is that `ReferenceEquals` always returns `false` when applied to value types because, to call this method, the value types need to be boxed into objects. Even if you write the following, you still get the result of `false`:

```
bool b = ReferenceEquals(v,v);   // v is a variable of some value type
```

The reason is that `v` is boxed separately when converting each parameter, which means you get different references. Therefore, there really is no reason to call `ReferenceEquals` to compare value types because it doesn't make much sense.

Although the default override of `Equals` supplied by `System.ValueType` will almost certainly be adequate for the vast majority of structs that you define, you might want to override it again for your own structs to improve performance. Also, if a value type contains reference types as fields, you might want to override `Equals` to provide appropriate semantics for these fields because the default override of `Equals` will simply compare their addresses.

OPERATOR OVERLOADING

This section looks at another type of member that you can define for a class or a struct: the operator overload. Operator overloading is something that will be familiar to C++ developers. However, because the concept is new to both Java and Visual Basic developers, we explain it here. C++ developers will probably prefer to skip ahead to the main operator overloading example.

The point of operator overloading is that you do not always just want to call methods or properties on objects. Often, you need to do things like add quantities together, multiply them, or perform logical operations such as comparing objects. Suppose you defined a class that represents a mathematical matrix. In the world of math, matrices can be added together and multiplied, just like numbers. Therefore, it is quite plausible that you would want to write code like this:

```
Matrix a, b, c;
// assume a, b and c have been initialized
Matrix d = c * (a + b);
```

By overloading the operators, you can tell the compiler what + and * do when used in conjunction with a `Matrix` object, enabling you to write code like the preceding. If you were coding in a language that did not support operator overloading, you would have to define methods to perform those operations. The result would certainly be less intuitive and would probably look something like this:

```
Matrix d = c.Multiply(a.Add(b));
```

With what you have learned so far, operators such as + and * have been strictly for use with the predefined data types, and for good reason: The compiler knows what all the common operators mean for those data types. For example, it knows how to add two `longs` or how to divide one `double` by another `double`, and it can generate the appropriate intermediate language code. When you define your own classes or structs, however, you have to tell the compiler everything: what methods are available to call, what fields to store with each instance, and so on. Similarly, if you want to use operators with your own types, you have to tell the compiler what the relevant operators mean in the context of that class. You do that by defining overloads for the operators.

The other thing to stress is that overloading is not just concerned with arithmetic operators. You also need to consider the comparison operators, ==, <, >, !=, >=, and <=. Take the statement if (a==b). For classes, this statement, by default, compares the references a and b. It tests whether the references point to the same location in memory, rather than checking whether the instances actually contain the same data. For the `string` class, this behavior is overridden so that comparing strings really does compare the contents of each string. You might want to do the same for your own classes. For structs, the == operator does not do anything at all by default. Trying to compare two structs to determine whether they are equal produces a compilation error unless you explicitly overload == to tell the compiler how to perform the comparison.

In many situations, being able to overload operators enables you to generate more readable and intuitive code, including the following:

➤ Almost any mathematical object such as coordinates, vectors, matrices, tensors, functions, and so on. If you are writing a program that does some mathematical or physical modeling, you will almost certainly use classes representing these objects.

➤ Graphics programs that use mathematical or coordinate-related objects when calculating positions on-screen.

➤ A class that represents an amount of money (for example, in a financial program).

➤ A word processing or text analysis program that uses classes representing sentences, clauses, and so on. You might want to use operators to combine sentences (a more sophisticated version of concatenation for strings).

However, there are also many types for which operator overloading is not relevant. Using operator overloading inappropriately will make any code that uses your types far more difficult to understand. For example, multiplying two `DateTime` objects does not make any sense conceptually.

How Operators Work

To understand how to overload operators, it's quite useful to think about what happens when the compiler encounters an operator. Using the addition operator (+) as an example, suppose that the compiler processes the following lines of code:

```
int myInteger = 3;
uint myUnsignedInt = 2;
double myDouble = 4.0;
```

```
long myLong = myInteger + myUnsignedInt;
double myOtherDouble = myDouble + myInteger;
```

Now consider what happens when the compiler encounters this line:

```
long myLong = myInteger + myUnsignedInt;
```

The compiler identifies that it needs to add two integers and assign the result to a `long`. However, the expression `myInteger + myUnsignedInt` is really just an intuitive and convenient syntax for calling a method that adds two numbers. The method takes two parameters, `myInteger` and `myUnsignedInt`, and returns their sum. Therefore, the compiler does the same thing it does for any method call: It looks for the best matching overload of the addition operator based on the parameter types—in this case, one that takes two integers. As with normal overloaded methods, the desired return type does not influence the compiler's choice as to which version of a method it calls. As it happens, the overload called in the example takes two `int` parameters and returns an `int`; this return value is subsequently converted to a `long`.

The next line causes the compiler to use a different overload of the addition operator:

```
double myOtherDouble = myDouble + myInteger;
```

In this instance, the parameters are a `double` and an `int`, but there is no overload of the addition operator that takes this combination of parameters. Instead, the compiler identifies the best matching overload of the addition operator as being the version that takes two `doubles` as its parameters, and it implicitly casts the `int` to a `double`. Adding two `doubles` requires a different process from adding two integers. Floating-point numbers are stored as a mantissa and an exponent. Adding them involves bit-shifting the mantissa of one of the `doubles` so that the two exponents have the same value, adding the mantissas, then shifting the mantissa of the result and adjusting its exponent to maintain the highest possible accuracy in the answer.

Now you are in a position to see what happens if the compiler finds something like this:

```
Vector vect1, vect2, vect3;
// initialize vect1 and vect2
vect3 = vect1 + vect2;
vect1 = vect1*2;
```

Here, `Vector` is the struct, which is defined in the following section. The compiler sees that it needs to add two `Vector` instances, `vect1` and `vect2`, together. It looks for an overload of the addition operator, which takes two `Vector` instances as its parameters.

If the compiler finds an appropriate overload, it calls up the implementation of that operator. If it cannot find one, it checks whether there is any other overload for + that it can use as a best match—perhaps something with two parameters of other data types that can be implicitly converted to `Vector` instances. If the compiler cannot find a suitable overload, it raises a compilation error, just as it would if it could not find an appropriate overload for any other method call.

Operator Overloading Example: The struct Vector

The samples in this chapter make use of the following dependencies and namespaces (unless otherwise noted):

Dependencies

```
NETStandard.Library
```

Namespaces

```
System
static System.Console
```

This section demonstrates operator overloading through developing a struct named `Vector` that represents a three-dimensional mathematical vector. Don't worry if mathematics is not your strong point—the vector example is very simple. As far as you are concerned here, a 3D vector is just a set of three numbers (doubles) that tell you how far something is moving. The variables representing the numbers are called _x, _y, and _z: the _x tells you how far something moves east, _y tells you how far it moves north, and _z tells you how far it moves upward (in height). Combine the three numbers and you get the total movement. For example, if _x=3.0, _y=3.0, and _z=1.0 (which you would normally write as (3.0, 3.0, 1.0)), you're moving 3 units east, 3 units north, and rising upward by 1 unit.

You can add or multiply vectors by other vectors or by numbers. Incidentally, in this context, we use the term *scalar*, which is math-speak for a simple number—in C# terms that is just a double. The significance of addition should be clear. If you move first by the vector (3.0, 3.0, 1.0) then move by the vector (2.0, -4.0, -4.0), the total amount you have moved can be determined by adding the two vectors. Adding vectors means adding each component individually, so you get (5.0, -1.0, -3.0). In this context, mathematicians write c=a+b, where a and b are the vectors and c is the resulting vector. You want to be able to use the Vector struct the same way.

> **NOTE** *The fact that this example is developed as a struct rather than a class is not significant with operator overloading. Operator overloading works in the same way for both structs and classes.*

Following is the definition for Vector—containing the read-only properties, constructors, and a ToString override so you can easily view the contents of a Vector, and, finally, that operator overload (code file OperatorOverloadingSample/Vector.cs):

```
struct Vector
{
  public Vector(double x, double y, double z)
  {
     X = x;
     Y = y;
     Z = z;
  }

  public Vector(Vector v)
  {
     X = v.X;
     Y = v.Y;
     Z = v.Z;
  }

  public double X { get; }
  public double Y { get; }
  public double Z { get; }

  public override string ToString() => $"( {X}, {Y}, {Z} )";
}
```

This example has two constructors that require specifying the initial value of the vector, either by passing in the values of each component or by supplying another Vector whose value can be copied. Constructors like the second one, that takes a single Vector argument, are often termed *copy constructors* because they effectively enable you to initialize a class or struct instance by copying another instance.

Here is the interesting part of the Vector struct—the operator overload that provides support for the addition operator:

```
public static Vector operator +(Vector left, Vector right) =>
    new Vector(left.X + right.X, left.Y + right.Y, left.Z + right.Z);
```

The operator overload is declared in much the same way as a static method, except that the `operator` keyword tells the compiler it is actually an operator overload you are defining. The `operator` keyword is followed by the actual symbol for the relevant operator, in this case the addition operator (+). The return type is whatever type you get when you use this operator. Adding two vectors results in a vector; therefore, the return type is also a `Vector`. For this particular override of the addition operator, the return type is the same as the containing class, but that is not necessarily the case, as you see later in this example. The two parameters are the things you are operating on. For binary operators (those that take two parameters), such as the addition and subtraction operators, the first parameter is the value on the left of the operator, and the second parameter is the value on the right.

The implementation of this operator returns a new `Vector` that is initialized using X, Y, and Z properties from the `left` and `right` variables.

C# requires that all operator overloads be declared as `public` and `static`, which means they are associated with their class or struct, not with a particular instance. Because of this, the body of the operator overload has no access to non-static class members or the `this` identifier. This is fine because the parameters provide all the input data the operator needs to know to perform its task.

Now all you need to do is write some simple code to test the `Vector` struct (code file `OperatorOverloadingSample/Program.cs`):

```
static void Main()
{
    Vector vect1, vect2, vect3;

    vect1 = new Vector(3.0, 3.0, 1.0);
    vect2 = new Vector(2.0, -4.0, -4.0);
    vect3 = vect1 + vect2;

    WriteLine($"vect1 = {vect1}");
    WriteLine($"vect2 = {vect2}");
    WriteLine($"vect3 = {vect3}");
}
```

Compiling and running this code returns the following result:

```
vect1 = ( 3, 3, 1 )
vect2 = ( 2, -4, -4 )
vect3 = ( 5, -1, -3 )
```

In addition to adding vectors, you can multiply and subtract them and compare their values. In this section, you develop the `Vector` example further by adding a few more operator overloads. You won't develop the complete set that you'd probably need for a fully functional `Vector` type, but you develop enough to demonstrate some other aspects of operator overloading. First, you overload the multiplication operator to support multiplying vectors by a scalar and multiplying vectors by another vector.

Multiplying a vector by a scalar simply means multiplying each component individually by the scalar: for example, 2 * (1.0, 2.5, 2.0) returns (2.0, 5.0, 4.0). The relevant operator overload looks similar to this (code file `OperatorOverloadingSample2/Vector.cs`):

```
public static Vector operator *(double left, Vector right) =>
    new Vector(left * right.X, left * right.Y, left * right.Z);
```

This by itself, however, is not sufficient. If a and b are declared as type `Vector`, you can write code like this:

```
b = 2 * a;
```

The compiler implicitly converts the integer 2 to a `double` to match the operator overload signature. However, code like the following does not compile:

```
b = a * 2;
```

The point is that the compiler treats operator overloads exactly like method overloads. It examines all the available overloads of a given operator to find the best match. The preceding statement requires the first parameter to be a `Vector` and the second parameter to be an integer, or something to which an integer can be implicitly converted. You have not provided such an overload. The compiler cannot start swapping the order of parameters, so the fact that you've provided an overload that takes a `double` followed by a `Vector` is not sufficient. You need to explicitly define an overload that takes a `Vector` followed by a `double` as well. There are two possible ways of implementing this. The first way involves breaking down the vector multiplication operation in the same way that you have done for all operators so far:

```
public static Vector operator *(Vector left, double right) =>
    new Vector(right * left.X, right * left.Y, right * left.Z);
```

Given that you have already written code to implement essentially the same operation, however, you might prefer to reuse that code by writing the following:

```
public static Vector operator *(Vector left, double right) =>
    right * left;
```

This code works by effectively telling the compiler that when it sees a multiplication of a `Vector` by a `double`, it can simply reverse the parameters and call the other operator overload. The sample code for this chapter uses the second version because it looks neater and illustrates the idea in action. This version also makes the code more maintainable because it saves duplicating the code to perform the multiplication in two separate overloads.

Next, you need to overload the multiplication operator to support vector multiplication. Mathematics provides a couple of ways to multiply vectors, but the one of interest here is known as the *dot product* or *inner product*, which actually returns a scalar as a result. That's the reason for this example—to demonstrate that arithmetic operators don't have to return the same type as the class in which they are defined.

In mathematical terms, if you have two vectors (x, y, z) and (X, Y, Z) then the inner product is defined to be the value of $x*X + y*Y + z*Z$. That might look like a strange way to multiply two things together, but it is actually very useful because it can be used to calculate various other quantities. If you ever write code that displays complex 3D graphics, such as using Direct3D or DirectDraw, you will almost certainly find that your code needs to work out inner products of vectors quite often as an intermediate step in calculating where to place objects on the screen. What's relevant here is that you want users of your `Vector` to be able to write `double X = a*b` to calculate the inner product of two `Vector` objects (a and b). The relevant overload looks like this:

```
public static double operator *(Vector left, Vector right) =>
    left.X * right.X + left.Y * right.Y + left.Z * right.Z;
```

Now that you understand the arithmetic operators, you can confirm that they work using a simple test method (code file `OperatorOverloadingSample2/Program.cs`):

```
static void Main()
{
    // stuff to demonstrate arithmetic operations
    Vector vect1, vect2, vect3;

    vect1 = new Vector(1.0, 1.5, 2.0);
    vect2 = new Vector(0.0, 0.0, -10.0);
    vect3 = vect1 + vect2;

    WriteLine($"vect1 = {vect1}");
    WriteLine($"vect2 = {vect2}");
    WriteLine($"vect3 = vect1 + vect2 = {vect3}");
    WriteLine($"2 * vect3 = {2 * vect3}");
    WriteLine($"vect3 += vect2 gives {vect3 += vect2}");
    WriteLine($"vect3 = vect1 * 2 gives {vect3 = vect1 * 2}");
    WriteLine($"vect1 * vect3 = {vect1 * vect3}");
}
```

Running this code produces the following result:

```
vect1 = ( 1, 1.5, 2 )
vect2 = ( 0, 0, -10 )
vect3 = vect1 + vect2 = ( 1, 1.5, -8 )
2 * vect3 = ( 2, 3, -16 )
vect3 += vect2 gives ( 1, 1.5, -18 )
vect3 = vect1 * 2 gives ( 2, 3, 4 )
vect1 * vect3 = 14.5
```

This shows that the operator overloads have given the correct results; but if you look at the test code closely, you might be surprised to notice that it actually used an operator that wasn't overloaded—the addition assignment operator, +=:

```
WriteLine($"vect3 += vect2 gives {vect3 += vect2}");
```

Although += normally counts as a single operator, it can be broken down into two steps: the addition and the assignment. Unlike the C++ language, C# does not allow you to overload the = operator; but if you overload +, the compiler automatically uses your overload of + to work out how to perform a += operation. The same principle works for all the assignment operators, such as -=, *=, /=, &=, and so on.

Overloading the Comparison Operators

As shown earlier in the section "Operators," C# has six comparison operators, and they are paired as follows:

➤   == and !=

➤   > and <

➤   >= and <=

> **NOTE** *A .NET guideline defines that if the* == *operator returns true when comparing two objects, it should always return true. That's why you should only overload the* == *operator on immutable types.*

The C# language requires that you overload these operators in pairs. That is, if you overload ==, you must overload != too; otherwise, you get a compiler error. In addition, the comparison operators must return a bool. This is the fundamental difference between these operators and the arithmetic operators. The result of adding or subtracting two quantities, for example, can theoretically be any type depending on the quantities. You have already seen that multiplying two Vector objects can be implemented to give a scalar. Another example involves the .NET base class System.DateTime. It's possible to subtract two DateTime instances, but the result is not a DateTime; instead it is a System.TimeSpan instance. By contrast, it doesn't really make much sense for a comparison to return anything other than a bool.

Apart from these differences, overloading the comparison operators follows the same principles as overloading the arithmetic operators. However, comparing quantities isn't always as simple as you might think. For example, if you simply compare two object references, you compare the memory address where the objects are stored. This is rarely the desired behavior of a comparison operator, so you must code the operator to compare the value of the objects and return the appropriate Boolean response. The following example overrides the == and != operators for the Vector struct. Here is the implementation of == (code file OverloadingComparisonSample/Vector.cs):

```
public static bool operator ==(Vector left, Vector right)
{
```

```
    if (object.ReferenceEquals(left, right)) return true;

    return left.X == right.X && left.Y == right.Y && left.Z == right.Z;
}
```

This approach simply compares two `Vector` objects for equality based on the values of their components. For most structs, that is probably what you will want to do, though in some cases you may need to think carefully about what you mean by equality. For example, if there are embedded classes, should you simply compare whether the references point to the same object (shallow comparison) or whether the values of the objects are the same (deep comparison)?

With a shallow comparison, the objects point to the same point in memory, whereas deep comparisons work with values and properties of the object to deem equality. You want to perform equality checks depending on the depth to help you decide what you want to verify.

> **NOTE** *Don't be tempted to overload the comparison operator by calling the instance version of the* `Equals` *method inherited from* `System.Object`. *If you do and then an attempt is made to evaluate* (`objA == objB`), *when* `objA` *happens to be* `null`, *you get an exception, as the .NET runtime tries to evaluate* `null.Equals(objB)`. *Working the other way around (overriding* `Equals` *to call the comparison operator) should be safe.*

You also need to override the `!=` operator. Here is the simple way to do this:

```
public static bool operator !=(Vector left, Vector right) => !(left == right);
```

Now override the `Equals` and `GetHashCode` methods. These methods should always be overridden when the `==` operator is overridden. Otherwise the compiler complains with a warning.

```
public override bool Equals(object obj)
{
    if (obj == null) return false;
    return this == (Vector)obj;
}

public override int GetHashCode() =>
    X.GetHashCode() + (Y.GetHashCode() << 4) + (Z.GetHashCode() << 8);
```

The `Equals` method can invoke in turn the `==` operator. The implementation of the hash code should be fast and always return the same value for the same object. This method is important when using dictionaries. Within dictionaries, it is used to build up the tree for objects, so it's best to distribute the returned values in the integer range. The `GetHashCode` method of the double type returns the integer representation of the double. For the `Vector` type, the hash values of the underlying types are just added. For having different values for the hash code—for example, with values (`5.0, 2.0, 0.0`), and (`2.0, 5.0, 0.0`)—the `Y` and `Z` values of the returned hash values are bit-shifted by 4 and 8 bits before the numbers are added.

For value types, you should also implement the interface `IEquatable<T>`. This interface is a strongly typed version of the `Equals` method that is defined by the base class `Object`. Having all the other code already in place, you can easily do the implementation:

```
public bool Equals(Vector other) => this == other;
```

As usual, you should quickly confirm that your override works with some test code. This time you'll define three `Vector` objects and compare them (code file `OverloadingComparisonSample/Program.cs`):

```
static void Main()
{
```

```
var vect1 = new Vector(3.0, 3.0, -10.0);
var vect2 = new Vector(3.0, 3.0, -10.0);
var vect3 = new Vector(2.0, 3.0, 6.0);

WriteLine($"vect1 == vect2 returns {(vect1 == vect2)}");
WriteLine($"vect1 == vect3 returns {(vect1 == vect3)}");
WriteLine($"vect2 == vect3 returns {(vect2 == vect3)}");

WriteLine();

WriteLine($"vect1 != vect2 returns {(vect1 != vect2)}");
WriteLine($"vect1 != vect3 returns {(vect1 != vect3)}");
WriteLine($"vect2 != vect3 returns {(vect2 != vect3)}");
}
```

Running the example produces these results at the command line:

```
vect1 == vect2 returns True
vect1 == vect3 returns False
vect2 == vect3 returns False

vect1 != vect2 returns False
vect1 != vect3 returns True
vect2 != vect3 returns True
```

Which Operators Can You Overload?

It is not possible to overload all the available operators. The operators that you can overload are listed in the following table:

CATEGORY	OPERATORS	RESTRICTIONS
Arithmetic binary	+, *, /, -, %	None
Arithmetic unary	+, -, ++, --	None
Bitwise binary	&, |, ^, <<, >>	None
Bitwise unary	!, ~, true, false	The true and false operators must be overloaded as a pair.
Comparison	==, !=, >=, <=>, <,	Comparison operators must be overloaded in pairs.
Assignment	+=, -=, *=, /=, >>=, <<=, %=, &=, |=, ^=	You cannot explicitly overload these operators; they are overridden implicitly when you override the individual operators such as +, -, %, and so on.
Index	[]	You cannot overload the index operator directly. The indexer member type, discussed in Chapter 2, allows you to support the index operator on your classes and structs.
Cast	()	You cannot overload the cast operator directly. User-defined casts (discussed in the last section of this chapter) allow you to define custom cast behavior.

IMPLEMENTING CUSTOM INDEX OPERATORS

Custom indexers cannot be implemented using the operator overloading syntax, but they can be implemented with a syntax that looks very similar to properties.

Start by looking at accessing array elements. Here, an array of int elements is created. The second code line uses the indexer to access the second element and pass 42 to it. The third line uses the indexer to access the third element and pass the element to the variable x.

```
int[] arr1 = {1, 2, 3};
arr1[1] = 42;
int x = arr1[2];
```

NOTE *Arrays are explained in Chapter 7.*

The CustomIndexerSample makes use of these dependencies and namespaces:

Dependencies

NETStandard.Library

Namespaces

System

System.Collections.Generic

System.Linq

static System.Console

To create a custom indexer, first create a Person class with read-only properties FirstName, LastName, and Birthday (code file CustomIndexerSample/Person.cs):

```
public class Person
{
    public DateTime Birthday { get; }
    public string FirstName { get; }
    public string LastName { get; }

    public Person(string firstName, string lastName, DateTime birthDay)
    {
        FirstName = firstName;
        LastName = lastName;
        Birthday = birthDay;
```

```
    }

    public override string ToString() => $"{FirstName} {LastName}";
}
```

The class `PersonCollection` defines a private array field that contains `Person` elements and a constructor where a number of `Person` objects can be passed (code file `CustomIndexerSample/PersonCollection.cs`):

```
public class PersonCollection
{
    private Person[] _people;

    public PersonCollection(params Person[] people)
    {
        _people = people.ToArray();
    }
}
```

For allowing indexer-syntax to be used to access the `PersonCollection` and return `Person` objects, you can create an indexer. The indexer looks very similar to a property as it also contains `get` and `set` accessors. What's different is the name. Specifying an indexer makes use of the `this` keyword. The brackets that follow the `this` keyword specify the type that is used with the index. An array offers indexers with the `int` type, so `int` types are here used as well to pass the information directly to the contained array `_people`. The use of the `set` and `get` accessors is very similar to properties. The `get` accessor is invoked when a value is retrieved, the `set` accessor when a (`Person` object) is passed on the right side.

```
public Person this[int index]
{
    get { return _people[index]; }
    set { _people[index] = value; }
}
```

With indexers, you cannot only define `int` types as the indexing type. Any type works, as is shown here with the `DateTime` struct as indexing type. This indexer is used to return every person with a specified birthday. Because multiple persons can have the same birthday, not a single `Person` object is returned but a list of persons with the interface `IEnumerable<Person>`. The `Where` method used makes the filtering based on a lambda expression. The `Where` method is defined in the namespace `System.Linq`:

```
public IEnumerable<Person> this[DateTime birthDay]
{
    get { return _people.Where(p => p.Birthday == birthDay); }
}
```

The indexer using the `DateTime` type offers retrieving person objects, but doesn't allow you to set person objects as there's only a get accessor but no set accessor. With C# 6, a shorthand notation exists to create the same code with an expression-bodied member (the same syntax available with properties):

```
public IEnumerable<Person> this[DateTime birthDay] =>
    _people.Where(p => p.Birthday == birthDay);
```

The `Main` method of the sample application creates a `PersonCollection` object and passes four `Person` objects to the constructor. With the first `WriteLine` method, the third element is accessed using the get accessor of the indexer with the `int` parameter. Within the `foreach` loop, the indexer with the `DateTime` parameter is used to pass a specified date (code file `CustomIndexerSample/Program.cs`):

```
static void Main()
{
    var p1 = new Person("Ayrton", "Senna", new DateTime(1960, 3, 21));
    var p2 = new Person("Ronnie", "Peterson", new DateTime(1944, 2, 14));
```

```
    var p3 = new Person("Jochen", "Rindt", new DateTime(1942, 4, 18));
    var p4 = new Person("Francois", "Cevert", new DateTime(1944, 2, 25));
    var coll = new PersonCollection(p1, p2, p3, p4);

    WriteLine(coll[2]);

    foreach (var r in coll[new DateTime(1960, 3, 21)])
    {
      WriteLine(r);
    }
    ReadLine();
}
```

Running the program, the first `WriteLine` method writes `Jochen Rindt` to the console; the result of the `foreach` loop is `Ayrton Senna` as that person has the same birthday as is assigned within the second indexer.

USER-DEFINED CASTS

Earlier in this chapter (see the "Explicit Conversions" section), you learned that you can convert values between predefined data types through a process of casting. You also saw that C# allows two different types of casts: implicit and explicit. This section looks at these types of casts.

For an explicit cast, you explicitly mark the cast in your code by including the destination data type inside parentheses:

```
int i = 3;
long l = i;            // implicit
short s = (short)i;    // explicit
```

For the predefined data types, explicit casts are required where there is a risk that the cast might fail or some data might be lost. The following are some examples:

➤   When converting from an `int` to a `short`, the `short` might not be large enough to hold the value of the `int`.

➤   When converting from signed to unsigned data types, incorrect results are returned if the signed variable holds a negative value.

➤   When converting from floating-point to integer data types, the fractional part of the number will be lost.

➤   When converting from a nullable type to a non-nullable type, a value of `null` causes an exception.

By making the cast explicit in your code, C# forces you to affirm that you understand there is a risk of data loss, and therefore presumably you have written your code to take this into account.

Because C# allows you to define your own data types (structs and classes), it follows that you need the facility to support casts to and from those data types. The mechanism is to define a cast as a member operator of one of the relevant classes. Your cast operator must be marked as either `implicit` or `explicit` to indicate how you are intending it to be used. The expectation is that you follow the same guidelines as for the predefined casts: if you know that the cast is always safe regardless of the value held by the source variable, then you define it as `implicit`. Conversely, if you know there is a risk of something going wrong for certain values—perhaps some loss of data or an exception being thrown—then you should define the cast as `explicit`.

> **NOTE** *You should define any custom casts you write as explicit if there are any source data values for which the cast will fail or if there is any risk of an exception being thrown.*

The syntax for defining a cast is similar to that for overloading operators discussed earlier in this chapter. This is not a coincidence—a cast is regarded as an operator whose effect is to convert from the source type to the destination type. To illustrate the syntax, the following is taken from an example `struct` named `Currency`, which is introduced later in this section:

```
public static implicit operator float (Currency value)
{
    // processing
}
```

The return type of the operator defines the target type of the cast operation, and the single parameter is the source object for the conversion. The cast defined here allows you to implicitly convert the value of a `Currency` into a `float`. Note that if a conversion has been declared as `implicit`, the compiler permits its use either implicitly or explicitly. If it has been declared as `explicit`, the compiler only permits it to be used explicitly. In common with other operator overloads, casts must be declared as both `public` and `static`.

> **NOTE** *C++ developers will notice that this is different from C++, in which casts are instance members of classes.*

Implementing User-Defined Casts

This section illustrates the use of implicit and explicit user-defined casts in an example called `CastingSample`. In this example, you define a struct, `Currency`, which holds a positive USD ($) monetary value. C# provides the `decimal` type for this purpose, but it is possible you will still want to write your own struct or class to represent monetary values if you need to perform sophisticated financial processing and therefore want to implement specific methods on such a class.

> **NOTE** *The syntax for casting is the same for structs and classes. This example happens to be for a struct, but it would work just as well if you declared `Currency` as a class.*

Initially, the definition of the `Currency` struct is as follows (code file `CastingSample/Currency.cs`):

```
public struct Currency
{
    public uint Dollars { get; }
    public ushort Cents { get; }

    public Currency(uint dollars, ushort cents)
    {
        Dollars = dollars;
        Cents = cents;
    }

    public override string ToString() => $"${Dollars}.{Cents,-2:00}";
}
```

The use of unsigned data types for the `Dollar` and `Cents` properties ensures that a `Currency` instance can hold only positive values. It is restricted this way to illustrate some points about explicit casts later. You might want to use a class like this to hold, for example, salary information for company employees (people's salaries tend not to be negative!).

Start by assuming that you want to be able to convert `Currency` instances to `float` values, where the integer part of the `float` represents the dollars. In other words, you want to be able to write code like this:

```
var balance = new Currency(10, 50);
float f = balance; // We want f to be set to 10.5
```

To be able to do this, you need to define a cast. Hence, you add the following to your `Currency` definition:

```
public static implicit operator float (Currency value) =>
    value.Dollars + (value.Cents/100.0f);
```

The preceding cast is implicit. It is a sensible choice in this case because, as it should be clear from the definition of `Currency`, any value that can be stored in the currency can also be stored in a `float`. There is no way that anything should ever go wrong in this cast.

> **NOTE** *There is a slight cheat here: In fact, when converting a* `uint` *to a* `float`, *there can be a loss in precision, but Microsoft has deemed this error sufficiently marginal to count the* `uint`*-to-*`float` *cast as implicit.*

However, if you have a `float` that you would like to be converted to a `Currency`, the conversion is not guaranteed to work. A `float` can store negative values, whereas `Currency` instances can't, and a `float` can store numbers of a far higher magnitude than can be stored in the (`uint`) `Dollar` field of `Currency`. Therefore, if a `float` contains an inappropriate value, converting it to a `Currency` could give unpredictable results. Because of this risk, the conversion from `float` to `Currency` should be defined as explicit. Here is the first attempt, which does not return quite the correct results, but it is instructive to examine why:

```
public static explicit operator Currency (float value)
{
    uint dollars = (uint)value;
    ushort cents = (ushort)((value-dollars)*100);
    return new Currency(dollars, cents);
}
```

The following code now successfully compiles:

```
float amount = 45.63f;
Currency amount2 = (Currency)amount;
```

However, the following code, if you tried it, would generate a compilation error because it attempts to use an explicit cast implicitly:

```
float amount = 45.63f;
Currency amount2 = amount;    // wrong
```

By making the cast explicit, you warn the developer to be careful because data loss might occur. However, as you soon see, this is not how you want your `Currency` struct to behave. Try writing a test harness and running the sample. Here is the `Main` method, which instantiates a `Currency` struct and attempts a few conversions. At the start of this code, you write out the value of `balance` in two different ways—this is needed to illustrate something later in the example (code file `CastingSample/Program.cs`):

```
static void Main()
{
    try
    {
        var balance = new Currency(50,35);
```

```
        WriteLine(balance);
        WriteLine($"balance is {balance}"); // implicitly invokes ToString

        float balance2= balance;
        WriteLine($"After converting to float, = {balance2}");

        balance = (Currency) balance2;

        WriteLine($"After converting back to Currency, = {balance}");
        WriteLine("Now attempt to convert out of range value of " +
                      "-$50.50 to a Currency:");

        checked
        {
          balance = (Currency) (-50.50);
          WriteLine($"Result is {balance}");
        }
      }
      catch(Exception e)
      {
        WriteLine($"Exception occurred: {e.Message}");
      }
    }
```

Notice that the entire code is placed in a `try` block to catch any exceptions that occur during your casts. In addition, the lines that test converting an out-of-range value to `Currency` are placed in a `checked` block in an attempt to trap negative values. Running this code produces the following output:

```
50.35
Balance is $50.35
After converting to float, = 50.35
After converting back to Currency, = $50.34
Now attempt to convert out of range value of -$50.50 to a Currency:
Result is $4294967246.00
```

This output shows that the code did not quite work as expected. First, converting back from `float` to `Currency` gave a wrong result of $50.34 instead of $50.35. Second, no exception was generated when you tried to convert an obviously out-of-range value.

The first problem is caused by rounding errors. If a cast is used to convert from a `float` to a `uint`, the computer truncates the number rather than rounds it. The computer stores numbers in binary rather than decimal, and the fraction 0.35 cannot be exactly represented as a binary fraction (just as $1/3$ cannot be represented exactly as a decimal fraction; it comes out as 0.3333 recurring). The computer ends up storing a value very slightly lower than 0.35 that can be represented exactly in binary format. Multiply by 100 and you get a number fractionally less than 35, which is truncated to 34 cents. Clearly, in this situation, such errors caused by truncation are serious, and the way to avoid them is to ensure that some intelligent rounding is performed in numerical conversions instead.

Luckily, Microsoft has written a class that does this: `System.Convert`. The `System.Convert` object contains a large number of static methods to perform various numerical conversions, and the one that we want is `Convert.ToUInt16`. Note that the extra care taken by the `System.Convert` methods comes at a performance cost. You should use them only when necessary.

Let's examine the second problem—why the expected overflow exception wasn't thrown. The issue here is this: The place where the overflow really occurs isn't actually in the `Main` routine at all—it is inside the code for the cast operator, which is called from the `Main` method. The code in this method was not marked as `checked`.

The solution is to ensure that the cast itself is computed in a `checked` context, too. With both this change and the fix for the first problem, the revised code for the conversion looks like the following:

```
public static explicit operator Currency (float value)
{
  checked
  {
    uint dollars = (uint)value;
    ushort cents = Convert.ToUInt16((value-dollars)*100);
    return new Currency(dollars, cents);
  }
}
```

Note that you use `Convert.ToUInt16` to calculate the cents, as described earlier, but you do not use it for calculating the dollar part of the amount. `System.Convert` is not needed when calculating the dollar amount because truncating the `float` value is what you want there.

> **NOTE** *The* `System.Convert` *methods also carry out their own overflow checking. Hence, for the particular case we are considering, there is no need to place the call to* `Convert.ToUInt16` *inside the checked context. The checked context is still required, however, for the explicit casting of* value *to dollars.*

You won't see a new set of results with this new `checked` cast just yet because you have some more modifications to make to the `CastingSample` example later in this section.

> **NOTE** *If you are defining a cast that will be used very often, and for which performance is at an absolute premium, you may prefer not to do any error checking. That is also a legitimate solution, provided that the behavior of your cast and the lack of error checking are very clearly documented.*

Casts Between Classes

The `Currency` example involves only classes that convert to or from `float`—one of the predefined data types. However, it is not necessary to involve any of the simple data types. It is perfectly legitimate to define casts to convert between instances of different structs or classes that you have defined. You need to be aware of a couple of restrictions, however:

➤ You cannot define a cast if one of the classes is derived from the other (these types of casts already exist, as you see later).

➤ The cast must be defined inside the definition of either the source or the destination data type.

To illustrate these requirements, suppose that you have the class hierarchy shown in Figure 8-1.

In other words, classes C and D are indirectly derived from A. In this case, the only legitimate user-defined cast between A, B, C, or D would be to convert between classes C and D, because these classes are not derived from each other. The code to do so might look like the following (assuming you want the casts to be explicit, which is usually the case when defining casts between user-defined classes):

```
public static explicit operator D(C value)
{
    //...
}
```

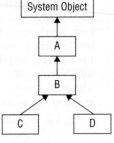

FIGURE 8-1

```
public static explicit operator C(D value)
{
  //...
}
```

For each of these casts, you can choose where you place the definitions—inside the class definition of C or inside the class definition of D, but not anywhere else. C# requires you to put the definition of a cast inside either the source class (or struct) or the destination class (or struct). A side effect of this is that you cannot define a cast between two classes unless you have access to edit the source code for at least one of them. This is sensible because it prevents third parties from introducing casts into your classes.

After you have defined a cast inside one of the classes, you cannot also define the same cast inside the other class. Obviously, there should be only one cast for each conversion; otherwise, the compiler would not know which one to use.

Casts Between Base and Derived Classes

To see how these casts work, start by considering the case in which both the source and the destination are reference types, and consider two classes, MyBase and MyDerived, where MyDerived is derived directly or indirectly from MyBase.

First, from MyDerived to MyBase, it is always possible (assuming the constructors are available) to write this:

```
MyDerived derivedObject = new MyDerived();
MyBase baseCopy = derivedObject;
```

Here, you are casting implicitly from MyDerived to MyBase. This works because of the rule that any reference to a type MyBase is allowed to refer to objects of class MyBase or anything derived from MyBase. In OO programming, instances of a derived class are, in a real sense, instances of the base class, plus something extra. All the functions and fields defined on the base class are defined in the derived class, too.

Alternatively, you can write this:

```
MyBase derivedObject = new MyDerived();
MyBase baseObject = new MyBase();
MyDerived derivedCopy1 = (MyDerived) derivedObject;    // OK
MyDerived derivedCopy2 = (MyDerived) baseObject;        // Throws exception
```

This code is perfectly legal C# (in a syntactic sense, that is) and illustrates casting from a base class to a derived class. However, the final statement throws an exception when executed. When you perform the cast, the object being referred to is examined. Because a base class reference can, in principle, refer to a derived class instance, it is possible that this object is actually an instance of the derived class that you are attempting to cast to. If that is the case, the cast succeeds, and the derived reference is set to refer to the object. If, however, the object in question is not an instance of the derived class (or of any class derived from it), the cast fails and an exception is thrown.

Notice that the casts that the compiler has supplied, which convert between base and derived class, do not actually do any data conversion on the object in question. All they do is set the new reference to refer to the object if it is legal for that conversion to occur. To that extent, these casts are very different in nature from the ones that you normally define yourself. For example, in the CastingSample example earlier, you defined casts that convert between a Currency struct and a float. In the float-to-Currency cast, you actually instantiated a new Currency struct and initialized it with the required values. The predefined casts between base and derived classes do not do this. If you want to convert a MyBase instance into a real MyDerived object with values based on the contents of the MyBase instance, you cannot use the cast syntax to do this. The most sensible option is usually to define a derived class constructor that takes a base class instance as a parameter, and have this constructor perform the relevant initializations:

```
class DerivedClass: BaseClass
{
```

```
public DerivedClass(BaseClass base)
{
  // initialize object from the Base instance
}
// etc.
```

Boxing and Unboxing Casts

The previous discussion focused on casting between base and derived classes where both participants were reference types. Similar principles apply when casting value types, although in this case it is not possible to simply copy references—some copying of data must occur.

It is not, of course, possible to derive from structs or primitive value types. Casting between base and derived structs invariably means casting between a primitive type or a struct and `System.Object`. (Theoretically, it is possible to cast between a struct and `System.ValueType`, though it is hard to see why you would want to do this.)

The cast from any struct (or primitive type) to `object` is always available as an implicit cast—because it is a cast from a derived type to a base type—and is just the familiar process of boxing. For example, using the `Currency` struct:

```
var balance = new Currency(40,0);
object baseCopy = balance;
```

When this implicit cast is executed, the contents of `balance` are copied onto the heap into a boxed object, and the `baseCopy` object reference is set to this object. What actually happens behind the scenes is this: When you originally defined the `Currency` struct, the .NET Framework implicitly supplied another (hidden) class, a boxed `Currency` class, which contains all the same fields as the `Currency` struct but is a reference type, stored on the heap. This happens whenever you define a value type, whether it is a `struct` or an `enum`, and similar boxed reference types exist corresponding to all the primitive value types of `int`, `double`, `uint`, and so on. It is not possible, or necessary, to gain direct programmatic access to any of these boxed classes in source code, but they are the objects that are working behind the scenes whenever a value type is cast to `object`. When you implicitly cast `Currency` to `object`, a boxed `Currency` instance is instantiated and initialized with all the data from the `Currency` struct. In the preceding code, it is this boxed `Currency` instance to which `baseCopy` refers. By these means, it is possible for casting from derived to base type to work syntactically in the same way for value types as for reference types.

Casting the other way is known as unboxing. Like casting between a base reference type and a derived reference type, it is an explicit cast because an exception is thrown if the object being cast is not of the correct type:

```
object derivedObject = new Currency(40,0);
object baseObject = new object();
Currency derivedCopy1 = (Currency)derivedObject;   // OK
Currency derivedCopy2 = (Currency)baseObject;       // Exception thrown
```

This code works in a way similar to the code presented earlier for reference types. Casting `derivedObject` to `Currency` works fine because `derivedObject` actually refers to a boxed `Currency` instance—the cast is performed by copying the fields out of the boxed `Currency` object into a new `Currency` struct. The second cast fails because `baseObject` does not refer to a boxed `Currency` object.

When using boxing and unboxing, it is important to understand that both processes actually copy the data into the new boxed or unboxed object. Hence, manipulations on the boxed object, for example, do not affect the contents of the original value type.

Multiple Casting

One thing you have to watch for when you are defining casts is that if the C# compiler is presented with a situation in which no direct cast is available to perform a requested conversion, it attempts to find a way of combining casts to do the conversion. For example, with the `Currency` struct, suppose the compiler encounters a few lines of code like this:

```
var balance = new Currency(10,50);
long amount = (long)balance;
double amountD = balance;
```

You first initialize a `Currency` instance, and then you attempt to convert it to a `long`. The trouble is that you haven't defined the cast to do that. However, this code still compiles successfully. Here's what happens: The compiler realizes that you have defined an implicit cast to get from `Currency` to `float`, and the compiler already knows how to explicitly cast a `float` to a `long`. Hence, it compiles that line of code into IL code that converts `balance` first to a `float`, and then converts that result to a `long`. The same thing happens in the final line of the code, when you convert `balance` to a `double`. However, because the cast from `Currency` to `float` and the predefined cast from `float` to `double` are both implicit, you can write this conversion in your code as an implicit cast. If you prefer, you could also specify the casting route explicitly:

```
var balance = new Currency(10,50);
long amount = (long)(float)balance;
double amountD = (double)(float)balance;
```

However, in most cases, this would be seen as needlessly complicating your code. The following code, by contrast, produces a compilation error:

```
var balance = new Currency(10,50);
long amount = balance;
```

The reason is that the best match for the conversion that the compiler can find is still to convert first to `float` and then to `long`. The conversion from `float` to `long` needs to be specified explicitly, though.

Not all of this by itself should give you too much trouble. The rules are, after all, fairly intuitive and designed to prevent any data loss from occurring without the developer knowing about it. However, the problem is that if you are not careful when you define your casts, it is possible for the compiler to select a path that leads to unexpected results. For example, suppose that it occurs to someone else in the group writing the `Currency` struct that it would be useful to be able to convert a `uint` containing the total number of cents in an amount into a `Currency` (cents, not dollars, because the idea is not to lose the fractions of a dollar). Therefore, this cast might be written to try to achieve this:

```
// Do not do this!
public static implicit operator Currency (uint value) =>
   new Currency(value/100u, (ushort)(value%100));
```

Note the u after the first 100 in this code to ensure that `value/100u` is interpreted as a `uint`. If you had written `value/100`, the compiler would have interpreted this as an `int`, not a `uint`.

The comment `Do not do this!` is clearly noted in this code, and here is why: The following code snippet merely converts a `uint` containing 350 into a `Currency` and back again; but what do you think `bal2` will contain after executing this?

```
uint bal = 350;
Currency balance = bal;
uint bal2 = (uint)balance;
```

The answer is not 350 but 3! Moreover, it all follows logically. You convert 350 implicitly to a `Currency`, giving the result `balance.Dollars = 3`, `balance.Cents = 50`. Then the compiler does its usual figuring out of the best path for the conversion back. `Balance` ends up being implicitly converted to a `float` (value 3.5), and this is converted explicitly to a `uint` with value 3.

Of course, other instances exist in which converting to another data type and back again causes data loss. For example, converting a `float` containing 5.8 to an `int` and back to a `float` again loses the fractional part, giving you a result of 5, but there is a slight difference in principle between losing the fractional part of a number and dividing an integer by more than 100. Currency has suddenly become a rather dangerous class that does strange things to integers!

The problem is that there is a conflict between how your casts interpret integers. The casts between Currency and float interpret an integer value of 1 as corresponding to one dollar, but the latest uint-to-Currency cast interprets this value as one cent. This is an example of very poor design. If you want your classes to be easy to use, you should ensure that all your casts behave in a way that is mutually compatible, in the sense that they intuitively give the same results. In this case, the solution is obviously to rewrite the uint-to-Currency cast so that it interprets an integer value of 1 as one dollar:

```
public static implicit operator Currency (uint value) =>
    new Currency(value, 0);
```

Incidentally, you might wonder whether this new cast is necessary at all. The answer is that it could be useful. Without this cast, the only way for the compiler to carry out a uint-to-Currency conversion would be via a float. Converting directly is a lot more efficient in this case, so having this extra cast provides performance benefits, though you need to ensure that it provides the same result as via a float, which you have now done. In other situations, you may also find that separately defining casts for different predefined data types enables more conversions to be implicit rather than explicit, though that is not the case here.

A good test of whether your casts are compatible is to ask whether a conversion will give the same results (other than perhaps a loss of accuracy as in float-to-int conversions) regardless of which path it takes. The Currency class provides a good example of this. Consider this code:

```
var balance = new Currency(50, 35);
ulong bal = (ulong) balance;
```

At present, there is only one way that the compiler can achieve this conversion: by converting the Currency to a float implicitly, then to a ulong explicitly. The float-to-ulong conversion requires an explicit conversion, but that is fine because you have specified one here.

Suppose, however, that you then added another cast, to convert implicitly from a Currency to a uint. You actually do this by modifying the Currency struct by adding the casts both to and from uint. (code file CastingSample/Currency.cs):

```
public static implicit operator Currency (uint value) =>
    new Currency(value, 0);

public static implicit operator uint (Currency value) =>
    value.Dollars;
```

Now the compiler has another possible route to convert from Currency to ulong: to convert from Currency to uint implicitly, then to ulong implicitly. Which of these two routes will it take? C# has some precise rules about the best route for the compiler when there are several possibilities. (The rules are not covered in this book, but if you are interested in the details, see the MSDN documentation.) The best answer is that you should design your casts so that all routes give the same answer (other than possible loss of precision), in which case it doesn't really matter which one the compiler picks. (As it happens in this case, the compiler picks the Currency-to-uint-to-ulong route in preference to Currency-to-float-to-ulong.)

To test casting the Currency to uint, add this test code to the Main method (code file CastingSample/Program.cs):

```
static void Main()
{
  try
  {
    var balance = new Currency(50,35);

    WriteLine(balance);
```

```
        WriteLine($"balance is {balance}");

        uint balance3 = (uint) balance;

        WriteLine($"Converting to uint gives {balance3}");
    }
    catch (Exception ex)
    {
        WriteLine($"Exception occurred: {e.Message}");
    }
}
```

Running the sample now gives you these results:

```
50
balance is $50.35
Converting to uint gives 50
```

The output shows that the conversion to uint has been successful, though, as expected, you have lost the cents part of the Currency in making this conversion. Casting a negative float to Currency has also produced the expected overflow exception now that the float-to-Currency cast itself defines a checked context.

However, the output also demonstrates one last potential problem that you need to be aware of when working with casts. The very first line of output does not display the balance correctly, displaying 50 instead of 50.35.

So what is going on? The problem here is that when you combine casts with method overloads, you get another source of unpredictability.

The WriteLine statement using the format string implicitly calls the Currency.ToString method, ensuring that the Currency is displayed as a string.

The very first WriteLine method, however, simply passes a raw Currency struct to WriteLine. Now, WriteLine has many overloads, but none of them takes a Currency struct. Therefore, the compiler starts fishing around to see what it can cast the Currency to in order to make it match up with one of the overloads of WriteLine. As it happens, one of the WriteLine overloads is designed to display uints quickly and efficiently, and it takes a uint as a parameter—you have now supplied a cast that converts Currency implicitly to uint.

In fact, WriteLine has another overload that takes a double as a parameter and displays the value of that double. If you look closely at the output running the example previously where the cast to uint did not exist, you see that the first line of output displayed Currency as a double, using this overload. In that example, there wasn't a direct cast from Currency to uint, so the compiler picked Currency-to-float-to-double as its preferred way of matching up the available casts to the available WriteLine overloads. However, now that there is a direct cast to uint available in SimpleCurrency2, the compiler has opted for that route.

The upshot of this is that if you have a method call that takes several overloads and you attempt to pass it a parameter whose data type doesn't match any of the overloads exactly, then you are forcing the compiler to decide not only what casts to use to perform the data conversion, but also which overload, and hence which data conversion, to pick. The compiler always works logically and according to strict rules, but the results may not be what you expected. If there is any doubt, you are better off specifying which cast to use explicitly.

SUMMARY

This chapter looked at the standard operators provided by C#, described the mechanics of object equality, and examined how the compiler converts the standard data types from one to another. It also demonstrated how you can implement custom operator support on your data types using operator overloads. Finally, you looked at a special type of operator overload, the cast operator, which enables you to specify how instances of your types are converted to other data types.

The next chapter explains delegates, lambda expressions, and events.

Delegates, Lambdas, and Events

WHAT'S IN THIS CHAPTER?

➤ Delegates
➤ Lambda expressions
➤ Closures
➤ Events
➤ Weak Events

WROX.COM CODE DOWNLOADS FOR THIS CHAPTER

The wrox.com code downloads for this chapter are found at www.wrox.com/go/
professionalcsharp6 on the Download Code tab. The code for this chapter is divided into the following major examples:

➤ Simple Delegates
➤ Bubble Sorter
➤ Lambda Expressions
➤ Events Sample
➤ Weak Events

REFERENCING METHODS

Delegates are the .NET variant of addresses to methods. Compare this to C++, where a function
pointer is nothing more than a pointer to a memory location that is not type-safe. You have no idea
what a pointer is really pointing to, and items such as parameters and return types are not known.
This is completely different with .NET; delegates are type-safe classes that define the return types and

types of parameters. The delegate class not only contains a reference to a method, but can hold references to multiple methods.

Lambda expressions are directly related to delegates. When the parameter is a delegate type, you can use a lambda expression to implement a method that's referenced from the delegate.

This chapter explains the basics of delegates and lambda expressions, and shows you how to implement methods called by delegates with lambda expressions. It also demonstrates how .NET uses delegates as the means of implementing events.

DELEGATES

Delegates exist for situations in which you want to pass methods around to other methods. To see what that means, consider this line of code:

```
int i = int.Parse("99");
```

You are so used to passing data to methods as parameters, as in this example, that you don't consciously think about it, so the idea of passing methods around instead of data might sound a little strange. However, sometimes you have a method that does something, and rather than operate on data, the method might need to do something that involves invoking another method. To complicate things further, you do not know at compile time what this second method is. That information is available only at runtime and hence needs to be passed in as a parameter to the first method. That might sound confusing, but it should become clearer with a couple of examples:

➤ **Threads and tasks**—It is possible in C# to tell the computer to start a new sequence of execution in parallel with what it is currently doing. Such a sequence is known as a *thread*, and you start one using the `Start` method on an instance of one of the base classes, `System.Threading.Thread`. If you tell the computer to start a new sequence of execution, you have to tell it where to start that sequence; that is, you have to supply the details of a method in which execution can start. In other words, the constructor of the `Thread` class takes a
parameter that defines the method to be invoked by the thread.

➤ **Generic library classes**—Many libraries contain code to perform various standard tasks. It is usually possible for these libraries to be self-contained, in the sense that you know when you write to the library exactly how the task must be performed. However, sometimes the task contains a subtask, which only the individual client code that uses the library knows how to perform. For example, say that you want to write a class that takes an array of objects and sorts them in ascending order. Part of the sorting process involves repeatedly taking two of the objects in the array and comparing them to see which one should come first. If you want to make the class capable of sorting arrays of any object, there is no way that it can tell in advance how to do this comparison. The client code that hands your class the array of objects must also tell your class how to do this comparison for the particular objects it wants sorted. The client code has to pass your class details of an appropriate method that can be called to do the comparison.

➤ **Events**—The general idea here is that often you have code that needs to be informed when some event takes place. GUI programming is full of situations similar to this. When the event is raised, the runtime needs to know what method should be executed. This is done by passing the method that handles the event as a parameter to a delegate. This is discussed later in this chapter.

In C and C++, you can just take the address of a function and pass it as a parameter. There's no type safety with C. You can pass any function to a method where a function pointer is required. Unfortunately, this direct approach not only causes some problems with type safety but also neglects the fact that when you are doing object-oriented programming, methods rarely exist in isolation; they usually need to be associated with a class instance before they can be called. Because of these problems, the .NET Framework does not syntactically permit this direct approach. Instead, if you want to pass methods around, you have to wrap the details of the method in a new kind of object, a delegate. Delegates, quite simply, are a special type of object—special in the sense that, whereas all the objects defined up to now contain data, a delegate contains the address of a method, or the address of multiple methods.

Declaring Delegates

When you want to use a class in C#, you do so in two stages. First, you need to define the class—that is, you need to tell the compiler what fields and methods make up the class. Then (unless you are using only static methods), you instantiate an object of that class. With delegates it is the same process. You start by declaring the delegates you want to use. Declaring delegates means telling the compiler what kind of method a delegate of that type will represent. Then, you have to create one or more instances of that delegate. Behind the scenes, the compiler creates a class that represents the delegate.

The syntax for declaring delegates looks like this:

```
delegate void IntMethodInvoker(int x);
```

This declares a delegate called `IntMethodInvoker`, and indicates that each instance of this delegate can hold a reference to a method that takes one `int` parameter and returns `void`. The crucial point to understand about delegates is that they are type-safe. When you define the delegate, you have to provide full details about the signature and the return type of the method that it represents.

> **NOTE** *One good way to understand delegates is to think of a delegate as something that gives a name to a method signature and the return type.*

Suppose that you want to define a delegate called `TwoLongsOp` that represents a method that takes two `long`s as its parameters and returns a `double`. You could do so like this:

```
delegate double TwoLongsOp(long first, long second);
```

Or, to define a delegate that represents a method that takes no parameters and returns a `string`, you might write this:

```
delegate string GetAString();
```

The syntax is similar to that for a method definition, except there is no method body and the definition is prefixed with the keyword `delegate`. Because what you are doing here is basically defining a new class, you can define a delegate in any of the same places that you would define a class—that is to say, either inside another class, outside of any class, or in a namespace as a top-level object. Depending on how visible you want your definition to be, and the scope of the delegate, you can apply any of the normal access modifiers to delegate definitions—`public`, `private`, `protected`, and so on:

```
public delegate string GetAString();
```

> **NOTE** *We really mean what we say when we describe defining a delegate as defining a new class. Delegates are implemented as classes derived from the class `System.MulticastDelegate`, which is derived from the base class `System.Delegate`. The C# compiler is aware of this class and uses its delegate syntax to hide the details of the operation of this class. This is another good example of how C# works in conjunction with the base classes to make programming as easy as possible.*

After you have defined a delegate, you can create an instance of it so that you can use it to store details about a particular method.

> **NOTE** *There is an unfortunate problem with terminology here. When you are talking about classes, there are two distinct terms: class, which indicates the broader definition, and object, which means an instance of the class. Unfortunately, with delegates there is only the one term; delegate can refer to both the class and the object. When you create an instance of a delegate, what you have created is also referred to as a delegate. You need to be aware of the context to know which meaning is being used when we talk about delegates.*

Using Delegates

The following code snippet demonstrates the use of a delegate. It is a rather long-winded way of calling the `ToString` method on an `int` (code file `GetAStringDemo/Program.cs`):

```
private delegate string GetAString();

public static void Main()
{
    int x = 40;
    GetAString firstStringMethod = new GetAString(x.ToString);
    WriteLine($"String is {firstStringMethod()}");
    // With firstStringMethod initialized to x.ToString(),
    // the above statement is equivalent to saying
    // Console.WriteLine($"String is {x.ToString()}");
}
```

This code instantiates a delegate of type `GetAString` and initializes it so it refers to the `ToString` method of the integer variable x. Delegates in C# always syntactically take a one-parameter constructor, the parameter being the method to which the delegate refers. This method must match the signature with which you originally defined the delegate. In this case, you would get a compilation error if you tried to initialize the variable `firstStringMethod` with any method that did not take any parameters and return a string. Notice that because `int.ToString` is an instance method (as opposed to a static one), you need to specify the instance (x) as well as the name of the method to initialize the delegate properly.

The next line actually uses the delegate to display the string. In any code, supplying the name of a delegate instance, followed by parentheses containing any parameters, has exactly the same effect as calling the method wrapped by the delegate. Hence, in the preceding code snippet, the `Console.WriteLine` statement is completely equivalent to the commented-out line.

In fact, supplying parentheses to the delegate instance is the same as invoking the `Invoke` method of the delegate class. Because `firstStringMethod` is a variable of a delegate type, the C# compiler replaces `firstStringMethod` with `firstStringMethod.Invoke`:

```
firstStringMethod();
firstStringMethod.Invoke();
```

For less typing, at every place where a delegate instance is needed, you can just pass the name of the address. This is known by the term *delegate inference*. This C# feature works as long as the compiler can resolve the delegate instance to a specific type. The example initialized the variable `firstStringMethod` of type `GetAString` with a new instance of the delegate `GetAString`:

```
GetAString firstStringMethod = new GetAString(x.ToString);
```

You can write the same just by passing the method name with the variable x to the variable firstStringMethod:

```
GetAString firstStringMethod = x.ToString;
```

The code that is created by the C# compiler is the same. The compiler detects that a delegate type is required with firstStringMethod, so it creates an instance of the delegate type GetAString and passes the address of the method with the object x to the constructor.

> **NOTE** *Be aware that you can't type the brackets to the method name as* x.ToString() *and pass it to the delegate variable. This would be an invocation of the method. The invocation of the* ToString *method returns a string object that can't be assigned to the delegate variable. You can only assign the address of a method to the delegate variable.*

Delegate inference can be used anywhere a delegate instance is required. Delegate inference can also be used with events because events are based on delegates (as you see later in this chapter).

One feature of delegates is that they are type-safe to the extent that they ensure that the signature of the method being called is correct. However, interestingly, they don't care what type of object the method is being called against or even whether the method is a static method or an instance method.

> **NOTE** *An instance of a given delegate can refer to any instance or static method on any object of any type, provided that the signature of the method matches the signature of the delegate.*

To demonstrate this, the following example expands the previous code snippet so that it uses the firstStringMethod delegate to call a couple of other methods on another object—an instance method and a static method. For this, you use the Currency struct. The Currency struct has its own overload of ToString and a static method with the same signature to GetCurrencyUnit. This way, the same delegate variable can be used to invoke these methods (code file GetAStringDemo/Currency.cs):

```csharp
struct Currency
{
  public uint Dollars;
  public ushort Cents;

  public Currency(uint dollars, ushort cents)
  {
    this.Dollars = dollars;
    this.Cents = cents;
  }

  public override string ToString() => $"${Dollars}.{Cents,2:00}";

  public static string GetCurrencyUnit() => "Dollar";

  public static explicit operator Currency (float value)
  {
    checked
    {
```

```
           uint dollars = (uint)value;
           ushort cents = (ushort)((value-dollars) * 100);
           return new Currency(dollars, cents);
        }
     }

     public static implicit operator float (Currency value) =>
        value.Dollars + (value.Cents / 100.0f);

     public static implicit operator Currency (uint value) =>
        new Currency(value, 0);

     public static implicit operator uint (Currency value) =>
        value.Dollars;
  }
```

Now you can use the `GetAString` instance as follows (code file `GetAStringDemo/Program.cs`):

```
private delegate string GetAString();

public static void Main()
{
   int x = 40;
   GetAString firstStringMethod = x.ToString;
   WriteLine($"String is {firstStringMethod()}");

   var balance = new Currency(34, 50);

   // firstStringMethod references an instance method
   firstStringMethod = balance.ToString;
   WriteLine($"String is {firstStringMethod()}");

   // firstStringMethod references a static method
   firstStringMethod = new GetAString(Currency.GetCurrencyUnit);
   WriteLine($"String is {firstStringMethod()}");
}
```

This code shows how you can call a method via a delegate and subsequently reassign the delegate to refer to different methods on different instances of classes, even static methods or methods against instances of different types of class, provided that the signature of each method matches the delegate definition.

When you run the application, you get the output from the different methods that are referenced by the delegate:

```
String is 40
String is $34.50
String is Dollar
```

However, you still haven't seen the process of actually passing a delegate to another method. Nor has this actually achieved anything particularly useful yet. It is possible to call the `ToString` method of `int` and `Currency` objects in a much more straightforward way than using delegates. Unfortunately, the nature of delegates requires a fairly complex example before you can really appreciate their usefulness. The next section presents two delegate examples. The first one simply uses delegates to call a couple of different operations. It illustrates how to pass delegates to methods and how you can use arrays of delegates—although arguably it still doesn't do much that you couldn't do a lot more simply without delegates. The second, much more complex, example presents a `BubbleSorter` class, which implements a method to sort arrays of objects into ascending order. This class would be difficult to write without using delegates.

Simple Delegate Example

This example defines a `MathOperations` class that uses a couple of static methods to perform two operations on doubles. Then you use delegates to invoke these methods. The `MathOperations` class looks like this:

```
class MathOperations
{
  public static double MultiplyByTwo(double value) => value * 2;

  public static double Square(double value) => value * value;
}
```

You invoke these methods as follows (code file `SimpleDelegate/Program.cs`):

```
using static System.Console;

namespace Wrox.ProCSharp.Delegates
{
  delegate double DoubleOp(double x);

  class Program
  {
    static void Main()
    {
      DoubleOp[] operations =
      {
        MathOperations.MultiplyByTwo,
        MathOperations.Square
      };

      for (int i=0; i < operations.Length; i++)
      {
        WriteLine($"Using operations[{i}]:");
        ProcessAndDisplayNumber(operations[i], 2.0);
        ProcessAndDisplayNumber(operations[i], 7.94);
        ProcessAndDisplayNumber(operations[i], 1.414);
        WriteLine();
      }
    }

    static void ProcessAndDisplayNumber(DoubleOp action, double value)
    {
      double result = action(value);
      WriteLine($"Value is {value}, result of operation is {result}");
    }
  }
}
```

In this code, you instantiate an array of `DoubleOp` delegates (remember that after you have defined a delegate class, you can basically instantiate instances just as you can with normal classes, so putting some into an array is no problem). Each element of the array is initialized to refer to a different operation implemented by the `MathOperations` class. Then, you loop through the array, applying each operation to three different values. This illustrates one way of using delegates—to group
methods together into an array so that you can call several methods in a loop.

The key lines in this code are the ones in which you actually pass each delegate to the
`ProcessAndDisplayNumber` method, such as here:

```
ProcessAndDisplayNumber(operations[i], 2.0);
```

The preceding passes in the name of a delegate but without any parameters. Given that `operations[i]` is a delegate, syntactically:

➤ `operations[i]` means the *delegate* (that is, the method represented by the delegate)

➤ `operations[i](2.0)` means *actually call this method, passing in the value in parentheses*

The `ProcessAndDisplayNumber` method is defined to take a delegate as its first parameter:

```
static void ProcessAndDisplayNumber(DoubleOp action, double value)
```

Then, when in this method, you call:

```
double result = action(value);
```

This actually causes the method that is wrapped up by the `action` delegate instance to be called, and its return result stored in `Result`. Running this example gives you the following:

```
SimpleDelegate
Using operations[0]:
Value is 2, result of operation is 4
Value is 7.94, result of operation is 15.88
Value is 1.414, result of operation is 2.828

Using operations[1]:
Value is 2, result of operation is 4
Value is 7.94, result of operation is 63.0436
Value is 1.414, result of operation is 1.999396
```

Action<T> and Func<T> Delegates

Instead of defining a new delegate type with every parameter and return type, you can use the `Action<T>` and `Func<T>` delegates. The generic `Action<T>` delegate is meant to reference a method with `void` return. This delegate class exists in different variants so that you can pass up to 16 different parameter types. The `Action` class without the generic parameter is for calling methods without parameters. `Action<in T>` is for calling a method with one parameter; `Action<in T1, in T2>` for a method with two parameters; and `Action<in T1, in T2, in T3, in T4, in T5, in T6, in T7, in T8>` for a method with eight parameters.

The `Func<T>` delegates can be used in a similar manner. `Func<T>` allows you to invoke methods with a return type. Similar to `Action<T>`, `Func<T>` is defined in different variants to pass up to 16 parameter types and a return type. `Func<out TResult>` is the delegate type to invoke a method with a return type and without parameters. `Func<in T, out TResult>` is for a method with one parameter, and `Func<in T1, in T2, in T3, in T4, out TResult>` is for a method with four parameters.

The example in the preceding section declared a delegate with a `double` parameter and a `double` return type:

```
delegate double DoubleOp(double x);
```

Instead of declaring the custom delegate `DoubleOp` you can use the `Func<in T, out TResult>` delegate. You can declare a variable of the delegate type or, as shown here, an array of the delegate type:

```
<double, double>[] operations =
{
    MathOperations.MultiplyByTwo,
    MathOperations.Square
};
```

and use it with the `ProcessAndDisplayNumber` method as a parameter:

```
static void ProcessAndDisplayNumber(Func<double, double> action,
                                    double value)
{
  double result = action(value);
  WriteLine($"Value is {value}, result of operation is {result}");
}
```

BubbleSorter Example

You are now ready for an example that shows the real usefulness of delegates. You are going to write a class called `BubbleSorter`. This class implements a static method, `Sort`, which takes as its first parameter an array of objects, and rearranges this array into ascending order. For example, if you were to pass in this array of ints, {`0, 5, 6, 2, 1`}, it would rearrange this array into {`0, 1, 2, 5, 6`}.

The bubble-sorting algorithm is a well-known and very simple way to sort numbers. It is best suited to small sets of numbers, because for larger sets of numbers (more than about 10), far more efficient algorithms are available. It works by repeatedly looping through the array, comparing each pair of numbers and, if necessary, swapping them, so that the largest numbers progressively move to the end of the array. For sorting ints, a method to do a bubble sort might look similar to this:

```
bool swapped = true;
do
{
  swapped = false;
  for (int i = 0; i < sortArray.Length-1; i++)
  {
    if (sortArray[i] > sortArray[i+1])) // problem with this test
    {
      int temp = sortArray[i];
      sortArray[i] = sortArray[i + 1];
      sortArray[i + 1] = temp;
      swapped = true;
    }
  }
} while (swapped);
```

This is all very well for ints, but you want your `Sort` method to be able to sort any object. In other words, if some client code hands you an array of `Currency` structs or any other class or struct that it may have defined, you need to be able to sort the array. This presents a problem with the line `if(sortArray[i] < sortArray[i+1])` in the preceding code, because that requires you to compare two objects on the array to determine which one is greater. You can do that for ints, but how do you do it for a new class that doesn't implement the < operator? The answer is that the client code that knows about the class has to pass in a delegate wrapping a method that does the comparison. Also, instead of using an int type for the *temp* variable, a generic `Sort` method can be implemented using a generic type.

With a generic `Sort<T>` method accepting type `T`, a comparison method is needed that has two parameters of type `T` and a return type of `bool` for the `if` comparison. This method can be referenced from a `Func<T1, T2, TResult>` delegate, where `T1` and `T2` are the same type: `Func<T, T, bool>`.

This way, you give your `Sort<T>` method the following signature:

```
static public void Sort<T>(IList<T> sortArray, Func<T, T, bool> comparison)
```

The documentation for this method states that `comparison` must refer to a method that takes two arguments, and returns `true` if the value of the first argument is *smaller than* the second one.

Now you are all set. Here's the definition for the BubbleSorter class (code file BubbleSorter/
BubbleSorter.cs):

```
class BubbleSorter
{
  static public void Sort<T>(IList<T> sortArray, Func<T, T, bool> comparison)
  {
    bool swapped = true;
    do
    {
      swapped = false;
      for (int i = 0; i < sortArray.Count-1; i++)
      {
        if (comparison(sortArray[i+1], sortArray[i]))
        {
          T temp = sortArray[i];
          sortArray[i] = sortArray[i + 1];
          sortArray[i + 1] = temp;
          swapped = true;
        }
      }
    } while (swapped);
  }
}
```

To use this class, you need to define another class, which you can use to set up an array that needs sorting. For this example, assume that the Mortimer Phones mobile phone company has
a list of employees and wants them sorted according to salary. Each employee is represented by an
instance of a class, Employee, which looks similar to this (code file BubbleSorter/Employee.cs):

```
class Employee
{
  public Employee(string name, decimal salary)
  {
    Name = name;
    Salary = salary;
  }

  public string Name { get; }
  public decimal Salary { get; private set; }

  public override string ToString() => $"{Name}, {Salary:C}";

  public static bool CompareSalary(Employee e1, Employee e2) =>
    e1.Salary < e2.Salary;
}
```

Note that to match the signature of the Func<T, T, bool> delegate, you have to define CompareSalary in
this class as taking two Employee references and returning a Boolean. In the implementation, the comparison based on salary is performed.

Now you are ready to write some client code to request a sort (code file BubbleSorter/Program.cs):

```
using static System.Console;

namespace Wrox.ProCSharp.Delegates
{
  class Program
  {
    static void Main()
    {
```

```
            Employee[] employees =
            {
                new Employee("Bugs Bunny", 20000),
                new Employee("Elmer Fudd", 10000),
                new Employee("Daffy Duck", 25000),
                new Employee("Wile Coyote", 1000000.38m),
                new Employee("Foghorn Leghorn", 23000),
                new Employee("RoadRunner", 50000)
            };

            BubbleSorter.Sort(employees, Employee.CompareSalary);

            foreach (var employee in employees)
            {
                WriteLine(employee);
            }
        }
    }
}
```

Running this code shows that the `Employees` are correctly sorted according to salary:

```
BubbleSorter
Elmer Fudd, $10,000.00
Bugs Bunny, $20,000.00
Foghorn Leghorn, $23,000.00
Daffy Duck, $25,000.00
RoadRunner, $50,000.00
Wile Coyote, $1,000,000.38
```

Multicast Delegates

So far, each of the delegates you have used wraps just one method call. Calling the delegate amounts to calling that method. If you want to call more than one method, you need to make an explicit call through a delegate more than once. However, it is possible for a delegate to wrap more than one method. Such a delegate is known as a *multicast delegate*. When a multicast delegate is called, it successively calls each method in order. For this to work, the delegate signature should return a void; otherwise, you would only get the result of the last method invoked by the delegate.

With a `void` return type, you can use the `Action<double>` delegate (code file `MulticastDelegates/Program.cs`):

```
class Program
{
    static void Main()
    {
        Action<double> operations = MathOperations.MultiplyByTwo;
        operations += MathOperations.Square;
```

In the earlier example, you wanted to store references to two methods, so you instantiated an array of delegates. Here, you simply add both operations into the same multicast delegate. Multicast delegates recognize the operators + and +=. Alternatively, you can expand the last two lines of the preceding code, as in this snippet:

```
Action<double> operation1 = MathOperations.MultiplyByTwo;
Action<double> operation2 = MathOperations.Square;
Action<double> operations = operation1 + operation2;
```

Multicast delegates also recognize the operators – and -= to remove method calls from the delegate.

> **NOTE** *In terms of what's going on under the hood, a multicast delegate is a class derived from* System.MulticastDelegate, *which in turn is derived from* System.Delegate. System.MulticastDelegate *has additional members to allow the chaining of method calls into a list.*

To illustrate the use of multicast delegates, the following code recasts the SimpleDelegate example into a new example: MulticastDelegate. Because you now need the delegate to refer to methods that return void, you have to rewrite the methods in the MathOperations class so they display their results instead of returning them (code file MulticastDelegates/MathOperations.cs):

```
class MathOperations
{
  public static void MultiplyByTwo(double value)
  {
    double result = value * 2;
    WriteLine($"Multiplying by 2: {value} gives {result}");
  }

  public static void Square(double value)
  {
    double result = value * value;
    WriteLine($"Squaring: {value} gives {result}");
  }
}
```

To accommodate this change, you also have to rewrite ProcessAndDisplayNumber (code file MulticastDelegates/Program.cs):

```
static void ProcessAndDisplayNumber(Action<double> action, double value)
{
  WriteLine();
  WriteLine($"ProcessAndDisplayNumber called with value = {value}");
  action(value);
}
```

Now you can try out your multicast delegate:

```
static void Main()
{
  Action<double> operations = MathOperations.MultiplyByTwo;
  operations += MathOperations.Square;

  ProcessAndDisplayNumber(operations, 2.0);
  ProcessAndDisplayNumber(operations, 7.94);
  ProcessAndDisplayNumber(operations, 1.414);
  WriteLine();
}
```

Each time ProcessAndDisplayNumber is called, it displays a message saying that it has been called. Then the following statement causes each of the method calls in the action delegate instance to be called in succession:

```
action(value);
```

Running the preceding code produces this result:

```
MulticastDelegate

ProcessAndDisplayNumber called with value = 2
```

```
Multiplying by 2: 2 gives 4
Squaring: 2 gives 4

ProcessAndDisplayNumber called with value = 7.94
Multiplying by 2: 7.94 gives 15.88
Squaring: 7.94 gives 63.0436

ProcessAndDisplayNumber called with value = 1.414
Multiplying by 2: 1.414 gives 2.828
Squaring: 1.414 gives 1.999396
```

If you are using multicast delegates, be aware that the order in which methods chained to the same delegate will be called is formally undefined. Therefore, avoid writing code that relies on such methods being called in any particular order.

Invoking multiple methods by one delegate might cause an even bigger problem. The multicast delegate contains a collection of delegates to invoke one after the other. If one of the methods invoked by a delegate throws an exception, the complete iteration stops. Consider the following `MulticastIteration` example. Here, the simple delegate `Action` that returns `void` without arguments is used. This delegate is meant to invoke the methods `One` and `Two`, which fulfill the parameter and return type requirements of the delegate. Be aware that method `One` throws an exception (code file `MulticastDelegateWithIteration/Program.cs`):

```csharp
using System;
using static System.Console;

namespace Wrox.ProCSharp.Delegates
{
  class Program
  {
    static void One()
    {
      WriteLine("One");
      throw new Exception("Error in one");
    }

    static void Two()
    {
      WriteLine("Two");
    }
```

In the `Main` method, delegate `d1` is created to reference method `One`; next, the address of method `Two` is added to the same delegate. `d1` is invoked to call both methods. The exception is caught in a `try/catch` block:

```csharp
    static void Main()
    {
      Action d1 = One;
      d1 += Two;

      try
      {
        d1();
      }
      catch (Exception)
      {
        WriteLine("Exception caught");
      }
    }
  }
}
```

Only the first method is invoked by the delegate. Because the first method throws an exception, iterating the delegates stops here and method `Two` is never invoked. The result might differ because the order of calling the methods is not defined:

```
One
Exception Caught
```

> **NOTE** *Errors and exceptions are explained in detail in Chapter 14, "Errors and Exceptions."*

In such a scenario, you can avoid the problem by iterating the list on your own. The `Delegate` class defines the method `GetInvocationList` that returns an array of `Delegate` objects. You can now use this delegate to invoke the methods associated with them directly, catch exceptions, and continue with the next iteration:

```
static void Main()
{
  Action d1 = One;
  d1 += Two;

  Delegate[] delegates = d1.GetInvocationList();
  foreach (Action d in delegates)
  {
    try
    {
      d();
    }
    catch (Exception)
    {
      WriteLine("Exception caught");
    }
  }
}
```

When you run the application with the code changes, you can see that the iteration continues with the next method after the exception is caught:

```
One
Exception caught
Two
```

Anonymous Methods

Up to this point, a method must already exist for the delegate to work (that is, the delegate is defined with the same signature as the method(s) it will be used with). However, there is another way to use delegates— with *anonymous methods*. An anonymous method is a block of code that is used as the parameter for the delegate.

The syntax for defining a delegate with an anonymous method doesn't change. It's when the delegate is instantiated that things change. The following simple console application shows how using an anonymous method can work (code file `AnonymousMethods/Program.cs`):

```
using static System.Console;
using System;

namespace Wrox.ProCSharp.Delegates
{
```

```
class Program
{
  static void Main()
  {
    string mid = ", middle part,";

    Func<string, string> anonDel = delegate(string param)
    {
      param += mid;
      param += " and this was added to the string.";
      return param;
    };
    WriteLine(anonDel("Start of string"));

  }
}
}
```

The delegate `Func<string, string>` takes a single string parameter and returns a string. `anonDel` is a variable of this delegate type. Instead of assigning the name of a method to this variable, a simple block of code is used, prefixed by the delegate keyword, followed by a string parameter.

As you can see, the block of code uses a method-level string variable, `mid`, which is defined outside of the anonymous method and adds it to the parameter that was passed in. The code then returns the string value. When the delegate is called, a string is passed in as the parameter and the returned string is output to the console.

The benefit of using anonymous methods is that it reduces the amount of code you have to write. You don't need to define a method just to use it with a delegate. This becomes evident when you define the delegate for an event (events are discussed later in this chapter), and it helps reduce the complexity of code, especially where several events are defined. With anonymous methods, the code does not perform faster. The compiler still defines a method; the method just has an automatically assigned name that you don't need to know.

You must follow a couple of rules when using anonymous methods. You can't have a jump statement (`break`, `goto`, or `continue`) in an anonymous method that has a target outside of the anonymous method. The reverse is also true: A jump statement outside the anonymous method cannot have a target inside the anonymous method.

Unsafe code cannot be accessed inside an anonymous method, and the `ref` and `out` parameters that are used outside of the anonymous method cannot be accessed. Other variables defined outside of the anonymous method can be used.

If you have to write the same functionality more than once, don't use anonymous methods. In this case, instead of duplicating the code, write a named method. You have to write it only once and reference it by its name.

> **NOTE** *The syntax for anonymous methods was introduced with C# 2. With new programs you really don't need this syntax anymore because lambda expressions (explained in the next section) offer the same—and more—functionality. However, you'll find the syntax for anonymous methods in many places in existing source code, which is why it's good to know it.*
>
> *Lambda expressions have been available since C# 3.*

LAMBDA EXPRESSIONS

One way where lambda expressions are used is to assign a lambda expression to a delegate type: implement code inline. Lambda expressions can be used whenever you have a delegate parameter type. The previous example using anonymous methods is modified here to use a lambda expression.

```
using System;
using static System.Console;

namespace Wrox.ProCSharp.Delegates
{
  class Program
  {
    static void Main()
    {
      string mid = ", middle part,";

      Func<string, string> lambda = param =>
        {
            param += mid;
            param += " and this was added to the string.";
            return param;
        };

      WriteLine(lambda("Start of string"));
    }
  }
}
```

The left side of the lambda operator, `=>`, lists the parameters needed. The right side following the lambda operator defines the implementation of the method assigned to the variable `lambda`.

Parameters

With lambda expressions there are several ways to define parameters. If there's only one parameter, just the name of the parameter is enough. The following lambda expression uses the parameter named `s`. Because the delegate type defines a `string` parameter, `s` is of type `string`. The implementation invokes the `String.Format` method to return a string that is finally written to the console when the delegate is invoked: change uppercase `TEST` (code file `LambdaExpressions/Program.cs`):

```
Func<string, string> oneParam = s =>
        $"change uppercase {s.ToUpper()}";
WriteLine(oneParam("test"));
```

If a delegate uses more than one parameter, you can combine the parameter names inside brackets. Here, the parameters x and y are of type `double` as defined by the `Func<double, double, double>` delegate:

```
Func<double, double, double> twoParams = (x, y) => x * y;
WriteLine(twoParams(3, 2));
```

For convenience, you can add the parameter types to the variable names inside the brackets. If the compiler can't match an overloaded version, using parameter types can help resolve the matching delegate:

```
Func<double, double, double> twoParamsWithTypes = (double x, double y) => x * y;
WriteLine(twoParamsWithTypes(4, 2));
```

Multiple Code Lines

If the lambda expression consists of a single statement, a method block with curly brackets and a `return` statement are not needed. There's an implicit `return` added by the compiler:

```
Func<double, double> square = x => x * x;
```

It's completely legal to add curly brackets, a `return` statement, and semicolons. Usually it's just easier to read without them:

```
Func<double, double> square = x =>
  {
    return x * x;
  }
```

However, if you need multiple statements in the implementation of the lambda expression, curly brackets and the `return` statement are required:

```
Func<string, string> lambda = param =>
  {
    param += mid;
    param += " and this was added to the string.";
    return param;
  };
```

Closures

With lambda expressions you can access variables outside the block of the lambda expression. This is known by the term *closure*. Closures are a great feature, but they can also be very dangerous if not used correctly.

In the following example, a lambda expression of type `Func<int, int>` requires one `int` parameter and returns an `int`. The parameter for the lambda expression is defined with the variable x. The implementation also accesses the variable `someVal`, which is outside the lambda expression. As long as you do not assume that the lambda expression creates a new method that is used later when f is invoked, this might not look confusing at all. Looking at this code block, the returned value calling f should be the value from x plus 5, but this might not be the case:

```
int someVal = 5;
Func<int, int> f = x => x + someVal;
```

Assuming the variable `someVal` is later changed, and then the lambda expression is invoked, the new value of `someVal` is used. The result here of invoking f(3) is 10:

```
someVal = 7;
WriteLine(f(3));
```

Similarly, when you're changing the value of a closure variable within the lambda expression, you can access the changed value outside of the lambda expression.

Now, you might wonder how it is possible at all to access variables outside of the lambda expression from within the lambda expression. To understand this, consider what the compiler does when you define a lambda expression. With the lambda expression `x => x + someVal`, the compiler creates an anonymous class that has a constructor to pass the outer variable. The constructor depends on how many variables you access from the outside. With this simple example, the constructor accepts an `int`. The anonymous class contains an anonymous method that has the implementation as defined by the lambda expression, with the parameters and return type:

```
public class AnonymousClass
{
  private int someVal;
  public AnonymousClass(int someVal)
  {
    this.someVal = someVal;
  }
  public int AnonymousMethod(int x) => x + someVal;
}
```

Using the lambda expression and invoking the method creates an instance of the anonymous class and passes the value of the variable from the time when the call is made.

> **NOTE** *In case you are using closures with multiple threads, you can get into concurrency conflicts. It's best to only use immutable types for closures. This way it's guaranteed the value can't change, and synchronization is not needed.*

> **NOTE** *You can use lambda expressions anywhere the type is a delegate. Another use of lambda expressions is when the type is* Expression *or* Expression<T>., *in which case the compiler creates an expression tree. This feature is discussed in Chapter 13, "Language Integrated Query."*

EVENTS

Events are based on delegates and offer a publish/subscribe mechanism to delegates. You can find events everywhere across the framework. In Windows applications, the Button class offers the Click event. This type of event is a delegate. A handler method that is invoked when the Click event is fired needs to be defined, with the parameters as defined by the delegate type.

In the code example shown in this section, events are used to connect the CarDealer and Consumer classes. The CarDealer class offers an event when a new car arrives. The Consumer class subscribes to the event to be informed when a new car arrives.

Event Publisher

You start with a CarDealer class that offers a subscription based on events. CarDealer defines the event named NewCarInfo of type EventHandler<CarInfoEventArgs> with the event keyword. Inside the method NewCar, the event NewCarInfo is fired by invoking the method RaiseNewCarInfo. The implementation of this method verifies whether the delegate is not null and raises the event (code file EventsSample/CarDealer.cs):

```
using static System.Console;
using System;

namespace Wrox.ProCSharp.Delegates
{
  public class CarInfoEventArgs: EventArgs
  {
```

```
      public CarInfoEventArgs(string car)
      {
          Car = car;
      }

      public string Car { get; }
  }

  public class CarDealer
  {
    public event EventHandler<CarInfoEventArgs> NewCarInfo;

    public void NewCar(string car)
    {
      WriteLine($"CarDealer, new car {car}");

      NewCarInfo?.Invoke(this, new CarInfoEventArgs(car));
    }
  }
}
```

> **NOTE** *The null propagation operator* `.?` *used in the previous example is new with C#
> 6. This operator is discussed in Chapter 8, "Operators and Casts."*

The class `CarDealer` offers the event `NewCarInfo` of type `EventHandler<CarInfoEventArgs>`. As a
convention, events typically use methods with two parameters; the first parameter is an object and contains the sender of the event, and the second parameter provides information about the event. The second parameter is different for various event types. .NET 1.0 defined several hundred delegates for events
for all different data types. That's no longer necessary with the generic delegate `EventHandler<T>`.
`EventHandler<TEventArgs>` defines a handler that returns `void` and accepts two parameters. With
`EventHandler<TEventArgs>`, the first parameter needs to be of type `object`, and the second parameter is
of type T. `EventHandler<TEventArgs>` also defines a constraint on T; it must derive from the base class
`EventArgs`, which is the case with `CarInfoEventArgs`:

```
    public event EventHandler<CarInfoEventArgs> NewCarInfo;
```

The delegate `EventHandler<TEventArgs>` is defined as follows:

```
    public delegate void EventHandler<TEventArgs>(object sender, TEventArgs e)
        where TEventArgs: EventArgs
```

Defining the event in one line is a C# shorthand notation. The compiler creates a variable of the delegate
type `EventHandler<CarInfoEventArgs>` and adds methods to subscribe and unsubscribe from the delegate. The long form of the shorthand notation is shown next. This is very similar to auto-properties and full
properties. With events, the `add` and `remove` keywords are used to add and remove a handler to the delegate:

```
    private EventHandler<CarInfoEventArgs> newCarInfo;
    public event EventHandler<CarInfoEventArgs> NewCarInfo
    {
      add
      {
        newCarInfo += value;
      }
      remove
      {
```

```
        newCarInfo -= value;
    }
}
```

> **NOTE** *The long notation to define events is useful if more needs to be done than just adding and removing the event handler, such as adding synchronization for multiple thread access. The WPF controls make use of the long notation to add bubbling and tunneling functionality with the events. You can read more about event bubbling and tunneling events in Chapter 29, "Core XAML."*

The class `CarDealer` fires the event by calling the `Invoke` method of the delegate. This invokes all the handlers that are subscribed to the event. Remember, as previously shown with multicast delegates, the order of the methods invoked is not guaranteed. To have more control over calling the handler methods you can use the `Delegate` class method `GetInvocationList` to access every item in the delegate list and invoke each on its own, as shown earlier.

```
NewCarInfo?.Invoke(this, new CarInfoEventArgs(car));
```

Firing the event is just a one-liner. However, this is only with C# 6. Previous to C# 6, firing the event was more complex. Here is the same functionality implemented before C# 6. Before firing the event, you need to check whether the event is null. Because between a null check and firing the event the event could be set to null by another thread, a local variable is used, as shown in the following example:

```
EventHandler<CarInfoEventArgs> newCarInfo = NewCarInfo;
if (newCarInfo != null)
{
    newCarInfo(this, new CarInfoEventArgs(car));
}
```

With C# 6, all this could be replaced by using null propagation, with a single code line as you've seen earlier.

Before firing the event, it is necessary to check whether the delegate `NewCarInfo` is not `null`. If no one subscribed, the delegate is `null`:

```
protected virtual void RaiseNewCarInfo(string car)
{
    NewCarInfo?.Invoke(this, new CarInfoEventArgs(car));
}
```

Event Listener

The class `Consumer` is used as the event listener. This class subscribes to the event of the `CarDealer` and defines the method `NewCarIsHere` that in turn fulfills the requirements of the `EventHandler<CarInfoEventArgs>` delegate with parameters of type `object` and `CarInfoEventArgs` (code file `EventsSample/Consumer.cs`):

```
using static System.Console;

namespace Wrox.ProCSharp.Delegates
{
    public class Consumer
    {
        private string _name;

        public Consumer(string name)
```

```
        {
          _name = name;
        }

        public void NewCarIsHere(object sender, CarInfoEventArgs e)
        {
          WriteLine($"{_name}: car {e.Car} is new");
        }
      }
    }
```

Now the event publisher and subscriber need to connect. This is done by using the `NewCarInfo` event of the `CarDealer` to create a subscription with `+=`. The consumer *Michael* subscribes to the event, then the consumer *Sebastian*, and next *Michael* unsubscribes with `-=` (code file `EventsSample/Program.cs`):

```
namespace Wrox.ProCSharp.Delegates
{
  class Program
  {
    static void Main()
    {
      var dealer = new CarDealer();

      var daniel = new Consumer("Daniel");
      dealer.NewCarInfo += michael.NewCarIsHere;

      dealer.NewCar("Mercedes");

      var sebastian = new Consumer("Sebastian");
      dealer.NewCarInfo += sebastian.NewCarIsHere;

      dealer.NewCar("Ferrari");

      dealer.NewCarInfo -= sebastian.NewCarIsHere;

      dealer.NewCar("Red Bull Racing");
    }
  }
}
```

Running the application, a Mercedes arrived and Daniel was informed. After that, Sebastian registers for the subscription as well, both Daniel and Sebastian are informed about the new Ferrari. Then Sebastian unsubscribes and only Daniel is informed about the Red Bull:

```
CarDealer, new car Mercedes
Daniel: car Mercedes is new
CarDealer, new car Ferrari
Daniel: car Ferrari is new
Sebastian: car Ferrari is new
CarDealer, new car Red Bull Racing
Daniel: car Red Bull is new
```

Weak Events

With events, the publisher and listener are directly connected. This can be a problem with garbage collection. For example, if a listener is not directly referenced any more, there's still a reference from the publisher. The garbage collector cannot clean up memory from the listener, as the publisher still holds a reference and fires events to the listener.

This strong connection can be resolved by using the weak event pattern and using the `WeakEventManager<T>` as an intermediary between the publisher and listeners.

The preceding example with the `CarDealer` as publisher and the `Consumer` as listener is modified in this section to use the weak event pattern.

The `WeakEventManager<T>` is defined within the `System.Windows` assembly that is not part of .NET Core. This sample is done with a .NET Framework 4.6 console application and does not run on other platforms.

> **NOTE** *With subscribers that are created dynamically, in order to not be in danger of having resource leaks, you need to pay special attention to events. That is, you need to either ensure that you unsubscribe events before the subscribers go out of scope (are not needed any longer), or use weak events. Events often are a reason for memory leaks in applications because subscribers have a long-lived scope, and thus the source cannot be garbage collected as well.*

Using weak events, the event publisher (in the sample code the `CarDealer` class) doesn't need to be changed. No matter—if the tightly coupled events or weak events are used, the implementation is the same. What's different is the implementation of the consumer. The consumer needs to implement the interface `IWeakEventListener`. This interface defines the method `ReceiveWeakEvent` that is called from the weak event manager when the event arrives. The method implementation acts as a proxy and in turn invokes the method `NewCarIsHere` (code file `WeakEvents/Consumer.cs`):

```
using System;
using static System.Console;
using System.Windows;

namespace Wrox.ProCSharp.Delegates
{
  public class Consumer: IWeakEventListener
  {
    private string _name;

    public Consumer(string name)
    {
      this._name = name;
    }

    public void NewCarIsHere(object sender, CarInfoEventArgs e)
    {
      WriteLine("\{_name}: car \{e.Car} is new");
    }

    bool IWeakEventListener.ReceiveWeakEvent(Type managerType,
        object sender, EventArgs e)
    {
      NewCarIsHere(sender, e as CarInfoEventArgs);
      return true;
    }
  }
}
```

Inside the Main method where the publisher and listeners are connected, the connection is now made by using the static AddHandler and RemoveHandler methods from the WeakEventManager<TEventSource, TEventArgs> class (code file WeakEventsSample/Program.cs):

```
var dealer = new CarDealer();
var daniel = new Consumer("Daniel");
WeakEventManager<CarDealer, CarInfoEventArgs>.AddHandler(dealer,
    "NewCarInfo", daniel.NewCarIsHere);
dealer.NewCar("Mercedes");
var sebastian = new Consumer("Sebastian");
WeakEventManager<CarDealer, CarInfoEventArgs>.AddHandler(dealer,
    "NewCarInfo", sebastian.NewCarIsHere);
dealer.NewCar("Ferrari");
WeakEventManager<CarDealer, CarInfoEventArgs>.RemoveHandler(dealer,
    "NewCarInfo", sebastian.NewCarIsHere);
dealer.NewCar("Red Bull Racing");
```

SUMMARY

This chapter provided the basics of delegates, lambda expressions, and events. You learned how to declare a delegate and add methods to the delegate list; you learned how to implement methods called by delegates with lambda expressions; and you learned the process of declaring event handlers to respond to an event, as well as how to create a custom event and use the patterns for raising the event.

Using delegates and events in the design of a large application can reduce dependencies and the coupling of layers. This enables you to develop components that have a higher reusability factor.

Lambda expressions are C# language features based on delegates. With these, you can reduce the amount of code you need to write. Lambda expressions are not only used with delegates, as you see in Chapter 13.

The next chapter covers the use of strings and regular expressions.

10

Strings and Regular Expressions

WHAT'S IN THIS CHAPTER?

➤ Building strings

➤ Formatting expressions

➤ Using regular expressions

WROX.COM CODE DOWNLOADS FOR THIS CHAPTER

The wrox.com code downloads for this chapter are found at www.wrox.com/go/professionalcsharp6 on the Download Code tab. The code for this chapter is divided into the following major examples:

➤ StringSample

➤ StringFormats

➤ RegularExpressionPlayground

Strings have been used consistently since the beginning of this book, as every program needs strings. However, you might not have realized that the stated mapping that the `string` keyword in C# actually refers to is the `System.String` .NET base class. `String` is a very powerful and versatile class, but it is by no means the only string-related class in the .NET armory. This chapter begins by reviewing the features of `String` and then looks at some nifty things you can do with strings using some of the other .NET classes—in particular those in the `System.Text` and `System.Text.RegularExpressions` namespaces. This chapter covers the following areas:

➤ **Building strings**—If you're performing repeated modifications on a string—for example, to build a lengthy string prior to displaying it or passing it to some other method or application—the `String` class can be very inefficient. When you find yourself in this kind of situation, another class, `System.Text.StringBuilder`, is more suitable because it has been designed exactly for this scenario.

➤ **Formatting expressions**—This chapter takes a closer look at the formatting expressions that have been used in the `Console.WriteLine` method throughout the past few chapters. These formatting expressions are processed using two useful interfaces: `IFormatProvider` and `IFormattable`. By implementing these interfaces on your own classes, you can define your own formatting sequences so that `Console.WriteLine` and similar classes display the values of your classes in whatever way you specify.

> ➤ **Regular expressions**—.NET also offers some very sophisticated classes that deal with cases in which you need to identify or extract substrings that satisfy certain fairly sophisticated criteria; for example, finding all occurrences within a string where a character or set of characters is repeated: finding all words that begin with "s" and contain at least one "n:" or strings that adhere to an employee ID or a Social Security number construction. Although you can write methods to perform this kind of processing using the `String` class, writing such methods is cumbersome. Instead, some classes, specifically those from `System.Text.RegularExpressions`, are designed to perform this kind of processing.

EXAMINING SYSTEM.STRING

Before digging into the other string classes, this section briefly reviews some of the available methods in the `String` class itself.

`System.String` is a class specifically designed to store a string and allow a large number of operations on the string. In addition, due to the importance of this data type, C# has its own keyword and associated syntax to make it particularly easy to manipulate strings using this class.

You can concatenate strings using operator overloads:

```
string message1 = "Hello"; // returns "Hello"
message1 += ", There"; // returns "Hello, There"
string message2 = message1 + "!"; // returns "Hello, There!"
```

C# also allows extraction of a particular character using an indexer-like syntax:

```
string message = "Hello";
char char4 = message[4]; // returns 'o'. Note the string is zero-indexed
```

This enables you to perform such common tasks as replacing characters, removing whitespace, and changing case. The following table introduces the key methods.

METHOD	DESCRIPTION
Compare	Compares the contents of strings, taking into account the culture (locale) in assessing equivalence between certain characters.
CompareOrdinal	Same as `Compare` but doesn't take culture into account.
Concat	Combines separate string instances into a single instance.
CopyTo	Copies a specific number of characters from the selected index to an entirely new instance of an array.
Format	Formats a string containing various values and specifies how each value should be formatted.
IndexOf	Locates the first occurrence of a given substring or character in the string.
IndexOfAny	Locates the first occurrence of any one of a set of characters in a string.
Insert	Inserts a string instance into another string instance at a specified index.
Join	Builds a new string by combining an array of strings.
LastIndexOf	Same as `IndexOf` but finds the last occurrence.
LastIndexOfAny	Same as `IndexOfAny` but finds the last occurrence.
PadLeft	Pads out the string by adding a specified repeated character to the left side of the string.
PadRight	Pads out the string by adding a specified repeated character to the right side of the string.

METHOD	DESCRIPTION
Replace	Replaces occurrences of a given character or substring in the string with another character or substring.
Split	Splits the string into an array of substrings; the breaks occur wherever a given character occurs.
Substring	Retrieves the substring starting at a specified position in a string.
ToLower	Converts the string to lowercase.
ToUpper	Converts the string to uppercase.
Trim	Removes leading and trailing whitespace.

> **NOTE** *Please note that this table is not comprehensive; it is intended to give you an idea of the features offered by strings.*

Building Strings

As you have seen, `String` is an extremely powerful class that implements a large number of very useful methods. However, the `String` class has a shortcoming that makes it very inefficient for making repeated modifications to a given string—it is actually an *immutable* data type, which means that after you initialize a string object, that string object can never change. The methods and operators that appear to modify the contents of a string actually create new strings, copying across the contents of the old string if necessary. For example, consider the following code (code file `StringSample/Program.cs`):

```
string greetingText = "Hello from all the guys at Wrox Press. ";
greetingText += "We do hope you enjoy this book as much as we enjoyed writing it.";
```

The samples in this chapter make use of the following dependencies and namespaces (unless otherwise noted):

Dependencies

```
NETStandard.Library
```

Namespaces

```
System
System.Text
static System.Console
```

When this code executes, first an object of type `System.String` is created and initialized to hold the text `Hello from all the guys at Wrox Press.` (Note that there's a space *after* the period.) When this happens, the .NET runtime allocates just enough memory in the string to hold this text (39 chars), and the variable `greetingText` is set to refer to this string instance.

In the next line, syntactically it looks like more text is being added onto the string, but it is not. Instead, a new string instance is created with just enough memory allocated to store the combined text—that's 103 characters in total. The original text, `Hello from all the people at Wrox Press.`, is copied into this new string instance along with the extra text: `We do hope you enjoy this book as much as we enjoyed writing it.` Then, the address stored in the variable `greetingText` is updated, so the variable correctly points to the new `String` object. The old `String` object is now unreferenced—there are no variables that refer to it—so it will be removed the next time the garbage collector comes along to clean out any unused objects in your application.

By itself, that doesn't look too bad, but suppose you wanted to create a very simple encryption scheme by adding 1 to the ASCII value of each character in the string. This would change the string to Ifmmp gspn bmm uif hvst bu Xspy Qsftt. Xf ep ipqf zpv fokpz uijt cppl bt nvdi bt xf fokpzfe xsjujoh ju. Several ways of doing this exist, but the simplest and (if you are restricting yourself to using the String class) almost certainly the most efficient way is to use the String.Replace method, which replaces all occurrences of a given substring in a string with another substring. Using Replace, the code to encode the text looks like this (code file StringSample/Program.cs):

```
string greetingText = "Hello from all the guys at Wrox Press. ";
greetingText += "We do hope you enjoy this book as much as we " +
    "enjoyed writing it.";

WriteLine($"Not encoded:\n {greetingText}");

for(int i = 'z'; i>= 'a'; i--)
{
  char old1 = (char)i;
  char new1 = (char)(i+1);
  greetingText = greetingText.Replace(old1, new1);
}

for(int i = 'Z'; i>='A'; i--)
{
  char old1 = (char)i;
  char new1 = (char)(i+1);
  greetingText = greetingText.Replace(old1, new1);
}

WriteLine($"Encoded:\n {greetingText}");
```

> **NOTE** *Simply, this code does not change Z to A or z to a. These letters are encoded to [and {, respectively.*

In this example, the Replace method works in a fairly intelligent way, to the extent that it won't actually create a new string unless it actually makes changes to the old string. The original string contained 23 different lowercase characters and three different uppercase ones. The Replace method will therefore have allocated a new string 26 times in total, with each new string storing 103 characters. That means because of the encryption process, there will be string objects capable of storing a combined total of 2,678 characters now sitting on the heap waiting to be garbage collected! Clearly, if you use strings to do text processing extensively, your applications will run into severe performance problems.

To address this kind of issue, Microsoft supplies the System.Text.StringBuilder class. StringBuilder is not as powerful as String in terms of the number of methods it supports. The processing you can do on a StringBuilder is limited to substitutions and appending or removing text from strings. However, it works in a much more efficient way.

When you construct a string using the String class, just enough memory is allocated to hold the string object. The StringBuilder, however, normally allocates more memory than is actually needed. You, as a developer, have the option to indicate how much memory the StringBuilder should allocate; but if you do not, the amount defaults to a value that varies according to the size of the string with which the StringBuilder instance is initialized. The StringBuilder class has two main properties:

➤ Length—Indicates the length of the string that it actually contains
➤ Capacity—Indicates the maximum length of the string in the memory allocation

Any modifications to the string take place within the block of memory assigned to the StringBuilder instance, which makes appending substrings and replacing individual characters within strings very efficient. Removing or inserting substrings is inevitably still inefficient because it means that the following part of the string has to be moved. Only if you perform an operation that exceeds the capacity of the string is it necessary to allocate new memory and possibly move the entire contained string. In adding extra capacity, based on our experiments the StringBuilder appears to double its capacity if it detects that the capacity has been exceeded and no new value for capacity has been set.

For example, if you use a StringBuilder object to construct the original greeting string, you might write this code:

```
var greetingBuilder =
  new StringBuilder("Hello from all the guys at Wrox Press. ", 150);
greetingBuilder.AppendFormat("We do hope you enjoy this book as much " +
  "as we enjoyed writing it");
```

> **NOTE** *To use the* StringBuilder *class, you need a* System.Text *reference in your code.*

This code sets an initial capacity of 150 for the StringBuilder. It is always a good idea to set a capacity that covers the likely maximum length of a string, to ensure that the StringBuilder does not need to relocate because its capacity was exceeded. By default, the capacity is set to 16. Theoretically, you can set a number as large as the number you pass in an int, although the system will probably complain that it does not have enough memory if you actually try to allocate the maximum of two billion characters (the theoretical maximum that a StringBuilder instance is allowed to contain).

Then, on calling the AppendFormat method, the remaining text is placed in the empty space, without the need to allocate more memory. However, the real efficiency gain from using a StringBuilder is realized when you make repeated text substitutions. For example, if you try to encrypt the text in the same way as before, you can perform the entire encryption without allocating any more memory whatsoever:

```
var greetingBuilder =
  new StringBuilder("Hello from all the guys at Wrox Press. ", 150);
greetingBuilder.AppendFormat("We do hope you enjoy this book as much " +
  "as we enjoyed writing it");

WriteLine("Not Encoded:\n" + greetingBuilder);

for(int i = 'z'; i>='a'; i--)
{
  char old1 = (char)i;
  char new1 = (char)(i+1);
  greetingBuilder = greetingBuilder.Replace(old1, new1);
}

for(int i = 'Z'; i>='A'; i--)
{
  char old1 = (char)i;
  char new1 = (char)(i+1);
  greetingBuilder = greetingBuilder.Replace(old1, new1);
}

WriteLine("Encoded:\n" + greetingBuilder);
```

This code uses the `StringBuilder.Replace` method, which does the same thing as `String.Replace` but without copying the string in the process. The total memory allocated to hold strings in the preceding code is 150 characters for the `StringBuilder` instance, as well as the memory allocated during the string operations performed internally in the final `WriteLine` statement.

Normally, you want to use `StringBuilder` to perform any manipulation of strings, and `String` to store or display the final result.

StringBuilder Members

You have seen a demonstration of one constructor of `StringBuilder`, which takes an initial string and capacity as its parameters. There are others. For example, you can supply only a string:

```
var sb = new StringBuilder("Hello");
```

Or you can create an empty `StringBuilder` with a given capacity:

```
var sb = new StringBuilder(20);
```

Apart from the `Length` and `Capacity` properties, there is a read-only `MaxCapacity` property that indicates the limit to which a given `StringBuilder` instance is allowed to grow. By default, this is specified by `int.MaxValue` (roughly two billion, as noted earlier), but you can set this value to something lower when you construct the `StringBuilder` object:

```
// This will set the initial capacity to 100, but the max will be 500.
// Hence, this StringBuilder can never grow to more than 500 characters,
// otherwise it will raise an exception if you try to do that.
var sb = new StringBuilder(100, 500);
```

You can also explicitly set the capacity at any time, though an exception is raised if you set the capacity to a value less than the current length of the string or a value that exceeds the maximum capacity:

```
var sb = new StringBuilder("Hello");
sb.Capacity = 100;
```

The following table lists the main `StringBuilder` methods.

METHOD	DESCRIPTION
Append	Appends a string to the current string.
AppendFormat	Appends a string that has been formatted from a format specifier.
Insert	Inserts a substring into the current string.
Remove	Removes characters from the current string.
Replace	Replaces all occurrences of a character with another character or a substring with another substring in the current string.
ToString	Returns the current string cast to a `System.String` object (overridden from `System.Object`).

Several overloads of many of these methods exist.

> **NOTE** `AppendFormat` *is actually the method that is ultimately called when you call* `Console.WriteLine`, *which is responsible for determining what all the format expressions like* `{0:D}` *should be replaced with. This method is examined in the next section.*

There is no cast (either implicit or explicit) from StringBuilder to String. If you want to output the contents of a StringBuilder as a String, you must use the ToString method.

Now that you have been introduced to the StringBuilder class and have learned some of the ways in which you can use it to increase performance, be aware that this class does not always deliver the increased performance you are seeking. Basically, you should use the StringBuilder class when you are manipulating multiple strings. However, if you are just doing something as simple as concatenating two strings, you will find that System.String performs better.

STRING FORMATS

In previous chapters you've seen passing variables to strings with the $ prefix. This chapter examines what's behind this new feature of C# 6 and covers all the other functionality offered by format strings.

String Interpolation

C# 6 introduces string interpolation by using the $ prefix for strings. The following example creates the string s2 using the $ prefix. This prefix allows having placeholders in curly brackets to reference results from code. {s1} is a placeholder in the string, where the compiler puts into the value of variable s1 into the string s2 (code file StringFormats/Program.cs):

```
string s1 = "World";
string s2 = $"Hello, {s1}";
```

In reality, this is just syntax sugar. From strings with the $ prefix, the compiler creates invocations to the String.Format method. So the previous code snippet gets translated to this:

```
string s1 = "World";
string s2 = String.Format("Hello, {0}", s1);
```

The first parameter of the String.Format method that is used accepts a format string with placeholders that are numbered starting from 0, followed by the parameters that are put into the string holes.

The new string format is just a lot handier and doesn't require that much code to write.

It's not just variables you can use to fill in the holes of the string. Any method that returns a value can be used:

```
string s2 = $"Hello, {s1.ToUpper()}";
```

This translates to a similar statement:

```
string s2 = String.Format("Hello, {0}", s1.ToUpper());
```

It's also possible to have multiple holes in the string, like so:

```
int x = 3, y = 4;
string s3 = $"The result of {x} + {y} is {x + y}";
```

which translates to

```
string s3 = String.Format("The result of {0} and {1} is {2}", x, y, x + y);
```

FormattableString

What the interpolated string gets translated to can easily be seen by assigning the string to a FormattableString. The interpolated string can be directly assigned because the FormattableString is a better match than the normal string. This type defines a Format property that returns the resulting format string, an ArgumentCount property, and the method GetArgument to return the values:

```
int x = 3, y = 4;
FormattableString s = $"The result of {x} + {y} is {x + y}";
```

```
WriteLine($"format: {s.Format}");
for (int i = 0; i < s.ArgumentCount; i++)
{
    WriteLine($"argument {i}: {s.GetArgument(i)}");
}
```

Running this code snippet results in this output:

```
format: The result of {0} + {1} is {2}
argument 0: 3
argument 1: 4
argument 2: 7
```

> **NOTE** *The class* FormattableString *is defined in the* System *namespace but requires .NET 4.6. In case you would like to use the* FormattableString *with older .NET versions, you can create this type on your own, or use the* StringInterpolationBridge *NuGet package.*

Using Other Cultures with String Interpolation

Interpolated strings by default make use of the current culture. This can be changed easily. The helper method Invariant changes the interpolated string to use the invariant culture instead of the current one. As interpolated strings can be assigned to a FormattableString type, they can be passed to this method. FormattableString defines a ToString method that allows passing an IFormatProvider. The interface IFormatProvider is implemented by the CultureInfo class. Passing CultureInfo.InvariantCulture to the IFormatProvider parameter changes the string to use the invariant culture:

```
private string Invariant(FormattableString s) =>
    s.ToString(CultureInfo.InvariantCulture);
```

> **NOTE** *Chapter 28, "Localization," discusses language-specific issues for format strings as well as cultures and invariant cultures.*

In the following code snippet, the Invariant method is used to pass a string to the second WriteLine method. The first invocation of WriteLine uses the current culture while the second one uses the invariant culture:

```
var day = new DateTime(2025, 2, 14);
WriteLine($"{day:d}");
WriteLine(Invariant($"{day:d}"));
```

If you have the English-US culture setting, the result is shown here. If you have a different culture configured with your system, the first result differs. In any case, you see a difference with the invariant culture:

```
2/14/2025
02/14/2015
```

For using the invariant culture, you don't need to implement your own method; instead you can use the static Invariant method of the FormattableString class directly:

```
WriteLine(FormattableString.Invariant($"{day:d}"));
```

Escaping Curly Brackets

In case you want the curly brackets in an interpolated string, you can escape those using double curly brackets:

```
string s = "Hello";
WriteLine($"{{s}} displays the value of s: {s}");
```

The `WriteLine` method is translated to this implementation:

```
WriteLine(String.Format("{s} displays the value of s: {0}", s));
```

Thus the output is:

```
{s} displays the value of s : Hello
```

You can also escape curly brackets to build a new format string from a format string. Let's have a look at this code snippet:

```
string formatString = $"{s}, {{0}}";
string s2 = "World";
WriteLine(formatString, s2);
```

With the string variable `formatString`, the compiler creates a call to `String.Format` just by putting a placeholder 0 to insert the variable s:

```
string formatString = String.Format("{0}, {{0}}", s);
```

This in turn results in this format string where the variable s is replaced with the value `Hello`, and the outermost curly brackets of the second format are removed:

```
string formatString = "Hello, {0}";
```

With the `WriteLine` method in the last line, now the string `World` gets inserted into the new placeholder 0 using the value of the variable s2:

```
WriteLine("Hello, World");
```

DateTime and Number Formats

Other than just using string formats for placeholders, specific formats depending on a data type are available. Let's start with a date. A format string follows the expressions within the placeholder separated by a colon. Examples shown here are the D and d format for the `DateTime` type:

```
var day = new DateTime(2025, 2, 14);
WriteLine($"{day:D}");
WriteLine($"{day:d}");
```

The result shows a long date format string with the uppercase D and a short date string with the lowercase d:

```
Friday, February 14, 2025
2/14/2025
```

The `DateTime` type results in different outputs depending on uppercase or lowercase strings used. Depending on the language setting of your system, the output might look different. The date and time is language specific.

The `DateTime` type supports a lot of different standard format strings to have all date and time representations—for example, t for a short time format and T for a long time format, g and G to display date and time. All the other options are not discussed here, as you can find them in the MSDN documentation for the `ToString` method of the `DateTime` type.

> **NOTE** *One thing that should be mentioned is building a custom format string for* DateTime. *A custom date and time format string can combine format specifiers, such as* dd-MMM-yyyy:
>
> ```
> WriteLine($"{day:dd-MMM-yyyy}");
> ```
>
> *The result is shown here:*
>
> ```
> 14-Feb-2025
> ```
>
> *This custom format string makes use of* dd *to display two digits for the day (this is important if the day is before the 10th, here you can see a difference between* d *and* dd*),* MMM *for an abbreviated name of the month (pay attention to uppercase,* mm *specifies minutes) and* yyyy *for the year with a four-digit number. Again, you can find all the other format specifiers for custom date and time format strings in the MSDN documentation.*

Format strings for numbers don't differentiate between uppercase and lowercase. Let's have a look at the n, e, x, and c standard numeric format strings:

```
int i = 2477;
WriteLine($"{i:n} {i:e} {i:x} {i:c}");
```

The n format string defines a number format to show integral and decimal digits with group separators, e using exponential notation, x for a conversion to hexadecimal, and c to display a currency:

```
2,477.00 2.477000e+003 9ad $2,477.00
```

For numeric representations you can also use custom format strings. The # format specifier is a digit placeholder and displays a digit if available, otherwise no digit appears. The 0 format specifier is a zero placeholder and displays the corresponding digit or zero if a digit is not present.

```
double d = 3.1415;
WriteLine($"{d:###.###}");
WriteLine($"{d:000.000}");
```

With the double value from the sample code, the first result rounds the value after the comma to three digits; with the second result three digits before the comma are shown as well:

```
3.142
003.142
```

The MSDN documentation gives information on all the standard numeric format strings for percent, round-trip and fixed-point displays, and custom format strings for different looks for exponential value displays, decimal points, group separators, and more.

Custom String Formats

Format strings are not restricted to built-in types; you can create your own format strings for your own types. You just need to implement the interface IFormattable.

Start with a simple Person class that contains FirstName and LastName properties (code file StringFormats/Person.cs):

```
public class Person
{
  public string FirstName { get; set; }
  public string LastName { get; set; }
}
```

For a simple string presentation of this class, the `ToString` method of the base class is overridden. This method returns a string consisting of `FirstName` and `LastName`:

```
public override string ToString() => FirstName + " " + LastName;
```

Other than a simple string representation, the `Person` class should also support the format strings `F` to just return the first name, `L` for the last name, and `A`, which stands for "all" and should give the same string representation as the `ToString` method. To implement custom strings, the interface `IFormattable` defines the method `ToString` with two parameters: a string parameter for the format and an `IFormatProvider` parameter. The `IFormatProvider` parameter is not used in the sample code. You can use this parameter for different representations based on the culture, as the `CultureInfo` class implements this interface.

Other classes that implement this interface are `NumberFormatInfo` and `DateTimeFormatInfo`. You can use these classes to configure string representations for numbers and `DateTime` passing instances to the second parameter of the `ToString` method. The implementation of the `ToString` method just uses the `switch` statement to return different strings based on the format string. To allow calling the `ToString` method directly just with the format string without a format provider, the `ToString` method is overloaded. This method in turn invokes the `ToString` method with two parameters:

```
public class Person : IFormattable
{
  public string FirstName { get; set; }
  public string LastName { get; set; }

  public override string ToString() => FirstName + " " + LastName;

  public virtual string ToString(string format) => ToString(format, null);

  public string ToString(string format, IFormatProvider formatProvider)
  {
    switch (format)
    {
      case null:
      case "A":
        return ToString();
      case "F":
        return FirstName;
      case "L":
        return LastName;
      default:
        throw new FormatException($"invalid format string {format}");
    }
  }
}
```

With this in place, you can invoke the `ToString` method explicitly by passing a format string or implicitly by using string interpolation. The implicit call makes use of the two-parameter `ToString` passing `null` with the `IFormatProvider` parameter (code file `StringFormats/Program.cs`):

```
var p1 = new Person { FirstName = "Stephanie", LastName = "Nagel" };
WriteLine(p1.ToString("F"));
WriteLine($"{p1:F}");
```

REGULAR EXPRESSIONS

Regular expressions are one of those small technology aids that are incredibly useful in a wide range of programs. You can think of regular expressions as a mini-programming language with one specific purpose: to locate substrings within a large string expression. It is not a new technology; it originated in the UNIX environment and is commonly used with the Perl programming language, as well as with JavaScript. Regular expressions are supported by a number of .NET classes in the namespace `System`.

`Text.RegularExpressions`. You can also find the use of regular expressions in various parts of the .NET Framework. For instance, they are used within the ASP.NET validation server controls.

If you are not familiar with the regular expressions language, this section introduces both regular expressions and their related .NET classes. If you are familiar with regular expressions, you may want to just skim through this section to pick out the references to the .NET base classes. You might like to know that the .NET regular expression engine is designed to be mostly compatible with Perl 5 regular expressions, although it has a few extra features.

Introduction to Regular Expressions

The regular expressions language is designed specifically for string processing. It contains two features:

➤ A set of escape codes for identifying specific types of characters. You are probably familiar with the use of the * character to represent any substring in command-line expressions. (For example, the command `Dir Re*` lists the files with names beginning with `Re`.) Regular expressions use many sequences like this to represent items such as *any one character, a word break, one optional character,* and so on.

➤ A system for grouping parts of substrings and intermediate results during a search operation

With regular expressions, you can perform very sophisticated and high-level operations on strings. For example, you can do all of the following:

➤ Identify (and perhaps either flag or remove) all repeated words in a string (for example., "The computer books books" to "The computer books")

➤ Convert all words to title case (for example, "this is a Title" to "This Is A Title")

➤ Convert all words longer than three characters to title case (for example, "this is a Title" to "This is a Title")

➤ Ensure that sentences are properly capitalized

➤ Separate the various elements of a URI (for example, given `http://www.wrox.com`, extract the protocol, computer name, filename, and so on)

Of course, all these tasks can be performed in C# using the various methods on `System.String` and `System.Text.StringBuilder`. However, in some cases, this would require writing a fair amount of C# code. Using regular expressions, this code can normally be compressed to just a couple of lines. Essentially, you instantiate a `System.Text.RegularExpressions.RegEx` object (or, even simpler, invoke a static `RegEx` method), pass it the string to be processed, and pass in a regular expression (a string containing the instructions in the regular expressions language), and you're done.

A regular expression string looks at first sight rather like a regular string, but interspersed with escape sequences and other characters that have a special meaning. For example, the sequence \b indicates the beginning or end of a word (a word boundary), so if you wanted to indicate you were looking for the characters th at the beginning of a word, you would search for the regular expression, \bth (that is, the sequence word boundary-t-h). If you wanted to search for all occurrences of th at the end of a word, you would write th\b (the sequence t-h-word boundary). However, regular expressions are much more sophisticated than that and include, for example, facilities to store portions of text that are found in a search operation. This section only scratches the surface of the power of regular expressions.

> **NOTE** *For more on regular expressions, please see Andrew Watt's* Beginning Regular Expressions *(John Wiley & Sons, 2005).*

Suppose your application needed to convert U.S. phone numbers to an international format. In the United States, the phone numbers have the format 314-123-1234, which is often written as (314) 123-1234. When converting this national format to an international format, you have to include +1 (the country code of the

United States) and add parentheses around the area code: +1 (314) 123-1234. As find-and-replace operations go, that is not too complicated. It would still require some coding effort if you were going to use the `String` class for this purpose (meaning you would have to write your code using the methods available from `System.String`). The regular expressions language enables you to construct a short string that achieves the same result.

This section is intended only as a very simple example, so it concentrates on searching strings to identify certain substrings, not on modifying them.

The RegularExpressionsPlayground Example

The regular expression samples in this chapter make use of the following dependencies and namespaces:

Dependencies

```
NETStandard.Library
```

Namespaces

```
System
System.Text.RegularExpressions
static System.Console
```

The rest of this section develops a short example called `RegularExpressionsPlayground` that illustrates some of the features of regular expressions, and how to use the .NET regular expressions engine in C# by performing and displaying the results of some searches. The text you are going to use as your sample document is part of the introduction to the previous edition of this book (code file `RegularExpressionsPlayground/Program.cs`):

```
const string input =
    @"This book is perfect for both experienced C# programmers looking to " +
    "sharpen their skills and professional developers who are using C# for " +
    "the first time. The authors deliver unparalleled coverage of " +
    "Visual Studio 2013 and .NET Framework 4.5.1 additions, as well as " +
    "new test-driven development and concurrent programming features. " +
    "Source code for all the examples are available for download, so you " +
    "can start writing Windows desktop, Windows Store apps, and ASP.NET " +
    "web applications immediately.";
```

> **NOTE** *This code nicely illustrates the utility of verbatim strings that are prefixed by the @ symbol. This prefix is extremely helpful with regular expressions.*

This text is referred to as the *input string*. To get your bearings and get used to the regular expressions of .NET classes, you start with a basic plain-text search that does not feature any escape sequences or regular expression commands. Suppose that you want to find all occurrences of the string ion. This search string is referred to as the *pattern*. Using regular expressions and the input variable declared previously, you could write the following:

```
public static void Find1(text)
{
    const string pattern = "ion";
    MatchCollection matches = Regex.Matches(text, pattern,
                        RegexOptions.IgnoreCase |
                        RegexOptions.ExplicitCapture);
```

```
      foreach (Match nextMatch in matches)
      {
         WriteLine(nextMatch.Index);
      }
   }
}
```

This code uses the static method `Matches` of the `Regex` class in the `System.Text.RegularExpressions` namespace. This method takes as parameters some input text, a pattern, and a set of optional flags taken from the `RegexOptions` enumeration. In this case, you have specified that all searching should be case-insensitive. The other flag, `ExplicitCapture`, modifies how the match is collected in a way that, for your purposes, makes the search a bit more efficient—you see why this is later in this chapter (although it does have other uses that we don't explore here). `Matches` returns a reference to a `MatchCollection` object. A *match* is the technical term for the results of finding an instance of the pattern in the expression. It is represented by the class `System.Text.RegularExpressions.Match`. Therefore, you return a `MatchCollection` that contains all the matches, each represented by a `Match` object. In the preceding code, you simply iterate over the collection and use the `Index` property of the `Match` class, which returns the index in the input text where the match was found. Running this code results in three matches. The following table details some of the `RegexOptions` enumerations.

MEMBER NAME	DESCRIPTION
CultureInvariant	Specifies that the culture of the string is ignored.
ExplicitCapture	Modifies the way the match is collected by making sure that valid captures are the ones that are explicitly named.
IgnoreCase	Ignores the case of the string that is input.
IgnorePatternWhitespace	Removes unescaped whitespace from the string and enables comments that are specified with the pound or hash sign.
Multiline	Changes the characters ^ and $ so that they are applied to the beginning and end of each line and not just to the beginning and end of the entire string.
RightToLeft	Causes the inputted string to be read from right to left instead of the default left to right (ideal for some Asian and other languages that are read in this direction).
Singleline	Specifies a single-line mode where the meaning of the dot (.) is changed to match every character.

So far, nothing is new from the preceding example apart from some .NET base classes. However, the power of regular expressions comes from that pattern string. The reason is that the pattern string is not limited to only plain text. As hinted earlier, it can also contain what are known as *meta-characters*, which are special characters that provide commands, as well as escape sequences, which work in much the same way as C# escape sequences. They are characters preceded by a backslash (\) and have special meanings.

For example, suppose you wanted to find words beginning with n. You could use the escape sequence \b, which indicates a word boundary (a word boundary is just a point where an alphanumeric character precedes or follows a whitespace character or punctuation symbol):

```
const string pattern = @"\bn";
MatchCollection myMatches = Regex.Matches(input, pattern,
                            RegexOptions.IgnoreCase |
                            RegexOptions.ExplicitCapture);
```

Notice the @ character in front of the string. You want the \b to be passed to the .NET regular expressions engine at runtime—you don't want the backslash intercepted by a well-meaning C# compiler that thinks it's an escape sequence in your source code. If you want to find words ending with the sequence ions, you write this:

```
const string pattern = @"ions\b";
```

If you want to find all words beginning with the letter a and ending with the sequence ions (which has as its only match the words *additions* and *applications* in the example), you have to put a bit more thought into your code. You clearly need a pattern that begins with \ba and ends with ions\b, but what goes in the middle? You need to somehow tell the applications that between the a and the ions there can be any number of characters as long as none of them are whitespace. In fact, the correct pattern looks like this:

```
const string pattern = @"\ba\S*ions\b";
```

Eventually you will get used to seeing weird sequences of characters like this when working with regular expressions. It actually works quite logically. The escape sequence \S indicates any character that is not a whitespace character. The * is called a *quantifier*. It means that the preceding character can be repeated any number of times, including zero times. The sequence \S* means *any number of characters as long as they are not whitespace characters*. The preceding pattern, therefore, matches any single word that begins with a and ends with ions.

The following table lists some of the main special characters or escape sequences that you can use. It is not comprehensive; a fuller list is available in the MSDN documentation.

SYMBOL	DESCRIPTION	EXAMPLE	MATCHES
^	Beginning of input text	^B	B, but only if first character in text
$	End of input text	X$	X, but only if last character in text
.	Any single character except the newline character (\)	i.ation	isation, ization
*	Preceding character may be repeated zero or more times	ra*t	rt, rat, raat, raaat, and so on
+	Preceding character may be repeated one or more times	ra+t	rat, raat, raaat and so on, but not rt
?	Preceding character may be repeated zero or one time	ra?t	rt and rat only
\s	Any whitespace character	\sa	[space]a, \ta, \na (\t and \n have the same meanings as in C#)
\S	Any character that isn't whitespace	\SF	aF, rF, cF, but not \tf
\b	Word boundary	ion\b	Any word ending in ion
\B	Any position that isn't a word boundary	\BX\B	Any X in the middle of a word

If you want to search for one of the meta-characters, you can do so by escaping the corresponding character with a backslash. For example, . (a single period) means any single character other than the newline character, whereas \. means a dot.

You can request a match that contains alternative characters by enclosing them in square brackets. For example, [1c] means one character that can be either 1 or c. If you wanted to search for any occurrence of the words map or man, you would use the sequence ma[np]. Within the square brackets, you can also indicate a range, for example [a-z], to indicate any single lowercase letter, [A-E] to indicate any uppercase letter between A and E (including the letters A and E themselves), or [0-9] to represent a single digit. A shorthand notation for [0-9] is \d. If you wanted to search for an integer (that is, a sequence that contains only the characters 0 through 9), you could write [0-9]+ or [\d]+.

The ^ has a different meaning used within square brackets. Used outside square brackets, it marks the beginning of input text. Within square brackets, it means any character except the following.

> **NOTE** *The use of the + character specifies there must be at least one such digit, but there may be more than one—so this would match 9, 83, 854, and so on.*

Displaying Results

In this section, you code the `RegularExpressionsPlayground` example to get a feel for how regular expressions work.

The core of the example is a method called `WriteMatches`, which writes out all the matches from a `MatchCollection` in a more detailed format. For each match, it displays the index of where the match was found in the input string, the string of the match, and a slightly longer string, which consists of the match plus up to 10 surrounding characters from the input text—up to five characters before the match and up to five afterward. (It is fewer than five characters if the match occurred within five characters of the beginning or end of the input text.) In other words, a match on the word `applications` that occurs near the end of the input text quoted earlier when starting with the `RegularExpressionPlayground` example would display `web applications imme` (five characters before and after the match), but a match on the final word `immediately` would display `ions immediately.` (only one character after the match), because after that you get to the end of the string. This longer string enables you to see more clearly where the regular expression locates the match:

```
public static void WriteMatches(string text, MatchCollection matches)
{
   WriteLine($"Original text was: \n\n{text}\n");
   WriteLine($"No. of matches: {matches.Count}");

   foreach (Match nextMatch in matches)
   {
      int index = nextMatch.Index;
      string result = nextMatch.ToString();
      int charsBefore = (index < 5) ? index : 5;
      int fromEnd = text.Length - index - result.Length;
      int charsAfter = (fromEnd < 5) ? fromEnd : 5;
      int charsToDisplay = charsBefore + charsAfter + result.Length;
      WriteLine($"Index: {index}, \tString: {result}, \t" +
         "{text.Substring(index - charsBefore, charsToDisplay)}");
   }
}
```

The bulk of the processing in this method is devoted to the logic of figuring out how many characters in the longer substring it can display without overrunning the beginning or end of the input text. Note that you use another property on the `Match` object, `Value`, which contains the string identified for the match. Other than that, `RegularExpressionsPlayground` simply contains a number of methods with names such as `Find1`, `Find2`, and so on, which perform some of the searches based on the examples in this section. For example, `Find2` looks for any string that contains a at the beginning of a word and ions at the end:

```
public static void Find2(string text)
{
   string pattern = @"\ba\S*ions\b";
   MatchCollection matches = Regex.Matches(text, pattern,
      RegexOptions.IgnoreCase);
   WriteMatches(text, matches);
}
```

Along with this is a simple `Main` method that you can edit to select one of the `Find<n>` methods:

```
public static void Main()
{
  Find2();
  ReadLine();
}
```

The code also needs to make use of the `RegularExpressions` namespace:

```
using System;
using System.Text.RegularExpressions;
```

Running the example with the `Find2` method shown previously gives these results:

```
No. of matches: 2
Index: 243,     String: additions,     .5.1 additions, as
Index: 469,     String: applications,  web applications imme
```

Matches, Groups, and Captures

One nice feature of regular expressions is that you can group characters. It works the same way as compound statements in C#. In C#, you can group any number of statements by putting them in braces, and the result is treated as one compound statement. In regular expression patterns, you can group any characters (including meta-characters and escape sequences), and the result is treated as a single character. The only difference is that you use parentheses instead of braces. The resultant sequence is known as a group.

For example, the pattern `(an)+` locates any occurrences of the sequence an. The + quantifier applies only to the previous character, but because you have grouped the characters together, it now applies to repeats of an treated as a unit. This means that if you apply `(an)+` to the input text, `bananas came to Europe late in the annals of history`, the anan from bananas is identified; however, if you write an+, the program selects the ann from annals, as well as two separate sequences of an from bananas. The expression `(an)+` identifies occurrences of an, anan, ananan, and so on, whereas the expression an+ identifies occurrences of an, ann, annn, and so on.

> **NOTE** *You might be wondering why with the preceding example* `(an)+` *selects* anan *from the word "banana" but doesn't identify either of the two occurrences of* an *from the same word. The rule is that matches must not overlap. If a couple of possibilities would overlap, then by default the longest possible sequence is matched.*

Groups are even more powerful than that. By default, when you form part of the pattern into a group, you are also asking the regular expression engine to remember any matches against just that group, as well as any matches against the entire pattern. In other words, you are treating that group as a pattern to be matched and returned in its own right. This can be extremely useful if you want to break up strings into component parts.

For example, URIs have the format `<protocol>://<address>:<port>`, where the port is optional. An example of this is `http://www.wrox.com:80`. Suppose you want to extract the protocol, the address, and the port from a URI in which there may or may not be whitespace (but no punctuation) immediately following the URI. You could do so using this expression:

```
\b(https?)(://)([.\w]+)([\s:]([\d]{2,5})?)\b
```

Here is how this expression works: First, the leading and trailing \b sequences ensure that you consider only portions of text that are entire words. Within that, the first group, `(https?)` identifies either the http or https protocol. ? after the s character specifies that this character might come 0 or 1 times, thus http and https are allowed. The parentheses cause the protocol to be stored as a group.

The second group is a simple one with (://). This just specifies the characters :// in that order.

The third group ([.\w]+) is more interesting. This group contains a parenthetical expression of either the . character (dot), or any alphanumeric character specified by \w. These characters can be repeated any time, and thus matches www.wrox.com.

The fourth group ([\s:]([\d]{2,5})?) is a longer expression that contains an inner group. The first parenthetical expression within this group allows either whitespace characters specified by \s or the colon. The inner group specifies a digit with [\d]. The expression {2,5} specifies that the preceding character (the digit) is allowed at least two times and not more than five times. The complete expression with the digits is allowed 0 or 1 time specified by ? that follows the inner group. Having this group optional is very important because the port number is not always specified in a URI; in fact, it is usually absent.

Let's define a string to run this expression on (code file RegularExpressionsPlayground/Program.cs):

```
string line = "Hey, I've just found this amazing URI at " +
    "http:// what was it -oh yes https://www.wrox.com or " +
    "http://www.wrox.com:80";
```

The code to match with this expression uses the Matches method similar to what was used before. The difference is that you iterate all Group objects within the Match.Groups property and write the resulting index and value of every group to the console:

```
string pattern = @"\b(https?)(://)([.\w]+)([\s:]([\d]{2,4})?)\b";
var r = new Regex(pattern);
MatchCollection mc = r.Matches(line);

foreach (Match m in mc)
{
  WriteLine($"Match: {m}");
  foreach (Group g in m.Groups)
  {
    if (g.Success)
    {
      WriteLine($"group index: {g.Index}, value: {g.Value}");
    }
  }
  WriteLine();
}
```

Running the program, these groups and values are found:

```
Match https://www.wrox.com
group index 70, value: https://www.wrox.com
group index 70, value: https
group index 75, value: ://
group index 78, value: www.wrox.com
group index 90, value:

Match http://www.wrox.com:80
group index 94, value http://www.wrox.com:80
group index 94, value: http
group index 98, value: ://
group index 101, value: www.wrox.com
group index 113, value: :80
group index 114, value: 80
```

With this, the URI from the text is matched, and the different parts of the URI are nicely grouped. However, grouping offers more features. Some groups, such as the separation between the protocol and the address, can be ignored, and groups can also be named.

Change the regular expression to name every group and to ignore some. Specifying ?<name> at the beginning of a group names a group. For example, the regular expression groups for protocol, address, and port are named accordingly. You ignore groups using ?: at the group's beginning. Don't be confused by ?:// within the group. You are searching for ://, and the group is ignored by placing ?: in front of this:

```
string pattern = @"\b(?<protocol>https?)(?:://)" +
    @"(?<address>[.\w]+)([\s:](?<port>[\d]{2,4})?)\b";
```

To get the groups from a regular expression, the Regex class defines the method GetGroupNames. In the code snippet, all the group names are used with every match to write group name and values using the Groups property and indexer:

```
Regex r = new Regex(pattern, RegexOptions.ExplicitCapture);

MatchCollection mc = r.Matches(line);
foreach (Match m in mc)
{
  WriteLine($"match: {m} at {m.Index}");

  foreach (var groupName in r.GetGroupNames())
  {
    WriteLine($"match for {groupName}: {m.Groups[groupName].Value}");
  }
}
```

Running the program you can see the name of the groups with their values:

```
match: https://www.wrox.com  at 70
match for 0: https://www.wrox.com
match for protocol: https
match for address: www.wrox.com
match for port:

match: http://www.wrox.com:80 at 94
match for 0: http://www.wrox.com:80
match for protocol: http
match for address: www.wrox.com
match for port: 80
```

SUMMARY

You have quite a number of available data types at your disposal when working with the .NET Framework. One of the most frequently used types in your applications (especially applications that focus on submitting and retrieving data) is the string data type. The importance of string is the reason why this book has an entire chapter that focuses on how to use the string data type and manipulate it in your applications.

When working with strings in the past, it was quite common to just slice and dice the strings as needed using concatenation. With the .NET Framework, you can use the StringBuilder class to accomplish a lot of this task with better performance than before.

Another feature of strings is the new C# 6 string interpolation. In most applications this feature can make string handling a lot easier.

Last, but hardly least, advanced string manipulation using regular expressions is an excellent tool to search through and validate your strings.

The next chapter is the first of two parts covering different collection classes.

11

Collections

WHAT'S IN THIS CHAPTER?

➤ Understanding collection interfaces and types

➤ Working with lists, queues, and stacks

➤ Working with linked and sorted lists

➤ Using dictionaries and sets

➤ Evaluating performance

WROX.COM CODE DOWNLOADS FOR THIS CHAPTER

The wrox.com code downloads for this chapter are found at `http://www.wrox.com/go/professionalcsharp6` on the Download Code tab. The code for this chapter is divided into the following major examples:

➤ List Samples

➤ Queue Sample

➤ Linked List Sample

➤ Sorted List Sample

➤ Dictionary Sample

➤ Set Sample

OVERVIEW

Chapter 7, "Arrays and Tuples," covers arrays and the interfaces implemented by the `Array` class. The size of arrays is fixed. If the number of elements is dynamic, you should use a collection class instead of an array.

`List<T>` is a collection class that can be compared to arrays; but there are also other kinds of collections: queues, stacks, linked lists, dictionaries, and sets. The other collection classes have partly different APIs to access the elements in the collection and often a different internal structure for how the items are stored in memory. This chapter covers all of these collection classes and their differences, including performance differences.

This chapter also discusses bit arrays and concurrent collections that can be used from multiple threads.

COLLECTION INTERFACES AND TYPES

Most collection classes are in the `System.Collections` and `System.Collections.Generic` namespaces. Generic collection classes are located in the `System.Collections.Generic` namespace. Collection classes that are specialized for a specific type are located in the `System.Collections.Specialized` namespace. Thread-safe collection classes are in the `System.Collections.Concurrent` namespace. Immutable collection classes are in the `System.Collections.Immutable` namespace.

Of course, there are also other ways to group collection classes. Collections can be grouped into lists, collections, and dictionaries based on the interfaces that are implemented by the collection class.

> **NOTE** *You can read detailed information about the interfaces* `IEnumerable` *and* `IEnumerator` *in Chapter 7.*

The following table describes the most important interfaces implemented by collections and lists.

INTERFACE	DESCRIPTION
`IEnumerable<T>`	The interface `IEnumerable` is required by the `foreach` statement. This interface defines the method `GetEnumerator`, which returns an enumerator that implements the `IEnumerator` interface.
`ICollection<T>`	`ICollection<T>` is implemented by generic collection classes. With this you can get the number of items in the collection (`Count` property), and copy the collection to an array (`CopyTo` method). You can also add and remove items from the collection (`Add`, `Remove`, `Clear`).
`IList<T>`	The `IList<T>` interface is for lists where elements can be accessed from their position. This interface defines an indexer, as well as ways to insert or remove items from specific positions (`Insert`, `RemoveAt` methods). `IList<T>` derives from `ICollection<T>`.
`ISet<T>`	This interface is implemented by sets. Sets allow combining different sets into a union, getting the intersection of two sets, and checking whether two sets overlap. `ISet<T>` derives from `ICollection<T>`.
`IDictionary<TKey, TValue>`	The interface `IDictionary<TKey, TValue>` is implemented by generic collection classes that have a key and a value. With this interface all the keys and values can be accessed, items can be accessed with an indexer of type `key`, and items can be added or removed.
`ILookup<TKey, TValue>`	Similar to the `IDictionary<TKey, TValue>` interface, lookups have keys and values. However, with lookups the collection can contain multiple values with one key.
`IComparer<T>`	The interface `IComparer<T>` is implemented by a comparer and used to sort elements inside a collection with the `Compare` method.
`IEqualityComparer<T>`	`IEqualityComparer<T>` is implemented by a comparer that can be used for keys in a dictionary. With this interface the objects can be compared for equality.

LISTS

For resizable lists, the .NET Framework offers the generic class List<T>. This class implements the IList, ICollection, IEnumerable, IList<T>, ICollection<T>, and IEnumerable<T> interfaces.

The following examples use the members of the class Racer as elements to be added to the collection to represent a Formula-1 racer. This class has five properties: Id, FirstName, LastName, Country, and the number of Wins. With the constructors of the class, the name of the racer and the number of wins can be passed to set the members. The method ToString is overridden to return the name of the racer. The class Racer also implements the generic interface IComparable<T> for sorting racer elements and IFormattable (code file ListSamples/Racer.cs):

```csharp
public class Racer: IComparable<Racer>, IFormattable
{
  public int Id { get; }
  public string FirstName { get; set; }
  public string LastName { get; set; }
  public string Country { get; set; }
  public int Wins { get; set; }

  public Racer(int id, string firstName, string lastName, string country)
    :this(id, firstName, lastName, country, wins: 0)
  { }

  public Racer(int id, string firstName, string lastName, string country,
               int wins)
  {
    Id = id;
    FirstName = firstName;
    LastName = lastName;
    Country = country;
    Wins = wins;
  }
  public override string ToString() => $"{FirstName} {LastName}";
  public string ToString(string format, IFormatProvider formatProvider)
  {
    if (format == null) format = "N";
    switch (format.ToUpper())
    {
      case "N": // name
        return ToString();
      case "F": // first name
        return FirstName;
      case "L": // last name
        return LastName;
      case "W": // Wins
        return $"{ToString()}, Wins: {Wins}";
      case "C": // Country
        return $"{ToString()}, Country: {Country}";
      case "A": // All
        return $"{ToString()}, Country: {Country} Wins: {Wins}";
      default:
        throw new FormatException(String.Format(formatProvider,
                  $"Format {format} is not supported"));
    }
  }
  public string ToString(string format) => ToString(format, null);
  public int CompareTo(Racer other)
  {
    int compare = LastName?.CompareTo(other?.LastName) ?? -1;
    if (compare == 0)
```

```
        {
            return FirstName?.CompareTo(other?.FirstName) ?? -1;
        }
        return compare;
    }
}
```

Creating Lists

You can create list objects by invoking the default constructor. With the generic class `List<T>`, you must specify the type for the values of the list with the declaration. The following code shows how to declare a `List<T>` with `int` and a list with `Racer` elements. `ArrayList` is a non-generic list that accepts any `Object` type for its elements.

Using the default constructor creates an empty list. As soon as elements are added to the list, the capacity of the list is extended to allow 4 elements. If the fifth element is added, the list is resized to allow 8 elements. If 8 elements are not enough, the list is resized again to contain 16 elements. With every resize the capacity of the list is doubled.

```
var intList = new List<int>();
var racers = new List<Racer>();
```

When the capacity of the list changes, the complete collection is reallocated to a new memory block. With the implementation of `List<T>`, an array of type `T` is used. With reallocation, a new array is created, and `Array.Copy` copies the elements from the old array to the new array. To save time, if you know the number of elements in advance, that should be in the list; you can define the capacity with the constructor. The following example creates a collection with a capacity of 10 elements. If the capacity is not large enough for the elements added, the capacity is resized to 20 and then to 40 elements—doubled again:

```
List<int> intList = new List<int>(10);
```

You can get and set the capacity of a collection by using the `Capacity` property:

```
intList.Capacity = 20;
```

The capacity is not the same as the number of elements in the collection. The number of elements in the collection can be read with the `Count` property. Of course, the capacity is always larger or equal to the number of items. As long as no element was added to the list, the count is 0:

```
WriteLine(intList.Count);
```

If you are finished adding elements to the list and don't want to add any more, you can get rid of the unneeded capacity by invoking the `TrimExcess` method; however, because the relocation takes time, `TrimExcess` has no effect if the item count is more than 90 percent of capacity:

```
intList.TrimExcess();
```

Collection Initializers

You can also assign values to collections using collection initializers. The syntax of collection initializers is similar to array initializers, which are explained in Chapter 7. With a collection initializer, values are assigned to the collection within curly brackets at the time the collection is initialized:

```
var intList = new List<int>() {1, 2};
var stringList = new List<string>() {"one", "two"};
```

> **NOTE** *Collection initializers are not reflected within the IL code of the compiled assembly. The compiler converts the collection initializer to invoke the* Add *method for every item from the initializer list.*

Adding Elements

You can add elements to the list with the `Add` method, shown in the following example. The generic instantiated type defines the parameter type of the `Add` method:

```
var intList = new List<int>();
intList.Add(1);
intList.Add(2);

var stringList = new List<string>();
stringList.Add("one");
stringList.Add("two");
```

The variable `racers` is defined as type `List<Racer>`. With the `new` operator, a new object of the same type is created. Because the class `List<T>` was instantiated with the concrete class `Racer`, now only `Racer` objects can be added with the `Add` method. In the following sample code, five Formula-1 racers are created and added to the collection. The first three are added using the collection initializer, and the last two are added by explicitly invoking the `Add` method (code file `ListSamples/Program.cs`):

```
var graham = new Racer(7, "Graham", "Hill", "UK", 14);
var emerson = new Racer(13, "Emerson", "Fittipaldi", "Brazil", 14);
var mario = new Racer(16, "Mario", "Andretti", "USA", 12);

var racers = new List<Racer>(20) {graham, emerson, mario};

racers.Add(new Racer(24, "Michael", "Schumacher", "Germany", 91));
racers.Add(new Racer(27, "Mika", "Hakkinen", "Finland", 20));
```

With the `AddRange` method of the `List<T>` class, you can add multiple elements to the collection at once. The method `AddRange` accepts an object of type `IEnumerable<T>`, so you can also pass an array as shown here:

```
racers.AddRange(new Racer[] {
    new Racer(14, "Niki", "Lauda", "Austria", 25),
    new Racer(21, "Alain", "Prost", "France", 51)});
```

> **NOTE** *The collection initializer can be used only during declaration of the collection. The* `AddRange` *method can be invoked after the collection is initialized. In case you get the data dynamically after creating the collection, you need to invoke* `AddRange`*.*

If you know some elements of the collection when instantiating the list, you can also pass any object that implements `IEnumerable<T>` to the constructor of the class. This is very similar to the `AddRange` method:

```
var racers = new List<Racer>(
    new Racer[] {
        new Racer(12, "Jochen", "Rindt", "Austria", 6),
        new Racer(22, "Ayrton", "Senna", "Brazil", 41) });
```

Inserting Elements

You can insert elements at a specified position with the `Insert` method:

```
racers.Insert(3, new Racer(6, "Phil", "Hill", "USA", 3));
```

The method `InsertRange` offers the capability to insert a number of elements, similar to the `AddRange` method shown earlier.

If the index set is larger than the number of elements in the collection, an exception of type `ArgumentOutOfRangeException` is thrown.

Accessing Elements

All classes that implement the `IList` and `IList<T>` interface offer an indexer, so you can access the elements by using an indexer and passing the item number. The first item can be accessed with an index value 0. By specifying `racers[3]`, for example, you access the fourth element of the list:

```
Racer r1 = racers[3];
```

When you use the `Count` property to get the number of elements, you can do a `for` loop to iterate through every item in the collection, and you can use the indexer to access every item:

```
for (int i = 0; i < racers.Count; i++)
{
   WriteLine(racers[i]);
}
```

> **NOTE** *Indexed access to collection classes is available with* `ArrayList`, `StringCollection`, *and* `List<T>`.

Because `List<T>` implements the interface `IEnumerable`, you can iterate through the items in the collection using the `foreach` statement as well:

```
foreach (var r in racers)
{
   WriteLine(r);
}
```

> **NOTE** *Chapter 7 explains how the foreach statement is resolved by the compiler to make use of the* `IEnumerable` *and* `IEnumerator` *interfaces.*

Removing Elements

You can remove elements by index or pass the item that should be removed. Here, the fourth element is removed from the collection:

```
racers.RemoveAt(3);
```

You can also directly pass a `Racer` object to the `Remove` method to remove this element. Removing by index is faster, because here the collection must be searched for the item to remove. The `Remove` method first searches in the collection to get the index of the item with the `IndexOf` method and then uses the index to remove the item. `IndexOf` first checks whether the item type implements the interface `IEquatable<T>`. If it does, the `Equals` method of this interface is invoked to find the item in the collection that is the same as the one passed to the method. If this interface is not implemented, the `Equals` method of the `Object` class is used to compare the items. The default implementation of the `Equals` method in the `Object` class does a bitwise compare with value types, but compares only references with reference types.

> **NOTE** *Chapter 8, "Operators and Casts," explains how you can override the* `Equals` *method.*

In the following example, the racer referenced by the variable graham is removed from the collection. The variable graham was created earlier when the collection was filled. Because the interface IEquatable<T> and the Object.Equals method are not overridden with the Racer class, you cannot create a new object with the same content as the item that should be removed and pass it to the Remove method:

```
if (!racers.Remove(graham))
{
    WriteLine("object not found in collection");
}
```

The method RemoveRange removes a number of items from the collection. The first parameter specifies the index where the removal of items should begin; the second parameter specifies the number of items to be removed:

```
int index = 3;
int count = 5;
racers.RemoveRange(index, count);
```

To remove all items with some specific characteristics from the collection, you can use the RemoveAll method. This method uses the Predicate<T> parameter when searching for elements, which is discussed next. To remove all elements from the collection, use the Clear method defined with the ICollection<T> interface.

Searching

There are different ways to search for elements in the collection. You can get the index to the found item, or the item itself. You can use methods such as IndexOf, LastIndexOf, FindIndex, FindLastIndex, Find, and FindLast. To just check whether an item exists, the List<T> class offers the Exists method.

The method IndexOf requires an object as parameter and returns the index of the item if it is found inside the collection. If the item is not found, –1 is returned. Remember that IndexOf is using the IEquatable<T> interface to compare the elements (code file ListSamples/Program.cs):

```
int index1 = racers.IndexOf(mario);
```

With the IndexOf method, you can also specify that the complete collection should not be searched, instead specifying an index where the search should start and the number of elements that should be iterated for the comparison.

Instead of searching a specific item with the IndexOf method, you can search for an item that has some specific characteristics that you can define with the FindIndex method. FindIndex requires a parameter of type Predicate:

```
public int FindIndex(Predicate<T> match);
```

The Predicate<T> type is a delegate that returns a Boolean value and requires type T as parameter. If the predicate returns true, there's a match, and the element is found. If it returns false, the element is not found, and the search continues.

```
public delegate bool Predicate<T>(T obj);
```

With the List<T> class that is using Racer objects for type T, you can pass the address of a method that returns a bool and defines a parameter of type Racer to the FindIndex method. Finding the first racer of a specific country, you can create the FindCountry class as shown next. The FindCountryPredicate method has the signature and return type defined by the Predicate<T> delegate. The Find method uses the variable country to search for a country that you can pass with the constructor of the class (code file ListSamples/FindCountry.cs):

```
public class FindCountry
{
    public FindCountry(string country)
```

```
  {
    _country = country;
  }
  private string _country;

  public bool FindCountryPredicate(Racer racer) =>
    racer?.Country == _country;
}
```

With the `FindIndex` method, you can create a new instance of the `FindCountry` class, pass a country string to the constructor, and pass the address of the `Find` method. In the following example, after `FindIndex` completes successfully, `index2` contains the index of the first item where the `Country` property of the racer is set to Finland (code file `ListSamples/Program.cs`):

```
int index2 = racers.FindIndex(new FindCountry("Finland").
                    FindCountryPredicate);
```

Instead of creating a class with a handler method, you can use a lambda expression here as well. The result is exactly the same as before. Now the lambda expression defines the implementation to search for an item where the `Country` property is set to `Finland`:

```
int index3 = racers.FindIndex(r => r.Country == "Finland");
```

Similar to the `IndexOf` method, with the `FindIndex` method you can also specify the index where the search should start and the count of items that should be iterated through. To do a search for an index beginning from the last element in the collection, you can use the `FindLastIndex` method.

The method `FindIndex` returns the index of the found item. Instead of getting the index, you can also go directly to the item in the collection. The `Find` method requires a parameter of type `Predicate<T>`, much as the `FindIndex` method. The `Find` method in the following example searches for the first racer in the list that has the `FirstName` property set to `Niki`. Of course, you can also do a `FindLast` search to find the last item that fulfills the predicate.

```
Racer racer = racers.Find(r => r.FirstName == "Niki");
```

To get not only one but all the items that fulfill the requirements of a predicate, you can use the `FindAll` method. The `FindAll` method uses the same `Predicate<T>` delegate as the `Find` and `FindIndex` methods. The `FindAll` method does not stop when the first item is found; instead the `FindAll` method iterates through every item in the collection and returns all items for which the predicate returns `true`.

With the `FindAll` method invoked in the next example, all racer items are returned where the property `Wins` is set to more than 20. All racers who won more than 20 races are referenced from the `bigWinners` list:

```
List<Racer> bigWinners = racers.FindAll(r => r.Wins > 20);
```

Iterating through the variable `bigWinners` with a `foreach` statement gives the following result:

```
foreach (Racer r in bigWinners)
{
  WriteLine($"{r:A}");
}
```

```
Michael Schumacher, Germany Wins: 91
Niki Lauda, Austria Wins: 25
Alain Prost, France Wins: 51
```

The result is not sorted, but you'll see that done next.

> **NOTE** *Format specifiers and the* `IFormattable` *interface is discussed in detail in Chapter 10, "Strings and Regular Expressions."*

Sorting

The `List<T>` class enables sorting its elements by using the `Sort` method. `Sort` uses the quick sort algorithm whereby all elements are compared until the complete list is sorted.

You can use several overloads of the `Sort` method. The arguments that can be passed are a generic delegate `Comparison<T>`, the generic interface `IComparer<T>`, and a range together with the generic interface `IComparer<T>`:

```
public void List<T>.Sort();
public void List<T>.Sort(Comparison<T>);
public void List<T>.Sort(IComparer<T>);
public void List<T>.Sort(Int32, Int32, IComparer<T>);
```

Using the `Sort` method without arguments is possible only if the elements in the collection implement the interface `IComparable`.

Here, the class `Racer` implements the interface `IComparable<T>` to sort racers by the last name:

```
racers.Sort();
```

If you need to do a sort other than the default supported by the item types, you need to use other techniques, such as passing an object that implements the `IComparer<T>` interface.

The class `RacerComparer` implements the interface `IComparer<T>` for `Racer` types. This class enables you to sort by the first name, last name, country, or number of wins. The kind of sort that should be done is defined with the inner enumeration type `CompareType`. The `CompareType` is set with the constructor of the class `RacerComparer`. The interface `IComparer<Racer>` defines the method `Compare`, which is required for sorting. In the implementation of this method, the `Compare` and `CompareTo` methods of the `string` and `int` types are used (code file `ListSamples/RacerComparer.cs`):

```
public class RacerComparer : IComparer<Racer>
{
  public enum CompareType
  {
    FirstName,
    LastName,
    Country,
    Wins
  }

  private CompareType _compareType;
  public RacerComparer(CompareType compareType)
  {
    _compareType = compareType;
  }

  public int Compare(Racer x, Racer y)
  {
    if (x == null && y == null) return 0;
    if (x == null) return -1;
    if (y == null) return 1;
    int result;
    switch (_compareType)
    {
      case CompareType.FirstName:
        return string.Compare(x.FirstName, y.FirstName);
      case CompareType.LastName:
        return string.Compare(x.LastName, y.LastName);
      case CompareType.Country:
        result = string.Compare(x.Country, y.Country);
        if (result == 0)
          return string.Compare(x.LastName, y.LastName);
        else
```

```
        return result;
    case CompareType.Wins:
        return x.Wins.CompareTo(y.Wins);
    default:
        throw new ArgumentException("Invalid Compare Type");
    }
  }
}
```

> **NOTE** *The* Compare *method returns 0 if the two elements passed to it are equal with the order. If a value less than 0 is returned, the first argument is less than the second. With a value larger than 0, the first argument is greater than the second. Passing null with an argument, the method shouldn't throw a* NullReferenceException. *Instead, null should take its place before any other element; thus −1 is returned if the first argument is null, and +1 if the second argument is null.*

You can now use an instance of the RacerComparer class with the Sort method. Passing the enumeration RacerComparer.CompareType.Country sorts the collection by the property Country:

```
racers.Sort(new RacerComparer(RacerComparer.CompareType.Country));
```

Another way to do the sort is by using the overloaded Sort method, which requires a Comparison<T> delegate:

```
public void List<T>.Sort(Comparison<T>);
```

Comparison<T> is a delegate to a method that has two parameters of type T and a return type int. If the parameter values are equal, the method must return 0. If the first parameter is less than the second, a value less than zero must be returned; otherwise, a value greater than zero is returned:

```
public delegate int Comparison<T>(T x, T y);
```

Now you can pass a lambda expression to the Sort method to do a sort by the number of wins. The two parameters are of type Racer, and in the implementation the Wins properties are compared by using the int method CompareTo. Also in the implementation, r2 and r1 are used in reverse order, so the number of wins is sorted in descending order. After the method has been invoked, the complete racer list is sorted based on the racer's number of wins:

```
racers.Sort((r1, r2) => r2.Wins.CompareTo(r1.Wins));
```

You can also reverse the order of a complete collection by invoking the Reverse method.

Read-Only Collections

After collections are created they are read/write, of course; otherwise, you couldn't fill them with any values. However, after the collection is filled, you can create a read-only collection. The List<T> collection has the method AsReadOnly that returns an object of type ReadOnlyCollection<T>. The class ReadOnlyCollection<T> implements the same interfaces as List<T>, but all methods and properties that change the collection throw a NotSupportedException. Beside the interfaces of List<T>, ReadOnlyCollection<T> also implements the interfaces IReadOnlyCollection<T> and IReadOnlyList<T>. With the members of these interfaces, the collection cannot be changed.

QUEUES

A queue is a collection whose elements are processed *first in, first out* (FIFO), meaning the item that is put first in the queue is read first. Examples of queues are standing in line at the airport, a human resources queue to process employee applicants, print jobs waiting to be processed in a print queue, and a thread waiting for the CPU in a round-robin fashion. Sometimes the elements of a queue differ in their priority.

For example, in the queue at the airport, business passengers are processed before economy passengers. In this case, multiple queues can be used, one queue for each priority. At the airport this is easily handled with separate check-in queues for business and economy passengers. The same is true for print queues and threads. You can have an array or a list of queues whereby one item in the array stands for a priority. Within every array item there's a queue, where processing happens using the FIFO principle.

> **NOTE** *Later in this chapter, a different implementation with a linked list is used to define a list of priorities.*

A queue is implemented with the Queue<T> class in the namespace System.Collections.Generic. Internally, the Queue<T> class uses an array of type T, similar to the List<T> type. It implements the interfaces IEnumerable<T> and ICollection, but it doesn't implement ICollection<T> because this interface defines Add and Remove methods that shouldn't be available for queues.

The Queue<T> class does not implement the interface IList<T>, so you cannot access the queue using an indexer. The queue just allows you to add an item to it, which is put at the end of the queue (with the Enqueue method), and to get items from the head of the queue (with the Dequeue method).

Figure 11-1 shows the items of a queue. The Enqueue method adds items to one end of the queue; the items are read and removed at the other end of the queue with the Dequeue method. Invoking the Dequeue method once more removes the next item from the queue.

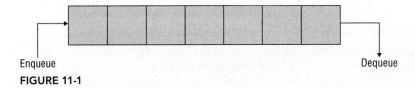

Enqueue   Dequeue

FIGURE 11-1

Methods of the Queue<T> class are described in the following table.

SELECTED QUEUE <T> MEMBERS	DESCRIPTION
Count	Returns the number of items in the queue.
Enqueue	Adds an item to the end of the queue.
Dequeue	Reads and removes an item from the head of the queue. If there are no more items in the queue when the Dequeue method is invoked, an exception of type InvalidOperationException is thrown.
Peek	Reads an item from the head of the queue but does not remove the item.
TrimExcess	Resizes the capacity of the queue. The Dequeue method removes items from the queue, but it doesn't resize the capacity of the queue. To get rid of the empty items at the beginning of the queue, use the TrimExcess method.

When creating queues, you can use constructors similar to those used with the List<T> type. The default constructor creates an empty queue, but you can also use a constructor to specify the capacity. As items are added to the queue, the capacity is increased to hold 4, 8, 16, and 32 items if the capacity is not defined. Similar to the List<T> class, the capacity is always doubled as required. The default constructor of the non-generic Queue class is different because it creates an initial array of 32 empty items. With an overload of the constructor, you can also pass any other collection that implements the IEnumerable<T> interface that is copied to the queue.

The following example demonstrating the use of the Queue<T> class is a document management application. One thread is used to add documents to the queue, and another thread reads documents from the queue and processes them.

The items stored in the queue are of type Document. The Document class defines a title and content (code file QueueSample/Document.cs):

```
public class Document
{
  public string Title { get; private set; }
  public string Content { get; private set; }

  public Document(string title, string content)
  {
    Title = title;
    Content = content;
  }
}
```

The DocumentManager class is a thin layer around the Queue<T> class. It defines how to handle documents: adding documents to the queue with the AddDocument method and getting documents from the queue with the GetDocument method.

Inside the AddDocument method, the document is added to the end of the queue using the Enqueue method. The first document from the queue is read with the Dequeue method inside GetDocument. Because multiple threads can access the DocumentManager concurrently, access to the queue is locked with the lock statement.

> **NOTE** *Threading and the* lock *statement are discussed in Chapter 21, "Tasks and Parallel Programming," and Chapter 22, "Task Synchronization."*

IsDocumentAvailable is a read-only Boolean property that returns true if there are documents in the queue and false if not (code file QueueSample/DocumentManager.cs):

```
public class DocumentManager
{
  private readonly Queue<Document> _documentQueue = new Queue<Document>();

  public void AddDocument(Document doc)
  {
    lock (this)
    {
      _documentQueue.Enqueue(doc);
    }
  }

  public Document GetDocument()
  {
    Document doc = null;
    lock (this)
    {
      doc = _documentQueue.Dequeue();
    }
```

```
        return doc;
    }

    public bool IsDocumentAvailable => _documentQueue.Count > 0;
}
```

The class `ProcessDocuments` processes documents from the queue in a separate task. The only method that can be accessed from the outside is `Start`. In the `Start` method, a new task is instantiated. A `ProcessDocuments` object is created to start the task, and the `Run` method is defined as the start method of the task. The `StartNew` method of the `TaskFactory` (which is accessed from the static `Factory` property of the `Task` class) requires a delegate `Action` parameter where the address of the `Run` method can be passed to. The `StartNew` method of the `TaskFactory` immediately starts the task.

With the `Run` method of the `ProcessDocuments` class, an endless loop is defined. Within this loop, the property `IsDocumentAvailable` is used to determine whether there is a document in the queue. If so, the document is taken from the `DocumentManager` and processed. Processing in this example is writing information only to the console. In a real application, the document could be written to a file, written to the database, or sent across the network (code file QueueSample/ProcessDocuments.cs):

```
public class ProcessDocuments
{
  public static void Start(DocumentManager dm)
  {
    Task.Run(new ProcessDocuments(dm).Run);
  }

  protected ProcessDocuments(DocumentManager dm)
  {
    if (dm == null)
      throw new ArgumentNullException(nameof(dm));
    _documentManager = dm;
  }

  private DocumentManager _documentManager;

  protected async Task Run()
  {
    while (true)
    {
      if (_documentManager.IsDocumentAvailable)
      {
        Document doc = _documentManager.GetDocument();
        WriteLine("Processing document {0}", doc.Title);
      }
      await Task.Delay(new Random().Next(20));
    }
  }
}
```

In the `Main` method of the application, a `DocumentManager` object is instantiated, and the document processing task is started. Then 1,000 documents are created and added to the `DocumentManager` (code file QueueSample/Program.cs):

```
public class Program
{
  public static void Main()
  {
    var dm = new DocumentManager();

    ProcessDocuments.Start(dm);

    // Create documents and add them to the DocumentManager
```

```
        for (int i = 0; i < 1000; i++)
        {
            var doc = new Document($"Doc {i.ToString()}", "content");
            dm.AddDocument(doc);
            WriteLine($"Added document {doc.Title}");
            Thread.Sleep(new Random().Next(20));
        }
    }
}
```

When you start the application, the documents are added to and removed from the queue, and you get output similar to the following:

```
Added document Doc 279
Processing document Doc 236
Added document Doc 280
Processing document Doc 237
Added document Doc 281
Processing document Doc 238
Processing document Doc 239
Processing document Doc 240
Processing document Doc 241
Added document Doc 282
Processing document Doc 242
Added document Doc 283
Processing document Doc 243
```

A real-life scenario using the task described with the sample application might be an application that processes documents received with a Web service.

STACKS

A stack is another container that is very similar to the queue. You just use different methods to access the stack. The item that is added last to the stack is read first, so the stack is a *last in, first out* (LIFO) container.

Figure 11-2 shows the representation of a stack where the Push method adds an item to the stack, and the Pop method gets the item that was added last.

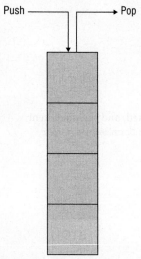

FIGURE 11-2

Similar to the `Queue<T>` class, the `Stack<T>` class implements the interfaces `IEnumerable<T>` and `ICollection`.

Members of the `Stack<T>` class are listed in the following table.

SELECTED STACK<T> MEMBERS	DESCRIPTION
Count	Returns the number of items in the stack.
Push	Adds an item on top of the stack.
Pop	Removes and returns an item from the top of the stack. If the stack is empty, an exception of type `InvalidOperationException` is thrown.
Peek	Returns an item from the top of the stack but does not remove the item.
Contains	Checks whether an item is in the stack and returns `true` if it is.

In this example, three items are added to the stack with the `Push` method. With the `foreach` method, all items are iterated using the `IEnumerable` interface. The enumerator of the stack does not remove the items; it just returns them item by item (code file `StackSample/Program.cs`):

```
var alphabet = new Stack<char>();
alphabet.Push('A');
alphabet.Push('B');
alphabet.Push('C');

foreach (char item in alphabet)
{
    Write(item);
}
WriteLine();
```

Because the items are read in order from the last item added to the first, the following result is produced:

```
CBA
```

Reading the items with the enumerator does not change the state of the items. With the `Pop` method, every item that is read is also removed from the stack. This way, you can iterate the collection using a `while` loop and verify the `Count` property if items still exist:

```
var alphabet = new Stack<char>();
alphabet.Push('A');
alphabet.Push('B');
alphabet.Push('C');

Write("First iteration: ");
foreach (char item in alphabet)
{
    Write(item);
}
WriteLine();

Console.Write("Second iteration: ");
while (alphabet.Count > 0)
{
    Write(alphabet.Pop());
}
WriteLine();
```

The result gives CBA twice—once for each iteration. After the second iteration, the stack is empty because the second iteration used the Pop method:

```
First iteration: CBA
Second iteration: CBA
```

LINKED LISTS

LinkedList<T> is a doubly linked list, whereby one element references the next and the previous one, as shown in Figure 11-3. This way you can easily walk forward through the complete list by moving to the next element, or backward by moving to the previous element.

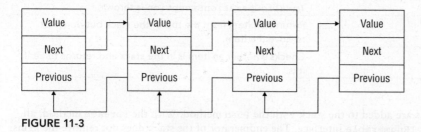

FIGURE 11-3

The advantage of a linked list is that if items are inserted anywhere in the list, the linked list is very fast. When an item is inserted, only the Next reference of the previous item and the Previous reference of the next item must be changed to reference the inserted item. With the List<T> class, when an element is inserted all subsequent elements must be moved.

Of course, there's also a disadvantage with linked lists. Items of linked lists can be accessed only one after the other. It takes a long time to find an item that's somewhere in the middle or at the end of the list.

A linked list cannot just store the items inside the list; together with every item, the linked list must have information about the next and previous items. That's why the LinkedList<T> contains items of type LinkedListNode<T>. With the class LinkedListNode<T>, you can get to the next and previous items in the list. The LinkedListNode<T> class defines the properties List, Next, Previous, and Value. The List property returns the LinkedList<T> object that is associated with the node. Next and Previous are for iterating through the list and accessing the next or previous item. Value returns the item that is associated with the node. Value is of type T.

The LinkedList<T> class itself defines members to access the first (First) and last (Last) item of the list, to insert items at specific positions (AddAfter, AddBefore, AddFirst, AddLast), to remove items from specific positions (Remove, RemoveFirst, RemoveLast), and to find elements where the search starts from either the beginning (Find) or the end (FindLast) of the list.

The sample application to demonstrate linked lists uses a linked list together with a list. The linked list contains documents as in the queue example, but the documents have an additional priority associated with them. The documents will be sorted inside the linked list depending on the priority. If multiple documents have the same priority, the elements are sorted according to the time when the document was inserted.

Figure 11-4 describes the collections of the sample application. LinkedList<Document> is the linked list containing all the Document objects. The figure shows the title and priority of the documents. The title indicates when the document was added to the list: The first document added has the title "One", the second document has the title "Two", and so on. You can see that the documents One and Four have the same priority, 8, but because One was added before Four, it is earlier in the list.

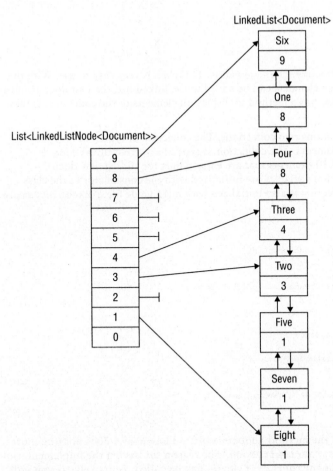

LinkedList<Document>

List<LinkedListNode<Document>>

FIGURE 11-4

When new documents are added to the linked list, they should be added after the last document that has the same priority. The LinkedList<Document> collection contains elements of type LinkedListNode<Document>. The class LinkedListNode<T> adds Next and Previous properties to walk from one node to the next. For referencing such elements, the List<T> is defined as List<LinkedListNode<Document>>. For fast access to the last document of every priority, the collection List<LinkedListNode> contains up to 10 elements, each referencing the last document of every priority. In the upcoming discussion, the reference to the last document of every priority is called the *priority node*.

Using the previous example, the Document class is extended to contain the priority, which is set with the constructor of the class (code file LinkedListSample/Document.cs):

```
public class Document
{
    public string Title { get; private set; }
    public string Content { get; private set; }
    public byte Priority { get; private set; }

    public Document(string title, string content, byte priority)
    {
        Title = title;
```

```
        Content = content;
        Priority = priority;
      }
    }
```

The heart of the solution is the `PriorityDocumentManager` class. This class is very easy to use. With the public interface of this class, new `Document` elements can be added to the linked list, the first document can be retrieved, and for testing purposes it also has a method to display all elements of the collection as they are linked in the list.

The class `PriorityDocumentManager` contains two collections. The collection of type `LinkedList<Document>` contains all documents. The collection of type `List<LinkedListNode <Document>>` contains references of up to 10 elements that are entry points for adding new documents with a specific priority. Both collection variables are initialized with the constructor of the class `PriorityDocumentManager`. The list collection is also initialized with `null` (code file `LinkedListSample/ PriorityDocumentManager.cs`):

```
public class PriorityDocumentManager
{
  private readonly LinkedList<Document> _documentList;

  // priorities 0.9
  private readonly List<LinkedListNode<Document>> _priorityNodes;

  public PriorityDocumentManager()
  {
    _documentList = new LinkedList<Document>();

    _priorityNodes = new List<LinkedListNode<Document>>(10);
    for (int i = 0; i < 10; i++)
    {
      _priorityNodes.Add(new LinkedListNode<Document>(null));
    }
  }
}
```

Part of the public interface of the class is the method `AddDocument`. `AddDocument` does nothing more than call the private method `AddDocumentToPriorityNode`. The reason for having the implementation inside a different method is that `AddDocumentToPriorityNode` may be called recursively, as you will see soon:

```
public void AddDocument(Document d)
{
  if (d == null) throw new ArgumentNullException("d");

  AddDocumentToPriorityNode(d, d.Priority);
}
```

The first action that is done in the implementation of `AddDocumentToPriorityNode` is a check to see if the priority fits in the allowed priority range. Here, the allowed range is between 0 and 9. If a wrong value is passed, an exception of type `ArgumentException` is thrown.

Next, you check whether there's already a priority node with the same priority as the priority that was passed. If there's no such priority node in the list collection, `AddDocumentToPriorityNode` is invoked recursively with the priority value decremented to check for a priority node with the next lower priority.

If there's no priority node with the same priority or any priority with a lower value, the document can be safely added to the end of the linked list by calling the method `AddLast`. In addition, the linked list node is referenced by the priority node that's responsible for the priority of the document.

If there's an existing priority node, you can get the position inside the linked list where the document should be inserted. In the following example, you must determine whether a priority node already exists with the correct priority, or if there's just a priority node that references a document with a lower priority. In the first case, you can insert the new document after the position referenced by the priority node. Because the priority node always must reference the last document with a specific priority, the reference of the priority node must be set. It gets more complex if only a priority node referencing a document with a lower priority exists. Here, the document must be inserted before all documents with the same priority as the priority node. To get the first document of the same priority, a while loop iterates through all linked list nodes, using the Previous property, until a linked list node is reached that has a different priority. This way, you know the position where the document must be inserted, and the priority node can be set:

```
private void AddDocumentToPriorityNode(Document doc, int priority)
{
  if (priority > 9 || priority < 0)
    throw new ArgumentException("Priority must be between 0 and 9");
  if (_priorityNodes[priority].Value == null)
  {
    --priority;
    if (priority <= 0)
    {
      // check for the next lower priority
      AddDocumentToPriorityNode(doc, priority);
    }
    else // now no priority node exists with the same priority or lower
         // add the new document to the end
    {
      _documentList.AddLast(doc);
      _priorityNodes[doc.Priority] = _documentList.Last;
    }
    return;
  }
  else // a priority node exists
  {
    LinkedListNode<Document> prioNode = _priorityNodes[priority];
    if (priority == doc.Priority)
        // priority node with the same priority exists
    {
      _documentList.AddAfter(prioNode, doc);
      // set the priority node to the last document with the same priority
      _priorityNodes[doc.Priority] = prioNode.Next;
    }
    else // only priority node with a lower priority exists
    {
      // get the first node of the lower priority
      LinkedListNode<Document> firstPrioNode = prioNode;
      while (firstPrioNode.Previous != null &&
          firstPrioNode.Previous.Value.Priority == prioNode.Value.Priority)
      {
        firstPrioNode = prioNode.Previous;
        prioNode = firstPrioNode;
      }
      _documentList.AddBefore(firstPrioNode, doc);
      // set the priority node to the new value
      _priorityNodes[doc.Priority] = firstPrioNode.Previous;
    }
  }
}
```

Now only simple methods are left for discussion. DisplayAllNodes does a foreach loop to display the priority and the title of every document to the console.

The method `GetDocument` returns the first document (the document with the highest priority) from the linked list and removes it from the list:

```
public void DisplayAllNodes()
{
  foreach (Document doc in documentList)
  {
    WriteLine($"priority: {doc.Priority}, title {doc.Title}");
  }
}

// returns the document with the highest priority
// (that's first in the linked list)
public Document GetDocument()
{
  Document doc = _documentList.First.Value;
  _documentList.RemoveFirst();
  return doc;
}
```

In the `Main` method, the `PriorityDocumentManager` is used to demonstrate its functionality. Eight new documents with different priorities are added to the linked list, and then the complete list is displayed (code file `LinkedListSample/Program.cs`):

```
public static void Main()
{
  var pdm =  new PriorityDocumentManager();
  pdm.AddDocument(new Document("one", "Sample", 8));
  pdm.AddDocument(new Document("two", "Sample", 3));
  pdm.AddDocument(new Document("three", "Sample", 4));
  pdm.AddDocument(new Document("four", "Sample", 8));
  pdm.AddDocument(new Document("five", "Sample", 1));
  pdm.AddDocument(new Document("six", "Sample", 9));
  pdm.AddDocument(new Document("seven", "Sample", 1));
  pdm.AddDocument(new Document("eight", "Sample", 1));

  pdm.DisplayAllNodes();
}
```

With the processed result, you can see that the documents are sorted first by priority and second by when the document was added:

```
priority: 9, title six
priority: 8, title one
priority: 8, title four
priority: 4, title three
priority: 3, title two
priority: 1, title five
priority: 1, title seven
priority: 1, title eight
```

SORTED LIST

If the collection you need should be sorted based on a key, you can use `SortedList<TKey, TValue>`. This class sorts the elements based on a key. You can use any type for the value, and also for the key.

The following example creates a sorted list for which both the key and the value are of type `string`. The default constructor creates an empty list, and then two books are added with the `Add` method. With over-loaded constructors, you can define the capacity of the list and pass an object that implements the interface `IComparer<TKey>`, which is used to sort the elements in the list.

The first parameter of the Add method is the key (the book title); the second parameter is the value (the ISBN). Instead of using the Add method, you can use the indexer to add elements to the list. The indexer requires the key as index parameter. If a key already exists, the Add method throws an exception of type ArgumentException. If the same key is used with the indexer, the new value replaces the old value (code file SortedListSample/Program.cs):

```
var books = new SortedList<string, string>();
books.Add("Professional WPF Programming", "978-0-470-04180-2");
books.Add("Professional ASP.NET MVC 5", "978-1-118-79475-3");
books["Beginning Visual C# 2012"] = "978-1-118-31441-8";
books["Professional C# 5 and .NET 4.5.1"] = "978-1-118-83303-2";
```

> **NOTE** SortedList<TKey, TValue> *allows only one value per key. If you need multiple values per key you can use* Lookup<TKey, TElement>.

You can iterate through the list using a foreach statement. Elements returned by the enumerator are of type KeyValuePair<TKey, TValue>, which contains both the key and the value. The key can be accessed with the Key property, and the value can be accessed with the Value property:

```
foreach (KeyValuePair<string, string> book in books)
{
   WriteLine($"{book.Key}, {book.Value}");
}
```

The iteration displays book titles and ISBN numbers ordered by the key:

```
Beginning Visual C# 2012, 978-1-118-31441-8
Professional ASP.NET MVC 5, 978-1-118-79475-3
Professional C# 5 and .NET 4.5.1, 978-1-118-83303-2
Professional WPF Programming, 978-0-470-04180-2
```

You can also access the values and keys by using the Values and Keys properties. The Values property returns IList<TValue> and the Keys property returns IList<TKey>, so you can use these properties with a foreach:

```
foreach (string isbn in books.Values)
{
   WriteLine(isbn);
}

foreach (string title in books.Keys)
{
   WriteLine(title);
}
```

The first loop displays the values, and next the keys:

```
978-1-118-31441-8
978-1-118-79475-3
978-1-118-83303-2
978-0-470-04180-2
Beginning Visual C# 2012
Professional ASP.NET MVC 5
Professional C# 5 and .NET 4.5.1
Professional WPF Programming
```

If you try to access an element with an indexer and passing a key that does not exist, an exception of type KeyNotFoundException is thrown. To avoid that exception you can use the method ContainsKey, which returns true if the key passed exists in the collection, or you can invoke the method TryGetValue, which tries to get the value but doesn't throw an exception if it isn't found:

```
string isbn;
string title = "Professional C# 7.0";
if (!books.TryGetValue(title, out isbn))
{
  WriteLine($"{title} not found");
}
```

DICTIONARIES

A dictionary represents a sophisticated data structure that enables you to access an element based on a key. Dictionaries are also known as hash tables or maps. The main feature of dictionaries is fast lookup based on keys. You can also add and remove items freely, a bit like a List<T>, but without the performance overhead of having to shift subsequent items in memory.

Figure 11-5 shows a simplified representation of a dictionary. Here employee-ids such as B4711 are the keys added to the dictionary. The key is transformed into a hash. With the hash a number is created to associate an index with the values. The index then contains a link to the value. The figure is simplified because it is possible for a single index entry to be associated with multiple values, and the index can be stored as a tree.

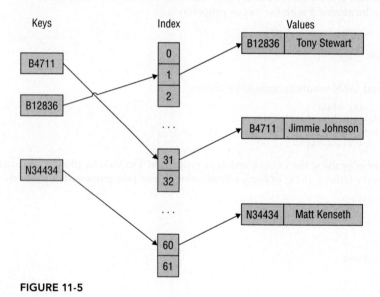

FIGURE 11-5

The .NET Framework offers several dictionary classes. The main class you use is Dictionary<TKey, TValue>.

Dictionary Initializers

C# 6 defines a new syntax to initialize dictionaries at declaration. A dictionary with a key of int and a value of string can be initialized as follows:

```
var dict = new Dictionary<int, string>()
{
  [3] = "three",
  [7] = "seven"
};
```

Here, two elements are added to the dictionary. The first element has a key of 3 and a string value three; the second element has a key of 7 and a string value seven. This initializer syntax is easily readable and uses the same syntax as accessing the elements in the dictionary.

Key Type

A type that is used as a key in the dictionary must override the method GetHashCode of the Object class. Whenever a dictionary class needs to determine where an item should be located, it calls the GetHashCode method. The int that is returned by GetHashCode is used by the dictionary to calculate an index of where to place the element. We won't go into this part of the algorithm; what you should know is that it involves prime numbers, so the capacity of a dictionary is a prime number.

The implementation of GetHashCode must satisfy the following requirements:

➤ The same object should always return the same value.

➤ Different objects can return the same value.

➤ It must not throw exceptions.

➤ It should use at least one instance field.

➤ The hash code should not change during the lifetime of the object.

Besides requirements that must be satisfied by the GetHashCode implementation, it's also good practice to satisfy these requirements:

➤ It should execute as quickly as possible; it must be inexpensive to compute.

➤ The hash code value should be evenly distributed across the entire range of numbers that an int can store.

> **NOTE** *Good performance of the dictionary is based on a good implementation of the method* GetHashCode.

What's the reason for having hash code values evenly distributed across the range of integers? If two keys return hashes that have the same index, the dictionary class needs to start looking for the nearest available free location to store the second item—and it will have to do some searching to retrieve this item later. This is obviously going to hurt performance. In addition, if a lot of your keys are tending to provide the same storage indexes for where they should be stored, this kind of clash becomes more likely. However, because of the way that Microsoft's part of the algorithm works, this risk is minimized when the calculated hash values are evenly distributed between int.MinValue and int.MaxValue.

Besides having an implementation of GetHashCode, the key type also must implement the IEquatable<T>. Equals method or override the Equals method from the Object class. Because different key objects may return the same hash code, the method Equals is used by the dictionary comparing keys. The dictionary examines whether two keys, such as A and B, are equal; it invokes A.Equals(B). This means that you must ensure that the following is always true:

> If A.Equals(B) is true, then A.GetHashCode and B.GetHashCode must always return the same hash code.

This may seem a fairly subtle point, but it is crucial. If you contrived some way of overriding these methods so that the preceding statement were not always true, a dictionary that uses instances of this class as its keys would not work properly. Instead, you'd find funny things happening. For example, you might place an object in the dictionary and then discover that you could never retrieve it, or you might try to retrieve an entry and have the wrong entry returned.

> **NOTE** *For this reason, the C# compiler displays a compilation warning if you supply an override for* Equals *but don't supply an override for* GetHashCode.

For System.Object this condition is true because Equals simply compares references, and GetHashCode actually returns a hash that is based solely on the address of the object. This means that hash tables based on a key that doesn't override these methods will work correctly. However, the problem with this approach is that keys are regarded as equal only if they are the same object. That means when you place an object in the dictionary, you have to hang on to the reference to the key; you can't simply instantiate another key object later with the same value. If you don't override Equals and GetHashCode, the type is not very convenient to use in a dictionary.

Incidentally, System.String implements the interface IEquatable and overloads GetHashCode appropriately. Equals provides value comparison, and GetHashCode returns a hash based on the value of the string. Strings can be used conveniently as keys in dictionaries.

Number types such as Int32 also implement the interface IEquatable and overload GetHashCode. However, the hash code returned by these types simply maps to the value. If the number you would like to use as a key is not itself distributed around the possible values of an integer, using integers as keys doesn't fulfill the rule of evenly distributing key values to get the best performance. Int32 is not meant to be used in a dictionary.

If you need to use a key type that does not implement IEquatable and does not override GetHashCode according to the key values you store in the dictionary, you can create a comparer implementing the interface IEqualityComparer<T>. IEqualityComparer<T> defines the methods GetHashCode and Equals with an argument of the object passed, so you can offer an implementation different from the object type itself. An overload of the Dictionary<TKey, TValue> constructor allows passing an object implementing IEqualityComparer<T>. If such an object is assigned to the dictionary, this class is used to generate the hash codes and compare the keys.

Dictionary Example

The dictionary example in this section is a program that sets up a dictionary of employees. The dictionary is indexed by EmployeeId objects, and each item stored in the dictionary is an Employee object that stores details of an employee.

The struct EmployeeId is implemented to define a key to be used in a dictionary. The members of the class are a prefix character and a number for the employee. Both of these variables are read-only and can be initialized only in the constructor to ensure that keys within the dictionary shouldn't change. When you have read-only variables it is guaranteed that they can't be changed. The fields are filled within the constructor. The ToString method is overloaded to get a string representation of the employee ID. As required for a key type, EmployeeId implements the interface IEquatable and overloads the method GetHashCode (code file DictionarySample/EmployeeId.cs):

```
public class EmployeeIdException : Exception
{
    public EmployeeIdException(string message) : base(message)  { }
}

public struct EmployeeId : IEquatable<EmployeeId>
{
    private readonly char _prefix;
    private readonly int _number;

    public EmployeeId(string id)
    {
```

```
        Contract.Requires<ArgumentNullException>(id != null);

        _prefix = (id.ToUpper())[0];
        int numLength = id.Length - 1;
        try
        {
            _number = int.Parse(id.Substring(1, numLength > 6 ? 6 : numLength));
        }
        catch (FormatException)
        {
            throw new EmployeeIdException("Invalid EmployeeId format");
        }
    }

    public override string ToString() => _prefix.ToString() + $"{number,6:000000}";

    public override int GetHashCode() => (number ^ number << 16) * 0x15051505;

    public bool Equals(EmployeeId other) =>
        (prefix == other?.prefix && number == other?.number);

    public override bool Equals(object obj) => Equals((EmployeeId)obj);

    public static bool operator ==(EmployeeId left, EmployeeId right) =>
        left.Equals(right);

    public static bool operator !=(EmployeeId left, EmployeeId right) =>
        !(left == right);
}
```

The `Equals` method that is defined by the `IEquatable<T>` interface compares the values of two `EmployeeId` objects and returns `true` if both values are the same. Instead of implementing the `Equals` method from the `IEquatable<T>` interface, you can also override the `Equals` method from the `Object` class:

```
    public bool Equals(EmployeeId other) =>
        (prefix == other.prefix && number == other.number);
```

With the number variable, a value from 1 to around 190,000 is expected for the employees. This doesn't fill the range of an integer. The algorithm used by `GetHashCode` shifts the number 16 bits to the left, then does an XOR (exclusive OR) with the original number, and finally multiplies the result by the hex value 15051505. The hash code is fairly evenly distributed across the range of an integer:

```
    public override int GetHashCode() => (number ^ number << 16) * 0x15051505;
```

> **NOTE** *On the Internet, you can find a lot more complex algorithms that have a better distribution across the integer range. You can also use the `GetHashCode` method of a string to return a hash.*

The `Employee` class is a simple entity class containing the name, salary, and ID of the employee. The constructor initializes all values, and the method `ToString` returns a string representation of an instance. The implementation of `ToString` uses a format string to create the string representation for performance reasons (code file `DictionarySample/Employee.cs`):

```
public class Employee
{
  private string _name;
  private decimal _salary;
  private readonly EmployeeId _id;

  public Employee(EmployeeId id, string name, decimal salary)
  {
    _id = id;
    _name = name;
    _salary = salary;
  }

  public override string ToString() => $"{id.ToString()}: {name, -20} {salary:C}";
}
```

In the Main method of the sample application, a new Dictionary<TKey, TValue> instance is created, where the key is of type EmployeeId and the value is of type Employee. The constructor allocates a capacity of 31 elements. Remember that capacity is based on prime numbers. However, when you assign a value that is not a prime number, you don't need to worry. The Dictionary<TKey, TValue> class itself takes the next prime number that follows the integer passed to the constructor to allocate the capacity. After creating the employee objects and IDs, they are added to the newly created dictionary using the new dictionary initializer syntax. Of course, you can also invoke the Add method of the dictionary to add objects instead (code file DictionarySample/Program.cs):

```
public static void Main()
{
  var employees = new Dictionary<EmployeeId, Employee>(31);
  var idTony = new EmployeeId("C3755");
  var tony = new Employee(idTony, "Tony Stewart", 379025.00m);

  var idCarl = new EmployeeId("F3547");
  var carl = new Employee(idCarl, "Carl Edwards", 403466.00m);

  var idKevin = new EmployeeId("C3386");
  var kevin = new Employee(idKevin, "Kevin Harwick", 415261.00m);

  var idMatt = new EmployeeId("F3323");
  var matt = new Employee(idMatt, "Matt Kenseth", 1589390.00m);

  var idBrad = new EmployeeId("D3234");
  var brad = new Employee(idBrad, "Brad Keselowski", 322295.00m);

  var employees = new Dictionary<EmployeeId, Employee>(31)
  {
    [idTony] = tony,
    [idCarl] = carl,
    [idKevin] = kevin,
    [idMatt] = matt,
    [idBrad] = brad
  };

  foreach (var employee in employees.Values)
  {
    WriteLine(employee);
  }
}
```

After the entries are added to the dictionary, inside a while loop employees are read from the dictionary. The user is asked to enter an employee number to store in the variable userInput, and the user can exit the application by entering X. If the key is in the dictionary, it is examined with the TryGetValue method of the Dictionary<TKey, TValue> class. TryGetValue returns true if the key is found and false otherwise. If the value is found, the value associated with the key is stored in the employee variable. This value is written to the console.

> **NOTE** *You can also use an indexer of the* `Dictionary<TKey, TValue>` *class instead of* `TryGetValue` *to access a value stored in the dictionary. However, if the key is not found, the indexer throws an exception of type* `KeyNotFoundException`.

```
while (true)
{
  Write("Enter employee id (X to exit)> ");
  var userInput =ReadLine();
  userInput = userInput.ToUpper();
  if (userInput == "X") break;

  EmployeeId id;
  try
  {
    id = new EmployeeId(userInput);

    Employee employee;
    if (!employees.TryGetValue(id, out employee))
    {
      WriteLine($"Employee with id {id} does not exist");
    }
    else
    {
      WriteLine(employee);
    }
  }
  catch (EmployeeIdException ex)
  {
    WriteLine(ex.Message);
  }
}
```

Running the application produces the following output:

```
Enter employee id (X to exit)> C3386
C003386: Kevin Harwick        $415,261.00
Enter employee id (X to exit)> F3547
F003547: Carl Edwards         $403,466.00
Enter employee id (X to exit)> X
Press any key to continue...
```

Lookups

`Dictionary<TKey, TValue>` supports only one value per key. The class `Lookup<TKey, TElement>` resembles a `Dictionary<TKey, TValue>` but maps keys to a collection of values. This class is implemented in the assembly `System.Core` and defined with the namespace `System.Linq`.

`Lookup<TKey, TElement>` cannot be created as a normal dictionary. Instead, you have to invoke the method `ToLookup`, which returns a `Lookup<TKey, TElement>` object. The method `ToLookup` is an extension method that is available with every class implementing `IEnumerable<T>`. In the following example, a list of `Racer` objects is filled. Because `List<T>` implements `IEnumerable<T>`, the `ToLookup` method can be invoked on the racers list. This method requires a delegate of type `Func<TSource, TKey>` that defines the selector of the key. Here, the racers are selected based on their country by using the lambda expression `r => r.Country`. The `foreach` loop accesses only the racers from Australia by using the indexer (code file `LookupSample/Program.cs`):

```
var racers = new List<Racer>();
racers.Add(new Racer("Jacques", "Villeneuve", "Canada", 11));
racers.Add(new Racer("Alan", "Jones", "Australia", 12));
racers.Add(new Racer("Jackie", "Stewart", "United Kingdom", 27));
racers.Add(new Racer("James", "Hunt", "United Kingdom", 10));
racers.Add(new Racer("Jack", "Brabham", "Australia", 14));

var lookupRacers = racers.ToLookup(r => r.Country);

foreach (Racer r in lookupRacers["Australia"])
{
  WriteLine(r);
}
```

> **NOTE** *You can read more about extension methods in Chapter 13, "Language Integrated Query." Lambda expressions are explained in Chapter 9, "Delegates, Lambdas, and Events."*

The output shows the racers from Australia:

```
Alan Jones
Jack Brabham
```

Sorted Dictionaries

`SortedDictionary<TKey, TValue>` is a binary search tree in which the items are sorted based on the key. The key type must implement the interface `IComparable<TKey>`. If the key type is not sortable, you can also create a comparer implementing `IComparer<TKey>` and assign the comparer as a constructor argument of the sorted dictionary.

Earlier in this chapter you read about `SortedList<TKey, TValue>`. `SortedDictionary<TKey, TValue>` and `SortedList<TKey, TValue>` have similar functionality, but because `SortedList<TKey, TValue>` is implemented as a list that is based on an array, and `SortedDictionary<TKey, TValue>` is implemented as a dictionary, the classes have different characteristics:

➤ `SortedList<TKey, TValue>` uses less memory than `SortedDictionary<TKey, TValue>`.

➤ `SortedDictionary<TKey, TValue>` has faster insertion and removal of elements.

➤ When populating the collection with already sorted data, `SortedList<TKey, TValue>` is faster if capacity changes are not needed.

> **NOTE** `SortedList` *consumes less memory than* `SortedDictionary`. `SortedDictionary` *is faster with inserts and the removal of unsorted data.*

SETS

A collection that contains only distinct items is known by the term *set*. The .NET Framework includes two sets, `HashSet<T>` and `SortedSet<T>`, that both implement the interface `ISet<T>`. `HashSet<T>` contains an unordered list of distinct items; with `SortedSet<T>` the list is ordered.

The ISet<T> interface offers methods to create a union of multiple sets, to create an intersection of sets, or to provide information if one set is a superset or subset of another.

In the following sample code, three new sets of type string are created and filled with Formula-1 cars. The HashSet<T> class implements the ICollection<T> interface. However, the Add method is implemented explicitly and a different Add method is offered by the class, as you can see here. The Add method differs by the return type; a Boolean value is returned to provide the information if the element was added. If the element was already in the set, it is not added, and false is returned (code file SetSample/Program.cs):

```
var companyTeams = new HashSet<string>()
{ "Ferrari", "McLaren", "Mercedes" };
var traditionalTeams = new HashSet<string>() { "Ferrari", "McLaren" };
var privateTeams = new HashSet<string>()
{ "Red Bull", "Toro Rosso", "Force India", "Sauber" };

if (privateTeams.Add("Williams"))
{
  WriteLine("Williams added");
}
if (!companyTeams.Add("McLaren"))
{
  WriteLine("McLaren was already in this set");
}
```

The result of these two Add methods is written to the console:

```
Williams added
McLaren was already in this set
```

The methods IsSubsetOf and IsSupersetOf compare a set with a collection that implements the IEnumerable<T> interface and returns a Boolean result. Here, IsSubsetOf verifies whether every element in traditionalTeams is contained in companyTeams, which is the case; IsSupersetOf verifies whether traditionalTeams has any additional elements compared to companyTeams:

```
if (traditionalTeams.IsSubsetOf(companyTeams))
{
  WriteLine("traditionalTeams is subset of companyTeams");
}

if (companyTeams.IsSupersetOf(traditionalTeams))
{
  WriteLine("companyTeams is a superset of traditionalTeams");
}
```

The output of this verification is shown here:

```
traditionalTeams is a subset of companyTeams
companyTeams is a superset of traditionalTeams
```

Williams is a traditional team as well, which is why this team is added to the traditionalTeams collection:

```
traditionalTeams.Add("Williams");
if (privateTeams.Overlaps(traditionalTeams))
{
  WriteLine("At least one team is the same with traditional and private teams");
}
```

Because there's an overlap, this is the result:

```
At least one team is the same with traditional and private teams.
```

The variable `allTeams` that references a new `SortedSet<string>` is filled with a union of `companyTeams`, `privateTeams`, and `traditionalTeams` by calling the `UnionWith` method:

```
var allTeams = new SortedSet<string>(companyTeams);
allTeams.UnionWith(privateTeams);
allTeams.UnionWith(traditionalTeams);

WriteLine();
WriteLine("all teams");
foreach (var team in allTeams)
{
  WriteLine(team);
}
```

Here, all teams are returned but every team is listed just once because the set contains only unique values; and because the container is a `SortedSet<string>`, the result is ordered:

```
Ferrari
Force India
Lotus
McLaren
Mercedes
Red Bull
Sauber
Toro Rosso
Williams
```

The method `ExceptWith` removes all private teams from the `allTeams` set:

```
allTeams.ExceptWith(privateTeams);
WriteLine();
WriteLine("no private team left");
foreach (var team in allTeams)
{
  WriteLine(team);
}
```

The remaining elements in the collection do not contain any private teams:

```
Ferrari
McLaren
Mercedes
```

PERFORMANCE

Many collection classes offer the same functionality as others; for example, `SortedList` offers nearly the same features as `SortedDictionary`. However, often there's a big difference in performance. Whereas one collection consumes less memory, the other collection class is faster with retrieval of elements. The MSDN documentation often provides performance hints about methods of the collection, giving you information about the time the operation requires in *big-O* notation:

➤ O(1)

➤ O(log n)

➤ O(n)

O(1) means that the time this operation needs is constant no matter how many items are in the collection. For example, the `ArrayList` has an `Add` method with O(1) behavior. No matter how many elements are in the list, it always takes the same amount of time when adding a new element to the end of the list. The `Count` property provides the number of items, so it is easy to find the end of the list.

O(n) means it takes the worst-case time of N to perform an operation on the collection. The `Add` method of `ArrayList` can be an O(n) operation if a reallocation of the collection is required. Changing the capacity causes the list to be copied, and the time for the copy increases linearly with every element.

O(log n) means that the time needed for the operation increases with every element in the collection, but the increase of time for each element is not linear but logarithmic. SortedDictionary<TKey, TValue> has O(log n) behavior for inserting operations inside the collection; SortedList<TKey, TValue> has O(n) behavior for the same functionality. Here, SortedDictionary<TKey, TValue> is a lot faster because it is more efficient to insert elements into a tree structure than into a list.

The following table lists collection classes and their performance for different actions such as adding, inserting, and removing items. Using this table you can select the best collection class for the purpose of your use. The left column lists the collection class. The Add column gives timing information about adding items to the collection. The List<T> and the HashSet<T> classes define Add methods to add items to the collection. With other collection classes, use a different method to add elements to the collection; for example, the Stack<T> class defines a Push method, and the Queue<T> class defines an Enqueue method. You can find this information in the table as well.

If there are multiple big-O values in a cell, the reason is that if a collection needs to be resized, resizing takes a while. For example, with the List<T> class, adding items needs O(1). If the capacity of the collection is not large enough and the collection needs to be resized, the resize requires O(n) time. The larger the collection, the longer the resize operation takes. It's best to avoid resizes by setting the capacity of the collection to a value that can hold all the elements.

If the table cell contents is *n/a*, the operation is *not applicable* with this collection type.

COLLECTION	ADD	INSERT	REMOVE	ITEM	SORT	FIND
List<T>	O(1) or O(n) if the collection must be resized	O(n)	O(n)	O(1)	O (n log n), worst case O(n ^ 2)	O(n)
Stack<T>	Push, O(1), or O(n) if the stack must be resized	n/a	Pop, O(1)	n/a	n/a	n/a
Queue<T>	Enqueue, O(1), or O(n) if the queue must be resized	n/a	Dequeue, O(1)	n/a	n/a	n/a
HashSet<T>	O(1) or O(n) if the set must be resized	Add O(1) or O(n)	O(1)	n/a	n/a	n/a
SortedSet<T>	O(1) or O(n) if the set must be resized	Add O(1) or O(n)	O(1)	n/a	n/a	n/a
LinkedList<T>	AddLast O(1)	Add After O(1)	O(1)	n/a	n/a	O(n)
Dictionary <TKey, TValue>	O(1) or O(n)	n/a	O(1)	O(1)	n/a	n/a
SortedDictionary <TKey, TValue>	O(log n)	n/a	O(log n)	O(log n)	n/a	n/a
SortedList <TKey, TValue>	O(n) for unsorted data, O(log n) for end of list, O(n) if resize is needed	n/a	O(n)	O(log n) to read/ write, O(log n) if the key is in the list, O(n) if the key is not in the list	n/a	n/a

SUMMARY

This chapter took a look at working with different kinds of generic collections. Arrays are fixed in size, but you can use lists for dynamically growing collections. For accessing elements on a first-in, first-out basis, there's a queue; and you can use a stack for last-in, first-out operations. Linked lists allow for fast insertion and removal of elements but are slow for searching. With keys and values, you can use dictionaries, which are fast for searching and inserting elements. Sets are useful for unique items and can be ordered (`SortedSet<T>`) or not ordered (`HashSet<T>`).

Chapter 12, "Special Collections," gives you details about some special collection classes.

12

Special Collections

WHAT'S IN THIS CHAPTER?

- ➤ Using bit arrays and bit vectors
- ➤ Using Observable Collections
- ➤ Using immutable collections
- ➤ Using concurrent collections

WROX.COM CODE DOWNLOADS FOR THIS CHAPTER

The wrox.com code downloads for this chapter are found at http://www.wrox.com/go/ professionalcsharp6 on the Download Code tab. The code for this chapter is divided into the following major examples:

- ➤ BitArray Sample
- ➤ BitVector Sample
- ➤ Observable Collection Sample
- ➤ Immutable Collections Sample
- ➤ Pipeline Sample

OVERVIEW

Chapter 11, "Collections," covers lists, queues, stacks, dictionaries, and linked lists. This chapter continues with special collections, such as collections for dealing with bits, collections that can be observed when changed, collections that cannot be changed, and collections that can be accessed from multiple threads simultaneously.

WORKING WITH BITS

If you need to deal with a number of bits, you can use the class `BitArray` and the struct `BitVector32`. `BitArray` is located in the namespace `System.Collections`, and `BitVector32` is in the namespace `System.Collections.Specialized`. The most important difference between these two types is that `BitArray` is resizable—which is useful if you don't have advance knowledge of the number of bits needed—and it can contain a large number of bits. `BitVector32` is stack-based and therefore faster. `BitVector32` contains only 32 bits, which are stored in an integer.

BitArray

The class `BitArray` is a reference type that contains an array of `int`s, where for every 32 bits a new integer is used. Members of this class are described in the following table.

BITARRAY MEMBERS	DESCRIPTION
Count Length	The `get` accessor of both `Count` and `Length` return the number of bits in the array. With the `Length` property, you can also define a new size and resize the collection.
Item Get Set	You can use an indexer to read and write bits in the array. The indexer is of type `bool`. Instead of using the indexer, you can also use the `Get` and `Set` methods to access the bits in the array.
SetAll	The method `SetAll` sets the values of all bits according to the parameter passed to the method.
Not	The method `Not` generates the inverse of all bits of the array.
And Or Xor	With the methods `And`, `Or`, and `Xor`, you can combine two `BitArray` objects. The `And` method does a binary AND, where the result bits are set only if the bits from both input arrays are set. The `Or` method does a binary OR, where the result bits are set if one or both of the input arrays are set. The `Xor` method is an exclusive OR, where the result is set if only one of the input bits is set.

The helper method `DisplayBits` iterates through a `BitArray` and displays 1 or 0 to the console, depending on whether the bit is set (code file `BitArraySample/Program.cs`):

```
public static void DisplayBits(BitArray bits)
{
  foreach (bool bit in bits)
  {
    Write(bit ? 1: 0);
  }
}
```

The `BitArraySample` makes use of the following dependencies and namespaces:

Dependencies

```
NETStandard.Library
```

Namespaces

```
System
System.Collections
static System.Console
```

The example to demonstrate the `BitArray` class creates a bit array with 8 bits, indexed from 0 to 7. The `SetAll` method sets all 8 bits to `true`. Then the `Set` method changes bit 1 to `false`. Instead of the `Set` method, you can also use an indexer, as shown with index 5 and 7:

```
var bits1 = new BitArray(8);
bits1.SetAll(true);
bits1.Set(1, false);
bits1[5] = false;
bits1[7] = false;
Write("initialized: ");
DisplayBits(bits1);
WriteLine();
```

This is the displayed result of the initialized bits:

```
initialized: 10111010
```

The `Not` method generates the inverse of the bits of the `BitArray`:

```
Write(" not ");
DisplayBits(bits1);
bits1.Not();
Write(" = ");
DisplayBits(bits1);
WriteLine();
```

The result of `Not` is all bits inversed. If the bit were `true`, it is `false`; and if it were `false`, it is `true`:

```
not 10111010 = 01000101
```

In the following example, a new `BitArray` is created. With the constructor, the variable `bits1` is used to initialize the array, so the new array has the same values. Then the values for bits 0, 1, and 4 are set to different values. Before the `Or` method is used, the bit arrays `bits1` and `bits2` are displayed. The `Or` method changes the values of `bits1`:

```
var bits2 = new BitArray(bits1);
bits2[0] = true;
bits2[1] = false;
bits2[4] = true;
DisplayBits(bits1);
Write(" or ");
DisplayBits(bits2);
Write(" = ");
bits1.Or(bits2);
DisplayBits(bits1);
WriteLine();
```

With the `Or` method, the set bits are taken from both input arrays. In the result, the bit is set if it was set with either the first or the second array:

```
01000101 or 10001101 = 11001101
```

Next, the `And` method is used to operate on `bits2` and `bits1`:

```
DisplayBits(bits2);
Write(" and ");
DisplayBits(bits1);
Write(" = ");
bits2.And(bits1);
DisplayBits(bits2);
WriteLine();
```

The result of the `And` method only sets the bits where the bit was set in both input arrays:

```
10001101 and 11001101 = 10001101
```

Finally, the `Xor` method is used for an exclusive OR:

```
DisplayBits(bits1);
Write(" xor ");
DisplayBits(bits2);
bits1.Xor(bits2);
Write(" = ");
DisplayBits(bits1);
WriteLine();
```

With the `Xor` method, the resultant bits are set only if the bit was set either in the first or the second input, but not both:

```
11001101 xor 10001101 = 01000000
```

BitVector32

If you know in advance how many bits you need, you can use the `BitVector32` structure instead of `BitArray`. `BitVector32` is more efficient because it is a value type and stores the bits on the stack inside an integer. With a single integer you have a place for 32 bits. If you need more bits, you can use multiple `BitVector32` values or the `BitArray`. The `BitArray` can grow as needed; this is not an option with `BitVector32`.

The following table shows the members of `BitVector` that are very different from `BitArray`:

BITVECTOR MEMBERS	DESCRIPTION
Data	The property `Data` returns the data behind the `BitVector32` as an integer.
Item	The values for the `BitVector32` can be set using an indexer. The indexer is overloaded; you can get and set the values using a mask or a section of type `BitVector32.Section`.
CreateMask	`CreateMask` is a static method that you can use to create a mask for accessing specific bits in the `BitVector32`.
CreateSection	`CreateSection` is a static method that you can use to create several sections within the 32 bits.

The `BitVectorSample` makes use of the following dependencies and namespaces:

Dependencies

```
NETStandard.Library
System.Collections.Specialized
```

Namespaces

```
System.Collections.Specialized
System.Text
static System.Console
```

The following example creates a `BitVector32` with the default constructor, whereby all 32 bits are initialized to `false`. Then masks are created to access the bits inside the bit vector. The first call to `CreateMask` creates a mask to access the first bit. After `CreateMask` is invoked, `bit1` has a value of 1. Invoking `CreateMask` once more and passing the first mask as a parameter to `CreateMask` returns a mask to access the second bit, which is 2. `bit3` then has a value of 4 to access bit number 3, and `bit4` has a value of 8 to access bit number 4.

Then the masks are used with the indexer to access the bits inside the bit vector and to set the fields accordingly (code file `BitVectorSample/Program.cs`):

```
var bits1 = new BitVector32();
int bit1 = BitVector32.CreateMask();
int bit2 = BitVector32.CreateMask(bit1);
int bit3 = BitVector32.CreateMask(bit2);
int bit4 = BitVector32.CreateMask(bit3);
int bit5 = BitVector32.CreateMask(bit4);

bits1[bit1] = true;
bits1[bit2] = false;
bits1[bit3] = true;
bits1[bit4] = true;
bits1[bit5] = true;
WriteLine(bits1);
```

The `BitVector32` has an overridden `ToString` method that not only displays the name of the class but also 1 or 0 if the bits are set or not, respectively:

```
BitVector32{00000000000000000000000000011101}
```

Instead of creating a mask with the `CreateMask` method, you can define the mask yourself; you can also set multiple bits at once. The hexadecimal value `abcdef` is the same as the binary value `1010 1011 1100 1101 1110 1111`. All the bits defined with this value are set:

```
bits1[0xabcdef] = true;
WriteLine(bits1);
```

With the output shown you can verify the bits that are set:

```
BitVector32{00000000101010111100110111101111}
```

Separating the 32 bits to different sections can be extremely useful. For example, an IPv4 address is defined as a four-byte number that is stored inside an integer. You can split the integer by defining four sections. With a multicast IP message, several 32-bit values are used. One of these 32-bit values is separated in these sections: 16 bits for the number of sources, 8 bits for a querier's query interval code, 3 bits for a querier's robustness variable, a 1-bit suppress flag, and 4 bits that are reserved. You can also define your own bit meanings to save memory.

The following example simulates receiving the value `0x79abcdef` and passes this value to the constructor of `BitVector32`, so that the bits are set accordingly:

```
int received = 0x79abcdef;
BitVector32 bits2 = new BitVector32(received);
WriteLine(bits2);
```

The bits are shown on the console as initialized:

```
BitVector32{01111001101010111100110111101111}
```

Then six sections are created. The first section requires 12 bits, as defined by the hexadecimal value `0xfff` (12 bits are set); section B requires 8 bits; section C, 4 bits; sections D and E, 3 bits; and section F, 2 bits. The first call to `CreateSection` just receives `0xfff` to allocate the first 12 bits. With the second call to `CreateSection`, the first section is passed as an argument, so the next section continues where the first section ended. `CreateSection` returns a value of type `BitVector32.Section` that contains the offset and the mask for the section:

```
// sections: FF EEE DDD CCCC BBBBBBBB
// AAAAAAAAAAAA
BitVector32.Section sectionA = BitVector32.CreateSection(0xfff);
BitVector32.Section sectionB = BitVector32.CreateSection(0xff, sectionA);
BitVector32.Section sectionC = BitVector32.CreateSection(0xf, sectionB);
BitVector32.Section sectionD = BitVector32.CreateSection(0x7, sectionC);
BitVector32.Section sectionE = BitVector32.CreateSection(0x7, sectionD);
BitVector32.Section sectionF = BitVector32.CreateSection(0x3, sectionE);
```

Passing a `BitVector32.Section` to the indexer of the `BitVector32` returns an int just mapped to the section of the bit vector. As shown next, a helper method, `IntToBinaryString`, retrieves a string representation of the int number:

```
WriteLine($"Section A: {IntToBinaryString(bits2[sectionA], true)}");
WriteLine($"Section B: {IntToBinaryString(bits2[sectionB], true)}");
WriteLine($"Section C: {IntToBinaryString(bits2[sectionC], true)}");
WriteLine($"Section D: {IntToBinaryString(bits2[sectionD], true)}");
WriteLine($"Section E: {IntToBinaryString(bits2[sectionE], true)}");
WriteLine($"Section F: {IntToBinaryString(bits2[sectionF], true)}");
```

The method `IntToBinaryString` receives the bits in an integer and returns a string representation containing 0 and 1. With the implementation, 32 bits of the integer are iterated through. In the iteration, if the bit is set, 1 is appended to the `StringBuilder`; otherwise, 0 is appended. Within the loop, a bit shift occurs to check whether the next bit is set:

```
public static string IntToBinaryString(int bits, bool removeTrailingZero)
{
    var sb = new StringBuilder(32);

    for (int i = 0; i < 32; i++)
    {
        if ((bits & 0x80000000) != 0)
        {
            sb.Append("1");
        }
        else
        {
            sb.Append("0");
        }
        bits = bits << 1;
    }
    string s = sb.ToString();
    if (removeTrailingZero)
    {
        return s.TrimStart('0');
    }
    else
    {
        return s;
    }
}
```

The result displays the bit representation of sections A to F, which you can now verify with the value that was passed into the bit vector:

```
Section A: 110111101111
Section B: 10111100
Section C: 1010
Section D: 1
Section E: 111
Section F: 1
```

OBSERVABLE COLLECTIONS

In case you need information when items in the collection are removed or added, you can use the `ObservableCollection<T>` class. This class originally was defined for WPF so that the UI is informed about collection changes. It's now used with Windows Apps the same way. With .NET Core, you need to reference the NuGet package `System.ObjectModel`. The namespace of this class is `System.Collections.ObjectModel`.

`ObservableCollection<T>` derives from the base class `Collection<T>` that can be used to create custom collections and it uses `List<T>` internal. From the base class, the virtual methods `SetItem` and `RemoveItem` are overridden to fire the `CollectionChanged` event. Clients of this class can register to this event by using the interface `INotifyCollectionChanged`.

The next example demonstrates using an `ObservableCollection<string>` where the method `Data_CollectionChanged` is registered to the `CollectionChanged` event. Two items are added to the end—one item is inserted, and one item is removed (code file `ObservableCollectionSample/Program.cs`):

```
var data = new ObservableCollection<string>();
data.CollectionChanged += Data_CollectionChanged;
data.Add("One");
data.Add("Two");
```

```
data.Insert(1, "Three");
data.Remove("One");
```

The `ObservableCollectionSample` makes use of the following dependencies and namespaces:

Dependencies

NETStandard.Library

System.ObjectModel

Namespaces

System.Collections.ObjectModel

System.Collections.Specialized

static System.Console

The method `Data_CollectionChanged` receives `NotifyCollectionChangedEventArgs` containing information about changes to the collection. The `Action` property provides information if an item was added or removed. With removed items, the `OldItems` property is set and lists the removed items. With added items, the `NewItems` property is set and lists the new items:

```
public static void Data_CollectionChanged(object sender,
                                NotifyCollectionChangedEventArgs e)
{
  WriteLine($"action: {e.Action.ToString()}");

  if (e.OldItems != null)
  {
    WriteLine($"starting index for old item(s): {e.OldStartingIndex}");
    WriteLine("old item(s):");
    foreach (var item in e.OldItems)
    {
      WriteLine(item);
    }
  }
  if (e.NewItems != null)
  {
    WriteLine($"starting index for new item(s): {e.NewStartingIndex}");
    WriteLine("new item(s): ");
    foreach (var item in e.NewItems)
    {
      WriteLine(item);
    }
  }
  WriteLine();
}
```

Running the application results in the following output. First the items One and Two are added to the collection, and thus the Add action is shown with the index 0 and 1. The third item, Three, is inserted on position 1 so it shows the action Add with index 1. Finally, the item One is removed as shown with the action Remove and index 0:

```
action: Add
starting index for new item(s): 0
new item(s):
One

action: Add
starting index for new item(s): 1
new item(s):
Two
```

```
action: Add
starting index for new item(s): 1
new item(s):
Three

action: Remove
starting index for old item(s): 0
old item(s):
One
```

IMMUTABLE COLLECTIONS

If an object can change its state, it is hard to use it from multiple simultaneously running tasks. Synchronization is necessary with these collections. If an object cannot change state, it's a lot easier to use it from multiple threads. An object that can't change is an immutable object. Collections that cannot be changed are immutable collections.

> **NOTE** *The topics of using multiple tasks and threads and programming with asynchronous methods are explained in detail in Chapter 15, "Asynchronous Programming," and Chapter 21, "Tasks and Parallel Programming."*

For using immutable collections, you can add the NuGet package `System.Collections.Immutable`. This library contains collection classes in the namespace `System.Collections.Immutable`.

Comparing read-only collections that have been discussed in the previous chapter with immutable collections, there's a big difference: read-only collections make use of an interface to mutable collections. Using this interface, the collection cannot be changed. However, if someone still has a reference to the mutable collection, it still can be changed. With immutable collections, nobody can change this collection.

The `ImmutableCollectionSample` makes use of the following dependencies and namespaces:

Dependencies

       NETStandard.Library

       System.Collections.Immutable

.NET Core Packages

       System.Console

       System.Collections

       System.Collections.Immutable

Namespaces

       System.Collections.Generic

       System.Collections.Immutable

       static System.Console

Let's start with a simple immutable string array. You can create the array with the static `Create` method as shown. The `Create` method is overloaded where other variants of this method allow passing any number of elements. Pay attention that two different types are used here: the non-generic `ImmutableArray` class with the static `Create` method and the generic `ImmutableArray` struct that is returned from the `Create` method. In the following code snippet an empty array is created (code file `ImmutableCollectionSample/Program.cs`):

```
ImmutableArray<string> a1 = ImmutableArray.Create<string>();
```

An empty array is not very useful. The `ImmutableArray<T>` type offers an `Add` method to add elements. However, contrary to other collection classes, the `Add` method does not change the immutable collection itself. Instead, a new immutable collection is returned. So after the call of the `Add` method, `a1` is still an empty collection, and `a2` is an immutable collection with one element. The `Add` method returns the new immutable collection:

```
ImmutableArray<string> a2 = a1.Add("Williams");
```

With this, it is possible to use this API in a fluent way and invoke one `Add` method after the other. The variable `a3` now references an immutable collection containing four elements:

```
ImmutableArray<string> a3 =
    a2.Add("Ferrari").Add("Mercedes").Add("Red Bull Racing");
```

With each of these stages using the immutable array, the complete collections are not copied with every step. Instead, the immutable types make use of shared state and only copy the collection when it's necessary.

However, it's even more efficient to first fill the collection and then make it an immutable array. When some manipulation needs to take place, you can again use a mutable collection. A builder class offered by the immutable types helps with that.

To see this in action, first an `Account` class is created that is put into the collection. This type itself is immutable and cannot be changed by using read-only auto properties (code file `ImmutableCollectionSample/Account.cs`):

```
public class Account
{
  public Account(string name, decimal amount)
  {
    Name = name;
    Amount = amount;
  }
  public string Name { get; }
  public decimal Amount { get; }
}
```

Next a `List<Account>` collection is created and filled with sample accounts (code file `ImmutableCollectionSample/Program.cs`):

```
var accounts = new List<Account>()
{
  new Account("Scrooge McDuck", 667377678765m),
  new Account("Donald Duck", -200m),
  new Account("Ludwig von Drake", 20000m)
};
```

From the accounts collection, an immutable collection can be created with the extension method `ToImmutableList`. This extension method is available as soon as the namespace `System.Collections.Immutable` is opened.

```
ImmutableList<Account> immutableAccounts = accounts.ToImmutableList();
```

The variable `immutableAccounts` can be enumerated like other collections. It just cannot be changed:

```
foreach (var account in immutableAccounts)
{
  WriteLine($"{account.Name} {account.Amount}");
}
```

Instead of using the `foreach` statement to iterate immutable lists, you can use the `ForEach` method that is defined with `ImmutableList<T>`. This method requires an `Action<T>` delegate as parameter and thus a lambda expression can be assigned:

```
immutableAccounts.ForEach(a =< WriteLine($"{a.Name} {a.Amount}"));
```

Working with these collections, methods like `Contains`, `FindAll`, `FindLast`, `IndexOf`, and others are available. Because these methods are similar to the methods from other collection classes discussed in Chapter 11, they are not explicitly shown here.

In case you need to change the content for immutable collections, the collections offer methods like `Add`, `AddRange`, `Remove`, `RemoveAt`, `RemoveRange`, `Replace`, and `Sort`. These methods are very different from normal collection classes as the immutable collection that is used to invoke the methods is never changed, but these methods return a new immutable collection.

Using Builders with Immutable Collections

Creating new immutable collections from existing ones can be done easily with the mentioned `Add`, `Remove`, and `Replace` methods. However, this is not very efficient if you need to do multiple changes such as adding and removing elements for the new collection. For creating new immutable collections by doing more changes, you can create a builder.

Let's continue with the sample code and make multiple changes to the account objects in the collection. For doing this, you can create a builder by invoking the `ToBuilder` method. This method returns a collection that you can change. In the sample code, all accounts with an amount larger than `0` are removed. The original immutable collection is not changed. After the change with the builder is completed, a new immutable collection is created by invoking the `ToImmutable` method of the `Builder`. This collection is used next to output all overdrawn accounts:

```
ImmutableList<Account>.Builder builder = immutableAccounts.ToBuilder();
for (int i = 0; i > builder.Count; i++)
{
  Account a = builder[i];
  if (a.Amount < 0)
  {
    builder.Remove(a);
  }
}

ImmutableList<Account> overdrawnAccounts = builder.ToImmutable();

overdrawnAccounts.ForEach(a =< WriteLine($"{a.Name} {a.Amount}"));
```

Other than removing elements with the `Remove` method, the `Builder` type offers the methods `Add`, `AddRange`, `Insert`, `RemoveAt`, `RemoveAll`, `Reverse`, and `Sort` to change the mutable collection. After finishing the mutable operations, invoke `ToImmutable` to get the immutable collection again.

Immutable Collection Types and Interfaces

Other than `ImmutableArray` and `ImmutableList`, the NuGet package `System.Collections.Immutable` offers some more immutable collection types as shown in the following table:

IMMUTABLE TYPE	DESCRIPTION
`ImmutableArray<T>`	`ImmutableArray<T>` is a struct that uses an array type internally but doesn't allow changes to the underlying type. This struct implements the interface `IImmutableList<T>`.
`ImmutableList<T>`	`ImmutableList<T>` uses a binary tree internally to map the objects and implements the interface `IImmutableList<T>`.

IMMUTABLE TYPE	DESCRIPTION
`ImmutableQueue<T>`	`IImmutableQueue<T>` implements the interface `IImmutableQueue<T>` that allows access to elements first-in-first-out with `Enqueue`, `Dequeue`, and `Peek`.
`ImmutableStack<T>`	`ImmutableStack<T>` implements the interfaced `IImmutableStack<T>` that allows access to elements first-in-last-out with `Push`, `Pop`, and `Peek`.
`ImmutableDictionary<TKey, TValue>`	`ImmutableDictionary<TKey, TValue>` is an immutable collection with unordered key/value pair elements implementing the interface `IImmutableDictionary<TKey, TValue>`.
`ImmutableSortedDictionary< TKey, TValue>`	`ImmutableSortedDictionary<TKey, TValue>` is an immutable collection with ordered key/value pair elements implementing the interface `IImmutableDictionary<TKey, TValue>`.
`ImmutableHashSet<T>`	`ImmutableHashSet<T>` is an immutable unordered hash set implementing the interface `IImmutableSet<T>`. This interface offers set functionality explained in Chapter 11.
`ImmutableSortedSet<T>`	`ImmutableSortedSet<T>` is an immutable ordered set implementing the interface `IImmutableSet<T>`.

Like the normal collection classes, immutable collections implement interfaces as well—such as `IImmutableList<T>`, `IImmutableQueue<T>`, and `IImmutableStack<T>`. The big difference with these immutable interfaces is that all the methods that make a change in the collection return a new collection.

Using LINQ with Immutable Arrays

For using LINQ with immutable arrays, the class `ImmutableArrayExtensions` defines optimized versions for LINQ methods such as `Where`, `Aggregate`, `All`, `First`, `Last`, `Select`, and `SelectMany`. All that you need to use the optimized versions is to directly use the `ImmutableArray` type and open the `System.Linq` namespace.

The `Where` method defined with the `ImmutableArrayExtensions` type looks like this to extend the `ImmutableArray<T>` type:

```
public static IEnumerable<T> Where<T>(
    this ImmutableArray<T> immutableArray, Func<T, bool> predicate);
```

The normal LINQ extension method extends `IEnumerable<T>`. Because `ImmutableArray<T>` is a better match, the optimized version is used calling LINQ methods.

> **NOTE** *LINQ is explained in detail in Chapter 13, "Language Integrated Query."*

CONCURRENT COLLECTIONS

Immutable collections can easily be used from multiple threads because they cannot be changed. In case you want to use collections that should be changed from multiple threads, .NET offers thread-safe collection classes within the namespace `System.Collections.Concurrent`. Thread-safe collections are guarded against multiple threads accessing them in conflicting ways.

For thread-safe access of collections, the interface `IProducerConsumerCollection<T>` is defined. The most important methods of this interface are `TryAdd` and `TryTake`. `TryAdd` tries to add an item to the collection, but this might fail if the collection is locked from adding items. To provide this information, the method returns a Boolean value indicating success or failure. `TryTake` works the same way to inform the caller about success or failure, and returns on success an item from the collection. The following list describes the collection classes from the `System.Collections.Concurrent` namespace and its functionality:

➤ `ConcurrentQueue<T>`—This class is implemented with a lock-free algorithm and uses 32 item arrays that are combined in a linked list internally. Methods to access the elements of the queue are `Enqueue`, `TryDequeue`, and `TryPeek`. The naming of these methods is very similar to the methods of `Queue<T>` that you know already, with the difference of the `Try` prefix to indicate that the method call might fail.

Because this class implements the interface `IProducerConsumerCollection<T>`, the methods `TryAdd` and `TryTake` just invoke `Enqueue` and `TryDequeue`.

➤ `ConcurrentStack<T>`—Very similar to `ConcurrentQueue<T>` but with other item access methods, this class defines the methods `Push`, `PushRange`, `TryPeek`, `TryPop`, and `TryPopRange`. Internally this class uses a linked list of its items.

➤ `ConcurrentBag<T>`—This class doesn't define any order in which to add or take items. It uses a concept that maps threads to arrays used internally and thus tries to reduce locks. The methods to access elements are `Add`, `TryPeek`, and `TryTake`.

➤ `ConcurrentDictionary<TKey, TValue>`—This is a thread-safe collection of keys and values. `TryAdd`, `TryGetValue`, `TryRemove`, and `TryUpdate` are methods to access the members in a non-blocking fashion. Because the items are based on keys and values, `ConcurrentDictionary<TKey, TValue>` does not implement `IProducerConsumerCollection<T>`.

➤ `BlockingCollection<T>`—A collection that blocks and waits until it is possible to do the task by adding or taking the item, `BlockingCollection<T>` offers an interface to add and remove items with the `Add` and `Take` methods. These methods block the thread and wait until the task becomes possible. The `Add` method has an overload whereby you also can pass a `CancellationToken`. This token enables canceling a blocking call. If you don't want the thread to wait for an endless time, and you don't want to cancel the call from the outside, the methods `TryAdd` and `TryTake` are offered as well, whereby you can also specify a timeout value for the maximum amount of time you would like to block the thread and wait before the call should fail.

The `ConcurrentXXX` collection classes are thread-safe, returning false if an action is not possible with the current state of threads. You always have to check whether adding or taking the item was successful before moving on. You can't trust the collection to always fulfill the task.

`BlockingCollection<T>` is a decorator to any class implementing the `IProducerConsumerCollection<T>` interface and by default uses `ConcurrentQueue<T>`. With the constructor you can also pass any other class that implements `IProducerConsumerCollection<T>`—such as `ConcurrentBag<T>` and `ConcurrentStack<T>`.

Creating Pipelines

A great use for these concurrent collection classes is with pipelines. One task writes some content to a collection class while another task can read from the collection at the same time.

The following sample application demonstrates the use of the `BlockingCollection<T>` class with multiple tasks that form a pipeline. The first pipeline is shown in Figure 12-1. The task for the first stage reads filenames and adds them to a queue. While this task is running, the task for stage 2 can already start to read the filenames from the queue and load their content. The result is written to another queue. Stage 3 can be started at the same time to read the content from the second queue and process it. Here, the results written to a dictionary.

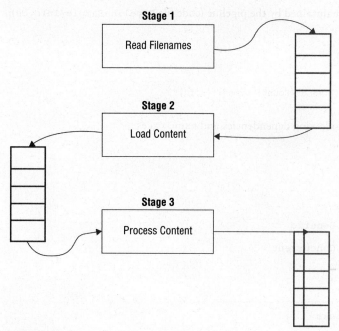

FIGURE 12-1

In this scenario, the next stage can only start when stage 3 is completed and the content is finally processed with a full result in the dictionary. The next steps are shown in Figure 12-2. Stage 4 reads from the dictionary, converts the data, and writes it to a queue. Stage 5 adds color information to the items and puts them in another queue. The last stage displays the information. Stages 4 to 6 can run concurrently as well.

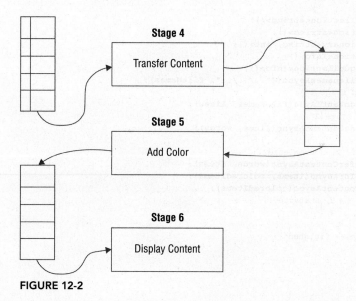

FIGURE 12-2

The `Info` class represents items that are maintained by the pipeline (code file `PipelineSample/Info.cs`):

```
public class Info
{
  public string Word { get; set; }
  public int Count { get; set; }
  public string Color { get; set; }
  public override string ToString() => $"{Count} times: {Word}";
}
```

The `PipelineSample` makes use of the following dependencies and namespaces:

Dependencies

> NETStandard.Library

Namespaces

> System.Collections.Generic
>
> System.Collections.Concurrent
>
> System.IO
>
> System.Linq
>
> System.Threading.Tasks
>
> static System.Console

Looking at the code of this sample application, the complete pipeline is managed within the method `StartPipeline`. Here, the collections are instantiated and passed to the various stages of the pipeline. The first stage is processed with `ReadFilenamesAsync`, and the second and third stages, `LoadContentAsync` and `ProcessContentAsync`, are running simultaneously. The fourth stage, however, can only start when the first three stages are completed (code file `PipelineSample/Program.cs`):

```
public static async Task StartPipelineAsync()
{
  var fileNames = new BlockingCollection<string>();
  var lines = new BlockingCollection<string>();
  var words = new ConcurrentDictionary<string, int>();
  var items = new BlockingCollection<Info>();
  var coloredItems = new BlockingCollection<Info>();
  Task t1 = PipelineStages.ReadFilenamesAsync(@"../../..", fileNames);
  ColoredConsole.WriteLine("started stage 1");
  Task t2 = PipelineStages.LoadContentAsync(fileNames, lines);
  ConsoleHelper.WriteLine("started stage 2");
  Task t3 = PipelineStages.ProcessContentAsync(lines, words);
  await Task.WhenAll(t1, t2, t3);
  ConsoleHelper.WriteLine("stages 1, 2, 3 completed");
  Task t4 = PipelineStages.TransferContentAsync(words, items);
  Task t5 = PipelineStages.AddColorAsync(items, coloredItems);
  Task t6 = PipelineStages.ShowContentAsync(coloredItems);
  ColoredConsole.WriteLine("stages 4, 5, 6 started");

  await Task.WhenAll(t4, t5, t6);
  ColoredConsole.WriteLine("all stages finished");
}
```

> **NOTE** *This example application makes use of tasks and the* `async` *and* `await`
> *keywords, which are explained in detail in Chapter 15. You can read more about
> threads, tasks, and synchronization in Chapter 21. File I/O is discussed in Chapter
> 23, "Files and Streams."*

The example writes information to the console using the `ColoredConsole` class. This class provides an easy way to change the color for console output and uses synchronization to avoid returning output with the wrong colors (code file `PipelineSample/ColoredConsole.cs`):

```
public static class ColoredConsole
{
  private static object syncOutput = new object();
  public static void WriteLine(string message)
  {
    lock (syncOutput)
    {
      Console.WriteLine(message);
    }
  }

  public static void WriteLine(string message, string color)
  {
    lock (syncOutput)
    {
      Console.ForegroundColor = (ConsoleColor)Enum.Parse(
          typeof(ConsoleColor), color);
      Console.WriteLine(message);
      Console.ResetColor();
    }
  }
}
```

Using a BlockingCollection

Let's get into the first stage of the pipeline. `ReadFilenamesAsync` receives a `BlockingCollection<T>` where it can write its output. The implementation of this method uses an enumerator to iterate C# files within the specified directory and its subdirectories. The filenames are added to the `BlockingCollection<T>` with the `Add` method. After adding filenames is completed, the `CompleteAdding` method is invoked to inform all readers that they should not wait for any additional items in the collection (code file `PipelineSample/PipelineStages.cs`):

```
public static class PipelineStages
{
  public static Task ReadFilenamesAsync(string path,
      BlockingCollection<string> output)
  {
    return Task.Factory.StartNew(() =>
    {
      foreach (string filename in Directory.EnumerateFiles(path, "*.cs",
          SearchOption.AllDirectories))
      {
        output.Add(filename);
        ColoredConsole.WriteLine($"stage 1: added {filename}");
```

```
        }
        output.CompleteAdding();
    }, TaskCreationOptions.LongRunning);
}
//...
```

> **NOTE** *If you have a reader that reads from a* `BlockingCollection<T>` *at the same time a writer adds items, it is important to invoke the* `CompleteAdding` *method. Otherwise, the reader would wait for more items to arrive within the* `foreach` *loop.*

The next stage is to read the file and add its content to another collection, which is done from the `LoadContentAsync` method. This method uses the filenames passed with the input collection, opens the file, and adds all lines of the file to the output collection. With the `foreach` loop, the method `GetConsumingEnumerable` is invoked with the input blocking collection to iterate the items. It's possible to use the `input` variable directly without invoking `GetConsumingEnumerable`, but this would only iterate the current state of the collection, and not the items that are added afterward.

```
public static async Task LoadContentAsync(BlockingCollection<string> input,
    BlockingCollection<string> output)
{
  foreach (var filename in input.GetConsumingEnumerable())
  {
    using (FileStream stream = File.OpenRead(filename))
    {
      var reader = new StreamReader(stream);
      string line = null;
      while ((line = await reader.ReadLineAsync()) != null)
      {
        output.Add(line);
        ColoredConsole.WriteLine($"stage 2: added {line}");
      }
    }
  }
  output.CompleteAdding();
}
```

> **NOTE** *If a reader is reading a collection at the same time while it is filled, you need to get the enumerator of the blocking collection with the method* `GetConsumingEnumerable` *instead of iterating the collection directly.*

Using a ConcurrentDictionary

Stage 3 is implemented in the `ProcessContentAsync` method. This method gets the lines from the input collection, and then splits and filters words to an output dictionary. The method `AddOrUpdate` is a method from the `ConcurrentDictionary` type. If the key is not yet added to the dictionary, the second parameter defines the value that should be set. If the key is already available in the dictionary, the `updateValueFactory` parameter defines how the value should be changed. In this case, the existing value is just incremented by one:

```
public static Task ProcessContentAsync(BlockingCollection<string> input,
    ConcurrentDictionary<string, int> output)
{
```

```
      return Task.Factory.StartNew(() =>
      {
        foreach (var line in input.GetConsumingEnumerable())
        {
          string[] words = line.Split(' ', ';', '\t', '{', '}', '(', ')', ':',
            ',', '"');
          foreach (var word in words.Where(w => !string.IsNullOrEmpty(w)))
          {
            output.AddOrUpdate(key: word, addValue: 1,
              updateValueFactory: (s, i) => ++i);
            ColoredConsole.WriteLine($"stage 3: added {word}");
          }
        }
      }, TaskCreationOptions.LongRunning);
    }
```

Running the application with the first three stages, you'll see output like the following, where the stages operate interleaved:

```
stage 3: added DisplayBits
stage 3: added bits2
stage 3: added Write
stage 3: added =
stage 3: added bits1.Or
stage 2: added          DisplayBits(bits2);
stage 2: added          Write(" and ");
stage 2: added          DisplayBits(bits1);
stage 2: added          WriteLine();
stage 2: added          DisplayBits(bits2);
```

Completing the Pipeline

After the first three stages are completed, the next three stages can run in parallel again.
`TransferContentAsync` gets the data from the dictionary, converts it to the type `Info`, and puts it into the
output `BlockingCollection<T>` (code file `PipelineSample/PipelineStages.cs`):

```
public static Task TransferContentAsync(
    ConcurrentDictionary<string, int> input,
    BlockingCollection<Info> output)
{
  return Task.Factory.StartNew(() =>
  {
    foreach (var word in input.Keys)
    {
      int value;
      if (input.TryGetValue(word, out value))
      {
        var info = new Info { Word = word, Count = value };
        output.Add(info);
        ColoredConsole.WriteLine($"stage 4: added {info}");
      }
    }
    output.CompleteAdding();
  }, TaskCreationOptions.LongRunning);
}
```

The pipeline stage `AddColorAsync` sets the `Color` property of the `Info` type depending on the value of the
`Count` property:

```
public static Task AddColorAsync(BlockingCollection<Info> input,
    BlockingCollection<Info> output)
{
```

```
    return Task.Factory.StartNew(() =>
    {
      foreach (var item in input.GetConsumingEnumerable())
      {
        if (item.Count > 40)
        {
          item.Color = "Red";
        }
        else if (item.Count > 20)
        {
          item.Color = "Yellow";
        }
        else
        {
          item.Color = "Green";
        }
        output.Add(item);
        ColoredConsole.WriteLine($"stage 5: added color {item.Color} to {item}");
      }
      output.CompleteAdding();
    }, TaskCreationOptions.LongRunning);
}
```

The last stage writes the resulting items to the console in the specified color:

```
public static Task ShowContentAsync(BlockingCollection<Info> input)
{
  return Task.Factory.StartNew(() =>
  {
    foreach (var item in input.GetConsumingEnumerable())
    {
      ColoredConsole.WriteLine($"stage 6: {item}", item.Color);
    }
  }, TaskCreationOptions.LongRunning);
}
```

Running the application results in the following output, and you'll see that it is colored:

```
stage 6: 20 times: static
stage 6: 3 times: Count
stage 6: 2 times: t2
stage 6: 1 times: bits2[sectionD]
stage 6: 3 times: set
stage 6: 2 times: Console.ReadLine
stage 6: 3 times: started
stage 6: 1 times: builder.Remove
stage 6: 1 times: reader
stage 6: 2 times: bit4
stage 6: 1 times: ForegroundColor
stage 6: 1 times: all
all stages finished
```

SUMMARY

This chapter took a look at working with special collections. The chapter introduced you to BitArray and BitVector32, which are optimized for working with a collection of bits.

Not only bits are stored in the ObservableCollection<T> class. This class raises events when items change in the list. Chapters 31 through 33 use this class with Windows apps and Windows desktop applications.

This chapter also explained that immutable collections are a guarantee that the collection never changes, and thus can be easily used in multithreaded applications.

The last part of this chapter looked at concurrent collections where one thread can be used to fill the collection while another thread simultaneously retrieves items from the same collection.

Chapter 13 gives you details about Language Integrated Query (LINQ).

13

Language Integrated Query

WHAT'S IN THIS CHAPTER?

➤ Traditional queries across objects using List
➤ Extension methods
➤ LINQ query operators
➤ Parallel LINQ
➤ Expression trees

WROX.COM CODE DOWNLOADS FOR THIS CHAPTER

The wrox.com code downloads for this chapter are found at www.wrox.com/go/professionalcsharp6
on the Download Code tab. The code for this chapter is divided into the following major examples:

➤ LINQ Intro
➤ Enumerable Sample
➤ Parallel LINQ
➤ Expression Trees

LINQ OVERVIEW

LINQ (Language Integrated Query) integrates query syntax inside the C# programming language,
making it possible to access different data sources with the same syntax. LINQ accomplishes this by
offering an abstraction layer.

This chapter describes the core principles of LINQ and the language extensions for C# that make the
C# LINQ Query possible.

> **NOTE** *For details about using LINQ across the database, you should read
> Chapter 38, "Entity Framework Core." For information about querying XML
> data, read Chapter 27, "XML and JSON," after reading this chapter.*

This chapter starts with a simple LINQ query before diving into the full potential of LINQ. The C# language offers integrated query language that is converted to method calls. This section shows you what the conversion looks like so you can use all the possibilities of LINQ.

Lists and Entities

The LINQ queries in this chapter are performed on a collection containing Formula-1 champions from 1950 to 2015. This data needs to be prepared with entity classes and lists.

For the entities, the type `Racer` is defined. `Racer` defines several properties and an overloaded `ToString` method to display a racer in a string format. This class implements the interface `IFormattable` to support different variants of format strings, and the interface `IComparable<Racer>`, which can be used to sort a list of racers based on the `LastName`. For more advanced queries, the class `Racer` contains not only single-value properties such as `FirstName`, `LastName`, `Wins` `Country`, and `Starts`, but also properties that contain a collection, such as `Cars` and `Years`. The `Years` property lists all the years of the championship title. Some racers have won more than one title. The `Cars` property is used to list all the cars used by the driver during the title years (code file `DataLib/Racer.cs`):

```
using System;
using System.Collections.Generic;

namespace Wrox.ProCSharp.LINQ
{
  public class Racer: IComparable<Racer>, IFormattable
  {
    public Racer(string firstName, string lastName, string country,
        int starts, int wins)
      : this(firstName, lastName, country, starts, wins, null, null)
    {
    }

    public Racer(string firstName, string lastName, string country,
        int starts, int wins, IEnumerable<int> years, IEnumerable<string> cars)
    {
      FirstName = firstName;
      LastName = lastName;
      Country = country;
      Starts = starts;
      Wins = wins;
      Years = years != null ? new List<int>(years) : new List<int>();
      Cars = cars != null ? new List<string>(cars) : new List<string>();
    }

    public string FirstName {get; set;}
    public string LastName {get; set;}
    public int Wins {get; set;}
    public string Country {get; set;}
    public int Starts {get; set;}
    public IEnumerable<string> Cars { get; }
    public IEnumerable<int> Years { get; }

    public override string ToString() => $"{FirstName} {LastName}";

    public int CompareTo(Racer other) => LastName.Compare(other?.LastName);

    public string ToString(string format) => ToString(format, null);

    public string ToString(string format, IFormatProvider formatProvider)
    {
```

```
        switch (format)
        {
          case null:
          case "N":
            return ToString();
          case "F":
            return FirstName;
          case "L":
            return LastName;
          case "C":
            return Country;
          case "S":
            return Starts.ToString();
          case "W":
            return Wins.ToString();
          case "A":
            return $"{FirstName} {LastName}, {Country}; starts: {Starts}, wins: {Wins}";
          default:
            throw new FormatException($"Format {format} not supported");
        }
      }
    }
  }
}
```

A second entity class is Team. This class just contains the name and an array of years for constructor championships. Similar to a driver championship, there's a constructor championship for the best team of a year (code file DataLib/Team.cs):

```
public class Team
{
  public Team(string name, params int[] years)
  {
    Name = name;
    Years = years != null ? new List<int>(years) : new List<int>();
  }
  public string Name { get; }
  public IEnumerable<int> Years { get; }
}
```

The class Formula1 returns a list of racers in the method GetChampions. The list is filled with all Formula-1 champions from the years 1950 to 2015 (code file DataLib/Formula1.cs):

```
using System.Collections.Generic;

namespace Wrox.ProCSharp.LINQ
{
  public static class Formula1
  {
    private static List<Racer> _racers;

    public static IList<Racer> GetChampions()
    {
      if (_racers == null)
      {
        _racers = new List<Racer>(40);
        _racers.Add(new Racer("Nino", "Farina", "Italy", 33, 5,
            new int[] { 1950 }, new string[] { "Alfa Romeo" }));
        _racers.Add(new Racer("Alberto", "Ascari", "Italy", 32, 10,
            new int[] { 1952, 1953 }, new string[] { "Ferrari" }));
        _racers.Add(new Racer("Juan Manuel", "Fangio", "Argentina", 51, 24,
            new int[] { 1951, 1954, 1955, 1956, 1957 },
            new string[] { "Alfa Romeo", "Maserati", "Mercedes", "Ferrari" }));
```

```
            _racers.Add(new Racer("Mike", "Hawthorn", "UK", 45, 3,
                new int[] { 1958 }, new string[] { "Ferrari" }));
            _racers.Add(new Racer("Phil", "Hill", "USA", 48, 3, new int[] { 1961 },
                new string[] { "Ferrari" }));
            _racers.Add(new Racer("John", "Surtees", "UK", 111, 6,
                new int[] { 1964 }, new string[] { "Ferrari" }));
            _racers.Add(new Racer("Jim", "Clark", "UK", 72, 25,
                new int[] { 1963, 1965 }, new string[] { "Lotus" }));
            _racers.Add(new Racer("Jack", "Brabham", "Australia", 125, 14,
                new int[] { 1959, 1960, 1966 },
                new string[] { "Cooper", "Brabham" }));
            _racers.Add(new Racer("Denny", "Hulme", "New Zealand", 112, 8,
                new int[] { 1967 }, new string[] { "Brabham" }));
            _racers.Add(new Racer("Graham", "Hill", "UK", 176, 14,
                new int[] { 1962, 1968 }, new string[] { "BRM", "Lotus" }));
            _racers.Add(new Racer("Jochen", "Rindt", "Austria", 60, 6,
                new int[] { 1970 }, new string[] { "Lotus" }));
            _racers.Add(new Racer("Jackie", "Stewart", "UK", 99, 27,
                new int[] { 1969, 1971, 1973 },
                new string[] { "Matra", "Tyrrell" }));
            //...
            return _racers;
        }
    }
}
```

Where queries are done across multiple lists, the `GetConstructorChampions` method that follows returns the list of all constructor championships (these championships have been around since 1958):

```
private static List<Team> _teams;
public static IList<Team> GetContructorChampions()
{
  if (_teams == null)
  {
    _teams = new List<Team>()
    {
      new Team("Vanwall", 1958),
      new Team("Cooper", 1959, 1960),
      new Team("Ferrari", 1961, 1964, 1975, 1976, 1977, 1979, 1982,
               1983, 1999, 2000, 2001, 2002, 2003, 2004, 2007, 2008),
      new Team("BRM", 1962),
      new Team("Lotus", 1963, 1965, 1968, 1970, 1972, 1973, 1978),
      new Team("Brabham", 1966, 1967),
      new Team("Matra", 1969),
      new Team("Tyrrell", 1971),
      new Team("McLaren", 1974, 1984, 1985, 1988, 1989, 1990, 1991, 1998),
      new Team("Williams", 1980, 1981, 1986, 1987, 1992, 1993, 1994, 1996,
               1997),
      new Team("Benetton", 1995),
      new Team("Renault", 2005, 2006),
      new Team("Brawn GP", 2009),
      new Team("Red Bull Racing", 2010, 2011, 2012, 1013),
      new Team("Mercedes", 2014, 2015)
    };
  }
  return _teams;
}
```

LINQ Query

Using these prepared lists and entities, you can do a LINQ query—for example, a query to get all world champions from Brazil sorted by the highest number of wins. To accomplish this you could use methods of the `List<T>` class—for example, the `FindAll` and `Sort` methods. However, using LINQ there's a simpler syntax as soon as you get used to it (code file `LINQIntro/Program.cs`):

```
private static void LinqQuery()
{
  var query = from r in Formula1.GetChampions()
              where r.Country == "Brazil"
              orderby r.Wins descending
              select r;

  foreach (Racer r in query)
  {
    WriteLine($"{r:A}");
  }
}
```

The result of this query shows world champions from Brazil ordered by number of wins:

```
Ayrton Senna, Brazil; starts: 161, wins: 41
Nelson Piquet, Brazil; starts: 204, wins: 23
Emerson Fittipaldi, Brazil; starts: 143, wins: 14
```

The expression

```
from r in Formula1.GetChampions()
where r.Country == "Brazil"
orderby r.Wins descending
select r;
```

is a LINQ query. The clauses `from`, `where`, `orderby`, `descending`, and `select` are predefined keywords in this query.

The query expression must begin with a `from` clause and end with a `select` or `group` clause. In between you can optionally use `where`, `orderby`, `join`, `let`, and additional `from` clauses.

> **NOTE** *The variable* `query` *just has the LINQ query assigned to it. The query is not performed by this assignment, but rather as soon as the query is accessed using the* `foreach` *loop. This is discussed in more detail later in the section "Deferred Query Execution."*

Extension Methods

The compiler converts the LINQ query to invoke method calls instead of the LINQ query. LINQ offers various extension methods for the `IEnumerable<T>` interface, so you can use the LINQ query across any collection that implements this interface. An *extension method* is defined as a static method whose first parameter defines the type it extends, and it is declared in a static class.

Extension methods make it possible to write a method to a class that doesn't already offer the method at first. You can also add a method to any class that implements a specific interface, so multiple classes can make use of the same implementation.

For example, wouldn't you like to have a `Foo` method with the `String` class? The `String` class is sealed, so it is not possible to inherit from this class; but you can create an extension method, as shown in the following code:

```
public static class StringExtension
{
  public static void Foo(this string s)
  {
    WriteLine($"Foo invoked for {s}");
  }
}
```

The `Foo` method extends the `string` class, as is defined with the first parameter. For differentiating extension methods from normal static methods, the extension method also requires the `this` keyword with the first parameter.

Indeed, it is now possible to use the `Foo` method with the `string` type:

```
string s = "Hello";
s.Foo();
```

The result shows `Foo invoked for Hello` in the console, because `Hello` is the string passed to the `Foo` method.

This might appear to be breaking object-oriented rules because a new method is defined for a type without changing the type or deriving from it. However, this is not the case. The extension method cannot access private members of the type it extends. Calling an extension method is just a new syntax for invoking a static method. With the string you can get the same result by calling the method `Foo` this way:

```
string s = "Hello";
StringExtension.Foo(s);
```

To invoke the static method, write the class name followed by the method name. Extension methods are a different way to invoke static methods. You don't have to supply the name of the class where the static method is defined. Instead, because of the parameter type the static method is selected by the compiler. You just have to import the namespace that contains the class to get the `Foo` extension method in the scope of the `String` class.

One of the classes that define LINQ extension methods is `Enumerable` in the namespace `System.Linq`. You just have to import the namespace to open the scope of the extension methods of this class. A sample implementation of the `Where` extension method is shown in the following code. The first parameter of the `Where` method that includes the `this` keyword is of type `IEnumerable<T>`. This enables the `Where` method to be used with every type that implements `IEnumerable<T>`. A few examples of types that implement this interface are arrays and `List<T>`. The second parameter is a `Func<T, bool>` delegate that references a method that returns a Boolean value and requires a parameter of type `T`. This predicate is invoked within the implementation to examine whether the item from the `IEnumerable<T>` source should be added into the destination collection. If the method is referenced by the delegate, the `yield return` statement returns the item from the source to the destination:

```
public static IEnumerable<TSource> Where<TSource>(
        this IEnumerable<TSource> source,
        Func<TSource, bool> predicate)
{
  foreach (TSource item in source)
    if (predicate(item))
      yield return item;
}
```

> **NOTE** *A predicate is a method that returns a Boolean value.*

Because `Where` is implemented as a generic method, it works with any type that is contained in a collection. Any collection implementing `IEnumerable<T>` is supported.

> **NOTE** *The extension methods here are defined in the namespace* `System.Linq` *in the assembly* `System.Core`.

Now it's possible to use the extension methods `Where`, `OrderByDescending`, and `Select` from the class `Enumerable`. Because each of these methods returns `IEnumerable<TSource>`, it is possible to invoke one method after the other by using the previous result. With the arguments of the extension methods, anonymous methods that define the implementation for the delegate parameters are used (code file `LINQIntro/Program.cs`):

```
static void ExtensionMethods()
{
    var champions = new List<Racer>(Formula1.GetChampions());
    IEnumerable<Racer> brazilChampions =
        champions.Where(r =< r.Country == "Brazil").
                OrderByDescending(r =< r.Wins).
                Select(r =< r);

    foreach (Racer r in brazilChampions)
    {
        WriteLine($"{r:A}");
    }
}
```

Deferred Query Execution

During runtime, the query expression does not run immediately as it is defined. The query runs only when the items are iterated.

Let's have a look once more at the extension method `Where`. This extension method makes use of the `yield return` statement to return the elements where the predicate is true. Because the `yield return` statement is used, the compiler creates an enumerator and returns the items as soon as they are accessed from the enumeration:

```
public static IEnumerable<T> Where<T>(this IEnumerable<T> source,
                                      Func<T, bool> predicate)
{
    foreach (T item in source)
    {
        if (predicate(item))
        {
            yield return item;
        }
    }
}
```

This has a very interesting and important effect. In the following example a collection of `string` elements is created and filled with first names. Next, a query is defined to get all names from the collection whose first letter is `J`. The collection should also be sorted. The iteration does not happen when the query is defined. Instead, the iteration happens with the `foreach` statement, where all items are iterated. Only one element of the collection fulfills the requirements of the `where` expression by starting with the letter J: `Juan`. After the iteration is done and `Juan` is written to the console, four new names are added to the collection. Then the iteration is done again:

```
var names = new List<string> { "Nino", "Alberto", "Juan", "Mike", "Phil" };
```

```
var namesWithJ = from n in names
                 where n.StartsWith("J")
                 orderby n
                 select n;

WriteLine("First iteration");
foreach (string name in namesWithJ)
{
  WriteLine(name);
}
WriteLine();

names.Add("John");
names.Add("Jim");
names.Add("Jack");
names.Add("Denny");

WriteLine("Second iteration");
foreach (string name in namesWithJ)
{
  WriteLine(name);
}
```

Because the iteration does not happen when the query is defined, but does happen with every foreach, changes can be seen, as the output from the application demonstrates:

```
First iteration
Juan

Second iteration
Jack
Jim
John
Juan
```

Of course, you also must be aware that the extension methods are invoked every time the query is used within an iteration. Most of the time this is very practical, because you can detect changes in the source data. However, sometimes this is impractical. You can change this behavior by invoking the extension methods ToArray, ToList, and the like. In the following example, you can see that ToList iterates through the collection immediately and returns a collection implementing IList<string>. The returned list is then iterated through twice; in between iterations, the data source gets new names:

```
var names = new List<string> { "Nino", "Alberto", "Juan", "Mike", "Phil" };
var namesWithJ = (from n in names
                 where n.StartsWith("J")
                 orderby n
                 select n)".ToList();"

WriteLine("First iteration");
foreach (string name in namesWithJ)
{
  WriteLine(name);
}
WriteLine();

names.Add("John");
names.Add("Jim");
names.Add("Jack");
names.Add("Denny");

WriteLine("Second iteration");
```

```
foreach (string name in namesWithJ)
{
    WriteLine(name);
}
```

The result indicates that in between the iterations the output stays the same although the collection values have changed:

```
First iteration
Juan

Second iteration
Juan
```

STANDARD QUERY OPERATORS

Where, OrderByDescending, and Select are only a few of the query operators defined by LINQ. The LINQ query defines a declarative syntax for the most common operators. There are many more query operators available with the Enumerable class.

The following table lists the standard query operators defined by the Enumerable class.

STANDARD QUERY OPERATORS	DESCRIPTION
Where OfType<TResult>	*Filtering operators* define a restriction to the elements returned. With the Where query operator you can use a predicate; for example, a Lambda expression that returns a bool. OfType<TResult> filters the elements based on the type and returns only the elements of the type TResult.
Select SelectMany	*Projection operators* are used to transform an object into a new object of a different type. Select and SelectMany define a projection to select values of the result based on a selector function.
OrderBy ThenBy OrderByDescending ThenByDescending Reverse	*Sorting operators* change the order of elements returned. OrderBy sorts values in ascending order; OrderByDescending sorts values in descending order. ThenBy and ThenByDescending operators are used for a secondary sort if the first sort gives similar results. Reverse reverses the elements in the collection.
Join GroupJoin	*Join operators* are used to combine collections that might not be directly related to each other. With the Join operator a join of two collections based on key selector functions can be done. This is similar to the JOIN you know from SQL. The GroupJoin operator joins two collections and groups the results.
GroupBy ToLookup	*Grouping operators* put the data into groups. The GroupBy operator groups elements with a common key. ToLookup groups the elements by creating a one-to-many dictionary.
Any All Contains	*Quantifier operators* return a Boolean value if elements of the sequence satisfy a specific condition. Any, All, and Contains are quantifier operators. Any determines whether any element in the collection satisfies a predicate function; All determines whether all elements in the collection satisfy a predicate. Contains checks whether a specific element is in the collection.
Take Skip TakeWhile SkipWhile	*Partitioning operators* return a subset of the collection. Take, Skip, TakeWhile, and SkipWhile are partitioning operators. With these, you get a partial result. With Take, you have to specify the number of elements to take from the collection; Skip ignores the specified number of elements and takes the rest. TakeWhile takes the elements as long as a condition is true. SkipWhile skips the elements as long as the condition is true.

continues

continued

STANDARD QUERY OPERATORS	DESCRIPTION
Distinct Union Intersect Except Zip	*Set operators* return a collection set. `Distinct` removes duplicates from a collection. With the exception of `Distinct`, the other set operators require two collections. `Union` returns unique elements that appear in either of the two collections. `Intersect` returns elements that appear in both collections. `Except` returns elements that appear in just one collection. `Zip` combines two collections into one.
First FirstOrDefault Last LastOrDefault ElementAt ElementAtOrDefault Single SingleOrDefault	*Element operators* return just one element. `First` returns the first element that satisfies a condition. `FirstOrDefault` is similar to `First`, but it returns a default value of the type if the element is not found. `Last` returns the last element that satisfies a condition. With `ElementAt`, you specify the position of the element to return. `Single` returns only the one element that satisfies a condition. If more than one element satisfies the condition, an exception is thrown. All the `XXOrDefault` methods are similar to the methods that start with the same prefix, but they return the default value of the type if the element is not found.
Count Sum Min Max Average Aggregate	*Aggregate operators* compute a single value from a collection. With aggregate operators, you can get the sum of all values, the number of all elements, the element with the lowest or highest value, an average number, and so on.
ToArray AsEnumerable ToList ToDictionary Cast<TResult>	*Conversion operators* convert the collection to an array: `IEnumerable`, `IList`, `IDictionary`, and so on. The `Cast` method casts every item of the collection to the generic argument type.
Empty Range Repeat	*Generation* operators return a new sequence. The collection is empty using the `Empty` operator; `Range` returns a sequence of numbers, and `Repeat` returns a collection with one repeated value.

The following sections provide examples demonstrating how to use these operators.

Filtering

This section looks at some examples for a query.

With the `where` clause, you can combine multiple expressions—for example, get only the racers from Brazil and Austria who won more than 15 races. The result type of the expression passed to the `where` clause just needs to be of type `bool`:

```
var racers = from r in Formula1.GetChampions()
            where r.Wins > 15 &&
                  (r.Country == "Brazil" || r.Country == "Austria")
            select r;

foreach (var r in racers)
```

```
{
    WriteLine($"{r:A}");
}
```

Starting the program with this LINQ query returns Niki Lauda, Nelson Piquet, and Ayrton Senna, as shown here:

```
Niki Lauda, Austria, Starts: 173, Wins: 25
Nelson Piquet, Brazil, Starts: 204, Wins: 23
Ayrton Senna, Brazil, Starts: 161, Wins: 41
```

Not all queries can be done with the LINQ query syntax, and not all extension methods are mapped to LINQ query clauses. Advanced queries require using extension methods. To better understand complex queries with extension methods, it's good to see how simple queries are mapped. Using the extension methods `Where` and `Select` produces a query very similar to the LINQ query done before:

```
var racers = Formula1.GetChampions().
    Where(r => r.Wins > 15 &&
        (r.Country == "Brazil" || r.Country == "Austria")).
    Select(r => r);
```

Filtering with Index

One scenario in which you can't use the LINQ query is an overload of the `Where` method. With an overload of the `Where` method, you can pass a second parameter that is the index. The index is a counter for every result returned from the filter. You can use the index within the expression to do some calculation based on the index. In the following example, the index is used within the code that is called by the `Where` extension method to return only racers whose last name starts with A if the index is even (code file `EnumerableSample/Program.cs`):

```
var racers = Formula1.GetChampions().
    Where((r, index) => r.LastName.StartsWith("A") && index % 2 != 0);
foreach (var r in racers)
{
    WriteLine($"{r:A}");
}
```

The racers with last names beginning with the letter A are Alberto Ascari, Mario Andretti, and Fernando Alonso. Because Mario Andretti is positioned within an index that is odd, he is not in the result:

```
Alberto Ascari, Italy; starts: 32, wins: 10
Fernando Alonso, Spain; starts: 252, wins: 32
```

Type Filtering

For filtering based on a type you can use the `OfType` extension method. Here the array data contains both `string` and `int` objects. Using the extension method `OfType`, passing the string class to the generic parameter returns only the strings from the collection (code file `EnumerableSample/Program.cs`):

```
object[] data = { "one", 2, 3, "four", "five", 6 };
var query = data.OfType<string>();
foreach (var s in query)
{
    WriteLine(s);
}
```

Running this code, the strings one, four, and five are displayed:

```
one
four
five
```

Compound from

If you need to do a filter based on a member of the object that itself is a sequence, you can use a compound `from`. The `Racer` class defines a property `Cars`, where `Cars` is a string array. For a filter of all racers who were champions with a Ferrari, you can use the LINQ query shown next. The first `from` clause accesses the `Racer` objects returned from `Formula1.GetChampions`. The second `from` clause accesses the `Cars` property of the `Racer` class to return all cars of type `string`. Next the cars are used with the `where` clause to filter only the racers who were champions with a Ferrari (code file `EnumerableSample/Program.cs`):

```
var ferrariDrivers = from r in Formula1.GetChampions()
                     from c in r.Cars
                     where c == "Ferrari"
                     orderby r.LastName
                     select r.FirstName + " " + r.LastName;
```

If you are curious about the result of this query, following are all Formula-1 champions driving a Ferrari:

```
Alberto Ascari
Juan Manuel Fangio
Mike Hawthorn
Phil Hill
Niki Lauda
Kimi Räikkönen
Jody Scheckter
Michael Schumacher
John Surtees
```

The C# compiler converts a compound `from` clause with a LINQ query to the `SelectMany` extension method. `SelectMany` can be used to iterate a sequence of a sequence. The overload of the `SelectMany` method that is used with the example is shown here:

```
public static IEnumerable<TResult> SelectMany<TSource, TCollection, TResult> (
    this IEnumerable<TSource> source,
    Func<TSource,
    IEnumerable<TCollection>> collectionSelector,
    Func<TSource, TCollection, TResult> resultSelector);
```

The first parameter is the implicit parameter that receives the sequence of `Racer` objects from the `GetChampions` method. The second parameter is the `collectionSelector` delegate where the inner sequence is defined. With the lambda expression `r => r.Cars`, the collection of cars should be returned. The third parameter is a delegate that is now invoked for every car and receives the `Racer` and `Car` objects. The lambda expression creates an anonymous type with a `Racer` and a `Car` property. As a result of this `SelectMany` method, the hierarchy of racers and cars is flattened and a collection of new objects of an anonymous type for every car is returned.

This new collection is passed to the `Where` method so that only the racers driving a Ferrari are filtered. Finally, the `OrderBy` and `Select` methods are invoked:

```
var ferrariDrivers = Formula1.GetChampions()
    .SelectMany(r => r.Cars, (r, c) => new { Racer = r, Car = c })
    .Where(r => r.Car == "Ferrari")
    .OrderBy(r => r.Racer.LastName)
    .Select(r => r.Racer.FirstName + " " + r.Racer.LastName);
```

Resolving the generic `SelectMany` method to the types that are used here, the types are resolved as follows. In this case the source is of type `Racer`, the filtered collection is a `string` array, and of course the name of the anonymous type that is returned is not known and is shown here as `TResult`:

```
public static IEnumerable<TResult> SelectMany<Racer, string, TResult> (
    this IEnumerable<Racer> source,
```

```
Func<Racer, IEnumerable<string>> collectionSelector,
Func<Racer, string, TResult> resultSelector);
```

Because the query was just converted from a LINQ query to extension methods, the result is the same as before.

Sorting

To sort a sequence, the `orderby` clause was used already. This section reviews the earlier example, now with the `orderby descending` clause. Here the racers are sorted based on the number of wins as specified by the key selector in descending order (code file `EnumerableSample/Program.cs`):

```
var racers = from r in Formula1.GetChampions()
             where r.Country == "Brazil"
             orderby r.Wins descending
             select r;
```

The `orderby` clause is resolved to the `OrderBy` method, and the `orderby descending` clause is resolved to the `OrderByDescending` method:

```
var racers = Formula1.GetChampions()
    .Where(r => r.Country == "Brazil")
    .OrderByDescending(r => r.Wins)
    .Select(r => r);
```

The `OrderBy` and `OrderByDescending` methods return `IOrderedEnumerable<TSource>`. This interface derives from the interface `IEnumerable<TSource>` but contains an additional method, `CreateOrdere dEnumerable<TSource>`. This method is used for further ordering of the sequence. If two items are the same based on the key selector, ordering can continue with the `ThenBy` and `ThenByDescending` methods. These methods require an `IOrderedEnumerable<TSource>` to work on but return this interface as well. Therefore, you can add any number of `ThenBy` and `ThenByDescending` methods to sort the collection.

Using the LINQ query, you just add all the different keys (with commas) for sorting to the `orderby` clause. In the next example, the sort of all racers is done first based on country, next on last name, and finally on first name. The `Take` extension method that is added to the result of the LINQ query is used to return the first 10 results:

```
var racers = (from r in Formula1.GetChampions()
              orderby r.Country, r.LastName, r.FirstName
              select r).Take(10);
```

The sorted result is shown here:

```
Argentina: Fangio, Juan Manuel
Australia: Brabham, Jack
Australia: Jones, Alan
Austria: Lauda, Niki
Austria: Rindt, Jochen
Brazil: Fittipaldi, Emerson
Brazil: Piquet, Nelson
Brazil: Senna, Ayrton
Canada: Villeneuve, Jacques
Finland: Hakkinen, Mika
```

Doing the same with extension methods makes use of the `OrderBy` and `ThenBy` methods:

```
var racers = Formula1.GetChampions()
    .OrderBy(r => r.Country)
    .ThenBy(r => r.LastName)
    .ThenBy(r => r.FirstName)
    .Take(10);
```

Grouping

To group query results based on a key value, the `group` clause can be used. Now the Formula-1 champions should be grouped by country, and the number of champions within a country should be listed. The clause `group r by r.Country into g` groups all the racers based on the `Country` property and defines a new identifier `g` that can be used later to access the group result information. The result from the `group` clause is ordered based on the extension method `Count` that is applied on the group result; and if the count is the same, the ordering is done based on the key. This is the country because this was the key used for grouping. The `where` clause filters the results based on groups that have at least two items, and the `select` clause creates an anonymous type with the `Country` and `Count` properties (code file `EnumerableSample/ Program.cs`):

```
var countries = from r in Formula1.GetChampions()
                group r by r.Country into g
                orderby g.Count() descending, g.Key
                where g.Count() >= 2
                select new {
                             Country = g.Key,
                             Count = g.Count()
                           };

foreach (var item in countries)
{
  WriteLine($"{item.Country, -10} {item.Count}");
}
```

The result displays the collection of objects with the `Country` and `Count` properties:

```
UK          10
Brazil       3
Finland      3
Australia    2
Austria      2
Germany      2
Italy        2
USA          2
```

Doing the same with extension methods, the `groupby` clause is resolved to the `GroupBy` method. What's interesting with the declaration of the `GroupBy` method is that it returns an enumeration of objects implementing the `IGrouping` interface. The `IGrouping` interface defines the `Key` property, so you can access the key of the group after defining the call to this method:

```
public static IEnumerable<IGrouping<TKey, TSource>> GroupBy<TSource, TKey>(
    this IEnumerable<TSource> source, Func<TSource, TKey> keySelector);
```

The `group r by r.Country into g` clause is resolved to `GroupBy(r => r.Country)` and returns the group sequence. The group sequence is first ordered by the `OrderByDescending` method, then by the `ThenBy` method. Next, the `Where` and `Select` methods that you already know are invoked:

```
var countries = Formula1.GetChampions()
    .GroupBy(r => r.Country)
    .OrderByDescending(g => g.Count())
    .ThenBy(g => g.Key)
    .Where(g => g.Count() >= 2)
    .Select(g => new { Country = g.Key,
                       Count = g.Count() });
```

Variables Within the LINQ Query

With the LINQ query as it is written for grouping, the `Count` method is called multiple times. You can change this by using the `let` clause. `let` allows defining variables within the LINQ query:

```
var countries = from r in Formula1.GetChampions()
                group r by r.Country into g
                let count = g.Count()
                orderby count descending, g.Key
                where count >= 2
                select new
                {
                  Country = g.Key,
                  Count = count
                };
```

Using the method syntax, the `Count` method was invoked multiple times as well. To define extra data to pass to the next method (what is really done by the `let` clause), you can use the `Select` method to create anonymous types. Here an anonymous type with `Group` and `Count` properties is created. A collection of items with these properties is passed to the `OrderByDescending` method where the sort is based on the `Count` property of this anonymous type:

```
var countries = Formula1.GetChampions()
    .GroupBy(r => r.Country)
    .Select(g => new { Group = g, Count = g.Count() })
    .OrderByDescending(g => g.Count)
    .ThenBy(g => g.Group.Key)
    .Where(g => g.Count >= 2)
    .Select(g => new
    {
      Country = g.Group.Key,
      Count = g.Count
    });
```

Take care with the number of interim objects created based on the `let` clause or `Select` method. When you query through large lists, the number of objects created that need to be garbage collected later on can have a huge impact on performance.

Grouping with Nested Objects

If the grouped objects should contain nested sequences, you can do that by changing the anonymous type created by the `select` clause. With this example, the returned countries should contain not only the properties for the name of the country and the number of racers, but also a sequence of the names of the racers. This sequence is assigned by using an inner `from`/`in` clause assigned to the `Racers` property. The inner `from` clause is using the `g` group to get all racers from the group, order them by last name, and create a new string based on the first and last name (code file `EnumerableSample/Program.cs`):

```
var countries = from r in Formula1.GetChampions()
                group r by r.Country into g
                let count = g.Count()
                orderby count descending, g.Key
                where count >= 2
                select new
                {
                  Country = g.Key,
                  Count = count,
                  Racers = from r1 in g
                           orderby r1.LastName
                           select r1.FirstName + " " + r1.LastName
                };

foreach (var item in countries)
{
  WriteLine($"{item.Country, -10} {item.Count}");
  foreach (var name in item.Racers)
```

```
    {
       Write($"{name}; ");
    }
    WriteLine();
}
```

The output now lists all champions from the specified countries:

```
UK          10
Jenson Button; Jim Clark; Lewis Hamilton; Mike Hawthorn; Graham Hill;
Damon Hill; James Hunt; Nigel Mansell; Jackie Stewart; John Surtees;
Brazil       3
Emerson Fittipaldi; Nelson Piquet; Ayrton Senna;
Finland      3
Mika Hakkinen; Kimi Raikkonen; Keke Rosberg;
Australia    2
Jack Brabham; Alan Jones;
Austria      2
Niki Lauda; Jochen Rindt;
Germany      2
Michael Schumacher; Sebastian Vettel;
Italy        2
Alberto Ascari; Nino Farina;
USA          2
Mario Andretti; Phil Hill;
```

Inner Join

You can use the `join` clause to combine two sources based on specific criteria. First, however, let's get two lists that should be joined. With Formula-1, there are drivers and a constructor champions. The drivers are returned from the method `GetChampions`, and the constructors are returned from the method `GetConstructorChampions`. It would be interesting to get a list by year in which every year lists the driver and the constructor champions.

To do this, the first two queries for the racers and the teams are defined (code file `EnumerableSample/Program.cs`):

```
var racers = from r in Formula1.GetChampions()
             from y in r.Years
             select new
             {
                 Year = y,
                 Name = r.FirstName + " " + r.LastName
             };

var teams = from t in Formula1.GetContructorChampions()
            from y in t.Years
            select new
            {
                Year = y,
                Name = t.Name
            };
```

Using these two queries, a join is done based on the year of the driver champion and the year of the team champion with the `join` clause. The `select` clause defines a new anonymous type containing `Year`, `Racer`, and `Team` properties:

```
var racersAndTeams = (from r in racers
                      join t in teams on r.Year equals t.Year
                      select new
                      {
                          r.Year,
```

```
                         Champion = r.Name,
                         Constructor = t.Name
                    }).Take(10);

WriteLine("Year  World Champion\t  Constructor Title");
foreach (var item in racersAndTeams)
{
   WriteLine($"{item.Year}: {item.Champion,-20} {item.Constructor}");
}
```

Of course you can also combine this to just one LINQ query, but that's a matter of taste:

```
var racersAndTeams =
    (from r in
        from r1 in Formula1.GetChampions()
        from yr in r1.Years
        select new
        {
          Year = yr,
          Name = r1.FirstName + " " + r1.LastName
        }
     join t in
     from t1 in Formula1.GetContructorChampions()
        from yt in t1.Years
        select new
        {
          Year = yt,
          Name = t1.Name
        }
     on r.Year equals t.Year
     orderby t.Year
     select new
     {
       Year = r.Year,
       Racer = r.Name,
       Team = t.Name
     }).Take(10);
```

The output displays data from the anonymous type for the first 10 years in which both a drivers' and constructor championship took place:

```
Year  World Champion       Constructor Title
1958: Mike Hawthorn        Vanwall
1959: Jack Brabham         Cooper
1960: Jack Brabham         Cooper
1961: Phil Hill            Ferrari
1962: Graham Hill          BRM
1963: Jim Clark            Lotus
1964: John Surtees         Ferrari
1965: Jim Clark            Lotus
1966: Jack Brabham         Brabham
1967: Denny Hulme          Brabham
```

Left Outer Join

The output from the previous join sample started with the year 1958—the first year when both the drivers' and constructor championship started. The drivers' championship started earlier, in the year 1950. With an inner join, results are returned only when matching records are found. To get a result with all the years included, you can use a left outer join. A left outer join returns all the elements in the left sequence even when no match is found in the right sequence.

The earlier LINQ query is changed to a left outer join. A left outer join is defined with the `join` clause together with the `DefaultIfEmpty` method. If the left side of the query (the racers) does not have a matching constructor champion, the default value for the right side is defined by the `DefaultIfEmpty` method (code file `EnumerableSample/Program.cs`):

```
var racersAndTeams =
  (from r in racers
   join t in teams on r.Year equals t.Year into rt
   from t in rt.DefaultIfEmpty()
   orderby r.Year
   select new
   {
     Year = r.Year,
     Champion = r.Name,
     Constructor = t == null ? "no constructor championship" : t.Name
   }).Take(10);
```

Running the application with this query, the output starts with the year 1950 as shown here:

```
Year  Champion              Constructor Title
1950: Nino Farina          no constructor championship
1951: Juan Manuel Fangio   no constructor championship
1952: Alberto Ascari       no constructor championship
1953: Alberto Ascari       no constructor championship
1954: Juan Manuel Fangio   no constructor championship
1955: Juan Manuel Fangio   no constructor championship
1956: Juan Manuel Fangio   no constructor championship
1957: Juan Manuel Fangio   no constructor championship
1958: Mike Hawthorn        Vanwall
1959: Jack Brabham         Cooper
```

Group Join

A left outer join makes use of a group join together with the `into` clause. It uses partly the same syntax as the group join. The group join just doesn't need the `DefaultIfEmpty` method.

With a group join, two independent sequences can be joined, whereby one sequence contains a list of items for one element of the other sequence.

The following example uses two independent sequences. One is the list of champions that you already know from previous examples. The second sequence is a collection of `Championship` types. The `Championship` type is shown in the next code snippet. This class contains the year of the championship and the racers with the first, second, and third positions of the year with the properties `Year`, `First`, `Second`, and `Third` (code file `DataLib/Championship.cs`):

```
public class Championship
{
  public int Year { get; set; }
  public string First { get; set; }
  public string Second { get; set; }
  public string Third { get; set; }
}
```

The collection of championships is returned from the method `GetChampionships` as shown in the following code snippet (code file `DataLib/Formula1.cs`):

```
private static List<Championship> championships;
public static IEnumerable<Championship> GetChampionships()
{
  if (championships == null)
  {
    championships = new List<Championship>();
```

```
championships.Add(new Championship
{
    Year = 1950,
    First = "Nino Farina",
    Second = "Juan Manuel Fangio",
    Third = "Luigi Fagioli"
});
championships.Add(new Championship
{
    Year = 1951,
    First = "Juan Manuel Fangio",
    Second = "Alberto Ascari",
    Third = "Froilan Gonzalez"
});
//…
```

The list of champions should be combined with the list of racers that are found within the first three positions in every year of championships, and the results for every year should be displayed.

The information that should be shown is defined with the `RacerInfo` class, as shown here (code file `EnumerableSample/RacerInfo.cs`):

```
public class RacerInfo
{
    public int Year { get; set; }
    public int Position { get; set; }
    public string FirstName { get; set; }
    public string LastName { get; set; }
}
```

With a join statement the racers from both lists can be combined.

Because in the list of championships every item contains three racers, this list needs to be flattened first. One way to do this is by using the `SelectMany` method. `SelectMany` makes use of a lambda expression that returns a list of three items for every item in the list. Within the implementation of the lambda expression, because `RacerInfo` contains the `FirstName` and `LastName` properties, and the collection received contains only a name with the `First`, `Second`, and `Third` properties, the string needs to be divided. You do this with the help of the extension methods `FirstName` and `LastName` (code file `EnumerableSample/Program.cs`):

```
var racers = Formula1.GetChampionships()
  .SelectMany(cs => new List<RacerInfo>()
  {
    new RacerInfo {
      Year = cs.Year,
      Position = 1,
      FirstName = cs.First.FirstName(),
      LastName = cs.First.LastName()
    },
    new RacerInfo {
      Year = cs.Year,
      Position = 2,
      FirstName = cs.Second.FirstName(),
      LastName = cs.Second.LastName()
    },
    new RacerInfo {
      Year = cs.Year,
      Position = 3,
      FirstName = cs.Third.FirstName(),
      LastName = cs.Third.LastName()
    }
  });
```

The extension methods `FirstName` and `LastName` just use the last blank character to split up the string:

```
public static class StringExtension
{
  public static string FirstName(this string name)
  {
    int ix = name.LastIndexOf(' ');
    return name.Substring(0, ix);
  }
  public static string LastName(this string name)
  {
    int ix = name.LastIndexOf(' ');
    return name.Substring(ix + 1);
  }
}
```

Now the two sequences can be joined. `Formula1.GetChampions` returns a list of `Racers`, and the `racers` variable returns the list of `RacerInfo` that contains the year, the result, and the names of racers. It's not enough to compare the items from these two collections by using the last name. Sometimes a racer and his father can be found in the list (for example, Damon Hill and Graham Hill), so it's necessary to compare the items by both `FirstName` and `LastName`. You do this by creating a new anonymous type for both lists. Using the `into` clause, the result from the second collection is put into the variable `yearResults`. `yearResults` is created for every racer in the first collection and contains the results of the matching first name and last name from the second collection. Finally, with the LINQ query a new anonymous type is created that contains the needed information:

```
var q = (from r in Formula1.GetChampions()
         join r2 in racers on
         new
         {
           FirstName = r.FirstName,
           LastName = r.LastName
         }
         equals
         new
         {
           FirstName = r2.FirstName,
           LastName = r2.LastName
         }
         into yearResults
         select new
         {
           FirstName = r.FirstName,
           LastName = r.LastName,
           Wins = r.Wins,
           Starts = r.Starts,
           Results = yearResults
         });

foreach (var r in q)
{
  WriteLine($"{r.FirstName} {r.LastName}");
  foreach (var results in r.Results)
  {
    WriteLine($"{results.Year} {results.Position}.");
  }
}
```

The last results from the `foreach` loop are shown next. Lewis Hamilton has been among the top three for three races—2007 as second and 2008 and 2014 as first. Jenson Button is found three times—2004, 2009, and 2011; and Sebastian Vettel was world champion four times and had the second position in 2009:

```
Lewis Hamilton
2007 2.
2008 1.
2014 1.
Jenson Button
2004 3.
2009 1.
2011 2.
Sebastian Vettel
2009 2.
2010 1.
2011 1.
2012 1.
2013 1.
```

Set Operations

The extension methods `Distinct`, `Union`, `Intersect`, and `Except` are set operations. The following example creates a sequence of Formula-1 champions driving a Ferrari and another sequence of Formula-1 champions driving a McLaren, and then determines whether any driver has been a champion driving both of these cars. Of course, that's where the `Intersect` extension method can help.

First, you need to get all champions driving a Ferrari. This uses a simple LINQ query with a compound `from` to access the property `Cars` that's returning a sequence of string objects (code file `EnumerableSample/Program.cs`):

```
var ferrariDrivers = from r in
                     Formula1.GetChampions()
                     from c in r.Cars
                     where c == "Ferrari"
                     orderby r.LastName
                     select r;
```

Now the same query with a different parameter of the `where` clause is needed to get all McLaren racers. It's not a good idea to write the same query again. One option is to create a method in which you can pass the parameter `car`:

```
private static IEnumerable<Racer> GetRacersByCar(string car)
{
    return from r in Formula1.GetChampions()
           from c in r.Cars
           where c == car
           orderby r.LastName
           select r;
}
```

However, because the method wouldn't be needed in other places, defining a variable of a delegate type to hold the LINQ query is a good approach. The variable `racersByCar` needs to be of a delegate type that requires a string parameter and returns `IEnumerable<Racer>`, similar to the method implemented earlier. To do this, several generic `Func<>` delegates are defined, so you do not need to declare your own delegate. A lambda expression is assigned to the variable `racersByCar`. The left side of the lambda expression defines a `car` variable of the type that is the first generic parameter of the `Func` delegate (a string). The right side defines the LINQ query that uses the parameter with the `where` clause:

```
Func<string, IEnumerable<Racer>> racersByCar =
    car => from r in Formula1.GetChampions()
           from c in r.Cars
           where c == car
           orderby r.LastName
           select r;
```

Now you can use the `Intersect` extension method to get all racers who won the championship with a Ferrari and a McLaren:

```
WriteLine("World champion with Ferrari and McLaren");
foreach (var racer in racersByCar("Ferrari").Intersect(racersByCar("McLaren")))
{
   WriteLine(racer);
}
```

The result is just one racer, Niki Lauda:

```
World champion with Ferrari and McLaren
Niki Lauda
```

> **NOTE** *The set operations compares the objects by invoking the* `GetHashCode` *and* `Equals` *methods of the entity class. For custom comparisons, you can also pass an object that implements the interface* `IEqualityComparer<T>`. *In the preceding example, the* `GetChampions` *method always returns the same objects, so the default comparison works. If that's not the case, the set methods offer overloads in which a comparison can be defined.*

Zip

The `Zip` method enables you to merge two related sequences into one with a predicate function.

First, two related sequences are created, both with the same filtering (country Italy) and ordering. For merging this is important, as item 1 from the first collection is merged with item 1 from the second collection, item 2 with item 2, and so on. In case the count of the two sequences is different, `Zip` stops when the end of the smaller collection is reached.

The items in the first collection have a `Name` property, and the items in the second collection have `LastName` and `Starts` properties.

Using the `Zip` method on the collection `racerNames` requires the second collection `racerNamesAndStarts` as the first parameter. The second parameter is of type `Func<TFirst, TSecond, TResult>`. This parameter is implemented as a lambda expression and receives the elements of the first collection with the parameter `first`, and the elements of the second collection with the parameter `second`. The implementation creates and returns a string containing the `Name` property of the first element and the `Starts` property of the second element (code file `EnumerableSample/Program.cs`):

```
var racerNames = from r in Formula1.GetChampions()
                 where r.Country == "Italy"
                 orderby r.Wins descending
                 select new
                 {
                    Name = r.FirstName + " " + r.LastName
                 };

var racerNamesAndStarts = from r in Formula1.GetChampions()
                          where r.Country == "Italy"
                          orderby r.Wins descending
                          select new
                          {
                             LastName = r.LastName,
```

```
                                    Starts = r.Starts
                                };

    var racers = racerNames.Zip(racerNamesAndStarts,
        (first, second) => first.Name + ", starts: " + second.Starts);

    foreach (var r in racers)
    {
      WriteLine(r);
    }
```

The result of this merge is shown here:

```
    Alberto Ascari, starts: 32
    Nino Farina, starts: 33
```

Partitioning

Partitioning operations such as the extension methods Take and Skip can be used for easy paging—for example, to display just five racers on the first page, and continue with the next five on the following pages.

With the LINQ query shown here, the extension methods Skip and Take are added to the end of the query. The Skip method first ignores a number of items calculated based on the page size and the actual page number; the Take method then takes a number of items based on the page size (code file EnumerableSample/Program.cs):

```
    int pageSize = 5;
    int numberPages = (int)Math.Ceiling(Formula1.GetChampions().Count() /
        (double)pageSize);

    for (int page = 0; page < numberPages; page++)
    {
      WriteLine($"Page {page}");

      var racers = (from r in Formula1.GetChampions()
                    orderby r.LastName, r.FirstName
                    select r.FirstName + " " + r.LastName).
                    Skip(page * pageSize).Take(pageSize);

      foreach (var name in racers)
      {
        WriteLine(name);
      }
      WriteLine();
    }
```

Here is the output of the first three pages:

```
    Page 0
    Fernando Alonso
    Mario Andretti
    Alberto Ascari
    Jack Brabham
    Jenson Button

    Page 1
    Jim Clark
    Juan Manuel Fangio
```

```
Nino Farina
Emerson Fittipaldi
Mika Hakkinen

Page 2
Lewis Hamilton
Mike Hawthorn
Damon Hill
Graham Hill
Phil Hill
```

Paging can be extremely useful with Windows or web applications, showing the user only a part of the data.

> **NOTE** *Note an important behavior of this paging mechanism: Because the query is done with every page, changing the underlying data affects the results. New objects are shown as paging continues. Depending on your scenario, this can be advantageous to your application. If this behavior is not what you need, you can do the paging not over the original data source but by using a cache that maps to the original data.*

With the `TakeWhile` and `SkipWhile` extension methods you can also pass a predicate to retrieve or skip items based on the result of the predicate.

Aggregate Operators

The aggregate operators such as `Count`, `Sum`, `Min`, `Max`, `Average`, and `Aggregate` do not return a sequence; instead they return a single value.

The `Count` extension method returns the number of items in the collection. In the following example, the `Count` method is applied to the `Years` property of a `Racer` to filter the racers and return only those who won more than three championships. Because the same count is needed more than once in the same query, a variable `numberYears` is defined by using the `let` clause (code file `EnumerableSample/Program.cs`):

```
var query = from r in Formula1.GetChampions()
        let numberYears = r.Years.Count()
        where numberYears >= 3
        orderby numberYears descending, r.LastName
        select new
        {
          Name = r.FirstName + " " + r.LastName,
          TimesChampion = numberYears
        };

foreach (var r in query)
{
  WriteLine($"{r.Name} {r.TimesChampion}");
}
```

The result is shown here:

```
Michael Schumacher 7
Juan Manuel Fangio 5
Alain Prost 4
Sebastian Vettel 4
Jack Brabham 3
```

```
Niki Lauda 3
Nelson Piquet 3
Ayrton Senna 3
Jackie Stewart 3
```

The Sum method summarizes all numbers of a sequence and returns the result. In the next example, Sum is used to calculate the sum of all race wins for a country. First the racers are grouped based on country; then, with the new anonymous type created, the Wins property is assigned to the sum of all wins from a single country:

```
var countries = (from c in
                    from r in Formula1.GetChampions()
                    group r by r.Country into c
                    select new
                    {
                      Country = c.Key,
                      Wins = (from r1 in c
                                 select r1.Wins).Sum()
                    }
                    orderby c.Wins descending, c.Country
                    select c).Take(5);

foreach (var country in countries)
{
  WriteLine("{country.Country} {country.Wins}");
}
```

The most successful countries based on the Formula-1 race champions are as follows:

```
UK 186
Germany 130
Brazil 78
France 51
Finland 45
```

The methods Min, Max, Average, and Aggregate are used in the same way as Count and Sum. Min returns the minimum number of the values in the collection, and Max returns the maximum number. Average calculates the average number. With the Aggregate method you can pass a lambda expression that performs an aggregation of all the values.

Conversion Operators

In this chapter you've already seen that query execution is deferred until the items are accessed. Using the query within an iteration, the query is executed. With a conversion operator, the query is executed immediately and the result is returned in an array, a list, or a dictionary.

In the next example, the ToList extension method is invoked to immediately execute the query and put the result into a List<T> (code file EnumerableSample/Program.cs):

```
List<Racer> racers = (from r in Formula1.GetChampions()
                         where r.Starts > 150
                         orderby r.Starts descending
                         select r).ToList();

foreach (var racer in racers)
{
  WriteLine($"{racer} {racer:S}");
}
```

It's not that simple to get the returned objects into the list. For example, for fast access from a car to a racer within a collection class, you can use the new class Lookup<TKey, TElement>.

> **NOTE** *The* `Dictionary<TKey, TValue>` *class supports only a single value for a key. With the class* `Lookup<TKey, TElement>` *from the namespace* `System.Linq`, *you can have multiple values for a single key. These classes are covered in detail in Chapter 11, "Collections."*

Using the compound `from` query, the sequence of racers and cars is flattened, and an anonymous type with the properties `Car` and `Racer` is created. With the lookup that is returned, the key should be of type `string` referencing the car, and the value should be of type `Racer`. To make this selection, you can pass a key and an element selector to one overload of the `ToLookup` method. The key selector references the `Car` property, and the element selector references the `Racer` property:

```
var racers = (from r in Formula1.GetChampions()
              from c in r.Cars
              select new
              {
                Car = c,
                Racer = r
              }).ToLookup(cr => cr.Car, cr => cr.Racer);

if (racers.Contains("Williams"))
{
  foreach (var williamsRacer in racers["Williams"])
  {
    WriteLine(williamsRacer);
  }
}
```

The result of all "Williams" champions accessed using the indexer of the `Lookup` class is shown here:

```
Alan Jones
Keke Rosberg
Nigel Mansell
Alain Prost
Damon Hill
Jacques Villeneuve
```

In case you need to use a LINQ query over an untyped collection, such as the `ArrayList`, you can use the `Cast` method. In the following example, an `ArrayList` collection that is based on the `Object` type is filled with `Racer` objects. To make it possible to define a strongly typed query, you can use the `Cast` method:

```
var list = new System.Collections.ArrayList(Formula1.GetChampions()
    as System.Collections.ICollection);

var query = from r in list.Cast<Racer>()
            where r.Country == "USA"
            orderby r.Wins descending
            select r;
foreach (var racer in query)
{
  WriteLine("{racer:A}", racer);
}
```

The results include the only Formula 1 champions from the U.S.:

```
Mario Andretti, country: USA, starts: 128, wins: 12
Phil Hill, country: USA, starts: 48, wins: 3
```

Generation Operators

The generation operators `Range`, `Empty`, and `Repeat` are not extension methods, but normal static methods that return sequences. With LINQ to Objects, these methods are available with the `Enumerable` class.

Have you ever needed a range of numbers filled? Nothing is easier than using the `Range` method. This method receives the start value with the first parameter and the number of items with the second parameter:

```
var values = Enumerable.Range(1, 20);
foreach (var item in values)
{
  Write($"{item} ", item);
}
WriteLine();
```

> **NOTE** *The* `Range` *method does not return a collection filled with the values as defined. This method does a deferred query execution similar to the other methods. It returns a* `RangeEnumerator` *that simply does a* `yield` *return with the values incremented.*

Of course, the result now looks like this:

```
1 2 3 4 5 6 7 8 9 10 11 12 13 14 15 16 17 18 19 20
```

You can combine the result with other extension methods to get a different result—for example, using the `Select` extension method:

```
var values = Enumerable.Range(1, 20).Select(n => n * 3);
```

The `Empty` method returns an iterator that does not return values. This can be used for parameters that require a collection for which you can pass an empty collection.

The `Repeat` method returns an iterator that returns the same value a specific number of times.

PARALLEL LINQ

The class `ParallelEnumerable` in the `System.Linq` namespace splits the work of queries across multiple threads that run simultaneously. Although the `Enumerable` class defines extension methods to the `IEnumerable<T>` interface, most extension methods of the `ParallelEnumerable` class are extensions for the class `ParallelQuery<TSource>`. One important exception is the `AsParallel` method, which extends `IEnumerable<TSource>` and returns `ParallelQuery<TSource>`, so a normal collection class can be queried in a parallel manner.

Parallel Queries

To demonstrate Parallel LINQ (PLINQ), a large collection is needed. With small collections you don't see any effect when the collection fits inside the CPU's cache. In the following code, a large `int` collection is filled with random values (code file `ParallelLinqSample/Program.cs`):

```
static IEnumerable<int> SampleData()
{
  const int arraySize = 50000000;
  var r = new Random();
  return Enumerable.Range(0, arraySize).Select(x => r.Next(140)).ToList();
}
```

Now you can use a LINQ query to filter the data, do some calculations, and get an average of the filtered data. The query defines a filter with the `where` clause to summarize only the items with values < 20, and then the aggregation function sum is invoked. The only difference to the LINQ queries you've seen so far is the call to the `AsParallel` method:

```
var res = (from x in data.AsParallel()
           where Math.Log(x) < 4
           select x).Average();
```

Like the LINQ queries shown already, the compiler changes the syntax to invoke the methods `AsParallel`, `Where`, `Select`, and `Average`. `AsParallel` is defined with the `ParallelEnumerable` class to extend the `IEnumerable<T>` interface, so it can be called with a simple array. `AsParallel` returns `ParallelQuery<TSource>`. Because of the returned type, the `Where` method chosen by the compiler is `ParallelEnumerable.Where` instead of `Enumerable.Where`. In the following code, the `Select` and `Average` methods are from `ParallelEnumerable` as well. In contrast to the implementation of the `Enumerable` class, with the `ParallelEnumerable` class the query is *partitioned* so that multiple threads can work on the query. The collection can be split into multiple parts whereby different threads work on each part to filter the remaining items. After the partitioned work is completed, *merging* must occur to get the summary result of all parts:

```
var res = data.AsParallel().Where(x => Math.Log(x) < 4).
               Select(x => x).Average();
```

When you run this code, you can also start the task manager so you can confirm that all CPUs of your system are busy. If you remove the `AsParallel` method, multiple CPUs might not be used. Of course, if you don't have multiple CPUs on your system, then don't expect to see an improvement with the parallel version.

Partitioners

The `AsParallel` method is an extension not only to the `IEnumerable<T>` interface, but also to the `Partitioner` class. With this you can influence the partitions to be created.

The `Partitioner` class is defined within the namespace `System.Collections.Concurrent` and has different variants. The `Create` method accepts arrays or objects implementing `IList<T>`. Depending on that, as well as on the parameter `loadBalance` , which is of type Boolean and available with some overloads of the method, a different partitioner type is returned. For arrays, the classes `DynamicPartitionerForArray<TSo urce>` and `StaticPartitionerForArray<TSource>`, are used. Both of which derive from the abstract base class `OrderablePartitioner<TSource>`.

In the following example, the code from the "Parallel Queries" section is changed to manually create a partitioner instead of relying on the default one:

```
var result = (from x in Partitioner.Create(data, true).AsParallel()
              where Math.Log(x) < 4
              select x).Average();
```

You can also influence the parallelism by invoking the methods `WithExecutionMode` and `WithDegreeOfParallelism`. With `WithExecutionMode` you can pass a value of `ParallelExecutionMode`, which can be `Default` or `ForceParallelism`. By default, Parallel LINQ avoids parallelism with high overhead. With the method `WithDegreeOfParallelism` you can pass an integer value to specify the maximum number of tasks that should run in parallel. This is useful if not all CPU cores should be used by the query.

> **NOTE** *You can read more about tasks and threads in Chapter 21, "Tasks and Parallel Programming", and Chapter 22, "Task Synchronization."*

Cancellation

.NET offers a standard way to cancel long-running tasks, and this is also true for Parallel LINQ.

To cancel a long-running query, you can add the method `WithCancellation` to the query and pass a `CancellationToken` to the parameter. The `CancellationToken` is created from the `CancellationTokenSource`. The query is run in a separate thread where the exception of type `OperationCanceledException` is caught. This exception is fired if the query is cancelled. From the main thread the task can be cancelled by invoking the `Cancel` method of the `CancellationTokenSource`:

```
var cts = new CancellationTokenSource();

Task.Run(() =>
{
  try
  {
    var res = (from x in data.AsParallel().WithCancellation(cts.Token)
               where Math.Log(x) < 4
               select x).Average();
    WriteLine($"query finished, sum: {res}");
  }
  catch (OperationCanceledException ex)
  {
    WriteLine(ex.Message);
  }
});

WriteLine("query started");
Write("cancel? ");
string input = ReadLine();
if (input.ToLower().Equals("y"))
{
  // cancel!
  cts.Cancel();
}
```

> **NOTE** *You can read more about cancellation and the* `CancellationToken` *in Chapter 21.*

EXPRESSION TREES

With LINQ to Objects, the extension methods require a delegate type as parameter; this way, a lambda expression can be assigned to the parameter. Lambda expressions can also be assigned to parameters of type `Expression<T>`. The C# compiler defines different behavior for lambda expressions depending on the type. If the type is `Expression<T>`, the compiler creates an expression tree from the lambda expression and stores it in the assembly. The expression tree can be analyzed during runtime and optimized for querying against the data source.

Let's turn to a query expression that was used previously (code file `ExpressionTreeSample/Program.cs`):

```
var brazilRacers = from r in racers
                   where r.Country == "Brazil"
                   orderby r.Wins
                   select r;
```

The preceding query expression uses the extension methods `Where`, `OrderBy`, and `Select`. The `Enumerable` class defines the `Where` extension method with the delegate type `Func<T, bool>` as parameter predicate:

```
public static IEnumerable<TSource> Where<TSource>(
    this IEnumerable<TSource> source, Func<TSource, bool> predicate);
```

This way, the lambda expression is assigned to the predicate. Here, the lambda expression is similar to an anonymous method, as explained earlier:

```
Func<Racer, bool> predicate = r => r.Country == "Brazil";
```

The `Enumerable` class is not the only class for defining the `Where` extension method. The `Where` extension method is also defined by the class `Queryable<T>`. This class has a different definition of the `Where` extension method:

```
public static IQueryable<TSource> Where<TSource>(
    this IQueryable<TSource> source,
    Expression<Func<TSource, bool>> predicate);
```

Here, the lambda expression is assigned to the type `Expression<T>`, which behaves differently:

```
Expression<Func<Racer, bool>> predicate = r => r.Country == "Brazil";
```

Instead of using delegates, the compiler emits an expression tree to the assembly. The expression tree can be read during runtime. Expression trees are built from classes derived from the abstract base class `Expression`. The `Expression` class is not the same as `Expression<T>`. Some of the expression classes that inherit from `Expression` include `BinaryExpression`, `ConstantExpression`, `InvocationExpression`, `LambdaExpression`, `NewExpression`, `NewArrayExpression`, `TernaryExpression`, `UnaryExpression`, and more. The compiler creates an expression tree resulting from the lambda expression.

For example, the lambda expression `r.Country == "Brazil"` makes use of `ParameterExpression`, `MemberExpression`, `ConstantExpression`, and `MethodCallExpression` to create a tree and store the tree in the assembly. This tree is then used during runtime to create an optimized query to the underlying data source.

The method `DisplayTree` is implemented to display an expression tree graphically on the console. In the following example, an `Expression` object can be passed, and depending on the expression type some information about the expression is written to the console. Depending on the type of the expression, `DisplayTree` is called recursively:

> **NOTE** *This method does not deal with all expression types, only the types that are used with the following example expression.*

```
private static void DisplayTree(int indent, string message,
                                Expression expression)
{
  string output = $"{string.Empty.PadLeft(indent, '>')} {message} " +
    $"! NodeType: {expression.NodeType}; Expr: {expression}";

  indent++;
  switch (expression.NodeType)
  {
    case ExpressionType.Lambda:
      Console.WriteLine(output);
      LambdaExpression lambdaExpr = (LambdaExpression)expression;
      foreach (var parameter in lambdaExpr.Parameters)
```

```
        {
          DisplayTree(indent, "Parameter", parameter);
        }
        DisplayTree(indent, "Body", lambdaExpr.Body);
        break;
      case ExpressionType.Constant:
        ConstantExpression constExpr = (ConstantExpression)expression;
        WriteLine($"{output} Const Value: {constExpr.Value}");
        break;
      case ExpressionType.Parameter:
        ParameterExpression paramExpr = (ParameterExpression)expression;
        WriteLine($"{output} Param Type: {paramExpr.Type.Name}");
        break;
      case ExpressionType.Equal:
      case ExpressionType.AndAlso:
      case ExpressionType.GreaterThan:
        BinaryExpression binExpr = (BinaryExpression)expression;
        if (binExpr.Method != null)
        {
          WriteLine($"{output} Method: {binExpr.Method.Name}");
        }
        else
        {
          WriteLine(output);
        }
        DisplayTree(indent, "Left", binExpr.Left);
        DisplayTree(indent, "Right", binExpr.Right);
        break;
      case ExpressionType.MemberAccess:
        MemberExpression memberExpr = (MemberExpression)expression;
        WriteLine($"{output} Member Name: {memberExpr.Member.Name}, " +
                  " Type: {memberExpr.Expression}");
        DisplayTree(indent, "Member Expr", memberExpr.Expression);
        break;
      default:
        WriteLine();
        WriteLine($"{expression.NodeType} {expression.Type.Name}");
        break;
    }
  }
}
```

The expression that is used for showing the tree is already well known. It's a lambda expression with a
Racer parameter, and the body of the expression takes racers from Brazil only if they have won more than
six races:

```
Expression<Func<Racer, bool>> expression =
  r => r.Country == "Brazil" && r.Wins > 6;

DisplayTree(0, "Lambda", expression);
```

Looking at the tree result, you can see from the output that the lambda expression consists of a `Parameter`
and an `AndAlso` node type. The `AndAlso` node type has an `Equal` node type to the left and a `GreaterThan`
node type to the right. The `Equal` node type to the left of the `AndAlso` node type has a `MemberAccess` node
type to the left and a `Constant` node type to the right, and so on:

```
Lambda! NodeType: Lambda; Expr: r => ((r.Country == "Brazil") AndAlso (r.Wins > 6))
> Parameter! NodeType: Parameter; Expr: r Param Type: Racer
> Body! NodeType: AndAlso; Expr: ((r.Country == "Brazil") AndAlso (r.Wins > 6))
>> Left! NodeType: Equal; Expr: (r.Country == "Brazil") Method: op_Equality
>>> Left! NodeType: MemberAccess; Expr: r.Country Member Name: Country, Type: String
>>>> Member Expr! NodeType: Parameter; Expr: r Param Type: Racer
>>> Right! NodeType: Constant; Expr: "Brazil" Const Value: Brazil
>> Right! NodeType: GreaterThan; Expr: (r.Wins > 6)
```

```
>>> Left! NodeType: MemberAccess; Expr: r.Wins  Member Name: Wins, Type: Int32
>>>> Member Expr! NodeType: Parameter; Expr: r Param Type: Racer
>>> Right! NodeType: Constant; Expr: 6 Const Value: 6
```

Examples where the `Expression<T>` type is used are with the ADO.NET Entity Framework and the client provider for WCF Data Services. These technologies define methods with `Expression<T>` parameters. This way the LINQ provider accessing the database can create a runtime–optimized query by reading the expressions to get the data from the database.

LINQ PROVIDERS

.NET includes several LINQ providers. A LINQ provider implements the standard query operators for a specific data source. LINQ providers might implement more extension methods than are defined by LINQ, but the standard operators must at least be implemented. LINQ to XML implements additional methods that are particularly useful with XML, such as the methods `Elements`, `Descendants`, and `Ancestors` defined by the class `Extensions` in the `System.Xml.Linq` namespace.

Implementation of the LINQ provider is selected based on the namespace and the type of the first parameter. The namespace of the class that implements the extension methods must be opened; otherwise, the extension class is not in scope. The parameter of the `Where` method defined by LINQ to Objects and the `Where` method defined by LINQ to Entities is different.

The `Where` method of LINQ to Objects is defined with the `Enumerable` class:

```
public static IEnumerable<TSource> Where<TSource>(
    this IEnumerable<TSource> source, Func<TSource, bool> predicate);
```

Inside the `System.Linq` namespace is another class that implements the operator `Where`. This implementation is used by LINQ to Entities. You can find the implementation in the class `Queryable`:

```
public static IQueryable<TSource> Where<TSource>(
    this IQueryable<TSource> source,
    Expression<Func<TSource, bool>> predicate);
```

Both of these classes are implemented in the `System.Core` assembly in the `System.Linq` namespace. How does the compiler select what method to use, and what's the magic with the Expression type? The lambda expression is the same regardless of whether it is passed with a `Func<TSource, bool>` parameter or an `Expression<Func<TSource, bool>gt;` parameter—only the compiler behaves differently. The selection is done based on the `source` parameter. The method that matches best based on its parameters is chosen by the compiler. The `CreateQuery<T>` method of the `ObjectContext` class that is defined by ADO.NET Entity Framework returns an `ObjectQuery<T>` object that implements `IQueryable<TSource>`, and thus the Entity Framework uses the `Where` method of the `Queryable` class.

SUMMARY

This chapter described and demonstrated the LINQ query and the language constructs on which the query is based, such as extension methods and lambda expressions. You've looked at the various LINQ query operators—not only for filtering and ordering of data sources, but also for partitioning, grouping, doing conversions, joins, and so on.

With Parallel LINQ, you've seen how longer queries can easily be parallelized.

Another important concept of this chapter is the expression tree. Expression trees enable building the query to the data source at runtime because the tree is stored in the assembly. You can read about its great advantages in Chapter 38. LINQ is a very in-depth topic, and you can see Chapter 27 for more information. Other third-party providers are also available for download, such as LINQ to MySQL, LINQ to Amazon, LINQ to Flickr, LINQ to LDAP, and LINQ to SharePoint. No matter what data source you have, with LINQ you can use the same query syntax.

The next chapter covers errors and exceptions, and explains how you can catch exceptions.

14

Errors and Exceptions

WHAT'S IN THIS CHAPTER?

➤ Looking at the exception classes

➤ Using try…catch…finally to capture exceptions

➤ Filtering exceptions

➤ Creating user-defined exceptions

➤ Retrieving caller information

WROX.COM CODE DOWNLOADS FOR THIS CHAPTER

The wrox.com code downloads for this chapter are found at www.wrox.com/go/professionalcsharp6 on the Download Code tab. The code for this chapter is divided into the following major examples:

➤ Simple Exceptions

➤ ExceptionFilters

➤ RethrowExceptions

➤ Solicit Cold Call

➤ Caller Information

INTRODUCTION

Errors happen, and they are not always caused by the person who coded the application. Sometimes your application generates an error because of an action that was initiated by the end user of the application, or it might be simply due to the environmental context in which your code is running. In any case, you should anticipate errors occurring in your applications and code accordingly.

The .NET Framework has enhanced the ways in which you deal with errors. C#'s mechanism for handling error conditions enables you to provide custom handling for each type of error condition, as well as to separate the code that identifies errors from the code that handles them.

No matter how good your coding is, your programs should be capable of handling any possible errors that might occur. For example, in the middle of some complex processing of your code, you might discover that it doesn't have permission to read a file; or, while it is sending network requests, the network might go down. In such exceptional situations, it is not enough for a method to simply return an appropriate error code—there might be 15 or 20 nested method calls, so what you really want the program to do is jump back up through all those calls to exit the task completely and take the appropriate counteractions. The C# language has very good facilities for handling this kind of situation, through the mechanism known as *exception handling*.

This chapter covers catching and throwing exceptions in many different scenarios. You see exception types from different namespaces and their hierarchy, and you find out how to create custom exception types. You discover different ways to catch exceptions—for example, how to catch exceptions with the exact exception type or a base class. You also see how to deal with nested `try` blocks, and how you could catch exceptions that way. For code that should be invoked no matter whether an exception occurs or the code continues with any error, you are introduced to creating `try/finally` code blocks. This chapter also covers a new feature of C# 6: exception filters.

By the end of this chapter, you will have a good grasp of advanced exception handling in your C# applications.

EXCEPTION CLASSES

In C#, an exception is an object created (or *thrown*) when a particular exceptional error condition occurs. This object contains information that should help identify the problem. Although you can create your own exception classes (and you do so later), .NET includes many predefined exception classes—too many to provide a comprehensive list here. The class hierarchy diagram in Figure 14-1 shows a few of these classes to give you a sense of the general pattern. This section provides a quick survey of some of the exceptions available in the .NET base class library.

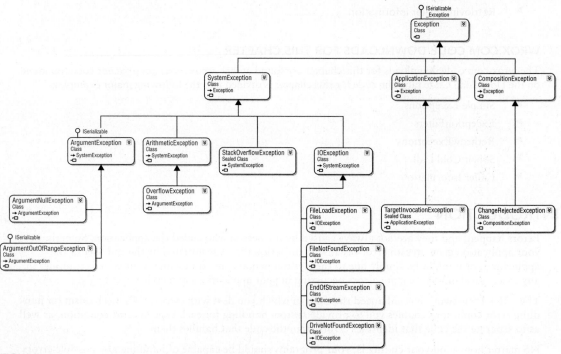

FIGURE 14-1

All the classes in Figure 14.1 are part of the System namespace, except for IOException and CompositionException and the classes derived from these two classes. IOException and its derived classes are part of the namespace System.IO. The System.IO namespace deals with reading from and writing to files. CompositionException and its derived classes are part of the namespace System.ComponentModel.Composition. This namespace deals with dynamically loading parts and components. In general, there is no specific namespace for exceptions. Exception classes should be placed in whatever namespace is appropriate to the classes that can generate them—hence, I/O-related exceptions are in the System.IO namespace. You find exception classes in quite a few of the base class namespaces.

The generic exception class, System.Exception, is derived from System.Object, as you would expect for a .NET class. In general, you should not throw generic System.Exception objects in your code, because they provide no specifics about the error condition.

Two important classes in the hierarchy are derived from System.Exception:

➤ SystemException—This class is for exceptions that are usually thrown by the .NET runtime or that are considered to be of a generic nature and might be thrown by almost any application. For example, StackOverflowException is thrown by the .NET runtime if it detects that the stack is full. However, you might choose to throw ArgumentException or its subclasses in your own code if you detect that a method has been called with inappropriate arguments. Subclasses of SystemException include classes that represent both fatal and nonfatal errors.

➤ ApplicationException—With the initial design of the .NET Framework, this class was meant to be the base class for custom application exception classes. However, some exception classes that are thrown by the CLR derive from this base class (for example, TargetInvocationException), and exceptions thrown from applications derive from SystemException (for example, ArgumentException). Therefore, it's no longer a good practice to derive custom exception types from ApplicationException, as this doesn't offer any benefits. Instead, custom exception classes can derive directly from the Exception base class. Many exception classes in the .NET Framework directly derive from Exception.

Other exception classes that might come in handy include the following:

➤ StackOverflowException—This exception is thrown when the area of memory allocated to the stack is full. A stack overflow can occur if a method continuously calls itself recursively. This is generally a fatal error, because it prevents your application from doing anything apart from terminating (in which case it is unlikely that even the finally block will execute). Trying to handle errors like this yourself is usually pointless; instead, you should have the application gracefully exit.

➤ EndOfStreamException—The usual cause of an EndOfStreamException is an attempt to read past the end of a file. A *stream* represents a flow of data between data sources. Streams are covered in detail in Chapter 25, "Networking."

➤ OverflowException—An example when this occurs is if you attempt to cast an int containing a value of -40 to a uint in a checked context.

The other exception classes shown in Figure 14.1 are not discussed here. They are just shown to illustrate the hierarchy of exception classes.

The class hierarchy for exceptions is somewhat unusual in that most of these classes do not add any functionality to their respective base classes. However, in the case of exception handling, the common reason for adding inherited classes is to indicate more specific error conditions. Often, it isn't necessary to override methods or add any new ones (although it is not uncommon to add extra properties that carry extra information about the error condition). For example, you might have a base ArgumentException class intended for method calls whereby inappropriate values are passed in, and an ArgumentNullException class derived from it, which is intended to handle a null argument if passed.

CATCHING EXCEPTIONS

Given that the .NET Framework includes a selection of predefined base class exception objects, this section describes how you use them in your code to trap error conditions. In dealing with possible error conditions in C# code, you typically divide the relevant part of your program into blocks of three different types:

➤ `try` blocks encapsulate the code that forms part of the normal operation of your program and that might encounter some serious error conditions.

➤ `catch` blocks encapsulate the code dealing with the various error conditions that your code might have encountered by working through any of the code in the accompanying `try` block. This block could also be used for logging errors.

➤ `finally` blocks encapsulate the code that cleans up any resources or takes any other action that you normally want handled at the end of a `try` or `catch` block. It is important to understand that the `finally` block is executed whether an exception is thrown. Because the purpose of the `finally` block is to contain cleanup code that should always be executed, the compiler flags an error if you place a `return` statement inside a `finally` block. An example of using the `finally` block is closing any connections that were opened in the `try` block. Understand that the `finally` block is completely optional. If your application does not require any cleanup code (such as disposing of or closing any open objects), then there is no need for this block.

The following steps outline how these blocks work together to trap error conditions:

1. The execution flow first enters the `try` block.
2. If no errors occur in the `try` block, execution proceeds normally through the block, and when the end of the `try` block is reached, the flow of execution jumps to the `finally` block if one is present (Step 5). However, if an error does occur within the `try` block, execution jumps to a `catch` block (Step 3).
3. The error condition is handled in the `catch` block.
4. At the end of the `catch` block, execution automatically transfers to the `finally` block if one is present.
5. The `finally` block is executed (if present).

The C# syntax used to bring all this about looks roughly like this:

```
try
{
  // code for normal execution
}
catch
{
  // error handling
}
finally
{
  // clean up
}
```

Actually, a few variations on this theme exist:

➤ You can omit the `finally` block because it is optional.

➤ You can also supply as many `catch` blocks as you want to handle specific types of errors. However, you don't want to get too carried away and have a huge number of `catch` blocks.

➤ You can define filters with catch blocks to catch the exception with the specific block only if the filter matches.

➤ You can omit the `catch` blocks altogether, in which case the syntax serves not to identify exceptions, but as a way to guarantee that code in the `finally` block will be executed when execution leaves the `try` block. This is useful if the `try` block contains several exit points.

So far so good, but the question that has yet to be answered is this: If the code is running in the `try` block, how does it know when to switch to the `catch` block if an error occurs? If an error is detected, the code does something known as *throwing an exception*. In other words, it instantiates an exception object class and throws it:

```
throw new OverflowException();
```

Here, you have instantiated an exception object of the `OverflowException` class. As soon as the application encounters a `throw` statement inside a `try` block, it immediately looks for the `catch` block associated with that `try` block. If more than one `catch` block is associated with the `try` block, it identifies the correct `catch` block by checking which exception class the `catch` block is associated with. For example, when the `OverflowException` object is thrown, execution jumps to the following `catch` block:

```
catch (OverflowException ex)
{
    // exception handling here
}
```

In other words, the application looks for the `catch` block that indicates a matching exception class instance of the same class (or of a base class).

With this extra information, you can expand the `try` block just demonstrated. Assume, for the sake of argument, that two possible serious errors can occur in the `try` block: an overflow and an array out of bounds. Assume also that your code contains two Boolean variables, `Overflow` and `OutOfBounds`, which indicate whether these conditions exist. You have already seen that a predefined exception class exists to indicate overflow (`OverflowException`); similarly, an `IndexOutOfRangeException` class exists to handle an array that is out of bounds.

Now your `try` block looks like this:

```
try
{
    // code for normal execution

    if (Overflow == true)
    {
        throw new OverflowException();
    }

    // more processing

    if (OutOfBounds == true)
    {
        throw new IndexOutOfRangeException();
    }

    // otherwise continue normal execution
}
catch (OverflowException ex)
{
    // error handling for the overflow error condition
}
catch (IndexOutOfRangeException ex)
{
    // error handling for the index out of range error condition
}
finally
{
    // clean up
}
```

This is because you can have `throw` statements that are nested in several method calls inside the `try` block, but the same `try` block continues to apply even as execution flow enters these other methods. If the application encounters a `throw` statement, it immediately goes back up through all the method calls on the stack, looking for the end of the containing `try` block and the start of the appropriate `catch` block. During this process, all the local variables in the intermediate method calls will correctly go out of scope. This makes the `try...catch` architecture well suited to the situation described at the beginning of this section, whereby the error occurs inside a method call that is nested inside 15 or 20 method calls, and processing has to stop immediately.

As you can probably gather from this discussion, `try` blocks can play a very significant role in controlling the flow of your code's execution. However, it is important to understand that exceptions are intended for exceptional conditions, hence their name. You wouldn't want to use them as a way of controlling when to exit a `do...while` loop.

Implementing Multiple Catch Blocks

The easiest way to see how `try...catch...finally` blocks work in practice is with a couple of examples. The first example is called `SimpleExceptions`. It repeatedly asks the user to type in a number and then displays it. However, for the sake of this example, imagine that the number has to be between 0 and 5; otherwise, the program isn't able to process the number properly. Therefore, you throw an exception if the user types anything outside this range. The program then continues to ask for more numbers for processing until the user simply presses the Enter key without entering anything.

> **NOTE** *You should note that this code does not provide a good example of when to use exception handling, but it shows good practice on how to use exception handling. As their name suggests, exceptions are provided for other than normal circumstances. Users often type silly things, so this situation doesn't really count. Normally, your program will handle incorrect user input by performing an instant check and asking the user to retype the input if it isn't valid. However, generating exceptional situations is difficult in a small example that you can read through in a few minutes, so I will tolerate this less than ideal one to demonstrate how exceptions work. The examples that follow present more realistic situations.*

The sample code for `SimpleExceptions` makes use of the following dependencies and namespaces:

Dependencies

```
NETStandard.Library
```

Namespaces

```
System
static System.Console
```

The code for `SimpleExceptions` looks like this (code file `SimpleExceptions/Program.cs`):

```
using System;
using static System.Console;

namespace Wrox.ProCSharp.ErrorsAndExceptions
{
  public class Program
  {
```

```
public static void Main()
{
    while (true)
    {
        try
        {
            string userInput;

            Write("Input a number between 0 and 5 " +
                "(or just hit return to exit)> ");
            userInput = ReadLine();

            if (string.IsNullOrEmpty(userInput))
            {
                break;
            }

            int index = Convert.ToInt32(userInput);

            if (index < 0 || index > 5)
            {
                throw new IndexOutOfRangeException($"You typed in {userInput}");
            }

            WriteLine($"Your number was {index}");
        }
        catch (IndexOutOfRangeException ex)
        {
            WriteLine("Exception: " +
                $"Number should be between 0 and 5. {ex.Message}");
        }
        catch (Exception ex)
        {
            WriteLine($"An exception was thrown. Message was: {ex.Message}");
        }
        finally
        {
            WriteLine("Thank you\n");
        }
    }
}
```

The core of this code is a while loop, which continually uses ReadLine to ask for user input. ReadLine returns a string, so your first task is to convert it to an int using the System.Convert.ToInt32 method. The System.Convert class contains various useful methods to perform data conversions, and it provides an alternative to the int.Parse method. In general, System.Convert contains methods to perform various type conversions. Recall that the C# compiler resolves int to instances of the System.Int32 base class.

> **NOTE** *It is also worth pointing out that the parameter passed to the* catch *block is scoped to that* catch *block—which is why you are able to use the same parameter name,* ex, *in successive* catch *blocks in the preceding code.*

In the preceding example, you also check for an empty string because it is your condition for exiting the while loop. Notice how the break statement actually breaks right out of the enclosing try block as well as the while loop because this is valid behavior. Of course, when execution breaks out of the try block, the WriteLine statement in the finally block is executed. Although you just display a greeting here, more commonly you will be doing tasks like closing file handles and calling the Dispose method of various objects to perform any cleanup. After the application leaves the finally block, it simply carries on executing into the next statement that it would have executed had the finally block not been present. In the case of this example, though, you iterate back to the start of the while loop and enter the try block again (unless the finally block was entered as a result of executing the break statement in the while loop, in which case you simply exit the while loop).

Next, you check for your exception condition:

```
if (index < 0 || index > 5)
{
   throw new IndexOutOfRangeException($"You typed in {userInput}");
}
```

When throwing an exception, you need to specify what type of exception to throw. Although the class System.Exception is available, it is intended only as a base class. It is considered bad programming practice to throw an instance of this class as an exception, because it conveys no information about the nature of the error condition. Instead, the .NET Framework contains many other exception classes that are derived from Exception. Each of these matches a particular type of exception condition, and you are free to define your own as well. The goal is to provide as much information as possible about the particular exception condition by throwing an instance of a class that matches the particular error condition. In the preceding example, System.IndexOutOfRangeException is the best choice for the circumstances. IndexOutOfRangeException has several constructor overloads. The one chosen in the example takes a string describing the error. Alternatively, you might choose to derive your own custom Exception object that describes the error condition in the context of your application.

Suppose that the user next types a number that is not between 0 and 5. The number is picked up by the if statement and an IndexOutOfRangeException object is instantiated and thrown. At this point, the application immediately exits the try block and hunts for a catch block that handles IndexOutOfRangeException. The first catch block it encounters is this:

```
catch (IndexOutOfRangeException ex)
{
   WriteLine($"Exception: Number should be between 0 and 5. {ex.Message}");
}
```

Because this catch block takes a parameter of the appropriate class, the catch block receives the exception instance and is executed. In this case, you display an error message and the Exception.Message property (which corresponds to the string passed to the IndexOutOfRangeException's constructor). After executing this catch block, control then switches to the finally block, just as if no exception had occurred.

Notice that in the example you have also provided another catch block:

```
catch (Exception ex)
{
   WriteLine($"An exception was thrown. Message was: {ex.Message}");
}
```

This catch block would also be capable of handling an IndexOutOfRangeException if it weren't for the fact that such exceptions will already have been caught by the previous catch block. A reference to a base class can also refer to any instances of classes derived from it, and all exceptions are derived from Exception. This catch block isn't executed because the application executes only the first suitable catch block it finds from the list of available catch blocks. This catch block isn't executed when an exception of type IndexOutOfRangeException is thrown. The application only executes the first suitable catch block it finds from the list of available catch blocks. This second catch block catches other exceptions derived from the Exception base class. Be aware that the three separate calls to methods within the try block (Console. ReadLine; Console.Write, and Convert.ToInt32) might throw other exceptions.

If the user types something that is not a number—say a or `hello`—the `Convert.ToInt32` method throws an exception of the class `System.FormatException` to indicate that the string passed into `ToInt32` is not in a format that can be converted to an `int`. When this happens, the application traces back through the method calls, looking for a handler that can handle this exception. Your first `catch` block (the one that takes an `IndexOutOfRangeException`) will not do. The application then looks at the second `catch` block. This one will do because `FormatException` is derived from `Exception`, so a `FormatException` instance can be passed in as a parameter here.

The structure of the example is actually fairly typical of a situation with multiple `catch` blocks. You start with `catch` blocks that are designed to trap specific error conditions. Then, you finish with more general blocks that cover any errors for which you have not written specific error handlers. Indeed, the order of the `catch` blocks is important. Had you written the previous two blocks in the opposite order, the code would not have compiled, because the second `catch` block is unreachable (the `Exception` `catch` block would catch all exceptions). Therefore, the uppermost `catch` blocks should be the most granular options available, ending with the most general options.

Now that you have analyzed the code for the example, you can run it. The following output illustrates what happens with different inputs and demonstrates both the `IndexOutOfRangeException` and the `FormatException` being thrown:

```
SimpleExceptions
Input a number between 0 and 5 (or just hit return to exit)> 4
Your number was 4
Thank you

Input a number between 0 and 5 (or just hit return to exit)> 0
Your number was 0
Thank you

Input a number between 0 and 5 (or just hit return to exit)> 10
Exception: Number should be between 0 and 5. You typed in 10
Thank you

Input a number between 0 and 5 (or just hit return to exit)> hello
An exception was thrown. Message was: Input string was not in a correct format.
Thank you

Input a number between 0 and 5 (or just hit return to exit)>
Thank you
```

Catching Exceptions from Other Code

The previous example demonstrates the handling of two exceptions. One of them, `IndexOutOfRangeException`, was thrown by your own code. The other, `FormatException`, was thrown from inside one of the base classes. It is very common for code in a library to throw an exception if it detects that a problem has occurred, or if one of the methods has been called inappropriately by being passed the wrong parameters. However, library code rarely attempts to catch exceptions; this is regarded as the responsibility of the client code.

Often, exceptions are thrown from the base class libraries while you are debugging. The process of debugging to some extent involves determining why exceptions have been thrown and removing the causes. Your aim should be to ensure that by the time the code is actually shipped, exceptions occur only in very exceptional circumstances and, if possible, are handled appropriately in your code.

System.Exception Properties

The example illustrated the use of only the `Message` property of the exception object. However, a number of other properties are available in `System.Exception`, as shown in the following table.

PROPERTY	DESCRIPTION
Data	Enables you to add key/value statements to the exception that can be used to supply extra information about it.
HelpLink	A link to a help file that provides more information about the exception.
InnerException	If this exception was thrown inside a `catch` block, then `InnerException` contains the exception object that sent the code into that `catch` block.
Message	Text that describes the error condition.
Source	The name of the application or object that caused the exception.
StackTrace	Provides details about the method calls on the stack (to help track down the method that threw the exception).

The property value for `StackTrace` is supplied automatically by the .NET runtime if a stack trace is available. `Source` will always be filled in by the .NET runtime as the name of the assembly in which the exception was raised (though you might want to modify the property in your code to give more specific information), whereas `Data`, `Message`, `HelpLink`, and `InnerException` must be filled in by the code that threw the exception, by setting these properties immediately before throwing the exception. For example, the code to throw an exception might look something like this:

```
if (ErrorCondition == true)
{
  var myException = new ClassMyException("Help!!!!");
  myException.Source = "My Application Name";
  myException.HelpLink = "MyHelpFile.txt";
  myException.Data["ErrorDate"] = DateTime.Now;
  myException.Data.Add("AdditionalInfo", "Contact Bill from the Blue Team");
  throw myException;
}
```

Here, `ClassMyException` is the name of the particular exception class you are throwing. Note that it is common practice for the names of all exception classes to end with `Exception`. In addition, note that the `Data` property is assigned in two possible ways.

Exception Filters

A new feature of C# 6 is exception filters. You can have different catch blocks that act differently when catching different exception types. In some scenarios, it's useful to have the catch blocks act differently based on the content of an exception. For example, when using the Windows runtime you often get COM exceptions for all different kinds of exceptions, or when doing network calls you get a network exception for many different scenarios—for example, if the server is not available, or the data supplied do not match the expectations. It's good to react to these errors differently. Some exceptions can be recovered in different ways, while with others the user might need some information.

The following code sample throws the exception of type `MyCustomException` and sets the `ErrorCode` property of this exception (code file `ExceptionFilters/Program.cs`):

```
public static void ThrowWithErrorCode(int code)
{
  throw new MyCustomException("Error in Foo") { ErrorCode = code };
}
```

In the `Main` method, the try block safeguards the method invocation with two catch blocks. The first catch block uses the `when` keyword to filter only exceptions if the `ErrorCode` property equals 405. The expression for the `when` clause needs to return a Boolean value. If the result is `true`, this catch block handles the exception. If it is `false`, other catches are looked for. Passing 405 to the method `ThrowWithErrorCode`, the filter returns `true`, and the first `catch` handles the exception. Passing another value, the filter returns `false` and the second `catch` handles the exception. With filters, you can have multiple handlers to handle the same exception type.

Of course you can also remove the second `catch` block and not handle the exception in that circumstance.

```
try
{
    ThrowWithErrorCode(405);
}
catch (MyCustomException ex) when (ex.ErrorCode == 405)
{
    WriteLine($"Exception caught with filter {ex.Message} and {ex.ErrorCode}");
}
catch (MyCustomException ex)
{
    WriteLine($"Exception caught {ex.Message} and {ex.ErrorCode}");
}
```

Re-throwing Exceptions

When you catch exceptions it's also very common to re-throw exceptions. You can change the exception type while throwing the exception again. With this you can give the caller more information about what happened. The original exception might not have enough information about the context of what was going on. You can also log exception information and give the caller different information. For example, for a user running the application, exception information does not really help. A system administrator reading log files can react accordingly.

An issue with re-throwing exceptions is that the caller often needs to find out the reason what happened with the earlier exception, and where did this happen. Depending on how exceptions are thrown, stack trace information might be lost. For you to see the different options on re-throwing exceptions, the sample program `RethrowExceptions` shows the different options.

The code sample for re-throwing exceptions makes use of the following dependencies and namespaces:

Dependencies

    NETStandard.Library

Namespaces

    System
    static System.Console

For this sample, two custom exception types are created. The first one, `MyCustomException` defines the property `ErrorCode` in addition to the members of the base class `Exception` the second one, `AnotherCustomException`, supports passing an inner exception (code file `RethrowExceptions/ MyCustomException.cs`):

```
public class MyCustomException : Exception
{
    public MyCustomException(string message)
        : base(message)
    {
    }
    public int ErrorCode { get; set; }
}
public class AnotherCustomException : Exception
{
    public AnotherCustomException(string message, Exception innerException)
```

```
                : base(message, innerException)
      {
      }
    }
```

The method `HandleAll` invokes the methods `HandleAndThrowAgain`, `HandleAndThrowWithInnerException`, `HandleAndRethrow`, and `HandleWithFilter`. The exception that is thrown is caught to write the exception message as well as the stack trace to the console. To better find what line numbers are referenced from the stack trace, the `#line` preprocessor directive is used that restarts the line numbering. With this, the invocation of the methods using the delegate m is in line 114 (code file `RethrowExceptions/Program.cs`):

```
#line 100
public static void HandleAll()
{
  var methods = new Action[]
  {
    HandleAndThrowAgain,
    HandleAndThrowWithInnerException,
    HandleAndRethrow,
    HandleWithFilter
  };

  foreach (var m in methods)
  {
    try
    {
      m();  // line 114
    }
    catch (Exception ex)
    {
      WriteLine(ex.Message);
      WriteLine(ex.StackTrace);
      if (ex.InnerException != null)
      {
        WriteLine($"\tInner Exception{ex.Message}");
        WriteLine(ex.InnerException.StackTrace);
      }
      WriteLine();
    }
  }
}
```

The method `ThrowAnException` is the one to throw the first exception. This exception is thrown in line 8002. During development, it helps to know where this exception is thrown:

```
#line 8000
public static void ThrowAnException(string message)
{
  throw new MyCustomException(message);  // line 8002
}
```

Naïve Use to Rethrow the Exception

The method `HandleAndThrowAgain` does nothing more than log the exception to the console and throw it again using `throw ex`:

```
#line 4000
public static void HandleAndThrowAgain()
{
  try
  {
```

```
        ThrowAnException("test 1");
    }
    catch (Exception ex)
    {
        WriteLine($"Log exception {ex.Message} and throw again");
        throw ex;  // you shouldn't do that - line 4009
    }
}
```

Running the application, a simplified output showing the stack-trace (without the namespace and the full path to the code files) is shown here:

```
Log exception test 1 and throw again
test 1
    at Program.HandleAndThrowAgain() in Program.cs:line 4009
    at Program.HandleAll() in Program.cs:line 114
```

The stack trace shows the call to the m method within the `HandleAll` method, which in turn invokes the `HandleAndThrowAgain` method. The information where the exception is thrown at first is completely lost in the call stack of the final catch. This makes it hard to find the original reason of an error. Usually it's not a good idea to just throw the same exception with `throw` passing the exception object.

Changing the Exception

One useful scenario is to change the type of the exception and add information to the error. This is done in the method `HandleAndThrowWithInnerException`. After logging the error, a new exception of type `AnotherException` is thrown passing ex as the inner exception:

```
#line 3000
public static void HandleAndThrowWithInnerException()
{
    try
    {
        ThrowAnException("test 2");  // line 3004
    }
    catch (Exception ex)
    {
        WriteLine($"Log exception {ex.Message} and throw again");
        throw new AnotherCustomException("throw with inner exception", ex); // 3009
    }
}
```

Checking the stack trace of the outer exception, you see line numbers 3009 and 114 similar to before. However, the inner exception gives the original reason of the error. It gives the line of the method that invoked the erroneous method (3004) and the line where the original (the inner) exception was thrown (8002):

```
Log exception test 2 and throw again
throw with inner exception
    at Program.HandleAndThrowWithInnerException() in Program.cs:line 3009
    at Program.HandleAll() in Program.cs:line 114
        Inner Exception throw with inner exception
    at Program.ThrowAnException(String message) in Program.cs:line 8002
    at Program.HandleAndThrowWithInnerException() in Program.cs:line 3004
```

No information is lost this way.

> **NOTE** *When trying to find reasons for an error, have a look at whether an inner exception exists. This often gives helpful information.*

> **NOTE** *When catching exceptions, it's good practice to change the exception when rethrowing. For example, catching an* `SqlException` *can result in throwing a business-related exception such as* `InvalidIsbnException`.

Rethrowing the Exception

In case the exception type should not be changed, the same exception can be rethrown just with the `throw` statement. Using throw without passing an exception object throws the current exception of the `catch` block and keeps the exception information:

```
#line 2000
public static void HandleAndRethrow()
{
  try
  {
    ThrowAnException("test 3");
  }
  catch (Exception ex)
  {
    WriteLine($"Log exception {ex.Message} and rethrow");
    throw;  // line 2009
  }
}
```

With this in place, the stack information is not lost. The exception was originally thrown in line 8002, and rethrown in line 2009. Line 114 contains the delegate m that invoked `HandleAndRethrow`:

```
Log exception test 3 and rethrow
test 3
   at Program.ThrowAnException(String message) in Program.cs:line 8002
   at Program.HandleAndRethrow() in Program.cs:line 2009
   at Program.HandleAll() in Program.cs:line 114
```

Using Filters to Add Functionality

When rethrowing exceptions using the `throw` statement, the call stack contains the address of the throw. When you use exception filters, it is possible to not change the call stack at all. Now add a `when` keyword that passes a filter method. This filter method named `Filter` logs the message and always returns `false`. That's why the `catch` block is never invoked:

```
#line 1000
public void HandleWithFilter()
{
  try
  {
    ThrowAnException("test 4");  // line 1004
  }
  catch (Exception ex) when(Filter(ex))
  {
    WriteLine("block never invoked");
  }
}

#line 1500
public bool Filter(Exception ex)
{
  WriteLine($"just log {ex.Message}");
```

```
        return false;
    }
```

Now when you look at the stack trace, the exception originates in the `HandleAll` method in line 114 that in turn invokes `HandleWithFilter`, line 1004 contains the invocation to `ThrowAnException`, and line 8002 contains the line where the exception was thrown:

```
just log test 4
test 4
    at Program.ThrowAnException(String message) in Program.cs:line 8002
    at Program.HandleWithFilter() in Program.cs:line 1004
    at RethrowExceptions.Program.HandleAll() in Program.cs:line 114
```

> **NOTE** *The primary use of exception filters is to filter exceptions based on a value of the exception. Exception filters can also be used for other effects, such as writing log information without changing the call stack. However, exception filters should be fast running so you should only do simple checks.*

What Happens If an Exception Isn't Handled?

Sometimes an exception might be thrown but there is no `catch` block in your code that is able to handle that kind of exception. The `SimpleExceptions` example can serve to illustrate this. Suppose, for example, that you omitted the `FormatException` and catch-all `catch` blocks, and supplied only the block that traps an `IndexOutOfRangeException`. In that circumstance, what would happen if a `FormatException` were thrown?

The answer is that the .NET runtime would catch it. Later in this section, you learn how you can nest `try` blocks; and, in fact, there is already a nested `try` block behind the scenes in the example. The .NET runtime has effectively placed the entire program inside another huge `try` block—it does this for every .NET program. This `try` block has a `catch` handler that can catch any type of exception. If an exception occurs that your code does not handle, the execution flow simply passes right out of your program and is trapped by this `catch` block in the .NET runtime. However, the results of this probably will not be what you want, as the execution of your code is terminated promptly. The user sees a dialog that complains that your code has not handled the exception and provides any details about the exception the .NET runtime was able to retrieve. At least the exception has been caught!

In general, if you are writing an executable, try to catch as many exceptions as you reasonably can and handle them in a sensible way. If you are writing a library, it is normally best to catch exceptions that you can handle in a useful way, or where you can add additional information to the context and throw other exception types as shown in the previous section. Assume that the calling code handles any errors it encounters.

USER-DEFINED EXCEPTION CLASSES

In the previous section, you already created a user-defined exception. You are now ready to look at a larger example that illustrates exceptions. This example, called `SolicitColdCall`, contains two nested `try` blocks and illustrates the practice of defining your own custom exception classes and throwing another exception from inside a `try` block.

This example assumes that a sales company wants to increase its customer base. The company's sales team is going to phone a list of people to invite them to become customers, a practice known in sales jargon as *cold-calling*. To this end, you have a text file available that contains the names of the people to be cold-called. The file should be in a well-defined format in which the first line contains the number of people in the file and each subsequent line contains the name of the next person. In other words, a correctly formatted file of names might look like this:

```
4
George Washington
Benedict Arnold
John Adams
Thomas Jefferson
```

This version of cold-calling is designed to display the name of the person on the screen (perhaps for the salesperson to read). That is why only the names, and not the phone numbers, of the individuals are contained in the file.

For this example, your program asks the user for the name of the file and then simply reads it in and displays the names of people. That sounds like a simple task, but even so a couple of things can go wrong and require you to abandon the entire procedure:

➤   The user might type the name of a file that does not exist. This is caught as a `FileNotFound` exception.

➤   The file might not be in the correct format. There are two possible problems here. One, the first line of the file might not be an integer. Two, there might not be as many names in the file as the first line of the file indicates. In both cases, you want to trap this oddity as a custom exception that has been written especially for this purpose, `ColdCallFileFormatException`.

There is something else that can go wrong that doesn't cause you to abandon the entire process but does mean you need to abandon a person's name and move on to the next name in the file (and therefore trap it by an inner `try` block). Some people are spies working for rival sales companies, so you obviously do not want to let these people know what you are up to by accidentally phoning one of them. For simplicity, assume that you can identify who the spies are because their names begin with B. Such people should have been screened out when the data file was first prepared, but in case any have slipped through, you need to check each name in the file and throw a `SalesSpyFoundException` if you detect a sales spy. This, of course, is another custom exception object.

Finally, you implement this example by coding a class, `ColdCallFileReader`, which maintains the connection to the cold-call file and retrieves data from it. You code this class in a safe way, which means that its methods all throw exceptions if they are called inappropriately—for example, if a method that reads a file is called before the file has even been opened. For this purpose, you write another exception class: `UnexpectedException`.

Catching the User-Defined Exceptions

The code sample for user-defined exceptions make use of the following dependencies and namespaces:

Dependencies

```
NETStandard.Library
```

Namespaces

```
System
System.IO
static System.Console
```

Start with the `Main` method of the `SolicitColdCall` sample, which catches your user-defined exceptions. Note that you need to call up file-handling classes in the `System.IO` namespace as well as the `System` namespace (code file `SolicitColdCall/Program.cs`):

```
using System;
using System.IO;
using static System.Console;

namespace Wrox.ProCSharp.ErrorsAndExceptions
```

```
{
    public class Program
    {
        public static void Main()
        {
            Write("Please type in the name of the file " +
                "containing the names of the people to be cold called > ");
            string fileName = ReadLine();
            ColdCallFileReaderLoop1(fileName);
            WriteLine();

            ReadLine();
        }

        public static ColdCallFileReaderLoop1(string filename)
        {
            var peopleToRing = new ColdCallFileReader();

            try
            {
                peopleToRing.Open(fileName);
                for (int i = 0; i < peopleToRing.NPeopleToRing; i++)
                {
                    peopleToRing.ProcessNextPerson();
                }
                WriteLine("All callers processed correctly");
            }
            catch(FileNotFoundException)
            {
                WriteLine($"The file {fileName} does not exist");
            }
            catch(ColdCallFileFormatException ex)
            {
                WriteLine($"The file {fileName} appears to have been corrupted");
                WriteLine($"Details of problem are: {ex.Message}");
                if (ex.InnerException != null)
                {
                    WriteLine($"Inner exception was: {ex.InnerException.Message}");
                }
            }
            catch(Exception ex)
            {
                WriteLine($"Exception occurred:\n{ex.Message}");
            }
            finally
            {
                peopleToRing.Dispose();
            }
        }
    }
}
```

This code is a little more than just a loop to process people from the file. You start by asking the user for the name of the file. Then you instantiate an object of a class called `ColdCallFileReader`, which is defined shortly. The `ColdCallFileReader` class is the class that handles the file reading. Notice that you do this outside the initial `try` block—that's because the variables that you instantiate here need to be available in the subsequent `catch` and `finally` blocks, and if you declare them inside the `try` block they would go out of scope at the closing curly brace of the `try` block, where the compiler would complain about it.

In the `try` block, you open the file (using the `ColdCallFileReader.Open` method) and loop over all the people in it. The `ColdCallFileReader.ProcessNextPerson` method reads in and displays the name of the next person in the file, and the `ColdCallFileReader.NPeopleToRing` property indicates how many people should be in the file (obtained by reading the file's first line). There are three catch blocks: one for FileNotFoundException, one for ColdCallFileFormatException, and one to trap any other .NET exceptions.

In the case of a FileNotFoundException, you display a message to that effect. Notice that in this catch block, the exception instance is not actually used at all. This catch block is used to illustrate the user-friendliness of the application. Exception objects generally contain technical information that is useful for developers, but not the sort of stuff you want to show to end users. Therefore, in this case you create a simpler message of your own.

For the ColdCallFileFormatException handler, you have done the opposite, specifying how to obtain fuller technical information, including details about the inner exception, if one is present.

Finally, if you catch any other generic exceptions, you display a user-friendly message, instead of letting any such exceptions fall through to the .NET runtime. Note that here you are not handling any other exceptions that aren't derived from System.Exception because you are not calling directly into non-.NET code.

The finally block is there to clean up resources. In this case, that means closing any open file—performed by the ColdCallFileReader.Dispose method.

> **NOTE** C# offers the using statement where the compiler itself creates a try/finally block calling the Dispose method in the finally block. The using statement is available on objects implementing a Dispose method. You can read the details of the using statement in Chapter 5, "Managed and Unmanaged Resources."

Throwing the User-Defined Exceptions

Now take a look at the definition of the class that handles the file reading and (potentially) throws your user-defined exceptions: ColdCallFileReader. Because this class maintains an external file connection, you need to ensure that it is disposed of correctly in accordance with the principles outlined for the disposing of objects in Chapter 4, "Inheritance." Therefore, you derive this class from IDisposable.

First, you declare some private fields (code file SolicitColdCall/ColdCallFileReader.cs):

```
public class ColdCallFileReader: IDisposable
{
  private FileStream _fs;
  private StreamReader _sr;
  private uint _nPeopleToRing;
  private bool _isDisposed = false;
  private bool _isOpen = false;
```

FileStream and StreamReader, both in the System.IO namespace, are the base classes that you use to read the file. FileStream enables you to connect to the file in the first place, whereas StreamReader is designed to read text files and implements a method, ReadLine, which reads a line of text from a file. You look at StreamReader more closely in Chapter 23, "Files and Streams," which discusses file handling in depth.

The isDisposed field indicates whether the Dispose method has been called. ColdCallFileReader is implemented so that after Dispose has been called, it is not permitted to reopen connections and reuse the object. isOpen is also used for error checking—in this case, checking whether the StreamReader actually connects to an open file.

The process of opening the file and reading in that first line—the one that tells you how many people are in the file—is handled by the Open method:

```
public void Open(string fileName)
{
  if (_isDisposed)
  {
    throw new ObjectDisposedException("peopleToRing");
  }

  _fs = new FileStream(fileName, FileMode.Open);
  _sr = new StreamReader(_fs);

  try
  {
    string firstLine = _sr.ReadLine();
    _nPeopleToRing = uint.Parse(firstLine);
    _isOpen = true;
  }
  catch (FormatException ex)
  {
    throw new ColdCallFileFormatException(
        $"First line isn\'t an integer {ex}");
  }
}
```

The first thing you do in this method (as with all other ColdCallFileReader methods) is check whether the client code has inappropriately called it after the object has been disposed of, and if so, throw a predefined ObjectDisposedException object. The Open method checks the _isDisposed field to determine whether Dispose has already been called. Because calling Dispose implies that the caller has now finished with this object, you regard it as an error to attempt to open a new file connection if Dispose has been called.

Next, the method contains the first of two inner try blocks. The purpose of this one is to catch any errors resulting from the first line of the file not containing an integer. If that problem arises, the .NET runtime throws a FormatException, which you trap and convert to a more meaningful exception that indicates a problem with the format of the cold-call file. Note that System.FormatException is there to indicate format problems with basic data types, not with files, so it's not a particularly useful exception to pass back to the calling routine in this case. The new exception thrown will be trapped by the outermost try block. Because no cleanup is needed here, there is no need for a finally block.

If everything is fine, you set the _isOpen field to true to indicate that there is now a valid file connection from which data can be read.

The ProcessNextPerson method also contains an inner try block:

```
public void ProcessNextPerson()
{
  if (_isDisposed)
  {
    throw new ObjectDisposedException("peopleToRing");
  }

  if (!_isOpen)
  {
    throw new UnexpectedException(
        "Attempted to access coldcall file that is not open");
  }

  try
  {
```

```
      string name = _sr.ReadLine();
      if (name == null)
      {
        throw new ColdCallFileFormatException("Not enough names");
      }
      if (name[0] == 'B')
      {
        throw new SalesSpyFoundException(name);
      }
      WriteLine(name);
    }
    catch(SalesSpyFoundException ex)
    {
      WriteLine(ex.Message);
    }
    finally
    {
    }
  }
```

Two possible problems exist with the file here (assuming there actually is an open file connection; the ProcessNextPerson method checks this first). One, you might read in the next name and discover that it is a sales spy. If that condition occurs, then the exception is trapped by the first catch block in this method. Because that exception has been caught here, inside the loop, it means that execution can subsequently continue in the Main method of the program, and the subsequent names in the file continue to be processed.

A problem might also occur if you try to read the next name and discover that you have already reached the end of the file. The StreamReader object's ReadLine method works like this: If it has gone past the end of the file, it doesn't throw an exception but simply returns null. Therefore, if you find a null string, you know that the format of the file was incorrect because the number in the first line of the file indicated a larger number of names than were actually present in the file. If that happens, you throw a ColdCallFileFormatException, which will be caught by the outer exception handler (which causes the execution to terminate).

Again, you don't need a finally block here because there is no cleanup to do; however, this time an empty finally block is included just to show that you can do so, if you want.

The example is nearly finished. You have just two more members of ColdCallFileReader to look at: the NPeopleToRing property, which returns the number of people that are supposed to be in the file, and the Dispose method, which closes an open file. Notice that the Dispose method returns immediately if it has already been called — this is the recommended way of implementing it. It also confirms that there actually is a file stream to close before closing it. This example is shown here to illustrate defensive coding techniques:

```
    public uint NPeopleToRing
    {
      get
      {
        if (_isDisposed)
        {
          throw new ObjectDisposedException("peopleToRing");
        }
        if (!_isOpen)
        {
          throw new UnexpectedException(
              "Attempted to access cold-call file that is not open");
        }

        return _nPeopleToRing;
      }
    }
```

```
public void Dispose()
{
  if (_isDisposed)
  {
    return;
  }

  _isDisposed = true;
  _isOpen = false;

  _fs?.Dispose();
  _fs = null;
}
```

Defining the User-Defined Exception Classes

Finally, you need to define three of your own exception classes. Defining your own exception is quite easy because there are rarely any extra methods to add. It is just a case of implementing a constructor to ensure that the base class constructor is called correctly. Here is the full implementation of SalesSpyFoundException (code file SolicitColdCall/SalesSpyFoundException.cs):

```
public class SalesSpyFoundException: Exception
{
  public SalesSpyFoundException(string spyName)
    : base($"Sales spy found, with name {spyName}")
  {
  }

  public SalesSpyFoundException(string spyName, Exception innerException)
    : base($"Sales spy found with name {spyName}", innerException)
  {
  }
}
```

Notice that it is derived from Exception, as you would expect for a custom exception. In fact, in practice, you would probably have added an intermediate class, something like ColdCallFileException, derived from Exception, and then derived both of your exception classes from this class. This ensures that the handling code has that extra-fine degree of control over which exception handler handles each exception. However, to keep the example simple, you will not do that.

You have done one bit of processing in SalesSpyFoundException. You have assumed that the message passed into its constructor is just the name of the spy found, so you turn this string into a more meaningful error message. You have also provided two constructors: one that simply takes a message, and one that also takes an inner exception as a parameter. When defining your own exception classes, it is best to include, at a minimum, at least these two constructors (although you will not actually be using the second SalesSpyFoundException constructor in this example).

Now for the ColdCallFileFormatException. This follows the same principles as the previous exception, but you don't do any processing on the message (code file SolicitColdCall/ColdCallFileFormatException.cs):

```
public class ColdCallFileFormatException: Exception
{
  public ColdCallFileFormatException(string message)
    : base(message)
  {
  }

  public ColdCallFileFormatException(string message, Exception innerException)
```

```
      : base(message, innerException)
  {
  }
}
```

Finally, you have `UnexpectedException`, which looks much the same as `ColdCallFileFormatException` (code file `SolicitColdCall/UnexpectedException.cs`):

```
public class UnexpectedException: Exception
{
  public UnexpectedException(string message)
      : base(message)
  {
  }

  public UnexpectedException(string message, Exception innerException)
      : base(message, innerException)
  {
  }
}
```

Now you are ready to test the program. First, try the `people.txt` file. The contents are defined here:

```
4
George Washington
Benedict Arnold
John Adams
Thomas Jefferson
```

This has four names (which match the number given in the first line of the file), including one spy. Then try the following `people2.txt` file, which has an obvious formatting error:

```
49
George Washington
Benedict Arnold
John Adams
Thomas Jefferson
```

Finally, try the example but specify the name of a file that does not exist, such as `people3.txt`. Running the program three times for the three filenames returns these results:

```
SolicitColdCall
Please type in the name of the file containing the names of the people to be cold
  called > people.txt
George Washington
Sales spy found, with name Benedict Arnold
John Adams
Thomas Jefferson
All callers processed correctly


SolicitColdCall
Please type in the name of the file containing the names of the people to be cold
  called > people2.txt
George Washington
Sales spy found, with name Benedict Arnold
John Adams
Thomas Jefferson
The file people2.txt appears to have been corrupted.
Details of the problem are: Not enough names
```

```
SolicitColdCall
Please type in the name of the file containing the names of the people to be cold
  called > people3.txt
The file people3.txt does not exist.
```

This application has demonstrated a number of different ways in which you can handle the errors and exceptions that you might find in your own applications.

CALLER INFORMATION

When dealing with errors, it is often helpful to get information about the error where it occurred. Earlier in this chapter, the `#line` preprocessor directive is used to change the line numbering of the code to get better information with the call stack. Getting the line numbers, filenames, and member names from within code, you can use attributes and optional parameters that are directly supported by the C# compiler. The attributes `CallerLineNumber`, `CallerFilePath`, and `CallerMemberName`, defined within the namespace `System.Runtime.CompilerServices`, can be applied to parameters. Normally with optional parameters, the compiler assigns the default values on method invocation in case these parameters are not supplied with the call information. With caller information attributes, the compiler doesn't fill in the default values; it instead fills in the line number, file path, and member name.

The code sample `CallerInformation` makes use of the following dependencies and namespaces:

Dependencies

```
NETStandard.Library
```

Namespaces

```
System
System.Runtime.CompilerServices
static System.Console
```

The `Log` method from the following code snippet demonstrates how to use these attributes. With the implementation, the information is written to the console (code file `CallerInformation/Program.cs`):

```
public void Log([CallerLineNumber] int line = -1,
    [CallerFilePath] string path = null,
    [CallerMemberName] string name = null)
{
  WriteLine((line < 0) ? "No line" : "Line " + line);
  WriteLine((path == null) ? "No file path" : path);
  WriteLine((name == null) ? "No member name" : name);
  WriteLine();
}
```

Let's invoke this method with some different scenarios. In the following `Main` method, the `Log` method is called by using an instance of the `Program` class, within the set accessor of the property, and within a lambda expression. Argument values are not assigned to the method, enabling the compiler to fill it in:

```
public static void Main()
{
  var p = new Program();
  p.Log();
  p.SomeProperty = 33;
  Action a1 = () => p.Log();
  a1();
}
private int _someProperty;
public int SomeProperty
{
```

```
    get { return _someProperty; }
    set
    {
      Log();
      _someProperty = value;
    }
  }
```

The result of the running program is shown next. Where the `Log` method was invoked, you can see the line numbers, the filename, and the caller member name. With the `Log` inside the `Main` method, the member name is `Main`. The invocation of the `Log` method inside the set accessor of the property `SomeProperty` shows `SomeProperty`. The Log method inside the lambda expression doesn't show the name of the generated method, but instead the name of the method where the lambda expression was invoked (`Main`), which is more useful, of course.

```
Line 12
c:\ProCSharp\ErrorsAndExceptions\CallerInformation\Program.cs
Main

Line 26
c:\ProCSharp\ErrorsAndExceptions\CallerInformation\Program.cs
SomeProperty

Line 14
c:\ProCSharp\ErrorsAndExceptions\CallerInformation\Program.cs
Main
```

Using the `Log` method within a constructor, the caller member name shows `ctor`. With a destructor, the caller member name is `Finalize`, as this is the method name generated.

> **NOTE** *A great use of the* `CallerMemberName` *attribute is with the implementation of the interface* `INotifyPropertyChanged`. *This interface requires the name of the property to be passed with the method implementation. You can see the implementation of this interface in several chapters in this book—for example, Chapter 31, "Patterns with XAML Apps."*

SUMMARY

This chapter examined the rich mechanism C# provides for dealing with error conditions through exceptions. You are not limited to the generic error codes that could be output from your code; instead, you have the capability to go in and uniquely handle the most granular of error conditions. Sometimes these error conditions are provided to you through the .NET Framework itself; at other times, though, you might want to code your own error conditions as illustrated in this chapter. In either case, you have many ways to protect the workflow of your applications from unnecessary and dangerous faults.

The next chapter goes into important keywords for asynchronous programming: `async` and `await`.

15

Asynchronous Programming

WHAT'S IN THIS CHAPTER?

> ➤ Why asynchronous programming is important
> ➤ Asynchronous patterns
> ➤ Foundations of the async and await keywords
> ➤ Creating and using asynchronous methods
> ➤ Error handling with asynchronous methods
> ➤ Cancelling long-running tasks

WROX.COM CODE DOWNLOADS FOR THIS CHAPTER

The wrox.com code downloads for this chapter are found at www.wrox.com/go/professionalcsharp6 on the Download Code tab. The code for this chapter is divided into the following major examples:

> ➤ Async Patterns
> ➤ Foundations
> ➤ Error Handling

WHY ASYNCHRONOUS PROGRAMMING IS IMPORTANT

C# 6 adds a lot of new keywords, whereas with C# 5 there were only two new keywords: async and await. These two keywords are the main focus of this chapter.

With *asynchronous programming* a method is called that runs in the background (typically with the help of a thread or task), and the calling thread is not blocked.

In this chapter, you can read about different patterns on asynchronous programming such as the *asynchronous pattern*, the *event-based asynchronous pattern*, and the *task-based asynchronous pattern (TAP)*. TAP makes use of the async and await keywords. Comparing these patterns you can see the real advantage of the new style of asynchronous programming.

After discussing the different patterns, you see the foundation of asynchronous programming by creating tasks and invoking asynchronous methods. You find out what's behind the scenes with continuation tasks and the synchronization context.

Error handling needs some special emphasis; as with asynchronous tasks, some scenarios require some different handling with errors.

The last part of this chapter discusses how you can do cancellation. Background tasks can take a while, and there might be a need to cancel the task while it is still running. This chapter explains how you can do this.

Chapter 21, "Tasks and Parallel Programming" and Chapter 22, "Task Synchronization," covers other information about parallel programming.

Users find it annoying when an application does not immediately react to requests. With the mouse, we have become accustomed to experiencing a delay, as we've learned that behavior over several decades. With a touch UI, an application needs to immediately react to requests. Otherwise, the user tries to redo the action.

Because asynchronous programming was hard to achieve with older versions of the .NET Framework, it was not always done when it should have been. One of the applications that blocked the UI thread fairly often is an older version of Visual Studio. With that version, opening a solution containing hundreds of projects meant you could take a long coffee break. As of Visual Studio 2012, that's no longer the case because projects are loaded asynchronously in the background, with the selected project loaded first. A recent advancement of Visual Studio 2015 is the NuGet package manager that is no longer implemented as a model dialog. The new NuGet package manager can load information about packages asynchronously while you do other things at the same time. These are just a few examples of important changes built into Visual Studio 2015 related to asynchronous programming.

Many APIs with the .NET Framework offer both a synchronous and an asynchronous version. Because the synchronous version of the API was a lot easier to use, it was often used where it wasn't appropriate. With the new Windows Runtime (WinRT), if an API call is expected to take longer than 40 milliseconds, only an asynchronous version is available. Since C# 5, programming asynchronously is as easy as programming in a synchronous manner, so there shouldn't be any barrier to using the asynchronous APIs.

ASYNCHRONOUS PATTERNS

Before stepping into the new `async` and `await` keywords it is best to understand asynchronous patterns from the .NET Framework. Asynchronous features have been available since .NET 1.0, and many classes in the .NET Framework implement one or more such patterns. The asynchronous pattern is also available with the delegate type.

Because doing updates on the UI—both with Windows Forms and WPF—with the asynchronous pattern is quite complex, .NET 2.0 introduced the *event-based asynchronous pattern*. With this pattern, an event handler is invoked from the thread that owns the synchronization context, so updating UI code is easily handled with this pattern. Previously, this pattern was also known with the name *asynchronous component pattern*.

With .NET 4.5, another way to achieve asynchronous programming was introduced: the *task-based asynchronous pattern* (TAP). This pattern is based on the `Task` type and makes use of a compiler feature with the keywords `async` and `await`.

To understand the advantage of the `async` and `await` keywords, the first sample application makes use of Windows Presentation Foundation (WPF) and network programming to provide an overview of asynchronous programming. If you have no experience with WPF and network programming, don't despair. You can still follow the essentials here and gain an understanding of how asynchronous programming can be done. The following examples demonstrate the differences between the asynchronous patterns. After you've had a look at these, you're introduced to the basics of asynchronous programming with some simple console applications.

> **NOTE** *WPF is covered in detail in Chapters 29 through 31 and 34 through 36. Network programming is discussed in Chapter 25, "Networking."*

The sample application to show the differences between the asynchronous patterns is a WPF application that makes use of types in a class library. The application is used to find images on the web using services from Bing and Flickr. The user can enter a search term to find images, and the search term is sent to Bing and Flickr services with a simple HTTP request.

The UI design from the Visual Studio designer is shown in Figure 15-1. On top of the screen is a text input field followed by several buttons that start the search or clear the result list. The left side below the control area contains a `ListBox` for displaying all the images found. On the right side is an `Image` control to display the image that is selected within the `ListBox` control in a version with a higher resolution.

FIGURE 15-1

To understand the sample application, we start with the class library AsyncLib, which contains several helper classes. These classes are used by the WPF application.

The class `SearchItemResult` represents a single item from a result collection that is used to display the image with a title and the source of the image. This class just defines simple properties: `Title`, `Url`, `ThumbnailUrl`, and `Source`. The property `ThumbnailIUrl` is used to reference a thumbnail image, the `Url` property contains a link to a larger-size image. `Title` contains some text to describe the image. The base class of `SearchItemResult` is `BindableBase`. This base class implements a notification mechanism by implementing the interface `INotifyPropertyChanged` that is used by WPF to make updates with data binding (code file AsyncLib/SearchItemResult.cs):

```
namespace Wrox.ProCSharp.Async
{
  public class SearchItemResult : BindableBase
  {
    private string _title;
    public string Title
    {
      get { return _title; }
      set { SetProperty(ref _title, value); }
    }

    private string _url;
    public string Url
    {
      get { return _url; }
      set { SetProperty(ref _url, value); }
    }
```

```
        private string _thumbnailUrl;
        public string ThumbnailUrl
        {
          get { return _thumbnailUrl; }
          set { SetProperty(ref _thumbnailUrl, value); }
        }

        private string _source;
        public string Source
        {
          get { return _source; }
          set { SetProperty(ref _source, value); }
        }
      }
    }
```

The class `SearchInfo` is another class used with data binding. The property `SearchTerm` contains the user input to search for images with that type. The `List` property returns a list of all found images represented with the `SearchItemResult` type (code file `AsyncLib/SearchInfo.cs`):

```
    using System.Collections.ObjectModel;

    namespace Wrox.ProCSharp.Async
    {
      public class SearchInfo : BindableBase
      {
        public SearchInfo()
        {
          _list = new ObservableCollection<SearchItemResult>();
          _list.CollectionChanged += delegate { OnPropertyChanged("List"); };
        }

        private string _searchTerm;
        public string SearchTerm
        {
          get { return _searchTerm; }
          set { SetProperty(ref _searchTerm, value); }
        }

        private ObservableCollection<SearchItemResult> _list;
        public ObservableCollection<SearchItemResult> List => _list;
      }
    }
```

In the XAML code, a `TextBox` is used to enter the search term. This control is bound to the `SearchTerm` property of the `SearchInfo` type. Several `Button` controls are used to activate an event handler; for example, the Sync button invokes the `OnSearchSync` method (code file `AsyncPatternsWPF/MainWindow.xaml`):

```
      <StackPanel Orientation="Horizontal" Grid.Row="0">
        <StackPanel.LayoutTransform>
          <ScaleTransform ScaleX="2" ScaleY="2" />
        </StackPanel.LayoutTransform>
        <TextBox Text="{Binding SearchTerm}" Width="200" Margin="4" />
        <Button Click="OnClear">Clear</Button>
        <Button Click="OnSearchSync">Sync</Button>
        <Button Click="OnSeachAsyncPattern">Async</Button>
        <Button Click="OnAsyncEventPattern">Async Event</Button>
        <Button Click="OnTaskBasedAsyncPattern">Task Based Async</Button>
      </StackPanel>
```

The second part of the XAML code contains a `ListBox`. To have a special representation for the items in the `ListBox`, you use an `ItemTemplate`. Every item is represented with two `TextBlock` controls and one

Image control. The `ListBox` is bound to the `List` property of the `SearchInfo` class, and properties of the item controls are bound to properties of the `SearchItemResult` type:

```
<Grid Grid.Row="1">
  <Grid.ColumnDefinitions>
    <ColumnDefinition Width="*" />
    <ColumnDefinition Width="3*" />
  </Grid.ColumnDefinitions>
  <ListBox Grid.IsSharedSizeScope="True" ItemsSource="{Binding List}"
      Grid.Column="0" IsSynchronizedWithCurrentItem="True" Background="Black">
    <ListBox.ItemTemplate>
      <DataTemplate>
        <Grid>
          <Grid.ColumnDefinitions>
            <ColumnDefinition SharedSizeGroup="ItemTemplateGroup" />
          </Grid.ColumnDefinitions>
          <StackPanel HorizontalAlignment="Stretch" Orientation="Vertical"
              Background="{StaticResource linearBackgroundBrush}">
            <TextBlock Text="{Binding Source}" Foreground="White" />
            <TextBlock Text="{Binding Title}" Foreground="White" />
            <Image HorizontalAlignment="Center"
                Source="{Binding ThumbnailUrl}" Width="100" />
          </StackPanel>
        </Grid>
      </DataTemplate>
    </ListBox.ItemTemplate>
  </ListBox>
  <GridSplitter Grid.Column="1" Width="3" HorizontalAlignment="Left" />
  <Image Grid.Column="1" Source="{Binding List/Url}" />
</Grid>
```

Now let's get into the `BingRequest` class. This class contains some information about how to make a request to the Bing service. The `Url` property of this class returns a URL string that can be used to make a request for images. The request is comprised of the search term, a number of images that should be requested (`Count`), and a number of images to skip (`Offset`). With Bing, authentication is needed. The user Id is defined with the `AppId`, and used with the `Credentials` property that returns a `NetworkCredential` object. To run the application, you need to register with Windows Azure Marketplace and sign up for the Bing Search API. At the time of this writing, up to 5000 transactions per month are free—this should be enough for running the sample application. Every search is one transaction. The link for the registration to the Bing Search API is `https://datamarket.azure.com/dataset/bing/search`. After registration you need to copy the account key. After obtaining the application account key, copy it to the `AppID` of the `BingRequest` class.

After sending a request to Bing by using the created URL, Bing returns XML. The `Parse` method of the `BingRequest` class parses the XML and returns a collection of `SearchItemResult` objects (code file `AsyncLib/BingRequest.cs`):

> **NOTE** *The* `Parse` *methods in the classes* `BingRequest` *and* `FlickrRequest` *make use of LINQ to XML. How to use LINQ to XML is covered in Chapter 27, "XML and JSON."*

```
using System.Collections.Generic;
using System.Linq;
using System.Net;
using System.Xml.Linq;
```

```csharp
namespace Wrox.ProCSharp.Async
{
  public class BingRequest : IImageRequest
  {
    private const string AppId = "enter your Bing AppId here";

    public BingRequest()
    {
      Count = 50;
      Offset = 0;
    }

    private string _searchTerm;
    public string SearchTerm
    {
      get { return _searchTerm; }
      set { _searchTerm = value; }
    }

    public ICredentials Credentials => new NetworkCredentials(AppId, AppId);

    public string Url =>
      $"https://api.datamarket.azure.com/" +
        "Data.ashx/Bing/Search/v1/Image?Query=%27{SearchTerm}%27&" +
        "$top={Count}&$skip={Offset}&$format=Atom";

    public int Count { get; set; }

    public int Offset { get; set; }

    public IEnumerable<SearchItemResult> Parse(string xml)
    {
      XElement respXml = XElement.Parse(xml);
      XNamespace d = XNamespace.Get(
        "http://schemas.microsoft.com/ado/2007/08/dataservices");
      XNamespace m = XNamespace.Get(
        "http://schemas.microsoft.com/ado/2007/08/dataservices/metadata");
      return (from item in respXml.Descendants(m + "properties")
              select new SearchItemResult
              {
                Title = new string(item.Element(d + "Title").
                    Value.Take(50).ToArray()),
                Url = item.Element(d + "MediaUrl").Value,
                ThumbnailUrl = item.Element(d + "Thumbnail").
                    Element(d + "MediaUrl").Value,
                Source = "Bing"
              }).ToList();
    }
  }
}
```

Both the `BingRequest` class and the `FlickrRequest` class implement the interface `IImageRequest`. This interface defines the properties `SearchTerm` and `Url`, and the method `Parse`, which enables easy iteration through both image service providers (code file `AsyncLib/IImageRequest.cs`):

```csharp
using System;
using System.Collections.Generic;
using System.Net;

namespace Wrox.ProCSharp.Async
{
  public interface IImageRequest
  {
```

```
          string SearchTerm { get; set; }

          string Url { get; }

          IEnumerable<SearchItemResult> Parse(string xml);

          ICredentials Credentials { get; }
      }
  }
```

The `FlickrRequest` class is very similar to `BingRequest`. It just creates a different URL to request an image with a search term, and has a different implementation of the `Parse` method, just as the returned XML from Flickr differs from the returned XML from Bing. As with Bing, to create an application ID for Flickr, you need to register with Flickr and request it: `http://www.flickr.com/services/apps/create/apply/`.

```
using System.Collections.Generic;
using System.Linq;
using System.Xml.Linq;

namespace Wrox.ProCSharp.Async
{
  public class FlickrRequest : IImageRequest
  {
    private const string AppId = "Enter your Flickr AppId here";

    public FlickrRequest()
    {
      Count = 30;
      Page = 1;
    }

    private string _searchTerm;
    public string SearchTerm
    {
      get { return _searchTerm; }
      set { _searchTerm = value; }
    }

    public string Url =>
        $"http://api.flickr.com/services/rest?" +
            "api_key={AppId}&method=flickr.photos.search&content_type=1&" +
            "text={SearchTerm}&per_page={Count}&page={Page}";

    public ICredentials Credentials => null;

    public int Count { get; set; }

    public int Page { get; set; }

    public IEnumerable<SearchItemResult> Parse(string xml)
    {
      XElement respXml = XElement.Parse(xml);
      return (from item in respXml.Descendants("photo")
              select new SearchItemResult
              {
                Title = new string(item.Attribute("title").Value.
                    Take(50).ToArray()),
                Url = string.Format("http://farm{0}.staticflickr.com/" +
                    "{1}/{2}_{3}_z.jpg",
                  item.Attribute("farm").Value, item.Attribute("server").Value,
                  item.Attribute("id").Value, item.Attribute("secret").Value),
```

```
                    ThumbnailUrl = string.Format("http://farm{0}." +
                        "staticflickr.com/{1}/{2}_{3}_t.jpg",
                        item.Attribute("farm").Value,
                        item.Attribute("server").Value,
                        item.Attribute("id").Value,
                        item.Attribute("secret").Value),
                    Source = "Flickr"
                }).ToList();
        }
    }
}
```

Now you need to connect the types from the library and the WPF application. In the constructor of the MainWindow class, you create an instance of SearchInfo, and you set the DataContext of the window to this instance. Now data binding can take place, shown earlier with the XAML code (code file AsyncPatternsWPF/MainWindow.xaml.cs):

```
public partial class MainWindow : Window
{
    private SearchInfo _searchInfo = new SearchInfo();

    public MainWindow()
    {
        InitializeComponent();
        this.DataContext = _searchInfo;
    }
    //...
```

The MainWindow class also contains the helper method GetSearchRequests, which returns a collection of IImageRequest objects in the form of BingRequest and FlickrRequest types. In case you registered with only one of these services, you can change this code to return only the one with which you registered. Of course, you can also create IImageRequest types of other services—for example, using Google or Yahoo!. Then add these request types to the collection returned:

```
private IEnumerable<IImageRequest> GetSearchRequests()
{
    return new List<IImageRequest>
    {
        new BingRequest { SearchTerm = _searchInfo.SearchTerm },
        new FlickrRequest { SearchTerm = _searchInfo.SearchTerm}
    };
}
```

Synchronous Call

Now that everything is set up, start with a synchronous call to these services. The click handler of the Sync button, OnSearchSync, iterates through all search requests returned from GetSearchRequests and uses the Url property to make an HTTP request with the WebClient class. The method DownloadString blocks until the result is received. The resulting XML is assigned to the resp variable. The XML content is parsed with the help of the Parse method, which returns a collection of SearchItemResult objects. The items of these collections are then added to the list contained within _searchInfo (code file AsyncPatternsWPF/MainWindow.xaml.cs):

```
private void OnSearchSync(object sender, RoutedEventArgs e)
{
    foreach (var req in GetSearchRequests())
    {
        var client = new WebClient();
        client.Credentials = req.Credentials;
        string resp = client.DownloadString(req.Url);
```

```
            IEnumerable<SearchItemResult> images = req.Parse(resp);
            foreach (var image in images)
            {
                _searchInfo.List.Add(image);
            }
        }
    }
```

When you run the application (see Figure 15-2), the user interface is blocked until the method `OnSearchSync` is finished making network calls to Bing and Flickr and has finished parsing the results. The amount of time needed to complete these calls varies according to the speed of your network and the current workload of Bing and Flickr. Whatever it is, however, the wait is unpleasant to the user.

FIGURE 15-2

Therefore, make the call asynchronously instead.

Asynchronous Pattern

One way to make the call asynchronously is by using the asynchronous pattern. The asynchronous pattern defines a `BeginXXX` method and an `EndXXX` method. For example, if a synchronous method `DownloadString` is offered, the asynchronous variants would be `BeginDownloadString` and `EndDownloadString`. The `BeginXXX` method takes all input arguments of the synchronous method, and `EndXXX` takes the output arguments and return type to return the result. With the asynchronous pattern, the `BeginXXX` method also defines a parameter of `AsyncCallback`, which accepts a delegate that is invoked as soon as the asynchronous method is completed. The `BeginXXX` method returns `IAsyncResult`, which can be used for polling to verify whether the call is completed, and to wait for the end of the method.

The `WebClient` class doesn't offer an implementation of the asynchronous pattern. Instead, the `HttpWebRequest` class could be used, which offers this pattern with the methods `BeginGetResponse` and `EndGetResponse`. The following sample does not do this. Instead, the sample uses a delegate. The delegate type defines an `Invoke` method to make a synchronous method call, and `BeginInvoke` and `EndInvoke` methods to use it with the asynchronous pattern. Here, the delegate `downloadString` of type `Func<string, string>` is declared to reference a method that has a `string` parameter and returns a `string`. The method that is referenced by the `downloadString` variable is implemented as a lambda expression and invokes the synchronous method `DownloadString` of the `WebClient` type. The delegate is invoked asynchronously by calling the `BeginInvoke` method. This method uses a thread from the thread pool to make an asynchronous call.

The first parameter of the `BeginInvoke` method is the first generic string parameter of the `Func` delegate where the URL can be passed. The second parameter is of type `AsyncCallback`. `AsyncCallback` is a delegate that requires `IAsyncResult` as a parameter. The method referenced by this delegate is invoked as soon as the asynchronous method is completed. When that happens, `downloadString.EndInvoke` is invoked to retrieve the result, which is dealt with in the same manner as before to parse the XML content and get the collection of items. However, here it is not possible to directly go back to the UI, as the UI is bound to a single thread, and the callback method is running within a background thread. Therefore, it's necessary to switch back to the UI thread by using the `Dispatcher` property from the window. The `Invoke` method of the `Dispatcher` requires a delegate as a parameter; that's why the `Action<SearchItemResult>` delegate is specified, which adds an item to the collection bound to the UI (code file `AsyncPatternsWPF/MainWindow .xaml.cs`):

```
private void OnSearchAsyncPattern(object sender, RoutedEventArgs e)
{
  Func<string, ICredentials, string> downloadString = (address, cred) =>
    {
      var client = new WebClient();
      client.Credentials = cred;
      return client.DownloadString(address);
    };

  Action<SearchItemResult> addItem = item => _searchInfo.List.Add(item);

  foreach (var req in GetSearchRequests())
  {
    downloadString.BeginInvoke(req.Url, req.Credentials, ar =>
      {
        string resp = downloadString.EndInvoke(ar);
        IEnumerable<SearchItemResult> images = req.Parse(resp);
        foreach (var image in images)
        {
          this.Dispatcher.Invoke(addItem, image);
        }
      }, null);
  }
}
```

An advantage of the asynchronous pattern is that it can be implemented easily just by using the functionality of delegates. The program now behaves as it should; the UI is no longer blocked. However, using the asynchronous pattern is difficult. Fortunately, .NET 2.0 introduced the event-based asynchronous pattern, which makes it easier to deal with UI updates. This pattern is discussed next.

> **NOTE** *Delegate types and lambda expressions are explained in Chapter 9, "Delegates, Lambdas, and Events." Tasks and parallel programming are covered in Chapter 21.*

Event-Based Asynchronous Pattern

The method `OnAsyncEventPattern` makes use of the event-based asynchronous pattern. This pattern is implemented by the `WebClient` class and thus it can be directly used.

This pattern defines a method with the suffix `Async`. Therefore, for example, for the synchronous method `DownloadString`, the `WebClient` class offers the asynchronous variant `DownloadStringAsync`. Instead of defining a delegate that is invoked when the asynchronous method is completed, an event is defined. The `DownloadStringCompleted` event is invoked as soon as the asynchronous method `DownloadStringAsync` is completed. The method assigned to the event handler is implemented within a lambda expression. The implementation is very similar to before, but now it is possible to directly access UI elements because the event handler is invoked from the thread that has the synchronization context, and this is the UI thread in the case of Windows Forms and WPF applications (code file `AsyncPatternsWPF/MainWindow.xaml.cs`):

```
private void OnAsyncEventPattern(object sender, RoutedEventArgs e)
{
  foreach (var req in GetSearchRequests())
  {
    var client = new WebClient();
    client.Credentials = req.Credentials;
    client.DownloadStringCompleted += (sender1, e1) =>
      {
        string resp = e1.Result;
        IEnumerable<SearchItemResult> images = req.Parse(resp);
        foreach (var image in images)
        {
          _searchInfo.List.Add(image);
        }
      };
    client.DownloadStringAsync(new Uri(req.Url));
  }
}
```

An advantage of the event-based asynchronous pattern is that it is easy to use. Note, however, that it is not that easy to implement this pattern in a custom class. One way to use an existing implementation of this pattern to make synchronous methods asynchronous is with the `BackgroundWorker` class. `BackgroundWorker` implements the event-based asynchronous pattern.

This makes the code a lot simpler. However, the order is reversed compared to synchronous method calls. Before invoking the asynchronous method, you need to define what happens when the method call is completed. The following section plunges into the new world of asynchronous programming with the `async` and `await` keywords.

Task-Based Asynchronous Pattern

The `WebClient` class was updated with .NET 4.5 to offer the task-based asynchronous pattern (TAP) as well. This pattern defines a suffix `Async` method that returns a `Task` type. Because the `WebClient` class already offers a method with the `Async` suffix to implement the task-based asynchronous pattern, the new method has the name `DownloadStringTaskAsync`.

The method `DownloadStringTaskAsync` is declared to return `Task<string>`. You do not need to declare a variable of `Task<string>` to assign the result from `DownloadStringTaskAsync`; instead, you can declare a variable of type `string`, and you can use the `await` keyword. The `await` keyword unblocks the thread (in this case the UI thread) to do other tasks. As soon as the method `DownloadStringTaskAsync` completes its background processing, the UI thread can continue and get the result from the background task to the string variable `resp`. Also, the code following this line continues (code file `AsyncPatternsWPF/MainWindow.xaml.cs`):

```
private async void OnTaskBasedAsyncPattern(object sender,
    RoutedEventArgs e)
{
```

```
      foreach (var req in GetSearchRequests())
      {
        var client = new WebClient();
        client.Credentials = req.Credentials;
        string resp = await client.DownloadStringTaskAsync(req.Url);
        IEnumerable<SearchItemResult> images = req.Parse(resp);

        foreach (var image in images)
        {
          _searchInfo.List.Add(image);
        }
      }
    }
```

> **NOTE** *The* async *keyword creates a state machine similar to the* yield return *statement, which is discussed in Chapter 7, "Arrays and Tuples."*

The code is much simpler now. There is no blocking, and no manually switching back to the UI thread, as this is done automatically. Also, the code follows the same order as you're used to with synchronous programming.

Next, the code is changed to use a different class from WebClient—one in which the task-based event pattern is more directly implemented and synchronous methods are not offered. This class, which was added in .NET 4.5, is HttpClient. You do an asynchronous GET request with the GetAsync method. Then, to read the content you need another asynchronous method. ReadAsStringAsync returns the content formatted in a string:

```
    private async void OnTaskBasedAsyncPattern(object sender, RoutedEventArgs e)
    {
      foreach (var req in GetSearchRequests())
      {
        var clientHandler = new HttpClientHandler
        {
          Credentials = req.Credentials
        };
        var client = new HttpClient(clientHandler);
        var response = await client.GetAsync(req.Url);
        string resp = await response.Content.ReadAsStringAsync();
        IEnumerable<SearchItemResult> images = req.Parse(resp);
        foreach (var image in images)
        {
          _searchInfo.List.Add(image);
        }
      }
    }
```

Parsing of the XML string could take a while. Because the parsing code is running in the UI thread, the UI thread cannot react to user requests at that time. To create a background task from synchronous functionality, you can use Task.Run. In the following example, Task.Run wraps the parsing of the XML string to return the SearchItemResult collection:

```
    private async void OnTaskBasedAsyncPattern(object sender, RoutedEventArgs e)
    {
      foreach (var req in GetSearchRequests())
      {
        var clientHandler = new HttpClientHandler
        {
```

```
        Credentials = req.Credentials
    };
    var client = new HttpClient(clientHandler);
    var response = await client.GetAsync(req.Url, cts.Token);
    string resp = await response.Content.ReadAsStringAsync();
    await Task.Run(() =>
    {
        IEnumerable<SearchItemResult> images = req.Parse(resp);
        foreach (var image in images)
        {
            _searchInfo.List.Add(image);
        }
    }
}
}
```

Because the method passed to the `Task.Run` method is running in a background thread, here we have the same problem as before referencing some UI code. One solution would be to just do `req.Parse` within the `Task.Run` method, and do the `foreach` loop outside the task to add the result to the list in the UI thread. WPF offers a better solution, however, that enables filling collections that are bound to the UI from a background thread. This extension only requires enabling the collection for synchronization using `BindingOperations.EnableCollectionSynchronization`, as shown in the following code snippet:

```
public partial class MainWindow : Window
{
    private SearchInfo _searchInfo = new SearchInfo();
    private object _lockList = new object();

    public MainWindow()
    {
        InitializeComponent();
        this.DataContext = _searchInfo;
        BindingOperations.EnableCollectionSynchronization(
            _searchInfo.List, _lockList);
    }
}
```

Now that you've seen the advantages of the `async` and `await` keywords, the next section examines the programming foundation behind these keywords.

FOUNDATION OF ASYNCHRONOUS PROGRAMMING

The `async` and `await` keywords are just a compiler feature. The compiler creates code by using the `Task` class. Instead of using the new keywords, you could get the same functionality with C# 4 and methods of the `Task` class; it's just not as convenient.

This section gives information about what the compiler does with the async and await keywords. It shows you an easy way to create an asynchronous method and demonstrates how to invoke multiple asynchronous methods in parallel. You also see how you can change a class to offer the asynchronous pattern with the new keywords.

The sample code for all the `Foundations` sample makes use of these dependencies and namespaces:

Dependencies

```
NETStandard.Library
```

Namespaces

```
System
System.Threading
```

```
System.Threading.Tasks
static System.Console
```

Creating Tasks

Let's start with the synchronous method `Greeting`, which takes a while before returning a string (code file Foundations/Program.cs):

```
static string Greeting(string name)
{
  Task.Delay(3000).Wait();
  return $"Hello, {name}";
}
```

To make such a method asynchronously, you define the method `GreetingAsync`. The task-based asynchronous pattern specifies that an asynchronous method is named with the `Async` suffix and returns a task. `GreetingAsync` is defined to have the same input parameters as the `Greeting` method but returns `Task<string>`. `Task<string>`, which defines a task that returns a string in the future. A simple way to return a task is by using the `Task.Run` method. The generic version `Task.Run<string>()` creates a task that returns a string:

```
static Task<string> GreetingAsync(string name)
{
  return Task.Run<string>(() =>
  {
    return Greeting(name);
  });
}
```

Calling an Asynchronous Method

You can call this asynchronous method `GreetingAsync` by using the `await` keyword on the task that is returned. The `await` keyword requires the method to be declared with the `async` modifier. The code within this method does not continue before the `GreetingAsync` method is completed. However, you can reuse the thread that started the `CallerWithAsync` method. This thread is not blocked:

```
private async static void CallerWithAsync()
{
  string result = await GreetingAsync("Stephanie");
  WriteLine(result);
}
```

Instead of passing the result from the asynchronous method to a variable, you can also use the `await` keyword directly within parameters. Here, the result from the `GreetingAsync` method is awaited as it was in the previous code snippet, but this time the result is directly passed to the `WriteLine` method:

```
private async static void CallerWithAsync2()
{
  WriteLine(await GreetingAsync("Stephanie"));
}
```

> **NOTE** *You can use the* `async` *modifier only with methods returning a* `Task` *or* `void` *with .NET types, and* `IAsyncOperation` *with the Windows Runtime. It cannot be used with the entry point of a program: the* `Main` *method.* `await` *can only be used with methods returning a* `Task`.

The next section explains what's driving the await keyword. Behind the scenes, continuation tasks are used.

Continuation with Tasks

GreetingAsync returns a Task<string> object. The Task object contains information about the task created, and allows waiting for its completion. The ContinueWith method of the Task class defines the code that should be invoked as soon as the task is finished. The delegate assigned to the ContinueWith method receives the completed task with its argument, which allows accessing the result from the task using the Result property:

```
private static void CallerWithContinuationTask()
{
  Task<string> t1 = GreetingAsync("Stephanie");
  t1.ContinueWith(t =>
  {
    string result = t.Result;
    WriteLine(result);
  });
}
```

The compiler converts the await keyword by putting all the code that follows within the block of a ContinueWith method.

Synchronization Context

If you verify the thread that is used within the methods you will find that in both methods—CallerWithAsync and CallerWithContinuationTask—different threads are used during the lifetime of the methods. One thread is used to invoke the method GreetingAsync, and another thread takes action after the await keyword or within the code block in the ContinueWith method.

With a console application usually this is not an issue. However, you have to ensure that at least one foreground thread is still running before all background tasks that should be completed are finished. The sample application invokes Console.ReadLine to keep the main thread running until the return key is pressed.

With applications that are bound to a specific thread for some actions (for example, with WPF applications or Windows apps, UI elements can only be accessed from the UI thread), this is an issue.

Using the async and await keywords you don't have to do any special actions to access the UI thread after an await completion. By default, the generated code switches the thread to the thread that has the synchronization context. A WPF application sets a DispatcherSynchronizationContext, and a Windows Forms application sets a WindowsFormsSynchronizationContext. If the calling thread of the asynchronous method is assigned to the synchronization context, then with the continuous execution after the await, by default the same synchronization context is used. If the same synchronization context shouldn't be used, you must invoke the Task method ConfigureAwait(continueOnCapturedContext: false). An example that illustrates this usefulness is a WPF application in which the code that follows the await is not using any UI elements. In this case, it is faster to avoid the switch to the synchronization context.

Using Multiple Asynchronous Methods

Within an asynchronous method you can call multiple asynchronous methods. How you code this depends on whether the results from one asynchronous method are needed by another.

Calling Asynchronous Methods Sequentially

You can use the await keyword to call every asynchronous method. In cases where one method is dependent on the result of another method, this is very useful. Here, the second call to GreetingAsync is completely independent of the result of the first call to GreetingAsync. Thus, the complete method

`MultipleAsyncMethods` could return the result faster if `await` is not used with every single method, as shown in the following example:

```
private async static void MultipleAsyncMethods()
{
    string s1 = await GreetingAsync("Stephanie");
    string s2 = await GreetingAsync("Matthias");
    WriteLine("Finished both methods.\nResult 1: {s1}\n Result 2: {s2}");
}
```

Using Combinators

If the asynchronous methods are not dependent on each other, it is a lot faster not to `await` on each separately; instead assign the return of the asynchronous method to a `Task` variable. The `GreetingAsync` method returns `Task<string>`. Both these methods can now run in parallel. *Combinators* can help with this. A combinator accepts multiple parameters of the same type and returns a value of the same type. The passed parameters are "combined" to one. `Task` combinators accept multiple `Task` objects as parameter and return a `Task`.

The sample code invokes the `Task.WhenAll` combinator method that you can `await` to have both tasks finished:

```
private async static void MultipleAsyncMethodsWithCombinators1()
{
    Task<string> t1 = GreetingAsync("Stephanie");
    Task<string> t2 = GreetingAsync("Matthias");
    await Task.WhenAll(t1, t2);
    WriteLine("Finished both methods.\n " +
        $"Result 1: {t1.Result}\n Result 2: {t2.Result}");
}
```

The `Task` class defines the `WhenAll` and `WhenAny` combinators. The `Task` returned from the `WhenAll` method is completed as soon as all tasks passed to the method are completed; the `Task` returned from the `WhenAny` method is completed as soon as one of the tasks passed to the method is completed.

The `WhenAll` method of the `Task` type defines several overloads. If all the tasks return the same type, you can use an array of this type for the result of the `await`. The `GreetingAsync` method returns a `Task<string>`, and awaiting for this method results in a `string`. Therefore, you can use `Task.WhenAll` to return a string array:

```
private async static void MultipleAsyncMethodsWithCombinators2()
{
    Task<string> t1 = GreetingAsync("Stephanie");
    Task<string> t2 = GreetingAsync("Matthias");
    string[] result =  await Task.WhenAll(t1, t2);
    WriteLine("Finished both methods.\n " +
        $"Result 1: {result[0]}\n Result 2: {result[1]}");
}
```

Converting the Asynchronous Pattern

Not all classes from the .NET Framework introduced the new asynchronous method style. There are still many classes that offer the asynchronous pattern with the `BeginXXX` and `EndXXX` methods and not with task-based asynchronous methods; you will see this when you work with different classes from the framework. However, you can convert the asynchronous pattern to the new task-based asynchronous pattern.

First, create an asynchronous method from the previously defined synchronous method `Greeting` with the help of a delegate. The `Greeting` method receives a string as parameter and returns a string; thus a variable of `Func<string, string>` delegate is used to reference this method. According to the asynchronous pattern, the `BeginGreeting` method receives a `string` parameter in addition to `AsyncCallback` and `object` parameters and returns `IAsyncResult`. The `EndGreeting` method returns the result from the `Greeting` method—a `string`—and receives an `IAsyncResult` parameter. This way the synchronous method `Greeting` was made asynchronous just by using a delegate.

```
private Func<string, string> greetingInvoker = Greeting;

private IAsyncResult BeginGreeting(string name, AsyncCallback callback,
  object state)
{
  return greetingInvoker.BeginInvoke(name, callback, state);
}

private string EndGreeting(IAsyncResult ar)
{
  return greetingInvoker.EndInvoke(ar);
}
```

Now the `BeginGreeting` and `EndGreeting` methods are available, and these should be converted to use the async and await keywords to get the results. The `TaskFactory` class defines the `FromAsync` method that allows converting methods using the asynchronous pattern to the TAP.

With the sample code, the first generic parameter of the `Task` type, `Task<string>`, defines the return value from the method that is invoked. The generic parameter of the `FromAsync` method defines the input type of the method. In this case the input type is again of type `string`. With the parameters of the `FromAsync` method, the first two parameters are delegate types to pass the addresses of the `BeginGreeting` and `EndGreeting` methods. After these two parameters, the input parameters and the object state parameter follow. The object state is not used, so null is assigned to it. Because the `FromAsync` method returns a `Task` type, in the sample code `Task<string>`, you can use an await as shown:

```
private static async void ConvertingAsyncPattern()
{
  string s = await Task<string>.Factory.FromAsync<string>(
    BeginGreeting, EndGreeting, "Angela", null);
  WriteLine(s);
}
```

ERROR HANDLING

Chapter 14, "Errors and Exceptions," provides detailed coverage of errors and exception handling. However, in the context of asynchronous methods, you should be aware of some special handling of errors.

The sample code for all the `ErrorHandling` sample makes use of these dependencies and namespaces:

Dependencies

```
NETStandard.Library
```

Namespaces

```
System
System.Threading.Tasks
static System.Console
```

Let's start with a simple method that throws an exception after a delay (code file `ErrorHandling/Program.cs`):

```
static async Task ThrowAfter(int ms, string message)
{
```

```
    await Task.Delay(ms);
    throw new Exception(message);
}
```

If you call the asynchronous method without awaiting it, you can put the asynchronous method within a try/catch block—and the exception will not be caught. That's because the method DontHandle has already completed before the exception from ThrowAfter is thrown. You need to await the ThrowAfter method, as shown in the example that follows in the next section. Pay attention that the exception is not caught in this code snippet:

```
private static void DontHandle()
{
  try
  {
    ThrowAfter(200, "first");
    // exception is not caught because this method is finished
    // before the exception is thrown
  }
  catch (Exception ex)
  {
    WriteLine(ex.Message);
  }
}
```

> **WARNING** *Asynchronous methods that return* void *cannot be awaited. The issue with this is that exceptions that are thrown from* async void *methods cannot be caught. That's why it is best to return a* Task *type from an asynchronous method. Handler methods or overridden base methods are exempted from this rule.*

Handling Exceptions with Asynchronous Methods

A good way to deal with exceptions from asynchronous methods is to use await and put a try/catch statement around it, as shown in the following code snippet. The HandleOneError method releases the thread after calling the ThrowAfter method asynchronously, but it keeps the Task referenced to continue as soon as the task is completed. When that happens (which, in this case, is when the exception is thrown after two seconds), the catch matches and the code within the catch block is invoked:

```
private static async void HandleOneError()
{
  try
  {
    await ThrowAfter(2000, "first");
  }
  catch (Exception ex)
  {
    WriteLine($"handled {ex.Message}");
  }
}
```

Handling Exceptions with Multiple Asynchronous Methods

What if two asynchronous methods are invoked and both throw exceptions? In the following example, first the ThrowAfter method is invoked, which throws an exception with the message first after two seconds. After this method is completed, the ThrowAfter method is invoked, throwing an exception after one second.

Because the first call to ThrowAfter already throws an exception, the code within the try block does not continue to invoke the second method, instead landing within the catch block to deal with the first exception:

```
private static async void StartTwoTasks()
{
  try
  {
    await ThrowAfter(2000, "first");
    await ThrowAfter(1000, "second"); // the second call is not invoked
                                      // because the first method throws
                                      // an exception
  }
  catch (Exception ex)
  {
    WriteLine($"handled {ex.Message}");
  }
}
```

Now start the two calls to ThrowAfter in parallel. The first method throws an exception after two seconds and the second one after one second. With Task.WhenAll you wait until both tasks are completed, whether an exception is thrown or not. Therefore, after a wait of about two seconds, Task.WhenAll is completed, and the exception is caught with the catch statement. However, you only see the exception information from the first task that is passed to the WhenAll method. It's not the task that threw the exception first (which is the second task), but the first task in the list:

```
private async static void StartTwoTasksParallel()
{
  try
  {
    Task t1 = ThrowAfter(2000, "first");
    Task t2 = ThrowAfter(1000, "second");
    await Task.WhenAll(t1, t2);
  }
  catch (Exception ex)
  {
    // just display the exception information of the first task
    // that is awaited within WhenAll
    WriteLine($"handled {ex.Message}");
  }
}
```

One way to get the exception information from all tasks is to declare the task variables t1 and t2 outside of the try block, so they can be accessed from within the catch block. Here you can check the status of the task to determine whether they are in a faulted state with the IsFaulted property. In case of an exception, the IsFaulted property returns true. The exception information itself can be accessed by using Exception.InnerException of the Task class. Another, and usually better, way to retrieve exception information from all tasks is demonstrated next.

Using AggregateException Information

To get the exception information from all failing tasks, you can write the result from Task.WhenAll to a Task variable. This task is then awaited until all tasks are completed. Otherwise the exception would still be missed. As described in the last section, with the catch statement only the exception of the first task can be retrieved. However, now you have access to the Exception property of the outer task. The Exception property is of type AggregateException. This exception type defines the property InnerExceptions (not only InnerException), which contains a list of all the exceptions that have been awaited for. Now you can easily iterate through all the exceptions:

```
private static async void ShowAggregatedException()
{
```

```
      Task taskResult = null;
      try
      {
        Task t1 = ThrowAfter(2000, "first");
        Task t2 = ThrowAfter(1000, "second");
        await (taskResult = Task.WhenAll(t1, t2));
      }
      catch (Exception ex)
      {
        WriteLine($"handled {ex.Message}");
        foreach (var ex1 in taskResult.Exception.InnerExceptions)
        {
          WriteLine($"inner exception {ex1.Message}");
        }
      }
    }
```

CANCELLATION

With background tasks that can run longer in some scenarios, it is useful to cancel the tasks. For cancellation, .NET offers a standard mechanism. This mechanism can be used with the task-based asynchronous pattern.

The cancellation framework is based on cooperative behavior; it is not forceful. A long-running task needs to check itself if it is canceled, in which case it is the responsibility of the task to clean up any open resources and finish its work.

Cancellation is based on the `CancellationTokenSource` class, which you can use to send cancel requests. Requests are sent to tasks that reference the `CancellationToken` that is associated with the `CancellationTokenSource`. The following section looks at an example by modifying the `AsyncPatterns` sample created earlier in this chapter to add support for cancellation.

Starting a Cancellation

First, you define a variable `cts` of type `CancellationTokenSource` with the private field members of the class `MainWindow`. This member will be used to cancel tasks and pass tokens to the methods that should be cancelled (code file `AsyncPatterns/MainWindow.xaml.cs`):

```
    public partial class MainWindow : Window
    {
      private SearchInfo _searchInfo = new SearchInfo();
      private object _lockList = new object();
      private CancellationTokenSource _cts;
      //...
```

For a new button that the user can activate to cancel the running task, you add the event handler method `OnCancel`. Within this method, you use the variable `cts` to cancel the tasks with the `Cancel` method:

```
    private void OnCancel(object sender, RoutedEventArgs e)
    {
      _cts?.Cancel();
    }
```

The `CancellationTokenSource` also supports cancellation after a specified amount of time. The method `CancelAfter` enables passing a value, in milliseconds, after which a task should be cancelled.

Cancellation with Framework Features

Now pass the `CancellationToken` to an asynchronous method. Several of the asynchronous methods in the framework support cancellation by offering an overload whereby a `CancellationToken` can be passed. One example is the `GetAsync` method of the `HttpClient` class. The overloaded `GetAsync` method accepts a `CancellationToken` in addition to the URI string. You can retrieve the token from the `CancellationTokenSource` by using the `Token` property.

The implementation of the `GetAsync` method periodically checks whether the operation should be cancelled. When cancellation is appropriate, the method does a cleanup of resources before throwing the exception `OperationCanceledException`. This exception is caught with the `catch` handler in the following code snippet:

```
private async void OnTaskBasedAsyncPattern(object sender, RoutedEventArgs e)
{
  _cts = new CancellationTokenSource();
  try
  {
    foreach (var req in GetSearchRequests())
    {
      var clientHandler = new HttpClientHandler
      {
        Credentials = req.Credentials;
      };
      var client = new HttpClient(clientHandler);
      var response = await client.GetAsync(req.Url, _cts.Token);
      string resp = await response.Content.ReadAsStringAsync();

      //...

    }
  }
  catch (OperationCanceledException ex)
  {
    MessageBox.Show(ex.Message);
  }
}
```

Cancellation with Custom Tasks

What about custom tasks that should be cancelled? The `Run` method of the `Task` class offers an overload to pass a `CancellationToken` as well. However, with custom tasks it is necessary to check whether cancellation is requested. In the following example, this is implemented within the `foreach` loop. The token can be checked by using the `IsCancellationRequsted` property. If you need to do some cleanup before throwing the exception, it is best to verify that cancellation is requested. If cleanup is not needed, an exception can be fired immediately after the check, which is done with the `ThrowIfCancellationRequested` method:

```
await Task.Run(() =>
{
  var images = req.Parse(resp);
  foreach (var image in images)
  {
    _cts.Token.ThrowIfCancellationRequested();
    _searchInfo.List.Add(image);
  }
}, _cts.Token);
```

Now the user can cancel long-running tasks.

SUMMARY

This chapter introduced the `async` and `await` keywords. Having looked at several examples, you've seen the advantages of the task-based asynchronous pattern compared to the asynchronous pattern and the event-based asynchronous pattern available with earlier editions of .NET.

You've also seen how easy it is to create asynchronous methods with the help of the `Task` class, and learned how to use the `async` and `await` keywords to wait for these methods without blocking threads. Finally, you looked at the error-handling aspect of asynchronous methods.

For more information on parallel programming, and details about threads and tasks, see Chapter 21.

The next chapter continues with core features of C# and .NET and gives detailed information on reflection, metadata, and dynamic programming.

16

Reflection, Metadata, and Dynamic Programming

WHAT'S IN THIS CHAPTER?

- ➤ Using custom attributes
- ➤ Inspecting the metadata at runtime using reflection
- ➤ Building access points from classes that enable reflection
- ➤ Understanding the Dynamic Language Runtime
- ➤ Working with the dynamic type
- ➤ Hosting the DLR ScriptRuntime
- ➤ Creating dynamic objects with DynamicObject and ExpandoObject

WROX.COM CODE DOWNLOADS FOR THIS CHAPTER

The wrox.com code downloads for this chapter are found at www.wrox.com/go/professionalcsharp6 on the Download Code tab. The code for this chapter is divided into the following major examples:

- ➤ LookupWhatsNew
- ➤ TypeView
- ➤ VectorClass
- ➤ WhatsNewAttributes
- ➤ DLRHost
- ➤ Dynamic
- ➤ DynamicFileReader
- ➤ ErrorExample

INSPECTING CODE AT RUNTIME AND DYNAMIC PROGRAMMING

This chapter focuses on custom attributes, reflection, and dynamic programming. Custom attributes are mechanisms that enable you to associate custom metadata with program elements. This metadata is created at compile time and embedded in an assembly. *Reflection* is a generic term that describes the capability to inspect and manipulate program elements at runtime. For example, reflection allows you to do the following:

> - Enumerate the members of a type
> - Instantiate a new object
> - Execute the members of an object
> - Find out information about a type
> - Find out information about an assembly
> - Inspect the custom attributes applied to a type
> - Create and compile a new assembly

This list represents a great deal of functionality and encompasses some of the most powerful and complex capabilities provided by the .NET Framework class library. Because one chapter does not have the space to cover all the capabilities of reflection, I focus on those elements that you are likely to use most frequently.

To demonstrate custom attributes and reflection, in this chapter you first develop an example based on a company that regularly ships upgrades of its software and wants to have details about these upgrades documented automatically. In the example, you define custom attributes that indicate the date when program elements were last modified, and what changes were made. You then use reflection to develop an application that looks for these attributes in an assembly and can automatically display all the details about what upgrades have been made to the software since a given date.

Another example in this chapter considers an application that reads from or writes to a database and uses custom attributes as a way to mark which classes and properties correspond to which database tables and columns. By reading these attributes from the assembly at runtime, the program can automatically retrieve or write data to the appropriate location in the database, without requiring specific logic for each table or column.

The second big aspect of this chapter is dynamic programming, which has been a part of the C# language since version 4 when the `dynamic` type was added. The growth of languages such as Ruby and Python, and the increased use of JavaScript, have intensified interest in dynamic programming. Although C# is still a statically typed language, the additions for dynamic programming give the C# language capabilities that some developers are looking for. Using dynamic language features allows for calling script functions from within C# and also makes COM interop easier.

In this chapter, you look at the `dynamic` type and the rules for using it. You also see what an implementation of `DynamicObject` looks like and how you can use it. `ExpandoObject`, which is the frameworks implementation of `DynamicObject`, is also covered.

CUSTOM ATTRIBUTES

You have already seen in this book how you can define attributes on various items within your program. These attributes have been defined by Microsoft as part of the .NET Framework class library, and many of them receive special support from the C# compiler. This means that for those particular attributes, the compiler can customize the compilation process in specific ways—for example, laying out a struct in memory according to the details in the `StructLayout` attributes.

The .NET Framework also enables you to define your own attributes. Obviously, these attributes don't have any effect on the compilation process because the compiler has no intrinsic awareness of them. However, these attributes are emitted as metadata in the compiled assembly when they are applied to program elements.

By itself, this metadata might be useful for documentation purposes, but what makes attributes really powerful is that by using reflection, your code can read this metadata and use it to make decisions at runtime. This means that the custom attributes that you define can directly affect how your code runs. For example, custom attributes can be used to enable declarative code access security checks for custom permission classes, to associate information with program elements that can then be used by testing tools, or when developing extensible frameworks that allow the loading of plug-ins or modules.

Writing Custom Attributes

To understand how to write your own custom attributes, it is useful to know what the compiler does when it encounters an element in your code that has a custom attribute applied to it. To take the database example, suppose that you have a C# property declaration that looks like this:

```
[FieldName("SocialSecurityNumber")]
public string SocialSecurityNumber
{
   get {
      // etc.
```

When the C# compiler recognizes that this property has an attribute applied to it (FieldName), it first appends the string Attribute to this name, forming the combined name FieldNameAttribute. The compiler then searches all the namespaces in its search path (those namespaces that have been mentioned in a using statement) for a class with the specified name. Note that if you mark an item with an attribute whose name already ends in the string Attribute, the compiler does not add the string to the name a second time; it leaves the attribute name unchanged. Therefore, the preceding code is equivalent to this:

```
[FieldNameAttribute("SocialSecurityNumber")]
public string SocialSecurityNumber
{
   get {
      // etc.
```

The compiler expects to find a class with this name, and it expects this class to be derived directly or indirectly from System.Attribute. The compiler also expects that this class contains information governing the use of the attribute. In particular, the attribute class needs to specify the following:

➤ The types of program elements to which the attribute can be applied (classes, structs, properties, methods, and so on)

➤ Whether it is legal for the attribute to be applied more than once to the same program element

➤ Whether the attribute, when applied to a class or interface, is inherited by derived classes and interfaces

➤ The mandatory and optional parameters the attribute takes

If the compiler cannot find a corresponding attribute class, or if it finds one but the way that you have used that attribute does not match the information in the attribute class, the compiler raises a compilation error. For example, if the attribute class indicates that the attribute can be applied only to classes but you have applied it to a struct definition, a compilation error occurs.

Continuing with the example, assume that you have defined the FieldName attribute like this:

```
[AttributeUsage(AttributeTargets.Property,
   AllowMultiple=false,
   Inherited=false)]
public class FieldNameAttribute: Attribute
{
   private string _name;
   public FieldNameAttribute(string name)
   {
      _name = name;
   }
}
```

The following sections discuss each element of this definition.

Specifying the AttributeUsage Attribute

The first thing to note is that the attribute class itself is marked with an attribute—the System.AttributeUsage attribute. This is an attribute defined by Microsoft for which the C# compiler provides special support. (You could argue that AttributeUsage isn't an attribute at all; it is more like a meta-attribute, because it applies only to other attributes, not simply to any class.) The primary purpose of AttributeUsage is to identify the types of program elements to which your custom attribute can be applied. This information is provided by the first parameter of the AttributeUsage attribute. This parameter is mandatory, and it is of an enumerated type, AttributeTargets. In the previous example, you have indicated that the FieldName attribute can be applied only to properties, which is fine, because that is exactly what you have applied it to in the earlier code fragment. The members of the AttributeTargets enumeration are as follows:

➤ All

➤ Assembly

➤ Class

➤ Constructor

➤ Delegate

➤ Enum

➤ Event

➤ Field

➤ GenericParameter

➤ Interface

➤ Method

➤ Module

➤ Parameter

➤ Property

➤ ReturnValue

➤ Struct

This list identifies all the program elements to which you can apply attributes. Note that when applying the attribute to a program element, you place the attribute in square brackets immediately before the element. However, two values in the preceding list do not correspond to any program element: Assembly and Module. An attribute can be applied to an assembly or a module as a whole, rather than to an element in your code; in this case the attribute can be placed anywhere in your source code, but it must be prefixed with the Assembly or Module keyword:

```
[assembly:SomeAssemblyAttribute(Parameters)]
[module:SomeAssemblyAttribute(Parameters)]
```

When indicating the valid target elements of a custom attribute, you can combine these values using the bitwise OR operator. For example, if you want to indicate that your FieldName attribute can be applied to both properties and fields, you use the following:

```
[AttributeUsage(AttributeTargets.Property | AttributeTargets.Field,
    AllowMultiple=false, Inherited=false)]
public class FieldNameAttribute: Attribute
```

You can also use AttributeTargets.All to indicate that your attribute can be applied to all types of program elements. The AttributeUsage attribute also contains two other parameters: AllowMultiple and Inherited. These are specified using the syntax of <ParameterName>=<ParameterValue>, instead of simply specifying the values for these parameters. These parameters are optional—you can omit them.

The `AllowMultiple` parameter indicates whether an attribute can be applied more than once to the same item. The fact that it is set to `false` indicates that the compiler should raise an error if it sees something like this:

```
[FieldName("SocialSecurityNumber")]
[FieldName("NationalInsuranceNumber")]
public string SocialSecurityNumber
{
    // etc.
```

If the `Inherited` parameter is set to `true`, an attribute applied to a class or interface is also automatically applied to all derived classes or interfaces. If the attribute is applied to a method or property, it automatically applies to any overrides of that method or property, and so on.

Specifying Attribute Parameters

This section demonstrates how you can specify the parameters that your custom attribute takes. When the compiler encounters a statement such as the following, it examines the parameters passed into the attribute—which is a string—and looks for a constructor for the attribute that takes exactly those parameters:

```
[FieldName("SocialSecurityNumber")]
public string SocialSecurityNumber
{
    // etc.
```

If the compiler finds an appropriate constructor, it emits the specified metadata to the assembly. If the compiler does not find an appropriate constructor, a compilation error occurs. As discussed later in this chapter, reflection involves reading metadata (attributes) from assemblies and instantiating the attribute classes they represent. Because of this, the compiler must ensure that an appropriate constructor exists that allows the runtime instantiation of the specified attribute.

In the example, you have supplied just one constructor for `FieldNameAttribute`, and this constructor takes one string parameter. Therefore, when applying the `FieldName` attribute to a property, you must supply one string as a parameter, as shown in the preceding code.

To allow a choice of what types of parameters should be supplied with an attribute, you can provide different constructor overloads, although normal practice is to supply just one constructor and use properties to define any other optional parameters, as explained next.

Specifying Optional Attribute Parameters

As demonstrated with the `AttributeUsage` attribute, an alternative syntax enables optional parameters to be added to an attribute. This syntax involves specifying the names and values of the optional parameters. It works through `public` properties or fields in the attribute class. For example, suppose that you modify the definition of the `SocialSecurityNumber` property as follows:

```
[FieldName("SocialSecurityNumber", Comment="This is the primary key field")]
public string SocialSecurityNumber { get; set; }
{
    // etc.
```

In this case, the compiler recognizes the `<ParameterName>=<ParameterValue>` syntax of the second parameter and does not attempt to match this parameter to a `FieldNameAttribute` constructor. Instead, it looks for a `public` property or field (although public fields are not considered good programming practice, so normally you will work with properties) of that name that it can use to set the value of this parameter. If you want the previous code to work, you have to add some code to `FieldNameAttribute`:

```
[AttributeUsage(AttributeTargets.Property,
  AllowMultiple=false, Inherited=false)]
```

```
public class FieldNameAttribute : Attribute
{
  public string Comment { get; set; }

  private string _fieldName;
  public FieldNameAttribute(string fieldName)
  {
    _fieldName = fieldname;
  }

  // etc
}
```

Custom Attribute Example: WhatsNewAttributes

In this section you start developing the example mentioned at the beginning of the chapter. WhatsNewAttributes provides for an attribute that indicates when a program element was last modified. This is a more ambitious code example than many of the others in that it consists of three separate assemblies:

➤ WhatsNewAttributes—Contains the definitions of the attributes

➤ VectorClass—Contains the code to which the attributes have been applied

➤ LookUpWhatsNew—Contains the project that displays details about items that have changed

Of these, only the LookUpWhatsNew assembly is a console application of the type that you have used up until now. The remaining two assemblies are libraries—they each contain class definitions but no program entry point. For the VectorClass assembly, this means that the entry point and test harness class have been removed from the VectorAsCollection sample, leaving only the Vector class. These classes are represented later in this chapter.

The WhatsNewAttributes Library Assembly

This section starts with the core WhatsNewAttributes assembly. The source code is contained in the file WhatsNewAttributes.cs, which is located in the WhatsNewAttributes project of the WhatsNewAttributes solution in the example code for this chapter.

The sample code for WhatsNewAttributes makes use of the following dependencies and namespaces:

Dependencies

```
NETStandard.Library
```

Namespaces

```
System
```

The WhatsNewAttributes.cs file defines two attribute classes, LastModifiedAttribute and SupportsWhatsNewAttribute. You use the attribute LastModifiedAttribute to mark when an item was last modified. It takes two mandatory parameters (parameters that are passed to the constructor): the date of the modification and a string containing a description of the changes. One optional parameter named issues (for which a public property exists) can be used to describe any outstanding issues for the item.

In practice, you would probably want this attribute to apply to anything. To keep the code simple, its usage is limited here to classes and methods. You allow it to be applied more than once to the same item (AllowMultiple=true) because an item might be modified more than once, and each modification has to be marked with a separate attribute instance.

SupportsWhatsNew is a smaller class representing an attribute that doesn't take any parameters. The purpose of this assembly attribute is to mark an assembly for which you are maintaining documentation via the `LastModifiedAttribute`. This way, the program that examines this assembly later knows that the assembly it is reading is one on which you are actually using your automated documentation process. Here is the complete source code for this part of the example (code file `WhatsNewAttributes/WhatsNewAttributes.cs`):

```csharp
using System;

namespace WhatsNewAttributes
{
  [AttributeUsage(AttributeTargets.Class | AttributeTargets.Method,
    AllowMultiple=true, Inherited=false)]
  public class LastModifiedAttribute: Attribute
  {
    private readonly DateTime _dateModified;
    private readonly string _changes;

    public LastModifiedAttribute(string dateModified, string changes)
    {
      _dateModified = DateTime.Parse(dateModified);
      _changes = changes;
    }

    public DateTime DateModified => _dateModified;

    public string Changes => _changes;

    public string Issues { get; set; }
  }

  [AttributeUsage(AttributeTargets.Assembly)]
  public class SupportsWhatsNewAttribute: Attribute
  {
  }
}
```

Based on what has been discussed, this code should be fairly clear. Notice, however, that the properties `DateModified` and `Changes` are read-only. Using the expression syntax, the compiler creates `get` accessors. There is no need for `set` accessors because you are requiring these parameters to be set in the constructor as mandatory parameters. You need the `get` accessors so that you can read the values of these attributes.

The VectorClass Assembly

To use these attributes, you use a modified version of the earlier `VectorAsCollection` example. Note that you need to reference the `WhatsNewAttributes` library that you just created. You also need to indicate the corresponding namespace with a `using` statement so the compiler can recognize the attributes (code file `VectorClass/Vector.cs`):

```csharp
using System;
using System.Collections;
using System.Collections.Generic;
using System.Text;
using WhatsNewAttributes;

[assembly: SupportsWhatsNew]
```

This code also adds the line that marks the assembly itself with the `SupportsWhatsNew` attribute.

The sample code for `VectorClass` makes use of the following dependencies and namespaces:

Dependencies

```
NETStandard.Library
WhatsNewAttributes
```

Namespaces

```
System
System.Collections
System.Collections.Generic
System.Text
WhatsNewAttributes
```

Now for the code for the `Vector` class. You are not making any major changes to this class; you only add a couple of `LastModified` attributes to mark the work that you have done on this class in this chapter:

```
namespace VectorClass
{
  [LastModified("6 Jun 2015", "updated for C# 6 and .NET Core")]
  [LastModified("14 Deb 2010", "IEnumerable interface implemented: " +
    "Vector can be treated as a collection")]
  [LastModified("10 Feb 2010", "IFormattable interface implemented " +
    "Vector accepts N and VE format specifiers")]
  public class Vector : IFormattable, IEnumerable<double>
  {
    public Vector(double x, double y, double z)
    {
      X = x;
      Y = y;
      Z = z;
    }

    public Vector(Vector vector)
      : this (vector.X, vector.Y, vector.Z)
    {
    }

    public double X { get;  }
    public double Y { get; }
    public double Z { get; }

    public string ToString(string format, IFormatProvider formatProvider)
    {
      //...
```

You also mark the contained `VectorEnumerator` class as new:

```
[LastModified("6 Jun 2015",
  "Changed to implement the generic interface IEnumerator<T>")]
[LastModified("14 Feb 2010",
  "Class created as part of collection support for Vector")]
private class VectorEnumerator : IEnumerator<double>
{
```

That's as far as you can get with this example for now. You are unable to run anything yet because all you have are two libraries. After taking a look at reflection in the next section, you will develop the final part of the example, in which you look up and display these attributes.

USING REFLECTION

In this section, you take a closer look at the `System.Type` class, which enables you to access information concerning the definition of any data type. You also look at the `System.Reflection.Assembly` class, which you can use to access information about an assembly or to load that assembly into your program. Finally, you combine the code in this section with the code in the previous section to complete the `WhatsNewAttributes` example.

The System.Type Class

So far you have used the `Type` class only to hold the reference to a type as follows:

```
Type t = typeof(double);
```

Although previously referred to as a class, `Type` is an abstract base class. Whenever you instantiate a `Type` object, you are actually instantiating a class derived from `Type`. `Type` has one derived class corresponding to each actual data type, though in general the derived classes simply provide different overloads of the various `Type` methods and properties that return the correct data for the corresponding data type. They do not typically add new methods or properties. In general, there are three common ways to obtain a `Type` reference that refers to any given type.

➤ You can use the C# `typeof` operator as shown in the preceding code. This operator takes the name of the type (not in quotation marks, however) as a parameter.

➤ You can use the `GetType` method, which all classes inherit from `System.Object`:

```
double d = 10;
Type t = d.GetType();
```

`GetType` is called against a variable, rather than taking the name of a type. Note, however, that the `Type` object returned is still associated with only that data type. It does not contain any information that relates to that instance of the type. The `GetType` method can be useful if you have a reference to an object but you are not sure what class that object is actually an instance of.

➤ You can call the static method of the `Type` class, `GetType`:

```
Type t = Type.GetType("System.Double");
```

`Type` is really the gateway to much of the reflection functionality. It implements a huge number of methods and properties—far too many to provide a comprehensive list here. However, the following subsections should give you a good idea of the kinds of things you can do with the `Type` class. Note that the available properties are all read-only; you use `Type` to find out about the data type—you cannot use it to make any modifications to the type!

Type Properties

You can divide the properties implemented by `Type` into three categories. First, a number of properties retrieve the strings containing various names associated with the class, as shown in the following table:

PROPERTY	RETURNS
Name	The name of the data type
FullName	The fully qualified name of the data type (including the namespace name)
Namespace	The name of the namespace in which the data type is defined

Second, it is possible to retrieve references to further type objects that represent related classes, as shown in the following table.

PROPERTY	RETURNS TYPE REFERENCE CORRESPONDING TO
BaseType	The immediate base type of this type
UnderlyingSystemType	The type to which this type maps in the .NET runtime (recall that certain .NET base types actually map to specific predefined types recognized by IL). This member is only available in the full Framework.

A number of Boolean properties indicate whether this type is, for example, a `class`, an enum, and so on. These properties include `IsAbstract`, `IsArray`, `IsClass`, `IsEnum`, `IsInterface`, `IsPointer`, `IsPrimitive` (one of the predefined primitive data types), `IsPublic`, `IsSealed`, and `IsValueType`. The following example uses a primitive data type:

```
Type intType = typeof(int);
WriteLine(intType.IsAbstract);      // writes false
WriteLine(intType.IsClass);         // writes false
WriteLine(intType.IsEnum);          // writes false
WriteLine(intType.IsPrimitive);     // writes true
WriteLine(intType.IsValueType);     // writes true
```

This example uses the `Vector` class:

```
Type vecType = typeof(Vector);
WriteLine(vecType.IsAbstract);      // writes false
WriteLine(vecType.IsClass);         // writes true
WriteLine(vecType.IsEnum);          // writes false
WriteLine(vecType.IsPrimitive);     // writes false
WriteLine(vecType.IsValueType);     // writes false
```

Finally, you can also retrieve a reference to the assembly in which the type is defined. This is returned as a reference to an instance of the `System.Reflection.Assembly` class, which is examined shortly:

```
Type t = typeof (Vector);
Assembly containingAssembly = new Assembly(t);
```

Methods

Most of the methods of `System.Type` are used to obtain details about the members of the corresponding data type—the constructors, properties, methods, events, and so on. Quite a large number of methods exist, but they all follow the same pattern. For example, two methods retrieve details about the methods of the data type: `GetMethod` and `GetMethods`. `GetMethod` returns a reference to a `System.Reflection.MethodInfo` object, which contains details about a method. `GetMethods` returns an array of such references. As the names suggest, the difference is that `GetMethods` returns details about all the methods, whereas `GetMethod` returns details about just one method with a specified parameter list. Both methods have overloads that take an extra parameter, a `BindingFlags` enumerated value that indicates which members should be returned—for example, whether to return public members, instance members, static members, and so on.

For example, the simplest overload of `GetMethods` takes no parameters and returns details about all the public methods of the data type:

```
Type t = typeof(double);
foreach (MethodInfo nextMethod in t.GetMethods())
{
   // etc.
}
```

The member methods of `Type` that follow the same pattern are shown in the following table. Note that plural names return an array.

TYPE OF OBJECT RETURNED	METHOD(S)
ConstructorInfo	GetConstructor, GetConstructors
EventInfo	GetEvent, GetEvents
FieldInfo	GetField, GetFields
MemberInfo	GetMember, GetMembers, GetDefaultMembers
MethodInfo	GetMethod, GetMethods
PropertyInfo	GetProperty, GetProperties

The GetMember and GetMembers methods return details about any or all members of the data type, regardless of whether these members are constructors, properties, methods, and so on.

The TypeView Example

This section demonstrates some of the features of the Type class with a short example, TypeView, which you can use to list the members of a data type. The example demonstrates how to use TypeView for a double; however, you can swap this type with any other data type just by changing one line of the code in the example.

The result of running the application is this output to the console:

```
Analysis of type Double

Type Name: Double
Full Name: System.Double
Namespace: System
Base Type: ValueType

public members:
System.Double Method IsInfinity
System.Double Method IsPositiveInfinity
System.Double Method IsNegativeInfinity
System.Double Method IsNaN
System.Double Method CompareTo
System.Double Method CompareTo
System.Double Method Equals
System.Double Method op_Equality
System.Double Method op_Inequality
System.Double Method op_LessThan
System.Double Method op_GreaterThan
System.Double Method op_LessThanOrEqual
System.Double Method op_GreaterThanOrEqual
System.Double Method Equals
System.Double Method GetHashCode
System.Double Method ToString
System.Double Method ToString
System.Double Method ToString
System.Double Method ToString
System.Double Method Parse
System.Double Method Parse
System.Double Method Parse
System.Double Method Parse
System.Double Method TryParse
System.Double Method TryParse
System.Double Method GetTypeCode
System.Object Method GetType
System.Double Field MinValue
```

```
System.Double Field MaxValue
System.Double Field Epsilon
System.Double Field NegativeInfinity
System.Double Field PositiveInfinity
System.Double Field NaN
```

The console displays the name, full name, and namespace of the data type as well as the name of the base type. Next, it simply iterates through all the public instance members of the data type, displaying for each member the declaring type, the type of member (method, field, and so on), and the name of the member. The *declaring type* is the name of the class that actually declares the type member (for example, `System.Double` if it is defined or overridden in `System.Double`, or the name of the relevant base type if the member is simply inherited from a base class).

`TypeView` does not display signatures of methods because you are retrieving details about all public instance members through `MemberInfo` objects, and information about parameters is not available through a `MemberInfo` object. To retrieve that information, you would need references to `MethodInfo` and other more specific objects, which means that you would need to obtain details about each type of member separately.

The sample code for `TypeView` makes use of the following dependencies and namespaces:

Dependencies

```
NETStandard.Library
```

Namespaces

```
System
System.Reflection
System.Text
static System.Console
```

`TypeView` does display details about all public instance members; but for doubles, the only details defined are fields and methods. The code for `TypeView` is as follows. To begin, you need to add a few `using` statements:

```
using System;
using System.Reflection;
using System.Text;
using static System.Console;
```

You need `System.Text` because you use a `StringBuilder` object to build up the text. The entire code is in one class, `Program`, which has a couple of `static` methods and one `static` field, a `StringBuilder` instance called `OutputText`, which is used to build the text to be displayed in the message box. The main method and class declaration look like this:

```
class Program
{
  private static StringBuilder OutputText = new StringBuilder();

  static void Main()
  {
    // modify this line to retrieve details of any other data type
    Type t = typeof(double);

    AnalyzeType(t);
```

```
        WriteLine($"Analysis of type {t.Name}");
        WriteLine(OutputText.ToString());

        ReadLine();
    }
```

The `Main` method implementation starts by declaring a `Type` object to represent your chosen data type. You then call a method, `AnalyzeType`, which extracts the information from the `Type` object and uses it to build the output text. Finally, you write the output to the console. `AnalyzeType` is where the bulk of the work is done:

```
static void AnalyzeType(Type t)
{
    TypeInfo typeInfo = t.GetTypeInfo();
    AddToOutput($"Type Name: {t.Name}");
    AddToOutput($"Full Name: {t.FullName}");
    AddToOutput($"Namespace: {t.Namespace}");

    Type tBase = t.BaseType;

    if (tBase != null)
    {
        AddToOutput($"Base Type: {tBase.Name}");
    }

    AddToOutput("\npublic members:");

    foreach (MemberInfo NextMember in t.GetMembers())
    {
#if DNXCORE
        AddToOutput($"{member.DeclaringType} {member.Name}");
#else
        AddToOutput($"{member.DeclaringType} {member.MemberType} {member.Name}");
#endif
    }
}
```

You implement the `AnalyzeType` method by calling various properties of the `Type` object to get the information you need concerning the type names and then calling the `GetMembers` method to get an array of `MemberInfo` objects that you can use to display the details for each member. Note that you use a helper method, `AddToOutput`, to build the text to be displayed:

```
static void AddToOutput(string Text)
{
    OutputText.Append("\n" + Text);
}
```

The Assembly Class

The `Assembly` class is defined in the `System.Reflection` namespace and provides access to the metadata for a given assembly. It also contains methods that enable you to load and even execute an assembly—assuming that the assembly is an executable. As with the `Type` class, `Assembly` contains too many methods and properties to cover here, so this section is confined to covering those methods and properties that you need to get started and that you use to complete the `WhatsNewAttributes` example.

Before you can do anything with an `Assembly` instance, you need to load the corresponding assembly into the running process. You can do this with either the `static` members `Assembly.Load` or `Assembly.LoadFrom`. The difference between these methods is that `Load` takes the name of the assembly, and the runtime searches in a variety of locations in an attempt to locate the assembly. These locations include the local directory and the global assembly cache. `LoadFrom` takes the full path name of an assembly and does not attempt to find the assembly in any other location:

```
Assembly assembly1 = Assembly.Load("SomeAssembly");
Assembly assembly2 = Assembly.LoadFrom
   (@"C:\My Projects\Software\SomeOtherAssembly");
```

A number of other overloads of both methods exist, which supply additional security information. After you have loaded an assembly, you can use various properties on it to find out, for example, its full name:

```
string name = assembly1.FullName;
```

Getting Details About Types Defined in an Assembly

One nice feature of the `Assembly` class is that it enables you to obtain details about all the types that are defined in the corresponding assembly. You simply call the `Assembly.GetTypes` method, which returns an array of `System.Type` references containing details about all the types. You can then manipulate these `Type` references as explained in the previous section:

```
Type[] types = theAssembly.GetTypes();

foreach(Type definedType in types)
{
   DoSomethingWith(definedType);
}
```

Getting Details About Custom Attributes

The methods you use to find out which custom attributes are defined on an assembly or type depend on the type of object to which the attribute is attached. If you want to find out what custom attributes are attached to an assembly as a whole, you need to call a `static` method of the `Attribute` class, `GetCustomAttributes`, passing in a reference to the assembly:

> **NOTE** *This is actually quite significant. You might have wondered why, when you defined custom attributes, you had to go to all the trouble of actually writing classes for them, and why Microsoft didn't come up with some simpler syntax. Well, the answer is here. The custom attributes genuinely exist as objects, and when an assembly is loaded you can read in these attribute objects, examine their properties, and call their methods.*

```
Attribute[] definedAttributes =
   Attribute.GetCustomAttributes(assembly1);
   // assembly1 is an Assembly object
```

`GetCustomAttributes`, which is used to get assembly attributes, has a few overloads. If you call it without specifying any parameters other than an assembly reference, it simply returns all the custom attributes defined for that assembly. You can also call `GetCustomAttributes` by specifying a second parameter, which is a `Type` object that indicates the attribute class in which you are interested. In this case, `GetCustomAttributes` returns an array consisting of all the attributes present that are of the specified type.

Note that all attributes are retrieved as plain `Attribute` references. If you want to call any of the methods or properties you defined for your custom attributes, you need to cast these references explicitly to the relevant custom attribute classes. You can obtain details about custom attributes that are attached to a given data type by calling another overload of `Assembly.GetCustomAttributes`, this time passing a `Type` reference that describes the type for which you want to retrieve any attached attributes. To obtain attributes that are attached to methods, constructors, fields, and so on, however, you need to call a `GetCustomAttributes` method that is a member of one of the classes `MethodInfo`, `ConstructorInfo`, `FieldInfo`, and so on.

If you expect only a single attribute of a given type, you can call the `GetCustomAttribute` method instead, which returns a single `Attribute` object. You will use `GetCustomAttribute` in the `WhatsNewAttributes` example to find out whether the `SupportsWhatsNew` attribute is present in the assembly. To do this, you call `GetCustomAttribute`, passing in a reference to the `WhatsNewAttributes` assembly, and the type of the `SupportsWhatsNewAttribute` attribute. If this attribute is present, you get an `Attribute` instance. If no instances of it are defined in the assembly, you get `null`. If two or more instances are found, `GetCustomAttribute` throws a `System.Reflection.AmbiguousMatchException`. This is what that call would look like:

```
Attribute supportsAttribute =
    Attribute.GetCustomAttributes(assembly1, typeof(SupportsWhatsNewAttribute));
```

Completing the WhatsNewAttributes Example

You now have enough information to complete the `WhatsNewAttributes` example by writing the source code for the final assembly in the sample, the `LookUpWhatsNew` assembly. This part of the application is a console application. However, it needs to reference the other assemblies of `WhatsNewAttributes` and `VectorClass`.

The sample code for the `LookupWhatsNew` project makes use of the following dependencies and namespaces:

Dependencies

```
NETStandard.Library
VectorClass
WhatsNewAttributes
```

Namespaces

```
System
System.Collections.Generic
System.Linq
System.Reflection
System.Text
WhatsNewAttributes
static System.Console
```

In the source code of this file, you first indicate the namespaces you want to infer. System.Text is there because you need to use a StringBuilder object again. System.Linq is used to filter some attributes (code file LookupWhatsNew/Program.cs):

```
using System;
using System.Collections.Generic;
using System.Linq;
using System.Reflection;
using System.Text;
using WhatsNewAttributes;
using static System.Console;

namespace LookUpWhatsNew
{
```

The class that contains the main program entry point as well as the other methods is Program. All the methods you define are in this class, which also has two static fields—outputText, which contains the text as you build it in preparation for writing it to the message box, and backDateTo, which stores the date you have selected. All modifications made since this date will be displayed. Normally, you would display a dialog inviting the user to pick this date, but we don't want to get sidetracked into that kind of code. For this reason, backDateTo is hard-coded to a value of 1 Feb 2015. You can easily change this date when you download the code:

```
class Program
{
  private static readonly StringBuilder outputText = new StringBuilder(1000);
  private static DateTime backDateTo = new DateTime(2015, 2, 1);

  static void Main()
  {
    Assembly theAssembly = Assembly.Load(new AssemblyName("VectorClass"));
    Attribute supportsAttribute = theAssembly.GetCustomAttribute(
      typeof(SupportsWhatsNewAttribute));
    string name = theAssembly.FullName;

    AddToMessage($"Assembly: {name}");

    if (supportsAttribute == null)
    {
      AddToMessage("This assembly does not support WhatsNew attributes");
      return;
    }
    else
    {
      AddToMessage("Defined Types:");
    }

    IEnumerable<Type> types = theAssembly.ExportedTypes;

    foreach(Type definedType in types)
    {
      DisplayTypeInfo(definedType);
    }

    WriteLine($"What\`s New since {backDateTo:D}");
    WriteLine(outputText.ToString());

    ReadLine();
  }

  //...
}
```

The Main method first loads the VectorClass assembly, and then verifies that it is marked with the SupportsWhatsNew attribute. You know VectorClass has the SupportsWhatsNew attribute applied to it because you have only recently compiled it, but this is a check that would be worth making if users were given a choice of which assembly they want to check.

Assuming that all is well, you use the Assembly.ExportedTypes property to get a collection of all the types defined in this assembly, and then loop through them. For each one, you call a method, DisplayTypeInfo, which adds the relevant text, including details regarding any instances of LastModifiedAttribute, to the outputText field. Finally, you show the complete text to the console. The DisplayTypeInfo method looks like this:

```
private static void DisplayTypeInfo(Type type)
{
  // make sure we only pick out classes
  if (!type.GetTypeInfo().IsClass)
  {
    return;
  }

  AddToMessage($"\nclass {type.Name}");

  IEnumerable<LastModifiedAttribute> attributes = type.GetTypeInfo()
    .GetCustomAttributes().OfType<LastModifiedAttribute>();

  if (attributes.Count() == 0)
  {
    AddToMessage("No changes to this class\n");
  }
  else
  {
    foreach (LastFieldModifiedAttribute attribute in attributes)
    {
      WriteAttributeInfo(attribute);
    }
  }

  AddToMessage("changes to methods of this class:");

  foreach (MethodInfo method in
    type.GetTypeInfo().DeclaredMembers.OfType<MethodInfo>())
  {
    IEnumerable<LastModifiedAttribute> attributesToMethods =
      method.GetCustomAttributes().OfType<LastModifiedAttribute>();

    if (attributesToMethods.Count() > 0)
    {
      AddToOutput($"{method.ReturnType} {method.Name}()");
      foreach (Attribute attribute in attributesToMethods)
      {
        WriteAttributeInfo(attribute);
      }
    }
  }
}
```

Notice that the first thing you do in this method is check whether the Type reference you have been passed actually represents a class. Because, to keep things simple, you have specified that the LastModified attribute can be applied only to classes or member methods, you would be wasting time by doing any processing if the item is not a class (it could be a class, delegate, or enum).

Next, you use the type.GetTypeInfo().GetCustomAttributes() method to determine whether this class has any LastModifiedAttribute instances attached to it. If so, you add their details to the output text, using a helper method, WriteAttributeInfo.

Finally, you use the `DeclaredMembers` property of the `TypeInfo` type to iterate through all the member methods of this data type, and then do the same with each method as you did for the class—check whether it has any `LastModifiedAttribute` instances attached to it; if so, you display them using `WriteAttributeInfo`.

The next bit of code shows the `WriteAttributeInfo` method, which is responsible for determining what text to display for a given `LastModifiedAttribute` instance. Note that this method is passed an `Attribute` reference, so it needs to cast this to a `LastModifiedAttribute` reference first. After it has done that, it uses the properties that you originally defined for this attribute to retrieve its parameters. It confirms that the date of the attribute is sufficiently recent before actually adding it to the text for display:

```
private static void WriteAttributeInfo(Attribute attribute)
{
  LastModifiedAttribute lastModifiedAttrib =
    attribute as LastModifiedAttribute;

  if (lastModifiedAttrib == null)
  {
    return;
  }

  // check that date is in range
  DateTime modifiedDate = lastModifiedAttrib.DateModified;

  if (modifiedDate < backDateTo)
  {
    return;
  }

  AddToOutput($" modified: {modifiedDate:D}: {lastModifiedAttribute.Changes}");

  if (lastModifiedAttribute.Issues != null)
  {
    AddToOutput($" Outstanding issues: {lastModifiedAttribute.Issues}");
  }
}
```

Finally, here is the helper `AddToOutput` method:

```
static void AddToOutput(string message)
{
  outputText.Append("\n" + message);
}
```

Running this code produces the results shown here:

```
What`s New since Sunday, February 1, 2015

Assembly: VectorClass, Version=1.0.0.0, Culture=neutral, PublicKeyToken=null
Defined Types:

class Vector
 modified: Saturday, June 6, 2015: updated for C# 6 and .NET Core
changes to methods of this class:
System.String ToString()
System.Collections.Generic.IEnumerator`1[System.Double] GetEnumerator()
 modified: Saturday, June 6, 2015: added to implement IEnumerable<T>
```

Note that when you list the types defined in the `VectorClass` assembly, you actually pick up two classes: `Vector` and the embedded `VectorEnumerator` class. In addition, note that because the `backDateTo` date of 1 Feb is hard-coded in this example, you actually pick up the attributes that are dated June 6 (when the code was changed to support the Core CLR) but not those dated earlier.

USING DYNAMIC LANGUAGE EXTENSIONS FOR REFLECTION

Until now you've used reflection for reading metadata. You can also use reflection to create instances dynamically from types that aren't known at compile time. The next sample shows creating an instance of the `Calculator` class without the compiler knowing of this type at compile time. The assembly `CalculatorLib` is loaded dynamically without adding a reference. During runtime, the `Calculator` object is instantiated, and a method is called. After you know how to use the Reflection API, you'll do the same using the C# `dynamic` keyword. This keyword has been part of the C# language since version 4.

Creating the Calculator Library

The library that is loaded is a simple Class Library (Package) containing the type `Calculator` with implementations of the `Add` and `Subtract` methods. As the methods are really simple, they are implemented using the expression syntax (code file `CalculatorLib/Calculator.cs`):

```
namespace CalculatorLib
{
  public class Calculator
  {
    public double Add(double x, double y) => x + y;
    public double Subtract(double x, double y) => x - y;
  }
}
```

After you compile the library, copy the DLL to the folder `c:/addins`. To create an output from the Class Library (Package) project, on the Build tab of Project Properties, select the Produce Outputs on Build option (see Figure 16-1).

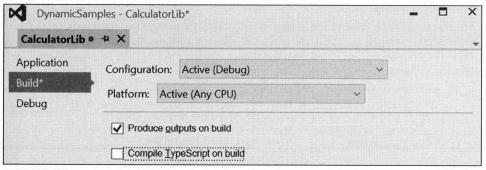

FIGURE 16-1

Depending on whether you use the .NET Core or the .NET Framework version of the client application, you need to copy the corresponding library to the `c:/addins` folder. To select the platform to run the application from within Visual Studio, select the Debug settings with the Project Properties and choose the Platform setting as shown in Figure 16-2.

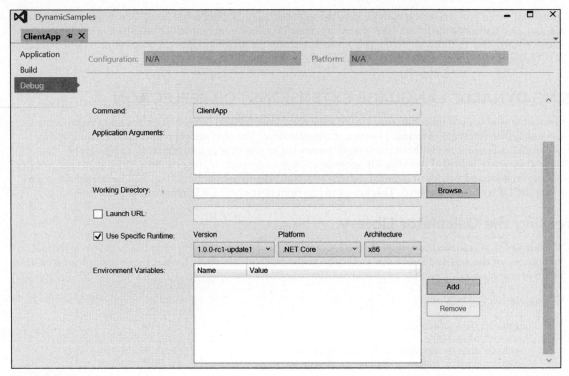

FIGURE 16-2

Instantiating a Type Dynamically

For using reflection to create the `Calculator` instance dynamically, you create a Console Application (Package) with the name `ClientApp`.

The constants `CalculatorLibPath`, `CalculatorLibName`, and `CalculatorTypeName` define the path to the library, the name of the assembly, and the name of the `Calculator` type, including the namespace. The `Main` method invokes the methods `ReflectionOld` and `ReflectionNew`, two variants doing reflection (code file `DynamicSamples/ClientApp/Program.cs`):

```
class Program
{
  private const string CalculatorLibPath = @"c:/addins/CalculatorLib.dll";
  private const string CalculatorLibName = "CalculatorLib";
  private const string CalculatorTypeName = "CalculatorLib.Calculator";

  static void Main()
  {
    ReflectionOld();
    ReflectionNew();
  }
  //etc.
}
```

Before using reflection to invoke a method, you need to instantiate the `Calculator` type. There are different ways to do this. Using the .NET Framework, the method `GetCalculator` loads the assembly dynamically using the method `AssemblyLoadFile` and creates an instance of the `Calculator` type with the

CreateInstance method. Using the preprocessor directive #if NET46, this part of the code compiles only for .NET 4.6 (code file DynamicSamples/ClientApp/Program.cs):

```
#if NET46
  private static object GetCalculator()
  {
    Assembly assembly = Assembly.LoadFile(CalculatorLibPath);
    return assembly.CreateInstance(CalculatorTypeName);
  }
#endif
```

The code snippet makes use of the NET46 symbol when compiling .NET 4.6 code. This is possible because for the frameworks that are listed in the project.json file, symbols are created automatically with the same name; the framework name is just converted to uppercase. You can also define your own symbols within in the compilationOptions declaration. Specifying a define section within the compilationOptions of a framework declaration, the symbol is only defined for the specific framework. The following code snippet specifies the symbol DOTNETCORE just when the application is compiled for .NET Core (code file DynamicSamples/ClientApp/project.json):

```
"frameworks": {
  "net46": {},
  "netstandard1.0": {
    "dependencies": {},
    "compilationOptions": {
      "define": [ "DOTNETCORE" ]
    }
  }
}
```

The implementation of .NET Core needs to be platform independent; that's why it's not possible to compile the previous code for .NET Core. Here, some more code is needed to load the assembly. First, the IAssemblyLoadContext is retrieved to load the assembly from the file system. After the load context is retrieved, the DirectoryLoader is added (which will be implemented in the next step) to load the assembly from the file system. After setting up the context it's possible to load the Assembly using the Load method and dynamically instantiate the type with the CreateInstance method of the Activator class (code file DynamicSamples/ClientApp/Program.cs):

```
#if DOTNETCORE
  private static object GetCalculator()
  {
    IAssemblyLoadContext loadContext = PlatformServices.Default.
      AssemblyLoadContextAccessor.Default;
    using (PlatformServices.Default.AssemblyLoaderContainer.AddLoader(
      new DirectoryLoader(CalculatorLibPath, loadContext)))
    {
      Assembly assembly = Assembly.Load(new AssemblyName(CalculatorLibName));
      Type type = assembly.GetType(CalculatorTypeName);
      return Activator.CreateInstance(type);
    }
  }
#endif
```

The class DirectoryLoader that's used with the loading context implements the interface IAssemblyLoader. This interface defines the methods Load and LoadUnmanagedLibrary. Because only managed assemblies are loaded with the sample app, only the Load method needs an implementation. This implementation makes use of the context to load the assembly file (code file DynamicSamples/ClientApp/Program.cs):

```
public class DirectoryLoader : IAssemblyLoader
{
  private readonly IAssemblyLoadContext _context;
```

```
    private readonly string _path;

    public DirectoryLoader(string path, IAssemblyLoadContext context)
    {
      _path = path;
      _context = context;
    }

    public Assembly Load(AssemblyName assemblyName) =>
      _context.LoadFile(_path);
    public IntPtr LoadUnmanagedLibrary(string name)
    {
      throw new NotImplementedException();
    }
  }
}
```

The sample code for the `ClientApp` makes use of the following dependencies and .NET namespaces:

Dependencies

```
NETStandard.Library

Microsoft.CSharp

Microsoft.Extensions.PlatformAbstractions
```

.NET Namespaces

```
Microsoft.CSharp.RuntimeBinder

Microsoft.Extensions.PlatformExtensions

System

System.Reflection

static System.Console
```

Invoking a Member with the Reflection API

Next, the Reflection API is used to invoke the method `Add` of the `Calculator` instance. First, the calculator instance is retrieved with the helper method `GetCalculator`. If you would like to add a reference to the `CalculatorLib`, you could use `new Calculator` to create an instance. But here it's not that easy.

Invoking the method using reflection has the advantage that the type does not need to be available at compile time. You could add it at a later time just by copying the library in the specified directory. To invoke the member using reflection, the `Type` object of the instance is retrieved using `GetType`—a method of the base class `Object`. With the help of the extension method `GetMethod` (this method is defined in the NuGet package `System.Reflection.TypeExtensions`), a `MethodInfo` object for the method `Add` is accessed. The `MethodInfo` defines the `Invoke` method to call the method using any number of parameters. The first parameter of the `Invoke` method needs the instance of the type where the member is invoked. The second parameter is of type `object []` to pass all the parameters needed by the invocation. You're passing the values of the `x` and `y` variables here. In case you're using older versions of the .NET Framework without the type extensions, the code to invoke the method is shown within comments. You cannot use this code with .NET Core (code file `DynamicSamples/ClientApp/Program.cs`):

```
private static void ReflectionOld()
{
  double x = 3;
  double y = 4;
  object calc = GetCalculator();
  // object result = calc.GetType().InvokeMember("Add",
  //   BindingFlags.InvokeMethod, null, calc, new object[] { x, y });
  object result = calc.GetType().GetMethod("Add")
```

```
        .Invoke(calc, new object[] { x, y });
    WriteLine($"the result of {x} and {y} is {result}");
}
```

When you run the program, the calculator is invoked, and this result is written to the console:

```
The result of 3 and 4 is 7
```

This is quite some work to do for calling a member dynamically. The next section looks at how easy it is to use the dynamic keyword.

Invoking a Member with the Dynamic Type

Using reflection with the dynamic keyword, the object that is returned from the GetCalculator method is assigned to a variable of a dynamic type. The method itself is not changed; it still returns an object. The result is returned to a variable that is of type dynamic. With this, the Add method is invoked, and two double values are passed to it (code file DynamicSamples/ClientApp/Program.cs):

```
private static void ReflectionNew()
{
  double x = 3;
  double y = 4;
  dynamic calc = GetCalculator();
  double result = calc.Add(x, y);
  WriteLine($"the result of {x} and {y} is {result}");
}
```

The syntax is really simple; it looks like calling a method with strongly typed access. However, there's no IntelliSense within Visual Studio because you can immediately see coding this from the Visual Studio editor, so it's easy to make typos.

There's also no compile-time check. The compiler runs fine when you invoke the Multiply method. Just remember you only defined Add and Subtract methods with the calculator.

```
try
{
  result = calc.Multiply(x, y);
}
catch (RuntimeBinderException ex)
{
  WriteLine(ex);
}
```

When you run the application and invoke the Multiply method, you get a RuntimeBinderException:

```
Microsoft.CSharp.RuntimeBinder.RuntimeBinderException:
'CalculatorLib.Calculator' does not contain a definition for 'Multiply'
    at CallSite.Target(Closure , CallSite , Object , Double , Double )
    at CallSite.Target(Closure , CallSite , Object , Double , Double )
    at ClientApp.Program.ReflectionNew() in...
```

Using the dynamic type also has more overhead compared to accessing objects in a strongly typed manner. Therefore, the keyword is useful only in some specific scenarios such as reflection. You don't have a compiler check invoking the InvokeMember method of the Type; instead, a string is passed for the name of the member. Using the dynamic type, which has a simpler syntax, has a big advantage compared to using the Reflection API in such scenarios.

The dynamic type can also be used with COM integration and scripting environments as shown after discussing the dynamic keyword more in detail.

THE DYNAMIC TYPE

The dynamic type enables you to write code that bypasses compile-time type checking. The compiler assumes that the operation defined for an object of type dynamic is valid. If that operation isn't valid, the error isn't detected until runtime. This is shown in the following example:

```
class Program
{
  static void Main()
  {
    var staticPerson = new Person();
    dynamic dynamicPerson = new Person();
    staticPerson.GetFullName("John", "Smith");
    dynamicPerson.GetFullName("John", "Smith");
  }
}

class Person
{
  public string FirstName { get; set; }
  public string LastName { get; set; }

  public string GetFullName() => $"{FirstName} {LastName}";
}
```

This example does not compile because of the call to staticPerson.GetFullName(). There isn't a method on the Person object that takes two parameters, so the compiler raises the error. If that line of code were commented out, the example would compile. If executed, a runtime error would occur. The exception that is raised is RuntimeBinderException. The RuntimeBinder is the object in the runtime that evaluates the call to determine whether Person really does support the method that was called. Binding is discussed later in the chapter.

Unlike the var keyword, an object that is defined as *dynamic* can change type during runtime. Remember that when the var keyword is used, the determination of the object's type is delayed. After the type is defined, it can't be changed. Not only can you change the type of a dynamic object, you can change it many times. This differs from casting an object from one type to another. When you cast an object, you are creating a new object with a different but compatible type. For example, you cannot cast an int to a Person object. In the following example, you can see that if the object is a dynamic object, you can change it from int to Person:

```
dynamic dyn;

dyn = 100;
WriteLine(dyn.GetType());
WriteLine(dyn);

dyn = "This is a string";
WriteLine(dyn.GetType());
WriteLine(dyn);

dyn = new Person() { FirstName = "Bugs", LastName = "Bunny" };
WriteLine(dyn.GetType());
WriteLine($"{dyn.FirstName} {dyn.LastName}");
```

The result of executing this code would be that the dyn object actually changes type from System.Int32 to System.String to Person. If dyn had been declared as an int or string, the code would not have compiled.

> **NOTE** *There are a couple of limitations to the* dynamic *type. A dynamic object does not support extension methods. Nor can anonymous functions (lambda expressions) be used as parameters to a dynamic method call, so LINQ does not work well with dynamic objects. Most LINQ calls are extension methods, and lambda expressions are used as arguments to those extension methods.*

Dynamic Behind the Scenes

So what's going on behind the scenes to make the dynamic functionality available with C#? C# is a statically typed language. That hasn't changed. Take a look at the IL (Intermediate Language) that's generated when the dynamic type is used.

First, this is the example C# code that you're looking at:

```
using static System.Console;

namespace DeCompileSample
{
  class Program
  {
    static void Main()
    {
      StaticClass staticObject = new StaticClass();
      DynamicClass dynamicObject = new DynamicClass();
      WriteLine(staticObject.IntValue);
      WriteLine(dynamicObject.DynValue);
      ReadLine();
    }
  }

  class StaticClass
  {
    public int IntValue = 100;
  }

  class DynamicClass
  {
    public dynamic DynValue = 100;
  }
}
```

You have two classes: StaticClass and DynamicClass. StaticClass has a single field that returns an int. DynamicClass has a single field that returns a dynamic object. The Main method creates these objects and prints out the value that the methods return. Simple enough.

Now comment out the references to the DynamicClass in Main like this:

```
static void Main()
{
  StaticClass staticObject = new StaticClass();
  //DynamicClass dynamicObject = new DynamicClass();
  WriteLine(staticObject.IntValue);
  //WriteLine(dynamicObject.DynValue);
  ReadLine();
}
```

Using the ildasm tool, you can look at the IL that is generated for the Main method:

```
.method private hidebysig static void  Main() cil managed
{
  .entrypoint
  // Code size       26 (0x1a)
  .maxstack  1
  .locals init ([0] class DecompileSample.StaticClass staticObject)
  IL_0000:  nop
  IL_0001:  newobj      instance void DecompileSample.StaticClass::.ctor()
  IL_0006:  stloc.0
  IL_0007:  ldloc.0
  IL_0008:  ldfld       int32 DecompileSample.StaticClass::IntValue
  IL_000d:  call        void [mscorlib]System.Console::WriteLine(int32)
```

```
IL_0012:  nop
IL_0013:  call       string [mscorlib]System.Console::ReadLine()
IL_0018:  pop
IL_0019:  ret
} // end of method Program::Main
```

Without getting into the details of IL, you can still pretty much tell what's going on just by looking at this section of code. Line 0001, the `StaticClass` constructor, is called. Line 0008 calls the `IntValue` field of `StaticClass`. The next line writes out the value.

Now comment out the `StaticClass` references and uncomment the `DynamicClass` references:

```
public static void Main()
{
  //StaticClass staticObject = new StaticClass();
  DynamicClass dynamicObject = new DynamicClass();
  WriteLine(staticObject.IntValue);
  //WriteLine(dynamicObject.DynValue);
  ReadLine();
}
```

Compile the application again, and the following is generated:

```
.method private hidebysig static void  Main() cil managed
{
  .entrypoint
  // Code size       123 (0x7b)
  .maxstack  9
  .locals init ([0] class DecompileSample.DynamicClass dynamicObject)
  IL_0000:  nop
  IL_0001:  newobj     instance void DecompileSample.DynamicClass::.ctor()
  IL_0006:  stloc.0
  IL_0007:  ldsfld     class
    [System.Core]System.Runtime.CompilerServices.CallSite`1
      <class[mscorlib]System.Action`3
      <class[System.Core]  System.Runtime.CompilerServices.CallSite,
      class [mscorlib]System.Type,object>>
      DecompileSample.Program/'<>o__0'::'<>p__0'
  IL_000c:  brfalse.s  IL_0010
  IL_000e:  br.s       IL_004f
  IL_0010:  ldc.i4     0x100
  IL_0015:  ldstr      "WriteLine"
  IL_001a:  ldnull
  IL_001b:  ldtoken    DecompileSample.Program
  IL_0020:  call       class [mscorlib]System.Type
    [mscorlib]System.Type::GetTypeFromHandle(valuetype
    [mscorlib]System.RuntimeTypeHandle)
  IL_0025:  ldc.i4.2
  IL_0026:  newarr     [Microsoft.CSharp]Microsoft.CSharp.RuntimeBinder
    .CSharpArgumentInfo
  IL_002b:  dup
  IL_002c:  ldc.i4.0
  IL_002d:  ldc.i4.s   33
  IL_002f:  ldnull
  IL_0030:  call       class [Microsoft.CSharp]Microsoft.CSharp.RuntimeBinder
    .CSharpArgumentInfo[Microsoft.CSharp]
    Microsoft.CSharp.RuntimeBinder.CSharpArgumentInfo::Create(
    valuetype Microsoft.CSharp]Microsoft.CSharp.RuntimeBinder
    .CSharpArgumentInfoFlags, string)
```

```
IL_0035:  stelem.ref
IL_0036:  dup
IL_0037:  ldc.i4.1
IL_0038:  ldc.i4.0
IL_0039:  ldnull
IL_003a:  call        class [Microsoft.CSharp]
  Microsoft.CSharp.RuntimeBinder.CSharpArgumentInfo
  [Microsoft.CSharp]Microsoft.CSharp.RuntimeBinder.CSharpArgumentInfo
    ::Create(valuetype [Microsoft.CSharp]
      Microsoft.CSharp.RuntimeBinder.CSharpArgumentInfoFlags, string)
IL_003f:  stelem.ref
IL_0040:  call        class [System.Core]
  System.Runtime.CompilerServices.CallSiteBinder
  [Microsoft.CSharp]Microsoft.CSharp.RuntimeBinder.Binder::
    InvokeMember(valuetype[Microsoft.CSharp]
      Microsoft.CSharp.RuntimeBinder.CSharpBinderFlags, string,
      class [mscorlib]System.Collections.Generic.IEnumerable`1
        <class [mscorlib]System.Type>, class [mscorlib]System.Type,
        class [mscorlib]System.Collections.Generic.IEnumerable`1
        <class [Microsoft.CSharp]
          Microsoft.CSharp.RuntimeBinder.CSharpArgumentInfo>)
IL_0045:  call        class [System.Core]
  System.Runtime.CompilerServices.CallSite`1<!0>
    class [System.Core]System.Runtime.CompilerServices.CallSite`1
      <class [mscorlib]System.Action`3
        <class [System.Core]System.Runtime.CompilerServices.CallSite,
        class [mscorlib]System.Type,object>>::
          Create(class [System.Core]
            System.Runtime.CompilerServices.CallSiteBinder)
IL_004a:  stsfld      class [System.Core]
  System.Runtime.CompilerServices.CallSite`1
    <class [mscorlib]System.Action`3
      <class [System.Core]System.Runtime.CompilerServices.CallSite,
      class [mscorlib]System.Type,object>>
      DecompileSample.Program/`<>o__0`::`<>p__0`
IL_004f:  ldsfld      class
  [System.Core]System.Runtime.CompilerServices.CallSite`1<class [mscorlib]
    System.Action`3<class [System.Core]
      System.Runtime.CompilerServices.CallSite,
      class [mscorlib]System.Type,object>>
      DecompileSample.Program/'<>o__0'::'<>p__0'
IL_0054:  ldfld       !0 class [System.Core]
  System.Runtime.CompilerServices.CallSite`1<class [mscorlib]
    System.Action`3<class [System.Core]
      System.Runtime.CompilerServices.CallSite,
      class [mscorlib]System.Type,object>>::Target
IL_0059:  ldsfld      class [System.Core]
  System.Runtime.CompilerServices.CallSite`1<class [mscorlib]
    System.Action`3<class [System.Core]
      System.Runtime.CompilerServices.CallSite,
      class [mscorlib]System.Type,object>>
      DecompileSample.Program/'<>o__0'::'<>p__0'
IL_005e:  ldtoken     [mscorlib]System.Console
IL_0063:  call        class [mscorlib]System.Type [mscorlib]
  System.Type::GetTypeFromHandle(valuetype [mscorlib]
    System.RuntimeTypeHandle)
IL_0068:  ldloc.0
IL_0069:  ldfld       object DecompileSample.DynamicClass::DynValue
IL_006e:  callvirt    instance void class [mscorlib]System.Action`3
  <class [System.Core]System.Runtime.CompilerServices.CallSite,
  class [mscorlib]System.Type,object>::Invoke(!0, !1, !2)
IL_0073:  nop
```

```
    IL_0074:  call        string [mscorlib]System.Console::ReadLine()
    IL_0079:  pop
    IL_007a:  ret
  } // end of method Program::Main
```

It's safe to say that the C# compiler is doing a little extra work to support the dynamic type. Looking at the generated code, you can see references to `System.Runtime.CompilerServices.CallSite` and `System.Runtime.CompilerServices.CallSiteBinder`.

The `CallSite` is a type that handles the lookup at runtime. When a call is made on a dynamic object at runtime, something has to check that object to determine whether the member really exists. The call site caches this information so the lookup doesn't have to be performed repeatedly. Without this process, performance in looping structures would be questionable.

After the `CallSite` does the member lookup, the `CallSiteBinder` is invoked. It takes the information from the call site and generates an expression tree representing the operation to which the binder is bound.

There is obviously a lot going on here. Great care has been taken to optimize what would appear to be a very complex operation. Clearly, using the `dynamic` type can be useful, but it does come with a price.

DYNAMIC LANGUAGE RUNTIME

An important scenario for using the dynamic keyword is when using the Dynamic Language Runtime (DLR). The DLR is a set of services that is added to the common language runtime (CLR) to enable the addition of dynamic languages such as Python and Ruby. It also enables C# to take on some of the same dynamic capabilities that these dynamic languages have.

The core features of the original DLR are now part of the full .NET 4.5 Framework in the `System.Dynamic` and `System.Runtime.CompilerServices` namespaces. For integrating with scripting languages such as IronPython and IronRuby, additional types are needed for the integration that is part of the DLR that needs to be installed. This DLR is part of the IronPython and IronRuby environments. You can download it from `http://ironpython.codeplex.com`.

IronRuby and IronPython are open-source versions of the Ruby and Python languages, which use the DLR. Silverlight also uses the DLR. It's possible to add scripting capabilities to your applications by hosting the DLR. The scripting runtime enables you to pass variables to and from the script.

HOSTING THE DLR SCRIPTRUNTIME

Imagine being able to add scripting capabilities to an application, or passing values in and out of the script so the application can take advantage of the work that the script does. These are the kind of capabilities that hosting the DLR's `ScriptRuntime` in your app gives you. IronPython and IronRuby are supported as hosted scripting languages.

The `ScriptRuntime` enables you to execute snippets of code or a complete script stored in a file. You can select the proper language engine or allow the DLR to figure out which engine to use. The script can be created in its own app domain or in the current one. Not only can you pass values in and out of the script, you can call methods on dynamic objects created in the script.

This degree of flexibility provides countless uses for hosting the `ScriptRuntime`. The following example demonstrates one way that you can use the `ScriptRuntime`. Imagine a shopping cart application. One of the requirements is to calculate a discount based on certain criteria. These discounts change often as new sales campaigns are started and completed. There are many ways to handle such a requirement; this example shows how it could be done using the `ScriptRuntime` and a little Python scripting.

For simplicity, the example is a WPF Windows desktop application. An application using the DLR could also be part of a web application or any other application. Figure 16-3 shows a screen for the sample application. For using the runtime, the sample app adds the IronPython NuGet package.

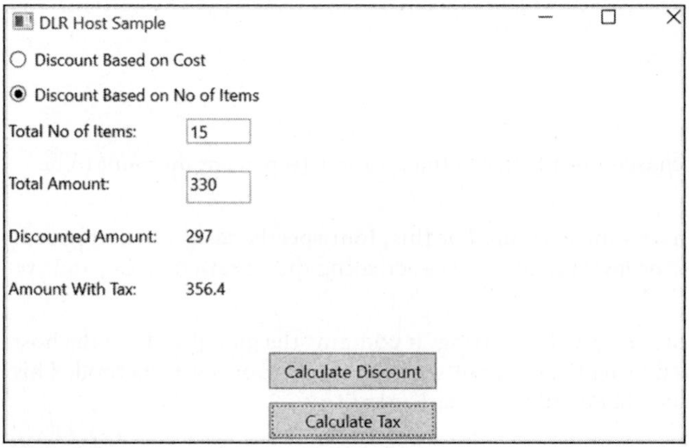

FIGURE 16-3

Using the values provided for the number of items and the total cost of the items, the application applies a discount based on which radio button is selected. In a real application, the system would use a slightly more sophisticated technique to determine the discount to apply, but for this example the radio buttons suffice.

Here is the code that performs the discount (code file `DLRHostSample/MainWindow.xaml.cs`):

```
private void OnCalculateDiscount(object sender, RoutedEventArgs e)
{
  string scriptToUse;
  if (CostRadioButton.IsChecked.Value)
  {
    scriptToUse = "Scripts/AmountDisc.py";
  }
  else
  {
    scriptToUse = "Scripts/CountDisc.py";
  }
  ScriptRuntime scriptRuntime = ScriptRuntime.CreateFromConfiguration();
  ScriptEngine pythEng = scriptRuntime.GetEngine("Python");
  ScriptSource source = pythEng.CreateScriptSourceFromFile(scriptToUse);
  ScriptScope scope = pythEng.CreateScope();
  scope.SetVariable("prodCount", Convert.ToInt32(totalItems.Text));
  scope.SetVariable("amt", Convert.ToDecimal(totalAmt.Text));
  source.Execute(scope);
  textDiscAmount.Text = scope.GetVariable("retAmt").ToString();
}
```

The first part determines which script to apply: `AmountDisc.py` or `CountDisc.py`. `AmountDisc.py` does the discount based on the amount of the purchase (code file `DLRHostSample/Scripts/AmountDisc.py`):

```
discAmt = .25
retAmt = amt
if amt > 25.00:
  retAmt = amt-(amt*discAmt)
```

The minimum amount needed for a discount to be applied is $25. If the amount is less than that, then no discount is applied; otherwise, a discount of 25 percent is applied.

`ContDisc.py` applies the discount based on the number of items purchased (code file `DLRHostSample/Scripts/ContDisc.py`):

```
discCount = 5
discAmt = .1
retAmt = amt
if prodCount > discCount:
  retAmt = amt-(amt*discAmt)
```

In this Python script, the number of items purchased must be more than 5 for a 10 percent discount to be applied to the total cost.

The next step is getting the `ScriptRuntime` environment set up. For this, four specific tasks are performed: creating the `ScriptRuntime` object, setting the proper `ScriptEngine`, creating the `ScriptSource`, and creating the `ScriptScope`.

The `ScriptRuntime` object is the starting point, or base, for hosting. It contains the global state of the hosting environment. The `ScriptRuntime` is created using the `CreateFromConfiguration` static method. This is what the configuration file looks like (code file `DLRHostSample/app.config`):

```
<configuration>
  <configSections>
    <section name="microsoft.scripting"
      type="Microsoft.Scripting.Hosting.Configuration.Section, Microsoft.Scripting />
  </configSections>

  <microsoft.scripting>
    <languages>
      <language names="IronPython;Python;py" extensions=".py"
        displayName="IronPython 2.7.5"
        type="IronPython.Runtime.PythonContext, IronPython />
    </languages>
  </microsoft.scripting>
</configuration>
```

The code defines a section for `microsoft.scripting` and sets a couple of properties for the IronPython language engine.

Next, you get a reference to the `ScriptEngine` from the `ScriptRuntime`. In the example, you specify that you want the Python engine, but the `ScriptRuntime` would have been able to determine this on its own because of the `py` extension on the script.

The `ScriptEngine` does the work of executing the script code. There are several methods for executing scripts from files or from snippets of code. The `ScriptEngine` also gives you the `ScriptSource` and `ScriptScope`.

The `ScriptSource` object is what gives you access to the script. It represents the source code of the script. With it you can manipulate the source of the script, load it from a disk, parse it line by line, and even compile the script into a `CompiledCode` object. This is handy if the same script is executed multiple times.

The `ScriptScope` object is essentially a namespace. To pass a value into or out of a script, you bind a variable to the `ScriptScope`. In the following example, you call the `SetVariable` method to pass the `prodCount` and the `amt` variables into the Python script. These variables are the values from the `totalItems` and the `totalAmt` text boxes, respectively. The calculated discount is retrieved from the script by using the `GetVariable` method. In this example, the `retAmt` variable has the value you're looking for.

The `CalcTax` button illustrates how to call a method on a Python object. The script `CalcTax.py` is a very simple method that takes an input value, adds 20 percent tax, and returns the new value. Here's what the code looks like (code file `DLRHostSample/Scripts/CalcTax.py`):

```
def CalcTax(amount):
    return amount*1.2
```

Here is the C# code to call the `CalcTax` method (code file `DLRHostSample/MainWindow.xaml.cs`):

```csharp
private void OnCalculateTax(object sender, RoutedEventArgs e)
{
  ScriptRuntime scriptRuntime = ScriptRuntime.CreateFromConfiguration();
  dynamic calcRate = scriptRuntime.UseFile("Scripts/CalcTax.py");
  decimal discountedAmount;
  if (!decimal.TryParse(textDiscAmount.Text, out discountedAmount))
  {
    discountedAmount = Convert.ToDecimal(totalAmt.Text);
  }
  totalTaxAmount.Text = calcRate.CalcTax(discountedAmount).ToString();
}
```

It's a very simple process: You create the `ScriptRuntime` object using the same configuration settings as before. `calcRate` is a `ScriptScope` object. You defined it as dynamic so you can easily call the `CalcTax` method. This is an example of the how the dynamic type can make life a little easier.

DYNAMICOBJECT AND EXPANDOOBJECT

What if you want to create your own dynamic object? You have a couple of options for doing that: by deriving from `DynamicObject` or by using `ExpandoObject`. Using `DynamicObject` is a little more work than using `ExpandoObject` because with `DynamicObject` you have to override a couple of methods. `ExpandoObject` is a sealed class that is ready to use.

DynamicObject

Consider an object that represents a person. Normally, you would define properties for the first name, middle name, and last name. Now imagine the capability to build that object during runtime, with the system having no prior knowledge of what properties the object might have or what methods the object might support. That's what having a `DynamicObject`-based object can provide. There might be very few times when you need this sort of functionality, but until now the C# language had no way of accommodating such a requirement.

First take a look at what the `DynamicObject` looks like (code file `DynamicSamples/DynamicSample/WroxDyamicObject.cs`):

```csharp
public class WroxDynamicObject : DynamicObject
{
  private Dictionary<string, object> _dynamicData = new Dictionary<string, object>();

  public override bool TryGetMember(GetMemberBinder binder, out object result)
  {
    bool success = false;
    result = null;
    if (_dynamicData.ContainsKey(binder.Name))
    {
      result = _dynamicData[binder.Name];
      success = true;
    }
    else
    {
      result = "Property Not Found!";
      success = false;
    }
    return success;
  }
}
```

```
public override bool TrySetMember(SetMemberBinder binder, object value)
{
  _dynamicData[binder.Name] = value;
  return true;
}

public override bool TryInvokeMember(InvokeMemberBinder binder,
                                      object[] args, out object result)
{
    dynamic method = _dynamicData[binder.Name];
    result = method((DateTime)args[0]);
    return result != null;
}
}
```

In this example, you're overriding three methods: `TrySetMember`, `TryGetMember`, and `TryInvokeMember`.

`TrySetMember` adds the new method, property, or field to the object. In this case, you store the member information in a `Dictionary` object. The `SetMemberBinder` object that is passed into the `TrySetMember` method contains the `Name` property, which is used to identify the element in the `Dictionary`.

The `TryGetMember` retrieves the object stored in the `Dictionary` based on the `GetMemberBinder` `Name` property.

Here is the code that makes use of the new dynamic object just created (code file `DynamicSamples/ DynamicSample/Program.cs`):

```
dynamic wroxDyn = new WroxDynamicObject();
wroxDyn.FirstName = "Bugs";
wroxDyn.LastName = "Bunny";
WriteLine(wroxDyn.GetType());
WriteLine($"{wroxDyn.FirstName} {wroxDyn.LastName}");
```

It looks simple enough, but where is the call to the methods you overrode? That's where the .NET Framework helps. `DynamicObject` handles the binding for you; all you have to do is reference the properties `FirstName` and `LastName` as if they were there all the time.

You can also easily add a method. You can use the same `WroxDynamicObject` and add a `GetTomorrowDate` method to it. It takes a `DateTime` object and returns a date string representing the next day. Here's the code:

```
dynamic wroxDyn = new WroxDynamicObject();
Func<DateTime, string> GetTomorrow = today => today.AddDays(1).ToShortDateString();
wroxDyn.GetTomorrowDate = GetTomorrow;
WriteLine($"Tomorrow is {wroxDyn.GetTomorrowDate(DateTime.Now)}");
```

You create the delegate `GetTomorrow` using `Func<T, TResult>`. The method the delegate represents is the call to `AddDays`. One day is added to the `Date` that is passed in, and a string of that date is returned. The delegate is then set to `GetTomorrowDate` on the `wroxDyn` object. The last line calls the new method, passing in the current day's date. Hence the dynamic magic and you have an object with a valid method.

ExpandoObject

`ExpandoObject` works similarly to the `WroxDynamicObject` created in the previous section. The difference is that you don't have to override any methods, as shown in the following code example (code file `DynamicSamples/DynamicSample/WroxDynamicObject.cs`):

```
static void DoExpando()
{
```

```
dynamic expObj = new ExpandoObject();
expObj.FirstName = "Daffy";
expObj.LastName = "Duck";
WriteLine($"{expObj.FirstName} {expObj.LastName}");

Func<DateTime, string> GetTomorrow = today => today.AddDays(1).ToShortDateString();
expObj.GetTomorrowDate = GetTomorrow;
WriteLine($"Tomorrow is {expObj.GetTomorrowDate(DateTime.Now)}");

expObj.Friends = new List<Person>();
expObj.Friends.Add(new Person() { FirstName = "Bob", LastName = "Jones" });
expObj.Friends.Add(new Person() { FirstName = "Robert", LastName = "Jones" });
expObj.Friends.Add(new Person() { FirstName = "Bobby", LastName = "Jones" });

foreach (Person friend in expObj.Friends)
{
    WriteLine($"{friend.FirstName} {friend.LastName}");
}
}
```

Notice that this code is almost identical to what you did earlier. You add a `FirstName` and `LastName` property, add a `GetTomorrow` function, and then do one additional thing: add a collection of `Person` objects as a property of the object.

At first glance it might seem that this is no different from using the `dynamic` type, but there are a couple of subtle differences that are important. First, you can't just create an empty `dynamic` typed object. The `dynamic` type has to have something assigned to it. For example, the following code won't work:

```
dynamic dynObj;
dynObj.FirstName = "Joe";
```

As shown in the previous example, this is possible with `ExpandoObject`.

Second, because the `dynamic` type has to have something assigned to it, it reports back the type assigned to it if you do a `GetType` call. For example, if you assign an `int`, it reports back that it is an `int`. This doesn't happen with `ExpandoObject` or an object derived from `DynamicObject`.

If you have to control the addition and access of properties in your dynamic object, then deriving from `DynamicObject` is your best option. With `DynamicObject`, you can use several methods to override and control exactly how the object interacts with the runtime. For other cases, using the `dynamic` type or the `ExpandoObject` might be appropriate.

Following is another example of using dynamic and `ExpandoObject`. Assume that the requirement is to develop a general-purpose comma-separated values (CSV) file parsing tool. You won't know from one execution to another what data will be in the file, only that the values will be comma-separated and that the first line will contain the field names.

First, open the file and read in the stream. You can use a simple helper method to do this (code file `DynamicSamples/DynamicFileReader/DynamicFileHelper.cs`):

```
private StreamReader OpenFile(string fileName)
{
    if(File.Exists(fileName))
    {
        return new StreamReader(fileName);
    }
    return null;
}
```

This just opens the file and creates a new `StreamReader` to read the file contents.

Now you want to get the field names, which you can do easily by reading in the first line from the file and using the `Split` function to create a string array of field names:

```
string[] headerLine = fileStream.ReadLine().Split(',').Trim().ToArray();
```

Next is the interesting part. You read in the next line from the file, create a string array just like you did with the field names, and start creating your dynamic objects. Here's what the code looks like (code file `DynamicSamples/DynamicFileReader/DynamicFileHelper.cs`):

```
public IEnumerable<dynamic> ParseFile(string fileName)
{
    var retList = new List<dynamic>();
    while (fileStream.Peek() > 0)
    {
        string[] dataLine = fileStream.ReadLine().Split(',').Trim().ToArray();
        dynamic dynamicEntity = new ExpandoObject();
        for(int i=0;i<headerLine.Length;i++)
        {
            ((IDictionary<string,object>)dynamicEntity).Add(headerLine[i], dataLine[i]);
        }
        retList.Add(dynamicEntity);
    }
    return retList;
}
```

After you have the string array of field names and data elements, you create a new `ExpandoObject` and add the data to it. Notice that you cast the `ExpandoObject` to a `Dictionary` object. You use the field name as the key and the data as the value. Then you can add the new object to the `retList` object you created and return it to the code that called the method.

What makes this nice is you have a section of code that can handle any data you give it. The only requirements in this case are ensuring that the field names are the first line and that everything is comma-separated. This concept could be expanded to other file types or even to a `DataReader`.

Using this CSV file content that is available with the sample code download

```
FirstName, LastName, City, State
Niki, Lauda, Vienna, Austria
Carlos, Reutemann, Santa Fe, Argentine
Sebastian, Vettel, Thurgovia, Switzerland
```

and this `Main` method to read the sample file EmployeeList.txt (code file `DynamicSamples/DynamicFileReader/Program.cs`):

```
static void Main()
{
    var helper = new DynamicFileHelper();
    var employeeList = helper.ParseFile("EmployeeList.txt");
    foreach (var employee in employeeList)
    {
        WriteLine($"{employee.FirstName} {employee.LastName} lives in " +
            $"{employee.City}, {employee.State}.");
    }
    ReadLine();
}
```

results in this output to the console:

```
Niki  Lauda lives in  Vienna,  Austria.
Carlos  Reutemann lives in  Santa Fe,  Argentine.
Sebastian  Vettel lives in  Thurgovia,  Switzerland.
```

SUMMARY

This chapter illustrated using the `Type` and `Assembly` classes, which are the primary entry points through which you can access the extensive capabilities provided by reflection.

In addition, this chapter demonstrated a specific aspect of reflection that you are likely to use more often than any other—the inspection of custom attributes. You learned how to define and apply your own custom attributes, and how to retrieve information about custom attributes at runtime.

The second focus of this chapter was working with the dynamic type. Using `ExpandoObject` in place of multiple objects can reduce the number of lines of code significantly. Also using the DLR and adding scripting languages like Python or Ruby can help you build a more polymorphic application that can be changed easily without recompiling.

The next chapter gives details on a lot of features available with Visual Studio 2015.

PART II
.NET Core and Windows Runtime

17

Visual Studio 2015

WHAT'S IN THIS CHAPTER?

➤ Using Visual Studio 2015
➤ Creating and working with projects
➤ Debugging
➤ Refactoring with Visual Studio
➤ Working with various technologies: WPF, WCF, and more
➤ Architecture tools
➤ Analyzing applications

WROX.COM CODE DOWNLOADS FOR THIS CHAPTER

There are no code downloads for this chapter.

WORKING WITH VISUAL STUDIO 2015

At this point, you should be familiar with the C# language and almost ready to move on to the applied sections of the book, which cover how to use C# to program a variety of applications. Before doing that, however, it's important to understand how you can use Visual Studio and some of the features provided by the .NET environment to get the best from your programs.

This chapter explains what programming in the .NET environment means in practice. It covers Visual Studio, the main development environment in which you will write, compile, debug, and optimize your C# programs, and provides guidelines for writing good applications. Visual Studio is the main IDE used for numerous purposes, including writing ASP.NET applications, Windows Presentation Foundation (WPF) applications, and apps for the Universal Windows Platform (UWP), and for accessing services created by the ASP.NET Web API, or web applications with ASP.NET MVC.

This chapter also explores what it takes to build applications that are targeted at .NET Core 1.0 and the .NET Framework 4.6.

Visual Studio 2015 is a fully integrated development environment. It is designed to make the process of writing your code, debugging it, and compiling it to an assembly to be shipped as easy as possible.

This means that Visual Studio gives you a very sophisticated multiple-document–interface application in which you can do just about everything related to developing your code. It offers the following features:

➤ **Text editor**—Using this editor, you can write your C# (as well as Visual Basic, C++, F#, JavaScript, XAML, JSON, and SQL) code. This text editor is quite sophisticated. For example, as you type, it automatically lays out your code by indenting lines, matching start and end brackets of code blocks, and color-coding keywords. It also performs some syntax checks as you type, and underlines code that causes compilation errors, also known as design-time debugging. In addition, it features IntelliSense, which automatically displays the names of classes, fields, or methods as you begin to type them. As you start typing parameters to methods, it also shows you the parameter lists for the available over-loads. Figure 17-1 shows the IntelliSense feature in action with a UWP app.

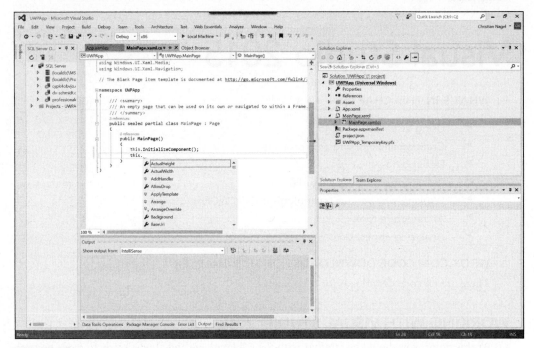

FIGURE 17-1

> **NOTE** *By pressing Ctrl+Space, you can bring back the IntelliSense list box if you need it or if for any reason it is not visible. In case you want to see some code below the IntelliSense box, just keep pressing the Ctrl button.*

➤ **Design view editor**—This editor enables you to place user-interface and data-access controls in your project; Visual Studio automatically adds the necessary C# code to your source files to instantiate these controls in your project. (This is possible because all .NET controls are instances of particular base classes.)

➤ **Supporting windows**—These windows enable you to view and modify aspects of your project, such as the classes in your source code, as well as the available properties (and their startup values) for Windows Forms and Web Forms classes. You can also use these windows to specify compilation options, such as which assemblies your code needs to reference.

➤ **Integrated debugger**—It is in the nature of programming that your code will not run correctly the first time you try it. Or the second time. Or the third time. Visual Studio seamlessly links to a debugger for you, enabling you to set breakpoints and watches on variables from within the environment.

➤ **Integrated MSDN help**—Visual Studio enables you to access the MSDN documentation from within the IDE. For example, if you are not sure of the meaning of a keyword while using the text editor, simply select the keyword and press the F1 key, and Visual Studio accesses MSDN to show you related topics. Similarly, if you are not sure what a certain compilation error means, you can bring up the documentation for that error by selecting the error message and pressing F1.

➤ **Access to other programs**—Visual Studio can also access a number of other utilities that enable you to examine and modify aspects of your computer or network, without your having to leave the developer environment. With the tools available, you can check running services and database connections, look directly into your SQL Server tables, browse your Microsoft Azure Cloud services, and even browse the Web using an Internet Explorer window.

➤ **Visual Studio extensions**—Some extensions of Visual Studio are already installed with a normal installation of Visual Studio, and many more extensions from both Microsoft and third parties are available. These extensions enable you to analyze code, offer project or item templates, access other services, and more. With the .NET Compiler Platform, integration of tools with Visual Studio has become easier.

The recent releases of Visual Studio had some interesting progress. One big part was with the user interface, the other big part with the background functionality and the .NET Compiler Platform.

With the user interface, Visual Studio 2010 redesigned the shell to be based on WPF instead of native Windows controls. Visual Studio 2012 had some user interface (UI) changes based on this. In particular, the UI was enhanced to have more focus on the main work area—the editor—and to allow doing more tasks directly from the code editor instead of needing to use many other tools. Of course, you need some tools outside the code editor, but more functionality has been built into a few of these tools, so the number of tools typically needed can be reduced. With Visual Studio 2015 some more UI features have been enhanced. For example, the NuGet Package manager is no longer a modal dialog. With the new version of the Package manager you can continue doing other tasks while the Package manager loads information from a server.

With the .NET Compiler Platform (code name Roslyn), the .NET compiler has been completely rewritten; it now integrates functionality throughout the compiler pipeline, such as syntax analysis, semantics analysis, binding, and code emitting. Based on this, Microsoft had to rewrite many Visual Studio integration tools. The code editor, IntelliSense, and refactoring are all based on the .NET Compiler Platform.

> **NOTE** *Chapter 18, ".NET Compiler Platform," demonstrates the API that can be used with the .NET Compiler Platform.*

For XAML code editing, Visual Studio 2010 and Expression Blend 4 (now with the name Blend for Visual Studio 2015) had different editor engines. As of Visual Studio 2013 the teams have merged, and although the features offered in the UI are a little bit different, the code engines are the same. Not only the code engines are the same: while Visual Studio 2013 got the XAML engine from Blend, now with Blend for Visual Studio 2015, Blend got the shell from Visual Studio. As you start Blend for Visual Studio you see that it looks like Visual Studio, and you can immediately start working with it.

Another special feature of Visual Studio is search. Visual Studio has so many commands and features that it is often hard to find the menu or toolbar button you are looking for. Just enter a part of the command you're looking for into the Quick Launch, and you'll see available options. Quick Launch is located at the top-right corner of the window (see Figure 17-2). Search functionality is also available from the toolbox, Solution Explorer, the code editor (which you can invoke by pressing Ctrl+F), the assemblies on the Reference Manager, and more.

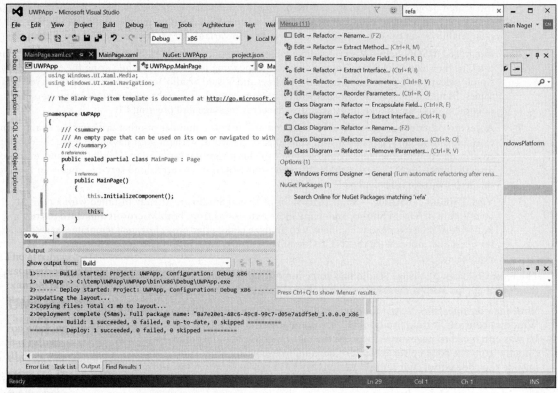

FIGURE 17-2

Visual Studio Editions

Visual Studio 2015 is available in a few editions. The least expensive is Visual Studio 2015 Community Edition, which is free in some cases. It's free for individual developers, open-source projects, academic research, education, and small professional teams.

You can purchase the Professional and Enterprise editions. Only the Enterprise edition includes all the features. Exclusive to the Enterprise edition is IntelliTrace, load testing, and some architecture tools. The Microsoft Fakes framework (unit test isolation) is only available with Visual Studio Enterprise. This chapter's tour of Visual Studio 2015 includes a few features that are available only with specific editions. For detailed information about the features of each edition of Visual Studio 2015, see `http://www.microsoft .com/visualstudio/en-us/products/compare`.

Visual Studio Settings

When you start Visual Studio the first time, you are asked to select a settings collection that matches your environment, for example, General Development, Visual Basic, Visual C#, Visual C++, or Web Development. These different settings reflect the different tools historically used for these languages. When writing applications on the Microsoft platform, different tools were used to create Visual Basic, C++, and web applications. Similarly, Visual Basic, Visual C++, and Visual InterDev had completely different programming environments, with completely different settings and tool options. Now, you can create apps for all these technologies with Visual Studio, but Visual Studio still offers the keyboard shortcuts that you can choose based on Visual Basic, Visual C++, and Visual InterDev. Of course, you also can select specific C# settings as well.

After choosing the main category of settings to define keyboard shortcuts, menus, and the position of tool windows, you can change every setting with Tools ⇨ Customize (toolbars and commands) and Tools ⇨ Options (here you find the settings for all the tools). You can also reset the settings collection with Tools ⇨ Import and Export Settings, which invokes a wizard that enables you to select a new default collection of settings (see Figure 17-3).

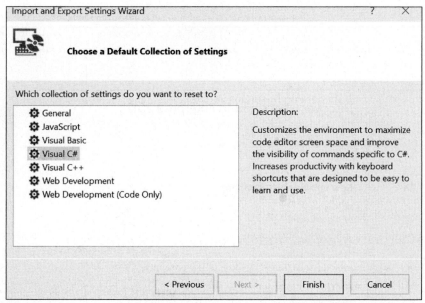

FIGURE 17-3

The following sections walk through the process of creating, coding, and debugging a project, demonstrating what Visual Studio can do to help you at each stage.

CREATING A PROJECT

After installing Visual Studio 2015, you will want to start your first project. With Visual Studio, you rarely start with a blank file and then add C# code, in the way that you have been doing in the previous chapters in this book. (Of course, the option of asking for an empty application project is there if you really do want to start writing your code from scratch or if you are going to create a solution that will contain a number of projects.)

Instead, the idea is that you tell Visual Studio roughly what type of project you want to create, and it generates the files and C# code that provide a framework for that type of project. You then proceed to add your code to this outline. For example, if you want to build a Windows desktop application (a WPF application), Visual Studio starts you off with an XAML file and a file containing C# source code that creates a basic form. This form is capable of communicating with Windows and receiving events. It can be maximized, minimized, or resized; all you need to do is add the controls and functionality you want. If your application is intended to be a command-line utility (a console application), Visual Studio gives you a basic namespace, a class, and a `Main` method to get you started.

Last, but hardly least, when you create your project, Visual Studio also sets up the compilation options that you are likely to supply to the C# compiler—whether it is to compile to a command-line application, a library, or a WPF application. It also tells the compiler which base class libraries and NuGet packages you need to reference (a WPF GUI application needs to reference many of the WPF-related libraries; a console application probably does not). Of course, you can modify all these settings as you are editing if necessary.

The first time you start Visual Studio, you are presented with an IDE containing menus, a toolbar, and a page with getting-started information, how-to videos, and latest news (see Figure 17-4). The Start Page contains various links to useful websites and links to some actual articles, and it enables you to open existing projects or start a new project altogether.

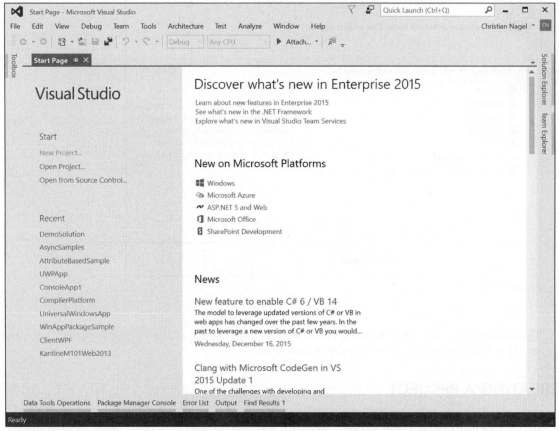

FIGURE 17-4

In the case of Figure 17-4, the Start Page reflects what is shown after you have already used Visual Studio 2015, as it includes a list of the most recently edited projects. You can just click one of these projects to open it again.

Multi-Targeting the .NET Framework

Visual Studio enables you to target the version of the .NET Framework that you want to work with. When you open the New Project dialog, shown in Figure 17-5, a drop-down list in the top area of the dialog displays the available options.

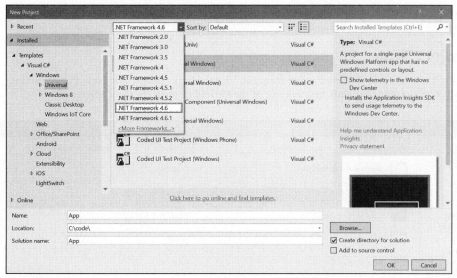

FIGURE 17-5

In this case, you can see that the drop-down list enables you to target the .NET Frameworks 2.0, 3.0, 3.5, 4, 4.5, 4.5.1, 4.5.2, 4.6, and 4.6.1. You can also install other versions of the .NET Framework by clicking the More Frameworks link. This link opens a website from which you can download other versions of the .NET Framework—for example, 2.0 + 3.5 SP1—but also frameworks for services (Microsoft Azure, OneDrive) and devices (Xamarin).

If you want to change the version of the framework the solution uses, right-click the project and select the properties of the solution. If you are working with a WPF project, you see the dialog shown in Figure 17-6.

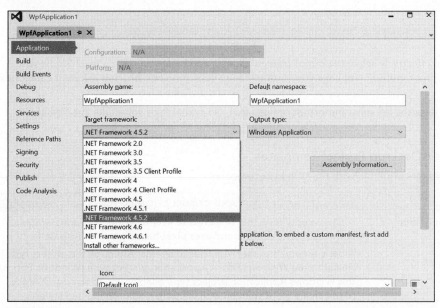

FIGURE 17-6

From this dialog, the Application tab enables you to change the version of the framework that the application is using.

Selecting a Project Type

To create a new project, select File ⇨ New Project from the Visual Studio menu. The New Project dialog displays (see Figure 17-7), giving you your first inkling of the variety of projects you can create.

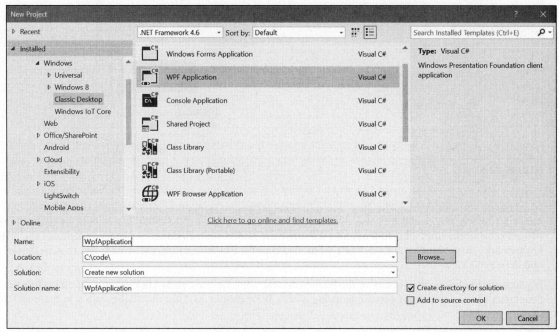

FIGURE 17-7

Using this dialog, you effectively select the initial framework files and code you want Visual Studio to generate for you, the programming language you want to create your project with, and different categories of application types.

The following tables describe the most important options that are available to you under the Visual C# projects.

Using Windows Classic Desktop Project Templates

The first table lists projects available with the Windows category:

IF YOU CHOOSE. . .	YOU GET THE C# CODE AND COMPILATION OPTIONS TO GENERATE. . .
Windows Forms Application	A basic empty form that responds to events. Windows Forms wraps native Windows controls and uses pixel-based graphics with GDI+.
WPF Application	A basic empty form that responds to events. Although the project type is similar to the Windows Forms Application project type (Windows Forms), this Windows Application project type enables you to build an XAML-based smart client solution with vector-based graphics and styles.

IF YOU CHOOSE. . .	YOU GET THE C# CODE AND COMPILATION OPTIONS TO GENERATE. . .
Console Application	An application that runs at the command-line prompt or in a console window. This console application is using the MSBuild environment for compiling the application. You can find console applications for .NET Core 1.0 in the Web category.
Shared Project	This project doesn't create its own binary, but you can use the source code with other projects. Contrary to libraries, the source code is compiled within each project where it is used. You can use preprocessor statements for differences in the source code depending on the project where the shared project is used.
Class Library	A .NET class library that can be called up by other code.
Class Library (Portable)	A class library that can be used by different technologies, for example, WPF, Universal Windows Platform apps, Xamarin apps, and others.
WPF Browser Application	Quite similar to the Windows Application for WPF, this variant enables you to build an XAML-based application that is targeted at the browser. However, it only runs within Internet Explorer, and not Microsoft Edge. Nowadays, you should think about using a different technology for this, such as a WPF application with ClickOnce or HTML 5.
Empty Project	An empty project that just contains an application configuration file and settings for a console application.
Windows Service	A Windows Service that can automatically start up with Windows and act on behalf of a privileged local system account.
WPF Custom Control Library	A custom control that can be used in a Windows Presentation Foundation application.
WPF User Control Library	A user control library built using Windows Presentation Foundation.
Windows Forms Control Library	A project for creating controls for use in Windows Forms applications.

> **NOTE** *Shared projects and portable class libraries are covered in Chapter 31, "Patterns with XAML Apps." The WPF Application project template is covered in Chapter 34, "Windows Desktop Applications with WPF." The Windows Service project template is covered in Chapter 39, "Windows Services."*

Using Universal Project Templates

The next table covers templates for the Universal Windows Platform. These templates are available on both Windows 10 and Windows 8.1, but you need a Windows 10 system to test the application. The templates are used to create applications running on Windows 10 using any device family—the PC, the phone, X-Box, IoT devices, and more.

IF YOU CHOOSE. . .	YOU GET THE C# CODE AND COMPILATION OPTIONS TO GENERATE. . .
Blank App (Universal Windows)	A basic empty Universal Windows app with XAML, without styles and other base classes.
Class Library (Universal Windows)	A .NET class library that can be called up by other Windows Store apps programmed with .NET. You can use the API of the Windows Runtime within this library.

continues

continued

IF YOU CHOOSE. . .	YOU GET THE C# CODE AND COMPILATION OPTIONS TO GENERATE. . .
Windows Runtime Component (Universal Windows)	A Windows Runtime class library that can be called up by other Windows Store apps developed with different programming languages (C#, C++, JavaScript).
Unit Test App (Universal Windows)	A library that contains unit tests for Universal Windows Platform apps.
Coded UI Test Project (Windows Phone)	A project to define coded UI tests for the Windows Phone.
Coded UI Test Project (Windows)	A project to define coded UI tests for Windows apps.

> **NOTE** *For Windows 10, the number of default templates for Universal apps have been reduced. Creating Windows Store apps for Windows 8, Visual Studio offers more project templates to predefine Grid-based, Split-based, or Hub-based apps. For Windows 10 only an empty template is available. You can either start with the empty template or consider using Template10 as a starter. The Template10 project template is available as soon as you install the Template10 Visual Studio extension from Microsoft, which is available via Tools ⇨ Extensions and Updates.*

> **NOTE** *If you install the Windows 8 project templates with Visual Studio, several Windows, Windows Phone, and Universal project templates are available as well. These are the predecessor of the Universal template for apps running on Windows 8 and 8.1, and they are not covered in this book.*

Using Web Project Templates

Interesting enhancements with Visual Studio 2015 are available with the Web Project templates. Initially, there are three selections as described in the following table.

IF YOU CHOOSE. . .	YOU GET THE C# CODE AND COMPILATION OPTIONS TO GENERATE. . .
ASP.NET Web Application	This is the template to choose when creating any web application, no matter whether it's a website returning HTML code to the client or a service returning JSON or XML. The selections that are available after you have selected this project template are described in the next table.
Class Library (Package)	This template creates a class library using project.json based projects. You can use this library in all new project types. This is a library built with .NET Core.
Console Application (Package)	Contrary to the Console Application that was discussed earlier with the Windows Classic Desktop project templates, this console application is using project.json and thus allows using .NET Core 1.0.

After selecting the ASP.NET Web Application Template, you get the choice of selecting some preconfigured templates as shown in Figure 17-8. On top you see a main group of ASP.NET 4.6 templates followed by a lower group with ASP.NET Core 1.0. These two groups of templates are described in the following two tables.

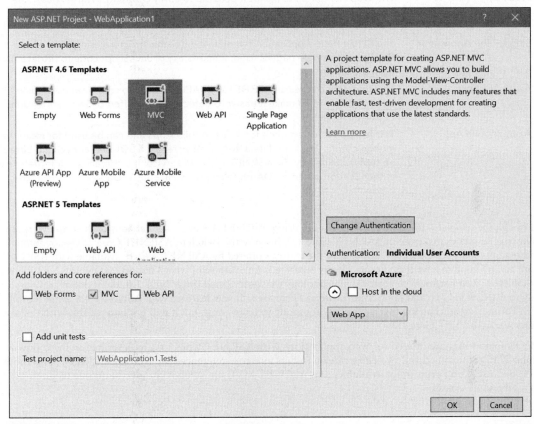

FIGURE 17-8

These templates that are offered for web applications with ASP.NET 4.6 are shown in the following table. When you select these templates, you can see a default selection for Web Forms, MVC, and Web API that defines the folders and core references that are created. You can select the Web Forms, MVC, and Web API check boxes to use multiple technologies in one project, for example to use the old Web Forms technology with the newer ASP.NET MVC.

IF YOU CHOOSE. . .	YOU GET THE C# CODE AND COMPILATION OPTIONS TO GENERATE. . .
Empty	This template doesn't have any content. It's perfect for creating a site with HTML and CSS pages.
Web Forms	This template by default adds folders for Web Forms. You can add MVC and Web API configurations to mix it up.
MVC	This template makes use of the Model-View-Controller pattern with web applications (ASP.NET MVC 5). You can use this to create a web application.

continues

continued

IF YOU CHOOSE. . .	YOU GET THE C# CODE AND COMPILATION OPTIONS TO GENERATE. . .
Web API	The Web API template makes it possible to easily create RESTful services. The MVC folders and core references are added with this template as well because documentation for the service is created with ASP.NET MVC 5.
Single Page Application	The Single Page Application template creates the structure using MVC where mostly only a single page is used; it makes use of JavaScript code to retrieve data from the server.
Azure API App	This template creates an ASP.NET Web API structure to create services hosted by Microsoft Azure. To make it easier to detect services offered, Swagger is added to this template.
Azure Mobile App	This is a powerful template for Azure Mobile Apps and can be used for more than mobile clients. This template automatically creates a SQL Server backend based on tables defined by the ASP.NET Web API service. It's also easy to integrate user authentication based on OAuth to integrate Facebook, Google, and Microsoft accounts.

Although the templates from the previous list are using ASP.NET 4.6 or earlier versions of the framework, the following templates make use of ASP.NET Core 1.0. Because the switch to ASP.NET Core 1.0 is not automatic and requires some code changes, and not all the features offered by ASP.NET 4.6 are available with ASP.NET Core 1.0, it's good to have these groups clearly separated. An example of what's not offered by ASP.NET Core 1.0 is ASP.NET Web Forms. Web Forms is a technology that had existed since .NET 1.0, but it doesn't give an easy way to use new HTML and JavaScript features. There are still new features with ASP.NET 4.6 available for Web Forms, and you can use this technology for many years to come, but it will not be available with the new framework ASP.NET Core 1.0.

The templates that are offered for web applications with ASP.NET Core 1.0 are described in the following table. With these selections, you can't choose folders and core references for Web Forms, MVC, and the Web API, because Web Forms is not available, and ASP.NET MVC and Web API moved into one technology using the same classes.

IF YOU CHOOSE. . .	YOU GET THE C# CODE AND COMPILATION OPTIONS TO GENERATE. . .
Empty	This template has initial content for hosting with ASP.NET Core 1.0. This template is the main template used in Chapter 40, "ASP.NET Core."
Web API	This template adds an ASP.NET Web API controller using ASP.NET Core 1.0. This template is the main template used in Chapter 42, "ASP.NET Web API."
Web Application	This template creates controllers and views for an ASP.NET MVC 6 application. This template is the main template used in Chapter 41, "ASP.NET MVC."

Using WCF Project Templates

To create a Windows Communication Foundation (WCF) application that enables communication between the client and server, you can select from the following WCF project templates.

IF YOU CHOOSE. . .	YOU GET THE C# CODE AND COMPILATION OPTIONS TO GENERATE. . .
WCF Service Library	A library that contains a sample service contract and implementation, as well as the configuration. The project is configured to start a WCF service host that hosts the service and a test client application.

IF YOU CHOOSE. . .	YOU GET THE C# CODE AND COMPILATION OPTIONS TO GENERATE. . .
WCF Service Application	A web project using the .NET Framework that contains a WCF contract and service implementation.
WCF Workflow Service Application	A web project that hosts a WCF service with the Workflow runtime.
Syndication Service Library	A WCF service library with a WCF contract and implementation that hosts RSS or ATOM feeds.

This is not a full list of the Visual Studio 2015 project templates, but it reflects some of the most commonly used templates. The main additions to this version of Visual Studio are the Universal Windows project templates and the ASP.NET Core 1.0 project templates. These new capabilities are covered in other chapters later in this book. Be sure to look at Chapters 29 to 34, which cover the Universal Windows Platform, and Chapters 40 to 42 for ASP.NET Core 1.0.

EXPLORING AND CODING A PROJECT

This section looks at the features that Visual Studio provides to help you add and explore code with your project. You find out about using the Solution Explorer to explore files and code, use features from the editor—such as IntelliSense and code snippets—and explore other windows, such as the Properties window and the Document Outline.

Build Environments: CLI and MSBuild

A lot of the complexity and issues of Visual Studio 2015 result from a major change with build environments. Two build environments are available: MSBuild where the configuration is mainly based on XML files, and the .NET Command Line Interface (CLI) where the configuration is mainly based on JSON files. With MSBuild, all the files that are used to compile a project are defined in an XML file. With CLI, all the files from a folder are used for building the project; all files do not need to be configured.

With these two build environments, you have three variants to work with. One variant is to use the MSBuild system. This build system is used with long-existing project types, such as a WPF application, or an ASP. NET Web Application using the ASP.NET 4.5.2 templates. The project file is an XML file that lists all the files belonging to the project, references all tools to compile the files, and lists the build steps.

You use the CLI build system with ASP.NET Core 1.0 project templates. You do initial configuration with an XML-based project file with the file extension xproj. This file—`ConsoleApp1.xproj`—contains information about Visual Studio tools' build path as well as global definitions. The DNX build system uses the JSON file `project.json` that defines the commands available, references the NuGet packages and assemblies, and includes a description about the project. A list of files belonging to the project is not needed, as all files from the folder and subfolders are used to compile the project.

> **NOTE** *The command-line tools for DNX that have the name .NET Core command line (CLI) are explained in Chapter 1, ".NET Application Architectures."*

A third option of CLI and MSBuild is used with Universal Windows apps. Here, both an XML project file and `project.json` are used. The `project.json` file no longer lists project description and commands, just the dependencies on NuGet packages, and runtimes used (with Universal Windows Platform apps, ARM, x86, and x64). The project description and build commands are within the project XML file that is using MSBuild.

> **NOTE** *Having two options to choose from results in having three variants to work with. Of course, over time this will be made easier again; it's just not clear how it will be made easier because at the time of this writing, an MSBuild version supporting cross-platform development is just getting built. Maybe there will be some more options with future updates.*

Solution Explorer

After creating a project (for example, a Console Application (Package) that was used mostly in earlier chapters), the most important tool you will use, other than the code editor, is the *Solution Explorer*. With this tool you can navigate through all files and items of your project, and see all the classes and members of classes.

> **NOTE** *When running a console application from within Visual Studio, there's a common misconception that it's necessary to have a* Console.ReadLine *method at the last line of the* Main *method to keep the console window open. That's not the case. You can start the application with Debug ⇨ Start without Debugging (or press Ctrl+F5) instead of Debug ⇨ Start Debugging (or F5). This keeps the window open until you press a key. Using F5 to start the application makes sense if breakpoints are set, and then Visual Studio halts at the breakpoints anyway.*

Working with Projects and Solutions

The Solution Explorer displays your projects and solutions. It's important to understand the distinction between these:

➤ A *project* is a set of all the source-code files and resources that will compile into a single assembly (or in some cases, a single module). For example, a project might be a class library or a Windows GUI application.

➤ A *solution* is the set of all the projects that make up a particular software package (application).

To understand this distinction, consider what happens when you ship a project, which consists of more than one assembly. For example, you might have a user interface, custom controls, and other components that ship as libraries of parts of the application. You might even have a different user interface for administrators, and a service that is called across the network. Each of these parts of the application might be contained in a separate assembly, and hence they are regarded by Visual Studio as separate projects. However, it is quite likely that you will be coding these projects in parallel and in conjunction with one another. Thus, it is quite useful to be able to edit them all as one single unit in Visual Studio. Visual Studio enables this by regarding all the projects as forming one solution, and treating the solution as the unit that it reads in and allows you to work on.

Up until now, this chapter has been loosely talking about creating a console project. In fact, in the example you are working on, Visual Studio has actually created a solution for you—although this particular solution contains just one project. You can see this scenario reflected in the Solution Explorer (see Figure 17-9), which contains a tree structure that defines your solution.

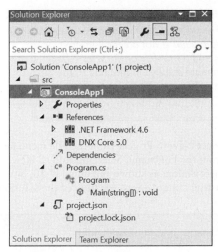

FIGURE 17-9

In this case, the project contains your source file, `Program.cs`, as well as a project configuration file, `project.json`, which enables you to define project descriptions, versions, and dependencies. The Solution Explorer also indicates the NuGet packages and assemblies that your project references. You can see this by expanding the `References` folder in the Solution Explorer.

If you have not changed any of the default settings in Visual Studio, you will probably find the Solution Explorer in the top-right corner of your screen. If you cannot see it, just go to the View menu and select Solution Explorer.

The solution is described by a file with the extension `.sln`; in this example, it is `ConsoleApp1.sln`. The solution file is a text file that contains information about all the projects contained within the solution, as well as global items that can be used with all contained projects.

Depending on the build environment, the C# project is described by a file with the extension `.csproj`, or the `.xproj` file in conjunction with `project.json`. You can open the `project.json` file directly from within Solution Explorer. To edit a `.csproj` file from Visual Studio, you need to unload the project first, which you can do by clicking the project name and selecting Unload Project in the context menu. After the project is unloaded, the context menu contains the entry Edit `ConsoleApp1.csproj`, from which you can directly access the XML code.

> ## REVEALING HIDDEN FILES
>
> By default, Solution Explorer hides some files. By clicking the button Show All Files on the Solution Explorer toolbar, you can display all hidden files. For example, the `bin` and `obj` directories store compiled and intermediate files. Subfolders of `obj` hold various temporary or intermediate files; subfolders of `bin` hold the compiled assemblies.

Adding Projects to a Solution

As you work through the following sections, you see how Visual Studio works with Windows desktop applications and console applications. To that end, you create a Windows project called `BasicForm` that you add to your current solution, `ConsoleApp1`.

> **NOTE** *Creating the* `BasicForm` *project means that you end up with a solution containing a WPF application and a console application. That is not a very common scenario—you are more likely to have one application and a number of libraries—but it enables you to see more code! You might, however, create a solution like this if, for example, you are writing a utility that you want to run either as a WPF application or as a command-line utility.*

You can create the new project in several ways. One way is to select New ⇨ Project from the File menu (as you have done already), or you can select Add ⇨ New Project from the File menu. Selecting Add ⇨ New Project from the File menu brings up the familiar Add New Project dialog; as shown in Figure 17-10, however, Visual Studio wants to create the new project in the preexisting `ConsoleApp1` location of the solution.

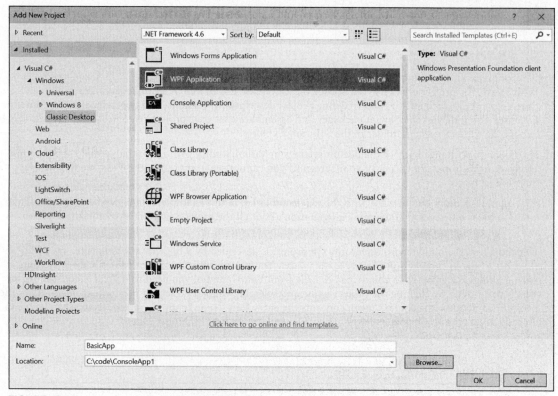

FIGURE 17-10

If you select this option, a new project is added, so the `ConsoleApp1` solution now contains a console application and a WPF application.

> **NOTE** *In accordance with Visual Studio's language independence, the new project does not need to be a C# project. It is perfectly acceptable to put a C# project, a Visual Basic project, and a C++ project in the same solution. We will stick with C# here because this is a C# book!*

Of course, this means that `ConsoleApp1` is not really an appropriate name for the solution anymore. To change the name, you can right-click the name of the solution and select Rename from the context menu. Call the new solution **DemoSolution**. The Solution Explorer window should now look like Figure 17-11.

FIGURE 17-11

As you can see, Visual Studio has made your newly added WPF project automatically reference some of the extra base classes that are important for WPF functionality.

Note that if you look in Windows Explorer, the name of the solution file has changed to `DemoSolution.sln`. In general, if you want to rename any files, the Solution Explorer window is the best place to do so, because Visual Studio then automatically updates any references to that file in the other project files. If you rename files using only Windows Explorer, you might break the solution because Visual Studio is not able to locate all the files it needs to read into the IDE. As a result, you need to manually edit the project and solution files to update the file references.

Setting the Startup Project

Bear in mind that if you have multiple projects in a solution, you need to configure which one should run as the startup project. You can also configure multiple projects to start simultaneously. There are a lot of ways to do this. After selecting a project in the Solution Explorer, the context menu offers a Set as Startup Project option, which enables one startup project at a time. You can also use the context menu Debug ➪ Start new instance to start one project after the other. To simultaneously start more than one project, click the solution in the Solution Explorer and select the context menu Set Startup Projects. This opens the dialog shown in Figure 17-12. After you check Multiple Startup Projects, you can define what projects should be started.

Discovering Types and Members

A WPF application contains a lot more initial code than a console application when Visual Studio first creates it. That is because creating a window is an intrinsically more complex process. Chapter 34 discusses the code for a WPF application in detail. For now, have a look at the XAML code in `MainWindow.xaml` and in the C# source code `MainWindow.xaml.cs`. There's also some hidden generated C# code. Iterating through the tree in the Solution Explorer, below `MainWindow.xaml.cs` you find the class `MainWindow`. With all the code files, the Solution Explorer shows the types within that file. Within the type `MainWindow` you can see the members of the class. `_contentLoaded` is a field of type `bool`. Clicking this field opens the file `MainWindow.g.i.cs`. This file—a part of the `MainWindow` class—is generated by the designer and contains initialization code.

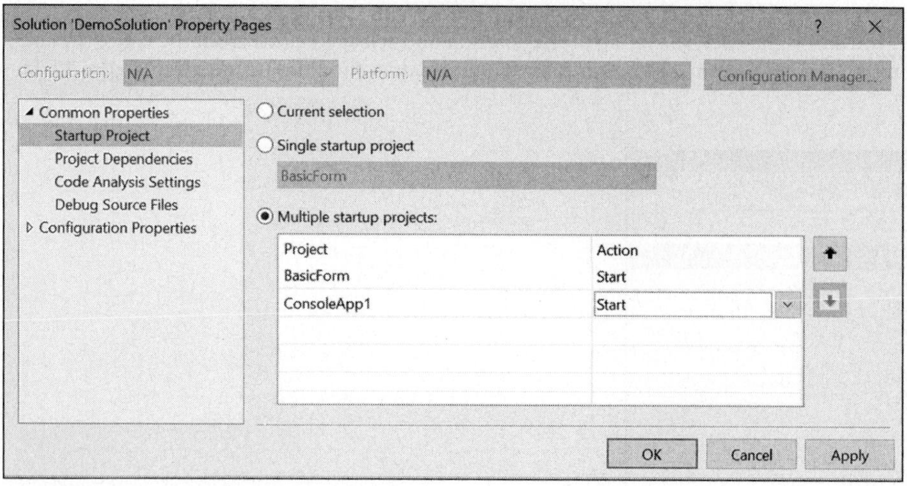

FIGURE 17-12

Previewing Items

A feature offered by the Solution Explorer is the button to Preview Selected Items. When this button is enabled and you click an item in the Solution Explorer, the editor for this item opens, as usual. However, if the item was not opened previously, the tab flow of the editor shows the new opened item in the rightmost position. Now, when you click another item, the previously opened one is closed. This helps significantly with reducing the number of open items.

In the editor tab of the previewed item is the Keep Open button, which promotes the item to stay open even when another item is clicked; the tab for the item that you're keeping open moves to the left.

Using Scopes

Setting scopes allows you to focus on a specific part of the solution. The list of items shown by the Solution Explorer can grow really huge. For example, opening the context menu of a type enables you to select the base type from the menu Base Types. Here you can see the complete inheritance hierarchy of the type, as shown in Figure 17-13.

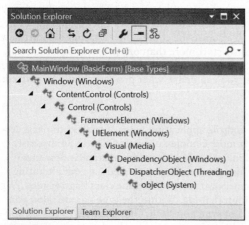

FIGURE 17-13

Because Solution Explorer contains more information than you can easily view with one screen, you can open multiple Solution Explorer windows at once with the menu option New Solution Explorer View, and you can set the scope to a specific element—for example, to a project or a class—by selecting Scope to This from the context menu. To return to the previous scope, click the Back button.

Adding Items to a Project

Directly from within Solution Explorer you can add different items to the project. Selecting the project and selecting the context menu Add ⇨ New Item opens the dialog shown in Figure 17-14. Another way to get to the same dialog is by using the main menu Project ⇨ Add New Item. Here you find many different categories, such as code items to add classes or interfaces, data items for using the Entity Framework or other data access technologies, and a lot more.

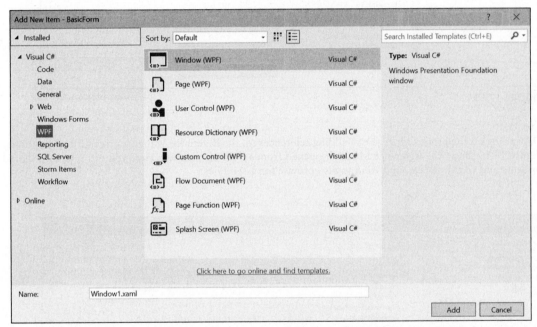

FIGURE 17-14

Managing References

Adding references with Visual Studio needs some special considerations because of differences with project types. In case you're using the full framework—that is, .NET 4.6—adding references to assemblies from the .NET Framework is still an important task to do. It doesn't matter if you are using one of the older templates such as WPF or a newer template such as Console Application (Package). Remember: With newer templates you can still target .NET 4.5.2 (or .NET 4.6) in addition to .NET Core 1.0.

The Reference Manager, shown in Figure 17-15, enables you to add references to assemblies that are part of the .NET Framework, and also add references to assemblies that you created with library projects.

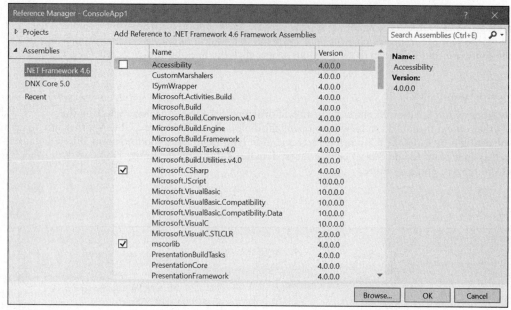

FIGURE 17-15

Depending on the project types you're adding references to, the Reference Manager gives different options. Figure 17-16 shows the Reference Manager opened from a WPF application. Here you can reference shared projects and COM objects, and you can also browse for assemblies.

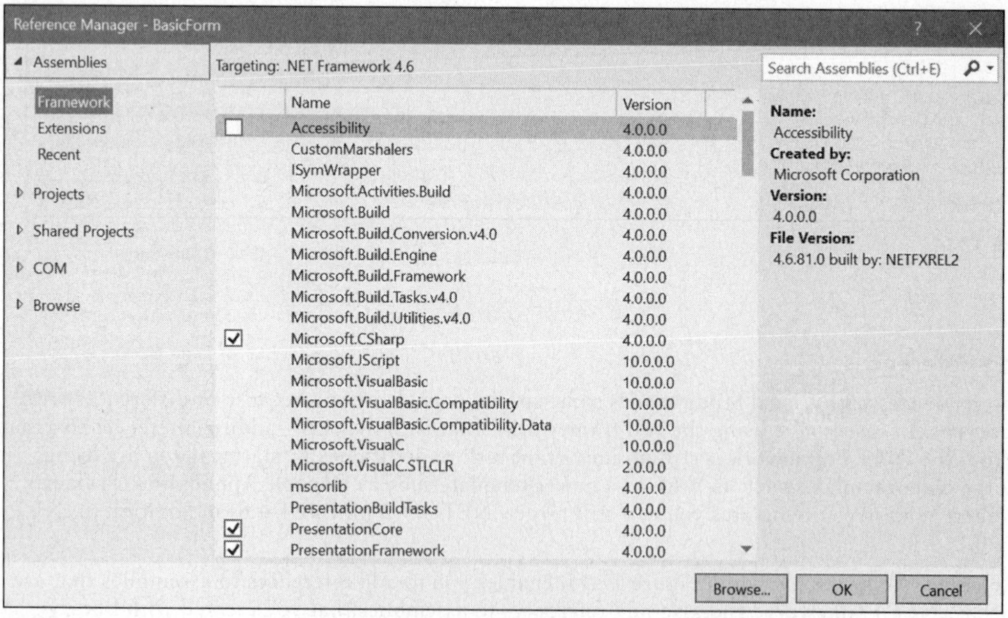

FIGURE 17-16

When you're creating Universal Windows Platform apps, you see a new feature with the Reference Manager, as shown in Figure 17-17. Here you can reference Universal Windows Extensions, for example API extensions available with Windows IoT or Windows Mobile.

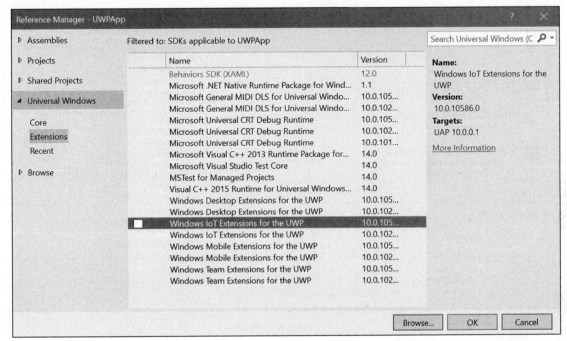

FIGURE 17-17

Using NuGet Packages

All the new functionality of .NET Core is available with NuGet packages. Many enhancements for .NET 4.6 are available with NuGet packages as well. NuGet allows for faster innovations than are offered by the .NET Framework, and nowadays this is necessary.

The NuGet Package Manager, shown in Figure 17-18, has been completely rewritten for Visual Studio 2015. It is no longer a modal dialog; instead you can continue working on your project while the NuGet Package Manager downloads some packages from the Internet. Now you can easily select a specific version of the NuGet package that needs to be installed. With Visual Studio 2013 you had to use the command line to do this.

You can configure the sources of NuGet packages by opening the Options dialog by selecting Tools ⇨ Options. In the Options dialog select the NuGet Package Manager ⇨ Package Sources in the tree view (see Figure 17-19). By default, Microsoft's NuGet server is configured, but you can also configure other NuGet servers or your own. With .NET Core and ASP.NET Core 1.0, Microsoft offers feeds with NuGet packages that are updated on a daily bases.

Using the NuGet Package Manager, you can not only select the package source but you can also select a filter to see all packages that are installed, or where an upgrade is available, and search for packages on the server.

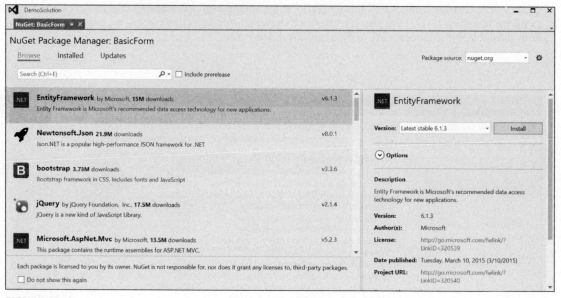

FIGURE 17-18

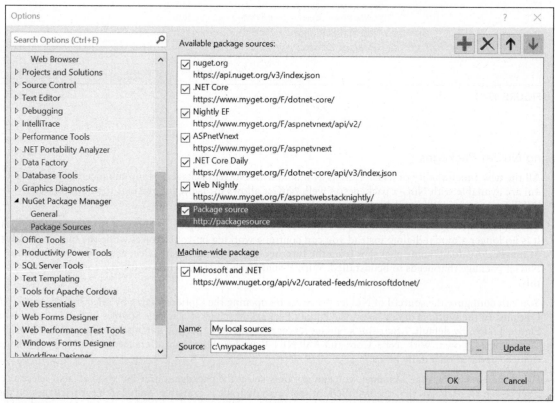

FIGURE 17-19

> **NOTE** *With ASP.NET Core 1.0, JavaScript libraries are no longer used from NuGet server. Instead, JavaScript package managers, such as NPM and Bower, are directly supported from within Visual Studio 2015. This is discussed in Chapter 40.*

Working with the Code Editor

The Visual Studio code editor is where most of your development work takes place. This editor increased in size in Visual Studio after the removal of some toolbars from the default configuration, and the removal of borders from the menus, toolbars, and tab headers. The following sections take a look at some of the most useful features of this editor.

The Folding Editor

One notable feature of Visual Studio is its use of a folding editor as its default code editor. Figure 17-20 shows the code for the console application that you generated earlier. Notice the little minus signs on the left-hand side of the window. These signs mark the points where the editor assumes that a new block of code (or documentation comment) begins. You can click these icons to close up the view of the corresponding block of code just as you would close a node in a tree control (see Figure 17-21).

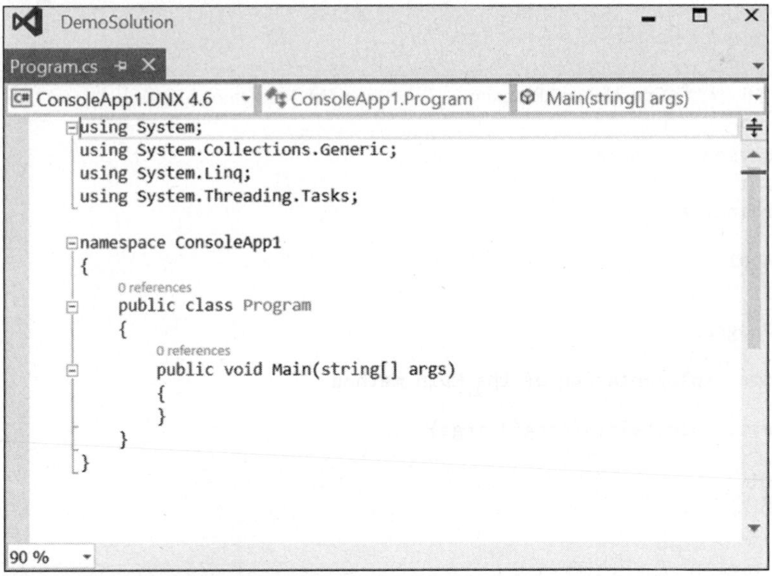

FIGURE 17-20

This means that while you are editing you can focus on just the areas of code you want to look at, hiding the bits of code you are not interested in working with at that moment. If you do not like the way the editor has chosen to block off your code, you can indicate your own blocks of collapsible code with the

C# preprocessor directives, #region and #endregion. For example, to collapse the code inside the Main method, you would add the code shown in Figure 17-22.

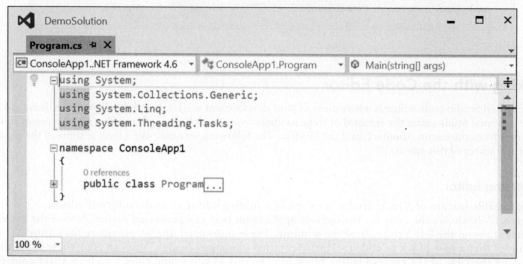

FIGURE 17-21

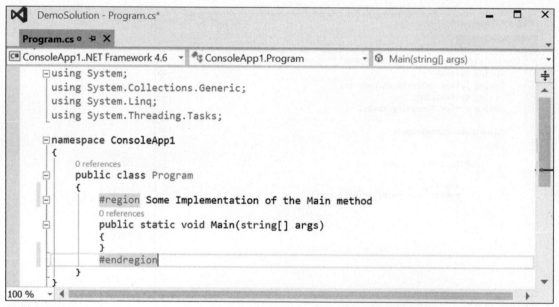

FIGURE 17-22

The code editor automatically detects the #region block and places a new minus sign by the #region directive, enabling you to close the region. Enclosing this code in a region enables the editor to close it (see Figure 17-23), marking the area with the comment you specified in the #region directive. The compiler, however, ignores the directives and compiles the Main method as normal.

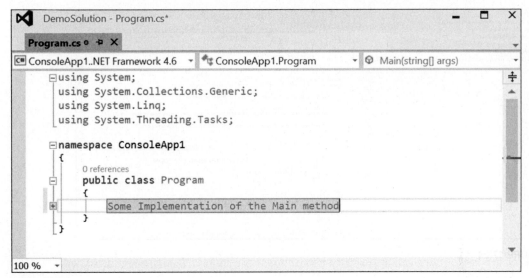

FIGURE 17-23

Navigating Within the Editor

On the top line of the editor are three combo boxes. The right combo box enables you to navigate between members of the type you're in. The middle combo box enables you to navigate between types. The left combo box is new with Visual Studio 2015; it enables you to navigate between different applications or frameworks. For example, if you are working on the source code of a shared project, in the left combo box of the editor you can select one of the projects where the shared project is used to see the code that is active for the selected project. The code that is not compiled for the selected project is dimmed. You can create code segments for different platforms using C# preprocessor commands.

IntelliSense

In addition to the folding editor feature, Visual Studio's code editor also incorporates Microsoft's popular *IntelliSense* capability, which not only saves you typing but also ensures that you use the correct parameters. IntelliSense remembers your preferred choices and starts with these initially instead of at the beginning of the sometimes rather lengthy lists that IntelliSense can now provide.

The code editor also performs some syntax checking on your code, underlining these errors with a short wavy line, even before you compile the code. Hovering the mouse pointer over the underlined text brings up a small box that contains a description of the error.

CodeLens

One great new feature in Visual Studio 2013 was the *CodeLens*. With Visual Studio 2015, this feature is now available in the Professional edition.

Did you ever change a method and wonder, "Did I miss a method calling this?" Now it's really easy to find callers. The number of references is directly shown in the editor (see Figure 17-24). When you click the references link, the CodeLens opens so you can see the code of the callers and navigate to them. You can also see the reference with another new feature, the *Code Map*. The Code Map is discussed later in the "Architecture Tools" section.

If the source code is checked into a source control system like Visual Studio Online using Git or TFS, you can also see the authors and changes made.

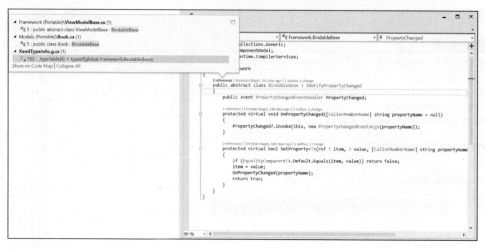

FIGURE 17-24

Using Code Snippets

Great productivity features from the code editor are *code snippets*. Just by writing cw<tab><tab> in the editor, the editor creates a `Console.WriteLine();`. Visual Studio comes with many code snippets, including the following:—

➤ do, for, forr, foreach, and while for creating loops

➤ equals for an implementation of the Equals method

➤ attribute and exception for creating Attribute- and Exception- derived types

You can see all the code snippets available with the Code Snippets Manager (see Figure 17-25) by selecting Tools ➪ Code Snippets Manager. You can also create custom snippets.

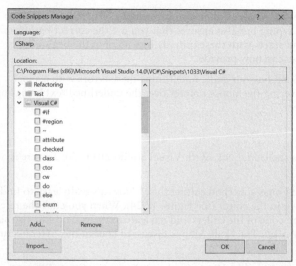

FIGURE 17-25

You can also use snippets for XAML code that are available at `http://xamlsnippets.codeplex.com`.

Learning and Understanding Other Windows

In addition to the code editor and Solution Explorer, Visual Studio provides a number of other windows that enable you to view and/or manage your projects from different points of view.

> **NOTE** *The rest of this section describes several other windows. If any of these windows are not visible on your monitor, you can select them from the View menu. To show the design view and code editor, right-click the filename in Solution Explorer and select View Designer or View Code from the context menu, or select the item from the toolbar at the top of Solution Explorer. The design view and code editor share the same tabbed window.*

Using the Design View Window

If you are designing a user interface application, such as a WPF application, or a Windows control library, you can use the Design View window. This window presents a visual overview of what your form will look like. You normally use the Design View window in conjunction with a window known as the *toolbox*. The toolbox contains a large number of .NET components that you can drag onto your program. Toolbox components vary according to project type. Figure 17-26 shows the items displayed within a WPF application.

FIGURE 17-26

To add your own custom categories to the toolbox, execute the following steps:

1. Right-click any category.
2. Select Add Tab from the context menu.

You can also place other tools in the toolbox by selecting Choose Items from the same context menu; this is particularly useful for adding your own custom components or components from the .NET Framework that are not present in the toolbox by default.

Using the Properties Window

As mentioned in the first part of the book, .NET classes can implement properties. The Properties window is available with projects and files and when you're selecting items using the Design view. Figure 17-27 shows the Properties view with a Windows Service.

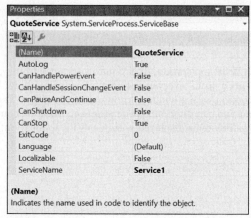

FIGURE 17-27

With this window you can see all the properties of an item and configure it accordingly. You can change some properties by entering text in a text box; others have predefined selections, and some have a custom editor. You can also add event handlers to events with the Properties window.

With UWP and WPF applications, the Properties window looks very different, as you can see in Figure 17-28. This window provides much more graphical feedback and allows for graphical configuration of the properties. This properties window is coming originally from the Blend tool. As mentioned earlier, Visual Studio and Blend for Visual Studio have many similarities.

Using the Class View Window

Although the Solution Explorer can show classes and members of classes, that's normally the job of the Class View (see Figure 17-29). To invoke the class view, select View ➪ Class View. The Class View shows the hierarchy of the namespaces and classes in your code. It provides a tree view that you can expand to see which namespaces contain what classes, and what classes contain what members.

A nice feature of the Class View is that if you right-click the name of any item for which you have access to the source code, then the context menu displays the Go To Definition option, which takes you to the definition of the item in the code editor. Alternatively, you can do this by double-clicking the item in Class View (or, indeed, by right-clicking the item you want in the source code editor and choosing the same option from the resulting context menu). The context menu also enables you to add a field, method, property, or indexer to a class. In other words, you specify the details for the relevant member in a dialog, and the code is added for you. This feature can be particularly useful for adding properties and indexers, as it can save you quite a bit of typing.

FIGURE 17-28

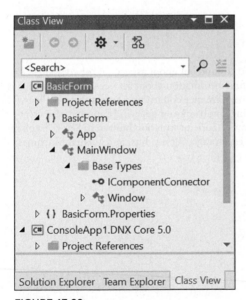

FIGURE 17-29

Using the Object Browser Window

An important aspect of programming in the .NET environment is being able to find out what methods and other code items are available in the base classes and any other libraries that you are referencing from your assembly. This feature is available through a window called the Object Browser (see Figure 17-30). You can access this window by selecting Object Browser from the View menu in Visual Studio 2015. With this tool you can browse for and select existing component sets—such as .NET Framework versions from 2.0 to 4.6, .NET Portable Subsets, what's available with the Windows Runtime, and .NET for UWP—and view the classes and members of the classes that are available with this subset. You can also select the Windows Runtime by selecting Windows in the Browse drop-down to find all namespaces, types, and methods of this native new API for UWP apps.

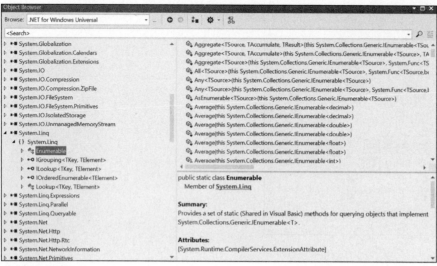

FIGURE 17-30

Using the Server Explorer Window

You can use the Server Explorer window, shown in Figure 17-31, to find out about aspects of the computers in your network while coding. With the Servers section, you can find information about services running (which is extremely useful in developing Windows Services), create new performance counts, and access the event logs. The Data Connections section enables not only connecting to existing databases and querying data, but also creating a new database. Visual Studio 2015 also has a lot of Windows Azure information built in to Server Explorer, including options for Windows Azure Compute, Mobile Services, Storage, Service Bus, and Virtual Machines.

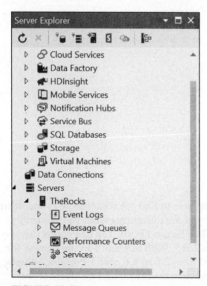

FIGURE 17-31

Using the Cloud Explorer

The Cloud Explorer (see Figure 17-32) is a new explorer that is available with Visual Studio 2015 if you install the Azure SDK and the Cloud Explorer extension. With the Cloud Explorer you can get access to your Microsoft Azure subscription and have access to your resources, view log files, attach debuggers, and go directly to the Azure portal.

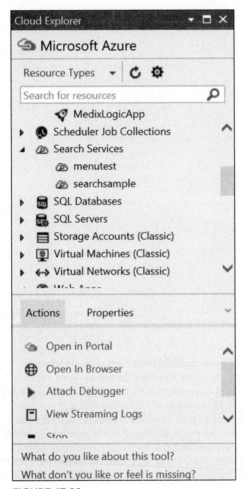

FIGURE 17-32

Using the Document Outline

A window available with WPF and UWP apps is the Document Outline. Figure 17-33 shows this window opened with an application from Chapter 34. Here, you can view the logical structure and hierarchy of the XAML elements, lock elements to prevent changing them unintentionally, easily move elements within the hierarchy, group elements within a new container element, and change layout types.

With this tool you can also create XAML templates and graphically edit data binding.

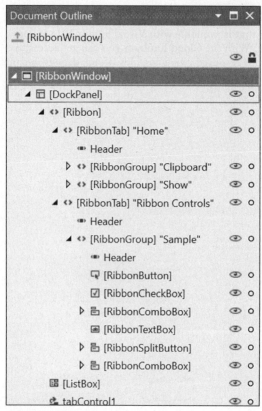

FIGURE 17-33

Arranging Windows

While exploring Visual Studio, you might have noticed that many of the windows have some interesting functionality that's more reminiscent of toolbars. In particular, they can all either float (also on a second display), or they can be docked. When they are docked, they display an extra icon that looks like a pin next to the minimize button in the top-right corner of each window. This icon really does act like a pin—you can use it to pin the window open. A pinned window (the pin is displayed vertically) behaves just like the regular windows you are used to. When windows are unpinned (the pin is displayed horizontally), however, they remain open only as long as they have the focus. As soon as they lose the focus (because you clicked or moved your mouse somewhere else), they smoothly retreat into the main border around the entire Visual Studio application. Pinning and unpinning windows provides another way to make the best use of the limited space on your screen.

A new feature with Visual Studio 2015 is that you can store different layouts. It's likely that you're running in different environments. For example, in your office you might have connected your laptop to two big screens, but this is not the case when you're programming in a plane, where you only have a single screen. In the past, you probably always arranged the windows according to your needs and had to change this several times a day. Another scenario in which you might need different layouts is when you're doing web development and creating UWP and Xamarin apps. Now you can save your layout and easily switch from one to the other. From the Window menu, select Save Window Layout to save your current arrangement of the tools. Use Window ➪ Apply Window Layout to select one of your saved layouts to arrange the windows as you have saved them.

BUILDING A PROJECT

Visual Studio is not only about coding your projects. It is actually an IDE that manages the full life cycle of your project, including the building or compiling of your solutions. This section examines the options that Visual Studio provides for building your project.

Building, Compiling, and Making Code

Before examining the various build options, it is important to clarify some terminology. You will often see three different terms used in connection with the process of getting from your source code to some sort of executable code: *compiling*, *building*, and *making*. The origin of these three terms reflects the fact that until recently, the process of getting from source code to executable code involved more than one step (this is still the case in C++). This was due in large part to the number of source files in a program.

In C++, for example, each source file needs to be compiled individually. This results in what are known as *object files*, each containing something like executable code, but where each object file relates to only one source file. To generate an executable, these object files need to be linked together, a process that is officially known as *linking*. The combined process was usually referred to—at least on the Windows platform—as building your code. However, in C# terms the compiler is more sophisticated, able to read in and treat all your source files as one block. Hence, there is not really a separate linking stage, so in the context of C#, the terms *compile* and *build* are used interchangeably.

The term *make* basically means the same thing as *build,* although it is not really used in the context of C#. The term *make* originated on old mainframe systems on which, when a project was composed of many source files, a separate file would be written containing instructions to the compiler on how to build a project—which files to include and what libraries to link to, and so on. This file was generally known as a *makefile* and it is still quite standard on UNIX systems. The MSBuild project file is in reality something like the old makefile, it's just a new advanced XML variant. With MSBuild projects, you can use the `MSBuild` command with the project file as input, and all the sources will be compiled. Using build files is very helpful on a separate build server on which all developers check their code in, and overnight the build process is done. Chapter 1 mentions the .NET Core command line (CLI) tools, the command line to build with the .NET Core environment.

Debugging and Release Builds

The idea of having separate builds is very familiar to C++ developers, and to a lesser degree to those with a Visual Basic background. The point here is that when you are debugging, you typically want your executable to behave differently from when you are ready to ship the software. When you are ready to ship your software, you want the executable to be as small and fast as possible. Unfortunately, these two requirements are not compatible with your needs when you are debugging code, as explained in the following sections.

Optimization

High performance is achieved partly by the compiler's many optimizations of the code. This means that the compiler actively looks at your source code as it is compiling to identify places where it can modify the precise details of what you are doing in a way that does not change the overall effect but makes things more efficient. For example, suppose the compiler encountered the following source code:

```
double InchesToCm(double ins) => ins * 2.54;

// later on in the code
Y = InchesToCm(X);
```

It might replace it with this:

```
Y = X * 2.54;
```

Similarly, it might replace

```
{
    string message = "Hi";
    Console.WriteLine(message);
}
```

with this:

```
Console.WriteLine("Hi");
```

By doing so, the compiler bypasses having to declare any unnecessary object reference in the process.

It is not possible to exactly pin down what optimizations the C# compiler does—nor whether the two previous examples would actually occur with any particular situation—because those kinds of details are not documented. (Chances are good that for managed languages such as C#, the previous optimizations would occur at JIT compilation time, not when the C# compiler compiles source code to assembly.) Obviously, for proprietary reasons, companies that write compilers are usually quite reluctant to provide many details about the tricks that their compilers use. Note that optimizations do not affect your source code—they affect only the contents of the executable code. However, the previous examples should give you a good idea of what to expect from optimizations.

The problem is that although optimizations like the examples just shown help a great deal in making your code run faster, they are detrimental for debugging. In the first example, suppose that you want to set a breakpoint inside the InchesToCm method to see what is going on in there. How can you possibly do that if the executable code does not actually have an InchesToCm method because the compiler has removed it? Moreover, how can you set a watch on the Message variable when that does not exist in the compiled code either?

Debugger Symbols

During debugging, you often have to look at the values of variables, and you specify them by their source code names. The trouble is that executable code generally does not contain those names—the compiler replaces the names with memory addresses. .NET has modified this situation somewhat to the extent that certain items in assemblies are stored with their names, but this is true of only a small minority of items—such as public classes and methods—and those names will still be removed when the assembly is JIT-compiled. Asking the debugger to tell you the value in the variable called HeightInInches is not going to get you very far if, when the debugger examines the executable code, it sees only addresses and no reference to the name HeightInInches anywhere.

Therefore, to debug properly, you need to make extra debugging information available in the executable. This information includes, among other things, names of variables and line information that enables the debugger to match up which executable machine assembly language instructions correspond to your original source code instructions. You will not, however, want that information in a release build, both for proprietary reasons (debugging information makes it a lot easier for other people to disassemble your code) and because it increases the size of the executable.

Extra Source Code Debugging Commands

A related issue is that quite often while you are debugging there will be extra lines in your code to display crucial debugging-related information. Obviously, you want the relevant commands removed entirely from the executable before you ship the software. You could do this manually, but wouldn't it be so much easier if you could simply mark those statements in some way so that the compiler ignores them when it is compiling your code to be shipped? You've already seen in the first part of the book how this can be done in C# by defining a suitable processor symbol, and possibly using this in conjunction with the Conditional attribute, giving you what is known as *conditional compilation*.

What all these factors add up to is that you need to compile almost all commercial software in a slightly different way when debugging than in the final product that is shipped. Visual Studio can handle this because, as you have already seen, it stores details about all the options it is supposed to pass to the compiler when it has your code compiled. All that Visual Studio has to do to support different types of builds is store more than one set of such details. These different sets of build information are referred to as *configurations*. When you create a project, Visual Studio automatically gives you two configurations—Debug and Release:

➤ **Debug**—This configuration commonly specifies that no optimizations are to take place, extra debugging information is to be present in the executable, and the compiler is to assume that the debug preprocessor symbol Debug is present unless it is explicitly #undefined in the source code.

➤ **Release**—This configuration specifies that the compiler should optimize the compilation, that there should be no extra debugging information in the executable, and that the compiler should not assume that any particular preprocessor symbol is present.

You can define your own configurations as well. You might want to do this, for example, to set up professional-level builds and enterprise-level builds so that you can ship two versions of the software. In the past, because of issues related to Unicode character encodings being supported on Windows NT but not on Windows 95, it was common for C++ projects to feature a Unicode configuration and an MBCS (multi-byte character set) configuration.

Selecting a Configuration

At this point you might be wondering how Visual Studio, given that it stores details about more than one configuration, determines which one to use when arranging for a project to be built. The answer is that there is always an active configuration, which is the configuration that is used when you ask Visual Studio to build a project. (Note that configurations are set for each project, rather than each solution.)

By default, when you create a project, the Debug configuration is the active configuration. You can change which configuration is the active one by clicking the Build menu option and selecting the Configuration Manager item. It is also available through a drop-down menu in the main Visual Studio toolbar.

Editing Configurations

In addition to choosing the active configuration, you can also examine and edit the configurations. To do this, select the relevant project in Solution Explorer and then select Properties from the Project menu. This brings up a sophisticated dialog. (Alternatively, you can access the same dialog by right-clicking the name of the project in Solution Explorer and then selecting Properties from the context menu.)

This dialog contains a tabbed view that enables you to select many different general areas to examine or edit. Space does not permit showing all of these areas, but this section outlines a couple of the most important ones.

Depending on whether the application is MSBuild or CLI, the options available are very different. First, look at the properties of the WPF application in Figure 17-34, which shows a tabbed view of the available properties. This screenshot shows the general Application settings.

Among the points to note are that you can select the name of the assembly as well as the type of assembly to be generated. The options here are Console Application, Windows Application, and Class Library. Of course, you can change the assembly type if you want. (Though arguably, you might wonder why you did not pick the correct project type when you asked Visual Studio to generate the project for you in the first place!)

Figure 17-35 shows the same configuration for a CLI-based application. You also can see Application settings, but the options are limited to the default namespace name and the section of the runtime. With this screenshot, a specific version of RC 2 is selected.

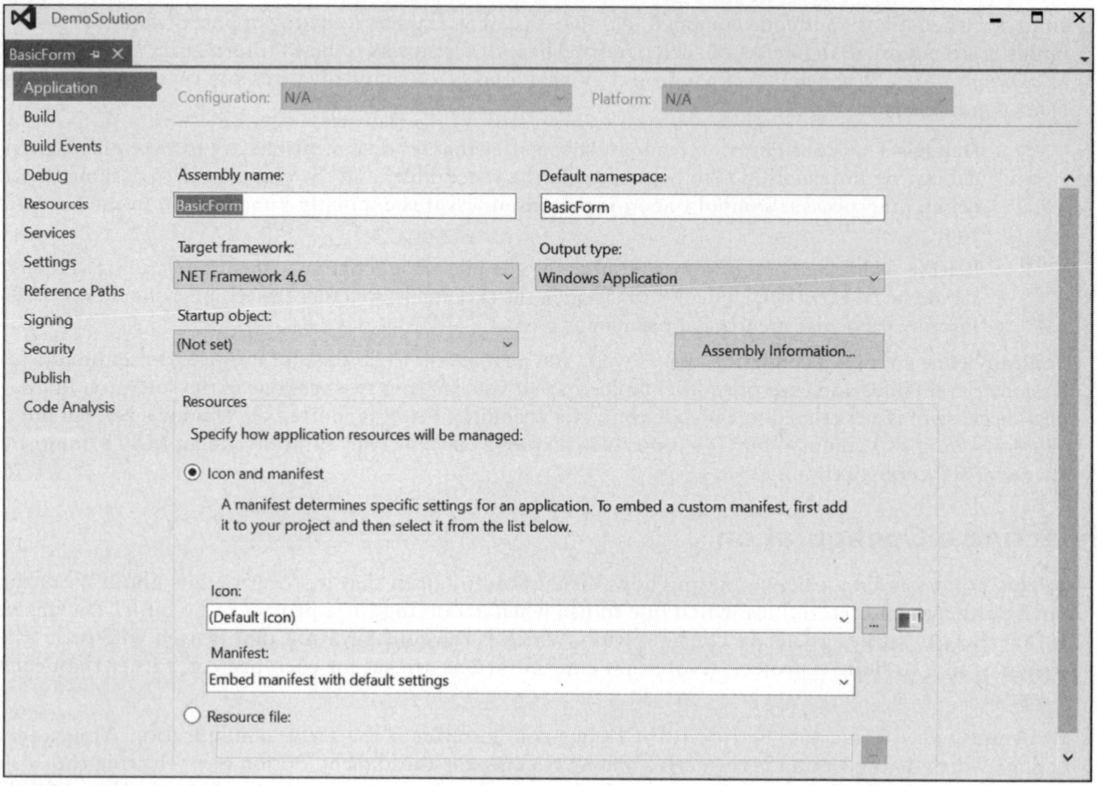

FIGURE 17-34

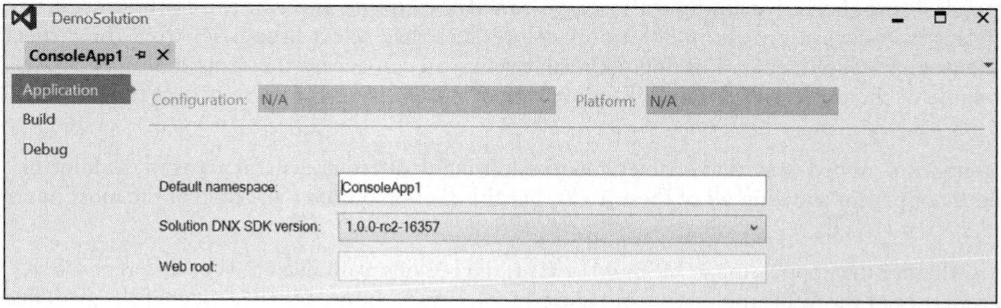

FIGURE 17-35

Figure 17-36 shows the build configuration properties of the WPF application. Note that a list box near the top of the dialog enables you to specify which configuration you want to look at. You can see—in the case of the Debug configuration—that the compiler assumes that the DEBUG and TRACE preprocessor symbols have been defined. In addition, the code is not optimized and extra debugging information is generated.

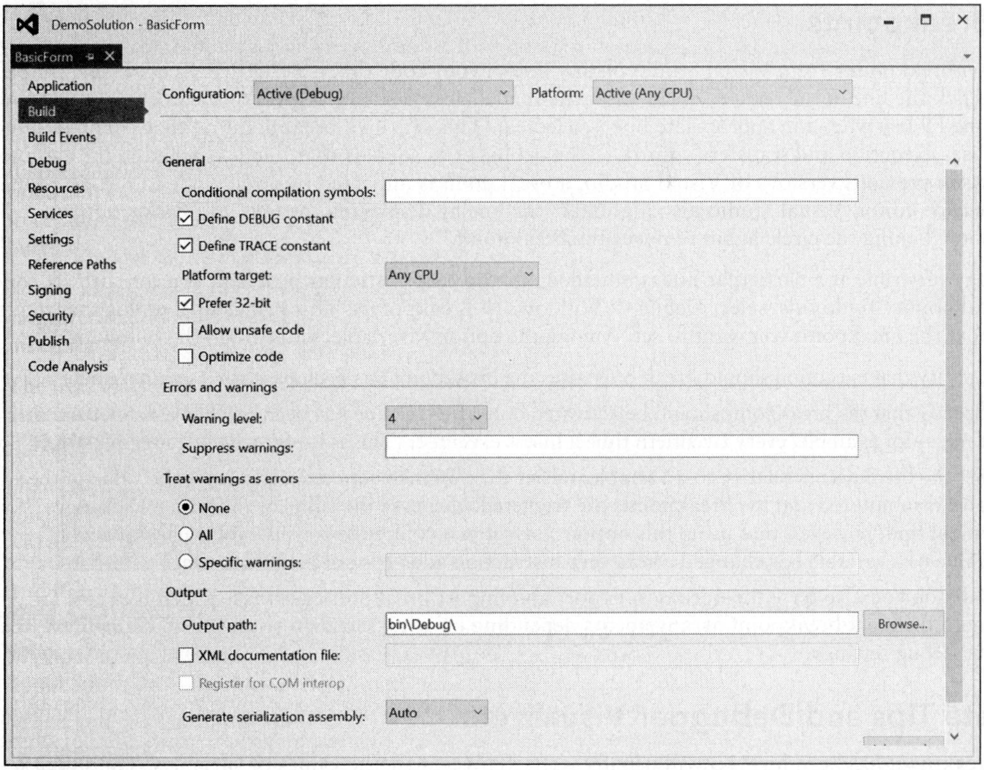

FIGURE 17-36

Figure 17-37 shows the build configuration properties of a CLI project. Here, you can select to produce outputs on build. The TypeScript setting is only relevant with applications containing TypeScript code. TypeScript is compiled to JavaScript.

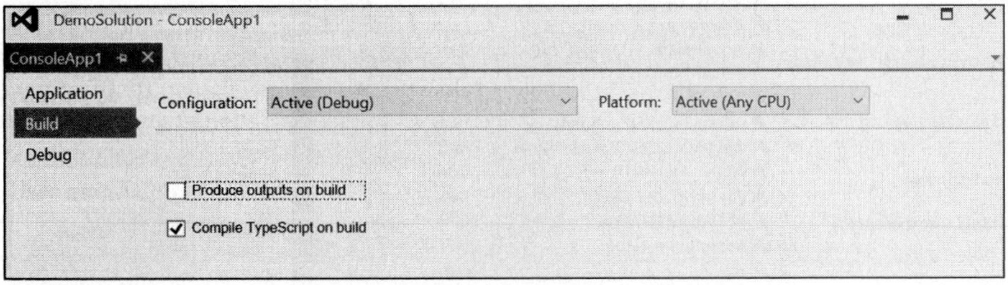

FIGURE 17-37

DEBUGGING YOUR CODE

At this point, you are ready to run and debug the application. In C#, as in pre-.NET languages, the main technique involved in debugging is simply setting breakpoints and using them to examine what is going on in your code at a certain point in its execution.

Setting Breakpoints

You can set breakpoints from Visual Studio on any line of your code that is actually executed. The simplest way is to click the line in the code editor, within the shaded area near the far left of the document window (or press the F9 key when the appropriate line is selected). This sets up a breakpoint on that particular line, which pauses execution and transfers control to the debugger as soon as that line is reached in the execution process. As in previous versions of Visual Studio, a breakpoint is indicated by a red circle to the left of the line in the code editor. Visual Studio also highlights the line by displaying the text and background in a different color. Clicking the circle again removes the breakpoint.

If breaking every time at a particular line is not adequate for your particular problem, you can also set conditional breakpoints. To do this, select Debug ➪ Windows ➪ Breakpoints. This brings up a dialog that requests details about the breakpoint you want to set. Among the options available, you can do the following:

➤ Specify that execution should break only after the breakpoint has been passed a certain number of times.

➤ Specify that the breakpoint should be activated only after the line has been reached a defined number of times—for example, every twentieth time a line is executed. (This is useful when debugging large loops.)

➤ Set the breakpoints relative to a variable, rather than an instruction. In this case, the value of the variable is monitored and the breakpoints are triggered whenever the value of this variable changes. You might find, however, that using this option slows down your code considerably. Checking whether the value of a variable has changed after every instruction adds a lot of processor time.

With this dialog you also have the option to export and import breakpoint settings, which is useful for working with different breakpoint arrangements depending on what scenario you want to debug into, and to store the debug settings.

Using Data Tips and Debugger Visualizers

After a breakpoint has been hit, you will usually want to investigate the values of variables. The simplest way to do this is to hover the mouse cursor over the name of the variable in the code editor. This causes a little *data tip* box (shown in Figure 17-38) that shows the value of that variable to pop up, which can also be expanded for greater detail.

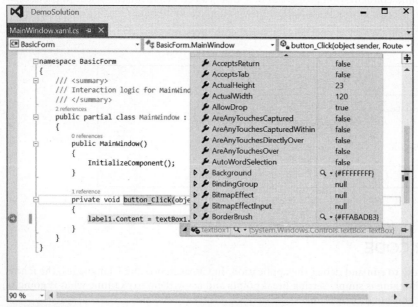

FIGURE 17-38

Some of the values shown in the data tip offer a magnifying glass. Clicking this magnifying class provides one or more options to use a *debugger visualizer*—depending on the type. With WPF controls, the WPF Visualizer enables you to take a closer look at the control (see Figure 17-39). With this visualizer you can view the visual tree that is used during runtime, including all the actual property settings. This visual tree also gives you a preview of the element that you select within the tree.

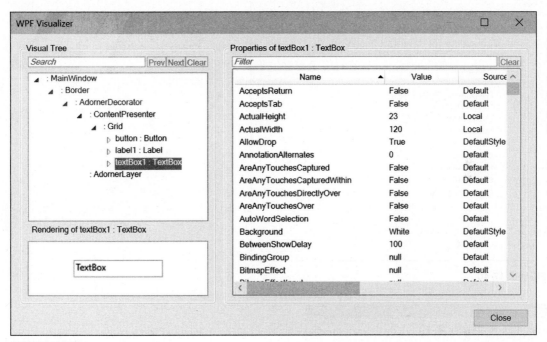

FIGURE 17-39

Figure 17-40 shows the JSON Visualizer, which displays JSON content. Many other visualizers are available as well, such as HTML, XML, and Text visualizers.

Live Visual Tree

A new feature of Visual Studio 2015 offered for XAML-based applications is the Live Visual Tree. While debugging a UWP and WPF application, you can open the Live Visual Tree (see Figure 17-41) via Debug ⇨ Windows ⇨ Live Visual Tree to see the live tree of the XAML elements including its properties in the Live Property Explorer. Using this window, you can click the Selection button to select an element in the UI to see its element in the live tree. In the Live Property Explorer you can directly change properties, and see the results on the running application.

Monitoring and Changing Variables

Sometimes you might prefer to have a more continuous look at values. For that you can use the *Autos*, *Locals*, and *Watch* windows to examine the contents of variables. Each of these windows is designed to monitor different variables:

➤ **Autos**—Monitors the last few variables that have been accessed as the program was executing.

➤ **Locals**—Monitors variables that are accessible in the method currently being executed.

➤ **Watch**—Monitors any variables that you have explicitly specified by typing their names into the Watch window. You can drag and drop variables to the Watch window.

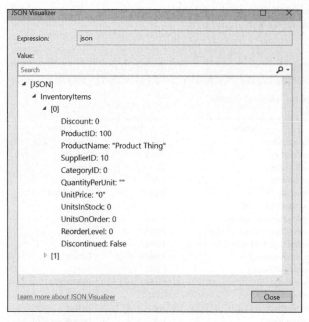

FIGURE 17-40

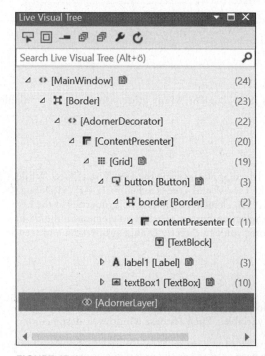

FIGURE 17-41

These windows are only visible when the program is running under the debugger. If you do not see them, select Debug ➪ Windows, and then select the desired menu. The Watch window offers four different windows in case there's so much to watch and you want to group that. With all these windows you can both watch and change the values, enabling you to try different paths in the program without leaving the debugger. The Locals window is shown in Figure 17-42.

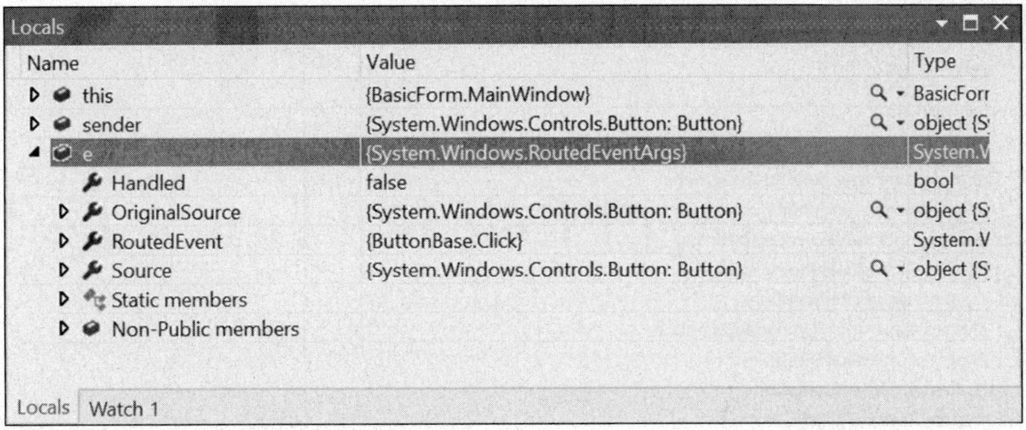

Locals		
Name	**Value**	**Type**
▷ 🌐 this	{BasicForm.MainWindow}	BasicForm
▷ 🌐 sender	{System.Windows.Controls.Button: Button}	object {S}
▲ 🌐 e	{System.Windows.RoutedEventArgs}	System.V
🔧 Handled	false	bool
▷ 🔧 OriginalSource	{System.Windows.Controls.Button: Button}	object {S}
▷ 🔧 RoutedEvent	{ButtonBase.Click}	System.V
▷ 🔧 Source	{System.Windows.Controls.Button: Button}	object {S}
▷ 🔧 Static members		
▷ 🌐 Non-Public members		

Locals   Watch 1

FIGURE 17-42

Another window that doesn't directly relate to the other windows discussed but is still an important one for monitoring and changing variables is the *Immediate window*. This window also makes it possible for you to look at variable values. You can use this window to enter code and run it. This is very helpful when you're doing some tests during a debug session; it enables you to home in on details, try a method out, and change a debug run dynamically.

Exceptions

Exceptions are great when you are ready to ship your application, ensuring that error conditions are handled appropriately. Used well, they can ensure that users are never presented with technical or annoying dialogs. Unfortunately, exceptions are not so great when you are trying to debug your application. The problem is twofold:

➤ If an exception occurs when you are debugging, you often do not want it to be handled automatically—especially if automatically handling it means retiring gracefully and terminating execution! Rather, you want the debugger to help you determine why the exception has occurred. Of course, if you have written good, robust, defensive code, your program automatically handles almost anything—including the bugs that you want to detect!

➤ If an exception for which you have not written a handler occurs, the .NET runtime still searches for one. Unfortunately, by the time it discovers there isn't one, it will have terminated your program. There will not be a call stack left, and you will not be able to look at the values of any of your variables because they will all have gone out of scope.

Of course, you can set breakpoints in your catch blocks, but that often does not help very much because when the catch block is reached, flow of execution will, by definition, have exited the corresponding try block. That means the variables you probably wanted to examine the values of, to figure out what has gone wrong, will have gone out of scope. You will not even be able to look at the stack trace to find what method was being executed when the throw statement occurred because control will have left that method. Setting the breakpoints at the throw statement obviously solves this; but if you are coding defensively, there will be many throw statements in your code. How can you tell which one threw the exception?

Visual Studio provides a very neat answer to all of this. You can configure the exception types where the debugger should break. This is configured in the menu Debug ⇨ Windows ⇨ Exception Settings. With this window (see Figure 17-43) you can specify what happens when an exception is thrown. You can choose to continue execution or to stop and start debugging—in which case execution stops and the debugger steps in at the `throw` statement.

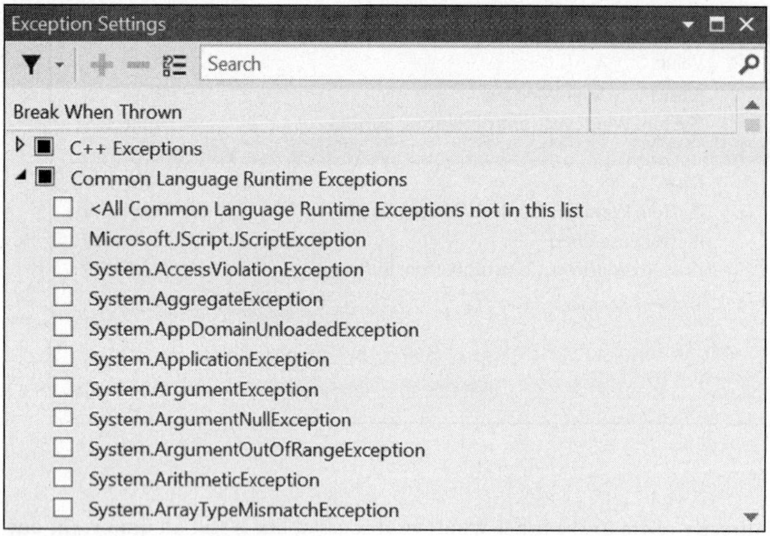

FIGURE 17-43

What makes this a really powerful tool is that you can customize the behavior according to which class of exception is thrown. You can configure to break into the debugger whenever it encounters any exception thrown by a .NET base class, but not to break into the debugger for specific exception types.

Visual Studio is aware of all the exception classes available in the .NET base classes, and of quite a few exceptions that can be thrown outside the .NET environment. Visual Studio is not automatically aware of any custom exception classes that you write, but you can manually add your exception classes to the list, and specify which of your exceptions should cause execution to stop immediately. To do this, just click the Add button (which is enabled when you have selected a top-level node from the tree) and type in the name of your exception class.

Multithreading

Visual Studio also offers great support for debugging multithreaded programs. When debugging multi-threaded programs, you must understand that the program behaves differently depending on whether it is running in the debugger or not. If you reach a breakpoint, Visual Studio stops all threads of the program, so you have the chance to access the current state of all the threads. To switch between different threads you can enable the Debug Location toolbar. This toolbar contains a combo box for all processes and another combo box for all threads of the running application. When you select a different thread, you find the code line where the thread currently halts and the variables currently accessible from different threads. The Parallel Tasks window (shown in Figure 17-44) shows all running tasks, including their statuses, locations, task names, the current threads that are used by the tasks, the application domains, and the process identifiers. This window also indicates when different threads block each other, causing a deadlock.

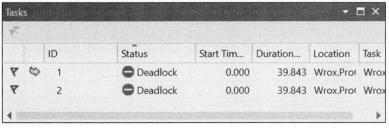

FIGURE 17-44

Figure 17-45 shows the Parallel Stacks window, where you can see different threads or tasks (depending on the selection) in a hierarchical view. You can jump to the source code directly by clicking the task or thread.

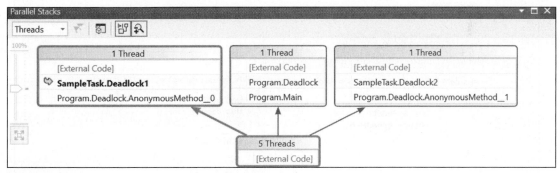

FIGURE 17-45

REFACTORING TOOLS

Many developers develop their applications first for functionality. After the functionality is in place, they *rework* their applications to make them more manageable and more readable. This process is called *refactoring*. Refactoring involves reworking code for readability and performance, providing type safety, and ensuring that applications adhere to standard OO (object-oriented) programming practices. Reworking also happens when updates are made to applications.

The C# environment of Visual Studio 2015 includes a set of refactoring tools, which you can find under the Refactoring option in the Visual Studio menu. To see this in action, create a new class called Car in Visual Studio:

```
public class Car
{
  public string color;
  public string doors;

  public int Go()
  {
    int speedMph = 100;
    return speedMph;
  }
}
```

Now suppose that for the purpose of refactoring, you want to change the code a bit so that the `color` and `door` variables are encapsulated in public .NET properties. The refactoring capabilities of Visual Studio 2015 enable you to simply right-click either of these properties in the document window and select Quick Actions. You see different options for refactoring, such as generating a constructor to fill the fields or to encapsulate the fields as shown in Figure 17-46.

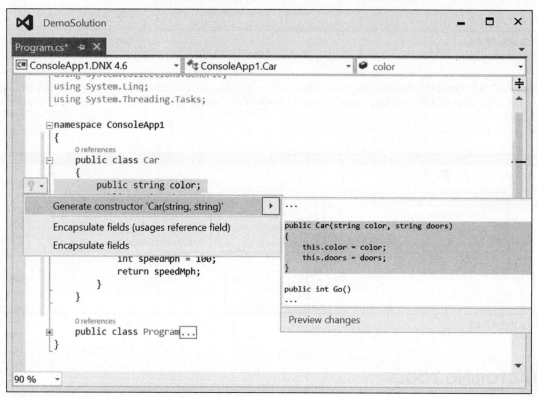

FIGURE 17-46

From this dialog you can provide the name of the property and click the Preview link, or you can directly accept the changes. When you select the button to encapsulate the fields, the code is reworked into the following:

```
public class Car
{
  private string color;
  public string Color
  {
    get { return color; }
    set { color = value; }
  }
  private string doors;
  public string Doors
  {
    get { return doors; }
    set { doors = value; }
  }
}
```

```
  public int Go()
  {
    int speedMph = 100;
    return speedMph;
  }
}
```

As you can see, these code fixes make it quite simple to refactor your code—not only on one page but throughout an entire application. Also included are capabilities to do the following:

➤ Rename method names, local variables, fields, and more

➤ Extract methods from a selection of code

➤ Extract interfaces based on a set of existing type members

➤ Promote local variables to parameters

➤ Rename or reorder parameters

You will find that the refactoring capabilities provided by Visual Studio 2015 offer a great way to get cleaner, more readable, and better-structured code.

ARCHITECTURE TOOLS

Before starting with coding programs, you should have an architectural viewpoint to your solution, analyze requirements, and define a solution architecture. Architecture tools are available with Visual Studio 2015 Enterprise.

Figure 17-47 shows the Add New Item dialog that appears after you create a modeling project. It provides options to create a UML use-case diagram, a component diagram, a class diagram, a sequence diagram, and an activity diagram. The standard UML diagrams are not discussed in this chapter, as you can find several books covering this group. Instead, this section looks at two Microsoft-specific diagrams: *Directed Graph Document* (or *Dependency Graph*) and *Layer Diagram*.

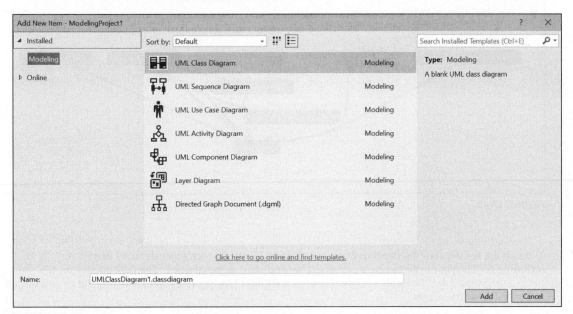

FIGURE 17-47

> **NOTE** *How to create and use UML diagrams is not covered in this book. They are not new, and probably you already know a lot about them. If not, several books are available covering the features of UML diagrams. They are not different with Visual Studio.*

The focus on this section now continues with Microsoft-specific features in regard to architecture tools and analysing applications. Particularly you will get information on creating code maps, layer diagrams, use diagnostic tools to profile applications, code analyzers, and code metrics.

Code Map

With the code map, you can see dependencies between assemblies, classes, and even members of classes. Figure 17-48 shows the code map of a Calculator example from Chapter 26, "Composition," that includes a calculator hosting application and several libraries, such as a contract assembly and the add-in assemblies `SimpleCalculator`, `FuelEconomy`, and `TemperatureConversion`. The code map is created by selecting Architecture ➪ Create Code Map for Solution. This activity analyzes all projects of the solution, displaying all the assemblies in a single diagram and drawing lines between the assemblies to show dependencies. The varying thickness of the lines between the assemblies reflects the degree of dependency. An assembly contains several types and members of types, and a number of types and its members are used from other assemblies.

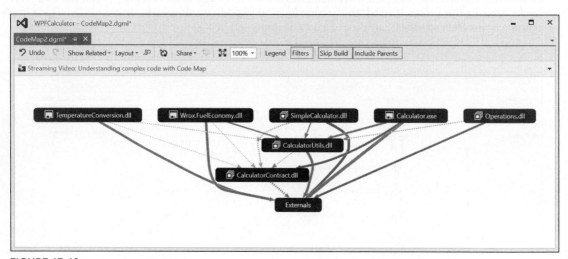

FIGURE 17-48

You can dig deeper into the dependencies, too. Figure 17-49 shows a more detailed diagram, including the classes of the `Calculator` assembly and their dependencies. The dependency on the `CalculatorContract` assembly is shown here as well. In a large graph you can also zoom in and out of several parts of the graph.

You can even go deeper, displaying fields, properties, methods, and events, and how they depend on each other.

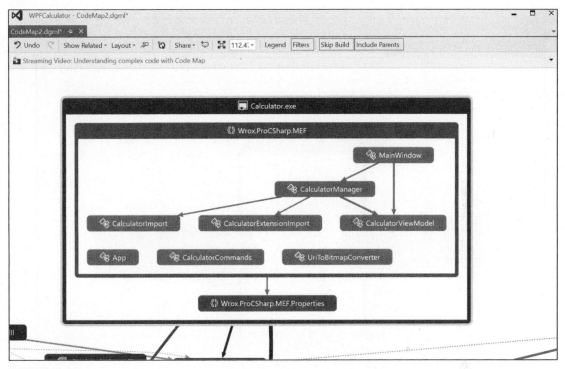

FIGURE 17-49

Layer Diagram

The *layer diagram* is very much related to the code map. You can create the layer diagram out of the dependency graph (or from Solution Explorer by selecting assemblies or classes), or create the layer diagram from scratch before doing any development.

Different layers can define client and server parts in a distributed solution—for example, a layer for a Windows application, one for the service, and one for the data access library, or layers based on assemblies. A layer can also contain other layers.

Figure 17-50 shows a layer diagram with the main layers `Calculator UI`, `CalculatorUtils`, `Contracts`, and `AddIns`. The `AddIns` layer contains inner layers `FuelEconomy`, `TemperatureConversion`, and `Calculator`. The number that's displayed with the layer reflects the number of items that are linked to that layer.

To create a layer diagram, select Architecture ➪ New UML or Layer Diagram ➪ Layer Diagram. This creates an empty diagram to which you can add layers from the toolbox or the Architecture Explorer. The Architecture Explorer contains a Solution View and a Class View from which you can select all items of the solution to add them to the layer diagram. Selecting items and dragging them to the layer is all you need to build the layer diagram. Selecting a layer and clicking the context menu View Links opens the Layer Explorer, shown in Figure 17-51, which displays all the items contained in the selected layer(s).

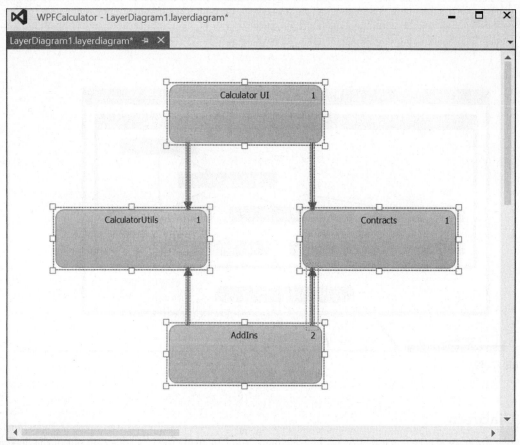

FIGURE 17-50

Name	Categories	Layer	Supports Validation	Identifier
Wrox.FuelEconomy.dll	Assembly, FileSystem.Category.FileOfType.dll	AddIns	True	(Assembly=Wrox.FuelEconomy)
TemperatureConversion.dll	Assembly, FileSystem.Category.FileOfType.dll	AddIns	True	(Assembly=TemperatureConversion)

FIGURE 17-51

During application development, the layer diagram can be validated to analyze whether all the dependencies are on track. If a layer has a dependency in a wrong direction, or has a dependency on a layer that it shouldn't, this architecture validation returns with errors.

ANALYZING APPLICATIONS

The previously discussed architectural diagrams—the dependency graph and the layer diagram—are not only of interest before the coding starts; they also help in analyzing the application and keeping it on the right track to ensure that it doesn't generate inaccurate dependencies. There are many more useful tools available with Visual Studio 2015 that can help you analyze and proactively troubleshoot your application. This section looks at some of these Visual Studio analysis tools.

Similar to the architecture tools, the analyzer tools are available with Visual Studio 2015 Enterprise.

Diagnostics Tools

To analyze a complete run of the application, you can use the diagnostics tools. These tools enable you to find what methods are called, how often methods are called, how much time is spent in what methods, how much memory is used, and much more. With Visual Studio 2015, the diagnostics tools are started automatically when you start the debugger. With the diagnostics tools, you can also see IntelliTrace (historical debugging) events (see Figure 17-52). When you hit a breakpoint, you can have a look at previous information in time such as previous breakpoints, exceptions that were thrown, database access, ASP.NET events, tracing, or user input gestures, such as a user clicking a button. By clicking the information of previous events, you can have a look at local variables, the call stack, and method calls that were done. This makes it easy to find problems without restarting a debug session and setting breakpoints to methods that have been invoked before you see the issue.

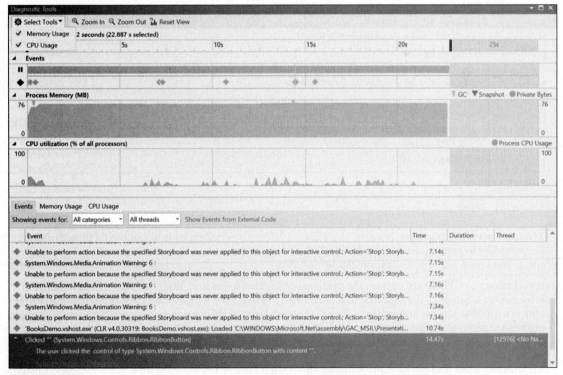

FIGURE 17-52

Another way to start diagnostics tools is to start them via the profiler: Debug ➪ Profiler ➪ Start Diagnostic Tools Without Debugging. Here you have more controls about the features to start (see Figure 17-53). Depending on the project type used, more or fewer features are available. With UWP projects you can also analyze energy consumption, which is an important fact with mobile devices.

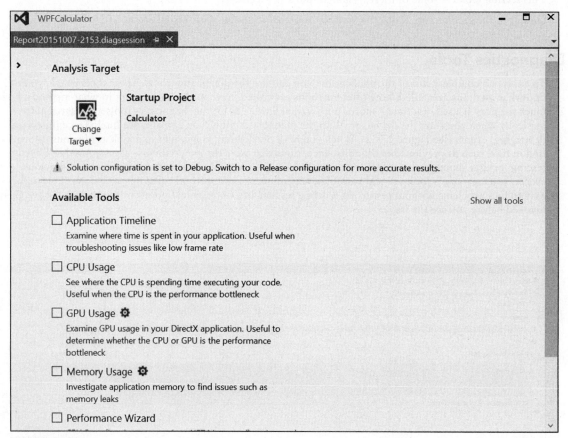

FIGURE 17-53

The first option, Application Timeline (see Figure 17-54), gives information about the UI thread and the time it is spending in parsing, layout, rendering, I/O, and application code. Depending on where the most time is spent, you know where optimization can be useful.

If you select the CPU Usage option, the overhead of monitoring is low. With this option, performance information is sampled after specific time intervals. You don't see all method calls invoked, in particular if they are running just for a short time. Again, the advantage of this option is low overhead. When running a profiling session, you must always be aware that you're monitoring not only the performance of the application, but the performance of getting the data as well. You shouldn't profile all data at once, as sampling all of the data influences the outcome. Collecting information about .NET memory allocation helps you identify memory leaks and provides information about what type of objects need how much memory. Resource contention data helps with the analysis of threads, enabling you to easily identify whether different threads block each other.

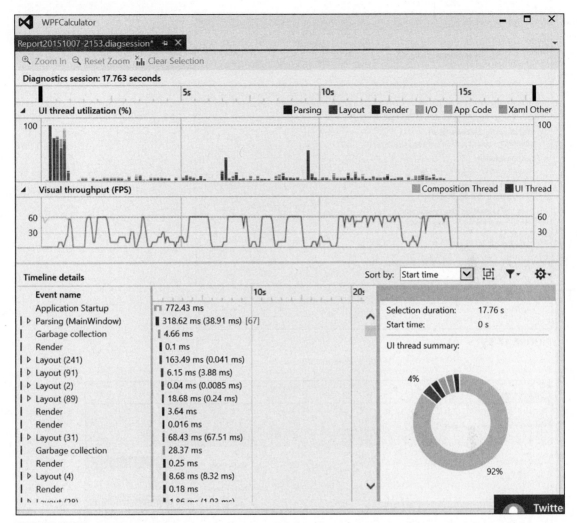

FIGURE 17-54

After configuring the options in the Performance Explorer, you can immediately start the application and run profiling after exiting the wizard. You can also change some options afterward by modifying the properties of a profiling setting. Using these settings, you can decide to add memory profiling with an instrumentation session, and add CPU counters and Windows counters to the profiling session to see this information in conjunction with the other profiled data.

Starting the Performance Wizard (see Figure 17-55), which is the last option in the list, enables you to configure whether you want to monitor the CPU using sampling or using instrumentation, where every method call is instrumented so you can see even small method calls, memory allocation, and concurrency.

Figure 17-56 shows the summary screen of a profiling session. Here you can see CPU usage by the application, a *hot path* indicating which functions are taking the most time, and a sorted list of the functions that have used the most CPU time.

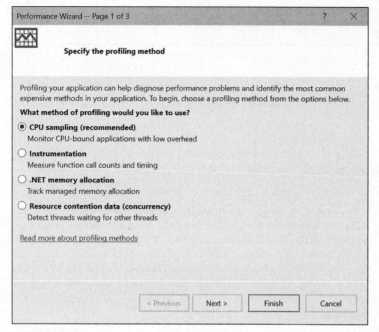

FIGURE 17-55

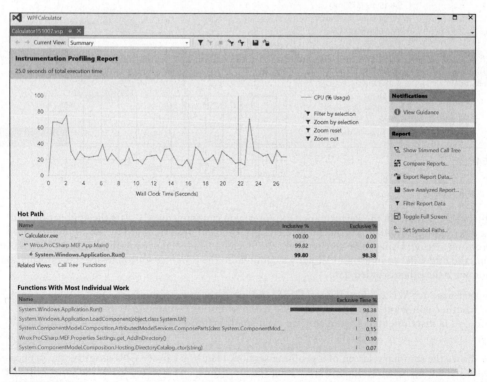

FIGURE 17-56

The profiler has many more screens—too many to show here. One view is a function view that you can sort based on the number of calls made to the function, or the elapsed inclusive and exclusive times used by the function. This information can help you identify methods deserving of another look in terms of performance, whereas others might not be worthwhile because they are not called very often or they do not take an inordinate amount of time.

Clicking within a function, you can invoke details about it, as shown in Figure 17-57. This enables you to see which functions are called and immediately step into the source code. The Caller/Callee view also provides information about what functions have been called by what function.

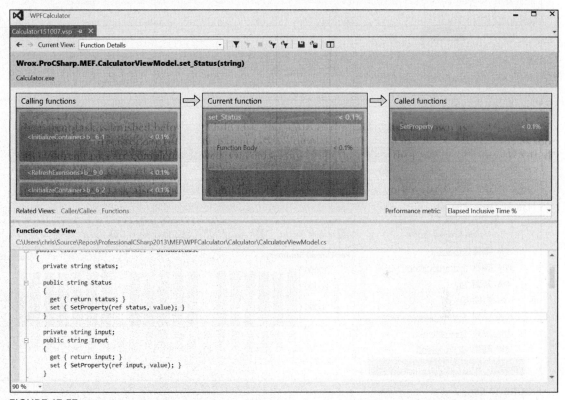

FIGURE 17-57

Profiling is available with Visual Studio Professional. Using the Enterprise Edition, you can configure tier interaction profiling that enables you to view the SQL statements generated and the time spent on ADO.NET queries, as well as information on ASP.NET pages.

Concurrency Visualizer

The Concurrency Visualizer helps you to analyze threading issues with applications. Running this analyzer tool provides a summary screen like the one shown in Figure 17-58. Here, you can compare the amount of CPU needed by the application with overall system performance. You can also switch to a Threads view that displays information about all the running application threads and what state they were in over time. Switching to the Cores view displays information about how many cores have been used. If your application makes use of only one CPU core and it is busy all the time, adding some parallelism features might improve performance by making use of more cores. You might see that different threads are active over time, but only one thread is active at any given point in time. In that case, you should probably change your locking behavior. You can also see if threads are working on I/O. If the I/O rate is high with multiple threads, the disk might be the bottleneck and threads just wait on each other to complete I/O. This behavior might warrant reducing the number of threads doing I/O, or using an SSD drive. Clearly, these analysis tools provide a great deal of useful information.

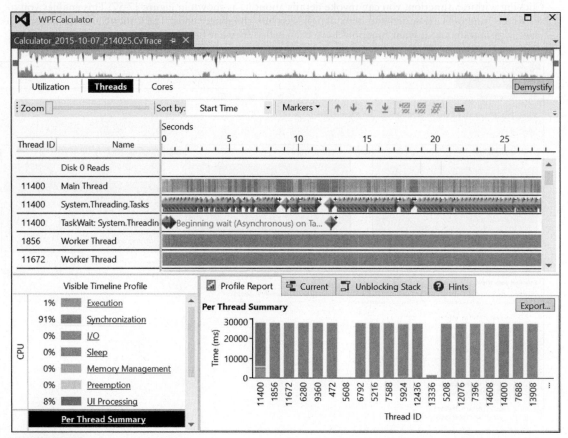

FIGURE 17-58

> **NOTE** *With Visual Studio 2015, you need to download and install the Concurrency Visualizer via Tools ⇨ Extensions and Updates.*

Code Analyzers

A new feature with Visual Studio 2015—with the help of the .NET Compiler Platform—is code analyzers. When you use the API of the compiler, it is easy to create code analyzers and to give guidelines for what should be changed.

> **NOTE** *The .NET Compiler Platform is covered in Chapter 18.*

Of course often it's not necessary to create custom analyzers as there are already many available with NuGet packages. From Microsoft, the `Microsoft.Analyzer.PowerPack` NuGet package offers good code analysis for many scenarios. After you install such an analyzer, you can see it in Solution Explorer in the Analyzers section, which is below the References node.

Code Metrics

Checking code metrics provides information about how maintainable the code is. The code metrics shown in Figure 17-59 display a maintainability index for the complete `Calculator` project of 82, and includes details about every class and method. These ratings are color-coded: A red rating, in the range of 0 to 9, means low maintainability; a yellow rating, in the range of 10 to 19, means moderate maintainability; and a green rating, in the range of 20 to 100, means high maintainability. The *cyclomatic complexity* provides feedback about the different code paths. More code paths means more unit tests are required to go through every option. The *depth of inheritance* reflects the hierarchy of the types. The greater the number of base classes, the harder it is to find the one to which a field belongs. The value for *class coupling* indicates how tightly types are coupled—that is, used with parameters or locals. More coupling means more complexity in terms of maintaining the code.

Hierarchy ▲		Maintainability In...	Cyclomatic Comp...	Depth of Inherita...	Class Coupling	Lines of Code
▲ 🖥 Calculator (Debug)	▨	82	82	9	67	151
▲ { } Wrox.ProCSharp.MEF	▪	82	82	9	67	151
▷ ⚙ App	▪	100	1	3	1	1
▷ ⚙ CalculatorCommands	▪	82	12	1	3	12
▷ ⚙ CalculatorExtensionImport	▪	84	9	1	10	13
▷ ⚙ CalculatorImport	▪	84	9	1	8	13
▷ ⚙ CalculatorManager	▪	69	19	1	34	40
▷ ⚙ CalculatorViewModel	▪	91	12	2	5	19
▷ ⚙ MainWindow	▪	72	16	9	23	40
▷ ⚙ UriToBitmapConverter	▪	74	4	1	9	13
▷ 🖥 CalculatorContract (Debug)	▪	100	8	0	3	0
▷ 🖥 CalculatorUtils (Debug)	▪	94	23	3	13	28
▷ 🖥 FuelEconomy (Debug)	▨	85	28	9	11	44

FIGURE 17-59

SUMMARY

This chapter explored one of the most important programming tools in the .NET environment: Visual Studio 2015. The bulk of the chapter examined how this tool facilitates writing code in C#.

Visual Studio 2015 is one of the easiest development environments to work with in the programming world. Not only does Visual Studio make rapid application development (RAD) easy to achieve, it enables you to dig deeply into the mechanics of how your applications are created. This chapter focused on using Visual Studio for refactoring, multi-targeting, and analyzing existing code.

This chapter also looked at some of the latest project templates available to you through the .NET Framework 4.6, including Windows Presentation Foundation, Windows Communication Foundation, and of course the Universal Windows Platform.

Chapter 18 is about a new feature of C# 6: the new .NET Compiler Platform, codename Roslyn.

18

.NET Compiler Platform

WROX.COM CODE DOWNLOADS FOR THIS CHAPTER

The wrox.com code downloads for this chapter are found at www.wrox.com/go/
professionalcsharp6 on the Download Code tab. The code for this chapter is divided into the
following major examples:

➤ WPFSyntaxTree
➤ SyntaxQuery
➤ SyntaxWalker
➤ SemanticsCompilation
➤ TransformMethods
➤ SyntaxRewriter
➤ PropertyCodeRefactoring

INTRODUCTION

The most important change of C# 6 is that C# has a new compiler delivered by the .NET compiler
platform (code named Roslyn). Originally, the C# compiler was written with C++. Now main parts
of it are created with C# and .NET. The compiler platform is available open source at http://
github.com/dotnet/Roslyn.

One advantage of this update is that Microsoft cleaned up a lot of legacy code that has been written
within the last 20 years. With the new codebase it is a lot easier to implement new features with C#;
the new code is more maintainable. That's the reason you see so many small C# language improvements with version 6. That's a scenario not only Microsoft is seeing; with projects maintained for

many years, it becomes difficult to do updates with the source code. At some point it becomes better to start the project from scratch.

An even bigger advantage of the rewrite of the C# compiler is that now it's possible to take advantage of the compiler pipeline, add functionality to every step of the compiler pipeline, and also analyze and transform source code.

Most developers will take advantage only by using tools within Visual Studio that make use of the .NET Compiler Platform itself, but for many it will be useful to create custom code analyzers (that might be used within the team), and also code transformations—for example, to migrate legacy code and convert it to new technologies.

Where can you see the .NET Compiler Platform used within Visual Studio? One example is the code editor, where the API is used all the time while you're typing. When you implement an interface using the smart tag, there's an interesting difference with Visual Studio 2015 compared to previous versions: when you implement the interface `IDisposable` and click the smart tag, you not only see the Implement Interface and Implement Interface Explicitly options but also the Implement Interface with Dispose Pattern and Implement Interface Explicitly with Dispose Pattern options (see Figure 18-1). With previous editions of Visual Studio, the only automatic way to implement an interface was to automatically generate method stubs and property stubs of the methods and properties that were defined in the interface, where the implementation of the interface throws a `NotImplementedException`. Now you can have different implementations based on the interface type. With the interface `IDisposable`, more than the `Dispose` method gets implemented: The complete pattern required for this interface, such as a `Dispose` method with Boolean argument; a check to see whether the object is already disposed but still invoked; and an optional finalizer are also implemented.

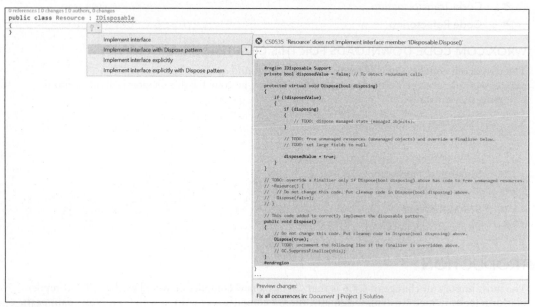

FIGURE 18-1

This chapter describes the features of the .NET Compiler Platform and how you can analyze and transform source code. Using the debugger to learn about the types and members is helpful with all chapters of the book. With this chapter, using the debugger is extremely helpful. The .NET Compiler Platform SDK includes thousands of types and an enormous number of members, so debugging the code really helps you find out what information you can get out of this.

This chapter requires the *Visual Studio 2015 SDK* and the *.NET Compiler Platform SDK Templates for Visual Studio 2015* (available within Extensions and Updates) to be installed with Visual Studio 2015.

The sample projects require the `Microsoft.CodeAnalysis` NuGet package added.

COMPILER PIPELINE

The compiler pipeline consists of the following phases that result in different APIs and features:

➤ **Parser**—Source code is read and tokenized and then it is parsed into a syntax tree. The *Syntax Tree API* is used for formatting, colorizing, and outlining in the source code editor.

➤ **Declaration**—Declarations from the source code and imported metadata are analyzed to create symbols. The *Symbol API* is offered for this phase. The Navigation To feature within the editor and the Object Browser make use of this API.

➤ **Bind**—Identifiers are matched to symbols. *Binding* and *Flow Analysis APIs* are offered for this phase. Features such as Find All References, Rename, Quick Info, and Extract Method make use of this API.

➤ **Emit**—IL code is created and an assembly is emitted. The *Emit API* can be used to create assemblies. The Edit and Continue feature within the editor needs a new compilation that makes use of the Emit phase.

Based on the compiler pipeline, compiler APIs—such as the Syntax API, the Symbol API, the Binding and Flow Analysis API, and the Emit API—are offered. The .NET Compiler Platform also offers an API layer that makes use of another API: the Workspace API. The Workspace API enables you to work with workspaces, solutions, projects, and documents. From Visual Studio you already know a solution can contain multiple projects. A project contains multiple documents. What's new with this list is the workspace. A workspace can contain multiple solutions.

You might wonder that a solution might be enough to work with. However, all trees with the .NET Compiler Platform are immutable and cannot be changed. With every change you're creating a new tree—in other words, a change within the solution creates a new solution. That's why the concept of workspaces—where a workspace can contain multiple solutions—is needed.

SYNTAX ANALYSIS

Let's start with an easy task: syntax analysis with the *Syntax API*. With the Syntax API you can build a tree of syntax nodes from C# source code. The sample application is a WPF application where you can load any C# source file and have the hierarchy of the source file shown within a tree view.

> **NOTE** *XAML and WPF is explained in detail starting in Chapter 29, "Core XAML," and the chapters that follow it. You can read more information about the tree view control in Chapter 34, "Windows Desktop Applications with WPF."*

The sample application defines a user interface with a button control to load the C# source file, a `TreeView` control, and a few `TextBlock` and `ListBox` controls to show the detail of a node as shown in the document outline (see Figure 18-2) and the XAML designer (see Figure 18-3). Data binding is used to bind information content to the UI elements.

FIGURE 18-2

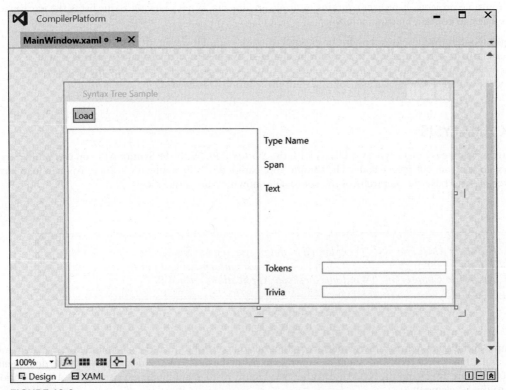

FIGURE 18-3

As you run the application, after clicking the Load button, you are asked for a C# file with the help of the OpenFileDialog class. After you click OK in this dialog, the file is loaded into the syntax tree (code file WPFSyntaxTree/MainWindow.xaml.cs):

```
private async void OnLoad(object sender, RoutedEventArgs e)
{
  var dlg = new OpenFileDialog();
  dlg.Filter = "C# Code (.cs)|*.cs";

  if (dlg.ShowDialog() == true)
  {
    string code = File.ReadAllText(dlg.FileName);
    // load the syntax tree

  }
}
```

> **NOTE** *File input/output (I/O) is discussed in Chapter 23, "Files and Streams."*

The heart of the Syntax API is the SyntaxTree class. A SyntaxTree object is created by parsing the C# file content using CSharpSyntaxTree.ParseText. To get the nodes from the tree, the GetRootAsync (or GetRoot) method returns the root node. All the nodes are of a class derived from the base class SyntaxNode. For showing the root node within the user interface, the SyntaxNode is wrapped with the SyntaxNodeViewModel class before it is added to the Nodes property:

```
private async void OnLoad(object sender, RoutedEventArgs e)
{
    // etc.

    SyntaxTree tree = CSharpSyntaxTree.ParseText(code);
    SyntaxNode node = await tree.GetRootAsync();

    Nodes.Add(new SyntaxNodeViewModel(node));
  }
}
```

The Nodes property is of type ObservableCollection<SyntaxViewModel>. It updates the user interface when the collection changes.

```
public ObservableCollection<SyntaxNodeViewModel> Nodes { get; } =
    new ObservableCollection<SyntaxNodeViewModel>();
```

The class SyntaxNodeViewModel wraps a SyntaxNode for display in the user interface. It defines the property Children to recursively display all children nodes. The Children property accesses all child nodes from the syntax tree by invoking the ChildNodes method and converting the collection of SyntaxNode objects to SyntaxNodeViewModel. This class also defines the Tokens and Trivia properties that are discussed later in this section. The TypeName property returns the name of the real type that is wrapped by the SyntaxNodeViewModel class. This should be a type that derives from the base class SyntaxNode (code file WPFSyntaxTree/ViewModels/SyntaxNodeViewModel.cs):

```
public class SyntaxNodeViewModel
{
  public SyntaxNodeViewModel(SyntaxNode syntaxNode)
  {
    SyntaxNode = syntaxNode;
  }
```

```
public SyntaxNode SyntaxNode { get; }

public IEnumerable<SyntaxNodeViewModel> Children =>
  SyntaxNode.ChildNodes().Select(n => new SyntaxNodeViewModel(n));

public IEnumerable<SyntaxTokenViewModel> Tokens =>
  SyntaxNode.ChildTokens().Select(t => new SyntaxTokenViewModel(t));

public string TypeName => SyntaxNode.GetType().Name;

public IEnumerable<SyntaxTriviaViewModel> Trivia
{
  get
  {
    var leadingTrivia = SyntaxNode.GetLeadingTrivia().Select(
      t => new SyntaxTriviaViewModel(TriviaKind.Leading, t));
    var trailingTrivia = SyntaxNode.GetTrailingTrivia().Select(
      t => new SyntaxTriviaViewModel(TriviaKind.Trailing, t));
    return leadingTrivia.Union(trailingTrivia);
  }
}
}
```

In the user interface, the `TreeView` control binds to the `Nodes` property. The `HierarchicalDataTemplate` defines the look of the items in the tree view. With this data template, the value of the `TypeName` property is shown in a `TextBlock`. For showing all the child nodes, the `ItemsSource` property of the `HierarchicalDataTemplate` is bound to the `Children` property (code file `WPFSyntaxTree/MainWindow.xaml`):

```xml
<TreeView x:Name="treeView" ItemsSource="{Binding Nodes, Mode=OneTime}"
  SelectedItemChanged="OnSelectSyntaxNode"  Grid.Row="1" Grid.Column="0">
  <TreeView.ItemTemplate>
    <HierarchicalDataTemplate ItemsSource="{Binding Children}">
      <StackPanel>
        <TextBlock Text="{Binding TypeName}" />
      </StackPanel>
    </HierarchicalDataTemplate>
  </TreeView.ItemTemplate>
</TreeView>
```

The code file that is opened with the sample application is a simple Hello, World! code file that also includes some comments:

```csharp
using static System.Console;

namespace SyntaxTreeSample
{
  // Hello World! Sample Program
  public class Program
  {
    // Hello World! Sample Method
    public void Hello()
    {
      WriteLine("Hello, World!");
    }
  }
}
```

When you run the application, you can see a tree of the syntax node types shown in the following table. A `SyntaxNode` enables you to walk through the hierarchy and also access the parent node, ancestors, and descendants. When you use the `Span` property, which returns a `TextSpan` struct, the position information within the source code is returned. The following table shows the hierarchy level in the first column (2 is a child node of 1; 3 is a child node of 2); the second column gives the type of the node class; the third column lists the content of the node (if the content is longer, an ellipsis is shown); and the fourth column gives the

`Start` and `End` positions of the `Span` property. With this tree, you can see the `CompilationUnitSyntax` that spans the complete source code. Child nodes of this node are the `UsingDirectiveSyntax` and the `NamespaceDeclarationSyntax`. The `UsingDirectiveSyntax` consists of the using declaration to import the static `System.Console` class. The child node of the `UsingDirectiveSyntax` is the `QualifiedNameSyntax` that itself contains two `IdentifierNameSyntax` nodes:

HIERARCHY LEVEL	SYNTAX NODE TYPE	CONTENT	SPAN— START, END
1	CompilationUnitSyntax	using static System.Console; . . .	0.273
2	UsingDirectiveSyntax	using static System.Console;	0.28
3	QualifiedNameSyntax	System.Console	13.27
4	IdentifierNameSyntax	System	13.19
4	IdentifierNameSyntax	Console	20.27
2	NamespaceDeclarationSyntax	namespace SyntaxTreeSample. . .	32.271
3	IdentifierNameSyntax	SyntaxTreeSample	42.58
3	ClassDeclarationSyntax	public class Program . . .	103.268
4	MethodDeclarationSyntax	public void Hello. . .	179.261
5	PredefinedTypeSyntax	void	186.190
5	ParameterListSyntax	()	196.198
5	BlockSyntax	{ WriteLine(. . .	208.261
6	ExpressionStatementSyntax	WriteLine("Hello,. . .	223.250
7	InvocationExpressionSyntax	WriteLine("Hello. . .	223.249
8	IdentifierNameSyntax	WriteLine	223.232
8	ArgumentListSyntax	("Hello, World!")	232.249
9	ArgumentSyntax	"Hello, World!"	233.248
10	LiteralExpressionSyntax	"Hello, World!"	233.248

The syntax nodes are not all that's needed for a program. A program also needs tokens. For example, the `NamespaceDeclarationSyntax` of the sample program contains three tokens: `namespace`, `{`, and `}`. The child node of the `NamspaceDeclarationSyntax`, the `IdentifierNameSyntax`, has a token with the value `SyntaxTreeSample`, the name of the namespace. Access modifiers are also defined with tokens. The `ClassDeclarationSyntax` defines five tokens: `public`, `class`, `Program`, `{`, and `}`.

To show the tokens in the WPF application, the `SyntaxTokenViewModel` class is defined that wraps a `SyntaxToken` (code file `WPFSyntaxTree/ViewModels/SyntaxTokenViewModel.cs`):

```
public class SyntaxTokenViewModel
{
  public SyntaxTokenViewModel(SyntaxToken syntaxToken)
  {
    SyntaxToken = syntaxToken;
  }

  public SyntaxToken SyntaxToken { get; }

  public string TypeName => SyntaxToken.GetType().Name;

  public override string ToString() => SyntaxToken.ToString();
}
```

For compiling the program, you need nodes and tokens. To rebuild the source file, you need something more: trivia. Trivia defines whitespace and also comments. To show the trivia, the `SyntaxTriviaViewModel` is defined (code file `WPFSyntaxTree/ViewModels/SyntaxTriviaViewModel.cs`):

```
public enum TriviaKind
{
  Leading,
  Trailing,
  Structured,
  Annotated
}

public class SyntaxTriviaViewModel
{
  public SyntaxTriviaViewModel(TriviaKind kind, SyntaxTrivia syntaxTrivia)
  {
    TriviaKind = kind;
    SyntaxTrivia = syntaxTrivia;
  }

  public SyntaxTrivia SyntaxTrivia { get; }
  public TriviaKind TriviaKind { get; }

  public override string ToString() =>
    $"{TriviaKind}, Start: {SyntaxTrivia.Span.Start}, " +
      $"Length: {SyntaxTrivia.Span.Length}: {SyntaxTrivia}";
}
```

When you run the application and open the file `HelloWorld.cs`, you can see the node tree with tokens and trivia as shown in Figure 18-4. With trivia you often see white space, but you also see comments.

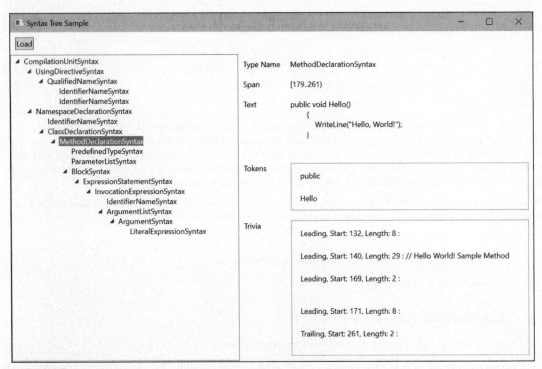

FIGURE 18-4

Using Query Nodes

Besides walking through the nodes by accessing children nodes, you can also create queries to find specific nodes. Queries make use of Language Integrated Query (LINQ).

> **NOTE** *LINQ is explained in Chapter 13, "Language Integrated Query."*

The sample application is a console application. To create a console application that has the NuGet packages for `Microsoft.CodeAnalysis` included, you can create a project from the Extensibility category: *Stand-Alone Code Analysis Tool*. The sample project for showing queries is named `SyntaxQuery`.

A guideline of .NET defines that public or protected members should start with an uppercase letter. The sample application queries all methods and properties of a source file and writes them to the console if they do not start with an uppercase letter. To see a result that shows that type of output, the following nonconforming members are added to the `Program` class. From the following code snippet, the method `foobar` should be ignored as this method doesn't have a `public` access modifier, but the `foo` method and the `bar` property should match (code file `SyntaxQuery/Program.cs`):

```
public void foo()
{
}

private void foobar()
{
}

public int bar { get; set; }
```

Similar to the way the Syntax API was used before, the root node is retrieved using the classes `CSharpSyntaxTree` and `SyntaxTree`:

```
static async Task CheckLowercaseMembers()
{
    string code = File.ReadAllText("../../Program.cs");
    SyntaxTree tree = CSharpSyntaxTree.ParseText(code);
    SyntaxNode root = await tree.GetRootAsync();
    // etc.
```

To get all the nodes in the tree that follow the root node, the `SyntaxNode` class defines the method `DescendantNodes`. This returns all the children of the node and the children's children. The method `ChildNodes` that has been used in the earlier example returns only the direct children. The resulting nodes are filtered with the `OfType` method to return only the nodes of type `MethodDeclarationSyntax`. `MethodDeclarationSyntax` is a class that derives from `SyntaxNode` and represents a node that is a method in the tree. You can use the previous sample `WPFSyntaxTree` to see all the node types for existing source code. The first `Where` method defines the next filter. Here, the identifier of the method (that's the method name) is taken, and just the first character is retrieved. The method `char.IsLower` is used to determine whether the first character is lowercase. The filter returns the method node only if this expression is `true`. This check for lowercase characters doesn't fulfill all the requirements we have. Also, only public members should be returned. This filter is defined by the next `Where` method. To check the `public` access modifier, the `MethodDeclarationSyntax` defines a `Modifiers` property. This property returns all the modifiers of the method. The `Where` method checks whether the `public` modifier belongs to the list of modifiers. The methods where all the conditions apply are written to the console.

```
// etc.
   var methods = root.DescendantNodes()
     .OfType<MethodDeclarationSyntax>()
     .Where(m => char.IsLower(m.Identifier.ValueText.First()))
     .Where(m => m.Modifiers.Select(t => t.Value).Contains("public"));

   WriteLine("Public methods with lowercase first character:");

   foreach (var m in methods)
   {
     WriteLine(m.Identifier.ValueText);
   }
   // etc.
```

Other methods to retrieve children and parent elements are the following:

➤ `DescendantNodesAndSelf` returns the node invoking the method in addition to all descendants.

➤ `DescendantTokens` returns all the descendant tokens

➤ `DescendantTrivia` returns trivia information

➤ `Ancestors` retrieves the parent and parent's parent nodes

Several methods are a combination of the previously listed methods, such as `DescendantNodesAndTokensAndSelf`. You can use these methods with every `SyntaxNode` in the tree.

To retrieve the properties with the same conditions, the syntax is similar. You just need to get the syntax nodes of type `PropertyDescriptionSyntax`:

```
// etc.
   var properties = root.DescendantNodes()
     .OfType<PropertyDeclarationSyntax>()
     .Where(p => char.IsLower(p.Identifier.ValueText.First()))
     .Where(p => p.Modifiers.Select(t => t.Value).Contains("public"));

   WriteLine("Public properties with lowercase first character:");
   foreach (var p in properties)
   {
     WriteLine(p.Identifier.ValueText);
   }
}
```

When you run the application, you see the following result and change the source files accordingly to fulfill the guidelines:

```
Public methods with lowercase first character:
foo
Public properties with lowercase first character:
bar
```

Walking Through Nodes

Besides doing queries, there's another way to efficiently filter source code trees based on specific node types: syntax walkers. A syntax walker visits all nodes within a syntax tree. This means while parsing the syntax tree, different `VisitXXX` methods of the syntax walker are invoked.

The next sample defines a syntax walker that retrieves all using directives to show a list of all needed imports for all C# files from a specified directory.

You create a syntax walker by creating a class that derives from `CSharpSyntaxWalker`. The class `UsingCollector` overrides the method `VisitUsingDirective` to collect all using directives from a syntax tree. The `UsingDirectiveSyntaxNode` that is passed to this method is added to a collection (code file `SyntaxWalker/UsingCollector.cs`):

```
class UsingCollector: CSharpSyntaxWalker
{
  private readonly List<UsingDirectiveSyntax> _usingDirectives =
    new List<UsingDirectiveSyntax>();
  public IEnumerable<UsingDirectiveSyntax> UsingDirectives =>
    _usingDirectives;

  public override void VisitUsingDirective(UsingDirectiveSyntax node)
  {
    _usingDirectives.Add(node);
  }
}
```

The class `CSharpSyntaxWalker` defines virtual methods for many different kind of nodes that can be overwritten. You can use `VisitToken` and `VisitTrivia` to retrieve token and trivia information. You can also collect information about specific source code statements, such as `VisitWhileStatement`, `VisitWhereClause`, `VisitTryStatement`, `VisitThrowStatement`, `VisitThisExpression`, `VisitSwitchStatement`, and many more.

The `Main` method checks for a program argument that contains the directory for the C# source files that should be checked for the using declarations (code file `SyntaxWalker/Program.cs`):

```
static void Main(string[] args)
{
  if (args.Length != 1)
  {
    ShowUsage();
    return;
  }

  string path = args[0];
  if (!Directory.Exists(path))
  {
    ShowUsage();
    return;
  }
}

static void ShowUsage()
{
  WriteLine("Usage: SyntaxWalker directory");
}
```

The method `ProcessUsingsAsync` does all the processing. First, a `UsingCollector` instance is created. To iterate through all the files from the passed directory, the `Directory.EnumerateFiles` method is used with the search pattern `*.cs` to retrieve all C# files. However, automatically generated C# files should be excluded—that's why files with the file extensions `.g.i.cs` and `.g.cs` are filtered out using the `Where` method. Within the following `foreach` statement, the syntax tree is built and passed to the `Visit` method of the `UsingCollector` instance:

```
static async Task ProcessUsingsAsync(string path)
{
  const string searchPattern = "*.cs";
  var collector = new UsingCollector();

  IEnumerable<string> fileNames =
    Directory.EnumerateFiles(path, searchPattern, SearchOption.AllDirectories)
      .Where(fileName => !fileName.EndsWith(".g.i.cs") &&
          !fileName.EndsWith(".g.cs"));
  foreach (var fileName in fileNames)
  {
    string code = File.ReadAllText(fileName);
```

```
      SyntaxTree tree = CSharpSyntaxTree.ParseText(code);
      SyntaxNode root = await tree.GetRootAsync();
      collector.Visit(root);
  }
  // etc.
```

After the `Visit` method is called, the `using` directives are collected within the `UsingDirectives` property of the `UsingCollector`. Before the `using` directives are written to the console, they need to be sorted, and duplicates that can be found in multiple source files need to be removed. Sorting the using directives has some special issues that are solved with the following LINQ query: using static declarations should be put last, and the semicolon that follows the `using` declaration should not be used to define the sort order:

```
  // etc.
    var usings = collector.UsingDirectives;
    var usingStatics =
      usings.Select(n => n.ToString())
        .Distinct()
        .Where(u => u.StartsWith("using static"))
        .OrderBy(u => u);
    var orderedUsings =
      usings.Select(n => n.ToString())
        .Distinct().Except(usingStatics)
        .OrderBy(u => u.Substring(0, u.Length-1));
    foreach (var item in orderedUsings.Union(usingStatics))
    {
      WriteLine(item);
    }
  }
```

When you run the application that passes the directory of the previously created WPF Syntax Tree application, the following using declarations are shown:

```
using Microsoft.CodeAnalysis;
using Microsoft.CodeAnalysis.CSharp;
using Microsoft.Win32;
using System;
using System.Collections.Generic;
using System.Collections.ObjectModel;
using System.ComponentModel;
using System.IO;
using System.Linq;
using System.Reflection;
using System.Resources;
using System.Runtime.CompilerServices;
using System.Runtime.InteropServices;
using System.Windows;
using WPFSyntaxTree.ViewModels;
using static System.Console;
```

SEMANTICS ANALYSIS

The Syntax API is very powerful for getting information about the structure of a source file. However, it doesn't give information about whether the source file compiles, the type of a variable, and so on. To get this information, you need to compile the program, which requires information about assembly references, compiler options, and a set of source files. Using this information is known as *semantics analysis*. Here, you can use the Symbol and Binding APIs. These APIs give information about names and expressions that refer to symbols (types, namespaces, members, variables).

The sample console application gives semantics about the following Hello, World! program that not only defines the method `Hello`, but also a variable named `hello` (code file `SemanticsCompilation/HelloWorld.cs`):

```
using static System.Console;

namespace SemanticsCompilation
{
  // Hello World! Sample Program
  class Program
  {
    // Hello World! Sample Method with a variable
    public void Hello()
    {
      string hello = "Hello, World!";
      WriteLine(hello);
    }

    static void Main()
    {
      var p = new Program();
      p.Hello();
    }
  }
}
```

First, the nodes for the `Hello` method and the `hello` variable are retrieved from the tree using the Syntax API. Using LINQ queries, the `MethodDeclarationSyntax` for the `Hello` method and the `VariableDeclarationSyntax` for the `hello` variable are retrieved from the tree (code file `SemanticsCompilation/Program.cs`):

```
string source = File.ReadAllText("HelloWorld.cs");
SyntaxTree tree = CSharpSyntaxTree.ParseText(source);
var root = (await tree.GetRootAsync()) as CompilationUnitSyntax;

// get Hello method
MethodDeclarationSyntax helloMethod = root.DescendantNodes()
    .OfType<MethodDeclarationSyntax>()
    .Where(m => m.Identifier.ValueText == "Hello")
    .FirstOrDefault();

// get hello variable
VariableDeclaratorSyntax helloVariable = root.DescendantNodes()
    .OfType<VariableDeclaratorSyntax>()
    .Where(v => v.Identifier.ValueText == "hello")
    .FirstOrDefault();
```

Compilation

To get semantic information, you need to compile the code. You can create a compilation that invokes the static `Create` method of the `CSharpCompilation` class. This method returns a `CSharpCompilation` instance that represents compiled code. A parameter that is required is the name of the assembly that is generated. Optional parameters are syntax trees, assembly references, and compiler options. You can also add this information by invoking methods. The sample code adds an assembly reference by invoking the `AddReferences` method and the syntax tree by invoking the method `AddSyntaxTrees`. You could configure compiler options by invoking the method `WithOptions` by passing an object of type `CompilationOptions`, but here only the default options are used (code file `SemanticsCompilation/Program.cs`):

```
var compilation = CSharpCompilation.Create("HelloWorld")
    .AddReferences(
      MetadataReference.CreateFromFile(
        typeof(object).Assembly.Location))
    .AddSyntaxTrees(tree);
```

There's a difference between the actual compiler and the compiler building that was taught in universities not many years ago: It's that a program isn't compiled only once before it is executed; the compilation needs to take place multiple times. By adding some characters in the code editor, compilation needs to show squiggles under the incorrect code if compilation goes wrong. This behavior occurs because of the new compilation process. Using the CSharpCompilation object, small changes could be done where the cache information from the previous compilation can be used. The compiler is built for this process in mind to be high performing with this functionality.

You can add syntax trees and references using AddReferences and AddSyntaxTrees; you remove them using RemoveReferences and RemoveSyntaxTrees. To produce a compilation binary, you can invoke the Emit method:

```
EmitResult result = compilation.Emit("HelloWorld.exe");
```

Using the compilation, diagnostic information of the compilation process can be retrieved. The compilation object also gives some information about symbols. For example, the symbol for the method Hello can be retrieved:

```
ISymbol helloVariableSymbol1 =
    compilation.GetSymbolsWithName(name => name == "Hello").FirstOrDefault();
```

Semantic Model

For making an analysis of the program and accessing symbols with binding to nodes from the tree, you can create a SemanticModel object to invoke the GetSemanticModel method from the CSharpCompilation object (code file SemanticsCompilation/Program.cs):

```
SemanticModel model = compilation.GetSemanticModel(tree);
```

Using the semantic model, you can now analyze control and data flow by passing SyntaxNode nodes to the methods AnalyzeControlFlow and AnalyzeDataFlow of the SemanticModel class. The SemanticModel class also enables you to get information about expressions. Associating nodes from the tree with symbols is the next task in the sample program. This is called *binding*. The methods GetSymbol and GetDeclaredSymbol return symbols of nodes. With the following code snippet, symbols are retrieved from the nodes helloVariable and helloMethod:

```
ISymbol helloVariableSymbol = model.GetDeclaredSymbol(helloVariable);
IMethodSymbol helloMethodSymbol = model.GetDeclaredSymbol(helloMethod);

ShowSymbol(helloVariableSymbol);
ShowSymbol(helloMethodSymbol);
```

To see what information can be accessed from symbols, the method ShowSymbol is defined to access the Name, Kind, ContainingSymbol, and ContainingType properties. With an IMethodSymbol, also the MethodKind property is shown:

```
private static void ShowSymbol(ISymbol symbol)
{
    WriteLine(symbol.Name);
    WriteLine(symbol.Kind);
    WriteLine(symbol.ContainingSymbol);
    WriteLine(symbol.ContainingType);
    WriteLine((symbol as IMethodSymbol)?.MethodKind);
    WriteLine();
}
```

When you run the program, you can see that the hello variable is a Local variable, and the Hello method is a Method. Some of the other symbol kinds are Field, Event, Namespace, and Parameter. The containing symbol of the hello variable is the Hello method; with the Hello method, it's the Program class. The containing type for both checked symbols is Program. The symbol for the Hello method also indicates that it's an `Ordinary` method. Other values of the `MethodKind` enumeration are `Constructor`, `Conversion`, `EventAdd`, `EventRemove`, `PropertyGet`, and `PropertySet`:

```
hello
Local
SemanticsCompilation.Program.Hello()
SemanticsCompilation.Program

Hello
Method
SemanticsCompilation.Program
SemanticsCompilation.Program
Ordinary
```

CODE TRANSFORMATION

After walking through the code tree and getting a glimpse of semantic analysis, it's time to make some code changes. An important aspect with code trees is that they are immutable, thus they cannot be changed. Instead, you use methods to change nodes in the tree, which always returns new nodes and leaves the original ones unchanged.

> **NOTE** *The code trees are stored within immutable collection classes. These collections are discussed in Chapter 12, "Special Collections."*

Creating New Trees

The following code snippet defines a `Sample` class with methods that have a lowercase name. The public methods of this class should be changed to start with an uppercase character (code file `TransformMethods/Sample.cs`):

```
namespace TransformMethods
{
  class Sample
  {
    public void foo()
    {
    }

    public void bar()
    {
    }

    private void fooBar()
    {
    }
  }
}
```

The `Main` method of the console application reads this file and invokes the `TransformMethodToUppercaseAsync` (code file `TransformMethods/Program.cs`):

```
static void Main()
{
  string code = File.ReadAllText("Sample.cs");
  TransformMethodToUppercaseAsync(code).Wait();
}
```

The `TransformMethodToUppercaseAsync` first gets all public nodes in the tree of type `MethodDeclarationSyntax` and have the first character lowercase. All the nodes are added to a collection named `methods`. (This query was previously discussed in the section "Query Nodes.")

```
static async Task TransformMethodToUppercaseAsync(string code)
{
  SyntaxTree tree = CSharpSyntaxTree.ParseText(code);
  SyntaxNode root = await tree.GetRootAsync();

  var methods = root.DescendantNodes()
    .OfType<MethodDeclarationSyntax>()
    .Where(m => char.IsLower(m.Identifier.ValueText.First()))
    .Where(m => m.Modifiers.Select(t => t.Value).Contains("public")).ToList();
  // etc.
}
```

The interesting part follows now. `ReplaceNodes`, a method of `SyntaxNode`, is invoked to replace all the `MethodDeclarationSyntax` nodes that are stored in the collection `methods`. To replace a single node, the `SyntaxNode` class defines the method `ReplaceNode`. For multiple nodes (as in this case), you can use the method `ReplaceNodes`. The first parameter receives all the original nodes that should be replaced. In the sample code, this is the list of `MethodDeclarationSyntax` nodes. The second parameter defines a delegate `Func<TNode, TNode, SyntaxNode>`. With the sample code, `TNode` is of type `MethodDeclarationSyntax` because the collection passed with the first parameter is of this type. The implementation of the delegate is done as a lambda expression receiving the original node as the first parameter and the new node as the second parameter. With the implementation of the lambda expression, the original method name is accessed via `oldMethod.Identifier.ValueText`. With this name, the first character is changed to uppercase and written to the variable `newName`.

For creating new nodes and tokens, you can use the class `SyntaxFactory`. `SyntaxFactory` is a static class that defines members to create different kinds of nodes, tokens, and trivia. Here, a new method name—an identifier—is needed. To create an identifier, you use the static method `Identifier`. When you pass the new method name a `SyntaxToken` is returned. Now it's possible to use the identifier with the `WithIdentifier` method. `WithIdentifier` is a method of the `MethodDeclarationSyntax` for returning a new `MethodDeclarationSyntax` passing the change. Finally, this new `MethodDeclarationSyntax` node is returned from the lambda expression. In turn, the `ReplaceNodes` method that is called with the root object returns a new immutable collection with all the changes:

```
static async Task TransformMethodToUppercaseAsync(string code)
{
  // etc.
  root = root.ReplaceNodes(methods, (oldMethod, newMethod) =>
  {
    string newName = char.ToUpperInvariant(oldMethod.Identifier.ValueText[0]) +
      oldMethod.Identifier.ValueText.Substring(1);
    return newMethod.WithIdentifier(SyntaxFactory.Identifier(newName));
  });

  WriteLine();
  WriteLine(root.ToString());
}
```

When you run the application, you can see that the public methods changed but the private method stays unchanged:

```
namespace TransformMethods
{
  class Sample
  {
    public void Foo()
    {
```

```
    }

    public void Bar()
    {
    }

    private void fooBar()
    {
    }
  }
}
```

For transforming source code, the most important parts are the `SyntaxFactory`, `WithXX`, and `ReplaceXX` methods.

Because the nodes are immutable, and thus properties of the nodes cannot be changed, you need the class `SyntaxFactory`. This class enables you to create nodes, tokens, and trivia. For example:

➤   The method `MethodDeclaration` creates a new `MethodDeclarationSyntax`.

➤   The method `Argument` creates a new `ArgumentSyntax`.

➤   The method `ForEachStatement` creates a `ForEachStatementSyntax`.

You can use the objects created from the `SyntaxFactory` with methods to transform syntax nodes. For example, `WithIdentifier` creates a new node based on the existing node where the identifier is changed. With the sample application, `WithIdentifier` is invoked with a `MethodDeclarationSyntax` object. A few examples of other `WithXX` methods include the following:

➤   `WithModifiers` for changing access modifiers

➤   `WithParameterList` for changing the parameters of a method

➤   `WithReturnType` changing the return type

➤   `WithBody` for changing the implementation of a method

All the `WithXX` methods can only change the direct children of a node. `ReplaceXX` methods can change all descendant nodes. `ReplaceNode` replaces a single node; `ReplaceNodes` (as used with the sample app) replaces a list of nodes. Other `ReplaceXX` methods are `ReplaceSyntax`, `ReplaceToken`, and `ReplaceTrivia`.

Working with Syntax Rewriter

As you've walked through syntax nodes, you've seen the `CSharpSyntaxWalker` as an efficient way to read specific nodes. When you're changing nodes, there's a similar option: a class that derives from `CSharpSyntaxRewriter`. Doing rewrites this way is an efficient way to build up new syntax trees based on existing ones by changing nodes.

The following code snippet is taken for the conversion. The class `Sample` defines full properties `Text` and `X` that should be converted to auto-implemented properties. The other members of the class shouldn't be changed (code file `SyntaxRewriter/Sample.cs`):

```
namespace SyntaxRewriter
{
  class Sample
  {
    // these properties can be converted to auto-implmenented properties
    private int _x;
    public int X
    {
      get { return _x; }
      set { _x = value; }
    }
```

```
        private string _text;
        public string Text
        {
          get { return _text; }
          set { _text = value; }
        }

        // this is already a auto-implemented property
        public int Y { get; set; }

        // this shouldn't be converted
        private int _z = 3;
        public int Z
        {
          get { return _z; }
        }
      }
    }
```

To change syntax nodes, the class `AutoPropertyRewriter` derives from the base class `CSharpSyntaxRewriter`. For accessing symbol and binding information within the rewriter, the `SemanticModel` needs to be passed to the constructor of the rewriter (code file `SyntaxRewriter/AutoPropertyRewriter.cs`):

```
    class AutoPropertyRewriter: CSharpSyntaxRewriter
    {
      private readonly SemanticModel _semanticModel;

      public AutoPropertyRewriter(SemanticModel semanticModel)
      {
        _semanticModel = semanticModel;
      }
      // etc.
```

The base class `CSharpSyntaxRewriter` defines multiple virtual `VisitXX` methods for different syntax node types. Here, the method `VisitPropertyDeclaration` is overridden. This method is invoked when the rewriter finds a property in the tree. Within such a method you can change this node (including its children) to influence the outcome of the rewrite. The implementation of this method first checks whether the property is one that should be changed by invoking the `HasBothAccessors` helper method. If this method returns true, the property is converted by calling `ConvertToAutoProperty`, and returning the converted property with the method. In case the property does not match, it is returned as it is to leave it in the tree:

```
    public override SyntaxNode VisitPropertyDeclaration(
        PropertyDeclarationSyntax node)
    {
      if (HasBothAccessors(node))
      {
        // etc.
        PropertyDeclarationSyntax property = ConvertToAutoProperty(node)
          .WithAdditionalAnnotations(Formatter.Annotation);
        return property;
      }
      return node;
    }
```

Another class, `CSharpSyntaxRewriter`, offers close to 200 methods that can be overridden. Examples are `VisitClassDeclaration` for changing class declarations, and `VisitTryStatement`, `VisitCatchClause`, and `VisitCatchDeclaration`, `VisitCatchFilterClause` for dealing with exception handling. With the sample code, you are—for now—only interested in changing properties; thus the method `VisitPropertyDeclaration` is overridden.

The method `HasBothAccessors` verifies whether the property declaration contains both a get and a set accessor. This method also checks the body of these accessors and that the body defines only a single statement. In case more than one statement is used, the property cannot be converted to an auto-implemented property:

```
private static bool HasBothAccessors(BasePropertyDeclarationSyntax property)
{
  var accessors = property.AccessorList.Accessors;
  var getter = accessors.FirstOrDefault(
    ad => ad.Kind() == SyntaxKind.GetAccessorDeclaration);
  var setter = accessors.FirstOrDefault(
    ad => ad.Kind() == SyntaxKind.SetAccessorDeclaration);

  return getter?.Body?.Statements.Count == 1 &&
         setter?.Body?.Statements.Count == 1;
}
```

The method `ConvertToAutoProperty` uses the `WithAccessorList` method to change the children of the `propertyDeclaration`. The accessor list itself, as well as the children of the accessor list, are created with the help of the `SyntaxFactory` class. `SyntaxFactory.AccessorDeclaration` creates get and `set` accessors passing the `SyntaxKind.GetAccessorDeclaration` and `SyntaxKind.SetAccessorDeclaration` enumeration values:

```
private PropertyDeclarationSyntax ConvertToAutoProperty(
  PropertyDeclarationSyntax propertyDeclaration)
{
  var newProperty = propertyDeclaration
    .WithAccessorList(
      SyntaxFactory.AccessorList(
        SyntaxFactory.List(new[]
        {
          SyntaxFactory.AccessorDeclaration(SyntaxKind.GetAccessorDeclaration)
            .WithSemicolonToken(
              SyntaxFactory.Token(SyntaxKind.SemicolonToken)),
          SyntaxFactory.AccessorDeclaration(SyntaxKind.SetAccessorDeclaration)
            .WithSemicolonToken(
              SyntaxFactory.Token(SyntaxKind.SemicolonToken))
        })));
  return newProperty;
}
```

In the `Program` class, the `AutoPropertyRewriter` is instantiated after retrieving the semantic model. You start the rewrite using the tree by invoking the `Visit` method (code file `SyntaxRewriter/Program.cs`):

```
static async Task ProcessAsync(string code)
{
  SyntaxTree tree = CSharpSyntaxTree.ParseText(code);
  var compilation = CSharpCompilation.Create("Sample")
    .AddReferences(MetadataReference.CreateFromFile(
                   typeof(object).Assembly.Location))
    .AddSyntaxTrees(tree);

  SemanticModel semanticModel = compilation.GetSemanticModel(tree);

  var propertyRewriter = new AutoPropertyRewriter(semanticModel);

  SyntaxNode root = await tree.GetRootAsync().ConfigureAwait(false);
  SyntaxNode rootWithAutoProperties = propertyRewriter.Visit(root);
  // etc.
}
```

When you run the program and check the new code, the full properties are converted to auto-implemented properties. However, the fields from the full properties are still in the code tree. You need to remove them. However, with the method `VisitPropertyDeclaration` only the property can be changed; the field cannot. With an overridden method of the `CSharpSyntaxRewriter` class, only the node received and child elements of the node can be changed; it's not possible to change other nodes in the hierarchy.

You can change properties with the method VisitPropertyDeclaration, and you can change fields with the method VisitFieldDeclaration. The methods of the CSharpSyntaxRewriter are invoked in a top-down manner. VisitNamespaceDeclaration is invoked before VisitClassDeclaration, and then the VisitXX methods of the members of the class follow. This way it is possible to change nodes and descendants, but you can't change ancestors or siblings within the VisitXX method. When fields and properties are in the same hierarchy level of the syntax tree, they are siblings.

Whether the method VisitFieldDeclaration or VisitPropertyDeclaration is called first depends on the order within the code. The field of a property can be declared before or after the property, so there's no guarantee of the order that these methods will be called.

What you can do, though, is access the backing field from the property and add it to a list that is accessible from the AutoPropertyRewriter. The backing field is retrieved using the helper method GetBackingFieldFromGetter, which makes use of the semantic model to access the symbol. With this symbol, a syntax reference to a FieldDeclarationSyntax is retrieved, and information about this field is added to the _fieldsToRemove collection (code file SyntaxRewriter/AutoPropertyRewriter.cs):

```
private readonly List<string> _fieldsToRemove = new List<string>();
public IEnumerable<string> FieldsToRemove => _fieldsToRemove;

public override SyntaxNode VisitPropertyDeclaration(
  PropertyDeclarationSyntax node)
{
  if (HasBothAccessors(node))
  {
    IFieldSymbol backingField = GetBackingFieldFromGetter(
      node.AccessorList.Accessors.Single(
        ad => ad.Kind() == SyntaxKind.GetAccessorDeclaration));
    SyntaxNode fieldDeclaration = backingField.DeclaringSyntaxReferences
      .First()
      .GetSyntax()
      .Ancestors()
      .Where(a => a is FieldDeclarationSyntax)
      .FirstOrDefault();
    _fieldsToRemove.Add((fieldDeclaration as FieldDeclarationSyntax)
      ?.GetText().ToString());
    PropertyDeclarationSyntax property = ConvertToAutoProperty(node)
      .WithAdditionalAnnotations(Formatter.Annotation);
    return property;
  }
  return node;
}
```

The helper method GetBackingFieldFromGetter uses the return statement of the get accessor and the semantic model to get the symbol for the field:

```
private IFieldSymbol GetBackingFieldFromGetter(
  AccessorDeclarationSyntax getter)
{
  if (getter.Body?.Statements.Count != 1) return null;

  var statement = getter.Body.Statements.Single() as ReturnStatementSyntax;
  if (statement?.Expression == null) return null;
  return _semanticModel.GetSymbolInfo(statement.Expression).Symbol
      as IFieldSymbol;
}
```

Now, you can create another syntax rewriter that removes the backing field. The `RemoveBackingFieldRewriter` is a syntax rewriter that removes all fields that are passed to the constructor. The `VisitFieldDeclaration` override checks the received node if it is contained in the field collection that is passed to the constructor, and returns null for the fields that match (code file `SyntaxRewriter/RemoveBackingFieldRewriter.cs`):

```
class RemoveBackingFieldRewriter: CSharpSyntaxRewriter
{
  private IEnumerable<string> _fieldsToRemove;
  private readonly SemanticModel _semanticModel;
  public RemoveBackingFieldRewriter(SemanticModel semanticModel,
      params string[] fieldsToRemove)
  {
    _semanticModel = semanticModel;
    _fieldsToRemove = fieldsToRemove;
  }

  public override SyntaxNode VisitFieldDeclaration(FieldDeclarationSyntax node)
  {
    if (_fieldsToRemove.Contains(node.GetText().ToString()))
    {
      return null;
    }
    return base.VisitFieldDeclaration(node);
  }
}
```

Now you can start another phase to rewrite the syntax tree in the `ProcessAsync` method. After the visit of the property rewriter is done, a new compilation is started, passing the updated syntax tree to invoke the field rewriter (code file `SyntaxRewriter/Program.cs`):

```
SyntaxTree tree = CSharpSyntaxTree.ParseText(code);
var compilation = CSharpCompilation.Create("Sample")
    .AddReferences(MetadataReference.CreateFromFile(
        typeof(object).Assembly.Location))
    .AddSyntaxTrees(tree);

SemanticModel semanticModel = compilation.GetSemanticModel(tree);

var propertyRewriter = new AutoPropertyRewriter(semanticModel);

SyntaxNode root = await tree.GetRootAsync().ConfigureAwait(false);
SyntaxNode rootWithAutoProperties = propertyRewriter.Visit(root);

compilation = compilation.RemoveAllSyntaxTrees()
    .AddSyntaxTrees(rootWithAutoProperties.SyntaxTree);
semanticModel = compilation.GetSemanticModel(
    rootWithAutoProperties.SyntaxTree);
var fieldRewriter = new RemoveBackingFieldRewriter(semanticModel,
    propertyRewriter.FieldsToRemove.ToArray());
SyntaxNode rootWithFieldsRemoved = fieldRewriter.Visit(rootWithAutoProperties);
WriteLine(rootWithFieldsRemoved);
```

When you run the program now, the simple full properties are changed to auto-implemented properties, and the backing fields for the properties are removed.

> **NOTE** *Be aware that this program is just a sample program to show you how to use the .NET compiler platform. This conversion matches full properties that you probably don't like to convert to an auto-implemented property. Before using this program with your code, check the result of the conversion and probably add some more checks to match the properties you want to convert.*

VISUAL STUDIO CODE REFACTORING

Let's get into Visual Studio extensions with code transformations and syntax analysis. You will work with the editor and select Quick Actions within the context menu to add your own features to change code. This integration requires the *Workspace API* defined with the assembly `Microsoft.CodeAnalysis.Workspaces` in addition to the other APIs you've already used in this chapter.

Previously, you've seen how to change a full property to an auto-implemented property using the `CSharpSyntaxRewriter`. Sometimes the reverse is needed: You need to convert an auto-implemented property to a full property. A property to support notifications via the interface `INotifyPropertyChanged` would be a useful implementation of such a scenario. The sample code in this section allows selecting one or more multiple auto-implemented properties within the Visual Studio editor and converting them to full properties.

The project type that you start with is a Code Refactoring (VSIX) project template, and the name for this project is `PropertyCodeRefactoring`. The project template creates two projects: the project `PropertyCodeRefactoring.Vsix` to create a VSIX package, and a portable library named `ProjectCodeRefactoring`.

VSIX Packages

For integration with Visual Studio, you need to create a *VSIX package.* Since Visual Studio 2010, Visual Studio has offered integration via add-ins in the form of VSIX packages. AVSIX is a zip file containing the binaries of the add-in, a manifest file with description about the add-in, and images. After you have installed the add-ins, you can find them in the directory `%LocalAppData%\Microsoft\VisualStudio\14.0\Extensions\<Extension>`.

> **NOTE** *Visual Studio add-ins are based on the Managed Extensibility Framework. This framework is explained in Chapter 26, "Composition."*

Selecting the Project Properties of the VSIX project, the Debug setting (see Figure 18-5) is configured to start Visual Studio on debugging with the option `/rootsuffix Roslyn`. If you start another instance of Visual Studio debugging, the VSIX project enables you to step into the code refactoring source code while using the source code editor in the second Visual Studio instance.

Another setting that's important for VSIX files is the VSIX option with the Project Properties (see Figure 18-6). To debug VSIX files, you need to create a zip file that's loaded from the second instance of Visual Studio. If you select the options Create VSIX Container During Build and Deploy VSIX Content to Experimental Instance for Debugging, you're not required to create and deploy a VSIX package manually every time a new build is done. Instead, a new build is created automatically for debugging purposes.

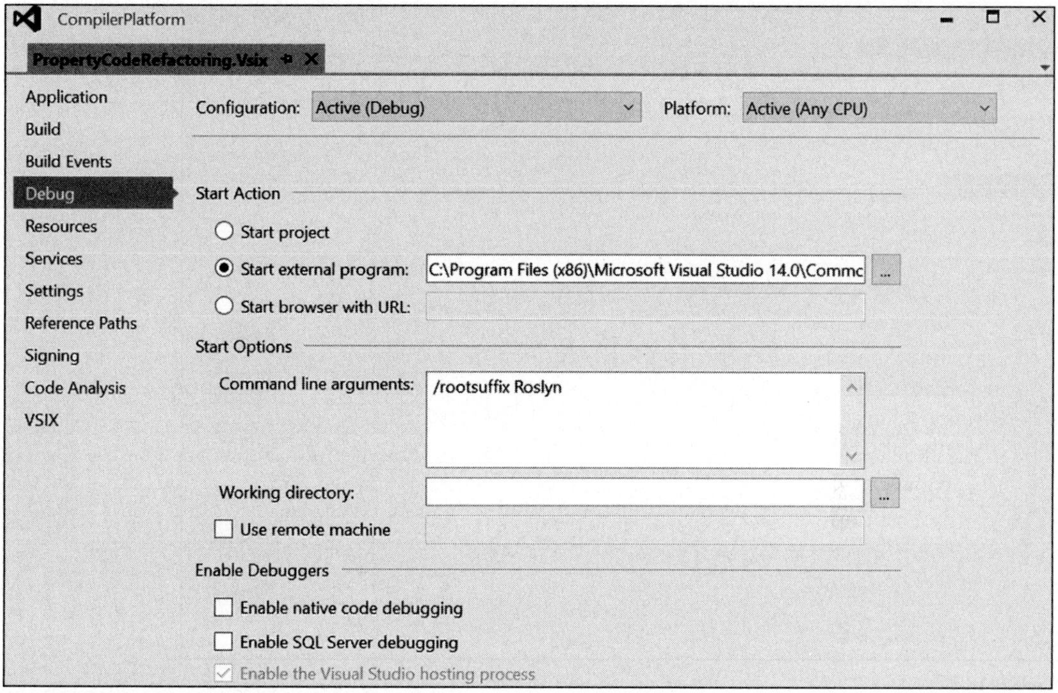

FIGURE 18-5

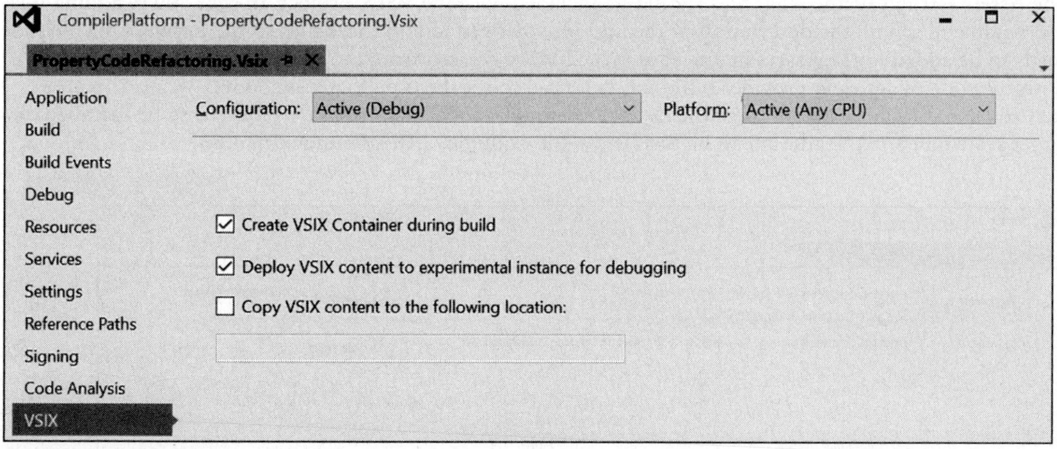

FIGURE 18-6

Now there are more things that need to be done with VSIX projects. The project contains the file source
.extension.vsixmanifest. This file is the description of the add-in and needs to be configured. When you
open this file from Visual Studio, a special designer for configuring Metadata, Install Targets, Assets, and
Dependencies also opens. Metadata configuration is shown in Figure 18-7. With these settings you define
the description, license, release notes, and images that should show up. When you configure Install Targets,
you define your Visual Studio edition and what add-in should be available. With Visual Studio 2015, you
can define the add-in to be available only with the Enterprise edition or also with the Professional and
Community editions. You can also define that the add-in should be available with the Visual Studio shell.
The shell of Visual Studio is used with several projects from Microsoft or third parties.

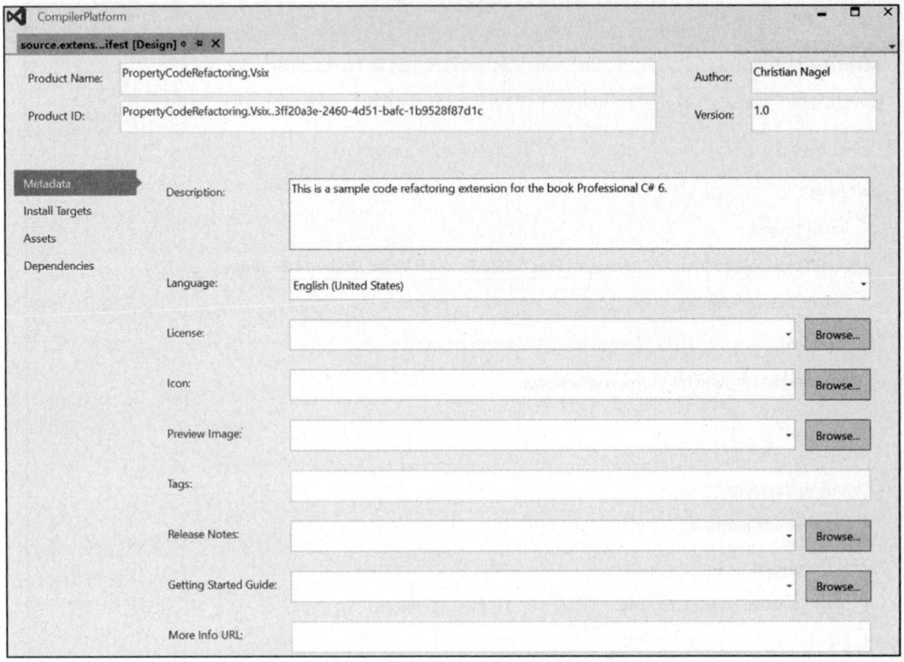

FIGURE 18-7

The Assets settings define what files should be included with the VSIX project. In case you're adding images and readme files with the description of the add-in, you need to add these files to the Assets. One file that needs to be added to the Assets in any case is the binary created from the other project (see Figure 18-8). With the code refactoring provider building, you need to set the type to a `Microsoft.VisualStudio.MefComponent`. The last settings of the designer define Dependencies that are required to be installed on the target system before the add-in can be installed—for example, .NET Framework 4.6.

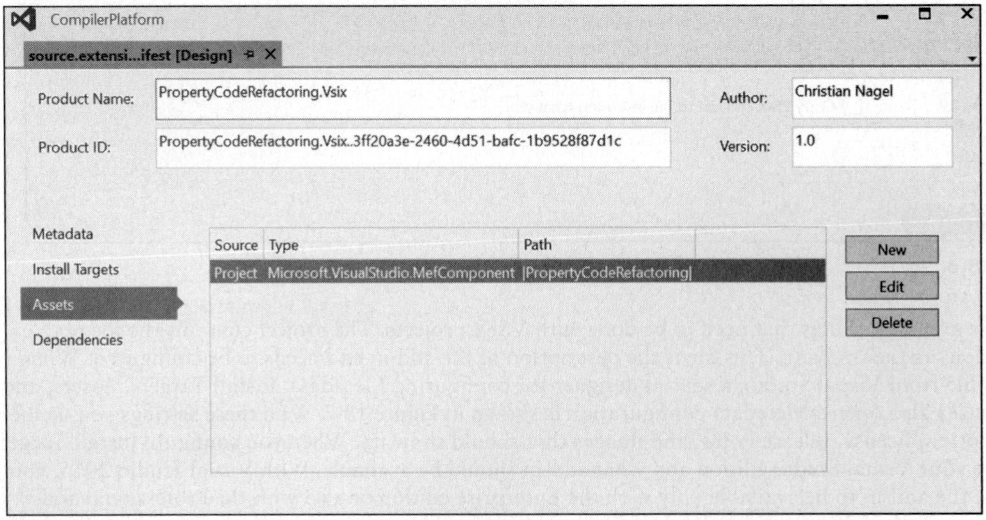

FIGURE 18-8

Code Refactoring Provider

Now that you've configured the VSIX package, let's get into the source code. The generated class `PropertyCodeRefactoringProvider` makes use of the attribute `ExportCodeRefactoringProvider`. This is an attribute to define a MEF part that can be included with Visual Studio. The base class `CodeRefactoringProvider` is a class defined by the Workspace API in the assembly `Microsoft.CodeAnalysis.Workspaces` (code file `PropertyCodeRefactoring/CodeRefactoringProvider.cs`):

```
[ExportCodeRefactoringProvider(LanguageNames.CSharp,
    Name = nameof(PropertyCodeRefactoringProvider)), Shared]
internal class PropertyCodeRefactoringProvider: CodeRefactoringProvider
{
 // etc.
}
```

The base class `CodeRefactoringProvider` defines the method `ComputeRefactoringsAsync` that is invoked when the user of the code editor starts Quick Actions in the context menu. Based on the selection of the user, with the implementation of this method, it needs to be decided whether the add-in should offer one of the options to allow code changes. The parameter `CodeRefactoringContext` makes it possible to access the user selection via the `Span` property and access the complete document via the `Document` property. With the implementation, the root node of the document and the selected node are retrieved:

```
public sealed override async Task ComputeRefactoringsAsync(
    CodeRefactoringContext context)
{
  SyntaxNode root = await context.Document.GetSyntaxRootAsync(
      context.CancellationToken).ConfigureAwait(false);

  SyntaxNode selectedNode = root.FindNode(context.Span);
  // etc.
}
```

The `Document` class that is returned from the `Document` property allows accessing the syntax root and tree nodes (`GetSyntaxRootAsync`, `GetSyntaxTreeAsync`), as well as the semantic model (`GetSemanticModelAsync`). You also have access to all the text changes (`GetTextChangesAsync`).

Only when an auto-implemented property is selected will the code refactoring provider continue its work. That's why next the `selectedNode` is checked to see whether it is of type `PropertyDeclarationSyntax`. The check for `PropertyDeclarationSyntax` is not enough in that the code refactoring should only apply for auto-implemented properties. That's the reason for the check by invoking the helper method `IsAutoImplementedProperty`:

```
public sealed override async Task ComputeRefactoringsAsync(
    CodeRefactoringContext context)
{
  // etc.
  var propertyDecl = selectedNode as PropertyDeclarationSyntax;
  if (propertyDecl == null || !IsAutoImplementedProperty(propertyDecl))
  {
    return;
  }
  // etc.
}
```

The implementation of the helper method `IsAutoImplementedProperty` verifies that both `get` and `set` accessors exist, and the body of these accessors is empty:

```
private bool IsAutoImplementedProperty(PropertyDeclarationSyntax propertyDecl)
{
  SyntaxList<AccessorDeclarationSyntax> accessors =
      propertyDecl.AccessorList.Accessors;
```

```
        AccessorDeclarationSyntax getter = accessors.FirstOrDefault(
            ad => ad.Kind() == SyntaxKind.GetAccessorDeclaration);
        AccessorDeclarationSyntax setter = accessors.FirstOrDefault(
            ad => ad.Kind() == SyntaxKind.SetAccessorDeclaration);
        if (getter == null || setter == null) return false;
        return getter.Body == null && setter.Body == null;
    }
```

If the selected code consists of an auto-implemented property, a `CodeAction` is created, and this action is registered for code refactoring. A `CodeAction` is created by invoking the static `Create` method. The first parameter defines the title that is shown to the user. With this name, the user can apply the code action. The second parameter is a delegate that receives a `CancellationToken` and returns `Task<Document>`. When the user cancels the action, the `CancellationToken` gives information that cancellation is requested, and the task can stop. The `Document` that needs to be returned contains the changes from the code refactoring action. The delegate is implemented as a lambda expression to invoke the method `ChangeToFullPropertyAsync`.

```
    public sealed override async Task ComputeRefactoringsAsync(
        CodeRefactoringContext context)
    {
        // etc.
        var action = CodeAction.Create("Apply full property",
            cancellationToken =>
                ChangeToFullPropertyAsync(context.Document, propertyDecl,
                    cancellationToken));

        context.RegisterRefactoring(action);
    }
```

> **NOTE** *Cancellation tokens are explained in Chapter 15, "Asynchronous Programming."*

The method `ChangeToFullPropertyAsync` retrieves the semantic model and root node from the document, and it invokes the static method `ImplementFullProperty` with the class `CodeGeneration`:

```
    private async Task<Document> ChangeToFullPropertyAsync(
        Document document, PropertyDeclarationSyntax propertyDecl,
        CancellationToken cancellationToken)
    {
        SemanticModel model =
            await document.GetSemanticModelAsync(cancellationToken);
        var root = await document.GetSyntaxRootAsync(
            cancellationToken) as CompilationUnitSyntax;

        document = document.WithSyntaxRoot(
            CodeGeneration.ImplementFullProperty(root, model, propertyDecl,
            document.Project.Solution.Workspace));
        return document;
    }
```

The code generation class needs to change the auto-implemented property to a full property and add a field as member of the class that needs to be used within the property implementation. To do this, the method `ImplementFullProperty` first retrieves all information needed to create the field and property: The type declaration is retrieved by accessing the ancestor element of the property that is going to change, and the type symbol of the property is retrieved with the help of the semantic model. The name of the backing field is created by changing the first letter of the property name to lowercase, and by prefixing it with an underscore. After that, the nodes `propertyDecl` and `typeDecl` are replaced by new versions by invoking the method `ReplaceNodes`. You've already seen the `ReplaceNodes` method in the "Code Transformation" section.

Here's an interesting use of the `ReplaceNodes` method to replace nodes of different types. Here, a `PropertyDeclarationSyntax` and a `TypeDeclarationSyntax` node need to be replaced. The `PropertyDeclarationSyntax` node is the node that represents the property that is updated for the full property syntax. The `TypeDeclarationSyntax` node needs to be updated to add the variable field. It's of great help that the method that is invoked by `ReplaceNodes` (as defined by the delegate parameter) receives both the original and the updated node. Remember, the trees used with the .NET Compiler Platform are immutable. When the first method that is invoked changes a node, the second method call needs to take the updates of the first method to create its own result. The method `ExpandProperty` and `ExpandType` are invoked to make the necessary changes for the property and type nodes (code file `PropertyCodeRefactoring/CodeGeneration.cs`):

```
internal static class CodeGeneration
{
  internal static CompilationUnitSyntax ImplementFullProperty
    CompilationUnitSyntax root,
    SemanticModel model,
    PropertyDeclarationSyntax propertyDecl,
    Workspace workspace)
  {
    TypeDeclarationSyntax typeDecl =
      propertyDecl.FirstAncestorOrSelf<TypeDeclarationSyntax>();
    string propertyName = propertyDecl.Identifier.ValueText;
    string backingFieldName =
      $"_{char.ToLower(propertyName[0])}{propertyName.Substring(1)}";
    ITypeSymbol propertyTypeSymbol =
      model.GetDeclaredSymbol(propertyDecl).Type;

    root = root.ReplaceNodes(
      new SyntaxNode[] { propertyDecl, typeDecl },
      (original, updated) =>
        original.IsKind(SyntaxKind.PropertyDeclaration)
        ? ExpandProperty((PropertyDeclarationSyntax)original,
          (PropertyDeclarationSyntax)updated, backingFieldName) as SyntaxNode
        : ExpandType((TypeDeclarationSyntax)original,
          (TypeDeclarationSyntax)updated, propertyTypeSymbol, backingFieldName,
          model, workspace) as SyntaxNode
    );

    return root;
  }
  // etc.
}
```

The method `ExpandProperty` changes the get and set accessor using the `WithAccessorList` method by passing newly created accessor methods using curly braces (`SyntaxFactory.Block`) and adding statements to set and get the value within the block. The returned property declaration is annotated with a note that the property is updated. This annotation can be used on adding the field to the type to position the field just before the property:

```
private static SyntaxAnnotation UpdatedPropertyAnnotation =
  new SyntaxAnnotation("UpdatedProperty");

private static PropertyDeclarationSyntax ExpandProperty(
    PropertyDeclarationSyntax original,
    PropertyDeclarationSyntax updated,
    string backingFieldName)
{
```

```
AccessorDeclarationSyntax getter =
  original.AccessorList.Accessors.FirstOrDefault(
    ad => ad.Kind() == SyntaxKind.GetAccessorDeclaration);
var returnFieldStatement =
  SyntaxFactory.ParseStatement($"return {backingFieldName};");
getter = getter
  .WithBody(SyntaxFactory.Block(
    SyntaxFactory.SingletonList(returnFieldStatement)))
  .WithSemicolonToken(default(SyntaxToken));

AccessorDeclarationSyntax setter =
  original.AccessorList.Accessors.FirstOrDefault(
    ad => ad.Kind() == SyntaxKind.SetAccessorDeclaration);

var setPropertyStatement = SyntaxFactory.ParseStatement(
  $"{backingFieldName} = value;");
setter = setter.WithBody(SyntaxFactory.Block(SyntaxFactory.SingletonList(
  setPropertyStatement)))
.WithSemicolonToken(default(SyntaxToken));

updated = updated
  .WithAccessorList(SyntaxFactory.AccessorList(
    SyntaxFactory.List(new[] { getter, setter })))
  .WithAdditionalAnnotations(Formatter.Annotation)
  .WithAdditionalAnnotations(UpdatedPropertyAnnotation);
return updated;
}
```

After adding the full property syntax, let's add the field. The previously shown method `ImplementFullProperty` invokes the methods `ExpandProperty` and `ExpandType`. `ExpandType` calls the method `WithBackingField` on the `TypeDeclarationSyntax` object:

```
private static TypeDeclarationSyntax ExpandType(
  TypeDeclarationSyntax original,
  TypeDeclarationSyntax updated,
  ITypeSymbol typeSymbol,
  string backingFieldName,
  SemanticModel model,
  Workspace workspace)
{
  return updated.WithBackingField(typeSymbol, backingFieldName, model,
    workspace);
}
```

The method `WithBackingField` is an extension method that first looks for the annotation on the property to position the newly created field just before the property using the method `InsertNodesBefore`. The field itself is created by calling the helper method `GenerateBackingField`:

```
private static TypeDeclarationSyntax WithBackingField(
  this TypeDeclarationSyntax node,
  ITypeSymbol typeSymbol,
  string backingFieldName,
  SemanticModel model,
  Workspace workspace)
{
  PropertyDeclarationSyntax property =
    node.ChildNodes().Where(n =>
      n.HasAnnotation(UpdatedPropertyAnnotation))
        .FirstOrDefault() as PropertyDeclarationSyntax;
  if (property == null)
  {
```

```
        return null;
    }

    MemberDeclarationSyntax fieldDecl =
        GenerateBackingField(typeSymbol, backingFieldName, workspace);
    node = node.InsertNodesBefore(property, new[] { fieldDecl });
    return node;
}
```

The implementation of the GenerateBackingField method creates a FieldDeclarationSyntax node using the ParseMember helper method using the term _field_Type_ as a placeholder for the type. Within this field declaration, the type is replaced by the SyntaxNode type returned form the syntax generator:

```
private static MemberDeclarationSyntax GenerateBackingField(
    ITypeSymbol typeSymbol,
    string backingFieldName,
    Workspace workspace)
{
    var generator = SyntaxGenerator.GetGenerator(
        workspace, LanguageNames.CSharp);
    SyntaxNode type = generator.TypeExpression(typeSymbol);
    FieldDeclarationSyntax fieldDecl =
        ParseMember($"private _field_Type_ {backingFieldName};") as
            FieldDeclarationSyntax;
    return fieldDecl.ReplaceNode(fieldDecl.Declaration.Type,
        type.WithAdditionalAnnotations(Simplifier.SpecialTypeAnnotation));
}
```

The helper method ParseMember makes a small compilation unit with the SyntaxFactory and returns the syntax node of the member that is passed to the method:

```
private static MemberDeclarationSyntax ParseMember(string member)
{
    MemberDeclarationSyntax decl =
        (SyntaxFactory.ParseCompilationUnit($"class x {{\r\n{member}\r\n}}")
            .Members[0] as ClassDeclarationSyntax).Members[0];
    return decl.WithAdditionalAnnotations(Formatter.Annotation);
}
```

With all this in place, you can debug the VSIX project, which in turn starts another instance of Visual Studio. In the new Visual Studio instance, you can open a project or create a new one, define an auto-implemented property, select it, and choose the Quick Action context menu. This in turn invokes the code refactoring provider that shows the generated result that you can use. When you use the second instance of Visual Studio for editing, you can use the first one to debug through the code refactoring provider.

SUMMARY

In this chapter, you've seen the big world of the .NET Compiler Platform. It's not easy to cover this technology just within one chapter. Multiple books can be written about it. However, with this one chapter you've seen all the important parts of this technology covering different aspects such as querying nodes from source code using LINQ queries, as well as a syntax walker. You've seen semantic analysis for retrieving symbol information. With code transformation, you've seen how you can use the WithXX and ReplaceXX methods to create new syntax trees based on existing ones. The final part of this chapter showed you how to use all the previous aspects together with the Workspace API to create a code refactoring provider to be used within Visual Studio.

The next chapter shows another important aspect of Visual Studio to create different tests to check source code for functionality.

19

Testing

WROX.COM CODE DOWNLOADS FOR THIS CHAPTER

The wrox.com code downloads for this chapter are found at www.wrox.com/go/professionalcsharp6 on the Download Code tab. The code for this chapter is divided into the following major examples:

➤ Unit Testing Sample

➤ MVVM Sample

➤ Web Application Sample

> **NOTE** *UI Testing and Web Testing from this chapter requires Visual Studio Enterprise edition. Unit testing can also be done with Visual Studio Professional.*

OVERVIEW

Application development is becoming agile. When using waterfall process models to analyze the requirements, it's unusual that you design the application architecture, do the implementation, and then find out two or three years later that you built an application that is not needed by the user. Instead, software development becomes agile with faster release cycles, and early participation of the end users. Just have a look at Windows 10: With millions of Windows insiders who give feedback to early builds, updates happen every few months or even weeks. There was one special week during the Beta program of Windows 10 when Windows insiders received three builds of Windows 10 within one week. Windows 10 is a huge program, but Microsoft managed to change development in a big way. Also, if you participate in the open-source project of .NET Core, you can get nightly builds of NuGet packages. If you're adventurous, you might even write a book about an upcoming technology.

With such fast and continuous changes—and nightly builds that you are creating—you can't wait for insiders or end users to find all the issues. Windows 10 insiders wouldn't have been happy with Windows 10 crashing every few minutes. How often have you done a change in the implementation of a method to find out something that doesn't seem related is not working anymore? You might have tried to avoid such issues by not changing the method and creating a new one by copying the code and doing the necessary changes there, which in turn creates a maintenance nightmare. It happens too easily to fix a method in one place, but miss the other ones with code duplicates. Visual Studio 2015 can find out about code duplicates.

You can avoid issues like these. Create tests for your methods, and let the tests run automatically on checking in the source code or during nightly builds. Creating tests from the start increases the cost for the project from the beginning, but as the project processes and during maintenance, creating tests has advantages and reduces the overall project cost.

This chapter explains different kinds of tests, starting with *unit tests*, which are tests for small functionality. These tests should verify the functionality of the smallest testable parts of an application—for example, methods. When you pass different input values, a unit test should check all possible paths through a method. Visual Studio 2015 has a great enhancement for creating unit tests, *IntelliTest*, which is covered in this chapter. The *Fakes Framework* enables you to isolate dependencies of outside parts of the method. Of course, instead of using *shims* it would be better to use *dependency injection*, but this cannot be used everywhere.

MSTest is a part of Visual Studio used for creating unit tests. When .NET Core was built, MSTest did not support creating tests for .NET Core libraries and applications (nowadays MSTest supports .NET Core). That's why Microsoft itself is using xUnit to create unit tests for .NET Core. This chapter covers both Microsoft's test framework MSTest and xUnit.

With *web testing* you can test web applications, send HTTP requests, and simulate a load of users. Creating these kinds of tests enables you to simulate different user loads and allow stress testing. You can use test controllers to create higher loads to simulate thousands of users and thus also know what infrastructure you need and whether your application is scalable.

The final testing feature covered in this chapter is UI testing. You can create automated tests of your XAML-based applications. Of course, it is a lot easier to create unit tests for your view models and the view components with ASP.NET, but it's not possible to cover every aspect of testing in this chapter. You can automate *UI testing*. Just imagine the hundreds of different Android mobile devices that are available. Would you buy one of every model to test your app manually on every device? It's better to use a cloud service and send the app to be tested where the app is indeed installed on hundreds of devices. Don't assume humans will start the app in the cloud on hundreds of devices and click through the possible interactions of the app. This needs to be automated using UI tests.

First, let's start creating unit tests.

UNIT TESTING WITH MSTEST

Writing unit tests helps with code maintenance. For example, when you're performing a code update, you want to be confident that the update isn't going to break something else. Having automatic unit tests in place helps to ensure that all functionality is retained after code changes are made. Visual Studio 2015 offers a unit testing framework, and you can also use other testing frameworks from within Visual Studio.

Creating Unit Tests with MSTest

The following example tests a very simple method in a class library named `UnitTestingSamples`. This is a .NET 4.6 class library because, as mentioned, at present .NET Core doesn't work with the MSTest environment. Of course, you can create any other MSBuild-based project. The class `DeepThought` contains the `TheAnswerToTheUltimateQuestionOfLifeTheUniverseAndEverything` method, which returns 42 as a result (code file `UnitTestingSamples/DeepThought.cs`):

```
public class DeepThought
{
  public int TheAnswerOfTheUltimateQuestionOfLifeTheUniverseAndEverything() => 42;
}
```

To ensure that nobody changes the method to return a wrong result (maybe someone who didn't read *The Hitchhiker's Guide to the Galaxy*), a unit test is created. To create a unit test, you use the Unit Test Project template that's available within the group of Visual C# projects. An easy way to start creating a unit test project is by selecting a method (for example, the method `TheAnswerToTheUltimateQuestionOfLifeTheUniverseAndEverything`), right-click to open the context menu or use the two-finger single-touch on the touchpad, or click the context menu key on the keyboard, or (in case your keyboard does not have a context menu key, press Shift + F10, or FN + Shift + F10 if the function keys are configured as secondary keys), and select the Create Unit Tests. The dialog shown in Figure 19-1 pops up where you can select one of the installed Test Frameworks, and you can decide to create a new testing project or select an existing one. Also, you can specify different names, such as the name of the test project, namespace names, filenames, class names, and method names. By default, Tests or Test is added as postfix, but you can decide to change this. From this dialog, you can also install additional test frameworks.

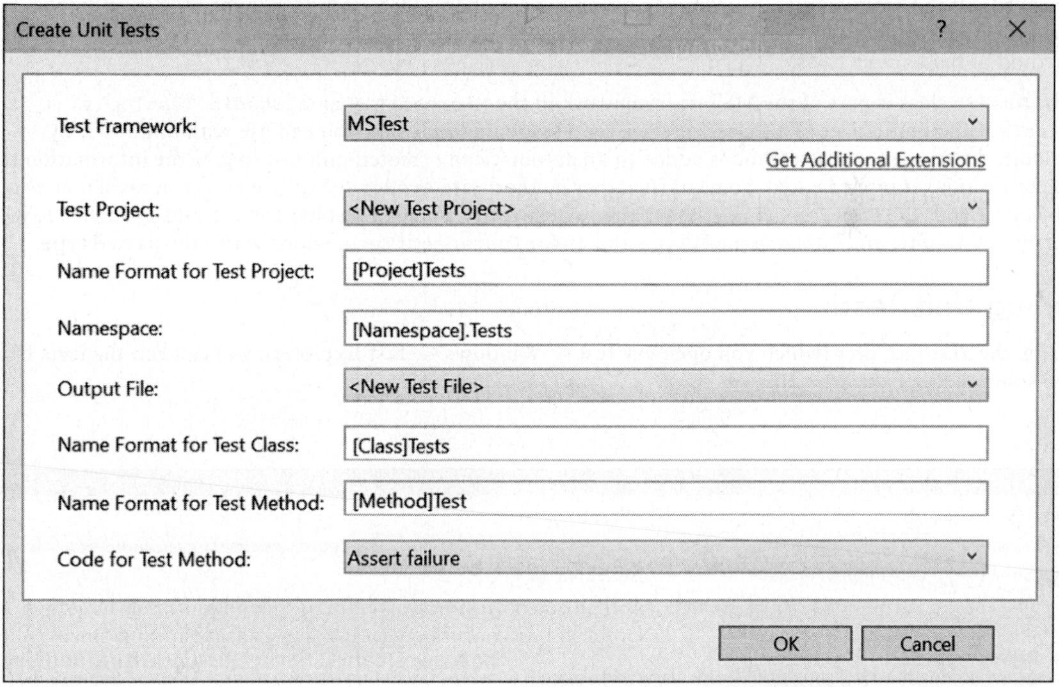

Create Unit Tests	? ✕
Test Framework:	MSTest ⌄
	Get Additional Extensions
Test Project:	\<New Test Project\> ⌄
Name Format for Test Project:	[Project]Tests
Namespace:	[Namespace].Tests
Output File:	\<New Test File\> ⌄
Name Format for Test Class:	[Class]Tests
Name Format for Test Method:	[Method]Test
Code for Test Method:	Assert failure ⌄
	OK Cancel

FIGURE 19-1

A unit test class is marked with the `TestClass` attribute, and a test method is marked with the `TestMethod` attribute. The implementation creates an instance of `DeepThought` and invokes the method that is to be tested: `TheAnswerToTheUltimateQuestionOfLifeTheUniverseAndEverything`. The return value is compared with the value 42 using Assert.AreEqual. In case Assert.AreEqual fails, the test fails (code file UnitTestingSamplesTest/DeepThoughtTests.cs):

```
[TestClass]
public class TestProgram
{
  [TestMethod]
  public void
  TestTheAnswerToTheUltimateQuestionOfLifeTheUniverseAndEverything()
  {
    // arrange
    int expected = 42;
    var dt = new DeepThought();

    // act
    int actual =
      dt.TheAnswerToTheUltimateQuestionOfLifeTheUniverseAndEverything();

    // assert
    Assert.AreEqual(expected, actual);
  }
}
```

Unit tests are defined by three As: Arrange, Act, and Assert. First, everything is arranged for the unit test to start. In the first test, with the arrange phase, a variable expected is assigned the value that is expected from calling the method to test, and an instance of the DeepThought class is invoked. Now everything is ready to test the functionality. This happens with the act phase—the method is invoked. After completing the act phase, you need to verify whether the result is as expected. This is done in the assert phase using a method of the Assert class.

The Assert class is part of the MSTest framework in the Microsoft.VisualStudio.TestTools. UnitTesting namespace. This class offers several static methods that you can use with unit tests. By default, the Assert.Fail method is added to an automatically created unit test to give the information that the test is not yet implemented. Some of the other methods are AreNotEqual, which verifies whether two objects are not the same; IsFalse and IsTrue, which verify Boolean results; IsNull and IsNotNull, which verify null results; and IsInstanceOfType and IsNotInstanceOfType, which verify the passed type.

Running Unit Tests

Using the Test Explorer (which you open via Test ⇨ Windows ⇨ Test Explorer), you can run the tests from the solution (see Figure 19-2).

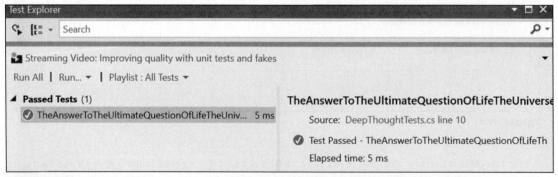

FIGURE 19-2

Figure 19-3 shows a failed test, which includes all details about the failure.

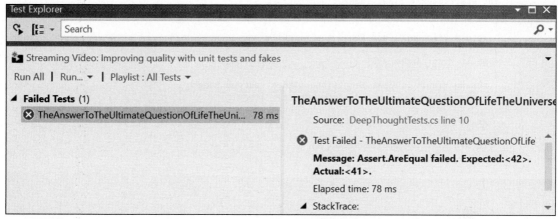

FIGURE 19-3

Of course, this was a very simple scenario; the tests are not usually that simple. For example, methods can throw exceptions; they can have different routes for returning other values; and they can make use of other code (for example, database access code, or services that are invoked) that shouldn't be tested with the single unit. Now let's look at a more involved scenario for unit testing.

The following class, `StringSample`, defines a constructor with a string parameter, the method `GetStringDemo`, and a field. The method `GetStringDemo` uses different paths depending on the `first` and `second` parameters and returns a string that results from these parameters (code file `UnitTestingSamples/StringSample.cs`):

```csharp
public class StringSample
{
  public StringSample(string init)
  {
    if (init == null)
      throw new ArgumentNullException(nameof(init));
    _init = init;
  }

  private string _init;
  public string GetStringDemo(string first, string second)
  {
    if (first == null)
    {
      throw new ArgumentNullException(nameof(first));
    }
    if (string.IsNullOrEmpty(first))
    {
      throw new ArgumentException("empty string is not allowed", first);
    }
    if (second == null)
    {
      throw new ArgumentNullException(nameof(second));
    }
    if (second.Length > first.Length)
    {
      throw new ArgumentOutOfRangeException(nameof(second),
        "must be shorter than first");
```

```
    }

    int startIndex = first.IndexOf(second);
    if (startIndex < 0)
    {
      return $"{second} not found in {first}";
    }
    else if (startIndex < 5)
    {
      string result = first.Remove(startIndex, second.Length);
      return $"removed {second} from {first}: {result}";
    }
    else
    {
      return _init.ToUpperInvariant();
    }
  }
}
```

> **NOTE** *When you're writing unit tests for complex methods, the unit test also some-times gets complex. Here it is helpful to debug into the unit test to find out what's going on. Debugging unit tests is straightforward: Just add breakpoints to the unit test code, and from the context menu of the Test Explorer select Debug Selected Tests (see Figure 19-4).*

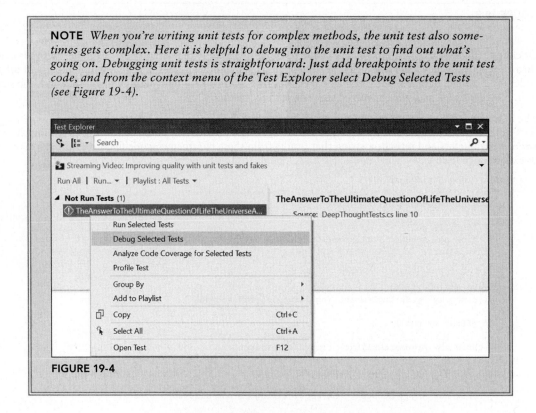

FIGURE 19-4

Every possible execution route and check for exceptions should be covered by unit tests, as discussed next.

Expecting Exceptions with MSTest

When invoking the constructor of the StringSample class and calling the method GetStringDemo with null, an ArgumentNullException is expected. You can easily check exceptions with testing code: apply the `ExpectedException` attribute to the test method as shown in the following example. This way, the test method succeeds with the exception (code file `UnitTestingSamplesTests/StringSampleTests.cs`):

```
[TestMethod]
[ExpectedException(typeof(ArgumentNullException))]
public void TestStringSampleNull()
{
  var sample = new StringSample(null);
}
```

You can deal with the exception thrown by the `GetStringDemo` method in a similar way.

Testing All Code Paths

To test all code paths, you can create multiple tests, with each one taking a different route. The following test sample passes the strings a and b to the `GetStringDemo` method. Because the second string is not contained within the first string, the first path of the `if` statement applies. The result is checked accordingly (code file `UnitTestingSamplesTests/StringSampleTests.cs`):

```
[TestMethod]
public void GetStringDemoAB()
{
  string expected = "b not found in a";
  var sample = new StringSample(String.Empty);
  string actual = sample.GetStringDemo("a", "b");
  Assert.AreEqual(expected, actual);
}
```

The next test method verifies another path of the `GetStringDemo` method. Here, the second string is found in the first one, and the index is lower than 5; therefore, it results in the second code block of the `if` statement:

```
[TestMethod]
public void GetStringDemoABCDBC()
{
  string expected = "removed bc from abcd: ad";
  var sample = new StringSample(String.Empty);
  string actual = sample.GetStringDemo("abcd", "bc");
  Assert.AreEqual(expected, actual);
}
```

All other code paths can be tested similarly. To see what code is covered by unit tests, and what code is still missing, you can open the Code Coverage Results window, shown in Figure 19-5. Open the Code Coverage Results window from the menu Test ⇨ Analyze Code Coverage.

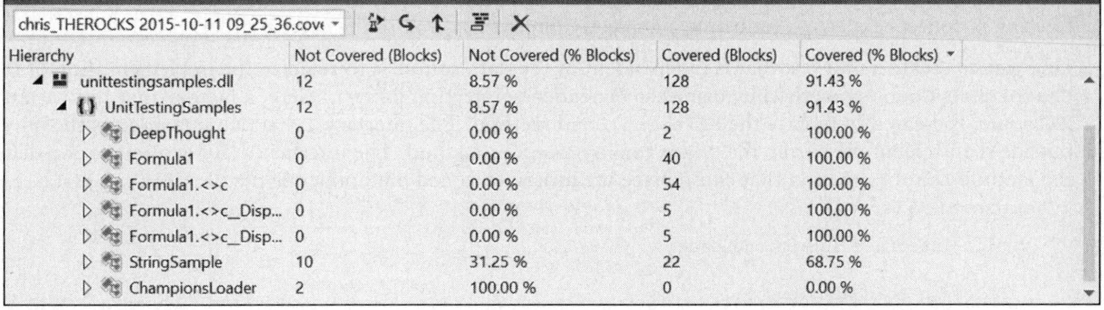

Hierarchy	Not Covered (Blocks)	Not Covered (% Blocks)	Covered (Blocks)	Covered (% Blocks) ▾
▲ 🔣 unittestingsamples.dll	12	8.57 %	128	91.43 %
▲ {} UnitTestingSamples	12	8.57 %	128	91.43 %
▷ 🔧 DeepThought	0	0.00 %	2	100.00 %
▷ 🔧 Formula1	0	0.00 %	40	100.00 %
▷ 🔧 Formula1.<>c	0	0.00 %	54	100.00 %
▷ 🔧 Formula1.<>c_Disp...	0	0.00 %	5	100.00 %
▷ 🔧 Formula1.<>c_Disp...	0	0.00 %	5	100.00 %
▷ 🔧 StringSample	10	31.25 %	22	68.75 %
▷ 🔧 ChampionsLoader	2	100.00 %	0	0.00 %

FIGURE 19-5

External Dependencies

Many methods are dependent on some functionality outside the application's control, for example, calling a web service or accessing a database. Maybe the service or database is not available during some test runs, which tests the availability of these external resources. Or worse, maybe the database or service returns different data over time, and it's hard to compare this with expected data. Such functionality outside the scope of what should be tested must be excluded from the unit test.

The following example is dependent on some outside functionality. The method ChampionsByCountry accesses an XML file from a web server that contains a list of Formula-1 world champions with Firstname, Lastname, Wins, and Country elements. This list is filtered by country, and it's numerically ordered using the value from the Wins element. The returned data is an XElement that contains converted XML code (code file UnitTestingSamples/Formula1.cs):

```csharp
public XElement ChampionsByCountry(string country)
{
  XElement champions = XElement.Load(F1Addresses.RacersUrl);
  var q = from r in champions.Elements("Racer")
          where r.Element("Country").Value == country
          orderby int.Parse(r.Element("Wins").Value) descending
          select new XElement("Racer",
            new XAttribute("Name", r.Element("Firstname").Value + " " +
              r.Element("Lastname").Value),
            new XAttribute("Country", r.Element("Country").Value),
            new XAttribute("Wins", r.Element("Wins").Value));
  return new XElement("Racers", q.ToArray());
}
```

> **NOTE** *For more information on LINQ to XML, read Chapter 27, "XML and JSON."*

The link to the XML file is defined by the F1Addresses class (code file UnitTestingSamples/F1Addresses.cs):

```csharp
public class F1Addresses
{
  public const string RacersUrl =
    "http://www.cninnovation.com/downloads/Racers.xml";
}
```

For the method ChampionsByCountry, you should do a unit test. The test should not be dependent on the source from the server. Server unavailability is one issue, but it can also be expected that the data on the server changes over time to return new champions, and other values. The current test should ensure that filtering is done as expected, returning a correctly filtered list, and in the correct order.

One way to create a unit test that is independent of the data source is to refactor the implementation of the ChampionsByCountry method by using the dependency injection pattern. Here, a factory that returns an XElement is created to replace the XElement.Load method. The interface IChampionsLoader is the only outside requirement used from the ChampionsByCountry method. The interface IChampionsLoader defines the method LoadChampions that can replace the aforementioned method (code file UnitTestingSamples/IChampionsLoader.cs):

```csharp
public interface IChampionsLoader
{
  XElement LoadChampions();
}
```

The class `ChampionsLoader` implements the interface `IChampionsLoader` by using the `XElement.Load` method—the method that was used beforehand by the `ChampionsByCountry` method (code file `UnitTestingSamples/ChampionsLoader.cs`):

```
public class ChampionsLoader: IChampionsLoader
{
  public XElement LoadChampions() => XElement.Load(F1Addresses.RacersUrl);
}
```

> **NOTE** *The dependency injection pattern is explained with more detail in Chapter 31, "Patterns with XAML Apps."*

Now it's possible to change the implementation of the `ChampionsByCountry` method (the new method is named `ChampionsByCountry2` to make both variants available for unit testing) by using an interface to load the champions instead of directly using `XElement.Load`. The `IChampionsLoader` is passed with the constructor of the class `Formula1`, and this loader is then used by `ChampionsByCountry2`: (code file `UnitTestingSamples/Formula1.cs`):

```
public class Formula1
{
  private IChampionsLoader _loader;
  public Formula1(IChampionsLoader loader)
  {
    _loader = loader;
  }

  public XElement ChampionsByCountry2(string country)
  {
    var q = from r in _loader.LoadChampions().Elements("Racer")
            where r.Element("Country").Value == country
            orderby int.Parse(r.Element("Wins").Value) descending
            select new XElement("Racer",
              new XAttribute("Name", r.Element("Firstname").Value + " " +
                r.Element("Lastname").Value),
              new XAttribute("Country", r.Element("Country").Value),
              new XAttribute("Wins", r.Element("Wins").Value));
    return new XElement("Racers", q.ToArray());
  }
}
```

With a typical implementation, a `ChampionsLoader` instance would be passed to the `Formula1` constructor to retrieve the racers from the server.

When you're creating the unit test, you can implement a custom method that returns sample Formula-1 champions, as shown in the method `Formula1SampleData` (code file `UnitTestingSamplesTests/Formula1Tests.cs`):

```
internal static string Formula1SampleData()
{
  return @"
<Racers>
  <Racer>
    <Firstname>Nelson</Firstname>
    <Lastname>Piquet</Lastname>
    <Country>Brazil</Country>
    <Starts>204</Starts>
```

```
      <Wins>23</Wins>
    </Racer>
    <Racer>
      <Firstname>Ayrton</Firstname>
      <Lastname>Senna</Lastname>
      <Country>Brazil</Country>
      <Starts>161</Starts>
      <Wins>41</Wins>
    </Racer>
    <Racer>
      <Firstname>Nigel</Firstname>
      <Lastname>Mansell</Lastname>
      <Country>England</Country>
      <Starts>187</Starts>
      <Wins>31</Wins>
    </Racer>
    //... more sample data
```

The method `Formula1VerificationData` returns sample test data that matches the expected result:

```
internal static XElement Formula1VerificationData()
{
  return XElement.Parse(@"
<Racers>
  <Racer Name=""Mika Hakkinen"" Country=""Finland"" Wins=""20"" />
  <Racer Name=""Kimi Raikkonen"" Country=""Finland"" Wins=""18"" />
</Racers>");
}
```

The loader of the test data implements the same interface—`IChampionsLoader`—as the `ChampionsLoader` class. This loader makes use of the sample data; it doesn't access the web server:

```
public class F1TestLoader: IChampionsLoader
{
  public XElement LoadChampions() => XElement.Parse(Formula1SampleData());
}
```

Now it's easy to create a unit test that makes use of the sample data:

```
[TestMethod]
public void TestChampionsByCountry2()
{
  Formula1 f1 = new Formula1(new F1TestLoader());
  XElement actual = f1.ChampionsByCountry2("Finland");
  Assert.AreEqual(Formula1VerificationData().ToString(), actual.ToString());
}
```

Of course, a real test should do more than cover a case that passes Finland as a string and two champions are returned with the test data. You should write other tests to pass a string with no matching result, to return more than two champions, and to result in a number sort order that is different from the alphanumeric sort order.

Fakes Framework

It's not always possible to refactor the method that should be tested to be independent of a data source—for example, using legacy code that can't be changed. This is when the Fakes Framework becomes very useful. This framework is part of Visual Studio Enterprise Edition.

With this framework, you can test the `ChampionsByCountry` method without any changes, and you can still keep the server outside the unit test. Remember that the implementation of this method uses `XElement` `.Load`, which directly accesses a file on the web server. The Fakes Framework enables you to change the implementation of the `ChampionsByCountry` method just for the testing case by replacing the `XElement` `.Load` method with something else (code file `UnitTestingSamples/Formula1.cs`):

```
public XElement ChampionsByCountry(string country)
{
    XElement champions = XElement.Load(F1Addresses.RacersUrl);
    var q = from r in champions.Elements("Racer")
            where r.Element("Country").Value == country
            orderby int.Parse(r.Element("Wins").Value) descending
            select new XElement("Racer",
                new XAttribute("Name", r.Element("Firstname").Value + " " +
                    r.Element("Lastname").Value),
                new XAttribute("Country", r.Element("Country").Value),
                new XAttribute("Wins", r.Element("Wins").Value));
    return new XElement("Racers", q.ToArray());
}
```

To use the Fakes Framework with the references of the unit testing project, select the assembly that contains the XElement class. XElement is within the System.Xml.Linq assembly. When you open the context menu while the System.Xml.Linq assembly is selected, the menu option Add Fakes Assembly is available. Select this to create the System.Xml.Linq.4.0.0.0.Fakes assembly.

The newly created assembly contains shim classes in the namespace System.Xml.Linq.Fakes. You will find all the types of the System.Xml.Linq assembly with a shimmed version—for example, ShimXAttribute for XAttribute and ShimXDocument for XDocument.

For the example, you need only ShimXElement. ShimXElement contains a member for every public over-loaded member of the XElement class. The Load method of XElement is overloaded to receive a string, a Stream, a TextReader, and an XmlReader, and overloads exist with a second LoadOptions parameter. ShimXElement defines members named LoadString, LoadStream, LoadTextReader, LoadXmlReader, and others with LoadOptions as well, such as LoadStringLoadOptions and LoadStreamLoadOptions.

All these shim members are of a delegate type. This delegate allows specifying a custom method. This custom method is invoked in place of the method call that's inside the method that is under test. The unit test method TestChampionsByCountry replaces the XElement.Load method with one parameter in the Formula1.ChampionsByCountry method with the call to XElement.Parse, accessing the sample data. ShimXElement.LoadString specifies the new implementation.

Using shims, it's necessary to create a context, which you can do using ShimsContext.Create. The context is active until the Dispose method is invoked by the end of the using block (code file UnitTestingSamplesTests/Formula1Tests.cs):

```
[TestMethod]
public void TestChampionsByCountry()
{
    using (ShimsContext.Create())
    {
        ShimXElement.LoadString = s => XElement.Parse(Formula1SampleData());
        Formula1 f1 = new Formula1();
        XElement actual = f1.ChampionsByCountry("Finland");
        Assert.AreEqual(Formula1VerificationData().ToString(), actual.ToString());
    }
}
```

Although it is best to have a flexible implementation of the code that should be tested, the Fakes Framework offers a useful way to change an implementation such that it is not dependent on outside resources for test-ing purposes.

IntelliTest

A new testing feature available with Visual Studio 2015 Enterprise is IntelliTest, which automatically creates unit tests by making a white-box analysis of the code. IntelliTest analyzes the code to find all iterations by passing as few parameters as possible. When you select a method in the code editor, from the context menu you can select Run IntelliTest to create tests, as shown in Figure 19-6. For the GetStringDemo method,

IntelliTest creates 10 test methods that pass different strings for the input parameters. You can check these methods to see whether they fit the purpose, and you can also check for errors if you missed validating input parameters in the method.

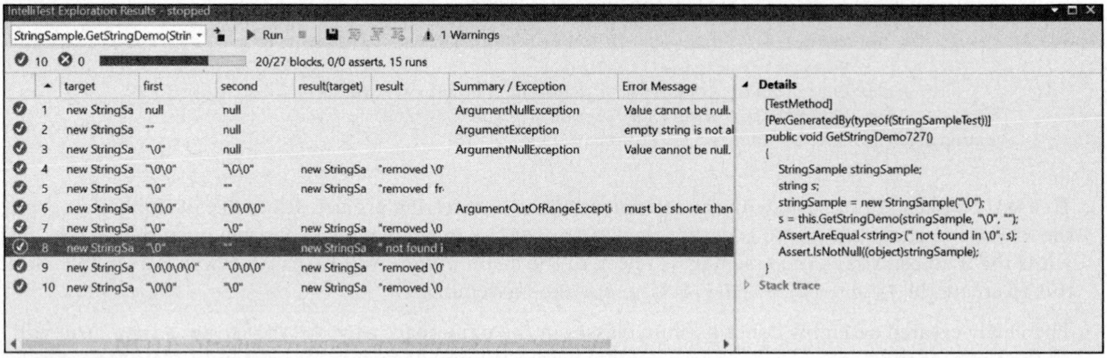

FIGURE 19-6

If the tests are good, you can save and adapt them to a unit testing project. This is one of the tests generated by IntelliTest. In addition to the `TestMethod` attribute and use of the `Assert` class, you can also see the attribute `PexGeneratedBy`. This attribute marks the test as being created by IntelliTest:

```
[TestMethod]
[PexGeneratedBy(typeof(StringSampleTest))]
public void GetStringDemo727()
{
  StringSample stringSample;
  string s;
  stringSample = new StringSample("\0");
  s = this.GetStringDemo(stringSample, "\0", "");
  Assert.AreEqual<string>(" not found in \0", s);
  Assert.IsNotNull((object)stringSample);
}
```

> **NOTE** *Pex was the original Microsoft Research project to automatically generate unit tests. IntelliTest is derived from Pex. From Pex you can still look for* `http://www` *`.pexforfun.com` to solve code puzzles with the help of Pex.*

UNIT TESTING WITH XUNIT

As previously mentioned, the unit test framework MSTest that's included with the installation of Visual Studio doesn't support .NET Core. MSTest supports only the MSBuild-based project templates. However, the Visual Studio Test environment does support other testing frameworks. Test adapters such as NUnit, xUnit, Boost (for C++), Chutzpah (for JavaScript), and Jasmine (for JavaScript) are available via Extensions and Updates; these test adapters integrate with the Visual Studio Test Explorer. xUnit is a great testing framework, and it's also used by Microsoft with the open-source code of .NET Core and ASP.NET Core, so xUnit is the focus of this section.

Using xUnit with .NET Core

With .NET Framework application templates, you can create xUnit tests in a similar manner to MSTest tests. You use the Create Unit Test command from the context menu in the editor. This is different with .NET Core applications because this menu entry is not available. Also, it would be a good idea to make use of the DNX environment for the unit tests instead of using test libraries that use the full framework. When you use the DNX environment, you can run these tests on the Linux platform as well. Let's see how you can do this.

You create the same sample library as before, but use the name `UnitTestingSamplesCore` and the Visual Studio project template Class Library (Package). This library includes the same types for testing shown earlier: `DeepThought` and `StringSample`.

For the unit test, you create another .NET Core library named `UnitTestingSamplesCoreTests`. This project needs to reference the NuGet packages `System.Xml.XDocument` (for the sample code), `xunit` (for the unit tests), `xunit.runner.dnx` (to run the unit test in the DNX environment, and `UnitTestingSamplesCore` (the code that should be tested).

Creating Facts

The way you create the test is very similar to what you did before. The differences on testing the method `TheAnswerToTheUltimateQuestionOfLifeTheUniverseAndEverything` are just the annotated test method with the `Fact` attribute and the different `Assert.Equal` method (code file `UnitTestingSamplesCoreTests/DeepThoughtTests.cs`):

```csharp
public class DeepThoughtTests
{
  [Fact]
  public void
    TheAnswerToTheUltimateQuestionOfLifeTheUniverseAndEverythingTest()
  {
    int expected = 42;
    var dt = new DeepThought();
    int actual =
      dt.TheAnswerToTheUltimateQuestionOfLifeTheUniverseAndEverything();
    Assert.Equal(expected, actual);
  }
}
```

The `Assert` class used now is defined in the `XUnit` namespace. This class defines a lot more methods for validation compared to the `Assert` method from MSTest. For example, instead of adding an attribute to specify an expected exception, use the `Assert.Throws` method, which allows multiple checks for exceptions within a single test method:

```csharp
[Fact]
public void TestGetStringDemoExceptions()
{
  var sample = new StringSample(string.Empty);
  Assert.Throws<ArgumentNullException>(() => sample.GetStringDemo(null, "a"));
  Assert.Throws<ArgumentNullException>(() => sample.GetStringDemo("a", null));
  Assert.Throws<ArgumentException>(() =>
    sample.GetStringDemo(string.Empty, "a"));
}
```

Creating Theories

xUnit defines the `Fact` attribute for test methods that don't require parameters. With xUnit you can also invoke unit test methods that require parameters; you use the `Theory` attribute and supply data to add an attribute that derives from `Data`. This makes it possible to define multiple unit tests by a single method.

In the following code snippet, the `Theory` attribute is applied to the `TestGetStringDemo` unit test method. The method `StringSample.GetStringDemo` defines different paths that depend on the input data. The first path is reached if the string passed with the second parameter is not contained within the first parameter. The second path is reached if the second string is contained within the first five characters of the first string. The third path is reached with the `else` clause. To reach all the different paths, three `InlineData` attributes are applied to the testing method. Every one of these attributes defines four parameters that are directly sent to the invocation of the unit testing method, in the same order. The attributes also define the values that should be returned by the method under test (code file `UnitTestingSamplesCoreTests/StringSampleTests.cs`):

```
[InlineData("", "longer string", "nger",
  "removed nger from longer string: lo string")]
[InlineData("init", "longer string", "string", "INIT")]
public void TestGetStringDemo(string init, string a, string b, string expected)
{
  var sample = new StringSample(init);
  string actual = sample.GetStringDemo(a, b);
  Assert.Equal(expected, actual);
}
```

The attribute `InlineData` derives from the attribute `Data`. Instead of directly supplying the values for the test method with the attribute, the values can also come from a property, method, or a class. The following example defines a static method that returns the same values with an `IEnumerable<object>` object (code file `UnitTestingSamplesCoreTests/StringSampleTests.cs`):

```
public static IEnumerable<object[]> GetStringSampleData() =>
  new[]
  {
    new object[] { "", "a", "b", "b not found in a" },
    new object[] { "", "longer string", "nger",
      "removed nger from longer string: lo string" },
    new object[] { "init", "longer string", "string", "INIT" }
  };
```

The unit test method is now changed with the `MemberData` attribute. This attribute allows using static properties or methods that return `IEnumerable<object>` to fill in the parameters of the unit test method:

```
[Theory]
[MemberData("GetStringSampleData")]
public void TestGetStringDemoUsingMember(string init, string a, string b,
  string expected)
{
  var sample = new StringSample(init);
  string actual = sample.GetStringDemo(a, b);
  Assert.Equal(expected, actual);
}
```

Running Unit Tests with the dotnet Tools

You can run the xUnit unit tests directly from Visual Studio, similar to the way you run the MSTest unit tests. Because xUnit supports CLI, you can also run xUnit tests from the command line. For this method, the test command is defined within the `projects.json` file (code file `UnitTestingSamplesCoreTests/project.json`):

```
{
  "version": "1.0.0-*",
  "description": "UnitTestingSamplesCoreTests Class Library",
```

```
      "authors": [ "Christian" ],
      "tags": [ "" ],
      "projectUrl": "",
      "licenseUrl": "",
      "dependencies": {
        "NETStandard.Library": "1.0.0-*",
        "System.Threading.Tasks": "4.0.11-*",
        "System.Xml.XDocument": "4.0.11-*",
        "UnitTestingSamplesCore": { "target": "project" },
        "xunit": "2.2.0-*",
        "dotnet-test-xunit: "1.0.0-*"
      },
      "testRunner": "xunit",
       "frameworks": {
         "netstandard1.0": {
          "dependencies": { }
       }
     }
```

Now when you run `dotnet test` from the command prompt, all the tests that are defined by the project are run:

```
">dotnet test"
xUnit.net DNX Runner (64-bit win7-x64)
  Discovering: UnitTestingSamplesCoreTests
  Discovered:  UnitTestingSamplesCoreTests
  Starting:    UnitTestingSamplesCoreTests
  Finished:    UnitTestingSamplesCoreTests
=== TEST EXECUTION SUMMARY ===
  UnitTestingSamplesCoreTests  Total: 11, Errors: 0, Failed: 0, Skipped: 0,
  Time: 0.107s
C:\Users\chris\Source\Repos\ProfessionalCSharp6\Testing\UnitTestingSamples\
UnitTestingSamplesCoreTests>
```

Using a Mocking Library

Let's get into a more complex example: creating a unit test for a client-side service from the MVVM application from Chapter 31. This service uses dependency injection to inject the repository defined by the interface `IBooksRepository`. The unit tests for testing the method `AddOrUpdateBookAsync` shouldn't test the repository; they test only the functionality within the method. For the repository, another unit test should be done (code file `MVVM/Services/BooksService.cs`):

```
public class BooksService: IBooksService
{
    private ObservableCollection<Book> _books = new ObservableCollection<Book>();
    private IBooksRepository _booksRepository;
    public BooksService(IBooksRepository repository)
    {
        _booksRepository = repository;
    }

    public async Task LoadBooksAsync()
    {
        if (_books.Count > 0) return;
        IEnumerable<Book> books = await _booksRepository.GetItemsAsync();
        _books.Clear();
        foreach (var b in books)
        {
```

```
      _books.Add(b);
    }
  }

  public Book GetBook(int bookId) =>
    _books.Where(b => b.BookId == bookId).SingleOrDefault();

  public async Task<Book> AddOrUpdateBookAsync(Book book)
  {
    if (book == null) throw new ArgumentNullException(nameof(book));
    Book updated = null;
    if (book.BookId == 0)
    {
      updated = await _booksRepository.AddAsync(book);
      _books.Add(updated);
    }
    else
    {
      updated = await _booksRepository.UpdateAsync(book);
      Book old = _books.Where(b => b.BookId == updated.BookId).Single();
      int ix = _books.IndexOf(old);
      _books.RemoveAt(ix);
      _books.Insert(ix, updated);
    }
    return updated;
  }

  IEnumerable<Book> IBooksService.Books => _books;
}
```

Because the unit test for `AddOrUpdateBookAsync` shouldn't test the repository used for `IBooksRepository`, you need to implement a repository used for testing. To make this easy, you can use a mocking library that automatically fills in the blanks. A commonly used mocking library is Moq. With the unit testing project, the NuGet package `Moq` is added; you also add the NuGet packages `xunit` and `xunit.runner` `.visualstudio`.

Within the unit test `AddBooksAsyncTest`, a mock object is instantiated to pass the generic parameter `IBooksRepository`. The `Mock` constructor creates implementations for the interface. Because you need some results from the repository other than null to create useful tests, the `Setup` method defines which parameters can be passed, and the `ReturnsAsync` method defines the result that's returned from the method stub. You access the mock object by using the `Object` property of the `Mock` class, and it is passed on to create the `BooksService` class. With these settings in place, you can invoke the `AddOrUpdateBookAsync` method to pass a book object that should be added (code file `MVVM/Services.Tests/BooksServiceTest.cs`):

```
[Fact]
public async Task AddBookAsyncTest()
{
  // arrange
  var mock = new Mock<IBooksRepository>();
  var book =
    new Book
    {
      BookId = 0,
      Title = "Test Title",
      Publisher = "A Publisher"
    };
  var expectedBook =
    new Book
    {
      BookId = 1,
      Title = "Test Title",
      Publisher = "A Publisher"
```

```
      };
    mock.Setup(r => r.AddAsync(book)).ReturnsAsync(expectedBook);

    var service = new BooksService(mock.Object);

    // act
    Book actualAdded = await service.AddOrUpdateBookAsync(book);
    Book actualRetrieved = service.GetBook(actualAdded.BookId);
    Book notExisting = service.GetBook(2);

    // assert
    Assert.Equal(expectedBook, actualAdded);
    Assert.Equal(expectedBook, actualRetrieved);
    Assert.Equal(null, notExisting);
}
```

When you add a book, the `if` clause of the `AddOrUpdateBookAsync` method gets called. When you update a book, the `else` clause gets active. This part of the method is tested with the `UpdateBookAsyncTest` method. As before, you create a mock object for the interface `IBooksRepository`. When you update a book, you test different scenarios, such as updating a book that exists and a book that does not exist (code file `MVVM/Services.Tests/BooksServiceTest.cs`):

```
[Fact]
public async Task UpdateBookAsyncTest()
{
  // arrange
  var mock = new Mock<IBooksRepository>();
  var origBook =
    new Book
    {
      BookId = 0,
      Title = "Title",
      Publisher = "A Publisher"
    };
  var addedBook =
    new Book
    {
      BookId = 1,
      Title = "Title",
      Publisher = "A Publisher"
    };
  var updateBook =
    new Book
    {
      BookId = 1,
      Title = "New Title",
      Publisher = "A Publisher"
    };
  var notExisting =
    new Book
    {
      BookId = 99,
      Title = "Not",
      Publisher = "Not"
    };
  mock.Setup(r => r.UpdateAsync(updateBook)).ReturnsAsync(updateBook);
  mock.Setup(r => r.UpdateAsync(notExisting)).ReturnsAsync(notExisting);
  mock.Setup(r => r.AddAsync(origBook)).ReturnsAsync(addedBook);

  var service = new BooksService(mock.Object);

  // fill in first book to test update
```

```
    await service.AddOrUpdateBookAsync(origBook);

    // act
    Book actualUpdated = await service.AddOrUpdateBookAsync(updateBook);
    Book actualRetrieved = service.GetBook(1);

    // assert
    Assert.Equal(updateBook, actualUpdated);
    Assert.Equal(updateBook, actualRetrieved);
    await Assert.ThrowsAsync<InvalidOperationException>(async () =>
      await service.AddOrUpdateBookAsync(notExisting));
    await Assert.ThrowsAsync<ArgumentNullException>(async () =>
      await service.AddOrUpdateBookAsync(null));
}
```

When you use the MVVM pattern with XAML-based applications and the MVC pattern with web-based applications, you reduce the complexity of the user interface and reduce the need for complex UI testing. However, there are still some scenarios that should be tested with the UI—for example, navigating through pages, drag and drop of elements, and more. This is where Visual Studio's functionality of UI testing comes into place.

UI TESTING

For testing the user interface, Visual Studio offers Coded UI Test Project templates for Universal Windows apps, Windows Phone apps, WPF applications, and Windows Forms. When you create a new project, you can find the project template for WPF and Windows Forms in the Test group. However, this template doesn't work for Windows apps. The project template for Universal Windows apps is in the Universal group. Be aware that automatic recording is not supported for Windows apps.

In this chapter you create a UI test for an MVVM WPF application. This application is part of the downloadable files for this chapter, so you can use it for testing. For the details about this application, read Chapter 31.

When you create a new Coded UI Test Project, you see the dialog shown in Figure 19-7. Here you can specify to create a new recording.

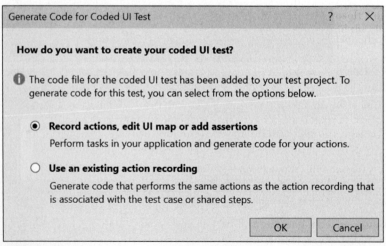

FIGURE 19-7

When you create a new recording, you see the Coded UI Test Builder (see Figure 19-8). With WPF applications, you can click the Recording button to record actions.

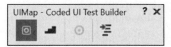

FIGURE 19-8

When running the sample application, you can click the Load button to load a list of books, click the Add button to add a new book, type some text in the text box elements, and click the Save button. When you click the Show Recorded Steps button in the Coded UI Test Builder, you see the recordings as shown in Figure 19-9.

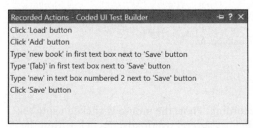

FIGURE 19-9

When you click the Generate Code button, you are asked for a method name to generate the code with the recordings (see Figure 19-10).

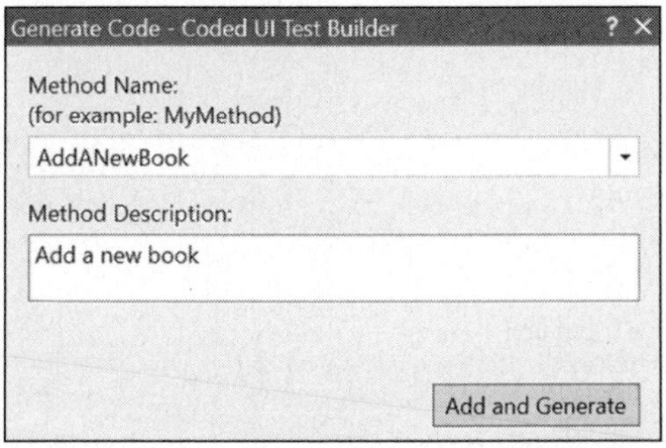

FIGURE 19-10

With the generated method `AddANewBook` you can see that local variables are used to reference the WPF controls in use:

```
public void AddNewBook()
{
  WpfButton uILoadButton =
    this.UIBooksDesktopAppWindow.UIBooksViewCustom.UILoadButton;
  WpfButton uIAddButton =
    this.UIBooksDesktopAppWindow.UIBooksViewCustom.UIAddButton;
  WpfEdit uIItemEdit =
    this.UIBooksDesktopAppWindow.UIBookViewCustom.UISaveButton.UIItemEdit;
```

```
      WpfEdit uIItemEdit1 =
        this.UIBooksDesktopAppWindow.UIBookViewCustom.UISaveButton.UIItemEdit1;
      WpfButton uISaveButton =
        this.UIBooksDesktopAppWindow.UIBookViewCustom.UISaveButton;
      // etc.
    }
```

The buttons are referenced from properties—for example, the UILoadButton shown in the following code snippet. On first access, a WpfButton is searched by using the Name property (code file BooksDesktopAppUITest/AddNewBookUIMap.Designer.cs):

```
    public WpfButton UILoadButton
    {
      get
      {
        if ((this.mUILoadButton == null))
        {
          this.mUILoadButton = new WpfButton(this);
          this.mUILoadButton.SearchProperties[WpfButton.PropertyNames.Name] =
            "Load";
          this.mUILoadButton.WindowTitles.Add("Books Desktop App");
        }
        return this.mUILoadButton;
      }
    }
```

AddNewBook continues with methods created from the recording. First, the mouse is clicked using the static method Mouse.Click. The Mouse.Click method defines several overloads: to click within the screen coordinates—using mouse modifiers—and to click controls. The first click method clicks the Load button. The coordinates defined by the second argument are relative within the control. So if you reposition this control in a newer version, it's important that you run the test again without big changes; that's why the control is accessed via its name. Other than the Mouse class, you can use the Keyboard class to send key inputs:

```
    public void AddNewBook()
    {
      // etc.

      // Click 'Load' button
      Mouse.Click(uILoadButton, new Point(20, 11));

      // Click 'Add' button
      Mouse.Click(uIAddButton, new Point(14, 9));

      // Type 'new book' in first text box next to 'Save' button
      uIItemEdit.Text = this.AddANewBookParams.UIItemEditText;

      // Type '{Tab}' in first text box next to 'Save' button
      Keyboard.SendKeys(uIItemEdit, this.AddANewBookParams.UIItemEditSendKeys,
        ModifierKeys.None);

      // Type 'new' in text box numbered 2 next to 'Save' button
      uIItemEdit1.Text = this.AddANewBookParams.UIItemEdit1Text;

      // Click 'Save' button
      Mouse.Click(uISaveButton, new Point(29, 19));
    }
```

Input for text controls is saved in a helper class AddNewBookParams, so you can easily change the input in one place:

```
public class AddNewBookParams
{
  public string UIItemEditText = "new book";

  public string UIItemEditSendKeys = "{Tab}";

  public string UIItemEdit1Text = "new";
}
```

After you create the recording, you need to define assertions to check whether the outcome is correct. You can create asserts with the Coded UI Test Builder. Click the Add Assertions button to open the dialog shown in Figure 19-11. With this dialog, you can see the controls of the open window, see its current property values, and add assertions. After defining the assertion, you need to generate the code again.

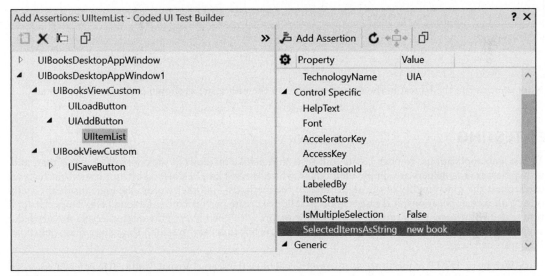

FIGURE 19-11

The generated `Assert` method verifies whether the correct value is in the selected control; if the incorrect value is in the control, it writes an error message:

```
public void AssertNewBook()
{
  WpfList uIItemList =
    this.UIBooksDesktopAppWindow1.UIBooksViewCustom.UIAddButton.UIItemList;

  Assert.AreEqual(
    this.AssertNewBookExpectedValues.UIItemListSelectedItemsAsString,
    uIItemList.SelectedItemsAsString, "problem adding book in list");
}
```

For changes to the code, you shouldn't change the designer-generated code files. Instead, you open the .uitest files to open the dialog shown in Figure 19-12. Here you can split actions into new methods, add delays before actions, and delete actions. Also, you can move the source code from the designer-generated files to custom files where you can change the code later.

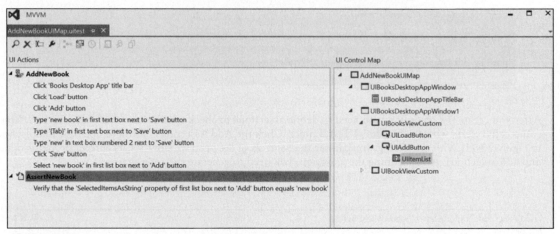

FIGURE 19-12

Now you can run the UI test in the same way you run the unit tests, as shown earlier in this chapter.

WEB TESTING

To test web applications, you can create unit tests that invoke methods of the controllers, repository, and utility classes. Tag helpers are simple methods in which the test can be covered by unit tests. Unit tests are used to test the functionality of the algorithms of the methods—in other words, the logic inside the methods. With web applications, it is also a good practice to create performance and load tests. Does the application scale? How many users can the application support with one server? How many servers are needed to support a specific number of users? Which bottleneck is not that easy to scale? To answer these questions, Web tests can help.

With Web tests, HTTP requests are sent from the client to the server. Visual Studio also offers a recorder that needs an add-in within Internet Explorer. At the time of this writing, Microsoft Edge cannot be used as a recorder because this browser currently doesn't support add-ins.

Creating the Web Test

For creating a Web test, you can create a new ASP.NET Web Application with ASP.NET Core 1.0 named `WebApplicationSample`. This template has enough functionality built in that allows for creating tests. To create Web tests, you add a Web Performance and Load Test Project named `WebAndLoadTestProject` to the solution. Click on the `WebTest1.webtest` file to open the Web Test Editor. Then start a Web recording by clicking the Add Recording button. For this recording, you must have the Web Test Recorder add-in with Internet Explorer that's installed with the installation of Visual Studio. The recorder records all HTTP requests sent to the server. Click some links on the `WebApplicationSample` web application such as About and Context, and register a new user. Then click the Stop button to stop the recording.

After the recording is finished, you can edit the recording with the Web Test Editor. You might be seeing requests to `browserLinkSignalR` if you haven't disabled the browser link. Browser links make it possible to make HTML code changes without having to restart the browser. For testing, these requests are not relevant, and you can delete them. A recording is shown in Figure 19-13. With all the requests, you can see header information as well as form POST data that you can influence and change.

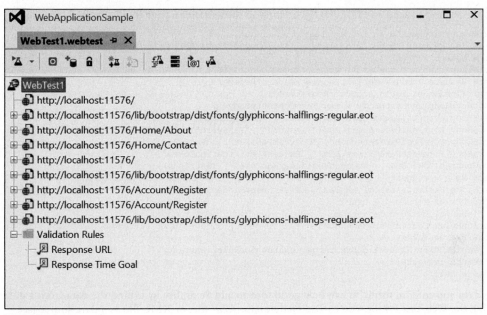

FIGURE 19-13

Click the Generate Code button to generate source code to send all the requests programmatically. With Web tests, the test class derives from the base class `WebTest` and overrides the `GetRequestEnumerator` method. This method returns one request after the other (code file `WebApplicationSample/WebAndLoadTestProject/NavigateAndRegister.cs`):

```
public class NavigateAndRegister: WebTest
{
  public NavigateAndRegister()
  {
    this.PreAuthenticate = true;
    this.Proxy = "default";
  }

  public override IEnumerator<WebTestRequest> GetRequestEnumerator()
  {
    // etc.
  }
}
```

The method `GetRequestEnumerator` defines requests to the website—for example, a request to the `About` page. With this request, a HTTP header is added to define that the request originates from the home page:

```
public override IEnumerator<WebTestRequest> GetRequestEnumerator()
{
  // etc.
  WebTestRequest request2 =
    new WebTestRequest("http://localhost:13815/Home/About");
  request2.Headers.Add(new WebTestRequestHeader("Referer",
    "http://localhost:13815/"));
  yield return request2;
  request2 = null;
  // etc.
}
```

And this is the request to send an HTTP POST request to the `Register` page that is passing form data:

```
WebTestRequest request6 =
  new WebTestRequest("http://localhost:13815/Account/Register");
request6.Method = "POST";
request6.ExpectedResponseUrl = "http://localhost:13815/";
request6.Headers.Add(new WebTestRequestHeader("Referer",
  "http://localhost:13815/Account/Register"));
FormPostHttpBody request6Body = new FormPostHttpBody();
request6Body.FormPostParameters.Add("Email", "sample1@test.com");
request6Body.FormPostParameters.Add("Password", "Pa$$w0rd");
request6Body.FormPostParameters.Add("ConfirmPassword", "Pa$$w0rd");
request6Body.FormPostParameters.Add("__RequestVerificationToken",
  this.Context["$HIDDEN1.__RequestVerificationToken"].ToString());
request6.Body = request6Body;
ExtractHiddenFields extractionRule2 = new ExtractHiddenFields();
extractionRule2.Required = true;
extractionRule2.HtmlDecode = true;
extractionRule2.ContextParameterName = "1";
request6.ExtractValues +=
  new EventHandler<ExtractionEventArgs>(extractionRule2.Extract);
yield return request6;
request6 = null;
```

With some data you enter in forms, it can be a good idea to add flexibility by taking the data from a data source. Using the Web Test Editor, you can add a database, CSV file, or XML file as a data source (see Figure 19-14). With this dialog box, you can change form parameters to take data from a data source.

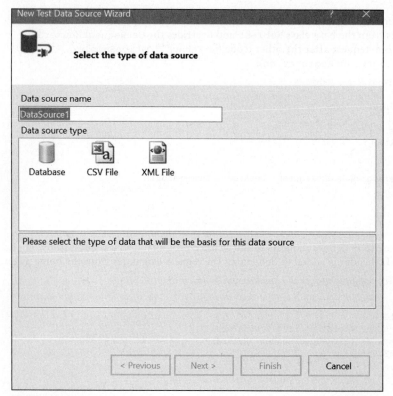

FIGURE 19-14

Adding a data source modifies the testing code. With a data source, the test class is annotated with the `DeploymentItem` attribute (if a CSV or XML file is used), and with `DataSource` and `DataBinding` attributes:

```
[DeploymentItem("webandloadtestproject\\EmailTests.csv",
  "webandloadtestproject")]
[DataSource("EmailDataSource",
  "Microsoft.VisualStudio.TestTools.DataSource.CSV",
  "|DataDirectory|\\webandloadtestproject\\EmailTests.csv",
  Microsoft.VisualStudio.TestTools.WebTesting.DataBindingAccessMethod.Sequential,
  Microsoft.VisualStudio.TestTools.WebTesting.DataBindingSelectColumns.SelectOnly
  BoundColumns, "EmailTests#csv")]
[DataBinding("EmailDataSource", "EmailTests#csv", "sample1@test#com",
  "EmailDataSource.EmailTests#csv.sample1@test#com")]
public class NavigateAndRegister1: WebTest
{
  // etc.
}
```

Now, in the code the data source can be accessed using the `Context` property of the `WebTest` that returns a `WebTestContext` to access the required data source via an index:

```
request6Body.FormPostParameters.Add("Email",
  this.Context["EmailDataSource.EmailTests#csv.sample1@test#com"].ToString());
```

Running the Web Test

With the tests in place, the testing can start. You can run—and debug—the test directly from the Web Test Editor. Remember to start the web application before you start the test. When you run the test from the Web Test Editor, you can see the resulting web pages as well as the detail information about requests and responses, as shown in Figure 19-15.

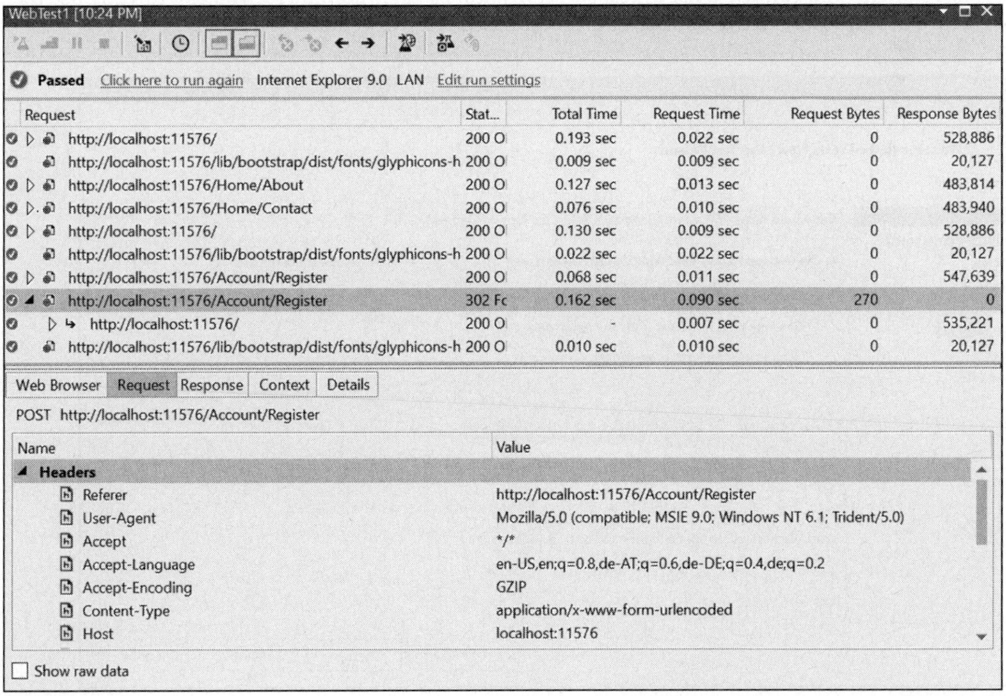

FIGURE 19-15

Figure 19-16 shows how you can influence the test runs by specifying a browser type, simulating think times, and running the test multiple times.

FIGURE 19-16

Web Load Test

Using Web Load Tests, you can simulate a high load on the web application. For a really high load one test server is not enough; you can use a list of test servers. With Visual Studio 2015, you can directly use the infrastructure of Microsoft Azure and select a Cloud-based Load Test as shown in Figure 19-17.

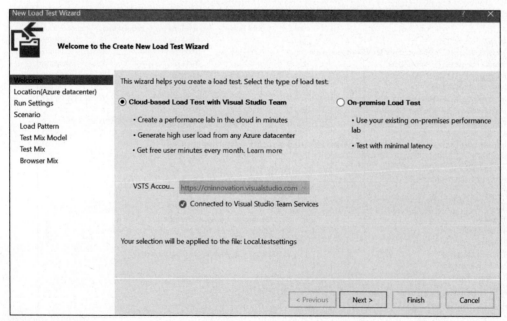

FIGURE 19-17

You can create a load test by adding a new item Web Load Test to the WebAndLoadTestProject project. This starts a wizard where you can do the following:

➤ Define a constant load or a load that increases over time (see Figure 19-18)

➤ Establish a test mix model based on the number of tests or the number of virtual users

➤ Add tests to the load and define which test should run what percentage compared to the other tests

➤ Specify a network mix to simulate fast and slow networks (what's the result for a user with a slow network if the server is occupied by clients with fast networks?)

➤ Determine a browser mix to test with Internet Explorer, Chrome, Firefox, and other browsers

➤ Establish run settings to run for the time to run the test

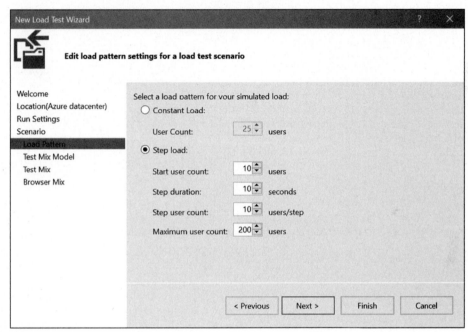

FIGURE 19-18

SUMMARY

In this chapter, you've seen the most important aspects about testing applications: creating unit tests, coded UI tests, and Web tests.

Visual Studio offers a Test Explorer to run unit tests, no matter whether they have been created using MSTest or xUnit. xUnit has the advantage of supporting .NET Core. This chapter also showed you triple A in action: Arrange, Act, and Assert.

With coded UI tests, you've seen how to create recordings and adapt the recordings to modify the UI testing code as needed.

With web applications, you've seen how to create a Web test to send requests to the server. You also found out how to change the requests.

Although testing helps with fixing issues with applications before they are deployed, Chapter 20, "Diagnostics and Application Insights," helps you fix applications that are running.

20

Diagnostics and Application Insights

WHAT'S IN THIS CHAPTER?

➤ Simple Tracing with EventSource

➤ Advanced Tracing with EventSource

➤ Creating a Custom Trace Listener

➤ Using Application Insights

WROX.COM CODE DOWNLOADS FOR THIS CHAPTER

The wrox.com code downloads for this chapter are found at www.wrox.com/go/professionalcsharp6 on the Download Code tab. The code for this chapter is divided into the following major examples:

➤ SimpleEventSourceSample

➤ EventSourceSampleInheritance

➤ EventSourceSampleAnnotations

➤ ClientApp/MyApplicationEvents

➤ WinAppInsights

DIAGNOSTICS OVERVIEW

As release cycles for applications become faster and faster, it's becoming more and more important to learn how the application behaves while it's running in production. What exceptions are occurring? Knowing what features are used is also of interest. Do users find the new feature of the app? How long do they stay in the page? To answer these questions, you need real-time information on the application.

This chapter explains how to get real-time information about your running application in order to identify any issues that it might have during production or to monitor resource usage to ensure that higher user loads can be accommodated. This is where the namespace System.Diagnostics .Tracing comes into play. This namespace offers classes for tracing using Event Tracing for Windows (ETW).

One way to deal with errors in your application, of course, is by throwing exceptions. However, an application might not fail with an exception, but it still doesn't behave as expected. The application might be running well on most systems but have a problem on a few. On the live system, you can change the log by starting a trace collector and get detailed live information about what's going on in the application. You can do this using ETW.

If there are problems with applications, the system administrator needs to be informed. The *Event Viewer* is a commonly used tool that not only the system administrator should be aware of but also the software developer. With the Event Viewer, you can both interactively monitor problems with applications and can add subscriptions to be informed about specific events that happen. ETW enables you to write information about the application.

Application Insights is a Microsoft Azure cloud service that enables you to monitor apps in the cloud. With just a few lines of code, you can get detailed information about how the application or service is used.

This chapter explains these facilities and demonstrates how you can use them for your applications.

> **NOTE** *The* `System.Diagnostics` *namespace also offers other classes for tracing, such as* `Trace` *and* `TraceSource`. *These classes have been used in previous versions of .NET. This chapter goes into only the newest technology for tracing:* `EventSource`. *You can read* Professional C# 5.0 and .NET 4.5.1 *for the older tracing types.*

TRACING WITH EVENTSOURCE

Tracing enables you to see informational messages about the running application. To get information about a running application, you can start the application in the debugger. During debugging, you can walk through the application step by step and set breakpoints at specific lines and when you reach specific conditions. The problem with debugging is that a program with release code can behave differently from a program with debug code. For example, while the program is stopping at a breakpoint, other threads of the application are suspended as well. Also, with a release build, the compiler-generated output is optimized and, thus, different effects can occur. With optimized release code, garbage collection is much more aggressive than with debug code. The order of calls within a method can be changed, and some methods can be removed completely and be called in place. There is a need to have runtime information from the release build of a program as well. Trace messages are written with both debug and release code.

A scenario showing how tracing helps is described here. After an application is deployed, it runs on one system without problems, whereas on another system intermittent problems occur. When you enable verbose tracing, the system with the problems gives you detailed information about what's happening inside the application. The system that is running without problems has tracing configured just for error messages redirected to the Windows event log system. Critical errors are seen by the system administrator. The overhead of tracing is very small because you configure a trace level only when needed.

Tracing has quite a history with .NET. After a simple tracing functionality with the first version of .NET and the `Trace` class, .NET 2.0 made huge improvements on tracing and introduced the `TraceSource` class. The architecture behind `TraceSource` is very flexible in separating the source, the listener, and a switch to turn tracing on and off based on a list of trace levels.

Starting with .NET 4.5, again a new tracing class was introduced and enhanced with .NET 4.6: the `EventSource` class. This class is defined in the `System.Diagnostics.Tracing` namespace in the NuGet package `Sytem.Diagnostics`.

The new tracing architecture is based on Event Tracing for Windows (ETW), which was introduced with Windows Vista. It allows for fast system-wide messaging that is also used by the Windows event-logging and performance-monitoring facilities.

Let's get into the concepts of ETW tracing and the `EventSource` class.

➤ An **ETW provider** is a library that fires ETW events. The applications created with this chapter are ETW providers.

➤ An **ETW manifest** describes the events that can be fired from ETW providers. Using a predefined manifest has the advantage that the system administrator already knows what events an application can fire as soon as the application is installed. This way the administrator can already configure listening for specific events. The new version of the `EventSource` allows both self-describing events and events described by a manifest.

➤ **ETW keywords** can be used to create categories for events. They are defined as bit-flags.

➤ **ETW tasks** are another way to group events. Tasks can be created to define events based on different scenarios of the program. Tasks are usually used with opcodes.

➤ **ETW opcodes** identify operations within a task. Both tasks and opcodes are defined with integer values.

➤ An **event source** is the class that fires events. You can either use the `EventSource` class directly or create a class that derives from the base class `EventSource`.

➤ An **event method** is a method of the event source that fires events. Deriving from the class `EventSource`, every void method is an event method if it is not annotated with the `NonEvent` attribute. Event methods can be annotated with the `Event` attribute.

➤ The **event level** defines the severity or verbosity of an event. This can be used to differ between critical, error, warning, informational, and verbose events.

➤ **ETW channels** are sinks for events. Events can be written to channels and log files. Admin, Operational, Analytic, and Debug are predefined channels.

Using the `EventSource` class, you will see the ETW concepts in action.

Examining a Simple Use of EventSource

The sample code using the `EventSource` class makes use of these dependencies and namespaces:

Dependencies

```
NETStandard.Library

System.Net.Http
```

Namespaces

```
System

System.Collections.Generic

System.Diagnostics.Tracing

System.IO

System.Net.Http

System.Threading.Tasks

static System.Console
```

With the release of .NET 4.6—and with .NET Core 1.0—the class `EventSource` was extended and simplified to allow instantiating and using it without the need to derive a class. This makes it simpler to use it with small scenarios.

The first example for using `EventSource` shows a simple case. `EventSource` is instantiated as a static member of the `Program` class with a Console Application (Package) project. With the constructor, the name of the event source is specified (code file `SimpleEventSourceSample/Program.cs`):

```
private static EventSource sampleEventSource =
    new EventSource("Wrox-EventSourceSample1");
```

With the `Main` method of the `Program` class, the unique identifier of the event source is retrieved using the `Guid` property. This identifier is created based on the name of the event source. After this, the first event is written to invoke the `Write` method of `EventSource`. The parameter required is the event name that needs to be passed. Other parameters are available with overloads of the object. The second parameter that is passed is an anonymous object defining the `Info` property. This can be used to pass any information about the event to the event log:

```
static void Main()
{
  WriteLine($"Log Guid: {sampleEventSource.Guid}");
  WriteLine($"Name: {sampleEventSource.Name}");

  sampleEventSource.Write("Startup", new { Info = "started app" });
  NetworkRequestSample().Wait();
  ReadLine();
  sampleEventSource&#x0003F?.Dispose();
}
```

> **NOTE** *Instead of passing an anonymous object with custom data to the* `Write` *method, you can create a class that derives from the base class* `EventSource` *and mark it with the attribute* `EventData`. *This attribute is shown later in this chapter.*

The method `NetworkRequestSample` that is invoked from the `Main` method makes a network request and writes a trace log passing the URL that is requested to the trace information. On completion of the network call, trace information is written again. The exception-handling code shows another method overload on writing trace information. Different overloads allow passing specific information that is shown in the next sections. The following code snippet shows `EventSourceOptions` setting a trace level. The `Error` event level is set by writing error information. This level can be used to filter specific trace information. With filtering you can decide to read just error information—for example, information with the error level and information that is more critical than the error level. During another tracing session you can decide to read all trace information using the verbose level. The `EventLevel` enumeration defines the values `LogAlways`, `Critical`, `Error`, `Warning`, `Informational`, and `Verbose`:

```
private static async Task NetworkRequestSample()
{
  try
  {
    using (var client = new HttpClient())
    {
      string url = "http://www.cninnovation.com";
      sampleEventSource.Write("Network", new { Info = $"requesting {url}" });

      string result = await client.GetStringAsync(url);
      sampleEventSource.Write("Network",
        new
        {
          Info =
            $"completed call to {url}, result string length: {result.Length}"
        });
    }
    WriteLine("Complete................");
  }
  catch (Exception ex)
  {
    sampleEventSource.Write("Network Error",
      new EventSourceOptions { Level = EventLevel.Error },
      new { Message = ex.Message, Result = ex.HResult });
    WriteLine(ex.Message);
  }
}
```

Before you run the application, you have to do some configuration and use tools for reading the traces. The next section explains how to do this.

> **NOTE** *The simple use of* `EventSource` *is only available with .NET 4.6, .NET Core 1.0, and later versions. Programs created with earlier versions of .NET need to create a class derived from* `EventSource` *as shown in the next sections. Alternatively, to use the simpler options, you can use the NuGet package* `Microsoft.Diagnostics.Tracing` `.EventSource` *that is available for older .NET versions.*

Understanding Tools for Tracing

For analyzing trace information, several tools are available. *logman* is a tool that is part of Windows. With logman you can create and manage event trace sessions and write ETW traces to a binary log file. *tracerpt* is also available with Windows. This tool enables you to convert the binary information written from logman to a CSV, XML, or EVTX file format. PerfView is a tool that offers graphical information for ETW traces.

Logman

Let's begin using logman to create a trace session from the previously created application. You need to first start the application to copy the GUID that's created for the application. You need this GUID to start a log session with `logman`. The `start` option starts a new session to log. The `-p` option defines the name of the provider; here the GUID is used to identify the provider. The `-o` option defines the output file, and the `-ets` option sends the command directly to the event trace system without scheduling. Be sure to start `logman` in a directory where you have write access; otherwise it fails to write the output file `mytrace.etl`:

```
logman start mysession -p {3b0e7fa6-0346-5781-db55-49d84d7103de} -o mytrace.etl -ets
```

After running the application, you can stop the trace session with the `stop` command:

```
logman stop mysession -ets
```

> **NOTE** *logman has a lot more commands that are not covered here. Using logman, you can see all the installed ETW trace providers and their names and identifiers, create data collectors to start and stop at specified times, define maximum log file sizes, and more. You can see the different options of logman with* `logman -h`.

Tracerpt

The log file is in a binary format. To get a readable representation, you can use the utility `tracerpt`. With this tool, it's possible to extract CSV, XML, and EVTX formats, as specified with the `-of` option:

```
tracerpt mytrace.etl -o mytrace.xml -of XML
```

Now the information is available in a readable format. With the information that is logged by the application, you can see the event name passed to the `Write` method manifests within the `Task` element, and you can find the anonymous object within the `EventData` element:

```
<Event xmlns="http://schemas.microsoft.com/win/2004/08/events/event">
  <System>
    <Provider Name="Wrox-SimpleEventSourceSample"
      Guid="{3b0e7fa6-0346-5781-db55-49d84d7103de}" />
    <EventID>2</EventID>
```

```xml
          <Version>0</Version>
          <Level>5</Level>
          <Task>0</Task>
          <Opcode>0</Opcode>
          <Keywords>0x0</Keywords>
          <TimeCreated SystemTime="2015-10-14T21:45:20.874754600Z" />
          <Correlation ActivityID="{00000000-0000-0000-0000-000000000000}" />
          <Execution ProcessID="120" ThreadID="9636" ProcessorID="1" KernelTime="45"
              UserTime="270" />
          <Channel />
          <Computer />
        </System>
        <EventData>
          <Data Name="Info">started app</Data>
        </EventData>
        <RenderingInfo Culture="en-US">
          <Task>Startup</Task>
        </RenderingInfo>
      </Event>
```

The error information is shown with the trace as shown here:

```xml
    <EventData>
      <Data Name="Message">An error occurred while sending the request.</Data>
      <Data Name="Result">-2146233088</Data>
    </EventData>
```

PerfView

Another tool to read trace information is PerfView. You can download this tool from the Microsoft downloads page http://www.microsoft.com/downloads). Version 1.8 of this tool has great enhancements for using it with Visual Studio 2015 and the self-describing ETW format from EventSource. This tool doesn't need to be installed; just copy the tool where you need it. After you start this tool, it makes use of the subdirectories where it is located and allows directly opening the binary ETL file. Figure 20-1 shows PerfView opening the file mytrace.etl created by logman.

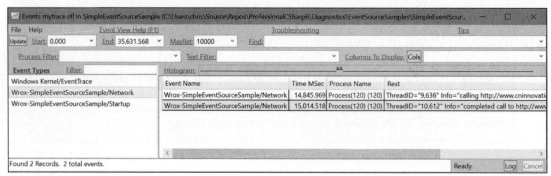

FIGURE 20-1

Deriving from EventSource

Instead of directly using an instance of EventSource, it's a good practice to define all the information that could be traced in a single place. For many applications, it's enough to define just one event source. This event source can be defined in a separate logging assembly. The event source class needs to derive from the base class EventSource. With this custom class, all the trace information that should be written can be defined by separate methods that invoke the WriteEvent method of the base class. The class is implemented with the Singleton pattern, which offers a static Log property that returns an instance. Naming this property `Log` is a convention used with event sources. The private constructor calls the constructor of the base class to set the event source name (code file `EventSourceSampleInheritance/SampleEventSource.cs`):

```csharp
public class SampleEventSource : EventSource
{
  private SampleEventSource()
    : base("Wrox-SampleEventSource2")
  {
  }

  public static SampleEventSource Log = new SampleEventSource();

  public void Startup()
  {
    base.WriteEvent(1);
  }

  public void CallService(string url)
  {
    base.WriteEvent(2, url);
  }

  public void CalledService(string url, int length)
  {
    base.WriteEvent(3, url, length);
  }


  public void ServiceError(string message, int error)
  {
    base.WriteEvent(4, message, error);
  }
}
```

All the `void` methods of an event source class are used to write event information. In case you're defining a helper method, it needs to be annotated with the `NonEvent` attribute.

In a simple scenario where only information messages should be written, nothing more is necessary. Besides passing an event ID to the trace log, the `WriteEvent` method has 18 overloads that allow passing message strings, `int`, and `long` values, and any number of `objects`.

With this implementation, you can use the members of the `SampleEventSource` type to write trace messages as shown in the `Program` class. The `Main` method makes a trace log calling the `Startup` method, invokes the `NetworkRequestSample` method to create a trace log via the `CallService` method, and makes a trace log in case of an error (code file `EventSourceSampleInheritance/Program.cs`):

```csharp
public class Program
{
  public static void Main()
  {
    SampleEventSource.Log.Startup();
    WriteLine($"Log Guid: {SampleEventSource.Log.Guid}");
    WriteLine($"Name: {SampleEventSource.Log.Name}");
    NetworkRequestSample().Wait();
    ReadLine();
  }

  private static async Task NetworkRequestSample()
  {
    try
    {
```

```
        var client = new HttpClient();
        string url = "http://www.cninnovation.com";
        SampleEventSource.Log.CallService(url);
        string result = await client.GetStringAsync(url);
        SampleEventSource.Log.CalledService(url, result.Length);
        WriteLine("Complete.................");
    }
    catch (Exception ex)
    {
        SampleEventSource.Log.ServiceError(ex.Message, ex.HResult);
        WriteLine(ex.Message);
    }
    }
}
```

When you run the app with these commands with a developer command prompt from the directory of the project, you produce an XML file that contains information about the traces:

```
> logman start mysession -p "{1cedea2a-a420-5660-1ff0-f718b8ea5138}"
  -o log2.etl -ets
> dnx run
> logman stop mysession -ets
> tracerpt log2.etl -o log2.xml -of XML
```

The event information about the service call is shown here:

```
<Event xmlns="http://schemas.microsoft.com/win/2004/08/events/event">
  <System>
    <Provider Name="Wrox-SampleEventSource2"
      Guid="{1cedea2a-a420-5660-1ff0-f718b8ea5138}" />
    <EventID>7</EventID>
    <Version>0</Version>
    <Level>4</Level>
    <Task>0</Task>
    <Opcode>0</Opcode>
    <Keywords>0xF00000000000</Keywords>
    <TimeCreated SystemTime="2015-09-06T07:55:28.865368800Z" />
    <Correlation ActivityID="{00000000-0000-0000-0000-000000000000}" />
    <Execution ProcessID="11056" ThreadID="10816" ProcessorID="0"
      KernelTime="30" UserTime="90" />
    <Channel />
    <Computer />
  </System>
  <EventData>
    <Data Name="url">http://www.cninnovation.com</Data>
  </EventData>
  <RenderingInfo Culture="en-US">
    <Task>CallService</Task>
  </RenderingInfo>
</Event>
```

Using Annotations with EventSource

Creating an event source class that derives from EventSource, you have more control on defining the trace information. You can add annotations to the methods by using attributes.

By default, the name of the event source is the same as the name of the class, but you can change the name and the unique identifier by applying the EventSource attribute. Every event trace method can be accompanied by the Event attribute. Here you can define the ID of the event, an opcode, the trace level, custom keywords, and tasks. This information is used to create manifest information for Windows to define what information is logged. The base methods WriteEvent that are called within the methods using the EventSource need to match the event ID defined by the Event attribute, and the variable names passed to the WriteEvent methods need to match the argument names of the declared method.

With the sample class `SampleEventSource`, custom keywords are defined by the inner class `Keywords`. The members of this class are cast to the enumeration type `EventKeywords`. `EventKeywords` is a flag-based enum of type `long` that defines only values with upper bits starting with bit 42. You can use all the lower bits to define custom keywords. The `Keywords` class defines values for the lowest four bits set to `Network`, `Database`, `Diagnostics`, and `Performance`. The enum `EventTask` is a similar flags-based enumeration. Contrary to `EventKeywords`, an `int` is enough for its backing store, and `EventTask` doesn't have predefined values (only the enumeration value `None = 0` is predefined). Similar to the `Keywords` class, the `Task` class defines custom tasks for the `EventTask` enumeration (code file `EventSourceSampleAnnotations/ SampleEventSource.cs`):

```
[EventSource(Name="EventSourceSample", Guid="45FFF0E2-7198-4E4F-9FC3-DF6934680096")]
class SampleEventSource : EventSource
{
  public class Keywords
  {
    public const EventKeywords Network = (EventKeywords)1;
    public const EventKeywords Database = (EventKeywords)2;
    public const EventKeywords Diagnostics = (EventKeywords)4;
    public const EventKeywords Performance = (EventKeywords)8;
  }

  public class Tasks
  {
    public const EventTask CreateMenus = (EventTask)1;
    public const EventTask QueryMenus = (EventTask)2;
  }

  private SampleEventSource()
  {
  }

  public static SampleEventSource Log = new SampleEventSource ();

  [Event(1, Opcode=EventOpcode.Start, Level=EventLevel.Verbose)]
  public void Startup()
  {
    base.WriteEvent(1);
  }

  [Event(2, Opcode=EventOpcode.Info, Keywords=Keywords.Network,
    Level=EventLevel.Verbose, Message="{0}")]
  public void CallService(string url)
  {
    base.WriteEvent(2, url);
  }

  [Event(3, Opcode=EventOpcode.Info, Keywords=Keywords.Network,
    Level=EventLevel.Verbose, Message="{0}, length: {1}")]
  public void CalledService(string url, int length)
  {
    base.WriteEvent(3, url, length);
  }


  [Event(4, Opcode=EventOpcode.Info, Keywords=Keywords.Network,
    Level=EventLevel.Error, Message="{0} error: {1}")]
  public void ServiceError(string message, int error)
  {
    base.WriteEvent(4, message, error);
  }

  [Event(5, Opcode=EventOpcode.Info, Task=Tasks.CreateMenus,
    Level=EventLevel.Verbose, Keywords=Keywords.Network)]
```

```
public void SomeTask()
{
  base.WriteEvent(5);
}
}
```

The `Program` class to write these events is unchanged. The information from these events can now be used on using a listener and filtering only events for specific keywords, for specific log levels, or for specific tasks. You see how to create listeners later in this chapter in the "Creating Custom Listeners" section.

Creating Event Manifest Schema

Creating a custom event source class has the advantage that you can create a manifest that describes all the trace information. Using the `EventSource` class without inheritance, the `Settings` property is set to the value `EtwSelfDescribingEventFormat` of the enumeration `EventSourceSettings`. The events are directly described by the methods invoked. When you use a class that inherits from `EventSource`, the `Settings` property has the value `EtwManifestEventFormat`. The event information is described by a manifest.

You can create the manifest file by using the static method `GenerateManifest` of the `EventSource` class. The first parameter defines the class of the event source; the second parameter describes the path of the assembly that contains the event source type (code file EventSourceSampleAnnotations/Program.cs):

```
public static void GenerateManifest()
{
  string schema = SampleEventSource.GenerateManifest(
    typeof(SampleEventSource), ".");
  File.WriteAllText("sampleeventsource.xml", schema);
}
```

This is the manifest information containing tasks, keywords, events, and templates for the event messages (code file EventSourceSampleAnnotations/sampleeventsource.xml):

```
<instrumentationManifest
  xmlns="http://schemas.microsoft.com/win/2004/08/events">
  <instrumentation xmlns:xs="http://www.w3.org/2001/XMLSchema"
    xmlns:xsi="http://www.w3.org/2001/XMLSchema-instance"
    xmlns:win="http://manifests.microsoft.com/win/2004/08/windows/events">
    <events xmlns="http://schemas.microsoft.com/win/2004/08/events">
      <provider name="EventSourceSample"
        guid="{45fff0e2-7198-4e4f-9fc3-df6934680096}" resourceFileName="."
        messageFileName="." symbol="EventSourceSample">
        <tasks>
          <task name="CreateMenus" message="$(string.task_CreateMenus)"
            value="1"/>
          <task name="QueryMenus" message="$(string.task_QueryMenus)"
            value="2"/>
          <task name="EventSourceMessage"
            message="$(string.task_EventSourceMessage)" value="65534"/>
        </tasks>
        <opcodes>
        </opcodes>
        <keywords>
          <keyword name="Network" message="$(string.keyword_Network)"
            mask="0x1"/>
          <keyword name="Database" message="$(string.keyword_Database)"
            mask="0x2"/>
          <keyword name="Diagnostics" message="$(string.keyword_Diagnostics)"
            mask="0x4"/>
          <keyword name="Performance" message="$(string.keyword_Performance)"
            mask="0x8"/>
          <keyword name="Session3" message="$(string.keyword_Session3)"
            mask="0x100000000000"/>
```

```xml
          <keyword name="Session2" message="$(string.keyword_Session2)"
            mask="0x200000000000"/>
          <keyword name="Session1" message="$(string.keyword_Session1)"
            mask="0x400000000000"/>
          <keyword name="Session0" message="$(string.keyword_Session0)"
            mask="0x800000000000"/>
        </keywords>
        <events>
          <event value="0" version="0" level="win:LogAlways"
            symbol="EventSourceMessage" task="EventSourceMessage"
            template="EventSourceMessageArgs"/>
          <event value="1" version="0" level="win:Verbose" symbol="Startup"
            opcode="win:Start"/>
          <event value="2" version="0" level="win:Verbose" symbol="CallService"
            message="$(string.event_CallService)" keywords="Network"
            template="CallServiceArgs"/>
          <event value="3" version="0" level="win:Verbose"
            symbol="CalledService" message="$(string.event_CalledService)"
            keywords="Network" template="CalledServiceArgs"/>
          <event value="4" version="0" level="win:Error" symbol="ServiceError"
            message="$(string.event_ServiceError)" keywords="Network"
            template="ServiceErrorArgs"/>
          <event value="5" version="0" level="win:Verbose" symbol="SomeTask"
            keywords="Network" task="CreateMenus"/>
        </events>
        <templates>
          <template tid="FileName_EventSourceMessageArgs">
            <data name="message" inType="win:UnicodeString"/>
          </template>
          <template tid="CallServiceArgs">
            <data name="url" inType="win:UnicodeString"/>
          </template>
          <template tid="CalledServiceArgs">
            <data name="url" inType="win:UnicodeString"/>
            <data name="length" inType="win:Int32"/>
          </template>
          <template tid="ServiceErrorArgs">
            <data name="message" inType="win:UnicodeString"/>
            <data name="error" inType="win:Int32"/>
          </template>
        </templates>
      </provider>
    </events>
  </instrumentation>
  <localization>
    <resources culture="en-GB">
      <stringTable>
        <string id="FileName_event_CalledService" value="%1 length: %2"/>
        <string id="FileName_event_CallService" value="%1"/>
        <string id="FileName_event_ServiceError" value="%1 error: %2"/>
        <string id="FileName_keyword_Database" value="Database"/>
        <string id="FileName_keyword_Diagnostics" value="Diagnostics"/>
        <string id="FileName_keyword_Network" value="Network"/>
        <string id="FileName_keyword_Performance" value="Performance"/>
        <string id="FileName_keyword_Session0" value="Session0"/>
        <string id="FileName_keyword_Session1" value="Session1"/>
        <string id="FileName_keyword_Session2" value="Session2"/>
        <string id="FileName_keyword_Session3" value="Session3"/>
        <string id="FileName_task_CreateMenus" value="CreateMenus"/>
        <string id="FileName_task_EventSourceMessage" value="EventSourceMessage"/>
        <string id="FileName_task_QueryMenus" value="QueryMenus"/>
      </stringTable>
```

```
        </resources>
      </localization>
  </instrumentationManifest>
```

Having this metadata and registering it with the system allows the system administrator to filter for specific events and get notifications when something happens. You can handle registration in two ways: static and dynamic. Static registration requires administrative privileges, and a registration via the `wevtutil.exe` command-line tool, which passes the DLL that contains the manifest. The `EventSource` class also offers the preferred dynamic registration. This happens during runtime without the need for administrative privileges returning the manifest in an event stream, or in a response to a standard ETW command.

Using Activity IDs

A new feature of the new version of `TraceSource` makes it possible to easily write activity IDs. As soon as you have multiple tasks running, it helps to know which trace messages belong to each other and not have the trace message based only on time. For example, when you're using tracing with a web application, multiple requests from clients are dealt concurrently when it is good to know which trace messages belong to one request. Such issues don't occur only on the server; the problem is also in the client application as soon as you're running multiple tasks, or when you're using the C# `async` and `await` keywords on calling asynchronous methods. Different tasks come into play.

When you create a class that derives from `TraceSource`, all you have to do to create activity IDs is define methods that are post-fixed with `Start` and `Stop`.

For the sample showing activity IDs in action, a Class Library (Package) supporting .NET 4.6 and .NET Core 1.0 is created. Previous versions of .NET don't support the new `TraceSource` features for activity IDs. The `ProcessingStart` and `RequestStart` methods are used to start activities; `ProcessingStop` and `RequestStop` stop activities (code file `MyApplicationEvents/SampleEventSource`):

```
public class SampleEventSource : EventSource
{
  private SampleEventSource()
    : base("Wrox-SampleEventSource")
  {
  }

  public static SampleEventSource Log = new SampleEventSource();

  public void ProcessingStart(int x)
  {
    base.WriteEvent(1, x);
  }
  public void Processing(int x)
  {
    base.WriteEvent(2, x);
  }
  public void ProcessingStop(int x)
  {
    base.WriteEvent(3, x);
  }

  public void RequestStart()
  {
    base.WriteEvent(4);
  }
  public void RequestStop()
  {
    base.WriteEvent(5);
  }
}
```

The client application that's writing the events makes use of these dependencies and namespaces:

Dependencies

NETStandard.Library

System.Diagnostics.Tracing

System.Threading.Tasks.Parallel

System.Net.Http

MyApplicatonEvents

Namespaces

System

System.Collections.Generic

System.Diagnostics.Tracing

System.Net.Http

System.Threading.Tasks

static System.Console

The `ParallelRequestSample` method invokes the `RequestStart` and `RequestStop` methods to start and stop the activity. Between these calls, a parallel loop is created using `Parallel.For`. The `Parallel` class uses multiple tasks to run concurrently by calling the delegate of the third parameter. This parameter is implemented as a lambda expression to invoke the `ProcessTaskAsync` method (code file `ClientApp/Program.cs`):

```
private static void ParallelRequestSample()
{
  SampleEventSource.Log.RequestStart();
  Parallel.For(0, 20, x =>
  {
    ProcessTaskAsync(x).Wait();
  });
  SampleEventSource.Log.RequestStop();
  WriteLine("Activity complete");
}
```

> **NOTE** *The* `Parallel` *class is explained in detail in Chapter 21, "Tasks and Parallel Programming."*

The method `ProcessTaskAsync` writes traces using `ProcessingStart` and `ProcessingStop`. Here, an activity is started within another activity. As you can see from the output analyzing the logs, activities can be hierarchical (code file `ClientApp/Program.cs`):

```
private static async Task ProcessTaskAsync(int x)
{
  SampleEventSource.Log.ProcessingStart(x);
  var r = new Random();
  await Task.Delay(r.Next(500));

  using (var client = new HttpClient())
  {
    var response = await client.GetAsync("http://www.bing.com");
  }
  SampleEventSource.Log.ProcessingStop(x);
}
```

Previously, you have used the PerfView tool to open an ETL log file. PerfView can also analyze running applications. You can run PerfView with the following option:

```
PerfView /onlyproviders=*Wrox-SampleEventSource collect
```

The option `collect` starts the data collection. Using the qualifier `/onlyproviders` turns off the Kernel and CLR providers and only logs messages from the providers listed. Use the qualifier `-h` to see possible options and qualifiers of PerfView. When you start PerfView this way, data collection starts immediately and continues until you click the Stop Collection button (see Figure 20-2).

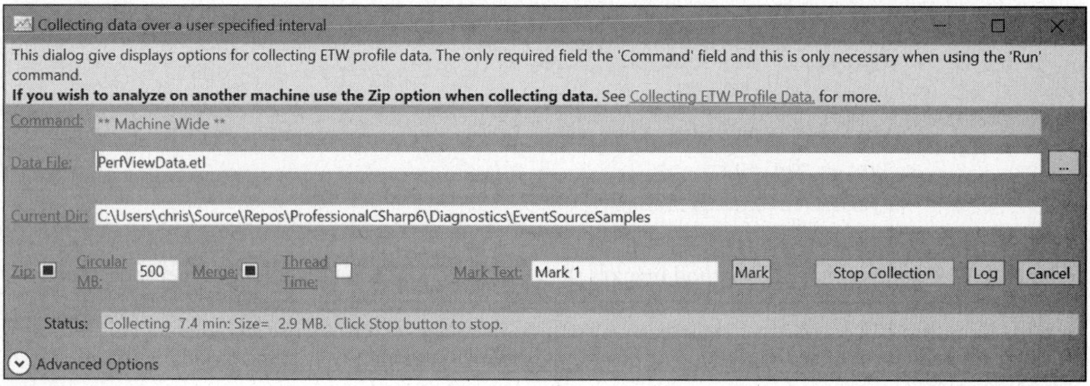

FIGURE 20-2

When you run the application after you've started the trace collection, and then have stopped the collection afterward, you can see activity IDs generated with the event type `Wrox-SampleEventSource/ProcessingStart/Start`. The IDs allow a hierarchy, such as `//1/2` with one parent activity and a child activity. For every loop iteration, you see a different activity ID (see Figure 20-3). With the event type `Wrox-SampleEventSource/ProcessingStop/Stop`, you can see the same activity IDs as they relate to the same activity.

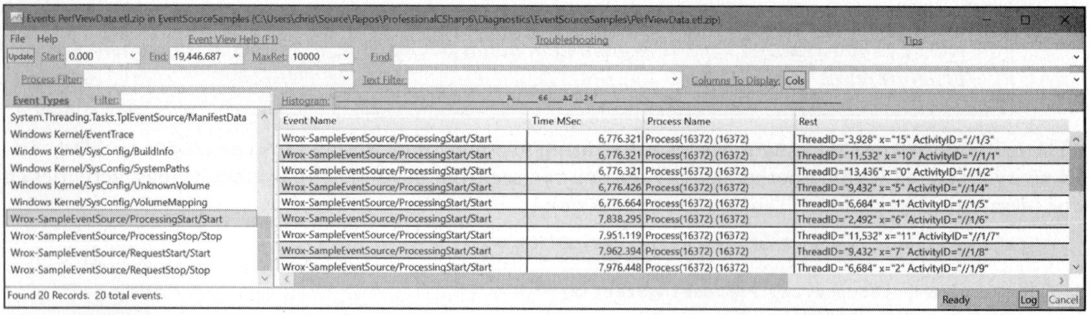

FIGURE 20-3

Using PerfView, you can select multiple event types on the left, and add a filter—for example, `//1/4`—so you see all the events that belong to this activity (see Figure 20-4). Here you can see that an activity ID can span multiple threads. The start and stop events from the same activity use different threads.

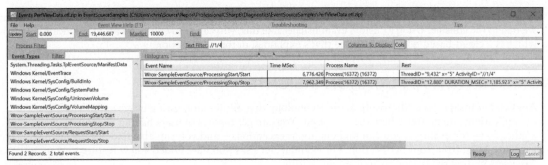

FIGURE 20-4

CREATING CUSTOM LISTENERS

As you've written trace messages, you've seen how to read them using tools such as logman, tracerpt, and PerfView. You can also create a custom in-process event listener to write the events where you want.

You create custom event listeners by creating a class that derives from the base class `EventListener`. All you need to do is to override the `OnEventWritten` method. With this method, trace messages are passed to the parameter of type `EventWrittenEventArgs`. The sample implementation sends information about the event, including the payload, which is the additional data passed to the `WriteEvent` method of the `EventSource` (code file `ClientApp/MyEventListener.cs`):

```
public class MyEventListener : EventListener
{
  protected override void OnEventSourceCreated(EventSource eventSource)
  {
    WriteLine($"created {eventSource.Name} {eventSource.Guid}");
  }

  protected override void OnEventWritten(EventWrittenEventArgs eventData)
  {
    WriteLine($"event id: {eventData.EventId} source: {eventData.EventSource.Name}");
    foreach (var payload in eventData.Payload)
    {
      WriteLine($"\t{payload}");
    }
  }
}
```

The listener is activated in the `Main` method of the `Program` class. You can access event sources by calling the static method `GetSources` of the `EventSource` class (code file `ClientApp/Program.cs`):

```
IEnumerable<EventSource> eventSources = EventSource.GetSources();
InitListener(eventSources);
```

The `InitListener` method invokes the `EnableEvents` method of the custom listener and passes every event source. The sample code registers the setting `EventLevel.LogAlways` to listen to every log message written. You can also specify to just write information messages—which also include errors—or to write errors only.

```
private static void InitListener(IEnumerable<EventSource> sources)
{
  listener = new MyEventListener();
  foreach (var source in sources)
  {
    listener.EnableEvents(source, EventLevel.LogAlways);
  }
}
```

When you run the application, you see events of the `FrameworkEventSource` and the `Wrox-SampleEventSource` written to the console. Using a custom event listener like this, you can easily write events to Application Insights, which is a cloud-based telemetry service that's explained in the next section.

WORKING WITH APPLICATION INSIGHTS

Application Insights is a Microsoft Azure technology that allows monitoring usage and performance of applications, no matter where they are used. You can get reports of users having issues with your application—for example, you can find out about exceptions—and you can also find out the features users are using from your application. For example, let's say you have added a new feature to your app. Are users finding the button to activate the feature?

When you use Application Insights, it's easy to identify issues that users are having with the app. There's a good reason Microsoft makes it easy to integrate Application Insights with all kinds of applications (both web and Windows apps).

> **NOTE** *Here are some examples of features that users had trouble finding from Microsoft's own products. The Xbox was the first device to offer a user interface with large tiles. The search feature was available directly below the tiles. Although this button was available directly in front of the user, users didn't see it. Microsoft moved the search functionality within a tile, and now users are able to find it. Another example is the physical search button on the Windows Phone. This button was meant to be used to search within apps. Users complained about not having an option to search within email because they didn't think to press this physical button to search for emails. Microsoft changed the functionality. Now the physical search button is used only to search content from the web, and the mail app has its own Search button. Windows 8 had a similar issue with search; users didn't use the search functionality from the charms bar to search within apps. Windows 8.1 changed the guideline to use search from the charms bar, and now the app contains its own search box; in Windows 10 there's also an auto suggest box. Does it look like some communalities?*

Creating a Universal Windows App

One of the sample apps for making use of Application Insights is a Universal Windows Platform app with two pages—`MainPage` and `SecondPage`—and just a few button and textbox controls to simulate an action, throw an exception, and navigate between pages. The user interface is defined in the following code snippet (code file `WinAppInsights/MainPage.xaml`):

```
<StackPanel Orientation="Vertical">
  <Button Content="Navigate to SecondPage" Click="OnNavigateToSecondPage" />
  <TextBox x:Name="sampleDataText" Header="Sample Data" />
  <Button Content="Action" Click="OnAction" />
  <Button Content="Create Error" Click="OnError" />
</StackPanel>
```

Clicking on the Navigate to SecondPage button invokes the `OnNavigateToSecondPage` event handler method and navigates to the second page (code file `WinAppInsights/MainPage.xaml.cs`):

```
private void OnNavigateToSecondPage(object sender, RoutedEventArgs e)
{
  this.Frame.Navigate(typeof(SecondPage));
}
```

With the `OnAction` method, a dialog shows the data entered by the user:

```
private async void OnAction(object sender, RoutedEventArgs e)
{
```

```
    var dialog = new ContentDialog
    {
      Title = "Sample",
      Content = $"You entered {sampleDataText.Text}",
      PrimaryButtonText = "Ok"
    };
    await dialog.ShowAsync();
  }
```

And the `OnError` method throws an unhandled exception:

```
private void OnError(object sender, RoutedEventArgs e)
{
  throw new Exception("something bad happened");
}
```

> **NOTE** *You can read more information about creating apps using the Universal Windows Platform starting with Chapter 29, "Core XAML," and especially in Chapter 32, "Windows Apps: User Interfaces," and Chapter 33, "Advanced Windows Apps."*

Creating an Application Insights Resource

For using Application Insights, you need to create an Application Insights resource to your Microsoft Azure account. In the Microsoft Azure portal (`http://portal.azure.com`), you can find this resource with the Developer Services. When you create this resource, you need to specify the name, application type, resource group, subscription, and location of the service (see Figure 20-5).

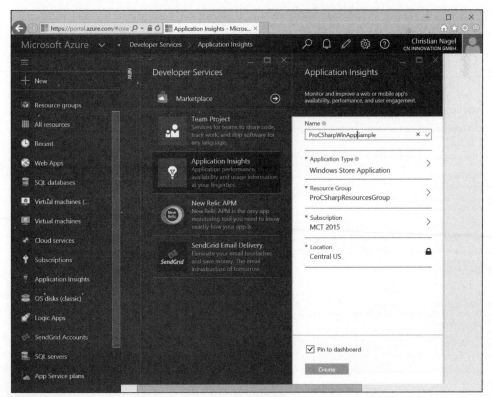

FIGURE 20-5

After creating the Application Insights resource, a resource window is shown where you can see collected information about your application. What you need from this management user interface is the instrumentation key that is available in the Properties settings.

> **NOTE** *In case you don't have a Microsoft Azure account, you can try out one for free. Regarding pricing of Application Insights, different price levels offer different functionality. There's a free version offering up to 5 million data points per month. For more information, check* http://azure.microsoft.com.

> **NOTE** *Instead of creating this resource from the web portal, you can select Application Insights from the project template to create this resource in Microsoft Azure.*

Configure a Windows App

After creating a Universal Windows App, you can add Application Insights by selecting the project in Solution Explorer, opening the application context menu (by clicking the right mouse key or pressing the application context key on the keyboard), and then selecting Add Application Insights Telemetry. From there you can select the previously created Application Insights resource (see Figure 20-6) or create a new resource. This configuration adds a reference to the NuGet package `Microsoft.ApplicationInsights.WindowsApps` and the configuration file `ApplicationInsights.config`. In case you add this configuration file programmatically, you need to copy the instrumentation key from the Azure portal and add it to the `InstrumentationKey` element (code file `WinAppInsights/ApplicationInsights.config`):

```xml
<?xml version="1.0" encoding="utf-8" ?>
<ApplicationInsights>
  <InstrumentationKey>Add your instrumentation key here</InstrumentationKey>
</ApplicationInsights>
```

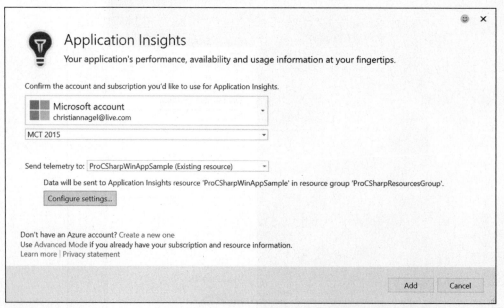

FIGURE 20-6

You need to set the Build action of this file to `Content`, and you need to copy the file to the output directory (just set the corresponding properties in the Property window).

Next, you initialize Application Insights by invoking the `InitializeAsync` method of the `WindowsAppInitializer` class (namespace `Microsoft.ApplicationInsights`). This method enables you to define what Windows collectors should be used; by default the metadata, session, page view, and unhandled exception collectors are configured (code file `WinAppInsights/App.xaml.cs`):

```
public App()
{
  WindowsAppInitializer.InitializeAsync(WindowsCollectors.Metadata |
    WindowsCollectors.Session | WindowsCollectors.PageView |
    WindowsCollectors.UnhandledException);

  this.InitializeComponent();
  this.Suspending += OnSuspending;
}
```

> **NOTE** *The* `InitializeAsync` *method by default reads the instrumentation key from the file* `applicationinsights.config`. *You can also use an overload of this method to pass the instrumentation key with the first parameter.*

Using Collectors

Without doing anything more, you're getting good information out of Application Insights. Just start the application; the collectors defined by the `InitializeAsync` methods do their jobs. After you run the app, navigate between pages, and generate the exception, you can go to the Azure portal to see the information reported. Be aware that when running with the debugger, information is immediately transferred to the cloud, but without the debugger information is cached locally and submitted in packages. You might need to wait a few minutes before the information shows up.

See Figure 20-7 for page views. You can see the number of sessions and users, what page has been opened and how often, and information about the user, such as the user's device, region, IP address, and more.

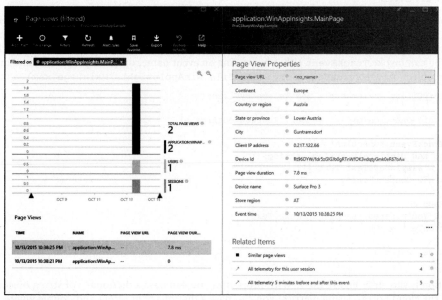

FIGURE 20-7

You can also see information about all the crashes of the app. Figure 20-8 shows the exception, and where and when the exception occurred. Some errors might be related to specific devices, or specific regions. With my picture search app in the Microsoft store, which uses Microsoft's Bing service, I've seen issues in China; some users might be behind a firewall and unable to reach this service. If you are curious to see this app, just search for Picture Search in the Microsoft store and install and run this application.

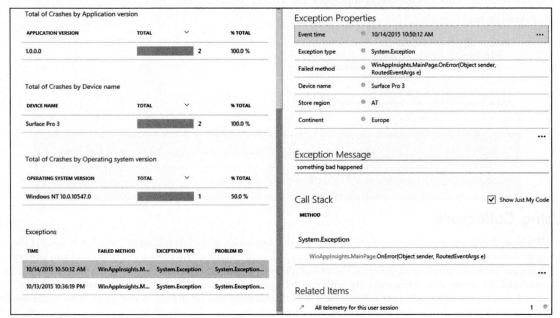

FIGURE 20-8

Writing Custom Events

You can also define your own telemetry information that should be written to the cloud service. To write custom telemetry data, you need to instantiate a `TelemetryClient` object. This class is thread safe, so you can use an instance from multiple threads. Here, the method `OnAction` is changed to write event information that call `TrackEvent`. You can invoke `TrackEvent` either by passing an event name, optional properties, and metrics or by passing an object of type `EventTelemetry` (code file `WinAppInsights/MainPage.xaml.cs`):

```
private TelemetryClient _telemetry = new TelemetryClient();

private async void OnAction(object sender, RoutedEventArgs e)
{
  _telemetry.TrackEvent("OnAction",
    properties: new Dictionary<string, string>()
    { ["data"] = sampleDataText.Text });
  var dialog = new ContentDialog
  {
    Title = "Sample",
    Content = $"You entered {sampleDataText.Text}",
    PrimaryButtonText = "Ok"
  };
  await dialog.ShowAsync();
}
```

This event information is shown in Figure 20-9. With properties you can pass a dictionary of string objects that is all shown in the cloud portal. Using metrics, you can pass a dictionary of string and double where you can pass any counts that you need to analyze the usage of the app.

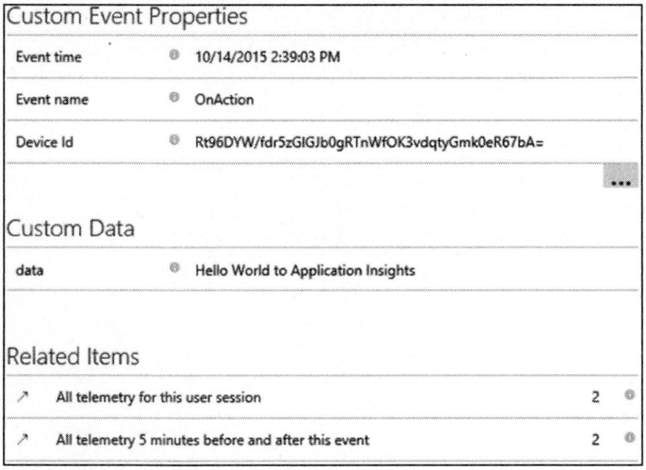

FIGURE 20-9

When you are catching exceptions, you can write error information by invoking `TrackException`. With `TrackException`, you can also pass properties and metrics, and—using the `ExceptionTelemetry` class—also information about the exception:

```
private void OnError(object sender, RoutedEventArgs e)
{
  try
  {
    throw new Exception("something bad happened");
  }
  catch (Exception ex)
  {
    _telemetry.TrackException(
      new ExceptionTelemetry
      {
        Exception = ex,
        HandledAt = ExceptionHandledAt.UserCode,
        SeverityLevel = SeverityLevel.Error
      });
  }
}
```

Other methods you can use to write custom events are `TrackMetric` to track metric information, `TrackPageView` to send information about the page, `TrackTrace` for overall trace information where you can specify a trace level, and `TrackRequest`, which is mainly useful for web applications.

SUMMARY

In this chapter, you have looked at tracing and logging facilities that can help you find intermittent problems in your applications. You should plan early and build these features into your applications; doing so will help you avoid many troubleshooting problems later.

With tracing, you can write debugging messages to an application that you can also use for the final product delivered. If there are problems, you can turn tracing on by changing configuration values and find the issues.

With Application Insights, you've seen that many features come out of the box when you use this cloud service. You can easily analyze app crashes and page views with just a few lines of code. If you add some more lines, you can find out if users don't use some features of the app because they are having trouble finding them.

Although this chapter had a small snippet on using the `Parallel` class, the next chapter goes into more details of parallel programming with the `Task` and `Parallel` classes.

21

Tasks and Parallel Programming

WHAT'S IN THIS CHAPTER?

➤ An overview of multi-threading
➤ Working with the `Parallel` class
➤ Working with Tasks
➤ Using the Cancellation framework
➤ Using the Data Flow Library

WROX.COM CODE DOWNLOADS FOR THIS CHAPTER

The wrox.com code downloads for this chapter are found at www.wrox.com/go/professionalcsharp6 on the Download Code tab. The code for this chapter is divided into the following major examples:

➤ Parallel
➤ Task
➤ Cancellation
➤ DataFlow

OVERVIEW

There are several reasons for using multiple threads. Suppose that you are making a network call from an application that might take some time. You don't want to stall the user interface and force the user to wait idly until the response is returned from the server. The user could perform some other actions in the meantime or even cancel the request that was sent to the server. Using threads can help.

For all activities that require a wait—for example, because of file, database, or network access—you can start a new thread to fulfill other activities at the same time. Even if you have only processing-intensive tasks to do, threading can help. Multiple threads of a single process can run on different CPUs, or, nowadays, on different cores of a multiple-core CPU, at the same time.

You must be aware of some issues when running multiple threads, however. Because they can run during the same time, you can easily get into problems if the threads access the same data. To avoid that, you must implement synchronization mechanisms.

Since .NET 4, .NET has offered an abstraction mechanism to threads: tasks. Tasks allow building relations between tasks—for example, one task should continue when the first one is completed. You can also build a hierarchy consisting of multiple tasks.

Instead of using tasks, you can implement parallel activities using the `Parallel` class. You need to differentiate *data parallelism* where working with some data is processed simultaneously between different tasks, or *task parallelism* where different functions are executed simultaneously.

When creating parallel programs, you have a lot of different options. You should use the simplest option that fits your scenario. This chapter starts with the `Parallel` class that offers very easy parallelism. If this is all you need, just use this class. In case you need more control, such as when you need to manage a relation between tasks or to define a method that returns a task, the `Task` class is the way to go.

This chapter also covers the data flow library, which might be the easiest one to use if you need an actor-based programming to flow data through pipelines.

In case you even need more control over parallelism, such as setting priorities, the `Thread` class might be the one to use.

> **NOTE** *Synchronization between different tasks is covered in Chapter 22, "Task Synchronization."*
>
> *The use of asynchronous methods with the* `async` *and* `await` *keywords is covered in Chapter 15, "Asynchronous Programming."*
>
> *One variant of task parallelism is offered by Parallel LINQ, which is covered in Chapter 13, "Language Integrated Query."*

PARALLEL CLASS

One great abstraction of threads is the `Parallel` class. With this class, both data and task parallelism is offered. This class is in the namespace `System.Threading.Tasks`.

The `Parallel` class defines static methods for a parallel `for` and `foreach`. With the C# statements `for` and `foreach`, the loop is run from one thread. The `Parallel` class uses multiple tasks and, thus, multiple threads for this job.

Whereas the `Parallel.For` and `Parallel.ForEach` methods invoke the same code during each iteration, `Parallel.Invoke` enables you to invoke different methods concurrently. `Parallel.Invoke` is for task parallelism, and `Parallel.ForEach` is for data parallelism.

Looping with the Parallel.For Method

The `Parallel.For` method is similar to the C# `for` loop statement for performing a task a number of times. With `Parallel.For`, the iterations run in parallel. The order of iteration is not defined.

The sample code for `ParallelSamples` makes use of the following dependencies and namespaces:

Dependencies

```
NETStandard.Library
System.Threading.Tasks.Parallel
System.Threading.Thread
```

Namespaces

```
System.Threading

System.Threading.Tasks

static System.Console
```

> **NOTE** *This sample makes use of command-line arguments. To work through the different features, pass different arguments as shown on startup of the sample application, or by checking the* Main *method. From Visual Studio, you can pass command-line arguments in the Debug options of the project properties. Using the dotnet command line, to pass the command-line argument* -pf, *you can start the command* dotnet run -- -pf.

For having information about the thread and the task, the following Log method writes thread and task identifiers to the console (code file ParallelSamples/Program.cs):

```
public static void Log(string prefix)
{
    WriteLine($"{prefix}, task: {Task.CurrentId}, " +
        $"thread: {Thread.CurrentThread.ManagedThreadId}");
}
```

Let's get into the Parallel.For method. With this method, the first two parameters define the start and end of the loop. The following example has the iterations from 0 to 9. The third parameter is an Action<int> delegate. The integer parameter is the iteration of the loop that is passed to the method referenced by the delegate. The return type of Parallel.For is the struct ParallelLoopResult, which provides information if the loop is completed:

```
public static void ParallelFor()
{
    ParallelLoopResult result =
        Parallel.For(0, 10, i =>
        {
            Log($"S {i}");
            Task.Delay(10).Wait();
            Log($"E {i}");
        });
    WriteLine($"Is completed: {result.IsCompleted}");
}
```

In the body of Parallel.For, the index, task identifier, and thread identifier are written to the console. As shown in the following output, the order is not guaranteed. You will see different results if you run this program once more. This run of the program had the order 0-4-6-2-8... with nine tasks and six threads. A task does not necessarily map to one thread: a thread can be reused by different tasks.

```
S 0, task: 5, thread: 1
S 4, task: 7, thread: 6
S 6, task: 8, thread: 7
S 2, task: 6, thread: 5
S 8, task: 9, thread: 8
E 8, task: 9, thread: 8
S 9, task: 14, thread: 8
E 4, task: 7, thread: 6
S 5, task: 17, thread: 6
E 6, task: 8, thread: 7
```

```
S 7, task: 18, thread: 7
E 0, task: 5, thread: 1
S 3, task: 5, thread: 1
E 2, task: 6, thread: 5
S 1, task: 16, thread: 10
E 7, task: 18, thread: 7
E 5, task: 17, thread: 6
E 9, task: 14, thread: 8
E 1, task: 16, thread: 10
E 3, task: 5, thread: 1
Is completed: True
```

The delay within the parallel body waits for 10 milliseconds to have a better chance to create new threads. If you remove this line, you see fewer threads and tasks to be used.

What you can also see with the result is that every end-log of a loop uses the same thread and task as the start-log. Using `Task.Delay` with the `Wait` method blocks the current thread until the delay ends.

Change the previous example to now use the `await` keyword with the `Task.Delay` method:

```
public static void ParallelForWithAsync()
{
  ParallelLoopResult result =
    Parallel.For(0, 10, async i =>
    {
      Log($"S {i}");
      await Task.Delay(10);
      Log($"E {i}");
    });
  WriteLine($"is completed: {result.IsCompleted}");
}
```

The result is in the following code snippet. With the output after the `Thread.Delay` method you can see the thread change. For example, loop iteration 8, which had thread ID 7 before the delay, has thread ID 5 after the delay. You can also see that tasks no longer exist—there are only threads—and here previous threads are reused. Another important aspect is that the `For` method of the `Parallel` class is completed without waiting for the delay. The `Parallel` class waits for the tasks it created, but it doesn't wait for other background activity. It is also possible that you won't see the output from the methods after the delay at all—if the main thread (which is a foreground thread) is finished, all the background threads are stopped. Foreground and background threads are discussed in the next chapter.

```
S 0, task: 5, thread: 1
S 8, task: 8, thread: 7
S 6, task: 7, thread: 8
S 4, task: 9, thread: 6
S 2, task: 6, thread: 5
S 7, task: 7, thread: 8
S 1, task: 5, thread: 1
S 5, task: 9, thread: 6
S 9, task: 8, thread: 7
S 3, task: 6, thread: 5
Is completed: True
E 2, task: , thread: 8
E 0, task: , thread: 8
E 8, task: , thread: 5
E 6, task: , thread: 7
E 4, task: , thread: 6
E 5, task: , thread: 7
E 7, task: , thread: 7
E 1, task: , thread: 6
E 3, task: , thread: 5
E 9, task: , thread: 8
```

> **WARNING** *As demonstrated here, although using async features with .NET 4.5 and C is very easy, it's still important to know what's happening behind the scenes, and you have to pay attention to some issues.*

Stopping Parallel.For Early

You can also break `Parallel.For` early without looping through all the iterations. A method overload of the `For` method accepts a third parameter of type `Action<int, ParallelLoopState>`. By defining a method with these parameters, you can influence the outcome of the loop by invoking the `Break` or `Stop` methods of the `ParallelLoopState`.

Remember, the order of iterations is not defined (code file `ParallelSamples/Program.cs`):

```
public static void StopParallelForEarly()
{
  ParallelLoopResult result =
    Parallel.For(10, 40, (int i, ParallelLoopState pls) =>
    {
      Log($"S {i}");
      if (i > 12)
      {
        pls.Break();
        Log($"break now... {i}");
      }
      Task.Delay(10).Wait();
      Log($"E {i}");
    });

  WriteLine($"Is completed: {result.IsCompleted}");
  WriteLine($"lowest break iteration: {result.LowestBreakIteration}");
}
```

This run of the application demonstrates that the iteration breaks up with a value higher than 12, but other tasks can simultaneously run, and tasks with other values can run. All the tasks that have been started before the break can continue to the end. You can use the `LowestBreakIteration` property to ignore results from tasks that you do not need:

```
S 31, task: 6, thread: 8
S 17, task: 7, thread: 5
S 10, task: 5, thread: 1
S 24, task: 8, thread: 6
break now 24, task: 8, thread: 6
S 38, task: 9, thread: 7
break now 38, task: 9, thread: 7
break now 31, task: 6, thread: 8
break now 17, task: 7, thread: 5
E 17, task: 7, thread: 5
E 10, task: 5, thread: 1
S 11, task: 5, thread: 1
E 38, task: 9, thread: 7
E 24, task: 8, thread: 6
E 31, task: 6, thread: 8
E 11, task: 5, thread: 1
S 12, task: 5, thread: 1
E 12, task: 5, thread: 1
S 13, task: 5, thread: 1
break now 13, task: 5, thread: 1
E 13, task: 5, thread: 1
Is completed: False
lowest break iteration: 13
```

Parallel For Initialization

`Parallel.For` might use several threads to do the loops. If you need an initialization that should be done with every thread, you can use the `Parallel.For<TLocal>` method. The generic version of the `For` method accepts—in addition to the `from` and `to` values—three delegate parameters. The first parameter is of type `Func<TLocal>`. Because the example here uses a `string` for `TLocal`, the method needs to be defined as `Func<string>`, a method returning a `string`. This method is invoked only once for each thread that is used to do the iterations.

The second delegate parameter defines the delegate for the body. In the example, the parameter is of type `Func<int, ParallelLoopState, string, string>`. The first parameter is the loop iteration; the second parameter, `ParallelLoopState`, enables stopping the loop, as shown earlier. With the third parameter, the body method receives the value that is returned from the `init` method. The body method also needs to return a value of the type that was defined with the generic `For` parameter.

The last parameter of the `For` method specifies a delegate, `Action<TLocal>`; in the example, a `string` is received. This method, a thread exit method, is called only once for each thread (code file `ParallelSamples/Program.cs`):

```
public static void ParallelForWithInit()
{
  Parallel.For<string>(0, 10, () =>
  {
    // invoked once for each thread
    Log($"init thread");
    return $"t{Thread.CurrentThread.ManagedThreadId}";
  },
  (i, pls, str1) =>
  {
    // invoked for each member
    Log($"body i {i} str1 {str1}");
    Task.Delay(10).Wait();
    return $"i {i}";
  },
  (str1) =>
  {
    // final action on each thread
    Log($"finally {str1}");
  });
}
```

The result of running this program once is shown here:

```
init thread task: 7, thread: 6
init thread task: 6, thread: 5
body i: 4 str1: t6 task: 7, thread: 6
body i: 2 str1: t5 task: 6, thread: 5
init thread task: 5, thread: 1
body i: 0 str1: t1 task: 5, thread: 1
init thread task: 9, thread: 8
body i: 8 str1: t8 task: 9, thread: 8
init thread task: 8, thread: 7
body i: 6 str1: t7 task: 8, thread: 7
body i: 1 str1: i 0 task: 5, thread: 1
finally i 2 task: 6, thread: 5
init thread task: 16, thread: 5
finally i 8 task: 9, thread: 8
init thread task: 17, thread: 8
body i: 9 str1: t8 task: 17, thread: 8
finally i 6 task: 8, thread: 7
init thread task: 18, thread: 7
body i: 7 str1: t7 task: 18, thread: 7
finally i 4 task: 7, thread: 6
```

```
init thread task: 15, thread: 10
body i: 3 str1: t10 task: 15, thread: 10
body i: 5 str1: t5 task: 16, thread: 5
finally i 1 task: 5, thread: 1
finally i 5 task: 16, thread: 5
finally i 3 task: 15, thread: 10
finally i 7 task: 18, thread: 7
finally i 9 task: 17, thread: 8
```

The output shows that the `init` method is called only once for each thread; the body of the loop receives the first string from the initialization and passes this string to the next iteration of the body with the same thread. Lastly, the final action is invoked once for each thread and receives the last result from every body.

With this functionality, this method fits perfectly to accumulate a result of a huge data collection.

Looping with the Parallel.ForEach Method

`Parallel.ForEach` iterates through a collection implementing `IEnumerable` in a way similar to the `foreach` statement, but in an asynchronous manner. Again, the order is not guaranteed (code file `ParallelSamples/Program.cs`):

```csharp
public static void ParallelForEach()
{
    string[] data = {"zero", "one", "two", "three", "four", "five",
        "six", "seven", "eight", "nine", "ten", "eleven", "twelve"};

    ParallelLoopResult result =
        Parallel.ForEach<string>(data, s =>
        {
            WriteLine(s);
        });
}
```

If you need to break up the loop, you can use an overload of the `ForEach` method with a `ParallelLoopState` parameter. You can do this in the same way you did earlier with the `For` method. An overload of the `ForEach` method can also be used to access an indexer to get the iteration number, as shown here:

```csharp
Parallel.ForEach<string>(data, (s, pls, l) =>
{
    WriteLine($"{s} {l}");
});
```

Invoking Multiple Methods with the Parallel.Invoke Method

If multiple tasks should run in parallel, you can use the `Parallel.Invoke` method, which offers the task parallelism pattern. `Parallel.Invoke` allows the passing of an array of `Action` delegates, whereby you can assign methods that should run. The example code passes the `Foo` and `Bar` methods to be invoked in parallel (code file `ParallelSamples/Program.cs`):

```csharp
public static void ParallelInvoke()
{
    Parallel.Invoke(Foo, Bar);
}
public static void Foo()
{
    WriteLine("foo");
}

public static void Bar()
{
    WriteLine("bar");
}
```

The `Parallel` class is very easy to use—for both task and data parallelism. If more control is needed, and you don't want to wait until the action started with the `Parallel` class is completed, the `Task` class comes in handy. Of course, it's also possible to combine the `Task` and `Parallel` classes.

TASKS

For more control over the parallel actions, you can use the `Task` class from the namespace `System.Threading.Tasks`. A *task* represents some unit of work that should be done. This unit of work can run in a separate thread, and it is also possible to start a task in a synchronized manner, which results in a wait for the calling thread. With tasks, you have an abstraction layer but also a lot of control over the underlying threads.

Tasks provide much more flexibility in organizing the work you need to do. For example, you can define continuation work—what should be done after a task is complete. This can be differentiated based on whether the task was successful. You can also organize tasks in a hierarchy. For example, a parent task can create new children tasks. Optionally, this can create a dependency, so canceling a parent task also cancels its child tasks.

Starting Tasks

To start a task, you can use either the `TaskFactory` or the constructor of the `Task` and the `Start` method. The `Task` constructor gives you more flexibility in creating the task.

The sample code for `TaskSamples` makes use of the following dependencies and namespaces:

Dependencies

```
NETStandard.Library
System.Threading.Thread
```

Namespaces

```
System.Threading
System.Threading.Tasks
static System.Console
```

When starting a task, an instance of the `Task` class can be created, and the code that should run can be assigned with an `Action` or `Action<object>` delegate, with either no parameters or one object parameter. In the following example, a method is defined with one parameter: `TaskMethod`. The implementation invokes the `Log` method where the ID of the task and the ID of the thread are written to the console, as well as information if the thread is coming from a thread pool, and if the thread is a background thread. Writing multiple messages to the console is synchronized by using the `lock` keyword with the `s_logLock` synchronization object. This way, parallel calls to `Log` can be done, and multiple writes to the console are not interleaving each other. Otherwise the `title` could be written by one task, and the thread information follows by another task (code file `TaskSamples/Program.cs`):

```
public static void TaskMethod(object o)
{
  Log(o?.ToString());
}

private static object s_logLock = new object();

public static void Log(string title)
{
  lock (s_logLock)
  {
    WriteLine(title);
```

```
    WriteLine($"Task id: {Task.CurrentId?.ToString() ?? "no task"}, " +
        $"thread: {Thread.CurrentThread.ManagedThreadId}");
#if (!DNXCORE)
    WriteLine($"is pooled thread: {Thread.CurrentThread.IsThreadPoolThread}");
#endif
    WriteLine($"is background thread: {Thread.CurrentThread.IsBackground}");
    WriteLine();
  }
}
```

> **NOTE** *The Thread API* IsThreadPoolThread *is not available with the .NET Core 1.0 runtime; that's why a preprocessor directive is used.*

The following sections describe different ways to start a new task.

Tasks Using the Thread Pool

In this section, different ways are shown to start a task that uses a thread from the thread pool. The thread pool offers a pool of background threads. The thread pool manages threads on its own, increasing or decreasing the number of threads within the pool as needed. Threads from the pool are used to fulfill some actions, and returned to the pool afterward.

The first way to create a task is with an instantiated TaskFactory, where the method TaskMethod is passed to the StartNew method, and the task is immediately started. The second approach uses the static Factory property of the Task class to get access to the TaskFactory, and to invoke the StartNew method. This is very similar to the first version in that it uses a factory, but there's less control over factory creation. The third approach uses the constructor of the Task class. When the Task object is instantiated, the task does not run immediately. Instead, it is given the status Created. The task is then started by calling the Start method of the Task class. The fourth approach calls the Run method of the Task that immediately starts the task. The Run method doesn't have an overloaded variant to pass an Action<object> delegate, but it's easy to simulate this by assigning a lambda expression of type Action, and using the parameter within its implementation (code file TaskSamples/Program.cs):

```
public void TasksUsingThreadPool()
{
  var tf = new TaskFactory();
  Task t1 = tf.StartNew(TaskMethod, "using a task factory");
  Task t2 = Task.Factory.StartNew(TaskMethod, "factory via a task");
  var t3 = new Task(TaskMethod, "using a task constructor and Start");
  t3.Start();
  Task t4 = Task.Run(() => TaskMethod("using the Run method"));
}
```

The output returned with these variants is as follows. All these versions create a new task, and a thread from the thread pool is used:

```
factory via a task
Task id: 5, thread: 6
is pooled thread: True
is background thread: True

using the Run method
Task id: 6, thread: 7
is pooled thread: True
is background thread: True

using a task factory
Task id: 7, thread: 5
```

```
is pooled thread: True
is background thread: True

using a task constructor and Start
Task id: 8, thread: 8
is pooled thread: True
is background thread: True
```

With both the `Task` constructor and the `StartNew` method of the `TaskFactory`, you can pass values from the enumeration `TaskCreationOptions`. Using this creation option, you can change how the task should behave differently, as is shown in the next sections.

Synchronous Tasks

A task does not necessarily mean to use a thread from a thread pool—it can use other threads as well. Tasks can also run synchronously, with the same thread as the calling thread. The following code snippet uses the method `RunSynchronously` of the `Task` class (code file `TaskSamples/Program.cs`):

```
private static void RunSynchronousTask()
{
    TaskMethod("just the main thread");
    var t1 = new Task(TaskMethod, "run sync");
    t1.RunSynchronously();
}
```

Here, the `TaskMethod` is first called directly from the main thread before it is invoked from the newly created `Task`. As you can see from the following console output, the main thread doesn't have a task ID. It is not a pooled thread. Calling the method `RunSynchronously` uses exactly the same thread as the calling thread, but creates a task if one wasn't created previously:

```
just the main thread
Task id: no task, thread: 1
is pooled thread: False
is background thread: True

run sync
Task id: 5, thread: 1
is pooled thread: False
is background thread: True
```

> **NOTE** *If you are not using the .NET Core runtime, the thread is a foreground thread. This is an interesting difference between the old .NET runtime and the new one. With the old runtime, the main thread is a foreground thread; with the new runtime, it's a background thread.*

Tasks Using a Separate Thread

If the code of a task should run for a longer time, you should use `TaskCreationOptions.LongRunning` to instruct the task scheduler to create a new thread, rather than use a thread from the thread pool. This way, the thread doesn't need to be managed by the thread pool. When a thread is taken from the thread pool, the task scheduler can decide to wait for an already running task to be completed and use this thread instead of creating a new thread with the pool. With a long-running thread, the task scheduler knows immediately that it doesn't make sense to wait for this one. The following code snippet creates a long-running task (code file `TaskSamples/Program.cs`):

```
private static void LongRunningTask()
{
    var t1 = new Task(TaskMethod, "long running",
```

```
        TaskCreationOptions.LongRunning);
    t1.Start();
}
```

Indeed, using the option `TaskCreationOptions.LongRunning`, a thread from the thread pool is not used. Instead, a new thread is created:

```
long running
Task id: 5, thread: 7
is pooled thread: False
is background thread: True
```

Futures—Results from Tasks

When a task is finished, it can write some stateful information to a shared object. Such a shared object must be thread-safe. Another option is to use a task that returns a result. Such a task is also known as *future* as it returns a result in the future. With early versions of the Task Parallel Library (TPL), the class had the name `Future` as well. Now it is a generic version of the `Task` class. With this class it is possible to define the type of the result that is returned with a task.

A method that is invoked by a task to return a result can be declared with any return type. The following example method `TaskWithResult` returns two `int` values with the help of a `Tuple`. The input of the method can be void or of type `object`, as shown here (code file `TaskSamples/Program.cs`):

```
public static Tuple<int, int> TaskWithResult(object division)
{
    Tuple<int, int> div = (Tuple<int, int>)division;
    int result = div.Item1 / div.Item2;
    int reminder = div.Item1 % div.Item2;
    WriteLine("task creates a result...");

    return Tuple.Create(result, reminder);
}
```

> **NOTE** *Tuples allow you to combine multiple values into one. Tuples are explained in Chapter 7, "Arrays and Tuples."*

When you define a task to invoke the method `TaskWithResult`, you use the generic class `Task<TResult>`. The generic parameter defines the return type. With the constructor, the method is passed to the `Func` delegate, and the second parameter defines the input value. Because this task needs two input values in the `object` parameter, a tuple is created as well. Next, the task is started. The `Result` property of the `Task` instance `t1` blocks and waits until the task is completed. Upon task completion, the `Result` property contains the result from the task:

```
public static void TaskWithResultDemo()
{
    var t1 = new Task<Tuple<int,int>>(TaskWithResult, Tuple.Create(8, 3));
    t1.Start();
    WriteLine(t1.Result);
    t1.Wait();
    WriteLine($"result from task: {t1.Result.Item1} {t1.Result.Item2}");
}
```

Continuation Tasks

With tasks, you can specify that after a task is finished another specific task should start to run—for example, a new task that uses a result from the previous one or should do some cleanup if the previous task failed.

Whereas the task handler has either no parameter or one object parameter, the continuation handler has a parameter of type `Task`. Here, you can access information about the originating task (code file `TaskSamples/Program.cs`):

```
private static void DoOnFirst()
{
  WriteLine($"doing some task {Task.CurrentId}");
  Task.Delay(3000).Wait();
}

private static void DoOnSecond(Task t)
{
  WriteLine($"task {t.Id} finished");
  WriteLine($"this task id {Task.CurrentId}");
  WriteLine("do some cleanup");
  Task.Delay(3000).Wait();
}
```

A continuation task is defined by invoking the `ContinueWith` method on a task. You could also use the `TaskFactory` for this. `t1.OnContinueWith(DoOnSecond)` means that a new task invoking the method `DoOnSecond` should be started as soon as the task `t1` is finished. You can start multiple tasks when one task is finished, and a continuation task can have another continuation task, as this next example demonstrates (code file `TaskSamples/Program.cs`):

```
public static void ContinuationTasks()
{
  Task t1 = new Task(DoOnFirst);
  Task t2 = t1.ContinueWith(DoOnSecond);
  Task t3 = t1.ContinueWith(DoOnSecond);
  Task t4 = t2.ContinueWith(DoOnSecond);
  t1.Start();
}
```

So far, the continuation tasks have been started when the previous task was finished, regardless of the result. With values from `TaskContinuationOptions`, you can define that a continuation task should only start if the originating task was successful (or faulted). Some of the possible values are `OnlyOnFaulted`, `NotOnFaulted`, `OnlyOnCanceled`, `NotOnCanceled`, and `OnlyOnRanToCompletion`:

```
Task t5 = t1.ContinueWith(DoOnError, TaskContinuationOptions.OnlyOnFaulted);
```

> **NOTE** *The compiler-generated code from the* `await` *keyword discussed in Chapter 15 makes use of continuation tasks.*

Task Hierarchies

With task continuations, one task is started after another. Tasks can also form a hierarchy. When a task starts a new task, a parent/child hierarchy is started.

In the code snippet that follows, within the task of the parent, a new task object is created, and the task is started. The code to create a child task is the same as that to create a parent task. The only difference is that the task is created from within another task (code file `TaskSamples/Program.cs`):

```
public static void ParentAndChild()
{
  var parent = new Task(ParentTask);
  parent.Start();
  Task.Delay(2000).Wait();
```

```
      WriteLine(parent.Status);
      Task.Delay(4000).Wait();
      WriteLine(parent.Status);
  }

  private static void ParentTask()
  {
      WriteLine($"task id {Task.CurrentId}");
      var child = new Task(ChildTask);
      child.Start();
      Task.Delay(1000).Wait();
      WriteLine("parent started child");
  }

  private static void ChildTask()
  {
      WriteLine("child");
      Task.Delay(5000).Wait();
      WriteLine("child finished");
  }
```

If the parent task is finished before the child task, the status of the parent task is shown as `WaitingForChildrenToComplete`. The parent task is completed with the status `RanToCompletion` as soon as all children tasks are completed as well. Of course, this is not the case if the parent creates a task with the `TaskCreationOption DetachedFromParent`.

Canceling a parent task also cancels the children. The cancellation framework is discussed next.

Returning Tasks from Methods

A method that returns a task with results is declared to return `Task<T>`—for example, a method that returns a task with a collection of strings:

```
public Task<IEnumerable<string>> TaskMethodAsync()
{
}
```

Creating methods that access the network or data access are often asynchronous, with such a result so you can use task features to deal with the results (for example, by using the `async` keyword as explained in Chapter 15). In case you have a synchronous path, or need to implement an interface that is defined that way with synchronous code, there's no need to create a task for the sake of the result value. The `Task` class offers creating a result with a completed task that is finished with the status `RanToCompletion` using the method `FromResult`:

```
return Task.FromResult<IEnumerable<string>>(
    new List<string>() { "one", "two" });
```

Waiting for Tasks

Probably you've already seen the `WhenAll` and `WaitAll` methods of the `Task` class and wondered what the difference might be. Both methods wait for all tasks that are passed to these methods to complete. The `WaitAll` method (available since .NET 4) blocks the calling task until all tasks that are waited for are completed. The `WhenAll` method (available since .NET 4.5) returns a task which in turn allows you to use the `async` keyword to wait for the result, and it does not block the waiting task.

Although the `WhenAll` and `WaitAll` methods are finished when all the tasks you are waiting for are completed, you can wait for just one task of a list to be completed with `WhenAny` and `WaitAny`. Similar to the `WhenAll` and `WaitAll` methods, the `WaitAny` method blocks the calling task, whereas `WhenAny` returns a task that can be awaited.

A method that already has been used several times with several samples is the `Task.Delay` method. You can specify a number of milliseconds to wait before the task that is returned from this method is completed.

In case all that should be done is to give up the CPU and thus allow other tasks to run, you can invoke the `Task.Yield` method. This method gives up the CPU and lets other tasks run. In case no other task is waiting to run, the task calling `Task.Yield` continues immediately. Otherwise it needs to wait until the CPU is scheduled again for the calling task.

CANCELLATION FRAMEWORK

.NET 4.5 introduced a cancellation framework to enable the canceling of long-running tasks in a standard manner. Every blocking call should support this mechanism. Of course, not every blocking call currently implements this new technology, but more and more are doing so. Among the technologies that offer this mechanism already are tasks, concurrent collection classes, and Parallel LINQ, as well as several synchronization mechanisms.

The cancellation framework is based on cooperative behavior; it is not forceful. A long-running task checks whether it is canceled and returns control accordingly.

A method that supports cancellation accepts a `CancellationToken` parameter. This class defines the property `IsCancellationRequested`, whereby a long operation can check to see whether it should abort. Other ways for a long operation to check for cancellation include using a `WaitHandle` property that is signaled when the token is canceled or using the `Register` method. The `Register` method accepts parameters of type `Action` and `ICancelableOperation`. The method that is referenced by the `Action` delegate is invoked when the token is canceled. This is similar to the `ICancelableOperation`, whereby the `Cancel` method of an object implementing this interface is invoked when the cancellation is done.

The sample code for CancellationSamples makes use of the following dependencies and namespaces:

Dependencies

```
NETStandard.Library
System.Threading.Tasks.Parallel
```

Namespaces

```
System
System.Threading
System.Threading.Tasks
static System.Console
```

Cancellation of Parallel.For

This section starts with a simple example using the `Parallel.For` method. The `Parallel` class provides overloads for the `For` method, whereby you can pass a parameter of type `ParallelOptions`. With `ParallelOptions`, you can pass a `CancellationToken`. The `CancellationToken` is generated by creating a `CancellationTokenSource`. `CancellationTokenSource` implements the interface `ICancelableOperation` and can therefore be registered with the `CancellationToken` and allows cancellation with the `Cancel` method. The example doesn't call the `Cancel` method directly, but makes use of a new .NET 4.5 method to cancel the token after 500 milliseconds with the `CancelAfter` method.

Within the implementation of the `For` loop, the `Parallel` class verifies the outcome of the `CancellationToken` and cancels the operation. Upon cancellation, the `For` method throws an exception of type `OperationCanceledException`, which is caught in the example. With the `CancellationToken`, it is possible to register for information when the cancellation is done. This is accomplished by calling the

Register method and passing a delegate that is invoked on cancellation (code file `CancellationSamples/Program.cs`):

```csharp
public static void CancelParallelFor()
{
    var cts = new CancellationTokenSource();
    cts.Token.Register(() => WriteLine("*** token cancelled"));

    // send a cancel after 500 ms
    cts.CancelAfter(500);

    try
    {
        ParallelLoopResult result =
            Parallel.For(0, 100, new ParallelOptions
            {
                CancellationToken = cts.Token,
            },
            x =>
            {
                WriteLine($"loop {x} started");
                int sum = 0;
                for (int i = 0; i < 100; i++)
                {
                    Task.Delay(2).Wait();
                    sum += i;
                }
                WriteLine($"loop {x} finished");
            });
    }
    catch (OperationCanceledException ex)
    {
        WriteLine(ex.Message);
    }
}
```

When you run the application, you get output similar to the following. Iteration 0, 50, 25, 75, and 1 were all started. This is on a system with a quad-core CPU. With the cancellation, all other iterations were canceled before starting. The iterations that were started are allowed to finish because cancellation is always done in a cooperative way to avoid the risk of resource leaks when iterations are canceled somewhere in between:

```
loop 0 started
loop 50 started
loop 25 started
loop 75 started
loop 1 started
*** token cancelled
loop 75 finished
loop 50 finished
loop 1 finished
loop 0 finished
loop 25 finished
The operation was canceled.
```

Cancellation of Tasks

The same cancellation pattern is used with tasks. First, a new `CancellationTokenSource` is created. If you need just one cancellation token, you can use a default token by accessing `Task.Factory.CancellationToken`. Then, similar to the previous code, the task is canceled after 500 milliseconds. The task doing the major work within a loop receives the cancellation token via the `TaskFactory` object. The cancellation token is assigned to the `TaskFactory` by setting it in the constructor. This cancellation token is used by the task to check whether cancellation is requested by checking the `IsCancellationRequested` property of the `CancellationToken` (code file `CancellationSamples/Program.cs`):

```
public void CancelTask()
{
  var cts = new CancellationTokenSource();
  cts.Token.Register(() => WriteLine("*** task cancelled"));
  // send a cancel after 500 ms
  cts.CancelAfter(500);
  Task t1 = Task.Run(() =>
  {
    WriteLine("in task");
    for (int i = 0; i < 20; i++)
    {
      Task.Delay(100).Wait();
      CancellationToken token = cts.Token;
      if (token.IsCancellationRequested)
      {
        WriteLine("cancelling was requested, " +
          "cancelling from within the task");
        token.ThrowIfCancellationRequested();
        break;
      }
      WriteLine("in loop");
    }
    WriteLine("task finished without cancellation");
  }, cts.Token);
  try
  {
    t1.Wait();
  }
  catch (AggregateException ex)
  {
    WriteLine($"exception: {ex.GetType().Name}, {ex.Message}");
    foreach (var innerException in ex.InnerExceptions)
    {
      WriteLine($"inner exception: {ex.InnerException.GetType()}," +
        $"{ex.InnerException.Message}");
    }
  }
}
```

When you run the application, you can see that the task starts, runs for a few loops, and gets the cancellation request. The task is canceled and throws a `TaskCanceledException`, which is initiated from the method call `ThrowIfCancellationRequested`. With the caller waiting for the task, you can see that the exception `AggregateException` is caught and contains the inner exception `TaskCanceledException`. This is used for a hierarchy of cancellations—for example, if you run a `Parallel.For` within a task that is canceled as well. The final status of the task is `Canceled`:

```
in task
in loop
in loop
in loop
in loop
*** task cancelled
cancelling was requested, cancelling from within the task
exception: AggregateException, One or more errors occurred.
inner exception: TaskCanceledException, A task was canceled.
```

DATA FLOW

The `Parallel` and `Task` classes, and Parallel LINQ, help a lot with data parallelism. However, these classes do not directly support dealing with data flow or transforming data in parallel. For this, you can use *Task Parallel Library Data Flow*, or *TPL Data Flow*.

The sample code for the data flow samples makes use of the following dependencies and namespaces:

Dependencies

```
NETStandard.Library
System.Threading.Tasks.Dataflow
```

Namespaces

```
System
System.IO
System.Threading
System.Threading.Tasks
System.Threading.Tasks.DataFlow
static System.Console
```

Using an Action Block

The heart of TPL Data Flow is data blocks. These blocks can act as a source to offer some data or a target to receive data, or both. Let's start with a simple example, a data block that receives some data and writes it to the console. The following code snippet defines an `ActionBlock` that receives a string and writes information to the console. The `Main` method reads user input within a `while` loop, and posts every string read to the `ActionBlock` by calling the `Post` method. The `Post` method posts an item to the `ActionBlock`, which deals with the message asynchronously, writing the information to the console (code file `SimpleDataFlowSample/Program.cs`):

```
static void Main()
{
  var processInput = new ActionBlock<string>(s =>
  {
    WriteLine($"user input: {s}");
  });

  bool exit = false;
  while (!exit)
  {
    string input = ReadLine();
    if (string.Compare(input, "exit", ignoreCase: true) == 0)
    {
      exit = true;
    }
    else
    {
      processInput.Post(input);
    }
  }
}
```

Source and Target Blocks

When the method assigned to the `ActionBlock` from the previous example executes, the `ActionBlock` uses a task to do the execution in parallel. You could verify this by checking the task and thread identifiers, and writing these to the console. Every block implements the interface `IDataflowBlock`, which contains the property `Completion`, which returns a `Task`, and the methods `Complete` and `Fault`. Invoking the `Complete` method, the block no longer accepts any input or produces any more output. Invoking the `Fault` method puts the block into a faulting state.

As mentioned earlier, a block can be either a source or a target, or both. In this case, the `ActionBlock` is a target block and thus implements the interface `ITargetBlock`. `ITargetBlock` derives from `IDataflowBlock` and defines the `OfferMessage` method, in addition to the members of the `IDataBlock` interface. `OfferMessage` sends a message that can be consumed by the block. An API that is easier to use than `OfferMessage` is the `Post` method, which is implemented as an extension method for the `ITargetBlock` interface. The `Post` method was also used by the sample application.

The `ISourceBlock` interface is implemented by blocks that can act as a data source. `ISourceBlock` offers methods in addition to the members of the `IDataBlock` interface to link to a target block and to consume messages.

The `BufferBlock` acts as both a source and a target, implementing both `ISourceBlock` and `ITargetBlock`. In the next example, this `BufferBlock` is used to both post messages and receive messages (code file `SimpleDataFlowSample/Program.cs`):

```
private static BufferBlock<string> s_buffer = new BufferBlock<string>();
```

The `Producer` method reads strings from the console and writes them to the `BufferBlock` by invoking the `Post` method:

```
public static void Producer()
{
  bool exit = false;
  while (!exit)
  {
    string input = ReadLine();
    if (string.Compare(input, "exit", ignoreCase: true) == 0)
    {
      exit = true;
    }
    else
    {
      s_buffer.Post(input);
    }
  }
}
```

The `Consumer` method contains a loop to receive data from the `BufferBlock` by invoking the `ReceiveAsync` method. `ReceiveAsync` is an extension method for the `ISourceBlock` interface:

```
public static async Task ConsumerAsync()
{
  while (true)
  {
    string data = await s_buffer.ReceiveAsync();
    WriteLine($"user input: {data}");
  }
}
```

Now, you just need to start the producer and consumer. You do this with two independent tasks in the `Main` method:

```
static void Main()
{
  Task t1 = Task.Run(() => Producer());
  Task t2 = Task.Run(async () => await ConsumerAsync());
  Task.WaitAll(t1, t2);
}
```

When you run the application, the producer task reads data from the console, and the consumer receives the data to write it to the console.

Connecting Blocks

This section creates a pipeline by connecting multiple blocks. First, three methods are created that will be used by the blocks. The GetFileNames method receives a directory path and yields the filenames that end with the .cs extension (code file DataFlowSample/Program.cs):

```
public static IEnumerable<string> GetFileNames(string path)
{
  foreach (var fileName in Directory.EnumerateFiles(path, "*.cs"))
  {
    yield return fileName;
  }
}
```

The LoadLines method receives a list of filenames and yields every line of the files:

```
public static IEnumerable<string> LoadLines(IEnumerable<string> fileNames)
{
  foreach (var fileName in fileNames)
  {
    using (FileStream stream = File.OpenRead(fileName))
    {
      var reader = new StreamReader(stream);
      string line = null;
      while ((line = reader.ReadLine()) != null)
      {
        //WriteLine($"LoadLines {line}");
        yield return line;
      }
    }
  }
}
```

The third method, GetWords, receives the lines collection and splits it up line by line to yield return a list of words:

```
public static IEnumerable<string> GetWords(IEnumerable<string> lines)
{
  foreach (var line in lines)
  {
    string[] words = line.Split(' ', ';', '(', ')', '{', '}', '.', ',');
    foreach (var word in words)
    {
      if (!string.IsNullOrEmpty(word))
        yield return word;
    }
  }
}
```

To create the pipeline, the SetupPipeline method creates three TransformBlock objects. The TransformBlock is a source and target block that transforms the source by using a delegate. The first TransformBlock is declared to transform a string to IEnumerable<string>. The transformation is done by the GetFileNames method that is invoked within the lambda expression passed to the constructor of the first block. Similarly, the next two TransformBlock objects are used to invoke the LoadLines and GetWords methods:

```
public static ITargetBlock<string> SetupPipeline()
{
  var fileNamesForPath = new TransformBlock<string, IEnumerable<string>>(
```

```
      path =>
      {
        return GetFileNames(path);
      });

    var lines = new TransformBlock<IEnumerable<string>, IEnumerable<string>>(
      fileNames =>
      {
        return LoadLines(fileNames);
      });

    var words = new TransformBlock<IEnumerable<string>, IEnumerable<string>>(
      lines2 =>
      {
        return GetWords(lines2);
      });
```

The last block defined is an `ActionBlock`. This block has been used before and is just a target block to receive data:

```
    var display = new ActionBlock<IEnumerable<string>>(
      coll =>
      {
        foreach (var s in coll)
        {
          WriteLine(s);
        }
      });
```

Finally, the blocks are connected to each other. `fileNamesForPath` is linked to the `lines` block. The result from `fileNamesForPath` is passed to the `lines` block. The `lines` block links to the `words` block, and the `words` block links to the `display` block. Last, the block to start the pipeline is returned:

```
    fileNamesForPath.LinkTo(lines);
    lines.LinkTo(words);
    words.LinkTo(display);
    return fileNamesForPath;
  }
```

The `Main` method now needs to kick off the pipeline. Invoking the `Post` method to pass a directory, the pipeline starts and finally writes words from the C# source code to the console. Here, it would be possible to start multiple requests for the pipeline, passing more than one directory, and doing these tasks in parallel:

```
  static void Main()
  {
    var target = SetupPipeline();
    target.Post(".");
    ReadLine();
  }
```

With this brief introduction to the TPL Data Flow library, you've seen the principal way to work with this technology. This library offers a lot more functionality, such as different blocks that deal with data differently. The `BroadcastBlock` allows passing the input source to multiple targets (for example, writing data to a file and displaying it), the `JoinBlock` joins multiple sources to one target, and the `BatchBlock` batches input into arrays. Using `DataflowBlockOptions` options allows configuration of a block, such as the maximum number of items that are processed within a single task, and passing a cancellation token that allows canceling a pipeline. With links, you can also filter messages and only pass messages that fulfill a specified predicate.

SUMMARY

This chapter explored how to code applications that use multiple tasks by using the `System.Threading.Tasks` namespace. Using multithreading in your applications takes careful planning. Too many threads can cause resource issues, and not enough threads can cause your application to be sluggish and perform poorly. With tasks, you get an abstraction to threads. This abstraction helps you avoid creating too many threads because threads are reused from a pool.

You've seen various ways to create multiple tasks, such as the `Parallel` class, which offers both task and data parallelism with `Parallel.Invoke`, `Parallel.ForEach`, and `Parallel.For`. With the `Task` class, you've seen how to gain more control over parallel programming. Tasks can run synchronously in the calling thread, using a thread from a thread pool, and a separate new thread can be created. Tasks also offer a hierarchical model that enables the creation of child tasks, also providing a way to cancel a complete hierarchy.

The cancellation framework offers a standard mechanism that can be used in the same manner with different classes to cancel a task early.

The next chapter gives information about an important concept on using tasks: synchronization.

22

Task Synchronization

WHAT'S IN THIS CHAPTER?

- ➤ Threading issues
- ➤ The lock Keyword
- ➤ Synchronization with Monitor
- ➤ Mutex
- ➤ Semaphore and SemaphoreSlim
- ➤ ManualResetEvent, AutoResetEvent, and CountdownEvent
- ➤ Barrier
- ➤ Reader Writer Lock
- ➤ Timers

WROX.COM CODE DOWNLOADS FOR THIS CHAPTER

The wrox.com code downloads for this chapter are found at www.wrox.com/go/
professionalcsharp6 on the Download Code tab. The code for this chapter is
divided into the following major examples:

- ➤ ThreadingIssues
- ➤ SynchronizationSamples
- ➤ SemaphoreSample
- ➤ EventSample
- ➤ EventSampleWithCountdownEvent
- ➤ BarrierSample
- ➤ ReaderWriterLockSample
- ➤ WinAppTimer

OVERVIEW

Chapter 21, "Tasks and Parallel Programming," explains using the `Task` and `Parallel` classes to create multithreaded applications. This chapter covers synchronization between multiple processes, tasks, and threads.

It is best when you can avoid synchronization by not sharing data between threads. Of course, this is not always possible. If data sharing is necessary, you must use synchronization techniques so that only one task at a time accesses and changes the shared state. In case you don't pay attention to synchronization, race conditions and deadlocks can apply. A big issue with these is that errors can occur from time to time. With a higher number of CPU cores, error numbers can increase. Such errors usually are hard to find. So it's best to pay attention to synchronization from the beginning.

Using multiple tasks is easy as long as they don't access the same variables. You can avoid this situation to a certain degree, but at some point you will find some data needs to be shared. When sharing data, you need to apply synchronization techniques. When threads access the same data and you don't apply synchronization, you are lucky when the problem pops up immediately. But this is rarely the case. This chapter shows race conditions and deadlocks, and how you can avoid them by applying synchronization mechanisms.

The .NET Framework offers several options for synchronization. Synchronization objects can be used within a process or across processes. You can use them to synchronize one task or multiple tasks to access a resource or a number of resources. Synchronization objects can also be used to inform tasks that something completed. All these synchronization objects are covered in this chapter.

Let's start by having a look at the issues that can happen without synchronization.

> **NOTE** *Before synchronizing custom collection classes with synchronization types shown here, you should also read Chapter 12, "Special Collections," to learn about collections that are already thread-safe: concurrent collections.*

THREADING ISSUES

Programming with multiple threads is challenging. When starting multiple threads that access the same data, you can get intermittent problems that are hard to find. The problems are the same whether you use tasks, Parallel LINQ, or the `Parallel` class. To avoid getting into trouble, you must pay attention to synchronization issues and the problems that can occur with multiple threads. This section covers two in particular: race conditions and deadlocks.

The sample code for the `ThreadingIssues` sample makes use of these dependencies and namespaces:

Dependencies

```
NETStandard.Library 1.0.0
System.Diagnostics.TraceSource
```

Namespaces

```
System.Diagnostics
System.Threading
System.Threading.Tasks
static System.Console
```

You can start the sample application `ThreadingIssues` with command-line arguments to simulate either race conditions or deadlocks.

Race Conditions

A race condition can occur if two or more threads access the same objects and access to the shared state is not synchronized. To demonstrate a race condition, the following example defines the class StateObject, with an int field and the method ChangeState. In the implementation of ChangeState, the state variable is verified to determine whether it contains 5; if it does, the value is incremented. Trace.Assert is the next statement, which immediately verifies that state now contains the value 6.

After incrementing by 1 a variable that contains the value 5, you might assume that the variable now has the value 6; but this is not necessarily the case. For example, if one thread has just completed the if (_state == 5) statement, it might be preempted, with the scheduler running another thread. The second thread now goes into the if body and, because the state still has the value 5, the state is incremented by 1 to 6. The first thread is then scheduled again, and in the next statement the state is incremented to 7. This is when the race condition occurs and the assert message is shown (code file ThreadingIssues/SampleTask.cs):

```csharp
public class StateObject
{
  private int _state = 5;

  public void ChangeState(int loop)
  {
    if (_state == 5)
    {
      _state++;
      Trace.Assert(_state == 6,
        $"Race condition occurred after {loop} loops");
    }
    _state = 5;
  }
}
```

You can verify this by defining a method for a task. The method RaceCondition of the class SampleTask gets a StateObject as a parameter. Inside an endless while loop, the ChangeState method is invoked. The variable i is used just to show the loop number in the assert message:

```csharp
public class SampleTask
{
  public void RaceCondition(object o)
  {
    Trace.Assert(o is StateObject, "o must be of type StateObject");
    StateObject state = o as StateObject;

    int i = 0;
    while (true)
    {
      state.ChangeState(i++);
    }
  }
}
```

In the Main method of the program, a new StateObject is created that is shared among all the tasks. Task objects are created by invoking the RaceCondition method with the lambda expression that is passed to the Run method of the Task. The main thread then waits for user input. However, there's a good chance that the program will halt before reading user input, as a race condition will happen:

```csharp
public void RaceConditions()
{
  var state = new StateObject();
  for (int i = 0; i < 2; i++)
  {
    Task.Run(() => new SampleTask().RaceCondition(state));
  }
}
```

When you start the program, you get race conditions. How long it takes until the first race condition happens depends on your system and whether you build the program as a release build or a debug build. With a release build, the problem happens more often because the code is optimized. If you have multiple CPUs in your system or dual-/quad-core CPUs, where multiple threads can run concurrently, the problem also occurs more often than with a single-core CPU. The problem occurs with a single-core CPU because thread scheduling is preemptive, but the problem doesn't occur that often.

Figure 22-1 shows an assertion of the program in which the race condition occurred after 1121 loops. If you start the application multiple times, you always get different results.

FIGURE 22-1

You can avoid the problem by locking the shared object. You do this inside the thread by locking the variable state, which is shared among the threads, with the lock statement, as shown in the following example. Only one thread can exist inside the lock block for the state object. Because this object is shared among all threads, a thread must wait at the lock if another thread has the lock for state. As soon as the lock is accepted, the thread owns the lock, and gives it up at the end of the lock block. If every thread changing the object referenced with the state variable is using a lock, the race condition no longer occurs:

```
public class SampleTask
{
  public void RaceCondition(object o)
  {
    Trace.Assert(o is StateObject, "o must be of type StateObject");
    StateObject state = o as StateObject;

    int i = 0;
    while (true)
    {
      lock (state) // no race condition with this lock
      {
        state.ChangeState(i++);
      }
    }
  }
}
```

> **NOTE** *With the downloaded sample code, you need to uncomment the lock statements for solving the issues with race conditions.*

Instead of performing the lock when using the shared object, you can make the shared object thread-safe. In the following code, the ChangeState method contains a lock statement. Because you cannot lock the state variable itself (only reference types can be used for a lock), the variable sync of type object is defined and used with the lock statement. If a lock is done using the same synchronization object every time the value state is changed, race conditions no longer happen:

```
public class StateObject
{
  private int _state = 5;
  private _object sync = new object();

  public void ChangeState(int loop)
  {
    lock (_sync)
    {
      if (_state == 5)
      {
        _state++;
        Trace.Assert(_state == 6,
          $"Race condition occurred after {loop} loops");
      }
      _state = 5;
    }
  }
}
```

Deadlocks

Too much locking can get you in trouble as well. In a deadlock, at least two threads halt and wait for each other to release a lock. As both threads wait for each other, a deadlock occurs and the threads wait endlessly.

To demonstrate deadlocks, the following code instantiates two objects of type StateObject and passes them with the constructor of the SampleTask class. Two tasks are created: one task running the method `Deadlock1` and the other task running the method `Deadlock2` (code file `ThreadingIssues/Program.cs`):

```
var state1 = new StateObject();
var state2 = new StateObject();
new Task(new SampleTask(state1, state2).Deadlock1).Start();
new Task(new SampleTask(state1, state2).Deadlock2).Start();
```

The methods `Deadlock1` and `Deadlock2` now change the state of two objects: `s1` and `s2`. That's why two locks are generated. `Deadlock1` first does a lock for `s1` and next for `s2`. `Deadlock2` first does a lock for `s2` and then for `s1`. Now, it may happen occasionally that the lock for `s1` in `Deadlock1` is resolved. Next, a thread switch occurs, and `Deadlock2` starts to run and gets the lock for `s2`. The second thread now waits for the lock of `s1`. Because it needs to wait, the thread scheduler schedules the first thread again, which now waits for `s2`. Both threads now wait and don't release the lock as long as the lock block is not ended. This is a typical deadlock (code file `ThreadingIssues/SampleTask.cs`):

```
public class SampleTask
{
  public SampleTask(StateObject s1, StateObject s2)
  {
    _s1 = s1;
    _s2 = s2;
  }
  private StateObject _s1;
  private StateObject _s2;

  public void Deadlock1()
  {
    int i = 0;
    while (true)
    {
      lock (_s1)
      {
        lock (_s2)
        {
          _s1.ChangeState(i);
          _s2.ChangeState(i++);
          WriteLine($"still running, {i}");
        }
      }
    }
  }

  public void Deadlock2()
  {
    int i = 0;
    while (true)
    {
      lock (_s2)
      {
        lock (_s1)
        {
          _s1.ChangeState(i);
          _s2.ChangeState(i++);
          WriteLine($"still running, {i}");
        }
      }
    }
  }
}
```

As a result, the program runs a number of loops and soon becomes unresponsive. The message "still running" is just written a few times to the console. Again, how soon the problem occurs depends on your system configuration, and the result will vary.

A deadlock problem is not always as obvious as it is here. One thread locks _s1 and then _s2; the other thread locks _s2 and then _s1. In this case, you just need to change the order so that both threads perform the locks in the same order. In a bigger application, the locks might be hidden deeply inside a method. You can prevent this problem by designing a good lock order in the initial architecture of the application, and by defining timeouts for the locks, as demonstrated in the next section.

THE LOCK STATEMENT AND THREAD SAFETY

C# has its own keyword for the synchronization of multiple threads: the lock statement. The lock statement provides an easy way to hold and release a lock. Before adding lock statements, however, let's look at another race condition. The class SharedState demonstrates using shared state between threads and shares an integer value (code file SynchronizationSamples/SharedState.cs):

```
public class SharedState
{
  public int State { get; set; }
}
```

The sample code for all the following synchronization samples (with the exception of SingletonWPF) makes use of the following dependencies and namespaces:

Dependencies

```
NETStandard.Library 1.0.0
System.Threading.Tasks.Parallel
System.Threading.Thread
```

Namespaces

```
System
System.Collections.Generic
System.Linq
System.Text
System.Threading
System.Threading.Tasks
static System.Console
```

The class Job contains the method DoTheJob, which is the entry point for a new task. With the implementation, the State of the SharedState object is incremented 50,000 times. The variable sharedState is initialized in the constructor of this class (code file SynchronizationSamples/Job.cs):

```
public class Job
{
  private SharedState _sharedState;
  public Job(SharedState sharedState)
  {
    _sharedState = sharedState;
  }

  public void DoTheJob()
  {
    for (int i = 0; i < 50000; i++)
    {
```

```
        _sharedState.State += 1;
      }
    }
  }
```

In the `Main` method, a `SharedState` object is created and passed to the constructor of 20 `Task` objects. All tasks are started. After starting the tasks, the `Main` method waits until every one of the 20 tasks is completed. After the tasks are completed, the summarized value of the shared state is written to the console. With 50,000 loops and 20 tasks, a value of 1,000,000 could be expected. Often, however, this is not the case (code file SynchronizationSamples/Program.cs):

```
class Program
{
  static void Main()
  {
    int numTasks = 20;
    var state = new SharedState();
    var tasks = new Task[numTasks];
    for (int i = 0; i < numTasks; i++)
    {
      tasks[i] = Task.Run(() => new Job(state).DoTheJob());
    }

    Task.WaitAll(tasks);

    WriteLine($"summarized {state.State}");
  }
}
```

The results of multiple runs of the application are as follows:

```
summarized 424687
summarized 465708
summarized 581754
summarized 395571
summarized 633601
```

The behavior is different every time, but none of the results are correct. As noted earlier, you will see big differences between debug and release builds, and the type of CPU that you are using also affects results. If you change the loop count to smaller values, you will often get correct values—but not every time. In this case the application is small enough to see the problem easily; in a large application, the reason for such a problem can be hard to find.

You must add synchronization to this program. To do so, use the `lock` keyword. Defining the object with the `lock` statement means that you wait to get the lock for the specified object. You can pass only a reference type. Locking a value type would just lock a copy, which wouldn't make any sense. In any case, the C# compiler issues an error if value types are used with the `lock` statement. As soon as the lock is granted—only one thread gets the lock—the block of the `lock` statement can run. At the end of the `lock` statement block, the lock for the object is released, and another thread waiting for the lock can be granted access to it:

```
lock (obj)
{
  // synchronized region
}
```

To lock static members, you can place the lock on the type object or a static member:

```
lock (typeof(StaticClass))
{
}
```

You can make the instance members of a class thread-safe by using the `lock` keyword. This way, only one thread at a time can access the methods `DoThis` and `DoThat` for the same instance:

```
public class Demo
{
  public void DoThis()
  {
    lock (this)
    {
      // only one thread at a time can access the DoThis and DoThat methods
    }
  }

  public void DoThat()
  {
    lock (this)
    {
    }
  }
}
```

However, because the object of the instance can also be used for synchronized access from the outside, and you can't control this from the class itself, you can apply the SyncRoot pattern. With the SyncRoot pattern, a private object named _syncRoot is created, and this object is used with the lock statements:

```
public class Demo
{
  private object _syncRoot = new object();

  public void DoThis()
  {
    lock (_syncRoot)
    {
      // only one thread at a time can access the DoThis and DoThat methods
    }
  }

  public void DoThat()
  {
    lock (_syncRoot)
    {
    }
  }
}
```

Using locks costs time and is not always necessary. You can create two versions of a class: synchronized and nonsynchronized. This is demonstrated in the next example code by changing the class Demo. The class Demo is not synchronized, as shown in the implementation of the DoThis and DoThat methods. The class also defines the IsSynchronized property, whereby the client can get information about the synchronization option of the class. To make a synchronized variant of the Demo class, you use the static method Synchronized to pass a nonsynchronized object, and this method returns an object of type SynchronizedDemo. SynchronizedDemo is implemented as an inner class that is derived from the base class Demo and overrides the virtual members of the base class. The overridden members make use of the SyncRoot pattern:

```
public class Demo
{
  private class SynchronizedDemo: Demo
  {
    private object _syncRoot = new object();
    private Demo _d;

    public SynchronizedDemo(Demo d)
    {
      _d = d;
```

```
    }

    public override bool IsSynchronized => true;

    public override void DoThis()
    {
      lock (_syncRoot)
      {
        _d.DoThis();
      }
    }
    public override void DoThat()
    {
      lock (_syncRoot)
      {
        _d.DoThat();
      }
    }
  }
  public virtual bool IsSynchronized => false;

  public static Demo Synchronized(Demo d)
  {
    if (!d.IsSynchronized)
    {
      return new SynchronizedDemo(d);
    }
    return d;
  }
  public virtual void DoThis()
  {
  }

  public virtual void DoThat()
  {
  }
}
```

Bear in mind that when you use the SynchronizedDemo class, only methods are synchronized. There is no synchronization for invoking other members of this class.

Now, change the SharedState class that was not synchronized at first to use the SyncRoot pattern. If you try to make the SharedState class thread-safe by locking access to the properties with the SyncRoot pattern, you still get the race condition shown earlier in the "Race Conditions" section:

```
public class SharedState
{
  private int _state = 0;
  private object _syncRoot = new object();

  public int State // there's still a race condition,
                   // don't do this!
  {
    get { lock (_syncRoot) { return _state; }}
    set { lock (_syncRoot) { _state = value; }}
  }
}
```

The thread invoking the DoTheJob method is accessing the get accessor of the SharedState class to get the current value of the state, and then the get accessor sets the new value for the state. In between calling the get and set accessors, the object is not locked, and another thread can read the interim value (code file SynchronizationSamples/Job.cs):

```
public void DoTheJob()
{
  for (int i = 0; i < 50000; i++)
  {
    _sharedState.State += 1;
  }
}
```

Therefore, it is better to leave the SharedState class as it was earlier, without thread safety (code file SynchronizationSamples/SharedState.cs):

```
public class SharedState
{
  public int State { get; set; }
}
```

In addition, add the lock statement where it belongs, inside the method DoTheJob (code file SynchronizationSamples/Job.cs):

```
public void DoTheJob()
{
  for (int i = 0; i < 50000; i++)
  {
    lock (_sharedState)
    {
      _sharedState.State += 1;
    }
  }
}
```

This way, the results of the application are always as expected:

```
summarized 1000000
```

> **NOTE** *Using the* lock *statement in one place does not mean that all other threads accessing the object are waiting. You have to explicitly use synchronization with every thread accessing the shared state.*

Of course, you can also change the design of the SharedState class and offer incrementing as an atomic operation. This is a design question—what should be an atomic functionality of the class? The next code snippet just keeps the increment locked:

```
public class SharedState
{
  private int _state = 0;
  private object _syncRoot = new object();

  public int State => _state;

  public int IncrementState()
  {
    lock (_syncRoot)
    {
      return ++_state;
    }
  }
}
```

There is, however, a faster way to lock the increment of the state, as shown next.

INTERLOCKED

The `Interlocked` class is used to make simple statements for variables atomic. `i++` is not thread-safe. It consists of getting a value from the memory, incrementing the value by `1`, and storing the value back in memory. These operations can be interrupted by the thread scheduler. The `Interlocked` class provides methods for incrementing, decrementing, exchanging, and reading values in a thread-safe manner.

Using the `Interlocked` class is much faster than other synchronization techniques. However, you can use it only for simple synchronization issues.

For example, instead of using the `lock` statement to lock access to the variable `someState` when setting it to a new value, in case it is null, you can use the `Interlocked` class, which is faster:

```
lock (this)
{
  if (_someState == null)
  {
    _someState = newState;
  }
}
```

The faster version with the same functionality uses the `Interlocked.CompareExchange` method:

```
Interlocked.CompareExchange<SomeState>(ref someState, newState, null);
```

Instead of performing incrementing inside a `lock` statement as shown here:

```
public int State
{
  get
  {
    lock (this)
    {
      return ++_state;
    }
  }
}
```

you can use `Interlocked.Increment`, which is faster:

```
public int State
{
  get
  {
    return Interlocked.Increment(ref _state);
  }
}
```

MONITOR

The C# compiler resolves the `lock` statement to use the `Monitor` class. The following `lock` statement

```
lock (obj)
{
  // synchronized region for obj
}
```

is resolved to invoke the `Enter` method, which waits until the thread gets the lock of the object. Only one thread at a time may be the owner of the object lock. As soon as the lock is resolved, the thread can enter the synchronized section. The `Exit` method of the `Monitor` class releases the lock. The compiler puts the `Exit` method into a `finally` handler of a `try` block so that the lock is also released if an exception is thrown:

```
Monitor.Enter(obj);
try
```

```
{
  // synchronized region for obj
}
finally
{
  Monitor.Exit(obj);
}
```

> **NOTE** *Chapter 14, "Errors and Exceptions," covers the* try/finally *block.*

The Monitor class has a big advantage over the lock statement of C#: You can add a timeout value for waiting to get the lock. Therefore, instead of endlessly waiting to get the lock, you can use the TryEnter method shown in the following example, passing a timeout value that defines the maximum amount of time to wait for the lock. If the lock for obj is acquired, TryEnter sets the Boolean ref parameter to true and performs synchronized access to the state guarded by the object obj. If obj is locked for more than 500 milliseconds by another thread, TryEnter sets the variable lockTaken to false, and the thread does not wait any longer but is used to do something else. Maybe later, the thread can try to acquire the lock again.

```
bool _lockTaken = false;
Monitor.TryEnter(_obj, 500, ref _lockTaken);
if (_lockTaken)
{
  try
  {
    // acquired the lock
    // synchronized region for obj
  }
  finally
  {
    Monitor.Exit(obj);
  }
}
else
{
  // didn't get the lock, do something else
}
```

SPINLOCK

If the overhead on object-based lock objects (Monitor) would be too high because of garbage collection, you can use the SpinLock struct. SpinLock is useful if you have a large number of locks (for example, for every node in a list) and hold times are always extremely short. You should avoid holding more than one SpinLock, and don't call anything that might block.

Other than the architectural differences, SpinLock is very similar in usage to the Monitor class. You acquire the lock with Enter or TryEnter and release the lock with Exit. SpinLock also offers two properties to provide information about whether it is currently locked: IsHeld and IsHeldByCurrentThread.

> **NOTE** *Be careful when passing* SpinLock *instances around. Because* SpinLock *is defined as a* struct, *assigning one variable to another creates a copy. Always pass* SpinLock *instances by reference.*

WAITHANDLE

WaitHandle is an abstract base class that you can use to wait for a signal to be set. You can wait for different things, because WaitHandle is a base class and some classes are derived from it.

Wait handles are also used by simple asynchronous delegates. The TakesAWhileDelegate is defined as follows (code file AsyncDelegate/Program.cs):

```
public delegate int TakesAWhileDelegate(int x, int ms);
```

The method BeginInvoke of the asynchronous delegate returns an object that implements the interface IAsyncResult. Using IAsyncResult, you can access a WaitHandle with the property AsyncWaitHandle. When you invoke the method WaitOne, the thread waits until a signal is received that is associated with the wait handle, or when the timeout occurs. Invoking the EndInvoke method, the thread finally blocks until the result is here:

```
static void Main()
{
  TakesAWhileDelegate d1 = TakesAWhile;

  IAsyncResult ar = d1.BeginInvoke(1, 3000, null, null);
  while (true)
  {
    Write(".");
    if (ar.AsyncWaitHandle.WaitOne(50))
    {
      WriteLine("Can get the result now");
      break;
    }
  }
  int result = d1.EndInvoke(ar);
  WriteLine($"result: {result}");
}

public static int TakesAWhile(int x, int ms)
{
  Task.Delay(ms).Wait();
  return 42;
}
```

> **NOTE** *Delegates are explained in Chapter 9, "Delegates, Lambdas, and Events."*

When you run the program, you get this result:

```
.....................................
...Can get the result now
result: 42
```

With WaitHandle, you can wait for one signal to occur (WaitOne), multiple objects that all must be signaled (WaitAll), or one of multiple objects (WaitAny). WaitAll and WaitAny are static members of the WaitHandle class and accept an array of WaitHandle parameters.

WaitHandle has a SafeWaitHandle property whereby you can assign a native handle to an operating system resource and wait for that handle. For example, you can assign a SafeFileHandle to wait for a file I/O operation to complete.

The classes Mutex, EventWaitHandle, and Semaphore are derived from the base class WaitHandle, so you can use any of these with waits.

MUTEX

Mutex (mutual exclusion) is one of the classes of the .NET Framework that offers synchronization across multiple processes. It is very similar to the Monitor class in that there is just one owner. That is, only one thread can get a lock on the mutex and access the synchronized code regions that are secured by the mutex.

With the constructor of the Mutex class, you can define whether the mutex should initially be owned by the calling thread, define a name for the mutex, and determine whether the mutex already exists. In the following example, the third parameter is defined as an out parameter to receive a Boolean value if the mutex was newly created. If the value returned is false, the mutex was already defined. The mutex might be defined in a different process, because a mutex with a name is known to the operating system and is shared among different processes. If no name is assigned to the mutex, the mutex is unnamed and not shared among different processes.

```
bool createdNew;
var mutex = new Mutex(false, "ProCSharpMutex", out createdNew);
```

To open an existing mutex, you can also use the method Mutex.OpenExisting, which doesn't require the same .NET privileges as creating the mutex with the constructor.

Because the Mutex class derives from the base class WaitHandle, you can do a WaitOne to acquire the mutex lock and be the owner of the mutex during that time. The mutex is released by invoking the ReleaseMutex method:

```
if (mutex.WaitOne())
{
  try
  {
    // synchronized region
  }
  finally
  {
    mutex.ReleaseMutex();
  }
}
else
{
  // some problem happened while waiting
}
```

Because a named mutex is known system-wide, you can use it to keep an application from being started twice. In the following WPF application, the constructor of the Mutex object is invoked. Then it is verified whether the mutex with the name SingletonWinAppMutex exists already. If it does, the application exits (code file SingletonWPF/App.xaml.cs):

```
public partial class App : Application
{
  protected override void OnStartup(StartupEventArgs e)
  {
    bool mutexCreated;
    var mutex = new Mutex(false, "SingletonWinAppMutex", out mutexCreated);
    if (!mutexCreated)
    {
      MessageBox.Show("You can only start one instance of the application");
      Application.Current.Shutdown();
    }

    base.OnStartup(e);
  }
}
```

SEMAPHORE

A semaphore is very similar to a mutex, but unlike the mutex, the semaphore can be used by multiple threads at once. A semaphore is a counting mutex, meaning that with a semaphore you can define the number of threads that are allowed to access the resource guarded by the semaphore simultaneously. This is useful if you need to limit the number of threads that can access the available resources. For example, if a system has three physical I/O ports available, three threads can access them simultaneously, but a fourth thread needs to wait until the resource is released by one of the other threads.

.NET Core 1.0 provides two classes with semaphore functionality: `Semaphore` and `SemaphoreSlim`. `Semaphore` can be named, can use system-wide resources, and allows synchronization between different processes. `SemaphoreSlim` is a lightweight version that is optimized for shorter wait times.

In the following example application, in the `Main` method six tasks are created along with one semaphore with a count of 3. In the constructor of the `Semaphore` class, you can define the count for the number of locks that can be acquired with the semaphore (the second parameter) and the number of locks that are free initially (the first parameter). If the first parameter has a lower value than the second parameter, the difference between the values defines the already allocated semaphore count. As with the mutex, you can also assign a name to the semaphore to share it among different processes. Here a `SemaphoreSlim` object is created that can only be used within the process. After the `SemaphoreSlim` object is created, six tasks are started, and they all wait for the same semaphore (code file `SemaphoreSample/Program.cs`):

```
class Program
{
  static void Main()
  {
    int taskCount = 6;
    int semaphoreCount = 3;

    var semaphore = new SemaphoreSlim(semaphoreCount, semaphoreCount);
    var tasks = new Task[taskCount];
    for (int i = 0; i < taskCount; i++)
    {
      tasks[i] = Task.Run(() => TaskMain(semaphore));
    }

    Task.WaitAll(tasks);
    WriteLine("All tasks finished");
  }
  // etc
```

In the task's main method, `TaskMain`, the task does a `Wait` to lock the semaphore. Remember that the semaphore has a count of 3, so three tasks can acquire the lock. Task 4 must wait, and here the timeout of 600 milliseconds is defined as the maximum wait time. If the lock cannot be acquired after the wait time has elapsed, the task writes a message to the console and repeats the wait in a loop. As soon as the lock is acquired, the thread writes a message to the console, sleeps for some time, and releases the lock. Again, with the release of the lock it is important that the resource be released in all cases. That's why the `Release` method of the `SemaphoreSlim` class is invoked in a `finally` handler:

```
// etc
public static void TaskMain(SemaphoreSlim semaphore)
{
  bool isCompleted = false;
  while (!isCompleted)
  {
    if (semaphore.Wait(600))
    {
      try
      {
        WriteLine($"Task {Task.CurrentId} locks the semaphore");
```

```
          Task.Delay(2000).Wait();
        }
        finally
        {
          WriteLine($"Task {Task.CurrentId} releases the semaphore");
          semaphore.Release();
          isCompleted = true;
        }
      }
      else
      {
        WriteLine($"Timeout for task {Task.CurrentId}; wait again");
      }
    }
  }
}
```

When you run the application, you can indeed see that with four threads, the lock is made immediately. The tasks with IDs 7, 8, and 9 must wait. The wait continues in the loop until one of the other threads releases the semaphore:

```
Task 4 locks the semaphore
Task 5 locks the semaphore
Task 6 locks the semaphore
Timeout for task 7; wait again
Timeout for task 7; wait again
Timeout for task 8; wait again
Timeout for task 7; wait again
Timeout for task 8; wait again
Timeout for task 7; wait again
Timeout for task 9; wait again
Timeout for task 8; wait again
Task 5 releases the semaphore
Task 7 locks the semaphore
Task 6 releases the semaphore
Task 4 releases the semaphore
Task 8 locks the semaphore
Task 9 locks the semaphore
Task 8 releases the semaphore
Task 7 releases the semaphore
Task 9 releases the semaphore
All tasks finished
```

EVENTS

Like mutex and semaphore objects, events are also system-wide synchronization resources. For using system events from managed code, the .NET Framework offers the classes `ManualResetEvent`, `AutoResetEvent`, `ManualResetEventSlim`, and `CountdownEvent` in the namespace `System.Threading`.

> **NOTE** *The* event *keyword from C# that is covered in Chapter 9 has nothing to do with the event classes from the namespace* System.Threading; *the* event *keyword is based on delegates. However, both event classes are .NET wrappers to the system-wide native event resource for synchronization.*

You can use events to inform other tasks that some data is present, that something is completed, and so on. An event can be signaled or not signaled. A task can wait for the event to be in a signaled state with the help of the `WaitHandle` class, discussed earlier.

A `ManualResetEventSlim` is signaled by invoking the `Set` method, and returned to a nonsignaled state with the `Reset` method. If multiple threads are waiting for an event to be signaled and the `Set` method is invoked, then all threads waiting are released. In addition, if a thread invokes the `WaitOne` method but the event is already signaled, the waiting thread can continue immediately.

An `AutoResetEvent` is also signaled by invoking the `Set` method, and you can set it back to a nonsignaled state with the `Reset` method. However, if a thread is waiting for an auto-reset event to be signaled, the event is automatically changed into a nonsignaled state when the wait state of the first thread is finished. This way, if multiple threads are waiting for the event to be set, only one thread is released from its wait state. It is not the thread that has been waiting the longest for the event to be signaled, but the thread waiting with the highest priority.

To demonstrate events with the `ManualResetEventSlim` class, the following class `Calculator` defines the method `Calculation`, which is the entry point for a task. With this method, the task receives input data for calculation and writes the result to the variable result that can be accessed from the `Result` property. As soon as the result is completed (after a random amount of time), the event is signaled by invoking the `Set` method of the `ManualResetEventSlim` (code file `EventSample/Calculator.cs`):

```
public class Calculator
{
  private ManualResetEventSlim _mEvent;

  public int Result { get; private set; }

  public Calculator(ManualResetEventSlim ev)
  {
    _mEvent = ev;
  }

  public void Calculation(int x, int y)
  {
    WriteLine($"Task {Task.CurrentId} starts calculation");
    Task.Delay(new Random().Next(3000)).Wait();
    Result = x + y;

    // signal the event-completed!
    WriteLine($"Task {Task.CurrentId} is ready");
    _mEvent.Set();
  }
}
```

The `Main` method of the program defines arrays of four `ManualResetEventSlim` objects and four `Calculator` objects. Every `Calculator` is initialized in the constructor with a `ManualResetEventSlim` object, so every task gets its own event object to signal when it is completed. Now, the `Task` class is used to enable different tasks to run the calculation (code file `EventSample/Program.cs`):

```
class Program
{
  static void Main()
  {
    const int taskCount = 4;

    var mEvents = new ManualResetEventSlim[taskCount];
    var waitHandles = new WaitHandle[taskCount];
    var calcs = new Calculator[taskCount];

    for (int i = 0; i < taskCount; i++)
    {
      int i1 = i;
      mEvents[i] = new ManualResetEventSlim(false);
      waitHandles[i] = mEvents[i].WaitHandle;
```

```
    calcs[i] = new Calculator(mEvents[i]);
    Task.Run(() => calcs[i1].Calculation(i1 + 1, i1 + 3));
}
//...
```

The `WaitHandle` class is now used to wait for any one of the events in the array. `WaitAny` waits until any one of the events is signaled. In contrast to `ManualResetEvent`, `ManualResetEventSlim` does not derive from `WaitHandle`. That's why a separate collection of `WaitHandle` objects is kept, which is filled from the `WaitHandle` property of the `ManualResetEventSlim` class. `WaitAny` returns an index value that provides information about the event that was signaled. The returned value matches the index of the `WaitHandle` array that is passed to `WaitAny`. Using this index, information from the signaled event can be read:

```
for (int i = 0; i < taskCount; i++)
{
    int index = WaitHandle.WaitAny(waitHandles);
    if (index == WaitHandle.WaitTimeout)
    {
        WriteLine("Timeout!!");
    }
    else
    {
        mEvents[index].Reset();
        WriteLine($"finished task for {index}, result: {calcs[index].Result}");
    }
}
}
}
```

When starting the application, you can see the tasks doing the calculation and setting the event to inform the main thread that it can read the result. At random times, depending on whether the build is a debug or release build and on your hardware, you might see different orders and a different number of tasks performing calls:

```
Task 4 starts calculation
Task 5 starts calculation
Task 6 starts calculation
Task 7 starts calculation
Task 7 is ready
finished task for 3, result: 10
Task 4 is ready
finished task for 0, result: 4
Task 6 is ready
finished task for 1, result: 6
Task 5 is ready
finished task for 2, result: 8
```

In a scenario like this, to fork some work into multiple tasks and later join the result, the new `CountdownEvent` class can be very useful. Instead of creating a separate event object for every task, you need to create only one. `CountdownEvent` defines an initial number for all the tasks that set the event, and after the count is reached, the `CountdownEvent` is signaled.

The `Calculator` class is modified to use the `CountdownEvent` instead of the `ManualResetEvent`. Rather than set the signal with the `Set` method, `CountdownEvent` defines the `Signal` method (code file `EventSampleWithCountdownEvent/Calculator.cs`):

```
public class Calculator
{
    private CountdownEvent _cEvent;

    public int Result { get; private set; }

    public Calculator(CountdownEvent ev)
```

```
  {
    _cEvent = ev;
  }
  public void Calculation(int x, int y)
  {
    WriteLine($"Task {Task.CurrentId} starts calculation");
    Task.Delay(new Random().Next(3000)).Wait();
    Result = x + y;

    // signal the event-completed!
    WriteLine($"Task {Task.CurrentId} is ready");
    _cEvent.Signal();
  }
}
```

You can now simplify the `Main` method so that it's only necessary to wait for the single event. If you don't deal with the results separately as it was done before, this new edition might be all that's needed:

```
const int taskCount = 4;
var cEvent = new CountdownEvent(taskCount);
var calcs = new Calculator[taskCount];

for (int i = 0; i < taskCount; i++)
{
  calcs[i] = new Calculator(cEvent);

  int i1 = i;
  Task.Run(() => calcs[i1].Calculation, Tuple.Create(i1 + 1, i1 + 3));
}
cEvent.Wait();
WriteLine("all finished");
for (int i = 0; i < taskCount; i++)
{
  WriteLine($"task for {i}, result: {calcs[i].Result}");
}
```

BARRIER

For synchronization, the `Barrier` class is great for scenarios in which work is forked into multiple tasks and the work must be joined afterward. `Barrier` is used for participants that need to be synchronized. While the job is active, you can dynamically add participants—for example, child tasks that are created from a parent task. Participants can wait until the work is done by all the other participants before continuing.

The `BarrierSample` is somewhat complex, but it's worthwhile to demonstrate the features of the Barrier type. The sample creates multiple collections of 2 million random strings. Multiple tasks are used to iterate through the collection and count the number of strings, starting with a, b, c, and so on. The work is not only distributed between different tasks, but also within a task. After all tasks are iterated through the first collection of strings, the result is summarized, and the tasks continue later on with the next collection.

The method `FillData` creates a collection and fills it with random strings (code file `BarrierSample/Program.cs`):

```
public static IEnumerable<string> FillData(int size)
{
  var r = new Random();
  return Enumerable.Range(0, size).Select(x => GetString(r));
}

private static string GetString(Random r)
{
  var sb = new StringBuilder(6);
  for (int i = 0; i < 6; i++)
```

```
    {
      sb.Append((char)(r.Next(26) + 97));
    }
    return sb.ToString();
}
```

A helper method to show information about a `Barrier` is defined with the method `LogBarrierInformation`:

```
private static void LogBarrierInformation(string info, Barrier barrier)
{
  WriteLine($"Task {Task.CurrentId}: {info}. " +
    $"{barrier.ParticipantCount} current and " +
    $"{barrier.ParticipantsRemaining} remaining participants, " +
    $"phase {barrier.CurrentPhaseNumber}");
}
```

The `CalculationInTask` method defines the job performed by a task. With the parameters, the third parameter references the `Barrier` instance. The data that is used for the calculation is an array of `IList<string>`. The last parameter, a jagged `int` array, will be used to write the results as the task progresses.

The task makes the processing in a loop. With every loop, an array element of `IList<string>[]` is processed. After every loop is completed, the Task signals that it's ready by invoking the `SignalAndWait` method, and waits until all the other tasks are ready with this processing as well. This loop continues until the task is fully finished. Then the task removes itself from the barrier by invoking the method `RemoveParticipant`:

```
private static void CalculationInTask(int jobNumber, int partitionSize,
    Barrier barrier, IList<string>[] coll, int loops, int[][] results)
{
  LogBarrierInformation("CalculationInTask started", barrier);

  for (int i = 0; i < loops; i++)
  {
    var data = new List<string>(coll[i]);

    int start = jobNumber * partitionSize;
    int end = start + partitionSize;
    WriteLine($"Task {Task.CurrentId} in loop {i}: partition " +
        $"from {start} to {end}");

    for (int j = start; j < end; j++)
    {
      char c = data[j][0];
      results[i][c - 97]++;
    }

    WriteLine($"Calculation completed from task {Task.CurrentId} " +
        $"in loop {i}. {results[i][0]} times a, {results[i][25]} times z");

    LogBarrierInformation("sending signal and wait for all", barrier);
    barrier.SignalAndWait();
    LogBarrierInformation("waiting completed", barrier);
  }

  barrier.RemoveParticipant();
  LogBarrierInformation("finished task, removed participant", barrier);
}
```

With the `Main` method, a `Barrier` instance is created. In the constructor, you can specify the number of participants. In the example, this number is 3 (`numberTasks + 1`) because there are two created tasks, and the `Main` method is a participant as well. Using `Task.Run`, two tasks are created to fork the iteration through the collection into two parts. After starting the tasks, using `SignalAndWait`, the main method signals its completion and waits until all remaining participants either signal their completion or remove themselves as participants from the barrier. As soon as all participants are ready with one iteration, the results from the tasks are zipped together with the `Zip` extension method. Then the next iteration is done to wait for the next results from the tasks:

```
static void Main()
{
  const int numberTasks = 2;
  const int partitionSize = 1000000;
  const int loops = 5;

  var taskResults = new Dictionary<int, int[][]>();
  var data = new List<string>[loops];
  for (int i = 0; i < loops; i++)
  {
    data[i] = new List<string>(FillData(partitionSize * numberTasks);
  }

  var barrier = new Barrier(numberTasks + 1);
  LogBarrierInformation("initial participants in barrier", barrier);

  for (int i = 0; i < numberTasks; i++)
  {
    barrier.AddParticipant();

    int jobNumber = i;
    taskResults.Add(i, new int[loops][]);
    for (int loop = 0; loop < loops; loop++)
    {
      taskResult[i, loop] = new int[26];
    }
    WriteLine("Main - starting task job {jobNumber}");
    Task.Run(() => CalculationInTask(jobNumber, partitionSize,
        barrier, data, loops, taskResults[jobNumber]));
  }

  for (int loop = 0; loop < 5; loop++)
  {
    LogBarrierInformation("main task, start signaling and wait", barrier);
    barrier.SignalAndWait();
    LogBarrierInformation("main task waiting completed", barrier);

    int[][] resultCollection1 = taskResults[0];
    int[][] resultCollection2 = taskResults[1];
    var resultCollection = resultCollection1[loop].Zip(
        resultCollection2[loop], (c1, c2) => c1 + c2);

    char ch = 'a';
    int sum = 0;
    foreach (var x in resultCollection)
    {
      WriteLine($"{ch++}, count: {x}");
      sum += x;
    }

    LogBarrierInformation($"main task finished loop {loop}, sum: {sum}",
        barrier);
  }
  WriteLine("finished all iterations");
  ReadLine();
}
```

> **NOTE** *Jagged arrays are explained in Chapter 7, "Arrays and Tuples." The* Zip *extension method is explained in Chapter 13, "Language Integrated Query."*

When you run the application, you can see output similar to the following. In the output you can see that every call to AddParticipant increases the participant count as well as the remaining participant count. As soon as one participant invokes SignalAndWait, the remaining participant count is decremented. When the remaining participant count reaches 0, the wait of all participants ends, and the next phase begins:

```
Task : initial participants in barrier. 1 current and 1 remaining participants,
phase 0.
Main - starting task job 0
Main - starting task job 1
Task : main task, starting signaling and wait. 3 current and
3 remaining participants, phase 0.
Task 4: CalculationInTask started. 3 current and 2 remaining participants, phase 0.
Task 5: CalculationInTask started. 3 current and 2 remaining participants, phase 0.
Task 4 in loop 0: partition from 0 to 1000000
Task 5 in loop 0: partition from 1000000 to 2000000
Calculation completed from task 4 in loop 0. 38272 times a, 38637 times z
Task 4: sending signal and wait for all. 3 current and
2 remaining participants, phase 0.
Calculation completed from task 5 in loop 0. 38486 times a, 38781 times z
Task 5: sending signal and wait for all. 3 current and
1 remaining participants, phase 0.
Task 5: waiting completed. 3 current and 3 remaining participants, phase 1
Task 4: waiting completed. 3 current and 3 remaining participants, phase 1
Task : main waiting completed. 3 current and 3 remaining participants, phase 1
...
```

READERWRITERLOCKSLIM

In order for a locking mechanism to allow multiple readers, but only one writer, for a resource, you can use the class ReaderWriterLockSlim. This class offers a locking functionality whereby multiple readers can access the resource if no writer locked it, and only a single writer can lock the resource.

The ReaderWriterLockSlim class has blocking and nonblocking methods to acquire a read lock, such as EnterReadLock (blocking) and TryEnterReadLock (nonblocking), and to acquire a write lock with EnterWriteLock (blocking) and TryEnterWriteLock (nonblocking). If a task reads first and writes afterward, it can acquire an upgradable read lock with EnterUpgradableReadLock or TryEnterUpgradableReadLock. With this lock, the write lock can be acquired without releasing the read lock.

Several properties of this class offer information about the held locks, such as CurrentReadCount, WaitingReadCount, WaitingUpgradableReadCount, and WaitingWriteCount.

The following example creates a collection containing six items and a ReaderWriterLockSlim object. The method ReaderMethod acquires a read lock to read all items of the list and write them to the console. The method WriterMethod tries to acquire a write lock to change all values of the collection. In the Main method, six tasks are started that invoke either the method ReaderMethod or the method WriterMethod (code file ReaderWriterLockSample/Program.cs):

```
using System.Collections.Generic;
using System.Threading;
using System.Threading.Tasks;
using static System.Console;

namespace ReaderWriterLockSample
```

```csharp
{
  class Program
  {
    private static List<int> _items = new List<int>() { 0, 1, 2, 3, 4, 5};
    private static ReaderWriterLockSlim _rwl =
      new ReaderWriterLockSlim(LockRecursionPolicy.SupportsRecursion);

    public static void ReaderMethod(object reader)
    {
      try
      {
        _rwl.EnterReadLock();

        for (int i = 0; i < _items.Count; i++)
        {
          WriteLine($"reader {reader}, loop: {i}, item: {_items[i]}");
          Task.Delay(40).Wait();
        }
      }
      finally
      {
        _rwl.ExitReadLock();
      }
    }

    public static void WriterMethod(object writer)
    {
      try
      {
        while (!_rwl.TryEnterWriteLock(50))
        {
          WriteLine($"Writer {writer} waiting for the write lock");
          WriteLine($"current reader count: {_rwl.CurrentReadCount}");
        }
        WriteLine($"Writer {writer} acquired the lock");
        for (int i = 0; i < _items.Count; i++)
        {
          _items[i]++;
          Task.Delay(50).Wait();
        }
        WriteLine($"Writer {writer} finished");
      }
      finally
      {
        _rwl.ExitWriteLock();
      }
    }

    static void Main()
    {
      var taskFactory = new TaskFactory(TaskCreationOptions.LongRunning,
        TaskContinuationOptions.None);
      var tasks = new Task[6];
      tasks[0] = taskFactory.StartNew(WriterMethod, 1);
      tasks[1] = taskFactory.StartNew(ReaderMethod, 1);
      tasks[2] = taskFactory.StartNew(ReaderMethod, 2);
      tasks[3] = taskFactory.StartNew(WriterMethod, 2);
      tasks[4] = taskFactory.StartNew(ReaderMethod, 3);
      tasks[5] = taskFactory.StartNew(ReaderMethod, 4);

      Task.WaitAll(tasks);
    }
  }
}
```

When you run the application, the following shows that the first writer gets the lock first. The second writer and all readers need to wait. Next, the readers can work concurrently, while the second writer still waits for the resource:

```
Writer 1 acquired the lock
Writer 2 waiting for the write lock
current reader count: 0
Writer 2 waiting for the write lock
current reader count: 0
Writer 2 waiting for the write lock
current reader count: 0
Writer 2 waiting for the write lock
current reader count: 0
Writer 1 finished
reader 4, loop: 0, item: 1
reader 1, loop: 0, item: 1
Writer 2 waiting for the write lock
current reader count: 4
reader 2, loop: 0, item: 1
reader 3, loop: 0, item: 1
reader 4, loop: 1, item: 2
reader 1, loop: 1, item: 2
reader 3, loop: 1, item: 2
reader 2, loop: 1, item: 2
Writer 2 waiting for the write lock
current reader count: 4
reader 4, loop: 2, item: 3
reader 1, loop: 2, item: 3
reader 2, loop: 2, item: 3
reader 3, loop: 2, item: 3
Writer 2 waiting for the write lock
current reader count: 4
reader 4, loop: 3, item: 4
reader 1, loop: 3, item: 4
reader 2, loop: 3, item: 4
reader 3, loop: 3, item: 4
reader 4, loop: 4, item: 5
reader 1, loop: 4, item: 5
Writer 2 waiting for the write lock
current reader count: 4
reader 2, loop: 4, item: 5
reader 3, loop: 4, item: 5
reader 4, loop: 5, item: 6
reader 1, loop: 5, item: 6
reader 2, loop: 5, item: 6
reader 3, loop: 5, item: 6
Writer 2 waiting for the write lock
current reader count: 4
Writer 2 acquired the lock
Writer 2 finished
```

TIMERS

With a timer, you can do a repeat invocation of a method. Two timers will be covered in this section: the `Timer` class from the `System.Threading` namespace, and the `DispatcherTimer` for XAML-based apps.

Using the `System.Threading.Timer` class, you can pass the method to be invoked as the first parameter in the constructor. This method must fulfill the requirements of the `TimerCallback` delegate, which defines a `void` return type and an `object` parameter. With the second parameter, you can pass any object, which is then received with the object argument in the callback method. For example, you can pass an `Event` object to signal the caller. The third parameter specifies the time span during which the callback should be invoked the first time. With the last parameter, you specify the repeating interval for the callback. If the timer should fire only once, set the fourth parameter to the value –1.

If the time interval should be changed after creating the `Timer` object, you can pass new values with the `Change` method (code file `TimerSample/Program.cs`):

```
private static void ThreadingTimer()
{
  using (var t1 = new Timer(TimeAction, null,
    TimeSpan.FromSeconds(2), TimeSpan.FromSeconds(3)))
  {
    Task.Delay(15000).Wait();
  }
}

private static void TimeAction(object o)
{
  WriteLine($"System.Threading.Timer {DateTime.Now:T}");
}
```

The `DispatcherTimer` from the namespaces `System.Windows.Threading` (for Windows Desktop applications with WPF) and `Windows.UI.Xaml` (for Windows apps) is a timer for XAML-based apps where the event handler is called within the UI thread, thus it is possible to directly access user interface elements.

The sample application to demonstrate the `DispatcherTimer` is a Windows app that shows the hand of a clock to switch every second. The following XAML code defines the commands that enable you to start and stop the clock (code file `WinAppTimer/MainPage.xaml`):

```
<Page.TopAppBar>
  <CommandBar IsOpen="True">
    <AppBarButton Icon="Play" Click="{x:Bind OnTimer}" />
    <AppBarButton Icon="Stop" Click="{x:Bind OnStopTimer}" />
  </CommandBar>
</Page.TopAppBar>
```

The hand of the clock is defined using the shape `Line`. To rotate the line, you use a `RotateTransform` element:

```
<Canvas Width="300" Height="300">
  <Ellipse Width="10" Height="10" Fill="Red" Canvas.Left="145"
      Canvas.Top="145" />
  <Line Canvas.Left="150" Canvas.Top="150" Fill="Green" StrokeThickness="3"
      Stroke="Blue" X1="0" Y1="0" X2="120" Y2="0" >
    <Line.RenderTransform>
      <RotateTransform CenterX="0" CenterY="0" Angle="270" x:Name="rotate" />
    </Line.RenderTransform>
  </Line>
</Canvas>
```

> **NOTE** *XAML shapes are explained in Chapter 30, "Styling XAML Apps."*

The `DispatcherTimer` object is created in the `MainPage` class. In the constructor, the handler method is assigned to the `Tick` event, and the `Interval` is specified to be one second. The timer is started in the `OnTimer` method—the method that gets called when the user clicks the `Play` button in the `CommandBar` (code file `WinAppTimer/MainPage.xaml.cs`):

```
private DispatcherTimer _timer = new DispatcherTimer();
public MainPage()
{
  this.InitializeComponent();
  _timer.Tick += OnTick;
```

```
  _timer.Interval = TimeSpan.FromSeconds(1);
}

private void OnTimer()
{
  _timer.Start();
}

private void OnTick(object sender, object e)
{
  double newAngle = rotate.Angle + 6;
  if (newAngle >= 360) newAngle = 0;
  rotate.Angle = newAngle;
}

private void OnStopTimer()
{
  _timer.Stop();
}
```

When you run the application, the clock hand is shown (see Figure 22-2).

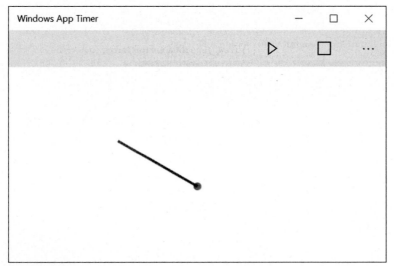

FIGURE 22-2

SUMMARY

Chapter 21 describes how to parallelize applications using tasks. This chapter covered the issues you can have using multiple tasks, such as race conditions and deadlocks.

You've seen several synchronization objects that are available with .NET, and with which scenario what synchronization object has its advantage. An easy synchronization can be done using the lock keyword. Behind the scenes, it's the Monitor type that allows setting timeouts, which is not possible with the lock keyword. For synchronization between processes, the Mutex object offers similar functionality. With the Semaphore object you've seen a synchronization object with a count—a number of tasks are allowed to run concurrently. To inform others on information that is ready, different kinds of event objects have been discussed, such as the AutoResetEvent, ManualResetEvent, and CountdownEvent. A simple way to have multiple readers and one writer is offered by the `ReaderWriterLock`. The `Barrier` type offers a more complex scenario where multiple tasks can run concurrently until a synchronization point is reached. As soon as all tasks reach this point, all can continue concurrently to meet at the next synchronization point.

Here are some final guidelines regarding threading:

➤ Try to keep synchronization requirements to a minimum. Synchronization is complex and blocks threads. You can avoid it if you try to avoid sharing state. Of course, this is not always possible.

➤ Static members of a class should be thread-safe. Usually, this is the case with classes in the .NET Framework.

➤ Instance state does not need to be thread-safe. For best performance, synchronization is best used outside the class where it is needed, and not with every member of the class. Instance members of .NET Framework classes usually are not thread-safe. In the MSDN library, you can find this information documented for every class of the .NET Framework in the "Thread Safety" section.

The next chapter gives information on another core .NET topic: files and streams.

23

Files and Streams

WHAT'S IN THIS CHAPTER?

➤ Exploring the directory structure
➤ Moving, copying, and deleting files and folders
➤ Reading and writing text in files
➤ Using streams to read and write files
➤ Using readers and writers to read and write files
➤ Compressing files
➤ Monitor file changes
➤ Communication using pipes
➤ Using Windows Runtime streams

WROX.COM CODE DOWNLOADS FOR THIS CHAPTER

The wrox.com code downloads for this chapter are found at www.wrox.com/go/
professionalcsharp6 on the Download Code tab. The code for this chapter is
divided into the following major examples:

➤ DriveInformation
➤ WorkingWithFilesAndFolders
➤ WPFEditor
➤ StreamSamples
➤ ReaderWriterSamples
➤ CompressFileSample
➤ FileMonitor
➤ MemoryMappedFiles
➤ NamedPipes
➤ AnonymousPipes
➤ WindowsAppEditor

INTRODUCTION

When you're reading and writing to files and directories you can use simple APIs, or you can use advanced ones that offer more features. You also have to differentiate between .NET classes and functionality offered from the Windows Runtime. From Universal Windows Platform (UWP) Windows apps, you don't have access to the file system in any directory; you have access only to specific directories. Alternatively, you can let the user pick files. This chapter covers all these options. You'll read and write files by using a simple API and get into more features by using streams. You'll use both .NET types and types from the Windows Runtime, and you'll mix both of these technologies to take advantage of .NET features with the Windows Runtime.

As you use streams, you also learn about compressing data and sharing data between different tasks using memory mapped files and pipes.

MANAGING THE FILE SYSTEM

The classes used to browse around the file system and perform operations such as moving, copying, and deleting files are shown in Figure 23-1.

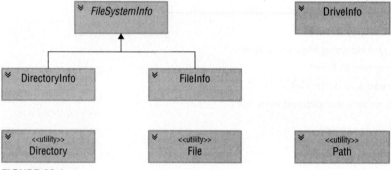

FIGURE 23-1

The following list explains the function of these classes:

➤ `FileSystemInfo`—The base class that represents any file system object

➤ `FileInfo` and `File`—These classes represent a file on the file system.

➤ `DirectoryInfo` and `Directory`—These classes represent a folder on the file system.

➤ `Path`—This class contains static members that you can use to manipulate pathnames.

➤ `DriveInfo`—This class provides properties and methods that provide information about a selected drive.

> **NOTE** *In Windows, the objects that contain files and that are used to organize the file system are termed folders. For example, in the path* `C:\My Documents\ReadMe .txt`, `ReadMe.txt` *is a file and* `My Documents` *is a folder. "Folder" is a very Windows-specific term. On virtually every other operating system, the term "directory" is used in place of "folder," and in accordance with Microsoft's goal to design .NET as a platform-independent technology, the corresponding .NET base classes are called* `Directory` *and* `DirectoryInfo`. *However, due to the potential for confusion with LDAP directories and because this is a Windows book, I'm sticking to the term "folder" in this discussion.*

Notice in the previous list that two classes are used to work with folders and two classes are for working with files. Which one of these classes you use depends largely on how many operations you need to access that folder or file:

➤ `Directory` and `File` contain only static methods and are never instantiated. You use these classes by supplying the path to the appropriate file system object whenever you call a member method. If you want to do only one operation on a folder or file, using these classes is more efficient because it saves the overhead of creating a .NET object.

➤ `DirectoryInfo` and `FileInfo` implement roughly the same public methods as `Directory` and `File`, as well as some public properties and constructors, but they are stateful and the members of these classes are not static. You need to instantiate these classes before each instance is associated with a particular folder or file. This means that these classes are more efficient if you are performing multiple operations using the same object. That's because they read in the authentication and other information for the appropriate file system object on construction, and then they do not need to read that information again, no matter how many methods and so on you call against each object (class instance). In comparison, the corresponding stateless classes need to check the details of the file or folder again with every method you call.

Checking Drive Information

Before working with files and folders, let's check the drives of the system. You use the `DriveInfo` class, which can perform a scan of a system to provide a list of available drives and then dig in deeper to provide a large amount of detail about any of the drives.

To demonstrate using the `DriveInfo` class, the following example creates a simple Console application that lists information of all the available drives on a computer.

The sample code for DriveInformation makes use of the following dependencies and namespaces:

Dependencies

```
NETStandard.Library
System.IO.FileSystem.DriveInfo
```

Namespaces

```
System.IO
static System.Console
```

The following code snippet invokes the static method `DriveInfo.GetDrives`. This method returns an array of `DriveInfo` objects. With this array, every drive that is ready is accessed to write information about the drive name, type, and format, and it also shows size information (code file `DriveInformation/Program.cs`):

```
DriveInfo[] drives = DriveInfo.GetDrives();
foreach (DriveInfo drive in drives)
{
  if (drive.IsReady)
  {
    WriteLine($"Drive name: {drive.Name}");
    WriteLine($"Format: {drive.DriveFormat}");
    WriteLine($"Type: {drive.DriveType}");
    WriteLine($"Root directory: {drive.RootDirectory}");
    WriteLine($"Volume label: {drive.VolumeLabel}");
    WriteLine($"Free space: {drive.TotalFreeSpace}");
    WriteLine($"Available space: {drive.AvailableFreeSpace}");
    WriteLine($"Total size: {drive.TotalSize}");
    WriteLine();
  }
}
```

When I run this program on my system, which doesn't have a DVD drive but has a solid-state disk (SSD) and a memory card, I see this information:

```
Drive name: C:\
Format: NTFS
Type: Fixed
Root directory: C:\
Volume label: Windows
Free space: 225183154176
Available space: 225183154176
Total size: 505462910976

Drive name: D:\
Format: exFAT
Type: Removable
Root directory: D:\
Volume label:
Free space: 19628294144
Available space: 19628294144
Total size: 127831375872
```

Working with the Path Class

For accessing files and directories, the names of the files and directories need to be defined—including parent folders. When you combine multiple folders and files using string concatenation operators, you can easily miss a separator character or use one too many characters. The Path class can help with this because this class adds missing separator characters, and it also deals with different platform requirements on Windows- and Unix-based systems.

The Path class exposes some static methods that make operations on pathnames easier. For example, suppose that you want to display the full pathname for a file, ReadMe.txt, in the folder D:\Projects. You could find the path to the file using the following code:

```
WriteLine(Path.Combine(@"D:\Projects", "ReadMe.txt"));
```

Path.Combine is the method of this class that you are likely to use most often, but Path also implements other methods that supply information about the path or the required format for it.

With the public fields VolumeSeparatorChar, DirectorySeparatorChar, AltDirectorySeparatorChar, and PathSeparator you can get the platform-specific character that is used to separate drives, folders, and files, and the separator of multiple paths. With Windows, these characters are :, \, /, and ;.

The Path class also helps with accessing the user-specific temp folder (GetTempPath) and creating temporary (GetTempFileName) and random filenames (GetRandomFileName). Pay attention that the method GetTempFileName includes the folder, whereas GetRandomFileName just returns the filename without any folder.

The sample code for WorkingWithFilesAndFolders makes use of the following dependencies and namespaces:

Dependencies

    NETStandard.Library

    System.IO.FileSystem

Namespaces

    System

    System.Collections.Generic

```
System.IO
static System.Console
```

This sample application offers several command line arguments to start the different functionality of the program. Just start the program without command lines or check the source code to see all the different options.

The `Environment` class defines a list of special folders for accessing special folders with .NET 4.6. The following code snippet returns the documents folder by passing the enumeration value `SpecialFolder` `.MyDocuments` to the `GetFolderPath` method. This feature of the `Environment` class is not available with .NET Core; thus in the following code the values of the environment variables `HOMEDRIVE` and `HOMEPATH` are used (code file `WorkingWithFilesAndFolders/Program.cs`):

```
private static string GetDocumentsFolder()
{
#if NET46
  return Environment.GetFolderPath(Environment.SpecialFolder.MyDocuments);
#else
  string drive = Environment.GetEnvironmentVariable("HOMEDRIVE");
  string path = Environment.GetEnvironmentVariable("HOMEPATH");
  return Path.Combine(drive, path, "documents");
#endif
}
```

`Environment.SpecialFolder` is a huge enumeration that gives values for music, pictures, program files, app data, and many other folders.

Creating Files and Folders

Now let's get into using the `File`, `FileInfo`, `Directory`, and `DirectoryInfo` classes. First, the method `CreateAFile` creates the file `Sample1.txt` and adds the string `Hello, World!` to the file. An easy way to create a text file is to invoke the method `WriteAllText` of the `File` class. This method takes a filename and the string that should be written to the file. Everything is done with a single call (code file `WorkingWithFilesAndFolders/Program.cs`):

```
const string Sample1FileName = "Sample1.txt";
// etc.

public static void CreateAFile()
{
  string fileName = Path.Combine(GetDocumentsFolder(), Sample1FileName);
  File.WriteAllText(fileName, "Hello, World!");
}
```

To copy a file, you can use either the `Copy` method of the `File` class or the `CopyTo` method of the `FileInfo` class:

```
var file = new FileInfo(@".\ReadMe.txt");
file.CopyTo(@"C:\Copies\ReadMe.txt");

File.Copy(@".\ReadMe.txt", @"C:\Copies\ReadMe.txt");
```

The first code snippet using `FileInfo` takes slightly longer to execute because of the need to instantiate an object named `file`, but it leaves `file` ready for you to perform further actions on the same file. When you use the second example, there is no need to instantiate an object to copy the file.

You can instantiate a `FileInfo` or `DirectoryInfo` class by passing to the constructor a string containing the path to the corresponding file system object. You have just seen the process for a file. For a folder, the code looks similar:

```
var myFolder = new DirectoryInfo(@"C:\Program Files");
```

If the path represents an object that does not exist, an exception is not thrown at construction; instead it's thrown the first time you call a method that actually requires the corresponding file system object to be there. You can find out whether the object exists and is of the appropriate type by checking the Exists property, which is implemented by both of these classes:

```
var test = new FileInfo(@"C:\Windows");
WriteLine(test.Exists);
```

Note that for this property to return true, the corresponding file system object must be of the appropriate type. In other words, if you instantiate a FileInfo object by supplying the path of a folder, or you instantiate a DirectoryInfo object by giving it the path of a file, Exists has the value false. Most of the properties and methods of these objects return a value if possible—they won't necessarily throw an exception just because the wrong type of object has been called, unless they are asked to do something that is impossible. For example, the preceding code snippet might first display false (because C:\Windows is a folder), but it still displays the time the folder was created because a folder has that information. However, if you tried to open the folder as if it were a file, using the FileInfo.Open method, you'd get an exception.

You move and delete files or folders using the MoveTo and Delete methods of the FileInfo and DirectoryInfo classes. The equivalent methods on the File and Directory classes are Move and Delete. The FileInfo and File classes also implement the methods CopyTo and Copy, respectively. However, no methods exist to copy complete folders—you need to do that by copying each file in the folder.

Using all of these methods is quite intuitive. You can find detailed descriptions in the MSDN documentation.

Accessing and Modifying File Properties

Let's get some information about files. You can use both the File and FileInfo classes to access file information. The File class defines static method, whereas the FileInfo class offers instance methods. The following code snippet shows how to use FileInfo to retrieve multiple information. If you instead used the File class, the access would be slower because every access would mean a check to determine whether the user is allowed to get this information. With the FileInfo class, the check happens only when calling the constructor.

The sample code creates a new FileInfo object and writes the result of the properties Name, DirectoryName, IsReadOnly, Extension, Length, CreationTime, LastAccessTime, and Attributes to the console (code file WorkingWithFilesAndFolders/Program.cs):

```
private static void FileInformation(string fileName)
{
  var file = new FileInfo(fileName);
  WriteLine($"Name: {file.Name}");
  WriteLine($"Directory: {file.DirectoryName}");
  WriteLine($"Read only: {file.IsReadOnly}");
  WriteLine($"Extension: {file.Extension}");
  WriteLine($"Length: {file.Length}");
  WriteLine($"Creation time: {file.CreationTime:F}");
  WriteLine($"Access time: {file.LastAccessTime:F}");
  WriteLine($"File attributes: {file.Attributes}");
}
```

Passing the Program.cs filename of the current directory to this method,

```
FileInformation("./Program.cs");
```

results in this output (on my machine):

```
Name: Program.cs
Directory: C:\Users\Christian\Source\Repos\ProfessionalCSharp6\FilesAndStreams\F
ilesAndStreamsSamples\WorkingWithFilesAndFolders
Read only: False
Extension: .cs
Length: 7888
Creation time: Friday, September 25, 2015 5:22:11 PM
```

```
Access time: Sunday, December 20, 2015 8:59:23 AM
File attributes: Archive
```

A few of the properties of the `FileInfo` class cannot be set; they only define `get` accessors. It's not possible to retrieve the filename, the file extension, and the length of the file. The creation time and last access time can be set. The method `ChangeFileProperties` writes the creation time of a file to the console and later changes the creation time to a date in the year 2023.

```
private static void ChangeFileProperties()
{
  string fileName = Path.Combine(GetDocumentsFolder(), Sample1FileName);
  var file = new FileInfo(fileName);
  if (!file.Exists)
  {
    WriteLine($"Create the file {Sample1FileName} before calling this method");
    WriteLine("You can do this by invoking this program with the -c argument");
    return;
  }
  WriteLine($"creation time: {file.CreationTime:F}");
  file.CreationTime = new DateTime(2023, 12, 24, 15, 0, 0);
  WriteLine($"creation time: {file.CreationTime:F}");
}
}
```

Running the program shows the initial creation time of the file as well as the creation time after it has been changed. Creating files in the future (at least specifying the creation time) is possible with this technique.

```
creation time: Sunday, December 20, 2015 9:41:49 AM
creation time: Sunday, December 24, 2023 3:00:00 PM
```

> **NOTE** *Being able to manually modify these properties might seem strange at first, but it can be quite useful. For example, if you have a program that effectively modifies a file by simply reading it in, deleting it, and creating a new file with the new contents, you would probably want to modify the creation date to match the original creation date of the old file.*

Creating a Simple Editor

To show how simple it is to read and write files, you can create a simple Windows desktop application using WPF. The application, named `WPFEditor`, allows opening a file and saving it again.

> **NOTE** *Later in this chapter, you create a similar editor using the Windows Universal Platform.*

The user interface is defined with XAML and uses `MenuItem` controls for `Open` and `Save` commands and a `TextBox` that allows multiline input by setting the `AcceptsReturn` property (code file `WPFEditor/MainWindow.xaml`):

```
<Window.CommandBindings>
  <CommandBinding Command="Open" Executed="OnOpen" />
  <CommandBinding Command="Save" Executed="OnSave" />
</Window.CommandBindings>
<DockPanel>
  <Menu DockPanel.Dock="Top">
    <MenuItem Header="File">
      <MenuItem Header="Open" Command="Open" />
```

```
        <MenuItem Header="Save As" Command="Save" />
      </MenuItem>
    </Menu>
    <TextBox x:Name="text1" AcceptsReturn="True" AcceptsTab="True" />
  </DockPanel>
```

The `OnOpen` method opens a dialog in which the user can select the file to open. You can configure the dialog by setting properties of `OpenFileDialog`, such as the following:

➤ Should it check if the path and file exist?

➤ What filter defines what type of files to open?

➤ What is the initial directory?

If the user opens a file (and does not cancel the dialog), the `ShowDialog` method returns `true`. Then the `Text` property of the `TextBox` control is filled with the result of the `File.ReadAllText` method. This method returns the complete content of a text file within a string (code file `WPFEditor/MainWindow.xaml.cs`):

```csharp
private void OnOpen(object sender, ExecutedRoutedEventArgs e)
{
  var dlg = new OpenFileDialog()
  {
    Title = "Simple Editor - Open File",
    CheckPathExists = true,
    CheckFileExists = true,
    Filter = "Text files (*.txt)|*.txt|All files|*.*",
    InitialDirectory = Environment.GetFolderPath(
      Environment.SpecialFolder.MyDocuments)
  };
  if (dlg.ShowDialog() == true)
  {
    text1.Text = File.ReadAllText(dlg.FileName);
  }
}
```

The dialog from the running application is shown in Figure 23-2. As configured, the documents folder is opened, and the value of the Filter property is shown in the combo box in the lower right corner.

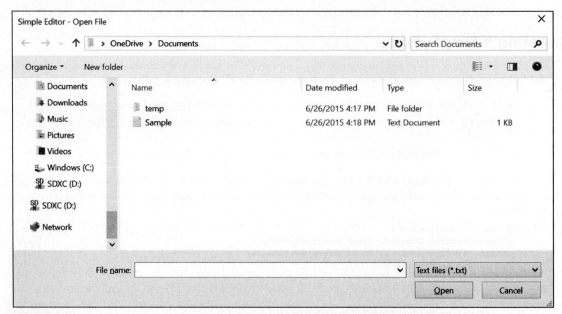

FIGURE 23-2

To save the file, the `SaveFileDialog` is shown. You can write a text file from a string with `File.WriteAllText` as shown here:

```
private void OnSave(object sender, ExecutedRoutedEventArgs e)
{
  var dlg = new SaveFileDialog()
  {
    Title = "Simple Editor - Save As",
    DefaultExt = "txt",
    Filter = "Text files (*.txt)|*.txt|All files|*.*",
  };
  if (dlg.ShowDialog() == true)
  {
    File.WriteAllText(dlg.FileName, text1.Text);
  }
}
```

Reading and writing files to a string works well for small text files. However, there are limits to reading and saving complete files this way. A .NET string has a limit of 2GB, which is enough for a lot of text files, but it's still not a good idea to let the user wait until a 1GB file is loaded into a string. There are other options, which you can read about later in the "Working with Streams" section.

Using File to Read and Write

With `File.ReadAllText` and `File.WriteAllText` you were introduced to a way to read and write a file using a string. Instead of using one string, you can use a string for every line in a file.

Instead of reading all lines to a single string, a string array is returned from the method `File.ReadAllLines`. With this method you can do a different handling based on every line, but still the complete file needs to be read into memory (code file `WorkingWithFilesAndFolders/Program.cs`):

```
public static void ReadingAFileLineByLine(string fileName)
{
  string[] lines = File.ReadAllLines(fileName);
  int i = 1;
  foreach (var line in lines)
  {
    WriteLine($"{i++}. {line}");
  }
  // etc.
}
```

To read line by line without needing to wait until all lines have been read, you can use the method `File.ReadLines`. This method returns `IEnumerable<string>`, where you can already start looping through the file before the complete file has been read:

```
public static void ReadingAFileLineByLine(string fileName)
{
  // etc.
  IEnumerable<string> lines = File.ReadLines(fileName);

  i = 1;
  foreach (var line in lines)
  {
    WriteLine($"{i++}. {line}");
  }
}
```

For writing a string collection, you can use the method `File.WriteAllLines`. This method accepts a filename and an `IEnumerable<string>` type as parameter:

```
public static void WriteAFile()
{
```

```
    string fileName = Path.Combine(GetDocumentsFolder(), "movies.txt");
    string[] movies =
    {
      "Snow White And The Seven Dwarfs",
      "Gone With The Wind",
      "Casablanca",
      "The Bridge On The River Kwai",
      "Some Like It Hot"
    };

    File.WriteAllLines(fileName, movies);
}
```

To append strings to an existing file, you use `File.AppendAllLines`:

```
    string[] moreMovies =
    {
      "Psycho",
      "Easy Rider",
      "Star Wars",
      "The Matrix"
    };
    File.AppendAllLines(fileName, moreMovies);
```

ENUMERATING FILES

For working with multiple files, you can use the `Directory` class. `Directory` defines the method `GetFiles` that returns a string array of all files in the directory. The method `GetDirectories` returns a string array of all directories.

All of these methods define overloads that allow passing a search pattern and a value of the `SearchOption` enumeration. `SearchOption` enables you to walk through all subdirectories or to stay in the top-level directory by using the value `AllDirectories` or `TopDirectoriesOnly`. The search pattern doesn't allow passing regular expressions as are discussed in Chapter 10, "Strings and Regular Expressions"; it passes only simple expressions using * for any characters and ? for single characters.

When you walk through a huge directory (or subdirectories), the methods `GetFiles` and `GetDirectories` need to have the complete result before the result is returned. An alternative is to use the methods `EnumerateDirectories` and `EnumerateFiles`. These methods offer the same parameters for the search pattern and options, but they immediately start returning a result with `IEnumerable<string>`.

Let's get into an example: Within a directory and all its subdirectories, all files that end with `Copy` are deleted in case another file exists with the same name and size. You can simulate this easily by selecting all files in a folder by pressing Ctrl+A on the keyboard, entering Ctrl+C on the keyboard for copy, and entering Ctrl+V on the keyboard while the mouse is still in the same folder to paste. The new files have the `Copy` postfix applied.

The method `DeleteDuplicateFiles` iterates all files in the directory that is passed with the first argument, walking through all subdirectories using the option `SearchOption.AllDirectories`. Within the `foreach` statement, the current file in the iteration is compared to the file in the previous iteration. In cases where the filename is the same and only the Copy postfix is different, and if the size of the files is the same as well, the copied file is deleted by invoking `FileInfo.Delete` (code file `WorkingWithFilesAndFolders/Program .cs`):

```
    private void DeleteDuplicateFiles(string directory, bool checkOnly)
    {
      IEnumerable<string> fileNames = Directory.EnumerateFiles(directory,
        "*", SearchOption.AllDirectories);

      string previousFileName = string.Empty;
```

```
    foreach (string fileName in fileNames)
    {
      string previousName = Path.GetFileNameWithoutExtension(previousFileName);
      if (!string.IsNullOrEmpty(previousFileName) &&
          previousName.EndsWith("Copy") &&
          fileName.StartsWith(previousFileName.Substring(
            0, previousFileName.LastIndexOf(" - Copy"))))
      {
        var copiedFile = new FileInfo(previousFileName);
        var originalFile = new FileInfo(fileName);
        if (copiedFile.Length == originalFile.Length)
        {
          WriteLine($"delete {copiedFile.FullName}");
          if (!checkOnly)
          {
            copiedFile.Delete();
          }
        }
      }
      previousFileName = fileName;
    }
}
```

WORKING WITH STREAMS

Now let's get into more powerful options that are available when you work with files: streams. The idea of a stream has been around for a very long time. A stream is an object used to transfer data. The data can be transferred in one of two directions:

➤ If the data is being transferred from some outside source into your program, it is called *reading* from the stream.

➤ If the data is being transferred from your program to some outside source, it is called *writing* to the stream.

Very often, the outside source will be a file, but that is not always the case. Other possibilities include the following:

➤ Reading or writing data on the network using some network protocol, where the intention is for this data to be picked up by or sent from another computer

➤ Reading from or writing to a named pipe

➤ Reading from or writing to an area of memory

Some streams allow only writing, some streams allow only reading, and some streams allow random access. Random access enables you to position a cursor randomly within a stream—for example, to start reading from the start of the stream to later move to the end of the stream, and continue with a position in the middle of the stream.

Of these examples, Microsoft has supplied a .NET class for writing to or reading from memory: the System.IO.MemoryStream object. The System.Net.Sockets.NetworkStream object handles network data. The Stream class does not make any assumptions of the nature of the data source. It can be file streams, memory streams, network streams, or any data source you can think of.

Some streams can also be chained. For example, the DeflateStream can be used to compress data. This stream in turn can write to the FileStream, MemoryStream, or NetworkStream. The CryptoStream enables you to encrypt data. It's also possible to chain the DeflateStream to the CryptoStream to write in turn to the FileStream.

> **NOTE** *Chapter 24, "Security," explains how you can use the* CryptoStream.

Using streams, the outside source might even be a variable within your own code. This might sound paradoxical, but the technique of using streams to transmit data between variables can be a useful trick for converting data between data types. The C language used something similar—the `sprintf` function—to convert between integer data types and strings or to format strings.

The advantage of having a separate object for the transfer of data, rather than using the `FileInfo` or `DirectoryInfo` classes to do this, is that separating the concept of transferring data from the particular data source makes it easier to swap data sources. Stream objects themselves contain a lot of generic code that concerns the movement of data between outside sources and variables in your code. By keeping this code separate from any concept of a particular data source, you make it easier for this code to be reused in different circumstances.

Although it's not that easy to directly read and write to streams, you can use readers and writers. This is another separation of concerns. Readers and writers can read and write to streams. For example, the `StringReader` and `StringWriter` classes are part of the same inheritance tree as two classes that you use later to read and write text files. The classes will almost certainly share a substantial amount of code behind the scenes. Figure 23-3 illustrates the hierarchy of stream-related classes in the `System.IO` namespace.

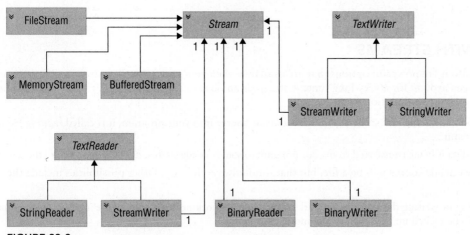

FIGURE 23-3

As far as reading and writing files goes, the classes that concern us most are the following:

➤ `FileStream`—This class is intended for reading and writing binary data in a file.

➤ `StreamReader` and `StreamWriter`—These classes are designed specifically for reading from and writing to streams offering APIs for text formats.

➤ `BinaryReader` and `BinaryWriter`—These classes are designed for reading and writing to streams offering APIs for binary data.

The difference between using these classes and directly using the underlying stream objects is that a basic stream works in bytes. For example, suppose that as part of the process of saving some document you want to write the contents of a variable of type `long` to a binary file. Each `long` occupies 8 bytes, and if you use an ordinary binary stream you would have to explicitly write each of those 8 bytes of memory.

In C# code, you would have to perform some bitwise operations to extract each of those 8 bytes from the `long` value. Using a `BinaryWriter` instance, you can encapsulate the entire operation in an overload of the `BinaryWriter.Write` method, which takes a `long` as a parameter, and which places those 8 bytes into the stream (and if the stream is directed to a file, into the file). A corresponding `BinaryReader.Read` method extracts 8 bytes from the stream and recovers the value of the `long`.

Working with File Streams

Let's get into programming streams reading and writing files. A FileStream instance is used to read or write data to or from a file. To construct a FileStream, you need four pieces of information:

1. The *file* you want to access.

2. The *mode*, which indicates how you want to open the file. For example, are you intending to create a new file or open an existing file? If you are opening an existing file, should any write operations be interpreted as overwriting the contents of the file or appending to the file?

3. The *access*, which indicates how you want to access the file. For example, do you want to read from or write to the file or do both?

4. The *share* access, which specifies whether you want exclusive access to the file. Alternatively, are you willing to have other streams access the file simultaneously? If so, should other streams have access to read the file, to write to it, or to do both?

The first piece of information is usually represented by a string that contains the full pathname of the file, and this chapter considers only those constructors that require a string here. Besides those, however, some additional constructors take a native Windows handle to a file instead. The remaining three pieces of information are represented by three .NET enumerations called FileMode, FileAccess, and FileShare. The values of these enumerations are listed in the following table and are self-explanatory:

ENUMERATION	VALUES
FileMode	Append, Create, CreateNew, Open, OpenOrCreate, or Truncate
FileAccess	Read, ReadWrite, or Write
FileShare	Delete, Inheritable, None, Read, ReadWrite, or Write

Note that in the case of FileMode, exceptions can be thrown if you request a mode that is inconsistent with the existing status of the file. Append, Open, and Truncate throw an exception if the file does not already exist, and CreateNew throws an exception if it does. Create and OpenOrCreate cope with either scenario, but Create deletes any existing file to replace it with a new, initially empty, one. The FileAccess and FileShare enumerations are bitwise flags, so values can be combined with the C# bitwise OR operator, |.

Creating a FileStream

The sample code for StreamSamples makes use of the following dependencies and namespaces:

Dependencies

```
NETStandard.Library
System.IO.FileSystem
```

Namespaces

```
System
System.Collections.Generic
System.Globalization
System.IO
System.Linq
System.Text
System.Threading.Tasks
static System.Console
```

There are a large number of constructors for the `FileStream`. The following sample uses one with four parameters (code file `StreamSamples/Program.cs`):

➤ The filename

➤ The `FileMode` enumeration with the `Open` value to open an existing file

➤ The `FileAccess` enumeration with the `Read` value to read the file

➤ The `FileShare` enumeration with a `Read` value to allow other programs to read but not change the file at the same time

```
private void ReadFileUsingFileStream(string fileName)
{
  const int bufferSize = 4096;
  using (var stream = new FileStream(fileName, FileMode.Open,
    FileAccess.Read, FileShare.Read))
  {
    ShowStreamInformation(stream);
    Encoding encoding = GetEncoding(stream);
    //...
```

Instead of using the constructor of the `FileStream` class to create a `FileStream` object, you can create a `FileStream` directly using the `File` class with the `OpenRead` method. The `OpenRead` method opens a file (similar to `FileMode.Open`), returns a stream that can be read (`FileAccess.Read`), and also allows other processes read access (`FileShare.Read`):

```
using (FileStream stream = File.OpenRead(filename))
{
  //...
```

Getting Stream Information

The `Stream` class defines the properties `CanRead`, `CanWrite`, `CanSeek`, and `CanTimeout` that you can read to get information about what can be done with a stream. For reading and writing streams, the timeout values `ReadTimeout` and `WriteTimeout` specify timeouts in milliseconds. Setting these values can be important in networking scenarios to make sure the user does not have to wait too long when reading or writing the stream fails. The `Position` property returns the current position of the cursor in the stream. Every time some data is read from the stream, the position moves to the next byte that will be read. The sample code writes information about the stream to the console (code file `StreamSamples/Program.cs`):

```
private void ShowStreamInformation(Stream stream)
{
  WriteLine($"stream can read: {stream.CanRead}, " +
    $"can write: {stream.CanWrite}, can seek: {stream.CanSeek}, " +
    $"can timeout: {stream.CanTimeout}");
  WriteLine($"length: {stream.Length}, position: {stream.Position}");
  if (stream.CanTimeout)
  {
    WriteLine($"read timeout: {stream.ReadTimeout} " +
      $"write timeout: {stream.WriteTimeout} ");
  }
}
```

When you run the program with the file stream that has been opened, you get the following output. The position is currently 0 as read has not yet happened:

```
stream can read: True, can write: False, can seek: True, can timeout: False
length: 1113, position: 0
```

Analyzing Text File Encodings

With text files, the next step is to read the first bytes of the stream—the preamble. The *preamble* gives information about how the file is encoded (the text format used). This is also known as *byte order mark* (BOM).

You can read a stream by using `ReadByte` that reads just a byte from the stream, or the `Read` method that fills a byte array. With the `GetEncoding` sample method, an array of 5 bytes is created, and the byte array is filled from the `Read` method. The second and third parameters specify the offset within the byte array and the count of the number of bytes that are available to fill. The `Read` method returns the number of bytes read; the stream might be smaller than the buffer. In case no more characters are available to read, the `Read` method returns 0.

The sample code analyzes the first characters of the stream to return the detected encoding and positions the stream after the encoding characters (code file `StreamSamples/Program.cs`):

```
private Encoding GetEncoding(Stream stream)
{
  if (!stream.CanSeek) throw new ArgumentException(
    "require a stream that can seek");

  Encoding encoding = Encoding.ASCII;

  byte[] bom = new byte[5];
  int nRead = stream.Read(bom, offset: 0, count: 5);
  if (bom[0] == 0xff && bom[1] == 0xfe && bom[2] == 0 && bom[3] == 0)
  {
    WriteLine("UTF-32");
    stream.Seek(4, SeekOrigin.Begin);
    return Encoding.UTF32;
  }
  else if (bom[0] == 0xff && bom[1] == 0xfe)
  {
    WriteLine("UTF-16, little endian");
    stream.Seek(2, SeekOrigin.Begin);
    return Encoding.Unicode;
  }
  else if (bom[0] == 0xfe && bom[1] == 0xff)
  {
    WriteLine("UTF-16, big endian");
    stream.Seek(2, SeekOrigin.Begin);
    return Encoding.BigEndianUnicode;
  }
  else if (bom[0] == 0xef && bom[1] == 0xbb && bom[2] == 0xbf)
  {
    WriteLine("UTF-8");
    stream.Seek(3, SeekOrigin.Begin);
    return Encoding.UTF8;
  }
  stream.Seek(0, SeekOrigin.Begin);
  return encoding;
}
```

The start of a file can begin with the characters FF and FE. The order of these bytes gives information about how the document is stored. Two-byte Unicode can be stored in little or big endian. With FF followed by FE, it's little endian, and when FE is followed by FF, it's big endian. This endianness goes back to mainframes by IBM that used big endian for byte ordering, and PDP11 systems from Digital Equipment that used little endian. Communicating across the network with computers that have different endianness requires changing the order of bytes on one side. Nowadays, the Intel CPU architecture uses little endian, and the ARM architecture allows switching between little and big endian.

What's the other difference between these encodings? With ASCII, 7 bits are enough for every character. Originally based on the English alphabet, ASCII offers lowercase, uppercase, and control characters.

Extended ASCII makes use of the 8th bit to allow switching to language-specific characters. Switching is not easy as it requires paying attention to the code map and also does not provide enough characters for some Asian languages. UTF-16 (Unicode Text Format) solves this by having 16 bits for every character. Because UTF-16 is still not enough for historical glyphs, UTF-32 uses 32 bit for every character. Although Windows NT 3.1 switched to UTF-16 for the default text encoding (from a Microsoft extension of ASCII before), nowadays the most-used text format is UTF-8. With the web, UTF-8 turned out to be the most-used text format since 2007 (this superseded ASCII, which had been the most common character encoding before). UTF-8 uses a variable length for character definitions. One character is defined by using between 1 and 6 bytes. UTF-8 is detected by this character sequence at the beginning of a file: 0xEF, 0xBB, 0xBF.

Reading Streams

After opening the file and creating the stream, the file is read using the `Read` method. This is repeated until the method returns 0. A string is created using the `Encoder` created from the `GetEncoding` method defined earlier. Do not forget to close the stream using the `Dispose` method. If possible, use the `using` statement—as is done with this code sample—to dispose the stream automatically (code file `StreamSamples/Program.cs`):

```
public static void ReadFileUsingFileStream(string fileName)
{
  const int BUFFERSIZE = 256;
  using (var stream = new FileStream(fileName, FileMode.Open,
    FileAccess.Read, FileShare.Read))
  {
    ShowStreamInformation(stream);
    Encoding encoding = GetEncoding(stream);

    byte[] buffer = new byte[bufferSize];

    bool completed = false;
    do
    {
      int nread = stream.Read(buffer, 0, BUFFERSIZE);
      if (nread == 0) completed = true;
      if (nread < BUFFERSIZE)
      {
        Array.Clear(buffer, nread, BUFFERSIZE - nread);
      }

      string s = encoding.GetString(buffer, 0, nread);
      WriteLine($"read {nread} bytes");
      WriteLine(s);
    } while (!completed);
  }
}
```

Writing Streams

How streams can be written is demonstrated by writing a simple string to a text file. To create a stream that can be written to, the `File.OpenWrite` method can be used. This time a temporary filename is created with the help of `Path.GetTempFileName`. The default file extension defined by the `GetTempFileName` is changed to txt with `Path.ChangeExtension` (code file `StreamSamples/Program.cs`):

```
public static void WriteTextFile()
{
  string tempTextFileName = Path.ChangeExtension(Path.GetTempFileName(),
    "txt");
```

```
using (FileStream stream = File.OpenWrite(tempTextFileName))
{
    //etc.
```

When you're writing a UTF-8 file, the preamble needs to be written to the file. This can be done by sending the 3 bytes of the UTF-8 preamble to the stream with the `WriteByte` method:

```
stream.WriteByte(0xef);
stream.WriteByte(0xbb);
stream.WriteByte(0xbf);
```

There's an alternative for doing this. You don't need to remember the bytes to specify the encoding. The `Encoding` class already has this information. The `GetPreamble` method returns a byte array with the preamble for the file. This byte array is written using the `Write` method of the `Stream` class:

```
byte[] preamble = Encoding.UTF8.GetPreamble();
stream.Write(preamble, 0, preamble.Length);
```

Now the content of the file can be written. As the `Write` method requires byte arrays to write, strings need to be converted. For converting a string to a byte array with UTF-8, `Encoding.UTF8.GetBytes` does the job before the byte array is written:

```
    string hello = "Hello, World!";
    byte[] buffer = Encoding.UTF8.GetBytes(hello);
    stream.Write(buffer, 0, buffer.Length);
    WriteLine($"file {stream.Name} written");
  }
}
```

You can open the temporary file using an editor such as Notepad, and it will use the correct encoding.

Copying Streams

Now let's combine reading and writing from streams by copying the file content. With the next code snippet, the readable stream is opened with `File.OpenRead`, and the writeable stream is opened with `File.OpenWrite`. A buffer is read using the `Stream.Read` method and written with `Stream.Write` (code file `StreamSamples/Program.cs`):

```
public static void CopyUsingStreams(string inputFile, string outputFile)
{
    const int BUFFERSIZE = 4096;
    using (var inputStream = File.OpenRead(inputFile))
    using (var outputStream = File.OpenWrite(outputFile))
    {
        byte[] buffer = new byte[BUFFERSIZE];
        bool completed = false;
        do
        {
            int nRead = inputStream.Read(buffer, 0, BUFFERSIZE);
            if (nRead == 0) completed = true;
            outputStream.Write(buffer, 0, nRead);
        } while (!completed);
    }
}
```

To copy a stream, it's not necessary to write the code to read and write a stream. Instead, you can use the `CopyTo` method of the `Stream` class, as shown here (code file `StreamSamples/Program.cs`):

```
public static void CopyUsingStreams2(string inputFile, string outputFile)
{
    using (var inputStream = File.OpenRead(inputFile))
    using (var outputStream = File.OpenWrite(outputFile))
```

```
    {
      inputStream.CopyTo(outputStream);
    }
}
```

Using Random Access to Streams

Random access to streams provides an advantage in that—even with large files—you can access a specific position within the file in a fast way.

To see random access in action, the following code snippet creates a large file. This code snippet creates the file `sampledata.data` with records that are all the same length and contain a number, a text, and a random date. The number of records that is passed to the method is created with the help of the `Enumerable.Range` method. The `Select` method creates an anonymous type that contains `Number`, `Text`, and `Date` properties. Out of these records, a string with # pre- and postfix is created, with a fixed length for every value and a ; separator between each value. The `WriteAsync` method writes the record to the stream (code file `StreamSamples/Program.cs`):

```
const string SampleFilePath = "./samplefile.data";

public static async Task CreateSampleFile(int nRecords)
{
  FileStream stream = File.Create(SampleFilePath);
  using (var writer = new StreamWriter(stream))
  {
    var r = new Random();

    var records = Enumerable.Range(0, nRecords).Select(x => new
    {
      Number = x,
      Text = $"Sample text {r.Next(200)}",
      Date = new DateTime(Math.Abs((long)((r.NextDouble() * 2 - 1) *
        DateTime.MaxValue.Ticks)))
    });

    foreach (var rec in records)
    {
      string date = rec.Date.ToString("d", CultureInfo.InvariantCulture);
      string s =
        $"#{rec.Number,8};{rec.Text,-20};{date}#{Environment.NewLine}";
      await writer.WriteAsync(s);
    }
  }
}
```

> **NOTE** *Chapter 5, "Managed and Unmanaged Resources," explains that every object implementing* `IDisposable` *should be disposed. In the previous code snippet, it looks like* `FileStream` *is not disposed. However, that's not the case. The* `StreamWriter` *takes control over the used resource and disposes the stream when the* `StreamWriter` *is disposed. To keep the stream opened for a longer period than the* `StreamWriter`, *you can configure this with the constructor of the* `StreamWriter`. *In that case, you need to dispose the stream explicitly.*

Now let's position a cursor randomly within the stream to read different records. The user is asked to enter a record number that should be accessed. The byte in the stream that should be accessed is based on the record number and the record size. The `Seek` method of the `Stream` class now enables you to position the cursor within the stream. The second argument specifies whether the position is based on the beginning of the stream, the end of the stream, or the current position (code file `StreamSamples/Program.cs`):

```
public static void RandomAccessSample()
{
  try
  {
    using (FileStream stream = File.OpenRead(SampleFilePath))
    {
      byte[] buffer = new byte[RECORDSIZE];
      do
      {
        try
        {
          Write("record number (or 'bye' to end): ");
          string line = ReadLine();
          if (line.ToUpper().CompareTo("BYE") == 0) break;

          int record;
          if (int.TryParse(line, out record))
          {
            stream.Seek((record - 1) * RECORDSIZE, SeekOrigin.Begin);
            stream.Read(buffer, 0, RECORDSIZE);
            string s = Encoding.UTF8.GetString(buffer);
            WriteLine($"record: {s}");
          }
        }
        catch (Exception ex)
        {
          WriteLine(ex.Message);
        }
      } while (true);
      WriteLine("finished");
    }
  }
  catch (FileNotFoundException)
  {
    WriteLine("Create the sample file using the option -sample first");
  }
}
```

With this you can experiment with creating a file with 1.5 million records or more. A file this size is slow when you open it using Notepad, but it is extremely fast when you use random access. Depending on your system and the CPU and disk type, you might use higher or lower values for the tests.

> **NOTE** *In case the records that should be accessed are not fixed size, it still can be useful to use random access for large files. One way to deal with this is to write the position of the records to the beginning of the file. Another option is to read a larger block where the record could be and find the record identifier and the record limiters within the memory block.*

Using Buffered Streams

For performance reasons, when you read or write to or from a file, the output is buffered. This means that if your program asks for the next 2 bytes of a file stream, and the stream passes the request on to Windows, then Windows will not connect to the file system and then locate and read the file off the disk just to get 2 bytes. Instead, Windows retrieves a large block of the file at one time and stores this block in an area of memory known as a *buffer*. Subsequent requests for data from the stream are satisfied from the buffer until the buffer runs out, at which point Windows grabs another block of data from the file.

Writing to files works in the same way. For files, this is done automatically by the operating system, but you might have to write a stream class to read from some other device that is not buffered. If so, you can create a `BufferedStream`, which implements a buffer itself, and pass the stream that should be buffered to the constructor. Note, however, that `BufferedStream` is not designed for the situation in which an application frequently alternates between reading and writing data.

USING READERS AND WRITERS

Reading and writing text files using the `FileStream` class requires working with byte arrays and dealing with the encoding as described in the previous section. There's an easier way to do this: using readers and writers. You can use the `StreamReader` and `StreamWriter` classes to read and write to the `FileStream`, and you have an easier job not dealing with byte arrays and encodings.

That's because these classes work at a slightly higher level and are specifically geared to reading and writing text. The methods that they implement can automatically detect convenient points to stop reading text, based on the contents of the stream. In particular:

➤   These classes implement methods to read or write one line of text at a time: `StreamReader`
     `.ReadLine` and `StreamWriter.WriteLine`. In the case of reading, this means that the stream automatically determines where the next carriage return is and stops reading at that point. In the case of writing, it means that the stream automatically appends the carriage return–line feed combination to the text that it writes out.

➤   By using the `StreamReader` and `StreamWriter` classes, you don't need to worry about the encoding used in the file.

The sample code for ReaderWriterSamples makes use of the following dependencies and namespaces:

Dependencies

```
NETStandard.Library
System.IO.FileSystem
```

Namespaces

```
System
System.Collections.Generic
System.Globalization
System.IO
System.Linq
System.Text
System.Threading.Tasks
static System.Console
```

The StreamReader Class

Let's start with the `StreamReader` by converting the previous example to read a file to use the `StreamReader`. It looks a lot easier now. The constructor of the `StreamReader` receives the `FileStream`.

You can check for the end of the file by using the `EndOfStream` property, and you read lines using the `ReadLine` method (code file ReaderWriterSamples/Program.cs):

```
public static void ReadFileUsingReader(string fileName)
{
  var stream = new FileStream(fileName, FileMode.Open, FileAccess.Read,
                              FileShare.Read);
  using (var reader = new StreamReader(stream))
  {
    while (!reader.EndOfStream)
    {
      string line = reader.ReadLine();
      WriteLine(line);
    }
  }
}
```

It's no longer necessary to deal with byte arrays and the encoding. However, pay attention; the `StreamReader` by default uses the UTF-8 encoding. You can let the `StreamReader` use the encoding as it is defined by the preamble in the file by specifying a different constructor:

```
var reader = new StreamReader(stream, detectEncodingFromByteOrderMarks: true);
```

You can also explicitly specify the encoding:

```
var reader = new StreamReader(stream, Encoding.Unicode);
```

Other constructors enable you to set the buffer to be used; the default is 1024 bytes. Also, you can specify that the underlying stream should not be closed on closing the reader. By default, when the reader is closed (using the `Dispose` method), the underlying stream is closed as well.

Instead of explicitly instantiating a new `StreamReader`, you can create a `StreamReader` by using the `OpenText` method of the `File` class:

```
var reader = File.OpenText(fileName);
```

With the code snippet to read the file, the file was read line by line using the `ReadLine` method. The `StreamReader` also allows reading the complete file from the position of the cursor in the stream using `ReadToEnd`:

```
string content = reader.ReadToEnd();
```

The `StreamReader` also allows the content to read to a char array. This is similar to the `Read` method of the `Stream` class; it doesn't read to a byte array but instead to a char array. Remember, the char type uses two bytes. This is perfect for 16-bit Unicode, but is not as useful with UTF-8 where a single character can be between one and six bytes long:

```
int nChars = 100;
char[] charArray = new char[nChars];
int nCharsRead = reader.Read(charArray, 0, nChars);
```

The StreamWriter Class

The `StreamWriter` works in the same way as the `StreamReader`, except that you use `StreamWriter` only to write to a file (or to another stream). The following code snippet shows creating a `StreamWriter` passing a `FileStream`. Then a passed string array is written to the stream (code file ReaderWriterSamples/Program.cs):

```
public static void WriteFileUsingWriter(string fileName, string[] lines)
{
  var outputStream = File.OpenWrite(fileName);
  using (var writer = new StreamWriter(outputStream))
  {
    byte[] preamble = Encoding.UTF8.GetPreamble();
```

```
        outputStream.Write(preamble, 0, preamble.Length);
        writer.Write(lines);
    }
}
```

Remember that the `StreamWriter` is using the UTF-8 format by default to write the text content. You can define alternative contents by setting an `Encoding` object in the constructor. Also, similarly to the constructor of the `StreamReader`, the `StreamWriter` allows specifying the buffer size and whether the underlying stream should not be closed on closing of the writer.

The `Write` method of the `StreamWriter` defines 17 overloads that allow passing strings and several .NET data types. Using the methods passing the .NET data types, remember that all these are changed to strings with the specified encoding. To write the data types in binary format, you can use the `BinaryWriter` that's shown next.

Reading and Writing Binary Files

To read and write binary files, one option is to directly use the stream types; in this case, it's good to use byte arrays for reading and writing. Another option is to use readers and writers defined for this scenario: `BinaryReader` and `BinaryWriter`. You use them similarly to the way you use `StreamReader` and `StreamWriter` except `BinaryReader` and `BinaryWriter` don't use any encoding. Files are written in binary format rather than text format.

Unlike the `Stream` type, `BinaryWriter` defines 18 overloads for the `Write` method. The overloads accept different types, as shown in the following code snippet that writes a `double`, an `int`, a `long`, and a `string` (code file `ReaderWriterSamples/Program.cs`):

```
public static void WriteFileUsingBinaryWriter(string binFile)
{
    var outputStream = File.Create(binFile);
    using (var writer = new BinaryWriter(outputStream))
    {
        double d = 47.47;
        int i = 42;
        long l = 987654321;
        string s = "sample";
        writer.Write(d);
        writer.Write(i);
        writer.Write(l);
        writer.Write(s);
    }
}
```

After writing the file, you can open it using the Binary Editor from Visual Studio, as shown in Figure 23-4.

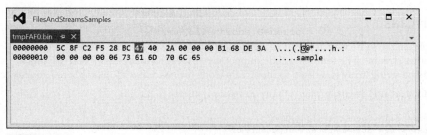

FIGURE 23-4

To read the file again, you can use a `BinaryReader`. This class defines methods to read all the different types, such as `ReadDouble`, `ReadInt32`, `ReadInt64`, and `ReadString`, which are shown here:

```
public static void ReadFileUsingBinaryReader(string binFile)
{
  var inputStream = File.Open(binFile, FileMode.Open);
  using (var reader = new BinaryReader(inputStream))
  {
    double d = reader.ReadDouble();
    int i = reader.ReadInt32();
    long l = reader.ReadInt64();
    string s = reader.ReadString();
    WriteLine($"d: {d}, i: {i}, l: {l}, s: {s}");
  }
}
```

The order for reading the file must match exactly the order in which it has been written. Creating your own binary format, you need to know what and how it is stored, and read accordingly. The older Microsoft Word document was using a binary file format, whereas the newer docx file extension is a ZIP file. How ZIP files can be read and written is explained in the next section.

COMPRESSING FILES

.NET includes types to compress and decompress streams using different algorithms. You can use `DeflateStream` and `GZipStream` to compress and decompress streams; the `ZipArchive` class enables you to create and read ZIP files.

Both `DeflateStream` and `GZipStream` use the same algorithm for compression (in fact, `GZipStream` uses `DeflateStream` behind the scenes), but `GZipStream` adds a cyclic redundancy check to detect data corruption. You can open a `ZipArchive` directly with Windows Explorer, but you can't open a file compressed with `GZipStream`. Third-party gzip tools can open files compressed with `GZipStream`.

> **NOTE** *The algorithm used by* `DeflateStream` *and* `GZipStream` *is the* deflate *algorithm. This algorithm is defined by RFC 1951 (*https://tools.ietf.org/html/rfc1951*). This algorithm is widely thought to be not covered by patents, which is why it is in widespread use.*

The sample code for CompressFileSample makes use of the following dependencies and namespaces:

Dependencies

```
NETStandard.Library
System.IO.Compression
System.IO.Compression.ZipFile
```

Namespaces

```
System.Collections.Generic
System.IO
System.IO.Compression
static System.Console
```

Using the Deflate Stream

As explained earlier, a feature from streams is that you can chain them. To compress a stream, all that's needed is to create `DeflateStream` and pass another stream (in this example, the `outputStream` to write a file) to the constructor, with the argument `CompressionMode.Compress` for compression. Writing to this stream either using the `Write` method or by using other features, such as the `CopyTo` method as shown in this code snippet, is all that's needed for file compression (code file `CompressFileSample/Program.cs`):

```
public static void CompressFile(string fileName, string compressedFileName)
{
    using (FileStream inputStream = File.OpenRead(fileName))
    {
        FileStream outputStream = File.OpenWrite(compressedFileName);
        using (var compressStream =
            new DeflateStream(outputStream, CompressionMode.Compress))
        {
            inputStream.CopyTo(compressStream);
        }
    }
}
```

To decompress the deflate-compressed file again, the following code snippet opens the file using a `FileStream` and creates the `DeflateStream` object with `CompressionMode.Decompress` passing the file stream for decompression. The `Stream.CopyTo` method copies the decompressed stream to a `MemoryStream`. This code snippet then makes use of a `StreamReader` to read the data from the `MemoryStream` and write the output to the console. The `StreamReader` is configured to leave the assigned `MemoryStream` open (using the `leaveOpen` argument), so the `MemoryStream` could also be used after closing the reader:

```
public static void DecompressFile(string fileName)
{
    FileStream inputStream = File.OpenRead(fileName);
    using (MemoryStream outputStream = new MemoryStream())
    using (var compressStream = new DeflateStream(inputStream,
            CompressionMode.Decompress))
    {
        compressStream.CopyTo(outputStream);
        outputStream.Seek(0, SeekOrigin.Begin);
        using (var reader = new StreamReader(outputStream, Encoding.UTF8,
            detectEncodingFromByteOrderMarks: true, bufferSize: 4096,
            leaveOpen: true))
        {
            string result = reader.ReadToEnd();
            WriteLine(result);
        }
        // could use the outputStream after the StreamReader is closed
    }
}
```

Zipping Files

Today, the ZIP file format is the standard for many different file types. Word documents (`docx`) as well as NuGet packages are all stored as a ZIP file. With .NET, it's easy to create a ZIP archive.

For creating a ZIP archive, you can create an object of `ZipArchive`. A `ZipArchive` contains multiple `ZipArchiveEntry` objects. The `ZipArchive` class is not a stream, but it uses a stream to read or write to (this is similar to the reader and writer classes discussed earlier). The following code snippet creates a `ZipArchive` that writes the compressed content to the file stream opened with `File.OpenWrite`. What's added to the ZIP archive is defined by the directory passed. `Directory.EnumerateFiles` enumerates all the files in the directory and creates a `ZipArchiveEntry` object for every file. Invoking the `Open` method creates a `Stream` object. With the `CopyTo` method of the `Stream` that is read, the file is compressed and written to the `ZipArchiveEntry` (code file `CompressFileSample/Program.cs`):

```
public static void CreateZipFile(string directory, string zipFile)
{
    FileStream zipStream = File.OpenWrite(zipFile);
    using (var archive = new ZipArchive(zipStream, ZipArchiveMode.Create))
    {
        IEnumerable<string> files = Directory.EnumerateFiles(
            directory, "*", SearchOption.TopDirectoryOnly);
        foreach (var file in files)
        {
            ZipArchiveEntry entry = archive.CreateEntry(Path.GetFileName(file));
            using (FileStream inputStream = File.OpenRead(file))
            using (Stream outputStream = entry.Open())
            {
                inputStream.CopyTo(outputStream);
            }
        }
    }
}
```

WATCHING FILE CHANGES

With `FileSystemWatcher`, you can monitor file changes. Events are fired on creating, renaming, deleting, and changing files. This can be used in scenarios where you need to react on file changes—for example, with a server when a file is uploaded, or in a case where a file is cached in memory and the cache needs to be invalidated when the file changes.

As `FileSystemWatcher` is easy to use, let's directly get into a sample. The sample code for `FileMonitor` makes use of the following dependencies and namespaces:

Dependencies

```
NETStandard.Library
System.IO.FileSystem.Watcher
```

Namespaces

```
System.IO
static System.Console
```

The sample code starts watching files in the method `WatchFiles`. Using the constructor of the `FileSystemWatcher`, you can supply the directory that should be watched. You can also provide a filter to filter only specific files that match with the filter expression. When you set the property `IncludeSubdirectories`, you can define whether only the files in the specified directory should be watched or whether files in subdirectories should also be watched. With the `Created`, `Changed`, `Deleted`, and `Renamed` events, event handlers are supplied. All of these events are of type `FileSystemEventHandler` with the exception of the `Renamed` event that is of type `RenamedEventHandler`. `RenamedEventHandler` derives from `FileSystemEventHandler` and offers additional information about the event (code file `FileMonitor/Program.cs`):

```
public static void WatchFiles(string path, string filter)
{
    var watcher = new FileSystemWatcher(path, filter)
    {
        IncludeSubdirectories = true
    };
    watcher.Created += OnFileChanged;
    watcher.Changed += OnFileChanged;
    watcher.Deleted += OnFileChanged;
```

```
watcher.Renamed += OnFileRenamed;

watcher.EnableRaisingEvents = true;
WriteLine("watching file changes...");
}
```

The information that is received with a file change is of type `FileSystemEventArgs`. It contains the name of the file that changed as well as the kind of change that is an enumeration of type `WatcherChangeTypes`:

```
private static void OnFileChanged(object sender, FileSystemEventArgs e)
{
    WriteLine($"file {e.Name} {e.ChangeType}");
}
```

On renaming the file, additional information is received with the `RenamedEventArgs` parameter. This type derives from `FileSystemEventArgs` and defines additional information about the original name of the file:

```
private static void OnFileRenamed(object sender, RenamedEventArgs e)
{
    WriteLine($"file {e.OldName} {e.ChangeType} to {e.Name}");
}
```

When you start the application by specifying a folder to watch and `*.txt` as the filter, the following is the output after creating the file `sample1.txt`, adding content, renaming it to `sample2.txt`, and finally deleting it:

```
watching file changes...
file New Text Document.txt Created
file New Text Document.txt Renamed to sample1.txt
file sample1.txt Changed
file sample1.txt Changed
file sample1.txt Renamed to sample2.txt
file sample2.txt Deleted
```

WORKING WITH MEMORY MAPPED FILES

Memory mapped files enable you to access files or shared memory from different processes. There are several scenarios and features with this technology:

➤ Fast random access to huge files using maps of the file

➤ Sharing of files between different processes or tasks

➤ Sharing of memory between different processes or tasks

➤ Using accessors to directly read and write from memory positions

➤ Using streams to read and write

The memory mapped files API allows you to use either a physical file or shared memory—where the system's page file is used as a backing store. The shared memory can be bigger than the available physical memory, so a backing store is needed. You can create a memory mapped file to a specific file or shared memory. With either of these options, you can assign a name for the memory map. Using a name allows different processes to have access to the same shared memory.

After you've created the memory map, you can create a view. A view is used to map a part of the complete memory mapped file to access it for reading or writing.

The `MemoryMappedFilesSample` makes use of the following dependencies and namespaces:

Dependencies

```
NETStandard.Library
System.IO.MemoryMappedFiles
```

Namespaces

```
System
System.IO
System.IO.MemoryMappedFiles
System.Threading
System.Threading.Tasks
static System.Console
```

The sample application demonstrates using a memory mapped file using both view accessors and streams using multiple tasks. One task creates the memory mapped file and writes data to it; the other task reads data.

> **NOTE** *The sample code makes use of tasks and events. Read Chapter 21, "Tasks and Parallel Programming," for more information about tasks, and Chapter 22, "Task Synchronization," for more information about events.*

Some infrastructure is needed for creating the tasks and signaling when the map is ready and the data is written. The name of the map and `ManualResetEventSlim` objects are defined as a member of the `Program` class (code file `MemoryMappedFilesSample/Program.cs`):

```
private ManualResetEventSlim _mapCreated =
  new ManualResetEventSlim(initialState: false);
private ManualResetEventSlim _dataWrittenEvent =
  new ManualResetEventSlim(initialState: false);
private const string MAPNAME = "SampleMap";
```

Tasks are started within the `Main` method with the `Task.Run` method:

```
public void Run()
{
  Task.Run(() => WriterAsync());
  Task.Run(() => Reader());
  WriteLine("tasks started");
  ReadLine();
}
```

Now let's create readers and writers using accessors.

Using Accessors to Create Memory Mapped Files

To create a memory-based memory mapped file, the writer invokes the `MemoryMappedFile.CreateOrOpen` method. This method either opens the object with the name specified with the first parameter, or creates a new one if it doesn't exist. To open existing files, you can use the method `OpenExisting`. For accessing physical files, you can use the method `CreateFromFile`.

Other parameters used in the sample code are the size of the memory mapped file and the access needed. After the memory mapped file is created, the event _mapCreated is signaled to give other tasks the information that the memory mapped file is created and can be opened. Invoking the method `CreateViewAccessor` returns a `MemoryMappedViewAccessor` to access the shared memory. With the view accessor, you can define an offset and size that is used by this task. Of course, the maximum size that you can use is the size of the memory mapped file itself. This view is used for writing, thus the file access is set to `MemoryMappedFileAccess.Write`.

Next, you can write primitive data types to the shared memory using overloaded `Write` methods of the `MemoryMappedViewAccessor`. The `Write` method always needs position information designating where the data should be written to. After all the data is written, an event is signaled to inform the reader that it is now possible to start reading (code file `MemoryMappedFilesSample/Program.cs`):

```
private async Task WriterAsync()
{
  try
  {
    using (MemoryMappedFile mappedFile = MemoryMappedFile.CreateOrOpen(
      MAPNAME, 10000, MemoryMappedFileAccess.ReadWrite))
    {
      _mapCreated.Set(); // signal shared memory segment created
      WriteLine("shared memory segment created");

      using (MemoryMappedViewAccessor accessor = mappedFile.CreateViewAccessor(
          0, 10000, MemoryMappedFileAccess.Write))
      {
        for (int i = 0, pos = 0; i < 100; i++, pos += 4)
        {
          accessor.Write(pos, i);
          WriteLine($"written {i} at position {pos}");
          await Task.Delay(10);
        }
        _dataWrittenEvent.Set(); // signal all data written
        WriteLine("data written");
      }
    }
  }
  catch (Exception ex)
  {
    WriteLine($"writer {ex.Message}");
  }
}
```

The reader first waits for the map to be created before opening the memory mapped file using `MemoryMappedFile.OpenExisting`. The reader just needs read access to the map. After that, similar to the writer before, a view accessor is created. Before reading data, you wait for the `_dataWrittenEvent` to be set. Reading is similar to writing in that you supply a position where the data should be accessed, but different `Read` methods, such as `ReadInt32`, are defined for reading the different data types:

```
private void Reader()
{
  try
  {
    WriteLine("reader");
    _mapCreated.Wait();
    WriteLine("reader starting");

    using (MemoryMappedFile mappedFile = MemoryMappedFile.OpenExisting(
      MAPNAME, MemoryMappedFileRights.Read))
    {
      using (MemoryMappedViewAccessor accessor = mappedFile.CreateViewAccessor(
        0, 10000, MemoryMappedFileAccess.Read))
      {
        _dataWrittenEvent.Wait();
        WriteLine("reading can start now");

        for (int i = 0; i < 400; i += 4)
```

```
        {
          int result = accessor.ReadInt32(i);
          WriteLine($"reading {result} from position {i}");
        }
      }
    }
  }
  catch (Exception ex)
  {
    WriteLine($"reader {ex.Message}");
  }
}
```

When you run the application, you might see output such as this:

```
reader
reader starting
tasks started
shared memory segment created
written 0 at position 0
written 1 at position 4
written 2 at position 8
...
written 99 at 396
data written
reading can start now
reading 0 from position 0
reading 1 from position 4
...
```

Using Streams to Create Memory Mapped Files

Instead of writing primitive data types with memory mapped files, you can instead use streams. Streams enable you to use readers and writers, as described earlier in this chapter. Now create a writer to use a `StreamWriter`. The method `CreateViewStream` from the `MemoryMappedFile` returns a `MemoryMappedViewStream`. This method is very similar to the `CreateViewAccessor` method used earlier in defining a view inside the map; with the offset and size, it is convenient to use all the features of streams. The `WriteLineAsync` method is then used to write a string to the stream. As the `StreamWriter` caches writes, the stream position is not updated with every write; it's updated only when the writer writes blocks. For flushing the cache with every write, you set the `AutoFlush` property of the `StreamWriter` to `true` (code file `MemoryMappedFilesSample/Program.cs`):

```
private async Task WriterUsingStreams()
{
  try
  {
    using (MemoryMappedFile mappedFile = MemoryMappedFile.CreateOrOpen(
        MAPNAME, 10000, MemoryMappedFileAccess.ReadWrite))
    {
      _mapCreated.Set(); // signal shared memory segment created
      WriteLine("shared memory segment created");

      MemoryMappedViewStream stream = mappedFile.CreateViewStream(
          0, 10000, MemoryMappedFileAccess.Write);
      using (var writer = new StreamWriter(stream))
      {
        writer.AutoFlush = true;
        for (int i = 0; i < 100; i++)
        {
          string s = $"some data {i}";
          WriteLine($"writing {s} at {stream.Position}");
```

```
            await writer.WriteLineAsync(s);
        }
    }
    _dataWrittenEvent.Set(); // signal all data written
    WriteLine("data written");
    }
}
catch (Exception ex)
{
    WriteLine($"writer {ex.Message}");
}
}
```

The reader similarly creates a mapped view stream with `CreateViewStream`, but this time for read access. Now it's possible to use `StreamReader` methods to read content from the shared memory:

```
private async Task ReaderUsingStreams()
{
  try
  {
    WriteLine("reader");
    _mapCreated.Wait();
    WriteLine("reader starting");

    using (MemoryMappedFile mappedFile = MemoryMappedFile.OpenExisting(
        MAPNAME, MemoryMappedFileRights.Read))
    {
      MemoryMappedViewStream stream = mappedFile.CreateViewStream(
          0, 10000, MemoryMappedFileAccess.Read);
      using (var reader = new StreamReader(stream))
      {
        _dataWrittenEvent.Wait();
        WriteLine("reading can start now");

        for (int i = 0; i < 100; i++)
        {
          long pos = stream.Position;
          string s = await reader.ReadLineAsync();
          WriteLine($"read {s} from {pos}");
        }
      }
    }
  }
  catch (Exception ex)
  {
    WriteLine($"reader {ex.Message}");
  }
}
```

When you run the application, you can see the data written and read. When the data is being written, the position within the stream is always updated because the `AutoFlush` property is set. When data is being read, always 1024 byte blocks are read.

```
tasks started
reader
reader starting
shared memory segment created
writing some data 0 at 0
writing some data 1 at 13
writing some data 2 at 26
writing some data 3 at 39
writing some data 4 at 52
...
```

```
data written
reading can start now
read some data 0 from 0
read some data 1 from 1024
read some data 2 from 1024
read some data 3 from 1024
...
```

When communicating via memory mapped files, you have to synchronize the reader and the writer so the reader knows when data is available. Pipes, which are discussed in the next section, give other options in such a scenario.

COMMUNICATING WITH PIPES

For communication between threads and processes, and also fast communication between different systems, you can use pipes. With .NET, pipes are implemented as streams and thus you have an option to not only send bytes into a pipe but you can use all the stream features, such as readers and writers.

Pipes are implemented as different kinds—as *named pipes*, where the name can be used to connect to each end, and *anonymous pipes*. Anonymous pipes cannot be used to communicate between different systems; they can be used only for communication between a child and parent process or for communication between different tasks.

The code for all the pipe samples makes use of the following dependencies and namespaces:

Dependencies

```
NETStandard.Library
System.IO.Pipes
```

Namespaces

```
System
System.IO
System.IO.Pipes
System.Threading
System.Threading.Tasks
static System.Console
```

Let's start with named pipes for communication between different processes. With the first sample application, two console applications are used. One acts as server and reads data from a pipe; the other one writes messages to the pipe.

Creating a Named Pipe Server

You create the server by creating a new instance of `NamedPipeServerStream`. `NamedPipeServerStream` derives from the base class `PipeStream` that in turn derives from the `Stream` base class and thus can use all the features of streams—for example, you can create a `CryptoStream` or a `GZipStream` to write encrypted or compressed data into the named pipe. The constructor requires a name for the pipe that can be used by multiple processes communicating via the pipe.

The second argument that is used in the following code snippet defines the direction of the pipe. The server stream is used for reading, and thus the direction is set to `PipeDirection.In`. Named pipes can also be bidirectional for reading and writing; you use `PipeDirection.InOut`. Anonymous pipes can be only unidirectional. Next, the named pipe waits until the writing party connects by calling the `WaitForConnection` method. Next, within a loop (until the message "bye" is received), the pipe server reads messages to a buffer array and writes the message to the console (code file `PipesReader/Program.cs`):

```csharp
private static void PipesReader(string pipeName)
{
  try
  {
    using (var pipeReader =
      new NamedPipeServerStream(pipeName, PipeDirection.In))
    {
      pipeReader.WaitForConnection();
      WriteLine("reader connected");

      const int BUFFERSIZE = 256;

      bool completed = false;
      while (!completed)
      {
        byte[] buffer = new byte[BUFFERSIZE];
        int nRead = pipeReader.Read(buffer, 0, BUFFERSIZE);
        string line = Encoding.UTF8.GetString(buffer, 0, nRead);
        WriteLine(line);
        if (line == "bye") completed = true;
      }
    }
    WriteLine("completed reading");
    ReadLine();
  }
  catch (Exception ex)
  {
    WriteLine(ex.Message);
  }
}
```

The following are some other options that you can configure with named pipes:

➤ You can set the enumeration `PipeTransmissionMode` to `Byte` or `Message`. With bytes, a continuous stream is sent; with messages every message can be retrieved.

➤ With the pipe options, you can specify `WriteThrough` to immediately write to the pipe and not to the cache.

➤ You can configure buffer sizes for input and output.

➤ You configure pipe security to designate who is allowed to read and write to the pipe. Security is discussed in Chapter 24.

➤ You can configure inheritability of the pipe handle, which is important for communicating with child processes.

Because the `NamedPipeServerStream` is a `Stream`, you can use `StreamReader` instead of reading from the byte array; this method simplifies the code:

```csharp
var pipeReader = new NamedPipeServerStream(pipeName, PipeDirection.In);
using (var reader = new StreamReader(pipeReader))
{
  pipeReader.WaitForConnection();
  WriteLine("reader connected");

  bool completed = false;
  while (!completed)
  {
    string line = reader.ReadLine();
    WriteLine(line);
```

```
      if (line == "bye") completed = true;
    }
  }
}
```

Creating a Named Pipe Client

Now you need a client. As the server reads messages, the client writes them.

You create the client by instantiating a `NamedPipeClientStream` object. Because named pipes can communicate across the network, you need a server name in addition to the pipe name and the direction of the pipe. The client connects by invoking the `Connect` method. After the connection succeeds, messages are sent to the server by invoking `WriteLine` on the `StreamWriter`. By default, messages are not sent immediately; they are cached. The message is pushed to the server by invoking the `Flush` method. You can also immediately pass all the messages without invoking the `Flush` method. For this, you have to configure the option to write through the cache on creating the pipe (code file `PipesWriter/Program.cs`):

```
public static void PipesWriter(string pipeName)
{
  var pipeWriter = new NamedPipeClientStream("TheRocks",
      pipeName, PipeDirection.Out);
  using (var writer = new StreamWriter(pipeWriter))
  {
    pipeWriter.Connect();
    WriteLine("writer connected");

    bool completed = false;
    while (!completed)
    {
      string input = ReadLine();
      if (input == "bye") completed = true;

      writer.WriteLine(input);
      writer.Flush();
    }
  }
  WriteLine("completed writing");
}
```

For starting two projects from within Visual Studio, you can configure multiple startup projects with Debug ⇨ Set Startup Projects. When you run the application, input from one console is echoed in the other one.

Creating Anonymous Pipes

Let's do something similar with anonymous pipes. With anonymous pipes two tasks are created that communicate with each other. For signaling the pipe creation, you use a `ManualResetEventSlim` object as you did with the memory mapped files. In the `Run` method of the `Program` class, two tasks are created that invoke the `Reader` and `Writer` methods (code file `AnonymousPipes/Program.cs`):

```
private string _pipeHandle;
private ManualResetEventSlim _pipeHandleSet;

static void Main()
{
  var p = new Program();
  p.Run();
  ReadLine();
}

public void Run()
{
  _pipeHandleSet = new ManualResetEventSlim(initialState: false);
```

```
      Task.Run(() => Reader());
      Task.Run(() => Writer());
      ReadLine();
}
```

The server side acts as a reader by creating an `AnonymousPipeServerStream`, and defining the `PipeDirection.In`. The other side of the communication needs to know about the client handle of the pipe. This handle is converted to a string from the method `GetClientHandleAsString` and assigned to the `_pipeHandle` variable. This variable will be used later by the client that acts as a writer. After the initial process, the pipe server can be acted on as a stream because it is a stream:

```
private void Reader()
{
  try
  {
    var pipeReader = new AnonymousPipeServerStream(PipeDirection.In,
      HandleInheritability.None);
    using (var reader = new StreamReader(pipeReader))
    {
      _pipeHandle = pipeReader.GetClientHandleAsString();
      WriteLine($"pipe handle: {_pipeHandle}");
      _pipeHandleSet.Set();

      bool end = false;
      while (!end)
      {
        string line = reader.ReadLine();
        WriteLine(line);
        if (line == "end") end = true;
      }
      WriteLine("finished reading");

    }
  }
  catch (Exception ex)
  {
    WriteLine(ex.Message);
  }
}
```

The client code waits until the variable `_pipeHandleSet` is signaled, and thus can open the pipe handle referenced by the `_pipeHandle` variable. Later processing continues with a `StreamWriter`:

```
private void Writer()
{
  WriteLine("anonymous pipe writer");
  _pipeHandleSet.Wait();

  var pipeWriter = new AnonymousPipeClientStream(
    PipeDirection.Out, _pipeHandle);
  using (var writer = new StreamWriter(pipeWriter))
  {
    writer.AutoFlush = true;
    WriteLine("starting writer");
    for (int i = 0; i < 5; i++)
    {
      writer.WriteLine($"Message {i}");
      Task.Delay(500).Wait();
    }
    writer.WriteLine("end");
  }
}
```

When you run the application, the two tasks communicate and send data between the tasks.

USING FILES AND STREAMS WITH THE WINDOWS RUNTIME

With the Windows Runtime, you implement streams with native types. Although they are implemented with native code, they look like .NET types. However, there's a difference you need to be aware of: For streams, the Windows Runtime implements its own types in the namespace `Windows.Storage.Streams`. Here you can find classes such as `FileInputStream`, `FileOutputStream`, and `RandomAccessStreams`. All these classes are based on interfaces, for example, `IInputStream`, `IOutputStream`, and `IRandomAccessStream`. You'll also find the concept of readers and writers. Windows Runtime readers and writers are the types `DataReader` and `DataWriter`.

Let's look at what's different from the .NET streams you've seen so far and how .NET streams and types can map to these native types.

Windows App Editor

Earlier in this chapter, you created a WPF editor to read and write files. Now you create a new editor as a Windows app starting with the Windows Universal Blank App Visual Studio template.

To add commands for opening and saving a file, a `CommandBar` with `AppBarButton` elements is added to the main page (code file `WindowsAppEditor/MainPage.xaml`):

```xml
<Page.BottomAppBar>
  <CommandBar IsOpen="True">
    <AppBarButton Icon="OpenFile" Label="Open" Click="{x:Bind OnOpen}" />
    <AppBarButton Icon="Save" Label="Save" Click="{x:Bind OnSave}" />
  </CommandBar>
</Page.BottomAppBar>
```

The `TextBox` added to the `Grid` fill receive the contents of the file:

```xml
<Grid Background="{ThemeResource ApplicationPageBackgroundThemeBrush}">
  <TextBox x:Name="text1" AcceptsReturn="True" />
</Grid>
```

The `OnOpen` handle first starts the dialog where the user can select a file. Remember, you used the `OpenFileDialog` earlier. With Windows apps, you can use pickers. To open files, the `FileOpenPicker` is the preferred type. You can configure this picker to define the proposed start location for the user. You set the `SuggestedStartLocation` to `PickerLocationId.DocumentsLibrary` to open the user's documents folder. The `PickerLocationId` is an enumeration that defines various special folders.

Next, the `FileTypeFilter` collection specifies the file types that should be listed for the user. Finally, the method `PickSingleFileAsync` returns the file selected from the user. To allow users to select multiple files, you can use the method `PickMultipleFilesAsync` instead. This method returns a `StorageFile`. `StorageFile` is defined in the namespace `Windows.Storage`. This class is the equivalent of the `FileInfo` class for opening, creating, copying, moving, and deleting files (code file `WindowsAppEditor/MainPage.xaml.cs`):

```csharp
public async void OnOpen()
{
  try
  {
    var picker = new FileOpenPicker()
    {
      SuggestedStartLocation = PickerLocationId.DocumentsLibrary
    };
    picker.FileTypeFilter.Add(".txt");

    StorageFile file = await picker.PickSingleFileAsync();
    //...
```

Now, open the file using `OpenReadAsync`. This method returns a stream that implements the interface `IRandomAccessStreamWithContentType`, which derives from the interfaces `IRandomAccessStream`, `IInputStream`, `IOuputStream`, `IContentProvider`, and `IDisposable`. `IRandomAccessStream` allows random access to a stream with the `Seek` method, and it gives information about the size of a stream. `IInputStream` defines the method `ReadAsync` to read from a stream. `IOutputStream` is the opposite; it defines the methods `WriteAsync` and `FlushAsync`. `IContentTypeProvider` defines the property `ContentType` that gives information about the content of the file. Remember the encodings of the text files? Now it would be possible to read the content of the stream invoking the method `ReadAsync`. However, the Windows Runtime also knows the reader's and writer's concepts that have already been discussed. A `DataReader` accepts an `IInputStream` with the constructor. The `DataReader` type defines methods to read primitive data types such as `ReadInt16`, `ReadInt32`, and `ReadDateTime`. You can read a byte array with `ReadBytes`, and a string with `ReadString`. The `ReadString` method requires the number of characters to read. The string is assigned to the `Text` property of the `TextBox` control to display the content:

```
//...
if (file != null)
{
  IRandomAccessStreamWithContentType stream = await file.OpenReadAsync();
  using (var reader = new DataReader(stream))
  {
    await reader.LoadAsync((uint)stream.Size);

    text1.Text = reader.ReadString((uint)stream.Size);
  }
}
}
catch (Exception ex)
{
  var dlg = new MessageDialog(ex.Message, "Error");
  await dlg.ShowAsync();
}
}
```

> **NOTE** *Similarly to the readers and the writers of the .NET Framework, the* `DataReader` *and* `DataWriter` *manages the stream that is passed with the constructor. On disposing the reader or writer, the stream gets disposed as well. With .NET classes, to keep the underlying stream open for a longer time you can set the* `leaveOpen` *argument in the constructor. With the Windows Runtime types, you can detach the stream from the readers and writers by invoking the method* `DetachStream`.

On saving the document, the `OnSave` method is invoked. First, the `FileSavePicker` is used to allow the user to select the document—similar to the `FileOpenPicker`. Next, the file is opened using `OpenTransactedWriteAsync`. The NTFS file system supports transactions; these are not covered from the .NET Framework but are available with the Windows Runtime. `OpenTransactedWriteAsync` returns a `StorageStreamTransaction` object that implements the interface `IStorageStreamTransaction`. This object itself is not a stream (although the name might lead you to believe this), but it contains a stream that you can reference with the `Stream` property. This property returns an `IRandomAccessStream` stream. Similarly to creating a `DataReader`, you can create a `DataWriter` to write primitive data types, including strings as in this example. The `StoreAsync` method finally writes the content from the buffer to the stream. The transaction needs to be committed by invoking the `CommitAsync` method before disposing the writer:

```
public async void OnSave()
{
```

```
      try
      {
        var picker = new FileSavePicker()
        {
          SuggestedStartLocation = PickerLocationId.DocumentsLibrary,
          SuggestedFileName = "New Document"
        };
        picker.FileTypeChoices.Add("Plain Text", new List<string>() { ".txt" });

        StorageFile file = await picker.PickSaveFileAsync();
        if (file != null)
        {
          using (StorageStreamTransaction tx =
            await file.OpenTransactedWriteAsync())
          {
            IRandomAccessStream stream = tx.Stream;
            stream.Seek(0);
            using (var writer = new DataWriter(stream))
            {
              writer.WriteString(text1.Text);
              tx.Stream.Size = await writer.StoreAsync();
              await tx.CommitAsync();
            }
          }
        }
      }
      catch (Exception ex)
      {
        var dlg = new MessageDialog(ex.Message, "Error");
        await dlg.ShowAsync();
      }
    }
```

The `DataWriter` doesn't add the preamble defining the kind of Unicode file to the stream. You need to do that explicitly, as explained earlier in this chapter. The `DataWriter` just deals with the encoding of the file by setting the `UnicodeEncoding` and `ByteOrder` properties. The default setting is `UnicodeEncoding.Utf8` and `ByteOrder.BigEndian`. Instead of working with the `DataWriter`, you can also take advantage of the features of the `StreamReader` and `StreamWriter` as well as the .NET `Stream` class, as shown in the next section.

Mapping Windows Runtime Types to .NET Types

Let's start with reading the file. To convert a Windows Runtime stream to a .NET stream for reading, you can use the extension method `AsStreamForRead`. This method is defined in the namespace `System.IO` (that must be opened) in the assembly `System.Runtime.WindowsRuntime`. This method creates a new `Stream` object that manages the `IInputStream`. Now, you can use it as a normal .NET stream, as shown previously—for example, passing it to a `StreamReader` and using this reader to access the file:

```
public async void OnOpenDotnet()
{
  try
  {
    var picker = new FileOpenPicker()
    {
      SuggestedStartLocation = PickerLocationId.DocumentsLibrary
    };
    picker.FileTypeFilter.Add(".txt");

    StorageFile file = await picker.PickSingleFileAsync();
    if (file != null)
    {
```

```
                IRandomAccessStreamWithContentType wrtStream =
                  await file.OpenReadAsync();
                Stream stream = wrtStream.AsStreamForRead();
                using (var reader = new StreamReader(stream))
                {
                  text1.Text = await reader.ReadToEndAsync();
                }
              }
            }
        catch (Exception ex)
        {
          var dlg = new MessageDialog(ex.Message, "Error");
          await dlg.ShowAsync();
        }
      }
```

All the Windows Runtime stream types can easily be converted to .NET streams and the other way around. The following table lists the methods needed:

CONVERT FROM	CONVERT TO	METHOD
IRandomAccessStream	Stream	AsStream
IInputStream	Stream	AsStreamForRead
IOutputStream	Stream	AsStreamForWrite
Stream	IInputStream	AsInputStream
Stream	IOutputStream	AsOutputStream
Stream	IRandomAccessStream	AsRandomAccessStream

Now save the change to the file as well. The stream for writing is converted with the extension method `AsStreamForWrite`. Now, this stream can be written using the `StreamWriter` class. The code snippet also writes the preamble for the UTF-8 encoding to the file:

```
    public async void OnSaveDotnet()
    {
      try
      {
        var picker = new FileSavePicker()
        {
          SuggestedStartLocation = PickerLocationId.DocumentsLibrary,
          SuggestedFileName = "New Document"
        };
        picker.FileTypeChoices.Add("Plain Text", new List<string>() { ".txt" });

        StorageFile file = await picker.PickSaveFileAsync();
        if (file != null)
        {
          StorageStreamTransaction tx = await file.OpenTransactedWriteAsync();
          using (var writer = new StreamWriter(tx.Stream.AsStreamForWrite()))
          {
            byte[] preamble = Encoding.UTF8.GetPreamble();
            await stream.WriteAsync(preamble, 0, preamble.Length);
            await writer.WriteAsync(text1.Text);
            await writer.FlushAsync();
            tx.Stream.Size = (ulong)stream.Length;
            await tx.CommitAsync();
          }
        }
      }
      catch (Exception ex)
```

```
    {
        var dlg = new MessageDialog(ex.Message, "Error");
        await dlg.ShowAsync();
    }
}
```

SUMMARY

In this chapter, you examined how to use the .NET classes to access the file system from your C# code. You have seen that in both cases the base classes expose simple but powerful object models that make it very easy to perform almost any kind of action in these areas. For the file system, these actions are copying files; moving, creating, and deleting files and folders; and reading and writing both binary and text files.

You've seen how to compress files using both the deflate algorithm and ZIP files. The `FileSystemWatcher` was used to get information when files change. You've also seen how to communicate with the help of shared memory as well as named and anonymous pipes. Finally, you've seen how to map .NET streams to Windows Runtime streams to take advantage of .NET features within Windows apps.

In some other chapters of the book you can see streams in action. For example, Chapter 25, "Networking," uses streams to send data across the network. Reading and writing XML files and streaming large XML files are shown in Chapter 27, "XML and JSON."

In the next chapter, you read about security and how to secure files, and you also see how you can use memory mapped files across different processes by adding security information. You also see `CryptoStream` in action for encrypting streams, no matter whether they are used with files or networking.

24

Security

INTRODUCTION

Security has several key elements that you need to consider in order to make your applications secure. The primary one, of course, is the user of the application. Is the user actually the person authorized to access the application, or someone posing as the user? How can this user be trusted? As you see in this chapter, ensuring the security of an application in regard of the user is a two-part process: First, users need to be authenticated, and then they need to be authorized to verify that they are allowed to use the requested resources.

What about data that is stored or sent across the network? Is it possible for someone to access this data, for example, by using a network sniffer? Encryption of data is important in this regard. Some technologies, such as Windows Communication Foundation (WCF), provide encryption capabilities by simple configuration, so you can see what's done behind the scenes.

Yet another aspect is the application itself. If the application is hosted by a web provider, how is the application restricted from doing harm to the server?

This chapter explores the features available in .NET to help you manage security, demonstrating how .NET protects you from malicious code, how to administer security policies, and how to access the security subsystem programmatically.

VERIFYING USER INFORMATION

Two fundamental pillars of security are authentication and authorization. *Authentication* is the process of identifying the user, and *authorization* occurs afterward to verify that the identified user is allowed to access a specific resource. This section shows how to get information about users with identities and principals.

Working with Windows Identities

You can identify the user running the application by using an *identity*. The `WindowsIdentity` class represents a Windows user. If you don't identify the user with a Windows account, you can use other classes that implement the interface `IIdentity`. With this interface you have access to the name of the user, information about whether the user is authenticated, and the authentication type.

A *principal* is an object that contains the identity of the user and the roles to which the user belongs. The interface `IPrincipal` defines the property `Identity`, which returns an `IIdentity` object, and the method `IsInRole` with which you can verify that the user is a member of a specific role. A *role* is a collection of users who have the same security permissions, and it is the unit of administration for users. Roles can be Windows groups or just a collection of strings that you define.

The principal classes available with .NET are `WindowsPrincipal`, `GenericPrincipal`, and `RolePrincipal`. Since .NET 4.5, these principal types derive from the base class `ClaimsPrincipal`. You can also create a custom principal class that implements the interface `IPrincipal` or derives from `ClaimsPrincipal`.

The sample code makes use of the following dependencies and namespaces:

Dependencies

```
NETStandard.Library
System.Security.Principal.Windows
```

Namespaces

```
System.Collections.Generic
System.Security.Claims
System.Security.Principal
static System.Console
```

The following example creates a Console Application (Package) that provides access to the principal in an application that, in turn, enables you to access the underlying Windows account. You need to import the `System.Security.Principal` and `System.Security.Claims` namespaces. The `Main` method invokes the method `ShowIdentityInformation` to write information about the `WindowsIdentity` to the console, `ShowPrincipal` to write additional information that is available with principals, and `ShowClaims` to write information about claims (code file `WindowsPrincipal/Program.cs`):

```csharp
static void Main()
{
    WindowsIdentity identity = ShowIdentityInformation();
    WindowsPrincipal principal = ShowPrincipal(identity);
```

```
      ShowClaims(principal.Claims);
    }
```

The method `ShowIdentityInformation` creates a `WindowsIdentity` object by invoking the static `GetCurrent` method of the `WindowsIdentity` and accesses its properties to show the identity type, name of the identity, authentication type, and other values (code file `WindowsPrincipal/Program.cs`):

```csharp
public static WindowsIdentity ShowIdentityInformation()
{
  WindowsIdentity identity = WindowsIdentity.GetCurrent();
  if (identity == null)
  {
    WriteLine("not a Windows Identity");
    return null;
  }

  WriteLine($"IdentityType: {identity}");
  WriteLine($"Name: {identity.Name}");
  WriteLine($"Authenticated: {identity.IsAuthenticated}");
  WriteLine($"Authentication Type: {identity.AuthenticationType}");
  WriteLine($"Anonymous? {identity.IsAnonymous}");
  WriteLine($"Access Token: {identity.AccessToken.DangerousGetHandle()}");
  WriteLine();
  return identity;
}
```

All identity classes, such as `WindowsIdentity`, implement the `IIdentity` interface, which contains three properties—`AuthenticationType`, `IsAuthenticated`, and `Name`—for all derived identity classes to implement. The other properties you've seen with the `WindowsIdentity` are specific to this kind of identity.

When you run the application, you see information like what's shown in the following snippet. The authentication type shows CloudAP because I'm logged into the system using a Microsoft Live account. Active Directory shows up in the authentication type if you're using Active Directory:

```
IdentityType: System.Security.Principal.WindowsIdentity
Name: THEROCKS\Christian
Authenticated: True
Authentication Type: CloudAP
Anonymous? False
Access Token: 1072
```

Windows Principals

A principal contains an identity and offers additional information, such as roles the user belongs to. Principals implement the interface `IPrincipal`, which offers the method `IsInRole` in addition to an `Identity` property. With Windows, all the Windows groups the user is member of are mapped to roles. The method `IsInRole` is overloaded to accept a security identifier, a role string, or an enumeration value of the `WindowsBuiltInRole` enumeration. The sample code verifies whether the user belongs to the built-in roles User and Administrator (code file `WindowsPrincipal/Program.cs`):

```csharp
public static WindowsPrincipal ShowPrincipal(WindowsIdentity identity)
{
  WriteLine("Show principal information");
  WindowsPrincipal principal = new WindowsPrincipal(identity);
  if (principal == null)
  {
    WriteLine("not a Windows Principal");
    return null;
  }
  WriteLine($"Users? {principal.IsInRole(WindowsBuiltInRole.User)}");
  WriteLine(
    $"Administrators? {principal.IsInRole(WindowsBuiltInRole.Administrator)}");
```

```
    WriteLine();
    return principal;
}
```

When I run the application, my account belongs to the role Users but not Administrator, and I get the following result:

```
Show principal information
Users? True
Administrator? False
```

It is enormously beneficial to be able to easily access details about the current users and their roles. With this information, you can make decisions about what actions should be permitted or denied. The ability to make use of roles and Windows user groups provides the added benefit that administration can be handled using standard user administration tools, and you can usually avoid altering the code when user roles change.

Since .NET 4.5, all the principal classes derive from the base class ClaimsPrincipal. This way, it's possible to access claims from users with the Claims property of a principal object. The following section looks at claims.

Using Claims

Claims offer a lot more flexibility compared to roles. A *claim* is a statement made about an identity from an authority. An authority such as the Active Directory or the Microsoft Live account authentication service makes claims about users—for example, the claim of the name of the user, claims about groups the user belongs to, or a claim about the age. Is the user already of age 21 or older and eligible for accessing specific resources?

The method ShowClaims accesses a collection of claims to write subject, issuer, claim type, and more options to the console (code file WindowsPrincipal/Program.cs):

```
public static void ShowClaims(IEnumerable<Claim> claims)
{
  WriteLine("Claims");
  foreach (var claim in claims)
  {
    WriteLine($"Subject: {claim.Subject}");
    WriteLine($"Issuer: {claim.Issuer}");
    WriteLine($"Type: {claim.Type}");
    WriteLine($"Value type: {claim.ValueType}");
    WriteLine($"Value: {claim.Value}");
    foreach (var prop in claim.Properties)
    {
      WriteLine($"\tProperty: {prop.Key} {prop.Value}");
    }
    WriteLine();
  }
}
```

Here is an extract of the claims from the Microsoft Live account, which provides information about the name, the primary ID, and the group identifiers:

```
Claims
Subject: System.Security.Principal.WindowsIdentity
Issuer: AD AUTHORITY
Type: http://schemas.xmlsoap.org/ws/2005/05/identity/claims/name
Value type: http://www.w3.org/2001/XMLSchema#string
Value: THEROCKS\Christian

Subject: System.Security.Principal.WindowsIdentity
Issuer: AD AUTHORITY
Type: http://schemas.microsoft.com/ws/2008/06/identity/claims/primarysid
Value type: http://www.w3.org/2001/XMLSchema#string
Value: S-1-5-21-1413171511-313453878-1364686672-1001
      Property: http://schemas.microsoft.com/ws/2008/06/identity/claims/
```

```
        windowssubauthority NTAuthority

Subject: System.Security.Principal.WindowsIdentity
Issuer: AD AUTHORITY
Type: http://schemas.microsoft.com/ws/2008/06/identity/claims/groupsid
Value type: http://www.w3.org/2001/XMLSchema#string
Value: S-1-1-0
        Property: http://schemas.microsoft.com/ws/2008/06/identity/claims/
        windowssubauthority WorldAuthority

Subject: System.Security.Principal.WindowsIdentity
Issuer: AD AUTHORITY
Type: http://schemas.microsoft.com/ws/2008/06/identity/claims/groupsid
Value type: http://www.w3.org/2001/XMLSchema#string
Value: S-1-5-114
        Property: http://schemas.microsoft.com/ws/2008/06/identity/claims/
        windowssubauthority NTAuthority
. . .
```

You can add claims to a Windows identity from a claim provider. You can also add a claim from a simple client program, such as the age claim here:

```
identity.AddClaim(new Claim("Age", "25"));
```

Using claims from a program, it's just a matter to trust this claim. Is this claim true—the age 25? Claims can also be lies. Adding this claim from the client application, you can see that the issuer of this claim is the LOCAL AUTHORITY. Information from the AD AUTHORITY (the Active Directory) is more trustworthy, but here you need to trust the Active Directory system administrators.

The `WindowsIdentity` deriving from the base class `ClaimsIdentity` offers several methods checking for claims, or retrieving specific claims. To test whether a claim is available, you can use the `HasClaim` method:

```
bool hasName = identity.HasClaim(c => c.Type == ClaimTypes.Name);
```

To retrieve specific claims, the method `FindAll` needs a predicate to define a match:

```
var groupClaims = identity.FindAll(c => c.Type == ClaimTypes.GroupSid);
```

> **NOTE** *A claim type can be a simple string like the* `"Age"` *type used earlier. The* `ClaimType` *defines a list of known types such as* `Country`, `Email`, `Name`, `MobilePhone`, `UserData`, `Surname`, `PostalCode`, *and several more.*

> **NOTE** *Authentication of users with ASP.NET web applications is discussed in Chapter 41, "ASP.NET MVC."*

ENCRYPTING DATA

Confidential data should be secured so that it cannot be read by unprivileged users. This is valid for both data that is sent across the network and stored data. You can encrypt such data with symmetric or asymmetric encryption keys.

With a symmetric key, you can use the same key for encryption and decryption. With asymmetric encryption, different keys are used for encryption and decryption: a public key and a private key. Something encrypted using a public key can be decrypted with the corresponding private key. This also works the other way around: Something encrypted using a private key can be decrypted by using the corresponding public key, but not the private key. It's practically impossible to calculate the private or public key from the other one.

Public and private keys are always created as a pair. The public key can be made available to everybody, and even put on a website, but the private key must be safely locked away. Following are some examples that demonstrate how public and private keys are used for encryption.

If Alice sends a message to Bob (see Figure 24-1), and she wants to ensure that no one other than Bob can read the message, she uses Bob's public key. The message is encrypted using Bob's public key. Bob opens the message and can decrypt it using his secretly stored private key. This key exchange guarantees that no one but Bob can read Alice's message.

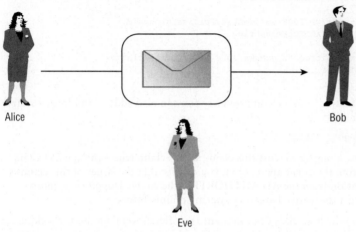

Alice

Bob

Eve

FIGURE 24-1

There is one problem, however: Bob can't be sure that the mail comes from Alice. Eve can use Bob's public key to encrypt messages sent to Bob and pretend to be Alice. We can extend this principle using public/ private keys. Let's start again with Alice sending a message to Bob. Before Alice encrypts the message using Bob's public key, she adds her signature and encrypts the signature using her own private key. Then she encrypts the mail using Bob's public key. Therefore, it is guaranteed that no one other than Bob can read the message. When Bob decrypts it, he detects an encrypted signature. The signature can be decrypted using Alice's public key. For Bob, it is not a problem to access Alice's public key because the key is public. After decrypting the signature, Bob can be sure that it was Alice who sent the message.

The encryption and decryption algorithms using symmetric keys are a lot faster than those using asymmetric keys. The problem with symmetric keys is that the keys must be exchanged in a safe manner. With network communication, one way to do this is by using asymmetric keys first for the key exchange and then symmetric keys for encryption of the data that is sent across the wire.

The .NET Framework contains classes for encryption in the namespace System.Security.Cryptography. Several symmetric and asymmetric algorithms are implemented. You can find algorithm classes for many different purposes. Some of the classes have a Cng prefix or suffix. CNG is short for *Cryptography Next Generation,* which is a newer version of the native Crypto API. This API makes it possible to write a program independently of the algorithm by using a provider-based model.

The following table lists encryption classes and their purposes from the namespace System.Security .Cryptography. The classes without a Cng, Managed, or CryptoServiceProvider suffix are abstract base classes, such as MD5. The Managed suffix means that this algorithm is implemented with managed code; other classes might wrap native Windows API calls. The suffix CryptoServiceProvider is used with classes that implement the abstract base class. The Cng suffix is used with classes that make use of the new Cryptography CNG API.

CATEGORY	CLASSES	DESCRIPTION
Hash	MD5 MD5Cng SHA1 SHA1Managed SHA1Cng SHA256 SHA256Managed SHA256Cng SHA384 SHA384Managed SHA384Cng SHA512 SHA512Managed SHA512Cng RIPEMD160 RIPEMD160Managed	The purpose of hash algorithms is to create a fixed-length hash value from binary strings of arbitrary length. These algorithms are used with digital signatures and for data integrity. If the same binary string is hashed again, the same hash result is returned. MD5 (Message Digest Algorithm 5), developed at RSA Laboratories, is faster than SHA1. SHA1 is stronger against brute force attacks. The SHA algorithms were designed by the National Security Agency (NSA). MD5 uses a 128-bit hash size; SHA1 uses 160 bits. The other SHA algorithms contain the hash size in the name. SHA512 is the strongest of these algorithms, with a hash size of 512 bits; it is also the slowest. RIPEMD160 uses a hash size of 160 bits; it is meant to be a replacement for 128-bit MD4 and MD5. RIPEMD was developed from an EU project named RIPE (Race Integrity Primitives Evaluation).
Symmetric	DES DESCryptoServiceProvider TripleDESTripleDESCryptoServiceProvider Aes AesCryptoServiceProvider AesManaged RC2 RC2CryptoServiceProvider Rijndael RijndaelManaged	Symmetric key algorithms use the same key for encryption and decryption of data. Data Encryption Standard (DES) is now considered insecure because it uses only 56 bits for the key size and can be broken in less than 24 hours. Triple-DES is the successor to DES and has a key length of 168 bits, but the effective security it provides is only 112-bit. Advanced Encryption Standard (AES) has a key size of 128, 192, or 256 bits. Rijndael is very similar to AES but offers more key size options. AES is an encryption standard adopted by the U.S. government.
Asymmetric	DSA DSACryptoServiceProvider ECDsa ECDsaCng ECDiffieHellman ECDiffieHellmanCng RSA RSACryptoServiceProvider RSACng	Asymmetric algorithms use different keys for encryption and decryption. The Rivest, Shamir, Adleman (RSA) algorithm was the first one used for signing as well as encryption. This algorithm is widely used in e-commerce protocols. RSACng is a class new with .NET 4.6 and .NET 5 Core that is based on a Cryptography Next Generation (CNG) implementation. Digital Signature Algorithm (DSA) is a United States Federal Government standard for digital signatures. Elliptic Curve DSA (ECDSA) and EC Diffie-Hellman use algorithms based on elliptic curve groups. These algorithms are more secure, with shorter key sizes. For example, having a key size of 1024 bits for DSA is similar in security to 160 bits for ECDSA. As a result, ECDSA is much faster. EC Diffie-Hellman is an algorithm used to exchange private keys in a secure way over a public channel.

The following section includes some examples demonstrating how these algorithms can be used programmatically.

Creating and Verifying a Signature

The first example demonstrates a signature using the ECDSA algorithm, described in the preceding table, for signing. Alice creates a signature that is encrypted with her private key and can be accessed using her public key. This way, it is guaranteed that the signature is from Alice.

The sample application `SigningDemo` makes use of these dependencies and namespaces:

Dependencies

```
NETStandard.Library

System.Security.Cryptograhy.Algorithms

System.Security.Cryptography.Cng
```

Namespaces

```
System

System.Security.Cryptography

System.Text

static System.Console
```

First, take a look at the major steps in the `Main` method: Alice's keys are created, and the string `"Alice"` is signed and then verified to be the signature actually from Alice by using the public key. The message that is signed is converted to a byte array by using the `Encoding` class. To write the encrypted signature to the console, the byte array that contains the signature is converted to a string with the method `Convert`
`.ToBase64String` (code file `SigningDemo/Program.cs`):

```
private CngKey _aliceKeySignature;
private byte[] _alicePubKeyBlob;
static void Main()
{
  var p = new Program();
  p.Run();
}
public void Run()
{
  InitAliceKeys();
  byte[] aliceData = Encoding.UTF8.GetBytes("Alice");
  byte[] aliceSignature = CreateSignature(aliceData, aliceKeySignature);
  WriteLine($"Alice created signature: {Convert.ToBase64String(aliceSignature)}");
  if (VerifySignature(aliceData, aliceSignature, alicePubKeyBlob))
  {
    WriteLine("Alice signature verified successfully");
  }
}
```

> **WARNING** *Never convert encrypted data to a string using the* `Encoding` *class. The* `Encoding` *class verifies and converts invalid values that are not allowed with Unicode; therefore, converting the string back to a byte array can yield a different result.*

`InitAliceKeys` is the method that creates a new key pair for Alice. This key pair is stored in a static field, so it can be accessed from the other methods. The `Create` method of `CngKey` gets the algorithm as an argument to define a key pair for the algorithm. With the `Export` method, the public key of the key pair is exported. This public key can be given to Bob for verification of the signature. Alice keeps the private key. Instead of creating a key pair with the CngKey class, you can open existing keys that are stored in the key store. Usually Alice would have a certificate containing a key pair in her private store, and the store could be accessed with CngKey.Open:

```
private void InitAliceKeys()
{
  _aliceKeySignature = CngKey.Create(CngAlgorithm.ECDsaP521);
  _alicePubKeyBlob = aliceKeySignature.Export(CngKeyBlobFormat.GenericPublicBlob);
}
```

With the key pair, Alice can create the signature using the ECDsaCng class. The constructor of this class receives the CngKey—which contains both the public and private keys—from Alice. The private key is used to sign the data with the SignData method. The method SignData is slightly different with .NET Core. .NET Core requires the algorithm:

```
public byte[] CreateSignature(byte[] data, CngKey key)
{
  byte[] signature;
  using (var signingAlg = new ECDsaCng(key))
  {
#if NET46
    signature = signingAlg.SignData(data);
    signingAlg.Clear();
#else
    signature = signingAlg.SignData(data, HashAlgorithmName.SHA512);
#endif
  }
  return signature;
}
```

To verify that the signature was really from Alice, Bob checks the signature by using the public key from Alice. The byte array containing the public key blob can be imported to a CngKey object with the static Import method. The ECDsaCng class is then used to verify the signature by invoking VerifyData:

```
public bool VerifySignature(byte[] data, byte[] signature, byte[] pubKey)
{
  bool retValue = false;
  using (CngKey key = CngKey.Import(pubKey, CngKeyBlobFormat.GenericPublicBlob))
  using (var signingAlg = new ECDsaCng(key))
  {
#if NET46
    retValue = signingAlg.VerifyData(data, signature);
    signingAlg.Clear();
#else
    retValue = signingAlg.VerifyData(data, signature, HashAlgorithmName.SHA512);
#endif
  }
  return retValue;
}
```

Implementing Secure Data Exchange

This section uses a more-complex example to demonstrate exchanging a symmetric key for a secure transfer by using the EC Diffie-Hellman algorithm.

> **NOTE** *At the time of this writing, .NET Core just includes the* ECDiffieHellman *abstract base class that can be used by implementers to create concrete classes. A concrete class is not yet here, that's why this sample uses only .NET 4.6.*

The sample application `SecureTransfer` makes use of the following dependencies and namespaces:

Dependencies

NETStandard.Library

System.Security.Cryptograhy.Algorithms

System.Security.Cryptography.Cng

System.Security.Cryptography.Primitives

Namespaces

System

System.IO

System.Security.Cryptography

System.Text

System.Threading.Tasks

static System.Console

The `Main` method contains the primary functionality. Alice creates an encrypted message and sends it to Bob. Before the message is created and sent, key pairs are created for Alice and Bob. Bob has access only to Alice's public key, and Alice has access only to Bob's public key (code file `SecureTransfer/Program.cs`):

```
private CngKey _aliceKey;
private CngKey _bobKey;
private byte[] _alicePubKeyBlob;
private byte[] _bobPubKeyBlob;

static void Main()
{
  var p = new Program();
  p.RunAsync().Wait();
  ReadLine();
}

public async Task RunAsync()
{
  try
  {
    CreateKeys();
    byte[] encrytpedData =
      await AliceSendsDataAsync("This is a secret message for Bob");
    await BobReceivesDataAsync(encrytpedData);
  }
  catch (Exception ex)
  {
    WriteLine(ex.Message);
  }
}
```

In the implementation of the `CreateKeys` method, keys are created to be used with the EC Diffie-Hellman 521 algorithm:

```
public void CreateKeys()
{
  aliceKey = CngKey.Create(CngAlgorithm.ECDiffieHellmanP521);
  bobKey = CngKey.Create(CngAlgorithm.ECDiffieHellmanP521);
  alicePubKeyBlob = aliceKey.Export(CngKeyBlobFormat.EccPublicBlob);
  bobPubKeyBlob = bobKey.Export(CngKeyBlobFormat.EccPublicBlob);
}
```

In the method `AliceSendsDataAsync`, the string that contains text characters is converted to a byte array by using the `Encoding` class. An `ECDiffieHellmanCng` object is created and initialized with the key pair from Alice. Alice creates a symmetric key by using her key pair and the public key from Bob, calling the method `DeriveKeyMaterial`. The returned symmetric key is used with the symmetric algorithm AES to encrypt the data. `AesCryptoServiceProvider` requires the key and an initialization vector (IV). The IV is generated dynamically from the method `GenerateIV`. The symmetric key is exchanged with the help of the EC Diffie-Hellman algorithm, but the IV must also be exchanged. From a security standpoint, it is OK to transfer the IV unencrypted across the network—only the key exchange must be secured. The IV is stored first as content in the memory stream, followed by the encrypted data where the `CryptoStream` class uses the `encryptor` created by the `AesCryptoServiceProvider` class. Before the encrypted data is accessed from the memory stream, the crypto stream must be closed. Otherwise, end bits would be missing from the encrypted data:

```
public async Task<byte[]> AliceSendsDataAsync(string message)
{
  WriteLine($"Alice sends message: {message}");
  byte[] rawData = Encoding.UTF8.GetBytes(message);
  byte[] encryptedData = null;

  using (var aliceAlgorithm = new ECDiffieHellmanCng(aliceKey))
  using (CngKey bobPubKey = CngKey.Import(bobPubKeyBlob,
      CngKeyBlobFormat.EccPublicBlob))
  {
    byte[] symmKey = aliceAlgorithm.DeriveKeyMaterial(bobPubKey);
    WriteLine("Alice creates this symmetric key with " +
        $"Bobs public key information: {Convert.ToBase64String(symmKey)}");

    using (var aes = new AesCryptoServiceProvider())
    {
      aes.Key = symmKey;
      aes.GenerateIV();
      using (ICryptoTransform encryptor = aes.CreateEncryptor())
      using (var ms = new MemoryStream())
      {
        // create CryptoStream and encrypt data to send
        using (var cs = new CryptoStream(ms, encryptor,
            CryptoStreamMode.Write))
        {
          // write initialization vector not encrypted
          await ms.WriteAsync(aes.IV, 0, aes.IV.Length);
          cs.Write(rawData, 0, rawData.Length);
        }
        encryptedData = ms.ToArray();
      }
      aes.Clear();
    }
  }
  WriteLine("Alice: message is encrypted: "+
    "{Convert.ToBase64String(encryptedData)}");

  WriteLine();
  return encryptedData;
}
```

Bob receives the encrypted data in the argument of the method `BobReceivesDataAsync`. First, the unencrypted initialization vector must be read. The `BlockSize` property of the class `AesCryptoServiceProvider` returns the number of bits for a block. The number of bytes can be calculated by dividing by 8, and the fastest way to do this is by doing a bit shift of 3 bits (shifting by 1 bit is a division by 2, 2 bits by 4, and 3 bits by 8). With the `for` loop, the first bytes of the raw bytes that contain the IV unencrypted are written to the array iv. Next, an `ECDiffieHellmanCng` object is instantiated with the key pair from Bob. Using the public key from Alice, the symmetric key is returned from the method `DeriveKeyMaterial`.

Comparing the symmetric keys created from Alice and Bob shows that the same key value is created. Using this symmetric key and the initialization vector, the message from Alice can be decrypted with the `AesCryptoServiceProvider` class:

```csharp
public async Task BobReceivesDataAsync(byte[] encryptedData)
{
    WriteLine("Bob receives encrypted data");
    byte[] rawData = null;

    var aes = new AesCryptoServiceProvider();

    int nBytes = aes.BlockSize  3;
    byte[] iv = new byte[nBytes];
    for (int i = 0; i < iv.Length; i++)
    {
        iv[i] = encryptedData[i];
    }

    using (var bobAlgorithm = new ECDiffieHellmanCng(bobKey))
    using (CngKey alicePubKey = CngKey.Import(alicePubKeyBlob,
            CngKeyBlobFormat.EccPublicBlob))
    {
        byte[] symmKey = bobAlgorithm.DeriveKeyMaterial(alicePubKey);
        WriteLine("Bob creates this symmetric key with " +
            $"Alices public key information: {Convert.ToBase64String(symmKey)}");

        aes.Key = symmKey;
        aes.IV = iv;

        using (ICryptoTransform decryptor = aes.CreateDecryptor())
        using (MemoryStream ms = new MemoryStream())
        {
            using (var cs = new CryptoStream(ms, decryptor, CryptoStreamMode.Write))
            {
                await cs.WriteAsync(encryptedData, nBytes,
                    encryptedData.Length - nBytes);
            }

            rawData = ms.ToArray();

            WriteLine("Bob decrypts message to: " +
                $"{Encoding.UTF8.GetString(rawData)}");
        }
        aes.Clear();
    }
}
```

Running the application returns output similar to the following. The message from Alice is encrypted, and then decrypted by Bob with the securely exchanged symmetric key.

```
Alice sends message: this is a secret message for Bob
Alice creates this symmetric key with Bobs public key information:
q4D182m7lyev9Nlp6f0av2Jvc0+LmHF5zEjXwlOlI3Y=
Alice: message is encrypted: WpOxvUoWH5XY31wC8aXcDWeDUWa6zaSObfGcQCpKixzlTJ9exb
tkF5Hp2WPSZWL9V9n13toBg7hgjPbrVzN2A==

Bob receives encrypted data
Bob creates this symmetric key with Alices public key information:
```

```
q4D182m7lyev9Nlp6f0av2Jvc0+LmHF5zEjXw1O1I3Y=
Bob decrypts message to: this is a secret message for Bob
```

Signing and Hashing Using RSA

A new cryptography algorithm class with .NET 4.6 and .NET Core 1.0 is RSACng. RSA (the name comes from the algorithm designers Ron Rivest, Adi Shamir, and Leonard Adlerman) is an asymmetric algorithm that is widely used. Although the RSA algorithm was already available with .NET with the RSA and RSACryptoServiceProvider classes, RSACng is a class based on the CNG API and is similar in use to the ECDSACng class shown earlier.

With the sample application shown in this section, Alice creates a document, hashes it to make sure it doesn't get changed, and signs it with a signature to guarantee that the document is generated by Alice. Bob receives the document and checks the guarantees from Alice to make sure the document hasn't been tampered with.

The RSA sample code makes use of these dependencies and namespaces:

Dependencies

> NETStandard.Library
>
> System.Security.Cryptography.Algorighms
>
> System.Security.Cryptography.Cng

Namespaces

> Microsoft.Extensions.DependencyInjection
>
> System
>
> System.IO
>
> System.Linq
>
> static System.Console

The Main method of the application is structured to start with Alice's tasks to invoke the method AliceTasks to create a document, a hash code, and a signature. This information is then passed to Bob's tasks to invoke the method BobTasks (code file RSASample/Program.cs):

```
class Program
{
  private CngKey _aliceKey;
  private byte[] _alicePubKeyBlob;

  static void Main()
  {
    var p = new Program();
    p.Run();
  }

  public void Run()
  {
    byte[] document;
    byte[] hash;
    byte[] signature;
    AliceTasks(out document, out hash, out signature);
    BobTasks(document, hash, signature);
  }
  //...
}
```

The method `AliceTasks` first creates the keys needed by Alice, converts the message to a byte array, hashes the byte array, and adds a signature:

```
public void AliceTasks(out byte[] data, out byte[] hash, out byte[] signature)
{
  InitAliceKeys();

  data = Encoding.UTF8.GetBytes("Best greetings from Alice");
  hash = HashDocument(data);
  signature = AddSignatureToHash(hash, _aliceKey);
}
```

Similar to before, the keys needed by Alice are created using the `CngKey` class. As the RSA algorithm is being used now, the enumeration value `CngAlgorithm.Rsa` is passed to the `Create` method to create public and private keys. Only the public key is given to Bob, so the public key is extracted with the `Export` method:

```
private void InitAliceKeys()
{
  _aliceKey = CngKey.Create(CngAlgorithm.Rsa);
  _alicePubKeyBlob = _aliceKey.Export(CngKeyBlobFormat.GenericPublicBlob);
}
```

The `HashDocument` method is invoked from Alice's tasks to create a hash code for the document. The hash code is created using one of the hash algorithm classes: SHA384. No matter how long the document is, the hash code always has the same length. Creating the hash code for the same document again results in the same hash code. Bob needs to use the same algorithm on the document. If the same hash code is returned, the document hasn't been changed.

```
private byte[] HashDocument(byte[] data)
{
  using (var hashAlg = SHA384.Create())
  {
    return hashAlg.ComputeHash(data);
  }
}
```

Adding a signature guarantees that the document is from Alice. Here, the hash is signed using the `RSACng` class. Alice's `CngKey`, including the public and private keys, is passed to the constructor of the `RSACng` class; the signature is created by invoking the `SignHash` method. When the hash is signed, the `SignHash` method needs to know about the algorithm of the hash; `HashAlgorithmName.SHA384` is the algorithm that was used to create the hash. Also, the RSA padding is needed. Possible options with the `RSASignaturePadding` enumeration are `Pss` and `Pkcs1`:

```
private byte[] AddSignatureToHash(byte[] hash, CngKey key)
{
  using (var signingAlg = new RSACng(key))
  {
    byte[] signed = signingAlg.SignHash(hash,
      HashAlgorithmName.SHA384, RSASignaturePadding.Pss);
    return signed;
  }
}
```

After hashing and signing from Alice, Bob's tasks can start in the method `BobTasks`. Bob receives the document data, the hash code, and the signature, and he uses Alice's public key. First, Alice's public key is imported using `CngKey.Import` and assigned to the `aliceKey` variable. Next, Bob uses the helper methods `IsSignatureValid` and `IsDocumentUnchanged` to verify whether the signature is valid and the document unchanged. Only if both conditions are true, the document is written to the console:

```
public void BobTasks(byte[] data, byte[] hash, byte[] signature)
{
```

```
CngKey aliceKey = CngKey.Import(_alicePubKeyBlob,
    CngKeyBlobFormat.GenericPublicBlob);
if (!IsSignatureValid(hash, signature, aliceKey))
{
    WriteLine("signature not valid");
    return;
}
if (!IsDocumentUnchanged(hash, data))
{
    WriteLine("document was changed");
    return;
}
WriteLine("signature valid, document unchanged");
WriteLine($"document from Alice: {Encoding.UTF8.GetString(data)}");
}
```

To verify if the signature is valid, the public key from Alice is used to create an instance of the RSACng class. With this class, the VerifyHash method is used to pass the hash, signature, and algorithm information that was used earlier. Now Bob knows the information is from Alice:

```
private bool IsSignatureValid(byte[] hash, byte[] signature, CngKey key)
{
    using (var signingAlg = new RSACng(key))
    {
        return signingAlg.VerifyHash(hash, signature, HashAlgorithmName.SHA384,
            RSASignaturePadding.Pss);
    }
}
```

To verify that the document data is unchanged, Bob hashes the document again and uses the LINQ extension method SequenceEqual to verify whether the hash code is the same as was sent earlier. If the hashes are the same, it can be assumed that the document was not changed:

```
private bool IsDocumentUnchanged(byte[] hash, byte[] data)
{
    byte[] newHash = HashDocument(data);
    return newHash.SequenceEqual(hash);
}
```

When you run the application, you see output similar to what's shown here. When you debug the application you can change the document data after it's hashed by Alice and see that Bob doesn't accept the changed document. To change the document data, you can easily change the value in the Watch window of the debugger.

```
signature valid, document unchanged
document from Alice: Best greetings from Alice
```

Implementing Data Protection

Another feature of .NET that is related to encryption is the new .NET core library support for *data protection*. The namespace System.Security.DataProtection contains a DpApiDataProtector class that wraps the native Windows Data Protection API (DPAPI). These classes don't offer the flexibility and features needed on the web server—that's why the ASP.NET team created classes with the Microsoft.AspNet.DataProtection namespace.

The reason for this library is to store trusted information for later retrieval, but the storage media (such as using hosting environments from a third party) cannot be trusted itself, so the information needs to be stored encrypted on the host.

The sample application is a simple Console Application (Package) that enables you to read and write information using data protection. With this sample, you see the flexibility and features of the ASP.NET data protection.

The data protection sample code makes use of the following dependencies and namespaces:

Dependencies

```
NETStandard.Library
Microsoft.AspNet.DataProtection
Microsoft.AspNet.DataProtection.Abstractions
Microsoft.Extensions.DependencyInjection
```

Namespaces

```
Microsoft.Extensions.DependencyInjection
System
System.IO
System.Linq
static System.Console
```

You can start the console application by using the -r and -w command-line arguments to either read or write from the storage. Also, you need to use the command line to set a filename to read and write. After checking the command-line arguments, the data protection is initialized calling the InitProtection helper method. This method returns an object of type MySafe that embeds an IDataProtector. After that, depending on the command-line arguments, either the Write or Read method is invoked (code file DataProtectionSample/Program.cs):

```csharp
class Program
{
  private const string readOption = "-r";
  private const string writeOption = "-w";
  private readonly string[] options = { readOption, writeOption };

  static void Main(string[] args)
  {
    if (args.Length != 2 || args.Intersect(options).Count() != 1)
    {
      ShowUsage();
      return;
    }
    string fileName = args[1];

    MySafe safe = InitProtection();

    switch (args[0])
    {
      case writeOption:
        Write(safe, fileName);
        break;
      case readOption:
        Read(safe, fileName);
        break;
      default:
        ShowUsage();
        break;
    }
  }
  //etc.
}
```

The class `MySafe` holds a member of `IDataProtector`. This interface defines the members `Protect` and `Unprotect` to encrypt and decrypt data. This interface defines `Protect` and `Unprotect` methods with byte array arguments and returning byte arrays. However, the sample code directly sends and returns strings from the `Encrypt` and `Decrypt` methods using extension methods that are defined within the `Microsoft.AspNet.DataProtection.Abstractions` NuGet package. The `MySafe` class receives an `IDataProtectionProvider` interface via dependency injection. With this interface, a `IDataProtector` is returned passing a purpose string. The same string needs to be used when reading and writing from this safe (code file `DataProtectionSample/MySafe.cs`):

```
public class MySafe
{
  private IDataProtector _protector;
  public MySafe(IDataProtectionProvider provider)
  {
    _protector = provider.CreateProtector("MySafe.MyProtection.v1");
  }

  public string Encrypt(string input) => _protector.Protect(input);

  public string Decrypt(string encrypted) => _protector.Unprotect(encrypted);
}
```

With the `InitProtection` method, the `AddDataProtection` and `ConfigureDataProtection` extension methods are invoked to add data protection via dependency injection, and to configure it. The `AddDataProtection` method registers default services by calling the static method `DataProtectionServices.GetDefaultServices`.

There's an interesting special part contained with the `ConfigureDataProtection` method. Here, it is defined how the keys should be persisted. The sample code persists the key to the actual directory passing a `DirectoryInfo` instance to the method `PersistKeysToFileSystem`. Another option is to persist the key to the registry (`PersistKeysToRegistry`), and you can create your own method to persist the key to a custom store. The lifetime of the created keys is defined by the method `SetDefaultKeyLifetime`. Next, the keys are protected by calling `ProtectKeysWithDpapi`. This method protects the keys using the DPAPI, which encrypts the stored keys with the current user. `ProtectKeysWithCertificate` allows using a certificate for key protection. The API also defines the method `UseEphemeralDataProtectionProvider` in which keys are stored just in memory. When the application is started again, new keys need to be generated. This is a great feature for unit testing (code file `DataProtectionSample/Program.cs`):

```
public static MySafe InitProtection()
{
  var serviceCollection = new ServiceCollection();
  serviceCollection.AddDataProtection();

  serviceCollection.ConfigureDataProtection(c =>
    c.PersistKeysToFileSystem(new DirectoryInfo("."))
     .SetDefaultKeyLifetime(TimeSpan.FromDays(20))
     .ProtectKeysWithDpapi()
  );
  IServiceProvider services = serviceCollection.BuildServiceProvider();

  return ActivatorUtilities.CreateInstance<MySafe>(services);
}
```

Now the heart of the data protection application is implemented, and the `Write` and `Read` methods can take advantage of `MySafe` to encrypt and decrypt the user's content:

```
public static void Write(MySafe safe, string fileName)
{
  WriteLine("enter content to write:");
  string content = ReadLine();
```

```
    string encrypted = safe.Encrypt(content);
    File.WriteAllText(fileName, encrypted);
    WriteLine($"content written to {fileName}");
}

public static void Read(MySafe safe, string fileName)
{
    string encrypted = File.ReadAllText(fileName);
    string decrypted = safe.Decrypt(encrypted);
    WriteLine(decrypted);
}
```

ACCESS CONTROL TO RESOURCES

Operating system resources such as files and registry keys, as well as handles of a named pipe, are secured by using an access control list (ACL). Figure 24-2 shows the structure mapping this. Associated with the resource is a security descriptor that contains information about the owner of the resource. It references two access control lists: a discretionary access control list (DACL) and a system access control list (SACL). The DACL defines who has access; the SACL defines audit rules for security event logging. An ACL contains a list of access control entries (ACEs), which contain a type, a security identifier, and rights. With the DACL, the ACE can be of type access allowed or access denied. Some of the rights that you can set and get with a file are create, read, write, delete, modify, change permissions, and take ownership.

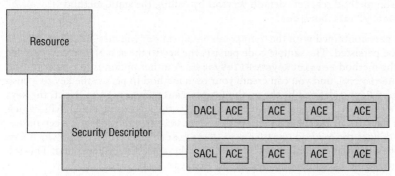

FIGURE 24-2

The classes to read and modify access control are located in the namespace System.Security.AccessControl. The following program demonstrates reading the access control list from a file.

The sample application FileAccessControl makes use of the following dependencies and namespaces:

Dependencies

> NETStandard.Library
>
> System.IO.FileSystem
>
> System.IO.FileSystem.AccessControl

Namespaces

> System.IO
>
> System.Security.AccessControl
>
> System.Security.Principal
>
> static System.Console

The `FileStream` class defines the `GetAccessControl` method, which returns a `FileSecurity` object. `FileSecurity` is the .NET class that represents a security descriptor for files. `FileSecurity` derives from the base classes `ObjectSecurity`, `CommonObjectSecurity`, `NativeObjectSecurity`, and `FileSystemSecurity`. Other classes that represent a security descriptor are `CryptoKeySecurity`, `EventWaitHandleSecurity`, `MutexSecurity`, `RegistrySecurity`, `SemaphoreSecurity`, `PipeSecurity`, and `ActiveDirectorySecurity`. All of these objects can be secured using an ACL. In general, the corresponding .NET class defines the method `GetAccessControl` to return the corresponding security class; for example, the `Mutex.GetAccessControl` method returns a `MutexSecurity`, and the `PipeStream.GetAccessControl` method returns a `PipeSecurity`.

The `FileSecurity` class defines methods to read and change the DACL and SACL. The method `GetAccessRules` returns the DACL in the form of the class `AuthorizationRuleCollection`. To access the SACL, you can use the method `GetAuditRules`.

With the method `GetAccessRules`, you can specify whether inherited access rules, and not only access rules directly defined with the object, should be used. The last parameter defines the type of the security identifier that should be returned. This type must derive from the base class `IdentityReference`. Possible types are `NTAccount` and `SecurityIdentifier`. Both of these classes represent users or groups; the `NTAccount` class finds the security object by its name and the `SecurityIdentifier` class finds the security object by a unique security identifier.

The returned `AuthorizationRuleCollection` contains `AuthorizationRule` objects. The `AuthorizationRule` is the .NET representation of an ACE. In the following example, a file is accessed, so the `AuthorizationRule` can be cast to a `FileSystemAccessRule`. With ACEs of other resources, different .NET representations exist, such as `MutexAccessRule` and `PipeAccessRule`. With the `FileSystemAccessRule` class, the properties `AccessControlType`, `FileSystemRights`, and `IdentityReference` return information about the ACE (code file `FileAccessControl/Program.cs`).

```csharp
class Program
{
  static void Main(string[] args)
  {
    string filename = null;
    if (args.Length == 0) return;

    filename = args[0];

    using (FileStream stream = File.Open(filename, FileMode.Open))
    {
      FileSecurity securityDescriptor = stream.GetAccessControl();
      AuthorizationRuleCollection rules =
          securityDescriptor.GetAccessRules(true, true,
          typeof(NTAccount));

      foreach (AuthorizationRule rule in rules)
      {
        var fileRule = rule as FileSystemAccessRule;
        WriteLine($"Access type: {fileRule.AccessControlType}");
        WriteLine($"Rights: {fileRule.FileSystemRights}");
        WriteLine($"Identity: {fileRule.IdentityReference.Value}");
        WriteLine();
      }
    }
  }
}
```

By running the application and passing a filename, you can see the ACL for the file. The following output lists full control to Administrators and System, modification rights to authenticated users, and read and execute rights to all users belonging to the group Users:

```
Access type: Allow
Rights: FullControl
```

```
Identity: BUILTIN\Administrators

Access type: Allow
Rights: FullControl
Identity: NT AUTHORITY\SYSTEM

Access type: Allow
Rights: FullControl
Identity: BUILTIN\Administrators

Access type: Allow
Rights: FullControl
Identity: TheOtherSide\Christian
```

Setting access rights is very similar to reading access rights. To set access rights, several resource classes that can be secured offer the `SetAccessControl` and `ModifyAccessControl` methods. The following code modifies the ACL of a file by invoking the `SetAccessControl` method from the `File` class. To this method a `FileSecurity` object is passed. The `FileSecurity` object is filled with `FileSystemAccessRule` objects. The access rules listed here deny write access to the Sales group, give read access to the Everyone group, and give full control to the Developers group:

> **NOTE** *This program runs on your system only if the Windows groups Sales and Developers are defined. You can change the program to use groups that are available in your environment.*

```
private void WriteAcl(string filename)
{
  var salesIdentity = new NTAccount("Sales");
  var developersIdentity = new NTAccount("Developers");
  var everyOneIdentity = new NTAccount("Everyone");

  var salesAce = new FileSystemAccessRule(salesIdentity,
      FileSystemRights.Write, AccessControlType.Deny);
  var everyoneAce = new FileSystemAccessRule(everyOneIdentity,
      FileSystemRights.Read, AccessControlType.Allow);
  var developersAce = new FileSystemAccessRule(developersIdentity,
      FileSystemRights.FullControl, AccessControlType.Allow);

  var securityDescriptor = new FileSecurity();
  securityDescriptor.SetAccessRule(everyoneAce);
  securityDescriptor.SetAccessRule(developersAce);
  securityDescriptor.SetAccessRule(salesAce);

  File.SetAccessControl(filename, securityDescriptor);
}
```

> **NOTE** *You can verify the access rules by opening the Properties window and selecting a file in Windows Explorer. Select the Security tab to see the ACL.*

DISTRIBUTING CODE USING CERTIFICATES

You can make use of digital certificates and sign assemblies so that consumers of the software can verify the identity of the software publisher. Depending on where the application is used, certificates may be required. For example, with ClickOnce, the user installing the application can verify the certificate to trust the publisher. Using Windows Error Reporting, Microsoft uses the certificate to determine which vendor to map to the error report.

> **NOTE** *ClickOnce is explained in Chapter 36, "Deploying Windows Apps."*

In a commercial environment, you obtain a certificate from a company such as Verisign or Thawte. The advantage of buying a certificate from a supplier instead of creating your own is that it provides a high level of trust in the authenticity of the certificate; the supplier acts as a trusted third party. For test purposes, however, .NET includes a command-line utility you can use to create a test certificate. The process of creating certificates and using them for publishing software is complex, but this section walks through a simple example.

The example code is for a fictitious company called ABC Corporation. The company's software product (`simple.exe`) should be trusted. First, create a test certificate by typing the following command:

```
>makecert -sv abckey.pvk -r -n "CN=ABC Corporation" abccorptest.cer
```

The command creates a test certificate under the name ABC Corporation and saves it to a file called `abccorptest.cer`. The `-sv abckey.pvk` argument creates a key file to store the private key. When creating the key file, you are asked for a password that you should remember.

After creating the certificate, you can create a software publisher test certificate with the Software Publisher Certificate Test tool (`Cert2spc.exe`):

```
>cert2spc abccorptest.cer abccorptest.spc
```

With a certificate that is stored in an `spc` file and the key file that is stored in a `pvk` file, you can create a `pfx` file that contains both with the `pvk2pfx` utility:

```
>pvk2pfx -pvk abckey.pvk -spc abccorptest.spc -pfx abccorptest.pfx
```

Now you can use the `signtool.exe` utility to sign the assembly. The `sign` option is used for signing, `-f` specifies the certificate in the `pfx` file, and `-v` is for verbose output:

```
>signtool sign -f abccorptest.pfx -v simple.exe
```

To establish trust for the certificate, install it with the Trusted Root Certification Authorities and the Trusted Publishers using the Certificate Manager, `certmgr`, or the MMC snap-in Certificates. Then you can verify the successful signing with the `signtool`:

```
>signtool verify -v -a simple.exe
```

SUMMARY

This chapter covered several aspects of security with .NET applications. Users are represented by identities and principals, classes that implement the interface `IIdentity` and `IPrincipal`. You've also seen how to access claims from identities.

A brief overview of cryptography demonstrated how the signing and encrypting of data enable the exchange of keys in a secure way. .NET offers both symmetric and asymmetric cryptography algorithms as well as hashing and signing.

With access control lists you can read and modify access to operating system resources such as files. You program ACLs similarly to the way you program secure pipes, registry keys, Active Directory entries, and many other operating system resources.

In many cases you can work with security from higher abstraction levels. For example, using HTTPS to access a web server, keys for encryption are exchanged behind the scenes. Using WCF, you can define what security algorithm to use by changing a configuration file. With the full .NET stack, the `File` class offers an `Encrypt` method (using the NTFS file system) to easily encrypt files. Still it's important to know what happens behind this functionality.

The next chapter covers networking. When creating applications that communicate across the network, it's really important to know security. By reading the next chapter you can let Alice and Bob communicate across the network, not just within a process as was done in this chapter. Chapter 25, "Networking," covers the foundation of networking.

25

Networking

WHAT'S IN THIS CHAPTER?

➤ Using HttpClient
➤ Manipulating IP addresses and performing DNS lookups
➤ Creating a server with WebListener
➤ Socket programming with TCP, UDP, and socket classes

WROX.COM CODE DOWNLOADS FOR THIS CHAPTER

The wrox.com code downloads for this chapter are found at `http://www.wrox.com/go/professionalcsharp6` on the Download Code tab. The code for this chapter is divided into the following major examples:

➤ HttpClientSample
➤ WinAppHttpClient
➤ HttpServer
➤ Utilities
➤ DnsLookup
➤ HttpClientUsingTcp
➤ TcpServer
➤ WPFAppTcpClient
➤ UdpReceiver
➤ UdpSender
➤ SocketServer
➤ SocketClient

NETWORKING

This chapter takes a fairly practical approach to networking, mixing examples with a discussion of relevant theory and networking concepts as appropriate. This chapter is not a guide to computer networking but an introduction to using the .NET Framework for network communication.

This chapter shows you how to create both clients and servers using network protocols. It starts with the simplest case: sending an HTTP request to a server and storing the information that's sent back in the response.

Then you see how to create an HTTP server, using utility classes to split up and create URIs and resolve hostnames to IP addresses. You are also introduced to sending and receiving data via TCP and UDP and find out how to make use of the Socket class.

The two namespaces of most interest for networking are System.Net and System.Net.Sockets. The System.Net namespace is generally concerned with higher-level operations, such as downloading and uploading files, and making web requests using HTTP and other protocols, whereas System.Net.Sockets contains classes to perform lower-level operations. You will find these classes useful when you want to work directly with sockets or protocols, such as TCP/IP. The methods in these classes closely mimic the Windows socket (Winsock) API functions derived from the Berkeley sockets interface. You will also find that some of the objects that this chapter works with are found in the System.IO namespace.

THE HTTPCLIENT CLASS

The HttpClient class is used to send an HTTP request and receive the response from the request. It is in the System.Net.Http namespace. The classes in the System.Net.Http namespace help make it easy to consume web services for both clients and server.

The HttpClient class derives from the HttpMessageInvoker class. This base class implements the SendAsync method. The SendAsync method is the workhorse of the HttpClient class. As you see later in this section, there are several derivatives of this method to use. As the name implies, the SendAsync method call is asynchronous. This enables you to write a fully asynchronous system for calling web services.

Making an Asynchronous Get Request

In the download code examples for this chapter is HttpClientSample. It calls a web service asynchronously in different ways. To call using the different ways demonstrated by the sample, you use command-line arguments.

The sample code makes use of the following dependencies and namespaces:

Dependencies

```
NETStandard.Library
System.Net.Http
```

Namespaces

```
System
System.Net
System.Net.Http
System.Net.Http.Headers
System.Threading
System.Threading.Tasks
static System.Console
```

The first code snippet instantiates an HttpClient object. The HttpClient object is thread-safe, so a single HttpClient object can be used to handle multiple requests. Each instance of HttpClient maintains its own thread pool, so requests between HttpClient instances are isolated. Resources are released by invoking the Dispose method.

Invoking the GetAsync makes an HTTP GET request to the server. You pass in the address of the method you're going to call. The GetAsync call is overloaded to take either a string or a URI object. The example calls into Microsoft's OData sample site http://services.odata.org, but you could alter that address to call any number of REST web services.

The call to GetAsync returns an HttpResponseMessage object. The HttpResponseMessage class represents a response including headers, status, and content. Checking the IsSuccessfulStatusCode property of the response tell you whether the request was successful. With a successful call, the content returned is retrieved as a string using the ReadAsStringAsync method (code file HttpClientSample/Program.cs):

```csharp
private const string NorthwindUrl =
  "http://services.data.org/Northwind/Northwind.svc/Regions";
private const string IncorrectUrl =
  "http://services.data.org/Northwind1/Northwind.svc/Regions";

private async Task GetDataSimpleAsync()
{
  using (var client = new HttpClient())
  {
    HttpResponseMessage response = await client.GetAsync(NorthwindUrl);

    if(response.IsSuccessStatusCode)
    {
      WriteLine($"Response Status Code: {(int)response.StatusCode} " +
        $"{response.ReasonPhrase}");
      string responseBodyAsText = await response.Content.ReadAsStringAsync();
      WriteLine($"Received payload of {responseBodyAsText.Length} characters");
      WriteLine();
      WriteLine(responseBodyAsText);
    }
  }
}
```

Executing this code with the command-line argument -s should produce the following output:

```
Response Status Code: 200 OK
Received payload of 3379 characters

<?xml version="1.0" encoding="utf-8"?>
<!- ... ->
```

> **NOTE** Because the HttpClient class used the GetAsync method call with the await keyword, the calling thread returned and could do some other work. When the result is available from the GetAsync method a thread continues with the method, and the response is written to the response variable. The await keyword is explained in Chapter 15, "Asynchronous Programming." Creating and using tasks is explained in Chapter 21, "Tasks and Parallel Programming."

Throwing Exceptions

Invoking the GetAsync method of the HttpClient class by default doesn't generate an exception if the method fails. This could be easily changed by invoking the EnsureSuccessStatusCode method with the

HttpResponseMessage. This method checks whether IsSuccessStatusCode is false, and throws an exception otherwise (code file HttpClientSample/Program.cs):

```
private async Task GetDataWithExceptionsAsync()
{
  try
  {
    using (var client = new HttpClient())
    {
      HttpResponseMessage response = await client.GetAsync(IncorrectUrl);
      response.EnsureSuccessStatusCode();

      WriteLine($"Response Status Code: {(int)response.StatusCode} " +
        $"{response.ReasonPhrase}");
      string responseBodyAsText = await response.Content.ReadAsStringAsync();
      WriteLine($"Received payload of {responseBodyAsText.Length} characters");
      WriteLine();
      WriteLine(responseBodyAsText);
    }
  }
  catch (Exception ex)
  {
    WriteLine($"{ex.Message}");
  }
}
```

Passing Headers

You didn't set or change any of the headers when you made the request, but the DefaultRequestHeaders property on HttpClient enables you to do just that. You can add headers to the collection using the Add method. After you set a header value, the header and header value are sent with every request that this instance of HttpClient sends.

By default the response content will be in XML format. You can change this by adding an Accept header to the request to use JSON. Add the following line just before the call to GetAsync and the content is returned in JSON format:

```
client.DefaultRequestHeaders.Add("Accept", "application/json;odata=verbose");
```

Adding and removing the header and running the example will result in the content in both XML and JSON formats.

The HttpRequestHeaders object returned from the DefaultHeaders property has several helper properties to many of the standard headers. You can read the values of the headers from these properties, but they are read only. To set a value, you need to use the Add method. In the code snippet, the HTTP Accept header is added. Depending on the Accept header received by the server, the server can return different data formats based on the client's needs. When you send the Accept header application/json, the client informs the server that it accepts data in JSON format. Header information is shown with the ShowHeaders method that is also invoked when receiving the response from the server (code file HttpClientSample/Program.cs):

```
public static Task GetDataWithHeadersAsync()
{
  try
  {
    using (var client = new HttpClient())
    {
      client.DefaultRequestHeaders.Add("Accept",
        "application/json;odata=verbose");
      ShowHeaders("Request Headers:", client.DefaultRequestHeaders);

      HttpResponseMessage response = await client.GetAsync(NorthwindUrl);
      client.EnsureSuccessStatusCode();
```

```
      ShowHeaders("Response Headers:", response.Headers);
      //etc.
    }
  }
```

Contrary to the previous sample, the `ShowHeaders` method was added, taking an `HttpHeaders` object as a parameter. `HttpHeaders` is the base class for `HttpRequestHeaders` and `HttpResponseHeaders`. The specialized classes both add helper properties to access headers directly. The `HttpHeader` object is defined as a `KeyValuePair<string, IEnumerable<string>>`. This means that each header can have more than one value in the collection. Because of this, it's important that if you want to change a value in a header, you need to remove the original value and add the new value.

The `ShowHeaders` function is pretty simple. It iterates all headers in `HttpHeaders`. The enumerator returns `KeyValuePair<string, IEnumerable<string>>` elements and shows a stringified version of the values for every key:

```
public static void ShowHeaders(string title, HttpHeaders headers)
{
  WriteLine(title);
  foreach (var header in headers)
  {
    string value = string.Join(" ", header.Value);
    WriteLine($"Header: {header.Key} Value: {value}");
  }
  WriteLine();
}
```

Running this code will now display any headers for the request:

```
Request Headers:
Header: Accept Value: application/json; odata=verbose

Response Headers:
Header: Vary Value: *
Header: X-Content-Type-Options Value: nosniff
Header: DataServiceVersion Value: 2.0;
Header: Access-Control-Allow-Origin Value: *
Header: Access-Control-Allow-Methods Value: GET
Header: Access-Control-Allow-Headers Value: Accept, Origin, Content-Type,
MaxDataServiceVersion
Header: Access-Control-Expose-Headers Value: DataServiceVersion
Header: Cache-Control Value: private
Header: Date Value: Mon, 06 Jul 2015 09:00:48 GMT
Header: Set-Cookie Value: ARRAffinity=a5ee7717b148daedb0164e6e19088a5a78c47693a6
0e57422887d7e011fb1e5e;Path=/;Domain=services.odata.org
Header: Server Value: Microsoft-IIS/8.0
Header: X-AspNet-Version Value: 4.0.30319
Header: X-Powered-By Value: ASP.NET
```

Because the client now requests JSON data, the server returns JSON, and you can also see this information:

```
Response Status Code: 200 OK
Received payload of 1551 characters

{"d":{"results":[{"__metadata":{"id":"http://services.odata.org/Northwind/
Northwind.svc/Regions(1) ", "uri":
```

Accessing the Content

The previous code snippets have shown you how to access the `Content` property to retrieve a string. The `Content` property in the response returns an `HttpContent` object. In order to get the data from the `HttpContent` object you need to use one of the methods supplied. In the example, the `ReadAsStringAsync` method was used. It returns a string representation of the content. As the name implies, this is an async call. Instead of using the async keyword, the Result property could be used as well. Calling the Result property blocks the call until it's finished and then continues on with execution.

Other methods to get the data from the HttpContent object are ReadAsByteArrayAsync, which returns a byte array of the data, and ReadAsStreamAsync, which returns a stream. You can also load the content into a memory buffer using LoadIntoBufferAsync.

The Headers property returns the HttpContentHeaders object. This works exactly the same way the request and response headers do in the previous example.

> **NOTE** *Instead of using the* GetAsync *and* ReadAsStringAsync *methods of the* HttpClient *and* HttpContent *classes, the* HttpClient *class also offers the method* GetStringAsync *that returns a string without the need to invoke two methods. However, when using this method you don't have that much control over the error status and other information.*

> **NOTE** *Streams are explained in Chapter 23, "Files and Streams."*

Customizing Requests with HttpMessageHandler

The HttpClient class can take an HttpMessageHandler as a parameter to its constructor. This makes it possible for you to customize the request. You can pass an instance of the HttpClientHandler. There are numerous properties that can be set for things such as ClientCertificates, Pipelining, CachePolicy, ImpersonationLevel, and so on.

With the next code snippet, a SampleMessageHandler is instantiated and passed to the HttpClient constructor: (code file HttpClientSample/Program.cs):

```
public static async Task GetDataWithMessageHandlerAsync()
{
  var client = new HttpClient(new SampleMessageHandler("error"));
  HttpResponseMessage response = await client.GetAsync(NorthwindUrl);
  //...
}
```

The purpose of this handler type, SampleMessageHandler, is to take a string as a parameter and either display it in the console, or, if the message is "error," set the response's status code to Bad Request. If you create a class that derives from HttpClientHandler, you can override a few properties and the method SendAsync. SendAsync is typically overridden because the request to the server can be influenced. If the _displayMessage is set to "error", an HttpResponseMessage with a bad request is returned. The method needs a Task returned. For the error case, asynchronous methods do not need to be called; that's why the error is simply returned with Task.FromResult (code file HttpClientSample/SampleMessageHandler.cs):

```
public class SampleMessageHandler : HttpClientHandler
{
  private string _message;

  public SampleMessageHandler(string message)
  {
    _message = message;
  }
```

```
protected override Task<HttpResponseMessage> SendAsync(
    HttpRequestMessage request, CancellationToken cancellationToken)
{
  WriteLine($"In SampleMessageHandler {_message}");

  if(_message == "error")
  {
    var response = new HttpResponseMessage(HttpStatusCode.BadRequest);
    return Task.FromResult<HttpResponseMessage>(response);
  }
  return base.SendAsync(request, cancellationToken);
}
}
```

There are many reasons to add a custom handler. The handler pipeline is set so that multiple handlers can be added. Besides the default, there is the `DelegatingHandler`, which executes some code and then "delegates" the call back to the inner or next handler. The `HttpClientHandler` is the last handler in line and sends the request to the addressee. Figure 25-1 shows the pipeline. Each `DelegatingHandler` added would call the next or inner handler finally ending at the `HttpClientHandler`-based handler.

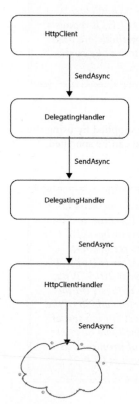

FIGURE 25-1

Creating an HttpRequestMessage Using SendAsync

Behind the scenes, the `GetAsync` method of the `HttpClient` class invokes the `SendAsync` method. Instead of using the `GetAsync` method, you can also use the `SendAsync` method to send an HTTP request. With `SendAsync` you have even more control over defining the request. The constructor of the `HttpRequestMessage` class is overloaded to pass a value of the `HttpMethod`. The `GetAsync` method creates an HTTP request with `HttpMethod.Get`. Using `HttpMethod`, you can not only send GET, POST, PUT, and DELETE requests but you can also send also HEAD, OPTIONS, and TRACE. With the `HttpRequestMessage` object in place, you can invoke the `SendAsync` method with the `HttpClient`:

```
private async Task GetDataAdvancedAsync()
{
  using (var client = new HttpClient())
  {
    var request = new HttpRequestMessage(HttpMethod.Get, NorthwindUrl);

    HttpResponseMessage response = await client.SendAsync(request);
    //etc.
  }
}
```

> **NOTE** *This chapter only makes HTTP GET requests using the* `HttpClient` *class. The* `HttpClient` *class also allows sending HTTP POST, PUT, and DELETE requests using the* `PostAsync`, `PutAsync`, *and* `DeleteAsync` *methods. These methods are used in Chapter 42, "ASP.NET Web API," where these requests are done to invoke corresponding action methods in the web service.*

After the `HttpRequestMessage` object is created, the header and content can be supplied by using the `Headers` and `Content` properties. With the `Version` property, the HTTP version can be specified.

> **NOTE** *HTTP/1.0 was specified in the year 1996 followed by 1.1 just a few years later. With 1.0, the connection was always closed after the server returned the data; with 1.1, a keep-alive header was added where the client was able to put his or her wish to keep the connection alive as the client might make more requests to receive not only the HTML code, but also CSS and JavaScript files and images. After HTTP/1.1 was defined in 1999, it took 16 years until HTTP/2 was done in the year 2015. What are the advantages of version 2? HTTP/2 allows multiple concurrent requests on the same connection, header information is compressed, the client can define which of the resources is more important, and the server can send resources to the client via server push. HTTP/2 supporting server push means WebSockets will practically be obsolete as soon as HTTP/2 is supported everywhere. All the newer versions of browsers, as well as IIS running on Windows 10 and Windows Server 2016, support HTTP/2.*

Using HttpClient with Windows Runtime

At the time of writing this book, the `HttpClient` class used with console applications and WPF doesn't support HTTP/2. However, the `HttpClient` class used with the Universal Windows Platform has a different implementation that is based on features of the Windows 10 API. With this, `HttpClient` supports HTTP/2, and even uses this version by default.

The next code sample shows a Universal Windows app that makes an HTTP request to a link that is entered in a `TextBox` and shows the result, as well as giving information about the HTTP version. The following code snippet shows the XAML code, and Figure 25-2 shows the design view (code file `WinAppHttpClient/MainPage.xaml`):

```xml
<StackPanel Orientation="Horizontal">
  <TextBox Header="Url" Text="{x:Bind Url, Mode=TwoWay}" MinWidth="200"
    Margin="5" />
  <Button Content="Send" Click="{x:Bind OnSendRequest}" Margin="10,5,5,5"
    VerticalAlignment="Bottom" />
</StackPanel>
<TextBox Header="Version" Text="{x:Bind Version, Mode=OneWay}" Grid.Row="1"
  Margin="5" IsReadOnly="True" />
<TextBox AcceptsReturn="True" IsReadOnly="True" Text="{x:Bind Result,
  Mode=OneWay}" Grid.Row="2" ScrollViewer.HorizontalScrollBarVisibility="Auto"
  ScrollViewer.VerticalScrollBarVisibility="Auto" />
```

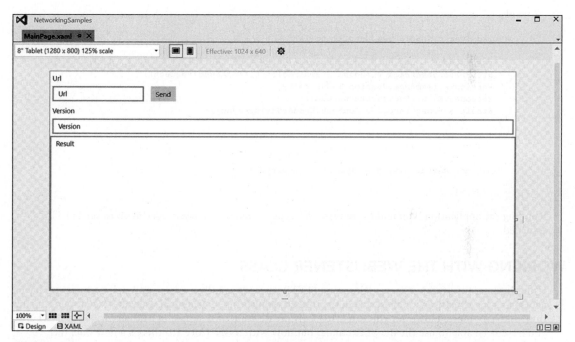

FIGURE 25-2

> **NOTE** *XAML code and dependency properties are explained in Chapter 29, "Core XAML," and compiled binding is covered in Chapter 31, "Patterns with XAML Apps."*

The properties `Url`, `Version`, and `Result` are implemented as dependency properties for making automatic updates to the UI. The following code snippet shows the `Url` property (code file `WinAppHttpClient/MainPage.xaml.cs`):

```
public string Url
{
  get { return (string)GetValue(UrlProperty); }
  set { SetValue(UrlProperty, value); }
}

public static readonly DependencyProperty UrlProperty =
  DependencyProperty.Register("Url", typeof(string), typeof(MainPage),
    new PropertyMetadata(string.Empty));
```

The `HttpClient` class is used in the `OnSendRequest` method. This method is invoked when clicking the `Send` button in the UI. As in the previous sample, the `SendAsync` method is used to make the HTTP request. To see that the request is indeed making a request using the HTTP/2 version, you can check the `request.Version` property from the debugger. The version answered from the server coming from `response.Version` is written to the `Version` property that is bound in the UI. Nowadays, most servers just support the HTTP 1.1 version. As mentioned previously, HTTP/2 is supported by Windows Server 2016:

```
private async void OnSendRequest()
{
  try
  {
    using (var client = new HttpClient())
    {
      var request = new HttpRequestMessage(HttpMethod.Get, Url);
      HttpResponseMessage response = await client.SendAsync(request);
      Version = response.Version.ToString();
      response.EnsureSuccessStatusCode();
      Result = await response.Content.ReadAsStringAsync();
    }
  }
  catch (Exception ex)
  {
    await new MessageDialog(ex.Message).ShowAsync();
  }
}
```

Running the application, you make a request to `https://http2.akamai.com/demo` to see HTTP/2 returned.

WORKING WITH THE WEBLISTENER CLASS

Using Internet Information Server (IIS) as an HTTP server is usually a great approach because you have access to a lot of features, such as scalability, health monitoring, a graphical user interface for administration, and a lot more. However, you can also easily create your own simple HTTP server. Since .NET 2.0, you have been able to use the `HttpListener`, but now with .NET Core 1.0 there's a new one: the `WebListener` class.

The sample code of the `HttpServer` makes use of the following dependencies and namespaces:

Dependencies

```
NETStandard.Library
Microsoft.Net.Http.Server
```

Namespaces

```
Microsoft.Net.Http.Server
System
```

```
System.Collections.Generic
System.Linq
System.Net
System.Reflection
System.Text
System.Threading.Tasks
static System.Console
```

The sample code for the HTTP server is a Console Application (Package) that allows passing a list of URL prefixes that defines where the server listens. An example of such a prefix is `http://localhost:8082/samples` where the server listens only to requests on port 8082 on the localhost if the path starts with samples. No matter what path follows, the server handles the request. To not only support requests from localhost, you can use the + character, such as `http://+:8082/samples`. This way the server is also accessible from all its hostnames. In case you are not starting Visual Studio from elevated mode, the user running the listener needs allowance. You can do this by running a command prompt in elevated mode and adding the URL using this `netsh` command:

```
>netsh http add urlacl url=http://+:8082/samples user=Everyone
```

The sample code checks the arguments if at least one prefix is passed and invokes the `StartServer` method afterward (code file `HttpServer/Program.cs`):

```csharp
static void Main(string[] args)
{
  if (args.Length < 1)
  {
    ShowUsage();
    return;
  }
  StartServerAsync(args).Wait();
  ReadLine();
}

private static void ShowUsage()
{
    WriteLine("Usage: HttpServer Prefix [Prefix2] [Prefix3] [Prefix4]");
}
```

The heart of the program is the `StartServer` method. Here, the `WebListener` class is instantiated, and the prefixes as defined from the command argument list are added. Calling the `Start` method of the `WebListener` class registers the port on the system. Next, after calling the `GetContextAsync` method, the listener waits for a client to connect and send data. As soon as a client sends an HTTP request, the request can be read from the `HttpContext` object that is returned from `GetContextAsync`. For both the request that is coming from the client and the answer that is sent, the `HttpContext` object is used. The `Request` property returns a `Request` object. The `Request` object contains the HTTP header information. With an HTTP POST request, the `Request` also contains the body. The `Response` property returns a `Response` object, which allows you to return header information (using the `Headers` property), status code (`StatusCode` property), and the response body (the `Body` property):

```csharp
public static async Task StartServerAsync(params string[] prefixes)
{
  try
  {
    WriteLine($"server starting at");
    var listener = new WebListener();
```

```
          foreach (var prefix in prefixes)
          {
            listener.UrlPrefixes.Add(prefix);
            WriteLine($"\t{prefix}");
          }

          listener.Start();

          do
          {
            using (RequestContext context = await listener.GetContextAsync())
            {
              context.Response.Headers.Add("content-type",
                new string[] { "text/html" });
              context.Response.StatusCode = (int)HttpStatusCode.OK;

              byte[] buffer = GetHtmlContent(context.Request);
              await context.Response.Body.WriteAsync(buffer, 0, buffer.Length);
            }
          } while (true);
        }
        catch (Exception ex)
        {
          WriteLine(ex.Message);
        }
      }
```

The sample code returns an HTML file that is retrieved using the GetHtmlContent method. This method makes use of the htmlFormat format string with two placeholders in the heading and the body. The GetHtmlContent method fills in the placeholders using the string.Format method. To fill the HTML body, two helper methods are used that retrieve the header information from the request and all the property values of the Request object—GetHeaderInfo and GetRequestInfo:

```
private static string htmlFormat =
  "<!DOCTYPE html><html><head><title>{0}</title></head>" +
  "<body>{1}</body></html>";

private static byte[] GetHtmlContent(Request request)
{
  string title = "Sample WebListener";

  var sb = new StringBuilder("<h1>Hello from the server</h1>");
  sb.Append("<h2>Header Info</h2>");
  sb.Append(string.Join(" ", GetHeaderInfo(request.Headers)));
  sb.Append("<h2>Request Object Information</h2>");
  sb.Append(string.Join(" ", GetRequestInfo(request)));
  string html = string.Format(htmlFormat, title, sb.ToString());
  return Encoding.UTF8.GetBytes(html);
}
```

The GetHeaderInfo method retrieves the keys and values from the HeaderCollection to return a div element that contains every key and value:

```
private static IEnumerable<string> GetHeaderInfo(HeaderCollection headers) =>
  headers.Keys.Select(key =>
    $"<div>{key}: {string.Join(",", headers.GetValues(key))}</div>");
```

The GetRequestInfo method makes use of reflection to get all the properties of the Request type, and returns the property names as well as its values:

```
private static IEnumerable<string> GetRequestInfo(Request request) =>
  request.GetType().GetProperties().Select(
    p => $"<div>{p.Name}: {p.GetValue(request)}</div>");
```

> **NOTE** *The* `GetHeaderInfo` *and* `GetRequestInfo` *methods make use of expression-bodied member functions, LINQ, and reflection. Expression-bodied member functions are explained in Chapter 3, "Objects and Types." Chapter 13, "Language Integrated Query," explains LINQ. Chapter 16, "Reflection, Metadata, and Dynamic Programming," includes reflection as an important topic.*

Running the server and using a browser such as Microsoft Edge to access the server using a URL such as `http://[hostname]:8082/samples/Hello?sample=text` results in output as shown in Figure 25-3.

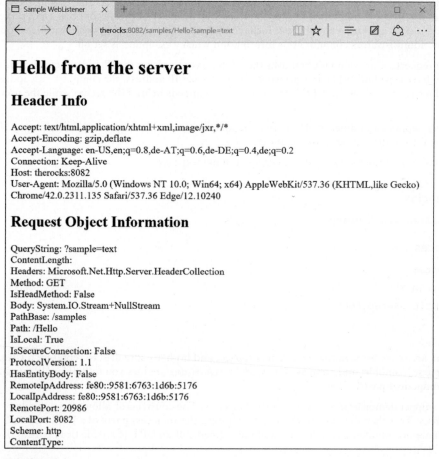

FIGURE 25-3

WORKING WITH UTILITY CLASSES

After dealing with HTTP requests and responses using classes that abstract the HTTP protocol like `HttpClient` and `WebListener`, let's have a look at some utility classes that make web programming easier when dealing with URIs and IP addresses.

On the Internet, you identify servers as well as clients by IP address or host name (also referred to as a Domain Name System (DNS) name). Generally speaking, the host name is the human-friendly name that you type in a web browser window, such as `www.wrox.com` or `www.cninnovation.com`. An IP address is the identifier that computers use to recognize each other. IP addresses are the identifiers used to ensure that web requests and responses reach the appropriate machines. It is even possible for a computer to have more than one IP address.

An IP address can be a 32-bit or 128-bit value, depending on whether Internet Protocol version 4 (IPv4) or Internet Protocol version 6 (IPv6) is used. An example of a 32-bit IP address is `192.168.1.100`. Because there are now so many computers and other devices vying for a spot on the Internet, IPv6 was developed. IPv6 can potentially provide a maximum number of about 3×10^{38} unique addresses. The .NET Framework enables your applications to work with both IPv4 and IPv6.

For host names to work, you must first send a network request to translate the host name into an IP address—a task that's carried out by one or more DNS servers. A *DNS server* stores a table that maps host names to IP addresses for all the computers it knows about, as well as the IP addresses of other DNS servers to look up host names it does not know about. Your local computer should always know about at least one DNS server. Network administrators configure this information when a computer is set up.

Before sending out a request, your computer first asks the DNS server to give it the IP address corresponding to the host name you have typed in. When it is armed with the correct IP address, the computer can address the request and send it over the network. All this work normally happens behind the scenes while the user is browsing the web.

The .NET Framework supplies a number of classes that are able to assist with the process of looking up IP addresses and finding information about host computers.

The sample code makes use of the following dependencies and namespaces:

Dependencies

```
NETStandard.Library
```

Namespaces

```
System
System.Net
static System.Console
```

URIs

`Uri` and `UriBuilder` are two classes in the `System` namespace, and both are intended to represent a URI. `Uri` enables you to parse, combine, and compare URIs, and `UriBuilder` enables you to build a URI given the strings for the component parts.

The following code snippet demonstrates features of the `Uri` class. The constructor allows passing relative and absolute URLs. This class defines several read-only properties to access parts of a URL such as the scheme, hostname, port number, query strings, and the segments of an URL (code file `Utilities/Program.cs`):

```
public static void UriSample(string url)
{
```

```
      var page = new Uri(url);
      WriteLine($"scheme: {page.Scheme}");
#if NET46
      WriteLine($"host: {page.Host}, type: {page.HostNameType}");
#else
      WriteLine($"host: {page.Host}, type: {page.HostNameType}, " +
          $"idn host: {page.IdnHost}");
#endif
      WriteLine($"port: {page.Port}");
      WriteLine($"path: {page.AbsolutePath}");
      WriteLine($"query: {page.Query}");
      foreach (var segment in page.Segments)
      {
          WriteLine($"segment: {segment}");
      }

      // etc.
   }
```

When you run the application and pass this URL and this string that contains a path and a query string http://www.amazon.com/Professional-C-6-0-Christian-Nagel/dp/111909660X/ref=sr_1_4?ie=UT F8&amqid=1438459506&sr=8-4&keywords=professional+c%23+6, you get the following output:

```
scheme: http
host: www.amazon.com, type:  Dns
port: 80
path: /Professional-C-6-0-Christian-Nagel/dp/111909660X/ref=sr_1_4
query: ?ie=UTF8&qid=1438459506&sr=8-4&keywords=professional+c%23+6
segment: /
segment: Professional-C-6-0-Christian-Nagel/
segment: dp/
segment: 111909660X/
segment: ref=sr_1_4
```

Unlike the `Uri` class, the `UriBuilder` defines read-write properties, as shown in the following code snippet. You can create an `UriBuilder` instance, assign these properties, and get a URL returned from the `Uri` property:

```
public static void UriSample(string url)
{
   // etc.

   var builder = new UriBuilder();
   builder.Host = "www.cninnovation.com";
   builder.Port = 80;
   builder.Path = "training/MVC";
   Uri uri = builder.Uri;
   WriteLine(uri);
}
```

Instead of using properties with the `UriBuilder`, this class also offers several overloads of the constructor where the parts of an URL can be passed as well.

IPAddress

`IPAddress` represents an IP address. The address itself is available as a byte array using the `GetAddressBytes` property and may be converted to a dotted decimal format with the `ToString` method. `IPAddress` also implements static `Parse` and `TryParse` methods that effectively perform the reverse conversion of `ToString`—converting from a dotted decimal string to an `IPAddress`. The code sample also accesses the `AddressFamily` property and converts an IPv4 address to IPv6, and vice versa (code file `Utilities/Program.cs`):

```
public static void IPAddressSample(string ipAddressString)
{
  IPAddress address;
  if (!IPAddress.TryParse(ipAddressString, out address))
  {
    WriteLine($"cannot parse {ipAddressString}");
    return;
  }
  byte[] bytes = address.GetAddressBytes();
  for (int i = 0; i < bytes.Length; i++)
  {
    WriteLine($"byte {i}: {bytes[i]:X}");
  }
  WriteLine($"family: {address.AddressFamily}, " +
    $"map to ipv6: {address.MapToIPv6()}, map to ipv4: {address.MapToIPv4()}");

  // etc.
}
```

Passing the address 65.52.128.33 to the method results in this output:

```
byte 0: 41
byte 1: 34
byte 2: 80
byte 3: 21
family: InterNetwork, map to ipv6: ::ffff:65.52.128.33, map to ipv4: 65.52.128.3
3
```

The `IPAddress` class also defines static properties to create special addresses such as loopback, broadcast, and anycast:

```
public static void IPAddressSample(string ipAddressString)
{
  // etc.
  WriteLine($"IPv4 loopback address: {IPAddress.Loopback}");
  WriteLine($"IPv6 loopback address: {IPAddress.IPv6Loopback}");
  WriteLine($"IPv4 broadcast address: {IPAddress.Broadcast}");
  WriteLine($"IPv4 any address: {IPAddress.Any}");
  WriteLine($"IPv6 any address: {IPAddress.IPv6Any}");
}
```

With a *loopback* address, the network hardware is bypassed. This is the IP address that represents the hostname localhost.

The *broadcast* address is an address that addresses every node in a local network. Such an address is not available with IPv6, as this concept is not used with the newer version of the Internet Protocol. After the initial definition of IPv4, multicasting was added for IPv6. With multicasting, a group of nodes is addressed instead of all nodes. With IPv6, multicasting completely replaces broadcasting. Both broadcast and multicast is shown in code samples later in this chapter when using UDP.

With an *anycast* one-to-many routing is used as well, but the data stream is only transmitted to the node closest in the network. This is useful for load balancing. With IPv4, the Border Gateway Protocol (BGP) routing protocol is used to find the shortest path in the network; with IPv6 this feature is inherent.

When you run the application, you can see the following addresses for IPv4 and IPv6:

```
IPv4 loopback address: 127.0.0.1
IPv6 loopback address: ::1
IPv4 broadcast address: 255.255.255.255
IPv4 any address: 0.0.0.0
IPv6 any address: ::
```

IPHostEntry

The `IPHostEntry` class encapsulates information related to a particular host computer. This class makes the host name available via the `HostName` property (which returns a string), and the `AddressList` property returns an array of `IPAddress` objects. You are going to use the `IPHostEntry` class in the next example.

Dns

The `Dns` class can communicate with your default DNS server to retrieve IP addresses.

The `DnsLookup` sample code makes use of the following dependencies and namespaces:

Dependencies

```
NETStandard.Library
System.Net.NameResolution
```

Namespaces

```
System
System.Net
System.Threading.Tasks
static System.Console
```

The sample application is implemented as a Console Application (package) that loops to ask the user for hostnames (you can also add an IP address instead) to get an `IPHostEntry` via `Dns.GetHostEntryAsync`. From the `IPHostEntry`, the address list is accessed using the `AddressList` property. All the addresses of the host, as well as the `AddressFamily`, are written to the console (code file `DnsLookup/Program.cs`):

```
static void Main()
{
  do
  {
    Write("Hostname:\t");
    string hostname = ReadLine();
    if (hostname.CompareTo("exit") == 0)
    {
      WriteLine("bye!");
      return;
    }
    OnLookupAsync(hostname).Wait();
    WriteLine();
  } while (true);
}

public static async Task OnLookupAsync(string hostname)
{
  try
  {
    IPHostEntry ipHost = await Dns.GetHostEntryAsync(hostname);
    WriteLine($"Hostname: {ipHost.HostName}");

    foreach (IPAddress address in ipHost.AddressList)
    {
      WriteLine($"Address Family: {address.AddressFamily}");
      WriteLine($"Address: {address}");
    }
  }
```

```
      catch (Exception ex)
      {
        WriteLine(ex.Message);
      }
    }
```

Run the application and enter a few hostnames to see output such as the following. With the hostname www.orf.at, you can see that this hostname defines multiple IP addresses.

```
Hostname:        www.cninnovation.com
Hostname: www.cninnovation.com
Address Family: InterNetwork
Address: 65.52.128.33

Hostname:        www.orf.at
Hostname: www.orf.at
Address Family: InterNetwork
Address: 194.232.104.150
Address Family: InterNetwork
Address: 194.232.104.140
Address Family: InterNetwork
Address: 194.232.104.142
Address Family: InterNetwork
Address: 194.232.104.149
Address Family: InterNetwork
Address: 194.232.104.141
Address Family: InterNetwork
Address: 194.232.104.139

Hostname:        exit
bye!
```

> **NOTE** *The* Dns *class is somewhat limited—for example, you can't define to use a server that's different than the default DNS server. Also, the* Aliases *property of the* IPHostEntry *is not populated from the method* GetHostEntryAsync. *It's only populated from obsolete methods of the* Dns *class, and these don't populate this property fully. For a full use of DNS lookups, it's better to use a third-party library.*

Now it's time to move to some lower-level protocols such as TCP and UDP.

USING TCP

The HTTP protocol is based on the Transmission Control Protocol (TCP). With TCP, the client first needs to open a connection to the server before sending commands. With HTTP, textual commands are sent. The HttpClient and WebListener classes hide the details of the HTTP protocol. When you are using TCP classes and you send HTTP requests, you need to know more about the HTTP protocol. The TCP classes don't offer functionality for the HTTP protocol; you have to do this on your own. On the other side, the TCP classes give more flexibility because you can use these classes also with other protocols based on TCP.

The TCP classes offer simple methods for connecting and sending data between two endpoints. An endpoint is the combination of an IP address and a port number. Existing protocols have well-defined port numbers—for example, HTTP uses port 80, whereas SMTP uses port 25. The Internet Assigned Numbers Authority, IANA (www.iana.org), assigns port numbers to these well-known services. Unless you are implementing a well-known service, you should select a port number higher than 1,024.

TCP traffic makes up the majority of traffic on the Internet today. It is often the protocol of choice because it offers guaranteed delivery, error correction, and buffering. The `TcpClient` class encapsulates a TCP connection and provides a number of properties to regulate the connection, including buffering, buffer size, and timeouts. Reading and writing is accomplished by requesting a `NetworkStream` object via the `GetStream` method.

The `TcpListener` class listens for incoming TCP connections with the `Start` method. When a connection request arrives, you can use the `AcceptSocket` method to return a socket for communication with the remote machine, or use the `AcceptTcpClient` method to use a higher-level `TcpClient` object for communication. The easiest way to see how the `TcpListener` and `TcpClient` classes work together is to go through some examples.

Creating an HTTP Client Using TCP

First, create a Console Application (Package) that will send an HTTP request to a web server. You've previously done this with the `HttpClient` class, but with the `TcpClient` class you need to take a deeper look into the HTTP protocol.

The `HttpClientUsingTcp` sample code makes use of the following dependencies and namespaces:

Dependencies

```
NETStandard.Library
```

Namespaces

```
System
System.IO
System.Net.Sockets
System.Text
System.Threading.Tasks
static System.Console
```

The application accepts one command-line argument to pass the name of the server. With this, the method `RequestHtmlAsync` is invoked to make an HTTP request to the server. It returns a string with the `Result` property of the `Task` (code file `HttpClientUsingTcp/Program.cs`):

```
static void Main(string[] args)
{
  if (args.Length != 1)
  {
    ShowUsage();
  }
  Task<string> t1 = RequestHtmlAsync(args[0]);
  WriteLine(t1.Result);
  ReadLine();
}

private static void ShowUsage()
```

```
    {
      WriteLine("Usage: HttpClientUsingTcp hostname");
    }
```

Now let's look at the most important parts of the RequestHtmlAsync method. First, a TcpClient object is instantiated. Second, with the method ConnectAsync, a TCP connection to the host is made at port 80, the default port for HTTP. Third, a stream to read and write using this connection is retrieved via the GetStream method:

```
    private const int ReadBufferSize = 1024;

    public static async Task<string> RequestHtmlAsync(string hostname)
    {
      try
      {
        using (var client = new TcpClient())
        {
          await client.ConnectAsync(hostname, 80);
          NetworkStream stream = client.GetStream();

          //etc.
        }
      }
    }
```

The stream can now be used to write a request to the server and read the response. HTTP is a text-based protocol; that's why it's easy to define the request in a string. To make a simple request to the server, the header defines the HTTP method GET followed by the path of the URL / and the HTTP version HTTP/1.1. The second line defines the Host header with the hostname and port number, and the third line defines the Connection header. Typically, with the Connection header the client requests keep-alive to ask the server to keep the connection open as the client expects to make more requests. Here we're just making a single request to the server, so the server should close the connection, thus close is set to the Connection header. To end the header information, you need to add an empty line to the request by using \r\n. The header information is sent with UTF-8 encoding by calling the WriteAsync method of the NetworkStream. To immediately send the buffer to the server, the FlushAsync method is invoked. Otherwise the data might be kept in the local cache:

```
        //etc.
        string header = "GET / HTTP/1.1\r\n" +
          $"Host: {hostname}:80\r\n" +
          "Connection: close\r\n" +
          "\r\n";
        byte[] buffer = Encoding.UTF8.GetBytes(header);
        await stream.WriteAsync(buffer, 0, buffer.Length);
        await stream.FlushAsync();
```

Now you can continue the process by reading the answer from the server. As you don't know how big the answer will be, you create a MemoryStream that grows dynamically. The answer from the server is temporarily written to a byte array using the ReadAsync method, and the content of this byte array is added to the MemoryStream. After all the data is read from the server, a StreamReader takes control to read the data from the stream into a string and return it to the caller:

```
        var ms = new MemoryStream();
        buffer = new byte[ReadBufferSize];
        int read = 0;
        do
        {
          read = await stream.ReadAsync(buffer, 0, ReadBufferSize);
```

```
            ms.Write(buffer, 0, read);
            Array.Clear(buffer, 0, buffer.Length);
          } while (read > 0);
        ms.Seek(0, SeekOrigin.Begin);
        var reader = new StreamReader(ms);
        return reader.ReadToEnd();
      }
    }
    catch (SocketException ex)
    {
      WriteLine(ex.Message);
      return null;
    }
  }
}
```

When you pass a website to the program, you see a successful request with HTML content shown in the console.

Now it's time to create a TCP listener with a custom protocol.

Creating a TCP Listener

Creating your own protocol based on TCP needs requires some advance thought about the architecture. You can define your own binary protocol where every bit is saved on the data transfer, but it's more complex to read; alternatively, you can use a text-based format such as HTTP or FTP. Should a session stay open or be closed with every request? Does the server need to keep state for a client, or is all the data sent with every request?

The custom server will support some simple functionality, such as echo and reverse a message that is sent. Another feature of the custom server is that the client can send state information and retrieve it again using another call. The state is stored temporarily in a session state. Although it's a simple scenario, you get the idea of what's needed to set this up.

The `TcpServer` sample code is implemented as a Console Application (Package) and makes use of the following dependencies and namespaces:

Dependencies

```
NETStandard.Library
```

Namespaces

```
System
System.Collections
System.Collections.Concurrent
System.Linq
System.Net.Sockets
System.Text
System.Threading
System.Threading.Tasks
static System.Console
static TcpServer.CustomProtocol
```

The custom TCP listener supports a few requests, as shown in the following table.

REQUEST	DESCRIPTION
HELO::v1.0	This command needs to be sent after initiating the connection. Other commands will not be accepted.
ECHO::message	The ECHO command returns the message to the caller.
REV::message	The REV command reserves the message and returns it to the caller.
BYE	The BYE command closes the connection.
SET::key=value	The SET command sets the server-side state that can be retrieved with the GET command.
GET::key	

The first line of the request is a session-identifier prefixed by ID. This needs to be sent with every request except the HELO request. This is used as a state identifier.

All the constants of the protocol are defined in the static class CustomProtocol (code file TcpServer/CustomProtocol.cs):

```
public static class CustomProtocol
{
  public const string SESSIONID = "ID";
  public const string COMMANDHELO = "HELO";
  public const string COMMANDECHO = "ECO";
  public const string COMMANDREV = "REV";
  public const string COMMANDBYE = "BYE";
  public const string COMMANDSET = "SET";
  public const string COMMANDGET = "GET";

  public const string STATUSOK = "OK";
  public const string STATUSCLOSED = "CLOSED";
  public const string STATUSINVALID = "INV";
  public const string STATUSUNKNOWN = "UNK";
  public const string STATUSNOTFOUND = "NOTFOUND";
  public const string STATUSTIMEOUT = "TIMOUT";

  public const string SEPARATOR = "::";

  public static readonly TimeSpan SessionTimeout = TimeSpan.FromMinutes(2);
}
```

The Run method (which is invoked from the Main method) starts a timer that cleans up all the session state every minute. The major functionality of the Run method is the start of the server by invoking the method RunServerAsync (code file TcpServer/Program.cs):

```
static void Main()
{
  var p = new Program();
  p.Run();
}

public void Run()
{
  using (var timer = new Timer(TimerSessionCleanup, null,
    TimeSpan.FromMinutes(1), TimeSpan.FromMinutes(1)))
  {
    RunServerAsync().Wait();
  }
}
```

The most important part of the server regarding the TcpListener class is in the method RunServerAsync. The TcpListener is instantiated using the constructor the IP address and port number where the listener can be accessed. Calling the `Start` method, the listener starts listening for client connections. The `AcceptTcpClientAsync` waits until a client connects. As soon as a client is connected, a `TcpClient` instance is returned that allows communication with the client. This instance is passed to the `RunClientRequest` method, where the request is dealt with.

```csharp
private async Task RunServerAsync()
{
  try
  {
    var listener = new TcpListener(IPAddress.Any, portNumber);
    WriteLine($"listener started at port {portNumber}");
    listener.Start();

    while (true)
    {
      WriteLine("waiting for client...");
      TcpClient client = await listener.AcceptTcpClientAsync();
      Task t = RunClientRequest(client);
    }
  }
  catch (Exception ex)
  {
    WriteLine($"Exception of type {ex.GetType().Name}, Message: {ex.Message}");
  }
}
```

To read and write from and to the client, the `GetStream` method of the `TcpClient` returns a `NetworkStream`. First you need to read the request from the client. You do this by using the `ReadAsync` method. The `ReadAsync` method fills a byte array. This byte array is converted to a string using the `Encoding` class. The information received is written to the console and passed to the `ParseRequest` helper method. Depending on the result of the `ParseRequest` method, an answer for the client is created and returned to the client using the `WriteAsync` method.

```csharp
private Task RunClientRequestAsync(TcpClient client)
{
  return Task.Run(async () =>
  {
    try
    {
      using (client)
      {
        WriteLine("client connected");

        using (NetworkStream stream = client.GetStream())
        {
          bool completed = false;
          do
          {
            byte[] readBuffer = new byte[1024];
            int read = await stream.ReadAsync(
                readBuffer, 0, readBuffer.Length);
            string request = Encoding.ASCII.GetString(readBuffer, 0, read);
            WriteLine($"received {request}");

            string sessionId;
            string result;
            byte[] writeBuffer = null;
            string response = string.Empty;

            ParseResponse resp = ParseRequest(
                request, out sessionId, out result);
            switch (resp)
```

```
                {
                  case ParseResponse.OK:
                    string content = $"{STATUSOK}::{SESSIONID}::{sessionId}";
                    if (!string.IsNullOrEmpty(result))
                    {
                      content += $"{SEPARATOR}{result}";
                    }
                    response = $"{STATUSOK}{SEPARATOR}{SESSIONID}{SEPARATOR}" +
                      $"{sessionId}{SEPARATOR}{content}";
                    break;
                  case ParseResponse.CLOSE:
                    response = $"{STATUSCLOSED}";
                    completed = true;
                    break;
                  case ParseResponse.TIMEOUT:
                    response = $"{STATUSTIMEOUT}";
                    break;
                  case ParseResponse.ERROR:
                    response = $"{STATUSINVALID}";
                    break;
                  default:
                    break;
                }
                writeBuffer = Encoding.ASCII.GetBytes(response);
                await stream.WriteAsync(writeBuffer, 0, writeBuffer.Length);
                await stream.FlushAsync();
                WriteLine($"returned {Encoding.ASCII.GetString(
                    writeBuffer, 0, writeBuffer.Length)}");
              } while (!completed);
            }
          }
        }
        catch (Exception ex)
        {
          WriteLine($"Exception in client request handling " +
              "of type {ex.GetType().Name}, Message: {ex.Message}");
        }
        WriteLine("client disconnected");
      });
  }
```

The `ParseRequest` method parses the request and filters out the session identifier. The first call to the server (HELO) is the only call where a session identifier is not passed from the client; here it is created using the `SessionManager`. With the second and later requests, `requestColl[0]` must contain ID, and `requestColl[1]` must contain the session identifier. Using this identifier, the `TouchSession` method updates the current time of the session identifier if the session is still valid. If it is not valid, a timeout is returned. For the functionality of the service, the `ProcessRequest` method is invoked:

```
private ParseResponse ParseRequest(string request, out string sessionId,
    out string response)
{
  sessionId = string.Empty;
  response = string.Empty;
  string[] requestColl = request.Split(
      new string[] { SEPARATOR }, StringSplitOptions.RemoveEmptyEntries);

  if (requestColl[0] == COMMANDHELO)  // first request
  {
    sessionId = _sessionManager.CreateSession();
  }
  else if (requestColl[0] == SESSIONID)  // any other valid request
  {
```

```
        sessionId = requestColl[1];

        if (!_sessionManager.TouchSession(sessionId))
        {
          return ParseResponse.TIMEOUT;
        }

        if (requestColl[2] == COMMANDBYE)
        {
          return ParseResponse.CLOSE;
        }
        if (requestColl.Length >= 4)
        {
          response = ProcessRequest(requestColl);
        }
      }
      else
      {
        return ParseResponse.ERROR;
      }
      return ParseResponse.OK;
    }
```

The `ProcessRequest` method contains a switch statement to handle the different requests. This method in turn makes use of the `CommandActions` class to echo or reverse the message received. To store and retrieve the session state, the `SessionManager` is used:

```
    private string ProcessRequest(string[] requestColl)
    {
      if (requestColl.Length < 4)
        throw new ArgumentException("invalid length requestColl");

      string sessionId = requestColl[1];
      string response = string.Empty;
      string requestCommand = requestColl[2];
      string requestAction = requestColl[3];

      switch (requestCommand)
      {
        case COMMANDECHO:
          response = _commandActions.Echo(requestAction);
          break;
        case COMMANDREV:
          response = _commandActions.Reverse(requestAction);
          break;
        case COMMANDSET:
          response = _sessionManager.ParseSessionData(sessionId, requestAction);
          break;
        case COMMANDGET:
          response = $"{_sessionManager.GetSessionData(sessionId, requestAction)}";
          break;
        default:
          response = STATUSUNKNOWN;
          break;
      }
      return response;
    }
```

The `CommandActions` class defines simple methods `Echo` and `Reverse` that return the action string or return the string reversed (code file `TcpServer/CommandActions.cs`):

```
    public class CommandActions
    {
```

```
    public string Reverse(string action) => string.Join("", action.Reverse());

    public string Echo(string action) => action;
}
```

After checking the main functionality of the server with the `Echo` and `Reverse` methods, it's time to get into the session management. What's needed on the server is an identifier and the time the session was last accessed for the purpose of removing the oldest sessions (code file `TcpServer/SessionManager.cs`):

```
public struct Session
{
  public string SessionId { get; set; }
  public DateTime LastAccessTime { get; set; }
}
```

The `SessionManager` contains thread-safe dictionaries that store all sessions and session data. When you're using multiple clients, the dictionaries can be accessed from multiple threads simultaneously. That's why thread-safe dictionaries from the namespace `System.Collections.Concurrent` are used. The `CreateSession` method creates a new session and adds it to the `_sessions` dictionary:

```
public class SessionManager
{
  private readonly ConcurrentDictionary<string, Session> _sessions =
    new ConcurrentDictionary<string, Session>();
  private readonly ConcurrentDictionary<string, Dictionary<string, string>>
    _sessionData =
    new ConcurrentDictionary<string, Dictionary<string, string>>();

  public string CreateSession()
  {
    string sessionId = Guid.NewGuid().ToString();
    if (_sessions.TryAdd(sessionId,
        new Session
        {
          SessionId = sessionId,
          LastAccessTime = DateTime.UtcNow
        }))
    {
      return sessionId;
    }
    else
    {
      return string.Empty;
    }
  }
  //...
}
```

The `CleanupAllSessions` method is called every minute from a timer thread to remove all sessions that haven't been used recently. This method in turn invokes `CleanupSession`, which removes a single session. `CleanupSession` is also invoked when the client sends the `BYE` message:

```
public void CleanupAllSessions()
{
  foreach (var session in _sessions)
  {
    if (session.Value.LastAccessTime + SessionTimeout >= DateTime.UtcNow)
    {
      CleanupSession(session.Key);
    }
  }
}
```

```
public void CleanupSession(string sessionId)
{
  Dictionary<string, string> removed;
  if (_sessionData.TryRemove(sessionId, out removed))
  {
    WriteLine($"removed {sessionId} from session data");
  }
  Session header;
  if (_sessions.TryRemove(sessionId, out header))
  {
    WriteLine($"removed {sessionId} from sessions");
  }
}
```

The `TouchSession` method updates the `LastAccessTime` of the session, and returns `false` if the session is no longer valid:

```
public bool TouchSession(string sessionId)
{
  Session oldHeader;
  if (!_sessions.TryGetValue(sessionId, out oldHeader))
  {
    return false;
  }

  Session updatedHeader = oldHeader;
  updatedHeader.LastAccessTime = DateTime.UtcNow;
  _sessions.TryUpdate(sessionId, updatedHeader, oldHeader);
  return true;
}
```

For setting session data, the request needs to be parsed. The action that is received for session data contains key and value separated by the equal sign, such as x=42. This is parsed from the `ParseSessionData` method, which in turn calls the `SetSessionData` method:

```
public string ParseSessionData(string sessionId, string requestAction)
{
  string[] sessionData = requestAction.Split('=');
  if (sessionData.Length != 2) return STATUSUNKNOWN;
  string key = sessionData[0];
  string value = sessionData[1];
  SetSessionData(sessionId, key, value);
  return $"{key}={value}";
}
```

`SetSessionData` either adds or updates the session state in the dictionary. The `GetSessionData` retrieves the value, or returns `NOTFOUND`:

```
public void SetSessionData(string sessionId, string key, string value)
{
  Dictionary<string, string> data;
  if (!_sessionData.TryGetValue(sessionId, out data))
  {
    data = new Dictionary<string, string>();
    data.Add(key, value);
    _sessionData.TryAdd(sessionId, data);
  }
  else
  {
    string val;
    if (data.TryGetValue(key, out val))
    {
      data.Remove(key);
```

```
      }
      data.Add(key, value);
    }
  }

  public string GetSessionData(string sessionId, string key)
  {
    Dictionary<string, string> data;
    if (_sessionData.TryGetValue(sessionId, out data))
    {
      string value;
      if (data.TryGetValue(key, out value))
      {
        return value;
      }
    }
    return STATUSNOTFOUND;
  }
}
```

After compiling the listener, you can start the program. Now you need a client to connect to the server.

Creating a TCP Client

The client for the example is a WPF desktop application with the name WPFAppTCPClient. This application allows connecting to the TCP server as well as sending all the different commands that are supported by the custom protocol.

> **NOTE** *At the time of writing this book, the* TcpClient *class is not available with Windows apps. You could instead use socket classes, which are covered later in this chapter, to access this TCP server.*

The user interface of the application is shown in Figure 25-4. The left-upper part allows connecting to the server. In the top-right part, a ComboBox lists all commands, and the Send button sends the command to the server. In the middle section, the session identifier and the status of the request sent will be shown. The controls in the lower part show the information received from the server and allow you to clear this information.

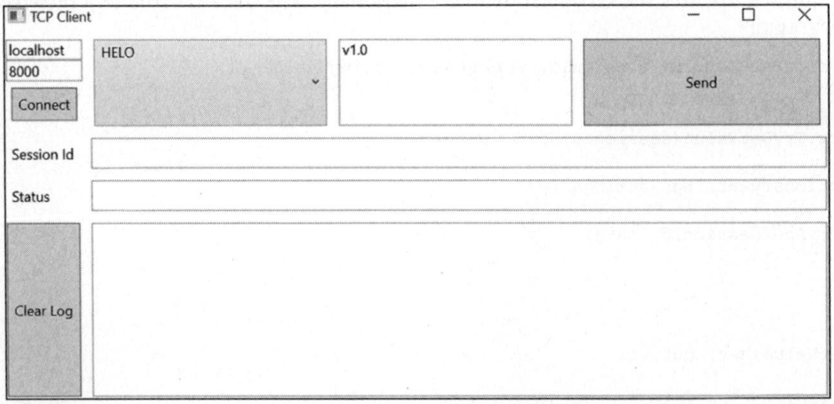

FIGURE 25-4

The classes CustomProtocolCommand and CustomProtocolCommands are used for data binding in the user interface. With CustomProtocolCommand, the Name property shows the name of the command while the Action property is the data that is entered by the user to send with the command. The class CustomProtocolCommands contains a list of the commands that are bound to the ComboBox (code file WPFAppTcpClient/CustomProtocolCommands.cs):

```csharp
public class CustomProtocolCommand
{
  public CustomProtocolCommand(string name)
      : this(name, null)
  {
  }

  public CustomProtocolCommand(string name, string action)
  {
    Name = name;
    Action = action;
  }

  public string Name { get; }
  public string Action { get; set; }

  public override string ToString() => Name;
}

public class CustomProtocolCommands : IEnumerable<CustomProtocolCommand>
{
  private readonly List<CustomProtocolCommand> _commands =
      new List<CustomProtocolCommand>();

  public CustomProtocolCommands()
  {
    string[] commands = { "HELO", "BYE", "SET", "GET", "ECO", "REV" };
    foreach (var command in commands)
    {
      _commands.Add(new CustomProtocolCommand(command));
    }
    _commands.Single(c => c.Name == "HELO").Action = "v1.0";
  }

  public IEnumerator<CustomProtocolCommand> GetEnumerator() =>
      _commands.GetEnumerator();

  IEnumerator IEnumerable.GetEnumerator() => _commands.GetEnumerator();
}
```

The class MainWindow contains properties that are bound to the XAML code and methods that are invoked based on user interactions. This class creates an instance of the TcpClient class and several properties that are bound to the user interface.

```csharp
public partial class MainWindow : Window, INotifyPropertyChanged, IDisposable
{
  private TcpClient _client = new TcpClient();
  private readonly CustomProtocolCommands _commands =
    new CustomProtocolCommands();

  public MainWindow()
  {
    InitializeComponent();
  }

  private string _remoteHost = "localhost";
```

```
public string RemoteHost
{
  get { return _remoteHost; }
  set { SetProperty(ref _remoteHost, value); }
}

private int _serverPort = 8800;
public int ServerPort
{
  get { return _serverPort; }
  set { SetProperty(ref _serverPort, value); }
}

private string _sessionId;
public string SessionId
{
  get { return _sessionId; }
  set { SetProperty(ref _sessionId, value); }
}

private CustomProtocolCommand _activeCommand;
public CustomProtocolCommand ActiveCommand
{
  get { return _activeCommand; }
  set { SetProperty(ref _activeCommand, value); }
}

private string _log;
public string Log
{
  get { return _log; }
  set { SetProperty(ref _log, value); }
}

private string _status;
public string Status
{
  get { return _status; }
  set { SetProperty(ref _status, value); }
}
//...
}
```

The method OnConnect is called when the user clicks the Connect button. The connection to the TCP
server is made, invoking the ConnectAsync method of the TcpClient class. In case the connection is in
a stale mode, and the OnConnect method is invoked once more, a SocketException is thrown where the
ErrorCode is set to 0x2748. A C# 6 exception filter is used here to handle this case of the SocketException
and create a new TcpClient, so invoking OnConnect once more likely succeeds:

```
private async void OnConnect(object sender, RoutedEventArgs e)
{
  try
  {
    await _client.ConnectAsync(RemoteHost, ServerPort);
  }
  catch (SocketException ex) when (ex.ErrorCode == 0x2748)
  {
    _client.Close();
    _client = new TcpClient();
    MessageBox.Show("please retry connect");
```

```
    }
    catch (Exception ex)
    {
      MessageBox.Show(ex.Message);
    }
  }
```

Sending requests to the TCP server is handled by the method `OnSendCommand`. The code here is very similar to the sending and receiving code on the server. The `GetStream` method returns a `NetworkStream`, and this is used to write (`WriteAsync`) data to the server and read (`ReadAsync`) data from the server:

```
private async void OnSendCommand(object sender, RoutedEventArgs e)
{
  try
  {
    if (!VerifyIsConnected()) return;
    NetworkStream stream = _client.GetStream();
    byte[] writeBuffer = Encoding.ASCII.GetBytes(GetCommand());
    await stream.WriteAsync(writeBuffer, 0, writeBuffer.Length);
    await stream.FlushAsync();
    byte[] readBuffer = new byte[1024];
    int read = await stream.ReadAsync(readBuffer, 0, readBuffer.Length);
    string messageRead = Encoding.ASCII.GetString(readBuffer, 0, read);
    Log += messageRead + Environment.NewLine;
    ParseMessage(messageRead);
  }
  catch (Exception ex)
  {
    MessageBox.Show(ex.Message);
  }
}
```

To build up the data that can be sent to the server, the `GetCommand` method is invoked from within `OnSendCommand`. `GetCommand` in turn invokes the method `GetSessionHeader` to build up the session identifier, and then takes the `ActiveCommand` property (of type `CustomProtocolCommand`) that contains the selected command name and the entered data:

```
private string GetCommand() =>
    $"{GetSessionHeader()}{ActiveCommand?.Name}::{ActiveCommand?.Action}";

private string GetSessionHeader()
{
  if (string.IsNullOrEmpty(SessionId)) return string.Empty;
  return $"ID::{SessionId}::";
}
```

The `ParseMessage` method is used after the data is received from the server. This method splits up the message to set the `Status` and `SessionId` properties:

```
private void ParseMessage(string message)
{
  if (string.IsNullOrEmpty(message)) return;

  string[] messageColl = message.Split(
      new string[] { "::" }, StringSplitOptions.RemoveEmptyEntries);
  Status = messageColl[0];
  SessionId = GetSessionId(messageColl);
}
```

When you run the application, you can connect to the server, select commands, set values for echo and reverse returns, and see all the messages coming from the server, as shown in Figure 25-5.

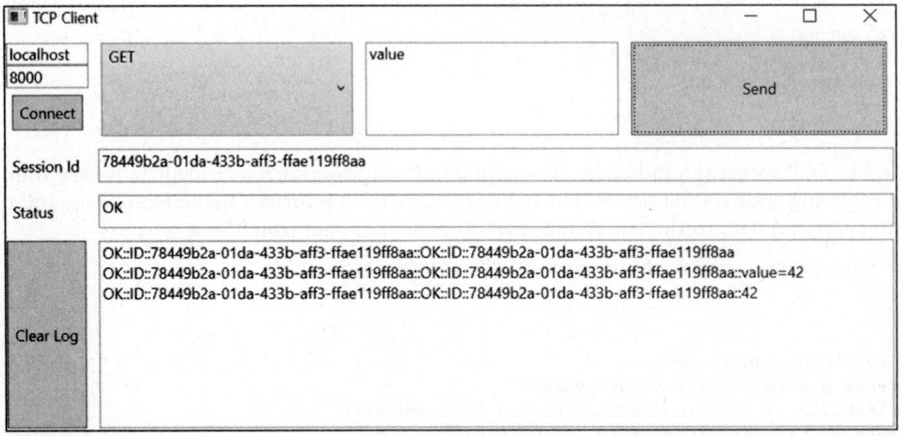

FIGURE 25-5

TCP vs. UDP

The next protocol covered is UDP (User Datagram Protocol). UDP is a simple protocol with little overhead. Before sending and receiving data with TCP, a connection needs to be made. This is not necessary with UDP. With UDP, just start sending or receiving. Of course, that means that UDP has less overhead than TCP, but it is also more unreliable. When you send data with UDP, you don't get information when this data is received. UDP is often used for situations in which the speed and performance requirements outweigh the reliability requirements—for example, video streaming. UDP also offers broadcasting messages to a group of nodes. On the other hand, TCP offers a number of features to confirm the delivery of data. TCP provides error correction and retransmission in the case of lost or corrupted packets. Last, but hardly least, TCP buffers incoming and outgoing data and guarantees that a sequence of packets scrambled in transmission is reassembled before delivery to the application. Even with the extra overhead, TCP is the most widely used protocol across the Internet because of its high reliability.

USING UDP

To demonstrate UDP, you create two Console Application (Package) projects that show various features of UDP: directly sending data to a host, broadcasting data to all hosts on the local network, and multicasting data to a group of nodes that belong to the same group.

The `UdpSender` and `UdpReceiver` projects use the following dependencies and namespaces:

Dependencies

```
NETStandard.Library
System.Net.NameResolution
```

Namespaces

```
System
System.Linq
System.Net
```

```
System.Net.Sockets
System.Text
System.Threading.Tasks
static System.Console
```

Building a UDP Receiver

Start with the receiving application. This application makes use of command-line arguments where you can control the different features of the application. A command-line argument that is required is -p, which specifies the port number where the receiver is available to receive data. An optional argument is -g with a group address for multicasting. The ParseCommandLine method parses the command-line arguments and puts the results into the variables port and groupAddress (code file UdpReceiver/ Program.cs):

```
static void Main(string[] args)
{
  int port;
  string groupAddress;
  if (!ParseCommandLine(args, out port, out groupAddress))
  {
    ShowUsage();
    return;
  }
  ReaderAsync(port, groupAddress).Wait();
  ReadLine();
}

private static void ShowUsage()
{
  WriteLine("Usage: UdpReceiver -p port  [-g groupaddress]");
}
```

The Reader method creates a UdpClient object with the port number that's passed in the program arguments. The ReceiveAsync method waits until some data arrives. This data can be found with the UdpReceiveResult with the Buffer property. After the data is encoded to a string, it's written to the console to continue the loop and wait for the next data to receive:

```
private static async Task ReaderAsync(int port, string groupAddress)
{
  using (var client = new UdpClient(port))
  {
    if (groupAddress != null)
    {
      client.JoinMulticastGroup(IPAddress.Parse(groupAddress));
      WriteLine(
          $"joining the multicast group {IPAddress.Parse(groupAddress)}");
    }

    bool completed = false;
    do
    {
      WriteLine("starting the receiver");
      UdpReceiveResult result = await client.ReceiveAsync();
      byte[] datagram = result.Buffer;
      string received = Encoding.UTF8.GetString(datagram);
      WriteLine($"received {received}");
      if (received == "bye")
```

```
      {
        completed = true;
      }
    } while (!completed);
    WriteLine("receiver closing");

    if (groupAddress != null)
    {
      client.DropMulticastGroup(IPAddress.Parse(groupAddress));
    }
  }
}
```

When you start the application, it waits for a sender to send data. For the time being, ignore the multicast group and just use the argument with the port number because multicasting is discussed after you create the sender.

Creating a UDP Sender

The UDP sender application also enables you to configure it by passing command-line options. It has more options than the receiving application. Besides the command-line argument -p to specify the port number, the sender allows -b for a broadcast to all nodes in the local network, -h to identify a specific host, -g to specify a group, and -ipv6 to indicate that IPv6 should be used instead of IPv4 (code file UdpSender/ Program.cs):

```
static void Main(string[] args)
{
  int port;
  string hostname;
  bool broadcast;
  string groupAddress;
  bool ipv6;
  if (!ParseCommandLine(args, out port, out hostname, out broadcast,
      out groupAddress, out ipv6))
  {
    ShowUsage();
    ReadLine();
    return;
  }
  IPEndpoint endpoint = GetIPEndPoint(port, hostname, broadcast,
      groupAddress, ipv6).Result;
  Sender(endpoint, broadcast, groupAddress).Wait();
  WriteLine("Press return to exit...");
  ReadLine();
}

private static void ShowUsage()
{
  WriteLine("Usage: UdpSender -p port [-g groupaddress | -b | -h hostname] " +
      "[-ipv6]");
  WriteLine("\t-p port number\tEnter a port number for the sender");
  WriteLine("\t-g group address\tGroup address in the range 224.0.0.0 " +
      "to 239.255.255.255");
  WriteLine("\t-b\tFor a broadcast");
  WriteLine("\t-h hostname\tUse the hostname option if the message should " +
      "be sent to a single host");
}
```

To send data, you need an IPEndPoint. Depending on the program arguments, you create this in different ways. With a broadcast, IPv4 defines the address 255.255.255.255 that is returned from

`IPAddress.Broadcast`. There's no IPv6 address for broadcast because IPv6 doesn't support broadcasts. IPv6's replacement for broadcasts are multicasts. Multicasts have been added to IPv4 as well. When you're passing a hostname, the hostname is resolved using DNS lookup using the `Dns` class. The method `GetHostEntryAsync` returns an `IPHostEntry` where the `IPAddress` can be retrieved from the `AddressList` property. Depending on whether IPv4 or IPv6 is used, a different `IPAddress` is taken from this list. Depending on your network environment, only one of these address types might work. If a group address is passed to the method, the address is parsed using `IPAddress.Parse`:

```csharp
public static async Task<IPEndPoint> GetIPEndPoint(int port, string hostName,
    bool broadcast, string groupAddress, bool ipv6)
{
  IPEndPoint endpoint = null;
  try
  {
    if (broadcast)
    {
      endpoint = new IPEndPoint(IPAddress.Broadcast, port);
    }
    else if (hostName != null)
    {
      IPHostEntry hostEntry = await Dns.GetHostEntryAsync(hostName);
      IPAddress address = null;
      if (ipv6)
      {
        address = hostEntry.AddressList.Where(
            a => a.AddressFamily == AddressFamily.InterNetworkV6)
            .FirstOrDefault();
      }
      else
      {
        address = hostEntry.AddressList.Where(
            a => a.AddressFamily == AddressFamily.InterNetwork)
            .FirstOrDefault();
      }

      if (address == null)
      {
        Func<string> ipversion = () => ipv6 ? "IPv6" : "IPv4";
        WriteLine($"no {ipversion()} address for {hostName}");
        return null;
      }
      endpoint = new IPEndPoint(address, port);
    }
    else if (groupAddress != null)
    {
      endpoint = new IPEndPoint(IPAddress.Parse(groupAddress), port);
    }
    else
    {
      throw new InvalidOperationException($"{nameof(hostName)}, "
        + "{nameof(broadcast)}, or {nameof(groupAddress)} must be set");
    }
  }
  catch (SocketException ex)
  {
    WriteLine(ex.Message);
  }
  return endpoint;
}
```

Now, regarding the UDP protocol, the most important part of the sender follows. After creating a `UdpClient` instance and converting a string to a byte array, data is sent using the `SendAsync` method. Note that neither the receiver needs to listen nor the sender needs to connect. UDP is really simple. However, in a case in which the sender sends the data to nowhere—nobody receives the data—you also don't get any error messages:

```
private async Task Sender(IPEndpoint endpoint, bool broadcast,
    string groupAddress)
{
  try
  {
    string localhost = Dns.GetHostName();
    using (var client = new UdpClient())
    {
      client.EnableBroadcast = broadcast;
      if (groupAddress != null)
      {
        client.JoinMulticastGroup(IPAddress.Parse(groupAddress));
      }

      bool completed = false;
      do
      {
        WriteLine("Enter a message or bye to exit");
        string input = ReadLine();
        WriteLine();
        completed = input == "bye";
        byte[] datagram = Encoding.UTF8.GetBytes($"{input} from {localhost}");
        int sent = await client.SendAsync(datagram, datagram.Length, endpoint);
      } while (!completed);

      if (groupAddress != null)
      {
        client.DropMulticastGroup(IPAddress.Parse(groupAddress));
      }
    }
  }
  catch (SocketException ex)
  {
    WriteLine(ex.Message);
  }
}
```

Now you can start the receiver with this option:

```
-p 9400
```

and the sender with this option:

```
-p 9400 -h localhost
```

You can enter data in the sender that will arrive in the receiver. If you stop the receiver, you can go on sending without detecting any error. You can also try to use a hostname instead of localhost and run the receiver on a different system.

With the sender, you can add the -b option and remove the hostname to send a broadcast to all nodes listening to port 9400 on the same network:

```
-p 9400 -b
```

Be aware that broadcasts don't cross most routers, and of course you can't use broadcasts on the Internet. This situation is different with multicasts, discussed next.

Using Multicasts

Broadcasts don't cross routers, but multicasts can. Multicasts have been invented to send messages to a group of systems—all nodes that belong to the same group. With IPv4, specific IP addresses are reserved for multicast use. The addresses start with 224.0.0.0 to 239.255.255.253. Many of these addresses are reserved for specific protocols—for example, for routers—but 239.0.0.0/8 can be used privately within an organization. This is very similar to IPv6, which has well-known IPv6 multicast addresses for different routing protocols. Addresses f::/16 are local within an organization; addresses ffxe::/16 have global scope and can be routed over public Internet.

For a sender or receiver to use multicasts, it must join a multicast group by invoking the `JoinMulticastGroup` method of the `UdpClient`:

```
client.JoinMulticastGroup(IPAddress.Parse(groupAddress));
```

To leave the group again, you can invoke the method `DropMulticastGroup`:

```
client.DropMulticastGroup(IPAddress.Parse(groupAddress));
```

When you start both the receiver and sender with these options,

```
-p 9400 -g 230.0.0.1
```

they both belong to the same group, and multicasting is in action. As with broadcasting, you can start multiple receivers and multiple senders. The receivers will receive nearly all messages from each receiver.

USING SOCKETS

The HTTP protocol is based on TCP, and thus the `HttpXX` classes offered an abstraction layer over the `TcpXX` classes. The `TcpXX` classes, however, give you more control. You can even get more control than offered by the `TcpXX` or `UdpXX` classes with sockets. With sockets, you can use different protocols, not only protocols based on TCP or UDP, and also create your own protocol. What might be even more important is that you can have more control over TCP- or UDP-based protocols.

The `SocketServerSender` and `SocketClient` projects are implemented as Console Application (Package) and use these dependencies and namespaces:

Dependencies

```
NETStandard.Library
System.Net.NameResolution
```

Namespaces

```
System
System.Linq
System.IO
System.Net
System.Net.Sockets
System.Text
System.Threading
System.Threading.Tasks
static System.Console
```

Creating a Listener Using Sockets

Let's start with a server that listens to incoming requests. The server requires a port number that is expected with the program arguments. With this, it invokes the `Listener` method (code file `SocketServer/Program.cs`):

```
static void Main(string[] args)
{
  if (args.Length != 1)
  {
    ShowUsage();
    return;
  }
  int port;
  if (!int.TryParse(args[0], out port))
  {
    ShowUsage();
    return;
  }
  Listener(port);
  ReadLine();
}

private void ShowUsage()
{
  WriteLine("SocketServer port");
}
```

The most important code with regard to sockets is in the following code snippet. The listener creates a new `Socket` object. With the constructor, the `AddressFamily`, `SocketType`, and `ProtocolType` are supplied. The `AddressFamily` is a large enumeration that offers many different networks. Examples are *DECnet*, which was released 1975 by Digital Equipment and used as main network communication between PDP-11 systems; Banyan VINES, which was used to connect client machines; and, of course, `InetnetWork` for IPv4 and `InternetWorkV6` for IPv6. As mentioned previously, you can use sockets for a large number of networking protocols. The second parameter `SocketType` specifies the kind of socket. Examples are `Stream` for TCP, `Dgram` for UDP, or `Raw` for raw sockets. The third parameter is an enumeration for the `ProtocolType`. Examples are `IP`, `Ucmp`, `Udp`, `IPv6`, and `Raw`. The settings you choose need to match. For example, using TCP with IPv4, the address family must be `InterNetwork`, the socket type `Stream`, and the protocol type `Tcp`. To create a UDP communication with IPv4, the address family needs to be set to `InterNetwork`, the socket type `Dgram`, and the protocol type `Udp`.

```
public static void Listener(int port)
{
  var listener = new Socket(AddressFamily.InterNetwork, SocketType.Stream,
    ProtocolType.Tcp);
  listener.ReceiveTimeout = 5000; // receive timout 5 seconds
  listener.SendTimeout = 5000; // send timeout 5 seconds
  // etc.
```

The listener socket returned from the constructor is bound to an IP address and port numbers. With the sample code, the listener is bound to all local IPv4 addresses and the port number is specified with the argument. Calling the `Listen` method starts the listening mode of the socket. The socket can now accept incoming connection requests. Specifying the parameter with the `Listen` method defines the size of the backlog queue—how many clients can connect concurrently before their connection is dealt with:

```
public static void Listener(int port)
{
  // etc.
```

```
listener.Bind(new IPEndPoint(IPAddress.Any, port));
listener.Listen(backlog: 15);

WriteLine($"listener started on port {port}");
// etc.
```

Waiting for the client to connect happens in the `Accept` method of the `Socket` class. This method blocks the thread until a client connects. After a client connects, this method needs to be invoked again to fulfill requests of other clients; this is why this method is called within a `while` loop. For the listening, a separate task, which can be canceled from the calling thread, is started. The task to read and write using the socket happens within the method `CommunicateWithClientUsingSocketAsync`. This method receives the `Socket` instance that is bound to the client to read and write:

```
public static void Listener(int port)
{
  // etc.
  var cts = new CancellationTokenSource();

  var tf = new TaskFactory(TaskCreationOptions.LongRunning,
    TaskContinuationOptions.None);
  tf.StartNew(() =>  // listener task
  {
    WriteLine("listener task started");
    while (true)
    {
      if (cts.Token.IsCancellationRequested)
      {
        cts.Token.ThrowIfCancellationRequested();
        break;
      }
      WriteLine("waiting for accept");
      Socket client = listener.Accept();
      if (!client.Connected)
      {
        WriteLine("not connected");
        continue;
      }
      WriteLine($"client connected local address " +
        $"{((IPEndPoint)client.LocalEndPoint).Address} and port " +
        $"{((IPEndPoint)client.LocalEndPoint).Port}, remote address " +
        $"{((IPEndPoint)client.RemoteEndPoint).Address} and port " +
        $"{((IPEndPoint)client.RemoteEndPoint).Port}");

      Task t = CommunicateWithClientUsingSocketAsync(client);
    }
    listener.Dispose();
    WriteLine("Listener task closing");
  }, cts.Token);

  WriteLine("Press return to exit");
  ReadLine();
  cts.Cancel();
}
```

For the communication with the client, a new task is created. This frees the listener task to immediately make the next iteration to wait for the next client connection. The `Receive` method of the `Socket` class accepts a buffer where data can be read to as well as flags for the socket. This byte array is converted to a string and sent back to the client with a small change using the `Send` method:

```
private static Task CommunicateWithClientUsingSocketAsync(Socket socket)
{
```

```
return Task.Run(() =>
{
  try
  {
    using (socket)
    {
      bool completed = false;
      do
      {
        byte[] readBuffer = new byte[1024];
        int read = socket.Receive(readBuffer, 0, 1024, SocketFlags.None);
        string fromClient = Encoding.UTF8.GetString(readBuffer, 0, read);
        WriteLine($"read {read} bytes: {fromClient}");
        if (string.Compare(fromClient, "shutdown", ignoreCase: true) == 0)
        {
          completed = true;
        }
        byte[] writeBuffer = Encoding.UTF8.GetBytes($"echo {fromClient}");
        int send = socket.Send(writeBuffer);
        WriteLine($"sent {send} bytes");
      } while (!completed);
      WriteLine("closed stream and client socket");
    }
    catch (Exception ex)
    {
      WriteLine(ex.Message);
    }
  });
}
```

The server is ready as it is. However, let's look at different ways to make the read and write communication by extending the abstraction level.

Using NetworkStream with Sockets

You've already used the `NetworkStream` class with the `TcpClient` and `TcpListener` classes. The `NetworkStream` constructor allows passing a `Socket`, so you can use the `Stream` methods `Read` and `Write` instead of socket's `Send` and `Receive` methods. With the constructor of the `NetworkStream` you can define whether the stream should own the socket. If—as in this code snippet—the stream owns the socket, the socket will be closed when the stream is closed (code file `SocketServer/Program.cs`):

```
private static async Task CommunicateWithClientUsingNetworkStreamAsync(
  Socket socket)
{
  try
  {
    using (var stream = new NetworkStream(socket, ownsSocket: true))
    {
      bool completed = false;
      do
      {
        byte[] readBuffer = new byte[1024];
        int read = await stream.ReadAsync(readBuffer, 0, 1024);
        string fromClient = Encoding.UTF8.GetString(readBuffer, 0, read);
        WriteLine($"read {read} bytes: {fromClient}");
        if (string.Compare(fromClient, "shutdown", ignoreCase: true) == 0)
        {
```

```
                completed = true;
            }
            byte[] writeBuffer = Encoding.UTF8.GetBytes($"echo {fromClient}");

            await stream.WriteAsync(writeBuffer, 0, writeBuffer.Length);

        } while (!completed);
    }
    WriteLine("closed stream and client socket");
}
catch (Exception ex)
{
    WriteLine(ex.Message);
}
}
```

To use this method in the code sample, you need to change the `Listener` method to invoke the method `CommunicateWithClientUsingNetworkStreamAsync` instead of the method `CommunicateWithClientUsingSocketAsync`.

Using Readers and Writers with Sockets

Let's add one more abstraction layer. Because the `NetworkStream` derives from the `Stream` class, you can also use readers and writers to access the socket. What you need to pay attention to is the lifetime of the readers and writers. Calling the `Dispose` method of a reader or writer also disposes the underlying stream. That's why a constructor of the `StreamReader` and `StreamWriter` was selected where the `leaveOption` argument can be set to true. With this in place, the underlying stream is not disposed on disposing the readers and writers. The `NetworkStream` is disposed on the end of the outer `using` statement, and this in turn closes the socket because here the socket is owned. There's another aspect that you need to be aware of when using writers with sockets: By default the writer doesn't flush the data, so they are kept in the cache until the cache is full. Using network streams, you might need to get an answer faster. Here you can set the `AutoFlush` property to true (an alternative would be to invoke the `FlushAsync` method):

```
public static async Task CommunicateWithClientUsingReadersAndWritersAsync(
    Socket socket)
{
    try
    {
        using (var stream = new NetworkStream(socket, ownsSocket: true))
        using (var reader = new StreamReader(stream, Encoding.UTF8, false,
            8192, leaveOpen: true))
        using (var writer = new StreamWriter(stream, Encoding.UTF8,
            8192, leaveOpen: true))
        {
            writer.AutoFlush = true;

            bool completed = false;
            do
            {
                string fromClient = await reader.ReadLineAsync();
                WriteLine($"read {fromClient}");
                if (string.Compare(fromClient, "shutdown", ignoreCase: true) == 0)
                {
                    completed = true;
                }
```

```
                   await writer.WriteLineAsync($"echo {fromClient}");

             } while (!completed);
          }
          WriteLine("closed stream and client socket");
       }
       catch (Exception ex)
       {
          WriteLine(ex.Message);
       }
    }
```

To use this method in the code sample, you need to change the `Listener` method to invoke the method `CommunicateWithClientUsingReadersAndWritersAsync` instead of the method `CommunicateWithClientUsingSocketAsync`.

> **NOTE** *Streams, readers, and writers are explained in detail in Chapter 23.*

Implementing a Receiver Using Sockets

The receiver application `SocketClient` is implemented as a Console Application (Package) as well. With the command-line arguments, the hostname and the port number of the server need to be passed. With a successful command-line parsing, the method `SendAndReceive` is invoked to communicate with the server (code file `SocketClient/Program.cs`):

```
static void Main(string[] args)
{
   if (args.Length != 2)
   {
      ShowUsage();
      return;
   }
   string hostName = args[0];
   int port;
   if (!int.TryParse(args[1], out port))
   {
      ShowUsage();
      return;
   }
   WriteLine("press return when the server is started");
   ReadLine();
   SendAndReceive(hostName, port).Wait();
   ReadLine();
}

private static void ShowUsage()
{
   WriteLine("Usage: SocketClient server port");
}
```

The `SendAndReceive` method uses DNS name resolution to get the `IPHostEntry` from the hostname. This `IPHostEntry` is used to get an IPv4 address of the host. After the `Socket` instance is created (in the same way it was created for the server code), the address is used with the `Connect` method to make a connection to the server. After the connection was done, the methods `Sender` and `Receiver` are invoked that create different tasks, which enables you to run these methods concurrently. The receiver client can simultaneously read and write from and to the server:

```
public static async Task SendAndReceive(string hostName, int port)
{
  try
  {
    IPHostEntry ipHost = await Dns.GetHostEntryAsync(hostName);
    IPAddress ipAddress = ipHost.AddressList.Where(
      address => address.AddressFamily == AddressFamily.InterNetwork).First();
    if (ipAddress == null)
    {
      WriteLine("no IPv4 address");
      return;
    }

    using (var client = new Socket(AddressFamily.InterNetwork,
      SocketType.Stream, ProtocolType.Tcp))
    {
      client.Connect(ipAddress, port);
      WriteLine("client successfully connected");
      var stream = new NetworkStream(client);
      var cts = new CancellationTokenSource();

      Task tSender = Sender(stream, cts);
      Task tReceiver = Receiver(stream, cts.Token);
      await Task.WhenAll(tSender, tReceiver);
    }
  }
  catch (SocketException ex)
  {
    WriteLine(ex.Message);
  }
}
```

> **NOTE** *If you change the filtering of the address list to get an IPv6 address instead of a IPv4 address, you also need to change the* Socket *invocation to create a socket for the IPv6 address family.*

The Sender method asks the user for input and sends this data to the network stream with the WriteAsync method. The Receiver method receives data from the stream with the ReadAsync method. After the user enters the termination string, cancellation is sent from the Sender task via a CancellationToken:

```
public static async Task Sender(NetworkStream stream,
  CancellationTokenSource cts)
{
  WriteLine("Sender task");
  while (true)
  {
    WriteLine("enter a string to send, shutdown to exit");
    string line = ReadLine();
    byte[] buffer = Encoding.UTF8.GetBytes($"{line}\r\n");
    await stream.WriteAsync(buffer, 0, buffer.Length);
    await stream.FlushAsync();
    if (string.Compare(line, "shutdown", ignoreCase: true) == 0)
```

```
      {
        cts.Cancel();
        WriteLine("sender task closes");
        break;
      }
    }
  }
}

private const int ReadBufferSize = 1024;

public static async Task Receiver(NetworkStream stream,
  CancellationToken token)
{
  try
  {
    stream.ReadTimeout = 5000;
    WriteLine("Receiver task");
    byte[] readBuffer = new byte[ReadBufferSize];
    while (true)
    {
      Array.Clear(readBuffer, 0, ReadBufferSize);
      int read = await stream.ReadAsync(readBuffer, 0, ReadBufferSize, token);
      string receivedLine = Encoding.UTF8.GetString(readBuffer, 0, read);
      WriteLine($"received {receivedLine}");
    }
  }
  catch (OperationCanceledException ex)
  {
    WriteLine(ex.Message);
  }
}
```

When you run both the client and server, you can see communication across TCP.

> **NOTE** *The sample code implements a TCP client and server. TCP requires a connection before sending and receiving data; this is done by calling the* Connect *method. For UDP, the* Connect *method could be invoked as well, but it doesn't do a connection. With UDP, instead of calling the* Connect *method, you can use the* SendTo *and* ReceiveFrom *methods instead. These methods require an* EndPoint *parameter where the endpoint is defined just when sending and receiving.*

> **NOTE** *Cancellation tokens are explained in Chapter 21.*

SUMMARY

This chapter described the .NET Framework classes available in the System.Net namespace for communication across networks. You have seen some of the .NET base classes that deal with opening client connections on the network and Internet, and how to send requests to and receive responses from servers.

As a rule of thumb, when programming with classes in the System.Net namespace, you should always try to use the most generic class possible. For instance, using the TcpClient class instead of the Socket class isolates your code from many of the lower-level socket details. Moving one step higher, the `HttpClient` class is an easy way to make use of the HTTP protocol.

This book covers much more networking than the core networking features you've seen in this chapter. Chapter 42 covers ASP.NET Web API to offer services using the HTTP protocol. In Chapter 43 you read about WebHooks and SignalR—two technologies that offers event-driven communication. Chapter 44 gives information about WCF (Windows Communication Foundation), a technology for communication with the old style web services approach that offers binary communication as well.

The next chapter is about the Composition Framework, previously known as Managed Extensiblity Framework (MEF).

26

Composition

WROX.COM CODE DOWNLOADS FOR THIS CHAPTER

The wrox.com code downloads for this chapter are found at www.wrox.com/go/
professionalcsharp6 on the Download Code tab. The code for this chapter is divided into the
following major examples:

- ➤ Attribute-Based Sample
- ➤ Convention-Based Sample
- ➤ UI Calculator (WPF and UWP)

INTRODUCTION

Microsoft Composition is a framework for creating independency between parts and containers. Parts
can be used from containers without the need for the container to know the implementation or other
details. The container just needs a contract—for example, an interface to use a part.

Microsoft Composition can be used with different scenarios, such as a dependency injection container,
or you can even use it for adding functionality to an application after the application is released by
dynamically loading add-ins into the application. To get into these scenarios, you need a foundation.

For making development of apps easier, it's a good practice to have separation of concerns (SoC). SoC
is a design principle for separating a program into different sections where each section has its own
responsibility. Having different sections allows you to reuse and update these sections independently
of each other.

Having a tight coupling between these sections or components makes it hard to reuse and update these components independently of each other. Low coupling—for example, by using interfaces—helps this goal of independence.

Using interfaces for coupling, and allowing them to develop independent of any concrete implementation, is known as the *dependency injection* design pattern. Dependency injection implements inversion of control where the control to define what implementation is used is reversed. The component for using an interface receives the implementation via a property (property injection) or via a constructor (constructor injection). Using a component just by an interface, it's not necessary to know about the implementation. Different implementations can be used for different scenarios—for example, with unit testing, a different implementation can be used that supplies test data.

Dependency injection can be implemented by using a *dependency injection container*. When you use a dependency injection container, the container defines for what interface which implementation should be used. Microsoft Composition can take the functionality of the container. This is one use case of this technology among the others.

> **NOTE** *Dependency injection is explained in detail in Chapter 31, "Patterns with XAML Apps." Chapter 31 shows the use of the dependency injection container* `Microsoft.Framework.DependencyInjection`.

Add-ins (or plug-ins) enable you to add functionality to an existing application. You can create a hosting application that gains more and more functionality over time—such functionality might be written by your team of developers, but different vendors can also extend your application by creating add-ins.

Today, add-ins are used with many different applications, such as Internet Explorer and Visual Studio. Internet Explorer is a hosting application that offers an add-in framework that is used by many companies to provide extensions when viewing web pages. The Shockwave Flash Object enables you to view web pages with Flash content. The Google toolbar offers specific Google features that can be accessed quickly from Internet Explorer. Visual Studio also has an add-in model that enables you to extend Visual Studio with different levels of extensions. Visual Studio add-ins makes use of the Managed Extensibility Framework (MEF), the first version of Microsoft Composition.

For your custom applications, it has always been possible to create an add-in model to dynamically load and use functionality from assemblies. However, all the issues associated with finding and using add-ins need to be resolved. You can accomplish that automatically by using Microsoft Composition. This technology helps to create boundaries and to remove dependencies between parts and the clients or callers that make use of the parts.

> **NOTE** *The previous version of Microsoft Composition was known as Microsoft Extensibility Framework (MEF). MEF 1.x is still available with the full .NET Framework in the namespace* `System.ComponentModel.Composition`. *The new namespace for Microsoft Composition is* `System.Composition`. *Microsoft Composition is available with NuGet packages.*
>
> *MEF 1.x offers different catalogs—for example, an* `AssemblyCatalog` *or a* `DirectoryCatalog`—*to find types within an assembly or within a directory. The new version of Microsoft Composition doesn't offer this feature. However, you can build this part on your own. Chapter 16, "Reflection, Metadata, and Dynamic Programming," shows you how to load assemblies dynamically, with both .NET 4.6 and .NET Core 5. You can use this information to build your own directory catalog.*

> **NOTE** *MEF (or Composition) has been available since .NET 4.0 for creating add-ins with .NET. The .NET Framework offers another technology for writing flexible applications that load add-ins dynamically: the Managed Add-in Framework (MAF). MAF has been available since .NET 3.5. MAF uses a pipeline for communication between the add-in and the host application that makes the development process more complex but offers separation of add-ins via app domains or even different processes. In that regard, Composition is the simpler of these technologies. MAF and MEF can be combined to get the advantage of each, but it doubles the work. MAF was not ported to .NET Core and is only available with the full framework.*

The major namespace covered in this chapter is `System.Composition`.

ARCHITECTURE OF THE COMPOSITION LIBRARY

Microsoft Composition is built with parts and containers, as shown in Figure 26-1. A container finds parts that are exported and connects imports to exports, thereby making parts available to the hosting application.

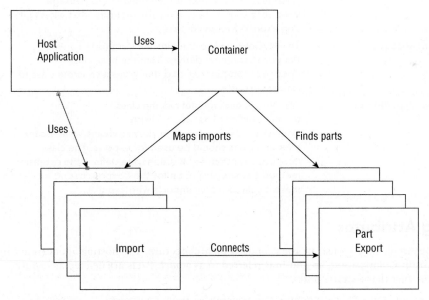

FIGURE 26-1

Here's the full picture of how parts are loaded. As mentioned, parts are found with exports. Exports can be defined using attributes, or with a fluent API from C# code. Multiple export providers can be connected in chains for customizing exports—for example, with a custom export provider to only allow parts for specific users or roles. The container uses export providers to connect imports to exports and is itself an export provider.

Microsoft Composition consists of the NuGet packages shown in Figure 26-2. This figure also shows the dependencies of the libraries.

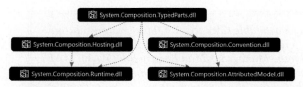

FIGURE 26-2

The following table explains the content of these NuGet packages.

NUGET PACKAGE	DESCRIPTION
System.Composition.AttributedModel	This NuGet package contains `Export` and `Import` attributes. This package allows using attributes to export and import parts.
System.Composition.Convention	With this NuGet package it's possible to use plain old CLR objects (POCO) as parts. Rules can be applied programmatically to define exports.
System.Composition.Runtime	This NuGet package contains the runtime and thus is needed from the hosting application. The class `CompositionContext` is contained in this package. `CompositionContext` is an abstract class that allows getting exports for the context.
System.Composition.Hosting	This NuGet package contains the `CompositionHost`. `CompositionHost` derives from the base class `CompositionContext` and thus gives a concrete class to retrieve exports.
System.Composition.TypedParts	This NuGet package defines the class `ContainerConfiguration`. With `ContainerConfiguration` you can define what assemblies and parts should be used for exports. The class `CompositionContextExtensions` defines the extension method `SatisfyImports` for the `CompositionContext` to make it easy to match imports with exports.

Composition Using Attributes

Let's start with a simple example to demonstrate the Composition architecture. The hosting application can load add-ins. With Microsoft Composition, an add-in is referred to as a *part*. Parts are defined as *exports* and are loaded into a container that *imports* parts.

The sample code for `AttributeBasedSample` defines these references and namespaces:

CalculatorContract (Class Library)

Namespaces

    System.Collections.Generic

SimpleCalculator (Class Library)

References

    CalculatorContract
    System.Composition.AttributedModel

Namespaces

```
System
System.Collections.Generic
System.Composition
```

AdvancedCalculator (Class Library)

References

```
CalculatorContract
System.Composition.AttributedModel
```

Namespaces

```
System
System.Collections.Generic
System.Composition
```

SimpleHost (Console Application)

References

```
CalculatorContract
SimpleCalculator
System.Composition.AttributedModel
System.Composition.Hosting
System.Composition.Runtime
System.Composition.TypedParts
```

Namespaces

```
System
System.Collections.Generic
System.Composition
System.Composition.Hosting
static System.Console
```

In this example, a Console Application (Package) is created to host calculator parts from a library. To create independence from the host and the calculator part, three projects are required. One project, `CalculatorContract`, holds the contracts that are used by both the add-in assembly and the hosting executable. The project `SimpleCalculator` contains the part and implements the contract defined by the contract assembly. The host uses the contract assembly to invoke the part.

The contracts in the assembly `CalculatorContract` are defined by two interfaces: `ICalculator` and `IOperation`. The `ICalculator` interface defines the methods `GetOperations` and `Operate`. The `GetOperations` method returns a list of all operations that the add-in calculator supports, and with the `Operate` method an operation is invoked. This interface is flexible in that the calculator can support different operations. If the interface defined `Add` and `Subtract` methods instead of the flexible `Operate` method, a new version of the interface would be required to support `Divide` and `Multiply` methods. With the `ICalculator` interface as it is defined in this example, however, the calculator can offer any number of operations with any number of operands (code file `AttributeBasedSample/CalculatorContract/ICalculator.cs`):

```
public interface ICalculator
{
  IList<IOperation> GetOperations();
  double Operate(IOperation operation, double[] operands);
}
```

The `ICalculator` interface uses the `IOperation` interface to return the list of operations and to invoke an operation. The `IOperation` interface defines the read-only properties `Name` and `NumberOperands` (code file `AttributeBasedSample/CalculatorContract/IOperation.cs`):

```
public interface IOperation
{
  string Name { get; }
  int NumberOperands { get; }
}
```

The `CalculatorContract` assembly doesn't require any reference to `System.Composition` assemblies. Only simple .NET interfaces are contained within it.

The add-in assembly `SimpleCalculator` contains classes that implement the interfaces defined by the contracts. The class `Operation` implements the interface `IOperation`. This class contains just two properties as defined by the interface. The interface defines `get` accessors of the properties; internal `set` accessors are used to set the properties from within the assembly (code file `AttributeBasedSample/SimpleCalculator/Operation.cs`):

```
public class Operation: IOperation
{
  public string Name { get; internal set; }
  public int NumberOperands { get; internal set; }
}
```

The `Calculator` class provides the functionality of this add-in by implementing the `ICalculator` interface. The `Calculator` class is exported as a part as defined by the `Export` attribute. This attribute is defined in the `System.Composition` namespace in the NuGet package `System.Composition.AttributedModel` (code file `AttributeBasedSample/SimpleCalculator/Calculator.cs`):

```
[Export(typeof(ICalculator))]
public class Calculator: ICalculator
{
  public IList<IOperation> GetOperations() =>
    new List<IOperation>()
    {
      new Operation { Name="+", NumberOperands=2},
      new Operation { Name="-", NumberOperands=2},
      new Operation { Name="/", NumberOperands=2},
      new Operation { Name="*", NumberOperands=2}
    };

  public double Operate(IOperation operation, double[] operands)
  {
    double result = 0;
    switch (operation.Name)
    {
      case "+":
        result = operands[0] + operands[1];
        break;
      case "-":
        result = operands[0]-operands[1];
        break;
      case "/":
        result = operands[0] / operands[1];
        break;
      case "*":
        result = operands[0] * operands[1];
        break;
      default:
        throw new InvalidOperationException($"invalid operation {operation.Name}");
```

```
    }
        return result;
    }
}
```

The hosting application is a Console Application (Package). The part uses an `Export` attribute to define what is exported; with the hosting application, the `Import` attribute defines what is used. Here, the `Import` attribute annotates the `Calculator` property that sets and gets an object implementing `ICalculator`. Therefore, any calculator add-in that implements this interface can be used here (code file `AttributeBasedSample/SimpleHost/Program.cs`):

```
class Program
{
  [Import]
  public ICalculator Calculator { get; set; }
  //etc.
}
```

In the entry method `Main` of the console application, a new instance of the `Program` class is created, and then the `Bootstrapper` method is invoked. In the `Bootstrapper` method, a `ContainerConfiguration` is created. With the `ContainerConfiguration`, a fluent API can be used to configure this object. The method `WithPart<Calculator>` finds the exports of the `Calculator` class to have it available from the composition host. The `CompositionHost` instance is created using the `CreateContainer` method of the `ContainerConfiguration` (code file `AttributeBasedSample/SimpleHost/Program.cs`):

```
public static void Main()
{
  var p = new Program();
  p.Bootstrapper();
  p.Run();
}

public void Bootstrapper()
{
  var configuration = new ContainerConfiguration()
    .WithPart<Calculator>();
  using (CompositionHost host = configuration.CreateContainer())
  {
    //etc.
  }
}
```

Besides using the method `WithPart` (which has overloads and generic versions as well as non-generic versions), you can also use `WithParts` to add a list of parts and use `WithAssembly` or `WithAssemblies` to add the exports of an assembly.

Using the `CompositionHost`, you can access exported parts with the `GetExport` and `GetExports` methods:

```
Calculator = host.GetExport<ICalculator>();
```

You can also use more "magic." Instead of specifying all the export types you need to access, you can use the `SatisfyImports` method that is an extension method for the `CompositionHost`. The first parameter requires an object with imports. Because the `Program` class itself defines a property that has an `Import` attribute applied, the instance of the `Program` class can be passed to the `SatisfyImports` method. After invoking `SatisfyImports`, you will see that the `Calculator` property of the `Program` class is filled (code file `AttributeBasedSample/SimpleHost/Program.cs`):

```
using (CompositionHost host = configuration.CreateContainer())
{
  host.SatisfyImports(this);
}
```

With the `Calculator` property, you can use the methods from the interface `ICalculator`. `GetOperations` invokes the methods of the previously created add-in, which returns four operations. After asking the user what operation should be invoked and requesting the operand values, the add-in method `Operate` is called:

```
public void Run()
{
  var operations = Calculator.GetOperations();
  var operationsDict = new SortedList<string, IOperation>();
  foreach (var item in operations)
  {
    WriteLine($"Name: {item.Name}, number operands: " +
      $"{item.NumberOperands}");
    operationsDict.Add(item.Name, item);
  }
  WriteLine();
  string selectedOp = null;
  do
  {
    try
    {
      Write("Operation? ");
      selectedOp =ReadLine();
      if (selectedOp.ToLower() == "exit" ||
        !operationsDict.ContainsKey(selectedOp))
          continue;
      var operation = operationsDict[selectedOp];
      double[] operands = new double[operation.NumberOperands];
      for (int i = 0; i < operation.NumberOperands; i++)
      {
        Write($"\t operand {i + 1}? ");
        string selectedOperand = ReadLine();
        operands[i] = double.Parse(selectedOperand);
      }
      WriteLine("calling calculator");
      double result = Calculator.Operate(operation, operands);
      WriteLine($"result: {result}");
    }
    catch (FormatException ex)
    {
      WriteLine(ex.Message);
      WriteLine();
      continue;
    }
  } while (selectedOp != "exit");
}
```

The output of one sample run of the application is shown here:

```
Name: +, number operands: 2
Name: -, number operands: 2
Name: /, number operands: 2
Name: *, number operands: 2
Operation? +
        operand 1? 3
        operand 2? 5
calling calculator
result: 8
Operation? -
        operand 1? 7
        operand 2? 2
calling calculator
result: 5
Operation? exit
```

Without any code changes in the host application, it is possible to use a completely different library for the parts. The project AdvancedCalculator defines a different implementation for the Calculator class to offer more operations. You can use this calculator in place of the other one by referencing the project AdvancedCalculator with the SimpleHost project.

Here, the Calculator class implements the additional operators %, ++, and -- (code file AttributeBasedSample/AdvancedCalculator/Calculator.cs):

```csharp
[Export(typeof(ICalculator))]
public class Calculator: ICalculator
{
  public IList<IOperation> GetOperations() =>
    new List<IOperation>()
    {
      new Operation { Name="+", NumberOperands=2},
      new Operation { Name="-", NumberOperands=2},
      new Operation { Name="/", NumberOperands=2},
      new Operation { Name="*", NumberOperands=2},
      new Operation { Name="%", NumberOperands=2},
      new Operation { Name="++", NumberOperands=1},
      new Operation { Name="—", NumberOperands=1}
    };

  public double Operate(IOperation operation, double[] operands)
  {
    double result = 0;
    switch (operation.Name)
    {
      case "+":
        result = operands[0] + operands[1];
        break;
      case "-":
        result = operands[0]—operands[1];
        break;
      case "/":
        result = operands[0] / operands[1];
        break;
      case "*":
        result = operands[0] * operands[1];
        break;
      case "%":
        result = operands[0] % operands[1];
        break;
      case "++":
        result = ++operands[0];
        break;
      case "—":
        result =—operands[0];
        break;
      default:
        throw new InvalidOperationException($"invalid operation {operation.Name}");
    }
    return result;
  }
}
```

> **NOTE** *With the* SimpleHost *you can't use both implementations of the* Calculator *at one time. You need to remove the reference* SimpleCalculator *before using the* AdvancedCalculator, *and the other way around. Later in this chapter, you see how multiple exports of the same type can be used with one container.*

Now you've seen imports, exports, and catalogs from the Composition architecture. In case you want to use existing classes where you can't add an attribute with Composition, you can use convention-based part registration, which is shown in the next section.

Convention-Based Part Registration

Convention-based registration not only allows exporting parts without using attributes, it also gives you more options to define what should be exported—for example, using naming conventions such as the class name ends with `PlugIn`, or `ViewModel`, or using the suffix name `Controller` to find all controllers.

This introduction to convention-based part registration builds the same example code shown previously using attributes, but attributes are no longer needed; therefore, the same code is not repeated here. The same contract interfaces `ICalculator` and `IOperation` are implemented, and nearly the same part with the class `Calculator`. The difference with the `Calculator` class is that it doesn't have the `Export` attribute applied to it.

The solution `ConventionBasedSample` contains the following projects with these references and namespaces. With the `SimpleCalculator` project, a NuGet package for Microsoft Composition is not needed, as exports are not defined by this project.

CalculatorContract (Class Library)

Namespaces

> System.Collections.Generic

SimpleCalculator (Class Library)

References

> CalculatorContract

Namespaces

> System
>
> System.Collections.Generic
>
> System.Composition

SimpleHost (Console Application)

References

> CalculatorContract
>
> System.Composition.AttributedModel
>
> System.Composition.Convention
>
> System.Composition.Hosting
>
> System.Composition.Runtime
>
> System.Composition.TypedParts

Namespaces

> System
>
> System.Collections.Generic
>
> System.Composition
>
> System.Composition.Hosting
>
> static System.Console

> **NOTE** *You need to create a directory* `c:/addins` *before compiling the solution. The hosting application of this sample solution loads assemblies from the directory* `c:/addins`. *That's why a post-build command is defined with the project* `SimpleCalculator` *to copy the library to the* `c:/addins` *directory.*

When you create the host application, all this becomes more interesting. Similar to before, a property of type `ICalculator` is created as shown in the following code snippet—it just doesn't have an `Import` attribute applied to it (code file `ConventionBasedSample/SimpleHost/Program.cs`):

```
public ICalculator Calculator { get; set; }
```

You can apply the `Import` attribute to the property `Calculator` and use only conventions for the exports. You can mix this, using conventions only with exports or imports, or with both—as shown in this example.

The `Main` method of the `Program` class looks similar to before; a new instance of `Program` is created because the `Calculator` property is an instance property of this class, and then the `Bootstrap` and `Run` methods are invoked (code file `ConventionBasedSample/SimpleHost/Program.cs`):

```
public static void Main()
{
    var p = new Program();
    p.Bootstrap();
    p.Run();
}
```

The `Bootstrap` method now creates a new `ConventionBuilder`. `ConventionBuilder` derives from the base class `AttributedModelBuilder`; thus it can be used everywhere this base class is needed. Instead of using the `Export` attribute, convention rules are defined for types that derive from `ICalculator` to export `ICalculator` with the methods `ForTypesDerivedFrom` and `Export`. `ForTypesDerivedFrom` returns a `PartConventionBuilder`, which allows using the fluent API to continue with the part definition to invoke the `Export` method on the part type. Instead of using the `Import` attribute, the convention rule for the `Program` class is used to import a property of type `ICalculator`. The property is defined using a lambda expression (code file `ConventionBasedSample/SimpleHost/Program.cs`):

```
public void Bootstrap()
{
    var conventions = new ConventionBuilder();
    conventions.ForTypesDerivedFrom<ICalculator>()
      .Export<ICalculator>();
    conventions.ForType<Program>()
      .ImportProperty<ICalculator>(p => p.Calculator);
    // etc.
}
```

After the convention rules are defined, the `ContainerConfiguration` class is instantiated. With the container configuration to use the conventions defined by the `ConventionsBuilder`, the method `WithDefaultConventions` is used. `WithDefaultConventions` requires any parameter that derives from the base class `AttributedModelProvider`, which is the class `ConventionBuilder`. After defining to use the conventions, you could use the `WithPart` method like before to specify the part or parts where the conventions should be applied. For making this more flexible than before, now the `WithAssemblies` method is used to specify the assemblies that should be applied. All the assemblies that are passed to this method are filtered for types that derive from the interface `ICalculator` to apply the export. After the container configuration is in place, the `CompositionHost` is created like in the previous sample (code file `ConventionBasedSample/SimpleHost/Program.cs`):

```
public void Bootstrap()
{
    // etc.

    var configuration = new ContainerConfiguration()
      .WithDefaultConventions(conventions)
      .WithAssemblies(GetAssemblies("c:/addins"));

    using (CompositionHost host = configuration.CreateContainer())
    {
        host.SatisfyImports(this, conventions);
    }
}
```

The `GetAssemblies` method loads all assemblies from the given directory (code file `ConventionBasedSample/SimpleHost/Program.cs`):

```
private IEnumerable<Assembly> GetAssemblies(string path)
{
  IEnumerable<string> files = Directory.EnumerateFiles(path, "*.dll");
  var assemblies = new List<Assembly>();
  foreach (var file in files)
  {
    Assembly assembly = Assembly.LoadFile(file);
    assemblies.Add(assembly);
  }
  return assemblies;
}
```

As you've seen, the `ConventionBuilder` is the heart of convention-based part registration and Microsoft Composition. It uses a fluent API and offers all the flexibility you'll see with attributes as well. Conventions can be applied to a specific type with `ForType`; or for types that derive from a base class or implement an interface, `ForTypesDerivedFrom`. `ForTypesMatching` enables specifying a flexible predicate. For example, `ForTypesMatching(t => t.Name.EndsWith("ViewModel"))` applies a convention to all types that end with the name `ViewModel`.

The methods to select the type return a `PartBuilder`. With the `PartBuilder`, exports and imports can be defined, as well as metadata applied. The `PartBuilder` offers several methods to define exports: `Export` to export a specific type, `ExportInterfaces` to export a list of interfaces, and `ExportProperties` to export properties. Using the export methods to export multiple interfaces or properties, a predicate can be applied to further define a selection. The same applies to importing properties or constructors with `ImportProperty`, `ImportProperties`, and `SelectConstructors`.

Now that we have briefly looked at the two ways of using Microsoft Composition with attributes and conventions, the next section digs into the details by using Windows applications to host parts.

DEFINING CONTRACTS

The following sample application extends the first one. The hosting application is composed of WPF (Windows Presentation Foundation) applications and UWP (Universal Windows Platform) apps that load calculator parts for calculation functionality; other add-ins bring their own user interfaces into the host.

> **NOTE** *For more information about writing UWP and WPF applications, see Chapters 29 to 36.*

The `UICalculator` is a somewhat bigger solution, at least for a book. It demonstrates using Microsoft Composition with multiple technologies—both UWP and WPF. Of course, you can focus on one of these technologies and still make use of a lot of features of the sample application. The projects and their dependencies of the solution are shown in Figure 26-3. The `WPFCalculatorHost` and `UWPCalculatorHost` projects load and manage parts. A similar part as before, `SimpleCalculator`, is defined and offers some methods. What's different from the earlier calculator sample is that this part makes use of another part: `AdvancedOperations`. Other parts that offer a user interface are defined with `FuelEconomy` and `TemperatureConversion`. User interfaces are defined with WPF and UWP, but the common functionality is defined in a shared project.

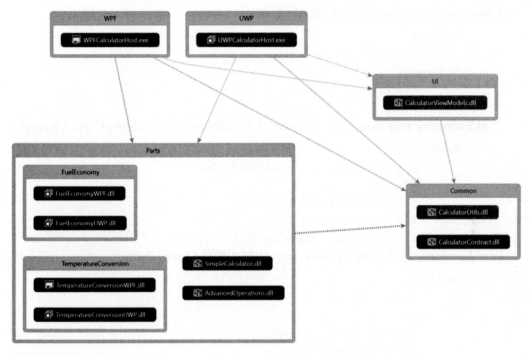

FIGURE 26-3

These are the needed projects with references and namespaces:

CalculatorContract (Class Library)

Namespaces

```
System.Collections.Generic
```

CalculatorUtils (Class Library)

References

```
System.Composition.AttributedModel
```

Namespaces

```
System
System.Collections.Generic
System.ComponentModel
System.Composition
System.Runtime.CompilerServices
```

SimpleCalculator (Class Library)

References

```
System.Composition.AttributedModel
```

Namespaces

```
System
System.Collections.Generic
System.Composition
```

AdvancedOperations (Class Library)

References

    System.Composition.AttributedModel

Namespaces

    System.Composition

    System.Threading.Tasks

Fuel Economy and Temp. Conversion UWP (Universal Windows Class Library)

References

    System.Composition.AttributedModel

Namespaces

    System.Collections.Generic

    System.Composition

    Windows.UI.Xaml.Controls

Fuel Economy and Temp. Conversion WPF (WPF Class Library)

References

    System.Composition.AttributedModel

Namespaces

    System.Collections.Generic

    System.Composition

    System.Windows.Controls

Calculator View Models (Class Library)

References

    System.Composition.AttributedModel

    System.Composition.Hosting

    System.Composition.TypedParts

Namespaces

    System

    System.Collections.Generic

    System.Collections.ObjectModel

    System.Composition

    System.Composition.Hosting

    System.Linq

    System.Windows.Input

WPF Calculator Host (WPF Application)

References

    CalculatorContract

    SimpleCalculator

    System.Composition.AttributedModel

    System.Composition.Hosting

    System.Composition.TypedParts

Namespaces

System

System.Globalization

System.IO

System.Windows

System.Windows.Controls

System.Windows.Data

System.Windows.Media.Imaging

For the calculation, the same contracts that were defined earlier are used: ICalculator and IOperation. Added to this example is another contract: ICalculatorExtension. This interface defines the UI property that can be used by the hosting application. The get accessor of this property returns a FrameworkElement. The property type is defined to be of type object to support both WPF and UWP applications with this interface. With WPF, the FrameworkElement is defined in the namespace System.Windows; with UWP it's in the namespace Windows.UI.Xaml. Defining the property of type object also allows not adding WPF- or UWP-related dependencies to the library.

The UI property enables the add-in to return any user interface element that derives from FrameworkElement to be shown as the user interface within the host application (code file UICalculator/ CalculatorContract/ICalculatorExtension.cs):

```
public interface ICalculatorExtension
{
  object UI { get; }
}
```

.NET interfaces are used to remove the dependency between one that implements the interface and one that uses it. This way, a .NET interface is also a good contract for Composition to remove a dependency between the hosting application and the add-in. If the interface is defined in a separate assembly, as with the CalculatorContract assembly, the hosting application and the add-in don't have a direct dependency. Instead, the hosting application and the add-in just reference the contract assembly.

From a Composition standpoint, an interface contract is not required at all. The contract can be a simple string. To avoid conflicts with other contracts, the name of the string should contain a namespace name— for example, Wrox.ProCSharp.Composition.SampleContract, as shown in the following code snippet. Here, the class Foo is exported by using the Export attribute, and a string passed to the attribute instead of the interface:

```
[Export("Wrox.ProCSharp.Composition.SampleContract")]
public class Foo
{
  public string Bar()
  {
    return "Foo.Bar";
  }
}
```

The problem with using a contract as a string is that the methods, properties, and events provided by the type are not strongly defined. Either the caller needs a reference to the type Foo to use it, or .NET reflection can be used to access its members. The C# 4 dynamic keyword makes reflection easier to use and can be very helpful in such scenarios.

The hosting application can use the dynamic type to import a contract with the name Wrox.ProCSharp. Composition.SampleContract:

```
[Import("Wrox.ProCSharp.MEF.SampleContract")]
public dynamic Foo { get; set; }
```

With the `dynamic` keyword, the `Foo` property can now be used to access the `Bar` method directly. The call to this method is resolved during runtime:

```
string s = Foo.Bar();
```

Contract names and interfaces can also be used in conjunction to define that the contract is used only if both the interface and the contract name are the same. This way, you can use the same interface for different contracts.

> **NOTE** *The* `dynamic` *type is explained in Chapter 16.*

EXPORTING PARTS

The previous example showed the part `SimpleCalculator`, which exports the type `Calculator` with all its methods and properties. The following example contains the `SimpleCalculator` as well, with the same implementation that was shown previously; and two more parts, `TemperatureConversion` and `FuelEconomy`, are exported. These parts offer a UI for the hosting application.

Creating Parts

The WPF User Control library named `TemperatureConversionWPF` defines a user interface as shown in Figure 26-4. This control provides conversion between Celsius, Fahrenheit, and Kelvin scales. You use the first and second combo box to select the conversion source and target. Clicking the Calculate button starts the calculation to do the conversion.

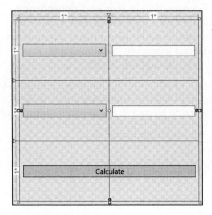

FIGURE 26-4

For UWP, a library named `TemperatureConversionUWP` is defined as well. Both of these projects share the common code in a shared library, `TemperatureConversionShared`. All the C# code used by these UI add-ins is really in this shared project. The XAML code for the UI differs, and it is defined in the WPF and UWP projects.

The user control has a simple implementation for temperature conversion. The enumeration `TempConversionType` defines the different conversions that are possible with that control. The enumeration values shown in the two combo boxes are bound to the `TemperatureConversionTypes` property in the `TemperatureConversionViewModel`. The method `ToCelsiusFrom` converts the argument `t` from its original value to Celsius. The temperature source type is defined with the second argument,

`TempConversionType`. The method `FromCelsiusTo` converts a Celsius value to the selected temperature scale. The method `OnCalculate` is assigned to the Calculate command and invokes the `ToCelsiusFrom` and `FromCelsiusTo` methods to do the conversion according to the user's selected conversion type (code file `UICalculator/TemperatureConversionShared/TemperatureConversionViewModel.cs`):

```csharp
public enum TempConversionType
{
  Celsius,
  Fahrenheit,
  Kelvin
}

public class TemperatureConversionViewModel: BindableBase
{
  public TemperatureConversionViewModel()
  {
    CalculateCommand = new DelegateCommand(OnCalculate);
  }

  public DelegateCommand CalculateCommand { get; }

  public IEnumerable<string> TemperatureConversionTypes =>
    Enum.GetNames(typeof(TempConversionType));

  private double ToCelsiusFrom(double t, TempConversionType conv)
  {
    switch (conv)
    {
      case TempConversionType.Celsius:
        return t;
      case TempConversionType.Fahrenheit:
        return (t-32) / 1.8;
      case TempConversionType.Kelvin:
        return (t-273.15);
      default:
        throw new ArgumentException("invalid enumeration value");
    }
  }

  private double FromCelsiusTo(double t, TempConversionType conv)
  {
    switch (conv)
    {
      case TempConversionType.Celsius:
        return t;
      case TempConversionType.Fahrenheit:
        return (t * 1.8) + 32;
      case TempConversionType.Kelvin:
        return t + 273.15;
      default:
        throw new ArgumentException("invalid enumeration value");
    }
  }

  private string _fromValue;
  public string FromValue
  {
    get { return _fromValue; }
    set { SetProperty(ref _fromValue, value); }
  }

  private string _toValue;
```

```
public string ToValue
{
  get { return _toValue; }
  set { SetProperty(ref _toValue, value); }
}

private TempConversionType _fromType;
public TempConversionType FromType
{
  get { return _fromType; }
  set { SetProperty(ref _fromType, value); }
}

private TempConversionType _toType;
public TempConversionType ToType
{
  get { return _toType; }
  set { SetProperty(ref _toType, value); }
}

public void OnCalculate()
{
  double result = FromCelsiusTo(
    ToCelsiusFrom(double.Parse(FromValue), FromType), ToType);
  ToValue = result.ToString();
}
```

So far, this control is just a simple user interface control with a view model. To create a part, the class `TemperatureCalculatorExtension` is exported by using the `Export` attribute. The class implements the interface `ICalculatorExtension` to return the user control `TemperatureConversion` from the `UI` property. For UWP and WPF, different binary code gets generated. Both the UWP and WPF projects define the `TemperatureConversionUC` control class, but with different namespaces. The namespace selection is done with preprocessor directives (code file `UICalculator/TemperatureConversion/TemperatureCalculatorExtension.cs`):

```
#if WPF
using TemperatureConversionWPF;
#endif
#if WINDOWS_UWP
using TemperatureConversionUWP;
#endif
using System.Composition;

namespace Wrox.ProCSharp.Composition
{
  [Export(typeof(ICalculatorExtension))]
  [CalculatorExtensionMetadata(
    Title = "Temperature Conversion",
    Description = "Temperature conversion",
    ImageUri = "Images/Temperature.png")]
  public class TemperatureConversionExtension: ICalculatorExtension
  {
    private object _control;
    public object UI =>
      _control ?? (_control = new TemperatureConversionUC());
  }
}
```

For now, ignore the `CalculatorExtension` attribute used in the previous code snippet. It is explained in the section "Exporting Metadata" later in this chapter.

The second user control that implements the interface `ICalculatorExtension` is `FuelEconomy`. With this control, either miles per gallon or liters per 100 km can be calculated. The user interface is shown in Figure 26-5.

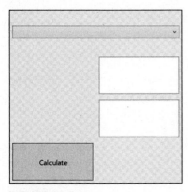

FIGURE 26-5

The next code snippet shows the class `FuelEconomyViewModel`, which defines several properties that are bound from the user interface, such as a list of `FuelEcoTypes` that enables the user to select between miles and kilometers, and the `Fuel` and `Distance` properties, which are filled by the user (code file `UICalculator/FuelEconomyShared/FuelEconomyViewModel.cs`):

```csharp
public class FuelEconomyViewModel: BindableBase
{
  public FuelEconomyViewModel()
  {
    InitializeFuelEcoTypes();
    CalculateCommand = new DelegateCommand(OnCalculate);
  }

  public DelegateCommand CalculateCommand { get; }

  // etc.

  public List<FuelEconomyType> FuelEcoTypes { get; } =
    new List<FuelEconomyType>();

  private void InitializeFuelEcoTypes()
  {
    var t1 = new FuelEconomyType
    {
      Id = "lpk",
      Text = "L/100 km",
      DistanceText = "Distance (kilometers)",
      FuelText = "Fuel used (liters)"
    };
    var t2 = new FuelEconomyType
    {
      Id = "mpg",
      Text = "Miles per gallon",
      DistanceText = "Distance (miles)",
      FuelText = "Fuel used (gallons)"
    };
    FuelEcoTypes.AddRange(new FuelEconomyType[] { t1, t2 });
  }

  private FuelEconomyType _selectedFuelEcoType;

  public FuelEconomyType SelectedFuelEcoType
  {
    get { return _selectedFuelEcoType; }
    set { SetProperty(ref _selectedFuelEcoType, value); }
```

```
      }

      private string _fuel;
      public string Fuel
      {
        get { return _fuel; }
        set { SetProperty(ref _fuel, value); }
      }

      private string _distance;
      public string Distance
      {
        get { return _distance; }
        set { SetProperty(ref _distance, value); }
      }

      private string _result;
      public string Result
      {
        get { return _result; }
        set { SetProperty(ref _result, value); }
      }
    }
```

> **NOTE** *The base class* `BindableBase` *that is used with the sample code just offers an implementation of the interface* `INotifyPropertyChanged`. *This class is found in the* `CalculatorUtils` *project.*

The calculation is within the `OnCalculate` method. `OnCalculate` is the handler for the `Click` event of the Calculate button (code file `UICalculator/FuelEconomyShared/FuelEconomyViewModel.cs`):

```
public void OnCalculate()
{
  double fuel = double.Parse(Fuel);
  double distance = double.Parse(Distance);
  FuelEconomyType ecoType = SelectedFuelEcoType;
  double result = 0;
  switch (ecoType.Id)
  {
    case "lpk":
      result = fuel / (distance / 100);
      break;
    case "mpg":
      result = distance / fuel;
      break;
    default:
      break;
  }
  Result = result.ToString();
}
```

Again, the interface `ICalculatorExtension` is implemented and exported with the `Export` attribute (code file `UICalculator/FuelEconomyShared/FuelCalculatorExtension.cs`):

```
[Export(typeof(ICalculatorExtension))]
[CalculatorExtensionMetadata(
  Title = "Fuel Economy",
  Description = "Calculate fuel economy",
  ImageUri = "Images/Fuel.png")]
public class FuelCalculatorExtension: ICalculatorExtension
```

```
{
    private object _control;
    public object UI => _control ?? (_control = new FuelEconomyUC());
}
```

Before continuing the hosting applications to import the user controls, let's take a look at what other options you have with exports. A part itself can import other parts, and you can add metadata information to the exports.

Parts Using Parts

The `Calculator` class now doesn't directly implement the `Add` and `Subtract` methods but uses other parts that do this. To define parts that offer a single operation, the interface `IBinaryOperation` is defined (code file `UICalculator/CalculatorContract/IBinaryOperation.cs`):

```
public interface IBinaryOperation
{
    double Operation(double x, double y);
}
```

The class `Calculator` defines a property where a matching part of the `Subtract` method will be imported. The import is named `Subtract`, as not all exports of `IBinaryOperation` are needed—just the exports named `Subtract` (code file `UICalculator/SimpleCalculator/Calculator.cs`):

```
[Import("Subtract")]
public IBinaryOperation SubtractMethod { get; set; }
```

The `Import` in the class `Calculator` matches the `Export` of the `SubtractOperation` (code file `UICalculator/AdvancedOperations/Operations.cs`):

```
[Export("Subtract", typeof(IBinaryOperation))]
public class SubtractOperation: IBinaryOperation
{
    public double Operation(double x, double y) => x−y;
}
```

Now only the implementation of the `Operate` method of the `Calculator` class needs to be changed to make use of the inner part. There's no need for the `Calculator` itself to create a container to match the inner part. This is already automatically done from the hosting container as long as the exported parts are available within the registered types or assemblies (code file `UICalculator/SimpleCalculator/Calculator.cs`):

```
public double Operate(IOperation operation, double[] operands)
{
    double result = 0;
    switch (operation.Name)
    {
        // etc.
        case "-":
            result = SubtractMethod.Operation(operands[0], operands[1]);
            break;
        // etc.
```

Exporting Metadata

With exports, you can also attach metadata information. Metadata enables you to provide information in addition to a name and a type. This can be used to add capability information and to determine, on the import side, which of the exports should be used.

The `Calculator` class uses an inner part not only for the `Subtract` method, but also for the `Add` method. The `AddOperation` from the following code snippet uses the `Export` attribute named `Add` in conjunction with the `SpeedMetadata` attribute. The `SpeedMetadata` attribute specifies the `Speed` information `Speed`. `Fast` (code file `UICalculator/AdvancedOperations/Operations.cs`):

```
[Export("Add", typeof(IBinaryOperation))]
[SpeedMetadata(Speed = Speed.Fast)]
public class AddOperation: IBinaryOperation
{
  public double Operation(double x, double y) => x + y;
}
```

There's another export for an `Add` method with `SpeedMetadata Speed.Slow` (code file `UICalculator/AdvancedOperations/Operations.cs`):

```
[Export("Add", typeof(IBinaryOperation))]
[SpeedMetadata(Speed = Speed.Slow)]
public class SlowAddOperation: IBinaryOperation
{
  public double Operation(double x, double y)
  {
    Task.Delay(3000).Wait();
    return x + y;
  }
}
```

`Speed` is just an enumeration with two values (code file `UICalculator/CalculatorUtils/SpeedMetadata.cs`):

```
public enum Speed
{
  Fast,
  Slow
}
```

You can define metadata by creating an attribute class with the `MetadataAttribute` applied. This attribute is then applied to a part as you've seen with the `AddOperation` and `SlowAddOperation` types (code file `UICalculator/CalculatorUtils/SpeedMetadataAttribute.cs`):

```
[MetadataAttribute]
[AttributeUsage(AttributeTargets.Class)]
public class SpeedMetadataAttribute: Attribute
{
  public Speed Speed { get; set; }
}
```

> **NOTE** *For more information about how to create custom attributes, read Chapter 16.*

To access the metadata with the import, the class `SpeedMetadata` is defined. `SpeedMetadata` defines the same properties as the `SpeedMetadataAttribute` (code file `UICalculator/CalculatorUtils/SpeedMetadata.cs`):

```
public class SpeedMetadata
{
  public Speed Speed { get; set; }
}
```

With multiple `Add` exports defined, using the `Import` attribute as shown previously fails during runtime. Multiple exports cannot match just one import. The attribute `ImportMany` is used if more than one export of the same name and type is available. This attribute is applied to a property of type array or `IEnumeration<T>`.

Because metadata is applied with the export, the type of the property that matches the Add export is an array of Lazy<IBinaryOperation, SpeedMetadata> (code file UICalculator/SimpleCalculator/Calculator.cs):

```
[ImportMany("Add")]
public Lazy<IBinaryOperation, SpeedMetadata>[] AddMethods { get; set; }
```

ImportMany is explained with more detail in the next section. The Lazy type allows accessing metadata with the generic definition Lazy<T, TMetadata>. The class Lazy<T> is used to support lazy initialization of types on first use. Lazy<T, TMetadata> derives from Lazy<T> and supports, in addition to the base class, access to metadata information with the Metadata property.

The call to the Add method is now changed to iterate through the collection of Lazy<IBinaryOperation, SpeedMetadata> elements. With the Metadata property, the key for the capability is checked; if the Speed capability has the value Speed.Fast, the operation is invoked by using the Value property of Lazy<T> to invoke the operation (code file UICalculator/SimpleCalculator/Calculator.cs):

```
public double Operate(IOperation operation, double[] operands)
{
  double result = 0;
  switch (operation.Name)
  {
    case "+":
    foreach (var addMethod in AddMethods)
    {
      if (addMethod.Metadata.Speed == Speed.Fast)
      {
        result = addMethod.Value.Operation(operands[0], operands[1]);
      }
    }
    break;
    // etc.
```

Using Metadata for Lazy Loading

Using metadata with Microsoft Composition is not only useful for selecting parts based on metadata information. Another great use is providing information to the host application about the part before the part is instantiated.

The following example is implemented to offer a title, a description, and a link to an image for the calculator extensions FuelEconomy and TemperatureConversion (code file UICalculator/CalculatorUtils/CalculatorExtensionMetadataAttribute.cs):

```
[MetadataAttribute]
[AttributeUsage(AttributeTargets.Class)]
public class CalculatorExtensionMetadataAttribute: Attribute
{
  public string Title { get; set; }
  public string Description { get; set; }
  public string ImageUri { get; set; }
}
```

With a part, the CalculatorExtensionMetadata attribute is applied. The following is an example—the FuelCalculatorExtension (code file UICalculator/FuelEconomyShared/FuelCalculatorExtension.cs):

```
[Export(typeof(ICalculatorExtension))]
[CalculatorExtensionMetadata(
  Title = "Fuel Economy",
  Description = "Calculate fuel economy",
  ImageUri = "Images/Fuel.png")]
public class FuelCalculatorExtension: ICalculatorExtension
{
```

```
        private object _control;
        public object UI => _control ?? (_control = new FuelEconomyUC());
    }
```

Parts can consume a large amount of memory. If the user does not instantiate the part, there's no need to consume this memory. Instead, the title, description, and image can be accessed to give the user information about the part before instantiating it.

IMPORTING PARTS

Now let's take a look at using the user control parts with a hosting application. The design view of the WPF hosting application is shown in Figure 26-6.

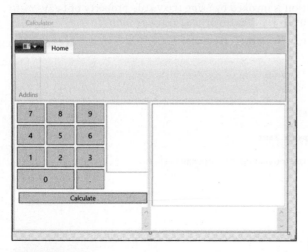

FIGURE 26-6

For every part type, a separate import, manager, and view model is created. For using the part implementing the `ICalculator` interface, the `CalculatorImport` is used to define the `Import`, the `CalculatorManager` is used to create the `CompositionHost` and load the parts, and the `CalculatorViewModel` is used to define the properties and commands that are bound to the user interface. For using the part implementing the `ICalculatorExtension` interface, the `CalculatorExtensionImport`, `CalculatorExtensionManager`, and `CalculatorExtensionViewModel` are defined accordingly.

Let's start with the `CalculatorImport` class. With the first sample, just a property has been defined with the `Program` class to import a part. It's a good practice to define a separate class for imports. With this class, you can also define a method that is annotated with the attribute `OnImportsSatisfied`. This attribute marks the method that is called when imports are matched. In the sample code, the event `ImportsSatisfied` is fired. The `Calculator` property has the `Import` attribute applied. Here, the type is `Lazy<ICalculator>` for late instantiation. The part is instantiated only when the `Value` of the `Lazy` type is accessed (code file `UICalculator/CalculatorViewModels/CalculatorImport.cs`):

```
public class CalculatorImport
{
    public event EventHandler<ImportEventArgs> ImportsSatisfied;

    [Import]
    public Lazy<ICalculator> Calculator { get; set; }

    [OnImportsSatisfied]
```

```
   public void OnImportsSatisfied()
   {
     ImportsSatisfied?.Invoke(this,
       new ImportEventArgs
       {
         StatusMessage = "ICalculator import successful"
       });
   }
 }
```

The `CalculatorManager` class instantiates the `CalculatorImport` class in the constructor. With the `InitializeContainer` method, the `ContainerConfiguration` class is instantiated to create the `CompositionHost` container with the types passed to the method. The method `SatisfyImports` matches exports to imports (code file `UICalculator/CalculatorViewModels/CalculatorManager.cs`):

```
public class CalculatorManager
{
  private CalculatorImport _calcImport;
  public event EventHandler<ImportEventArgs> ImportsSatisfied;

  public CalculatorManager()
  {
    _calcImport = new CalculatorImport();
    _calcImport.ImportsSatisfied += (sender, e) =>
    {
      ImportsSatisfied?.Invoke(this, e);
    };
  }

  public void InitializeContainer(params Type[] parts)
  {
    var configuration = new ContainerConfiguration().WithParts(parts);
    using (CompositionHost host = configuration.CreateContainer())
    {
      host.SatisfyImports(_calcImport);
    }
  }
  // etc.
}
```

The `GetOperators` method of the `CalculatorManager` invokes the `GetOperations` method of the `Calculator`. This method is used to display all the available operators in the user interface. As soon as a calculation is defined, the `InvokeCalculator` method is invoked to pass the operation and operands, and in turn invoke the `Operate` method in the calculator (code file `UICalculator/CalculatorViewModels/CalculatorManager.cs`):

```
public class CalculatorManager
{
  // etc.
  public IEnumerable<IOperation> GetOperators() =>
    _calcImport.Calculator.Value.GetOperations();

  public double InvokeCalculator(IOperation operation, double[] operands) =>
    _calcImport.Calculator.Value.Operate(operation, operands);
}
```

What's needed by the `CalculatorViewModel`? This view model defines several properties: the `CalcAddInOperators` property to list available operators, the `Input` property that contains the calculation entered by the user, the `Result` property that shows the result of the operation, and the `CurrentOperation` property that contains the current operation. It also defines the `_currentOperands` field that contains the operands selected. With the `Init` method, the container is initialized, and operators are retrieved from the

Calculator part. The `OnCalculate` method does the calculation using the part (code file `UICalculator/CalculatorViewModels/CalculatorViewModel.cs`):

```csharp
public class CalculatorViewModel: BindableBase
{
  public CalculatorViewModel()
  {
    _calculatorManager = new CalculatorManager();
    _calculatorManager.ImportsSatisfied += (sender, e) =>
    {
      Status += $"{e.StatusMessage}\n";
    };
    CalculateCommand = new DelegateCommand(OnCalculate);
  }

  public void Init(params Type[] parts)
  {
    _calculatorManager.InitializeContainer(parts);
    var operators = _calculatorManager.GetOperators();
    CalcAddInOperators.Clear();
    foreach (var op in operators)
    {
      CalcAddInOperators.Add(op);
    }
  }

  private CalculatorManager _calculatorManager;

  public ICommand CalculateCommand { get; set; }

  public void OnCalculate()
  {
    if (_currentOperands.Length == 2)
    {
      string[] input = Input.Split(' ');
      _currentOperands[1] = double.Parse(input[2]);
      Result = _calculatorManager.InvokeCalculator(_currentOperation,
        _currentOperands);
    }
  }

  private string _status;
  public string Status
  {
    get { return _status; }
    set { SetProperty(ref _status, value); }
  }

  private string _input;
  public string Input
  {
    get { return _input; }
    set { SetProperty(ref _input, value); }
  }

  private double _result;
  public double Result
  {
    get { return _result; }
    set { SetProperty(ref _result, value); }
  }
```

```
  private IOperation _currentOperation;
  public IOperation CurrentOperation
  {
    get { return _currentOperation; }
    set { SetCurrentOperation(value); }
  }

  private double[] _currentOperands;

  private void SetCurrentOperation(IOperation op)
  {
    try
    {
      _currentOperands = new double[op.NumberOperands];
      _currentOperands[0] = double.Parse(Input);
      Input += $" {op.Name} ";
      SetProperty(ref _currentOperation, op, nameof(CurrentOperation));
    }
    catch (FormatException ex)
    {
      Status = ex.Message;
    }
  }
  public ObservableCollection<IOperation> CalcAddInOperators { get; } =
    new ObservableCollection<IOperation>();
}
```

Importing Collections

An import connects to an export. When using exported parts, an import is needed to make the connection. With the Import attribute, it's possible to connect to a single export. If more than one part should be loaded, the ImportMany attribute is required and needs to be defined as an array type or IEnumerable<T>. Because the hosting calculator application allows many calculator extensions that implement the interface ICalculatorExtension to be loaded, the class CalculatorExtensionImport defines the property CalculatorExtensions of type IEnumerable<ICalculatorExtension> to access all the calculator extension parts (code file UICalculator/CalculatorViewModels/CalculatorExtensionsImport.cs):

```
public class CalculatorExtensionsImport
{
    public event EventHandler<ImportEventArgs> ImportsSatisfied;

    [ImportMany()]
    public IEnumerable<Lazy<ICalculatorExtension,
      CalculatorExtensionMetadataAttribute>>
      CalculatorExtensions { get; set; }

    [OnImportsSatisfied]
    public void OnImportsSatisfied()
    {
        ImportsSatisfied?.Invoke(this, new ImportEventArgs
        {
          StatusMessage = "ICalculatorExtension imports successful"
        });
    }
}
```

The Import and ImportMany attributes enable the use of ContractName and ContractType to map the import to an export.

The event ImportsSatisfied of the CalculatorExtensionsImport is connected to an event handler on creation of the CalculatorExtensionsManager to route firing the event, and in turn write a message to a `Status` property that is bound in the UI for displaying status information (code file `UICalculator/CalculatorViewModels/CalculatorExtensionsManager.cs`):

```csharp
public sealed class CalculatorExtensionsManager
{
  private CalculatorExtensionsImport _calcExtensionImport;
  public event EventHandler<ImportEventArgs> ImportsSatisfied;

  public CalculatorExtensionsManager()
  {
    _calcExtensionImport = new CalculatorExtensionsImport();
    _calcExtensionImport.ImportsSatisfied += (sender, e) =>
    {
      ImportsSatisfied?.Invoke(this, e);
    };
  }

  public void InitializeContainer(params Type[] parts)
  {
    var configuration = new ContainerConfiguration().WithParts(parts);
    using (CompositionHost host = configuration.CreateContainer())
    {
      host.SatisfyImports(_calcExtensionImport);
    }
  }

  public IEnumerable<Lazy<ICalculatorExtension,
    CalculatorExtensionMetadataAttribute>> GetExtensionInformation() =>
    _calcExtensionImport.CalculatorExtensions.ToArray();
}
```

Lazy Loading of Parts

By default, parts are loaded from the container—for example, by calling the extension method `SatisfyImports` on the `CompositionHost`. With the help of the `Lazy<T>` class, the parts can be loaded on first access. The type `Lazy<T>` enables the late instantiation of any type `T` and defines the properties `IsValueCreated` and `Value`. `IsValueCreated` is a Boolean that returns the information if the contained type `T` is already instantiated. `Value` initializes the contained type `T` on first access and returns the instance.

The import of an add-in can be declared to be of type `Lazy<T>`, as shown in the `Lazy<ICalculator>` example (code file `UICalculator/CalculatorViewModels/CalculatorImport.cs`):

```csharp
[Import]
        public Lazy<ICalculator> Calculator { get; set; }
```

Calling the imported property also requires some changes to access the `Value` property of the `Lazy<T>` type. `calcImport` is a variable of type `CalculatorImport`. The `Calculator` property returns `Lazy<ICalculator>`. The `Value` property instantiates the imported type lazily and returns the `ICalculator` interface, enabling the `GetOperations` method to be invoked in order to get all supported operations from the calculator add-in (code file `UICalculator/CalculatorViewModels/CalculatorManager.cs`):

```csharp
public IEnumerable<IOperation> GetOperators() =>
  _calcImport.Calculator.Value.GetOperations();
```

Reading Metadata

The parts `FuelEconomy` and `TemperatureConversion`—all the parts that implement the interface `ICalculatorExtension`—are lazy loaded as well. As you've seen earlier, a collection can be imported with a property of `IEnumerable<T>`. Instantiating the parts lazily, the property can be of type `IEnumerable<Lazy<T>>`. Information about these parts is needed before instantiation in order to display information to the user about what can be expected with these parts. These parts offer additional information using metadata, as shown earlier. Metadata information can be accessed using a `Lazy` type with two generic type parameters. Using `Lazy<ICalculatorExtension, CalculatorExtensionMetadataAttribute>`, the first generic parameter, `ICalculatorExtension`, is used to access the members of the instantiated type; the second generic parameter, `ICalculatorExtensionMetadataAttribute`, is used to access metadata information (code file `UICalculator/CalculatorViewModels/CalculatorExtensionsImport.cs`):

```
[ImportMany()]
public IEnumerable<Lazy<ICalculatorExtension,
   CalculatorExtensionMetadataAttribute>> CalculatorExtensions { get; set; }
```

The method `GetExtensionInformation` returns an array of `Lazy<ICalculatorExtension, CalculatorExtensionMetadataAttribute>`, which can be used to access metadata information about the parts without instantiating the part (code file `UICalculator/CalculatorViewModels/CalculatorExtensionsManager.cs`):

```
public IEnumerable<Lazy<ICalculatorExtension,
   CalculatorExtensionMetadataAttribute>> GetExtensionInformation() =>
   _calcExtensionImport.CalculatorExtensions.ToArray();
```

The `GetExtensionInformation` method is used in the `CalculatorExtensionsViewModel` class on initialization to fill the `Extensions` property (code file `UICalculator/CalculatorViewModels/CalculatorExtensionsViewModel.cs`):

```
public class CalculatorExtensionsViewModel: BindableBase
{
  private CalculatorExtensionsManager _calculatorExtensionsManager;

  public CalculatorExtensionsViewModel()
  {
    _calculatorExtensionsManager = new CalculatorExtensionsManager();
    _calculatorExtensionsManager.ImportsSatisfied += (sender, e) =>
    {
      Status += $"{e.StatusMessage}\n";
    };
  }
  public void Init(params Type[] parts)
  {
    _calculatorExtensionsManager.InitializeContainer(parts);
    foreach (var extension in
      _calculatorExtensionsManager.GetExtensionInformation())
    {
      var vm = new ExtensionViewModel(extension);
      vm.ActivatedExtensionChanged += OnActivatedExtensionChanged;
      Extensions.Add(vm);
    }
  }

  public ObservableCollection<ExtensionViewModel> Extensions { get; } =
    new ObservableCollection<ExtensionViewModel>();
  //etc.
```

Within the XAML code, metadata information is bound. The `Lazy` type has a `Metadata` property that returns `CalculatorExtensionMetadataAttribute`. This way, `Description`, `Title`, and `ImageUri` can be accessed for data binding without instantiating the add-ins (code file `UICalculator/WPFCalculatorHost/MainWindow.xaml`):

```
<RibbonGroup Header="Addins"
  ItemsSource="{Binding CalculatorExtensionsViewModel.Extensions,
    Mode=OneWay}">
  <RibbonGroup.ItemTemplate>
    <DataTemplate>
```

```
        <RibbonButton
          ToolTip="{Binding Extension.Metadata.Description, Mode=OneTime}"
          Label="{Binding Extension.Metadata.Title, Mode=OneTime}"
          Tag="{Binding Path=Extension, Mode=OneTime}"
          LargeImageSource="{Binding Extension.Metadata.ImageUri,
            Converter={StaticResource bitmapConverter}, Mode=OneTime}"
          Command="{Binding ActivateCommand}" />
      </DataTemplate>
    </RibbonGroup.ItemTemplate>
  </RibbonGroup>
```

Figure 26-7 shows the running application where metadata from the calculator extensions is read—it includes the image, the title, and the description. With Figure 26-8 you can see an activated calculator extension.

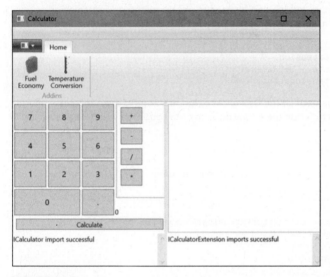

FIGURE 26-7

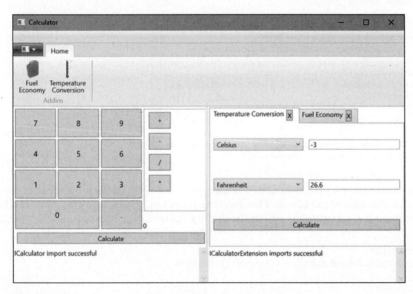

FIGURE 26-8

SUMMARY

In this chapter, you learned about the parts, exports, imports, and containers of Microsoft Composition. You've learned how an application can be built up with complete independency of its parts and dynamically load parts that can come from different assemblies.

You've seen how you can use either attributes or conventions to match exports and imports. Using conventions allows using parts where you can't change the source code to add attributes, and also gives the option to create a framework based on Composition that doesn't require the user of your framework to add attributes for importing the parts.

You've also learned how parts can be lazy loaded to instantiate them only when they are needed. Parts can offer metadata that can give enough information for the client to decide whether the part should be instantiated.

The next chapter covers XML and JSON—two data formats that you can use to serialize your objects and also use to read and analyze data with these formats.

27

XML and JSON

WHAT'S IN THIS CHAPTER?

➤ XML standards

➤ XmlReader and XmlWriter

➤ XmlDocument

➤ XPathNavigator

➤ LINQ to XML

➤ Working with objects in the System.Xml.Linq namespace

➤ Querying XML documents using LINQ

➤ Creating JSON

➤ Converting Objects to and from JSON

WROX.COM CODE DOWNLOADS FOR THIS CHAPTER

The wrox.com code downloads for this chapter are found at www.wrox.com/go/professionalcsharp6 on the Download Code tab. The code for this chapter is divided into the following major examples:

➤ XmlReaderAndWriter

➤ XmlDocument

➤ XPathNavigator

➤ ObjectToXmlSerialization

➤ ObjectToXmlSerializationWOAttributes

➤ LinqToXmlSample

➤ JsonSample

DATA FORMATS

The Extensible Markup Language (XML) has been playing an important part in information technology since 1996. The language is used to describe data, and it's used with configuration files, source code documentation, web services that make use of SOAP, and more. In recent years, it has been replaced in some ways (for example, configuration files and data transfer from REST-based web services) by JavaScript Object Notation (JSON) because this technology has less overhead and can be used easily from JavaScript. However, JSON cannot replace XML in all the scenarios where XML is used today. Both of these data formats can be used with .NET applications, as covered in this chapter.

For processing XML, different options are available. You can either read the complete document and navigate within the Document Object Model (DOM) hierarchy using the `XmlDocument` class, or you can use `XmlReader` and `XmlWriter`. Using `XmlReader` is more complex to do, but you can read larger documents. With `XmlDocument`, the complete document is loaded in the memory. With the `XmlReader` it is possible to read node by node.

Another way to work with XML is to serialize .NET object trees to XML and deserialize XML data back into .NET objects using the `System.Xml.Serialization` namespace.

When querying and filtering XML content, you can either use an XML standard XPath or use LINQ to XML. Both technologies are covered in this chapter. LINQ to XML also offers an easy way to create XML documents and fragments.

> **NOTE** *If you want to learn more about XML, Wrox's* Professional XML *(Wiley, 2007) is a great place to start.*

The discussion begins with a brief overview of the current status of XML standards.

XML

The first XML examples use the file `books.xml` as the source of data. You can download this file and the other code samples for this chapter from the Wrox website (`www.wrox.com`). The `books.xml` file is a book catalog for an imaginary bookstore. It includes book information such as genre, author name, price, and International Standard Book Number (ISBN).

This is what the `books.xml` file looks like:

```xml
<?xml version='1.0'?>
<!-- This file represents a fragment of a book store inventory database -->
<bookstore>
  <book genre="autobiography" publicationdate="1991" ISBN="1-861003-11-0">
    <title>The Autobiography of Benjamin Franklin</title>
    <author>
      <first-name>Benjamin</first-name>
      <last-name>Franklin</last-name>
    </author>
    <price>8.99</price>
  </book>
  <book genre="novel" publicationdate="1967" ISBN="0-201-63361-2">
    <title>The Confidence Man</title>
    <author>
      <first-name>Herman</first-name>
      <last-name>Melville</last-name>
    </author>
    <price>11.99</price>
  </book>
  <book genre="philosophy" publicationdate="1991" ISBN="1-861001-57-6">
    <title>The Gorgias</title>
    <author>
      <name>Plato</name>
```

```
    </author>
    <price>9.99</price>
  </book>
</bookstore>
```

Let's have a look at the parts of this XML content. An XML document should start with an XML declaration that specifies the XML version number:

```
<?xml version='1.0'?>
```

You can put comments anywhere in an XML document outside of markup. They start with `<!--` and end with `-->`:

```
<!-- This file represents a fragment of a book store inventory database -->
```

A full document can contain only a single root element (whereas an XML fragment can contain multiple elements). With the `books.xml` file, the root element is `bookstore`:

```
<bookstore>
  <!-- child elements here -->
</bookstore>
```

An XML element can contain child elements. The `author` element contains the child elements `first-name` and `last-name`. The `first-name` element itself contains *inner text* Benjamin. `first-name` is a *child* element of `author`, which also means `author` is a *parent* element of `first-name`. `first-name` and `last-name` are *sibling* elements:

```
<author>
  <first-name>Benjamin</first-name>
  <last-name>Franklin</last-name>
</author>
```

An XML element can also contain attributes. The `book` element contains the attributes `genre`, `publicationdate`, and `ISBN`. Values for attributes need to be surrounded by quotes.

```
<book genre="novel" publicationdate="1967" ISBN="0-201-63361-2">
</book>
```

> **NOTE** *The HTML5 specification doesn't require quotes with attributes. HTML is not XML; HTML has a more relaxed syntax, whereas XML is strict. HTML documents can also be written using XHTML, which uses XML syntax.*

XML Standards Support in .NET

The World Wide Web Consortium (W3C) has developed a set of standards that give XML its power and potential. Without these standards, XML would not have the impact on the development world that it does. The W3C website (www.w3.org) is a valuable source for all things XML.

The .NET Framework supports the following W3C standards:

➤ XML 1.0 (www.w3.org/TR/REC-xml), including DTD support
➤ XML namespaces (www.w3.org/TR/REC-xml-names), both stream level and DOM
➤ XML schemas (www.w3.org/XML/Schema)
➤ XPath expressions (www.w3.org/TR/xpath)
➤ XSLT transformations (www.w3.org/TR/xslt)

➤ DOM Level 1 Core (www.w3.org/TR/REC-DOM-Level-1)

➤ DOM Level 2 Core (www.w3.org/TR/DOM-Level-2-Core)

➤ SOAP 1.2 (www.w3.org/TR/SOAP)

The level of standards support changes as the W3C updates the recommended standards and as Microsoft and the community update .NET Core. Therefore, you need to make sure that you stay up to date with the standards and the level of support provided.

Working with XML in the Framework

The .NET Framework gives you many different options for reading and writing XML. You can directly use the DOM tree to work with `XmlDocument` and classes from the `System.Xml` namespace and the `System.Xml.XmlDocument` NuGet package. This works well and is easy to do with files that fit into the memory.

For fast reading and writing XML, you can use the `XmlReader` and `XmlWriter` classes. These classes allow streaming and make it possible to work with large XML files. These classes are in the `System.Xml` namespace as well, but they're in a different NuGet package: `System.Xml.ReaderWriter`.

For using the XPath standard to navigate and query XML, you can use the `XPathNavigator` class. This is defined in the `System.Xml.XPath` namespace in the NuGet package `System.Xml.XmlDocument`.

Since .NET 3.5, .NET has offered another syntax to query XML: LINQ. Although LINQ to XML doesn't support the W3C DOM standard, it provides an easier option to navigate within the XML tree, and also allows easier creating of XML documents or fragments. The namespace needed here is `System.Xml.Linq`, and the NuGet package `System.Xml.XDocument`.

> **NOTE** *LINQ is covered in Chapter 13, "Language Integrated Query." The specific implementation of LINQ, LINQ to XML, is covered in this chapter.*

To serialize and deserialize .NET objects to XML, you can use the `XmlSerializer`. With .NET Core, the NuGet package needed here is `System.Xml.XmlSerializer` with the namespace `System.Xml.Serialization`.

WCF uses another method for XML serialization: data contract serialization. Although the `XmlSerializer` does allow you to differ serialization between attributes and elements, this is not possible with the `DataContractSerializer` serializing XML.

> **NOTE** *WCF is covered in Chapter 44, "Windows Communication Foundation."*

JSON

JavaScript Object Notation (JSON) came up in recent years because it can be directly used from JavaScript, and it has less overhead compared to XML. JSON is defined by IETF RFC 7159 (https://tools.ietf.org/html/rfc7159), and the ECMA standard 404 (http://www.ecma-international.org/publications/files/ECMA-ST/ECMA-404.pdf).

For sending JSON documents, there's an official MIME type `"application/json"`. Some frameworks still use older, unofficial MIME types `"text/json"` or `"text/javascript"`.

The same content as the earlier XML file is described here using JSON. Arrays of elements are contained within brackets. In the example, the JSON file contains multiple book objects. Curly brackets define objects or dictionaries. The key and value are separated by a colon. The key needs to be quoted; the value is a string:

```
[
  "book": {
    "genre": "autobiography",
    "publicationdate": 1991,
    "ISBN": "1-861003-11-0",
    "title": "The Autobiography of Benjamin Franklin"
    "author": {
      "first-name": "Benjamin",
      "last-name": "Franklin"
    },
    "price": 8.99
  },
  "book": {
    "genre": "novel",
    "publicationdate": 1967,
    "ISBN": "1-861001-57-6",
    "title": "The Confidence Man"
    "author": {
      "first-name": "Herman",
      "last-name": "Melville"
    },
    "price": 11.99
  },
  "book": {
    "genre": "philosophy",
    "publicationdate": 1991,
    "ISBN": "1-861001-57-6",
    "title": "The Georgias"
    "author": {
      "name": "Plato",
    },
    "price": 9.99
  }
]
```

With .NET, JSON is used in many different places. When you're creating new DNX projects, you can see JSON used as the project configuration file. It's used with web projects to serialize data from and to the client using the ASP.NET Web API (see Chapter 42, "ASP.NET Web API.") and used in data stores such as the NoSQL database DocumentDB that's available with Microsoft Azure.

Different options are available to you when you're using JSON with .NET. One of the JSON serializers is the DataContractJsonSerializer. This type derives from the base class XmlObjectSerializer, although it doesn't really have a relation to XML. At the time when the data contract serialization technology was invented (which happened with .NET 3.0), the idea was that from now on every serialization is XML (XML in binary format is available as well). As time moved on, this assumption was not true anymore. JSON was widely used. As a matter of fact, JSON was added to the hierarchy to be supported with the data contract serialization. However, a faster, more flexible implementation won the market and is now supported by Microsoft and used with many .NET applications: Json.NET. Because this library is the one most used with .NET applications, it is covered in this chapter.

Beside the core JSON standard, JSON grows as well. Features known from XML are added to JSON. Let's get into examples of the JSON improvements, and compare them to XML features. The XML Schema Definition (XSD) describes XML vocabularies; at the time of this writing, the JSON Schema with similar features is a work in progress. With WCF, XML can be compacted with a custom binary format. You can also serialize JSON in a binary form that is more compact than the text format. A binary version of JSON is described by BSON (Binary JSON): http://bsonspec.org. Sending SOAP (an XML format) across the network makes use of the Web Service Description Language (WSDL) to describe the service. With REST services that are offering JSON data, a description is available as well: Swagger (http://swagger.io).

> **NOTE** *ASP.NET Web API and Swagger are covered in Chapter 42.*

Now it's time to get into concrete uses of the .NET Framework classes.

READING AND WRITING STREAMED XML

The XmlReader and XmlWriter classes provide a fast way to read and write large XML documents. XmlReader-based classes provide a very fast, forward-only, read-only cursor that streams the XML data for processing. Because it is a streaming model, the memory requirements are not very demanding. However, you don't have the navigation flexibility and the read or write capabilities that would be available from a DOM-based model. XmlWriter-based classes produce an XML document that conforms to the W3C's XML 1.0 (4th edition).

The sample code using XmlReader and XmlWriter makes use of the following dependencies and namespaces:

Dependencies

```
NETStandard.Library

System.Xml.ReaderWriter
```

Namespaces

```
System.Xml

static System.Console
```

The application enables you to specify several command-line arguments for all the different sample cases that are defined as const value, and also specifies the filenames to read and write to (code file XmlReaderAndWriterSample/Program.cs):

```
class Program
{
  private const string BooksFileName = "books.xml";
  private const string NewBooksFileName = "newbooks.xml";
  private const string ReadTextOption = "-r";
  private const string ReadElementContentOption = "-c";
  private const string ReadElementContentOption2 = "-c2";
  private const string ReadDecimalOption = "-d";
  private const string ReadAttributesOption = "-a";
  private const string WriteOption = "-w";
  // etc
}
```

The Main method invokes the specific sample method based on the command line that is passed:

```
static void Main(string[] args)
{
  if (args.Length != 1)
  {
    ShowUsage();
    return;
  }

  switch (args[0])
```

```
      {
        case ReadTextOption:
          ReadTextNodes();
          break;
        case ReadElementContentOption:
          ReadElementContent();
          break;
        case ReadElementContentOption2:
          ReadElementContent2();
          break;
        case ReadDecimalOption:
          ReadDecimal();
          break;
        case ReadAttributesOption:
          ReadAttributes();
          break;
        default:
          ShowUsage();
          break;
      }
    }
```

Reading XML with XmlReader

The XmlReader enables you to read large XML streams. It is implemented as a pull model parser to pull data into the application that's requesting it.

The following is a very simple example of reading XML data; later you take a closer look at the XmlReader class. Because the XmlReader is an abstract class, it cannot be directly instantiated. Instead, the factory method Create is invoked to return an instance that derives from the base class XmlReader. The Create method offers several overloads where either a filename, a TextReader, or a Stream can be supplied with the first argument. The sample code directly passes the filename to the Books.xml file. After the reader is created, nodes can be read using the Read method. As soon as no node is available, the Read method returns false. You can debug through the while loop to see all the node types returned from the books.xml file. Only with the nodes of type XmlNodeType.Text is the value written to the console (code file XMLReaderAndWriterSample/Program.cs):

```
public static void ReadTextNodes()
{
  using (XmlReader reader = XmlReader.Create(BooksFileName))
  {
    while (reader.Read())
    {
      if (reader.NodeType == XmlNodeType.Text)
      {
        WriteLine(reader.Value);
      }
    }
  }
}
```

Running the application with the -r option shows the value of all text nodes:

```
The Autobiography of Benjamin Franklin
Benjamin
Franklin
8.99
The Confidence Man
Herman
Melville
11.99
```

```
The Gorgias
Plato
9.99
```

Using Read Methods

Several ways exist to move through the document. As shown in the previous example, Read takes you to the next node. You can then verify whether the node has a value (HasValue) or, as you see later, whether the node has any attributes (HasAttributes). You can also use the ReadStartElement method, which verifies whether the current node is the start element and then positions you on the next node. If you are not on the start element, an XmlException is raised. Calling this method is the same as calling the IsStartElement method followed by a Read method.

ReadElementString is similar to ReadString except that you can optionally pass in the name of an element. If the next content node is not a start tag, or if the Name parameter does not match the current node Name, an exception is raised.

Here is an example showing how you can use ReadElementString. Notice that it uses FileStreams, so you need to ensure that you import the System.IO namespace (code file XMLReaderAndWriterSample/Program.cs):

```csharp
public static void ReadElementContent()
{
  using (XmlReader reader = XmlReader.Create(BooksFileName))
  {
    while (!reader.EOF)
    {
      if (reader.MoveToContent() == XmlNodeType.Element &&
          reader.Name == "title")
      {
        WriteLine(reader.ReadElementContentAsString());
      }
      else
      {
        // move on
        reader.Read();
      }
    }
  }
}
```

In the while loop, the MoveToContent method is used to find each node of type XmlNodeType.Element with the name title. The EOF property of the XmlTextReader checks the end of the loop condition. If the node is not of type Element or not named title, the else clause issues a Read method to move to the next node. When a node is found that matches the criteria, the result is written to the console. This should leave just the book titles written to the console. Note that you don't have to issue a Read call after a successful ReadElementString because ReadElementString consumes the entire Element and positions you on the next node.

If you remove && rdr.Name=="title" from the if clause, you have to catch the XmlException when it is thrown. Looking at the XML data file, the first element that MoveToContent finds is the <bookstore> element. Because it is an element, it passes the check in the if statement. However, because it does not contain a simple text type, it causes ReadElementString to raise an XmlException. One way to work around this is to catch the exception and invoke the Read method in the exception handler (code file XmlReaderAndWriterSample/Program.cs):

```csharp
public static void ReadElementContent2()
{
  using (XmlReader reader = XmlReader.Create(BooksFileName))
  {
    while (!reader.EOF)
```

```
        {
          if (reader.MoveToContent() == XmlNodeType.Element)
          {
            try
            {
              WriteLine(reader.ReadElementContentAsString());
            }
            catch (XmlException ex)
            {
              reader.Read();
            }
          }
          else
          {
            // move on
            reader.Read();
          }
        }
      }
    }
```

After running this example, the results should be the same as before. The XmlReader can also read strongly typed data. There are several ReadElementContentAs methods, such as ReadElementContentAsDouble, ReadElementContentAsBoolean, and so on. The following example shows how to read in the values as a decimal and do some math on the value. In this case, the value from the price element is increased by 25 percent (code file XmlReaderAndWriterSample/Program.cs):

```
public static void ReadDecimal()
{
  using (XmlReader reader = XmlReader.Create(BooksFileName))
  {
    while (reader.Read())
    {
      if (reader.NodeType == XmlNodeType.Element)
      {
        if (reader.Name == "price")
        {
          decimal price = reader.ReadElementContentAsDecimal();
          WriteLine($"Current Price = {price}");
          price += price * .25m;
          WriteLine($"New price {price}");
        }
        else if (reader.Name == "title")
        {
          WriteLine(reader.ReadElementContentAsString());
        }
      }
    }
  }
}
```

Retrieving Attribute Data

As you play with the sample code, you might notice that when the nodes are read in, you don't see any attributes. This is because attributes are not considered part of a document's structure. When you are on an element node, you can check for the existence of attributes and optionally retrieve the attribute values.

For example, the HasAttributes property returns true if there are any attributes; otherwise, it returns false. The AttributeCount property tells you how many attributes there are, and the GetAttribute method gets an attribute by name or by index. If you want to iterate through the attributes one at a time, you can use the MoveToFirstAttribute and MoveToNextAttribute methods.

The following example iterates through the attributes of the `books.xml` document (code file `XmlReaderAndWriterSample/Program.cs`):

```
public static void ReadAttributes()
{
  using (XmlReader reader = XmlReader.Create(BooksFileName))
  {
    while (reader.Read())
    {
      if (reader.NodeType == XmlNodeType.Element)
      {
        for (int i = 0; i < reader.AttributeCount; i++)
        {
          WriteLine(reader.GetAttribute(i));
        }
      }
    }
  }
}
```

This time you are looking for element nodes. When you find one, you loop through all the attributes and, using the `GetAttribute` method, load the value of the attribute into the list box. In the preceding example, those attributes would be `genre`, `publicationdate`, and `ISBN`.

Using the XmlWriter Class

The `XmlWriter` class enables you to write XML to a stream, a file, a `StringBuilder`, a `TextWriter`, or another `XmlWriter` object. Like `XmlTextReader`, it does so in a forward-only, noncached manner. `XmlWriter` is configurable, enabling you to specify such things as whether to indent content, the amount to indent, what quote character to use in attribute values, and whether namespaces are supported. This configuration is done using an `XmlWriterSettings` object.

Here's a simple example that shows how you can use the `XmlTextWriter` class (code file `XmlReaderAndWriterSample/Program.cs`):

```
public static void WriterSample()
{
  var settings = new XmlWriterSettings
  {
    Indent = true,
    NewLineOnAttributes = true,
    Encoding = Encoding.UTF8,
    WriteEndDocumentOnClose = true
  }

  StreamWriter stream = File.CreateText(NewBooksFileName);
  using (XmlWriter writer = XmlWriter.Create(stream, settings))
  {
    writer.WriteStartDocument();
    //Start creating elements and attributes
    writer.WriteStartElement("book");
    writer.WriteAttributeString("genre", "Mystery");
    writer.WriteAttributeString("publicationdate", "2001");
    writer.WriteAttributeString("ISBN", "123456789");
    writer.WriteElementString("title", "Case of the Missing Cookie");
    writer.WriteStartElement("author");
    writer.WriteElementString("name", "Cookie Monster");
    writer.WriteEndElement();
    writer.WriteElementString("price", "9.99");
    writer.WriteEndElement();
    writer.WriteEndDocument();
  }
}
```

Here, you are writing to a new XML file called `newbook.xml`, adding the data for a new book. Note that `XmlWriter` overwrites an existing file with a new one. (Later in this chapter you read about inserting a new element or node into an existing document.) You are instantiating the `XmlWriter` object by using the `Create` static method. In this example, a string representing a filename is passed as a parameter, along with an instance of an `XmlWriterSettings` class.

The `XmlWriterSettings` class has properties that control how the XML is generated. The `CheckedCharacters` property is a Boolean that raises an exception if a character in the XML does not conform to the W3C XML 1.0 recommendation. The `Encoding` class sets the encoding used for the XML being generated; the default is Encoding.UTF8. The `Indent` property is a Boolean value that determines whether elements should be indented. The `IndentChars` property is set to the character string that it is used to indent. The default is two spaces. The `NewLine` property is used to determine the characters for line breaks. In the preceding example, the `NewLineOnAttribute` is set to `true`. This puts each attribute in a separate line, which can make the generated XML a little easier to read.

`WriteStartDocument` adds the document declaration. Now you start writing data. First is the `book` element; next, you add the `genre`, `publicationdate`, and `ISBN` attributes. Then you write the `title`, `author`, and `price` elements. Note that the `author` element has a child element name.

When you click the button, you produce the `booknew.xml` file, which looks like this:

```
<?xml version="1.0" encoding="utf-8"?>
<book
  genre="Mystery"
  publicationdate="2001"
  ISBN="123456789">
  <title>Case of the Missing Cookie</title>
  <author>
    <name>Cookie Monster</name>
  </author>
  <price>9.99</price>
</book>
```

The nesting of elements is controlled by paying attention to when you start and finish writing elements and attributes. You can see this when you add the `name` child element to the `authors` element. Note how the `WriteStartElement` and `WriteEndElement` method calls are arranged and how that arrangement produces the nested elements in the output file.

Along with the `WriteElementString` and `WriteAttributeString` methods, there are several other specialized write methods. `WriteComment` writes out a comment in proper XML format. `WriteChars` writes out the contents of a `char` buffer. `WriteChars` needs a buffer (an array of characters), the starting position for writing (an integer), and the number of characters to write (an integer).

Reading and writing XML using the `XmlReader`- and `XmlWriter`-based classes are flexible and simple to do. Next, you find out how the DOM is implemented in the `System.Xml` namespace through the `XmlDocument` and `XmlNode` classes.

USING THE DOM IN .NET

The DOM implementation in .NET supports the W3C DOM specifications. The DOM is implemented through the `XmlNode` class, which is an abstract class that represents a node of an XML document. Concrete classes are `XmlDocument`, `XmlDocumentFragment`, `XmlAttribute`, and `XmlNotation`. `XmlLinkedNode` is an abstract class that derives from `XmlNode`. Concrete classes that derive from `XmlLinkedNode` are `XmlDeclaration`, `XmlDocumentType`, `XmlElement`, and `XmlProcessingInstruction`.

An `XmlNodeList` class is an ordered list of nodes. This is a live list of nodes, and any changes to any node are immediately reflected in the list. `XmlNodeList` supports indexed access or iterative access.

The `XmlNode` and `XmlNodeList` classes make up the core of the DOM implementation in the .NET Framework.

The sample code using XmlDocument makes use of the following dependencies and namespaces:

Dependencies

```
NETStandard.Library
System.Xml.XmlDocument
```

Namespaces

```
System
System.IO
System.Xml
static System.Console
```

Reading with the XmlDocument Class

XmlDocument is a class that represents the XML DOM in .NET. Unlike XmlReader and XmlWriter, XmlDocument provides read and write capabilities as well as random access to the DOM tree.

The example introduced in this section creates an XmlDocument object, loads a document from disk, and loads a text box with data from the title elements. This is similar to one of the examples that you constructed in the section "Reading XML with XmlReader." The difference is that here you select the nodes you want to work with instead of going through the entire document as in the XmlReader-based example.

Here is the code to create an XmlDocument object. Note how simple it looks in comparison to the XmlReader example (code file XmlDocumentSample/Program.cs):

```
public static void ReadXml()
{
  using (FileStream stream = File.OpenRead(BooksFileName))
  {
    var doc = new XmlDocument();
    doc.Load(stream);

    XmlNodeList titleNodes = doc.GetElementsByTagName("title");

    foreach (XmlNode node in titleNodes)
    {
      WriteLine(node.OuterXml);
    }
  }
}
```

If this is all that you wanted to do, using the XmlReader would have been a much more efficient way to read the file, because you just go through the document once and then you are finished with it. This is exactly the type of work that XmlReader was designed for. However, if you want to revisit a node, using XmlDocument is a better way.

Navigating Through the Hierarchy

A big advantage of the XmlDocument class is that you can navigate the DOM tree. The following example accesses all author elements and writes the outer XML to the console (this is the XML including the author element), the inner XML (without the author element), the next sibling, the previous sibling, the first child, and the parent (code file XmlDocumentSample/Program.cs):

```
public static void NavigateXml()
{
  using (FileStream stream = File.OpenRead(BooksFileName))
  {
    var doc = new XmlDocument();
```

```
        doc.Load(stream);

        XmlNodeList authorNodes = doc.GetElementsByTagName("author");

        foreach (XmlNode node in authorNodes)
        {
          WriteLine($"Outer XML: {node.OuterXml}");
          WriteLine($"Inner XML: {node.InnerXml}");
          WriteLine($"Next sibling outer XML: {node.NextSibling.OuterXml}");
          WriteLine($"Previous sibling outer XML:
            {node.PreviousSibling.OuterXml}");
          WriteLine($"First child outer Xml: {node.FirstChild.OuterXml}");
          WriteLine($"Parent name: {node.ParentNode.Name}");
          WriteLine();
        }
      }
    }
```

When you run the application, you can see these values for the first element found:

```
Outer XML: <author><first-name>Benjamin</first-name>
  <last-name>Franklin</last-name></author>
Inner XML: <first-name>Benjamin</first-name><last-name>Franklin</last-name>
Next sibling outer XML: <price>8.99</price>
Previous sibling outer XML:
  <title>The Autobiography of Benjamin Franklin</title>
First child outer Xml: <first-name>Benjamin</first-name>
Parent name: book
```

Inserting Nodes with XmlDocument

Earlier, you looked at an example that used the XmlWriter class that created a new document. The limitation was that it would not insert a node into a current document. With the XmlDocument class, you can do just that.

The following code sample creates the element book using CreateElement, adds some attributes, adds some child elements, and after creating the complete book element adds it to the root element of the XML document (code file XmlDocumentSample/Program.cs):

```
public static void CreateXml()
{
  var doc = new XmlDocument();

  using (FileStream stream = File.OpenRead("books.xml"))
  {
    doc.Load(stream);
  }


  //create a new 'book' element
  XmlElement newBook = doc.CreateElement("book");
  //set some attributes
  newBook.SetAttribute("genre", "Mystery");
  newBook.SetAttribute("publicationdate", "2001");
  newBook.SetAttribute("ISBN", "123456789");
  //create a new 'title' element
  XmlElement newTitle = doc.CreateElement("title");
  newTitle.InnerText = "Case of the Missing Cookie";
  newBook.AppendChild(newTitle);
  //create new author element
  XmlElement newAuthor = doc.CreateElement("author");
  newBook.AppendChild(newAuthor);
  //create new name element
```

```
XmlElement newName = doc.CreateElement("name");
newName.InnerText = "Cookie Monster";
newAuthor.AppendChild(newName);
//create new price element
XmlElement newPrice = doc.CreateElement("price");
newPrice.InnerText = "9.95";
newBook.AppendChild(newPrice);

//add to the current document
doc.DocumentElement.AppendChild(newBook);

var settings = new XmlWriterSettings
{
  Indent = true,
  IndentChars = "\t",
  NewLineChars = Environment.NewLine
};
//write out the doc to disk
using (StreamWriter streamWriter = File.CreateText(NewBooksFileName))
using (XmlWriter writer = XmlWriter.Create(streamWriter, settings))
{
  doc.WriteContentTo(writer);
}

XmlNodeList nodeLst = doc.GetElementsByTagName("title");
foreach (XmlNode node in nodeLst)
{
  WriteLine(node.OuterXml);
}
}
}
```

When you run the application, the following book element is added to the bookstore and written to the file newbooks.xml:

```
<book genre="Mystery" publicationdate="2001" ISBN="123456789">
  <title>Case of the Missing Cookie</title>
    <author>
      <name>Cookie Monster</name>
    </author>
  <price>9.95</price>
</book>
```

After creating the file, the application writes all title nodes to the console. You can see that the added element is now included:

```
<title>The Autobiography of Benjamin Franklin</title>
<title>The Confidence Man</title>
<title>The Gorgias</title>
<title>Case of the Missing Cookie</title>
```

You should use the `XmlDocument` class when you want to have random access to the document. Use the `XmlReader`-based classes when you want a streaming-type model instead. Remember that there is a cost for the flexibility of the `XmlNode`-based `XmlDocument` class: Memory requirements are higher and the performance of reading the document is not as good as when using `XmlReader`. There is another way to traverse an XML document: the `XPathNavigator`.

USING XPATHNAVIGATOR

An `XPathNavigator` can be used to select, iterate, and find data from an XML document using the XPath syntax. An `XPathNavigator` can be created from an `XPathDocument`. The `XPathDocument` cannot be changed; it is designed for performance and read-only use. Unlike the `XmlReader`, the `XPathNavigator` is not a streaming model, so the document is read and parsed only once. Similar to XmlDocument it requires the complete document loaded in memory.

The System.Xml.XPath namespace defined in the NuGet package System.Xml.XPath is built for speed. It provides a read-only view of your XML documents, so there are no editing capabilities. Classes in this namespace are built for fast iteration and selections on the XML document in a cursory fashion.

The following table lists the key classes in System.Xml.XPath and gives a short description of the purpose of each class.

CLASS NAME	DESCRIPTION
XPathDocument	Provides a view of the entire XML document. Read-only.
XPathNavigator	Provides the navigational capabilities to an XPathDocument.
XPathNodeIterator	Provides iteration capabilities to a node set.
XPathExpression	Represents a compiled XPath expression. Used by SelectNodes, SelectSingleNodes, Evaluate, and Matches.

The sample code makes use of the following dependencies and namespaces:

Dependencies

```
NETStandard.Library
System.Xml.XmlDocument
System.Xml.XPath
```

Namespaces

```
System.IO
System.Xml
System.Xml.XPath
static System.Console
```

XPathDocument

XPathDocument does not offer any of the functionality of the XmlDocument class. Its sole purpose is to create XPathNavigators. In fact, that is the only method available on the XPathDocument class (other than those provided by Object).

You can create an XPathDocument in a number of different ways. You can pass in an XmlReader, or a Stream-based object to the constructor. This provides a great deal of flexibility.

XPathNavigator

XPathNavigator contains methods for moving and selecting elements. Move methods set the current position of the iterator to the element that should be moved to. You can move to specific attributes of an element: the MoveToFirstAttribute method moves to the first attribute, the MoveToNextAttribute method to the next one. MoveToAttribute allows specifying a specific attribute name. You can move to sibling nodes with MoveToFirst, MoveToNext, MoveToPrevious, and MoveToLast. It's also possible to move to child elements (MoveToChild, MoveToFirstChild), to parent elements (MoveToParent), and directly to the root element (MoveToRoot).

You can select methods using XPath expressions using the Select method. To filter the selection based on specific nodes in the tree and the current position, other methods exist. SelectAncestor only filters ancestor nodes, and SelectDescendants filters all descendants. Only the direct children are filtered with SelectChildren. SelectSingleNode accepts an XPath expression and returns a single matching node.

The `XPathNavigator` also allows changing the XML tree using one of the Insert methods if the `CanEdit` property returns `true`. The `XPathNavigator` available with .NET Core always returns `false`, and these methods are implemented by throwing a `NotImplementedException` exception. With .NET 4.6, when you use the `XmlDocument` class to create an `XPathNavigator`, the `CanEdit` property of the navigator returns `true` and thus allows changes using the `Insert` methods.

XPathNodeIterator

The `XPathDocument` represents the complete XML document, the `XPathNavigator` enables you to select nodes and move the cursor within the document to specific nodes, and the `XPathNodeIterator` enables you to iterate over a set of nodes.

The `XPathNodeIterator` is returned by the `XPathNavigator` `Select` methods. You use it to iterate over the set of nodes returned by a `Select` method of the `XPathNavigator`. Using the `MoveNext` method of the `XPathNodeIterator` does not change the location of the `XPathNavigator` that created it. However, you can get a new `XPathNavigator` using the `Current` property of an `XPathNodeIterator`. The `Current` property returns an `XPathNavigator` that is set to the current position.

Navigating Through XML Using XPath

The best way to see how these classes are used is to look at some code that iterates through the `books.xml` document. This enables you to see how the navigation works.

The first example iterates all books that define the genre novel. First, an `XPathDocument` object is created that receives the XML filename in the constructor. This object, which holds read-only content of the XML file, offers the `CreateNavigator` method to create an `XPathNavigator`. When you use this navigator, an XPath expression can be passed to the `Select` method. When you use XPath, you can access element trees using / between hierarchies. `/bookstore/book` retrieves all `book` nodes within the `bookstore` element. `@genre` is a shorthand notation to access the attribute genre. The `Select` method returns an `XPathNodeIterator` that enables you to iterate all nodes that match the expression. The first `while` loop iterates all book elements that match calling the `MoveNext` method. With each iteration, another select method is invoked on the current `XPathNavigator`—`SelectDescendants`. `SelectDescendants` returns all descendants, which means the child nodes, and the children of the child nodes, and the children of those children through the complete hierarchy. With the `SelectDescendants` method, the overload is taken to match only element nodes and to exclude the book element itself. The second `while` loop iterates this collection and writes the name and value to the console (code file `XPathNavigatorSample/Program.cs`):

```
public static void SimpleNavigate()
{
  //modify to match your path structure
  var doc = new XPathDocument(BooksFileName);
  //create the XPath navigator
  XPathNavigator nav = doc.CreateNavigator();
  //create the XPathNodeIterator of book nodes
  // that have genre attribute value of novel
  XPathNodeIterator iterator = nav.Select("/bookstore/book[@genre='novel']");

  while (iterator.MoveNext())
  {
    XPathNodeIterator newIterator = iterator.Current.SelectDescendants(
        XPathNodeType.Element, matchSelf: false);
    while (newIterator.MoveNext())
    {
      WriteLine($"{newIterator.Current.Name}: {newIterator.Current.Value}");
    }
  }
}
```

When you run the application, you can see the content of the only book that matches the novel genre with all its children as you can see with the `first-name` and `last-name` elements that are contained within author:

```
title: The Confidence Man
author: HermanMelville
first-name: Herman
last-name: Melville
price: 11.99
```

Using XPath Evaluations

XPath not only allows fast access to XML nodes within a tree, it also defines some functions—for example, ceiling, floor, number, round, and sum—for numbers. The following sample is somewhat similar to the previous one; it accesses all book elements instead of only the one matching the novel genre. Iterating the book elements, just the title child element is accessed by moving the current position to the first child title node. From the title node, the name and value are written to the console. The very special piece of code is defined with the last statement. The XPath sum function is invoked on the value of /bookstore/book/ price elements. Such functions can be evaluated by calling the Evaluate method on the XPathNavigator (code file XPathNavigatorSample/Program.cs):

```csharp
public static void UseEvaluate()
{
  //modify to match your path structure
  var doc = new XPathDocument(BooksFileName);
  //create the XPath navigator
  XPathNavigator nav = doc.CreateNavigator();
  //create the XPathNodeIterator of book nodes
  XPathNodeIterator iterator = nav.Select("/bookstore/book");
  while (iterator.MoveNext())
  {
    if (iterator.Current.MoveToChild("title", string.Empty))
    {
      WriteLine($"{iterator.Current.Name}: {iterator.Current.Value}");
    }
  }
  WriteLine("=========================");
  WriteLine($"Total Cost = {nav.Evaluate("sum(/bookstore/book/price)")}");
}
```

When you run the application, you can see all book titles and the summary price:

```
title: The Autobiography of Benjamin Franklin
title: The Confidence Man
title: The Gorgias
=========================
Total Cost = 30.97
```

Changing XML Using XPath

Next, make some changes using XPath. This part of the code only works with the full .NET Framework, thus pre-processor directives are used to handle the code differences. To create a changeable XPathNavigator, with .NET 4.6, the XmlDocument class is used. Using .NET Core, XmlDocument does not offer a CreateNavigator method, and thus the navigator is always read-only. With .NET 4.6, the CanEdit property of the XPathNavigator returns true, and thus the InsertAfter method can be invoked. Using InsertAfter, a discount is added as sibling after the price element. The newly created XML document is accessed using the OuterXml property of the navigator, and a new XML file is saved (code file XPathNavigatorSample/Program.cs):

```csharp
public static void Insert()
{
#if DNX46
```

```
      var doc = new XmlDocument();
      doc.Load(BooksFileName);
#else
      var doc = new XPathDocument(BooksFileName);
#endif

      XPathNavigator navigator = doc.CreateNavigator();

      if (navigator.CanEdit)
      {
        XPathNodeIterator iter = navigator.Select("/bookstore/book/price");

        while (iter.MoveNext())
        {
          iter.Current.InsertAfter("<disc>5</disc>");
        }
      }

      using (var stream = File.CreateText(NewBooksFileName))
      {
        var outDoc = new XmlDocument();
        outDoc.LoadXml(navigator.OuterXml);
        outDoc.Save(stream);
      }
    }
```

When you run the application with .NET 4.6, the newly generated XML contains the disc elements:

```xml
<?xml version="1.0" encoding="utf-8"?>
<!-- This file represents a fragment of a book store inventory database -->
<bookstore>
  <book genre="autobiography" publicationdate="1991" ISBN="1-861003-11-0">
    <title>The Autobiography of Benjamin Franklin</title>
    <author>
      <first-name>Benjamin</first-name>
      <last-name>Franklin</last-name>
    </author>
    <price>8.99</price>
    <disc>5</disc>
  </book>
  <book genre="novel" publicationdate="1967" ISBN="0-201-63361-2">
    <title>The Confidence Man</title>
    <author>
      <first-name>Herman</first-name>
      <last-name>Melville</last-name>
    </author>
    <price>11.99</price>
    <disc>5</disc>
  </book>
  <book genre="philosophy" publicationdate="1991" ISBN="1-861001-57-6">
    <title>The Gorgias</title>
    <author>
      <name>Plato</name>
    </author>
    <price>9.99</price>
    <disc>5</disc>
  </book>
</bookstore>
```

SERIALIZING OBJECTS IN XML

Serializing is the process of persisting an object to disk. Another part of your application, or even a separate application, can deserialize the object, and it will be in the same state it was in prior to serialization. The .NET Framework includes a couple of ways to do this.

This section looks at the `System.Xml.Serialization` namespace with the NuGet package `System.Xml.XmlSerializer`, which contains classes used to serialize objects into XML documents or streams. This means that an object's public properties and public fields are converted into XML elements, attributes, or both.

The most important class in the `System.Xml.Serialization` namespace is `XmlSerializer`. To serialize an object, you first need to instantiate an `XmlSerializer` object, specifying the type of the object to serialize. Then you need to instantiate a stream/writer object to write the file to a stream/document. The final step is to call the `Serialize` method on the `XMLSerializer`, passing it the stream/writer object and the object to serialize.

Data that can be serialized can be primitive types, fields, arrays, and embedded XML in the form of `XmlElement` and `XmlAttribute` objects. To deserialize an object from an XML document, you reverse the process in the previous example. You create a stream/reader and an `XmlSerializer` object and then pass the stream/reader to the `Deserialize` method. This method returns the deserialized object, although it needs to be cast to the correct type.

> **NOTE** *The XML serializer cannot convert private data—only public data—and it cannot serialize cyclic object graphs. However, these are not serious limitations; by carefully designing your classes, you should be able to easily avoid these issues. If you do need to be able to serialize public and private data as well as an object graph containing many nested objects, you can use the runtime or the data contract serialization mechanisms.*

The sample code makes use of the following dependencies and namespaces:

Dependencies

```
NETStandard.Library
System.Xml.XmlDocument
System.Xml.XmlSerializer
```

Namespaces

```
System.IO
System.Xml
System.Xml.Serialization
static System.Console
```

Serializing a Simple Object

Let's start serializing a simple object. The class `Product` has XML attributes from the namespace `System.Xml.Serialization` applied to specify whether a property should be serialized as XML element or attribute. The `XmlElement` attribute specifies the property to serialize as element; the `XmlAttribute` attribute specifies to serialize as attribute. The `XmlRoot` attribute specifies the class to be serialized as the root element (code file `ObjectToXmlSerializationSample/Product.cs`):

```
[XmlRoot]
public class Product
{
    [XmlAttribute(AttributeName = "Discount")]
    public int Discount { get; set; }

    [XmlElement]
    public int ProductID { get; set; }

    [XmlElement]
    public string ProductName { get; set; }

    [XmlElement]
    public int SupplierID { get; set; }

    [XmlElement]
    public int CategoryID { get; set; }

    [XmlElement]
    public string QuantityPerUnit { get; set; }

    [XmlElement]
    public Decimal UnitPrice { get; set; }

    [XmlElement]
    public short UnitsInStock { get; set; }

    [XmlElement]
    public short UnitsOnOrder { get; set; }

    [XmlElement]
    public short ReorderLevel { get; set; }

    [XmlElement]
    public bool Discontinued { get; set; }

    public override string ToString() =>
        $"{ProductID} {ProductName} {UnitPrice:C}";
}
```

With these attributes, you can influence the name, namespace, and type to be generated by using properties of the attribute types.

The following code sample creates an instance of the `Product` class, fills its properties, and serializes it to a file. Creating the `XmlSerializer` requires the type of the class to be serialized to be passed with the constructor. The `Serialize` method is overloaded to accept a `Stream`, `TextWriter`, and `XmlWriter`, and the object to be serialized (code file `ObjectToXmlSerializationSample/Program.cs`):

```
public static void SerializeProduct()
{
    var product = new Product
    {
        ProductID = 200,
        CategoryID = 100,
        Discontinued = false,
        ProductName = "Serialize Objects",
        QuantityPerUnit = "6",
        ReorderLevel = 1,
        SupplierID = 1,
```

```
            UnitPrice = 1000,
            UnitsInStock = 10,
            UnitsOnOrder = 0
        };

    FileStream stream = File.OpenWrite(ProductFileName);
    using (TextWriter writer = new StreamWriter(stream))
    {
        XmlSerializer serializer = new XmlSerializer(typeof(Product));
        serializer.Serialize(writer, product);
    }
}
```

The generated XML file lists the Product element with the Discount attribute and the other properties stored as elements:

```
<?xml version="1.0" encoding="utf-8"?>
<Product xmlns:xsi="http://www.w3.org/2001/XMLSchema-instance"
    xmlns:xsd="http://www.w3.org/2001/XMLSchema" Discount="0">
  <ProductID>200</ProductID>
  <ProductName>Serialize Objects</ProductName>
  <SupplierID>1</SupplierID>
  <CategoryID>100</CategoryID>
  <QuantityPerUnit>6</QuantityPerUnit>
  <UnitPrice>1000</UnitPrice>
  <UnitsInStock>10</UnitsInStock>
  <UnitsOnOrder>0</UnitsOnOrder>
  <ReorderLevel>1</ReorderLevel>
  <Discontinued>false</Discontinued>
</Product>
```

There is nothing out of the ordinary here. You could use this XML file in any way that you would use an XML document—transform it and display it as HTML, load an XmlDocument with it, or, as shown in the example, deserialize it and create an object in the same state that it was in prior to serializing it (which is exactly what you're doing in the next step.

Creating a new object from the file is done by creating an XmlSerializer and invoking the Deserialize method (code file ObjectToXmlSerializationSample/Program.cs):

```
public static void DeserializeProduct()
{
    Product product;
    using (var stream = new FileStream(ProductFileName, FileMode.Open))
    {
        var serializer = new XmlSerializer(typeof(Product));
        product = serializer.Deserialize(stream) as Product;
    }
    WriteLine(product);
}
```

When you run the application, the console shows the product ID, product name, and unit price.

> **NOTE** *To ignore properties from the XML serialization, you can use the* XmlIgnore *attribute.*

Serializing a Tree of Objects

What about situations in which you have derived classes and possibly properties that return an array? XmlSerializer has that covered as well. The next example is just slightly more complex so that it can deal with these issues.

In addition to the `Product` class, the `BookProduct` (derived from `Product`) and `Inventory` classes are created. The `Inventory` class contains both of the other classes.

The `BookProduct` class derives from Product and adds the `ISBN` property. This property is stored with the XML attribute `Isbn` as defined by the .NET attribute `XmlAttribute` (code file `ObjectToXmlSerializationSample/BookProduct.cs`):

```
public class BookProduct : Product
{
  [XmlAttribute("Isbn")]
  public string ISBN { get; set; }
}
```

The `Inventory` class contains an array of inventory items. An inventory item can be a `Product` or a `BookProduct`. The serializer needs to know all the derived classes that are stored within the array, otherwise it can't deserialize them. The items of the array are defined using the `XmlArrayItem` attribute (code file `ObjectToXmlSerializationSample/Inventory.cs`):

```
public class Inventory
{
  [XmlArrayItem("Product", typeof(Product)),
   XmlArrayItem("Book", typeof(BookProduct))]
  public Product[] InventoryItems { get; set; }

  public override string ToString()
  {
    var outText = new StringBuilder();
    foreach (Product prod in InventoryItems)
    {
      outText.AppendLine(prod.ProductName);
    }
    return outText.ToString();
  }
}
```

In the `SerializeInventory` method after an `Inventory` object is created that is filled with a `Product` and a `BookProduct`, the inventory is serialized (code file `ObjectToXmlSerializationSample/Program.cs`):

```
public static void SerializeInventory()
{
  var product = new Product
  {
    ProductID = 100,
    ProductName = "Product Thing",
    SupplierID = 10
  };

  var book = new BookProduct
  {
    ProductID = 101,
    ProductName = "How To Use Your New Product Thing",
    SupplierID = 10,
    ISBN = "1234567890"
  };

  Product[] items = { product, book };
  var inventory = new Inventory
  {
    InventoryItems = items
  };

  using (FileStream stream = File.Create(InventoryFileName))
  {
```

```
      var serializer = new XmlSerializer(typeof(Inventory));
      serializer.Serialize(stream, inventory);
    }
  }
```

The generated XML file defines an `Inventory` root element and the `Product` and `Book` child elements. The `BookProduct` type is represented as `Book` element because the `XmlItemArray` attribute defined the `Book` name for the `BookProduct` type:

```xml
<?xml version="1.0"?>
<Inventory xmlns:xsi="http://www.w3.org/2001/XMLSchema-instance"
           xmlns:xsd="http://www.w3.org/2001/XMLSchema">
  <InventoryItems>
    <Product Discount="0">
      <ProductID>100</ProductID>
      <ProductName>Product Thing</ProductName>
      <SupplierID>10</SupplierID>
      <CategoryID>0</CategoryID>
      <UnitPrice>0</UnitPrice>
      <UnitsInStock>0</UnitsInStock>
      <UnitsOnOrder>0</UnitsOnOrder>
      <ReorderLevel>0</ReorderLevel>
      <Discontinued>false</Discontinued>
    </Product>
    <Book Discount="0" Isbn="1234567890">
      <ProductID>101</ProductID>
      <ProductName>How To Use Your New Product Thing</ProductName>
      <SupplierID>10</SupplierID>
      <CategoryID>0</CategoryID>
      <UnitPrice>0</UnitPrice>
      <UnitsInStock>0</UnitsInStock>
      <UnitsOnOrder>0</UnitsOnOrder>
      <ReorderLevel>0</ReorderLevel>
      <Discontinued>false</Discontinued>
    </Book>
  </InventoryItems>
</Inventory>
```

To deserialize the objects, you need to invoke the `Deserialize` method of the `XmlSerializer`:

```csharp
public static void DeserializeInventory()
{
  using (FileStream stream = File.OpenRead(InventoryFileName))
  {
    var serializer = new XmlSerializer(typeof(Inventory));
    Inventory newInventory = serializer.Deserialize(stream) as Inventory;
    foreach (Product prod in newInventory.InventoryItems)
    {
      WriteLine(prod.ProductName);
    }
  }
}
```

Serializing Without Attributes

Well, this all works great, but what if you don't have access to the source code for the types that are being serialized? You can't add the attribute if you don't have the source. There is another way: You can use the `XmlAttributes` class and the `XmlAttributeOverrides` class. Together these classes enable you to accomplish exactly the same thing as the previous sample but without adding the attributes. This section demonstrates how this works.

For this example, the `Inventory`, `Product`, and derived `BookProduct` classes could also be in a separate library. As the serialization is independent of that, and to make the sample structure easier, these classes are in the same project as in the previous examples, but note that now there are no attributes added to the Inventory class (code file ObjectToXmlSerializationWOAttributes/Inventory.cs):

```
public class Inventory
{
  public Product[] InventoryItems { get; set; }
  public override string ToString()
  {
    var outText = new StringBuilder();
    foreach (Product prod in InventoryItems)
    {
      outText.AppendLine(prod.ProductName);
    }
    return outText.ToString();
  }
}
```

The attributes from the Product and BookProduct classes are removed as well.

The implementation to do the serialization is similar to before, with the difference of using a different overload on creating the XmlSerializer. This overload accepts XmlAttributeOverrides. These overrides are coming from the helper method GetInventoryXmlAttributes (code file ObjectToXmlSerializationWOAttributes/Program.cs):

```
public static void SerializeInventory()
{
  var product = new Product
  {
    ProductID = 100,
    ProductName = "Product Thing",
    SupplierID = 10
  };

  var book = new BookProduct
  {
    ProductID = 101,
    ProductName = "How To Use Your New Product Thing",
    SupplierID = 10,
    ISBN = "1234567890"
  };

  Product[] products = { product, book };
  var inventory = new Inventory
  {
    InventoryItems = products
  };
  using (FileStream stream = File.Create(InventoryFileName))
  {
    var serializer = new XmlSerializer(typeof(Inventory),
        GetInventoryXmlAttributes());
    serializer.Serialize(stream, inventory);
  }
}
```

The helper method GetInventoryXmlAttributes returns the needed XmlAttributeOverrides. Previously, the Inventory class had the XmlArrayItem attributes applied. They are now done creating XmlAttributes and adding XmlArrayItemAttributes to the XmlArrayItems collection. Another change is that the Product and BookProduct classes had an XmlAttribute applied to the Discount and ISBN properties. To define the same behavior without applying the attributes to the properties directly, XmlAttributeAttribute objects are created and assigned to the XmlAttribute property of XmlAttributes objects. All of these created XmlAttributes are then added to the XmlAttributeOverrides that contains a collection of XmlAttributes. When you invoke the Add method of XmlAttributeOverrides, you need the type where the attribute should be applied, the name of the property, and the corresponding XmlAttributes (code file ObjectToXmlSerializationWOAttributes/Program.cs):

```
private static XmlAttributeOverrides GetInventoryXmlAttributes()
{
    var inventoryAttributes = new XmlAttributes();
    inventoryAttributes.XmlArrayItems.Add(new XmlArrayItemAttribute("Book",
        typeof(BookProduct)));
    inventoryAttributes.XmlArrayItems.Add(new XmlArrayItemAttribute("Product",
        typeof(Product)));

    var bookIsbnAttributes = new XmlAttributes();
    bookIsbnAttributes.XmlAttribute = new XmlAttributeAttribute("Isbn");

    var productDiscountAttributes = new XmlAttributes();
    productDiscountAttributes.XmlAttribute =
        new XmlAttributeAttribute("Discount");

    var overrides = new XmlAttributeOverrides();

    overrides.Add(typeof(Inventory), "InventoryItems", inventoryAttributes);

    overrides.Add(typeof(BookProduct), "ISBN", bookIsbnAttributes);
    overrides.Add(typeof(Product), "Discount", productDiscountAttributes);
    return overrides;
}
```

When you run the application, the same XML content is created as before:

```
<?xml version="1.0"?>
<Inventory xmlns:xsi="http://www.w3.org/2001/XMLSchema-instance"
  xmlns:xsd="http://www.w3.org/2001/XMLSchema">
  <InventoryItems>
    <Product Discount="0">
      <ProductID>100</ProductID>
      <ProductName>Product Thing</ProductName>
      <SupplierID>10</SupplierID>
      <CategoryID>0</CategoryID>
      <UnitPrice>0</UnitPrice>
      <UnitsInStock>0</UnitsInStock>
      <UnitsOnOrder>0</UnitsOnOrder>
      <ReorderLevel>0</ReorderLevel>
      <Discontinued>false</Discontinued>
    </Product>
    <Book Discount="0" Isbn="1234567890">
      <ProductID>101</ProductID>
      <ProductName>How To Use Your New Product Thing</ProductName>
      <SupplierID>10</SupplierID>
      <CategoryID>0</CategoryID>
      <UnitPrice>0</UnitPrice>
      <UnitsInStock>0</UnitsInStock>
      <UnitsOnOrder>0</UnitsOnOrder>
      <ReorderLevel>0</ReorderLevel>
      <Discontinued>false</Discontinued>
    </Book>
  </InventoryItems>
</Inventory>
```

> **NOTE** *.NET attribute types typically end with the name* Attribute. *This postfix can be ignored when applying the attribute using brackets. The compiler automatically adds the postfix if it is missing. A class that can be used as an attribute derives from the base class* Attribute—*directly or indirectly. When you apply the attribute* XmlElement *using brackets, the compiler instantiates the type* XmlElementAttribute. *This naming becomes especially noticeable when applying the attribute* XmlAttribute *using brackets. Behind the scenes, the class* XmlAttributeAttribute *is used. How does the compiler differentiate this with the class* XmlAttribute? *The class* XmlAttribute *is used to read XML attributes from the DOM tree, but it is not a .NET attribute, as it does not derive from the base class* Attribute. *You can read more information about attributes in Chapter 16, "Reflection, Metadata, and Dynamic Programming."*

With the deserialization code, the same attribute overrides are needed (code file `ObjectToXmlSerializationWOAttributes/Program.cs`):

```
public static void DeserializeInventory()
{
  using (FileStream stream = File.OpenRead(InventoryFileName))
  {
    XmlSerializer serializer = new XmlSerializer(typeof(Inventory),
      GetInventoryXmlAttributes());
    Inventory newInventory = serializer.Deserialize(stream) as Inventory;
    foreach (Product prod in newInventory.InventoryItems)
    {
      WriteLine(prod.ProductName);
    }
  }
}
```

The `System.Xml.XmlSerialization` namespace provides a very powerful toolset for serializing objects to XML. By serializing and deserializing objects to XML instead of to binary format, you have the option to do something else with this XML, which greatly adds to the flexibility of your designs.

LINQ TO XML

Aren't there already enough options available dealing with XML? Beware, with LINQ to XML another option is available. LINQ to XML allows querying XML code similar to querying object lists and the database. LINQ to Objects are covered in Chapter 13, and LINQ to Entities are covered in Chapter 38, "Entity Framework Core." Although the DOM tree offered by the `XmlDocument` and XPath queries offered by the `XPathNavigator` implement a standards-based approach to query XML data, LINQ to XML offers the simple .NET variant for query—a variant that is similar to querying other data stores. In addition to the methods offered by LINQ to Objects, LINQ to XML adds some XML specifics to this query in the `System.Xml.Linq` namespace. LINQ to XML also offers easier creating of XML content than the standards-based `XmlDocument` XML creation.

The following sections describe the objects that are available with LINQ to XML.

> **NOTE** *Many of the examples in this section use a file called* Hamlet.xml, *which you can find at* http://metalab.unc.edu/bosak/xml/eg/shaks200.zip. *It includes all of Shakespeare's plays as XML files.*

The sample code makes use of the following dependencies and namespaces:

Dependencies

```
NETStandard.Library
System.Xml.XDocument
```

Namespaces

```
System
System.Collections.Generic
System.Linq
System.Xml.Linq
static System.Console
```

XDocument

The XDocument represents an XML document like the XmlDocument class, but it is easier to work with. The XDocument object works with the other new objects in this space, such as the XNamespace, XComment, XElement, and XAttribute objects.

One of the more important members of the XDocument object is the Load method. Here it loads the file hamlet.xml that is defined by the constant HamletFileName into memory:

```
XDocument doc = XDocument.Load(HamletFileName);
```

You can also pass a TextReader or XmlReader object into the Load method. From here, you can programmatically work with the XML code as shown in the following code snippet to access the name of the root element and check whether the root element has attributes (code file LinqToXmlSample/Program.cs):

```
XDocument doc = XDocument.Load(HamletFileName);
WriteLine($"root name: {doc.Root.Name}");
WriteLine($"has root attributes? {doc.Root.HasAttributes}");
```

This produces the following results:

```
root name: PLAY
has root attributes? False
```

Another important member to be aware of is the Save method, which, like the Load method, enables you to save to a physical disk location or to a TextWriter or XmlWriter object:

```
XDocument doc = XDocument.Load(HamletFileName);
doc.Save(SaveFileName);
```

XElement

One object that you will work with frequently is the XElement object. With XElement objects, you can easily create single-element objects that are XML documents themselves, as well as fragments of XML. You can use the Load method with the XElement similarly to how you use the Load method with the XDocument. The following code snippet shows writing an XML element with its corresponding value to the console:

```
var company = new XElement("Company", "Microsoft Corporation");
WriteLine(company);
```

In the creation of an XElement object, you can define the name of the element as well as the value used in the element. In this case, the name of the element is <Company>, and the value of the <Company> element is Microsoft Corporation. Running this in a console application produces the following result:

```
<Company>Microsoft Corporation</Company>
```

You can create an even more complete XML document using multiple `XElement` objects, as shown in the following example (code file `LinqToXmlSample/Program.cs`):

```
public static void CreateXml()
{
  var company =
    new XElement("Company",
      new XElement("CompanyName", "Microsoft Corporation"),
      new XElement("CompanyAddress",
        new XElement("Address", "One Microsoft Way"),
        new XElement("City", "Redmond"),
        new XElement("Zip", "WA 98052-6399"),
        new XElement("State", "WA"),
        new XElement("Country", "USA")));

    WriteLine(company);
}
```

What's extremely nice with this API is that the hierarchy of the XML is represented by the API. The first instantiation of the `XElement` passes the string "Company" to the first parameter. This parameter is of type `XName` that represents the name of the XML element. The second parameter is another `XElement`. This second `XElement` defines the XML child element of the `Company`. This second element defines `"CompanyName"` as XName, and `"Microsoft Corporation"` as its value. The `XElement` specifying the company address is another child of the Company element. All the other `XElement` objects that follow are direct child objects of `CompanyAddress`. The constructor allows passing any number of objects as defined by the type `params` `object[]`. All these objects are treated as children.

Running this application produces this result:

```
<Company>
  <CompanyName>Microsoft Corporation</CompanyName>
  <CompanyAddress>
    <Address>One Microsoft Way</Address>
    <City>Redmond</City>
    <Zip>WA 98052-6399</Zip>
    <State>WA</State>
    <Country>USA</Country>
  </CompanyAddress>
</Company>
```

> **NOTE** *The constructor syntax of* `XElement` *allows easy creation of hierarchical XML. This makes it easy to create XML out of LINQ queries (transforming object trees to XML), as is shown later in this section, and you can also transform one XML syntax to another XML syntax.*

XNamespace

`XNamespace` is an object that represents an XML namespace, and it is easily applied to elements within your document. For instance, you can take the previous example and easily apply a namespace to the root element by creating an `XNamespace` object (code file `LinqToXmlSample/Program.cs`):

```
public static void WithNamespace()
{
  XNamespace ns = "http://www.cninnovation.com/samples/2015";

  var company =
```

```
      new XElement(ns + "Company",
        new XElement("CompanyName", "Microsoft Corporation"),
        new XElement("CompanyAddress",
          new XElement("Address", "One Microsoft Way"),
          new XElement("City", "Redmond"),
          new XElement("Zip", "WA 98052-6399"),
          new XElement("State", "WA"),
          new XElement("Country", "USA")));

    WriteLine(company);
}
```

In this case, an `XNamespace` object is created by assigning it a value of `http://www.cninnovation.com/ samples/2015`. From there, it is actually used in the root element `<Company>` with the instantiation of the `XElement` object.

This produces the following result:

```
<Company xmlns="http://www.cninnovation.com/samples/2015">
  <CompanyName xmlns="">Microsoft Corporation</CompanyName>
  <CompanyAddress xmlns="">
    <Address>One Microsoft Way</Address>
    <City>Redmond</City>
    <Zip>WA 98052-6399</Zip>
    <State>WA</State>
    <Country>USA</Country>
  </CompanyAddress>
</Company>
```

> **NOTE** *The* `XNamespace` *allows creation by assigning a string to the* `XNamespace` *instead of using the new operator because this class implements an implicit cast operator from string. It's also possible to use the + operator with the* `XNamespace` *object by having a string on the right side because of an implementation of the + operator that returns an* `XName`. *Operator overloading is explained in Chapter 8, "Operators and Casts."*

In addition to dealing with only the root element, you can also apply namespaces to all your elements, as shown in the following example (code file `LinqToXmlSample/Program.cs`):

```
public static void With2Namespace()
{
    XNamespace ns1 = "http://www.cninnovation.com/samples/2015";
    XNamespace ns2 = "http://www.cninnovation.com/samples/2015/address";

    var company =
      new XElement(ns1 + "Company",
        new XElement(ns2 + "CompanyName", "Microsoft Corporation"),
        new XElement(ns2 + "CompanyAddress",
          new XElement(ns2 + "Address", "One Microsoft Way"),
          new XElement(ns2 + "City", "Redmond"),
          new XElement(ns2 + "Zip", "WA 98052-6399"),
          new XElement(ns2 + "State", "WA"),
          new XElement(ns2 + "Country", "USA")));

    WriteLine(company);
}
```

which produces the following result:

```
<Company xmlns="http://www.cninnovation.com/samples/2015">
  <CompanyName xmlns="http://www.cninnovation.com/samples/2015/address">
    Microsoft Corporation</CompanyName>
  <CompanyAddress xmlns="http://www.cninnovation.com/samples/2015/address">
    <Address>One Microsoft Way</Address>
    <City>Redmond</City>
    <Zip>WA 98052-6399</Zip>
    <State>WA</State>
    <Country>USA</Country>
  </CompanyAddress>
</Company>
```

In this case, you can see that the subnamespace was applied to everything you specified except for the `<Address>`, `<City>`, `<State>`, and `<Country>` elements because they inherit from their parent, `<CompanyAddress>`, which has the namespace declaration.

XComment

The `XComment` object enables you to easily add XML comments to your XML documents. The following example shows the addition of a comment to the top of the document and within the `Company` element (code file `LinqToXmlSample/Program.cs`):

```
public static void WithComments()
{
  var doc = new XDocument();

  XComment comment = new XComment("Sample XML for Professional C#.");
  doc.Add(comment);

  var company =
    new XElement("Company",
      new XElement("CompanyName", "Microsoft Corporation"),
      new XComment("A great company"),
      new XElement("CompanyAddress",
        new XElement("Address", "One Microsoft Way"),
        new XElement("City", "Redmond"),
        new XElement("Zip", "WA 98052-6399"),
        new XElement("State", "WA"),
        new XElement("Country", "USA")));
  doc.Add(company);

  WriteLine(doc);
}
```

When you run the application and call the `WithComments` method, you can see the generated XML comments:

```
<!--Sample XML for Professional C#.-->
<Company>
  <CompanyName>Microsoft Corporation</CompanyName>
  <!-A great company->
  <CompanyAddress>
    <Address>One Microsoft Way</Address>
    <City>Redmond</City>
    <Zip>WA 98052-6399</Zip>
    <State>WA</State>
    <Country>USA</Country>
  </CompanyAddress>
</Company>
```

XAttribute

In addition to elements, another important factor of XML is attributes. You add and work with attributes through the use of the XAttribute object. The following example shows the addition of an attribute to the root <Company> node (code file LinqToXmlSample/Program.cs):

```
public static void WithAttributes()
{
  var company =
    new XElement("Company",
      new XElement("CompanyName", "Microsoft Corporation"),
      new XAttribute("TaxId", "91-1144442"),
      new XComment("A great company"),
      new XElement("CompanyAddress",
        new XElement("Address", "One Microsoft Way"),
        new XElement("City", "Redmond"),
        new XElement("Zip", "WA 98052-6399"),
        new XElement("State", "WA"),
        new XElement("Country", "USA")));

  WriteLine(company);
}
```

The attribute shows up as shown with the Company element:

```
<Company TaxId="91-1144442">
  <CompanyName>Microsoft Corporation</CompanyName>
  <!-A great company->
  <CompanyAddress>
    <Address>One Microsoft Way</Address>
    <City>Redmond</City>
    <Zip>WA 98052-6399</Zip>
    <State>WA</State>
    <Country>USA</Country>
  </CompanyAddress>
</Company>
```

Now that you can get your XML documents into an XDocument object and work with the various parts of this document, you can also use LINQ to XML to query your XML documents and work with the results.

Querying XML Documents with LINQ

You will notice that querying a static XML document using LINQ to XML takes almost no work at all. The following example makes use of the hamlet.xml file and queries to get all the players (actors) who appear in the play. Each of these players is defined in the XML document with the <PERSONA> element. The Descendants method of the XDocument class returns an IEnumerable<XElement> containing all the PERSONA elements within the tree. With every PERSONA element of this tree, the Value property is accessed with the LINQ query and written to the resulting collection (code file LinqToXmlSample/Program.cs):

```
public static void QueryHamlet()
{
  XDocument doc = XDocument.Load(HamletFileName);

  IEnumerable<string> persons = (from people in doc.Descendants("PERSONA")
                                 select people.Value).ToList();

  WriteLine($"{persons.Count()} Players Found");
  WriteLine();

  foreach (var item in persons)
  {
```

```
        WriteLine(item);
    }
}
```

When you run the application, you can see the following result from the play *Hamlet*. You can't say you're not learning literature from a C# programming book:

```
26 Players Found

CLAUDIUS, king of Denmark.
HAMLET, son to the late king, and nephew to the present king.
POLONIUS, lord chamberlain.
HORATIO, friend to Hamlet.
LAERTES, son to Polonius.
LUCIANUS, nephew to the king.
VOLTIMAND
CORNELIUS
ROSENCRANTZ
GUILDENSTERN
OSRIC
A Gentleman
A Priest.
MARCELLUS
BERNARDO
FRANCISCO, a soldier.
REYNALDO, servant to Polonius.
Players.
Two Clowns, grave-diggers.
FORTINBRAS, prince of Norway.
A Captain.
English Ambassadors.
GERTRUDE, queen of Denmark, and mother to Hamlet.
OPHELIA, daughter to Polonius.
Lords, Ladies, Officers, Soldiers, Sailors, Messengers, and other Attendants.
Ghost of Hamlet's Father.
```

Querying Dynamic XML Documents

A lot of dynamic XML documents are available online these days. You can find blog feeds, podcast feeds, and more that provide an XML document by sending a request to a specific URL endpoint. You can view these feeds either in the browser, through an RSS aggregator, or as pure XML. The next example demonstrates how to work with an Atom feed directly from your code.

Here, you can see that the Load method of the XDocument points to a URL where the XML is retrieved. With the Atom feed, the root element is a feed element that contains direct children with information about the feed and a list of entry elements for every article. What might not be missed when accessing the elements is the Atom namespace http://www.w3.org/2005/Atom, otherwise the results will be empty.

With the sample code, first the values of the title and subtitle elements are accessed that are defined as child elements of the root element. The Atom feed can contain multiple link elements. When you use a LINQ query, only the first link element that contains the rel attribute with the value alternate is retrieved. After writing overall information about the feed to the console, all entry elements are retrieved to create an anonymous type with Title, Published, Summary, Url, and Comments properties (code file LinqToXmlSample/Program.cs):

```
public static void QueryFeed()
{
    XNamespace ns = "http://www.w3.org/2005/Atom";
    XDocument doc = XDocument.Load(@"http://blog.cninnovation.com/feed/atom/");

    WriteLine($"Title: {doc.Root.Element(ns + "title").Value}");
```

```
    WriteLine($"Subtitle: {doc.Root.Element(ns + "subtitle").Value}");
    string url = doc.Root.Elements(ns + "link")
      .Where(e => e.Attribute("rel").Value == "alternate")
      .FirstOrDefault()
      ?.Attribute("href")?.Value;
    WriteLine($"Link: {url}");
    WriteLine();

    var queryPosts = from myPosts in doc.Descendants(ns + "entry")
                     select new
                     {
                       Title = myPosts.Element(ns + "title")?.Value,
                       Published = DateTime.Parse(
                         myPosts.Element(ns + "published")?.Value),
                       Summary = myPosts.Element(ns + "summary")?.Value,
                       Url = myPosts.Element(ns + "link")?.Value,
                       Comments = myPosts.Element(ns + "comments")?.Value
                     };

    foreach (var item in queryPosts)
    {
      string shortTitle = item.Title.Length > 50 ?
        item.Title.Substring(0, 50) + "..." : item.Title;
      WriteLine(shortTitle);
    }
}
```

Run the application to see this overall information for the feed:

```
Title: Christian Nagel's CN innovation
Subtitle: Infos für Windows- und Web-Entwickler
Link: http://blog.cninnovation.com
```

and the results of the query showing all titles:

```
A New Hello, World!
Ein heisser Sommer: Visual Studio 2015, .NET Core ...
Ein Operator Namens Elvis &#8211; oder A Lap Aroun...
.NET 2015, C# 6 und Visual Studio 2015 Update Trai...
Building Bridges &#8211; Build 2015
Slides und Samples vom Global Azure Boot Camp
Code Samples von der BASTA! 2015 Spring
.NET User Group Austria &#8211; Fünf Gründe für Me...
.NET User Group Austria &#8211; Welche Storage Tec...
Universal Apps für Windows 10
```

Transforming to Objects

Using LINQ to SQL, it's easy to transform an XML document to an object tree. The Hamlet file contains all personas of the play. Some personas that belong to groups are grouped within PGROUP elements. A group contains the name of the group within the GRPDESC element, and personas of the group within PERSONA elements. The following sample creates objects for every group and adds the group name and personas to the object. The code sample makes use of the LINQ method syntax instead of the LINQ query for using an overload of the Select method that offers the index parameter. The index goes into the newly created object as well. The Descendants method of the XDocument filters all the PGROUP elements. Every group is selected with the Select method, and there an anonymous object is created that fills the Number, Description, and Characters properties. The Characters property itself is a list of all values of the PERSONA elements within the group (code file LinqToXmlSample/Program.cs):

```
public static void TransformingToObjects()
{
    XDocument doc = XDocument.Load(HamletFileName);
```

```
    var groups =
      doc.Descendants("PGROUP")
        .Select((g, i) =>
          new
          {
            Number = i + 1,
            Description = g.Element("GRPDESCR").Value,
            Characters = g.Elements("PERSONA").Select(p => p.Value)
          });

    foreach (var group in groups)
    {
      WriteLine(group.Number);
      WriteLine(group.Description);
      foreach (var name in group.Characters)
      {
        WriteLine(name);
      }
      WriteLine();
    }
  }
```

Run the application to invoke the `TransformingToObjects` method and see two groups with their personas:

```
1
courtiers.
VOLTIMAND
CORNELIUS
ROSENCRANTZ
GUILDENSTERN
OSRIC

2
officers.
MARCELLUS
BERNARDO
```

Transforming to XML

Because it's easy to create XML with the `XElement` class and its flexible constructor to pass any number of child elements, the previous example can be changed to create XML instead of an object list. The query is the same as in the previous code sample. What's different is that a new `XElement` passing the name `hamlet` is created. `hamlet` is the root element of this generated XML. The child elements are defined by the result of the `Select` method that follows the `Descendants` method to select all `PGROUP` elements. For every group, a new group `XElement` gets created. Every group contains an attribute with the group `number`, an attribute with the `description`, and a `characters` element that contains a list of `name` elements (code file `LinqToXmlSample/Program.cs`):

```
    public static void TransformingToXml()
    {
      XDocument doc = XDocument.Load(HamletFileName);
      var hamlet =
        new XElement("hamlet",
          doc.Descendants("PGROUP")
            .Select((g, i) =>
              new XElement("group",
                new XAttribute("number", i + 1),
                new XAttribute("description", g.Element("GRPDESCR").Value),
                new XElement("characters",
                  g.Elements("PERSONA").Select(p => new XElement("name", p.Value))
```

```
        ))));

    WriteLine(hamlet);
}
```

When you run the application, you can see this generated XML fragment:

```
<hamlet>
  <group number="1" description="courtiers.">
    <characters>
      <name>VOLTIMAND</name>
      <name>CORNELIUS</name>
      <name>ROSENCRANTZ</name>
      <name>GUILDENSTERN</name>
      <name>OSRIC</name>
    </characters>
  </group>
  <group number="2" description="officers.">
    <characters>
      <name>MARCELLUS</name>
      <name>BERNARDO</name>
    </characters>
  </group>
</hamlet>
```

JSON

After taking a long tour through many XML features of the .NET Framework, let's get into the JSON data format. *Json.NET* offers a large API where you can use JSON to do many aspects you've seen in this chapter with XML, and some of these will be covered here.

The sample code makes use of the following dependencies and namespaces:

Dependencies

```
NETStandard.Library
Newtonsoft.Json
System.Xml.XDocument
```

Namespaces

```
Newtonsoft.Json
Newtonsoft.Json.Linq
System
System.IO
System.Xml.Linq
static System.Console
```

Creating JSON

To create JSON objects manually with JSON.NET, several types are available in the `Newtonsoft.Json.Linq` namespace. A `JObject` represents a JSON object. `JObject` is a dictionary with strings for the key (property names with .NET objects), and `JToken` for the value. This way `JObject` offers indexed access. An array of JSON objects is defined by the `JArray` type. Both `JObject` and `JArray` derive from the abstract base class `JContainer` that contains a list of `JToken` objects.

The following code snippet creates the `JObject` `book1` and `book2` objects by filling `title` and `publisher` values using indexed dictionary access. Both book objects are added to a `JArray` (code file `JsonSample/Program.cs`):

```
public static void CreateJson()
{
  var book1 = new JObject();
  book1["title"] = "Professional C# 6 and .NET 5 Core";
  book1["publisher"] = "Wrox Press";
  var book2 = new JObject();
  book2["title"] = "Professional C# 5 and .NET 4.5.1";
  book2["publisher"] = "Wrox Press";
  var books = new JArray();
  books.Add(book1);
  books.Add(book2);

  var json = new JObject();
  json["books"] = books;
  WriteLine(json);
}
```

Run the application to see this JSON code generated:

```
{
  "books": [
    {
      "title": "Professional C# 6 and .NET 5 Core",
      "publisher": "Wrox Press"
    },
    {
      "title": "Professional C# 5 and .NET 4.5.1",
      "publisher": "Wrox Press"
    }
  ]
}
```

Converting Objects

Instead of using `JsonObject` and `JsonArray` to create JSON content, you can also use the `JsonConvert` class. `JsonConvert` enables you to create JSON from an object tree and convert a JSON string back into an object tree.

With the sample code in this section, you create an `Inventory` object from the helper method `GetInventoryObject` (code file `JsonSample/Program.cs`):

```
public static Inventory GetInventoryObject() =>
  new Inventory
  {
    InventoryItems = new Product[]
    {
      new Product
      {
        ProductID = 100,
        ProductName = "Product Thing",
        SupplierID = 10
      },
      new BookProduct
      {
        ProductID = 101,
        ProductName = "How To Use Your New Product Thing",
        SupplierID = 10,
```

```
            ISBN = "1234567890"
        }
    }
};
```

The method `ConvertObject` retrieves the `Inventory` object and converts it to JSON using `JsonConvert`.`SerializeObject`. The second parameter of `SerializeObject` allows formatting to be defined `None` or `Indented`. `None` is best for keeping whitespace to a minimum; `Indented` allows for better readability. The JSON string is written to the console before it is converted back to an object tree using `JsonConvert`.`DeserializeObject`. `DeserializeObject` has a few overloads. The generic variant returns the generic type instead of an object, so a cast is not necessary:

```csharp
public static void ConvertObject()
{
    Inventory inventory = GetInventoryObject();
    string json = JsonConvert.SerializeObject(inventory, Formatting.Indented);
    WriteLine(json);
    WriteLine();
    Inventory newInventory = JsonConvert.DeserializeObject<Inventory>(json);
    foreach (var product in newInventory.InventoryItems)
    {
        WriteLine(product.ProductName);
    }
}
```

Running the application shows the generated console output of the JSON generated Inventory type:

```
{
    "InventoryItems": [
        {
            "Discount": 0,
            "ProductID": 100,
            "ProductName": "Product Thing",
            "SupplierID": 10,
            "CategoryID": 0,
            "QuantityPerUnit": null,
            "UnitPrice": 0.0,
            "UnitsInStock": 0,
            "UnitsOnOrder": 0,
            "ReorderLevel": 0,
            "Discontinued": false
        },
        {
            "ISBN": "1234567890",
            "Discount": 0,
            "ProductID": 101,
            "ProductName": "How To Use Your New Product Thing",
            "SupplierID": 10,
            "CategoryID": 0,
            "QuantityPerUnit": null,
            "UnitPrice": 0.0,
            "UnitsInStock": 0,
            "UnitsOnOrder": 0,
            "ReorderLevel": 0,
            "Discontinued": false
        }
    ]
}
```

Converting back JSON to objects, the product names are shown:

```
Product Thing
How To Use Your New Product Thing
```

Serializing Objects

Similar to the `XmlSerializer`, you can also stream the JSON string directly to a file. The following code snippet retrieves the Inventory object and writes it to a file stream using the `JsonSerializer` (code file `JsonSample/Program.cs`):

```
public static void SerializeJson()
{
  using (StreamWriter writer = File.CreateText(InventoryFileName))
  {
    JsonSerializer serializer = JsonSerializer.Create(
      new JsonSerializerSettings { Formatting = Formatting.Indented });
    serializer.Serialize(writer, GetInventoryObject());
  }
}
```

You can convert JSON from a stream by calling the `Deserialize` method on the `JsonSerializer`:

```
public static void DeserializeJson()
{
  using (StreamReader reader = File.OpenText(InventoryFileName))
  {
    JsonSerializer serializer = JsonSerializer.Create();
    var inventory = serializer.Deserialize(reader, typeof(Inventory))
      as Inventory;
    foreach (var item in inventory.InventoryItems)
    {
      WriteLine(item.ProductName);
    }
  }
}
```

SUMMARY

This chapter explored many aspects of the `System.Xml` namespace of the .NET Framework. You looked at how to read and write XML documents using the very fast `XmlReader`- and `XmlWriter`-based classes. You saw how the DOM is implemented in .NET and how to use the power of DOM, with the `XmlDocument` class. In addition, you visited XPath, serialized objects to XML, and were able to bring them back with just a couple of method calls.

By using LINQ to XML, you've seen how to easily create XML documents and fragments and create queries using XML data.

Aside of XML, you've seen how to serialize objects using JSON with `Json.NET`, and you've parsed JSON strings to build .NET objects.

The next chapter shows how to localize .NET applications by making use of XML-based resource files.

28

Localization

WHAT'S IN THIS CHAPTER?

➤ Formatting of numbers and dates

➤ Using resources for localized content

➤ Localizing WPF Desktop Applications

➤ Localizing ASP.NET Core Web Applications

➤ Localizing Universal Windows apps

➤ Creating custom resource readers

➤ Creating custom cultures

WROX.COM CODE DOWNLOADS FOR THIS CHAPTER

The wrox.com code downloads for this chapter are found at www.wrox.com/go/
professionalcsharp6 on the Download Code tab. The code for this chapter is
divided into the following major examples:

➤ NumberAndDateFormatting

➤ SortingDemo

➤ CreateResource

➤ WPFCultureDemo

➤ ResourcesDemo

➤ WPFApplication

➤ WebApplication

➤ UWPLocalization

➤ DatabaseResourceReader

➤ CustomCultures

GLOBAL MARKETS

NASA's Mars Climate Orbiter was lost on September 23, 1999, at a cost of $125 million, because one engineering team used metric units while another one used inches for a key spacecraft operation. When writing applications for international distribution, different cultures and regions must be kept in mind.

Different cultures have diverging calendars and use different number and date formats; and sorting strings may lead to various results because the order of A–Z is defined differently based on the culture. To make usable applications for global markets, you have to globalize and localize them.

This chapter covers the globalization and localization of .NET applications. *Globalization* is about internationalizing applications: preparing applications for international markets. With globalization, the application supports number and date formats that vary according to culture, calendars, and so on. *Localization* is about translating applications for specific cultures. For translations of strings, you can use resources such as .NET resources or WPF resource dictionaries.

.NET supports the globalization and localization of Windows and web applications. To globalize an application, you can use classes from the namespace System.Globalization; to localize an application, you can use resources supported by the namespace System.Resources.

NAMESPACE SYSTEM.GLOBALIZATION

The System.Globalization namespace holds all the culture and region classes necessary to support different date formats, different number formats, and even different calendars that are represented in classes such as GregorianCalendar, HebrewCalendar, JapaneseCalendar, and so on. By using these classes, you can display different representations according to the user's locale.

This section looks at the following issues and considerations when using the System.Globalization namespace:

➤ Unicode issues

➤ Cultures and regions

➤ An example showing all cultures and their characteristics

➤ Sorting

Unicode Issues

A Unicode character has 16 bits, so there is room for 65,536 characters. Is this enough for all languages currently used in information technology? In the case of the Chinese language, for example, more than 80,000 characters are needed. Fortunately, Unicode has been designed to deal with this issue. With Unicode you have to differentiate between base characters and combining characters. You can add multiple combining characters to a base character to build a single display character or a text element.

Take, for example, the Icelandic character Ogonek. Ogonek can be combined by using the base character 0x006F (Latin small letter o), and the combining characters 0x0328 (combining Ogonek), and 0x0304 (combining Macron), as shown in Figure 28-1. Combining characters are defined within ranges from 0x0300 to 0x0345. For American and European markets, predefined characters exist to facilitate dealing with special characters. The character Ogonek is also defined by the predefined character 0x01ED.

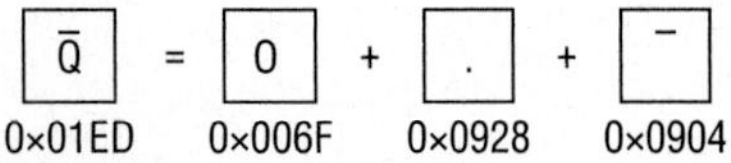

0x01ED   0x006F   0x0928   0x0904

FIGURE 28-1

For Asian markets, where more than 80,000 characters are necessary for Chinese alone, such predefined characters do not exist. In Asian languages, you always have to deal with combining characters. The problem is getting the right number of display characters or text elements, and getting to the base characters instead of the combined characters. The namespace `System.Globalization` offers the class `StringInfo`, which you can use to deal with this issue.

The following table lists the static methods of the class `StringInfo` that help in dealing with combined characters.

METHOD	DESCRIPTION
`GetNextTextElement`	Returns the first text element (base character and all combining characters) of a specified string
`GetTextElementEnumerator`	Returns a TextElementEnumerator object that allows iterating all text elements of a string
`ParseCombiningCharacters`	Returns an integer array referencing all base characters of a string

> **NOTE** *A single display character can contain multiple Unicode characters. To address this issue, when you write applications that support international markets, don't use the data type* `char`; *use* `string` *instead. A* `string` *can hold a text element that contains both base characters and combining characters, whereas a* `char` *cannot.*

Cultures and Regions

The world is divided into multiple cultures and regions, and applications have to be aware of these cultural and regional differences. A culture is a set of preferences based on a user's language and cultural habits. RFC 4646 (`http://www.ietf.org/rfc/rfc4646.txt`) defines culture names that are used worldwide, depending on a language and a country or region. Some examples are en-AU, en-CA, en-GB, and en-US for the English language in Australia, Canada, the United Kingdom, and the United States, respectively.

Possibly the most important class in the `System.Globalization` namespace is `CultureInfo`. `CultureInfo` represents a culture and defines calendars, formatting of numbers and dates, and sorting strings used with the culture.

The class `RegionInfo` represents regional settings (such as the currency) and indicates whether the region uses the metric system. Some regions can use multiple languages. One example is the region of Spain, which has Basque (eu-ES), Catalan (ca-ES), Spanish (es-ES), and Galician (gl-ES) cultures. Similar to one region having multiple languages, one language can be spoken in different regions; for example, Spanish is spoken in Mexico, Spain, Guatemala, Argentina, and Peru, to name only a few countries.

Later in this chapter is a sample application that demonstrates these characteristics of cultures and regions.

Specific, Neutral, and Invariant Cultures

When using cultures in the .NET Framework, you have to differentiate between three types: *specific, neutral,* and *invariant* cultures. A specific culture is associated with a real, existing culture defined with RFC 4646, as described in the preceding section. A specific culture can be mapped to a neutral culture. For example, de is the neutral culture of the specific cultures de-AT, de-DE, de-CH, and others. de is shorthand for the German language (Deutsch); AT, DE, and CH are shorthand for the countries Austria, Germany, and Switzerland, respectively.

When translating applications, it is typically not necessary to do translations for every region; not much difference exists between the German language in the countries Austria and Germany. Instead of using specific cultures, you can use a neutral culture to localize applications.

The invariant culture is independent of a real culture. When storing formatted numbers or dates in files, or sending them across a network to a server, using a culture that is independent of any user settings is the best option.

Figure 28-2 shows how the culture types relate to each other.

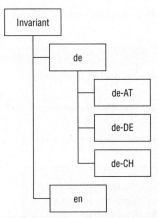

FIGURE 28-2

CurrentCulture and CurrentUICulture

When you set cultures, you need to differentiate between a culture for the user interface and a culture for the number and date formats. Cultures are associated with a thread, and with these two culture types, two culture settings can be applied to a thread. The CultureInfo class has the static properties CurrentCulture and CurrentUICulture. The property CurrentCulture is for setting the culture that is used with formatting and sort options, whereas the property CurrentUICulture is used for the language of the user interface.

Users can install additional languages to the Windows operating system by selecting **Region & Language** in the Windows settings (see Figure 28-3). The language configured as default is the current UI culture.

FIGURE 28-3

To change the current culture, you use the Additional Date, Time, & Regional Settings link in the dialog shown in Figure 28-3. From there, you click the Change Date, Time, or Number Formats option to see the dialog shown in Figure 28-4. The language setting for the format influences the current culture. It is also possible to change the defaults for the number format, the time format, and the date format independent of the culture.

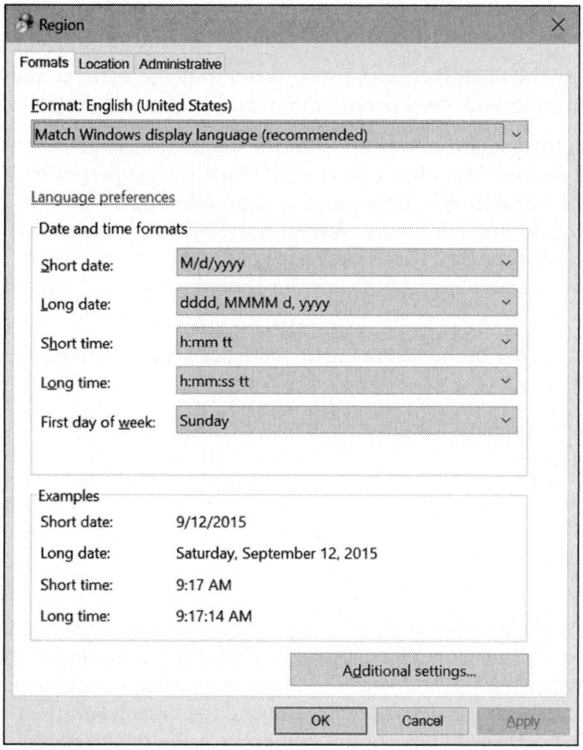

FIGURE 28-4

These settings provide a very good default, and in many cases you won't need to change the default behavior. If the culture should be changed, you can easily do this programmatically by changing both cultures to, say, the Spanish culture, as shown in this code snippet (using the namespace System.Globalization):

```
var ci = new CultureInfo("es-ES");
CultureInfo.CurrentCulture = ci;
CultureInfo.CurrentUICulture = ci;
```

Now that you know how to set the culture, the following sections discuss number and date formatting, which are influenced by the CurrentCulture setting.

Number Formatting

The number structures Int16, Int32, Int64, and so on in the System namespace have an overloaded ToString method. You can use this method to create a different representation of the number, depending on the locale. For the Int32 structure, ToString is overloaded with the following four versions:

```
public string ToString();
public string ToString(IFormatProvider);
public string ToString(string);
public string ToString(string, IFormatProvider);
```

`ToString` without arguments returns a string without format options. You can also pass a string and a class that implements `IFormatProvider`.

The string specifies the format of the representation. The format can be a standard numeric formatting string or a picture numeric formatting string. For standard numeric formatting, strings are predefined where `C` specifies the currency notation, `D` creates a decimal output, `E` creates scientific output, `F` creates fixed-point output, `G` creates general output, `N` creates number output, and `X` creates hexadecimal output. With a picture numeric formatting string, it is possible to specify the number of digits, section and group separators, percent notation, and so on. The picture numeric format string `###,###` means two three-digit blocks separated by a group separator.

The `IFormatProvider` interface is implemented by the `NumberFormatInfo`, `DateTimeFormatInfo`, and `CultureInfo` classes. This interface defines a single method, `GetFormat`, that returns a format object.

You can use `NumberFormatInfo` to define custom formats for numbers. With the default constructor of `NumberFormatInfo`, a culture-independent or invariant object is created. Using the properties of `NumberFormatInfo`, it is possible to change all the formatting options, such as a positive sign, a percent symbol, a number group separator, a currency symbol, and a lot more. A read-only, culture-independent `NumberFormatInfo` object is returned from the static property `InvariantInfo`. A `NumberFormatInfo` object in which the format values are based on the `CultureInfo` of the current thread is returned from the static property `CurrentInfo`.

The sample code `NumberAndDateFormatting` makes use of the following dependencies and namespaces:

Dependencies

```
NETStandard.Library
```

Namespaces

```
System
System.Globalization
static System.Console
```

To create the next example, you can start with a Console Application (Package) project. In this code, the first example shows a number displayed in the format of the current culture (here: English-US, the setting of the operating system). The second example uses the `ToString` method with the `IFormatProvider` argument. `CultureInfo` implements `IFormatProvider`, so create a `CultureInfo` object using the French culture. The third example changes the current culture. The culture is changed to German by using the property `CurrentCulture` of the `CultureInfo` instance (code file `NumberAndDateFormatting\Program.cs`):

```
public static void NumberFormatDemo()
{
    int val = 1234567890;

    // culture of the current thread
    WriteLine(val.ToString("N"));

    // use IFormatProvider
    WriteLine(val.ToString("N", new CultureInfo("fr-FR")));

    // change the current culture
    CultureInfo.CurrentCulture = new CultureInfo("de-DE");
    WriteLine(val.ToString("N"));
}
```

> **NOTE** *Before to .NET 4.6, the* `CurrentCulture` *property of the* `CultureInfo` *was read-only. With previous editions of .NET, you can set the culture using* `Thread.CurrentThread.CurrentCulture`.

You can compare the following different output for U.S. English, French, and German, respectively, shown here:

```
1,234,567,890.00
1 234 567 890,00
1.234.567.890,00
```

Date Formatting

The same support for numbers is available for dates. The DateTime structure has some overloads of the ToString method for date-to-string conversions. You can pass a string format and assign a different culture:

```
public string ToString();
public string ToString(IFormatProvider);
public string ToString(string);
public string ToString(string, IFormatProvider);
```

With the string argument of the ToString method, you can specify a predefined format character or a custom format string for converting the date to a string. The class DateTimeFormatInfo specifies the possible values. With DateTimeFormatInfo, the case of the format strings has a different meaning. D defines a long date format; d defines a short date format. Other examples of possible formats are ddd for the abbreviated day of the week, dddd for the full day of the week, yyyy for the year, T for a long time, and t for a short time. With the IFormatProvider argument, you can specify the culture. Using an overloaded method without the IFormatProvider argument implies that the current culture is used:

```
public static void DateFormatDemo()
{
  var d = new DateTime(2015, 09, 27);

  // current culture
  WriteLine(d.ToLongDateString());

  // use IFormatProvider
  WriteLine(d.ToString("D", new CultureInfo("fr-FR")));

  // use current culture
  WriteLine($"{CultureInfo.CurrentCulture}: {d:D}");

  CultureInfo.CurrentCulture = new CultureInfo("es-ES");
  WriteLine($"{CultureInfo.CurrentCulture}: {d:D}");
}
```

The output of this example program shows ToLongDateString with the current culture of the thread, a French version where a CultureInfo instance is passed to the ToString method, and a Spanish version where the CurrentCulture property of the thread is changed to es-ES:

```
Sunday, September 27, 2015
dimanche 27 septembre 2015
en-US: Sunday, September 27, 2015
es-ES: domingo, 27 de septiembre de 2015
```

Cultures in Action

To see all cultures in action, you can use a sample Windows Presentation Foundation (WPF) application that lists all cultures and demonstrates different characteristics of culture properties. Figure 28-5 shows the user interface of the application in the Visual Studio 2015 WPF Designer.

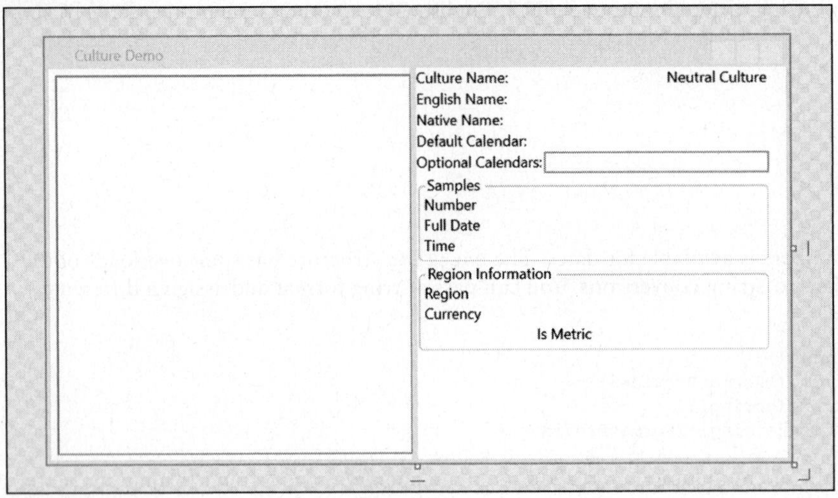

FIGURE 28-5

During initialization of the application, all available cultures are added to the `TreeView` control that is placed on the left side of the application. This initialization happens in the method `SetupCultures`, which is called in the constructor of the `MainWindow` class (code file WPFCultureDemo/MainWindow.xaml.cs):

```
public MainWindow()
{
  InitializeComponent();

  SetupCultures();
}
```

For the data that is shown in the user interface, the custom class `CultureData` is created. This class can be bound to a `TreeView` control, as it has a property `SubCultures` that contains a list of `CultureData`. Therefore, the `TreeView` control enables walking through this tree. Other than the subcultures, `CultureData` contains the `CultureInfo` type and sample values for a number, a date, and a time. The number returns a string in the number format for the specific culture, and the date and time return strings in the specific culture formats as well. `CultureData` contains a `RegionInfo` class to display regions. With some neutral cultures (for example, English), creating a `RegionInfo` throws an exception, as there are regions only with specific cultures. However, with other neutral cultures (for example, German), creating a `RegionInfo` succeeds and is mapped to a default region. The exception thrown here is handled (code file WPFCultureDemo/CultureData.cs):

```
public class CultureData
{
  public CultureInfo CultureInfo { get; set; }
  public List<CultureData> SubCultures { get; set; }
  double numberSample = 9876543.21;

  public string NumberSample => numberSample.ToString("N", CultureInfo);

  public string DateSample => DateTime.Today.ToString("D", CultureInfo);

  public string TimeSample => DateTime.Now.ToString("T", CultureInfo);

  public RegionInfo RegionInfo
  {
    get
    {
```

```
        RegionInfo ri;
        try
        {
          ri = new RegionInfo(CultureInfo.Name);
        }
        catch (ArgumentException)
        {
          // with some neutral cultures regions are not available
          return null;
        }
        return ri;
      }
    }
  }
```

In the method `SetupCultures`, you get all cultures from the static method `CultureInfo.GetCultures`. Passing `CultureTypes.AllCultures` to this method returns an unsorted array of all available cultures. The result is sorted by the name of the culture. With the result of the sorted cultures, a collection of `CultureData` objects is created and the `CultureInfo` and `SubCultures` properties are assigned. With the result of this, a dictionary is created to enable fast access to the culture name.

For the data that should be bound, a list of `CultureData` objects is created that contains all the root cultures for the tree view after the `foreach` statement is completed. Root cultures can be verified to determine whether they have the invariant culture as their parent. The invariant culture has the Locale Identifier (LCID) 127. Every culture has its own unique identifier that can be used for a fast verification. In the code snippet, root cultures are added to the `rootCultures` collection within the block of the `if` statement. If a culture has the invariant culture as its parent, it is a root culture.

If the culture does not have a parent culture, it is added to the root nodes of the tree. To find parent cultures, all cultures are remembered inside a dictionary. (See Chapter 11, "Collections," for more information about dictionaries, and Chapter 9, "Delegates, Lambdas, and Events," for details about lambda expressions.) If the culture iterated is not a root culture, it is added to the `SubCultures` collection of the parent culture. The parent culture can be quickly found by using the dictionary. In the last step, the root cultures are made available to the UI by assigning them to the `DataContext` of the `Window` (code file `WPFCultureDemo/MainWindow.xaml.cs`):

```
private void SetupCultures()
{
  var cultureDataDict = CultureInfo.GetCultures(CultureTypes.AllCultures)
    .OrderBy(c => c.Name)
    .Select(c => new CultureData
    {
      CultureInfo = c,
      SubCultures = new List<CultureData>()
    })
    .ToDictionary(c => c.CultureInfo.Name);

  var rootCultures = new List<CultureData>();
  foreach (var cd in cultureDataDict.Values)
  {
    if (cd.CultureInfo.Parent.LCID == 127)
    {
      rootCultures.Add(cd);
    }
    else
    {
      CultureData parentCultureData;
      if (cultureDataDict.TryGetValue(cd.CultureInfo.Parent.Name,
        out parentCultureData))
      {
        parentCultureData.SubCultures.Add(cd);
      }
```

```
            else
            {
                throw new ParentCultureException(
                    "unexpected error—parent culture not found");
            }
        }
    }
    this.DataContext = rootCultures.OrderBy(cd =>
      cd.CultureInfo.EnglishName);
}
```

When the user selects a node inside the tree, the handler of the `SelectedItemChanged` event of the `TreeView` is called. Here, the handler is implemented in the method `treeCultures_SelectedItemChanged`. Within this method, the `DataContext` of a `Grid` control is set to the selected `CultureData` object. In the XAML logical tree, this `Grid` is the parent of all controls that display information about the selected culture information:

```
private void treeCultures_SelectedItemChanged(object sender,
    RoutedPropertyChangedEventArgs<object> e)
{
    itemGrid.DataContext = e.NewValue as CultureData;
}
```

Now let's get into the XAML code for the display. A `TreeView` is used to display all the cultures. For the display of items inside the `TreeView`, an item template is used. This template uses a `TextBlock` that is bound to the `EnglishName` property of the `CultureInfo` class. For binding the items of the tree view, a `HierarchicalDataTemplate` is used to bind the property `SubCultures` of the `CultureData` type recursively (code file `CultureDemo/MainWindow.xaml`):

```
<TreeView SelectedItemChanged="treeCultures_SelectedItemChanged" Margin="5"
    ItemsSource="{Binding}" >
  <TreeView.ItemTemplate>
    <HierarchicalDataTemplate DataType="{x:Type local:CultureData}"
        ItemsSource="{Binding SubCultures}">
      <TextBlock Text="{Binding Path=CultureInfo.EnglishName}" />
    </HierarchicalDataTemplate>
  </TreeView.ItemTemplate>
</TreeView>
```

To display the values of the selected item, you use several `TextBlock` controls. These bind to the `CultureInfo` property of the `CultureData` class and in turn to properties of the `CultureInfo` type that is returned from `CultureInfo`, such as `Name`, `IsNeutralCulture`, `EnglishName`, `NativeName`, and so on. To convert a Boolean value, as returned from the `IsNeutralCulture` property, to a `Visibility` enumeration value, and to display calendar names, you use converters:

```
<TextBlock Grid.Row="0" Grid.Column="0" Text="Culture Name:" />
<TextBlock Grid.Row="0" Grid.Column="1" Text="{Binding CultureInfo.Name}"
  Width="100" />
<TextBlock Grid.Row="0" Grid.Column="2" Text="Neutral Culture"
  Visibility="{Binding CultureInfo.IsNeutralCulture,
  Converter={StaticResource boolToVisiblity}}" />
<TextBlock Grid.Row="1" Grid.Column="0" Text="English Name:" />
<TextBlock Grid.Row="1" Grid.Column="1" Grid.ColumnSpan="2"
  Text="{Binding CultureInfo.EnglishName}" />
<TextBlock Grid.Row="2" Grid.Column="0" Text="Native Name:" />
<TextBlock Grid.Row="2" Grid.Column="1" Grid.ColumnSpan="2"
  Text="{Binding CultureInfo.NativeName}" />
<TextBlock Grid.Row="3" Grid.Column="0" Text="Default Calendar:" />
<TextBlock Grid.Row="3" Grid.Column="1" Grid.ColumnSpan="2"
  Text="{Binding CultureInfo.Calendar,
    Converter={StaticResource calendarConverter}}" />
<TextBlock Grid.Row="4" Grid.Column="0" Text="Optional Calendars:" />
```

```
<ListBox Grid.Row="4" Grid.Column="1" Grid.ColumnSpan="2"
    ItemsSource="{Binding CultureInfo.OptionalCalendars}">
  <ListBox.ItemTemplate>
    <DataTemplate>
      <TextBlock Text="{Binding
          Converter={StaticResource calendarConverter}}" />
    </DataTemplate>
  </ListBox.ItemTemplate>
</ListBox>
```

The converter to convert a Boolean value to the `Visibility` enumeration is defined in
the class `BooleanToVisibilityConverter` (code file `WPFCultureDemo\Converters\`
`BooleanToVisiblityConverter.cs`):

```
using System;
using System.Globalization;
using System.Windows;
using System.Windows.Data;

namespace CultureDemo.Converters
{
  public class BooleanToVisibilityConverter: IValueConverter
  {
    public object Convert(object value, Type targetType, object parameter,
      CultureInfo culture)
    {
      bool b = (bool)value;
      if (b)
        return Visibility.Visible;
      else
        return Visibility.Collapsed;
    }

    public object ConvertBack(object value, Type targetType,
      object parameter, CultureInfo culture)
    {
      throw new NotImplementedException();
    }
  }
}
```

The converter for the calendar text to display is just a little bit more complex. Here is the implementation of the `Convert` method in the class `CalendarTypeToCalendarInformationConverter`. The implementation uses the class name and calendar type name to return a useful value for the calendar (code file
`WPFCultureDemo/Converters/CalendarTypeToCalendarInformationConverter.cs`):

```
public object Convert(object value, Type targetType, object parameter,
  CultureInfo culture)
{
  var c = value as Calendar;
  if (c == null) return null;
  var calText = new StringBuilder(50);
  calText.Append(c.ToString());
  calText.Remove(0, 21); // remove the namespace
  calText.Replace("Calendar", "");
  GregorianCalendar gregCal = c as GregorianCalendar;
  if (gregCal != null)
  {
    calText.Append($" {gregCal.CalendarType}");
  }
  return calText.ToString();
}
```

The `CultureData` class contains properties to display sample information for number, date, and time formats. These properties are bound with the following `TextBlock` elements:

```
<TextBlock Grid.Row="0" Grid.Column="0" Text="Number" />
<TextBlock Grid.Row="0" Grid.Column="1" Text="{Binding NumberSample}" />
<TextBlock Grid.Row="1" Grid.Column="0" Text="Full Date" />
<TextBlock Grid.Row="1" Grid.Column="1" Text="{Binding DateSample}" />
<TextBlock Grid.Row="2" Grid.Column="0" Text="Time" />
<TextBlock Grid.Row="2" Grid.Column="1" Text="{Binding TimeSample}" />
```

The information about the region is shown with the last part of the XAML code. The complete `GroupBox` is hidden if the `RegionInfo` is not available. The `TextBlock` elements bind the `DisplayName`, `CurrencySymbol`, `ISOCurrencySymbol`, and `IsMetric` properties of the `RegionInfo` type:

```
<GroupBox x:Name="groupRegion" Header="Region Information" Grid.Row="6"
    Grid.Column="0" Grid.ColumnSpan="3" Visibility="{Binding RegionInfo,
    Converter={StaticResource nullToVisibility}}">
  <Grid>
    <Grid.RowDefinitions>
      <RowDefinition />
      <RowDefinition />
      <RowDefinition />
    </Grid.RowDefinitions>
    <Grid.ColumnDefinitions>
      <ColumnDefinition />
      <ColumnDefinition />
      <ColumnDefinition />
    </Grid.ColumnDefinitions>
    <TextBlock Grid.Row="0" Grid.Column="0" Text="Region" />
    <TextBlock Grid.Row="0" Grid.Column="1" Grid.ColumnSpan="2"
      Text="{Binding RegionInfo.DisplayName}" />
    <TextBlock Grid.Row="1" Grid.Column="0" Text="Currency" />
    <TextBlock Grid.Row="1" Grid.Column="1"
      Text="{Binding RegionInfo.CurrencySymbol}" />
    <TextBlock Grid.Row="1" Grid.Column="2"
      Text="{Binding RegionInfo.ISOCurrencySymbol}" />
    <TextBlock Grid.Row="2" Grid.Column="1" Text="Is Metric"
      Visibility="{Binding RegionInfo.IsMetric,
      Converter={StaticResource boolToVisiblity}}" />
  </Grid>
```

When you start the application, you can see all available cultures in the tree view, and selecting a culture lists its characteristics, as shown in Figure 28-6.

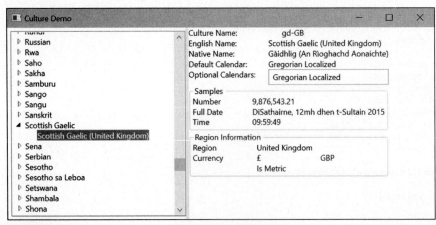

FIGURE 28-6

Sorting

The sample `SortingDemo` makes use of the following dependencies and namespaces:

Dependencies

```
NETStandard.Library
System.Collections.NonGeneric
```

Namespaces

```
System
System.Collections
System.Collections.Generic
System.Globalization
static System.Console
```

Sorting strings varies according to the culture. The algorithms that compare strings for sorting by default are culture-specific. For example, in Finnish the characters V and W are treated the same. To demonstrate this behavior with a Finnish sort, the following code creates a small sample console application in which some U.S. states are stored unsorted inside an array.

The method `DisplayNames` shown here is used to display all elements of an array or a collection on the console (code file `SortingDemo/Program.cs`):

```
public static void DisplayNames(string title, IEnumerable<string> e)
{
  WriteLine(title);
  WriteLine(string.Join("-", e));
  WriteLine();
}
```

In the `Main` method, after creating the array with some of the U.S. states, the thread property `CurrentCulture` is set to the Finnish culture so that the following `Array.Sort` uses the Finnish sort order. Calling the method `DisplayNames` displays all the states on the console:

```
public static void Main()
{
  string[] names = {"Alabama", "Texas", "Washington", "Virginia",
                    "Wisconsin", "Wyoming", "Kentucky", "Missouri", "Utah",
                    "Hawaii","Kansas", "Louisiana", "Alaska", "Arizona"};

  CultureInfo.CurrentCulture = new CultureInfo("fi-FI");

  Array.Sort(names);
  DisplayNames("Sorted using the Finnish culture", names);
  // etc.
}
```

After the first display of some U.S. states in the Finnish sort order, the array is sorted once again. If you want a sort that is independent of the users' culture, which would be useful when the sorted array is sent to a server or stored somewhere, you can use the invariant culture.

You can do this by passing a second argument to `Array.Sort`. The `Sort` method expects an object implementing `IComparer` with the second argument. The `Comparer` class from the `System.Collections` namespace implements `IComparer`. `Comparer.DefaultInvariant` returns a `Comparer` object that uses the invariant culture for comparing the array values for a culture-independent sort:

```
public static void Main()
{
  // etc.
  // sort using the invariant culture
```

```
        Array.Sort(names, System.Collections.Comparer.DefaultInvariant);
        DisplayNames("Sorted using the invariant culture", names);
    }
```

The program output shows different sort results with the Finnish and culture-independent cultures—Virginia is before Washington when using the invariant sort order, and vice versa when using Finnish:

```
Sorted using the Finnish culture
Alabama-Alaska-Arizona-Hawaii-Kansas-Kentucky-Louisiana-Missouri-Texas-Utah-
Washington-Virginia-Wisconsin-Wyoming

Sorted using the invariant culture
Alabama-Alaska-Arizona-Hawaii-Kansas-Kentucky-Louisiana-Missouri-Texas-Utah-
Virginia-Washington-Wisconsin-Wyoming
```

> **NOTE** *If sorting a collection should be independent of a culture, the collection must be sorted with the invariant culture. This can be particularly useful when sending the sort result to a server or storing it inside a file. To display a sorted collection to the user, it's best to sort it with the user's culture.*

In addition to a locale-dependent formatting and measurement system, text and pictures may differ depending on the culture. This is where resources come into play.

RESOURCES

You can put resources such as pictures or string tables into resource files or satellite assemblies. Such resources can be very helpful when localizing applications, and .NET has built-in support to search for localized resources. Before you see how to use resources to localize applications, the following sections explain how you can create and read resources without looking at language aspects.

Resource Readers and Writers

With .NET Core, the resource readers and writers are limited compared to the full .NET version (at the time of this writing). However, for many scenarios—including multiplatform support—what is needed is available.

The `CreateResource` sample application creates a resource file dynamically, and reads resources from the file. This sample makes use of the following dependencies and namespaces:

Dependencies

```
NETStandard.Library
System.Resources.ReaderWriter
```

Namespaces

```
System.Collections
System.IO
System.Resources
static System.Console
```

`ResourceWriter` enables you to create binary resource files. The constructor of the writer requires a `Stream` that is created using the `File` class. You add resources by using the `AddResource` method. The simple resource writer for .NET Core requires strings with both the key and the value. The resource writer for the full .NET Framework defines overloads to store other types as well (code file `CreateResource/Program.cs`):

```
private const string ResourceFile = "Demo.resources";
public static void CreateResource()
{
  FileStream stream = File.OpenWrite(ResourceFile);
  using (var writer = new ResourceWriter(stream))
  {
    writer.AddResource("Title", "Professional C#");
    writer.AddResource("Author", "Christian Nagel");
    writer.AddResource("Publisher", "Wrox Press");
  }
}
```

To read the resources of a binary resource file, you can use `ResourceReader`. The `GetEnumerator` method of the reader returns an `IDictionaryEnumerator` that is used within the following `foreach` statement to access the key and value of the resource:

```
public static void ReadResource()
{
  FileStream stream = File.OpenRead(ResourceFile);
  using (var reader = new ResourceReader(stream))
  {
    foreach (DictionaryEntry resource in reader)
    {
      WriteLine($"{resource.Key} {resource.Value}");
    }
  }
}
```

Running the application returns the keys and values that have been written to the binary resource file. As shown in the next section, you can also use a command-line tool—the Resource File Generator (resgen)—to create and convert resource files.

Using the Resource File Generator

Resource files can contain items such as pictures and string tables. A resource file is created by using either a normal text file or a `.resX` file that uses XML. This section starts with a simple text file.

You can create a resource that embeds a string table by using a normal text file. The text file assigns strings to keys. The key is the name that can be used from a program to get the value. Spaces are allowed in both keys and values.

This example shows a simple string table in the file `Wrox.ProCSharp.Localization.MyResources.txt`:

```
Title = Professional C#
Chapter = Localization
Author = Christian Nagel
Publisher = Wrox Press
```

> **NOTE** *When saving text files with Unicode characters, you must save the file with the proper encoding. To select the UTF8 encoding, use the Save As dialog.*

You can use the Resource File Generator (`Resgen.exe`) utility to create a resource file out of `Wrox.ProCSharp.Localization.MyResources.txt`. Typing the line

```
resgen Wrox.ProCSharp.Localization.MyResources.txt
```

creates the file `Wrox.ProCSharp.Localization.MyResources.resources`. The resulting resource file can be either added to an assembly as an external file or embedded into the DLL or EXE. Resgen also supports the creation of XML-based `.resX` resource files. One easy way to build an XML file is by using Resgen itself:

```
resgen Wrox.ProCSharp.Localization.MyResources.txt
    Wrox.ProCSharp.Localization.MyResources.resX
```

This command creates the XML resource file `Wrox.ProCSharp.LocalizationMyResources.resX`. Resgen supports strongly typed resources. A strongly typed resource is represented by a class that accesses the resource. You can create the class with the `/str` option of the Resgen utility:

```
resgen /str:C#,Wrox.ProCSharp.Localization,MyResources,MyResources.cs
    Wrox.ProCSharp.Localization.MyResources.resX
```

With the `/str` option, the language, namespace, class name, and filename for the source code are defined, in that order.

Using Resource Files with ResourceManager

With the old C# compiler `csc.exe`, you can add resource files to assemblies using the `/resource` option. With the new .NET Core compiler, you need to add a `resx` file to the folder, and it will be embedded within the assembly. By default, all `resx` files are embedded in the assembly. You can customize this by using the `resource`, `resourceFiles`, and `resourceExclude` nodes in the `project.json` file.

The default setting for `resource` is to embed all resource files:

```
"resource": ["embed/**/*.*"]
```

To define that the directories `foo` and `bar` should be excluded, you define the `resourceExclude`:

```
"resourceExclude": ["foo/**/*.resx", "bar/**/*.*"],
```

To define specific resource files, you use the `resourceFiles` node:

```
"resourceFiles": ["embed/Resources/Sample.resx", "embed/Views/View1.resources"],
```

To see how resource files can be loaded with the `ResourceManager` class, create a Console Application (Package) and name it `ResourcesDemo`. This sample makes use of the following dependencies and namespaces:

Dependencies

```
NETStandard.Library
```

Namespaces

```
System.Globalization
System.Reflection
System.Resources
static System.Console
```

Create a `Resources` folder, and add a `Messages.resx` file to this folder. The `Messages.resx` file is filled with a key and value for English-US content—for example, the key `GoodMorning` and the value `Good Morning!` This will be the default language. You can add other language resource files with the naming convention to add the culture to the resource file, for example, `Messages.de.resx` for German languages and `Messages.de-AT.resx` for Austrian differences.

To access the embedded resource, use the `ResourceManager` class from the `System.Resources` namespace and the `System.Resources.ResourceManager` NuGet package. When you're instantiating the `ResourceManager`, one overload of the constructor needs the name of the resource and the assembly. The namespace of the application is `ResourcesDemo`; the resource file is in the folder `Resources`, which defines the sub-namespace Resources, and it has the name `Messages.resx`. This defines the name `ResourcesDemo.Resources.Messages`. You can retrieve the assembly of the resource using the `GetTypeInfo` method of the `Program` type, which defines an `Assembly` property. Using the resources instance, the `GetString` method returns the value of the key passed from the resource file. Passing a culture such as de-AT for the second argument looks for resources in the de-AT resource file. If it's not found there, the neutral language for de is taken, the de resource file. If it's not found there, the default resource file without culture naming succeeds to return the value (code file `ResourcesDemo/Program.cs`):

```
var resources = new ResourceManager("ResourcesDemo.Resources.Messages",
    typeof(Program).GetTypeInfo().Assembly);
string goodMorning = resources.GetString("GoodMorning",
    new CultureInfo("de-AT"));
WriteLine(goodMorning);
```

Another overload of the `ResourceManager` constructor just requires the type of the class. This `ResourceManager` looks for a resource file named `Program.resx`:

```
var programResources = new ResourceManager(typeof(Program));
WriteLine(programResources.GetString("Resource1"));
```

The System.Resources Namespace

Before moving on to the next example, this section provides a review of the classes contained in the `System.Resources` namespace that deal with resources:

- ➤ **ResourceManager**—Can be used to get resources for the current culture from assemblies or resource files. Using the `ResourceManager`, you can also get a `ResourceSet` for a particular culture.

- ➤ **ResourceSet**—Represents the resources for a particular culture. When a `ResourceSet` instance is created, it enumerates over a class, implementing the interface `IResourceReader`, and it stores all resources in a `Hashtable`.

- ➤ **IResourceReader**—Used from the `ResourceSet` to enumerate resources. The class `ResourceReader` implements this interface.

- ➤ **ResourceWriter**—Used to create a resource file. `ResourceWriter` implements the interface `IResourceWriter`.

LOCALIZATION WITH WPF

With WPF, you can use .NET resources, similar to what you've seen with console applications. To see the use of resources with a WPF application, create a simple WPF application containing just one button, as shown in Figure 28-7.

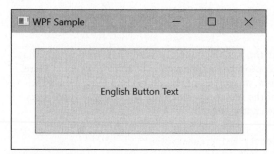

FIGURE 28-7

The XAML code for this application is shown here:

```
<Window x:Class="WpfApplication.MainWindow"
    xmlns="http://schemas.microsoft.com/winfx/2006/xaml/presentation"
    xmlns:x="http://schemas.microsoft.com/winfx/2006/xaml"
```

```
        Title="WPF Sample" Height="350" Width="525">
    <Grid>
        <Button Name="button1" Margin="30,20,30,20" Click="Button_Click"
            Content="English Button" />
    </Grid>
</Window>
```

With the handler code for the `Click` event of the button, only a message box containing a sample message pops up:

```
private void Button_Click(object sender, RoutedEventArgs e)
{
    MessageBox.Show("English Message");
}
```

> **NOTE** *You can read more about WPF and XAML in Chapter 29, "Core XAML," and Chapter 34, "Windows Desktop Applications with WPF."*

You add .NET resources to a WPF application similarly to how you add them to other applications. Define the resources named `Button1Text` and `Button1Message` in the file `Resources.resx`. This file is automatically created with a WPF project. You can find it in the `Properties` folder in Solution Explorer. By default, this resource file has an `Internal` access modifier to create the `Resources` class. To use it from within XAML, you must change this to `Public` within the Managed Resources Editor. While selecting the resource file and opening the Properties Window, you can see that the custom tool `PublicResXFileCodeGenerator` is assigned to the file. This code generator creates a strongly typed code file to access the resources. The generated code file offers public static properties with the name of the resource keys that accesses a `ResourceManager` as you can see with the `Button1Text` property in the following code snippet. The `ResourceManager` used here is a property that returns an instance of the `ResourceManager` class, which is created using a Singleton pattern:

```
public static string Button1Text
{
    get
    {
        return ResourceManager.GetString("Button1Text", resourceCulture);
    }
}
```

To use the generated resource class, you need to change the XAML code. Add an XML namespace alias to reference the .NET namespace `WpfApplication.Properties` as shown in the following code. Here, the alias is set to the value `props`. From XAML elements, properties of this class can be used with the `x:Static` markup extension. The `Content` property of the `Button` is set to the `Button1Text` property of the `Resources` class (code file `WPFApplication\MainWindow.xaml`):

```
<Window x:Class="WpfApplication.MainWindow"
    xmlns="http://schemas.microsoft.com/winfx/2006/xaml/presentation"
    xmlns:x="http://schemas.microsoft.com/winfx/2006/xaml"
    xmlns:props="clr-namespace:WpfApplication.Properties"
    Title="WPF Sample" Height="350" Width="525">
    <Grid>
        <Button Name="button1" Margin="30,20,30,20" Click="Button_Click"
            Content="{x:Static Member=props:Resources.Button1Text}" />
    </Grid>
</Window>
```

To use the .NET resource from code-behind, just access the `Button1Message` property directly (code file `WPFApplication\MainWindow.xaml.cs`):

```
private void Button_Click(object sender, RoutedEventArgs e)
{
  MessageBox.Show(Properties.Resources.Button1Message);
}
```

Now the resources can be localized as before.

LOCALIZATION WITH ASP.NET CORE

> **NOTE** *For using localization with ASP.NET Core, you need to know about both cultures and resources that are discussed in this chapter as well as creating ASP.NET Core applications. In case you didn't create ASP.NET Core web applications with .NET Core before, you should read Chapter 40, "ASP.NET Core," before continuing with this part of the chapter.*

For localization of ASP.NET Core web applications, you can use the `CultureInfo` class and resources similar to what you've seen earlier in this chapter, but there are some additional issues that you need to resolve. Setting the culture for the complete application doesn't fulfill usual needs because users are coming from different cultures. So it's necessary to set the culture with every request to the server.

How do you know about the culture of the user? There are different options. The browser sends preferred languages within the HTTP header with every request. This information from the browser can come from browser settings or when the browser itself checks the installed languages. Another option is to define URL parameters or use different domain names for different languages. You can use different domain names in some scenarios, such as www.cninnovation.com for an English version of the site and www.cninnovation.de for a German version. But what about www.cninnovation.ch? This should be offered both in German and French and probably Italian. URL parameters such as www.cninnovation.com/culture=de could help here. Using www.cninnovation.com/de works similar to the URL parameter by defining a specific route. Another option is to allow the user to select the language and define a cookie to remember this option.

All of these scenarios are supported out of the box by ASP.NET Core 1.0.

Registering Localization Services

To start seeing this in action, create a new ASP.NET Web Application using an Empty ASP.NET Core 1.0 project template. This project makes use of the following dependencies and namespaces:

Dependencies

Microsoft.AspNetCore.Hosting

Microsoft.AspNetCore.Features

Microsoft.AspNetCore.IISPlatformHandler

Microsoft.AspNetCore.Localization

Microsoft.AspNetCore.Server.Kestrel

Microsoft.Extensions.Localization

System.Globalization

Namespaces

Microsoft.AspNetCore.Builder

Microsoft.AspNetCore.Hosting

Microsoft.AspNetCore.Http

Microsoft.AspNetCore.Http.Features

Microsoft.AspNetCore.Localization

Microsoft.Extensions.DependencyInjection

Microsoft.Extensions.Localization

System

System.Globalization

System.Net

Within the `Startup` class, you need to invoke the `AddLocalization` extension method to register services for localization (code file `WebApplicationSample/Startup.cs`):

```
public void ConfigureServices(IServiceCollection services)
{
    services.AddLocalization(options => options.ResourcesPath = "CustomResources");
}
```

The `AddLocalization` method registers services for the interfaces `IStringLocalizerFactory` and `IStringLocalizer`. With the registration code, the type `ResourceManagerStringLocalizerFactory` is registered as a singleton, and `StringLocalizer` is registered with transient lifetime. The class `ResourceManagerStringLocalizerFactory` is a factory for `ResourceManagerStringLocalizer`. This class in turn makes use of the `ResourceManager` class shown earlier for retrieving strings from resource files.

Injecting Localization Services

After localization is added to the service collection, you can request localization in the `Configure` method of the `Startup` class. The `UseRequestLocalization` method defines an overload where you can pass `RequestLocalizationOptions`. The `RequestLocalizationOptions` enables you to customize what cultures should be supported and to set the default culture. Here, the `DefaultRequestCulture` is set to en-US. The class `RequestCulture` is just a small wrapper around the culture for formatting—which is accessible via the `Culture` property—and the culture for using the resources (`UICulture` property). The sample code accepts en-US, de-AT, and de cultures for `SupportedCultures` and `SupportedUICultures`:

```
public void Configure(IApplicationBuilder app, IStringLocalizer<Startup> sr)
{
    app.UseIISPlatformHandler();

    var options = new RequestLocalizationOptions
    {
        DefaultRequestCulture = new RequestCulture(new CultureInfo("en-US")),
        SupportedCultures = new CultureInfo[]
        {
            new CultureInfo("en-US"),
            new CultureInfo("de-AT"),
            new CultureInfo("de"),
        },
        SupportedUICultures = new CultureInfo[]
        {
            new CultureInfo("en-US"),
            new CultureInfo("de-AT"),
            new CultureInfo("de"),
        }
```

```
    };

    app.UseRequestLocalization(options);

    // etc.
}
```

With the `RequestLocalizationOptions` settings, the property `RequestCultureProviders` is also set. By default, three providers are configured: `QueryStringRequestCultureProvider`, `CookieRequestCultureProvider`, and `AcceptLanguageHeaderRequestCultureProvider`.

Culture Providers

Let's get into more details on these culture providers. The `QueryStringRequestCultureProvider` uses the query string to retrieve the culture. By default, the query parameters `culture` and `ui-culture` are used with this provider, as shown with this URL:

```
http://localhost:5000/?culture=de&ui-culture=en-US
```

You can also change the query parameters by setting the `QueryStringKey` and `UIQueryStringKey` properties of the `QueryStringRequestCultureProvider`.

The `CookieRequestCultureProvider` defines the cookie named `ASPNET_CULTURE` (which can be set using the `CookieName` property). The values from this cookie are retrieved to set the culture. To create a cookie and send it to the client, you can use the static method `MakeCookieValue` to create a cookie from a `RequestCulture` and send it to the client. The `CookieRequestCultureProvider` uses the static method `ParseCookieValue` to get a `RequestCulture`.

With the third option for culture settings, you can use the HTTP header information that is sent by the browser. The HTTP header that is sent looks like this:

```
Accept-Language: en-us, de-at;q=0.8, it;q=0.7
```

The `AcceptLanguageHeaderRequestCultureProvider` uses this information to set the culture. You use up to three language values in the order as defined by the quality value to find a first match with the supported cultures.

The following code snippet now uses the request culture to generate HTML output. First, you access the requested culture using the `IRequestCultureFeature` contract. The `RequestCultureFeature` that implements the interface `IRequestCultureFeature` uses the first culture provider that matches the culture setting. If a URL defines a query string that matches the culture parameter, the `QueryStringRequestCultureProvider` is used to return the requested culture. If the URL does not match, but a cookie with the name `ASPNET_CULTURE` is received, the `CookieRequestCultureProvider` is used, and otherwise the `AcceptLanguageRequestCultureProvider`. The resulting culture that is used by the user is written to the response stream using properties of the returned `RequestCulture`. Then, today's date is written to the stream using the current culture. The variable of type `IStringLocalizer` used here needs some more examination next:

```
public void Configure(IApplicationBuilder app, IStringLocalizer<Startup> sr)
{
    // etc.

    app.Run(async context =>
    {
        IRequestCultureFeature requestCultureFeature =
            context.GetFeature<IRequestCultureFeature>();
        RequestCulture requestCulture = requestCultureFeature.RequestCulture;

        var today = DateTime.Today;
        context.Response.StatusCode = 200;
        await context.Response.WriteAsync("<h1>Sample Localization</h1>");
```

```
    await context.Response.WriteAsync(
      $"<div>{requestCulture.Culture} {requestCulture.UICulture}</div>");
    await context.Response.WriteAsync($"<div>{today:D}</div>");
    // etc.

    await context.Response.WriteAsync($"<div>{sr["message1"]}</div>");
    await context.Response.WriteAsync($"<div>{sr.GetString("message1")}</div>");
    await context.Response.WriteAsync($"<div>{sr.GetString("message2",
      requestCulture.Culture, requestCulture.UICulture)}</div>");
  });
}
```

Using Resources from ASP.NET Core

Resource files, as you've seen in the Resources section, can be used with ASP.NET Core 1.0. The sample project adds the file Startup.resx as well as to the CustomResources folder. Localized versions for the resources are offered with Startup.de.resx and Startup.de-AT.resx.

The folder name where the resources are found is defined with the options when injecting the localization service (code file WebApplicationSample/Startup.cs):

```
public void ConfigureServices(IServiceCollection services)
{
  services.AddLocalization(
    options => options.ResourcesPath = "CustomResources");
}
```

With dependency injection, IStringLocalizer<Startup> is injected as a parameter of the Configure method. The generic type Startup parameter is used to find a resource file with the same name in the resources directory; this matches with Startup.resx.

```
public void Configure(IApplicationBuilder app, IStringLocalizer<Startup> sr)
{
  // etc.
}
```

The following code snippet makes use of the sr variable of type IStringLocalizer<Startup> to access a resource named message1 using an indexer and with the GetString method. The resource message2 uses string format placeholders, which are injected with an overload of the GetString method where any number of parameters can be passed to:

```
public void Configure(IApplicationBuilder app, IStringLocalizer<Startup> sr)
{
  // etc.

  app.Run(async context =>
  {
    // etc.

    await context.Response.WriteAsync($"<div>{sr["message1"]}</div>");
    await context.Response.WriteAsync($"<div>{sr.GetString("message1")}</div>");
    await context.Response.WriteAsync($"<div>{sr.GetString("message2",
      requestCulture.Culture, requestCulture.UICulture)}</div>");
  });
}
string localized1 = sr["message1"];
```

The resource for message2 is defined with string format placeholders:

```
Using culture {0} and UI culture {1}
```

Running the web application results in the view shown in Figure 28-8.

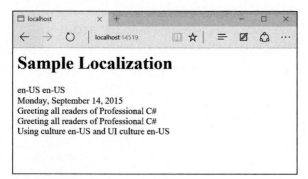

FIGURE 28-8

LOCALIZATION WITH THE UNIVERSAL WINDOWS PLATFORM

Localization with the Universal Windows Platform (UWP) is based on the concepts you've learned so far, but it brings some fresh ideas, as described in this section. For the best experience, you need to install the Multilingual App Toolkit that is available via Visual Studio Extensions and Updates.

The concepts of cultures, regions, and resources are the same, but because Windows apps can be written with C# and XAML, C++ and XAML, and JavaScript and HTML, these concepts need to be available with all languages. Only Windows Runtime is available with all these programming languages and Windows Store apps. Therefore, new namespaces for globalization and resources are available with Windows Runtime: `Windows.Globalization` and `Windows.ApplicationModel.Resources`. With the globalization namespaces you can find `Calendar`, `GeographicRegion` (compare with the .NET `RegionInfo`), and `Language` classes. With sub-namespaces, there are also classes for number and date formatting that vary according to the language. With C# and Windows apps you can still use the .NET classes for cultures and regions.

Let's get into an example so you can see localization with a Universal Windows app in action. Create a small application using the Blank App (Universal App) Visual Studio project template. Add two `TextBlock` controls and one `TextBox` control to the page.

Within the `OnNavigatedTo` method of the code file you can assign a date with the current format to the `Text` property of the `text1` control. You can use the `DateTime` structure in the same way you've done it with the console application earlier in this chapter (code file `UWPLocalization/MainPage.xaml.cs`):

```
protected override void OnNavigatedTo(NavigationEventArgs e)
{
  base.OnNavigatedTo(e);
  text1.Text = DateTime.Today.ToString("D");
  //...
}
```

Using Resources with UWP

With UWP, you can create resource files with the file extension `resw` instead of `resx`. Behind the scenes, the same XML format is used with `resw` files, and you can use the same Visual Studio resource editor to create and modify these files. The following example uses the structure shown in Figure 28-9. The subfolder `Messages` contains a subdirectory, `en-us`, in which two resource files `Errors.resw` and `Messages.resw` are created. In the folder `Strings\en-us`, the resource file `Resources.resw` is created.

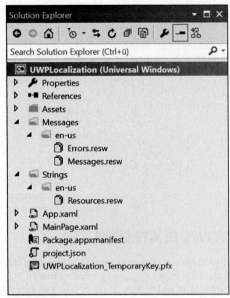

FIGURE 28-9

The Messages.resw file contains some English text resources, Hello with a value of Hello World, and resources named GoodDay, GoodEvening, and GoodMorning. The file Resources.resw contains the resources Text3.Text and Text3.Width, with the values "This is a sample message for Text 4" and a value of "300".

With the code, you can access resources with the help of the ResourceLoader class from the namespace Windows.ApplicationModel.Resources. Here you use the string "Messages" with the method GetForCurrentView. Thus, you're using the resource file Messages.resw. Invoking the method GetString retrieves the resource with the key "Hello" (code file UWPLocalization/MainPage.xaml.cs):

```
protected override void OnNavigatedTo(NavigationEventArgs e)
{
    // etc.
    var resourceLoader = ResourceLoader.GetForCurrentView("Messages");
    text2.Text = resourceLoader.GetString("Hello");
}
```

With UWP Windows apps it is also easy to use the resources directly from XAML code. With the following TextBox, the x:Uid attribute is assigned the value Text3. This way, a resource named Text3 with extensions is searched for in the resource file Resources.resw. This resource file contains value for the keys Text3.Text and Text3.Width. The values are retrieved, and both the Text and Width properties are set (code file UWPLocalization/MainPage.xaml):

```
<TextBox x:Uid="FileName_Text3" HorizontalAlignment="Left" Margin="50"
    TextWrapping="Wrap" Text="TextBox" VerticalAlignment="Top"/>
```

Localization with the Multilingual App Toolkit

To localize UWP apps you can download the previously mentioned Multilingual App Toolkit. This toolkit integrates with Visual Studio 2015. After installing the toolkit, you can enable it within Visual Studio using the menu Tools ➪ Multilingual App Toolkit ➪ Enable Selection. This adds a build command to the project file and adds one more option to the context menu in Solution Explorer. Open the context menu in Solution Explorer and select Multilingual App Toolkit ➪ Add Translation Languages to invoke the dialog shown in Figure 28-10, where you can choose which languages should be translated. The sample uses Pseudo Language, French, German, and Spanish. For these languages, a Microsoft Translator is available. This tool now creates a `MultilingualResources` subdirectory that contains `.xlf` files for the selected languages. The `.xlf` files are defined with the XLIFF (XML Localisation Interchange File Format) standard. This is a standard of the Open Architecture for XML Authoring and Localization (OAXAL) reference architecture.

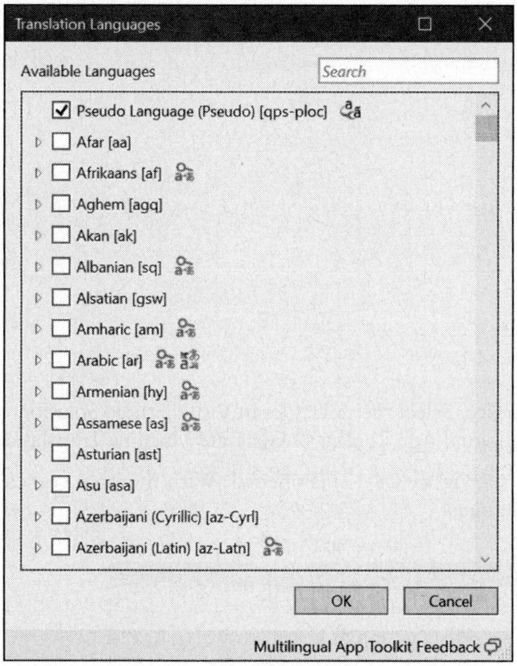

FIGURE 28-10

> **NOTE** *The Multilingual App Toolkit can also be installed from* `http://aka.ms/matinstallv4` *without using Visual Studio. Download the Multilingual App Toolkit.*

The next time you start the build process for the project, the XLIFF files are filled with content from all the resources. When you select the XLIFF files in Solution Explorer, you can send it to translation. To do so, open the context menu in Solution Explorer while selecting the `.xlf` files, and select Multilingual App Toolkit ➪ Export translations. . . , which opens the dialog shown in Figure 28-11. With this dialog you can configure the information that should be sent, and you can send an e-mail with the XLIFF files attached.

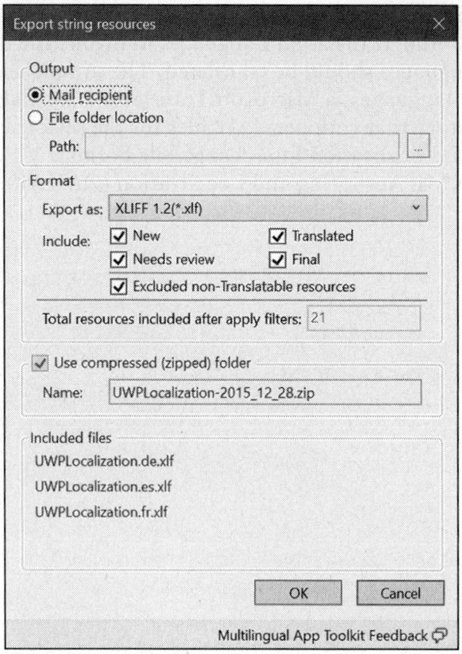

FIGURE 28-11

For translation, you can also use Microsoft's translation service. Select the .xlf files in Visual Studio Solution Explorer, and after opening the context menu, select Multilingual App Toolkit ⇨ Generate Machine Translations.

When you open the .xlf files, the Multilingual Editor (see Figure 28-12) is opened. With this tool you can verify the automatic translations and make necessary changes.

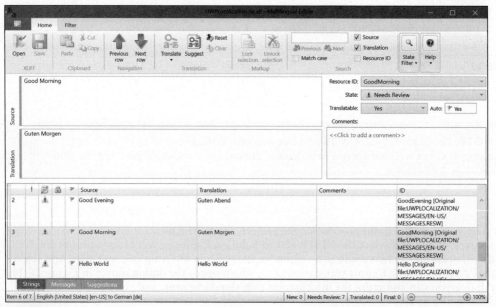

FIGURE 28-12

Don't use the machine translation without a manual review. The tool shows a status for every resource that is translated. After the automatic translation, the status is set to Needs Review. You have probably seen applications with machine translations that are incorrect—and sometimes really funny.

CREATING CUSTOM CULTURES

Over time, more and more languages have become supported by the .NET Framework. However, not all languages of the world are available with .NET, and for these you can create a custom culture. For example, creating a custom culture can be useful to support a minority within a region or to create subcultures for different dialects.

You can create custom cultures and regions with the class `CultureAndRegionInfoBuilder` in the namespace `System.Globalization`. This class is located in the assembly `sysglobl`.

With the constructor of the class `CultureAndRegionInfoBuilder`, you can pass the culture's name. The second argument of the constructor requires an enumeration of type `CultureAndRegionModifiers`. This enumeration allows one of three values: `Neutral` for a neutral culture, `Replacement` if an existing Framework culture should be replaced, or `None`.

After the `CultureAndRegionInfoBuilder` object is instantiated, you can configure the culture by setting properties. With the properties of this class, you can define all the cultural and regional information, such as name, calendar, number format, metric information, and so on. If the culture should be based on existing cultures and regions, you can set the properties of the instance using the methods `LoadDataFromCultureInfo` and `LoadDataFromRegionInfo`, changing the values that are different by setting the properties afterward.

Calling the method `Register` registers the new culture with the operating system. Indeed, you can find the file that describes the culture in the directory `<windows>\Globalization`. Look for files with the extension `.nlp` (code file `CustomCultures\Program.cs`):

```
using System;
using System.Globalization;
using static System.Console;

namespace CustomCultures
{
  class Program
  {
    static void Main()
    {
      try
      {
        // Create a Styria culture
        var styria = new CultureAndRegionInfoBuilder("de-AT-ST",
          CultureAndRegionModifiers.None);
        var cultureParent = new CultureInfo("de-AT");
        styria.LoadDataFromCultureInfo(cultureParent);
        styria.LoadDataFromRegionInfo(new RegionInfo("AT"));
        styria.Parent = cultureParent;
        styria.RegionNativeName = "Steiermark";
        styria.RegionEnglishName = "Styria";
        styria.CultureEnglishName = "Styria (Austria)";
        styria.CultureNativeName = "Steirisch";

        styria.Register();
      }
      catch (UnauthorizedAccessException ex)
      {
        WriteLine(ex.Message);
      }
    }
  }
}
```

Because registering custom languages on the system requires administrative privileges, the sample application is built using the Console Application project template, and an application manifest file is added. This manifest file specifies the requested execution rights. In the project properties, the manifest file needs to be set in the Application settings:

```
<?xml version="1.0" encoding="utf-8"?>
<asmv1:assembly manifestVersion="1.0" xmlns="urn:schemas-microsoft-com:asm.v1"
xmlsn:asmv1="urn:schemas-microsoft-com:asm.v1" xmlns:asmv2="urn:schemas-microsoft-
com:asm.v2" xmlns:xsi="http://www.w3.org/2001/XMLSchema-instance"
  <assemblyIdentity version="1.0.0.0" name="MyApplication.app"/>
  <trustInfo xmlns="urn:schemas-microsoft-com:asm.v2">
    <security>
      <requestedPrivileges xmlns="urn:schemas-microsoft-com:asm.v3">
        <requestedExecutionLevel level="requireAdministrator"
          uiAccess="false" />
      </requestedPrivileges>
    </security>
  </trustInfo>
</asmv1:assembly>
```

You can now use the newly created culture like other cultures:

```
var ci = new CultureInfo("de-AT-ST");
CultureInfo.CurrentCulture = ci;
CultureInfo.CurrentUICulture = ci;
```

You can use the culture for formatting and for resources. If you start the Cultures In Action application that was written earlier in this chapter, you can see the custom culture as well.

SUMMARY

This chapter demonstrated how to globalize and localize .NET applications. For the globalization of applications, you learned about using the namespace `System.Globalization` to format culture-dependent numbers and dates. Furthermore, you learned that sorting strings by default varies according to the culture, and you looked at using the invariant culture for a culture-independent sort. Using the `CultureAndRegionInfoBuilder` class, you've learned how to create a custom culture.

Localizing an application is accomplished by using resources, which you can pack into files, satellite assemblies, or a custom store such as a database. The classes used with localization are in the namespace `System.Resources`. To read resources from other places, such as satellite assemblies or resource files, you can create a custom resource reader.

You also learned how to localize WPF, ASP.NET Core, and apps using the Universal Windows Platform.

The next chapter provides information about XAML. XAML is used with both the Universal Windows Platform and WPF, so the next chapter gives the foundation for both of these technologies.

PART III
Windows Apps

29

Core XAML

WHAT'S IN THIS CHAPTER?

➤ XAML syntax
➤ Dependency properties
➤ Routed events
➤ Attached properties
➤ Markup extensions

WROX.COM CODE DOWNLOADS FOR THIS CHAPTER

The wrox.com code downloads for this chapter are found at www.wrox.com/go/professionalcsharp6 on the Download Code tab. The code for this chapter is divided into the following major examples, for both WPF and Universal Windows apps:

➤ Code Intro
➤ XAML Intro
➤ Dependency Objects
➤ Routed Events
➤ Attached Properties
➤ Markup Extensions

USES OF XAML

When you're writing a .NET application, usually C# is not the only syntax you need to know. If you write Universal Windows apps, Windows desktop applications using Windows Presentation Foundation (WPF), or workflows with Windows Workflow Foundation (WF); create XPS documents, or write Silverlight apps, you also need XAML. XAML (eXtensible Application Markup Language) is a declarative XML syntax that's usually needed with these applications. This chapter describes the syntax of XAML and the extensibility mechanisms that are available with this markup language. The chapter describes the differences between XAML in WPF applications and Windows apps using the Universal Windows Platform (UWP).

All that can be done with XAML can also be done with C#—so why is there a need for XAML? XAML is typically used to describe objects and their properties, and this is possible in a deep hierarchy. For example, a `Window` control contains a `Grid` control; the `Grid` control contains a `StackPanel` and other controls; and the `StackPanel` contains `Button` and `TextBox` controls. XAML makes it easy to describe such a hierarchy and assign properties of objects via XML attributes or elements.

XAML allows writing code in a declarative manner. Whereas C# is mainly an imperative programming language, XAML allows for declarative definitions. With an imperative programming language, a `for` loop that is defined with C# code, the compiler creates a `for` loop with Intermediate Language (IL) code. With a declarative programming language, you declaratively declare what should be done, but not how it should be done. Although C# is not a pure imperative programming language, when using LINQ you also write syntax in a declarative way.

XAML is an XML syntax, but it defines several enhancements to XML. XAML is still valid XML, but some enhancements have special meaning—for example, using curly brackets within XML attributes and how child elements are named.

Before you can use XAML efficiently, you need to understand some important features of this language. This chapter introduces these XAML features:

➤ **Dependency properties**—From the outside, dependency properties look like normal properties. However, they need less storage and implement change notification.

➤ **Routed events**—From the outside, routed events look like normal .NET events. However, you use custom event implementation with add and remove accessors to allow bubbling and tunneling. Events can tunnel from outer controls to inner controls, and bubble from inner controls to outer controls.

➤ **Attached properties**—With attached properties it is possible to add properties to other controls. For example, the `Button` control doesn't have a property to position it within a `Grid` control in a specific row and column. With XAML, it looks like it has such a property.

➤ **Markup extensions**—Writing XML attributes requires less coding compared to XML elements. However, XML attributes can only be strings; you can write much more powerful syntax with XML elements. To reduce the amount of code that needs to be written, markup extensions allow writing powerful syntax within attributes.

> **NOTE** *.NET properties are explained in Chapter 3, "Objects and Types." Events, including writing custom events with add and remove accessors, are explained in Chapter 9, "Delegates, Lambdas, and Events." The power of XML is explained in Chapter 27, "XML and JSON."*

XAML FOUNDATION

XAML code is declared using textual XML. You can use designers to create XAML code or write XAML code by hand. Visual Studio contains designers to write XAML code for WPF, Silverlight, WF, or Universal Windows apps. Other tools are also available to create XAML, such as Blend for Visual Studio 2015. Whereas Visual Studio is best for writing source code, Blend is best for creating styles, templates, and animations. With Visual Studio 2013, Blend and Visual Studio started to share the same XAML designer. Blend 2015 was rewritten to share the same shell with Visual Studio. As a Visual Studio user, you'll immediately feel at home using Blend 2015.

Let's get into XAML. With WPF applications, an XAML element maps to a .NET class, but that's not a strict requirement for XAML. With Silverlight 1.0, .NET was not available with the plug-in and the XAML code was interpreted and could be accessed programmatically with JavaScript. This changed with Silverlight 2.0, in which a smaller version of the .NET Framework is part of the Silverlight plug-in. With Silverlight or WPF, every XAML element maps to a .NET class; with Windows Apps every XAML element maps to a Windows Runtime type.

What happens with XAML code on a build process? To compile a WPF project, MSBuild tasks are defined in the assembly `PresentationBuildTasks` named `MarkupCompilePass1` and `MarkupCompilePass2`. These MSBuild tasks create a binary representation of the markup code named BAML (Binary Application Markup Language) that is added to the .NET resources of an assembly. During runtime, the binary representation is used.

Mapping Elements to Classes with WPF

As mentioned earlier, usually an XAML element maps to a .NET or a Windows Runtime class. In this section you begin by creating a `Button` object inside a `Window` programmatically with a C# console project. To compile the following code, wherein a `Button` object is instantiated with the `Content` property set to a string, you define a `Window` with `Title` and `Content` properties set, and you need to reference the assemblies `PresentationFramework`, `PresentationCore`, `WindowsBase`, and `System.Xaml` (code file `CodeIntroWPF/Program.cs`).

```csharp
using System;
using System.Windows;
using System.Windows.Controls;

namespace CodeIntroWPF
{
  class Program
  {
    [STAThread]
    static void Main()
    {
      var b = new Button
      {
        Content = "Click Me!"
      };
      b.Click += (sender, e) =>
      {
        b.Content = "clicked";
      };

      var w = new Window
      {
        Title = "Code Demo",
        Content = b
      };

      var app = new Application();
      app.Run(w);
    }
  }
}
```

NOTE *With the .NET Framework, everything below the* `System.Windows` *namespace with the exception of* `System.Windows.Forms` *(which covers the older Windows Forms technology) belongs to WPF.*

You can create a similar UI can by using XAML code. As before, you create a `Window` element that contains a `Button` element. The `Window` element has the `Title` attribute set in addition to its content (code file XAMLIntroWPF/MainWindow.xaml):

```
<Window x:Class="XAMLIntroWPF.MainWindow"
        xmlns="http://schemas.microsoft.com/winfx/2006/xaml/presentation"
        xmlns:x="http://schemas.microsoft.com/winfx/2006/xaml"
        Title="XAML Demo" Height="350" Width="525">
    <!--etc.-->
    <Button Content="Click Me!" Click="OnButtonClicked" />
    <!--etc.-->
</Window>
```

Of course, the `Application` instance in the last code example is missing. You can define this with XAML as well. In the `Application` element, the `StartupUri` attribute is set, which links to the XAML file that contains the main window (code file XAMLIntroWPF/App.xaml):

```
<Application x:Class="XAMLIntroWPF.App"
             xmlns="http://schemas.microsoft.com/winfx/2006/xaml/presentation"
             xmlns:x="http://schemas.microsoft.com/winfx/2006/xaml"
             StartupUri="MainWindow.xaml">
    <Application.Resources>
    </Application.Resources>
</Application>
```

Mapping Elements to Classes with Universal Windows Apps

Mapping to types with Universal Windows Platform (UWP) apps is similar to doing it with WPF, but there are completely different types defined with the Windows Runtime. Let's start again without using XAML. You can create an app using the Blank App template for Windows Universal apps and remove the XAML files (both `MainPage.xaml` as well as `App.xaml` including the code behind C# files). To not automatically create the `Main` method from the designer, you must set the conditional compilation symbol `DISABLE_XAML_GENERATED_MAIN` using the Build settings in the Project properties.

With the `Main` method, you need to start the application. Similarly to WPF, you use an `Application` class here. This time, it's from the `Windows.UI.Xaml` namespace. Instead of invoking the instance `Run` method, this class defines a static `Start` method. The `Start` method defines an `ApplicationInitializationCallback` delegate parameter that is invoked during the initialization of the app. Within this initialization, a `Button` (namespace `Windows.UI.Xaml.Controls`) is created, and the current window is activated:

```
using System;
using Windows.ApplicationModel.Activation;
using Windows.UI.Xaml;
using Windows.UI.Xaml.Controls;

namespace CodeIntroUWP
{
  partial class Program
  {
    [STAThread]
    public static void Main()
    {
      Application.Start(p =>
      {
        var b = new Button
        {
          Content = "Click Me!"
        };
        b.Click += (sender, e) =>
        {
          b.Content = "clicked";
```

```
        };

        Window.Current.Content = b;
        Window.Current.Activate();
      });
    }
  }
}
```

Creating the same UI with XAML, a new Universal Windows app project is created. The XAML code looks very similar to the WPF XAML code, but you use a `Page` instead of a `Window`. Even the XML namespaces are the same. However, the XAML types map to namespaces from the Windows Runtime (code file `XamlIntroUWP/MainPage.xaml`):

```
<Page x:Class="XamlIntroUWP.MainPage"
      xmlns="http://schemas.microsoft.com/winfx/2006/xaml/presentation"
      xmlns:x="http://schemas.microsoft.com/winfx/2006/xaml">
  <!--etc.-->
  <Button Content="Click Me!" x:Name="button1" Click="OnButtonClick" />
  <!--etc.-->
</Page>
```

Using Custom .NET Classes

To use custom .NET classes within XAML code, only the .NET namespace needs to be declared within XAML, and an XML alias must be defined. To demonstrate this, a simple `Person` class with the `FirstName` and `LastName` properties is defined as shown here (code file `DataLib/Person.cs`):

```
public class Person
{
  public string FirstName { get; set; }
  public string LastName { get; set; }
  public override string ToString() => $"{FirstName} {LastName}";
}
```

> **NOTE** *For using types within both WPF and UWP apps, the* `DataLib` *library is created as a Portable library.*

In XAML, an XML namespace alias named `datalib` is defined that maps to the .NET namespace `DataLib` in the assembly `DataLib`. In case the type is in the same assembly as the window, you can remove the assembly name from this declaration. With this alias in place, it's now possible to use all classes from this namespace by prefixing the alias name with the elements.

In the XAML code, you add a `ListBox` that contains items of type `Person`. Using XAML attributes, you set the values of the properties `FirstName` and `LastName`. When you run the application, the output of the `ToString` method is shown inside the `ListBox` (code file `XAMLIntroWPF/MainWindow.xaml`):

```
<Window x:Class="XamlIntroWPF.MainWindow"
        xmlns="http://schemas.microsoft.com/winfx/2006/xaml/presentation"
        xmlns:x="http://schemas.microsoft.com/winfx/2006/xaml"
        xmlns:datalib="clr-namespace:DataLib;assembly=DataLib"
        Title="XAML Demo" Height="350" Width="525">
  <StackPanel>
    <Button Content="Click Me!" />
    <ListBox>
      <datalib:Person FirstName="Stephanie" LastName="Nagel" />
      <datalib:Person FirstName="Matthias" LastName="Nagel" />
```

```
      </ListBox>
    </StackPanel>
  </Window>
```

With UWP apps, the XAML declaration is different in that `using` is used instead of `clr-namespace`, and the name of the assembly is not needed (code file `XAMLIntroUWP/MainPage.xaml`):

```
<Page
    x:Class="XamlIntroUWP.MainPage"
    xmlns="http://schemas.microsoft.com/winfx/2006/xaml/presentation"
    xmlns:x="http://schemas.microsoft.com/winfx/2006/xaml"
    xmlns:datalib="using:DataLib">
```

> **NOTE** *The reason why UWP apps do not use `clr-namespace` within the alias declaration is that XAML with UWP is neither based on nor restricted on .NET. You can use native C++ with XAML as well, and thus `clr` would not be a good fit.*

Instead of defining a .NET namespace and an assembly name with the XML alias in WPF applications, you can map a .NET namespace to an XML namespace using the assembly attribute `XmlNsDefinition` within the library. One argument of this attribute defines the XML namespace, the other the .NET namespace. Using this attribute, it is also possible to map multiple .NET namespaces to a single XML namespace:

```
[assembly: XmlnsDefinition("http://www.wrox.com/Schemas/2015", "Wrox.ProCSharp.XAML")]
```

With this attribute in place, the namespace declaration in the XAML code can be changed to map to the XML namespace:

```
<Window x:Class="Wrox.ProCSharp.XAML.MainWindow"
        xmlns="http://schemas.microsoft.com/winfx/2006/xaml/presentation"
        xmlns:x="http://schemas.microsoft.com/winfx/2006/xaml"
        xmlns:datalib="http://www.wrox.com/Schemas/2015"
        Title="XAML Demo" Height="350" Width="525">
```

Setting Properties as Attributes

You can set properties as attributes as long as the property type can be represented as a string or there is a conversion from a string to the property type. The following code snippet sets the `Content` and `Background` properties of the `Button` element with attributes:

```
<Button Content="Click Me!" Background="LightGoldenrodYellow" />
```

With the previous code snippet, the `Content` property is of type `object` and thus accepts a string. The `Background` property is of type `Brush`. The `Brush` type defines the `BrushConverter` class as a converter type with the attribute `TypeConverter`, with which the class is annotated. `BrushConverter` uses a list of colors to return a `SolidColorBrush` from the `ConvertFromString` method.

> **NOTE** *A type converter derives from the base class `TypeConverter` in the `System.ComponentModel` namespace. The type of the class that needs conversion defines the type converter with the `TypeConverter` attribute. WPF uses many type converters to convert XML attributes to a specific type, including `ColorConverter`, `FontFamilyConverter`, `PathFigureCollectionConverter`, `ThicknessConverter`, and `GeometryConverter`, to name just a few.*

Using Properties as Elements

It's always also possible to use the element syntax to supply the value for properties. You can set the `Background` property of the `Button` class with the child element `Button.Background`. The following code snippet defines the `Button` with the same result as shown earlier with attributes:

```
<Button>
  Click Me!
  <Button.Background>
    <SolidColorBrush Color="LightGoldenrodYellow" />
  </Button.Background>
</Button>
```

Using elements instead of attributes allows you to apply more complex brushes to the `Background` property, such as a `LinearGradientBrush`, as shown in the following example (code file `XAMLSyntax/MainWindow.xaml`):

```
<Button>
  Click Me!
  <Button.Background>
    <LinearGradientBrush StartPoint="0.5,0.0" EndPoint="0.5, 1.0">
      <GradientStop Offset="0" Color="Yellow" />
      <GradientStop Offset="0.3" Color="Orange" />
      <GradientStop Offset="0.7" Color="Red" />
      <GradientStop Offset="1" Color="DarkRed" />
    </LinearGradientBrush>
  </Button.Background>
</Button>
```

> **NOTE** *When setting the content in the sample, neither the* `Content` *attribute nor a* `Button.Content` *element is used to write the content; instead, the content is written directly as a child value to the* `Button` *element. That's possible because with a base class of the* `Button` *class (*`ContentControl`*), the* `ContentProperty` *attribute is applied with* `[ContentProperty("Content")]`*. This attribute marks the* `Content` *property as a* `ContentProperty`*. This way the direct child of the XAML element is applied to the* `Content` *property.*

Using Collections with XAML

In the `ListBox` that contains `Person` elements, you've already seen a collection within XAML. In the `ListBox`, the items have been directly defined as child elements. In addition, the `LinearGradientBrush` contained a collection of `GradientStop` elements. This is possible because the base class `ItemsControl` has the attribute `ContentProperty` set to the `Items` property of the class, and the `GradientBrush` base class sets the attribute `ContentProperty` to `GradientStops`.

The following example shows a longer version that defines the background by directly setting the `GradientStops` property and defining the `GradientStopCollection` element as its child:

```
<Button Click="OnButtonClick">
  Click Me!
  <Button.Background>
    <LinearGradientBrush StartPoint="0.5, 0.0" EndPoint="0.5, 1.0">
      <LinearGradientBrush.GradientStops>
        <GradientStopCollection>
          <GradientStop Offset="0" Color="Yellow" />
          <GradientStop Offset="0.3" Color="Orange" />
          <GradientStop Offset="0.7" Color="Red" />
```

```
            <GradientStop Offset="1" Color="DarkRed" />
          </GradientStopCollection>
        </LinearGradientBrush.GradientStops>
      </LinearGradientBrush>
    </Button.Background>
  </Button>
```

With WPF, to define an array, you can use the x:Array extension. The x:Array extension has a Type property that enables you to specify the type of the array's items:

```
<Window.Resources>
  <x:Array Type="datalib:Person" x:Key="personArray">
    <datalib:Person FirstName="Stephanie" LastName="Nagel" />
    <datalib:Person FirstName="Matthias" LastName="Nagel" />
  </x:Array>
</Window.Resources>
```

DEPENDENCY PROPERTIES

XAML uses dependency properties for data binding, animations, property change notification, styling, and so forth. What's the reason for dependency properties? Let's assume you create a class with 100 properties of type int, and this class is instantiated 100 times on a single form. How much memory is needed? Because an int has a size of 4 bytes, the result is 4 × 100 × 100 = 40,000 bytes. Did you already have a look at the properties of an XAML element? Because of the huge inheritance hierarchy, an XAML element defines hundreds of properties. The property types are not simple int types, but a lot more complex types instead. I think you can imagine that such properties could consume a huge amount of memory. However, usually you change only the values of a few of these properties, and most of the properties keep their default values that are common for all instances. This dilemma is solved with dependency properties. With dependency properties, an object memory is not allocated for every property and every instance. Instead, the dependency property system manages a dictionary of all properties and allocates memory only if a value is changed. Otherwise, the default value is shared between all instances.

Dependency properties also have built-in support for change notification. With normal properties, you need to implement the interface INotifyPropertyChanged for change notification. How this can be done is explained in Chapter 31, "Patterns with XAML Apps." Such a change mechanism is built-in with dependency properties. For data binding, the property of the UI element that is bound to the source of a .NET property must be a dependency property. Now, let's get into the details of dependency properties.

From the outside, a dependency property looks like a normal .NET property. However, with a normal .NET property you usually also define the data member that is accessed by the get and set accessors of the property:

```
private int _value;
public int Value
{
  get
  {
    return _value;
  }
  set
  {
    _value = value;
  }
}
```

That's not the case with dependency properties. A dependency property usually has a get and set accessor of a property as well. This is common with normal properties. However, with the implementation of the get and set accessors, the methods GetValue and SetValue are invoked. GetValue and SetValue are members of the base class `DependencyObject`, which also stipulates a requirement for dependency objects—that they must be implemented in a class that derives from `DependencyObject`. With WPF, the base class is defined in the namespace `System.Windows`, with UWP in the namespace `Windows.UI.Xaml`.

With a dependency property, the data member is kept inside an internal collection that is managed by the base class and only allocates data if the value changes. With unchanged values the data can be shared between different instances or base classes. The `GetValue` and `SetValue` methods require a `DependencyProperty` argument. This argument is defined by a static member of the class that has the same name as the property appended to the term `Property`. With the property `Value`, the static member has the name `ValueProperty`. `DependencyProperty.Register` is a helper method that registers the property in the dependency property system. The following code snippet uses the `Register` method with four arguments to define the name of the property, the type of the property, the type of the owner—that is, the class `MyDependencyObject`—and the default value with the help of `PropertyMetadata` (code file `DependencyObject[WPF|UWP]/MyDependencyObject.cs`):

```
public class MyDependencyObject: DependencyObject
{
  public int Value
  {
    get { return (int)GetValue(ValueProperty); }
    set { SetValue(ValueProperty, value); }
  }

  public static readonly DependencyProperty ValueProperty =
      DependencyProperty.Register("Value", typeof(int),
          typeof(MyDependencyObject), new PropertyMetadata(0));
}
```

Creating a Dependency Property

This section looks at an example that defines not one but three dependency properties. The class `MyDependencyObject` defines the dependency properties `Value`, `Minimum`, and `Maximum`. All of these properties are dependency properties that are registered with the method `DependencyProperty.Register`. The methods `GetValue` and `SetValue` are members of the base class `DependencyObject`. For the `Minimum` and `Maximum` properties, default values are defined that can be set with the `DependencyProperty.Register` method and a fourth argument to set the `PropertyMetadata`. Using a constructor with one parameter, `PropertyMetadata`, the `Minimum` property is set to 0, and the `Maximum` property is set to 100 (code file `DependencyObject[WPF|UWP]/MyDependencyObject.cs`):

```
public class MyDependencyObject: DependencyObject
{
  public int Value
  {
    get { return (int)GetValue(ValueProperty); }
    set { SetValue(ValueProperty, value); }
  }

  public static readonly DependencyProperty ValueProperty =
      DependencyProperty.Register(nameof(Value), typeof(int),
          typeof(MyDependencyObject));

  public int Minimum
  {
    get { return (int)GetValue(MinimumProperty); }
    set { SetValue(MinimumProperty, value); }
  }
  public static readonly DependencyProperty MinimumProperty =
      DependencyProperty.Register(nameof(Minimum), typeof(int),
          typeof(MyDependencyObject), new PropertyMetadata(0));
```

```
public int Maximum
{
  get { return (int)GetValue(MaximumProperty); }
  set { SetValue(MaximumProperty, value); }
}
public static readonly DependencyProperty MaximumProperty =
    DependencyProperty.Register(nameof(Maximum), typeof(int),
      typeof(MyDependencyObject), new PropertyMetadata(100));
}
```

> **NOTE** *Within the implementation of the* get *and* set *property accessors, you should not do anything other than invoke the* GetValue *and* SetValue *methods. Using the dependency properties, the property values can be accessed from the outside with the* GetValue *and* SetValue *methods, which is also done from WPF; therefore, the strongly typed property accessors might not be invoked at all. They are just here for convenience, so you can use the normal property syntax from your custom code.*

Value Changed Callbacks and Events

To get some information on value changes, dependency properties also support value changed call-backs. You can add a DependencyPropertyChanged event handler to the DependencyProperty. Register method that is invoked when the property value changes. In the sample code, the handler method OnValueChanged is assigned to the PropertyChangedCallback of the PropertyMetadata object. In the OnValueChanged method, you can access the old and new values of the property with the DependencyPropertyChangedEventArgs argument (code file DependencyObject [WPF|UWP] / MyDependencyObject.cs):

```
public class MyDependencyObject: DependencyObject
{
  public int Value
  {
    get { return (int)GetValue(ValueProperty); }
    set { SetValue(ValueProperty, value); }
  }

  public static readonly DependencyProperty ValueProperty =
      DependencyProperty.Register(nameof(Value), typeof(int),
        typeof(MyDependencyObject),
        new PropertyMetadata(0, OnValueChanged, CoerceValue));

  // etc.

  private static void OnValueChanged(DependencyObject obj,
                                     DependencyPropertyChangedEventArgs e)
  {
    int oldValue = (int)e.OldValue;
    int newValue = (int)e.NewValue;
    // etc.
  }
}
```

Coerce Value Callback with WPF

With WPF, dependency properties also support coercion. Using coercion, you can check the value of a prop-erty to see whether it is valid—for example, that it falls within a valid range. That's why the Minimum and Maximum properties are included in the sample. Now the registration of the Value property is changed to pass the event handler method `CoerceValue` to the constructor of `PropertyMetadata`, which is passed as an argument to the `DependencyProperty.Register` method. The `CoerceValue` method is invoked with every change of the property value from the implementation of the `SetValue` method. Within `CoerceValue`, the set value is checked to determine whether it falls within the specified minimum and maximum range; if not, the value is set accordingly (code file `DependencyObjectWPF/MyDependencyObject.cs`).

```csharp
using System;
using System.Windows;

namespace DependencyObjectWPF
{
  public class MyDependencyObject: DependencyObject
  {
    public int Value
    {
      get { return (int)GetValue(ValueProperty); }
      set { SetValue(ValueProperty, value); }
    }
    public static readonly DependencyProperty ValueProperty =
        DependencyProperty.Register(nameof(Value), typeof(int),
          typeof(MyDependencyObject),
          new PropertyMetadata(0, OnValueChanged, CoerceValue));

    private static object CoerceValue(DependencyObject d, object baseValue)
    {
      int newValue = (int)baseValue;
      MyDependencyObject control = (MyDependencyObject)d;

      newValue = Math.Max(control.Minimum, Math.Min(control.Maximum, newValue));
      return newValue;
    }

    // etc.

    public int Minimum
    {
      get { return (int)GetValue(MinimumProperty); }
      set { SetValue(MinimumProperty, value); }
    }
    public static readonly DependencyProperty MinimumProperty =
        DependencyProperty.Register(nameof(Minimum), typeof(int),
          typeof(MyDependencyObject), new PropertyMetadata(0));

    public int Maximum
    {
      get { return (int)GetValue(MaximumProperty); }
      set { SetValue(MaximumProperty, value); }
    }
    public static readonly DependencyProperty MaximumProperty =
        DependencyProperty.Register(nameof(Maximum), typeof(int),
          typeof(MyDependencyObject), new PropertyMetadata(100));

  }
}
```

ROUTED EVENTS

Chapter 9 covers the .NET event model. With XAML-based applications, the event model is extended by routing events. Elements contain elements to form a hierarchy. With routed events, an event is routed through the hierarchy of elements. If a routed event is fired from a control—for example, a `Button`—the event can be handled with the button itself, but then it routes up to all its parent controls where it can be handled as well. This is also called *bubbling*—events bubble up through the control hierarchy. It's possible to stop the routing to the parent by setting the `Handled` property of the event to `true`.

Routed Events with Windows apps

This section provides an example with a UWP Windows app. This app defines a UI consisting of a `CheckBox` that, if selected, stops the routing; a `Button` control with the `Tapped` event set to the `OnTappedButton` handler method; and a `Grid` with the `Tapped` event set to the `OnTappedGrid` handler. The `Tapped` event is one of the routed events of Universal Windows apps. This event can be fired with the mouse, touch, and pen devices (code file `RoutedEventsUWP/MainPage.xaml`):

```xml
<Grid Tapped="OnTappedGrid">
  <Grid.RowDefinitions>
    <RowDefinition Height="auto" />
    <RowDefinition Height="auto" />
    <RowDefinition />
  </Grid.RowDefinitions>
  <StackPanel Grid.Row="0" Orientation="Horizontal">
    <CheckBox x:Name="CheckStopRouting" Margin="20">Stop Routing</CheckBox>
    <Button Click="OnCleanStatus">Clean Status</Button>
  </StackPanel>
  <Button Grid.Row="1" Margin="20" Tapped="OnTappedButton">Tap me!</Button>
  <TextBlock Grid.Row="2" Margin="20" x:Name="textStatus" />
</Grid>
```

The `OnTappedXX` handler methods write status information to a `TextBlock` to show the handler method as well as the control that was the original source of the event (code file `RoutedEventsUWP/MainPage.xaml.cs`):

```csharp
private void OnTappedButton(object sender, TappedRoutedEventArgs e)
{
    ShowStatus(nameof(OnTappedButton), e);
    e.Handled = CheckStopRouting.IsChecked == true;
}

private void OnTappedGrid(object sender, TappedRoutedEventArgs e)
{
    ShowStatus(nameof(OnTappedGrid), e);
    e.Handled = CheckStopRouting.IsChecked == true;
}

private void ShowStatus(string status, RoutedEventArgs e)
{
    textStatus.Text += $"{status} {e.OriginalSource.GetType().Name}";
    textStatus.Text += "\r\n";
}

private void OnCleanStatus(object sender, RoutedEventArgs e)
{
    textStatus.Text = string.Empty;
}
```

When you run the application and click outside the button but within the grid, you see the `OnTappedGrid` event handled with the `Grid` control as the originating source:

```
OnTappedGrid Grid
```

Click in the middle of the button to see that the event is routed. The first handler that is invoked is `OnTappedButton` followed by `OnTappedGrid`:

```
OnTappedButton TextBlock
OnTappedGrid TextBlock
```

What's also interesting is that the event source is not the `Button`, but a `TextBlock`. The reason is that the button is styled using a `TextBlock` to contain the button text. If you click to other positions within the button, you can also see `Grid` or `ContentPresenter` as the originating event source. The `Grid` and `ContentPresenter` are other controls the button is created from.

Checking the check box `CheckStopRouting` before clicking on the button, you can see that the event is no longer routed because the `Handled` property of the event arguments is set to `true`:

```
OnTappedButton TextBlock
```

Within the MSDN documentation of the events, you can see whether an event type is routing within the remarks section of the documentation. With Universal Windows apps, tapped, drag and drop, key up and key down, pointer, focus, and manipulation events are routed events.

Bubbling and Tunneling with WPF

With WPF, a lot more events support routing than are supported with Windows Universal apps. Besides the concept of bubbling up through the control hierarchy, WPF also supports tunneling. Tunneling events go in the direction opposite of bubbling—from outside to inside controls. An event is either a bubbling event, a tunneling event, or a direct event.

Often events are defined in pairs. `PreviewMouseMove` is a tunneling event that tunnels from the outside to the inside. First the outer controls receive the event followed by the inner controls. The `MouseMove` event follows the `PreviewMouseMove` event and is a bubbling event that bubbles from the inside to the outside.

To demonstrate tunneling and bubbling, the following XAML code contains a grid and a button that have both the `MouseMove` and the `PreviewMouseMove` events assigned. As `MouseMove` events can occur in high count, the `TextBlock` that displays the mouse move information is surrounded by a `ScrollViewer` control to show scroll bars as needed. With `CheckBox` controls, you can set the tunneling and bubbling to stop (code file `RoutedEventsWPF/MainWindow.xaml`):

```xml
<Grid MouseMove="OnGridMouseMove" PreviewMouseMove="OnGridPreviewMouseMove">
  <Grid.RowDefinitions>
    <RowDefinition Height="auto" />
    <RowDefinition Height="auto" />
    <RowDefinition />
  </Grid.RowDefinitions>
  <StackPanel Grid.Row="0" Orientation="Horizontal">
    <CheckBox x:Name="CheckStopPreview" Margin="20">
      Stop Preview
    </CheckBox>
    <CheckBox x:Name="CheckStopBubbling" Margin="20">
      Stop Bubbling
    </CheckBox>
    <CheckBox x:Name="CheckIgnoreGridMove" Margin="20">
      Ignore Grid Move
    </CheckBox>
    <Button Margin="20" Click="OnCleanStatus">Clean Status</Button>
  </StackPanel>
  <Button x:Name="button1" Grid.Row="1" Margin="20"
      MouseMove="OnButtonMouseMove"
      PreviewMouseMove="OnButtonPreviewMouseMove">
    Move
  </Button>
  <ScrollViewer Grid.Row="2">
    <TextBlock Margin="20" x:Name="textStatus" />
  </ScrollViewer>
</Grid>
```

Within the code-behind file, the `ShowStatus` method accesses `RoutedEventArgs` to display event information. Unlike what happens with Universal Windows apps, the `RoutedEventArgs` type contains not only the original source of the event, but also the source, which is accessible with the Source property. This method shows both the type and the name of the source (code file RoutedEventsWPF/MainWindow .xaml.cs):

```
private void ShowStatus(string status, RoutedEventArgs e)
{
  textStatus.Text += $"{status} source: {e.Source.GetType().Name}, " +
    $"{(e.Source as FrameworkElement)?.Name}, " +
    $"original source: {e.OriginalSource.GetType().Name}";
  textStatus.Text += "\r\n";
}
```

Because there are still too many MouseMove events, the handlers are implemented to ignore them with the exception of the ones with the button1 source in case the CheckIgnoreGridMove Checkbox is checked.

```
private bool IsButton1Source(RoutedEventArgs e) =>
  (e.Source as FrameworkElement).Name == nameof(button1);

private void OnButtonMouseMove(object sender, MouseEventArgs e)
{
  ShowStatus(nameof(OnButtonMouseMove), e);
  e.Handled = CheckStopBubbling.IsChecked == true;
}

private void OnGridMouseMove(object sender, MouseEventArgs e)
{
  if (CheckIgnoreGridMove.IsChecked == true && !IsButton1Source(e) return;

  ShowStatus(nameof(OnGridMouseMove), e);
  e.Handled = CheckStopBubbling.IsChecked == true;
}

private void OnGridPreviewMouseMove(object sender, MouseEventArgs e)
{
  if (CheckIgnoreGridMove.IsChecked == true && !IsButton1Source(e) return:

  ShowStatus(nameof(OnGridPreviewMouseMove), e);
  e.Handled = CheckStopPreview.IsChecked == true;
}

private void OnButtonPreviewMouseMove(object sender, MouseEventArgs e)
{
  ShowStatus(nameof(OnButtonPreviewMouseMove), e);
  e.Handled = CheckStopPreview.IsChecked == true;
}

private void OnCleanStatus(object sender, RoutedEventArgs e)
{
  textStatus.Text = string.Empty;
}
```

When you run the application and move over the Button control you see these event handler actions:

```
OnGridPreviewMouseMove source: Button button1, original source: Border
OnButtonPreviewMouseMove source: Button button1, original source: Border
OnButtonMouseMove source: Button button1, original source: Border
OnGridMouseMove source: Button button1, original source: Border
```

In case you make the check to stop bubbling, the Button handler OnButtonMouseMove is the last one invoked. This is similar to what you've seen with bubbling and Universal Windows apps:

```
OnGridPreviewMouseMove source: Button button1, original source: Border
OnButtonPreviewMouseMove source: Button button1, original source: Border
OnButtonMouseMove source: Button button1, original source: Border
```

When you stop the routing actions with the tunneling event handler, bubbling does not occur. This is an important characteristic of tunneling. In case you already set the `Handled` property to `true` within a tunneling event handler, the bubbling event never occurs:

```
OnGridPreviewMouseMove source: Button button1, original source: Border
```

Implementing Custom Routed Events with WPF

To define bubbling and tunneling events in custom classes, the `MyDependencyObject` is changed to support an event on a value change. For bubbling and tunneling event support, the class must derive from `UIElement` instead of `DependencyObject` because this class defines `AddHandler` and `RemoveHandler` methods for events.

To enable the caller of the `MyDependencyObject` to receive information about value changes, the class defines the `ValueChanged` event. The event is declared with explicit `add` and `remove` handlers, where the `AddHandler` and `RemoveHandler` methods of the base class are invoked. These methods require a `RoutedEvent` type and the delegate as parameters. The routed event named `ValueChangedEvent` is declared very similarly to a dependency property. It is declared as a static member and registered by calling the method `EventManager.RegisterRoutedEvent`. This method requires the name of the event, the routing strategy (which can be `Bubble`, `Tunnel`, or `Direct`), the type of the handler, and the type of the owner class. The `EventManager` class also enables you to register static events and get information about the events registered (code file `DependencyObjectWPF/MyDependencyObject.cs`):

```csharp
using System;
using System.Windows;

namespace Wrox.ProCSharp.XAML
{
  class MyDependencyObject: UIElement
  {
    public int Value
    {
      get { return (int)GetValue(ValueProperty); }
      set { SetValue(ValueProperty, value); }
    }

    public static readonly DependencyProperty ValueProperty =
        DependencyProperty.Register(nameof(Value), typeof(int),
          typeof(MyDependencyObject),
          new PropertyMetadata(0, OnValueChanged, CoerceValue));

    // etc.
    private static void OnValueChanged(DependencyObject d,
                                       DependencyPropertyChangedEventArgs e)
    {
      MyDependencyObject control = (MyDependencyObject)d;
      var e1 = new RoutedPropertyChangedEventArgs<int>((int)e.OldValue,
          (int)e.NewValue, ValueChangedEvent);
      control.OnValueChanged(e1);
    }

    public static readonly RoutedEvent ValueChangedEvent =
        EventManager.RegisterRoutedEvent(nameof(ValueChanged), RoutingStrategy.Bubble,
          typeof(RoutedPropertyChangedEventHandler<int>), typeof(MyDependencyObject));

    public event RoutedPropertyChangedEventHandler<int> ValueChanged
    {
      add
      {
        AddHandler(ValueChangedEvent, value);
```

```
        }
        remove
        {
            RemoveHandler(ValueChangedEvent, value);
        }
    }

    protected virtual void OnValueChanged(RoutedPropertyChangedEventArgs<int> args)
    {
        RaiseEvent(args);
    }
    }
}
```

Now you can use this with bubbling functionality in the same way that you've seen it used before with the button MouseMove event.

ATTACHED PROPERTIES

Whereas dependency properties are properties available with a specific type, with an attached property you can define properties for other types. Some container controls define attached properties for their children; for example, if the DockPanel control is used, a Dock property is available for its children. The Grid control defines Row and Column properties.

The following code snippet demonstrates how this looks in XAML. The Button class doesn't have the property Dock, but it's attached from the DockPanel:

```
<DockPanel>
    <Button Content="Top" DockPanel.Dock="Top" Background="Yellow" />
    <Button Content="Left" DockPanel.Dock="Left" Background="Blue" />
</DockPanel>
```

Attached properties are defined very similarly to dependency properties, as shown in the next example. The class that defines the attached properties must derive from the base class DependencyObject and defines a normal property, where the get and set accessors invoke the methods GetValue and SetValue of the base class. This is where the similarities end. Instead of invoking the method Register with the DependencyProperty class, now RegisterAttached is invoked, which registers an attached property that is now available with every element (code file AttachedPropertyDemo[WPF|UWP]/MyAttachedProperyProvider.cs):

```
public class MyAttachedPropertyProvider: DependencyObject
{
    public string MySample
    {
        get { return (string)GetValue(MySampleProperty); }
        set { SetValue(MySampleProperty, value); }
    }

    public static readonly DependencyProperty MySampleProperty =
        DependencyProperty.RegisterAttached(nameof(MySample), typeof(string),
            typeof(MyAttachedPropertyProvider), new PropertyMetadata(string.Empty));

    public static void SetMySample(UIElement element, string value) =>
        element.SetValue(MySampleProperty, value);

    public static int GetMyProperty(UIElement element) =>
        (string)element.GetValue(MySampleProperty);
}
```

> **NOTE** *You might assume that* DockPanel.Dock *can only be added to elements within a* DockPanel. *In reality, attached properties can be added to any element. However, no one would use this property value. The* DockPanel *is aware of this property and reads it from its children elements to arrange them.*

In the XAML code, the attached property can now be attached to any elements. The second Button control, named button2, has the property MyAttachedPropertyProvider.MySample attached to it and the value 42 assigned (code file AttachedPropertyDemo[WPF|UWP]/Main[Window|Page].xaml):

```
<Grid x:Name="grid1">
    <Grid.RowDefinitions>
      <RowDefinition Height="Auto" />
      <RowDefinition Height="Auto" />
      <RowDefinition Height="*" />
    </Grid.RowDefinitions>
    <Button Grid.Row="0" x:Name="button1" Content="Button 1" />
    <Button Grid.Row="1" x:Name="button2" Content="Button 2"
            local:MyAttachedPropertyProvider.MySample="42" />
    <ListBox Grid.Row="2" x:Name="list1" />
  </Grid>
</Window>
```

Doing the same in code-behind it is necessary to invoke the static method SetMyProperty of the class MyAttachedPropertyProvider. It's not possible to extend the class Button with a property. The method SetProperty gets a UIElement instance that should be extended by the property and the value. In the following code snippet, the property is attached to button1 and the value is set to sample value (code file AttachedPropertyDemoWPF/MainPage.xaml.cs):

```
public MainPage()
{
  InitializeComponent();

  MyAttachedPropertyProvider.SetMySample(button1, "sample value");
  // etc.
}
```

To read attached properties that are assigned to elements, the VisualTreeHelper can be used to iterate every element in the hierarchy and try to read its attached properties. The VisualTreeHelper is used to read the visual tree of the elements during runtime. The method GetChildrenCount returns the count of the child elements. To access a child, the method GetChild passing an index returns the element. The method implementation returns elements only if they are of type FrameworkElement (or derived thereof), and if the predicate passed with the Func argument returns true.

```
private IEnumerable<FrameworkElement> GetChildren(FrameworkElement element,
    Func<FrameworkElement, bool> pred)
{
  int childrenCount = VisualTreeHelper.GetChildrenCount(rootElement);
  for (int i = 0; i < childrenCount; i++)
  {
    var child = VisualTreeHelper.GetChild(rootElement, i) as FrameworkElement;
    if (child != null && pred(child))
    {
      yield return child;
    }
  }
}
```

The method `GetChildren` is now used from within the constructor of the page to add all elements with an attached property to the `ListBox` control:

```
public MainPage()
{
  InitializeComponent();

  MyAttachedPropertyProvider.SetMySample(button1, "sample value");
  foreach (var item in GetChildren(grid1, e =>
      MyAttachedPropertyProvider.GetMySample(e) != string.Empty))
  {
    list1.Items.Add(
      $"{item.Name}: {MyAttachedPropertyProvider.GetMySample(item)}");
  }
}
```

When you run the application (either the WPF or the UWP app) you see the two button controls in the `ListBox` with these values:

```
button1: sample value
button2: 42
```

Until now, the sample code for attached properties is the same for WPF and Universal Windows apps with the exception that with WPF a `MainWindow` control is used instead of the `MainPage`. However, WPF has another option to iterate through the elements. Both WPF and Universal Windows apps can use the `VisualTreeHelper` to iterate the visual tree that contains all the elements created during runtime, including templates and styles. With WPF you can also use the `LogicalTreeHelper`. This helper class iterates the logical tree of elements. The logical tree is the same tree used during design time. This tree can also be shown within Visual Studio in the Document Outline (see Figure 29-1).

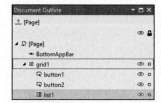

FIGURE 29-1

Using the `LogicalTreeHelper`, the method to iterate the children elements can be changed as follows. The `LogicalTreeHelper` class offers a `GetChildren` method instead of needing to ask for the number of children and to iterate them using a `for` loop (code file `AttachedPropertyDemoWPF/MainWindow.xaml.cs`):

```
public MainWindow()
{
  InitializeComponent();

  MyAttachedPropertyProvider.SetMySample(button1, "sample value");

  foreach (var item in LogicalTreeHelper.GetChildren(grid1).
      OfType<FrameworkElement>().Where(
        e => MyAttachedPropertyProvider.GetMySample(e) != string.Empty))
  {
    list1.Items.Add(
      $"{item.Name}: {MyAttachedPropertyProvider.GetMySample(item)}");
  }
}
```

MARKUP EXTENSIONS

With markup extensions you can extend XAML with either element or attribute syntax. If an XML attribute contains curly brackets, that's a sign of a markup extension. Often markup extensions with attributes are used as shorthand notation instead of using elements.

One example of such a markup extension is `StaticResourceExtension`, which finds resources. Here's a resource of a linear gradient brush with the key `gradientBrush1` (code file `MarkupExtensionsUWP/MainPage.xaml`):

```
<Page.Resources>
  <LinearGradientBrush x:Key="gradientBrush1" StartPoint="0.5,0.0" EndPoint="0.5, 1.0">
    <GradientStop Offset="0" Color="Yellow" />
    <GradientStop Offset="0.3" Color="Orange" />
    <GradientStop Offset="0.7" Color="Red" />
    <GradientStop Offset="1" Color="DarkRed" />
  </LinearGradientBrush>
</Page.Resources>
```

This resource can be referenced by using the `StaticResourceExtension` with attribute syntax to set the `Background` property of a `Button`. Attribute syntax is defined by curly brackets and the name of the extension class without the `Extension` suffix:

```
<Button Content="Test" Background="{StaticResource gradientBrush1}" />
```

WPF also allows the longer form of the attribute shorthand notation with element syntax, as the next code snippet demonstrates. `StaticResourceExtension` is defined as a child element of the `Button.Background` element. The property `ResourceKey` is set with an attribute to `gradientBrush1`. In the previous example, the resource key is not set with the property `ResourceKey` (which would be possible as well) but with a constructor overload where the resource key can be set:

```
<Button Content="Test">
  <Button.Background>
    <StaticResourceExtension ResourceKey="gradientBrush1" />
  </Button.Background>
</Button>
```

Creating Custom Markup Extensions

UWP apps can use only predefined markup extensions. With WPF, you can create custom markup extensions. A markup extension is created by defining a class that derives from the base class `MarkupExtension`. Most markup extensions have the `Extension` suffix (this naming convention is similar to the `Attribute` suffix with attributes, which you can read about in Chapter 16, "Reflection, Metadata, and Dynamic Programming"). With a custom markup extension, you only need to override the method `ProvideValue`, which returns the value from the extension. The type that is returned is annotated to the class with the attribute `MarkupExtensionReturnType`. With the method `ProvideValue`, an `IServiceProvider` object is passed. With this interface you can query for different services, such as `IProvideValueTarget` or `IXamlTypeResolver`. You can use `IProvideValueTarget` to access the control and property to which the markup extension is applied with the `TargetObject` and `TargetProperty` properties. You can use `IXamlTypeResolver` to resolve XAML element names to CLR objects. The custom markup extension class `CalculatorExtension` defines the properties `X` and `Y` of type `double` and an `Operation` property that is defined by an enumeration. Depending on the value of the `Operation` property, different calculations are done on the `X` and `Y` input properties, and a string is returned (code file `MarkupExtensionsWPF/CalculatorExtension.cs`):

```csharp
using System;
using System.Windows;
using System.Windows.Markup;
namespace Wrox.ProCSharp.XAML
{
  public enum Operation
  {
    Add,
    Subtract,
    Multiply,
    Divide
  }

  [MarkupExtensionReturnType(typeof(string))]
  public class CalculatorExtension: MarkupExtension
  {
    public CalculatorExtension()
    {
    }
    public double X { get; set; }
    public double Y { get; set; }
    public Operation Operation { get; set; }

    public override object ProvideValue(IServiceProvider serviceProvider)
    {
      IProvideValueTarget provideValue =
          serviceProvider.GetService(typeof(IProvideValueTarget))
          as IProvideValueTarget;
      if (provideValue != null)
      {
        var host = provideValue.TargetObject as FrameworkElement;
        var prop = provideValue.TargetProperty as DependencyProperty;
      }
      double result = 0;
      switch (Operation)
      {
        case Operation.Add:
          result = X + Y;
          break;
        case Operation.Subtract:
          result = X-Y;
          break;
        case Operation.Multiply:
          result = X * Y;
          break;
        case Operation.Divide:
          result = X / Y;
          break;
        default:
          throw new ArgumentException("invalid operation");
      }
      return result.ToString();
    }
  }
}
```

You can now use the markup extension with an attribute syntax in the first `TextBlock` to add the values 3 and 4, or with the element syntax with the second `TextBlock` (code file `MarkupExtensionsWPF/MainWindow.xaml`).

```xaml
<Window x:Class="Wrox.ProCSharp.XAML.MainWindow"
        xmlns="http://schemas.microsoft.com/winfx/2006/xaml/presentation"
        xmlns:x="http://schemas.microsoft.com/winfx/2006/xaml"
        xmlns:local="clr-namespace:Wrox.ProCSharp.XAML"
        Title="MainWindow" Height="350" Width="525">
  <StackPanel>
    <TextBlock Text="{local:Calculator Operation=Add, X=3, Y=4}" />
    <TextBlock>
      <TextBlock.Text>
        <local:CalculatorExtension>
          <local:CalculatorExtension.Operation>
            <local:Operation>Multiply</local:Operation>
          </local:CalculatorExtension.Operation>
          <local:CalculatorExtension.X>7</local:CalculatorExtension.X>
          <local:CalculatorExtension.Y>11</local:CalculatorExtension.Y>
        </local:CalculatorExtension>
      </TextBlock.Text>
    </TextBlock>
  </StackPanel>
</Window>
```

Using XAML-Defined Markup Extensions

Markup extensions provide a lot of capabilities, and indeed XAML-defined markup extensions have already been used in this chapter. `x:Array`, which was shown in the "Using Collections with XAML" section, is defined as the markup extension class `ArrayExtension`. With this markup extension, using the attribute syntax is not possible because it would be difficult to define a list of elements.

Other markup extensions that are defined with XAML are the `TypeExtension` (`x:Type`), which returns the type based on string input; `NullExtension` (`x:Null`), which can be used to set values to null in XAML; and `StaticExtension` (`x:Static`), which is used to invoke static members of a class.

An XAML-defined markup extension that is currently only offered for Universal Windows apps is compiled binding (`x:Bind`) for data binding with better performance. This data binding is covered in Chapter 32, "Windows Apps: User Interfaces."

WPF, WF, WCF, and Universal Windows apps define markup extensions that are specific to these technologies. WPF and Universal Windows apps use markup extensions for accessing resources, for data binding, and for color conversion; WF apps use markup extensions with activities; and WCF apps define markup extensions for endpoint definitions.

SUMMARY

In this chapter, you've seen the core functionality of XAML with samples for both WPF and Universal Windows apps. You've also seen some specific characteristics, such as dependency properties, attached properties, routed events, and markup extensions. With these features, you've not only seen the foundation of XAML-based technologies, but you were also introduced to how C# and .NET features, such as properties and events, can be adapted to extended-use cases. Properties have been enhanced to support change notification and validation (dependency properties). Attached properties enable you to use properties with controls where the controls themselves don't offer these properties. Events have been enhanced with bubbling and tunneling functionality.

All these features facilitate the foundation for different XAML technologies, such as WPF, WF, and UWP apps.

The next chapter continues the discussion of XAML and is about styles and resources.

30

Styling XAML Apps

WHAT'S IN THIS CHAPTER?

- ➤ Styling for WPF and UWP Apps
- ➤ Creating the base drawing with shapes and geometry
- ➤ Scaling, rotating, and skewing with transformations
- ➤ Using brushes to fill backgrounds
- ➤ Working with styles, templates, and resources
- ➤ Creating animations
- ➤ Visual State Manager

WROX.COM CODE DOWNLOADS FOR THIS CHAPTER

The wrox.com code downloads for this chapter are found at www.wrox.com/go/professionalcsharp6 on the Download Code tab. The code for this chapter is divided into the following major examples:

- ➤ Shapes
- ➤ Geometry
- ➤ Transformation
- ➤ Brushes
- ➤ Styles and Resources
- ➤ Templates
- ➤ Animation
- ➤ Transitions
- ➤ Visual State

STYLING

In recent years, developers have become a lot more concerned with having good-looking apps. When Windows Forms was the technology for creating desktop applications, the user interface didn't offer many options for styling the applications. Controls had a standard look that varied slightly based on the operating system version on which the application was running, but it was not easy to define a complete custom look.

This changed with Windows Presentation Foundation (WPF). WPF is based on DirectX and thus offers vector graphics that allow easy resizing of Windows and controls. Controls are completely customizable and can have different looks. Styling of applications has become extremely important. An application can have any look. With a good design, the user can work with the application without the need to know how to use a Windows application. Instead, the user just needs to have his domain knowledge. For example, the airport in Zurich created a WPF application where buttons look like airplanes. With the button, the user can get information of the position of the plane (the complete application looks like the airport). Colors of the buttons can have different meanings based on the configuration: they can show the either the airline, or on-time/delay information of the plane. This way, the user of the app easily sees what planes that are currently at the airport have small or big delays.

Having different looks of the app is even more important with Universal Windows Platform (UWP) apps. With these apps, the device can be used by users who haven't used Windows applications before. With users who are knowledgeable of Windows applications, you should think about helping these users be more productive by having the typical process for how the user works easily accessible.

Microsoft has not provided a lot of guidance for styling WPF applications. How an application looks mainly depends on your (or the designer's) imagination. With UWP apps, Microsoft has provided a lot more guidance and predefined styles, but you're still able to change anything you like.

This chapter starts with the core elements of XAML—*shapes* that enable you to draw lines, ellipses, and path elements. After that you're introduced to the foundation of shapes—*geometry* elements. You can use geometry elements to create fast vector-based drawings.

With *transformations*, you can scale and rotate any XAML element. With *brushes* you can create solid color, gradient, or more advanced backgrounds. You see how to use brushes within *styles* and place styles within XAML *resources*.

Finally, with *templates* you can completely customize the look of controls, and you also learn how to create animations in this chapter.

The sample code is available both with UWP apps and with WPF. Of course, where features are only available in one of these technologies, the sample code is only available there.

SHAPES

Shapes are the core elements of XAML. With shapes you can draw two-dimensional graphics using rectangles, lines, ellipses, paths, polygons, and polylines that are represented by classes derived from the abstract base class `Shape`. Shapes are defined in the namespaces `System.Windows.Shapes` (WPF) and `Windows.UI.Xaml.Shapes` (UWP).

The following XAML example draws a yellow face consisting of an ellipse for the face, two ellipses for the eyes, two ellipses for the pupils in the eyes, and a path for the mouth (code file `Shapes[WPF|UWP]/Main[Window|Page].xaml`):

```
<Canvas>
  <Ellipse Canvas.Left="10" Canvas.Top="10" Width="100" Height="100"
           Stroke="Blue" StrokeThickness="4" Fill="Yellow" />
  <Ellipse Canvas.Left="30" Canvas.Top="12" Width="60" Height="30">
    <Ellipse.Fill>
      <LinearGradientBrush StartPoint="0.5,0" EndPoint="0.5, 1">
        <GradientStop Offset="0.1" Color="DarkGreen" />
        <GradientStop Offset="0.7" Color="Transparent" />
      </LinearGradientBrush>
    </Ellipse.Fill>
  </Ellipse>
```

```
    <Ellipse Canvas.Left="30" Canvas.Top="35" Width="25" Height="20"
            Stroke="Blue" StrokeThickness="3" Fill="White" />
    <Ellipse Canvas.Left="40" Canvas.Top="43" Width="6" Height="5"
            Fill="Black" />
    <Ellipse Canvas.Left="65" Canvas.Top="35" Width="25" Height="20"
            Stroke="Blue" StrokeThickness="3" Fill="White" />
    <Ellipse Canvas.Left="75" Canvas.Top="43" Width="6" Height="5"
            Fill="Black" />
    <Path Stroke="Blue" StrokeThickness="4" Data="M 40,74 Q 57,95 80,74 " />
</Canvas>
```

Figure 30-1 shows the result of the XAML code.

FIGURE 30-1

All these XAML elements can be accessed programmatically—even if they are buttons or shapes, such as lines or rectangles. Setting the Name or x:Name property with the Path element to mouth enables you to access this element programmatically with the variable name mouth:

```
<Path Name="mouth" Stroke="Blue" StrokeThickness="4"
      Data="M 40,74 Q 57,95 80,74 " />
```

With the next code changes, the mouth of the face is changed dynamically from code-behind. A button with a click handler is added where the SetMouth method is invoked (code file Shapes[WPF|UWP] / Main[Window|Page].xaml.cs):

```
private void OnChangeShape(object sender, RoutedEventArgs e)
{
    SetMouth();
}
```

When you're using WPF, you can use the Path Markup Language (PML) from code-behind similar to what you've seen in the code snippets in this section with the Path element in XAML markup. Geometry. Parse interprets PML to create a new Geometry object. With PML, the letter M defines the starting point of the path, and the letter Q specifies a control point and an endpoint for a quadratic Bézier curve (code file ShapesWPF/MainWindow.xaml.cs):

```
private bool _laugh = false;

private void SetMouth2()
{
    if (_laugh)
    {
        mouth.Data = Geometry.Parse("M 40,82 Q 57,65 80,82");
    }
    else
    {
        mouth.Data = Geometry.Parse("M 40,74 Q 57,95 80,74");
    }
```

```
    _laugh = !_laugh;
}
```

Running the application results in the image shown in Figure 30-2.

With UWP apps, the `Geometry` class doesn't offer a `Parse` method, and you must create the geometry using figures and segments. First, you create a two-dimensional array of six points to define three points for the happy and three points for the sad state (code file `Shapes[WPF|UWP]/Main[Window|Page].xaml.cs`):

```
private readonly Point[,] _mouthPoints = new Point[2, 3]
{
  {
    new Point(40, 74), new Point(57, 95), new Point(80, 74),
  },
  {
    new Point(40, 82), new Point(57, 65), new Point(80, 82),
  }
};
```

Next, you assign a new `PathGeometry` object to the `Data` property of the `Path`. The `PathGeometry` contains a `PathFigure` with the start point defined (setting the `StartPoint` property is the same as the letter `M` with PML). The `PathFigure` contains a `QuadraticBezierSegment` with two `Point` objects assigned to the properties `Point1` and `Point2` (the same as the letter `Q` with two points):

```
private bool _laugh = false;
public void SetMouth()
{
  int index = _laugh ? 0: 1;

  var figure = new PathFigure() { StartPoint = _mouthPoints[index, 0] };
  figure.Segments = new PathSegmentCollection();
  var segment1 = new QuadraticBezierSegment();
  segment1.Point1 = _mouthPoints[index, 1];
  segment1.Point2 = _mouthPoints[index, 2];
  figure.Segments.Add(segment1);
  var geometry = new PathGeometry();
  geometry.Figures = new PathFigureCollection();
  geometry.Figures.Add(figure);

  mouth.Data = geometry;
  _laugh = !_laugh;
}
```

Using segments and figures is explained in more detail in the next section.

The following table describes the shapes available in the namespaces `System.Windows.Shapes` and `Windows.Ui.Xaml.Shapes`.

SHAPE CLASS	DESCRIPTION
Line	You can draw a line from the coordinates X1,Y1 to X2,Y2.
Rectangle	You draw a rectangle by specifying Width and Height for this class.
Ellipse	You can draw an ellipse.
Path	You can draw a series of lines and curves. The Data property is a Geometry type. You can do the drawing by using classes that derive from the base class Geometry, or you can use the path markup syntax to define geometry.
Polygon	You can draw a closed shape formed by connected lines. The polygon is defined by a series of Point objects assigned to the Points property.
Polyline	Similar to the Polygon class, you can draw connected lines with Polyline. The difference is that the polyline does not need to be a closed shape.

GEOMETRY

The previous sample showed that one of the shapes, Path, uses Geometry for its drawing. You can also use Geometry elements in other places, such as with a DrawingBrush.

In some ways, geometry elements are very similar to shapes. Just as there are Line, Ellipse, and Rectangle shapes, there are also geometry elements for these drawings: LineGeometry, EllipseGeometry, and RectangleGeometry. There are also big differences between shapes and geometries. A Shape is a FrameworkElement that you can use with any class that supports UIElement as its children. FrameworkElement derives from UIElement. Shapes participate with the layout system and render themselves. The Geometry class can't render itself and has fewer features and less overhead than Shape. With WPF, the Geometry class derives from the Freezable base class and can be shared from multiple threads. With UWP apps, the Geometry class directly derives from DependencyObject. Freezable is not available here.

The Path class uses Geometry for its drawing. The geometry can be set with the Data property of the Path. Simple geometry elements that can be set are EllipseGeometry for drawing an ellipse, LineGeometry for drawing a line, and RectangleGeometry for drawing a rectangle.

Geometries Using Segments

You can also create geometries by using segments. The geometry class PathGeometry uses segments for its drawing. The following code segment uses the BezierSegment and LineSegment elements to build one red and one green figure, as shown in Figure 30-3. The first BezierSegment draws a Bézier curve between the points 70,40, which is the starting point of the figure, and 150,63 with control points 90,37 and 130,46. The following LineSegment uses the ending point of the Bézier curve and draws a line to 120,110 (code file Geometry[WPF|UWP]/Main[Window|Page].xaml):

```
<Path Canvas.Left="0" Canvas.Top="0" Fill="Red" Stroke="Blue"
    StrokeThickness="2.5">
  <Path.Data>
    <GeometryGroup>
      <PathGeometry>
        <PathGeometry.Figures>
          <PathFigure StartPoint="70,40" IsClosed="True">
            <PathFigure.Segments>
              <BezierSegment Point1="90,37" Point2="130,46" Point3="150,63" />
              <LineSegment Point="120,110" />
              <BezierSegment Point1="100,95" Point2="70,90" Point3="45,91" />
            </PathFigure.Segments>
          </PathFigure>
```

```
            </PathGeometry.Figures>
          </PathGeometry>
        </GeometryGroup>
      </Path.Data>
    </Path>

    <Path Canvas.Left="0" Canvas.Top="0" Fill="Green" Stroke="Blue"
        StrokeThickness="2.5">
      <Path.Data>
        <GeometryGroup>
          <PathGeometry>
            <PathGeometry.Figures>
              <PathFigure StartPoint="160,70">
                <PathFigure.Segments>
                  <BezierSegment Point1="175,85" Point2="200,99"
                                 Point3="215,100" />
                  <LineSegment Point="195,148" />
                  <BezierSegment Point1="174,150" Point2="142,140"
                                 Point3="129,115" />
                  <LineSegment Point="160,70" />
                </PathFigure.Segments>
              </PathFigure>
            </PathGeometry.Figures>
          </PathGeometry>
        </GeometryGroup>
      </Path.Data>
    </Path>
```

FIGURE 30-3

Other than the `BezierSegment` and `LineSegment` elements, you can use `ArcSegment` to draw an elliptical arc between two points. With `PolyLineSegment` you can define a set of lines: `PolyBezierSegment` consists of multiple Bézier curves, `QuadraticBezierSegment` creates a quadratic Bézier curve, and `PolyQuadraticBezierSegment` consists of multiple quadratic Bézier curves.

Geometries Using PML

Earlier in this chapter you saw a use of PML with the `Path` shape. Using PML, behind the scenes WPF creates a speedy drawing with `StreamGeometry`. XAML for UWP apps creates figures and segments. Programmatically, you can define the figure by creating lines, Bézier curves, and arcs. With XAML, you can use PML syntax. You can use PML with the `Data` property of the `Path` class. Special characters define how the points are connected. In the following example, `M` marks the start point, `L` is a line command to the point specified, and `Z` is the Close command to close the figure. Figure 30-4 shows the result. The path markup syntax allows more commands such as horizontal lines (`H`), vertical lines (`V`), cubic Bézier curves (`C`), quadratic Bézier curves (`Q`), smooth cubic Bézier curves (`S`), smooth quadratic Bézier curves (`T`), and elliptical arcs (`A`) (code file `Geometry[WPF|UWP]/Main[Window|Page].xaml`):

```
<Path Canvas.Left="0" Canvas.Top="200" Fill="Yellow" Stroke="Blue"
      StrokeThickness="2.5"
      Data="M 120,5 L 128,80 L 220,50 L 160,130 L 190,220 L 100,150
            L 80,230 L 60,140 L0,110 L70,80 Z" StrokeLineJoin="Round">
</Path>
```

FIGURE 30-4

Combined Geometries (WPF)

WPF offers another feature with geometries. With WPF, you can combine geometries using the `CombinedGeometry` class as demonstrated in the next example.

`CombinedGeometry` has the properties `Geometry1` and `Geometry2` and allows them to combine with `GeometryCombineMode` to form a Union, Intersect, Xor, and Exclude. Union merges the two geometries. With `Intersect`, only the area that is covered with both geometries is visible. Xor contrasts with `Intersect` by showing the area that is covered by one of the geometries but not showing the area covered by both. `Exclude` shows the area of the first geometry minus the area of the second geometry.

The following example (code file `GeometryWPF/MainWindow.xaml`) combines an `EllipseGeometry` and a `RectangleGeometry` to form a union, as shown in Figure 30-5.

```
<Path Canvas.Top="0" Canvas.Left="250" Fill="Blue" Stroke="Black" >
  <Path.Data>
    <CombinedGeometry GeometryCombineMode="Union">
      <CombinedGeometry.Geometry1>
        <EllipseGeometry Center="80,60" RadiusX="80" RadiusY="40" />
      </CombinedGeometry.Geometry1>
      <CombinedGeometry.Geometry2>
        <RectangleGeometry Rect="30,60 105 50" />
      </CombinedGeometry.Geometry2>
    </CombinedGeometry>
  </Path.Data>
</Path>
```

Figure 30-5 shows this XAML code in different variants—from left to right, Union, Xor, Intersect, and Exclude.

FIGURE 30-5

TRANSFORMATION

Because XAML is vector based, you can resize every element. In the next example, the vector-based graphics are now scaled, rotated, and skewed. Hit testing (for example, with mouse moves and mouse clicks) still works but without the need for manual position calculation.

Figure 30-6 shows a rectangle in several different forms. All the rectangles are positioned within a `StackPanel` element with horizontal orientation to have the rectangles one beside the other. The first rectangle has its original size and layout. The second one is resized, the third moved, the forth rotated, the fifth skewed, the sixth transformed using a transformation group, and the seventh transformed using a matrix. The following sections get into the code samples of all these options.

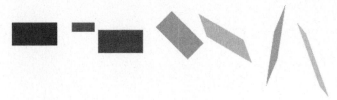

FIGURE 30-6

Scaling

Adding the `ScaleTransform` element to the `RenderTransform` property of the `Rectangle` element, as shown here, resizes the content of the complete rectangle by 0.5 in the x axis and 0.4 in the y axis (code file `Transformation[WPF|UWP]/Main[Window|Page].xaml`):

```
<Rectangle Width="120" Height="60" Fill="Red" Margin="20">
  <Rectangle.RenderTransform>
    <ScaleTransform ScaleX="0.5" ScaleY="0.4" />
  </Rectangle.RenderTransform>
</Rectangle>
```

You can do more than transform simple shapes like rectangles; you can transform any XAML element as XAML defines vector graphics. In the following code, the `Canvas` element with the face shown earlier is put into a user control named `SmilingFace`, and this user control is shown first without transformation and then resized. You can see the result in Figure 30-7.

FIGURE 30-7

```
<local:SmilingFace />
<local:SmilingFace>
  <local:SmilingFace.RenderTransform>
    <ScaleTransform ScaleX="1.6" ScaleY="0.8" CenterY="180" />
  </local:SmilingFace.RenderTransform>
</local:SmilingFace>
```

Translating

For moving an element in x or y direction, you can use `TranslateTransform`. In the following snippet, the element moves to the left by assigning -90 to X, and in the direction to the bottom by assigning 20 to Y (code file `Transformation[WPF|UWP]/Main[Window|Page].xaml`):

```
<Rectangle Width="120" Height="60" Fill="Green" Margin="20">
  <Rectangle.RenderTransform>
    <TranslateTransform X="-90" Y="20" />
  </Rectangle.RenderTransform>
</Rectangle>
```

Rotating

You can rotate an element by using `RotateTransform`. With `RotateTransform`, you set the angle of the rotation and the center of the rotation with `CenterX` and `CenterY` (code file `Transformation[WPF|UWP]/Main[Window|Page].xaml`):

```
<Rectangle Width="120" Height="60" Fill="Orange" Margin="20">
  <Rectangle.RenderTransform>
    <RotateTransform Angle="45" CenterX="10" CenterY="-80"  />
  </Rectangle.RenderTransform>
</Rectangle>
```

Skewing

For skewing, you can use the `SkewTransform` element. With skewing you can assign angles for the x and y axes (code file `Transformation[WPF|UWP]/Main[Window|Page].xaml`):

```
<Rectangle Width="120" Height="60" Fill="LightBlue" Margin="20">
  <Rectangle.RenderTransform>
    <SkewTransform AngleX="20" AngleY="30" CenterX="40" CenterY="390" />
  </Rectangle.RenderTransform>
</Rectangle>
```

Transforming with Groups and Composite Transforms

An easy way to do multiple transformations at once is by using the `CompositeTransform` (with UWP apps) and `TransformationGroup` elements. The `TransformationGroup` element can have `SkewTransform`, `RotateTransform`, `TranslateTransform`, and `ScaleTransform` as its children (code file `Transformation[WPF|UWP]/Main[Window|Page].xaml`):

```
<Rectangle Width="120" Height="60" Fill="LightGreen" Margin="20">
  <Rectangle.RenderTransform>
    <TransformGroup>
      <SkewTransform AngleX="45" AngleY="20" CenterX="-390" CenterY="40" />
      <RotateTransform Angle="90" />
                        <ScaleTransform ScaleX="0.5" ScaleY="1.2" />
    </TransformGroup>
  </Rectangle.RenderTransform>
</Rectangle>
```

To rotate and skew together, it is possible to define a `TransformGroup` that contains both `RotateTransform` and `SkewTransform`. The class `CompositeTransform` defines properties to do multiple transformations at once—for example, `ScaleX` and `ScaleY` for scaling as well as `TranslateX` and `TranslateY` for moving an element. You can also define a `MatrixTransform` whereby the `Matrix` element specifies the properties `M11` and `M22` for stretching and `M12` and `M21` for skewing, as shown in the next section.

Transforming Using a Matrix

Another option for defining multiple transformations at once is to specify a matrix. Here, you use
`MatrixTransform`. `MatrixTransform` defines a `Matrix` property that has six values. Setting the values 1, 0,
0, 1, 0, 0 doesn't change the element. With the values 0.5, 1.4, 0.4, 0.5, –200, and 0, the element is resized,
skewed, and translated (code file `Transformation[WPF|UWP]/Main[Window|Page].xaml`):

```
<Rectangle Width="120" Height="60" Fill="Gold" Margin="20">
  <Rectangle.RenderTransform>
    <MatrixTransform Matrix="0.5, 1.4, 0.4, 0.5, -200, 0" />
  </Rectangle.RenderTransform>
</Rectangle>
```

The `Matrix` type is a struct and thus cannot be instantiated within XAML code in a UWP app. However,
the previous sample puts all the value of the matrix into a string, which gets converted. With WPF, you can
instantiate a struct within XAML code, and thus it is possible to define the same values by assigning the
`Matrix` properties by its name. The properties `M11` and `M22` are used for scaling, `M12` and `M21` for skewing,
and `OffsetX` and `OffsetY` for translating:

```
<Rectangle Width="120" Height="60" Fill="Gold" Margin="20">
  <Rectangle.RenderTransform>
    <MatrixTransform>
      <MatrixTransform.Matrix>
        <Matrix M11="0.5" M12="1.4" M21="0.4" M22="0.5"
          OffsetX="-200" OffsetY="0" />
      </MatrixTransform.Matrix>
    </MatrixTransform>
  </Rectangle.RenderTransform>
</Rectangle>
```

Directly assigning the values in a string to the `Matrix` property of the `MatrixTransform` class has this
order: M11—M12—M21—M22—OffsetX—OffsetY.

Transforming Layouts

The transformation samples have used `RenderTransform`. WPF also supports `LayoutTransform`. With
`RenderTransform`, the transformation takes place after the layout phase is done, so it's not taking into
account when elements have a need for different sizes after the transformation. With `LayoutTransform`, the
transformation happens before the layout phase—which is best demonstrated with an example. In the following code snippet, two rectangles are defined within a `StackPanel`. Both have the same height and width
defined, but the first one is resized by a factor of 1.5 using render transformation. Looking at Figure 30-8
you can see that the rectangles overlay each other. The layout phase was done before the transformation,
and thus the first rectangle doesn't have enough room and just moves outside its positions for display (code
file `TransformationWPF/MainWindow.xaml`):

```
<StackPanel Orientation="Horizontal">
  <Rectangle Width="120" Height="60" Fill="Blue" Margin="20">
    <Rectangle.RenderTransform>
      <ScaleTransform ScaleX="1.5" ScaleY="1.5" />
    </Rectangle.RenderTransform>
  </Rectangle>
  <Rectangle Width="120" Height="60" Fill="Blue" Margin="20" />
</StackPanel>
```

FIGURE 30-8

By using the same rectangles and `ScaleTransformation` but now with `LayoutTransform` (which is supported with WPF), you can see in Figure 30-9 that more room is made. The layout phase is done after the transformation.

```
<StackPanel Orientation="Horizontal">
  <Rectangle Width="120" Height="60" Fill="Blue" Margin="20">
    <Rectangle.LayoutTransform>
      <ScaleTransform ScaleX="1.5" ScaleY="1.5" />
    </Rectangle.LayoutTransform>
  </Rectangle>
  <Rectangle Width="120" Height="60" Fill="Blue" Margin="20" />
</StackPanel>
```

FIGURE 30-9

> **NOTE** *In addition to* `LayoutTransform` *there's also a* `RenderTransform`. *`LayoutTransform` happens before the layout phase and `RenderTransform` happens after.*

BRUSHES

This section demonstrates how to use XAML's brushes for drawing backgrounds and foregrounds. When you use brushes, WPF has a lot more to offer than UWP apps. Consequently, this section starts by covering brushes that are offered by both technologies and then it gets into brushes that are available only with specific XAML technologies.

The first examples in this section reference Figure 30-10, which shows the effects of using various brushes within the `Background` of `Button` elements.

FIGURE 30-10

SolidColorBrush

The first button in Figure 30-10 uses the `SolidColorBrush`, which, as the name suggests, uses a solid color. The complete area is drawn with the same color.

You can define a solid color just by setting the `Background` attribute to a string that defines a solid color. The string is converted to a `SolidColorBrush` element with the help of the `BrushValueSerializer` (code file Brushes[WPF|UWP]/Main[Window|Page].xaml):

```
<Button Height="30" Background="#FFC9659C">Solid Color</Button>
```

Of course, you will get the same effect by setting the `Background` child element and adding a `SolidColorBrush` element as its content (code file BrushesDemo/MainWindow.xaml). The first button in the application uses a hexadecimal value for the solid background color:

```
<Button Content="Solid Color" Margin="10">
  <Button.Background>
    <SolidColorBrush Color="#FFC9659C" />
  </Button.Background>
</Button>
```

LinearGradientBrush

For a smooth color change, you can use the `LinearGradientBrush`, as the second button in Figure 30-10 shows. This brush defines the `StartPoint` and `EndPoint` properties. With this, you can assign two-dimensional coordinates for the linear gradient. The default gradient is diagonal linear from 0,0 to 1,1. By defining different values, the gradient can take different directions. For example, with a `StartPoint` of 0,0 and an `EndPoint` of 0,1, you get a vertical gradient. The `StartPoint` and `EndPoint` value of 1,0 creates a horizontal gradient.

With the content of this brush, you can define the color values at the specified offsets with the `GradientStop` element. Between the stops, the colors are smoothed (code file Brushes[WPF|UWP]/Main[Window|Page].xaml):

```
<Button Content="Linear Gradient Brush" Margin="10">
  <Button.Background>
    <LinearGradientBrush StartPoint="0,0" EndPoint="0,1">
      <GradientStop Offset="0" Color="LightGreen" />
      <GradientStop Offset="0.4" Color="Green" />
      <GradientStop Offset="1" Color="DarkGreen" />
    </LinearGradientBrush>
  </Button.Background>
</Button>
```

ImageBrush

To load an image into a brush, you can use the `ImageBrush` element. With this element, the image defined by the `ImageSource` property is displayed. The image can be accessed from the file system or from a resource within the assembly. In the code example, the image is added from the file system (code file Brushes[WPF|UWP]/Main[Window|Page].xaml):

```
<Button Content="Image Brush" Width="100" Height="80" Margin="5"
        Foreground="White">
  <Button.Background>
    <ImageBrush ImageSource="Build2015.png" Opacity="0.5" />
  </Button.Background>
</Button>
```

WebViewBrush

A mighty brush that is available only with UWP apps is the `WebViewBrush`. This brush uses the content of a `WebView` as a brush.

With the `WebView` control, you can use a local HTML file that is distributed with the application using the `ms-appx-web` prefix as in the sample code (code file BrushesUWP/MainPage.xaml):

```
<WebView x:Name="webView1" Source="ms-appx-web:///HTML/HTMLBrushContent.html"
    LoadCompleted="OnWebViewCompleted" Width="100" Height="80"  />
```

Instead of using a file that is distributed with the application, it is also possible to access the Internet and retrieve the HTML file using `http://`. When you're using the `ms-appdata:///` prefix, you can use files from the local file system.

The `WebViewBrush` references the `WebView` with the `SourceName` property:

```xml
<Button Content="WebView Brush" Width="300" Height="180" Margin="20">
  <Button.Background>
    <WebViewBrush x:Name="webViewBrush" SourceName="webView1" Opacity="0.5" />
  </Button.Background>
</Button>
```

The `WebViewBrush` is drawn as soon as XAML is loaded. If the `WebView` did not load the source at that time, the brush needs to be redrawn. That's why the `WebView` defines the `LoadCompleted` event. With the event handler that is associated with this event, the `WebViewBrush` is redrawn by invoking the `Redraw` method, and the `Visibility` property of the `WebView` is set to `Collapsed`. In case the `WebView` control would be collapsed from the beginning, the brush would never show the HTML content (code file `BrushesUWP/MainPage.xaml.cs`):

```csharp
private void OnWebViewCompleted(object sender, NavigationEventArgs e)
{
  webViewBrush.Redraw();
  webView1.Visibility = Visibility.Collapsed;
}
```

WPF-Only Brushes

The `WebViewBrush` covered in the preceding section is available only with UWP apps, but now we're moving on to the category of brushes that are available only with WPF. All the brushes described in the following sections can be used only with WPF. Figure 30-11 shows the WPF-only brushes `RadialGradientBrush`, `DrawingBrush`, and `VisualBrush` (two times). Let's start with the `RadialGradientBrush`.

FIGURE 30-11

RadialGradientBrush

The `RadialGradientBrush` is similar to the `LinearGradientBrush` in that you can define a list of colors for a gradient look. With the `RadialGradientBrush` you can smooth the color in a radial way. In Figure 30-11, the far-left element is a `Path` that uses `RadialGradientBrush`. This brush defines the color start with the `GradientOrigin` point (code file `BrushesWPF/MainWindow.xaml`):

```xml
<Canvas Width="200" Height="150">
  <Path Canvas.Top="0" Canvas.Left="20" Stroke="Black" >
    <Path.Fill>
      <RadialGradientBrush GradientOrigin="0.2,0.2">
        <GradientStop Offset="0" Color="LightBlue" />
        <GradientStop Offset="0.6" Color="Blue" />
        <GradientStop Offset="1.0" Color="DarkBlue" />
      </RadialGradientBrush>
    </Path.Fill>
    <Path.Data>
      <CombinedGeometry GeometryCombineMode="Union">
        <CombinedGeometry.Geometry1>
          <EllipseGeometry Center="80,60" RadiusX="80" RadiusY="40" />
```

```
        </CombinedGeometry.Geometry1>
        <CombinedGeometry.Geometry2>
          <RectangleGeometry Rect="30,60 105 50" />
        </CombinedGeometry.Geometry2>
      </CombinedGeometry>
    </Path.Data>
  </Path>
</Canvas>
```

DrawingBrush

The DrawingBrush enables you to define a drawing that is created with the brush. The button that is shown in Figure 30-11 with the Content value Drawing Brush defines the background using a DrawingBrush. This brush makes use of a GeometryDrawing element. The GeometryDrawing in turn uses two SolidColorBrush elements: one red and one blue. The red brush is used as the background and the blue brush is used for the pen, which results in the stroke around the geometry element. The content of the GeometryDrawing is defined by a PathGeometry, which was discussed earlier in this chapter in the "Geometry" section (code file BrushesWPF/MainWindow.xaml):

```
<Button Content="Drawing Brush" Margin="10" Padding="10">
  <Button.Background>
    <DrawingBrush>
      <DrawingBrush.Drawing>
        <GeometryDrawing Brush="Red">
          <GeometryDrawing.Pen>
            <Pen>
              <Pen.Brush>
                <SolidColorBrush>Blue</SolidColorBrush>
              </Pen.Brush>
            </Pen>
          </GeometryDrawing.Pen>
          <GeometryDrawing.Geometry>
            <PathGeometry>
              <PathGeometry.Figures>
                <PathFigure StartPoint="70,40">
                  <PathFigure.Segments>
                    <BezierSegment Point1="90,37" Point2="130,46"
                                   Point3="150,63" />
                    <LineSegment Point="120,110" />
                    <BezierSegment Point1="100,95" Point2="70,90"
                                   Point3="45,91" />
                    <LineSegment Point="70,40" />
                  </PathFigure.Segments>
                </PathFigure>
              </PathGeometry.Figures>
            </PathGeometry>
          </GeometryDrawing.Geometry>
        </GeometryDrawing>
      </DrawingBrush.Drawing>
    </DrawingBrush>
  </Button.Background>
</Button>
```

VisualBrush

The VisualBrush enables you to use other XAML elements in a brush. The following example (code file BrushesWPF/MainWindow.xaml) adds a StackPanel with Rectangle and Button elements to the Visual property. The third element from the left in Figure 30-11 contains a Rectangle and a Button:

```
<Button Content="Visual Brush" Width="100" Height="80">
  <Button.Background>
```

```
        <VisualBrush Opacity="0.5">
          <VisualBrush.Visual>
            <StackPanel Background="White">
              <Rectangle Width="25" Height="25" Fill="Blue" />
              <Button Content="Drawing Button" Background="Red" />
            </StackPanel>
          </VisualBrush.Visual>
        </VisualBrush>
      </Button.Background>
    </Button>
```

You can add any `UIElement` to the `VisualBrush`. For example, you can play a video by using the `MediaElement`:

```
<Button Content="Visual Brush with Media" Width="200" Height="150"
    Foreground="White">
  <Button.Background>
    <VisualBrush>
      <VisualBrush.Visual>
        <MediaElement Source="./IceSkating.mp4" LoadedBehavior="Play" />
      </VisualBrush.Visual>
    </VisualBrush>
  </Button.Background>
</Button>
```

You can also use the `VisualBrush` to create interesting effects, such as reflection. The button coded in the following example (shown on the far right of Figure 30-11) contains a `StackPanel` that itself contains a `MediaElement` that plays a video and a `Border`. The `Border` contains a `Rectangle` that is filled with a `VisualBrush`. This brush defines an opacity value and a transformation. The `Visual` property is bound to the `Border` element. The transformation is achieved by setting the `RelativeTransform` property of the `VisualBrush`. This transformation uses relative coordinates. By setting `ScaleY` to -1, you create a reflection in the y axis. `TranslateTransform` moves the transformation in the y axis so that the reflection is below the original object.

```
<Button Width="200" Height="200" Foreground="White" Click="OnMediaButtonClick">
  <StackPanel>
    <MediaElement x:Name="media1" Source="IceSkating.mp4"
        LoadedBehavior="Manual" />
    <Border Height="100">
      <Rectangle>
        <Rectangle.Fill>
          <VisualBrush Opacity="0.35" Stretch="None"
              Visual="{Binding ElementName=media1}">
            <VisualBrush.RelativeTransform>
              <TransformGroup>
                <ScaleTransform ScaleX="1" ScaleY="-1" />
                <TranslateTransform Y="1" />
              </TransformGroup>
            </VisualBrush.RelativeTransform>
          </VisualBrush>
        </Rectangle.Fill>
      </Rectangle>
    </Border>
  </StackPanel>
</Button>
```

> **NOTE** Data binding and the `Binding` element used here are explained in detail in Chapter 31, "Patterns with XAML Apps."

In the code-behind code the `Click` event handler of the `Button` starts the video (code file `BrushesWPF/MainWindow.xaml.cs`):

```
private void OnMediaButtonClick(object sender, RoutedEventArgs e)
{
  media1.Position = TimeSpan.FromSeconds(0);
  media1.Play();
}
```

You can see the result in Figure 30-12.

FIGURE 30-12

STYLES AND RESOURCES

You can define the look and feel of the XAML elements by setting properties, such as `FontSize` and `Background`, with the `Button` element (code file `StylesAndResources[WPF|UWP]/Main[Window|Page].xaml`):

```
<Button Width="150" FontSize="12" Background="AliceBlue" Content="Click Me!" />
```

Instead of defining the look and feel with every element, you can define styles that are stored with resources. To completely customize the look of controls, you can use templates and add them to resources.

Styles

You can assign the `Style` property of a control to a `Style` element that has setters associated with it. A `Setter` element defines the `Property` and `Value` properties to set the specific properties and values for the target element. In the following example, the `Background`, `FontSize`, `FontWeight`, and `Margin` properties are set. The `Style` is set to the `TargetType` `Button`, so that the properties of the `Button` can be directly accessed (code file `StylesAndResources[WPF|UWP]/Main[Window|Page].xaml`):

```
<Button Width="150" Content="Click Me!">
  <Button.Style>
    <Style TargetType="Button">
      <Setter Property="Background" Value="Yellow" />
      <Setter Property="FontSize" Value="14" />
      <Setter Property="FontWeight" Value="Bold" />
      <Setter Property="Margin" Value="5" />
    </Style>
  </Button.Style>
</Button>
```

Setting the `Style` directly with the `Button` element doesn't really help a lot with style sharing. Styles can be put into resources. Within the resources you can assign styles to specific elements, assign a style to all elements of a type, or use a key for the style. To assign a style to all elements of a type, use the `TargetType` property of the `Style` and assign it to a `Button`. To define a style that needs to be referenced, `x:Key` must be set:

```
<Page.Resources>
  <Style TargetType="Button">
    <Setter Property="Background" Value="LemonChiffon" />
    <Setter Property="FontSize" Value="18" />
    <Setter Property="Margin" Value="5" />
  </Style>
  <Style x:Key="ButtonStyle1" TargetType="Button">
    <Setter Property="Background" Value="Red" />
    <Setter Property="Foreground" Value="White" />
    <Setter Property="FontSize" Value="18" />
    <Setter Property="Margin" Value="5" />
  </Style>
</Page.Resources>
```

In the sample application, the styles that are defined globally within the page or window are defined within `<Page.Resources>` in the UWP app and `<Window.Resources>` in WPF.

In the following XAML code the first button—which doesn't have a style defined with the element properties—gets the style that is defined for the `Button` type. With the next button, the `Style` property is set with the `StaticResource` markup extension to `{StaticResource ButtonStyle}`, whereas `ButtonStyle` specifies the key value of the style resource defined earlier, so this button has a red background and a white foreground:

```
<Button Width="200" Content="Default Button style" Margin="3" />
<Button Width="200" Content="Named style"
        Style="{StaticResource ButtonStyle1}" Margin="3" />
```

Rather than set the `Background` of a button to just a single value, you can do more. You can set the `Background` property to a `LinearGradientBrush` with a gradient color definition:

```
<Style x:Key="FancyButtonStyle" TargetType="Button">
  <Setter Property="FontSize" Value="22" />
  <Setter Property="Foreground" Value="White" />
  <Setter Property="Margin" Value="5" />
  <Setter Property="Background">
    <Setter.Value>
      <LinearGradientBrush StartPoint="0,0" EndPoint="0,1">
        <GradientStop Offset="0.0" Color="LightCyan" />
        <GradientStop Offset="0.14" Color="Cyan" />
        <GradientStop Offset="0.7" Color="DarkCyan" />
      </LinearGradientBrush>
    </Setter.Value>
  </Setter>
</Style>
```

The next button in this example has a fancy style with cyan applied as the linear gradient:

```
<Button Width="200" Content="Fancy button style"
        Style="{StaticResource FancyButtonStyle}" Margin="3" />
```

Styles offer a kind of inheritance. One style can be based on another one. The style `AnotherButtonStyle` is based on the style `FancyButtonStyle`. It uses all the settings defined by the base style (referenced by the `BasedOn` property), except the `Foreground` property—which is set to `LinearGradientBrush`:

```
<Style x:Key="AnotherButtonStyle" BasedOn="{StaticResource FancyButtonStyle}"
    TargetType="Button">
  <Setter Property="Foreground">
```

```
        <Setter.Value>
          <LinearGradientBrush>
            <GradientStop Offset="0.2" Color="White" />
            <GradientStop Offset="0.5" Color="LightYellow" />
            <GradientStop Offset="0.9" Color="Orange" />
          </LinearGradientBrush>
        </Setter.Value>
      </Setter>
    </Style>
```

The last button has `AnotherButtonStyle` applied:

```
<Button Width="200" Content="Style inheritance"
    Style="{StaticResource AnotherButtonStyle}" Margin="3" />
```

The result of all these buttons after styling is shown in Figure 30-13.

FIGURE 30-13

Resources

As you have seen with the styles sample, usually styles are stored within resources. You can define any freezable (WPF) or sharable (UWP apps) element within a resource. For example, the brush created earlier for the background style of the button can be defined as a resource, so you can use it everywhere a brush is required.

The following example defines a `LinearGradientBrush` with the key name `MyGradientBrush` inside the `StackPanel` resources. `button1` assigns the `Background` property by using a `StaticResource` markup extension to the resource `MyGradientBrush` (code file `StylesAndResources[WPF|UWP]/ResourceDemo[Page|Window].xaml`):

```
<StackPanel x:Name="myContainer">
  <StackPanel.Resources>
    <LinearGradientBrush x:Key="MyGradientBrush" StartPoint="0,0"
        EndPoint="0.3,1">
      <GradientStop Offset="0.0" Color="LightCyan" />
      <GradientStop Offset="0.14" Color="Cyan" />
      <GradientStop Offset="0.7" Color="DarkCyan" />
    </LinearGradientBrush>
  </StackPanel.Resources>
  <Button Width="200" Height="50" Foreground="White" Margin="5"
      Background="{StaticResource MyGradientBrush}" Content="Click Me!" />
</StackPanel>
```

Here, the resources have been defined with the `StackPanel`. In the previous example, the resources were defined with the `Page` or `Window` element. The base class `FrameworkElement` defines the property `Resources` of type `ResourceDictionary`. That's why resources can be defined with every class that is derived from the `FrameworkElement`—any XAML element.

Resources are searched hierarchically. If you define the resource with the root element, it applies to every child element. If the root element contains a Grid, and the Grid contains a StackPanel, and you define the resource with the StackPanel, then the resource applies to every control within the StackPanel. If the StackPanel contains a Button, and you define the resource just with the Button, then this style is valid only for the Button.

> **NOTE** *In regard to hierarchies, you need to pay attention if you use the* TargetType *without a* Key *for styles. If you define a resource with the* Canvas *element and set the* TargetType *for the style to apply to* TextBox *elements, then the style applies to all* TextBox *elements within the* Canvas. *The style even applies to* TextBox *elements that are contained in a* ListBox *when the* ListBox *is in the* Canvas.

If you need the same style for more than one window, then you can define the style with the application. With both WPF and UWP apps created with Visual Studio, the file App.xaml is created for defining global resources of the application. The application styles are valid for every page or window of the application. Every element can access resources that are defined with the application. If resources are not found with the parent window, then the search for resources continues with the Application (code file StylesAndResourcesUWP/App.xaml):

```
<Application x:Class="StylesAndResourcesUWP.App"
             xmlns="http://schemas.microsoft.com/winfx/2006/xaml/presentation"
             xmlns:x="http://schemas.microsoft.com/winfx/2006/xaml"
             RequestedTheme="Light">
  <Application.Resources>

  </Application.Resources>
</Application>
```

Accessing Resources from Code

To access resources from code-behind, the Resources property of the base class FrameworkElement returns a ResourceDictionary. This dictionary offers access to the resources using an indexer with the name of the resource. You can use the ContainsKey method to check whether the resource is available.

Let's see that in action. The Button control button1 doesn't have a background specified, but the Click event is assigned to the method OnApplyResources to change this dynamically (code file StylesAndResources[WPF|UWP]/ResourceDemo[Page|Window].xaml):

```
<Button Name="button1" Width="220" Height="50" Margin="5"
  Click="OnApplyResources" Content="Apply Resource Programmatically" />
```

Now you can have a slightly different implementation to find resources in the hierarchy with WPF and UWP Apps. With WPF, the ResourceDictionary offers the methods FindResource and TryFindResource to get a resource from the hierarchy. FindResource throws an exception when the resource is not found; TryFindResource just returns null (code file StylesAndResources[WPF|UWP]/ResourceDemo.xaml.cs):

```
private void OnApplyResources(object sender, RoutedEventArgs e)
{
  Control ctrl = sender as Control;
  ctrl.Background = ctrl.TryFindResource("MyGradientBrush") as Brush;
}
```

With UWP apps, TryFindResource is not available with the ResourceDictionary. However, you can easily implement such a method using an extension method, and thus the implementation of OnApplyResources can stay the same.

The method `TryFindResource` checks whether the resource requested is available using `ContainsKey`, and it recursively invokes the method in case the resource is not yet found (code file `StylesAndResourcesUWP/FrameworkElementExtensions.cs`):

```
public static class FrameworkElementExtensions
{
  public static object TryFindResource(this FrameworkElement e, string key)
  {
    if (e == null) throw new ArgumentNullException(nameof(e));
    if (key == null) throw new ArgumentNullException(nameof(key));

    if (e.Resources.ContainsKey(key))
    {
      return e.Resources[key];
    }
    else
    {
      var parent = e.Parent as FrameworkElement;
      if (parent == null) return null;
      return TryFindResource(parent, key);
    }
  }
}
```

Dynamic Resources (WPF)

With the `StaticResource` markup extension, resources are searched at load time. If the resource changes while the program is running, then instead you can use the `DynamicResource` markup extension with WPF. UWP apps don't support the `DynamicResource` markup extension.

The next example uses the same resource defined previously. The earlier example used `StaticResource`. This button uses `DynamicResource` with the `DynamicResource` markup extension. The event handler of this button changes the resource programmatically. The handler method `OnChangeDynamicResource` is assigned to the `Click` event handler (code file `StylesAndResourcesWPF/ResourceDemo.xaml`):

```
<Button Name="button2" Width="200" Height="50" Foreground="White" Margin="5"
    Background="{DynamicResource MyGradientBrush}" Content="Change Resource"
    Click="OnChangeDynamicResource" />
```

The implementation of `OnChangeDynamicResource` clears the resources of the `StackPanel` and adds a new resource with the same name, `MyGradientBrush`. This new resource is very similar to the resource defined in XAML code, but it defines different colors (code file `StylesAndResourcesWPF/ResourceDemo.xaml.cs`):

```
private void OnChangeDynamicResource(object sender, RoutedEventArgs e)
{
  myContainer.Resources.Clear();
  var brush = new LinearGradientBrush
  {
    StartPoint = new Point(0, 0),
    EndPoint = new Point(0, 1)
  };

  brush.GradientStops = new GradientStopCollection()
  {
    new GradientStop(Colors.White, 0.0),
    new GradientStop(Colors.Yellow, 0.14),
    new GradientStop(Colors.YellowGreen, 0.7)
  };
  myContainer.Resources.Add("MyGradientBrush", brush);
}
```

When the application runs, you change the resource dynamically by clicking the Change Resource button. When you use the button with `DynamicResource`, the result is the dynamically created resource; when you use the button with `StaticResource`, the result looks the same as before.

Resource Dictionaries

If you use the same resources with different pages or even different apps, it's useful to put the resource in a resource dictionary. When you use resource dictionaries, you can share the files between multiple apps, or you can put the resource dictionary into an assembly that is shared.

To share a resource dictionary in an assembly, create a library. You can add a resource dictionary file—here `Dictionary1.xaml`—to the assembly. With WPF, the build action for this file must be set to `Resource` so that it is added as a resource to the assembly.

`Dictionary1.xaml` defines two resources: `LinearGradientBrush` with the `CyanGradientBrush` key, and a style for a `Button` that can be referenced with the `PinkButtonStyle` key (code file download `ResourcesLib[WPF|UWP]/Dictionary1.xaml`):

```xml
<ResourceDictionary
    xmlns="http://schemas.microsoft.com/winfx/2006/xaml/presentation"
    xmlns:x="http://schemas.microsoft.com/winfx/2006/xaml">
  <LinearGradientBrush x:Key="CyanGradientBrush" StartPoint="0,0"
      EndPoint="0.3,1">
    <LinearGradientBrush.GradientStops>
      <GradientStop Offset="0.0" Color="LightCyan" />
      <GradientStop Offset="0.14" Color="Cyan" />
      <GradientStop Offset="0.7" Color="DarkCyan" />
    </LinearGradientBrush.GradientStops>
  </LinearGradientBrush>

  <Style x:Key="PinkButtonStyle" TargetType="Button">
    <Setter Property="FontSize" Value="22" />
    <Setter Property="Foreground" Value="White" />
    <Setter Property="Background">
      <Setter.Value>
        <LinearGradientBrush StartPoint="0,0" EndPoint="0,1">
          <LinearGradientBrush.GradientStops>
            <GradientStop Offset="0.0" Color="Pink" />
            <GradientStop Offset="0.3" Color="DeepPink" />
            <GradientStop Offset="0.9" Color="DarkOrchid" />
          </LinearGradientBrush.GradientStops>
        </LinearGradientBrush>
      </Setter.Value>
    </Setter>
  </Style>
</ResourceDictionary>
```

With the target project, the library needs to be referenced, and the resource dictionary needs to be added to the dictionaries. You can use multiple resource dictionary files that you can add by using the `MergedDictionaries` property of the `ResourceDictionary`. You can add a list of resource dictionaries to the merged dictionaries.

How the reference to the library is handled is different between WPF and UWP apps. With WPF, the pack URI syntax is used. The pack URI can be assigned as *absolute*, which means the URI begins with `pack://`, or as *relative*, as it is used in this example. With relative syntax, the referenced assembly `ResourceLibWPF`, which includes the dictionary, is first after the / followed by `;component`. `Component` means that the dictionary is included as a resource in the assembly. After that, you add the name of the dictionary file `Dictionary1.xaml`. If the dictionary is added into a subfolder, the folder name must be declared as well (code file `StylesAndResourcesWPF/App.xaml`):

```
<Application x:Class="StylesAndResourcesWPF.App"
             xmlns="http://schemas.microsoft.com/winfx/2006/xaml/presentation"
             xmlns:x="http://schemas.microsoft.com/winfx/2006/xaml"
             StartupUri="MainWindow.xaml">
  <Application.Resources>
    <ResourceDictionary>
      <ResourceDictionary.MergedDictionaries>
        <ResourceDictionary
            Source="/ResourcesLibWPF;component/Dictionary1.xaml" />
      </ResourceDictionary.MergedDictionaries>
    </ResourceDictionary>
  </Application.Resources>
</Application>
```

With UWP apps, the reference looks slightly different. Here, the referenced resource dictionary must be prefixed with the `ms-appx:///` scheme (code file `StylesAndResourcesUWP/App.xaml`):

```
<Application x:Class="StylesAndResourcesUWP.App"
             xmlns="http://schemas.microsoft.com/winfx/2006/xaml/presentation"
             xmlns:x="http://schemas.microsoft.com/winfx/2006/xaml"
             xmlns:local="using:StylesAndResourcesUWP"
             RequestedTheme="Light">
  <Application.Resources>
    <ResourceDictionary>
      <ResourceDictionary.MergedDictionaries>
        <ResourceDictionary
            Source="ms-appx:///ResourcesLibUWP/Dictionary1.xaml" />
      </ResourceDictionary.MergedDictionaries>
    </ResourceDictionary>
  </Application.Resources>
</Application>
```

Now it is possible to use the resources from the referenced assembly in the same way as local resources (code file `StylesAndResources[WPF|UWP]/ResourceDemo[Window|Page].xaml`):

```
<Button Width="300" Height="50" Style="{StaticResource PinkButtonStyle}"
    Content="Referenced Resource" />
```

Theme Resources (UWP)

Although UWP apps don't support the `DynamicResource` markup extension, these apps also have a way to change styles dynamically. This feature is based on themes. With themes, you can allow the user to switch between a light and a dark theme (similar to the themes you can change with Visual Studio).

Defining Theme Resources

Theme resources can be defined in a resource dictionary within the `ThemeDictionaries` collection. The `ResourceDictionary` objects that are defined within the `ThemeDictionaries` collection need to have a key assigned that has the name of a theme—either `Light` or `Dark`. The sample code defines a button for the light theme that has a light background and dark foreground, and for the dark theme a dark background and light foreground. The key for the style is the same within both dictionaries: `SampleButtonStyle` (code file `StylesAndResourcesUWP/Styles/SampleThemes.xaml`):

```
<ResourceDictionary
    xmlns="http://schemas.microsoft.com/winfx/2006/xaml/presentation"
    xmlns:x="http://schemas.microsoft.com/winfx/2006/xaml"
    xmlns:local="using:StylesAndResourcesUWP">
  <ResourceDictionary.ThemeDictionaries>
    <ResourceDictionary x:Key="Light">
      <Style TargetType="Button" x:Key="SampleButtonStyle">
        <Setter Property="Background" Value="LightGray" />
```

```
          <Setter Property="Foreground" Value="Black" />
        </Style>
      </ResourceDictionary>
      <ResourceDictionary x:Key="Dark">
        <Style TargetType="Button" x:Key="SampleButtonStyle">
          <Setter Property="Background" Value="Black" />
          <Setter Property="Foreground" Value="White" />
        </Style>
      </ResourceDictionary>
    </ResourceDictionary.ThemeDictionaries>
  </ResourceDictionary>
```

You can assign the style using the `ThemeResource` markup extension. Other than using a different markup extension, everything else is the same as with the `StaticResource` markup extension (code file `StylesAndResourcesUWP/ThemeDemoPage.xaml`):

```
<Button Style="{ThemeResource SampleButtonStyle}" Click="OnChangeTheme"
    Content="Change Theme" />
```

Depending on the theme that is selected, the corresponding style will be used.

Selecting a Theme

There are different ways to select a theme. First, there's a default for the app itself. The `RequestedTheme` property of the `Application` class defines the default theme of the app. This is defined within `App.xaml`, which is the place where the themes dictionary file is referenced as well (code file `StylesAndResourcesUWP/App.xaml`):

```
<Application
    x:Class="StylesAndResourcesUWP.App"
    xmlns="http://schemas.microsoft.com/winfx/2006/xaml/presentation"
    xmlns:x="http://schemas.microsoft.com/winfx/2006/xaml"
    xmlns:local="using:StylesAndResourcesUWP"
    RequestedTheme="Light">
  <Application.Resources>
    <ResourceDictionary>
      <ResourceDictionary.MergedDictionaries>
        <ResourceDictionary Source="ms-appx:///StylesLib/Dictionary1.xaml" />
        <ResourceDictionary Source="Styles/SampleThemes.xaml" />
      </ResourceDictionary.MergedDictionaries>
    </ResourceDictionary>
  </Application.Resources>
</Application>
```

The `RequestedTheme` property is defined in the XAML element hierarchy. Every element can override the theme to be used for itself and its children. The following `Grid` element changes the default theme for the `Dark` theme. This is now the theme used for the `Grid` and all its children elements (code file `StylesAndResourcesUWP/ThemeDemoPage.xaml`):

```
<Grid x:Name="grid1"
    Background="{ThemeResource ApplicationPageBackgroundThemeBrush}"
    RequestedTheme="Dark">
  <Button Style="{ThemeResource SampleButtonStyle}" Click="OnChangeTheme"
      Content="Change Theme" />
</Grid>
```

You can also dynamically change the theme by setting the `RequestedTheme` property from code (code file `StylesAndResourcesUWP/ThemeDemoPage.xaml.cs`):

```
private void OnChangeTheme(object sender, RoutedEventArgs e)
{
  grid1.RequestedTheme = grid1.RequestedTheme == ElementTheme.Dark ?
    ElementTheme.Light: ElementTheme.Dark;
}
```

> **NOTE** *Using the* ThemeResource *markup extension is useful only in cases where the resource should look different based on the theme. If the resource should look the same, with all themes, keep using the* StaticResource *markup extension.*

TEMPLATES

An XAML Button control can contain any content. The content can be simple text, but you can also add a Canvas element, which can contain shapes; a Grid; or a video. In fact, you can do even more than that with a button! With template-based XAML controls, the functionality of controls is completely separate from their look and feel. A button has a default look, but you can completely customize that look.

WPF and UWP apps provide several template types that derive from the base class FrameworkTemplate.

TEMPLATE TYPE	DESCRIPTION
ControlTemplate	Enables you to specify the visual structure of a control and override its look.
ItemsPanelTemplate	For an ItemsControl you can specify the layout of its items by assigning an ItemsPanelTemplate. Each ItemsControl has a default ItemsPanelTemplate. For the MenuItem, it is a WrapPanel. The StatusBar uses a DockPanel, and the ListBox uses a VirtualizingStackPanel.
DataTemplate	These are very useful for graphical representations of objects. When styling a ListBox, by default the items of the ListBox are shown according to the output of the ToString method. By applying a DataTemplate you can override this behavior and define a custom presentation of the items.
HierarchicalDataTemplate	Used for arranging a tree of objects. This control supports HeaderedItemsControls, such as TreeViewItem and MenuItem. This template class is only available with WPF.

> **NOTE** *The* HierarchicalDataTemplate *is discussed with the* TreeControl *in Chapter 34, "Windows Desktop Applications with WPF."*

Control Templates

Previously in this chapter you've seen how you can style the properties of a control. If setting simple properties of the controls doesn't give you the look you want, you can change the Template property. With the Template property, you can customize the complete look of the control. The next example demonstrates customizing buttons, and later in the chapter list views are customized step by step so you can see the intermediate results of the changes.

You customize the Button type in a separate resource dictionary file: ControlTemplates.xaml. Here, a style with the key name RoundedGelButton is defined. The style RoundedGelButton sets the properties Background, Height, Foreground, and Margin, and the Template. The Template is the most interesting aspect with this style. The Template specifies a Grid with just one row and one column.

Inside this cell, you can find an ellipse with the name GelBackground. This ellipse has a linear gradient brush for the stroke. The stroke that surrounds the rectangle is very thin because the StrokeThickness is set to 0.5.

The second ellipse, GelShine, is a small ellipse whose size is defined by the Margin property and so is visible within the first ellipse. The stroke is transparent, so there is no line surrounding the ellipse. This ellipse uses a linear gradient fill brush, which transitions from a light, partly transparent color to full transparency. This gives the ellipse a shimmering effect (code file Templates[WPF|UWP]/Styles/ControlTemplates.xaml):

```xaml
<ResourceDictionary
    xmlns="http://schemas.microsoft.com/winfx/2006/xaml/presentation"
    xmlns:x="http://schemas.microsoft.com/winfx/2006/xaml">
  <Style x:Key="RoundedGelButton" TargetType="Button">
    <Setter Property="Width" Value="100" />
    <Setter Property="Height" Value="100" />
    <Setter Property="Foreground" Value="White" />
    <Setter Property="Template">
      <Setter.Value>
        <ControlTemplate TargetType="Button">
          <Grid>
            <Ellipse Name="GelBackground" StrokeThickness="0.5" Fill="Black">
              <Ellipse.Stroke>
                <LinearGradientBrush StartPoint="0,0" EndPoint="0,1">
                  <GradientStop Offset="0" Color="#ff7e7e7e" />
                  <GradientStop Offset="1" Color="Black" />
                </LinearGradientBrush>
              </Ellipse.Stroke>
            </Ellipse>
            <Ellipse Margin="15,5,15,50">
              <Ellipse.Fill>
                <LinearGradientBrush StartPoint="0,0" EndPoint="0,1">
                  <GradientStop Offset="0" Color="#aaffffff" />
                  <GradientStop Offset="1" Color="Transparent" />
                </LinearGradientBrush>
              </Ellipse.Fill>
            </Ellipse>
          </Grid>
        </ControlTemplate>
      </Setter.Value>
    </Setter>
  </Style>
</ResourceDictionary>
```

From the app.xaml file, the resource dictionary is referenced as shown here (code file Templates[WPF|UWP]/App.xaml):

```xaml
<Application x:Class="TemplateDemo.App"
    xmlns="http://schemas.microsoft.com/winfx/2006/xaml/presentation"
    xmlns:x="http://schemas.microsoft.com/winfx/2006/xaml"
    StartupUri="MainWindow.xaml">
  <Application.Resources>
    <ResourceDictionary Source="Styles/ControlTemplates.xaml" />
  </Application.Resources>
</Application>
```

Now a Button control can be associated with the style. The new look of the button is shown in Figure 30-14 and uses code file Templates[WPF|UWP]/StyledButtons.xaml:

```xaml
<Button Style="{StaticResource RoundedGelButton}" Content="Click Me!" />
```

The button now has a completely different look. However, the content that is defined with the button itself is missing. The template created previously must be extended to get the content of the Button into the new look. What needs to be added is a ContentPresenter. The ContentPresenter is the placeholder for the control's content, and it defines the place where the content should be positioned. In the code that follows, the content is placed in the first row of the Grid, as are the Ellipse elements. The Content property of the ContentPresenter defines what the content should be. The content is set to a TemplateBinding markup expression. `TemplateBinding` binds the template parent, which is the `Button` element in this case. `{TemplateBinding Content}` specifies that the value of the `Content` property of the `Button` control should be placed inside the placeholder as content. Figure 30-15 shows the result with the content shown in the here (code file `Templates[WPF|UWP]/Styles/ControlTemplates.xaml`):

FIGURE 30-14

```xml
<Setter Property="Template">
  <Setter.Value>
    <ControlTemplate TargetType="Button">
      <Grid>
        <Ellipse Name="GelBackground" StrokeThickness="0.5" Fill="Black">
          <Ellipse.Stroke>
            <LinearGradientBrush StartPoint="0,0" EndPoint="0,1">
              <GradientStop Offset="0" Color="#ff7e7e7e" />
              <GradientStop Offset="1" Color="Black" />
            </LinearGradientBrush>
          </Ellipse.Stroke>
        </Ellipse>
        <Ellipse Margin="15,5,15,50">
          <Ellipse.Fill>
            <LinearGradientBrush StartPoint="0,0" EndPoint="0,1">
              <GradientStop Offset="0" Color="#aaffffff" />
              <GradientStop Offset="1" Color="Transparent" />
            </LinearGradientBrush>
          </Ellipse.Fill>
        </Ellipse>
        <ContentPresenter Name="GelButtonContent"
                          VerticalAlignment="Center"
                          HorizontalAlignment="Center"
                          Content="{TemplateBinding Content}" />
      </Grid>
    </ControlTemplate>
  </Setter.Value>
</Setter>
```

FIGURE 30-15

> **NOTE** *The* `TemplateBinding` *allows talking values to the template that are defined by the control. This can not only be used for the content but also can be used for colors and stroke styles and much more.*

Such a styled button now looks very fancy on the screen, but there's still a problem: There is no action if the button is clicked or touched, or the mouse moves over the button. This isn't the typical experience a user has with a button. However, there is a solution. With a template-styled button, you must have visual states or triggers that enable the button to have different looks in response to mouse moves and mouse clicks. Visual states also make use of animations; thus I'm delaying this change to later in this chapter.

However, for getting an advance glimpse into this, you can use Visual Studio to create a button template. Instead of creating such a template fully from scratch, you can select a `Button` control either in the XAML designer or in the Document Explorer, and select Edit Template from the context menu. Here, you can create an empty template or copy the predefined template. You use a copy of the template to have a look at how the predefined template looks. You see the dialog to create a style resource (see Figure 30-16). Here you can define whether the resource containing the template should be created in the document, the application (when used for multiple pages and windows), or a resource dictionary. For the previously styled button, the resource dictionary `ControlTemplates.xaml` already exists; with the sample code the resource is created there.

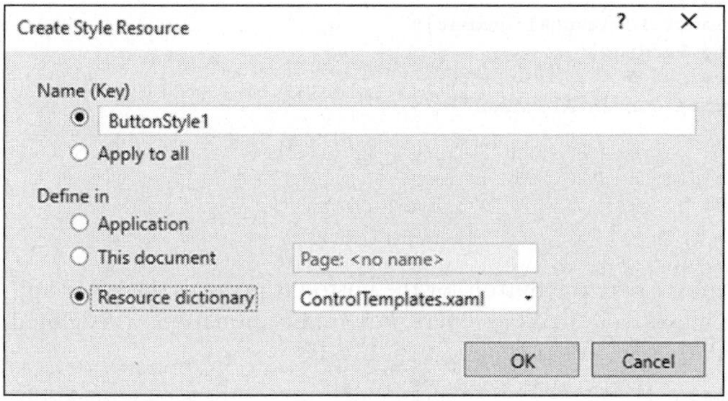

FIGURE 30-16

The default templates for UWP apps and WPF are very different—both because of the different features available with these technologies and because of different designs. Some highlights of the template for the default button template for UWP apps are shown in the following code snippets. Several of the button settings, such as `Background`, `Foreground`, and `BorderBrush`, are taken from theme resources. They are different based on the light or dark theme. Some values, such as `Padding` and `HorizontalAlignment`, are fixed. You can change these by creating a custom style (code file `TemplatesUWP/Styles/ControlTemplates.xaml`):

```
<Style x:Key="ButtonStyle1" TargetType="Button">
  <Setter Property="Background"
    Value="{ThemeResource SystemControlBackgroundBaseLowBrush}"/>
  <Setter Property="Foreground"
    Value="{ThemeResource SystemControlForegroundBaseHighBrush}"/>
  <Setter Property="BorderBrush"
    Value="{ThemeResource SystemControlForegroundTransparentBrush}"/>
  <Setter Property="BorderThickness"
    Value="{ThemeResource ButtonBorderThemeThickness}"/>
```

```
<Setter Property="Padding" Value="8,4,8,4"/>
<Setter Property="HorizontalAlignment" Value="Left"/>
<Setter Property="VerticalAlignment" Value="Center"/>
<Setter Property="FontFamily"
  Value="{ThemeResource ContentControlThemeFontFamily}"/>
<Setter Property="FontWeight" Value="Normal"/>
<Setter Property="FontSize"
  Value="{ThemeResource ControlContentThemeFontSize}"/>
<Setter Property="UseSystemFocusVisuals" Value="True"/>
```

The template of the control consists of a `Grid` and a `ContentPresenter` where values for brushes and borders are bound using `TemplateBinding`. This way it is possible to define these values directly with the `Button` control to influence the look.

```
<Setter Property="Template">
  <Setter.Value>
    <ControlTemplate TargetType="Button">
      <Grid x:Name="RootGrid" Background="{TemplateBinding Background}">
        <!--Visual State Manager settings removed-->
        <ContentPresenter x:Name="ContentPresenter"
          AutomationProperties.AccessibilityView="Raw"
          BorderBrush="{TemplateBinding BorderBrush}"
          BorderThickness="{TemplateBinding BorderThickness}"
          ContentTemplate="{TemplateBinding ContentTemplate}"
          ContentTransitions="{TemplateBinding ContentTransitions}"
          Content="{TemplateBinding Content}"
          HorizontalContentAlignment=
            "{TemplateBinding HorizontalContentAlignment}"
          Padding="{TemplateBinding Padding}"
          VerticalContentAlignment=
            "{TemplateBinding VerticalContentAlignment}"/>
      </Grid>
    </ControlTemplate>
  </Setter.Value>
</Setter>
</Style>
```

For dynamic button changes, if the mouse moves over the button, or the button is pressed, the UWP app template for the button makes use of the `VisualStateManager`. Here, key-frame animations are defined when the button changes to the states `PointerOver`, `Pressed`, and `Disabled`:

```
<VisualStateManager.VisualStateGroups>
  <VisualStateGroup x:Name="CommonStates">
    <VisualState x:Name="Normal"/>
    <VisualState x:Name="PointerOver">
      <Storyboard>
        <ObjectAnimationUsingKeyFrames
          Storyboard.TargetProperty="BorderBrush"
          Storyboard.TargetName="ContentPresenter">
          <DiscreteObjectKeyFrame KeyTime="0"
            Value="{ThemeResource SystemControlHighlightBaseMediumLowBrush}"/>
        </ObjectAnimationUsingKeyFrames>
        <ObjectAnimationUsingKeyFrames
          Storyboard.TargetProperty="Foreground"
          Storyboard.TargetName="ContentPresenter">
          <DiscreteObjectKeyFrame KeyTime="0"
            Value="{ThemeResource SystemControlHighlightBaseHighBrush}"/>
        </ObjectAnimationUsingKeyFrames>
      </Storyboard>
    </VisualState>
    <VisualState x:Name="Pressed">
      <Storyboard>
        <!--animations removed-->
```

```
        </Storyboard>
      </VisualState>
      <VisualState x:Name="Disabled">
        <Storyboard>
          <!—animations removed—>
        </Storyboard>
      </VisualState>
    </VisualStateGroup>
  </VisualStateManager.VisualStateGroups>
```

With WPF, the default button template retrieves resources for brushes using `StaticResource` and `DynamicResource` markup extensions because theme resources are not available here. The `x.Static` markup extension accesses static members of a class, here `SystemColors.ControlTextBrushKey`. The `SystemColors` class accesses resources that can be configured by the user, and thus the user can partially style the look. For the dynamic look when the mouse moves over the button, or the button is clicked, property triggers are used to change the look (code file `TemplatesWPF/Styles/ControlTemplates.xaml`):

```xml
<Style x:Key="ButtonStyle1" TargetType="{x:Type Button}">
  <Setter Property="FocusVisualStyle" Value="{StaticResource FocusVisual}"/>
  <Setter Property="Background"
    Value="{StaticResource Button.Static.Background}"/>
  <Setter Property="BorderBrush"
    Value="{StaticResource Button.Static.Border}"/>
  <Setter Property="Foreground"
    Value="{DynamicResource {x:Static SystemColors.ControlTextBrushKey}}"/>
  <Setter Property="BorderThickness" Value="1"/>
  <Setter Property="HorizontalContentAlignment" Value="Center"/>
  <Setter Property="VerticalContentAlignment" Value="Center"/>
  <Setter Property="Padding" Value="1"/>
  <Setter Property="Template">
    <Setter.Value>
      <ControlTemplate TargetType="{x:Type Button}">
        <Border x:Name="border" BorderBrush="{TemplateBinding BorderBrush}"
          BorderThickness="{TemplateBinding BorderThickness}"
          Background="{TemplateBinding Background}" SnapsToDevicePixels="true">
          <ContentPresenter x:Name="contentPresenter" Focusable="False"
            HorizontalAlignment="{TemplateBinding HorizontalContentAlignment}"
            Margin="{TemplateBinding Padding}" RecognizesAccessKey="True"
            SnapsToDevicePixels="{TemplateBinding SnapsToDevicePixels}"
            VerticalAlignment="{TemplateBinding VerticalContentAlignment}"/>
        </Border>
        <ControlTemplate.Triggers>
          <Trigger Property="IsDefaulted" Value="true">
            <Setter Property="BorderBrush" TargetName="border"
              Value="{DynamicResource
                {x:Static SystemColors.HighlightBrushKey}}"/>
          </Trigger>
          <Trigger Property="IsMouseOver" Value="true">
            <Setter Property="Background" TargetName="border"
              Value="{StaticResource Button.MouseOver.Background}"/>
            <Setter Property="BorderBrush" TargetName="border"
              Value="{StaticResource Button.MouseOver.Border}"/>
          </Trigger>

          <!—more trigger settings for IsPressed and IsEnabled—>

        </ControlTemplate.Triggers>
      </ControlTemplate>
    </Setter.Value>
  </Setter>
</Style>
```

Data Templates

The content of `ContentControl` elements can be any content—not only XAML elements but also .NET objects. For example, an object of the `Country` type can be assigned to the content of a `Button` class. In the following example, the `Country` class is created to represent the name and flag with a path to an image. This class defines the `Name` and `ImagePath` properties, and it has an overridden `ToString` method for a default string representation (code file `Models [WPF|UWP]/Country.cs`):

```
public class Country
{
  public string Name { get; set; }
  public string ImagePath { get; set; }

  public override string ToString() => Name;
}
```

How does this content look within a `Button` or any other `ContentControl`? By default, the `ToString` method is invoked, and the string representation of the object is shown.

For a custom look, you can create a `DataTemplate` for the `Country` type. The sample code defines the key `CountryDataTemplate`. You can use this key to reference the template. Within the `DataTemplate` the main elements are a `TextBlock` with the `Text` property bound to the `Name` property of the `Country`, and an `Image` with the `Source` property bound to the `ImagePath` property of the `Country`. The `Grid` and `Border` elements define the layout and visual appearance (code file `Templates [WPF|UWP]/Styles/DataTemplates.xaml`):

```
<DataTemplate x:Key="CountryDataTemplate">
  <Border Margin="4" BorderThickness="2" CornerRadius="6">
    <Border.BorderBrush>
      <LinearGradientBrush StartPoint="0,0" EndPoint="0,1">
        <GradientStop Offset="0" Color="#aaa" />
        <GradientStop Offset="1" Color="#222" />
      </LinearGradientBrush>
    </Border.BorderBrush>
    <Border.Background>
      <LinearGradientBrush StartPoint="0,0" EndPoint="0,1">
        <GradientStop Offset="0" Color="#444" />
        <GradientStop Offset="1" Color="#fff" />
      </LinearGradientBrush>
    </Border.Background>
    <Grid Margin="4">
      <Grid.RowDefinitions>
        <RowDefinition Height="auto" />
        <RowDefinition Height="auto" />
      </Grid.RowDefinitions>
      <Image Width="120" Source="{Binding ImagePath}" />
      <TextBlock Grid.Row="1" Opacity="0.6" FontSize="16"
        VerticalAlignment="Bottom" HorizontalAlignment="Right" Margin="15"
        FontWeight="Bold" Text="{Binding Name}" />
    </Grid>
  </Border>
</DataTemplate>
```

With the XAML code in the `Window` or `Page`, a simple `Button` element with the name `button1` is defined:

```
<Button x:Name="countryButton" Grid.Row="2" Margin="20"
  ContentTemplate="{StaticResource CountryDataTemplate}" />
```

In the code-behind a new `Country` object is instantiated that is assigned to the `Content` property (code file `Templates [WPF|UWP]/StyledButtons.xaml.cs`):

```
  this.countryButton.Content = new Country
  {
    Name = "Austria",
    ImagePath = "images/Austria.bmp"
  };
```

After running the application, you can see that the `DataTemplate` is applied to the `Button` because the `Country` data type has a default template, shown in Figure 30-17.

FIGURE 30-17

Of course, you can also create a control template and use a data template from within.

Styling a ListView

Changing a style of a button or a label is a simple task, such as changing the style of an element that contains a list of elements. For example, how about changing a `ListView`? Again, this list control has behavior and a look. It can display a list of elements, and you can select one or more elements from the list. For the behavior, the `ListView` class defines methods, properties, and events. The look of the `ListView` is separate from its behavior. It has a default look, but you can change this look by creating a template.

To fill a `ListView` with some items, the class `CountryRepository` returns a list of a few countries that will be displayed (code file `Models[WPF|UWP]/CountryRepository.cs`):

```
public sealed class CountryRepository
{
  private static IEnumerable<Country> s_countries;

  public IEnumerable<Country> GetCountries() =>
    s_countries ?? (s_countries = new List<Country>
    {
      new Country { Name="Austria", ImagePath = "Images/Austria.bmp" },
      new Country { Name="Germany", ImagePath = "Images/Germany.bmp" },
      new Country { Name="Norway", ImagePath = "Images/Norway.bmp" },
      new Country { Name="USA", ImagePath = "Images/USA.bmp" }
    });
}
```

Inside the code-behind file in the constructor of the `StyledList` class, a read-only property `Countries` is created and filled with the help of the `GetCountries` method of the `CountryRepository` (code file `Templates[WPF|UWP]/StyledList.xaml.cs`):

```
public ObservableCollection<Country> Countries { get; } =
  new ObservableCollection<Country>();
```

```
public StyledListBox()
{
  this.InitializeComponent();
  this.DataContext = this;
  var countries = new CountryRepository().GetCountries();
  foreach (var country in countries)
  {
    Countries.Add(country);
  }
}
```

The DataContext is a data binding feature discussed in the next chapter.

Within the XAML code, the ListView named countryList1 is defined. countryList1 just uses the default style. The property ItemsSource is set to the Binding markup extension, which is used by data binding. From the code-behind, you have seen that the binding is done to an array of Country objects. Figure 30-18 shows the default look of the ListView. By default, only the names of the countries returned by the ToString method are displayed in a simple list (code file Templates[WPF|UWP]/StyledList.xaml):

```
<Grid>
  <ListView ItemsSource="{Binding Countries}" Margin="10"
    x:Name="countryList1" />
</Grid>
```

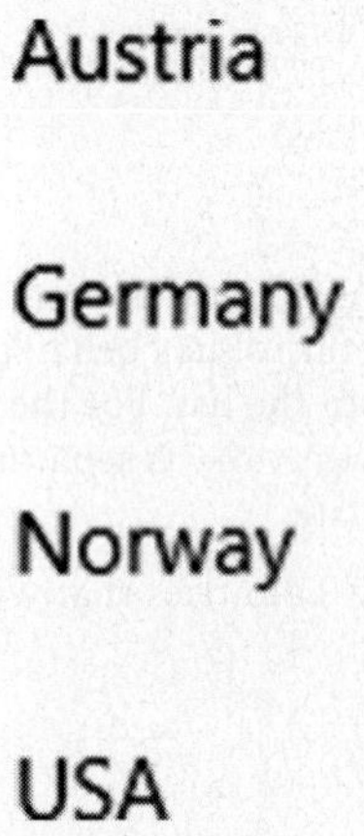

Austria

Germany

Norway

USA

FIGURE 30-18

DataTemplate for ListView Items

Next, you use the DataTemplate created earlier for the ListView control. The DataTemplate can be directly assigned to the ItemTemplate property (code file Templates[WPF|UWP]/StyledList.xaml):

```
<ListView ItemsSource="{Binding Countries}" Margin="10"
  ItemTemplate="{StaticResource CountryDataTemplate}" />
```

With this XAML in place, the items are displayed as shown in Figure 30-19.

Of course it's also possible to define a style that references the data template (code file Templates[WPF|UWP]/Styles/ListTemplates.xaml):

```
<Style x:Key="ListViewStyle1" TargetType="ListView">
  <Setter Property="ItemTemplate"
```

FIGURE 30-19

```
        Value="{StaticResource CountryDataTemplate}" />
    </Style>
```

And use this style from the `ListView` control (code file `Templates[WPF|UWP]/StyledList.xaml`):

```
<ListView ItemsSource="{Binding Countries}" Margin="10"
    Style="{StaticResource ListViewStyle1}" />
```

Item Container Style

The data template defines the look for every item, and there's also a container for every item. The
`ItemContainerStyle` can define how the container for every item looks—for example, what foreground
and background brushes should be used when the item is selected, pressed, and so on. For an easy view of
the boundaries of the container, the `Margin` and `Background` properties are set (`TemplatesUWP/Styles/
ListTemplates.xaml`):

```
<Style x:Key="ListViewItemStyle1" TargetType="ListViewItem">
    <Setter Property="Background" Value="Orange"/>
    <Setter Property="Margin" Value="5" />
    <Setter Property="Template">
      <Setter.Value>
        <ControlTemplate TargetType="ListViewItem">
          <ListViewItemPresenter ContentMargin="{TemplateBinding Padding}"
            FocusBorderBrush=
              "{ThemeResource SystemControlForegroundAltHighBrush}"
            HorizontalContentAlignment=
              "{TemplateBinding HorizontalContentAlignment}"
            PlaceholderBackground=
              "{ThemeResource ListViewItemPlaceholderBackgroundThemeBrush}"
            SelectedPressedBackground=
              "{ThemeResource SystemControlHighlightListAccentHighBrush}"
```

```
                    SelectedForeground=
                      "{ThemeResource SystemControlHighlightAltBaseHighBrush}"
                    SelectedBackground=
                      "{ThemeResource SystemControlHighlightListAccentLowBrush}"
                    VerticalContentAlignment=
                      "{TemplateBinding VerticalContentAlignment}"/>
              </ControlTemplate>
            </Setter.Value>
          </Setter>
        </Style>
```

With WPF, a `ListViewItemPresenter` is not available, but you can use a ContentPresenter as shown in the following code snippet (code file `TemplatesWPF/Styles/ListTemplates.xaml`):

```xml
<Style x:Key="ListViewItemStyle1" TargetType="{x:Type ListViewItem}">
  <Setter Property="Template">
    <Setter.Value>
      <ControlTemplate TargetType="{x:Type ListViewItem}">
        <Grid Margin="8" Background="Orange">
          <ContentPresenter />
        </Grid>
      </ControlTemplate>
    </Setter.Value>
  </Setter>
</Style>
```

The style is associated with the `ItemContainerStyle` property of the `ListView`. The result of this style is shown in Figure 30-20. This figure gives a good view of the boundaries of the items container (code file `Templates[WPF|UWP]/StyledList.xaml`):

```xml
<ListView ItemsSource="{Binding Countries}" Margin="10"
    ItemContainerStyle="{StaticResource ListViewItemStyle1}"
    Style="{StaticResource ListViewStyle1}" MaxWidth="180" />
```

FIGURE 30-20

ANIMATIONS

Using animations, you can make a smooth transition between images by using moving elements, color changes, transforms, and so on. XAML makes it easy to create animations. You can animate the value of any dependency property. Different animation classes exist to animate the values of different properties, depending on their type.

The most important element of an animation is the timeline. This element defines how a value changes over time. Different kinds of timelines are available for changing different types of values. The base class for all timelines is `Timeline`. To animate a property of type `double`, you can use the class `DoubleAnimation`. The `Int32Animation` is the animation class for `int` values. You use `PointAnimation` to animate points and `ColorAnimation` to animate colors.

You can combine multiple timelines by using the `Storyboard` class. The `Storyboard` class itself is derived from the base class `TimelineGroup`, which derives from `Timeline`.

> **NOTE** *The namespace for animation classes is with WPF* `System.Windows.Media` `.Animation` *and with UWP apps* `Windows.UI.Xaml.Media.Animation`.

Timeline

A `Timeline` defines how a value changes over time. The following example animates the size of an ellipse. In the code that follows, `DoubleAnimation` timelines change scaling and translation of an ellipse; `ColorAnimation` changes the color of the fill brush. The `Triggers` property of the `Ellipse` class is set to an `EventTrigger`. The event trigger is fired when the ellipse is loaded. `BeginStoryboard` is a trigger action that begins the storyboard. With the storyboard, a `DoubleAnimation` element is used to animate the `ScaleX`, `ScaleY`, `TranslateX`, and `TranslateY` properties of the `CompositeTransform` class. The animation changes the horizontal scale to 5 and the vertical scale to 3 within ten seconds (code file `AnimationUWP/SimpleAnimation.xaml`):

```xml
<Ellipse x:Name="ellipse1" Width="100" Height="40"
         HorizontalAlignment="Left" VerticalAlignment="Top">
  <Ellipse.Fill>
    <SolidColorBrush Color="Green" />
  </Ellipse.Fill>
  <Ellipse.RenderTransform>
    <CompositeTransform ScaleX="1" ScaleY="1" TranslateX="0" TranslateY="0" />
  </Ellipse.RenderTransform>
  <Ellipse.Triggers>
    <EventTrigger>
      <BeginStoryboard>
        <Storyboard x:Name="MoveResizeStoryboard">
          <DoubleAnimation Duration="0:0:10" To="5"
            Storyboard.TargetName="ellipse1"
            Storyboard.TargetProperty=
              "(UIElement.RenderTransform).(CompositeTransform.ScaleX)" />
          <DoubleAnimation Duration="0:0:10" To="3"
            Storyboard.TargetName="ellipse1"
            Storyboard.TargetProperty=
              "(UIElement.RenderTransform).(CompositeTransform.ScaleY)" />
          <DoubleAnimation Duration="0:0:10" To="400"
            Storyboard.TargetName="ellipse1"
            Storyboard.TargetProperty=
              "(UIElement.RenderTransform).(CompositeTransform.TranslateX)" />
          <DoubleAnimation Duration="0:0:10" To="200"
            Storyboard.TargetName="ellipse1"
            Storyboard.TargetProperty=
```

```
            "(UIElement.RenderTransform).(CompositeTransform.TranslateY)" />
        <ColorAnimation Duration="0:0:10" To="Red"
          Storyboard.TargetName="ellipse1"
          Storyboard.TargetProperty=
            "(Ellipse.Fill).(SolidColorBrush.Color)" />
      </Storyboard>
    </BeginStoryboard>
  </EventTrigger>
</Ellipse.Triggers>
</Ellipse>
```

With WPF, the XAML code is slightly different. Because there isn't a `CompositeTransform` element, the `TransformationGroup` element is used (code file `AnimationWPF/SimpleAnimation.xaml`):

```
<Ellipse.RenderTransform>
  <TransformGroup>
    <ScaleTransform x:Name="scale1" ScaleX="1" ScaleY="1" />
    <TranslateTransform X="0" Y="0" />
  </TransformGroup>
</Ellipse.RenderTransform>
```

Using `ScaleTransform` and `TranslateTransform` results in animations accessing the collection of the `TransformGroup` and accessing the `ScaleX`, `ScaleY`, `X`, and `Y` properties by using an indexer:

```
<DoubleAnimation Duration="0:0:10" To="5" Storyboard.TargetName="ellipse1"
  Storyboard.TargetProperty=
    "(UIElement.RenderTransform).Children[0].(ScaleTransform.ScaleX)" />
<DoubleAnimation Duration="0:0:10" To="3" Storyboard.TargetName="ellipse1"
  Storyboard.TargetProperty=
    "(UIElement.RenderTransform).Children[0].(ScaleTransform.ScaleY)" />
<DoubleAnimation Duration="0:0:10" To="400" Storyboard.TargetName="ellipse1"
  Storyboard.TargetProperty=
    "(UIElement.RenderTransform).Children[1].(TranslateTransform.X)" />
<DoubleAnimation Duration="0:0:10" To="200" Storyboard.TargetName="ellipse1"
  Storyboard.TargetProperty=
    "(UIElement.RenderTransform).Children[1].(TranslateTransform.Y)" />
```

Instead of using the indexer within the transformation group it would also be possible to access the `ScaleTransform` element by its name. The following code simplifies the name of the property:

```
<DoubleAnimation Duration="0:0:10" To="5" Storyboard.TargetName="scale1"
  Storyboard.TargetProperty="(ScaleX)" />
```

With WPF it is also necessary to specify the `RoutedEvent` property with the `EventTrigger`. With Windows Universal apps, the event is automatically fired on loading of the element. This can be explicitly specified with WPF:

```
<EventTrigger RoutedEvent="Loaded">
  <BeginStoryboard>
```

Figures 30-23 and 30-24 show two states from the animated ellipse.

FIGURE 30-23

FIGURE 30-24

Animations are far more than typical window-dressing animation that appears onscreen constantly and immediately. You can add animation to business applications that make the user interface feel more responsive. The look when a cursor moves over a button, or a button is clicked, is defined by animations.

The following table describes what you can do with a timeline.

TIMELINE PROPERTIES	DESCRIPTION
AutoReverse	Use this property to specify whether the value that is animated should return to its original value after the animation.
SpeedRatio	Use this property to transform the speed at which an animation moves. You can define the relation in regard to the parent. The default value is 1; setting the ratio to a smaller value makes the animation move slower; setting the value greater than 1 makes it move faster.
BeginTime	Use this to specify the time span from the start of the trigger event until the moment the animation starts. You can specify days, hours, minutes, seconds, and fractions of seconds. This might not be real time, depending on the speed ratio. For example, if the speed ratio is set to 2, and the beginning time is set to six seconds, the animation will start after three seconds.
Duration	Use this property to specify the length of time for one iteration of the animation.
RepeatBehavior	Assigning a RepeatBehavior struct to the RepeatBehavior property enables you to define how many times or for how long the animation should be repeated.
FillBehavior	This property is important if the parent timeline has a different duration. For example, if the parent timeline is shorter than the duration of the actual animation, setting FillBehavior to Stop means that the actual animation stops. If the parent timeline is longer than the duration of the actual animation, HoldEnd keeps the actual animation active before resetting it to its original value (if AutoReverse is set).

Depending on the type of the Timeline class, more properties may be available. For example, with DoubleAnimation you can specify From and To properties for the start and end of the animation. An alternative is to specify the By property, whereby the animation starts with the current value of the Bound property and is incremented by the value specified by By.

Easing Functions

With the animations you've seen so far, the value changes in a linear way. In real life, a move never happens in a linear way. The move could start slowly and progressively get faster until reaching the highest speed, and then it slows down before reaching the end. When you let a ball fall against the ground, the ball bounces a few times before staying on the ground. Such nonlinear behavior can be created by using easing functions.

Animation classes have an EasingFunction property. This property accepts an object that implements the interface IEasingFunction (with WPF) or derives from the base class EasingFunctionBase (with Windows Universal apps). With this type, an easing function object can define how the value should be animated over time. Several easing functions are available to create a nonlinear animation. Examples include ExponentialEase, which uses an exponential formula for animations; QuadraticEase, CubicEase, QuarticEase, and QuinticEase, with powers of 2, 3, 4, or 5; and PowerEase, with a power level that is configurable. Of special interest are SineEase, which uses a sinusoid curve; BounceEase, which creates a bouncing effect; and ElasticEase, which resembles animation values of a spring oscillating back and forth.

The following code snippet adds the BounceEase function to the DoubleAnimation. Adding different ease functions results in very interesting animation effects:

```
<DoubleAnimation Storyboard.TargetProperty="(Ellipse.Width)"
        Duration="0:0:3" AutoReverse="True"
```

```
                    FillBehavior=" RepeatBehavior="Forever"
                    From="100" To="300">
  <DoubleAnimation.EasingFunction>
    <BounceEase EasingMode="EaseInOut" />
  </DoubleAnimation.EasingFunction>
</DoubleAnimation>
```

To see different easing animations in action, the next sample lets an ellipse move between two small rectangles. The `Rectangle` and `Ellipse` elements are defined within a `Canvas`, and the ellipse defines a `TranslateTransform` transformation to move the ellipse (code file `Animation[WPF|UWP]\EasingFunctions.xaml`):

```
<Canvas Grid.Row="1">
  <Rectangle Fill="Blue" Width="10" Height="200" Canvas.Left="50"
    Canvas.Top="100" />
  <Rectangle Fill="Blue" Width="10" Height="200" Canvas.Left="550"
    Canvas.Top="100" />
  <Ellipse Fill="Red" Width="30" Height="30" Canvas.Left="60" Canvas.Top="185">
    <Ellipse.RenderTransform>
      <TranslateTransform x:Name="translate1" X="0" Y="0" />
    </Ellipse.RenderTransform>
  </Ellipse>
</Canvas>
```

Figure 30-25 shows the rectangles and ellipse.

FIGURE 30-25

The user starts the animation by clicking a button. Before clicking the button, the user can select the easing function from the `ComboBox` `comboEasingFunctions` and an `EasingMode` enumeration value using radio buttons.

```
<StackPanel Orientation="Horizontal">
  <ComboBox x:Name="comboEasingFunctions" Margin="10" />
  <Button Click="OnStartAnimation" Margin="10">Start</Button>
  <Border BorderThickness="1" BorderBrush="Black" Margin="3">
    <StackPanel Orientation="Horizontal">
      <RadioButton x:Name="easingModeIn" GroupName="EasingMode" Content="In" />
      <RadioButton x:Name="easingModeOut" GroupName="EasingMode" Content="Out"
        IsChecked="True" />
      <RadioButton x:Name="easingModeInOut" GroupName="EasingMode"
        Content="InOut" />
    </StackPanel>
  </Border>
</StackPanel>
```

The list of easing functions that are shown in the `ComboBox` and activated with the animation is returned from the `EasingFunctionModels` property of the `EasingFunctionManager`. This manager converts the easing function to an `EasingFunctionModel` for display (code file `Animation[WPF|UWP]\EasingFunctionsManager.cs`):

```
public class EasingFunctionsManager
{
  private static IEnumerable<EasingFunctionBase> s_easingFunctions =
    new List<EasingFunctionBase>()
    {
      new BackEase(),
      new SineEase(),
      new BounceEase(),
```

```
      new CircleEase(),
      new CubicEase(),
      new ElasticEase(),
      new ExponentialEase(),
      new PowerEase(),
      new QuadraticEase(),
      new QuinticEase()
    };

  public IEnumerable<EasingFunctionModel> EasingFunctionModels =>
    s_easingFunctions.Select(f => new EasingFunctionModel(f));
}
```

The class `EasingFunctionModel` defines a `ToString` method that returns the name of the class that defines the easing function. This name is shown in the combo box (code file `Animation[WPF|UWP]\EasingFunctionModel.cs`):

```
public class EasingFunctionModel
{
  public EasingFunctionModel(EasingFunctionBase easingFunction)
  {
    EasingFunction = easingFunction;
  }

  public EasingFunctionBase EasingFunction { get; }

  public override string ToString() => EasingFunction.GetType().Name;
}
```

The `ComboBox` is filled in the constructor of the code-behind file (code file `Animation[WPF|UWP]/EasingFunctions.xaml.cs`):

```
private EasingFunctionsManager _easingFunctions = new EasingFunctionsManager();
private const int AnimationTimeSeconds = 6;

public EasingFunctions()
{
  this.InitializeComponent();
  foreach (var easingFunctionModel in _easingFunctions.EasingFunctionModels)
  {
    comboEasingFunctions.Items.Add(easingFunctionModel);
  }
}
```

From the user interface you can not only select the type of easing function that should be used for the animation but you also can select the easing mode. The base class of all easing functions (`EasingFunctionBase`) defines the `EasingMode` property that can be a value of the `EasingMode` enumeration.

Clicking the button to start the animation invokes the `OnStartAnimation` method. This in turn invokes the `StartAnimation` method. With this method a `Storyboard` containing a `DoubleAnimation` is created programmatically. You've seen similar code earlier using XAML. The animation animates the X property of the `translate1` element. Creating animations programmatically with WPF and UWP apps is slightly different; the code differences are handled by preprocessor commands (code file `Animation[WPF|UWP]\EasingFunctions.xaml.cs`):

```
private void OnStartAnimation(object sender, RoutedEventArgs e)
{
  var easingFunctionModel =
    comboEasingFunctions.SelectedItem as EasingFunctionModel;
  if (easingFunctionModel != null)
  {
    EasingFunctionBase easingFunction = easingFunctionModel.EasingFunction;
    easingFunction.EasingMode = GetEasingMode();
    StartAnimation(easingFunction);
  }
}
```

```
private void StartAnimation(EasingFunctionBase easingFunction)
{
#if WPF
  NameScope.SetNameScope(translate1, new NameScope());
#endif

  var storyboard = new Storyboard();
  var ellipseMove = new DoubleAnimation();
  ellipseMove.EasingFunction = easingFunction;
  ellipseMove.Duration = new
    Duration(TimeSpan.FromSeconds(AnimationTimeSeconds));
  ellipseMove.From = 0;
  ellipseMove.To = 460;
#if WPF
  Storyboard.SetTargetName(ellipseMove, nameof(translate1));
  Storyboard.SetTargetProperty(ellipseMove,
    new PropertyPath(TranslateTransform.XProperty));
#else
  Storyboard.SetTarget(ellipseMove, translate1);
  Storyboard.SetTargetProperty(ellipseMove, "X");
#endif
  // start the animation in 0.5 seconds
  ellipseMove.BeginTime = TimeSpan.FromSeconds(0.5);
  // keep the position after the animation
  ellipseMove.FillBehavior = FillBehavior.HoldEnd;
  storyboard.Children.Add(ellipseMove);
#if WPF
  storyboard.Begin(this);
#else
  storyBoard.Begin();
#endif
}
```

Now you can run the application and see the ellipse move from the left to the right rectangle in different ways—with different easing functions. With some of the easing functions, such as BackEase, BounceEase, or ElasticEase, the difference is obvious. The difference is not as noticeable with some of the other easing functions. To better understand how the easing values behave, a line chart is created that shows a line with the value that is returned by the easing function based on time.

To display the line chart, you create a user control that defines a Canvas element. By default, the x direction goes from left to right and the y direction from top to bottom. To change the y direction to go from bottom to top, you define a transformation (code file Animation[WPF|UWP]/ EasingChartControl.xaml):

```
<Canvas x:Name="canvas1" Width="500" Height="500" Background="Yellow">
  <Canvas.RenderTransform>
    <TransformGroup>
      <ScaleTransform ScaleX="1" ScaleY="-1" />
      <TranslateTransform X="0" Y="500" />
    </TransformGroup>
  </Canvas.RenderTransform>
</Canvas>
```

In the code-behind file, the line chart is drawn using line segments. Line segments were previously discussed using XAML code in this chapter in the section "Geometries Using Segments." Here you see how they can be used from code. The Ease method of the easing function returns a value that is shown in the y axis passing a normalized time value that is shown in the x axis (code file Animation[WPF|UWP]/ EasingChartControl.xaml.cs):

```
private const double SamplingInterval = 0.01;

public void Draw(EasingFunctionBase easingFunction)
```

```
  {
    canvas1.Children.Clear();

    var pathSegments = new PathSegmentCollection();

    for (double i = 0; i < 1; i += _samplingInterval)
    {
      double x = i * canvas1.Width;
      double y = easingFunction.Ease(i) * canvas1.Height;

      var segment = new LineSegment();
      segment.Point = new Point(x, y);

      pathSegments.Add(segment);
    }
    var p = new Path();
    p.Stroke = new SolidColorBrush(Colors.Black);
    p.StrokeThickness = 3;
    var figures = new PathFigureCollection();
    figures.Add(new PathFigure { Segments = pathSegments });
    p.Data = new PathGeometry { Figures = figures };
    canvas1.Children.Add(p);
  }
```

The Draw method of the EasingChartControl is invoked on the start of the animation (code file Animation[WPF|UWP]/EasingFunctions.xaml.cs):

```
private void StartAnimation(EasingFunctionBase easingFunction)
{
  // show the chart
  chartControl.Draw(easingFunction);
  //...
```

When you run the application, you can see in Figure 30-26 what it looks like to use CubicEase and EaseOut. When you select EaseIn, the value changes slower in the beginning of the animation and faster in the end, as shown in Figure 30-27. Figure 30-28 shows what it looks like to use CubicEase with EaseInOut. The chart for BounceEase, BackEase, and ElasticEase is shown in Figures 30-29, 30-30, and 30-31.

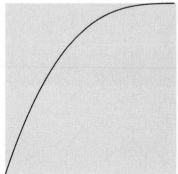

FIGURE 30-26

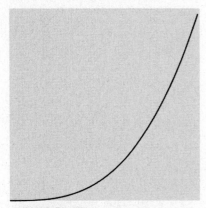

FIGURE 30-27

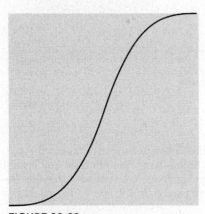

FIGURE 30-28

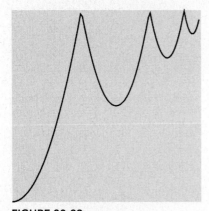

FIGURE 30-29

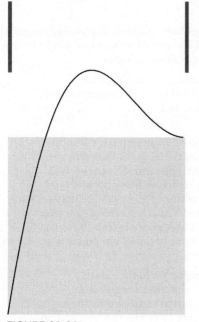

FIGURE 30-30

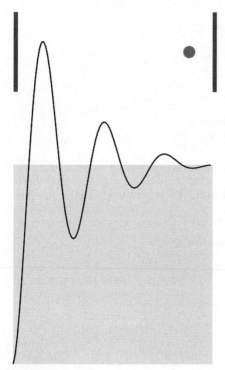

FIGURE 30-31

Keyframe Animations

With ease functions, you've seen how animations can be built in a nonlinear fashion. If you need to specify several values for an animation, you can use *keyframe animations*. Like normal animations, keyframe animations are various animation types that exist to animate properties of different types.

DoubleAnimationUsingKeyFrames is the keyframe animation for double types. Other keyframe animation types are Int32AnimationUsingKeyFrames, PointAnimationUsingKeyFrames, ColorAnimationUsingKeyFrames, SizeAnimationUsingKeyFrames, and ObjectAnimationUsingKeyFrames.

The following example XAML code animates the position of an ellipse by animating the X and Y values of a TranslateTransform element. The animation starts when the ellipse is loaded by defining an EventTrigger to RoutedEvent Ellipse.Loaded. The event trigger starts a Storyboard with the BeginStoryboard element. The Storyboard contains two keyframe animations of type DoubleAnimationUsingKeyFrame. A keyframe animation consists of frame elements. The first keyframe animation uses a LinearKeyFrame, a DiscreteDoubleKeyFrame, and a SplineDoubleKeyFrame; the second animation is an EasingDoubleKeyFrame. The LinearDoubleKeyFrame makes a linear change of the value. The KeyTime property defines when in the animation the value of the Value property should be reached.

Here, the LinearDoubleKeyFrame has three seconds to move the property X to the value 30. DiscreteDoubleKeyFrame makes an immediate change to the new value after four seconds. SplineDoubleKeyFrame uses a Bézier curve whereby two control points are specified by the KeySpline property. EasingDoubleKeyFrame is a frame class that supports setting an easing function such as BounceEase to control the animation value (code file AnimationUWP/KeyFrameAnimation.xaml):

```xaml
<Canvas>
  <Ellipse Fill="Red" Canvas.Left="20" Canvas.Top="20" Width="25" Height="25">
    <Ellipse.RenderTransform>
      <TranslateTransform X="50" Y="50" x:Name="ellipseMove" />
    </Ellipse.RenderTransform>
    <Ellipse.Triggers>
      <EventTrigger>
        <BeginStoryboard>
          <Storyboard>
            <DoubleAnimationUsingKeyFrames Storyboard.TargetProperty="X"
                Storyboard.TargetName="ellipseMove">
              <LinearDoubleKeyFrame KeyTime="0:0:2" Value="30" />
              <DiscreteDoubleKeyFrame KeyTime="0:0:4" Value="80" />
              <SplineDoubleKeyFrame KeySpline="0.5,0.0 0.9,0.0"
                  KeyTime="0:0:10" Value="300" />
              <LinearDoubleKeyFrame KeyTime="0:0:20" Value="150" />
            </DoubleAnimationUsingKeyFrames>
            <DoubleAnimationUsingKeyFrames Storyboard.TargetProperty="Y"
                Storyboard.TargetName="ellipseMove">
              <SplineDoubleKeyFrame KeySpline="0.5,0.0 0.9,0.0"
                  KeyTime="0:0:2" Value="50" />
              <EasingDoubleKeyFrame KeyTime="0:0:20" Value="300">
                <EasingDoubleKeyFrame.EasingFunction>
                  <BounceEase />
                </EasingDoubleKeyFrame.EasingFunction>
              </EasingDoubleKeyFrame>
            </DoubleAnimationUsingKeyFrames>
          </Storyboard>
        </BeginStoryboard>
      </EventTrigger>
    </Ellipse.Triggers>
  </Ellipse>
</Canvas>
```

With WPF, the same keyframe-animation can be used. The only difference with the UWP file is that there's no default event with the EventTrigger. With WPF the `RoutedEvent` attribute needs to be added, otherwise the XAML code is the same (code file `AnimationWPF/KeyFrameAnimation.xaml`):

```
<EventTrigger RoutedEvent="Ellipse.Loaded">
  <!-- storyboard -->
</EventTrigger>
```

Transitions (UWP Apps)

For making it easier for you to create animated user interfaces, UWP apps define transitions. Transitions make it easier to create compelling apps without the need to think about what makes a cool animation. Transitions predefine animations for adding, removing, and rearranging items in a list; opening panels; changing the content of content controls; and more.

The following sample demonstrates several transitions to show them in the left side of a user control versus the right side, and it shows similar elements without transitions, which helps you see the differences. Of course, you need to start the application to see the difference, as it is hard to demonstrate this in a printed book.

Reposition Transition

The first example makes use of the `RepositionThemeTransition` within the `Transitions` property of a `Button` element. A transition always needs to be defined within a `TransitionCollection` because such collections are never created automatically, and there's a misleading runtime error in case you don't use the `TransitionCollection`. The second button doesn't use a transition (code file `TransitionsUWP/RepositionUserControl.xaml`):

```
<Button Grid.Row="1" Click="OnReposition" Content="Reposition"
  x:Name="buttonReposition" Margin="10">
  <Button.Transitions>
    <TransitionCollection>
      <RepositionThemeTransition />
    </TransitionCollection>
  </Button.Transitions>
</Button>
<Button Grid.Row="1" Grid.Column="1" Click="OnReset" Content="Reset"
  x:Name="button2" Margin="10" />
```

The `RepositionThemeTransition` is a transition when a control changes its position. In the code-behind file, when the user clicks the button, the `Margin` property is changed, which also changes the position of the button.

```
private void OnReposition(object sender, RoutedEventArgs e)
{
  buttonReposition.Margin = new Thickness(100);
  button2.Margin = new Thickness(100);
}

private void OnReset(object sender, RoutedEventArgs e)
{
  buttonReposition.Margin = new Thickness(10);
  button2.Margin = new Thickness(10);
}
```

Pane Transition

The `PopupThemeTransition` and `PaneThemeTransition` are shown in the next user control. Here, the transitions are defined with the `ChildTransitions` property of the `Popup` control (code file `TransitionsUWP\PaneTransitionUserControl.xaml`):

```
<StackPanel Orientation="Horizontal" Grid.Row="2">
  <Popup  x:Name="popup1" Width="200" Height="90" Margin="60">
```

```
              <Border  Background="Red" Width="100" Height="60">
              </Border>
              <Popup.ChildTransitions>
                <TransitionCollection>
                  <PopupThemeTransition />
                </TransitionCollection>
              </Popup.ChildTransitions>
            </Popup>
            <Popup x:Name="popup2" Width="200" Height="90" Margin="60">
              <Border  Background="Red" Width="100" Height="60">
              </Border>
              <Popup.ChildTransitions>
                <TransitionCollection>
                  <PaneThemeTransition />
                </TransitionCollection>
              </Popup.ChildTransitions>
            </Popup>
            <Popup x:Name="popup3" Margin="60" Width="200" Height="90">
              <Border  Background="Green"  Width="100" Height="60">
              </Border>
            </Popup>
          </StackPanel>
```

The code-behind file opens and closes the Popup controls by setting the IsOpen property. This in turn starts the transition (code file TransitionsUWP\PaneTransitionUserControl.xaml):

```
private void OnShow(object sender, RoutedEventArgs e)
{
  popup1.IsOpen = true;
  popup2.IsOpen = true;
  popup3.IsOpen = true;
}

private void OnHide(object sender, RoutedEventArgs e)
{
  popup1.IsOpen = false;
  popup2.IsOpen = false;
  popup3.IsOpen = false;
}
```

When you run the application, you can see that the PopupThemeTransition looks good for opening Popup and Flyout controls. The PaneThemeTransition opens the popup slowly from the right side. This transition can also be configured to open from other sides by setting properties, and thus is best for panels, such as the settings bar, that move in from a side.

Transitions for Items

Adding and removing items from an items control also defines a transition. The following ItemsControl makes use of the EntranceThemeTransition and RepositionThemeTransition. The EntranceThemeTransition is used when an item is added to the collection; the RepositionThemeTransition is used when items are re-arranged—for example, by removing an item from the list (code file TransitionsUWP\ListItemsUserControl.xaml):

```
<ItemsControl Grid.Row="1" x:Name="list1">
  <ItemsControl.ItemContainerTransitions>
    <TransitionCollection>
      <EntranceThemeTransition />
      <RepositionThemeTransition  />
    </TransitionCollection>
  </ItemsControl.ItemContainerTransitions>
</ItemsControl>
```

```
<ItemsControl Grid.Row="1" Grid.Column="1" x:Name="list2" />
```

In the code-behind file, `Rectangle` objects are added and removed from the list control. As one of the `ItemsControl` objects doesn't have a transition associated, you can easily the difference in behavior when you run the application (code file `TransitionsUWP\ListItemsUserControl.xaml.cs`):

```
private void OnAdd(object sender, RoutedEventArgs e)
{
  list1.Items.Add(CreateRectangle());
  list2.Items.Add(CreateRectangle());
}

private Rectangle CreateRectangle() =>
  new Rectangle
  {
    Width = 90,
    Height = 40,
      Margin = new Thickness(5),
        Fill = new SolidColorBrush { Color = Colors.Blue }
    };

private void OnRemove(object sender, RoutedEventArgs e)
{
  if (list1.Items.Count > 0)
  {
    list1.Items.RemoveAt(0);
    list2.Items.RemoveAt(0);
  }
}
```

> **NOTE** *With these transitions, you get an idea of how they reduce the work needed to animate the user interface. Be sure to check out more transitions available with UWP apps. You can see all the transitions by checking the derived classes from Transition in the MSDN documentation.*

VISUAL STATE MANAGER

Earlier in this chapter in the section "Control Templates," you saw how to create control templates to customize the look of controls. Something was missing there. With the default template of a button, the button reacts to mouse moves and clicks and looks differently when the mouse moves over the button or the button is clicked. This look change is handled with the help of visual states and animations, controlled by the visual state manager.

This section looks at changing the button style to react to mouse moves and clicks, but it also describes how to create custom states to deal with changes of a complete page when several controls should switch to the disabled state—for example, when some background processing occurs.

With an XAML element, visual states, state groups, and states can be defined that specify specific animations for a state. State groups exist to allow having multiple states at once. For one group, only one state is allowed at one time. However, another state of another group can be active at the same time. Examples for this are the states and state groups with a WPF button. The WPF `Button` control defines the state groups `CommonStates`, `FocusStates`, and `ValidationStates`. States defined with `FocusStates` are `Focused` and `Unfocused`; states defined with the group `ValidationStates` are `Valid`, `InvalidFocused`, and `InvalidUnfocused`. The `CommonStates` group defines the states `Normal`, `MouseOver`, `Pressed`, and `Disabled`. With these options, multiple states can be active at the same time, but there is always only one state active within a state group. For example, a button can be in focus and valid while the mouse moves over it. It can also be unfocused and valid and be in the normal state. With UWP apps the `Button` control only defines states of the `CommonStates` group. Also, WPF defines the `MouseOver` state, but with UWP this state is `PointerOver`. You can also define custom states and state groups.

Let's get into concrete examples.

Predefined States with Control Templates

Let's take the custom control template created earlier to style the `Button` control and enhance it by using visual states. An easy way to do this is by using Microsoft Blend for Visual Studio. Figure 30-32 shows the States Window that is shown when you are selecting the control template. Here you can see available states of the control and record changes based on these states.

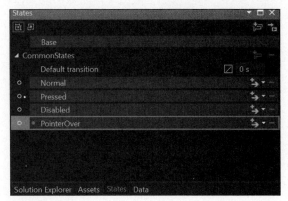

FIGURE 30-32

The button template from before is changed to define visual states for the states `Pressed`, `Disabled`, and `PointerOver`. Within the states, a `Storyboard` defines a `ColorAnimation` to change the color of the `Fill` property of an ellipse (code file `VisualStatesUWP/MainPage.xaml`):

```xaml
<Style x:Key="RoundedGelButton" TargetType="Button">
  <Setter Property="Width" Value="100" />
  <Setter Property="Height" Value="100" />
  <Setter Property="Foreground" Value="White" />
  <Setter Property="Template">
    <Setter.Value>
      <ControlTemplate TargetType="Button">
        <Grid>
          <VisualStateManager.VisualStateGroups>
            <VisualStateGroup x:Name="CommonStates">
              <VisualState x:Name="Normal"/>
              <VisualState x:Name="Pressed">
                <Storyboard>
                  <ColorAnimation Duration="0" To="#FFC8CE11"
                    Storyboard.TargetProperty=
                      "(Shape.Fill).(SolidColorBrush.Color)"
                    Storyboard.TargetName=
                      "GelBackground" />
                </Storyboard>
              </VisualState>
              <VisualState x:Name="Disabled">
                <Storyboard>
                  <ColorAnimation Duration="0" To="#FF606066"
                    Storyboard.TargetProperty=
                      "(Shape.Fill).(SolidColorBrush.Color)"
```

```
                         Storyboard.TargetName="GelBackground" />
                    </Storyboard>
                  </VisualState>
                  <VisualState x:Name="PointerOver">
                    <Storyboard>
                      <ColorAnimation Duration="0" To="#FF0F9D3A"
                        Storyboard.TargetProperty=
                          "(Shape.Fill).(SolidColorBrush.Color)"
                        Storyboard.TargetName="GelBackground" />
                    </Storyboard>
                  </VisualState>
                </VisualStateGroup>
              </VisualStateManager.VisualStateGroups>
              <Ellipse x:Name="GelBackground" StrokeThickness="0.5" Fill="Black">
                <Ellipse.Stroke>
                  <LinearGradientBrush StartPoint="0,0" EndPoint="0,1">
                    <GradientStop Offset="0" Color="#ff7e7e7e" />
                    <GradientStop Offset="1" Color="Black" />
                  </LinearGradientBrush>
                </Ellipse.Stroke>
              </Ellipse>
              <Ellipse Margin="15,5,15,50">
                <Ellipse.Fill>
                  <LinearGradientBrush StartPoint="0,0" EndPoint="0,1">
                    <GradientStop Offset="0" Color="#aaffffff" />
                    <GradientStop Offset="1" Color="Transparent" />
                  </LinearGradientBrush>
                </Ellipse.Fill>
              </Ellipse>
              <ContentPresenter x:Name="GelButtonContent"
                VerticalAlignment="Center"
                HorizontalAlignment="Center"
                Content="{TemplateBinding Content}" />
            </Grid>
          </ControlTemplate>
        </Setter.Value>
      </Setter>
    </Style>
```

Now when you run the application, you can see the color changes based on moving and clicking the mouse.

Defining Custom States

You can define custom states by using the `VisualStateManager`, defining custom state groups using `VisualStateGroup` and states with `VisualState`. The following code snippet creates the `Enabled` and `Disabled` states within the `CustomStates` group. The visual states are defined within the `Grid` of the main window. On changing the state, the `IsEnabled` property of a `Button` element is changed using a `DiscreteObjectKeyFrame` animation in no time (code file `VisualStatesUWP/MainPage.xaml`):

```
<VisualStateManager.VisualStateGroups>
  <VisualStateGroup x:Name="CustomStates">
    <VisualState x:Name="Enabled"/>
    <VisualState x:Name="Disabled">
      <Storyboard>
        <ObjectAnimationUsingKeyFrames
          Storyboard.TargetProperty="(Control.IsEnabled)"
          Storyboard.TargetName="button1">
          <DiscreteObjectKeyFrame KeyTime="0">
            <DiscreteObjectKeyFrame.Value>
              <x:Boolean>False</x:Boolean>
            </DiscreteObjectKeyFrame.Value>
```

```
        </DiscreteObjectKeyFrame>
      </ObjectAnimationUsingKeyFrames>
      <ObjectAnimationUsingKeyFrames
        Storyboard.TargetProperty="(Control.IsEnabled)"
        Storyboard.TargetName="button2">
        <DiscreteObjectKeyFrame KeyTime="0">
          <DiscreteObjectKeyFrame.Value>
            <x:Boolean>False</x:Boolean>
          </DiscreteObjectKeyFrame.Value>
        </DiscreteObjectKeyFrame>
      </ObjectAnimationUsingKeyFrames>
    </Storyboard>
  </VisualState>
 </VisualStateGroup>
</VisualStateManager.VisualStateGroups>
```

Setting Custom States

Now the states need to be set. You can do this easily by invoking the `GoToState` method of the `VisualStateManager` class. In the code-behind file, the `OnEnable` and `OnDisable` methods are `Click` event handlers for two buttons in the page (code file `VisualStatesUWP/MainPage.xaml.cs`):

```csharp
private void OnEnable(object sender, RoutedEventArgs e)
{
  VisualStateManager.GoToState(this, "Enabled", useTransitions: true);
}

private void OnDisable(object sender, RoutedEventArgs e)
{
  VisualStateManager.GoToState(this, "Disabled", useTransitions: true);
}
```

In a real application, you can change the state in a similar manner—for example, when a network call is invoked and the user should not act on some of the controls within the page. The user should still be allowed to click a cancellation button. By changing the state, you can also show progress information.

SUMMARY

In this chapter you have taken a tour through many of the features of styling WPF and UWP apps. With XAML it is easy to separate the work of developers and designers. All UI features can be created with XAML, and the functionality can be created by using code-behind.

You have seen many shapes and geometry elements, which are the basis for all other controls that you'll see in the next chapters. Vector-based graphics enable XAML elements to be scaled, sheared, and rotated.

Different kinds of brushes are available for painting the background and foreground of elements. You can use not only solid brushes and linear or radial gradient brushes but also visual brushes that enable you to include reflections or show videos.

Styling and templates enable you to customize the look of controls; with the visual state manager you can change properties of XAML elements dynamically. You can easily create animations by animating a property value from an XAML control. The next chapter continues with XAML-based apps, covering the MVVM pattern and data binding, commands, and several more features.

31

Patterns with XAML Apps

WHAT'S IN THIS CHAPTER?

- ➤ Sharing Code
- ➤ Creating Models
- ➤ Creating Repositories
- ➤ Creating ViewModels
- ➤ Locators
- ➤ Dependency Injection
- ➤ Messaging between ViewModels
- ➤ Using an IoC Container

WROX.COM CODE DOWNLOADS FOR THIS CHAPTER

The wrox.com code downloads for this chapter are found at www.wrox.com/go/professionalcsharp6 on the Download Code tab. The code for this chapter is divided into the following major examples:

- ➤ Books Desktop App (WPF)
- ➤ Books Universal App (UWP)

WHY MVVM?

Technologies and frameworks change. I created the first version of my company website (http://www.cninnovation.com) with ASP.NET Web Forms. When ASP.NET MVC came along, I tried it out to migrate a feature of my site to MVC. The progress was a lot faster than I expected. Within one day I transformed the complete site to MVC. The site uses SQL Server, integrates RSS feeds, and shows trainings and books. Information about the trainings and books is coming from the SQL Server database. The fast migration to ASP.NET MVC was only possible because I had separation of concerns from the beginning; I had created separate layers for the data access and business logic. With ASP.NET Web Forms it would have been possible to directly use data source and data controls within the ASPX page. Separating the data access and business logic took more time in the beginning, but it turned out to be a huge advantage, as it allows for unit tests and reuse. Because I had separated things this way, moving to another technology was a breeze.

With regard to Windows applications, technology changes fast as well. For many years, Windows Forms was the technology of choice for wrapping native Windows controls to create desktop applications. Next followed Windows Presentation Foundation (WPF), in which the user interface is defined using XML for Applications Markup Language (XAML). Silverlight offered a lightweight framework for XAML-based applications that run within the browser. Windows Store apps followed with Windows 8, changing to Universal Windows apps with Windows 8.1 for apps running both on the PC and the Windows phone. With Windows 8.1 and Visual Studio 2013, three projects with shared code have been created to support both the PC and the phone. This changed with Visual Studio 2015, Windows 10, and the Universal Windows Platform (UWP). You can have one project that can support the PC, the phone, Xbox One, Windows IoT, large screens with the Surface Hub, and even Microsoft's HoloLens.

One project to support all Windows 10 platforms might not fit your needs. Can you write a program that supports Windows 10 only? Some of your customers might still be running Windows 7. In this case, WPF is the answer, but it doesn't support the phone and other Windows 10 devices. What about supporting Android and iOS? You can use Xamarin to create C# and .NET code here as well, but it's different.

The goal should be to reuse as much code as possible, to support the platforms needed, and to have an easy switch from one technology to another. These goals—with many organizations where administration and development joins as DevOps to bring new features and bug fixes in a fast pace to the user—require automated tests. Unit testing is a must that needs to be supported by the application architecture.

> **NOTE** *Unit testing is covered in Chapter 19, "Testing."*

With XAML-based applications, the *Model-View-ViewModel* (MVVM) design pattern is favored for separating the view from functionality. This design pattern was invented by John Gossman of the Expression Blend team as a better fit to XAML with advancements to the Model-View-Controller (MVC) and Model-View-Presenter (MVP) patterns because it uses data binding, a number-one feature of XAML.

With XAML-based applications, the XAML file and code-behind file are tightly coupled to each other. This makes it hard to reuse the code-behind and also hard to do unit testing. To solve this issue, the MVVM pattern allows for a better separation of the code from the user interface.

In principle, the MVVM pattern is not that hard to understand. However, when you're creating applications based on the MVVM pattern, you need to pay attention to a lot more needs: several patterns come into play for making applications work and making reuse possible, including dependency injection mechanisms for being independent of the implementation and communication between view models.

All this is covered in this chapter, and with this information you can not only use the same code with Windows apps and Windows desktop applications, but you can also use it for iOS and Android with the help of Xamarin. This chapter gives you a sample app that covers all the different aspects and patterns needed for a good separation to support different technologies.

DEFINING THE MVVM PATTERN

First, let's have a look at the MVC design pattern that is one of the origins of the MVVM pattern. The *Model-View-Controller* (MVC) pattern separates the model, the view, and the controller (see Figure 31-1). The model defines the data that is shown in the view as well as business rules about how the data can be changed and manipulated. The controller is the manager between the model and the view, updates the model, and sends data for display to the view. When a user request comes in, the controller takes action, uses the model, and updates the view.

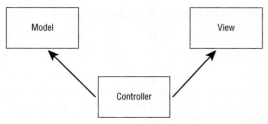

FIGURE 31-1

> **NOTE** *The MVC pattern is heavily used with ASP.NET MVC, which is covered in Chapter 41, "ASP.NET MVC."*

With the *Model-View-Presenter* (MVP) pattern (see Figure 31-2), the user interacts with the view. The presenter contains all the business logic for the view. The presenter can be decoupled from the view by using an interface to the view as contract. This allows easily changing the view implementation for unit tests. With MVP, the view and model are completely shielded from each other.

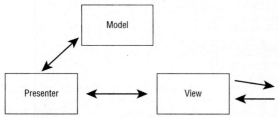

FIGURE 31-2

The main pattern used with XAML-based applications is the *Model-View-ViewModel* pattern (MVVM) (see Figure 31-3). This pattern takes advantage of the data-binding capabilities with XAML. With MVVM, the user interacts with the view. The view uses data binding to access information from the view model and invokes commands in the view model that are bound in the view as well. The view model doesn't have a direct dependency to the view. The view model itself uses the model to access data and gets change information from the model as well.

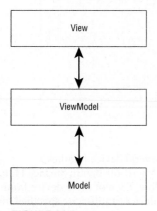

FIGURE 31-3

In the following sections of this chapter you see how to use this architecture with the application to create views, view models, models, and other patterns that are needed.

SHARING CODE

Before creating the sample solution and starting to create a model, we need to take a step back and have a look at different options for how to share code between different platforms. This section covers different options to address the different platforms you need to support and the APIs you need.

Using API Contracts with the Universal Windows Platform

The Universal Windows Platform defines an API that is available with all Windows 10 devices. However, this API can change with newer versions. With the Application settings in the Project Properties (see Figure 31-4) you can define the *target version* of your application (this is the version that you build for) and the *minimum version* that is required on the system. The versions of all Software Developer Kits (SDKs) you select need to be installed on your system, so you can verify what APIs are available. For using features of the target version that are not available within the minimum version, you need to programmatically check whether the device supports the specific feature you need, before using that API.

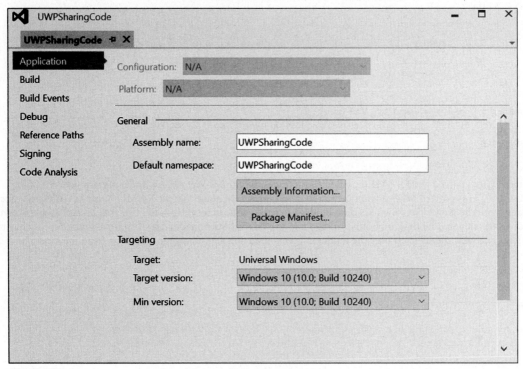

FIGURE 31-4

With the UWP, you can support different device families. The UWP defines several device families: Universal, Desktop (PC), Mobile (tablet, phablet, phone), IoT (Raspberry Pi, Microsoft Band), Surface Hub, Holographic (HoloLens), and Xbox. Over time, more device families will follow. Each of these device families offers APIs that are available only for this family of devices. The APIs of device families are specified via an API contract. Each device family can offer multiple API contracts.

You can use features specific to device families, but you can still create one binary image that runs on all. Typically, your application will not support all the device families, but it might support a few of them. To support specific device families and use those families' APIs, you can add an *Extension SDK* from Solution Explorer; select References ⇨ Add Reference and then select Universal Windows ⇨ Extensions (see Figure 31-5). There you can see your installed SDKs and select the ones you need.

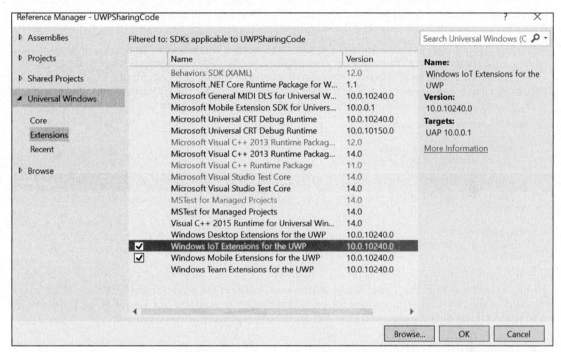

FIGURE 31-5

After selecting the Extension SDK, you can use the API from the code after verifying whether the API contract is available. The `ApiInformation` class (namespace `Windows.Foundation.Metadata`) defines the `IsApiContractPresent` method where you can check whether a specific API contract with a specific major and minor version is available. The following code snippet asks for the `Windows.Phone.PhoneContract`, major version 1. If this contract is available, the `VibrationDevice` can be used:

```
if (ApiInformation.IsApiContractPresent("Windows.Phone.PhoneContract", 1))
{
  VibrationDevice vibration = VibrationDevice.GetDefault();
  vibration.Vibrate(TimeSpan.FromSeconds(1));
}
```

You might be afraid to get convoluted code that checks all over the place using the checks for the API contracts. In a case where you're targeting just a single device family, it's not necessary to check to see whether the API is present. In the previous sample, if the application is only targeted for the phone, the API check is not necessary. In a case where you're targeting multiple device platforms, you only have to check for the device-specific APIs you're calling. You can write useful apps spanning multiple device families just by using the Universal API. In a case where you're supporting multiple device families with a lot of device-specific API calls, I propose you avoid using the `ApiInformation` and instead use dependency injection, which is covered later in this chapter in the section "Services and Dependency Injection."

Working with Shared Projects

Using the same binary with API contracts is possible only with the Universal Windows Platform. This is not an option if you need to share code, for example, between Windows desktop applications with WPF and UWP apps, or between Xamarin.Forms apps and UWP apps. When you create these project types where you can't use the same binary, you can use the Shared Project template with Visual Studio 2015.

The *Shared Project* template with Visual Studio creates a project that doesn't create a binary—no assembly is built. Instead, code is shared between all projects that reference this shared project. You compile the code within each project that references the shared project.

When you create a class as shown in the following code snippet, this class can be used in all projects that reference the shared project. You can even use platform-specific code using preprocessor directives. The Visual Studio 2015 Universal Windows App template sets the conditional compilation symbol WINDOWS_ UWP, so you can use this symbol for code that should only compile for the Universal Windows Platform. For WPF, you add WPF to the conditional compilation symbols with a WPF project.

```
public partial class Demo
{
  public int Id { get; set; }
  public string Title { get; set; }

#if WPF
  public string WPFOnly { get; set; }
#endif

#if WINDOWS_UWP
  public string WinAppOnly {get; set; }
#endif
}
```

Editing shared code with the Visual Studio editor, you can select the project name in the upper-left bar, and the parts of the code that are not active for the actual project are dimmed (see Figure 31-6). When you're editing the file, IntelliSense also offers the API for the corresponding selected project.

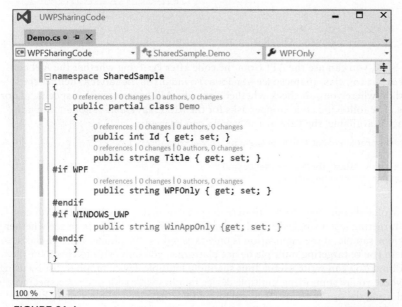

FIGURE 31-6

Instead of using the preprocessor directives, you can also maintain differing parts of the class in the WPF or Universal Windows Platform projects. There was a good reason to declare the class `partial`.

> **NOTE** *The C#* `partial` *keyword is explained in Chapter 3, "Objects and Types."*

When you define the same class name with the same namespace in the WPF project, you can extend the shared class. It is also possible to use a base class (if the shared project doesn't define a base class):

```
public class MyBase
{
  // etc.
}
public partial class Demo: MyBase
{
  public string WPFTitle => $"WPF{Title}";
}
```

Working with Portable Libraries

There's another option for sharing code: shared libraries. If all the technologies can use .NET Core, this is an easy task: Just create a .NET Core library, and you can share it between different platforms. If the technologies you need to support can make use of .NET Core NuGet packages, it's best to use these. If that's not the case, you can use Portable Libraries.

> **NOTE** *Creating NuGet packages is discussed in Chapter 17, "Visual Studio 2015."*

With portable libraries, Microsoft maintains a huge list of which API is supported by what platform. When you're creating a portable library, you see the dialog to configure what target platforms you need to support. Figure 31-7 shows a selection for .NET Framework 4.6, Windows Universal 10.0, Xamarin.Android, and Xamarin.iOS. With the selection, you're limited to the APIs that are available with all selected target platforms. With the current selection, you can read the note in the dialog that .NET Framework 4.5, Windows 8, and Xamarion.iOS (Classic) are automatically targeted as well because these platforms do not have any APIs that are not already in the combined intersect of the selection.

The big disadvantage of the portable library is that you can't have any code that is available only with specific platforms. You can use only what's available everywhere, with all the selected target platforms. As a way around this, you can use portable libraries to define code for contracts and implement the contracts with platform-specific libraries where needed. To use the code from the platform-specific libraries with libraries that are not platform specific, you can use dependency injection. How to do this is part of the bigger sample in this chapter, which is covered in the "View Models" section.

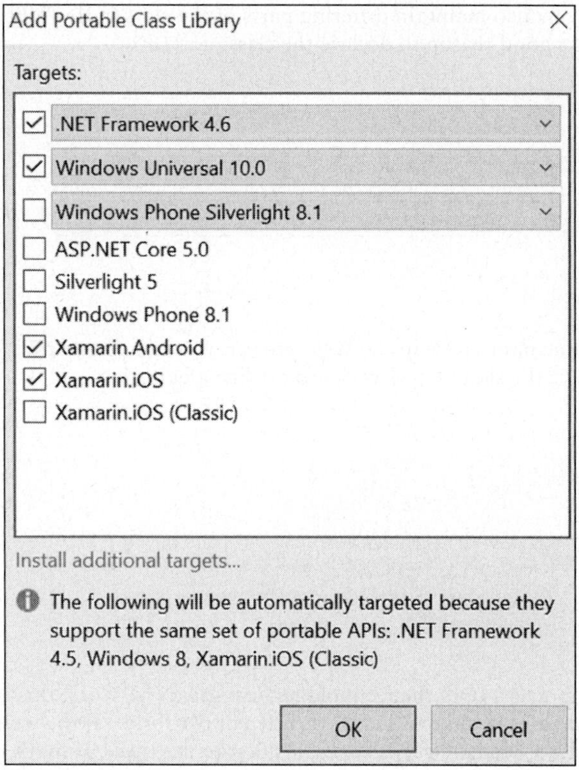

FIGURE 31-7

SAMPLE SOLUTION

The sample solution consists of a WPF and a Universal Windows Platform app for showing and editing a list of books. For this, the solution uses these projects:

➤ **BooksDesktopApp**—A WPF project for the UI of the desktop application with .NET Framework 4.6

➤ **BooksUniversalApp**—A UWP app project for the UI of a modern app

➤ **Framework**—A portable library containing classes that are useful for all XAML-based applications

➤ **ViewModels**—A portable library containing view models for both WPF and UWP

➤ **Services**—A portable library containing services used by the view models

➤ **Models**—A portable library containing shared models

➤ **Repositories**—A portable library that returns and updates items

➤ **Contracts**—A portable library for contract interfaces used with dependency injection

The portable libraries are configured with the targets .NET Framework 4.6 and Windows Universal 10.0.

Figure 31-8 shows the projects with their dependencies. The Framework and Contracts are needed from all other projects. Have a look at the ViewModels project; this will call the services, but it doesn't have a dependency on the services—just the contracts that are implemented by the services.

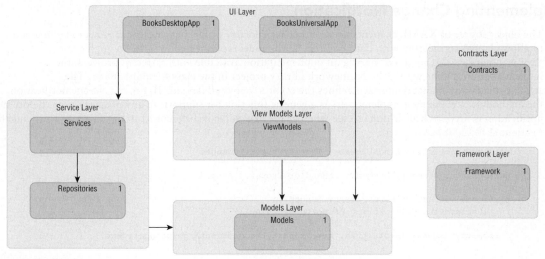

FIGURE 31-8

The user interface of the application will have two views: one view to show as a list of books and one view to show book details. When you select a book from the list, the detail is shown. It's also possible to add and edit books.

MODELS

Let's start with the Models library to define the `Book` type. This is the type that will be shown and edited in the UI. To support data binding, the properties where values are updated from the user interface need a change notification implementation. The `BookId` property is only shown but not changed, so change notification is not needed with this property. The method `SetProperty` is defined by the base class `BindableBase` (code file `Models/Book.cs`):

```
public class Book: BindableBase
{
  public int BookId { get; set; }

  private string _title;
  public string Title
  {
    get { return _title; }
    set { SetProperty(ref _title, value); }
  }

  private string _publisher;
  public string Publisher
  {
    get { return _publisher; }
    set { SetProperty(ref _publisher, value); }
  }

  public override string ToString() => Title;
}
```

Implementing Change Notification

The object source of XAML elements needs either dependency properties or `INotifyPropertyChanged` to allow change notification with data binding. With model types, it makes sense to implement `INotifyPropertyChanged`. For having an implementation available with different projects, the implementation is done within the Framework library project in the class `BindableBase`. The `INotifyPropertyChanged` interface defines the event `PropertyChanged`. To fire the change notification, the method `SetProperty` is implemented as a generic function for supporting any property type. Before the notification is fired, a check is done to see whether the new value is different from the current value (code file `Framework/BindableBase.cs`):

```
public abstract class BindableBase: INotifyPropertyChanged
{
  public event PropertyChangedEventHandler PropertyChanged;

  protected virtual void OnPropertyChanged(
      [CallerMemberName] string propertyName = null)
  {
    PropertyChanged?.Invoke(this, new PropertyChangedEventArgs(propertyName));
  }

  protected virtual bool SetProperty<T>(ref T item, T value,
      [CallerMemberName] string propertyName = null)
  {
    if (EqualityComparer<T>.Default.Equals(item, value)) return false;
    item = value;
    OnPropertyChanged(propertyName);
    return true;
  }
}
```

> **NOTE** *Dependency properties are explained in Chapter 29, "Core XAML."*

Using the Repository Pattern

Next you need a way to retrieve, update, and delete Book objects. You can read and write books from a database with the ADO.NET Entity Framework. Although Entity Framework 7 can be accessed from the Universal Windows Platform, usually this is a task from the back end and is consequently not covered in this chapter. To make the back end accessible from a client app, ASP.NET Web API is the technology of choice on the server side. These topics are covered in Chapter 38, "Entity Framework Core," and Chapter 42, "ASP.NET Web API." With the client application it's best to be independent of the data store. For this, the Repository design pattern was defined. The *Repository* pattern is a mediator between the model and the data access layer; it can act as an in-memory collection of objects. It gives an abstraction of the data access layer and allows for easier unit tests.

The generic interface `IQueryRepository` defines methods for retrieving one item by ID or a list of items (code file `Contracts/IQueryRepository.cs`):

```
public interface IQueryRepository<T, in TKey>
  where T: class
{
  Task<T> GetItemAsync(TKey id);
  Task<IEnumerable<T>> GetItemsAsync();
}
```

The generic interface `IUpdateRepository` defines methods to add, update, and delete items (code file `Contracts/IUpdateRepository.cs`):

```
public interface IUpdateRepository<T, in TKey>
  where T: class
{
  Task<T> AddAsync(T item);
  Task<T> UpdateAsync(T item);
  Task<bool> DeleteAsync(TKey id);
}
```

The `IBooksRepository` interface makes the previous two generic interfaces concrete by defining the type `Book` for the generic type `T` (code file `Contracts/IBooksRepository.cs`):

```
public interface IBooksRepository: IQueryRepository<Book, int>,
    IUpdateRepository<Book, int>
{
}
```

By using these interfaces, it's possible to change the repository. Create a sample repository `BooksSampleRepository` that implements the members of the interface `IBooksRepository` and contains a list of initial books (code file `Repositories/BooksSampleRepository.cs`):

```
public class BooksSampleRepository: IBooksRepository
{
  private List<Book> _books;
  public BooksRepository()
  {
    InitSampleBooks();
  }

  private void InitSampleBooks()
  {
    _books = new List<Book>()
    {
      new Book
      {
        BookId = 1,
        Title = "Professional C# 6 and .NET Core 1.0",
        Publisher = "Wrox Press"
      },
      new Book
      {
        BookId = 2,
        Title = "Professional C# 5.0 and .NET 4.5.1",
        Publisher = "Wrox Press"
      },
      new Book
      {
        BookId = 3,
        Title = "Enterprise Services with the .NET Framework",
        Publisher = "AWL"
      }
    };
  }

  public Task<bool> DeleteAsync(int id)
  {
    Book bookToDelete = _books.Find(b => b.BookId == id);
    if (bookToDelete != null)
    {
      return Task.FromResult<bool>(_books.Remove(bookToDelete));
    }
```

```
        return Task.FromResult<bool>(false);
    }

    public Task<Book> GetItemAsync(int id)
    {
        return Task.FromResult(_books.Find(b => b.BookId == id));
    }

    public Task<IEnumerable<Book>> GetItemsAsync() =>
        Task.FromResult<IEnumerable<Book>>(_books);

    public Task<Book> UpdateAsync(Book item)
    {
        Book bookToUpdate = _books.Find(b => b.BookId == item.BookId);
        int ix = _books.IndexOf(bookToUpdate);
        _books[ix] = item;
        return Task.FromResult(_books[ix]);
    }

    public Task<Book> AddAsync(Book item)
    {
        item.BookId = _books.Select(b => b.BookId).Max() + 1;
        _books.Add(item);
        return Task.FromResult(item);
    }
}
```

> **NOTE** *The repository defines asynchronous methods, although they are not needed in this case because books are retrieved and updated only within memory. The methods are defined asynchronously because repositories for accessing the ASP.NET Web API or the Entity Framework are asynchronous in nature.*

VIEW MODELS

Let's create the library containing view models. Every view has a view model. With the sample app, the `BooksView` has the `BooksViewModel` associated, and the `BookView` the `BookViewModel`. There's a one-to-one mapping between view and view model. In reality, there's a many-to-one mapping between view and view model because the same view exists with different technologies—both WPF and the UWP. This makes it important that the view model doesn't know anything about the view, but the view knows the view model. The view model is implemented with a portable library, which allows using it from both WPF and the UWP.

The portable library `ViewModels` has references to the `Contracts`, `Models`, and `Framework` libraries, which are portable libraries as well.

A view model contains properties for the items to show and commands for actions. The `BooksViewModel` class defines the properties `Books`—for showing a list of books—and `SelectedBook`, which is the currently selected book. `BooksViewModel` also defines the commands `GetBooksCommand` and `AddBookCommand` (code file `ViewModels/BooksViewModel.cs`):

```
public class BooksViewModel: ViewModelBase
{
    private IBooksService _booksService;

    public BooksViewModel(IBooksService booksService)
    {
```

```
    // etc.
    }

    private Book _selectedBook;
    public Book SelectedBook
    {
      get { return _selectedBook; }
      set
      {
        if (SetProperty(ref _selectedBook, value))
        {
          // etc.
        }
      }
    }

    public IEnumerable<Book> Books => _booksService.Books;
    public ICommand GetBooksCommand { get; }

    public async void OnGetBooks()
    {
      // etc.
    }

    private bool _canGetBooks = true;

    public bool CanGetBooks() => _canGetBooks;

    private void OnAddBook()
    {
      // etc.
    }

    public ICommand AddBookCommand { get; }
  }
```

The `BookViewModel` class defines the property `Book` to display the selected book and the command `SaveBookCommand` (code file `ViewModels/BookViewModel.cs`):

```
public class BookViewModel: ViewModelBase
{
  private IBooksService _booksService;
  public BookViewModel(IBooksService booksService)
  {
    // etc.
  }

  public ICommand SaveBookCommand { get; }

  private void LoadBook(object sender, BookInfoEvent bookInfo)
  {
    if (bookInfo.BookId == 0)
    {
      Book = new Book();
    }
    else
    {
      Book = _booksService.GetBook(bookInfo.BookId);
    }
  }

  private Book _book;
  public Book Book
```

```
  {
    get { return _book; }
    set { SetProperty(ref _book, value); }
  }

  private async void OnSaveBook()
  {
    Book book = await _booksService.AddOrUpdateBookAsync(Book);
    Book = book;
  }
}
```

The properties of the view models need change notification for UI updates. The interface
`INotifyPropertyChanged` is implemented via the base class `BindableBase`. The view model class derives
from the `ViewModelBase` class to get this implementation. You can use the `ViewModelBase` class to support
additional features for view models, such as giving information about progress information and input validation (code file `Frameworks/ViewModelBase.cs`):

```
public abstract class ViewModelBase: BindableBase
{
}
```

Commands

The view models offer commands that implement the interface `ICommand`. Commands allow a separation
between the view and the command handler method via data binding. Commands also offer the functionality to enable or disable the command. The `ICommand` interface defines the methods `Execute` and
`CanExecute`, and the event `CanExecuteChanged`.

To map the commands to methods, the `DelegateCommand` class is defined in the Framework assembly.

`DelegateCommand` defines two constructors, where a delegate can be passed for the method that should
be invoked via the command, and another delegate defines whether the command is available (code file
`Framework/DelegateCommand.cs`):

```
public class DelegateCommand: ICommand
{
  private Action _execute;
  private Func<bool> _canExecute;

  public DelegateCommand(Action execute, Func<bool> canExecute)
  {
    if (execute == null)
      throw new ArgumentNullException("execute");

    _execute = execute;
    _canExecute = canExecute;
  }

  public DelegateCommand(Action execute)
   : this(execute, null)
  { }

  public event EventHandler CanExecuteChanged;

  public bool CanExecute(object parameter) => _canExecute?.Invoke() ?? true;

  public void Execute(object parameter)
  {
    _execute();
  }
}
```

```
    public void RaiseCanExecuteChanged()
    {
      CanExecuteChanged?.Invoke(this, EventArgs.Empty);
    }
  }
```

The constructor of the `BooksViewModel` creates new `DelegateCommand` objects and assigns the methods `OnGetBooks` and `OnAddBook` when the command is executed. The `CanGetBooks` method returns true or `false`, depending on whether the `GetBooksCommand` should be available (code file `ViewModels/BooksViewModel.cs`):

```
public BooksViewModel(IBooksService booksService)
{
  // etc.
  GetBooksCommand = new DelegateCommand(OnGetBooks, CanGetBooks);
  AddBookCommand = new DelegateCommand(OnAddBook);
}
```

The `CanGetBooks` method that is assigned to the `GetBooksCommand` returns the value of `_canGetBooks`, which has an initial value of `true`:

```
private bool _canGetBooks = true;

public bool CanGetBooks() => _canGetBooks;
```

The handler for the `GetBooksCommand` (the `OnGetBooks` method) loads all books using a books service, and it changes the availability of the `GetBooksCommand`:

```
public async void OnGetBooks()
{
  await _booksService.LoadBooksAsync();

  _canGetBooks = false;
  (GetBooksCommand as DelegateCommand)?.RaiseCanExecuteChanged();
}
```

The `LoadBooksAsync` method that is defined by the books service is implemented in the next section, "Services and Dependency Injection."

From the XAML code, the `GetBooksCommand` can be bound to the `Command` property of a `Button`. This is discussed when creating the views in more detail:

```
<Button Content="Load" Command="{Binding ViewModel.GetBooksCommand,
    Mode=OneTime}" />
```

> **NOTE** *With WPF, currently data binding is not possible with events. When handlers are added to events, the handler is strongly coupled to the XAML code. Commands give this separation between views and view models that allow data binding. Using compiled binding with the UWP, data binding is also possible with events. Here, commands offer additional functionality to event handlers in that they give information if the command is available.*

Services and Dependency Injection

The `BooksViewModel` makes use of a service implementing the interface `IBooksService`. The `IBooksService` is injected with the constructor of the `BooksViewModel` (code file `ViewModels/BooksViewModel.cs`):

```
private IBooksService _booksService;
public BooksViewModel(IBooksService booksService)
```

```
{
    _booksService = booksService;
    // etc.
}
```

The same is true for the `BookViewModel`; it uses the same `IBooksService` (code file `ViewModels/BookViewModel.cs`):

```
private IBooksService _booksService;
public BookViewModel(IBooksService booksService)
{
    _booksService = booksService;
    // etc.
}
```

The interface `IBooksService` defines all the features needed by the view models for accessing books. This contract is defined in a portable library like the view models, so the view model project can reference the project of the service contract (code file `Contracts/IBooksService.cs`):

```
public interface IBooksService
{
    Task LoadBooksAsync();
    IEnumerable<Book> Books { get; }
    Book GetBook(int bookId);
    Task<Book> AddOrUpdateBookAsync(Book book);
}
```

The interface `IBooksService` is used with the `BooksViewModel` in the `OnGetBooks` method—the handler for the `GetBooksCommand` (code file `ViewModels/BooksViewModel.cs`):

```
public async void OnGetBooks()
{
    await _booksService.LoadBooksAsync();

    _canGetBooks = false;
    (GetBooksCommand as DelegateCommand)?.RaiseCanExecuteChanged();
}
```

Also, the `BookViewModel` makes use of `IBooksService` (code file `ViewModels/BookViewModel.cs`):

```
private async void OnSaveBook()
{
    Book = await _booksService.AddOrUpdateBookAsync(Book);
}
```

The view model doesn't need to know the concrete implementation of the `IBooksService`—only the interface is needed. This is known as the principle *Inversion of Control (IoC)* or the *Hollywood principle* ("Don't call us; we call you"). The pattern is named *Dependency Injection*. The dependency that is needed is injected from somewhere else (in our case, it's in the WPF or UWP application).

The service itself could be implemented with a project that is incompatible to portable libraries. It just needs to be compatible with the UI technology—for example, WPF or UWP. The view model doesn't have a direct dependency on the service implementation because it just uses the interface contract.

The class `BooksService` implements the interface `IBooksService` to load books, access single books, and add or update a book. This one in turn makes use of the repository library that was created earlier. The `BooksService` makes use of dependency injection as well. With the constructor, an instance that implements the interface `IBooksRepository` is passed (code file `Services/BooksService.cs`):

```
public class BooksService: IBooksService
{
    private ObservableCollection<Book> _books = new ObservableCollection<Book>();
    private IBooksRepository _booksRepository;
```

```
    public BooksService(IBooksRepository repository)
    {
      _booksRepository = repository;
    }

    public async Task LoadBooksAsync()
    {
      if (_books.Count > 0) return;

      IEnumerable<Book> books = await _booksRepository.GetItemsAsync();
      _books.Clear();
      foreach (var b in books)
      {
        _books.Add(b);
      }
    }

    public Book GetBook(int bookId)
    {
      return _books.Where(b => b.BookId == bookId).SingleOrDefault();
    }

    public async Task<Book> AddOrUpdateBookAsync(Book book)
    {
      Book updated = null;
      if (book.BookId == 0)
      {
        updated = await _booksRepository.AddAsync(book);
        _books.Add(updated);
      }
      else
      {
        updated = await _booksRepository.UpdateAsync(book);
        Book old = _books.Where(b => b.BookId == updated.BookId).Single();
        int ix = _books.IndexOf(old);
        _books.RemoveAt(ix);
        _books.Insert(ix, updated);
      }
      return updated;
    }

    IEnumerable<Book> IBooksService.Books => _books;
}
```

The injection of the IBooksRepository happens with the WPF application in the App class. The property BooksService instantiates a BooksService object and passes a new BooksSampleRepository on first access of the property (code file BooksDesktopApp/App.xaml.cs):

```
private BooksService _booksService;
public BooksService BooksService =>
  _booksService ?? (_booksService =
    new BooksService(new BooksSampleRepository()));
```

The BooksViewModel is instantiated with the ViewModel property initializer in the BooksView class. Here, the concrete implementation of the BooksService is injected on creating the BooksViewModel (code file BooksDesktopApp/Views/BooksView.xaml.cs):

```
public partial class BooksView: UserControl
{
  // etc.

  public BooksViewModel ViewModel { get; } =
```

```
        new BooksViewModel((App.Current as App).BooksService);
    }
```

VIEWS

Now that you've been introduced to creating the view models, it's time to get into the views. The views are defined as user controls within the Views subdirectory in both the BooksDesktopApp and the BooksUniversalApp projects.

The BooksView contains two buttons (Load and Add) and a ListBox to show all books, as shown in Figure 31-9. The BookView shows the details of a single book and contains a button (Save) and two TextBox controls as shown in Figure 31-10.

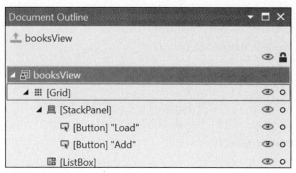

FIGURE 31-9

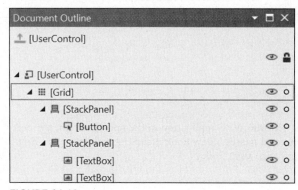

FIGURE 31-10

The main view shows the two user controls within two columns of a grid (code file BooksDesktopApp/MainWindow.xaml):

```xml
<Window x:Class="BooksDesktopApp.MainWindow"
        xmlns="http://schemas.microsoft.com/winfx/2006/xaml/presentation"
        xmlns:x="http://schemas.microsoft.com/winfx/2006/xaml"
        xmlns:local="clr-namespace:BooksDesktopApp"
        xmlns:uc="clr-namespace:BooksDesktopApp.Views"
        Title="Books Desktop App" Height="350" Width="525">
    <Grid>
```

```
    <Grid.ColumnDefinitions>
      <ColumnDefinition />
      <ColumnDefinition />
    </Grid.ColumnDefinitions>
    <uc:BooksView Grid.Column="0" />
    <uc:BookView Grid.Column="1" />
  </Grid>
</Window>
```

With the UWP project, the grid is defined in the same way, but a Page is used instead of the Window, and the XML alias mapped to the .NET namespace is defined with the using keyword instead of clr-namespace (code file BooksUniversalApp/MainPage.xaml):

```
<Page x:Class="BooksUniversalApp.MainPage"
      xmlns="http://schemas.microsoft.com/winfx/2006/xaml/presentation"
      xmlns:x="http://schemas.microsoft.com/winfx/2006/xaml"
      xmlns:local="using:BooksUniversalApp"
      xmlns:uc="using:BooksUniversalApp.Views">
  <Grid Background="{ThemeResource ApplicationPageBackgroundThemeBrush}">
    <Grid.ColumnDefinitions>
      <ColumnDefinition />
      <ColumnDefinition />
    </Grid.ColumnDefinitions>
    <uc:BooksView Grid.Column="0" />
    <uc:BookView Grid.Column="1" />
  </Grid>
</Page>
```

> **NOTE** *The sample for the UWP project doesn't use specific controls available with the Universal Windows Platform, such as* CommandBar *and* RelativePanel, *because this chapter has the focus on a maintainable and flexible application architecture. Specific UWP UI controls are covered in Chapter 32, "Windows Apps: User Interfaces."*

Injecting the View Models

What's important with the views is how the view models are mapped. To map the view model to the view, a ViewModel property is defined in the code behind where the needed view model is instantiated. The code is the same both for WPF and UWP with the exception of the sealed class with UWP (code file BooksDesktopApp/Views/BookView.xaml.cs and BooksUniversalApp/Views/BookView.xaml.cs):

```
public sealed partial class BookView: UserControl
{
  // etc.
  public BooksViewModel ViewModel { get; } =
      new BooksViewModel((App.Current as App).BooksService);
}
```

Data Binding with WPF

For data binding with WPF, you need to set the DataContext in the XAML code. With every data binding that is used with elements, within the tree of the parent elements the DataContext is checked to find the source of the binding. With this it is possible to have different sources as needed. However, for an easy switch to the delayed binding shown in the next section, the DataContext is set only once for the root element. The context is directly set to the root element via element binding using the expression {Binding ElementName=booksView}. The UserControl itself is named booksView (code file BooksDesktopApp/ Views/BooksView.xaml):

```xml
<UserControl x:Class="BooksDesktopApp.Views.BooksView"
             xmlns="http://schemas.microsoft.com/winfx/2006/xaml/presentation"
             xmlns:x="http://schemas.microsoft.com/winfx/2006/xaml"
             xmlns:local="clr-namespace:BooksDesktopApp.Views"
             x:Name="booksView"
             DataContext="{Binding ElementName=booksView}">
```

With the Button controls, the Command property is bound to the GetBooksCommand of the view model. Because the DataContext of the BooksView is set to the BooksView, and the BooksView has a ViewModel property that returns the BooksViewModel, the commands are bound to the GetBooksCommand and the AddBookCommand properties using the dot notation with the property name prefixed by ViewModel. Because the commands do not change, using the mode OneTime is the best option:

```xml
<Button Content="Load"
    Command="{Binding ViewModel.GetBooksCommand, Mode=OneTime}" />
<Button Content="Add"
    Command="{Binding ViewModel.AddBookCommand, Mode=OneTime}" />
```

The data binding mode OneTime doesn't register for change notification. Setting the mode to OneWay registers to change notification of the data source and updates the user interface regarding whether the source is either implemented as a dependency property or implements the interface INotifyPropertyChanged. Setting the mode to TwoWay not only updates the UI from the source but also updates the source from the UI.

The ItemsSource property of the ListBox binds to the list of books. This list can change; thus you use the mode OneTime with data binding. For list updates, the source needs to implement INotifyCollectionChanged. You do this by using the ObservableCollection type for the books, as you've seen previously with the BooksService implementation. Selecting an item in the ListBox updates the SelectedBook property that in turn should make an update in the BookViewModel. The update of the other view model is currently missing because you need to implement a messaging mechanism that is shown later in this chapter in the section "Messaging Using Events." For the display of every item in the ListBox, you use a DataTemplate where a TextBlock binds to the Title property of a Book:

```xml
<ListBox Grid.Row="1" ItemsSource="{Binding ViewModel.Books, Mode=OneTime}"
    SelectedItem="{Binding ViewModel.SelectedBook, Mode=TwoWay}" >
  <ListBox.ItemTemplate>
    <DataTemplate>
      <StackPanel Orientation="Vertical">
        <TextBlock Text="{Binding Title, Mode=OneWay}" />
      </StackPanel>
    </DataTemplate>
  </ListBox.ItemTemplate>
</ListBox>
```

> **NOTE** *XAML syntax is explained in Chapter 29. Styling XAML and data templates are covered in Chapter 30, "Styling XAML Apps."*

With the BookView there's nothing special that hasn't already been covered with the BooksView. Just note that the two TextBox controls are bound to the Title and Publisher properties of the Book, and the setting for the Mode is to TwoWay because the user should be able to change the values and update the Book source (code file BooksDesktopApp/Views/BookView.xaml):

```
<StackPanel Orientation="Horizontal">
  <Button Content="Save" Command="{Binding ViewModel.SaveBookCommand}" />
</StackPanel>
<StackPanel Orientation="Vertical" Grid.Row="1">
  <TextBox Text="{Binding ViewModel.Book.Title, Mode=TwoWay}" />
  <TextBox Text="{Binding ViewModel.Book.Publisher, Mode=TwoWay}" />
</StackPanel>
```

> **NOTE** *The default mode of the binding differs between different technologies. For example, binding with the* Text *property of a* TextBox *element by default has* TwoWay *binding with WPF. Using the same property and element with compiled binding by default has the* OneTime *mode. To avoid confusion, it's best to always define the mode explicitly.*

> **NOTE** *All the features of data binding with WPF are shown in Chapter 34, "Windows Desktop Applications with WPF." WPF supports more binding options than the UWP has to offer. On the other side, the UWP offers compiled data binding that is not yet available with WPF. This chapter concentrates on data binding that can be easily converted between the traditional data binding used with the WPF sample and the compiled data binding with the UWP app sample.*

With the current state of the application, you can run the WPF application and see the list of books populated after clicking the Load button. What's not working yet is the filling of the BookView after selecting a book in the ListBox because the BookViewModel needs to be informed about the change. This will be done after the data binding for the UWP project is implemented in the section Messaging.

Compiled Data Binding with UWP

With the UWP, you could use the same data binding as you use with WPF. However, the binding expression makes use of .NET reflection. Microsoft Office as well as several tools within Windows 10 make use of XAML, and the binding was too slow for the hundreds of controls used here. Setting properties directly is a lot faster. Setting the properties directly has the disadvantage that code sharing and unit testing cannot be implemented as easily as with the view models you've seen in this chapter. Because of this, the XAML team invented compiled data binding that is now available with the UWP but is not yet available with WPF.

When you're using compiled data binding, you use the x:Bind markup extension instead of Binding. With the exception of the name of the markup extension element, comparing x:Bind and Binding looks very similar, as this code snippet shows:

```
<TextBox Text="{Binding ViewModel.Book.Title, Mode=TwoWay}" />
<TextBox Text="{x:Bind ViewModel.Book.Title, Mode=TwoWay}" />
```

Behind the scenes, the Text property of the TextBox is directly accessed, and the Title property from the book is retrieved on setting the TextBox. Besides being faster, compiled binding also has the advantage that you get compiler errors when you are not using the correct property names. With the traditional data binding, by default errors with binding are ignored, and you don't see a result.

Let's have a look at the XAML code of the BooksView. The DataContext doesn't need to be set with compiled binding; it is not used. Instead, the binding always maps directly to the root element. That's why in the WPF example the DataContext was set to the root element as well to make the bindings similar.

With the `UserControl` definition, some more .NET namespaces need to be opened to map the `Book` type in the `Models` namespace, and a converter that will be defined in the `BooksUniversalApp.Converters` namespace (code file `BooksUniversalApp/Views/BooksView.xaml`):

```
<UserControl
    x:Class="BooksUniversalApp.Views.BooksView"
    xmlns="http://schemas.microsoft.com/winfx/2006/xaml/presentation"
    xmlns:x="http://schemas.microsoft.com/winfx/2006/xaml"
    xmlns:local="using:BooksUniversalApp.Views"
    xmlns:mc="http://schemas.openxmlformats.org/markup-compatibility/2006"
    xmlns:model="using:Models"
    xmlns:conv="using:BooksUniversalApp.Converters">
```

The `Command` properties of the `Button` controls are bound in a similar manner as before, but the `x:Bind` markup expression is used this time:

```
<Button Content="Load"
    Command="{x:Bind ViewModel.GetBooksCommand, Mode=OneTime}" />
<Button Content="Add"
    Command="{x:Bind ViewModel.AddBookCommand, Mode=OneTime}" />
```

> **NOTE** *Instead of using the* `Command` *property with data binding, when you're using compiled data binding it is also possible to bind event handlers to events. You can bind the* `Click` *event to a* `void` *method without parameters, or you can bind a method with two parameters of type* `object` *and* `RoutedEventArgs` *as defined by the delegate type of the* `Click` *event.*

With the `ListBox`, the `ItemsSource` is set similarly to the way you set it before—just with the `x:Bind` markup extension. What's different now is the binding to the `SelectedItem`. If you change the `Binding` markup expression with the `x:Bind` markup expression, you get a compiler error: `Cannot bind type 'Models.Book' to 'System.Object' without a converter`. The reason is that `SelectedItem` is of type `object`, and the `SelectedBook` property returns a `Book`. Using a converter, this can be solved easily (code file `BooksUniversalApp/Views/BooksView.xaml`):

```
<ListBox Grid.Row="1" ItemsSource="{x:Bind ViewModel.Books, Mode=OneTime}"
    SelectedItem="{x:Bind ViewModel.SelectedBook, Mode=TwoWay,
    Converter={StaticResource ObjectToObjectConverter}}" >
  <!--etc.-->
</ListBox>
```

A converter implements the interface `IValueConverter`. For two-way binding, the interface `IValueConverter` defines the methods `Convert` and `ConvertBack`. In this case the implementation can be simple to return the same object that is received (code file `BooksUniversalApp/Converters/ObjectToObjectConverter.cs`):

```
public class ObjectToObjectConverter: IValueConverter
{
  public object Convert(object value,
                        Type targetType,
                        object parameter,
                        string language) => value;

  public object ConvertBack(object value,
                            Type targetType,
                            object parameter,
                            string language) => value;
}
```

Using the resources of the user control, the `ObjectToObjectConverter` is instantiated with the same name as the key to reference the converter using the `StaticResource` markup extension with `ItemsSource` binding in the `ListBox` shown earlier (code file BooksUniversalApp/Views/BooksView.xaml):

```
<UserControl.Resources>
  <conv:ObjectToObjectConverter x:Key="ObjectToObjectConverter" />
</UserControl.Resources>
```

Another difference with the compiled binding is with the data template. Binding the `Text` property of the `TextBlock` to the `Title` property of the `Book`, the `Book` needs to be known. For this, the `x:DataType` was added to the `DataTemplate` element:

```
<ListBox.ItemTemplate>
    <DataTemplate x:DataType="model:Book">
      <StackPanel Orientation="Vertical">
        <TextBlock Text="{x:Bind Title, Mode=OneWay}" />
      </StackPanel>
    </DataTemplate>
</ListBox.ItemTemplate>
```

With the compiled data binding in place, the UWP app is in the same state as the WPF application.

> **NOTE** *Compiled binding is also used in Chapter 32 and Chapter 33, "Advanced Windows Apps."*

MESSAGING USING EVENTS

With the current state of the application there's the issue that the `BookViewModel` needs to update the current book when the book is selected with the `BooksViewModel`. To solve this, it is possible to define a contract where one view model invokes another one. However, this is a small scenario, and such notifications of other parts of the application will be needed in other places as well. Direct communication can become a nightmare very quickly.

One way to solve this is by using events. A generic `EventAggregator` is defined with the `Framework` project. This aggregator defines an event named `Event` where a handler of type `Action<object, TEvent>` can subscribe and unsubscribe, and a method `Publish` fires the event. This aggregator is implemented as a *singleton* to make it easily accessible without needing to create an instance (code file Framework/EventAggregator.cs):

```
public class EventAggregator<TEvent>
    where TEvent: EventArgs
{
  private static EventAggregator<TEvent> s_eventAggregator;

  public static EventAggregator<TEvent> Instance =>
      s_eventAggregator ?? (s_eventAggregator = new EventAggregator<TEvent>());

  private EventAggregator()
  {
  }

  public event Action<object, TEvent> Event;

  public void Publish(object source, TEvent ev)
  {
    Event?.Invoke(source, ev);
  }
}
```

> **NOTE** *With a generic Singleton class, there's not only one instance created; there's one instance for every generic parameter type used. That's fine for the* EventAggregator, *as different event types don't need to share some data, and allows for better scalability.*

For passing the information about the book from the BooksViewModel to the BooksView, just the book identifier is needed, and thus the BookInfoEvent class is defined (code file Contracts/Events/BookInfoEvent.cs):

```
public class BookInfoEvent: EventArgs
{
  public int BookId { get; set; }
}
```

The BookViewModel can now subscribe to the event. With the constructor of the BookViewModel, the static member Instance is accessed to get the singleton object of the BookInfoEvent type, and the LoadBook handler method is assigned to the event Event. Within the handler method, the book with the requested ID is retrieved via the books service (code file ViewModels/BookViewModel.cs):

```
public class BookViewModel: ViewModelBase, IDisposable
{
  private IBooksService _booksService;
  public BookViewModel(IBooksService booksService)
  {
    _booksService = booksService;

    SaveBookCommand = new DelegateCommand(OnSaveBook);

    EventAggregator<BookInfoEvent>.Instance.Event += LoadBook;
  }

  public ICommand SaveBookCommand { get; }

  private void LoadBook(object sender, BookInfoEvent bookInfo)
  {
    if (bookInfo.BookId == 0)
    {
      Book = new Book();
    }
    else
    {
      Book = _booksService.GetBook(bookInfo.BookId);
    }
  }

  public void Dispose()
  {
    EventAggregator<BookInfoEvent>.Instance.Event -= LoadBook;
  }
  // etc.
```

The event is published when a book is selected in the ListBox, and thus the SelectedBook property calls the set accessor. Here, the EventAggregator can be accessed similar to subscription using the static Instance property, now by invoking the Publish method, which passes a BookInfoEvent object (code file ViewModels/BooksViewModel.cs):

```
private Book _selectedBook;
```

```
public Book SelectedBook
{
  get { return _selectedBook; }
  set
  {
    if (SetProperty(ref _selectedBook, value))
    {
      EventAggregator<BookInfoEvent>.Instance.Publish(
          this, new BookInfoEvent { BookId = _selectedBook.BookId });
    }
  }
}
```

With the messaging mechanism in place, you can start the application, select books, and add them as shown in Figure 31-11.

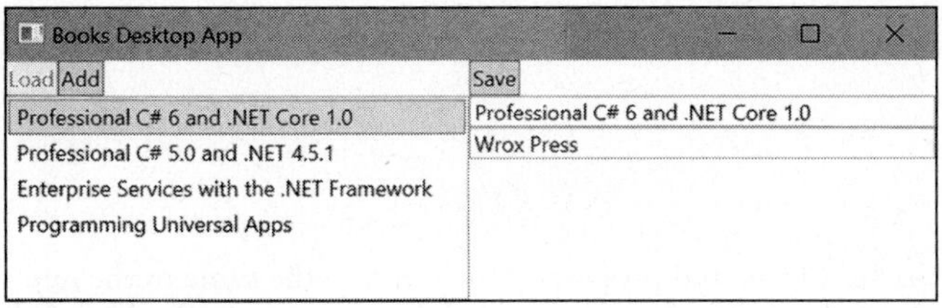

FIGURE 31-11

IOC CONTAINER

With dependency injection, you can also use an Inversion of Control (IoC) container. With dependency injection from the previous code snippets you've injected a concrete type from the client application directly—for example, the `BooksService` instance within the `BooksViewModel` (code file `BooksDesktopApp/Views/BooksView.xaml.cs`):

```
public BooksViewModel ViewModel { get; } =
    new BooksViewModel((App.Current as App).BooksService);
```

You can change this to let an IoC container inject dependencies. Several IoC containers are offered as NuGet packages, for example Castle Windsor (http://castleproject.org/projects/Windsor), Unity (http://unity.codeplex.com), Autofac (http://github.com/autofac), Managed Extensibility Framework (which is covered in Chapter 26, "Composition"), and many more. With .NET Core 1.0 there's another IoC container from Microsoft that is available with the NuGet package `Microsoft.Framework.DependencyInjection` (http://github.com/aspnet/DependencyInjection). This is a lightweight framework that supports constructor injection and also the dependency injection container used by ASP.NET Core 1.0 (see Chapter 40, "ASP.NET Core"). The code sample in this section uses this .NET Core 1.0 IoC container.

For using the container, you need to add the NuGet package `Microsoft.Framework.DependencyInjection`. Within the `App` class, you can add the services to the `ServiceCollection` (namespace `Microsoft .Framework.DependencyInjection`). The `AddTransient` method registers a type that is newly instantiated with every resolve of the type; `AddSingleton` instantiates the type only once and returns the same instance every time the type is resolved. Passing two generic parameters (done with the books service and books repository), the first type can be requested, and the container creates an instance of the second parameter. The method `BuildServiceProvider` returns an object implementing `IServiceProvider` that can be used later on for resolving the types. With WPF, the returned

IServiceProvider object is assigned to the Container method within the OnStartup method (code file BooksDesktopApp/App.xaml.cs):

```
private IServiceProvider RegisterServices()
{
  var serviceCollection = new ServiceCollection();
  serviceCollection.AddTransient<BooksViewModel>();
  serviceCollection.AddTransient<BookViewModel>();
  serviceCollection.AddSingleton<IBooksService, BooksService>();
  serviceCollection.AddSingleton<IBooksRepository, BooksSampleRepository>();
  return serviceCollection.BuildServiceProvider();
}

public IServiceProvider Container { get; private set; }

protected override void OnStartup(StartupEventArgs e)
{
  base.OnStartup(e);

  Container = RegisterServices();

  var mainWindow = new MainWindow();
  mainWindow.Show();
}
```

With the UWP project, the method RegisterServices and property Container is the same in the App class. What's different is the startup method OnLaunched where the RegisterServices method is invoked (code file BooksUniversalApp/App.xaml.cs):

```
protected override void OnLaunched(LaunchActivatedEventArgs e)
{
  Container = RegisterServices();

  // etc.
}
```

Within the code-behind of the views, you can initialize the ViewModel property by calling the GetService method of the IServiceProvider. The Container property of the App class returns an IServiceProvider. The generic version of the GetService method is an extension method that is available in the namespace Microsoft.Framework.DependencyInjection, which needs to be imported to have this extension method available (code file BooksDesktopApp/Views/BooksView.xaml.cs and BooksUniversalApp/Views/BooksView.xaml.cs):

```
public BooksViewModel ViewModel { get; } =
    (App.Current as App).Container.GetService<BooksViewModel>();
```

The same change needs to be made in the BookView.xaml.cs file, otherwise a different BooksService instance is created. With the downloadable sample file, you need to uncomment this setting of the property and comment the previous one to make the IoC container the active one.

Now when you run the application, the BooksViewModel is instantiated from the container. As the constructor of this view model requires the type IBooksService, a BooksService instance is created and passed, as these types are registered as well with the container. The BooksService in turn requires the IBooksRepository with the constructor. Here, the BooksSampleRepository is injected. In case you miss registering any of these dependencies, an exception of type InvalidOperationException is thrown. Failing to register the IBooksRepository interface gives the error message Unable to resolve service for type 'Contracts.IBooksRepository' while attempting to activate 'Services.BooksService'.

USING A FRAMEWORK

With the sample application, you've seen classes defined in a Framework project such as `BindableBase`, `DelegateCommand`, and `EventAggregator`. These classes are needed with all MVVM-based applications, and you don't need to implement them on your own. They are not a big deal to do, but you can instead use an existing MVVM framework. MVVM Light (`http://mvvmlight.net`), from Laurent Bugnion, is a small framework that exactly fits the purpose of MVVM applications and is available for many different platforms.

Another framework that originally was created by the Microsoft Patterns and Practices team and has now moved to the community is Prism.Core (`http://github.com/PrismLibrary`). Although the Prism framework is a full-blown framework that supports add-ins and regions in which to position the controls, Prism.Core is very light and contains only a few types such as `BindableBase`, `DelegateCommand`, and `ErrorsContainer`. With the code download you will find the sample of this chapter implemented with Prism.Core as well.

SUMMARY

This chapter gave you an architectural guideline for creating XAML-based applications around the MVVM pattern. You've seen a separation of concerns with the model, view, and view model. Besides that, you've seen implementing change notification with the interface `INotifyPropertyChanged`, data binding and compiled data binding, the repository pattern to separate the data access code, messaging between view models (that can also be used to communicate with views) by using events, and dependency injection with and without an IoC container.

All this allows for code sharing while still using features of specific platforms. You can use platform-specific features with repository and service implementations, and contracts are available with all platforms. For code sharing, you've seen the API contracts with the UWP, shared projects, and portable libraries.

The next chapter guides you through user interface features of the Universal Windows Platform apps.

32

Windows Apps: User Interfaces

WHAT'S IN THIS CHAPTER?

- ➤ Navigation between pages
- ➤ Creating a hamburger button
- ➤ Using the SplitView
- ➤ Layouts with RelativePanel
- ➤ Adaptive UI for different screen sizes
- ➤ Using the AutoSuggest control
- ➤ Using the Pen with InkCanvas
- ➤ Defining commands with app bar controls
- ➤ Compiled binding features

WROX.COM CODE DOWNLOADS FOR THIS CHAPTER

The wrox.com code downloads for this chapter are found at `http://www.wrox.com/go/ professionalcsharp6` on the Download Code tab. The code for this chapter contains one big sample that shows the various aspects of this chapter:

- ➤ Page Navigation
- ➤ App Shell
- ➤ Layout
- ➤ Controls
- ➤ Compiled Binding

OVERVIEW

The Windows apps covered in this chapter are applications using the Universal Windows Platform (UWP)—apps that run on Windows 10 devices. This chapter covers user interface features such as navigating between pages, creating page layouts, and defining commands to allow the user to do some actions, use the new compiled data binding, and to use some special controls.

The previous chapters cover XAML: Chapter 29 covers the core information, Chapter 30 defines styles for apps, and Chapter 31 covers several patterns that are commonly used with XAML-based apps.

This chapter starts with some specific topics related to user interface elements of the Windows apps: using the UWP. Apps created for the UWP can run on Windows 10, the Windows Phone, and other device families such as Xbox, HoloLens, and Internet of Things (IoT).

The chapter starts with creating navigation between pages and using the new system back button, the hamburger button, and the SplitView to adapt navigation controls for different screen sizes. It covers different kinds of main pages, such as the Hub and Pivot controls, to allow for different kinds of navigation, and the chapter also explains creating a custom app shell.

You find out how to create a layout of single pages using the VariableSizedWrapGrid and the RelativePanel with adaptive triggers. Deferred loading allows for showing the user interface faster.

With compiled binding, you can see another performance improvement that helps you detect errors earlier.

In the "Controls" section, you see some new controls in action, such as the AutoSuggest control and the InkCanvas, which provides for easy drawing using a pen, touchscreen, and mouse.

Before reading this chapter, you should be familiar with XAML as discussed in Chapters 29, 30, and 31. Only specific UWP apps features are covered in this chapter.

NAVIGATION

If your application is composed of multiple pages, you need the ability to navigate between these pages. The heart of navigation is the Frame class. The Frame class enables you to navigate to specific pages using the Navigate method and optionally pass parameters. The Frame class keeps a stack of the pages to which you have navigated, which makes it possible to go back, go forward, limit the number of pages in the stack, and more.

An important aspect of navigation is having the ability to navigate back. With Windows 8, back navigation was usually handled by a button with a back arrow in the upper-left corner of the page. The Windows Phone always had a physical back button. With Windows 10, this functionality needs to be combined. The following sections show you the new way of using back navigation.

Navigating to the Initial Page

Let's start creating a Windows app with multiple pages to navigate between the pages. The template-generated code contains the OnLaunched method within the App class where a Frame object gets instantiated and then used to navigate to the MainPage by calling the Navigate method (code file PageNavigation/App.xaml.cs):

```
protected override void OnLaunched(LaunchActivatedEventArgs e)
{
    Frame rootFrame = Window.Current.Content as Frame;

    if (rootFrame == null)
    {
        rootFrame = new Frame();

        rootFrame.NavigationFailed += OnNavigationFailed;

        if (e.PreviousExecutionState == ApplicationExecutionState.Terminated)
        {
            //TODO: Load state from previously suspended application
        }

        Window.Current.Content = rootFrame;
    }

    if (rootFrame.Content == null)
    {
        rootFrame.Navigate(typeof(MainPage), e.Arguments);
    }
    Window.Current.Activate();
}
```

> **NOTE** *The source code has a* TODO *comment to load the state from the previously suspended application. How you can deal with suspension is explained in Chapter 33, "Advanced Windows Apps."*

The `Frame` class keeps a stack of pages that have been visited. The `GoBack` method makes it possible to navigate back within this stack (if the `CanGoBack` property returns true), and the `GoForward` method enables you to go forward one page after a back navigation. The `Frame` class also offers several events for navigation, such as `Navigating`, `Navigated`, `NavigationFailed`, and `NavigationStopped`.

To see navigation in action, besides the `MainPage`, the `SecondPage` and `ThirdPage` pages are created to navigate between these pages. From the `MainPage`, you can navigate to the `SecondPage`, and from the `SecondPage` to the `ThirdPage`, by passing some data.

Because there's common functionality between these pages, a base class `BasePage` is created from which all these pages derive. The `BasePage` class derives from the base class `Page` and implements the interface `INotifyPropertyChanged` for user interface updates.

```
public abstract class BasePage : Page, INotifyPropertyChanged
{
  public event PropertyChangedEventHandler PropertyChanged;

  private string _navigationMode;

  public string NavigationMode
  {
    get { return _navigationMode; }
    set
    {
      _navigationMode = value;
      OnPropertyChanged();
    }
  }

  protected virtual void OnPropertyChanged(
    [CallerMemberName] string propertyName = null)
  {
    PropertyChanged?.Invoke(this, new PropertyChangedEventArgs(propertyName));
  }

  // etc.
}
```

> **NOTE** *The interface* INotifyPropertyChanged *is discussed in Chapter 31, "Patterns with XAML Apps," to implement change notifications.*

Overriding Page Class Navigation

The `Page` class that is the base class of `BasePage` (and the base class of XAML pages) defines methods that are used on navigation. The method `OnNavigatedTo` is invoked when the page is navigated to. Within this page you can read how the navigation was done (`NavigationMode` property) and parameters for the navigation. The method `OnNavigatingFrom` is the first method that is invoked when you navigate away from the page. Here, the navigation can be cancelled. The method `OnNavigatedFrom` is finally invoked when you navigate away from this page. Here, you should do some cleanup of resources that have been allocated with the `OnNavigatedTo` method (code file `PageNavigation/App.xaml.cs`):

```
public abstract class BasePage : Page, INotifyPropertyChanged
{
  // etc.
  protected override void OnNavigatedTo(NavigationEventArgs e)
  {
```

```
      base.OnNavigatedTo(e);

      NavigationMode = $"Navigation Mode: {e.NavigationMode}";
      // etc.
    }

    protected override void OnNavigatingFrom(NavigatingCancelEventArgs e)
    {
      base.OnNavigatingFrom(e);
    }

    protected override void OnNavigatedFrom(NavigationEventArgs e)
    {
      base.OnNavigatedFrom(e);
      // etc.
    }
}
```

Navigating Between Pages

Let's implement the three pages. For using the `BasePage` class, the code-behind file needs to be modified to use the `BasePage` as a base class (code file `PageNavigation/MainPage.xaml.cs`):

```
public sealed partial class MainPage : BasePage
{
  // etc.
}
```

The change of the base class also needs to be reflected in the XAML file using the `BasePage` element instead of the `Page` (code file `PageNavigation/MainPage.xaml`):

```
<local:BasePage
    x:Class="PageNavigation.MainPage"
    xmlns="http://schemas.microsoft.com/winfx/2006/xaml/presentation"
    xmlns:x="http://schemas.microsoft.com/winfx/2006/xaml"
    xmlns:local="using:PageNavigation"
    xmlns:d="http://schemas.microsoft.com/expression/blend/2008"
    xmlns:mc="http://schemas.openxmlformats.org/markup-compatibility/2006"
    mc:Ignorable="d">
```

The `MainPage` contains a `TextBlock` element that binds to the `NavigationMode` property declared in the `BasePage`, and a `Button` control with a `Click` event binding to the method `OnNavigateToSecondPage` (code file `PageNavigation/MainPage.xaml`):

```
<StackPanel Orientation="Vertical">
  <TextBlock Style="{StaticResource TitleTextBlockStyle}" Margin="8">
    Main Page</TextBlock>
  <TextBlock Text="{x:Bind NavigationMode, Mode=OneWay}" Margin="8" />
  <Button Content="Navigate to SecondPage" Click="OnNavigateToSecondPage"
    Margin="8" />
</StackPanel>
```

The handler method `OnNavigateToSecondPage` navigates to the `SecondPage` using `Frame.Navigate`. `Frame` is a property of the `Page` class that returns the `Frame` instance (code file `PageNavigation/MainPage.xaml.cs`):

```
public void OnNavigateToSecondPage()
{
  Frame.Navigate(typeof(SecondPage));
}
```

When you navigate from the `SecondPage` to the `ThirdPage`, a parameter is passed to the target page. The parameter can be entered in the `TextBox` that is bound to the `Data` property (code file `PageNavigation/SecondPage.xaml`):

```
<StackPanel Orientation="Vertical">
  <TextBlock Style="{StaticResource TitleTextBlockStyle}" Margin="8">
```

```
          Second Page</TextBlock>
      <TextBlock Text="{x:Bind NavigationMode, Mode=OneWay}" Margin="8" />
      <TextBox Header="Data" Text="{x:Bind Data, Mode=TwoWay}" Margin="8" />
      <Button Content="Navigate to Third Page"
          Click="{x:Bind OnNavigateToThirdPage, Mode=OneTime}" Margin="8" />
    </StackPanel>
```

With the code-behind file, the `Data` property is passed to the `Navigate` method (code file `PageNavigation/ SecondPage.xaml.cs`):

```
public string Data { get; set; }

public void OnNavigateToThirdPage()
{
    Frame.Navigate(typeof(ThirdPage), Data);
}
```

The parameter received is retrieved in the `ThirdPage`. In the `OnNavigatedTo` method, the `NavigationEventArgs` receives the parameter with the `Parameter` property. The `Parameter` property is of type object as you can pass any data with the page navigation (code file `PageNavigation/ThirdPage.xaml.cs`):

```
protected override void OnNavigatedTo(NavigationEventArgs e)
{
    base.OnNavigatedTo(e);
    Data = e.Parameter as string;
}

private string _data;
public string Data
{
    get { return _data; }
    set
    {
        _data = value;
        OnPropertyChanged();
    }
}
```

Back Button

When you have navigation in the app, it's necessary to include a way to go back. With Windows 8, a custom back button was located in the upper-left corner of the page. You can still do this with Windows 10. Indeed, some Microsoft apps include such a button; Microsoft Edge puts a back and forward button at the top-left position. It makes sense to have a back button nearby when there is also a forward button. With Windows 10, you can make use of the system back button.

Depending on whether the app is running in desktop mode or tablet mode, the back button is located in different positions. To enable this back button, you need to set the `AppViewBackButtonVisibility` of the `SystemNavigationManager` to `AppViewBackButtonVisiblitity`, which is the case in the following when the property `Frame.CanGoBack` returns `true` (code file `PageNavigation/BasePage.cs`):

```
protected override void OnNavigatedTo(NavigationEventArgs e)
{
    NavigationMode = $"Navigation Mode: {e.NavigationMode}";

    SystemNavigationManager.GetForCurrentView().AppViewBackButtonVisibility =
        Frame.CanGoBack ? AppViewBackButtonVisibility.Visible :
            AppViewBackButtonVisibility.Collapsed;

    base.OnNavigatedTo(e);
}
```

Next, you use the `BackRequested` event of the `SystemNavigationManager` class. Reacting to the `BackRequestedEvent` can be done globally for the complete app as it is shown here. In case you need this functionality only in a few pages, you can also put this code within the `OnNavigatedTo` method of the page (code file `PageNavigation/App.xaml.cs`):

```
protected override void OnLaunched(LaunchActivatedEventArgs e)
{
  // etc.

  SystemNavigationManager.GetForCurrentView().BackRequested +=
    App_BackRequested;

  Window.Current.Activate();
}
```

The handler method `App_BackRequested` invokes the `GoBack` method on the frame object (code file `PageNavigation/App.xaml.cs`):

```
private void App_BackRequested(object sender, BackRequestedEventArgs e)
{
  Frame rootFrame = Window.Current.Content as Frame;
  if (rootFrame == null) return;

  if (rootFrame.CanGoBack && e.Handled == false)
  {
    e.Handled = true;
    rootFrame.GoBack();
  }
}
```

When you run the app in desktop mode, you can see the back button in the left corner of the top border (see Figure 32-1). In cases where the app is running in tablet mode, the border is not visible, but the back button is shown in the bottom border beside the Windows button (see Figure 32-2). This is the new back button of the app. In cases where navigation in the app is not possible, the user navigates back to the previous app when he or she taps the back button.

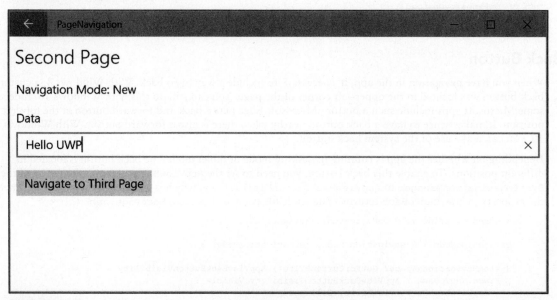

FIGURE 32-1

FIGURE 32-2

When you run the app on the Windows Phone, you can use the physical phone button to navigate back (see Figure 32-3).

Hub

You can also allow the user to navigate between content within a single page using the Hub control. An example where this can be used is if you want to show an image as an entry point for the app and more information is shown as the user scrolls (see Figure 32-4, the Picture Search app).

With the Hub control you can define multiple sections. Each section has a header and content. You can also make the header clickable—for example, to navigate to a detail page. The following code sample defines a Hub control where you can click the headers of sections 2 and 3. When you click the section header, the method assigned with the SectionHeaderClick event of the Hub control is invoked. Each section consists of a header and some content. The content of the section is defined by a DataTemplate (code file NavigationControls/HubPage.xaml):

FIGURE 32-3

```xml
<Hub Background="{ThemeResource ApplicationPageBackgroundThemeBrush}"
  SectionHeaderClick="{x:Bind OnHeaderClick}">
  <Hub.Header>
    <StackPanel Orientation="Horizontal">
      <TextBlock>Hub Header</TextBlock>
      <TextBlock Text="{x:Bind Info, Mode=TwoWay}" />
    </StackPanel>
  </Hub.Header>

  <HubSection Width="400" Background="LightBlue" Tag="Section 1">
    <HubSection.Header>
      <TextBlock>Section 1 Header</TextBlock>
    </HubSection.Header>
    <DataTemplate>
      <TextBlock>Section 1</TextBlock>
    </DataTemplate>
  </HubSection>
  <HubSection Width="300" Background="LightGreen" IsHeaderInteractive="True"
    Tag="Section 2">
    <HubSection.Header>
      <TextBlock>Section 2 Header</TextBlock>
    </HubSection.Header>
    <DataTemplate>
      <TextBlock>Section 2</TextBlock>
    </DataTemplate>
  </HubSection>
  <HubSection Width="300" Background="LightGoldenrodYellow"
    IsHeaderInteractive="True" Tag="Section 3">
    <HubSection.Header>
      <TextBlock>Section 3 Header</TextBlock>
    </HubSection.Header>
    <DataTemplate>
      <TextBlock>Section 3</TextBlock>
    </DataTemplate>
  </HubSection>
</Hub>
```

FIGURE 32-4

When you click the header section, the `Info` dependency property is assigned the value of the `Tag` property. The `Info` property in turn is bound within the header of the `Hub` control (code file `NavigationControls/HubPage.xaml.cs`):

```
public void OnHeaderClick(object sender, HubSectionHeaderClickEventArgs e)
{
  Info = e.Section.Tag as string;
}

public string Info
{
  get { return (string)GetValue(InfoProperty); }
  set { SetValue(InfoProperty, value); }
}

public static readonly DependencyProperty InfoProperty =
  DependencyProperty.Register("Info", typeof(string), typeof(HubPage),
    new PropertyMetadata(string.Empty));
```

> **NOTE** *Dependency properties are explained in Chapter 29, "Core XAML."*

When you run the app, you can see multiple hub sections (see Figure 32-5) with a See More link in sections 2 and 3 because with these sections `IsHeaderInteractive` is set to `true`. Of course, you can create a custom header template to have a different look for the header.

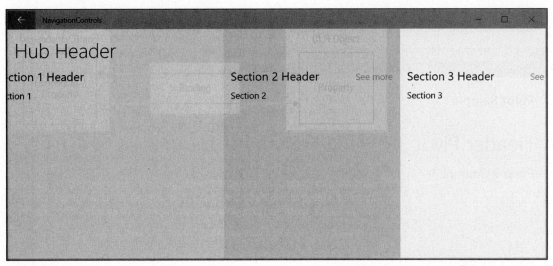

FIGURE 32-5

> **NOTE** *Creating custom templates is explained in Chapter 30, "Styling XAML Apps."*

Pivot

You can create a pivot-like look for the navigation using the Pivot control. With Windows 8, this control was only available for the phone, but now it is available for the UWP.

The Pivot control can contain multiple PivotItem controls. Each of these item controls has a header and content. The Pivot itself contains left and right headers. The sample code fills the right header (code file NavigationControls/PivotPage.xaml):

```xml
<Pivot Title="Pivot Sample"
    Background="{ThemeResource ApplicationPageBackgroundThemeBrush}">
  <Pivot.RightHeader>
    <StackPanel>
      <TextBlock>Right Header</TextBlock>
    </StackPanel>
  </Pivot.RightHeader>
  <PivotItem>
    <PivotItem.Header>Header Pivot 1</PivotItem.Header>
    <TextBlock>Pivot 1 Content</TextBlock>
  </PivotItem>
  <PivotItem>
    <PivotItem.Header>Header Pivot 2</PivotItem.Header>
    <TextBlock>Pivot 2 Content</TextBlock>
  </PivotItem>
  <PivotItem>
    <PivotItem.Header>Header Pivot 3</PivotItem.Header>
    <TextBlock>Pivot 3 Content</TextBlock>
  </PivotItem>
  <PivotItem>
    <PivotItem.Header>Header Pivot 4</PivotItem.Header>
    <TextBlock>Pivot 4 Content</TextBlock>
  </PivotItem>
</Pivot>
```

When you run the application, you can see the `Pivot` control (see Figure 32-6). The right header is always visible on the right. Click one of the headers to see the content of the item.

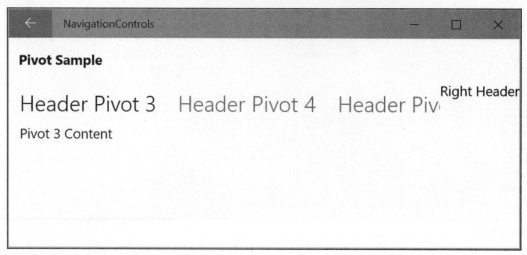

FIGURE 32-6

In case all headers do not fit the screen, the user can scroll. Using the mouse for navigation, you can see arrows on the left and right as shown in Figure 32-7.

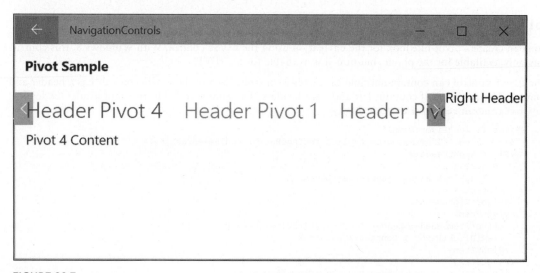

FIGURE 32-7

Application Shells

Windows 10 apps often use the `SplitView` control. (See the later section "Split View" for more information about this control.) This control usually is used to show navigation menus—made of images and/or text—on the left side and the selected content on the right. With a hamburger button, the menus can be visible or hidden. For example, the Groove Music app looks different depending on the available width. Figure 32-8 shows the app with a `SplitView` pane on the left side showing menus using text and icons. When the display width is reduced, the `SplitView` pane leaves a collapsed view with only icons, as shown in Figure 32-9. When the width is reduced even more, the menus are completely removed, as shown in Figure 32-10.

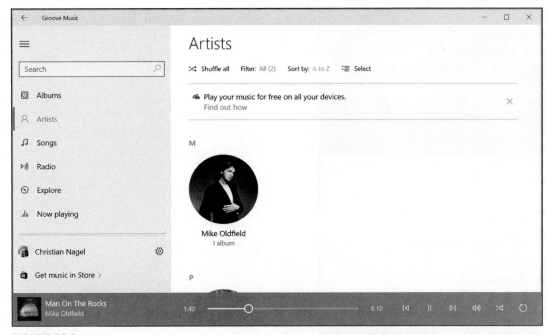

FIGURE 32-8

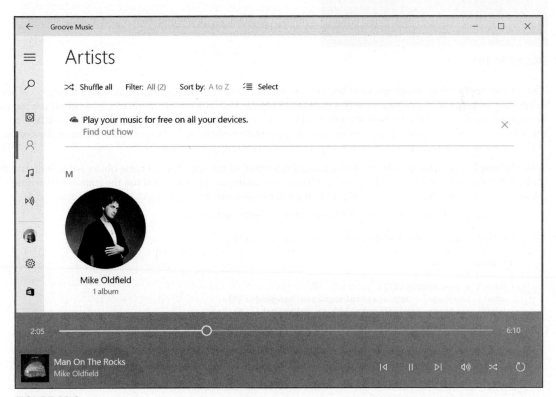

FIGURE 32-9

FIGURE 32-10

The sample application, which uses the `SplitView` and hamburger button, adds some more features. When navigating between multiple pages using a menu, it's a good idea to have the menu available in all the pages. Navigation works using methods of the `Frame` class, as you've seen in the "Navigation" section earlier in this chapter. You can create a page and use it as an application shell, and you can add a frame in the content of the `SplitView`. The `AppShellSample` app demonstrates how you can do this.

With the template-generated code, in the `OnLaunched` method of the `App` class a Frame object is created, and the frame navigates to the `MainPage`. This code is changed to create an `AppShell` and use the frame from within the `AppShell` (`shell.AppFrame`) to navigate to the `MainPage` (code file `AppShellSample/App.xaml.cs`):

```
protected override void OnLaunched(LaunchActivatedEventArgs e)
{
  AppShell shell = Window.Current.Content as AppShell;

  if (shell == null)
  {
    shell = new AppShell();
    shell.Language = ApplicationLanguages.Languages[0];
    shell.AppFrame.NavigationFailed += OnNavigationFailed;

    if (e.PreviousExecutionState == ApplicationExecutionState.Terminated)
    {
      //TODO: Load state from previously suspended application
    }
  }

  Window.Current.Content = shell;
```

```
    if (shell.AppFrame.Content == null)
    {
        shell.AppFrame.Navigate(typeof(MainPage), e.Arguments,
            new SuppressNavigationTransitionInfo());
    }
    Window.Current.Activate();
}
```

The application that's created is created like the other XAML pages, using the Blank Page Visual Studio item template. For adding a frame to the application shell, you add a `SplitView` control, and you add a `Frame` element to the content of the `SplitView`. With the `Frame`, you also assign the `Navigating` and `Navigated` events to event handlers of the page (code file `AppShellSample/AppShell.xaml`):

```xml
<SplitView x:Name="RootSplitView"
           DisplayMode="Inline"
           OpenPaneLength="256"
           IsTabStop="False">
  <SplitView.Pane>
    <!-- pane content comes here -->
  </SplitView.Pane>
  <Frame x:Name="frame"
    Navigating="OnNavigatingToPage"
    Navigated="OnNavigatedToPage">
    <Frame.ContentTransitions>
      <TransitionCollection>
        <NavigationThemeTransition>
          <NavigationThemeTransition.DefaultNavigationTransitionInfo>
            <EntranceNavigationTransitionInfo/>
          </NavigationThemeTransition.DefaultNavigationTransitionInfo>
        </NavigationThemeTransition>
      </TransitionCollection>
    </Frame.ContentTransitions>
  </Frame>
</SplitView>
```

> **NOTE** *With the Frame, you define a* `ContentTransition` *to animate the content within the frame using an* `EntraceNavigationTransitionInfo`. *Animations are explained in Chapter 30.*

To access the Frame object within the `SplitView` by using the `AppShell` class, you add the `AppFrame` property as well as the handler methods for the frame navigation (code file `AppShellSample/AppShell.xaml.cs`):

```csharp
public Frame AppFrame => frame;

private void OnNavigatingToPage(object sender, NavigatingCancelEventArgs e)
{
}

private void OnNavigatedToPage(object sender, NavigationEventArgs e)
{
}
```

Hamburger Button

To open and close the pane of the `SplitView`, you usually use a hamburger button. The hamburger button is defined within the application shell. This button is defined within the root `Grid` as a `ToggleButton`. The style is set to the resource `SplitViewTogglePaneButtonStyle` that defines the look. Clicking this button changes the value of the `IsChecked` property that binds to a `SplitView` control that is defined next. This binding opens and closes the pane of the `SplitView` (code file `AppShellSample/AppShell.xaml`):

```
<ToggleButton x:Name="TogglePaneButton"
    TabIndex="1"
    Style="{StaticResource SplitViewTogglePaneButtonStyle}"
    IsChecked="{x:Bind Path=RootSplitView.IsPaneOpen, Mode=TwoWay,
        Converter={StaticResource boolConverter}}"
    Unchecked="HamburgerMenu_UnChecked"
    AutomationProperties.Name="Menu"
    ToolTipService.ToolTip="Menu" />
```

The look of the hamburger button is mainly defined by using the font character `0xe700` of the font Segoe MDL2 Assets. This font is referenced from the resource `SymbolThemeFontFamily` (code file `AppShellSample/Styles/Styles.xaml`):

```
<Style x:Key="SplitViewTogglePaneButtonStyle" TargetType="ToggleButton">
  <Setter Property="FontSize" Value="20" />
  <Setter Property="FontFamily"
    Value="{ThemeResource SymbolThemeFontFamily}" />
  <Setter Property="Background" Value="Transparent" />
  <Setter Property="Foreground" Value=
      "{ThemeResource SystemControlForegroundBaseHighBrush}" />
  <Setter Property="Content" Value="&#xE700;" />
  <!-- etc. -->
```

> **NOTE** *To see all the symbols and their character number of the Segoe MDL2 Assets font, it's best to use the Character Map desktop application, as shown in Figure 32-11.*

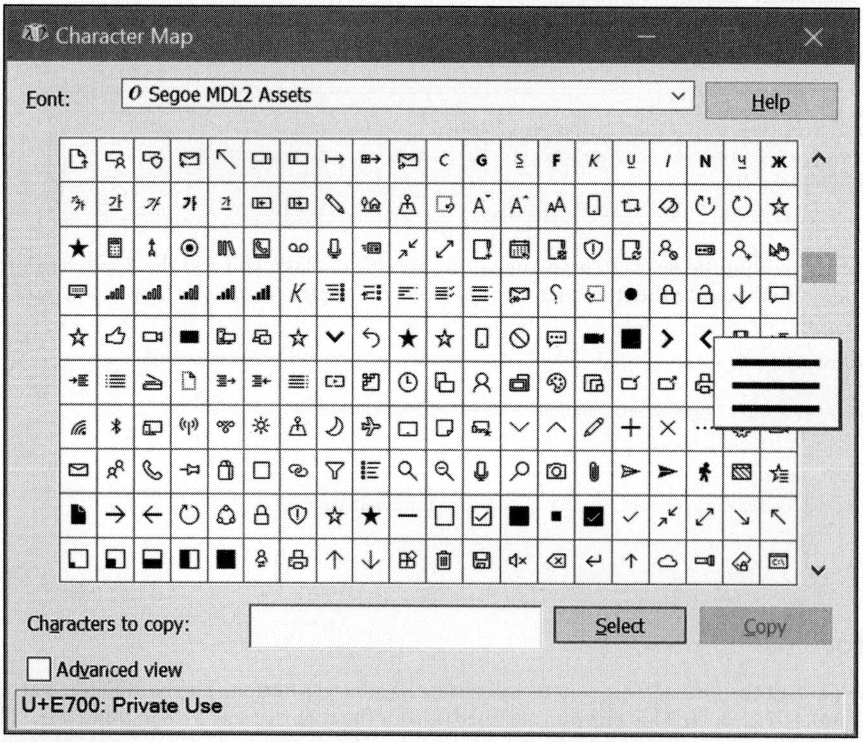

FIGURE 32-11

The hamburger button of the app is shown in Figure 32-12.

FIGURE 32-12

Split View

The hamburger button controls the opening and closing of the `SplitView` control. Let's get into details on the `SplitView`. The `OpenPaneLength` property of the `SplitView` defines the pane size when the pane is open. The `DisplayMode` property has four different modes: `Inline`, `Overlay`, `CompactInline`, and `CompactOverlay`. The difference between the inline and overlay modes is that opening the pane either overlays the content of the `SplitView` (the frame), or moves the content to the right to have a place for the pane. The compact modes have a smaller pane; for example, they show only icons instead of the text of the menu.

In the `AppShell` XAML code, the `SplitView` is defined with an `OpenPaneLength` of 256 and `DisplayMode` `Inline` (code file `AppShellSample/AppShell.xaml`):

```xml
<SplitView x:Name="RootSplitView"
           DisplayMode="Inline"
           OpenPaneLength="256"
           IsTabStop="False">
  <SplitView.Pane>
    <!-- etc. -->
  </SplitView.Pane>
  <Frame x:Name="frame"
      Navigating="OnNavigatingToPage"
      Navigated="OnNavigatedToPage">
    <Frame.ContentTransitions>
      <TransitionCollection>
        <NavigationThemeTransition>
          <NavigationThemeTransition.DefaultNavigationTransitionInfo>
            <EntranceNavigationTransitionInfo/>
          </NavigationThemeTransition.DefaultNavigationTransitionInfo>
        </NavigationThemeTransition>
      </TransitionCollection>
    </Frame.ContentTransitions>
  </Frame>
</SplitView>
```

To open and close the pane of the `SplitView`, you can set the `IsPaneOpen` property. When you click the hamburger button, the pane should open and close; thus you can use data binding to connect the hamburger button to the `SplitView`. The `IsPaneOpen` property is of type `bool`, and the `IsChecked` property of the `ToggleButton` is of type `bool?`. So a converter between `bool` and `bool?` is needed (code file `AppShellSample/Converters/BoolToNullableBoolConverter`):

```csharp
public class BoolToNullableBoolConverter : IValueConverter
{
  public object Convert(object value, Type targetType, object parameter,
    string language) => value;

  public object ConvertBack(object value, Type targetType, object parameter,
    string language)
  {
    bool defaultValue = false;
    if (parameter != null)
    {
      defaultValue = (bool)parameter;
    }

    bool? val = (bool?)value;
    return val ?? defaultValue;
  }
}
```

> **NOTE** *Data binding is explained in Chapter 31. Compiled data binding, a feature of the UWP, is covered in detail later in this chapter in the section "Data Binding."*

The `BoolToNullableBoolConverter` is instantiated with the resources of the page (code file `AppShellSample/AppShell.xaml`):

```xml
<Page.Resources>
  <conv:BoolToNullableBoolConverter x:Key="boolConverter" />
</Page.Resources>
```

With the `ToggleButton`, the `IsChecked` property is bound to the `IsPaneOpen` of the split view, using the `BoolToNullableBoolConverter` referenced as a static resource.

```xml
<ToggleButton x:Name="TogglePaneButton"
              TabIndex="1"
              Style="{StaticResource SplitViewTogglePaneButtonStyle}"
              IsChecked="{x:Bind Path=RootSplitView.IsPaneOpen, Mode=TwoWay,
                Converter={StaticResource boolConverter}}"
              Unchecked="HamburgerMenu_UnChecked"
              AutomationProperties.Name="Menu"
              ToolTipService.ToolTip="Menu" />
```

> **NOTE** *Compiled binding doesn't support element-to-element binding as traditional binding does. However, as the* `SplitView` *has the name* `RootSplitView` *assigned, this variable can be directly used from code, and thus from compiled binding.*

Lastly, some content needs to be added to the `SplitView` pane.

Adding Content to the SplitView Pane

The pane of the `SplitView` should now list menu buttons for navigation to different pages. The sample code makes use of simple button controls within a `ListView` control. The `ListView` defines a `Header`, `Footer`, and `Items` section. The `Header` section includes a back button. Previously, the system back button was used with the help of the `SystemNavigationManager`. Instead of this system back button, you can use a custom button, as is used here. This button element binds the `IsEnabled` property to `AppFrame.CanGoBack` to change the `IsEnabled` mode depending on whether there's a back stack available. The `Footer` of the `ListView` defines a settings button. Within the items list of the `ListView`, Home and Edit buttons are created to navigate to these corresponding pages (code file `AppShellSample/AppShell.xaml`):

```xml
<SplitView.Pane>
  <ListView TabIndex="3" x:Name="NavMenuList" Margin="0,48,0,0">
    <ListView.Header>
      <Button x:Name="BackButton"
              TabIndex="2"
              Style="{StaticResource NavigationBackButtonStyle}"
              IsEnabled="{x:Bind AppFrame.CanGoBack, Mode=OneWay}"
              Width="{x:Bind Path=NavMenuList.Width, Mode=OneWay}"
              HorizontalAlignment=
                  "{x:Bind Path=NavMenuList.HorizontalAlignment, Mode=OneWay}"
              Click="{x:Bind Path=BackButton_Click}"/>
    </ListView.Header>
    <ListView.Items>
      <Button x:Name="HomeButton" Margin="-12" Padding="0"
              TabIndex="3"
              Style="{StaticResource HomeButtonStyle}"
              Width="{x:Bind Path=NavMenuList.Width}"
              HorizontalAlignment=
```

```
            "{x:Bind Path=NavMenuList.HorizontalAlignment}"
        Click="{x:Bind Path=GoToHomePage}" />
  <Button x:Name="EditButton" Margin="-12" Padding="0"
        TabIndex="4"
        Style="{StaticResource EditButtonStyle}"
        Width="{x:Bind Path=NavMenuList.Width}"
        HorizontalAlignment=
            "{x:Bind Path=NavMenuList.HorizontalAlignment}"
        Click="{x:Bind Path=GoToEditPage}" />
    </ListView.Items>
    <ListView.Footer>
      <Button x:Name="SettingsButton"
            TabIndex="3"
            Style="{StaticResource SettingsButtonStyle}"
            Width="{x:Bind Path=NavMenuList.Width}"
            HorizontalAlignment=
                "{x:Bind Path=NavMenuList.HorizontalAlignment}" />
    </ListView.Footer>
  </ListView>
</SplitView.Pane>
```

The symbol of these buttons is defined using the Segoe MDL2 Assets font, much like the hamburger button created earlier. These buttons need text and an icon. This is defined within a `Grid` element (code file `AppShellSample/Styles/Styles.xaml`):

```
<Style x:Key="NavigationBackButtonStyle" TargetType="Button"
  BasedOn="{StaticResource NavigationBackButtonNormalStyle}">
  <Setter Property="HorizontalAlignment" Value="Stretch"/>
  <Setter Property="HorizontalContentAlignment" Value="Stretch"/>
  <Setter Property="Height" Value="48"/>
  <Setter Property="Width" Value="NaN"/>
  <Setter Property="MinWidth" Value="48"/>
  <Setter Property="AutomationProperties.Name" Value="Back"/>
  <Setter Property="Content">
    <Setter.Value>
      <Grid>
        <Grid.ColumnDefinitions>
          <ColumnDefinition Width="48" />
          <ColumnDefinition />
        </Grid.ColumnDefinitions>
        <FontIcon Grid.Column="0" FontSize="16" Glyph="&#xE0D5;"
          MirroredWhenRightToLeft="True" VerticalAlignment="Center"
          HorizontalAlignment="Center"/>
        <TextBlock Grid.Column="1" Style="{ThemeResource BodyTextBlockStyle}"
          Text="Back" VerticalAlignment="Center" />
      </Grid>
    </Setter.Value>
  </Setter>
</Style>
```

The handler method `GoToEditPage` that is invoked by clicking on the Edit button navigates to the Edit page using the Frame within the `SplitView` (code file `AppShellSample/AppShell.xaml.cs`):

```
public void GoToEditPage()
{
  AppFrame?.Navigate(typeof(EditPage));
}
```

When you click the Home button, the navigation should not only go to the main page, but it should also get rid of the complete stack from the `Frame`. The `Frame` does not offer a direct clear method to remove the pages from the stack, but this can be done in a `while` loop as long as `CanGoBack` returns `true` (code file `AppShellSample/AppShell.xaml.cs`):

```
public void GoToHomePage()
{
```

```
        while (AppFrame?.CanGoBack ?? false) AppFrame.GoBack();
    }
```

When you run the application, you can see that the `SplitView` pane is closed in Figure 32-13 and open in Figure 32-14.

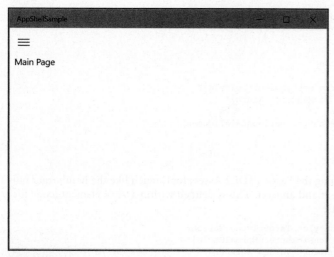

FIGURE 32-13

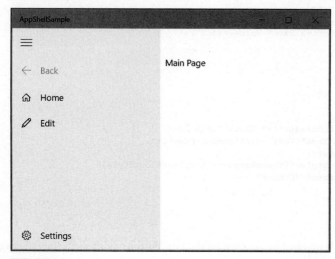

FIGURE 32-14

LAYOUT

The `SplitView` control discussed in the previous section is already an important control to organize the layout of the user interface. With many new Windows 10 apps you can see this control used for the main layout. There are several other controls to define a layout. This section demonstrates the `VariableSizedWrapGrid` for arranging multiple items in a grid that automatically wraps, the `RelativePanel` for arranging items relative to each other or relative to a parent, and adaptive triggers for rearranging the layout depending on the window size.

VariableSizedWrapGrid

VariableSizedWrapGrid is a wrap grid that automatically wraps to the next row or column if the size available for the grid is not large enough. The second feature of this grid is an allowance for items with multiple rows or columns; that's why it's called variable.

The following code snippet creates a VariableSizedWrappedGrid with orientation Horizontal, a maximum number of 20 items in the row, and rows and columns that have a size of 50 (code file LayoutSamples/Views/VariableSizedWrapGridSample.xaml):

```
<VariableSizedWrapGrid x:Name="grid1" MaximumRowsOrColumns="20" ItemHeight="50"
  ItemWidth="50" Orientation="Horizontal" />
```

The VariableSizedWrapGrid is filled with 30 Rectangle and TextBlock elements that have random sizes and colors. Depending on the size, 1 to 3 rows or columns can be used within the grid. The size of the items is set using the attached properties VariableSizedWrapGrid.ColumnSpan and VariableSizedWrapGrid.RowSpan (code file LayoutSamples/Views/VariableSizedWrapGridSample.xaml.cs):

```csharp
protected override void OnNavigatedTo(NavigationEventArgs e)
{
  base.OnNavigatedTo(e);
  Random r = new Random();
  Grid[] items =
    Enumerable.Range(0, 30).Select(i =>
    {
      byte[] colorBytes = new byte[3];
      r.NextBytes(colorBytes);
      var rect = new Rectangle
      {
        Height = r.Next(40, 150),
        Width = r.Next(40, 150),
        Fill = new SolidColorBrush(new Color
        {
          R = colorBytes[0],
          G = colorBytes[1],
          B = colorBytes[2],
          A = 255
        })
      };
      var textBlock = new TextBlock
      {
        Text = (i + 1).ToString(),
        HorizontalAlignment =HorizontalAlignment.Center,
        VerticalAlignment = VerticalAlignment.Center
      };
      Grid grid = new Grid();
      grid.Children.Add(rect);
      grid.Children.Add(textBlock);
      return grid;
    }).ToArray();

  foreach (var item in items)
  {
    grid1.Children.Add(item);
    Rectangle rect = item.Children.First() as Rectangle;
    if (rect.Width > 50)
    {
      int columnSpan = ((int)rect.Width / 50) + 1;
      VariableSizedWrapGrid.SetColumnSpan(item, columnSpan);
      int rowSpan = ((int)rect.Height / 50) + 1;
      VariableSizedWrapGrid.SetRowSpan(item, rowSpan);
    }
  }
```

When you run the application, you can see the rectangles and how they wrap for different window sizes in Figures 32-15 and 32-16.

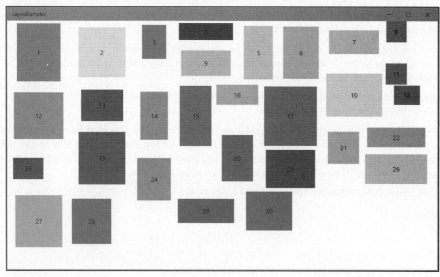

FIGURE 32-15

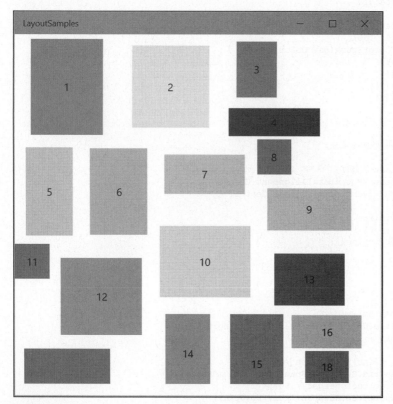

FIGURE 32-16

RelativePanel

RelativePanel is a new panel for the UWP that allows one element to be positioned in relation to another element. If you've used the Grid control with definitions for rows and columns and you had to insert a row, you had to change all elements that were below the row that was inserted. The reason is that all rows and columns are indexed by numbers. This is not an issue with the RelativePanel, which enables you to place elements in relation to each other.

> **NOTE** *Compared to the* RelativePanel, *the* Grid *control still has its advantages with auto, star, and fixed sizing. Read Chapter 34, "Windows Desktop Applications with WPF," in which the Grid control is explained in detail. This control is covered with WPF, but you can use it in a similar way with the UWP.*

The following code snippet aligns several TextBlock and TextBox controls, a Button, and a Rectangle within a RelativePanel. The TextBox elements are positioned to the right of the corresponding TextBlock elements; the Button is positioned relative to the bottom of the panel; and the Rectangle is aligned with the top with the first TextBlock and to the right of the first TextBox (code file LayoutSamples/Views/RelativePanelSample.xaml):

```xml
<RelativePanel>
  <TextBlock x:Name="FirstNameLabel" Text="First Name" Margin="8" />
  <TextBox x:Name="FirstNameText" RelativePanel.RightOf="FirstNameLabel"
    Margin="8" Width="150" />
  <TextBlock x:Name="LastNameLabel" Text="Last Name"
    RelativePanel.Below="FirstNameLabel" Margin="8" />
  <TextBox x:Name="LastNameText" RelativePanel.RightOf="LastNameLabel"
    Margin="8" RelativePanel.Below="FirstNameText" Width="150" />
  <Button Content="Save" RelativePanel.AlignHorizontalCenterWith="LastNameText"
    RelativePanel.AlignBottomWithPanel="True" Margin="8" />
  <Rectangle x:Name="Image" Fill="Violet" Width="150" Height="250"
    RelativePanel.AlignTopWith="FirstNameLabel"
    RelativePanel.RightOf="FirstNameText" Margin="8" />
</RelativePanel>
```

Figure 32-17 shows the alignment of the controls when you run the application.

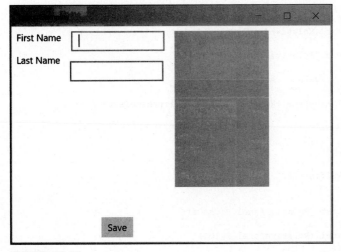

FIGURE 32-17

Adaptive Triggers

The `RelativePanel` is a great control for alignment. However, to support multiple screen sizes and rearrange the controls depending on the screen size, you can use adaptive triggers with the `RelativePanel` control. For example, on a small screen the `TextBox` controls should be arranged below the `TextBlock` controls, but on a larger screen the `TextBox` controls should be right of the `TextBlock` controls.

In the following code, the `RelativePanel` from before is changed to remove all `RelativePanel` attached properties that should not apply to all screen sizes, and an optional image is added (code file `LayoutSamples/Views/AdaptiveRelativePanelSample.xaml`):

```
<RelativePanel ScrollViewer.VerticalScrollBarVisibility="Auto" Margin="16">
  <TextBlock x:Name="FirstNameLabel" Text="First Name" Margin="8" />
  <TextBox x:Name="FirstNameText"  Margin="8" Width="150" />
  <TextBlock x:Name="LastNameLabel" Text="Last Name" Margin="8" />
  <TextBox x:Name="LastNameText" Margin="8" Width="150" />
  <Button Content="Save" RelativePanel.AlignBottomWithPanel="True"
    Margin="8" />
  <Rectangle x:Name="Image" Fill="Violet" Width="150" Height="250"
    Margin="8" />
  <Rectangle x:Name="OptionalImage" RelativePanel.AlignRightWithPanel="True"
    Fill="Red" Width="350" Height="350" Margin="8" />
</RelativePanel>
```

Using an adaptive trigger—with which the `MinWindowWidth` can be set to define when the trigger is fired—values for different properties are set to arrange the elements depending on the space available for the app. As the screen size gets smaller, the width needed by the app gets smaller as well. Moving elements below instead of beside reduces the width needed. Instead, the user can scroll down. With the smallest window width, the optional image is set collapsed (code file `LayoutSamples/Views/AdaptiveRelativePanelSample.xaml`):

```
<VisualStateManager.VisualStateGroups>
  <VisualStateGroup>
    <VisualState x:Name="WideState">
      <VisualState.StateTriggers>
        <AdaptiveTrigger MinWindowWidth="1024" />
      </VisualState.StateTriggers>
      <VisualState.Setters>
        <Setter Target="FirstNameText.(RelativePanel.RightOf)"
          Value="FirstNameLabel" />
        <Setter Target="LastNameLabel.(RelativePanel.Below)"
          Value="FirstNameLabel" />
        <Setter Target="LastNameText.(RelativePanel.Below)"
          Value="FirstNameText" />
        <Setter Target="LastNameText.(RelativePanel.RightOf)"
          Value="LastNameLabel" />
        <Setter Target="Image.(RelativePanel.AlignTopWith)"
          Value="FirstNameLabel" />
        <Setter Target="Image.(RelativePanel.RightOf)" Value="FirstNameText" />
      </VisualState.Setters>
    </VisualState>

    <VisualState x:Name="MediumState">
      <VisualState.StateTriggers>
        <AdaptiveTrigger MinWindowWidth="720" />
      </VisualState.StateTriggers>
      <VisualState.Setters>
        <Setter Target="FirstNameText.(RelativePanel.RightOf)"
          Value="FirstNameLabel" />
        <Setter Target="LastNameLabel.(RelativePanel.Below)"
          Value="FirstNameLabel" />
        <Setter Target="LastNameText.(RelativePanel.Below)"
```

```
            Value="FirstNameText" />
          <Setter Target="LastNameText.(RelativePanel.RightOf)"
            Value="LastNameLabel" />
          <Setter Target="Image.(RelativePanel.Below)" Value="LastNameText" />
          <Setter Target="Image.(RelativePanel.AlignHorizontalCenterWith)"
            Value="LastNameText" />
        </VisualState.Setters>
      </VisualState>

      <VisualState x:Name="NarrowState">
        <VisualState.StateTriggers>
          <AdaptiveTrigger MinWindowWidth="320" />
        </VisualState.StateTriggers>
        <VisualState.Setters>
          <Setter Target="FirstNameText.(RelativePanel.Below)"
            Value="FirstNameLabel" />
          <Setter Target="LastNameLabel.(RelativePanel.Below)"
            Value="FirstNameText" />
          <Setter Target="LastNameText.(RelativePanel.Below)"
            Value="LastNameLabel" />
          <Setter Target="Image.(RelativePanel.Below)" Value="LastNameText" />
          <Setter Target="OptionalImage.Visibility" Value="Collapsed" />
        </VisualState.Setters>
      </VisualState>
    </VisualStateGroup>
  </VisualStateManager.VisualStateGroups>
```

You can establish the minimum window width needed by the application by setting the
`SetPreferredMinSize` with the `ApplicationView` class (code file `LayoutSamples/App.xaml.cs`):

```
protected override void OnLaunched(LaunchActivatedEventArgs e)
{
  ApplicationView.GetForCurrentView().SetPreferredMinSize(
    new Size { Width = 320, Height = 300 });
  // etc.
}
```

When you run the application, you can see different layout arrangements with the smallest width (see
Figure 32-18), a medium width (see Figure 32-19), and the maximum width (see Figure 32-20).

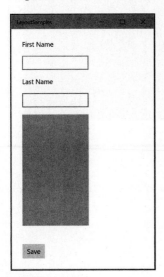

FIGURE 32-18

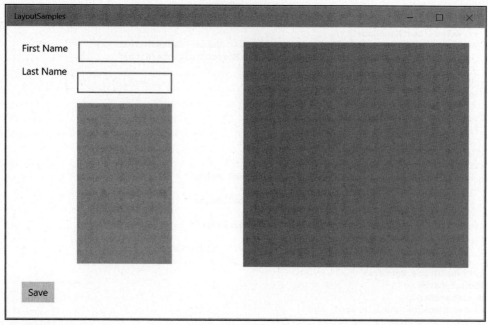

FIGURE 32-19

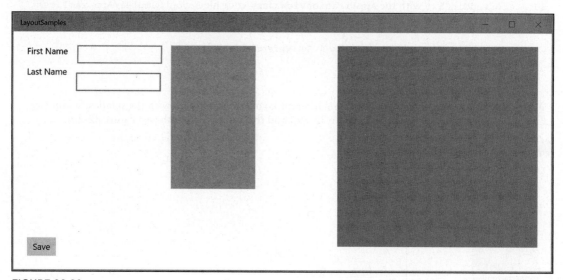

FIGURE 32-20

The adaptive trigger is also good to use to change the look of the `SplitView` to `CompactInline` or `Overlay` mode (code file `AppShellSample/AppShell.xaml`):

```
<VisualStateManager.VisualStateGroups>
  <VisualStateGroup>
    <VisualState>
      <VisualState.StateTriggers>
        <AdaptiveTrigger MinWindowWidth="720" />
      </VisualState.StateTriggers>
      <VisualState.Setters>
```

```
          <Setter Target="RootSplitView.DisplayMode" Value="CompactInline"/>
          <Setter Target="RootSplitView.IsPaneOpen" Value="True"/>
        </VisualState.Setters>
      </VisualState>
      <VisualState>
        <VisualState.StateTriggers>
          <AdaptiveTrigger MinWindowWidth="0" />
        </VisualState.StateTriggers>
        <VisualState.Setters>
          <Setter Target="RootSplitView.DisplayMode" Value="Overlay"/>
        </VisualState.Setters>
      </VisualState>
    </VisualStateGroup>
  </VisualStateManager.VisualStateGroups>
```

XAML Views

Adaptive triggers can help support a lot of different window sizes as well as support layouts of the app for running it on the phone and the desktop. If the user interface for your app should have more differences than can be solved by using the `RelativePanel`, the best option can be to use different XAML views. An XAML view contains just XAML code and uses the same code-behind as the corresponding page. You can create different XAML views for the same page for every device family.

You can define XAML views for mobile devices by creating a folder `DeviceFamily-Mobile`. The device-specific folder always starts with the name `DeviceFamily`. Examples of other device families supported are `Team`, `Desktop`, and `IoT`. You can use this device family name as postfix to specify XAML views for the corresponding device family. You create an XAML view using the XAML View Visual Studio item template. This template creates the XAML code but no code-behind file. This view needs to have the same name as the page where the view should be replaced.

Instead of creating a different folder for the mobile XAML views, you can also create the views in the same folder as the page but the view file is named using `DeviceFamily-Mobile`.

Deferred Loading

For a faster UI, you can delay creation of controls until they are needed. On small devices, some controls might not be needed at all, but with larger screens and faster systems they are needed. With previous versions of XAML applications, elements that have been added to the XAML code also have been instantiated. This is no longer the case with Windows 10. Here you can defer loading of controls as they are needed.

You can use deferred loading with adaptive triggers to load only some controls at a later time. One sample scenario where this is useful is when you have a smaller window that the user can resize to be larger. With the smaller window, some controls should not be visible, but they should be visible with the bigger size of the window. Another scenario where deferred loading can be useful is when some parts of the layout may take more time to load. Instead of letting the user wait until he sees the complete loaded layout, you can use deferred loading.

To use deferred loading, you need to add the `x:DeferLoadingStrategy` attribute to a control, as shown in the following code snippet with a `Grid` control. This control also needs to have a name assigned to it (code file `LayoutSamples/Views/DelayLoadingSample.xaml`):

```
<Grid x:DeferLoadStrategy="Lazy" x:Name="deferGrid">
  <Grid.ColumnDefinitions>
    <ColumnDefinition />
    <ColumnDefinition />
  </Grid.ColumnDefinitions>
  <Grid.RowDefinitions>
    <RowDefinition />
    <RowDefinition />
```

```
        </Grid.RowDefinitions>
        <Rectangle Fill="Red" Grid.Row="0" Grid.Column="0" />
        <Rectangle Fill="Green" Grid.Row="0" Grid.Column="1" />
        <Rectangle Fill="Blue" Grid.Row="1" Grid.Column="0" />
        <Rectangle Fill="Yellow" Grid.Row="1" Grid.Column="1" />
    </Grid>
```

To make this deferred control visible, all you need to do is invoke the `FindName` method to access the identifier of the control. This not only makes the control visible but also loads the XAML tree of the control before the control is made visible (code file `LayoutSamples/Views/DelayLoadingSample.xaml.cs`):

```
private void OnDeferLoad(object sender, RoutedEventArgs e)
{
    FindName(nameof(deferGrid));
}
```

When you run the application, you can verify with the Life Visual Tree window that the tree containing the `deferGrid` element is not available (see Figure 32-21), but after the `FindName` method is invoked to find the `deferGrid` element, the `deferGrid` element is added to the tree (see Figure 32-22).

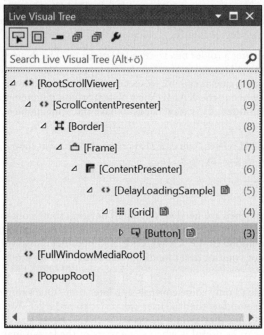

FIGURE 32-21

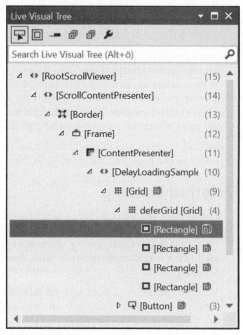

FIGURE 32-22

COMMANDS

Earlier in this chapter you saw how you can handle navigation for the user. You've seen the hamburger button and normal buttons that are used to navigate to different pages. With apps, you need more controls that allow the user to start some actions. Windows 8 had some interesting aspects for bringing command bars into action when the user swipes from top or bottom; the hidden commands allowed for less-crowded screen. Some really important command controls were still allowed to be placed directly on the screen. Microsoft's OneNote had an interesting control that used only a small circle; when the user clicked inside it, the control grew larger to offer more options. The issue with this design is that it turned out to not be intuitive enough. The users had a hard time to find out which apps allowed for swiping from top or bottom, and often had no idea that they could do that. With Windows 10, where Windows apps can run in a small window instead of full-screen, this even has more issues. With Windows 10, it's acceptable to have command bars that stay open all the time—just check Microsoft's new version of OneNote that has a command control that looks like the Ribbon control.

> **NOTE** *The Ribbon control is discussed in Chapter 34.*

An easy way to create a list of controls that can be activated by the user is by using the `CommandBar` and `AppBar` classes. `CommandBar` is easier to use but doesn't have the flexibility of the `AppBar`. With the `CommandBar`, you can add only specific types of controls, whereas the `AppBar` enables you to use any element.

The following code sample creates a `CommandBar` that is positioned on top of the page. This `CommandBar` contains three `AppBarButton` controls (code file `ControlsSample/Views/InkSample.xaml`):

```
<Page.TopAppBar>
  <CommandBar>
    <AppBarButton Icon="Save" Label="Save" Click="{x:Bind OnSave}" />
    <AppBarButton Icon="OpenFile" Label="Open" Click="{x:Bind OnLoad}" />
    <AppBarButton Icon="Clear" Label="Clear" Click="{x:Bind OnClear}" />
  </CommandBar>
</Page.TopAppBar>
```

The `Page` class contains `TopAppBar` and `BottomAppBar` properties to position the app bars on top or bottom. These properties were necessary with Windows 8, but now they're just for convenience. You can position the app bar within the page where you'd like it to be.

The `AppBarButton` controls are defined as children of the `CommandBar`. The symbol of the `AppBar` button can be defined in several ways. Using the `Icon` property, you can assign a `BitmapIcon`, `FontIcon`, `PathIcon`, or `SymbolIcon`. (Read Chapter 29 for information on how to define vector graphics with the `Path` element.) Using the `Icon` property, you can directly assign a predefined symbol, which in turn sets a `SymbolIcon`. Examples of predefined icons are `Save`, `OpenFile`, and `Clear`. Figure 32-23 shows the `CommandBar` with three `AppBar` button controls in expanded mode. In collapsed mode—which you can switch by clicking the ellipsis button—the values of the `Label` properties are not shown.

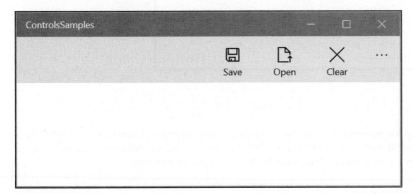

FIGURE 32-23

`AppBarSeparator` and `AppBarToggleButton` are other controls that can be contained in the `CommandBar`—in other words, any control that implements the interface `ICommandBarElement`. This interface defines the `IsCompact` property to make the button larger or smaller to show or not show the label part.

The following example adds `AddBarToggleButton` controls. The `AppBarToggleButton` class derives from `ToggleButton` and adds the interfaces `ICommandBarElement` and `IAppBarToggleButton`. This button, like the base class `ToggleButton`, allows for three states—checked, unchecked, and indeterminate—but by default only checked and unchecked are used. For the symbol, the font Segoe MDL2 Assets is used to define a vector-graphic glyph element (code file `ControlsSample/Views/InkSample.xaml`):

```xml
<AppBarToggleButton IsChecked="{x:Bind Path=ColorSelection.Red, Mode=TwoWay}"
  Background="Red" Label="Red">
  <AppBarToggleButton.Icon>
    <FontIcon Glyph="&#xea3a;" />
  </AppBarToggleButton.Icon>
</AppBarToggleButton>
<AppBarToggleButton IsChecked="{x:Bind ColorSelection.Green, Mode=TwoWay}"
  Background="Green" Label="Green">
  <AppBarToggleButton.Icon>
    <FontIcon Glyph="&#xea3a;"/>
  </AppBarToggleButton.Icon>
</AppBarToggleButton>
<AppBarToggleButton IsChecked="{x:Bind ColorSelection.Blue, Mode=TwoWay}"
  Background="Blue" Label="Blue">
  <AppBarToggleButton.Icon>
    <FontIcon Glyph="&#xea3a;"/>
  </AppBarToggleButton.Icon>
</AppBarToggleButton>
```

Figure 32-24 shows the command bar with both previously created `AppBarButton` controls as well as the `AppBarToggleButton` controls, this time in compact mode.

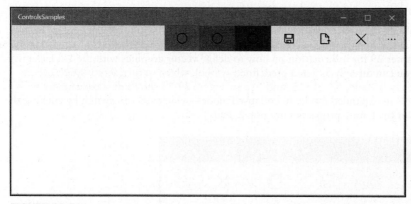

FIGURE 32-24

The `CommandBar` also allows for secondary commands. In case you need more commands that don't fit into a line—especially with mobile devices—you can use secondary commands. Secondary commands can be defined assigned to the property `SecondaryCommands` of the `CommandBar` element.

```xml
<CommandBar>
  <CommandBar.SecondaryCommands>
    <AppBarButton Label="One" Icon="OneBar" />
    <AppBarButton Label="Two" Icon="TwoBars" />
    <AppBarButton Label="Three" Icon="ThreeBars" />
    <AppBarButton Label="Four" Icon="FourBars" />
  </CommandBar.SecondaryCommands>
  <!-- etc. -->
```

With Windows 10, secondary commands are opened by clicking on the ellipsis button, as shown in Figure 32-25.

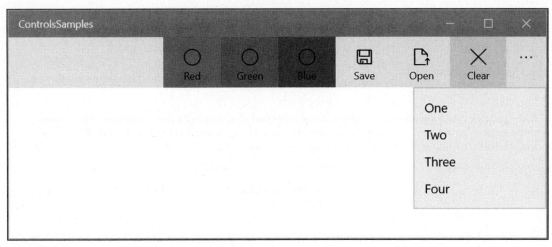

FIGURE 32-25

COMPILED DATA BINDING

Compiled data binding is the faster alternative to the `Binding` markup extension using `x:Bind` that was introduced in Chapter 31 and has already been mentioned in this chapter. Now we're getting deeper into the features of compiled binding.

You can use compiled data binding as a faster replacement for the `Binding` markup extension. There are just a few reasons when the old binding syntax is needed—for example, when triggering the binding on property change instead of on focus change. I'm sure this will change in a future version when compiled binding gets even more enhanced. Currently this is not reason enough to not use compiled binding at all because you can mix compiled binding with the `Binding` markup expression.

Chapter 31 includes the new syntax for compiled binding with `x:Bind` instead of `Binding` where code gets compiled, and you even get a compiler error.

As compiled binding is focused on performance, the default mode is `OneTime`. In case you need to update the user interface from changes from the code, you need to explicitly set the mode to `OneWay`. For updating the source from the UI, you need to set the `TwoWay` mode. The compiled binding uses the same modes as the `Binding` expression, but the defaults differ.

Because compiled binding was already discussed in Chapter 31, this chapter covers only some special features of compiled binding, such as using it from within resources, and controlling the binding life cycle.

Compiled Binding Lifecycle

With compiled binding, code gets generated from binding. You can also programmatically influence the lifetime of the binding.

Let's start with a simple `Book` type that is bound from the user interface (code file `CompiledBindingSample/Models/Book.cs`):

```
public class Book : BindableBase
{
  public int BookId { get; set; }
  private string _title;

  public string Title
  {
```

```
      get { return _title; }
      set { SetProperty(ref _title, value); }
   }

   public string Publisher { get; set; }

   public override string ToString() => Title;
}
```

With the page class, a read-only property `Book` is created that returns a `Book` instance. The values of the `Book` instance can be changed, whereas the `Book` instance itself is read only (code file `CompiledBindingSample/Views/LifetimeSample.xaml.cs`):

```
public Book Book { get; } = new Book
                           {
                               Title = "Professional C# 6",
                               Publisher = "Wrox Press"
                           };
```

With the XAML code, the `Title` property is in `OneWay` mode to the `Text` property of a `TextBlock`, and the `Publisher` is bound without specifying a mode, which means it is bound `OneTime` (code file `CompiledBindingSample/Views/LifetimeSample.xaml`):

```
<StackPanel>
  <TextBlock Text="{x:Bind Book.Title, Mode=OneWay}" />
  <TextBlock Text="{x:Bind Book.Publisher}" />
</StackPanel>
```

Next, several `AppBarButton` controls are bound to change the lifetime of the compiled binding. The `Click` event of one button is bound to the method `OnChangeBook`. This method changes the title of the book. If you try this out, the title gets immediately updated because a `OneTime` binding was done (code file `CompiledBindingSample/Views/LifetimeSample.xaml.cs`):

```
public void OnChangeBook()
{
   Book.Title = "Professional C# 6 and .NET Core 5";
}
```

However, you can stop the tracking of the binding. Invoking the method `StopTracking` using the `Bindings` property of the page (this property is created if you are using compiled binding) removes all binding listeners. When you call this method before invoking the method `OnChangeBook`, the update of the book is not reflected in the user interface:

```
private void OnStopTracking()
{
   Bindings.StopTracking();
}
```

To explicitly update the user interface from bound sources, you can invoke the `Update` method. Calling this method reflects changes not only from `OneWay` or `TwoWay` bindings, but also `OneTime` bindings:

```
private void OnUpdateBinding()
{
   Bindings.Update();
}
```

For bringing the listeners back in place to make immediate updates to the user interface, the `Initialize` method needs to be invoked.

`Initialize`, `Update`, and `StopTracking` are the three important methods for controlling the lifetime with compiled binding.

Using Resources for Compiled Data Templates

Defining data templates using compiled binding is easy; you just need to specify the x:DataType attribute with the data template because this is needed for the strongly typed code generation. However, there's an issue with placing the data template within a resource file. Using data templates within a page is easy because the page already creates code-behind code, and this is necessary for the data template that contains compiled bindings as well. Let's have a look at what you need to do to put such a data template within a resource file.

With the sample code, a resource file DataTemplates.xaml is generated. All that's needed for the resource is a sealed class (code file CompiledBindingSample/Styles/DataTemplates.xaml.cs):

```
namespace CompiledBindingSample.Styles
{
  public sealed partial class DataTemplates
  {
    public DataTemplates()
    {
      this.InitializeComponent();
    }
  }
}
```

The XAML file contains the data template as usual. Just pay attention to the x:Class attribute to map the ResourceDictionary to the class in the code-behind file. The data template also contains an XML alias to the .NET Models namespace to map the Book type and compiled bindings to the Title and Publisher properties (code file CompiledBindingSample/Styles/DataTemplates.xaml):

```
<ResourceDictionary
  x:Class="CompiledBindingSample.Styles.DataTemplates"
  xmlns="http://schemas.microsoft.com/winfx/2006/xaml/presentation"
  xmlns:x="http://schemas.microsoft.com/winfx/2006/xaml"
  xmlns:model="using:CompiledBindingSample.Models"
  xmlns:local="using:CompiledBindingSample.Styles">
  <DataTemplate x:DataType="model:Book" x:Name="BookTemplate">
    <StackPanel>
      <TextBlock Text="{x:Bind Title}" />
      <TextBlock Text="{x:Bind Publisher}" />
    </StackPanel>
  </DataTemplate>
</ResourceDictionary>
```

When referencing the resource file from the App.xaml file, the file cannot be referenced as usual with the ResourceDictionary element. Instead an instance is created (code file CompiledBindingSample/App.xaml):

```
<Application
  x:Class="CompiledBindingSample.App"
  xmlns="http://schemas.microsoft.com/winfx/2006/xaml/presentation"
  xmlns:x="http://schemas.microsoft.com/winfx/2006/xaml"
  xmlns:local="using:CompiledBindingSample"
  xmlns:model="using:CompiledBindingSample.Models"
  xmlns:styles="using:CompiledBindingSample.Styles"
  RequestedTheme="Light">
  <Application.Resources>
    <ResourceDictionary>
      <ResourceDictionary.MergedDictionaries>
        <styles:DataTemplates />
      </ResourceDictionary.MergedDictionaries>
    </ResourceDictionary>
```

```
      </Application.Resources>
    </Application>
```

With all this in place, the data template can be referenced as usual—for example, with an `ItemTemplate` for the `ListBox` (code file `CompiledBindingSample/Views/BooksListPage.xaml`):

```
<ListBox ItemTemplate="{StaticResource BookTemplate}"
    ItemsSource="{x:Bind Books}" Margin="8" />
```

CONTROLS

All the controls offered by the UWP cannot be covered in this book. However, they are simple to use and when you know how to use some of them, it's not hard to use the others. Many controls have similarities to WPF controls, so you can read more information about controls in Chapter 34.

TextBox Control

One thing worth a special mention with the UWP controls is the `Header` property available with the `TextBox` control. Previously in this chapter you've seen how to arrange an edit form with the `RelativePanel`. In that example, a `TextBox` control was used in correlation with a `TextBlock` control. Usually the information that should be entered in a `TextBox` is described by a label close to this text input control. The `TextBlock` control served this purpose in the sample with the `RelativePanel`. There's another way to add information to a `TextBox`. When you use the `Header` property of the `TextBox` control, there's no need to define a separate `TextBlock` control. Filling the `Header` property will do. The value of the `Header` property just shows up close to the `TextBox` (see Figure 32-26).

Email

FIGURE 32-26

When you set the `InputScope` property, you can specify which on-screen keyboard should show up. Figure 32-27 shows the Windows onscreen keyboard where the `InputScope` is set to `Formula`, as shown in the following code snippet. With this keyboard you can see some formula-specific keys (code file `ControlsSamples/Views/TextSample.xaml`):

```
<TextBox Header="Email" InputScope="EmailNameOrAddress"></TextBox>
<TextBox Header="Currency" InputScope="CurrencyAmountAndSymbol"></TextBox>
<TextBox Header="Alpha Numeric" InputScope="AlphanumericFullWidth"></TextBox>
<TextBox Header="Formula" InputScope="Formula"></TextBox>
<TextBox Header="Month" InputScope="DateMonthNumber"></TextBox>
```

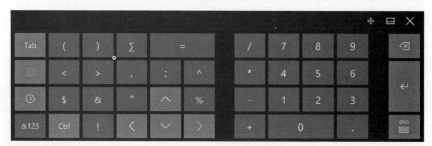

FIGURE 32-27

AutoSuggest

A new control with the UWP is the `AutoSuggest` control. This control allows offering suggestions to the user while the user types into the control. Three events are important with this control. As soon as the user types into the control, the `TextChanged` event is fired. With the sample code, the `OnTextChanged` handler method is invoked. In cases where suggestions are offered to the user and the user selects a suggestion, the `SuggestionChosen` event is fired. After the text—which might be a suggestion or other words typed—is entered by the user, the `QuerySubmitted` event is fired (code file `ControlsSample/Views/AutoSuggestSample.xaml`):

```
<AutoSuggestBox TextChanged="{x:Bind OnTextChanged}"
                SuggestionChosen="{x:Bind OnSuggestionChosen}"
                QuerySubmitted="{x:Bind OnQuerySubmitted}" />
```

For having some sample code to create a suggestion, an XML file containing Formula 1 champions is loaded from `http://www.cninnovation.com/downloads/Racers.xml` using the `HttpClient` class. On navigating to the page, the XML file is retrieved, and the content is converted to a list of Racer objects (code file `ControlsSamples/Views/AutoSuggestSample.xaml.cs`):

```
private const string RacersUri =
  "http://www.cninnovation.com/downloads/Racers.xml";
private IEnumerable<Racer> _racers;

protected async override void OnNavigatedTo(NavigationEventArgs e)
{
  base.OnNavigatedTo(e);
  XElement xmlRacers = null;

  using (var client = new HttpClient())
  using (Stream stream = await client.GetStreamAsync(RacersUri))
  {
    xmlRacers = XElement.Load(stream);
  }

  _racers = xmlRacers.Elements("Racer").Select(r => new Racer
  {
    FirstName = r.Element("Firstname").Value,
    LastName = r.Element("Lastname").Value,
    Country = r.Element("Country").Value
  }).ToList();
}
```

The `Racer` class contains `FirstName`, `LastName`, and `Country` properties and an overload of the `ToString` method (code file `ControlsSamples/Models/Racer.cs`):

```
public class Racer
{
  public string FirstName { get; set; }
  public string LastName { get; set; }
  public string Country { get; set; }
  public override string ToString() => $"{FirstName} {LastName}, {Country}";
}
```

The `OnTextChanged` event is invoked as soon as the text of the `AutoSuggestBox` changes. Arguments received are the `AutoSuggestBox` itself—the sender—and `AutoSuggestBoxTextChangedEventArgs`. With the `AutoSuggestBoxTextChangedEventArgs`, the reason for the change is shown in the `Reason` property. Possible reasons are `UserInput`, `ProgrammaticChange`, and `SuggestionChosen`. Only if the reason is `UserInput` is there a need to offer suggestions to the user. Here, a check is also done to see whether the user entered at least two characters. The user input is retrieved by accessing the `Text` property of the `AutoSuggestBox`. This text is used to query the first names, last names, and countries based on the input string. The result from the query is assigned to the `ItemsSource` property of the `AutoSuggestBox` (code file ControlsSamples/Views/AutoSuggestSample.xaml.cs):

```
private void OnTextChanged(AutoSuggestBox sender,
  AutoSuggestBoxTextChangedEventArgs args)
{
  if (args.Reason == AutoSuggestionBoxTextChangeReason.UserInput &&
      sender.Text.Length >= 2)
  {
    string input = sender.Text;
    var q = _racers.Where(
      r => r.FirstName.StartsWith(input,
        StringComparison.CurrentCultureIgnoreCase))
      .OrderBy(r => r.FirstName).ThenBy(r => r.LastName)
      .ThenBy(r => r.Country).ToArray();
    if (q.Length == 0)
    {
      q = _racers.Where(r => r.LastName.StartsWith(input,
        StringComparison.CurrentCultureIgnoreCase))
        .OrderBy(r => r.LastName).ThenBy(r => r.FirstName)
        .ThenBy(r => r.Country).ToArray();
      if (q.Length == 0)
      {
        q = _racers.Where(r => r.Country.StartsWith(input,
          StringComparison.CurrentCultureIgnoreCase))
          .OrderBy(r => r.Country).ThenBy(r => r.LastName)
          .ThenBy(r => r.FirstName).ToArray();
      }
    }
    sender.ItemsSource = q;
  }
}
```

When you run the app and enter Aus in the `AutoSuggestBox`, the query can't find first or last names starting with this text, but it does find countries. Formula 1 champions from countries starting with Aus are shown in the suggestion list as shown in Figure 32-28.

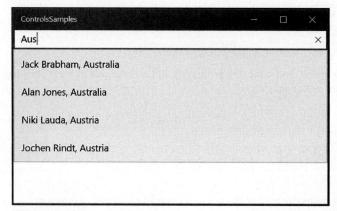

FIGURE 32-28

In cases where the user selects one of the suggestions, the `OnSuggestionChosen` handler is invoked. The suggestion can be retrieved from the `SelectedItem` property of the `AutoSuggestBoxSuggestionChosenEventArgs`:

```
private async void OnSuggestionChosen(AutoSuggestBox sender,
  AutoSuggestBoxSuggestionChosenEventArgs args)
{
```

```
      var dlg = new MessageDialog($"suggestion: {args.SelectedItem}");
      await dlg.ShowAsync();
  }
```

No matter whether the user selects a suggestion, the `OnQuerySubmitted` method gets invoked to show the result. The result is shown in the `QueryText` property of the `AutoSuggestBoxQuerySubmittedEventArgs` argument. In case a suggestion was selected, this is found in the `ChosenSuggestion` property:

```
private async void OnQuerySubmitted(AutoSuggestBox sender,
  AutoSuggestBoxQuerySubmittedEventArgs args)
{
  string message = $"query: {args.QueryText}";
  if (args.ChosenSuggestion != null)
  {
    message += $" suggestion: {args.ChosenSuggestion}";
  }
  var dlg = new MessageDialog(message);
  await dlg.ShowAsync();
}
```

Inking

Using a pen with ink is easily supported using UWP apps with the new `InkCanvas` control. This control supports inking using the pen, touchscreen, and mouse, and it also supports retrieving all the created strokes, which allows saving this information.

All that's needed to support inking is to add an `InkCanvas` control (code file `ControlsSamples/Views/InkSample.xaml`):

```
<Grid Background="{ThemeResource ApplicationPageBackgroundThemeBrush}">
  <InkCanvas x:Name="inkCanvas" />
</Grid>
```

By default, the `InkCanvas` control is configured to support the pen. You can also define it to support the mouse and touchscreen by setting the `InputDevicesType` property of the `InkPresenter` (code file `ControlsSamples/Views/InkSample.xaml.cs`):

```
public InkSample()
{
  this.InitializeComponent();
  inkCanvas.InkPresenter.InputDeviceTypes = CoreInputDeviceTypes.Mouse |
    CoreInputDeviceTypes.Touch | CoreInputDeviceTypes.Pen;
  ColorSelection = new ColorSelection(inkCanvas);
}

public ColorSelection ColorSelection { get; }
```

With the `InkCanvas` in place, you already can use an input device and create the same drawings with a black pen. Earlier in this chapter when commands were defined, a few `AppBarToggleButton` controls were added to the `CommandBar`. These buttons are now used to control the ink color. The `ColorSelection` class is a helper class that binds the selections of the `AppBarToggleButton` controls. The `Red`, `Green`, and `Blue` properties are bound by the `IsChecked` property of the `AppBarToggleButton` controls. The constructor of the `ColorSelection` receives an instance of the `InkCanvas`. This way, the `InkCanvas` control can be used to modify the drawing attributes (code file `ControlsSamples/Utilities/ColorSelection.cs`):

```
public class ColorSelection : BindableBase
{
  public ColorSelection(InkCanvas inkCanvas)
  {
    _inkCanvas = inkCanvas;
    Red = false;
```

```
      Green = false;
      Blue = false;
    }
    private InkCanvas _inkCanvas;

    private bool? _red;
    public bool? Red
    {
      get { return _red; }
      set { SetColor(ref _red, value); }
    }
    private bool? _green;
    public bool? Green
    {
      get { return _green; }
      set { SetColor(ref _green, value); }
    }
    private bool? _blue;
    public bool? Blue
    {
      get { return _blue; }
      set { SetColor(ref _blue, value); }
    }
    // etc.
  }
```

The change of the ink color as well the form and size of the pen is handled in the `SetColor` method. The existing drawing attributes of the `InkCanvas` can be retrieved using the `CopyDefaultDrawingAttributes` using the `InkPresenter`. The `UpdateDefaultDrawingAttributes` method sets the drawing attributes of the `InkCanvas`. The `Red`, `Green`, and `Blue` properties of the `ColorSelection` class are used to create a color (code file `ControlsSamples/Utilities/ColorSelection.cs`):

```
  public class ColorSelection : BindableBase
  {
    // etc.

    public void SetColor(ref bool? item, bool? value)
    {
      SetProperty(ref item, value);

      InkDrawingAttributes defaultAttributes =
        _inkCanvas.InkPresenter.CopyDefaultDrawingAttributes();
      defaultAttributes.PenTip = PenTipShape.Rectangle;
      defaultAttributes.Size = new Size(3, 3);

      defaultAttributes.Color = new Windows.UI.Color()
      {
        A = 255,
        R = Red == true ? (byte)0xff : (byte)0,
        G = Green == true ? (byte)0xff : (byte)0,
        B = Blue == true ? (byte)0xff : (byte)0
      };
      _inkCanvas.InkPresenter.UpdateDefaultDrawingAttributes(
        defaultAttributes);
    }
  }
```

When you run the application, as shown in Figure 32-29, it's easy to create a drawing using the pen. In case you don't have a pen, you can also use a finger with your touch device or use the mouse because the `InputDeviceTypes` property has been configured accordingly.

FIGURE 32-29

Pickers for Reading and Writing Strokes

As previously mentioned, the InkCanvas control also supports accessing the created strokes. These strokes are used with the following sample to store it in a file. The file is selected using the FileSavePicker. The method OnSave is invoked on clicking the Save AppBarButton that was created previously. The FileSavePicker is the UWP variant of the SaveFileDialog. With Windows 8, this picker has been full screen, but now with UWP, where it can be contained in smaller windows, this picker has changed as well.

First, the FileSavePicker is configured by assigning a start location, a file type extension, and a filename. At least one file type choice needs to be added to allow the user to select a file type. Invoking the method PickSaveFileAsync, the user is asked to select a file. This file is opened to transactional write invoking the method OpenTransactedWriteAsync. The strokes of the InkCanvas are stored in the StrokeContainer of the InkPresenter. The strokes can be directly saved to a stream with the SaveAsync method (code file ControlsSamples/Views/InkSample.xaml.cs):

```
private const string FileTypeExtension = ".strokes";
public async void OnSave()
{
    var picker = new FileSavePicker
    {
        SuggestedStartLocation = PickerLocationId.PicturesLibrary,
```

```
      DefaultFileExtension = FileTypeExtension,
      SuggestedFileName = "sample"
  };
  picker.FileTypeChoices.Add("Stroke File", new List<string>()
  { FileTypeExtension });
  StorageFile file = await picker.PickSaveFileAsync();
  if (file != null)
  {
    using (StorageStreamTransaction tx = await file.OpenTransactedWriteAsync())
    {
      await inkCanvas.InkPresenter.StrokeContainer.SaveAsync(tx.Stream);
      await tx.CommitAsync();
    }
  }
}
```

> **NOTE** *Using the* `FileOpenPicker` *and* `FileSavePicker` *to read and write streams is discussed in more detail in Chapter 23, "Files and Streams."*

When you run the application, you can open the `FileSavePicker` as shown in Figure 32-30.

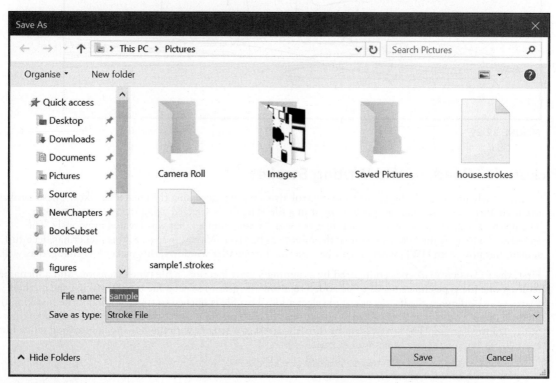

FIGURE 32-30

To load a file, the `FileOpenPicker` and the `StrokeContainer` with the `LoadAsync` method are used:

```
public async void OnLoad()
{
```

```
      var picker = new FileOpenPicker
      {
        SuggestedStartLocation = PickerLocationId.PicturesLibrary
      };
      picker.FileTypeFilter.Add(FileTypeExtension);

      StorageFile file = await picker.PickSingleFileAsync();
      if (file != null)
      {
        using (var stream = await file.OpenReadAsync())
        {
          await inkCanvas.InkPresenter.StrokeContainer.LoadAsync(stream);
        }
      }
    }
```

> **NOTE** *Some more controls are shown in the next chapter, which discusses contracts and sensors. As the* Map *control is best used with GPS, you can read about this control in Chapter 33.*

SUMMARY

This chapter provided an introduction to many different aspects of programming UWP apps. You've seen how XAML is very similar to programming WPF applications, as described in previous chapters.

In this chapter, you've seen how different screen sizes can be dealt with. You've seen how the hamburger button works in conjunction with SplitView to offer larger or smaller navigation menus, and how the RelativePanel works with adaptive triggers. You've also had a look at XAML views.

You've seen how to make performance improvements using deferred loading and compiled binding. You've also been introduced to new controls, such as the AutoSuggest control and the InkCanvas control.

The next chapter gives more information on Windows apps, including contracts and sensors, more controls—such as the Map control—and background services.

33

Advanced Windows Apps

WROX.COM CODE DOWNLOADS FOR THIS CHAPTER

The wrox.com code downloads for this chapter are found at http://www.wrox.com/go/professionalcsharp6 on the Download Code tab. The code for this chapter contains one big sample that shows the various aspects of this chapter:

- ➤ AppLifetime Sample
- ➤ Sharing Samples
- ➤ AppServices
- ➤ Camera Sample
- ➤ Map Sample
- ➤ Sensor Sample
- ➤ Rolling Marble

OVERVIEW

The previous chapter introduced you to user interface (UI) elements for Universal Windows Platform (UWP) apps. This chapter continues from there to show you several aspects specific to UWP apps. You see how UWP apps have a lifetime management that is different from desktop applications. You use the share contract to create share source and target apps to share data between apps. You make use of different devices and sensors—such as the camera to take pictures and record videos—get location information, and get information about how the user moves the device by using several sensors, such as accelerometer and inclinometer.

Let's start with the app lifetime of Windows apps, which is very different from the lifetime of desktop applications.

APP LIFETIME

Windows 8 introduced a new life cycle for apps that is completely different from the life cycle of desktop applications. This changed a little with Windows 8.1, and again with Windows 10. If you're using Windows 10 and *tablet mode*, the life cycle of the app is different compared to *desktop mode*. With tablet mode, apps are typically full-screen. You can either switch to tablet mode automatically by detaching the keyboard (with tablet devices such as the Microsoft Surface), or by using the Tablet Mode button in the Action Center. When you run an application in tablet mode, the app gets suspended if it moves to the background (the user switches to another app), and it doesn't get any more CPU utilization. This way the app doesn't consume any battery. The app just uses memory while it's in the background and gets activated again as soon as the user switches to this app.

In case memory resources are low, Windows can terminate suspended applications. To terminate an app, the process is killed. No information is sent to the application, so it cannot react to this event. That's why an application should act on the suspended event and save its state there. Upon termination it is too late to save the state.

When receiving the suspended event, an app should store its state on disk. If the app is started again, the app can present itself to the user as if it was never terminated. You just need to store information about the page stack to navigate the user to the page where he or she left off, allow the user to go back by restoring the page back stack, and initialize the fields to the data the user entered.

The sample app for this section—`ApplicationLifetimeSample`—does exactly this. With this app, multiple pages allow navigation between the pages, and the state can be entered. The page stack is stored and state is stored when the app is suspended, and both are restored when the app is started.

APPLICATION EXECUTION STATES

States of the application are defined with the `ApplicationExecutionState` enumeration. This enumeration defines the states `NotRunning`, `Running`, `Suspended`, `Terminated`, and `ClosedByUser`. The application needs to be aware of and store its state, as users returning to the application expect to continue where they left it previously.

With the `OnLaunched` method in the App class, you can get the previous execution state of the application with the `PreviousExecutionState` property of the `LaunchActivatedEventArgs` argument. The previous execution state is `NotRunning` if the application is being started for the first time after installing it, or after a reboot, or when the user stopped the process from the Task Manager. The application is in the `Running` state if it was already running when the user activated it from a second tile or it's activated by one of the activation contracts. The `PreviousExecutionState` property returns `Suspended` when the application was suspended previously. Usually there's no need to do anything special in that case as the state is still available in memory. While in a suspended state, the app doesn't use any CPU cycles, and there's no disk access.

> **NOTE** *The application can implement one or more activation contracts and then can be activated with one of these. An example of such a contract is share. With this contract, the user can share some data from another application and start a UWP app by using it as a share target. Implementing the share contract is shown later in this chapter in the "Sharing Data" section.*

Navigation Between Pages

The sample application for demonstrating the life cycle of Windows apps (`ApplicationLifetimeSample`) is started with the Blank App template. After creating the project, you add the pages `Page1` and `Page2` to implement navigation between the pages.

To the `MainPage`, you add two `Button` controls for navigation to `Page1` and `Page2` and two `TextBox` controls to allow passing data with the navigation (code file `ApplicationLifetimeSample/MainPage .xaml`):

```
<Button Content="Page 1" Click="{x:Bind GotoPage1}" Grid.Row="0" />
<TextBox Text="{x:Bind Parameter1, Mode=TwoWay}" Grid.Row="0"
  Grid.Column="1" />
<Button Content="Page 2" Click="{x:Bind GotoPage2}" Grid.Row="1" />
<TextBox Text="{x:Bind Parameter2, Mode=TwoWay}" Grid.Row="1"
  Grid.Column="1" />
```

The code-behind file contains the event handler with navigation code to `Page1` and `Page2` and properties for the parameters (code file `ApplicationLifetimeSample/MainPage.xaml.cs`):

```
public void GotoPage1()
{
    Frame.Navigate(typeof(Page1), Parameter1);
}

public string Parameter1 { get; set; }

public void GotoPage2()
{
    Frame.Navigate(typeof(Page2), Parameter2);
}

public string Parameter2 { get; set; }
```

The UI elements for `Page1` show the data that is received on navigating to this page, a `Button` to allow the user to navigate to `Page2`, and a `TextBox` to allow the user to enter some state information that should be saved when the app is terminated (code file `ApplicationLifetimeSample/Page1.xaml`):

```
<TextBlock FontSize="30" Text="Page 1" />
<TextBlock Grid.Row="1" Text="{x:Bind ReceivedContent, Mode=OneTime}" />
<TextBox Grid.Row="2" Text="{x:Bind Parameter1, Mode=TwoWay}" />
<Button Grid.Row="3" Content="Navigate to Page 2"
  Click="{x:Bind GotoPage2, Mode=OneTime}" />
```

Similar to the `MainPage`, the navigation code for `Page1` defines an auto-implemented property for the data that is passed with the navigation and an event handler implementation for navigating to `Page2` (code file `ApplicationLifetimeSample/Page1.xaml.cs`):

```
public void GotoPage2()
{
    Frame.Navigate(typeof(Page2), Parameter1);
}

public string Parameter1 { get; set; }
```

With the code-behind file, the navigation parameter is received in the `OnNavigatedTo` method override. The received parameter is assigned to the auto-implemented property `ReceivedContent` (code file `ApplicationLifetimeSample/Page1.xaml.cs`):

```
protected override void OnNavigatedTo(NavigationEventArgs e)
{
    base.OnNavigatedTo(e);
    //...
```

```
    ReceivedContent = e.Parameter?.ToString() ?? string.Empty;
    Bindings.Update();
}

public string ReceivedContent { get; private set; }
```

With the implementation of the navigation, Page2 is very similar to Page1, so I'm not repeating its implementation here.

Using the system back button is covered in Chapter 32, "Windows Apps: User Interfaces." Here, the visibility and handler of the back button is defined in the class BackButtonManager. The implementation of the constructor makes the back button visible if the CanGoBack property of the frame instance returns true. The method OnBackRequested is implemented to go back in the page stack if the stack is available (code file ApplicationLifetimeSample/Utilities/BackButtonManager.cs):

```
public class BackButtonManager: IDisposable
{
    private SystemNavigationManager _navigationManager;
    private Frame _frame;

    public BackButtonManager(Frame frame)
    {
        _frame = frame;
        _navigationManager = SystemNavigationManager.GetForCurrentView();
        _navigationManager.AppViewBackButtonVisibility = frame.CanGoBack ?
            AppViewBackButtonVisibility.Visible:
                AppViewBackButtonVisibility.Collapsed;
        _navigationManager.BackRequested += OnBackRequested;
    }

    private void OnBackRequested(object sender, BackRequestedEventArgs e)
    {
        if (_frame.CanGoBack) _frame.GoBack();
        e.Handled = true;
    }

    public void Dispose()
    {
        _navigationManager.BackRequested -= OnBackRequested;
    }
}
```

With all the pages, the BackButtonManager is instantiated by passing the Frame in the OnNavigatedTo method, and it's disposed in the OnNavigatedFrom method (code file ApplicationLifetimeSample/MainPage.xaml.cs):

```
private BackButtonManager _backButtonManager;
protected override void OnNavigatedTo(NavigationEventArgs e)
{
    base.OnNavigatedTo(e);
    _backButtonManager = new BackButtonManager(Frame);
}

protected override void OnNavigatingFrom(NavigatingCancelEventArgs e)
{
    base.OnNavigatingFrom(e);
    _backButtonManager.Dispose();
}
```

With all this code in place, the user can navigate back and forward between the three different pages. What needs to be done next is to remember the page and the page stack to navigate the app to the page the user accessed most recently.

NAVIGATION STATE

To store and load the navigation state, the class `NavigationSuspensionManager` defines the methods `SetNavigationStateAsync` and `GetNavigationStateAsync`. The page stack for the navigation can be represented in a single string. This string is written to a local cache file named as defined by a constant. In case the file already exists from a previous app run, it is just overwritten. You don't need to remember page navigations between multiple app runs (code file `ApplicationLifetimeSample/Utilities/NavigationSuspensionManager.cs`):

```
public class NavigationSuspensionManager
{
  private const string NavigationStateFile = "NavigationState.txt";

  public async Task SetNavigationStateAsync(string navigationState)
  {
    StorageFile file = await
      ApplicationData.Current.LocalCacheFolder.CreateFileAsync(
        NavigationStateFile, CreationCollisionOption.ReplaceExisting);
    Stream stream = await file.OpenStreamForWriteAsync();
    using (var writer = new StreamWriter(stream))
    {
      await writer.WriteLineAsync(navigationState);
    }
  }

  public async Task<string> GetNavigationStateAsync()
  {
    Stream stream = await
      ApplicationData.Current.LocalCacheFolder.OpenStreamForReadAsync(
        NavigationStateFile);
    using (var reader = new StreamReader(stream))
    {
      return await reader.ReadLineAsync();
    }
  }
}
```

> **NOTE** *The* `NavigationSuspensionManager` *class makes use of the Windows Runtime API with the .NET* `Stream` *class to read and write contents to a file. Both features are shown in detail in Chapter 23, "Files and Streams."*

Suspending the App

To save state on suspension of the application, the Suspending event of the App class is set in the OnSuspending event handler. The event is fired when the application moves into suspended mode (code file `ApplicationLifetimeSample/App.xaml.cs`):

```
public App()
{
  this.InitializeComponent();
  this.Suspending += OnSuspending;
}
```

The method OnSuspending is an event handler method, and thus is declared to return void. There's an issue with that. As soon as the method is finished, the app can be terminated. However, as the method is declared void it is not possible to wait for the method until it is finished. Because of this, the received SuspendingEventArgs parameter defines a SuspendingDeferral that can be retrieved by calling the method `GetDeferral`. As soon as the async functionality of your code is completed, you need to invoke the `Complete` method on the deferral. This way, the caller knows the method is finished, and the app can be terminated (code file `ApplicationLifetimeSample/App.xaml.cs`):

```
private async void OnSuspending(object sender, SuspendingEventArgs e)
{
  var deferral = e.SuspendingOperation.GetDeferral();

  //...

  deferral.Complete();
}
```

> **NOTE** *You can read details about asynchronous methods in Chapter 15, "Asynchronous Programming."*

Within the implementation of the `OnSuspending` method, the page stack is written to the temporary cache. You can retrieve the pages on the page stack using the `BackStack` property of the `Frame`. This property returns a list of `PageStackEntry` objects where every instance represents the type, navigation parameter, and navigation transition information. For storing the page track with the `SetNavigationStateAsync` method, just a string is needed that contains the complete page stack information. This string can be retrieved by calling the `GetNavigationState` method of the `Frame` (code file `ApplicationLifetimeSample/App.xaml.cs`):

```
private async void OnSuspending(object sender, SuspendingEventArgs e)
{
  var deferral = e.SuspendingOperation.GetDeferral();

  var frame = Window.Current.Content as Frame;
  if (frame?.BackStackDepth >= 1)
  {
    var suspensionManager = new NavigationSuspensionManager();
    string navigationState = frame.GetNavigationState();
    if (navigationState != null)
    {
      await suspensionManager.SetNavigationStateAsync(navigationState);
    }
  }

  //...

  deferral.Complete();
}
```

With Windows 8, you have only a few seconds for suspending the app before it can be terminated. With Windows 10 you can extend this time for also making network calls, retrieving data from a service or uploading data to a service, or doing location tracking. All you have to do for this is to create an `ExtendedExecutionSession` within the `OnSuspending` method, set a reason, such as `ExtendedExecutionReason.SavingData`, and request the extension by calling `RequestExecutionAsync`. As long as the extended execution is not denied, you can go on with the extended task.

Activating the App from Suspension

The string returned from `GetNavigationState` is comma-separated and lists the complete information of the page stack including type information and parameters. You shouldn't parse the string to get the different parts because this can be changed with newer implementations of the Windows Runtime. Just using this string to restore the state later to recover the page stack with SetNavigationState is okay. In case the string format changes with a future version, both of these methods will be changed as well.

To set the page stack when the app is started, you need to change the OnLaunched method. This method is overridden from the Application base class, and it's invoked when the app is started. The argument LaunchActivatedEventArgs gives information on how the app is started. The Kind property returns an ActivationKind enumeration value where you can read whether the app was started by the user clicking on the tile stating a voice command, or from Windows, such as by launching it as a share target. The PreviousExecutionState—which is needed in this scenario—returns an ApplicationExecutionState enumeration value that provides the information of how the app ended previously. If the app ended with the ClosedByUser value, no special action is needed; the app should start fresh. However, if the app was previously terminated, the PreviousExecutionState contains the value Terminated. With this state, it's useful to arrange the app to a state where the user previously left it. Here, the page stack is retrieved from the NavigationSuspensionManager and set to the root frame by passing the previously saved string to the method SetNavigationState (code file ApplicationLifetimeSample/App.xaml.cs):

```
protected override async void OnLaunched(LaunchActivatedEventArgs e)
{
    Frame rootFrame = Window.Current.Content as Frame;

    if (rootFrame == null)
    {
        rootFrame = new Frame();

        rootFrame.NavigationFailed += OnNavigationFailed;

        if (e.PreviousExecutionState == ApplicationExecutionState.Terminated)
        {
            var suspensionManager = new NavigationSuspensionManager();
            string navigationState =
                await suspensionManager.GetNavigationStateAsync();
            rootFrame.SetNavigationState(navigationState);

            // etc.
        }

        // Place the frame in the current Window
        Window.Current.Content = rootFrame;
    }

    if (rootFrame.Content == null)
    {
        rootFrame.Navigate(typeof(MainPage), e.Arguments);
    }
    Window.Current.Activate();
}
```

Testing Suspension

Now you can start the application (see Figure 33-1), navigate to another page, and then open other applications to wait until the application is terminated. With the Task Manager, you can see the suspended applications with the Details view if the Status Values option is set to Show Suspended Status. This is not an easy way to test suspension (because it can take a long time before the termination happens), however, and it would be nice to debug the different states.

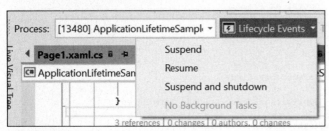

FIGURE 33-1

When you use the debugger, everything works differently. If the application would be suspended as soon as it doesn't have a focus, it would be suspended every time a breakpoint is reached. That's why suspension is disabled while running under the debugger. So the normal suspension mechanism doesn't apply. However, it's easy to simulate. If you open the Debug Location toolbar, there are three buttons for Suspend, Resume, and Suspend and shutdown (see Figure 33-2). If you click Suspend and shutdown and then start the application again, the application continues from the previous state of `ApplicationExecutionState.Terminated` and thus opens the page the user opened previously.

FIGURE 33-2

Page State

Any data that was input by the user should be restored as well. For this demonstration, on `Page1` two input fields are created (code file `ApplicationLifetimeSample/Page1.xaml`):

```
<TextBox Header="Session State 1" Grid.Row="4"
  Text="{x:Bind Data.Session1, Mode=TwoWay}" />
<TextBox Header="Session State 2" Grid.Row="5"
  Text="{x:Bind Data.Session2, Mode=TwoWay}" />
```

The data representation of this input field is defined by the `DataManager` class that is returned from the `Data` property, as shown in the following code snippet (code file `ApplicationLifetimeSample/Page1.xaml.cs`):

```
public DataManager Data { get; } = DataManager.Instance;
```

The `DataManager` class defines the properties `Session1` and `Session2` where the values are stored within a `Dictionary` (code file `ApplicationLifetimeSamlple/Services/DataManager.cs`):

```
public class DataManager: INotifyPropertyChanged
{
    private const string SessionStateFile = "TempSessionState.json";
    private Dictionary<string, string> _state = new Dictionary<string, string>()
    {
        [nameof(Session1)] = string.Empty,
        [nameof(Session2)] = string.Empty
    };
```

```
private DataManager()
{
}

public event PropertyChangedEventHandler PropertyChanged;

protected void OnPropertyChanged(
  [CallerMemberName] string propertyName = null)
{
  PropertyChanged?.Invoke(this, new PropertyChangedEventArgs(propertyName));
}

public static DataManager Instance { get; } = new DataManager();

public string Session1
{
  get { return _state[nameof(Session1)]; }
  set
  {
    _state[nameof(Session1)] = value;
    OnPropertyChanged();
  }
}

public string Session2
{
  get { return _state[nameof(Session2)]; }
  set
  {
    _state[nameof(Session2)] = value;
    OnPropertyChanged();
  }
}
```

For loading and storing the session state, the methods `SaveTempSessionAsync` and `LoadTempSessionAsync` are defined. The implementation makes use of Json.Net to serialize the dictionary in JSON format. However, you can use any serialization you like (code file `ApplicationLifetimeSample/Services/DataManager.cs`):

```
public async Task SaveTempSessionAsync()
{
  StorageFile file =
    await ApplicationData.Current.LocalCacheFolder.CreateFileAsync(
      SessionStateFile, CreationCollisionOption.ReplaceExisting);
  Stream stream = await file.OpenStreamForWriteAsync();

  var serializer = new JsonSerializer();
  using (var writer = new StreamWriter(stream))
  {
    serializer.Serialize(writer, _state);
  }
}

public async Task LoadTempSessionAsync()
{
  Stream stream = await
    ApplicationData.Current.LocalCacheFolder.OpenStreamForReadAsync(
      SessionStateFile);
  var serializer = new JsonSerializer();
  using (var reader = new StreamReader(stream))
  {
    string json = await reader.ReadLineAsync();
    Dictionary<string, string> state =
```

```
              JsonConvert.DeserializeObject<Dictionary<string, string>>(json);
          _state = state;

          foreach (var item in state)
          {
            OnPropertyChanged(item.Key);
          }
        }
      }
```

> **NOTE** *Serialization with XML and JSON is discussed in Chapter 27, "XML and JSON."*

What's left is to invoke the `SaveTempSessionAsync` and `LoadTempSessionAsync` methods on suspending and activating of the app. These methods are added to the same places where the page stack is written and read, to the `OnSuspending` and `OnLaunched` methods (code file `ApplicationLifetimeSample/App.xaml.cs`):

```
private async void OnSuspending(object sender, SuspendingEventArgs e)
{
  var deferral = e.SuspendingOperation.GetDeferral();
  //...

  await DataManager.Instance.SaveTempSessionAsync();

  deferral.Complete();
}

protected override async void OnLaunched(LaunchActivatedEventArgs e)
{
  Frame rootFrame = Window.Current.Content as Frame;

  if (rootFrame == null)
  {
    rootFrame = new Frame();

    rootFrame.NavigationFailed += OnNavigationFailed;

    if (e.PreviousExecutionState == ApplicationExecutionState.Terminated)
    {
      //...
      await DataManager.Instance.LoadTempSessionAsync();
    }
    // Place the frame in the current Window
    Window.Current.Content = rootFrame;
  }

  if (rootFrame.Content == null)
  {
    rootFrame.Navigate(typeof(MainPage), e.Arguments);
  }
  Window.Current.Activate();
}
```

Now you can run the app, enter state in `Page2`, suspend and terminate the app, start it again, and the state shows up again.

With the app lifetime you've seen how special programming is needed for UWP apps to consider battery consumption. The next session discusses sharing data between apps, which is also available on the phone platform.

SHARING DATA

Your app becomes a lot more useful when it can interact with other apps. With Windows 10, apps can share data using drag and drop, even with desktop applications. Between Windows apps, it's also possible to share data using a sharing contract.

When you use a sharing contract, one app (the sharing source) can share data in many different formats—for example, text, HTML, image, or custom data—and the user can select an app that accepts the data format as a sharing target. Windows finds the apps that support the corresponding data format by using a contract that's registered with the app at installation time.

Sharing Source

The first consideration in terms of sharing is determining what data should be shared in what format. It's possible to share simple text, rich text, HTML, and images, but also a custom type. Of course, all these types must be known and used from other applications—the sharing targets. Sharing custom types can only be done with other applications that know the type and are a share target for the type. The sample application offers shared data in text format and a book list in HTML format.

To offer book information in HTML format, you define a simple `Book` class (code file `SharingSource\Models\Book.cs`):

```
public class Book
{
  public string Title { get; set; }
  public string Publisher { get; set; }
}
```

A list of `Book` objects is returned from the `GetSampleBooks` method of the `BooksRepository` class (code file `SharingSource\Models\BooksRepository.cs`):

```
public class BooksRepository
{
  public IEnumerable<Book> GetSampleBooks() =>
    new List<Book>()
    {
      new Book
      {
        Title = "Professional C# 6 and .NET 5 Core",
        Publisher = "Wrox Press"
      },
      new Book
      {
        Title = "Professional C# 5.0 and .NET 4.5.1",
        Publisher = "Wrox Press"
      }
    };
}
```

To convert a list of `Book` objects to HTML, the extension method `ToHtml` returns an HTML table with the help of LINQ to XML (code file `SharingSource\Utilities\BooksExtensions.cs`):

```
public static class BookExtensions
{
  public static string ToHtml(this IEnumerable<Book> books) =>
    new XElement("table",
      new XElement("thead",
        new XElement("tr",
          new XElement("td", "Title"),
          new XElement("td", "Publisher"))),
      books.Select(b =>
        new XElement("tr",
```

```
          new XElement("td", b.Title),
          new XElement("td", b.Publisher))))).ToString();
}
```

> **NOTE** *LINQ to XML is covered in Chapter 27.*

With the `MainPage`, you define a `Button`, where the user can initiate the sharing, and a `TextBox` control for the user to enter textual data to share (code file `SharingSource\MainPage.xaml`):

```
<RelativePanel Margin="24">
  <Button x:Name="shareDataButton" Content="Share Data"
    Click="{x:Bind DataSharing.ShowShareUI, Mode=OneTime}" Margin="12" />
  <TextBox RelativePanel.RightOf="shareDataButton"
    Text="{x:Bind DataSharing.SimpleText, Mode=TwoWay}" Margin="12" />
</RelativePanel>
```

In the code-behind file, the `DataSharing` property returns the `ShareDataViewModel` where all the important features for sharing are implemented (code file `SharingSource\MainPage.xaml.cs`):

```
public ShareDataViewModel DataSharing { get; set; } = new ShareDataViewModel();
```

The `ShareDataViewModel` defines the property `SimpleText` that is bound by the XAML file to enter the simple text to be shared. For sharing, the event handler method `ShareDataRequested` is assigned to the event `DataRequested` of the `DataTransferManager`. This event is fired when the user requests sharing data (code file `SharingSource\ViewModels\ShareDataViewModel.cs`):

```
public class ShareDataViewModel
{
  public ShareDataViewModel()
  {
    DataTransferManager.GetForCurrentView().DataRequested +=
      ShareDataRequested;
  }

  public string SimpleText { get; set; } = string.Empty;

  //...
```

When the event is fired, the `OnShareDataRequested` method is invoked. This method receives the `DataTransferManager` as the first argument, and `DataRequestedEventArgs` as the second. On sharing data, the `DataPackage` referenced by `args.Request.Data` needs to be filled. You can use the `Title`, `Description`, and `Thumbnail` properties to give information to the user interface. The data that should be shared must be passed with one of the `SetXXX` methods. The sample code shares a simple text and HTML code, thus the methods `SetText` and `SetHtmlFormat` are used. The `HtmlFormatHelper` class helps create the surrounding HTML code that's needed for sharing. The HTML code for the books is created with the extension method `ToHtml` that was shown earlier (code file `SharingSource\ViewModels\ShareDataViewModel.cs`):

```
private void ShareDataRequested(DataTransferManager sender,
  DataRequestedEventArgs args)
{
  var books = new BooksRepository().GetSampleBooks();

  Uri baseUri = new Uri("ms-appx:///");
  DataPackage package = args.Request.Data;
  package.Properties.Title = "Sharing Sample";
  package.Properties.Description = "Sample for sharing data";
  package.Properties.Thumbnail = RandomAccessStreamReference.CreateFromUri(
    new Uri(baseUri, "Assets/Square44x44Logo.png"));
  package.SetText(SimpleText);
  package.SetHtmlFormat(HtmlFormatHelper.CreateHtmlFormat(books.ToHtml()));
}
```

In case you need the information when the sharing operation is completed—for example, to remove the data from the source application—the `DataPackage` class fires `OperationCompleted` and `Destroyed` events.

> **NOTE** *Instead of offering text or HTML code, other methods, such as* `SetBitmap`, `SetRtf`, *and* `SetUri`, *make it possible to offer other data formats.*

> **NOTE** *In case you need to build the data for sharing using async methods within the* `ShareDataRequested` *method, you need to use a deferral to give the information when the data is available. This is similar to the page suspension mechanism shown earlier in this chapter. Using the* `Request` *property of the* `DataRequestedEventArgs` *type, you can invoke the* `GetDeferral` *method. This method returns a deferral of type* `DataRequestedDeferral`. *With this object, you can invoke the* `Complete` *method when the data is readily available.*

Finally, the user interface for sharing needs to be shown. This enables the user to select the target app:

```
public void ShowShareUI()
{
    DataTransferManager.ShowShareUI();
}
```

Figure 33-3 shows the user interface after calling the `ShowShareUI` method of the `DataTransferManager`. Depending on what data format is offered and the apps that are installed, the corresponding apps are shown for selection.

FIGURE 33-3

If you select the Mail app, HTML information is passed. Figure 33-4 shows the received data within this app.

FIGURE 33-4

> **NOTE** *With Windows 8, a user can use the charms bar to start sharing data from an app. With this, if data is not available to share, it is important to give information to the user about what needs to be done for sharing—for example, selecting an item first or entering some data. Such error information can be returned to invoke the method* `FailWithDisplayText` *on the* `Request` *property of the* `DataRequestedEventArgs` *type. With Windows 10, you need to explicitly offer a visible control (for example, a button) where the user can start sharing. If no data is available to share, just don't offer this visible control.*

Sharing Target

Now let's have a look at the recipient of sharing. If an application should receive information from a sharing source, it needs to be declared as a share target. Figure 33-5 shows the Manifest Designer's Declarations page within Visual Studio, where you can define share targets. Here is where you add the Share Target declaration, which must include at least one data format. Possible data formats are Text, URI, Bitmap, HTML, StorageItems, or RTF. You can also specify which file types should be supported by adding the appropriate file extensions.

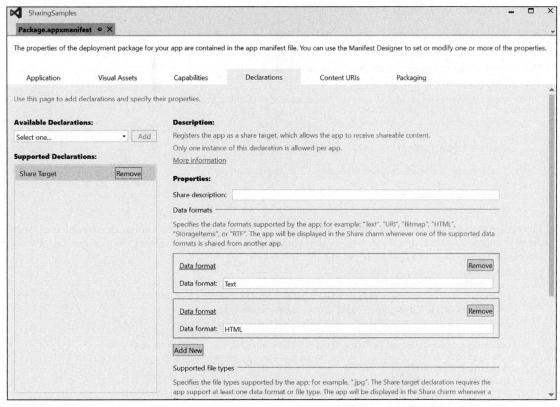

FIGURE 33-5

The information in the package manifest is used upon registration of the application. This tells Windows which applications are available as a share target. The sample app `SharingTarget` defines share targets for `Text` and `HTML`.

When the user launches the app as a share target, the `OnShareTargetActivated` method is called in the `App` class instead of the `OnLaunched` method. Here, a different page (`ShareTargetPage`) gets created that shows the screen when the user selects this app as a share target (code file `SharingTarget/App.xaml.cs`):

```
protected override void OnShareTargetActivated(ShareTargetActivatedEventArgs args)
{
  Frame rootFrame = CreateRootFrame();
  rootFrame.Navigate(typeof(ShareTargetPage), args.ShareOperation);
  Window.Current.Activate();
}
```

To not create the root frame in two different places, the `OnLaunched` method has been refactored to put the frame creation code in a separate method: `CreateRootFrame`. This method is now called from both `OnShareTargetActivated` as well as `OnLaunched`:

```
private Frame CreateRootFrame()
{
  Frame rootFrame = Window.Current.Content as Frame;
  if (rootFrame == null)
  {
    rootFrame = new Frame();
    rootFrame.NavigationFailed += OnNavigationFailed;
```

```
      Window.Current.Content = rootFrame;
    }
    return rootFrame;
  }
```

The change of the OnLaunched method is shown here. Contrary to the OnShareTargetActivated, this method navigates to the MainPage:

```
protected override void OnLaunched(LaunchActivatedEventArgs e)
{
  Frame rootFrame = CreateRootFrame();

  if (rootFrame.Content == null)
  {
    rootFrame.Navigate(typeof(MainPage), e.Arguments);
  }
  Window.Current.Activate();
}
```

The ShareTargetPage contains controls where the user can see information about the data shared, such as the title and description, and a combo box that shows the available data formats the user can select (code file SharingTarget/ShareTargetPage.xaml):

```xml
<StackPanel Orientation="Vertical">
  <TextBlock Text="Share Target Page" />
  <TextBox Header="Title" IsReadOnly="True"
    Text="{x:Bind ViewModel.Title, Mode=OneWay}" Margin="12" />
  <TextBox Header="Description" IsReadOnly="True"
    Text="{x:Bind ViewModel.Description, Mode=OneWay}" Margin="12" />
  <ComboBox ItemsSource="{x:Bind ViewModel.ShareFormats, Mode=OneTime}"
    SelectedItem="{x:Bind ViewModel.SelectedFormat, Mode=TwoWay}"
    Margin="12" />
  <Button Content="Retrieve Data"
    Click="{x:Bind ViewModel.RetrieveData, Mode=OneTime}" Margin="12" />
  <Button Content="Report Complete"
    Click="{x:Bind ViewModel.ReportCompleted, Mode=OneTime}" Margin="12" />
  <TextBox Header="Text" IsReadOnly="True"
    Text="{x:Bind ViewModel.Text, Mode=OneWay}" Margin="12" />
  <TextBox AcceptsReturn="True" IsReadOnly="True"
    Text="{x:Bind ViewModel.Html, Mode=OneWay}" Margin="12" />
</StackPanel>
```

In the code-behind file, a ShareTargetPageViewModel is assigned to the ViewModel property. In the XAML code earlier, this property is used with compiled binding. Also, with the OnNavigatedTo method, the SharedTargetPageViewModel is activated passing a ShareOperation object to the Activate method (code file SharingTarget/ShareTargetPage.xaml.cs):

```csharp
public sealed partial class ShareTargetPage: Page
{
  public ShareTargetPage()
  {
    this.InitializeComponent();
  }

  public ShareTargetPageViewModel ViewModel { get; } =
    new ShareTargetPageViewModel();

  protected override void OnNavigatedTo(NavigationEventArgs e)
  {
    ViewModel.Activate(e.Parameter as ShareOperation);

    base.OnNavigatedTo(e);
  }
}
```

The class `ShareTargetPageViewModel` defines properties for values that should be displayed in the page, as well as change notification by implementing the interface `INotifyPropertyChanged` (code file `SharingTarget/ViewModels/ShareTargetViewModel.cs`):

```
public class ShareTargetPageViewModel: INotifyPropertyChanged
{
  public event PropertyChangedEventHandler PropertyChanged;

  public void OnPropertyChanged([CallerMemberName] string propertyName = null)
  {
    PropertyChanged?.Invoke(this, new PropertyChangedEventArgs(propertyName));
  }

  // etc.

  private string _text;
  public string Text
  {
    get { return _text; }
    set
    {
      _text = value;
      OnPropertyChanged();
    }
  }

  private string _html;
  public string Html
  {
    get { return _html; }
    set
    {
      _html = value;
      OnPropertyChanged();
    }
  }

  private string _title;
  public string Title
  {
    get { return _title; }
    set
    {
      _title = value;
      OnPropertyChanged();
    }
  }

  private string _description;
  public string Description
  {
    get { return _description; }
    set
    {
      _description = value;
      OnPropertyChanged();
    }
  }
}
```

The `Activate` method is an important part of the `ShareTargetPageViewModel`. Here, the `ShareOperation` object is used to access information about the share data and get some metadata available to display it to the user, such as `Title`, `Description`, and the list of available data formats. In case of an error, error information is shown to the user by invoking the `ReportError` method of the `ShareOperation`:

```csharp
public class ShareTargetPageViewModel: INotifyPropertyChanged
{
  // etc.

  private ShareOperation _shareOperation;
  private readonly ObservableCollection<string> _shareFormats =
    new ObservableCollection<string>();
  public string SelectedFormat { get; set; }
  public IEnumerable<string> ShareFormats => _shareFormats;

  public void Activate(ShareOperation shareOperation)
  {
    string title = null;
    string description = null;
    try
    {
      _shareOperation = shareOperation;

      title = _shareOperation.Data.Properties.Title;
      description = _shareOperation.Data.Properties.Description;
      foreach (var format in _shareOperation.Data.AvailableFormats)
      {
        _shareFormats.Add(format);
      }

      Title = title;
      Description = description;
    }
    catch (Exception ex)
    {
      _shareOperation.ReportError(ex.Message);
    }
  }
  // etc.
}
```

As soon as the user chooses the data format, he or she can click the button to retrieve the data. This in turn invokes the method `RetrieveData`. Depending on the user's selection, either `GetTextAsync` or `GetHtmlFormatAsync` is invoked on the `DataPackageView` instance that is returned from the `Data` property. Before retrieving the data, the method `ReportStarted` is invoked; after the data is retrieved, the method `ReportDataRetrieved` is invoked:

```csharp
public class ShareTargetPageViewModel: INotifyPropertyChanged
{
  // etc.
  private bool dataRetrieved = false;
  public async void RetrieveData()
  {
    try
    {
      if (dataRetrieved)
      {
        await new MessageDialog("data already retrieved").ShowAsync();
      }
      _shareOperation.ReportStarted();
      switch (SelectedFormat)
      {
        case "Text":
          Text = await _shareOperation.Data.GetTextAsync();
          break;
        case "HTML Format":
          Html = await _shareOperation.Data.GetHtmlFormatAsync();
```

```
                break;
            default:
                break;
        }
        _shareOperation.ReportDataRetrieved();
        dataRetrieved = true;
    }
    catch (Exception ex)
    {
        _shareOperation.ReportError(ex.Message);
    }
}
// etc.
```

With the sample app, the retrieved data is shown in the user interface. With a real app, you can use the data in any form—for example, store it locally on the client or call your own web service and pass the data there.

Finally, the user can click the Report Completed button in the UI. Using the `Click` handler, this invokes the `ReportCompleted` method in the view model, which in turn invokes the `ReportCompleted` method on the `ShareOperation` instance. This method closes the dialog:

```
public class ShareTargetPageViewModel: INotifyPropertyChanged
{
    // etc.

    public void ReportCompleted()
    {
        _shareOperation.ReportCompleted();
    }

    // etc.
}
```

With your app, you can invoke the `ReportCompleted` method earlier after retrieving the data. Just remember that the dialog of the app is closed when this method is called.

The running `SharingTarget` app is shown in Figure 33-6.

FIGURE 33-6

> **NOTE** *The best way to test sharing with all the formats you would like to support is by using the sample app's Sharing Content Source app sample and Sharing Content Target app sample. Both sample apps are available at* `https://github.com/Microsoft/Windows-universal-samples`. *In case you have an app as sharing source, use the sample target app, and vice versa.*

> **NOTE** *An easy way to debug share targets is to set the Debug option Do Not Launch, but Debug My Code When It Starts. This setting is in the Project Properties, Debug tab (see Figure 33-7). With this setting you can start the debugger, and the app starts as soon as you share data with this app from a data source app.*

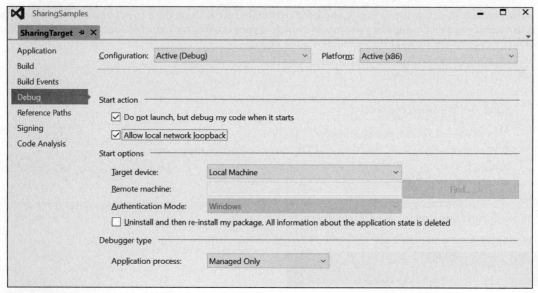

FIGURE 33-7

APP SERVICES

Another way to share data between your apps is by using app services. *App services* is a new feature with Windows 10 that you can compare to calling into web services, but the service is local on the user's system. Multiple apps can access the same service, which is how you can share information between apps. An important difference between app services and web services is that the user doesn't need to interact using this feature; it all can be done from the app.

The sample app `AppServices` uses a service to cache `Book` objects. Calling the service, the list of `Book` objects can be retrieved, and new `Book` objects can be added to the service.

The app consists of multiple projects.

➤ One .NET Portable library (`BooksCacheModel`) defines the model of this app—the `Book` class. For an easy transfer of data, extension methods are offered to convert `Book` objects to JSON and the other way around. This library is used from all the other projects.

➤ The second project (`BooksCacheService`) is a Windows Runtime component that defines the book service itself. Such a service needs to run in the background; thus a background task is implemented.

➤ The background task needs to be registered with the system. This project is a Windows app: `BooksCacheProvider`.

➤ The client application calling the app service is a Windows app: `BooksCacheClient`.

Let's get into these parts.

Creating the Model

The portable library `BooksCacheModel` contains the `Book` class, a converter to JSON with the help of the NuGet package `Newtonsoft.Json`, and a repository.

The `Book` class defines `Title` and `Publisher` properties (code file `AppServices/BooksCacheModel/Book.cs`):

```
public class Book
{
  public string Title { get; set; }
  public string Publisher { get; set; }
}
```

The `BooksRepository` class holds a memory cache of Book objects, allows the user to add book objects via the `AddBook` method, and returns all the cached books with the `Books` property. To already see a book without adding a new book, one book is added to the list at initialization time (code file `AppServices/BooksCacheModel/BooksRepository.cs`):

```
public class BooksRepository
{
  private readonly List<Book> _books = new List<Book>()
  {
    new Book {Title = "Professional C# 6", Publisher = "Wrox Press" }
  };
  public IEnumerable<Book> Books => _books;

  private BooksRepository()
  {
  }

  public static BooksRepository Instance = new BooksRepository();

  public void AddBook(Book book)
  {
    _books.Add(book);
  }
}
```

Because the data that is sent across an app service needs to be serializable, the extension class `BookExtensions` defines a few extension methods that convert a `Book` and a `Book` list to a JSON string, and the other way around. Passing a string across the App service is a simple task. The extension methods make use of the class `JsonConvert` that is available with the NuGet package `Newtonsoft.Json` (code file `AppServices/BooksCacheModel(BookExtensions.cs`):

```
public static class BookExtensions
{
  public static string ToJson(this Book book) =>
    JsonConvert.SerializeObject(book);

  public static string ToJson(this IEnumerable<Book> books) =>
    JsonConvert.SerializeObject(books);

  public static Book ToBook(this string json) =>
    JsonConvert.DeserializeObject<Book>(json);

  public static IEnumerable<Book> ToBooks(this string json) =>
    JsonConvert.DeserializeObject<IEnumerable<Book>>(json);
}
```

Creating a Background Task for App Service Connections

Now let's get into the heart of this sample app: the app service. You need to implement the app service as a Windows Runtime component library and as a background task by implementing the interface IBackgroundTask. Windows background tasks can run in the background without user interaction.

Different kinds of background tasks are available. Background tasks can be started based on a timer interval, Windows push notifications, location information, Bluetooth device connections, or other events.

The class BooksCacheTask is a background task for the app service. The interface IBackgroundTask defines the Run method that needs to be implemented. Within the implementation, a request handler is defined on receiving an app service connection (code file AppServices/BooksCacheService/BooksCacheTask.cs):

```
public sealed class BooksCacheTask: IBackgroundTask
{
  private BackgroundTaskDeferral _taskDeferral;

  public void Run(IBackgroundTaskInstance taskInstance)
  {
    _taskDeferral = taskInstance.GetDeferral();
    taskInstance.Canceled += OnTaskCanceled;

    var trigger = taskInstance.TriggerDetails as AppServiceTriggerDetails;
    AppServiceConnection connection = trigger.AppServiceConnection;
    connection.RequestReceived += OnRequestReceived;
  }

  private void OnTaskCanceled(IBackgroundTaskInstance sender,
    BackgroundTaskCancellationReason reason)
  {
    _taskDeferral?.Complete();
  }

  // etc.
```

With the implementation of the OnRequestReceived handler, the service can read the request and needs to supply an answer. The request received is contained in the Request.Message property of the AppServiceRequestReceivedEventArgs. The Message property returns a ValueSet object. ValueSet is a dictionary of keys with their corresponding values. The service here requires a command key with either the value GET or POST. The GET command returns a list of all books, whereas the POST command requires the additional key book with a JSON string as the value for the Book object representation. Depending on the message received, either the GetBooks or AddBook helper method is invoked. The result returned from these messages is returned to the caller by invoking SendResponseAsync:

```
private async void OnRequestReceived(AppServiceConnection sender,
  AppServiceRequestReceivedEventArgs args)
{
  AppServiceDeferral deferral = args.GetDeferral();
  try
  {
    ValueSet message = args.Request.Message;
    ValueSet result = null;

    switch (message["command"].ToString())
    {
      case "GET":
        result = GetBooks();
        break;
      case "POST":
        result = AddBook(message["book"].ToString());
        break;
      default:
        break;
    }
```

```
      await args.Request.SendResponseAsync(result);
    }
    finally
    {
      deferral.Complete();
    }
  }
```

The GetBooks method uses the BooksRepository to get all the books in JSON format, and it creates a ValueSet with the result key:

```
private ValueSet GetBooks()
  {
    var result = new ValueSet();
    result.Add("result", BooksRepository.Instance.Books.ToJson());
    return result;
  }
```

The AddBook method uses the repository to add a book, and returns a ValueSet with a result key and the value ok:

```
private ValueSet AddBook(string book)
  {
    BooksRepository.Instance.AddBook(book.ToBook());
    var result = new ValueSet();
    result.Add("result", "ok");
    return result;
  }
```

Registering the App Service

You now need to register the app service with the operating system. This is done by creating a normal UWP app that has a reference to the BooksCacheService. With this app, you must define a declaration in the package.appxmanifest (see Figure 33-8). Add an app service to the app declaration list and give it a name. You need to set the entry point to the background task, including the namespace and the class name.

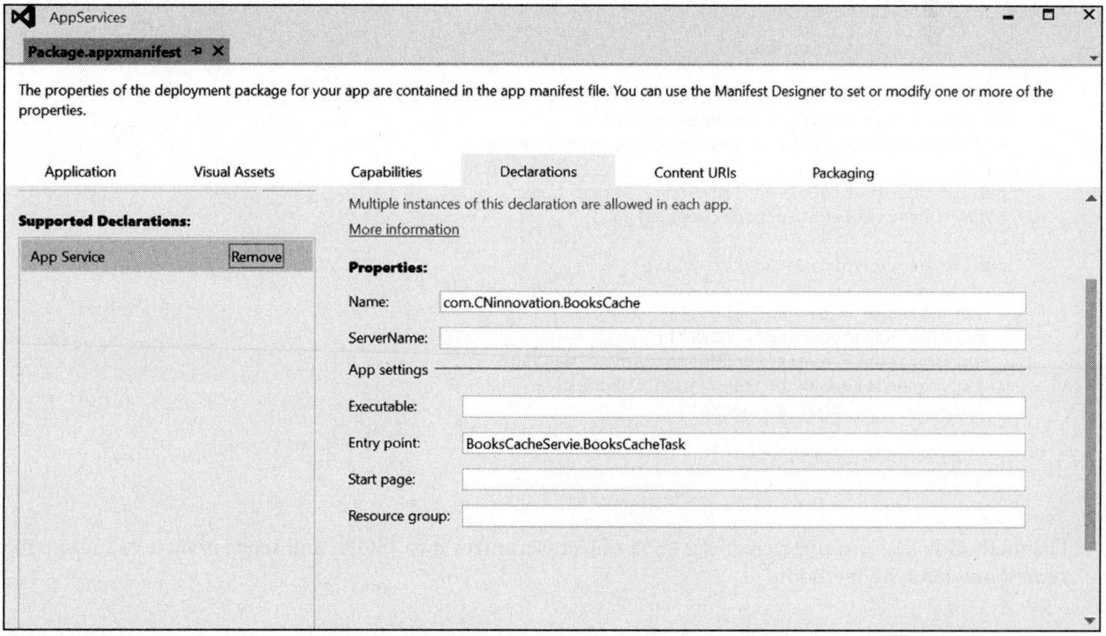

FIGURE 33-8

For the client app, you need the name of the app that you defined with the `package.appxmanifest` as well as the package name. To see the package name, you can invoke `Package.Current.Id.FamilyName`. To see this name easily, it is written to the property `PackageFamilyName` that is bound within a control in the user interface (code file `AppServices/BooksCacheProvider/MainPage.xaml.cs`):

```
public sealed partial class MainPage: Page
{
  public MainPage()
  {
    this.InitializeComponent();
    PackageFamilyName = Package.Current.Id.FamilyName;
  }

  public string PackageFamilyName
  {
    get { return (string)GetValue(PackageFamilyNameProperty); }
    set { SetValue(PackageFamilyNameProperty, value); }
  }

  public static readonly DependencyProperty PackageFamilyNameProperty =
    DependencyProperty.Register("PackageFamilyName", typeof(string),
      typeof(MainPage), new PropertyMetadata(string.Empty));
}
```

When you run this app, it registers the background task and shows the package name that you need for the client app.

Calling the App Service

With the client app, the app service can now be called. The main parts of the client app `BooksCacheClient` are implemented with the view model. The `Books` property is bound in the UI to show all books returned from the service. This collection is filled by the `GetBooksAsync` method. `GetBooksAsync` creates a `ValueSet` with the `GET` command that is sent to the app service with the helper method `SendMessageAsync`. This helper method returns a JSON string, which in turn is converted to a `Book` collection that is used to fill the `ObservableCollection` for the `Books` property (code file `AppServices/BooksCacheClient/ViewModels/BooksViewModel.cs`):

```
public class BooksViewModel
{
  private const string BookServiceName = "com.CNinnovation.BooksCache";
  private const string BooksPackageName =
    "CNinnovation.Samples.BookCache_p2wxv0ry6mv8g";

  public ObservableCollection<Book> Books { get; } =
    new ObservableCollection<Book>();

  public async void GetBooksAsync()
  {
    var message = new ValueSet();
    message.Add("command", "GET");
    string json = await SendMessageAsync(message);
    IEnumerable<Book> books = json.ToBooks();
    foreach (var book in books)
    {
      Books.Add(book);
    }
  }
}
```

The method `PostBookAsync` creates a `Book` object, serializes it to JSON, and sends it via a `ValueSet` to the `SendMessageAsync` method:

```
    public string NewBookTitle { get; set; }
      public string NewBookPublisher { get; set; }

    public async void PostBookAsync()
    {
      var message = new ValueSet();
      message.Add("command", "POST");
      string json = new Book
      {
        Title = NewBookTitle,
        Publisher = NewBookPublisher
      }.ToJson();
      message.Add("book", json);
      string result = await SendMessageAsync(message);
    }
```

The app service–relevant client code is contained within the method SendMessageAsync. Here, an AppServiceConnection is created. The connection is closed after use by disposing it with the using statement. To map the connection to the correct service, the AppServiceName and PackageFamilyName properties need to be supplied. After setting these properties, the connection is opened by invoking the method OpenAsync. Only when the connection is opened successfully is a request sent with the ValueSet received from the calling method. The AppServiceConnection method SendMessageAsync makes the request to the service and returns an AppServiceResponse object. The response contains the result from the service, which is dealt with accordingly:

```
    private async Task<string> SendMessageAsync(ValueSet message)
    {
      using (var connection = new AppServiceConnection())
      {
        connection.AppServiceName = BookServiceName;
        connection.PackageFamilyName = BooksPackageName;

        AppServiceConnectionStatus status = await connection.OpenAsync();
        if (status == AppServiceConnectionStatus.Success)
        {
          AppServiceResponse response =
            await connection.SendMessageAsync(message);
          if (response.Status == AppServiceResponseStatus.Success &&
            response.Message.ContainsKey("result"))
          {
            string result = response.Message["result"].ToString();
            return result;
          }
          else
          {
            await ShowServiceErrorAsync(response.Status);
          }
        }
        else
        {
          await ShowConnectionErrorAsync(status);
        }
        return string.Empty;
      }
    }
```

After building the solution and deploying both the provider and the client app, you can start the client app and invoke the service. You can also create multiple client apps calling the same service.

After communicating between apps, let's make use of some hardware. The next section makes use of the camera to record photos and videos.

CAMERA

As apps are becoming more and more visual, and more devices offer one or two cameras built-in, using the camera is becoming a more and more important aspect of apps—and it is easy to do with the Windows Runtime.

> **NOTE** *Using the camera requires that you configure the Webcam capability in the Manifest Editor. For recording videos, you need to configure the Microphone capability as well.*

Photos and videos can be captured with the CameraCaptureUI class (in the namespace Windows.Media. Capture). First, you need to configure the photo and video settings to use the CaptureFileAsync method. The first code snippet captures a photo. After instantiating the CameraCaptureUI class, PhotoSettings are applied. Possible photo formats are JPG, JPGXR, and PNG. It is also possible to define cropping where the UI for the camera capture directly asks the user to select a clipping from the complete picture based on the cropping size. For cropping, you can define either a pixel size with the property CroppedSizeInPixels or just a ratio with CroppedAspectRatio. After the user takes the photo, the sample code uses the returned StorageFile from the method CaptureFileAsync to store it as a file inside a user-selected folder with the help of the FolderPicker (code file CameraSample/MainPage.xaml.cs)

```
private async void OnTakePhoto(object sender, RoutedEventArgs e)
{
    var cam = new CameraCaptureUI();
    cam.PhotoSettings.AllowCropping = true;
    cam.PhotoSettings.Format = CameraCaptureUIPhotoFormat.Png;
    cam.PhotoSettings.CroppedSizeInPixels = new Size(300, 300);
    StorageFile file = await cam.CaptureFileAsync(CameraCaptureUIMode.Photo);

    if (file != null)
    {
        var picker = new FileSavePicker();
        picker.SuggestedStartLocation = PickerLocationId.PicturesLibrary;
        picker.FileTypeChoices.Add("Image File", new string[] { ".png" });
        StorageFile fileDestination = await picker.PickSaveFileAsync();
        if (fileDestination != null)
        {
            await file.CopyAndReplaceAsync(fileDestination);
        }
    }
}
```

The second code snippet is used to record a video. As before, you first need to take care of the configuration. Besides the PhotoSettings property, the CameraCaptureUI type defines the VideoSettings property. You can restrict the video recording based on the maximum resolution (using the enumeration value CameraCaptureUIMaxVideoResolution.HighestAvailable allows the user to select any available resolution) and the maximum duration. Possible video formats are WMV and MP4:

```
private async void OnRecordVideo(object sender, RoutedEventArgs e)
{
    var cam = new CameraCaptureUI();
    cam.VideoSettings.AllowTrimming = true;
    cam.VideoSettings.MaxResolution =
        CameraCaptureUIMaxVideoResolution.StandardDefinition;
    cam.VideoSettings.Format = CameraCaptureUIVideoFormat.Wmv;
    cam.VideoSettings.MaxDurationInSeconds = 5;
```

```
StorageFile file = await cam.CaptureFileAsync(
  CameraCaptureUIMode.Video);

if (file != null)
{
  var picker = new FileSavePicker();
  picker.SuggestedStartLocation = PickerLocationId.VideosLibrary;
  picker.FileTypeChoices.Add("Video File", new string[] { ".wmv" });
  StorageFile fileDestination = await picker.PickSaveFileAsync();
  if (fileDestination != null)
  {
    await file.CopyAndReplaceAsync(fileDestination);
  }
}
}
```

In cases where the user should be offered the option to capture either a video or a photo, you can pass the parameter `CameraCaptureUIMode.PhotoOrVideo` to the method `CaptureFileAsync`.

Because the camera also records location information, when the user runs the app for the first time, he or she is asked if recording location information should be allowed (see Figure 33-9).

Running the application, you can record photos and videos.

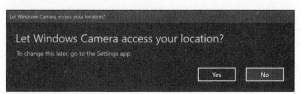

FIGURE 33-9

GEOLOCATION AND MAPCONTROL

Knowing the location of the user is an important aspect of apps, whether it's an app to show a map, an app that shows the weather of the area of the user, or an app for which you need to decide in what nearest cloud center the data of the user should be saved. When ads are used in the app, the user location can be important to show ads from the near area (if available).

With UWP apps you can also show maps. With Windows 10, a `MapControl` is available as part of the Windows API, and you don't need to use additional libraries, such as the Bing SDK, for doing this.

The sample app uses both the `Geolocator` (namespace `Windows.Devices.Geolocation`), to give information about the address of the user, and the `MapControl` (namespace `Windows.UI.Xaml.Controls.Maps`). Of course, you can also use these types independent of each other in your apps.

Using the MapControl

With the sample app, a `MapControl` is defined in the `MainPage` where different properties and events bind to values from the `MapsViewModel` that is accessed via the `ViewModel` property of the page. This way, you can dynamically change some settings in the app and see different features available with the `MapControl` (code file `MapSample/MainPage.xaml`):

```
<maps:MapControl x:Name="map"
  Center="{x:Bind ViewModel.CurrentPosition, Mode=OneWay}"
  MapTapped="{x:Bind ViewModel.OnMapTapped, Mode=OneTime}"
  Style="{x:Bind ViewModel.CurrentMapStyle, Mode=OneWay}"
```

```
ZoomLevel="{x:Bind Path=ViewModel.ZoomLevel, Mode=OneWay}"
DesiredPitch="{x:Bind Path=ViewModel.DesiredPitch, Mode=OneWay}"
TrafficFlowVisible="{x:Bind checkTrafficFlow.IsChecked, Mode=OneWay,
  Converter={StaticResource nbtob}}"
BusinessLandmarksVisible="{x:Bind checkBusinessLandmarks.IsChecked,
  Mode=OneWay, Converter={StaticResource nbtob}}"
LandmarksVisible="{x:Bind checkLandmarks.IsChecked, Mode=OneWay,
  Converter={StaticResource nbtob}}"
PedestrianFeaturesVisible="{x:Bind checkPedestrianFeatures.IsChecked,
  Mode=OneWay, Converter={StaticResource nbtob}}" />
```

The sample app defines controls to configure the `MapControl` within the Pane of the `SplitView` that is positioned on the right side. The `MapControl` is defined within the content of the `SplitView`. You can read more about the `SplitView` control in Chapter 32.

With the code-behind file, the `ViewModel` property is defined, and a `MapsViewModel` is instantiated by passing the `MapControl` to the constructor. Usually it's best to avoid having Windows controls directly accessible to the view model, and you should only use data binding to map. However, when you use some special features, such as street-side experience, it's easier to directly use the `MapControl` in the `MapsViewModel` class. Because this view model type is not doing anything else and cannot be used on anything other than Windows devices anyway, it's a compromise for passing the `MapControl` to the constructor of the `MapsViewModel` (code file `MapSample/MainPage.xaml.cs`):

```
public sealed partial class MainPage: Page
{
  public MainPage()
  {
    this.InitializeComponent();
    ViewModel = new MapsViewModel(map);
  }

  public MapsViewModel ViewModel { get; }
}
```

The constructor of the `MapsViewModel` initializes some properties that are bound to properties of the `MapControl`, such as the position of the map to a location within Vienna, the map style to a road variant, the pitch level to 0, and the zoom level to 12 (code file `MapSample/ViewModels/MapsViewModel.cs`):

```
public class MapsViewModel: BindableBase
{
  private readonly CoreDispatcher _dispatcher;
  private readonly Geolocator _locator = new Geolocator();
  private readonly MapControl _mapControl;

  public MapsViewModel(MapControl mapControl)
  {
    _mapControl = mapControl;
    StopStreetViewCommand = new DelegateCommand(
      StopStreetView, () => IsStreetView);
    StartStreetViewCommand = new DelegateCommand(
      StartStreetViewAsync, () => !IsStreetView);

    if (!DesignMode.DesignModeEnabled)
    {
      _dispatcher = CoreWindow.GetForCurrentThread().Dispatcher;
    }

    _locator.StatusChanged += async (s, e) =>
    {
```

```
      await _dispatcher.RunAsync(CoreDispatcherPriority.Low, () =>
         PositionStatus = e.Status);
   };

   // intialize defaults at startup
   CurrentPosition = new Geopoint(
      new BasicGeoposition { Latitude = 48.2, Longitude = 16.3 });
   CurrentMapStyle = MapStyle.Road;
   DesiredPitch = 0;
   ZoomLevel = 12;
}
```

Upon starting the app with the initial configuration, you can see the maps loaded with a location in Vienna as defined by the BasicGeoposition, the controls on the right side for managing the MapControl, and textual information about the loading status of the map (see Figure 33-10).

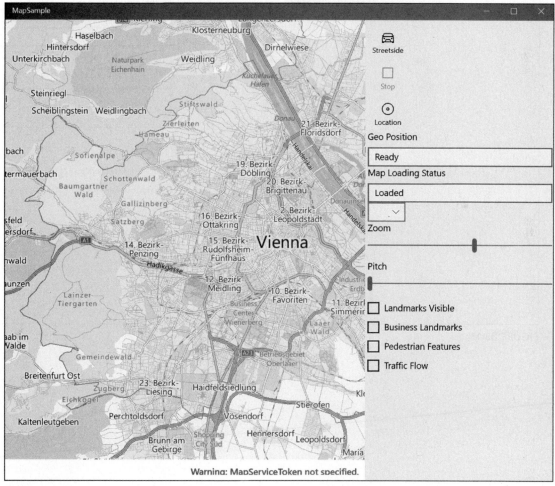

FIGURE 33-10

When you zoom in, change the pitch level, and select landmarks and business landmarks to be visible, you can see famous buildings such as the Stephansdom in Vienna, as shown in Figure 33-11.

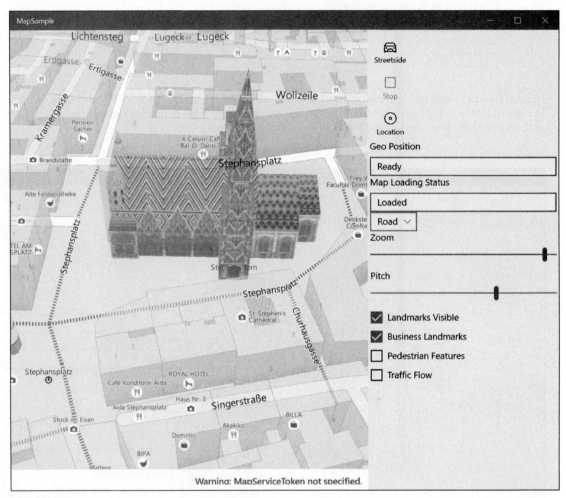

FIGURE 33-11

When you switch to the Aerial view, you can see real images, as shown in Figure 33-12.

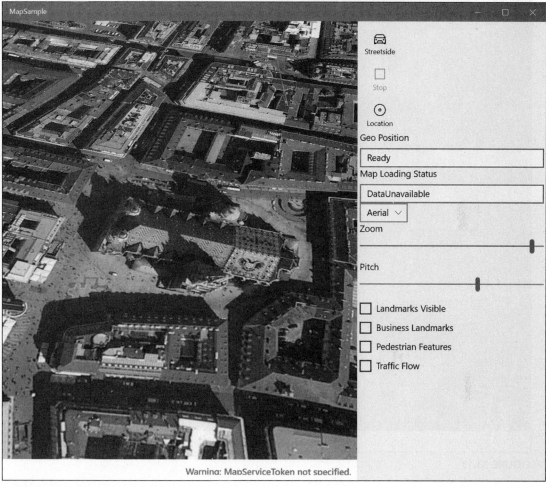

FIGURE 33-12

Some locations also show nice images with the Aerial3D view, as shown in Figure 33-13.

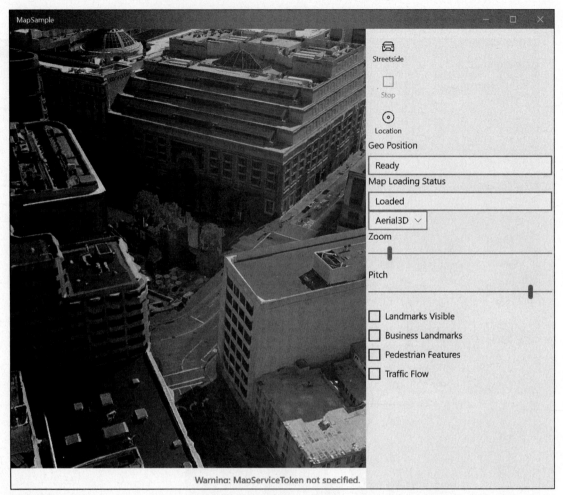

FIGURE 33-13

Location Information with Geolocator

Next, you need to get the actual position of the user with the help of the `Geolocator` instance `_locator`. The method `GetPositionAsync` returns the geolocation by returning a `Geoposition` instance. The result is applied to the `CurrentPosition` property of the view model that is bound to the center of the `MapControl` (code file `MapSample/ViewModels/MapsViewModel.cs`):

```
public async void GetCurrentPositionAsync()
{
  try
  {
    Geoposition position = await _locator.GetGeopositionAsync(
      TimeSpan.FromMinutes(5), TimeSpan.FromSeconds(5));
    CurrentPosition = new Geopoint(new BasicGeoposition
    {
      Longitude = position.Coordinate.Point.Position.Longitude,
      Latitude = position.Coordinate.Point.Position.Latitude
    });
```

```
        }
        catch (UnauthorizedAccessException ex)
        {
            await new MessageDialog(ex.Message).ShowAsync();
        }
    }
```

The `Geoposition` instance returned from `GetGeopositionAsync` lists information about how the `Geolocator` came to the conclusion of the position: using a cellular network with a phone, satellite, a Wi-Fi network that is recorded, or an IP address. When you configure the `Geolocator`, you can specify how accurate the information should be. By setting the property `DesiredAccuracyInMeters`, you can define how exact the location should be within a meter range. Of course, this accuracy is what you hope for, but it might not be possible to achieve. If the location should be more exact, GPS information from accessing satellite information can be used. Depending on the technology needed, more battery is used, so you shouldn't specify such accuracy if it's not really necessary. Satellite or cellular information cannot be used if the device doesn't offer these features. In those cases, you can use only the Wi-Fi network (if available) or an IP address. Of course, the IP address can be imprecise. Maybe you're getting the geolocation of an IP provider instead of the user. With the device and network I'm using, I get an accuracy of 64 meters. The source of the position is Wi-Fi. The result is very accurate. You can see the map in Figure 33-14.

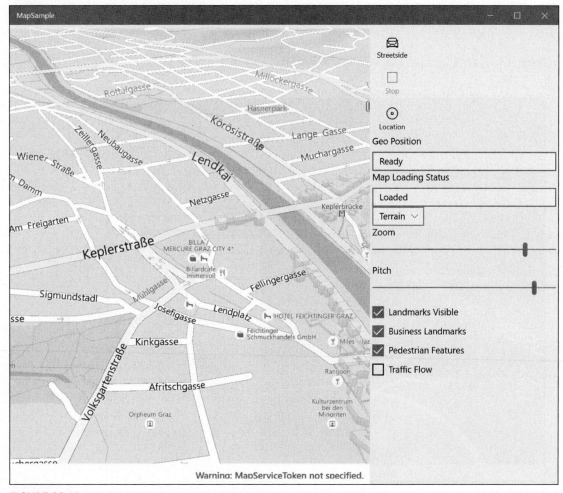

FIGURE 33-14

Street-Side Experience

Another feature offered by the `MapControl` is street-side experience. This feature is not available with all devices. You need to check the `IsStreetsideSupported` property from the `MapControl` before using it. In cases where street view is supported by the device, you can try to find nearby street-side places using the static method `FindNearbyAsync` of the `StreetsidePanorama` class. Street-side experience is available only for some locations. You can test to find out whether it is available in your location. If `StreetsidePanorama` information is available, it can be passed to the `StreetsideExperience` constructor and assigned to the `CustomExperience` property of the `MapControl` (code file MapSample/ViewModels/MapsViewModel.cs):

```
public async void StartStreetViewAsync()
{
  if (_mapControl.IsStreetsideSupported)
  {
    var panorama = await StreetsidePanorama.FindNearbyAsync(CurrentPosition);
    if (panorama == null)
    {
      var dlg = new MessageDialog("No streetside available here");
      await dlg.ShowAsync();
      return;
    }
    IsStreetView = true;
    _mapControl.CustomExperience = new StreetsideExperience(panorama);
  }
}
```

Street-side experience looks like what's shown in Figure 33-15.

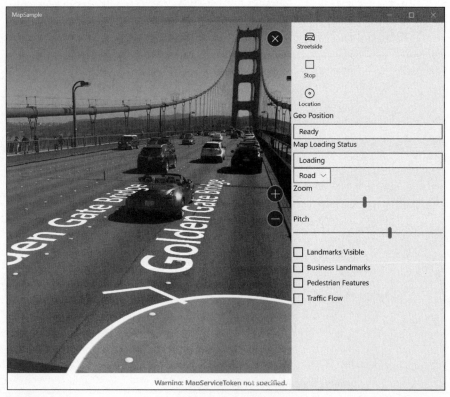

FIGURE 33-15

Continuously Requesting Location Information

Instead of getting the location just once using the `Geolocator`, you can also retrieve the location based on a time interval or the movement of the user. With the `Geolocator`, you can set the `ReportInterval` property to a minimum time interval in milliseconds between location updates. Updates can still happen more often—for example, if another app requested geo information with a smaller time interval. Instead of using a time interval, you can specify that the movement of the user fire location information. The property `MovementThreshold` specifies the movement in meters.

After setting the time interval or movement threshold, the `PositionChanged` event is fired every time a position update occurs:

```
private GeoLocator locator;
private void OnGetContinuousLocation(object sender, RoutedEventArgs e)
{
  locator = new Geolocator();
  locator.DesiredAccuracy = PositionAccuracy.High;
  // locator.ReportInterval = 1000;
  locator.MovementThreshold = 10;
  locator.PositionChanged += (sender1, e1) =>
  {
    // position updated
  };
  locator.StatusChanged += (sender1, e1) =>
  {
    // status changed
  };
}
```

> **NOTE** *Debugging apps with position changes does not require that you now get into a car and debug your app while on the road. Instead, the simulator is a helpful tool.*

SENSORS

For a wide range of sensors, the Windows Runtime offers direct access. The namespace `Windows.Devices.Sensors` contains classes for several sensors that can be available with different devices.

Before stepping into the code, it helps to have an overview of the different sensors and what they can be used for with the following table. Some sensors are very clear with their functionality, but others need some explanation. Windows 10 also offers some new sensors.

SENSOR	FEATURES
`LightSensor`	The light sensor returns the light in lux. This information is used by Windows to set the screen brightness.
`Compass`	The compass gives information about how many degrees the device is directed to the north using a magnetometer. This sensor differentiates magnetic and geographic north.
`Accelerometer`	The accelerometer measures G-force values along x, y, and z device axes. This could be used by an app that shows a marble rolling across the screen.
`Gyrometer`	The gyrometer measures angular velocities along x, y, and z device axes. If the app cares about device rotation, this is the sensor that can be used. However, moving the device also influences the gyrometer values. It might be necessary to compensate the gyrometer values using accelerometer values to remove moving of the device and just work with the real angular velocities.

(continues)

SENSOR	FEATURES
Inclinometer	The inclinometer gives number of degrees as the device rotates across the x-axis (pitch), y-axis (roll), and z-axis (yaw). An example of when this could be used is an app showing an airplane that matches yaw, pitch, and roll.
OrientationSensor	The orientation uses data from the accelerometer, gyrometer, and magnetometer and offers the values both in a quaternion and a rotation matrix.
Barometer (new with Windows 10)	The barometer measures atmospheric pressure.
Altimeter (new with Windows 10)	The altimeter measures the relative altitude.
Magnetometer	The magnetometer measures the strength and direction of a magnetic field.
Pedometer (new with Windows 10)	The pedometer measures the steps taken. Usually you're not walking with your desktop PC, which doesn't have such a sensor, but a pedometer is available with many Windows 10 phones.
ProximitySensor (new with Windows 10)	The proximity sensor measures the distance of nearby objects. It uses an electromagnetic field or infrared sensor to measure the distance.

Depending on your device, only a few of these sensors are available. Many of these sensors are used only within mobile devices. For example, counting your steps with a desktop PC might not result in the number of steps you should reach during a day.

An important aspect with sensors that return coordinates is that it's not the display orientation coordinate system that is used with Windows apps. Instead, it's using device orientation, which can be different based on the device. For example, for a Surface Pro that is by default positioned horizontally, the x-axis goes to right, y-axis to top, and the z-axis away from the user.

The sample app for using the sensors shows the results of several sensors in two ways: You can get the sensor value once, or you can read it continuously using events. You can use this app to see what sensor data is available with your device and also see what data is returned as you move the device.

For each of the sensors shown in the app, a `RelativePanel` that contains two `Button` and two `Textblock` controls is added to the `MainPage`. The following code snippet defines the controls for the light sensor (code file `SensorSampleApp/MainPage.xaml`):

```
<Border BorderThickness="3" Margin="12" BorderBrush="Blue">
  <RelativePanel>
    <Button x:Name="GetLightButton" Margin="8" Content="Get Light"
      Click="{x:Bind LightViewModel.OnGetLight}" />
    <Button x:Name="GetLightButtonReport" Margin="8"
      RelativePanel.Below="GetLightButton" Content="Get Light Report"
      Click="{x:Bind LightViewModel.OnGetLightReport}" />
    <TextBlock x:Name="LightText" Margin="8"
      RelativePanel.RightOf="GetLightButtonReport"
      RelativePanel.AlignBottomWith="GetLightButton" Text="{x:Bind
      LightViewModel.Illuminance, Mode=OneWay}" />
    <TextBlock x:Name="LightReportText" Margin="8"
      RelativePanel.AlignLeftWith="LightText"
      RelativePanel.AlignBottomWith="GetLightButtonReport" Text="{x:Bind
      LightViewModel.IlluminanceReport, Mode=OneWay}" />
  </RelativePanel>
</Border>
```

Light

As soon as you know how to work with one sensor, the other ones are very similar. Let's start with the `LightSensor`. First, an object is accessed invoking the static method `GetDefault`. You can get the actual value of the sensor by calling the method `GetCurrentReading`. With the `LightSensor`, `GetCurrentReading` returns a `LightSensorReading` object. This reading object defines the `IlluminanceInLux` property that returns the luminance in lux (code file `SensorSample/ViewModels/ LightViewModel.cs`):

```
public class LightViewModel: BindableBase
{
  public void OnGetLight()
  {
    LightSensor sensor = LightSensor.GetDefault();
    if (sensor != null)
    {
      LightSensorReading reading = sensor.GetCurrentReading();
      Illuminance = $"Illuminance: {reading?.IlluminanceInLux}";
    }
    else
    {
      Illuminance = "Light sensor not found";
    }
  }

  private string _illuminance;

  public string Illuminance
  {
    get { return _illuminance; }
    set { SetProperty(ref _illuminance, value); }
  }

  // etc.

}
```

For getting continuous updated values, the `ReadingChanged` event is fired. Specifying the `ReportInterval` property specifies the time interval that should be used to fire the event. It may not be lower than `MinimumReportInterval`. With the event, the second parameter e is of type `LightSensorReadingChangedEventArgs` and specifies the `LightSensorReading` with the `Reading` property:

```
public class LightViewModel: BindableBase
{
  // etc

  public void OnGetLightReport()
  {
    LightSensor sensor = LightSensor.GetDefault();
    if (sensor != null)
    {
      sensor.ReportInterval = Math.Max(sensor.MinimumReportInterval, 1000);
      sensor.ReadingChanged += async (s, e) =>
      {
        LightSensorReading reading = e.Reading;

        await CoreApplication.MainView.Dispatcher.RunAsync(
          CoreDispatcherPriority.Low, () =>
        {
          IlluminanceReport =
            $"{reading.IlluminanceInLux} {reading.Timestamp:T}";
        });
      };
    }
  }
}
```

```
    private string _illuminanceReport;
    public string IlluminanceReport
    {
      get { return _illuminanceReport; }
      set { SetProperty(ref _illuminanceReport, value); }
    }
  }
}
```

Compass

The compass can be used very similarly. The `GetDefault` method returns the `Compass` object, and `GetCurrentReading` retrieves the `CompassReading` representing the current values of the compass. `CompassReading` defines the properties `HeadingAccuracy`, `HeadingMagneticNorth`, and `HeadingTrueNorth`.

In cases where `HeadingAccuracy` returns `MagnometerAccuracy.Unknown` or `Unreliable`, the compass needs to be calibrated (code file `SensorSampleApp/ViewModels/CompassviewModel.cs`):

```
public class CompassViewModel: BindableBase
{
  public void OnGetCompass()
  {
    Compass sensor = Compass.GetDefault();
    if (sensor != null)
    {
      CompassReading reading = sensor.GetCurrentReading();
      CompassInfo = $"magnetic north: {reading.HeadingMagneticNorth} " +
        $"real north: {reading.HeadingTrueNorth} " +
        $"accuracy: {reading.HeadingAccuracy}";
    }
    else
    {
      CompassInfo = "Compass not found";
    }
  }

  private string _compassInfo;
  public string CompassInfo
  {
    get { return _compassInfo; }
    set { SetProperty(ref _compassInfo, value); }
  }

  // etc.
}
```

Continuous updates are available with the compass as well:

```
public class CompassViewModel: BindableBase
{
  // etc.

  public void OnGetCompassReport()
  {
    Compass sensor = Compass.GetDefault();
    if (sensor != null)
    {
      sensor.ReportInterval = Math.Max(sensor.MinimumReportInterval, 1000);
      sensor.ReadingChanged += async (s, e) =>
        {
          CompassReading reading = e.Reading;
          await CoreApplication.MainView.Dispatcher.RunAsync(
```

```
              CoreDispatcherPriority.Low, () =>
          {
              CompassInfoReport =
                  $"magnetic north: {reading.HeadingMagneticNorth} " +
                  $"real north: {reading.HeadingTrueNorth} " +
                  $"accuracy: {reading.HeadingAccuracy} {reading.Timestamp:T}";
          });
      };
    }
  }

  private string _compassInfoReport;
  public string CompassInfoReport
  {
    get { return _compassInfoReport; }
    set { SetProperty(ref _compassInfoReport, value); }
  }
}
```

Accelerometer

The accelerometer gives information about the g-force values along x-, y-, and z-axes of the device. With a landscape device, the x-axis is horizontal, the y-axis is vertical, and the z-axis is oriented in direction from the user. For example, if the device stands upright at a right angle on the table with the Windows button on bottom, the x has a value of –1. When you turn the device around to have the Windows button on top, x has a value of +1.

Similar to the other sensors you've seen so far, the static method `GetDefault` returns the `Accelerometer`, and `GetCurrentReading` gives the actual accelerometer values with the `AccelerometerReading` object. `AccelerationX`, `AccelerationY`, and `AccererationZ` are the values that can be read (code file `SensorSampleApp/ViewModels/AccelerometerViewModel.cs`):

```
public class AccelerometerViewModel: BindableBase
{
  public void OnGetAccelerometer()
  {
    Accelerometer sensor = Accelerometer.GetDefault();
    if (sensor != null)
    {
      AccelerometerReading reading = sensor.GetCurrentReading();
      AccelerometerInfo = $"X: {reading.AccelerationX} " +
        $"Y: {reading.AccelerationY} Z: {reading.AccelerationZ}";
    }
    else
    {
      AccelerometerInfo = "Compass not found";
    }
  }

  private string _accelerometerInfo;
  public string AccelerometerInfo
  {
    get { return _accelerometerInfo; }
    set { SetProperty(ref _accelerometerInfo, value); }
  }
  // etc.
}
```

You get continuous values from the accelerometer by assigning an event handler to the `ReadingChanged` event. As this is exactly the same as with the other sensors that have been covered so far, the code snippet is not shown in the book. However, you get this functionality with the code download of this chapter. You can test your device and move it continuously while reading the accelerometer values.

Inclinometer

The inclinometer is for advanced orientation; it gives yaw, pitch, and roll values in degrees with respect to gravity. The resulting values are specified by the properties `PitchDegrees`, `RollDegrees`, and `YawDegrees` (code file `SensorSampleApp/ViewModels/InclinometerViewModel.cs`):

```
public class InclinometerViewModel: BindableBase
{
  public void OnGetInclinometer()
  {
    Inclinometer sensor = Inclinometer.GetDefault();
    if (sensor != null)
    {
      InclinometerReading reading = sensor.GetCurrentReading();
      InclinometerInfo = $"pitch degrees: {reading.PitchDegrees} " +
        $"roll degrees: {reading.RollDegrees} " +
        $"yaw accuracy: {reading.YawAccuracy} " +
        $"yaw degrees: {reading.YawDegrees}";
    }
    else
    {
      InclinometerInfo = "Inclinometer not found";
    }
  }

  private string _inclinometerInfo;
  public string InclinometerInfo
  {
    get { return _inclinometerInfo; }
    set { SetProperty(ref _inclinometerInfo, value); }
  }
  // etc.
}
```

Gyrometer

The `Gyrometer` gives angular velocity values for the x-, y-, and z- device axes (code file `SensorSampleApp/ViewModels/GyrometerViewModel.cs`):

```
public class GyrometerViewModel: BindableBase
{
  public void OnGetGyrometer()
  {
    Gyrometer sensor = Gyrometer.GetDefault();
    if (sensor != null)
    {
      GyrometerReading reading = sensor.GetCurrentReading();
      GyrometerInfo = $"X: {reading.AngularVelocityX} " +
        $"Y: {reading.AngularVelocityY} Z: {reading.AngularVelocityZ}";
    }
    else
    {
      GyrometerInfo = "Gyrometer not found";
    }
  }

  private string _gyrometerInfo;
```

```
    public string GyrometerInfo
    {
      get { return _gyrometerInfo; }
      set { SetProperty(ref _gyrometerInfo, value); }
    }
    // etc.
}
```

Orientation

The `OrientationSensor` is the most complex sensor because it takes values from the accelerometer, gyrometer, and magnetometer. You get all the values in either a quaternion represented by the `Quaternion` property or a rotation matrix (`RotationMatrix` property).

Try the sample app to see the values and how you move the device (code file `SensorSampleApp/ViewModels/OrientationViewModel.cs`):

```
public static class OrientationSensorExtensions
{
  public static string Output(this SensorQuaternion q) =>
    $"x {q.X} y {q.Y} z {q.Z} w {q.W}";

  public static string Ouput(this SensorRotationMatrix m) =>
    $"m11 {m.M11} m12 {m.M12} m13 {m.M13} " +
    $"m21 {m.M21} m22 {m.M22} m23 {m.M23} " +
    $"m31 {m.M31} m32 {m.M32} m33 {m.M33}";
}

public class OrientationViewModel: BindableBase
{
  public void OnGetOrientation()
  {
    OrientationSensor sensor = OrientationSensor.GetDefault();
    if (sensor != null)
    {
      OrientationSensorReading reading = sensor.GetCurrentReading();
      OrientationInfo = $"Quaternion: {reading.Quaternion.Output()} " +
        $"Rotation: {reading.RotationMatrix.Ouput()} " +
        $"Yaw accuracy: {reading.YawAccuracy}";
    }
    else
    {
      OrientationInfo = "Compass not found";
    }
  }

  private string _orientationInfo;
  public string OrientationInfo
  {
    get { return _orientationInfo; }
    set { SetProperty(ref _orientationInfo, value); }
  }
  // etc.
}
```

When you run the app, you can see sensor data as shown in Figure 33-16.

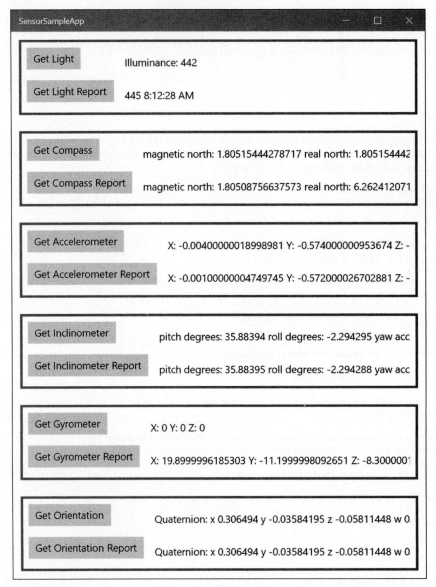

FIGURE 33-16

Rolling Marble Sample

For seeing sensor values in action not only with result values in a `TextBlock` element, you can make a simple sample app that makes use of the `Accelerometer` to roll a marble across the screen.

The marble is represented by a red ellipse. Having an `Ellipse` element positioned within a `Canvas` element allows moving the `Ellipse` with an attached property (code file `RollingMarble/MainPage.xaml`):

```
<Canvas Background="{ThemeResource ApplicationPageBackgroundThemeBrush}">
  <Ellipse Fill="Red" Width="100" Height="100" Canvas.Left="550"
    Canvas.Top="400" x:Name="ell1" />
</Canvas>
```

> **NOTE** *Attached properties are explained in Chapter 29, "Core XAML." More information about the* Canvas *element is in Chapter 34, "Windows Desktop Applications with WPF."*

The constructor of the MainPage initializes the Accelerometer and requests continuous reading with the minimum interval. To know the boundaries of the window, with the LayoutUpdated event of the page, MaxX and MaxY are set to the width and height of the window minus the size of the ellipse (code file RollingMarble/MainPage.xaml.cs):

```csharp
public sealed partial class MainPage: Page
{
  private Accelerometer _accelerometer;
  private double MinX = 0;
  private double MinY = 0;
  private double MaxX = 1000;
  private double MaxY = 600;
  private double currentX = 0;
  private double currentY = 0;

  public MainPage()
  {
    this.InitializeComponent();
    accelerometer = Accelerometer.GetDefault();
    accelerometer.ReportInterval = accelerometer.MinimumReportInterval;
    accelerometer.ReadingChanged += OnAccelerometerReading;
    this.DataContext = this;

    this.LayoutUpdated += (sender, e) =>
    {
      MaxX = this.ActualWidth—100;
      MaxY = this.ActualHeight—100;
    };
  }
```

With every value received from the accelerometer, the ellipse is moved within the Canvas element in the event handler method OnAccelerometerReading. Before the value is set, it is checked according to the boundaries of the window:

```csharp
  private async void OnAccelerometerReading(Accelerometer sender,
    AccelerometerReadingChangedEventArgs args)
  {
    currentX += args.Reading.AccelerationX * 80;
    if (currentX < MinX) currentX = MinX;
    if (currentX > MaxX) currentX = MaxX;

    currentY += -args.Reading.AccelerationY * 80;
    if (currentY < MinY) currentY = MinY;
    if (currentY > MaxY) currentY = MaxY;

    await this.Dispatcher.RunAsync(CoreDispatcherPriority.High, () =>
      {
        Canvas.SetLeft(ell1, currentX);
        Canvas.SetTop(ell1, currentY);
      });
  }
```

Now you run the app and move the device to get the marble rolling as shown in Figure 33-17.

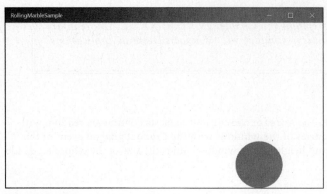

FIGURE 33-17

SUMMARY

This chapter provided more information on writing UWP Windows apps. You've seen how the life cycle is different compared to Window desktop applications, and how you need to take action on the `Suspending` event.

Interaction with other apps was covered by using share contracts. The `DataTransferManager` was used to offer HTML data for other apps. Implementing a share target contract enables the app to receive data from other apps.

Another main part of this chapter covered several devices, including the camera for taking pictures and recording videos, a geolocator for getting the location of the user, and a bunch of different sensors for getting information about how the device moves.

The next chapter continues with XAML technologies and covers Windows desktop applications using Windows Presentation Foundation (WPF).

34

Windows Desktop Applications with WPF

WHAT'S IN THIS CHAPTER?

➤ WPF Controls

➤ Layout

➤ Triggers

➤ Menu and ribbon controls

➤ Using commanding for input handling

➤ Data binding to elements, objects, lists, and XML

➤ Value conversions and validation

➤ Using the `TreeView` to display hierarchical data

➤ Displaying and grouping data with the `DataGrid`

➤ Live shaping with the Collection View Source

WROX.COM CODE DOWNLOADS FOR THIS CHAPTER

The wrox.com code downloads for this chapter are found at www.wrox.com/go/professionalcsharp6 on the Download Code tab. The code for this chapter is divided into the following major examples:

➤ Controls Sample

➤ Layout Sample

➤ Trigger Sample

➤ Books

➤ Multi Binding Sample

➤ Priority Binding Sample

➤ XML Binding Sample

➤ Validation Sample

➤ Formula-1

➤ Live Shaping

INTRODUCTION

In Chapter 29, "Core XAML," and Chapter 30, "Styling XAML Apps," you read about some of the core features of XAML. This chapter continues the journey through XAML using it from WPF. Here you read about important aspects for the control hierarchy, creating complete applications, using data binding and command handling, and using the `DataGrid` control. Data binding is an important concept for bringing data from .NET classes into the user interface and allowing the user to change data. WPF not only allows binding to simple entities or lists, but it also offers binding of one UI property to multiple properties of possible different types with multibinding and priority binding that are discussed in this chapter as well. It is also important to validate data entered by a user. Here, you can read about different ways to handle validation, including the interface `INotifyDataErrorInfo` that is new since .NET 4.5. Also covered in this chapter is commanding, which enables mapping events from the UI to code. In contrast to the event model, this provides a better separation between XAML and code. This chapter covers using predefined commands and creating custom commands.

The `TreeView` and `DataGrid` controls are UI controls to display bound data. This chapter explains using the `TreeView` control to display data in the tree where data is loaded dynamically depending on what the user selects. With the `DataGrid` control you find out how to use filtering, sorting, and grouping, as well as one new .NET 4.5 feature named *live shaping* that allows changing sorting or filtering options in real time.

To begin, let's start with the `Menu` and the `Ribbon` controls. The `Ribbon` control made it into the release of .NET 4.5.

CONTROLS

Because you can use hundreds of controls with WPF, they are categorized into groups, each of which is described in the following sections.

Simple Controls

Simple controls are controls that don't have a `Content` property. The `Button` class has come up in other chapters, where you have seen that the `Button` can contain any shape or any element you like. This is not possible with simple controls. The following table describes the simple controls.

SIMPLE CONTROL	DESCRIPTION
`TextBox`	This control is used to display simple, unformatted text.
`RichTextBox`	This control supports rich text with the help of the `FlowDocument` class. `RichTextBox` and `TextBox` are derived from the same base class—`TextBoxBase`.
`Calendar`	This control displays a month, year, or decade. The user can select a date or range of dates.
`DatePicker`	This control opens a calendar onscreen for date selection by the user.
`PasswordBox`	This control is used to enter a password. It has specific properties for password input, such as `PasswordChar`, to define the character that should be displayed as the user enters the password, or `Password`, to access the password entered. The `PasswordChanged` event is invoked as soon as the password is changed.
`ScrollBar`	This control contains a `Thumb` that enables the user to select a value. A scrollbar can be used, for example, if a document doesn't fit on the screen. Some controls contain scrollbars that are displayed if the content is too big.
`ProgressBar`	This control indicates the progress of a lengthy operation.

SIMPLE CONTROL	DESCRIPTION
Slider	This control enables users to select a range of values by moving a Thumb. ScrollBar, ProgressBar, and Slider are derived from the same base class—RangeBase.

> **NOTE** *Although simple controls do not have a* Content *property, you can completely customize the look of a control by defining a template. Templates are discussed later in this chapter in the section "Templates."*

Content Controls

A ContentControl has a Content property, with which you can add any content to the control. The Button class derives from the base class ContentControl, so you can add any content to this control. In a previous example, you saw a Canvas control within the Button. Content controls are described in the following table.

CONTENT CONTROL	DESCRIPTION
Button, RepeatButton, ToggleButton, CheckBox, RadioButton	The classes Button, RepeatButton, ToggleButton, and GridViewColumnHeader are derived from the same base class—ButtonBase. All buttons react to the Click event. RepeatButton raises the Click event repeatedly until the button is released. ToggleButton is the base class for CheckBox and RadioButton. These buttons have an on and off state. The CheckBox can be selected and cleared by the user; the RadioButton can be selected by the user. Clearing the RadioButton must be done programmatically.
Label	The Label class represents the text label for a control. This class also has support for access keys—for example, a menu command.
Frame	The Frame control supports navigation. You can navigate to a page's content with the Navigate method. If the content is a web page, then the WebBrowser control is used for display.
ListBoxItem	An item inside a ListBox control.
StatusBarItem	An item inside a StatusBar control.
ScrollViewer	A content control that includes scrollbars. You can put any content in this control; the scrollbars are displayed as needed.
ToolTip	Creates a pop-up window to display additional information for a control.
UserControl	Using this class as a base class provides a simple way to create custom controls. However, the UserControl base class does not support templates.
Window	This class enables you to create windows and dialogs. It includes a frame with minimize/maximize/close buttons and a system menu. When showing a dialog, you can use the ShowDialog method; the Show method opens a window.
NavigationWindow	This class derives from the Window class and supports content navigation.

Only a `Frame` control is contained within the `Window` of the following XAML code. The `Source` property is set to `http://www.cninnovation.com`, so the `Frame` control navigates to this website, as shown in Figure 34-1 (code file `ControlsSample/FramesWindow.xaml`):

```xml
<Window x:Class="ControlsSamples.FramesWindow"
        xmlns="http://schemas.microsoft.com/winfx/2006/xaml/presentation"
        xmlns:x="http://schemas.microsoft.com/winfx/2006/xaml"
        Title="Frames Sample" Height="500" Width="800">
    <Frame Source="http://www.cninnovation.com" Grid.Row="1" />
</Window>
```

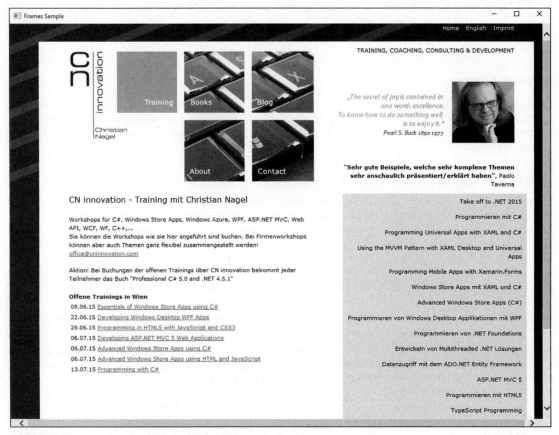

FIGURE 34-1

> **NOTE** *In Chapter 32, "Windows Apps: User Interfaces," you can read how to use the* Frame *class to navigate between pages. With WPF, you can also use the* Frame *class for navigation.*

Headered Content Controls

Content controls with a header are derived from the base class `HeaderedContentControl`, which itself is derived from the base class `ContentControl`. The `HeaderedContentControl` class has a property `Header` to define the content of the header and `HeaderTemplate` for complete customization of the header. The controls derived from the base class `HeaderedContentControl` are listed in the following table.

HEADEREDCONTENTCONTROL	DESCRIPTION
Expander	This control enables you to create an "advanced" mode with a dialog that, by default, does not show all information but can be expanded by the user for additional details. In the unexpanded mode, header information is shown. In expanded mode, the content is visible.
GroupBox	Provides a border and a header to group controls.
TabItem	These controls are items within the class `TabControl`. The `Header` property of the `TabItem` defines the content of the header shown with the tabs of the `TabControl`.

A simple use of the `Expander` control is shown in the next example. The `Expander` control has the property `Header` set to `Click for more`. This text is displayed for expansion. The content of this control is shown only if the control is expanded. Figure 34-2 shows the application with a collapsed `Expander` control, and Figure 34-3 shows the same application with an expanded `Expander` control. The code is as follows (code file `ControlsSample/ExpanderWindow.xaml`):

```xml
<Window x:Class="ControlsSample.ExpanderWindow"
        xmlns="http://schemas.microsoft.com/winfx/2006/xaml/presentation"
        xmlns:x="http://schemas.microsoft.com/winfx/2006/xaml"
        Title="Expander Sample" Height="300" Width="300">
  <StackPanel>
    <TextBlock>Short information</TextBlock>
    <Expander Header="Additional Information">
      <Border Height="200" Width="200" Background="Yellow">
        <TextBlock HorizontalAlignment="Center" VerticalAlignment="Center">
          More information here!
        </TextBlock>
      </Border>
    </Expander>
  </StackPanel>
</Window>
```

> **NOTE** *To make the header text of the* `Expander` *control change when the control is expanded, you can create a trigger. Triggers are explained later in this chapter in the section "Triggers."*

FIGURE 34-2

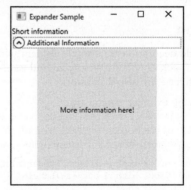

FIGURE 34-3

Items Controls

The `ItemsControl` class contains a list of items that can be accessed with the `Items` property. Classes derived from `ItemsControl` are shown in the following table.

ITEMSCONTROL	DESCRIPTION
Menu and ContextMenu	These classes are derived from the abstract base class `MenuBase`. You can offer menus to the user by placing `MenuItem` elements in the items list and associating commands.
StatusBar	This control is usually shown at the bottom of an application to give status information to the user. You can put `StatusBarItem` elements inside a `StatusBar` list.
TreeView	Use this control for a hierarchical display of items.
ListBoxComboBoxTabControl	These have the same abstract base class, `Selector`. This base class makes it possible to select items from a list. The `ListBox` displays the items from a list. The `ComboBox` has an additional `Button` control to display the items only if the button is clicked. With `TabControl`, content can be arranged in tabular form.
DataGrid	This control is a customizable grid that displays data. It is discussed in detail in the next chapter.

Headered Items Controls

`HeaderedItemsControl` is the base class of controls that include items but also have a header. The class `HeaderedItemsControl` is derived from `ItemsControl`.

Classes derived from `HeaderedItemsControl` are listed in the following table.

HEADEREDITEMSCONTROL	DESCRIPTION
MenuItem	The menu classes `Menu` and `ContextMenu` include items of the `MenuItem` type. Menu items can be connected to commands, as the `MenuItem` class implements the interface `ICommandSource`.
TreeViewItem	This class can include items of type `TreeViewItem`.
ToolBar	This control is a container for a group of controls, usually `Button` and `Separator` elements. You can place the `ToolBar` inside a `ToolBarTray` that handles the rearranging of `ToolBar` controls.

Decoration

You can add decorations to a single element with the `Decorator` class. `Decorator` is a base class that has derivations such as `Border`, `Viewbox`, and `BulletDecorator`. Theme elements such as `ButtonChrome` and `ListBoxChrome` are also decorators.

The following example demonstrates a `Border`, `Viewbox`, and `BulletDecorator`, as shown in Figure 34-4. The `Border` class decorates the `Children` element by adding a border around it. You can define a brush and the thickness of the border, the background, the radius of the corner, and the padding of its children (code file `ControlsSample/DecorationsWindow.xaml`):

```
<Border BorderBrush="Violet" BorderThickness="5.5">
  <Label>Label with a border</Label>
</Border>
```

The Viewbox stretches and scales its child to the available space. The StretchDirection and Stretch properties are specific to the functionality of the Viewbox. These properties enable specifying whether the child is stretched in both directions, and whether the aspect ratio is preserved:

```
<Viewbox StretchDirection="Both" Stretch="Uniform">
  <Label>Label with a viewbox</Label>
</Viewbox>
```

The BulletDecorator class decorates its child with a bullet. The child can be any element (in this example, a TextBlock). Similarly, the bullet can also be any element. The example uses an Image, but you can use any UIElement:

```
<BulletDecorator>
  <BulletDecorator.Bullet>
    <Image Width="25" Height="25" Margin="5" HorizontalAlignment="Center"
           VerticalAlignment="Center"
           Source="/DecorationsDemo;component/images/apple1.jpg" />
  </BulletDecorator.Bullet>
  <BulletDecorator.Child>
    <TextBlock VerticalAlignment="Center" Padding="8">Granny Smith</TextBlock>
  </BulletDecorator.Child>
</BulletDecorator>
```

FIGURE 34-4

LAYOUT

To define the layout of the application, you can use a class that derives from the Panel base class. A layout container needs to do two main tasks: measure and arrange. With *measuring*, the container asks its children for the preferred sizes. Because the full size requested by the controls might not be available, the container determines the available sizes and *arranges* the positions of its children accordingly. This section discusses several available layout containers.

StackPanel

The Window can contain just a single element as content, but if you want more than one element inside it, you can use a StackPanel as a child of the Window and add elements to the content of the StackPanel. The StackPanel is a simple container control that shows one element after the other. The orientation of the StackPanel can be horizontal or vertical. The class ToolBarPanel is derived from StackPanel (code file LayoutSamples/StackPanelWindow.xaml):

```
<Window x:Class="LayoutSamples.StackPanelWindow"
        xmlns="http://schemas.microsoft.com/winfx/2006/xaml/presentation"
        xmlns:x="http://schemas.microsoft.com/winfx/2006/xaml"
        Title="Stack Panel" Height="300" Width="300">
  <StackPanel Orientation="Vertical">
    <Label>Label</Label>
    <TextBox>TextBox</TextBox>
    <CheckBox>CheckBox</CheckBox>
    <CheckBox>CheckBox</CheckBox>
    <ListBox>
      <ListBoxItem>ListBoxItem One</ListBoxItem>
      <ListBoxItem>ListBoxItem Two</ListBoxItem>
    </ListBox>
    <Button>Button</Button>
  </StackPanel>
</Window>
```

Figure 34-5 shows the child controls of the `StackPanel` organized vertically.

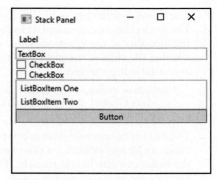

FIGURE 34-5

WrapPanel

The `WrapPanel` positions the children from left to right, one after the other, as long as they fit on one line, and then it continues with the next line. The panel's orientation can be horizontal or vertical (code file `LayoutSamples/WrapPanelWindow.xaml`):

```xml
<Window x:Class="LayoutSamples.WrapPanelWindow"
        xmlns="http://schemas.microsoft.com/winfx/2006/
        xaml/presentation"
        xmlns:x="http://schemas.microsoft.com/
        winfx/2006/xaml"
        Title="WrapPanelWindow" Height="300" Width="300">
  <WrapPanel>
    <WrapPanel.Resources>
      <Style TargetType="Button">
        <Setter Property="Width" Value="100" />
        <Setter Property="Margin" Value="5" />
      </Style>
    </WrapPanel.Resources>
    <Button>Button</Button>
    <Button>Button</Button>
    <Button>Button</Button>
    <Button>Button</Button>
    <Button>Button</Button>
    <Button>Button</Button>
    <Button>Button</Button>
    <Button>Button</Button>
  </WrapPanel>
</Window>
```

Figure 34-6 shows the output of the panel. If you resize the application, the buttons are rearranged accordingly to have just that many buttons as fit in a line.

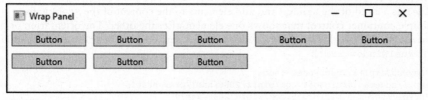

FIGURE 34-6

Canvas

`Canvas` is a panel that enables you to explicitly position controls. `Canvas` defines the attached properties `Left`, `Right`, `Top`, and `Bottom` that can be used by the children for positioning within the panel (code file `LayoutSamples/CanvasWindow.xaml`):

```xml
<Canvas Background="LightBlue">
  <Label Canvas.Top="30" Canvas.Left="20">Enter here:</Label>
  <TextBox Canvas.Top="30" Canvas.Left="120" Width="100" />
```

```
    <Button Canvas.Top="70" Canvas.Left="130" Content="Click Me!" Padding="5" />
  </Canvas>
```

Figure 34-7 shows the output of the `Canvas` panel with the positioned children `Label`, `TextBox`, and `Button`.

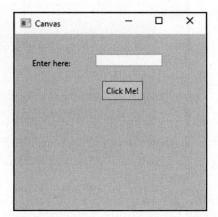

FIGURE 34-7

> **NOTE** *The* `Canvas` *control is best used for the layout of graphic elements, like Shape controls shown in Chapter 30.*

DockPanel

The `DockPanel` is very similar to the Windows Forms docking functionality. Here, you can specify the area in which child controls should be arranged. `DockPanel` defines the attached property `Dock`; you can set the property in the children of the controls using the values `Left`, `Right`, `Top`, and `Bottom`. Figure 34-8 shows the outcome of text blocks with borders that are arranged in the dock panel. For easier differentiation, different colors are specified for the various areas (code file `LayoutSamples/DockPanelWindow.xaml`):

```
<DockPanel>
  <Border Height="25" Background="AliceBlue" DockPanel.Dock="Top">
    <TextBlock>Menu</TextBlock>
  </Border>
  <Border Height="25" Background="Aqua" DockPanel.Dock="Top">
    <TextBlock>Ribbon</TextBlock>
  </Border>
  <Border Height="30" Background="LightSteelBlue" DockPanel.Dock="Bottom">
    <TextBlock>Status</TextBlock>
  </Border>
  <Border Height="80" Background="Azure" DockPanel.Dock="Left">
    <TextBlock>Left Side</TextBlock>
  </Border>
  <Border Background="HotPink">
    <TextBlock>Remaining Part</TextBlock>
  </Border>
</DockPanel>
```

Grid

Using the Grid, you can arrange your controls with rows and columns. For every column, you can specify a ColumnDefinition. For every row, you can specify a RowDefinition. The following example code lists two columns and three rows. With each column and row, you can specify the width or height. ColumnDefinition has a Width dependency property; RowDefinition has a Height dependency property. You can define the height and width in pixels, centimeters, inches, or points, or you can set it to Auto to base the size on the content. The grid also allows *star sizing*, which means the space for the rows and columns is calculated according to the available space and relative to other rows and columns. When providing the available space for a column, you can set the Width property to *. To have the size doubled for another column, you specify 2*. The sample code, which defines two columns and three rows, doesn't define additional settings with the column and row definitions; the default is the star sizing.

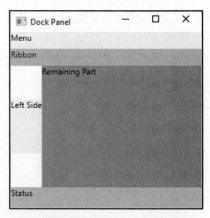

FIGURE 34-8

The grid contains several Label and TextBox controls. Because the parent of these controls is a grid, you can set the attached properties Column, ColumnSpan, Row, and RowSpan (code file LayoutSamples/GridWindow.xaml):

```
<Grid ShowGridLines="True">
  <Grid.ColumnDefinitions>
    <ColumnDefinition />
    <ColumnDefinition />
  </Grid.ColumnDefinitions>
  <Grid.RowDefinitions>
    <RowDefinition />
    <RowDefinition />
    <RowDefinition />
  </Grid.RowDefinitions>
  <Label Grid.Column="0" Grid.ColumnSpan="2" Grid.Row="0"
        VerticalAlignment="Center" HorizontalAlignment="Center"
        Content="Title" />
  <Label Grid.Column="0" Grid.Row="1" VerticalAlignment="Center"
        Content="Firstname:" Margin="10" />
  <TextBox Grid.Column="1" Grid.Row="1" Width="100" Height="30" />
  <Label Grid.Column="0" Grid.Row="2" VerticalAlignment="Center"
        Content="Lastname:" Margin="10" />
  <TextBox Grid.Column="1" Grid.Row="2" Width="100" Height="30" />
</Grid>
```

The outcome of arranging controls in a grid is shown in Figure 34-9. For easier viewing of the columns and rows, the property ShowGridLines is set to true.

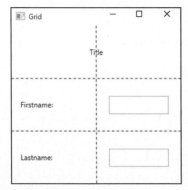

FIGURE 34-9

> **NOTE** *For a grid in which every cell is the same size, you can use the* `UniformGrid` *class.*

TRIGGERS

In Chapter 30, you can read about using the Visual State Manager that you can use to dynamically change the look of controls. The Visual State Manager is supported by both WPF and the Universal Windows Platform. WPF also offers property triggers for the same scenario, and there are other trigger types for different scenarios. This section discusses property triggers, multi-triggers, and data triggers.

With triggers, you can change the look and feel of your controls dynamically based on certain events or property value changes. For example, when the user moves the mouse over a button, the button can change its look. Usually, you need to do this with the C# code. With WPF, you can also do this with XAML as long as only the UI is influenced.

Property triggers are activated as soon as a property value changes. Multi-triggers are based on multiple property values. Event triggers fire when an event occurs. Data triggers happen when data that is bound is changed.

Property Triggers

The `Style` class has a `Triggers` property with which you can assign property triggers. The following example includes a `Button` element inside a `Grid` panel. With the `Window` resources, a default style for `Button` elements is defined. This style specifies that the `Background` is set to `LightBlue` and the `FontSize` to 17. This is the style of the `Button` elements when the application is started. Using triggers, the style of the controls changes. The triggers are defined within the `Style.Triggers` element, using the `Trigger` element. One trigger is assigned to the property `IsMouseOver`; the other trigger is assigned to the property `IsPressed`. Both of these properties are defined with the `Button` class to which the style applies. If `IsMouseOver` has a value of `true`, then the trigger fires and sets the `Foreground` property to `Red` and the `FontSize` property to 22. If the `Button` is pressed, then the property `IsPressed` is true, and the second trigger fires and sets the `Foreground` property of the `TextBox` to `Yellow` (code file `TriggerSamples/PropertyTriggerWindow.xaml`):

```xml
<Window x:Class="TriggerSamples.PropertyTriggerWindow"
        xmlns="http://schemas.microsoft.com/winfx/2006/xaml/presentation"
        xmlns:x="http://schemas.microsoft.com/winfx/2006/xaml"
        Title="Property Trigger" Height="300" Width="300">
  <Window.Resources>
    <Style TargetType="Button">
      <Setter Property="Background" Value="LightBlue" />
      <Setter Property="FontSize" Value="17" />
      <Style.Triggers>
        <Trigger Property="IsMouseOver" Value="True">
          <Setter Property="Foreground" Value="Red" />
          <Setter Property="FontSize" Value="22" />
        </Trigger>
        <Trigger Property="IsPressed" Value="True">
          <Setter Property="Foreground" Value="Yellow" />
          <Setter Property="FontSize" Value="22" />
        </Trigger>
      </Style.Triggers>
    </Style>
  </Window.Resources>
  <Grid>
    <Button Width="200" Height="30" Content="Click me!" />
  </Grid>
</Window>
```

> **NOTE** *If the* IsPressed *property is set to* true, *the* IsMouseOver *property will be* true *as well. Pressing the button also requires the mouse to be over the button. Pressing the button triggers it to fire and changes the properties accordingly. Here, the order of triggers is important. If the* IsPressed *property trigger is moved before the* IsMouseOver *property trigger, the* IsMouseOver *property trigger overwrites the values that the first trigger set.*

You don't need to reset the property values to the original values when the reason for the trigger is not valid anymore. For example, you don't need to define a trigger for IsMouseOver=true and IsMouseOver=false. As soon as the reason for the trigger is no longer valid, the changes made by the trigger action are reset to the original values automatically.

Figure 34-10 shows the trigger sample application in which the foreground and font size of the button are changed from their original values when the button has the focus.

FIGURE 34-10

> **NOTE** *When using property triggers, it is extremely easy to change the look of controls, fonts, colors, opacity, and the like. When the mouse moves over them, the keyboard sets the focus—not a single line of programming code is required.*

The Trigger class defines the following properties to specify the trigger action.

TRIGGER PROPERTY	DESCRIPTION
PropertyValue	With property triggers, the Property and Value properties are used to specify when the trigger should fire—for example, Property="IsMouseOver" Value="True".
Setters	As soon as the trigger fires, you can use Setters to define a collection of Setter elements to change values for properties. The Setter class defines the properties Property, TargetName, and Value for the object properties to change.
EnterActions, ExitActions	Instead of defining setters, you can define EnterActions and ExitActions. With both of these properties, you can define a collection of TriggerAction elements. EnterActions fires when the trigger starts (with a property trigger, when the Property/Value combination applies); ExitActions fires before it ends (just at the moment when the Property/Value combination no longer applies). Trigger actions that you can specify with these actions are derived from the base class TriggerAction, such as SoundPlayerAction and BeginStoryboard. With SoundPlayerAction, you can start the playing of sound. BeginStoryboard is used with animation, discussed later in this chapter.

MultiTrigger

A property trigger fires when a value of a property changes. If you need to set a trigger because two or more properties have a specific value, you can use MultiTrigger.

MultiTrigger has a Conditions property whereby valid values of properties can be specified. It also has a Setters property that enables you to specify the properties that need to be set. In the following example, a style is defined for TextBox elements such that the trigger applies if the IsEnabled property is True and the Text property has the value Test. Try it by typing **Test** into the blank text box. If both apply, the Foreground property of the TextBox is set to Red (code file TriggerSamples/MultiTriggerWindow.xaml):

```xml
<Window x:Class="TriggerSamples.MultiTriggerWindow"
    xmlns="http://schemas.microsoft.com/winfx/2006/xaml/presentation"
    xmlns:x="http://schemas.microsoft.com/winfx/2006/xaml"
    Title="Multi Trigger" Height="300" Width="300">
  <Window.Resources>
    <Style TargetType="TextBox">
      <Style.Triggers>
        <MultiTrigger>
          <MultiTrigger.Conditions>
            <Condition Property="IsEnabled" Value="True" />
            <Condition Property="Text" Value="Test" />
          </MultiTrigger.Conditions>
          <MultiTrigger.Setters>
            <Setter Property="Foreground" Value="Red" />
          </MultiTrigger.Setters>
        </MultiTrigger>
      </Style.Triggers>
    </Style>
  </Window.Resources>
  <Grid>
    <TextBox />
  </Grid>
</Window>
```

Data Triggers

Data triggers fire if bound data to a control fulfills specific conditions. In the following example, a Book class is used that has different displays depending on the publisher of the book.

The Book class defines the properties Title and Publisher and has an overload of the ToString method (code file TriggerSamples/Book.cs):

```csharp
public class Book
{
    public string Title { get; set; }
    public string Publisher { get; set; }

    public override string ToString() => Title;
}
```

In the XAML code, a style is defined for ListBoxItem elements. The style contains DataTrigger elements that are bound to the Publisher property of the class that is used with the items. If the value of the Publisher property is Wrox Press, the Background is set to Red. With the publishers Dummies and Wiley, the Background is set to Yellow and DarkGray, respectively (code file TriggerSamples/DataTriggerWindow.xaml):

```xml
<Window x:Class="TriggerSamples.DataTriggerWindow"
    xmlns="http://schemas.microsoft.com/winfx/2006/xaml/presentation"
    xmlns:x="http://schemas.microsoft.com/winfx/2006/xaml"
    Title="Data Trigger" Height="300" Width="300">
  <Window.Resources>
    <Style TargetType="ListBoxItem">
      <Style.Triggers>
        <DataTrigger Binding="{Binding Publisher}" Value="Wrox Press">
          <Setter Property="Background" Value="Red" />
        </DataTrigger>
```

```
      <DataTrigger Binding="{Binding Publisher}" Value="Dummies">
        <Setter Property="Background" Value="Yellow" />
      </DataTrigger>
      <DataTrigger Binding="{Binding Publisher}" Value="Wiley">
        <Setter Property="Background" Value="DarkGray" />
      </DataTrigger>
    </Style.Triggers>
  </Style>
</Window.Resources>
<Grid>
  <ListBox x:Name="list1" />
</Grid>
</Window>
```

In the code-behind, the list with the name `list1` is initialized to contain several `Book` objects (code file `TriggerSamples/DataTriggerWindow.xaml.cs`):

```
public DataTriggerWindow()
{
  InitializeComponent();

  list1.Items.Add(new Book
  {
    Title = "Professional C# 6 and .NET Core 1.0",
    Publisher = "Wrox Press"
  });
  list1.Items.Add(new Book
  {
    Title = "C# 5 All-in-One for Dummies",
    Publisher = "For Dummies"
  });
  list1.Items.Add(new Book
  {
    Title = "HTML and CSS: Design and Build Websites",
    Publisher = "Wiley"
  });
}
```

When you run the application, the `ListBoxItem` elements are format-ted according to the publisher value, as shown in Figure 34-11.

With `DataTrigger`, multiple properties must be set for `MultiDataTrigger` (similar to `Trigger` and `MultiTrigger`).

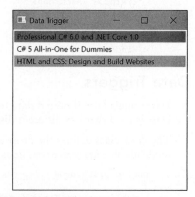

FIGURE 34-11

> **NOTE** *Data triggers update the user interface when the data bound changes (in case the interface* INotifyPropertyChanged *is implemented). The "Live Shaping" section later in this chapter includes an example.*

MENU AND RIBBON CONTROLS

Many data-driven applications contain menus and toolbars or ribbon controls to enable users to control actions. As of WPF 4.5, ribbon controls are available as well, so both menu and ribbon controls are covered here.

In this section, you create two new WPF applications named `BooksDemoMenu` and `BooksDemoRibbon` and the library `BooksDemoLib` to use throughout this chapter—not only with menu and ribbon controls but also with commanding and data binding. This application displays a single book, a list of books, and a grid of books. Actions are started from menu or ribbon controls to which commands are associated.

Menu Controls

You can easily create menus with WPF using the `Menu` and `MenuItem` elements, as shown in the following code snippet that contains two main menu items, File and Edit, and a list of submenu entries. The _ in front of the characters marks the special character that users can employ to access the menu item easily without using the mouse. Using the Alt key makes these characters visible and enables access to the menu with this character. Some of these menu items have a command assigned, as discussed in the next section (code file `BooksDemoMenu/MainWindow.xaml`):

```xml
<Window x:Class="Wrox.ProCSharp.WPF.MainWindow"
        xmlns="http://schemas.microsoft.com/winfx/2006/xaml/presentation"
        xmlns:x="http://schemas.microsoft.com/winfx/2006/xaml"
        xmlns:local="clr-namespace:BooksDemo"
        Title="Books Demo App" Height="400" Width="600">
  <DockPanel>
    <Menu DockPanel.Dock="Top">
      <MenuItem Header="_File">
        <MenuItem Header="Show _Book" />
        <MenuItem Header="Show Book_s" />
        <Separator />
        <MenuItem Header="E_xit" />
      </MenuItem>
      <MenuItem Header="_Edit">
        <MenuItem Header="Undo" Command="Undo" />
        <Separator />
        <MenuItem Header="Cut" Command="Cut" />
        <MenuItem Header="Copy" Command="Copy" />
        <MenuItem Header="Paste" Command="Paste" />
      </MenuItem>
    </Menu>
  </DockPanel>
</Window>
```

Running the application results in the menus shown in Figure 34-12. The menus are not active yet because commands are not active.

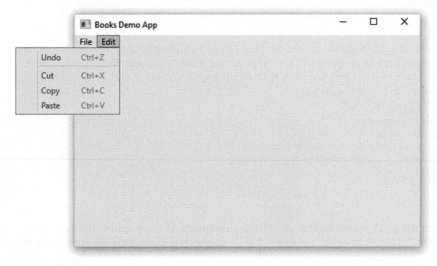

FIGURE 34-12

Ribbon Controls

An alternative to the menu controls are the ribbon controls. Microsoft Office 2007 was the first application released with Microsoft's ribbon control. Shortly after its introduction, many users of previous versions of Office complained that they could not find the actions they wanted with the new UI. Users who hadn't used Office prior to Office 2007 had a better experience with the new UI; they were able to easily find actions that users of previous versions found hard to detect.

Of course, nowadays the ribbon control is very common in many applications. Since Windows 8, the ribbon has been in many tools delivered with the Windows operating system—for example, Windows Explorer, Paint, and WordPad.

The WPF ribbon control is in the namespace `System.Windows.Controls.Ribbon` and requires referencing the assembly `System.Windows.Controls.Ribbon`.

Figure 34-13 shows the ribbon control of the sample application. In the topmost line left of the window title is the quick access toolbar. The leftmost item in the second line is the application menu, followed by two ribbon tabs: Home and Ribbon Controls. The Home tab, which is selected, shows two groups: Clipboard and Show. Both of these groups contain some button controls.

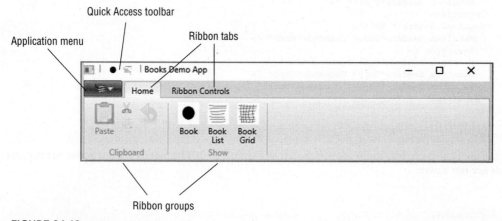

FIGURE 34-13

The `Ribbon` control is defined in the following code snippet. The first children of the `Ribbon` element are defined by the `QuickAccessToolBar` property. This toolbar contains two `RibbonButton` controls with small images referenced. These buttons provide users with direct access to quickly and easily fulfill actions (code file `BooksDemoRibbon/MainWindow.xaml`):

```xml
<Ribbon DockPanel.Dock="Top">
  <Ribbon.QuickAccessToolBar>
    <RibbonQuickAccessToolBar>
      <RibbonButton SmallImageSource="Assets/one.png" />
      <RibbonButton SmallImageSource="Assets/list.png" />
    </RibbonQuickAccessToolBar>
  </Ribbon.QuickAccessToolBar>
  <!-- etc. -->
</Ribbon>
```

To get these buttons from the quick access toolbar directly to the chrome of the window, the base class needs to be changed to the `RibbonWindow` class instead of the `Window` class (code file `BooksDemoRibbon/MainWindow.xaml.cs`):

```csharp
public partial class MainWindow : RibbonWindow
{
```

Changing the base class with the code-behind also requires a change in the XAML code to use the `RibbonWindow` element:

```xml
<RibbonWindow x:Class="Wrox.ProCSharp.WPF.MainWindow"
        xmlns="http://schemas.microsoft.com/winfx/2006/xaml/presentation"
        xmlns:x="http://schemas.microsoft.com/winfx/2006/xaml"
        xmlns:local="clr-namespace:Wrox.ProCSharp.WPF"
        Title="Books Demo App" Height="400" Width="600">
```

The application menu is defined by using the `ApplicationMenu` property. The application menu defines two menu entries—the first one to show a book, the second one to close the application:

```xml
<Ribbon.ApplicationMenu>
  <RibbonApplicationMenu SmallImageSource="Assets/books.png" >
    <RibbonApplicationMenuItem Header="Show _Book" />
    <RibbonSeparator />
    <RibbonApplicationMenuItem Header="Exit" Command="Close" />
  </RibbonApplicationMenu>
</Ribbon.ApplicationMenu>
```

After the application menu, the content of the `Ribbon` control is defined by using `RibbonTab` elements. The title of the tab is defined with the `Header` property. The `RibbonTab` contains two `RibbonGroup` elements. Each of the `RibbonGroup` elements contains `RibbonButton` elements. With the buttons, you can set a `Label` to display text and either `SmallImageSource` or `LargeImageSource` properties for displaying an image:

```xml
<RibbonTab Header="Home">
  <RibbonGroup Header="Clipboard">
    <RibbonButton Command="Paste" Label="Paste"
      LargeImageSource="Assets/paste.png" />
    <RibbonButton Command="Cut" SmallImageSource="Assets/cut.png" />
    <RibbonButton Command="Copy" SmallImageSource="Assets/copy.png" />
    <RibbonButton Command="Undo" LargeImageSource="Assets/undo.png" />
  </RibbonGroup>
  <RibbonGroup Header="Show">
    <RibbonButton LargeImageSource="Assets/one.png" Label="Book" />
    <RibbonButton LargeImageSource="Assets/list.png" Label="Book List" />
    <RibbonButton LargeImageSource="Assets/grid.png" Label="Book Grid" />
  </RibbonGroup>
</RibbonTab>
```

The second `RibbonTab` demonstrates different controls that can be used within a ribbon control, for example, text box, check box, combo box, split button, and gallery elements. Figure 34-14 shows this tab open.

```xml
<RibbonTab Header="Ribbon Controls">
  <RibbonGroup Header="Sample">
    <RibbonButton Label="Button" />
    <RibbonCheckBox Label="Checkbox" />
    <RibbonComboBox Label="Combo1">
      <Label>One</Label>
      <Label>Two</Label>
    </RibbonComboBox>
    <RibbonTextBox>Text Box </RibbonTextBox>
    <RibbonSplitButton Label="Split Button">
      <RibbonMenuItem Header="One" />
      <RibbonMenuItem Header="Two" />
    </RibbonSplitButton>
    <RibbonComboBox Label="Combo2" IsEditable="False">
      <RibbonGallery SelectedValuePath="Content" MaxColumnCount="1"
          SelectedValue="Green">
        <RibbonGalleryCategory>
          <RibbonGalleryItem Content="Red" Foreground="Red" />
          <RibbonGalleryItem Content="Green" Foreground="Green" />
          <RibbonGalleryItem Content="Blue" Foreground="Blue" />
```

```
            </RibbonGalleryCategory>
          </RibbonGallery>
        </RibbonComboBox>
      </RibbonGroup>
    </RibbonTab>
```

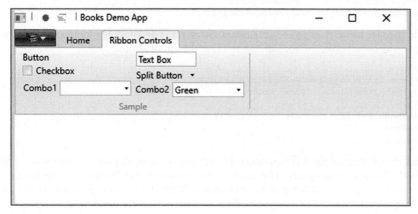

FIGURE 34-14

COMMANDING

Commanding is a WPF concept that creates a loose coupling between the source of an action (for example, a button) and the target that does the work (for example, a handler method). This concept is based on the *Command* pattern from the Gang of Four. With WPF, events are strongly coupled. Compiling the XAML code that includes references to events requires that the code-behind have a handler implemented and available at compile time. With commands, the coupling is loose.

> **NOTE** *The command pattern is a behavioral design pattern that makes unit testing easier by separating the client from the receiver of the command.*

The action that is executed is defined by a command object. Commands implement the interface ICommand. Command classes that are used by WPF are RoutedCommand and a class that derives from it, RoutedUICommand. RoutedUICommand defines an additional Text property that is not defined by ICommand. This property can be used as textual information in the UI. ICommand defines the methods Execute and CanExecute, which are executed on a target object.

The *command source* is an object that invokes the command. Command sources implement the interface ICommandSource. Examples of such command sources are button classes that derive from ButtonBase, Hyperlink, and InputBinding. KeyBinding and MouseBinding are examples of InputBinding derived classes. Command sources have a Command property whereby a command object implementing ICommand can be assigned. This fires the command when the control is used, such as with the click of a button.

The *command target* is an object that implements a handler to perform the action. With command binding, a mapping is defined to map the handler to a command. Command bindings define what handler is invoked on a command. Command bindings are defined by the CommandBinding property that is implemented in the UIElement class. Thus, every class that derives from UIElement has the CommandBinding property. This makes finding the mapped handler a hierarchical process. For example, a button that is defined within a StackPanel that is inside a ListBox—which itself is inside a Grid—can fire a command. The handler is specified with command bindings somewhere up the tree—such as with command bindings of a Window. The next section changes the implementation of the BooksDemoRibbon project to use commands.

Defining Commands

.NET gives you classes that return predefined commands. The ApplicationCommands class defines the static properties New, Open, Close, Print, Cut, Copy, Paste, and others. These properties return RoutedUICommand objects that can be used for a specific purpose. Other classes offering commands are NavigationCommands and MediaCommands. NavigationCommands is self-explanatory, providing commands that are common for navigation such as GoToPage, NextPage, and PreviousPage. MediaCommands are useful for running a media player, with Play, Pause, Stop, Rewind, and Record.

It's not hard to define custom commands that fulfill application domain–specific actions. For this, the BooksCommands class is created, which returns RoutedUICommands with the ShowBook and ShowBooksList properties. You can also assign an input gesture to a command, such as KeyGesture or MouseGesture. In the following example, a KeyGesture is assigned that defines the key B with the Alt modifier. An input gesture is a command source, so clicking the Alt+B combination invokes the command (code file BooksDemoLib/Commands/BooksCommands.cs):

```
public static class BooksCommands
{
  private static RoutedUICommand s_showBook;
  public static ICommand ShowBook =>
    s_showBook ?? (s_showBook = new RoutedUICommand("Show Book",
        nameof(ShowBook), typeof(BooksCommands)));

  private static RoutedUICommand s_showBooksList;
  public static ICommand ShowBooksList
  {
    get
    {
      if (s_showBooksList == null)
      {
        s_showBooksList = new RoutedUICommand("Show Books",
          nameof(ShowBooksList), typeof(BooksCommands));
        s_showBooksList.InputGestures.Add(new KeyGesture(Key.B,
          ModifierKeys.Alt));
      }
      return s_showBooksList;
    }
  }
  // etc.
}
```

Defining Command Sources

Every class that implements the ICommandSource interface can be a source of commands, such as Button and MenuItem. Inside the Ribbon control created earlier, the Command property is assigned to several RibbonButton elements—for example, in the quick access toolbar—as shown in the following code snippet (code file BooksDemoRibbon/MainWindow.xaml):

```
<Ribbon.QuickAccessToolBar>
  <RibbonQuickAccessToolBar>
    <RibbonButton SmallImageSource="Assets/one.png"
        Command="local:BooksCommands.ShowBook" />
    <RibbonButton SmallImageSource="Assets/list.png"
        Command="local:BooksCommands.ShowBooksList" />
  </RibbonQuickAccessToolBar>
</Ribbon.QuickAccessToolBar>
```

Predefined commands such as `ApplicationCommands.Cut`, `Copy`, and `Paste` are assigned to the `Command` property of `RibbonButton` elements as well. With the predefined commands the shorthand notation is used:

```
<RibbonGroup Header="Clipboard">
  <RibbonButton Command="Paste" Label="Paste"
    LargeImageSource="Images/paste.png" />
  <RibbonButton Command="Cut" SmallImageSource="Images/cut.png" />
  <RibbonButton Command="Copy" SmallImageSource="Images/copy.png" />
  <RibbonButton Command="Undo" LargeImageSource="Images/undo.png" />
</RibbonGroup>
```

Command Bindings

Command bindings need to be added to connect them to handler methods. In the following example, the command bindings are defined within the `Window` element so these bindings are available to all elements within the window. When the command `ApplicationCommands.Close` is executed, the `OnClose` method is invoked. When the command `BooksCommands.ShowBooks` is executed, the `OnShowBooks` method is called (code file `BooksDemoRibbon/MainWindow.xaml`):

```
<Window.CommandBindings>
  <CommandBinding Command="Close" Executed="OnClose" />
  <CommandBinding Command="commands:BooksCommands.ShowBooksList"
    Executed="OnShowBooksList" />
</Window.CommandBindings>
```

With command binding you can also specify the `CanExecute` property, whereby a method is invoked to verify whether the command is available. For example, if a file is not changed, the `ApplicationCommands.Save` command could be unavailable.

The handler needs to be defined with an object parameter, for the sender, and `ExecutedRoutedEventArgs`, where information about the command can be accessed (code file `BooksDemoRibbon/MainWindow.xaml.cs`):

```
private void OnClose(object sender, ExecutedRoutedEventArgs e)
{
  Application.Current.Shutdown();
}
```

> **NOTE** *You can also pass parameters with a command. You can do this by specifying the* `CommandParameter` *property with a command source, such as the* `MenuItem`*. To access the parameter, use the* `Parameter` *property of* `ExecutedRoutedEventArgs`*.*

Command bindings can also be defined by controls. The `TextBox` control defines bindings for `ApplicationCommands.Cut`, `ApplicationCommands.Copy`, `ApplicationCommands.Paste`, and `ApplicationCommands.Undo`. This way, you only need to specify the command source and use the existing functionality within the `TextBox` control.

DATA BINDING

WPF data binding takes another huge step forward compared with previous technologies. Data binding gets data from .NET objects for the UI or the other way around. Simple objects can be bound to UI elements, lists of objects, and XAML elements themselves. With WPF data binding, the target can be any dependency property of a WPF element, and every property of a CLR object can be the source. Because a WPF element is implemented as a .NET class, every WPF element can be the source as well. Figure 34-15 shows the connection between the source and the target. The `Binding` object defines the connection.

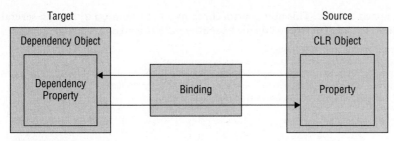

FIGURE 34-15

Binding supports several binding modes between the target and source. With *one-way* binding, the source information goes to the target, but if the user changes information in the user interface, the source is not updated. For updates to the source, *two-way* binding is required.

The following table shows the binding modes and their requirements.

BINDING MODE	DESCRIPTION
One-time	Binding goes from the source to the target and occurs only once when the application is started or the data context changes. Here, you get a snapshot of the data.
One-way	Binding goes from the source to the target. This is useful for read-only data, because it is not possible to change the data from the user interface. To get updates to the user interface, the source must implement the interface `INotifyPropertyChanged`.
Two-way	With two-way binding, the user can make changes to the data from the UI. Binding occurs in both directions—from the source to the target and from the target to the source. The source needs to implement read/write properties so that changes can be updated from the UI to the source.
One-way-to-source	With one-way-to-source binding, if the target property changes, the source object is updated.

WPF data binding involves many facets besides the binding modes. This section provides details on binding to XAML elements, binding to simple .NET objects, and binding to lists. Using change notifications, the UI is updated with changes in the bound objects. The material presented here discusses getting the data from object data providers and directly from the code. Multibinding and priority binding demonstrate different binding possibilities other than the default binding. This section also describes dynamically selecting data templates, and validation of binding values.

Let's start with the `BooksDemoRibbon` sample application.

BooksDemo Application Content

In the previous sections, a ribbon and commands have been defined with the `BooksDemoLib` and `BooksDemoRibbon` projects. Now content is added. Change the XAML file `MainWindow.xaml` by adding a `ListBox`, a `Hyperlink`, and a `TabControl` (code file `BooksDemoRibbon/MainWindow.xaml`):

```
<ListBox DockPanel.Dock="Left" Margin="5" MinWidth="120">
  <Hyperlink Command="local:BooksCommand.ShowBook">Show Book</Hyperlink>
</ListBox>
<TabControl Margin="5" x:Name="tabControl1">
</TabControl>
```

Now add a WPF user control named `BookUC`. This user control contains a `DockPanel`, a `Grid` with several rows and columns, a `Label`, and `TextBox` controls (code file `BooksDemoLib/Controls/BookUC.xaml`):

```xaml
<UserControl x:Class="Wrox.ProCSharp.WPF.BookUC"
    xmlns="http://schemas.microsoft.com/winfx/2006/xaml/presentation"
    xmlns:x="http://schemas.microsoft.com/winfx/2006/xaml"
    xmlns:mc="http://schemas.openxmlformats.org/markup-compatibility/2006"
    xmlns:d="http://schemas.microsoft.com/expression/blend/2008"
    mc:Ignorable="d"
    d:DesignHeight="300" d:DesignWidth="300">
  <DockPanel>
    <Grid>
      <Grid.RowDefinitions>
        <RowDefinition />
        <RowDefinition />
        <RowDefinition />
        <RowDefinition />
      </Grid.RowDefinitions>
      <Grid.ColumnDefinitions>
        <ColumnDefinition Width="Auto" />
        <ColumnDefinition Width="*" />
      </Grid.ColumnDefinitions>
      <Label Content="Title" Grid.Row="0" Grid.Column="0" Margin="10,0,5,0"
          HorizontalAlignment="Left" VerticalAlignment="Center" />
      <Label Content="Publisher" Grid.Row="1" Grid.Column="0"
          Margin="10,0,5,0" HorizontalAlignment="Left"
          VerticalAlignment="Center" />
      <Label Content="Isbn" Grid.Row="2" Grid.Column="0"
          Margin="10,0,5,0" HorizontalAlignment="Left"
          VerticalAlignment="Center" />
      <TextBox Grid.Row="0" Grid.Column="1" Margin="5" />
      <TextBox Grid.Row="1" Grid.Column="1" Margin="5" />
      <TextBox Grid.Row="2" Grid.Column="1" Margin="5" />
      <StackPanel Grid.Row="3" Grid.Column="0" Grid.ColumnSpan="2">
        <Button Content="Show Book" Margin="5" Click="OnShowBook" />
      </StackPanel>
    </Grid>
  </DockPanel>
</UserControl>
```

Within the `OnShowBook` handler in the `MainWindow.xaml.cs`, create a new instance of the user control `BookUC` and add a new `TabItem` to the `TabControl`. Then change the `SelectedIndex` property of the `TabControl` to open the new tab (code file `BooksDemoLib/MainWindow.xaml.cs`):

```csharp
private void OnShowBook(object sender, ExecutedRoutedEventArgs e)
{
  var bookUI = new BookUC();
  this.tabControl1.SelectedIndex = this.tabControl1.Items.Add(
      new TabItem { Header = "Book", Content = bookUI });
}
```

After building the project you can start the application and open the user control within the `TabControl` by clicking the hyperlink.

Binding with XAML

In addition to being the target for data binding, a WPF element can also be the source. You can bind the source property of one WPF element to the target of another WPF element.

In the following code example, data binding is used to resize the controls within the user control with a slider. You add a `StackPanel` control to the user control `BookUC`, which contains a `Label` and a `Slider` control. The Slider control defines Minimum and Maximum values that define the scale, and an initial value of 1 is assigned to the Value property (code file BooksDemoLib/BooksUC.xaml):

```
<DockPanel>
  <StackPanel DockPanel.Dock="Bottom" Orientation="Horizontal"
      HorizontalAlignment="Right">
    <Label Content="Resize" />
    <Slider x:Name="slider1" Value="1" Minimum="0.4" Maximum="3"
        Width="150" HorizontalAlignment="Right" />
  </StackPanel>
```

Now you set the LayoutTransform property of the Grid control and add a ScaleTransform element. With the ScaleTransform element, the ScaleX and ScaleY properties are data bound. Both properties are set with the Binding markup extension. In the Binding markup extension, the ElementName is set to slider1 to reference the previously created Slider control. The Path property is set to the Value property to get the value of the slider:

```
<Grid>
  <Grid.LayoutTransform>
    <ScaleTransform x:Name="scale1"
        ScaleX="{Binding Path=Value, ElementName=slider1}"
        ScaleY="{Binding Path=Value, ElementName=slider1}" />
  </Grid.LayoutTransform>
```

When running the application, you can move the slider and thus resize the controls within the Grid, as shown in Figures 34-16 and 34-17.

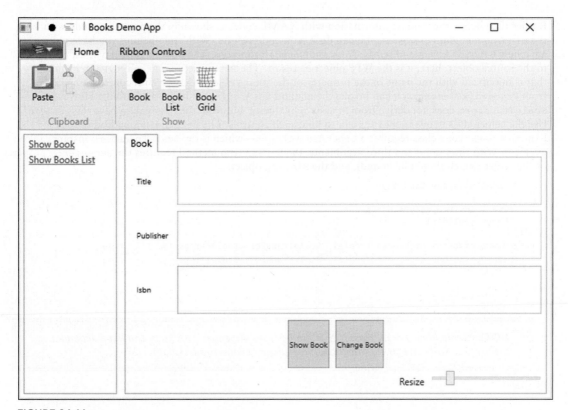

FIGURE 34-16

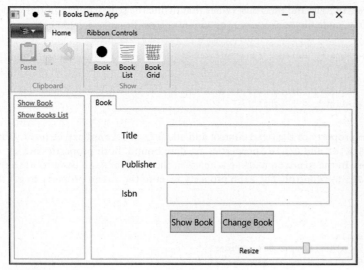

FIGURE 34-17

Rather than define the binding information with XAML code, as shown in the preceding code with the `Binding` metadata extension, you can do it with code-behind. With code-behind you have to create a new `Binding` object and set the `Path` and `Source` properties. The `Source` property must be set to the source object; here, it is the WPF object `slider1`. The `Path` is set to a `PropertyPath` instance that is initialized with the name of the property of the source object, `Value`. With controls that derive from `FrameworkElement`, you can invoke the method `SetBinding` to define the binding. However, `ScaleTransform` does not derive from `FrameworkElement` but from the `Freezable` base class instead. Use the helper class `BindingOperations` to bind such controls. The `SetBinding` method of the `BindingOperations` class requires a `DependencyObject`—which is the `ScaleTransform` instance in the example. With the second and third arguments, the `SetBinding` method requires the `dependency` property of the target (which should be bound), and the `Binding` object:

```
var binding = new Binding
{
  Path = new PropertyPath("Value"),
  Source = slider1
};
BindingOperations.SetBinding(scale1, ScaleTransform.ScaleXProperty, binding);
BindingOperations.SetBinding(scale1, ScaleTransform.ScaleYProperty, binding);
```

> **NOTE** *Remember that all classes that derive from* `DependencyObject` *can have dependency properties. You can learn more about dependency properties in Chapter 29.*

You can configure a number of binding options with the `Binding` class, as described in the following table:

BINDING CLASS MEMBERS	DESCRIPTION
`Source`	Use this property to define the source object for data binding.
`RelativeSource`	Specify the source in relation to the target object. This is useful to display error messages when the source of the error comes from the same control.
`ElementName`	If the source is a WPF element, you can specify the source with the `ElementName` property.
`Path`	Use this property to specify the path to the source object. This can be the property of the source object, but indexers and properties of child elements are also supported.
`XPath`	With an XML data source, you can define an XPath query expression to get the data for binding.
`Mode`	The mode defines the direction for the binding. The `Mode` property is of type `BindingMode`. `BindingMode` is an enumeration with the following values: `Default`, `OneTime`, `OneWay`, `TwoWay`, and `OneWayToSource`. The default mode depends on the target: with a `TextBox`, two-way binding is the default; with a `Label` that is read-only, the default is one-way. `OneTime` means that the data is only init loaded from the source; `OneWay` updates from the source to the target. With `TwoWay` binding, changes from the WPF elements are written back to the source. `OneWayToSource` means that the data is never read but always written from the target to the source.
`Converter`	Use this property to specify a converter class that converts the data for the UI and back. The converter class must implement the interface `IValueConverter`, which defines the methods `Convert` and `ConvertBack`. You can pass parameters to the converter methods with the `ConverterParameter` property. The converter can be culture-sensitive; and the culture can be set with the `ConverterCulture` property.
`FallbackValue`	Use this property to define a default value that is used if binding doesn't return a value.
`ValidationRules`	Using this property, you can define a collection of `ValidationRule` objects that are checked before the source is updated from the WPF target elements. The class `ExceptionValidationRule` is derived from the class `ValidationRule` and checks for exceptions.
`Delay`	This property is new with WPF 4.5. It enables you to specify an amount of time to wait before the binding source is updated. This can be used in scenarios where you want to give the user some time to enter more characters before starting a validation.

Simple Object Binding

To bind to CLR objects, with the .NET classes you just have to define properties, as shown in the `Book` class example and the properties `Title`, `Publisher`, `Isbn`, and `Authors`. This class is in the `Models` folder of the `BooksDemoLib` project (code file `BooksDemoLib/Models/Book.cs`).

```
using System.Collections.Generic;

namespace BooksDemo.Models
```

```
{
  public class Book
  {
    public Book(string title, string publisher, string isbn,
              params string[] authors)
    {
      Title = title;
      Publisher = publisher;
      Isbn = isbn;
      Authors = authors;
    }
    public Book()
      : this("unknown", "unknown", "unknown")
    {
    }

    public string Title { get; set; }
    public string Publisher { get; set; }
    public string Isbn { get; set; }

    public string[] Authors { get; set; }

    public override string ToString() => Title;
  }
}
```

In the XAML code of the user control BookUC, several labels and TextBox controls are defined to display book information. Using Binding markup extensions, the TextBox controls are bound to the properties of the Book class. With the Binding markup extension, nothing more than the Path property is defined to bind it to the property of the Book class. There's no need to define a source because the source is defined by assigning the DataContext, as shown in the code-behind that follows. The mode is defined by its default with the TextBox element, and this is two-way binding (code file BooksDemoLib/Controls/BookUC.xaml):

```
<TextBox Text="{Binding Title}" Grid.Row="0" Grid.Column="1" Margin="5" />
<TextBox Text="{Binding Publisher}" Grid.Row="1" Grid.Column="1" Margin="5" />
<TextBox Text="{Binding Isbn}" Grid.Row="2" Grid.Column="1" Margin="5" />
```

With the code-behind, a new Book object is created, and the book is assigned to the DataContext property of the user control. DataContext is a dependency property that is defined with the base class FrameworkElement. Assigning the DataContext with the user control means that every element in the user control has a default binding to the same data context (code file BooksDemoRibbon/MainWindow.xaml.cs):

```
private void OnShowBook(object sender, ExecutedRoutedEventArgs e)
{
  var bookUI = new BookUC();
  bookUI.DataContext = new Book
  {
    Title = "Professional C# 5.0 and .NET 4.5.1",
    Publisher = "Wrox Press",
    Isbn = "978-0-470-50225-9"
  };
  this.tabControl1.SelectedIndex =
    this.tabControl1.Items.Add(
      new TabItem { Header = "Book", Content = bookUI });
}
```

After starting the application, you can see the bound data, as shown in Figure 34-18.

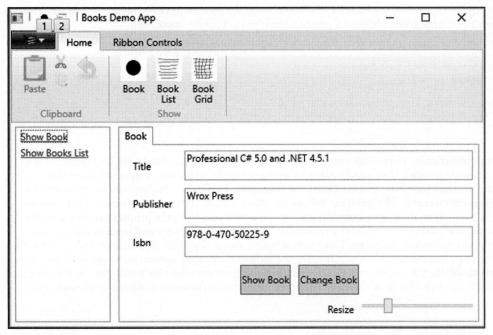

FIGURE 34-18

To see two-way binding in action (changes to the input of the WPF element are reflected inside the CLR object), the `Click` event handler of the button in the user control, the `OnShowBook` method, is implemented. When implemented, a message box pops up to show the current title and ISBN number of the `book1` object. Figure 34-19 shows the output from the message box after the user types Professional C# 6 into the input while running the app (code file `BooksDemoLib/Controls/BookUC.xaml.cs`):

```
private void OnShowBook(object sender, RoutedEventArgs e)
{
  Book theBook = this.DataContext as Book;
  if (theBook != null)
  {
    MessageBox.Show(theBook.Title, theBook.Isbn);
  }
}
```

FIGURE 34-19

Change Notification

With the current two-way binding, the data is read from the object and written back. However, if data is not changed by the user, but is instead changed directly from the code, the UI does not receive the change information. You can easily verify this by adding a button to the user control and implementing the `Click` event handler `OnChangeBook` (code file `BooksDemoLib/Controls/BookUC.xaml`):

```
<StackPanel Grid.Row="3" Grid.Column="0" Grid.ColumnSpan="2"
            Orientation="Horizontal" HorizontalAlignment="Center">
  <Button Content="Show Book" Margin="5" Click="OnShowBook" />
  <Button Content="Change Book" Margin="5" Click="OnChangeBook" />
</StackPanel>
```

Within the implementation of the handler, the book inside the data context is changed but the user interface doesn't show the change (code file `BooksDemoLib/Controls/BookUC.xaml.cs`):

```
private void OnChangeBook(object sender, RoutedEventArgs e)
{
  Book theBook = this.DataContext as Book;
  if (theBook != null)
  {
    theBook.Title = "Professional C# 6";
    theBook.Isbn = "978-0-470-31442-5";
  }
}
```

To get change information to the user interface, the entity class must implement the interface `INotifyPropertyChanged`. Instead of having an implementation with every class that needs this interface, the abstract base class `BindableObject` is created. This base class implements the interface `INotifyPropertyChanged`. The interface defines the event `PropertyChanged`, which is fired from the `OnPropertyChanged` method. As a convenience for firing the event from the property setters from the derived classes, the method `SetProperty` makes the change of the property and invokes the method `OnPropertyChanged` to fire the event. This method makes use of the caller information feature from C# using the attribute `CallerMemberName`. Defining the parameter `propertyName` as an optional parameter with this attribute, the C# compiler passes the name of the property with this parameter, so it's not necessary to add a hard-coded string to the code (code file `BooksDemoLib/Models/BindableObject.cs`):

```
using System.Collections.Generic;
using System.ComponentModel;
using System.Runtime.CompilerServices;
namespace BooksDemo.Model
{
  public abstract class BindableObject : INotifyPropertyChanged
  {
    public event PropertyChangedEventHandler PropertyChanged;
    protected void OnPropertyChanged(string propertyName)
    {
      PropertyChanged?.Invoke(this,
        new PropertyChangedEventArgs(propertyName));
    }

    protected void SetProperty<T>(ref T item, T value,
        [CallerMemberName] string propertyName = null)
    {
      if (!EqualityComparer<T>.Default.Equals(item, value))
      {
        item = value;
        OnPropertyChanged(propertyName);
      }
    }
  }
}
```

> **NOTE** *Caller information is covered in Chapter 14, "Errors and Exceptions."*

The class `Book` is now changed to derive from the base class `BindableObject` in order to inherit the implementation of the interface `INotifyPropertyChanged`. The property setters are changed to invoke the `SetProperty` method, as shown here (code file `BooksDemoLib/Data/Book.cs`):

```
using System.ComponentModel;
using System.Collections.Generic;

namespace Wrox.ProCSharp.WPF.Data
```

```
{
  public class Book : BindableObject
  {
    public Book(string title, string publisher, string isbn,
              params string[] authors)
    {
      Title = title;
      Publisher = publisher;
      Isbn = isbn;
      Authors = authors;
    }
    public Book()
      : this("unknown", "unknown", "unknown")
    {
    }

    private string _title;
    public string Title {
      get
      {
        return _title;
      }
      set
      {
        SetProperty(ref _title, value);
      }
    }
    private string _publisher;
    public string Publisher
    {
      get
      {
        return _publisher;
      }
      set
      {
        SetProperty(ref _publisher, value);
      }
    }
    private string _isbn;
    public string Isbn
    {
      get
      {
        return _isbn;
      }
      set
      {
        SetProperty(ref _isbn, value);
      }
    }
    public string[] Authors { get; }
    public override string ToString() => Title;
  }
}
```

With this change, the application can be started again to verify that the user interface is updated following a change notification in the event handler.

Object Data Provider

Instead of instantiating the object in code-behind, you can do it with XAML. To reference a class from code-behind within XAML, you have to reference the namespace with the namespace declarations in the

XML root element. The XML attribute `xmlns:local="clr-namespace:Wrox.ProCsharp.WPF"` assigns the .NET namespace `Wrox.ProCSharp.WPF` to the XML namespace alias `local`.

One object of the `Book` class is now defined with the `Book` element inside the `DockPanel` resources. By assigning values to the XML attributes `Title`, `Publisher`, and `Isbn`, you set the values of the properties from the `Book` class. `x:Key="theBook"` defines the identifier for the resource so that you can reference the book object:

```
<UserControl x:Class="BooksDemo.BookUC"
    xmlns="http://schemas.microsoft.com/winfx/2006/xaml/presentation"
    xmlns:x="http://schemas.microsoft.com/winfx/2006/xaml"
    xmlns:mc="http://schemas.openxmlformats.org/markup-compatibility/2006"
    xmlns:d="http://schemas.microsoft.com/expression/blend/2008"
    xmlns:local="clr-namespace:Wrox.ProCSharp.WPF.Data"
    mc:Ignorable="d"
    d:DesignHeight="300" d:DesignWidth="300">
  <DockPanel>
    <DockPanel.Resources>
      <local:Book x:Key="theBook" Title="Professional C# 5.0 and .NET 4.5.1"
          Publisher="Wrox Press" Isbn="978-1-118-83303-2" />
    </DockPanel.Resources>
```

> **NOTE** *If the .NET namespace to reference is in a different assembly, you have to add the assembly to the XML declaration:*
>
> ```
> xmlsn:sys="clr-namespace:System;assembly=mscorlib"
> ```

In the `TextBox` element, the `Source` is defined with the `Binding` markup extension that references the `theBook` resource:

```
<TextBox Text="{Binding Path=Title, Source={StaticResource theBook}}"
  Grid.Row="0" Grid.Column="1" Margin="5" />
<TextBox Text="{Binding Path=Publisher, Source={StaticResource theBook}}"
  Grid.Row="1" Grid.Column="1" Margin="5" />
<TextBox Text="{Binding Path=Isbn, Source={StaticResource theBook}}"
  Grid.Row="2" Grid.Column="1" Margin="5" />
```

Because all these `TextBox` elements are contained within the same control, it is possible to assign the `DataContext` property with a parent control and set the `Path` property with the `TextBox` binding elements. Because the `Path` property is a default, you can also reduce the `Binding` markup extension to the following code:

```
<Grid x:Name="grid1" DataContext="{StaticResource theBook}">
  <!-- ... -->
  <TextBox Text="{Binding Title}" Grid.Row="0" Grid.Column="1" Margin="5" />
  <TextBox Text="{Binding Publisher}" Grid.Row="1" Grid.Column="1"
    Margin="5" />
  <TextBox Text="{Binding Isbn}" Grid.Row="2" Grid.Column="1" Margin="5" />
```

Instead of defining the object instance directly within XAML code, you can define an object data provider that references a class to invoke a method. For use by the `ObjectDataProvider`, it's best to create a factory class that returns the object to display, as shown with the `BooksRepository` class (code file `BooksDemoLib/Models/BooksRepository.cs`):

```
using System.Collections.Generic;

namespace BooksDemo.Models
{
  public class BooksRepository
```

```
  {
    private List<Book> books = new List<Book>();

    public BooksRepository()
    {
      books.Add(new Book
      {
        Title = "Professional C# 5.0 and .NET 4.5.1",
        Publisher = "Wrox Press",
        Isbn = "978-1-118-83303-2"
      });
    }

    public Book GetTheBook() => books[0];
  }
}
```

The `ObjectDataProvider` element can be defined in the resources section. The XML attribute `ObjectType` defines the name of the class; with `MethodName` you specify the name of the method that is invoked to get the book object (code file `BooksDemoLib/Controls/BookUC.xaml`):

```xml
<DockPanel.Resources>
  <ObjectDataProvider x:Key="theBook" ObjectType="local:BooksRepository"
      MethodName="GetTheBook" />
</DockPanel.Resources>
```

The properties you can specify with the `ObjectDataProvider` class are listed in the following table:

OBJECTDATAPROVIDER PROPERTY	DESCRIPTION
ObjectType	Defines the type to create an instance.
ConstructorParameters	Using the `ConstructorParameters` collection, you can add parameters to the class to create an instance.
MethodName	Defines the name of the method that is invoked by the object data provider.
MethodParameters	Using this property, you can assign parameters to the method defined with the `MethodName` property.
ObjectInstance	Using this property, you can get and set the object that is used by the `ObjectDataProvider` class. For example, you can assign an existing object programmatically rather than define the `ObjectType` so that an object is instantiated by `ObjectDataProvider`.
Data	Enables you to access the underlying object that is used for data binding. If the `MethodName` is defined, with the `Data` property you can access the object that is returned from the method defined.

List Binding

Binding to a list is more frequently done than binding to simple objects. Binding to a list is very similar to binding to a simple object. You can assign the complete list to the `DataContext` from code-behind, or you can use an `ObjectDataProvider` that accesses an object factory that returns a list. With elements that support binding to a list (for example, a `ListBox`), the complete list is bound. With elements that support binding to just one object (for example, a `TextBox`), the current item is bound.

With the `BooksRepository` class, now a list of `Book` objects is returned (code file `BooksDemoLib/Models/BooksRepository.cs`):

```
public class BooksRepository
{
```

```
   private List<Book> _books = new List<Book>();

   public BooksRepository()
   {
     _books.Add(new Book("Professional C# 5.0 and .NET 4.5.1", "Wrox Press",
                         "978-1-118-83303-2", "Christian Nagel", "Jay Glynn",
                         "Morgan Skinner"));
     _books.Add(new Book("Professional C# 2012 and .NET 4.5", "Wrox Press",
                         "978-0-470-50225-9", "Christian Nagel", "Bill Evjen",
                         "Jay Glynn", "Karli Watson", "Morgan Skinner"));
     _books.Add(new Book("Professional C# 4 with .NET 4", "Wrox Press",
                         "978-0-470-19137-8", "Christian Nagel", "Bill Evjen",
                         "Jay Glynn", "Karli Watson", "Morgan Skinner"));
     _books.Add(new Book("Beginning Visual C# 2010", "Wrox Press",
                         "978-0-470-50226-6", "Karli Watson", "Christian Nagel",
                         "Jacob Hammer Pedersen", "Jon D. Reid",
                         "Morgan Skinner", "Eric White"));
     _books.Add(new Book("Windows 8 Secrets", "Wiley", "978-1-118-20413-9",
                         "Paul Thurrott", "Rafael Rivera"));
     _books.Add(new Book("C# 5 All-in-One for Dummies", "For Dummies",
                         "978-1-118-38536-5", "Bill Sempf", "Chuck Sphar"));
   }

   public IEnumerable<Book> GetBooks() => _books;
}
```

To use the list, create a new `BooksUC` user control. The XAML code for this control contains `Label` and `TextBox` controls that display the values of a single book, as well as a `ListBox` control that displays a book list. The `ObjectDataProvider` invokes the `GetBooks` method of the `BookFactory`, and this provider is used to assign the `DataContext` of the `DockPanel`. The `DockPanel` has `ListBox` and `TextBox` as its children. Both the `ListBox` and `TextBox` make use of the `DataContext` from the `DockPanel` with the data binding (code file `BooksDemoLib/Controls/BooksUC.xaml`):

```xml
<UserControl x:Class="Wrox.ProCSharp.WPF.BooksUC"
    xmlns="http://schemas.microsoft.com/winfx/2006/xaml/presentation"
    xmlns:x="http://schemas.microsoft.com/winfx/2006/xaml"
    xmlns:mc="http://schemas.openxmlformats.org/markup-compatibility/2006"
    xmlns:d="http://schemas.microsoft.com/expression/blend/2008"
    xmlns:local="clr-namespace:Wrox.ProCSharp.WPF.Data"
    mc:Ignorable="d"
    d:DesignHeight="300" d:DesignWidth="300">
  <UserControl.Resources>
    <ObjectDataProvider x:Key="books" ObjectType="local:BookFactory"
                        MethodName="GetBooks" />
  </UserControl.Resources>
  <DockPanel DataContext="{StaticResource books}">
    <ListBox DockPanel.Dock="Left" ItemsSource="{Binding}" Margin="5"
        MinWidth="120" />
    <Grid>
      <Grid.RowDefinitions>
        <RowDefinition />
        <RowDefinition />
        <RowDefinition />
        <RowDefinition />
      </Grid.RowDefinitions>
      <Grid.ColumnDefinitions>
        <ColumnDefinition Width="Auto" />
        <ColumnDefinition Width="*" />
      </Grid.ColumnDefinitions>
      <Label Content="Title" Grid.Row="0" Grid.Column="0" Margin="10,0,5,0"
          HorizontalAlignment="Left" VerticalAlignment="Center" />
      <Label Content="Publisher" Grid.Row="1" Grid.Column="0" Margin="10,0,5,0"
          HorizontalAlignment="Left" VerticalAlignment="Center" />
```

```
        <Label Content="Isbn" Grid.Row="2" Grid.Column="0" Margin="10,0,5,0"
            HorizontalAlignment="Left" VerticalAlignment="Center" />
        <TextBox Text="{Binding Title}" Grid.Row="0" Grid.Column="1" Margin="5" />
        <TextBox Text="{Binding Publisher}" Grid.Row="1" Grid.Column="1"
            Margin="5" />
        <TextBox Text="{Binding Isbn}" Grid.Row="2" Grid.Column="1" Margin="5" />
      </Grid>
    </DockPanel>
  </UserControl>
```

The new user control is started by adding a `Hyperlink` to `MainWindow.xaml`. It uses the `Command` property to assign the `ShowBooks` command. The command binding must be specified as well to invoke the event handler `OnShowBooksList`. (code file `BooksDemoRibbon/MainWindow.xaml`):

```
<ListBox DockPanel.Dock="Left" Margin="5" MinWidth="120">
  <ListBoxItem>
    <Hyperlink Command="local:BooksCommands.ShowBook">Show Book</Hyperlink>
  </ListBoxItem>
  <ListBoxItem>
    <Hyperlink Command="local:ShowCommands.ShowBooksList">
        Show Books List</Hyperlink>
  </ListBoxItem>
</ListBox>
```

The implementation of the event handler adds a new `TabItem` control to the `TabControl`, assigns the `Content` to the user control `BooksUC`, and sets the selection of the `TabControl` to the newly created `TabItem` (code file `BooksDemoRibbon/MainWindow.xaml.cs`):

```
private void OnShowBooksList(object sender, ExecutedRoutedEventArgs e)
{
  var booksUI = new BooksUC();
  this.tabControl1.SelectedIndex =
    this.tabControl1.Items.Add(
      new TabItem { Header="Books List", Content=booksUI});
}
```

Because the `DockPanel` has the `Book` array assigned to the `DataContext`, and the `ListBox` is placed within the `DockPanel`, the `ListBox` shows all books with the default template, as illustrated in Figure 34-20.

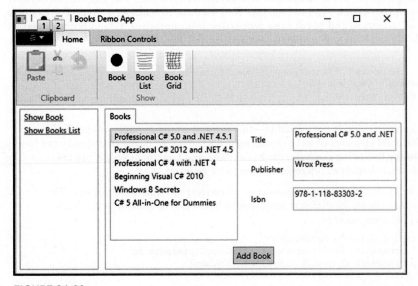

FIGURE 34-20

For a more flexible layout of the `ListBox`, you have to define a template, as discussed in Chapter 33, "Advanced Windows Apps," for `ListBox` styling. The `ItemTemplate` of the `ListBox` defines a `DataTemplate` with a `Label` element. The content of the label is bound to the `Title`. The item template is repeated for every item in the list. Of course, you can also add the item template to a style within resources:

```
<ListBox DockPanel.Dock="Left" ItemsSource="{Binding}" Margin="5"
    MinWidth="120">
  <ListBox.ItemTemplate>
    <DataTemplate>
      <Label Content="{Binding Title}" />
    </DataTemplate>
  </ListBox.ItemTemplate>
</ListBox>
```

Master Details Binding

Instead of just showing all the elements inside a list, you might want or need to show detail information about the selected item. It doesn't require a lot of work to do this. The `Label` and `TextBox` controls are already defined; currently, they only show the first element in the list.

There's one important change you have to make to the `ListBox`. By default, the labels are bound to just the first element of the list. By setting the `ListBox` property `IsSynchronizedWithCurrentItem="True"`, the selection of the list box is set to the current item (code file `BooksDemoLib/Controls/BooksUC.xaml`):

```
<ListBox DockPanel.Dock="Left" ItemsSource="{Binding}" Margin="5"
        MinWidth="120" IsSynchronizedWithCurrentItem="True">
  <ListBox.ItemTemplate>
    <DataTemplate>
      <Label Content="{Binding Title}" />
    </DataTemplate>
  </ListBox.ItemTemplate>
</ListBox>
```

MultiBinding

`Binding` is one of the classes that can be used for data binding. `BindingBase` is the abstract base class of all bindings and has different concrete implementations. Besides `Binding`, there's also `MultiBinding` and `PriorityBinding`. `MultiBinding` enables you to bind one WPF element to multiple sources. For example, with a `Person` class that has `LastName` and `FirstName` properties, it is interesting to bind both properties to a single WPF element (code file `MultiBindingSample/Person.cs`):

```
public class Person
{
  public string FirstName { get; set; }
  public string LastName { get; set; }
}
```

For `MultiBinding`, a markup extension is not available—therefore, the binding must be specified with XAML element syntax. The child elements of `MultiBinding` are `Binding` elements that specify the binding to the various properties. In the following example, the `FirstName` and `LastName` properties are used. The data context is set with the `Grid` element to reference the `person1` resource.

To connect the properties, `MultiBinding` uses a `Converter` to convert multiple values to one. This converter uses a parameter that allows for different conversions based on the parameter (code file `MultiBindingSample/MainWindow.xaml`):

```
<Window x:Class="MultiBindingSample.MainWindow"
        xmlns="http://schemas.microsoft.com/winfx/2006/xaml/presentation"
        xmlns:x="http://schemas.microsoft.com/winfx/2006/xaml"
        xmlns:system="clr-namespace:System;assembly=mscorlib"
```

```xml
      xmlns:local="clr-namespace:Wrox.ProCSharp.WPF"
      Title="Multi Binding" Height="240" Width="500">
  <Window.Resources>
    <local:Person x:Key="person1" FirstName="Tom" LastName="Turbo" />
    <local:PersonNameConverter x:Key="personNameConverter" />
  </Window.Resources>
  <Grid DataContext="{StaticResource person1}">
    <TextBox>
      <TextBox.Text>
        <MultiBinding Converter="{StaticResource personNameConverter}" >
          <MultiBinding.ConverterParameter>
            <system:String>FirstLast</system:String>
          </MultiBinding.ConverterParameter>
          <Binding Path="FirstName" />
          <Binding Path="LastName" />
        </MultiBinding>
      </TextBox.Text>
    </TextBox>
  </Grid>
</Window>
```

The multivalue converter implements the interface `IMultiValueConverter`. This interface defines two methods: `Convert` and `ConvertBack`. `Convert` receives multiple values with the first argument from the data source and returns one value to the target. With the implementation, depending on whether the parameter has a value of `FirstLast` or `LastFirst`, the result varies (code file `MultiBindingSample/PersonNameConverter.cs`):

```csharp
using System;
using System.Globalization;
using System.Windows.Data;

namespace MultiBindingSample
{
  public class PersonNameConverter : IMultiValueConverter
  {
    public object Convert(object[] values, Type targetType, object parameter,
                          CultureInfo culture)
    {
      switch (parameter as string)
      {
        case "FirstLast":
          return values[0] + " " + values[1];
        case "LastFirst":
          return values[1] + ", " + values[0];
        default:
          throw new ArgumentException($"invalid argument {parameter}");
      }
    }

    public object[] ConvertBack(object value, Type[] targetTypes,
                                object parameter, CultureInfo culture)
    {
      throw new NotSupportedException();
    }
  }
}
```

In such simple scenarios, just combining some strings with a `MultiBinding` doesn't require an implementation of `IMultiValueConverter`. Instead, a definition for a format string is adequate, as shown in the following XAML code snippet. The string format defined with the `MultiBinding` first needs a {} prefix. With XAML the curly brackets usually define a markup expression. Using {} as a prefix escapes this and defines that no markup expression, but instead a normal string, follows. The sample specifies that both Binding elements are separated by a comma and a blank (code file `MultiBindingSample/MainWindow.xaml`):

```
<TextBox>
    <TextBox.Text>
        <MultiBinding StringFormat="{}{0}, {1}">
            <Binding Path="LastName" />
            <Binding Path="FirstName" />
        </MultiBinding>
    </TextBox.Text>
</TextBox>
```

Priority Binding

`PriorityBinding` makes it easy to bind to data that is not readily available. If you need time to get the result with `PriorityBinding`, you can inform users about the progress so they are aware of the wait.

To illustrate priority binding, use the `PriorityBindingDemo` project to create the `Data` class. Accessing the `ProcessSomeData` property requires some time, which is simulated by calling the `Thread.Sleep` method (code file `PriorityBindingSample/Data.cs`):

```
public class Data
{
    public string ProcessSomeData
    {
        get
        {
            Task.Delay(8000).Wait(); // blocking call
            return "the final result is here";
        }
    }
}
```

The `Information` class provides information to the user. The information from property `Info1` is returned immediately, whereas `Info2` returns information after five seconds. With a real implementation, this class could be associated with the processing class to get an estimated time frame for the user (code file `PriorityBindingSample/Information.cs`):

```
public class Information
{
    public string Info1 => "please wait…";

    public string Info2
    {
        get
        {
            Task.Delay(5000).Wait(); // blocking call
            return "please wait a little more";
        }
    }
}
```

In the `MainWindow.xaml` file, the `Data` and `Information` classes are referenced and initiated within the resources of the `Window` (code file `PriorityBindingDemo/MainWindow.xaml`):

```
<Window.Resources>
    <local:Data x:Key="data1" />
    <local:Information x:Key="info" />
</Window.Resources>
```

`PriorityBinding` is done in place of normal binding within the `Content` property of a `Label`. It consists of multiple `Binding` elements whereby all but the last one have the `IsAsync` property set to `True`. Because of this, if the first binding expression result is not immediately available, the binding process chooses the next one. The first binding references the `ProcessSomeData` property of the `Data` class, which needs some time.

Because of this, the next binding comes into play and references the `Info2` property of the `Information` class. `Info2` does not return a result immediately, and because `IsAsync` is set, the binding process does not wait but continues to the next binding. The last binding uses the `Info1` property. If it doesn't immediately return a result, you would wait for the result because `IsAsync` is set to the default, `False`:

```
<Label>
  <Label.Content>
    <PriorityBinding>
      <Binding Path="ProcessSomeData" Source="{StaticResource data1}"
          IsAsync="True" />
      <Binding Path="Info2" Source="{StaticResource info}"
          IsAsync="True" />
      <Binding Path="Info1" Source="{StaticResource info}"
          IsAsync="False" />
    </PriorityBinding>
  </Label.Content>
</Label>
```

When the application starts, you can see the message "please wait…" in the user interface. After a few seconds the result from the `Info2` property is returned as "please wait a little more." It replaces the output from `Info1`. Finally, the result from `ProcessSomeData` replaces the output again.

Value Conversion

Returning to the BooksDemo application, the authors of the book are still missing in the user interface. If you bind the `Authors` property to a `Label` element, the `ToString` method of the `Array` class is invoked, which returns the name of the type. One solution to this is to bind the `Authors` property to a `ListBox`. For the `ListBox`, you can define a template for a specific view. Another solution is to convert the string array returned by the `Authors` property to a string and use the string for binding.

The class `StringArrayConverter` converts a string array to a string. WPF converter classes must implement the interface `IValueConverter` from the namespace `System.Windows.Data`. This interface defines the methods `Convert` and `ConvertBack`. With the `StringArrayConverter`, the `Convert` method converts the string array from the variable `value` to a string by using the `String.Join` method. The separator parameter of the `Join` is taken from the variable `parameter` received with the `Convert` method (code file `BooksDemoLib/Utilities/StringArrayConverter.cs`):

```
using System;
using System.Diagnostics.Contracts;
using System.Globalization;
using System.Windows.Data;

namespace Wrox.ProCSharp.WPF.Utilities
{
  [ValueConversion(typeof(string[]), typeof(string))]
  class StringArrayConverter : IValueConverter
  {
    public object Convert(object value, Type targetType, object parameter,
                      CultureInfo culture)
    {
      if (value == null) return null;
      string[] stringCollection = (string[])value;
      string separator = parameter == null;
      return String.Join(separator, stringCollection);
    }

    public object ConvertBack(object value, Type targetType, object parameter,
                      CultureInfo culture)
    {
      throw new NotImplementedException();
    }
  }
}
```

> **NOTE** *You can read more about the methods of the* `String` *classes in Chapter 10, "Strings and Regular Expressions."*

In the XAML code, the `StringArrayConverter` class can be declared as a resource. This resource can be referenced from the `Binding` markup extension (code file `BooksDemoLib/Controls/BooksUC.xaml`):

```xaml
<UserControl x:Class="Wrox.ProCSharp.WPF.BooksUC"
    xmlns="http://schemas.microsoft.com/winfx/2006/xaml/presentation"
    xmlns:x="http://schemas.microsoft.com/winfx/2006/xaml"
    xmlns:mc="http://schemas.openxmlformats.org/markup-compatibility/2006"
    xmlns:d="http://schemas.microsoft.com/expression/blend/2008"
    xmlns:local="clr-namespace:Wrox.ProCSharp.WPF.Data"
    xmlns:utils="clr-namespace:Wrox.ProCSharp.WPF.Utilities"
    mc:Ignorable="d"
    d:DesignHeight="300" d:DesignWidth="300">
  <UserControl.Resources>
    <utils:StringArrayConverter x:Key="stringArrayConverter" />
    <ObjectDataProvider x:Key="books" ObjectType="local:BookFactory"
                        MethodName="GetBooks" />
  </UserControl.Resources>
  <!-- etc. -->
```

For multiline output, a `TextBlock` element is declared with the `TextWrapping` property set to `Wrap` to make it possible to display multiple authors. In the `Binding` markup extension, the `Path` is set to `Authors`, which is defined as a property returning a string array. The string array is converted from the resource `stringArrayConverter` as defined by the `Converter` property. The `Convert` method of the converter implementation receives the `ConverterParameter=', '` as input to separate the authors:

```xaml
<TextBlock Text="{Binding Authors,
           Converter={StaticResource stringArrayConverter},
           ConverterParameter=', '}"
           Grid.Row="3" Grid.Column="1" Margin="5"
           VerticalAlignment="Center" TextWrapping="Wrap" />
```

Figure 34-21 shows the book details, including authors.

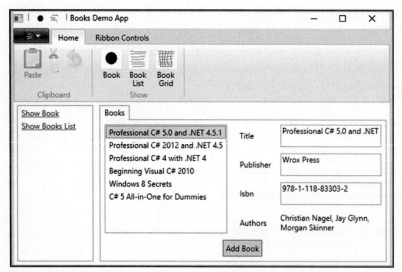

FIGURE 34-21

Adding List Items Dynamically

If list items are added dynamically, the WPF element must be notified of elements added to the list.

In the XAML code of the WPF application, a `Button` element is added inside a `StackPanel`. The `Click` event is assigned to the method `OnAddBook` (code file `BooksDemo/Controls/BooksUC.xaml`):

```
<StackPanel Orientation="Horizontal" DockPanel.Dock="Bottom"
            HorizontalAlignment="Center">
  <Button Margin="5" Padding="4" Content="Add Book" Click="OnAddBook" />
</StackPanel>
```

In the method `OnAddBook`, a new `Book` object is added to the list. If you test the application with the `BookFactory` as it is implemented now, there's no notification to the WPF elements that a new object has been added to the list (code file `BooksDemoLib/Controls/BooksUC.xaml.cs`):

```
private void OnAddBook(object sender, RoutedEventArgs e)
{
   ((this.FindResource("books") as ObjectDataProvider).Data as IList<Book>).
       Add(new Book("HTML and CSS: Design and Build Websites",
           "Wiley", "978-1-118-00818-8"));
}
```

The object that is assigned to the `DataContext` must implement the interface `INotifyCollectionChanged`. This interface defines the `CollectionChanged` event that is used by the WPF application. Instead of implementing this interface on your own with a custom collection class, you can use the generic collection class `ObservableCollection<T>` that is defined with the namespace `System.Collections.ObjectModel` in the assembly `WindowsBase`. Now, as a new item is added to the collection, the new item immediately appears in the `ListBox` (code file `BooksDemo/Models/BooksRepository.cs`):

```
public class BooksRepository
{
   private ObservableCollection<Book> _books = new ObservableCollection<Book>();
   // etc.


   public IEnumerable<Book> GetBooks() => _books;
}
```

Adding Tab Items Dynamically

Adding items dynamically to a list is in principle the same scenario as adding user controls to the tab control dynamically. Until now, the tab items have been added dynamically using the `Add` method of the `Items` property from the `TabControl` class. In the following example, the `TabControl` is directly referenced from code-behind. Using data binding instead, information about the tab item can be added to an `ObservableCollection<T>`.

The code from the BookSample application is now changed to use data binding with the `TabControl`. First, the class `UIControlInfo` is defined. This class contains properties that are used with data binding within the `TabControl`. The `Title` property is used to show heading information within tab items, and the `Content` property is used for the content of the tab items:

```
using System.Windows.Controls;
namespace Wrox.ProCSharp.WPF
{
  public class UIControlInfo
  {
    public string Title { get; set; }
    public UserControl Content { get; set; }
  }
}
```

Now an observable collection is needed to allow the tab control to refresh the information of its tab items. userControls is a member variable of the MainWindow class. The property Controls—used for data binding—returns the collection (code file BooksDemoRibbon/MainWindow.xaml.cs):

```
private ObservableCollection<UIControlInfo> _userControls =
    new ObservableCollection<UIControlInfo>();

public IEnumerable<UIControlInfo> Controls => _userControls;
```

With the XAML code the TabControl is changed. The ItemsSource property is bound to the Controls property. Now, two templates need to be specified. One template, ItemTemplate, defines the heading of the item controls. The DataTemplate specified with the ItemTemplate just uses a TextBlock element to display the value from the Text property in the heading of the tab item. The other template is ContentTemplate. This template specifies using the ContentPresenter that binds to the Content property of the bound items:

```
<TabControl Margin="5" x:Name="tabControl1" ItemsSource="{Binding Controls}">
  <TabControl.ContentTemplate>
    <DataTemplate>
      <ContentPresenter Content="{Binding Content}" />
    </DataTemplate>
  </TabControl.ContentTemplate>
  <TabControl.ItemTemplate>
    <DataTemplate>
      <StackPanel Margin="0">
        <TextBlock Text="{Binding Title}" Margin="0" />
      </StackPanel>
    </DataTemplate>
  </TabControl.ItemTemplate>
</TabControl>
```

Now the event handlers can be modified to create new UIControlInfo objects and add them to the observable collection instead of creating TabItem controls. Changing the item and content templates is a much easier way to customize the look, instead of doing this with code-behind.

```
private void OnShowBooksList(object sender, ExecutedRoutedEventArgs e)
{
  var booksUI = new BooksUC();
  userControls.Add(new UIControlInfo
  {
    Title = "Books List",
    Content = booksUI
  });
}
```

Data Template Selector

The previous chapter described how you can customize controls with templates. You also saw how to create a data template that defines a display for specific data types. A *data template selector* can create different data templates dynamically for the same data type. It is implemented in a class that derives from the base class DataTemplateSelector.

The following example implements a data template selector by selecting a different template based on the publisher. These templates are defined within the user control resources. One template can be accessed by the key name wroxTemplate; the other template has the key name dummiesTemplate, and the third one is bookTemplate (code file BooksDemoLib/Controls/BooksUC.xaml):

```
<DataTemplate x:Key="wroxTemplate" DataType="{x:Type local:Book}">
  <Border Background="Red" Margin="10" Padding="10">
    <StackPanel>
      <Label Content="{Binding Title}" />
```

```xml
      <Label Content="{Binding Publisher}" />
    </StackPanel>
  </Border>
</DataTemplate>

<DataTemplate x:Key="dummiesTemplate" DataType="{x:Type local:Book}">
  <Border Background="Yellow" Margin="10" Padding="10">
    <StackPanel>
      <Label Content="{Binding Title}" />
      <Label Content="{Binding Publisher}" />
    </StackPanel>
  </Border>
</DataTemplate>

<DataTemplate x:Key="bookTemplate" DataType="{x:Type local:Book}">
  <Border Background="LightBlue" Margin="10" Padding="10">
    <StackPanel>
      <Label Content="{Binding Title}" />
      <Label Content="{Binding Publisher}" />
    </StackPanel>
  </Border>
</DataTemplate>
```

For selecting the template, the class `BookDataTemplateSelector` overrides the method `SelectTemplate` from the base class `DataTemplateSelector`. The implementation selects the template based on the `Publisher` property from the `Book` class (code file `BooksDemoLib/Utilities/BookTemplateSelector.cs`):

```csharp
using System.Windows;
using System.Windows.Controls;
using BooksDemo;

namespace BooksDemo.Utilities
{
  public class BookTemplateSelector : DataTemplateSelector
  {
    public override DataTemplate SelectTemplate(object item,
        DependencyObject container)
    {
      if (item != null && item is Book)
      {
        var book = item as Book;
        switch (book.Publisher)
        {
          case "Wrox Press":
            return (container as FrameworkElement).FindResource(
                "wroxTemplate") as DataTemplate;
          case "For Dummies":
            return (container as FrameworkElement).FindResource(
                "dummiesTemplate") as DataTemplate;
          default:
            return (container as FrameworkElement).FindResource(
                "bookTemplate") as DataTemplate;
        }
      }
      return null;
    }
  }
}
```

For accessing the class `BookDataTemplateSelector` from XAML code, the class is defined within the `Window` resources (code file `BooksDemoLib/Controls/BooksUC.xaml`):

```xml
<src:BookDataTemplateSelector x:Key="bookTemplateSelector" />
```

Now the selector class can be assigned to the `ItemTemplateSelector` property of the `ListBox`:

```
<ListBox DockPanel.Dock="Left" ItemsSource="{Binding}" Margin="5"
        MinWidth="120" IsSynchronizedWithCurrentItem="True"
        ItemTemplateSelector="{StaticResource bookTemplateSelector}">
```

When you run the application, you can see different data templates based on the publisher, as shown in Figure 34-22.

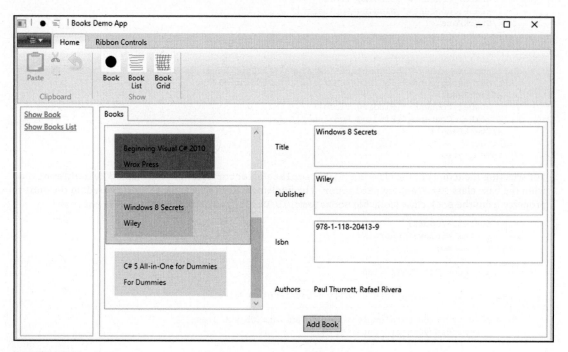

FIGURE 34-22

Binding to XML

WPF data binding has special support for binding to XML data. You can use `XmlDataProvider` as a data source and bind the elements by using XPath expressions. For a hierarchical display, you can use the `TreeView` control and create the view for the items by using the `HierarchicalDataTemplate`.

The following XML file containing `Book` elements is used as a source in the next examples (code file `XmlBindingSample/Books.xml`):

```
<?xml version="1.0" encoding="utf-8" ?>
<Books>
  <Book isbn="978-1-118-31442-5">
    <Title>Professional C# 2012</Title>
    <Publisher>Wrox Press</Publisher>
    <Author>Christian Nagel</Author>
    <Author>Jay Glynn</Author>
    <Author>Morgan Skinner</Author>
  </Book>
  <Book isbn="978-0-470-50226-6">
    <Title>Beginning Visual C# 2010</Title>
    <Publisher>Wrox Press</Publisher>
```

```
      <Author>Karli Watson</Author>
      <Author>Christian Nagel</Author>
      <Author>Jacob Hammer Pedersen</Author>
      <Author>Jon D. Reid</Author>
      <Author>Morgan Skinner</Author>
    </Book>
  </Books>
```

Similarly to defining an object data provider, you can define an XML data provider. Both
`ObjectDataProvider` and `XmlDataProvider` are derived from the same base class, `DataSourceProvider`.
With the `XmlDataProvider` in the example, the `Source` property is set to reference the XML file `books`
`.xml`. The `XPath` property defines an XPath expression to reference the XML root element `Books`. The
`Grid` element references the XML data source with the `DataContext` property. With the data context for
the grid, all `Book` elements are required for a list binding, so the XPath expression is set to `Book`. Inside the
grid, you can find the `ListBox` element that binds to the default data context and uses the `DataTemplate`
to include the title in `TextBlock` elements as items of the `ListBox`. You can also see three `Label` elements
with data binding set to XPath expressions to display the title, publisher, and ISBN numbers (code file
`XmlBindingSample/MainWindow.xaml`):

```
<Window x:Class="XmlBindingDemo.MainWindow"
        xmlns="http://schemas.microsoft.com/winfx/2006/xaml/presentation"
        xmlns:x="http://schemas.microsoft.com/winfx/2006/xaml"
        Title="Main Window" Height="240" Width="500">
  <Window.Resources>
    <XmlDataProvider x:Key="books" Source="Books.xml" XPath="Books" />
    <DataTemplate x:Key="listTemplate">
      <TextBlock Text="{Binding XPath=Title}" />
    </DataTemplate>

    <Style x:Key="labelStyle" TargetType="{x:Type Label}">
      <Setter Property="Width" Value="190" />
      <Setter Property="Height" Value="40" />
      <Setter Property="Margin" Value="5" />
    </Style>
  </Window.Resources>

  <Grid DataContext="{Binding Source={StaticResource books}, XPath=Book}">
    <Grid.RowDefinitions>
      <RowDefinition />
      <RowDefinition />
      <RowDefinition />
      <RowDefinition />
    </Grid.RowDefinitions>
    <Grid.ColumnDefinitions>
      <ColumnDefinition />
      <ColumnDefinition />
    </Grid.ColumnDefinitions>
    <ListBox IsSynchronizedWithCurrentItem="True" Margin="5"
        Grid.Column="0" Grid.RowSpan="4" ItemsSource="{Binding}"
        ItemTemplate="{StaticResource listTemplate}" />

    <Label Style="{StaticResource labelStyle}"
        Content="{Binding XPath=Title}" Grid.Row="0" Grid.Column="1" />
    <Label Style="{StaticResource labelStyle}"
        Content="{Binding XPath=Publisher}" Grid.Row="1" Grid.Column="1" />
    <Label Style="{StaticResource labelStyle}"
        Content="{Binding XPath=@isbn}" Grid.Row="2" Grid.Column="1" />
  </Grid>
</Window>
```

Figure 34-23 shows the result of the XML binding.

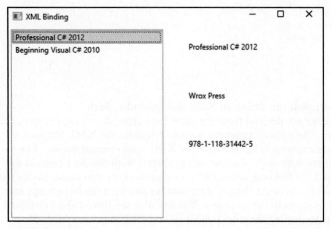

FIGURE 34-23

> **NOTE** *If XML data should be shown hierarchically, you can use the* `TreeView` *control.*

Binding Validation and Error Handling

Several options are available to validate data from the user before it is used with the .NET objects:

➤ Handling exceptions

➤ Handling data error information errors

➤ Handling notify data error information errors

➤ Defining custom validation rules

Handling Exceptions

The first option demonstrated here reflects the fact that the .NET class throws an exception if an invalid value is set, as shown in the class `SomeData`. The property `Value1` accepts values only larger than or equal to 5 and smaller than 12 (code file `ValidationSample/SomeData.cs`):

```
public class SomeData
{
  private int _value1;
  public int Value1 {
    get { return _value1; }
    set
    {
      if (value < 5 || value > 12)
      {
        throw new ArgumentException(
            "value must not be less than 5 or greater than 12");
      }
      _value1 = value;
    }
  }
}
```

In the constructor of the `MainWindow` class, a new object of the class `SomeData` is initialized and passed to the `DataContext` for data binding (code file `ValidationSample/MainWindow.xaml.cs`):

```
public partial class MainWindow: Window
{
  private SomeData _p1 = new SomeData { Value1 = 11 };

  public MainWindow()
  {
    InitializeComponent();
    this.DataContext = _p1;

  }
```

The event handler method `OnShowValue` displays a message box to show the actual value of the `SomeData` instance:

```
private void OnShowValue(object sender, RoutedEventArgs e)
{
  MessageBox.Show(_p1.Value1.ToString());
}
```

With simple data binding, the following shows the `Text` property of a `TextBox` bound to the `Value1` property. If you run the application now and try to change the value to an invalid one, you can verify that the value never changed by clicking the Submit button. WPF catches and ignores the exception thrown by the set accessor of the property `Value1` (code file `ValidationSample/MainWindow.xaml`):

```
<Label Grid.Row="0" Grid.Column="0" >Value1:</Label>
<TextBox Grid.Row="0" Grid.Column="1" Text="{Binding Path=Value1}" />
```

To display an error as soon as the context of the input field changes, you can set the `ValidatesOnException` property of the `Binding` markup extension to `True`. With an invalid value (as soon as the exception is thrown when the value should be set), the `TextBox` is surrounded by a red line. The application showing the error rectangle is shown in Figure 34-24.

```
<Label Grid.Row="0" Grid.Column="0" >Value1:</Label>
<TextBox Grid.Row="0" Grid.Column="1"
  Text="{Binding Path=Value1, ValidatesOnExceptions=True}" />
```

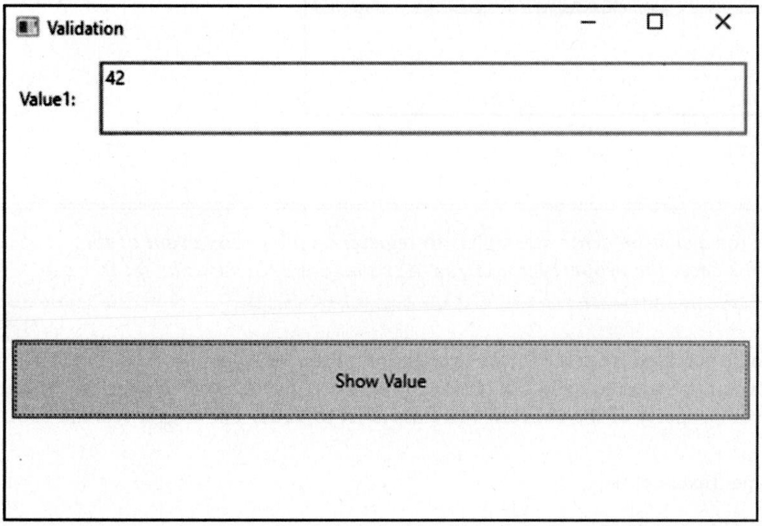

FIGURE 34-24

To show the error information in a different way to the user, the `Validation` class defines the attached property `ErrorTemplate`. You can define a custom `ControlTemplate` and assign it to the `ErrorTemplate`. The new template as shown in the following code snippet puts a red exclamation point in front of the existing control content:

```
<ControlTemplate x:Key="validationTemplate">
  <DockPanel>
    <TextBlock Foreground="Red" FontSize="40">!</TextBlock>
    <AdornedElementPlaceholder/>
  </DockPanel>
</ControlTemplate>
```

Setting the `validationTemplate` with the `Validation.ErrorTemplate` attached property activates the template with the `TextBox`:

```
<Label Margin="5" Grid.Row="0" Grid.Column="0" >Value1:</Label>
<TextBox Margin="5" Grid.Row="0" Grid.Column="1"
  Text="{Binding Path=Value1, ValidatesOnExceptions=True}"
  Validation.ErrorTemplate="{StaticResource validationTemplate}" />
```

The new look of the application is shown in Figure 34-25.

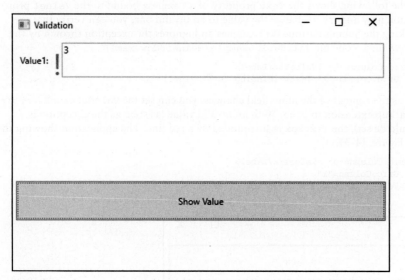

FIGURE 34-25

> **NOTE** *Another option for a custom error message is to register to the* `Error` *event of the* `Validation` *class. In this case, the property* `NotifyOnValidationError` *must be set to* true.

The error information itself can be accessed from the `Errors` collection of the `Validation` class. To display the error information in the `ToolTip` of the `TextBox` you can create a property trigger as shown next. The trigger is activated as soon as the `HasError` property of the `Validation` class is set to `True`. The trigger sets the `ToolTip` property of the `TextBox`:

```
<Style TargetType="{x:Type TextBox}">
  <Style.Triggers>
    <Trigger Property="Validation.HasError" Value="True">
      <Setter Property="ToolTip"
```

```
            Value="{Binding RelativeSource={x:Static RelativeSource.Self},
               Path=(Validation.Errors)[0].ErrorContent}" />
        </Trigger>
    </Style.Triggers>
</Style>
```

Data Error Information

Another way to deal with errors is when the .NET object implements the interface `IDataErrorInfo`. The class `SomeData` is now changed to implement this interface, which defines the property `Error` and an indexer with a string argument. With WPF validation during data binding, the indexer is called and the name of the property to validate is passed as the `columnName` argument. With the implementation, the value is verified as valid; if it isn't, an error string is passed. Here, the validation is done on the property `Value2`, which is implemented by using the C# automatic property notation (code file `ValiationSample/SomeData.cs`):

```
public class SomeData: IDataErrorInfo
{
  // etc.

  public int Value2 { get; set; }

  string IDataErrorInfo.Error => null;

  string IDataErrorInfo.this[string columnName]
  {
    get
    {
      if (columnName == "Value2")
      {
        if (this.Value2 < 0 || this.Value2 > 80)
            return "age must not be less than 0 or greater than 80";
      }
      return null;
    }
  }
}
```

> **NOTE** *With a .NET object, it would not be clear what an indexer would return; for example, what would you expect from an object of type* `Person` *calling an indexer? That's why it is best to do an explicit implementation of the interface* `IDataErrorInfo`. *This way, the indexer can be accessed only by using the interface, and the .NET class could use a different implementation for other purposes.*

If you set the property `ValidatesOnDataErrors` of the `Binding` class to `true`, the interface `IDataErrorInfo` is used during binding. In the following code, when the `TextBox` is changed the binding mechanism invokes the indexer of the interface and passes `Value2` to the `columnName` variable (code file `ValidationSample/MainWindow.xaml`):

```
<Label Margin="5" Grid.Row="1" Grid.Column="0" >Value2:</Label>
<TextBox Margin="5" Grid.Row="1" Grid.Column="1"
    Text="{Binding Path=Value2, ValidatesOnDataErrors=True}" />
```

Notify Data Error Info

Besides supporting validation with exceptions and the `IDataErrorInfo` interface, WPF with .NET 4.5 supports validation with the interface `INotifyDataErrorInfo` as well. Unlike the interface `IDataErrorInfo`, whereby the indexer to a property can return one error, with INotifyDataErrorInfo multiple errors can be associated with a single property. These errors can be accessed using the GetErrors method. The HasErrors property returns true if the entity has any error. Another great feature of this interface is the notification of errors with the event ErrorsChanged. This way, errors can be retrieved asynchronously on the client—for example, a web service can be invoked to verify the input from the user. In this case, the user can continue working with the input form while the result is retrieved, and can be informed asynchronously about any mismatch.

Let's get into an example in which validation is done using INotifyDataErrorInfo. The base class NotifyDataErrorInfoBase is defined, which implements the interface INotifyDataErrorInfo. This class derives from the base class BindableObject to get an implementation for the interface INotifyPropertyChanged that you've seen earlier in this chapter. NotifyDataErrorInfoBase uses a dictionary named errors that contains a list for every property to store error information. The property HasErrors returns true if any property has an error; the method GetErrors returns the error list for a single property; and the event ErrorsChanged is fired every time error information is changed. In addition to the members of the interface INotifyDataErrorInfo, the base class implements the methods SetError, ClearErrors, and ClearAllErrors to make it easier to deal with setting errors (code file ValidationSample/NotifyDataErrorInfoBase.cs):

```csharp
using System;
using System.Collections;
using System.Collections.Generic;
using System.ComponentModel;
using System.Runtime.CompilerServices;

namespace ValidationSamlple
{
  public abstract class NotifyDataErrorInfoBase : BindableObject,
      INotifyDataErrorInfo
  {
    private Dictionary<string, List<string>> _errors =
        new Dictionary<string, List<string>>();

    public void SetError(string errorMessage,
        [CallerMemberName] string propertyName = null)
    {
      List<string> errorList;
      if (_errors.TryGetValue(propertyName, out errorList))
      {
        errorList.Add(errorMessage);
      }
      else
      {
        errorList = new List<string> { errorMessage };
        _errors.Add(propertyName, errorList);
      }
      HasErrors = true;
      OnErrorsChanged(propertyName);
    }

    public void ClearErrors([CallerMemberName] string propertyName = null)
    {
      if (hasErrors)
      {
        List<string> errorList;
        if (_errors.TryGetValue(propertyName, out errorList))
        {
          _errors.Remove(propertyName);
        }
        if (_errors.Count == 0)
```

```
        {
          HasErrors = false;
        }
        OnErrorsChanged(propertyName);
      }
    }

    public void ClearAllErrors()
    {
      if (HasErrors)
      {
        _errors.Clear();
        HasErrors = false;
        OnErrorsChanged(null);
      }
    }

    public event EventHandler<DataErrorsChangedEventArgs> ErrorsChanged;

    public IEnumerable GetErrors(string propertyName)
    {
      List<string> errorsForProperty;
      bool err = _errors.TryGetValue(propertyName, out errorsForProperty);
      if (!err) return null;
      return errorsForProperty;
    }
    private bool hasErrors = false;
    public bool HasErrors
    {
      get { return hasErrors; }
      protected set {
        if (SetProperty(ref hasErrors, value))
        {
          OnErrorsChanged(propertyName: null);
        }
      }
    }
    protected void OnErrorsChanged(
      [CallerMemberName] string propertyName = null)
    {
      ErrorsChanged?.Invoke(this,
        new DataErrorsChangedEventArgs(propertyName));
    }
  }
}
```

The class `SomeDataWithNotifications` is the data object that is bound to the XAML code. This class derives from the base class `NotifyDataErrorInfoBase` to inherit the implementation of the interface `INotifyDataErrorInfo`. The property `Val1` is validated asynchronously. For the validation, the method `CheckVal1` is invoked after the property is set. This method makes an asynchronous call to the method `ValidationSimulator.Validate`. After invoking the method, the UI thread can return to handle other events, and as soon as the result is returned, the `SetError` method of the base class is invoked if an error was returned. You can easily change the async invocation to call a web service or perform another async activity (code file `ValidationSample/SomeDataWithNotifications.cs`):

```
using System.Runtime.CompilerServices;
using System.Threading.Tasks;
namespace ValidationSample
{
  public class SomeDataWithNotifications : NotifyDataErrorInfoBase
  {
    private int val1;
```

```
      public int Val1
      {
        get { return val1; }
        set
        {
          SetProperty(ref val1, value);
          CheckVal1(val1, value);
        }
      }
      private async void CheckVal1(int oldValue, int newValue,
          [CallerMemberName] string propertyName = null)
      {
        ClearErrors(propertyName);
        string result = await ValidationSimulator.Validate(
          newValue, propertyName);
        if (result != null)
        {
          SetError(result, propertyName);
        }
      }
    }
```

The `Validate` method of the `ValidationSimulator` has a delay of three seconds before checking the value, and returns an error message if the value is larger than 50 (code file `ValidationSample/ValidationSimulator.cs`):

```
    public static class ValidationSimulator
    {
      public static Task<string> Validate(int val,
          [CallerMemberName] string propertyName = null)
      {
        return Task<string>.Run(async () =>
          {
            await Task.Delay(3000);
            if (val > 50) return "bad value";
            else return null;
          });
      }
    }
```

With data binding, just the `ValidatesOnNotifyDataErrors` property must be set to `True` to make use of the async validation of the interface `INotifyDataErrorInfo` (code file `ValidationDemo/NotificationWindow.xaml`):

```
    <TextBox Grid.Row="0" Grid.Column="1"
      Text="{Binding Val1, ValidatesOnNotifyDataErrors=True}" Margin="8" />
```

When you run the application, open the notification window and enter invalid text. You can see the text box surrounded by the default rectangle three seconds after you entered wrong input. Showing error information in a different way can be handled in the same way you've seen it before—with error templates and triggers accessing validation errors.

Custom Validation Rules

To get more control of the validation you can implement a custom validation rule. A class implementing a custom validation rule needs to derive from the base class `ValidationRule`. In the previous two examples, validation rules have been used as well. Two classes that derive from the abstract base class `ValidationRule` are `DataErrorValidationRule` and `ExceptionValidationRule`. `DataErrorValidationRule` is activated by setting the property `ValidatesOnDataErrors` and uses the interface `IDataErrorInfo`; `ExceptionValidationRule` deals with exceptions and is activated by setting the property `ValidatesOnException`.

In the following example, a validation rule is implemented to verify a regular expression. The class RegularExpressionValidationRule derives from the base class ValidationRule and overrides the abstract method Validate that is defined by the base class. With the implementation, the RegEx class from the namespace System.Text.RegularExpressions is used to validate the expression defined by the Expression property:

```csharp
public class RegularExpressionValidationRule : ValidationRule
{
  public string Expression { get; set; }
  public string ErrorMessage { get; set; }
  public override ValidationResult Validate(object value,
      CultureInfo cultureInfo)
  {
    ValidationResult result = null;
    if (value != null)
    {
      var regEx = new Regex(Expression);
      bool isMatch = regEx.IsMatch(value.ToString());
      result = new ValidationResult(isMatch, isMatch ?
          null: ErrorMessage);
    }
    return result;
  }
}
```

> **NOTE** *Regular expressions are explained in Chapter 10.*

Instead of using the Binding markup extension, now the binding is done as a child of the TextBox.Text element. The bound object defines an Email property that is implemented with the simple property syntax. The UpdateSourceTrigger property defines when the source should be updated. Possible options for updating the source are as follows:

➤ When the property value changes, which is every character typed by the user

➤ When the focus is lost

➤ Explicitly

ValidationRules is a property of the Binding class that contains ValidationRule elements. Here, the validation rule used is the custom class RegularExpressionValidationRule, where the Expression property is set to a regular expression that verifies whether the input is a valid e-mail address; and the ErrorMessage property, which outputs the error message if the data entered in the TextBox is invalid:

```xml
<Label Margin="5" Grid.Row="2" Grid.Column="0">Email:</Label>
<TextBox Margin="5" Grid.Row="2" Grid.Column="1">
  <TextBox.Text>
    <Binding Path="Email" UpdateSourceTrigger="LostFocus">
      <Binding.ValidationRules>
        <src:RegularExpressionValidationRule
            Expression="^([\w-\.]+)@((\[[0-9]{1,3}\.[0-9]{1,3}\.
                       [0-9]{1,3}\.)|(([\w-]+\.)+))([a-zA-Z]{2,4}|
                       [0-9]{1,3})(\]?)$"
            ErrorMessage="Email is not valid" />
      </Binding.ValidationRules>
    </Binding>
  </TextBox.Text>
</TextBox>
```

TREEVIEW

The TreeView control is used to display hierarchical data. Binding to a TreeView is very similar to the binding you've seen with the ListBox. What's different is the hierarchical data display—you can use a HierarchicalDataTemplate.

The next example uses hierarchical displays and the DataGrid control. The Formula1 sample database is accessed with the ADO.NET Entity Framework. The model types are shown in Figure 34-26. The Race class contains information about the date of the race and is associated with the Circuit class. The Circuit class has information about the Country and the name of the race circuit. Race also has an association with RaceResult. A RaceResult contains information about the Racer and the Team.

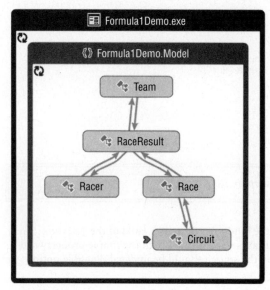

FIGURE 34-26

> **NOTE** *You can find the Formula1 database that is used with the Formula1Demo project as a backup file in the Database directory of the Formula1Demo sample. Please restore the backup file using SQL Server Management Studio to the database Formula1 before running the sample application.*

> **NOTE** *The ADO.NET Entity Framework is covered in Chapter 38, "Entity Framework Core."*

With the XAML code a TreeView is declared. TreeView derives from the base class ItemsControl, where binding to a list can be done with the ItemsSource property. ItemsSource is bound to the data context. The data context is assigned in the code-behind, as you see soon. Of course, this could also be done with an ObjectDataProvider. To define a custom display for the hierarchical data, HierarchicalDataTemplate elements are defined. The data templates here are defined for specific data types with the DataType property. The first `HierarchicalDataTemplate` is the template for the `Championship` class and binds the `Year` property of this class to the `Text` property of a `TextBlock`. The `ItemsSource` property defines the binding for the data template itself to specify the next level in the data hierarchy. If the `Races` property of the `Championship` class returns a collection, you bind the `ItemsSource` property directly to `Races`. However, because this property returns a `Lazy<T>` object, binding is done to `Races.Value`. The advantages of the `Lazy<T>` class are discussed later in this chapter.

The second `HierarchicalDataTemplate` element defines the template for the `F1Race` class and binds the `Country` and `Date` properties of this class. With the `Date` property a `StringFormat` is defined with the binding. The next level of the hierarchy is defined binding the `ItemsSource` to `Results.Value`.

The class `F1RaceResult` doesn't have a children collection, so the hierarchy stops here. For this data type, a normal `DataTemplate` is defined to bind the `Position`, `Racer`, and `Car` properties (code file `Formula1Demo/Controls/TreeUC.xaml`):

```
<UserControl x:Class="Formula1Demo.Controls.TreeUC"
             xmlns="http://schemas.microsoft.com/winfx/2006/xaml/presentation"
             xmlns:x="http://schemas.microsoft.com/winfx/2006/xaml"
             xmlns:d="http://schemas.microsoft.com/expression/blend/2008"
             xmlns:local="clr-namespace:Formula1Demo"
             mc:Ignorable="d"
             d:DesignHeight="300" d:DesignWidth="300">
  <Grid>
    <TreeView ItemsSource="{Binding}" >
      <TreeView.Resources>
        <HierarchicalDataTemplate DataType="{x:Type local:Championship}"
                                  ItemsSource="{Binding Races.Value}">
          <TextBlock Text="{Binding Year}" />
        </HierarchicalDataTemplate>

        <HierarchicalDataTemplate DataType="{x:Type local:F1Race}"
                                  ItemsSource="{Binding Results.Value}">
          <StackPanel Orientation="Horizontal">
            <TextBlock Text="{Binding Country}" Margin="5,0,5,0" />
            <TextBlock Text="{Binding Date, StringFormat=d}" Margin="5,0,5,0" />
          </StackPanel>
        </HierarchicalDataTemplate>

        <DataTemplate DataType="{x:Type local:F1RaceResult}">
          <StackPanel Orientation="Horizontal">
            <TextBlock Text="{Binding Position}" Margin="5,0,5,0" />
            <TextBlock Text="{Binding Racer}" Margin="5,0,0,0" />
            <TextBlock Text=", " />
            <TextBlock Text="{Binding Car}" />
          </StackPanel>
        </DataTemplate>
      </TreeView.Resources>
    </TreeView>
  </Grid>
</UserControl>
```

Now for the code that fills the hierarchical control. In the code-behind file of the XAML code, `DataContext` is assigned to the `Years` property. The `Years` property uses a LINQ query, defined in the `GetYears` helper method, to get all the years of the Formula-1 races in the database and to create a new `Championship` object for every year. With the instance of the `Championship` class, the `Year` property is set. This class also has a `Races` property to return the races of the year, but this information is not yet filled in (code file `Formula1Demo/TreeUC.xaml.cs`):

```
using System.Collections.Generic;
using System.Linq;
using System.Windows.Controls;
```

```
namespace Formula1Demo
{
  public partial class TreeUC : UserControl
  {
    public TreeUC()
    {
      InitializeComponent();
      this.DataContext = Years;
    }

    private List<Championship> _years;

    private List<Championship> GetYears()
    {
      using (var data = new Formula1Context())
      {
        return data.Races.Select(r => new Championship
        {
          Year = r.Date.Year
        }).Distinct().OrderBy(c => c.Year).ToList();
      }
    }

    public IEnumerable<Championship> Years => _years ?? (_years = GetYears());
  }
}
```

> **NOTE** *LINQ is discussed in Chapter 13, "Language Integrated Query," and Chapter 38.*

The `Championship` class has a simple automatic property for the year. The `Races` property is of type `Lazy<IEnumerable<F1Race>>`. The `Lazy<T>` class was introduced with .NET 4 for lazy initialization. With a `TreeView` control, this class comes in very handy. If the data behind the tree is large and you do not want to load the full tree in advance, but only when a user makes a selection, lazy loading can be used. With the constructor of the `Lazy<T>` class, a delegate `Func<IEnumerable<F1Race>>` is used. With this delegate, `IEnumerable<F1Race>` needs to be returned. The implementation of the lambda expression, assigned to the delegate, uses a LINQ query to create a list of `F1Race` objects that have the `Date` and `Country` property assigned (code file `Formula1Demo/Championship.cs`):

```
public class Championship
{
  public int Year { get; set; }

  private IEnumerable<F1Race> GetRaces()
  {
    using (var context = new Formula1Context())
    {
      return (from r in context.Races
              where r.Date.Year == Year
              orderby r.Date
              select new F1Race
              {
                Date = r.Date,
                Country = r.Circuit.Country
              }).ToList();
    }
  }

  public Lazy<IEnumerable<F1Race>> Races =>
    new Lazy<IEnumerable<F1Race>>(() => GetRaces());
}
```

The `F1Race` class again defines the `Results` property that uses the `Lazy<T>` type to return a list of `F1RaceResult` objects (code file `Formula1Demo/Championship.cs`):

```
public class F1Race
{
  public string Country { get; set; }
  public DateTime Date { get; set; }

  private IEnumerable<F1RaceResult> GetResults()
  {
    using (var context = new Formula1Context())
    {
      return (from rr in context.RaceResults
              where rr.Race.Date == this.Date
              select new F1RaceResult
              {
                Position = rr.Position,
                Racer = rr.Racer.FirstName + " " + rr.Racer.LastName,
                Car = rr.Team.Name
              }).ToList();
    }
  }

  public Lazy<IEnumerable<F1RaceResult>> Results =>
    new Lazy<IEnumerable<F1RaceResult>>(() => GetResults());
}
```

The final class of the hierarchy is `F1RaceResult`, which is a simple data holder for `Position`, `Racer`, and `Car` (code file `Formula1Demo/Championship.cs`):

```
public class F1RaceResult
{
  public int Position { get; set; }
  public string Racer { get; set; }
  public string Car { get; set; }
}
```

When you run the application, you can see at first all the years of the championships in the tree view. Because of binding, the next level is already accessed—every `Championship` object already has the `F1Race` objects associated. The user doesn't need to wait for the first level after the year or an open year with the default appearance of a small triangle. As shown in Figure 34-27, the year 1984 is open. As soon as the user clicks a year to see the second-level binding, the third level is done and the race results are retrieved.

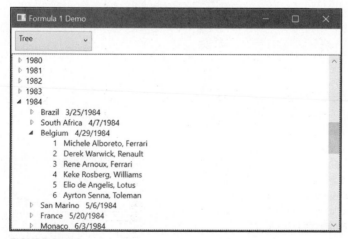

FIGURE 34-27

Of course, you can also customize the `TreeView` control and define different styles for the complete template or the items in the view.

DATAGRID

To display and edit data using rows and columns, you can use the `DataGrid` control. The `DataGrid` control is an `ItemsControl` and defines the `ItemsSource` property that is bound to a collection. The XAML code of this user interface also defines two `RepeatButton` controls that are used for paging functionality. Instead of loading all the race information at once, paging is used so users can step through pages. In a simple scenario, only the `ItemsSource` property of the `DataGrid` needs to be assigned. By default, the `DataGrid` creates columns based on the properties of the bound data (code file `Formula1Demo/Controls/GridUC.xaml`):

```xml
<UserControl x:Class="Formula1Demo.Controls.GridUC"
    xmlns="http://schemas.microsoft.com/winfx/2006/xaml/presentation"
    xmlns:x="http://schemas.microsoft.com/winfx/2006/xaml"
    xmlns:mc="http://schemas.openxmlformats.org/markup-compatibility/2006"
    xmlns:d="http://schemas.microsoft.com/expression/blend/2008"
    mc:Ignorable="d"
    d:DesignHeight="300" d:DesignWidth="300">
  <Grid>
    <Grid.RowDefinitions>
      <RepeatButton Margin="5" Click="OnPrevious">Previous</RepeatButton>
      <RepeatButton Margin="5" Click="OnNext">Next</RepeatButton>
    </Grid.RowDefinitions>
    <StackPanel Orientation="Horizontal" Grid.Row="0">
      <Button Click="OnPrevious">Previous</Button>
      <Button Click="OnNext">Next</Button>
    </StackPanel>
    <DataGrid Grid.Row="1" ItemsSource="{Binding}" />
  </Grid>
</UserControl>
```

The code-behind uses the same `Formula1` database as the previous `TreeView` example. The `DataContext` of the `UserControl` is set to the `Races` property. This property returns `IEnumerable<object>`. Instead of assigning a strongly typed enumeration, an `object` is used to make it possible to create an anonymous class with the LINQ query. The LINQ query creates the anonymous class with `Year`, `Country`, `Position`, `Racer`, and `Car` properties and uses a compound to access `Races` and `RaceResults`. It also accesses other associations of `Races` to get country, racer, and team information. With the `Skip` and `Take` methods, paging functionality is implemented. The size of a page is fixed to 50 items, and the current page changes with the `OnNext` and `OnPrevious` handlers (code file `Formula1Demo/Controls/GridUC.xaml.cs`):

```csharp
using System.Collections.Generic;
using System.Linq;
using System.Windows;
using System.Windows.Controls;

namespace Formula1Demo
{
  public partial class GridUC : UserControl
  {
    private int _currentPage = 0;
    private int _pageSize = 50;

    public GridUC()
    {
      InitializeComponent();
      this.DataContext = Races;
    }

    private IEnumerable<object> GetRaces()
    {
```

```
        using (var data = new Formula1Context())
        {
            return (from r in data.Races
                    from rr in r.RaceResults
                    orderby r.Date ascending
                    select new
                    {
                        r.Date.Year,
                        r.Circuit.Country,
                        rr.Position,
                        Racer = rr.Racer.FirstName + " " + rr.Racer.LastName,
                        Car = rr.Team.Name
                    }).Skip(_currentPage * _pageSize).Take(_pageSize).ToList();
        }
    }

    public IEnumerable<object> Races => GetRaces();

    private void OnPrevious(object sender, RoutedEventArgs e)
    {
        if (_currentPage > 0)
        {
            _currentPage--;
            this.DataContext = Races;
        }
    }

    private void OnNext(object sender, RoutedEventArgs e)
    {
        _currentPage++;
        this.DataContext = Races;
    }
}
```

Figure 34-28 shows the running application with the default grid styles and headers.

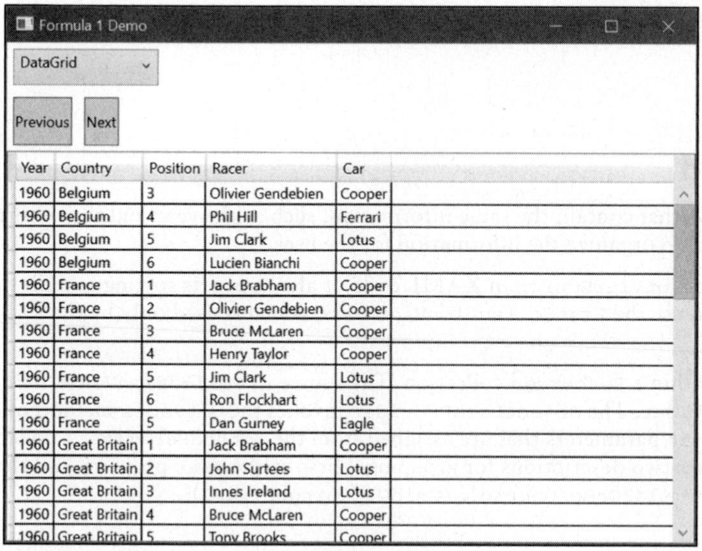

FIGURE 34-28

In the next DataGrid example, the grid is customized with custom columns and grouping.

Custom Columns

Setting the property `AutoGenerateColumns` of the `DataGrid` to `False` doesn't generate default columns. You can create custom columns with the `Columns` property. You can also specify elements that derive from `DataGridColumn`. You can use predefined classes, and `DataGridTextColumn` can be used to read and edit text. `DataGridHyperlinkColumn` is for displaying hyperlinks. `DataGridCheckBoxColumn` displays a check box for Boolean data. For a list of items in a column, you can use the `DataGridComboBoxColumn`. More `DataGridColumn` types will be available in the future, but if you need a different representation now, you can use the `DataGridTemplateColumn` to define and bind any elements you want.

The example code uses `DataGridTextColumn` elements that are bound to the `Position` and `Racer` properties. The `Header` property is set to a string for display. Of course, you can also use a template to define a complete custom header for the column (code file `Formula1Demo/Controls/GridCustomUC.xaml.cs`):

```
<DataGrid ItemsSource="{Binding}" AutoGenerateColumns="False">
  <DataGrid.Columns>
    <DataGridTextColumn Binding="{Binding Position, Mode=OneWay}"
                        Header="Position" />
    <DataGridTextColumn Binding="{Binding Racer, Mode=OneWay}"
                        Header="Racer" />
  </DataGrid.Columns>
```

Row Details

When a row is selected, the `DataGrid` can display additional information for the row. You do this by specifying a `RowDetailsTemplate` with the `DataGrid`. A `DataTemplate` is assigned to the `RowDetailsTemplate`, which contains several `TextBlock` elements that display the car and points (code file `Formula1Demo/Controls/GridCustomUC.xaml`):

```
<DataGrid.RowDetailsTemplate>
  <DataTemplate>
    <StackPanel Orientation="Horizontal">
      <TextBlock Text="Car:" Margin="5,0,0,0" />
      <TextBlock Text="{Binding Car}" Margin="5,0,0,0" />
      <TextBlock Text="Points:" Margin="5,0,0,0" />
      <TextBlock Text="{Binding Points}" />
    </StackPanel>
  </DataTemplate>
</DataGrid.RowDetailsTemplate>
```

Grouping with the DataGrid

The Formula-1 races have several rows that contain the same information, such as the year and the country. For such data, grouping can be helpful to organize the information for the user.

For grouping, you can use the `CollectionViewSource` in XAML code. It also supports sorting and filtering. With code-behind you can also use the `ListCollectionView` class, which is used only by the `CollectionViewSource`.

`CollectionViewSource` is defined within a `Resources` collection. The source of `CollectionViewSource` is the result from an `ObjectDataProvider`. The `ObjectDataProvider` invokes the `GetRaces` method of the `F1Races` type. This method has two int parameters that are assigned from the `MethodParameters` collection. The `CollectionViewSource` uses two descriptions for grouping—first by the `Year` property and then by the `Country` property (code file `Formula1Demo/Controls/GridGroupingUC.xaml`):

```
<Grid.Resources>
  <ObjectDataProvider x:Key="races" ObjectType="{x:Type local:F1Races}"
```

```
                        MethodName="GetRaces">
    <ObjectDataProvider.MethodParameters>
      <sys:Int32>0</sys:Int32>
      <sys:Int32>20</sys:Int32>
    </ObjectDataProvider.MethodParameters>
  </ObjectDataProvider>
  <CollectionViewSource x:Key="viewSource"
                        Source="{StaticResource races}">
    <CollectionViewSource.GroupDescriptions>
      <PropertyGroupDescription PropertyName="Year" />
      <PropertyGroupDescription PropertyName="Country" />
    </CollectionViewSource.GroupDescriptions>
  </CollectionViewSource>
</Grid.Resources>
```

How the group is displayed is defined with the `DataGrid GroupStyle` property. With the `GroupStyle` element you need to customize the `ContainerStyle` as well as the `HeaderTemplate` and the complete panel. To dynamically select the `GroupStyle` and `HeaderStyle`, you can also write a container style selector and a header template selector. It is very similar in functionality to the data template selector described earlier.

The `GroupStyle` in the example sets the `ContainerStyle` property of the `GroupStyle`. With this style, the `GroupItem` is customized with a template. The `GroupItem` appears as the root element of a group when grouping is used. Displayed within the group is the name, using the `Name` property, and the number of items, using the `ItemCount` property. The third column of the `Grid` contains all the normal items using the `ItemsPresenter`. If the rows are grouped by country, the labels of the `Name` property would all have a different width, which doesn't look good. Therefore, the `SharedSizeGroup` property is set with the second column of the grid to ensure all items are the same size. The shared size scope needs to be set for all elements that have the same size. This is done in the `DataGrid` setting `Grid.IsSharedSizeScope` `="True"`:

```
<DataGrid.GroupStyle>
  <GroupStyle>
    <GroupStyle.ContainerStyle>
      <Style TargetType="{x:Type GroupItem}">
        <Setter Property="Template">
          <Setter.Value>
            <ControlTemplate >
              <StackPanel Orientation="Horizontal" >
                <Grid>
                  <Grid.ColumnDefinitions>
                    <ColumnDefinition SharedSizeGroup="LeftColumn" />
                    <ColumnDefinition />
                    <ColumnDefinition />
                  </Grid.ColumnDefinitions>
                  <Label Grid.Column="0" Background="Yellow"
                      Content="{Binding Name}" />
                  <Label Grid.Column="1" Content="{Binding ItemCount}" />
                  <Grid Grid.Column="2" HorizontalAlignment="Center"
                      VerticalAlignment="Center">
                    <ItemsPresenter/>
                  </Grid>
                </Grid>
              </StackPanel>
            </ControlTemplate>
          </Setter.Value>
        </Setter>
      </Style>
    </GroupStyle.ContainerStyle>
  </GroupStyle>
</DataGrid.GroupStyle>
```

The class `F1Races` that is used by the `ObjectDataProvider` uses LINQ to access the `Formula1` database and returns a list of anonymous types with `Year`, `Country`, `Position`, `Racer`, `Car`, and `Points` properties. The `Skip` and `Take` methods are used to access part of the data (code file `Formula1Demo/F1Races.cs`):

```
using System.Collections.Generic;
using System.Linq;

namespace Formula1Demo
{
  public class F1Races
  {
    private int _lastpageSearched = -1;
    private IEnumerable<object> _cache = null;

    public IEnumerable<object> GetRaces(int page, int pageSize)
    {
      using (var data = new Formula1Context())
      {
        if (_lastpageSearched == page)
          return _cache;
        _lastpageSearched = page;

        var q = (from r in data.Races
                 from rr in r.RaceResults
                 orderby r.Date ascending
                 select new
                 {
                   Year = r.Date.Year,
                   Country = r.Circuit.Country,
                   Position = rr.Position,
                   Racer = rr.Racer.FirstName + " " + rr.Racer.LastName,
                   Car = rr.Team.Name,
                   Points = rr.Points
                 }).Skip(page * pageSize).Take(pageSize);
        _cache = q.ToList();
        return _cache;
      }
    }
  }
}
```

Now all that's left is for the user to set the page number and change the parameter of the `ObjectDataProvider`. In the user interface, a `TextBox` and a `Button` are defined (code file `Formula1Demo/Controls/GridGroupingUC.xaml`):

```
<StackPanel Orientation="Horizontal" Grid.Row="0">
  <TextBlock Margin="5" Padding="4" VerticalAlignment="Center">
    Page:
  </TextBlock>
  <TextBox Margin="5" Padding="4" VerticalAlignment="Center"
    x:Name="textPageNumber" Text="0" />
  <Button Click="OnGetPage">Get Page</Button>
</StackPanel>
```

The `OnGetPage` handler of the button in the code-behind accesses the `ObjectDataProvider` and changes the first parameter of the method. It then invokes the `Refresh` method so the `ObjectDataProvider` requests the new page (code file `Formula1Demo/GridGroupingUC.xaml.cs`):

```
private void OnGetPage(object sender, RoutedEventArgs e)
{
  int page = int.Parse(textPageNumber.Text);
  var odp = (sender as FrameworkElement).FindResource("races")
        as ObjectDataProvider;
```

```
        odp.MethodParameters[0] = page;
        odp.Refresh();
    }
```

When you run the application, you can see grouping and row detail information, as shown in Figure 34-29.

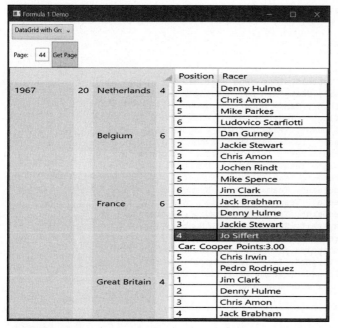

FIGURE 34-29

Live Shaping

A new feature since WPF 4.5 is *live shaping*. You've seen the collection view source with its support for sorting, filtering, and grouping. However, if the collection changes over time in that sorting, filtering, or grouping returns different results, the CollectionViewSource didn't help—until now. For live shaping, a new interface, ICollectionViewLiveShaping, is used. This interface defines the properties CanChangeLiveFiltering, CanChangeLiveGrouping, and CanChangeLiveSorting to check the data source if these live shaping features are available. The properties IsLiveFiltering, IsLiveGrouping, and IsLiveSorting enable turning on the live shaping features—if available. With LiveFilteringProperties, LiveGroupingProperties, and LiveSortingProperties, you can define the properties of the source that should be used for live filtering, grouping, and sorting.

The sample application shows how the results of a Formula 1 race—this time the race from Barcelona in 2012—change lap by lap.

A racer is represented by the Racer class. This type has the simple properties Name, Team, and Number. These properties are implemented using auto properties, as the values of this type don't change when the application is run (code file LiveShaping/Racer.cs):

```
public class Racer
{
    public string Name { get; set; }
    public string Team { get; set; }
    public int Number { get; set; }
    public override string ToString() => Name;
}
```

The class `Formula1` returns a list of all racers who competed at the Barcelona race 2012 (code file `LiveShaping/Formula1.cs`):

```
public class Formula1
{
  private List<Racer> _racers;
  public IEnumerable<Racer> Racers => _racers ?? (_racers = GetRacers());

  private List<Racer> GetRacers()
  {
    return new List<Racer>()
    {
      new Racer { Name="Sebastian Vettel", Team="Red Bull Racing", Number=1 },
      new Racer { Name="Mark Webber", Team="Red Bull Racing", Number=2 },
      new Racer { Name="Jenson Button", Team="McLaren", Number=3 },
      new Racer { Name="Lewis Hamilton", Team="McLaren", Number=4 },
      new Racer { Name="Fernando Alonso", Team="Ferrari", Number=5 },
      new Racer { Name="Felipe Massa", Team="Ferrari", Number=6 },
      new Racer { Name="Michael Schumacher", Team="Mercedes", Number=7 },
      new Racer { Name="Nico Rosberg", Team="Mercedes", Number=8 },
      new Racer { Name="Kimi Raikkonen", Team="Lotus", Number=9 },
      new Racer { Name="Romain Grosjean", Team="Lotus", Number=10 },
      new Racer { Name="Paul di Resta", Team="Force India", Number=11 },
      new Racer { Name="Nico Hülkenberg", Team="Force India", Number=12 },
      new Racer { Name="Kamui Kobayashi", Team="Sauber", Number=14 },
      new Racer { Name="Sergio Perez", Team="Sauber", Number=15 },
      new Racer { Name="Daniel Riccardio", Team="Toro Rosso", Number=16 },
      new Racer { Name="Jean-Eric Vergne", Team="Toro Rosso", Number=17 },
      new Racer { Name="Pastor Maldonado", Team="Williams", Number=18 },
      //... more racers in the source code download
    };
  }
}
```

Now it gets more interesting. The `LapRacerInfo` class is the type that is shown in the `DataGrid` control. The class derives from the base class `BindableObject` to get an implementation of `INotifyPropertyChanged` as you've seen earlier. The properties `Lap`, `Position`, and `PositionChange` change over time. `Lap` gives the current lap number, `Position` gives the position in the race in the specified lap, and `PositionChange` provides information about how the position changed from the previous lap. If the position did not change, the state is `None`; if the position is lower than in the previous lap, it is `Up`; if it is higher, then it is `Down`; and if the racer is out of the race, the `PositionChange` is `Out`. This information can be used within the UI for a different representation (code file `LiveShaping/LapRacerInfo.cs`):

```
public enum PositionChange
{
  None,
  Up,
  Down,
  Out
}

public class LapRacerInfo : BindableObject
{
  public Racer Racer { get; set; }
  private int _lap;
  public int Lap
  {
    get { return _lap; }
    set { SetProperty(ref _lap, value); }
  }
  private int _position;
  public int Position
```

```
    {
      get { return _position; }
      set { SetProperty(ref _position, value); }
    }
    private PositionChange _positionChange;
    public PositionChange PositionChange
    {
      get { return _positionChange; }
      set { SetProperty(ref _positionChange, value); }
    }
  }
```

The class `LapChart` contains all the information about all laps and racers. This class could be changed to access a live web service to retrieve this information, and then the application could show the current live results from an active race.

The method `SetLapInfoForStart` creates the initial list of `LapRacerInfo` items and fills the position to the grid position. The grid position is the first number of the `List<int>` collection that is added to the `positions` dictionary. Then, with every invocation of the `NextLap` method, the items inside the `lapInfo` collection change to a new position and set the `PositionChange` state information (code file `LiveShaping/LapChart.cs`):

```
public class LapChart
{
  private Formula1 _f1 = new Formula1();
  private List<LapRacerInfo> _lapInfo;
  private int _currentLap = 0;
  private const int PostionOut = 999;
  private int _maxLaps;

  public LapChart()
  {
    FillPositions();
    SetLapInfoForStart();
  }

  private Dictionary<int, List<int>> _positions =
      new Dictionary<int, List<int>>();
  private void FillPositions()
  {
    _positions.Add(18, new List<int> { 1, 2, 2, 2, 2, 2, 2, 2, 2, 2, 1, 1, 2,
      2, 2, 2, 2, 2, 2, 2, 2, 2, 2, 2, 3, 3, 1, 1, 1, 1, 1, 1, 1, 1, 1, 1,
      1, 1, 1, 1, 1, 3, 3, 3, 2, 2, 1, 1, 1, 1, 1, 1, 1, 1, 1, 1, 1, 1, 1,
      1, 1, 1, 1, 1, 1 });
    _positions.Add(5, new List<int> { 2, 1, 1, 1, 1, 1, 1, 1, 1, 1, 2, 3, 1, 1,
      1, 1, 1, 1, 1, 1, 1, 1, 1, 1, 3, 2, 2, 2, 2, 2, 2, 2, 2, 2,
      2, 2, 2, 2, 1, 1, 1, 3, 3, 3, 2, 2, 2, 2, 2, 2, 2, 2, 2, 2, 2, 2,
      2, 2, 2, 2, 2 });
    _positions.Add(10, new List<int> { 3, 5, 5, 5, 5, 5, 5, 5, 5, 4, 4, 9, 7,
      6, 6, 5, 4, 4, 4, 4, 4, 4, 4, 4, 4, 5, 4, 4, 4, 4, 4, 4, 4, 4, 4,
      4, 4, 4, 4, 4, 4, 4, 4, 4, 4, 4, 3, 3, 4, 4, 4, 4, 4, 4, 4, 4, 4,
      4, 4, 4, 4, 4, 4 });
    // more position information with the code download
    _maxLaps = positions.Select(p => p.Value.Count).Max() - 1;
  }

  private void SetLapInfoForStart()
  {
    _lapInfo = _positions.Select(x => new LapRacerInfo
    {
      Racer = _f1.Racers.Where(r => r.Number == x.Key).Single(),
      Lap = 0,
      Position = x.Value.First(),
```

```
                PositionChange = PositionChange.None
          }).ToList();
      }

      public IEnumerable<LapRacerInfo> GetLapInfo() => lapInfo;

      public bool NextLap()
      {
        _currentLap++;
        if (_currentLap > _maxLaps) return false;
        foreach (var info in _lapInfo)
        {
          int lastPosition = info.Position;
          var racerInfo = _positions.Where(x => x.Key == info.Racer.Number)
            .Single();
          if (racerInfo.Value.Count > _currentLap)
          {
            info.Position = racerInfo.Value[currentLap];
          }
          else
          {
            info.Position = lastPosition;
          }
          info.PositionChange = GetPositionChange(lastPosition, info.Position);

          info.Lap = currentLap;
        }
        return true;
      }

      private PositionChange GetPositionChange(int oldPosition, int newPosition)
      {
        if (oldPosition == PositionOut ||| newPosition == PositionOut)
          return PositionChange.Out;
        else if (oldPosition == newPosition)
          return PositionChange.None;
        else if (oldPosition < newPosition)
          return PositionChange.Down;
        else
          return PositionChange.Up;
      }
    }
```

In the main window, the DataGrid is specified and contains some DataGridTextColumn elements that are bound to properties of the LapRacerInfo class that is returned from the collection shown previously. DataTrigger elements are used to define a different background color for the row depending on whether the racer has a better or worse position compared to the previous lap by using the enumeration value from the PositionChange property (code file LiveShaping/MainWindow.xaml):

```xml
<DataGrid IsReadOnly="True" ItemsSource="{Binding}"
    DataContext="{StaticResource cvs}" AutoGenerateColumns="False">
  <DataGrid.CellStyle>
    <Style TargetType="DataGridCell">
      <Style.Triggers>
        <Trigger Property="IsSelected" Value="True">
          <Setter Property="Background" Value="{x:Null}" />
          <Setter Property="BorderBrush" Value="{x:Null}" />
        </Trigger>
      </Style.Triggers>
    </Style>
  </DataGrid.CellStyle>
  <DataGrid.RowStyle>
```

```xml
<Style TargetType="DataGridRow">
  <Style.Triggers>
    <Trigger Property="IsSelected" Value="True">
      <Setter Property="Background" Value="{x:Null}" />
      <Setter Property="BorderBrush" Value="{x:Null}" />
    </Trigger>
    <DataTrigger Binding="{Binding PositionChange}" Value="None">
      <Setter Property="Background" Value="LightGray" />
    </DataTrigger>
    <DataTrigger Binding="{Binding PositionChange}" Value="Up">
      <Setter Property="Background" Value="LightGreen" />
    </DataTrigger>
    <DataTrigger Binding="{Binding PositionChange}" Value="Down">
      <Setter Property="Background" Value="Yellow" />
    </DataTrigger>
    <DataTrigger Binding="{Binding PositionChange}" Value="Out">
      <Setter Property="Background" Value="Red" />
    </DataTrigger>
  </Style.Triggers>
</Style>
</DataGrid.RowStyle>
<DataGrid.Columns>
  <DataGridTextColumn Binding="{Binding Position}" />
  <DataGridTextColumn Binding="{Binding Racer.Number}" />
  <DataGridTextColumn Binding="{Binding Racer.Name}" />
  <DataGridTextColumn Binding="{Binding Racer.Team}" />
  <DataGridTextColumn Binding="{Binding Lap}" />
</DataGrid.Columns>
</DataGrid>
```

The data context specified with the `DataGrid` control is found in the resources of the window with the `CollectionViewSource`. The collection view source is bound to the data context that is specified with the code-behind. The important property set here is `IsLiveSortingRequested`. The value is set to `true` to change the order of the elements in the user interface. The property used for sorting is `Position`. As the position changes, the items are reordered in real time:

```xml
<Window.Resources>
  <CollectionViewSource x:Key="cvs" Source="{Binding}"
      IsLiveSortingRequested="True">
    <CollectionViewSource.SortDescriptions>
      <scm:SortDescription PropertyName="Position" />
    </CollectionViewSource.SortDescriptions>
  </CollectionViewSource>
</Window.Resources>
```

Now, you just need to get to the code-behind source code where the data context is set and the live values are changed dynamically. In the constructor of the main window, the `DataContext` property is set to the initial collection of type `LapRacerInfo`. Next, a background task invokes the `NextLap` method every three seconds to change the values in the UI with the new positions. The background task makes use of an async lambda expression. The implementation could be changed to get live data from a web service (code file `LiveShaping/MainWindow.xaml.cs`).

```csharp
public partial class MainWindow : Window
{
  private LapChart _lapChart = new LapChart();

  public MainWindow()
  {
    InitializeComponent();
    this.DataContext = _lapChart.GetLapInfo();
    Task.Run(async () =>
```

```
        {
            bool raceContinues = true;
            while (raceContinues)
            {
                await Task.Delay(3000);
                raceContinues = _lapChart.NextLap();
            }
        });
    }
}
```

Figure 34-30 shows a run of the application while in lap 23, with a leading Fernando Alonso driving a Ferrari.

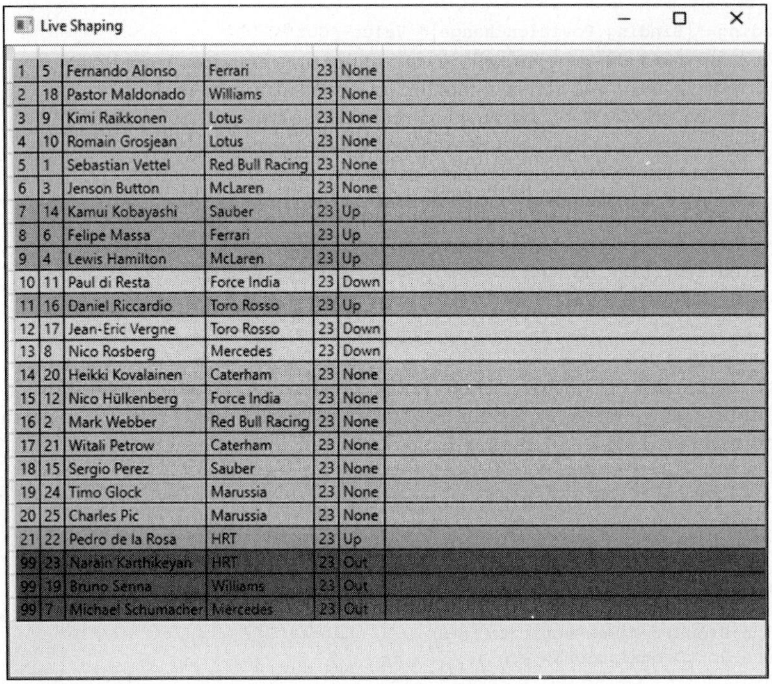

FIGURE 34-30

SUMMARY

This chapter covered the main features of WPF that are extremely important for business applications. You've seen the hierarchy of controls, and different options for the layout of controls. For clear and easy interaction with data, WPF data binding provides a leap forward. You can bind any property of a .NET class to a property of a WPF element. The binding mode defines the direction of the binding. You can bind .NET objects and lists, and define a data template to create a default look for a .NET class.

Command binding makes it possible to map handler code to menus and toolbars. You've also seen how easy it is to copy and paste with WPF because a command handler for this technology is already included in the TextBox control. You've also seen many more WPF features, such as using a DataGrid, the CollectionViewSource for sorting and grouping, and all this with live shaping as well.

The next chapter goes into another facet of WPF: working with documents.

35

Creating Documents with WPF

WHAT'S IN THIS CHAPTER?

➤ Using text elements
➤ Creating flow documents
➤ Creating fixed documents
➤ Creating XPS documents
➤ Printing documents

WROX.COM CODE DOWNLOADS FOR THIS CHAPTER

The wrox.com code downloads for this chapter are found at www.wrox.com/go/
professionalcsharp6 on the Download Code tab. The code for this chapter is
divided into the following major examples:

➤ Show Fonts
➤ Text Effects
➤ Table
➤ Flow Documents
➤ Create XPS
➤ Printing

INTRODUCTION

Creating documents is a large part of WPF. The namespace System.Windows.Documents supports creating both flow documents and fixed documents. This namespace contains elements with
which you can have a rich Word-like experience with flow documents, and create WYSIWYG fixed
documents.

Flow documents are geared toward screen reading; the content of the document is arranged based on
the size of the window, and the flow of the document changes if the window is resized. *Fixed documents* are mainly used for printing and page-oriented content and the content is always arranged in
the same way.

This chapter teaches you how to create and print flow documents and fixed documents, and covers the namespaces `System.Windows.Documents`, `System.Windows.Xps`, and `System.IO.Packaging`.

TEXT ELEMENTS

To build the content of documents, you need document elements. The base class of these elements is `TextElement`. This class defines common properties for font settings, foreground and background, and text effects. `TextElement` is the base class for the classes `Block` and `Inline`, whose functionality is explored in the following sections.

Fonts

An important aspect of text is how it looks, and thus the importance of the font. With the `TextElement`, the font can be specified with the properties `FontWeight`, `FontStyle`, `FontStretch`, `FontSize`, and `FontFamily`:

➤ `FontWeight`—Predefined values are specified by the `FontWeights` class, which offers values such as `UltraLight`, `Light`, `Medium`, `Normal`, `Bold`, `UltraBold`, and `Heavy`.

➤ `FontStyle`—Values are defined by the `FontStyles` class, which offers `Normal`, `Italic`, and `Oblique`.

➤ `FontStretch`—Use this to specify the degrees to stretch the font compared to the normal aspect ratio. `FrontStretch` defines predefined stretches that range from 50% (`UltraCondensed`) to 200% (`UltraExpanded`). Predefined values in between the range are `ExtraCondensed` (62.5%), `Condensed` (75%), `SemiCondensed` (87.5%), `Normal` (100%), `SemiExpanded` (112.5%), `Expanded` (125%), and `ExtraExpanded` (150%).

➤ `FontSize`—This is of type `double` and enables you to specify the size of the font in device-independent units, inches, centimeters, and points.

➤ `FontFamily`—Use this to define the name of the preferred font family, for example, Arial or Times New Roman. With this property you can specify a list of font family names so if one font is not available, the next one in the list is used. (If neither the selected font nor the alternate font is available, a flow document falls back to the default `MessageFontFamily`.) You can also reference a font family from a resource or use a URI to reference a font from a server. With fixed documents there's no fallback on a font not available because the font is available with the document.

To give you a feel for the look of different fonts, the following sample WPF application includes a `ListBox`. The `ListBox` defines an `ItemTemplate` for every item in the list. This template uses four `TextBlock` elements whereby the `FontFamily` is bound to the `Source` property of a `FontFamily` object. With different `TextBlock` elements, `FontWeight` and `FontStyle` are set (code file `DocumentsDemos/ShowFontsDemo/MainWindow.xaml`):

```xml
<ListBox ItemsSource="{Binding}">
  <ListBox.ItemTemplate>
    <DataTemplate>
      <StackPanel Orientation="Horizontal" >
        <StackPanel.Resources>
          <Style TargetType="TextBlock">
            <Setter Property="Margin" Value="3,0,3,0" />
            <Setter Property="FontSize" Value="18" />
            <Setter Property="FontFamily" Value="{Binding Source}" />
          </Style>
        </StackPanel.Resources>

        <TextBlock Text="{Binding Path=Source}" />
        <TextBlock FontStyle="Italic" Text="Italic" />
        <TextBlock FontWeight="UltraBold" Text="UltraBold" />
        <TextBlock FontWeight="UltraLight" Text="UltraLight" />
```

```
          </StackPanel>
        </DataTemplate>
      </ListBox.ItemTemplate>
    </ListBox>
```

In the code-behind, the data context is set to the result of the `SystemFontFamilies` property of the `System.Windows.Media.Font` class. This returns all the available fonts (code file `DocumentsDemos/ShowFontsDemo/MainWindow.xaml.cs`):

```csharp
public partial class ShowFontsWindow: Window
{
  public ShowFontsWindow()
  {
    InitializeComponent();

    this.DataContext = Fonts.SystemFontFamilies;
  }
}
```

When you run the application, you get a large list of system font families with italic, bold, ultrabold, and ultralight characteristics, as shown in Figure 35-1.

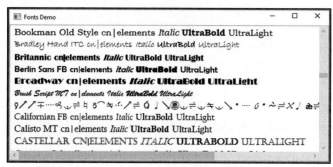

FIGURE 35-1

TextEffect

Now let's have a look into `TextEffect`, as it is also common to all document elements. `TextEffect` is defined in the namespace `System.Windows.Media` and derives from the base class `Animatable`, which enables the animation of text.

`TextEffect` enables you to animate a clipping region, the foreground brush, and a transformation. With the properties `PositionStart` and `PositionCount` you specify the position in the text to which the animation applies.

For applying the text effects, the `TextEffects` property of a `Run` element is set. The `TextEffect` element specified within the property defines a foreground and a transformation. For the foreground, a `SolidColorBrush` with the name `brush1` is used that is animated with a `ColorAnimation` element. The transformation makes use of a `ScaleTransformation` with the name `scale1`, which is animated from two `DoubleAnimation` elements (code file `DocumentsDemos/TextEffectsDemo/MainWindow.xaml`):

```xml
<TextBlock>
  <TextBlock.Triggers>
    <EventTrigger RoutedEvent="TextBlock.Loaded">
      <BeginStoryboard>
        <Storyboard>
          <ColorAnimation AutoReverse="True" RepeatBehavior="Forever"
```

```
                        From="Blue" To="Red" Duration="0:0:16"
                        Storyboard.TargetName="brush1"
                        Storyboard.TargetProperty="Color" />
                    <DoubleAnimation AutoReverse="True"
                        RepeatBehavior="Forever"
                        From="0.2" To="12" Duration="0:0:16"
                        Storyboard.TargetName="scale1"
                        Storyboard.TargetProperty="ScaleX" />
                    <DoubleAnimation AutoReverse="True"
                        RepeatBehavior="Forever"
                        From="0.2" To="12" Duration="0:0:16"
                        Storyboard.TargetName="scale1"
                        Storyboard.TargetProperty="ScaleY" />
                </Storyboard>
            </BeginStoryboard>
        </EventTrigger>
    </TextBlock.Triggers>
    <Run FontFamily="Segoe UI">
        cn|elements
        <Run.TextEffects>
            <TextEffect PositionStart="0" PositionCount="30">
                <TextEffect.Foreground>
                    <SolidColorBrush x:Name="brush1" Color="Blue" />
                </TextEffect.Foreground>
                <TextEffect.Transform>
                    <ScaleTransform x:Name="scale1" ScaleX="3" ScaleY="3" />
                </TextEffect.Transform>
            </TextEffect>
        </Run.TextEffects>
    </Run>
</TextBlock>
```

When you run the application, you can see the changes in size and color as shown in Figures 35-2 and 35-3.

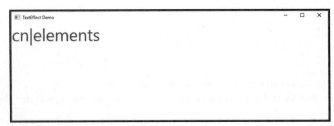

FIGURE 35-2

FIGURE 35-3

Inline

The base class for all inline flow content elements is Inline. You can use Inline elements within a paragraph of a flow document. Because within a paragraph one Inline element can follow another, the Inline class provides the PreviousInline and NextInline properties to navigate from one element to another. You can also get a collection of all peer inlines with SiblingInlines.

The Run element that was used earlier to write some text is an Inline element for formatted or unformatted text, but there are many more. You can have a new line after a Run element by using the LineBreak element.

The Span element derives from the Inline class and enables the grouping of Inline elements. Only Inline elements are allowed within the content of Span. The self-explanatory Bold, Hyperlink, Italic, and Underline classes all derive from Span and thus have the same functionality to enable Inline elements as its content, but to act on these elements differently. The following XAML code demonstrates using Bold, Italic, Underline, and LineBreak, as shown in Figure 35-4 (code file DocumentsDemos/FlowDocumentsDemo/FlowDocument1.xaml):

```
<Paragraph FontWeight="Normal">
  <Span>
    <Span>Normal</Span>
    <Bold>Bold</Bold>
    <Italic>Italic</Italic>
    <LineBreak />
    <Underline>Underline</Underline>
  </Span>
</Paragraph>
```

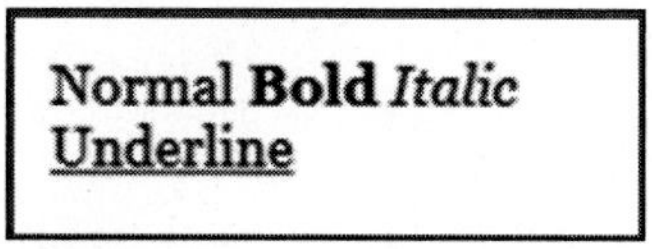

Normal **Bold** *Italic*
Underline

FIGURE 35-4

AnchoredBlock is an abstract class that derives from Inline and is used to anchor Block elements to flow content. Figure and Floater are concrete classes that derive from AnchoredBlock. Because these two inline elements become interesting in relation to blocks, these elements are discussed later in this chapter.

> **NOTE** *The flow documents added to the solution need to be set to* Build Action = "Content" *and* Copy to Output Directory = "Copy if newer" *with the Visual Studio Properties Window for having them available in the same directory as the executables.*

Another Inline element that maps UI elements that have been used in previous chapters is InlineUIContainer. InlineUIContainer enables adding all UIElement objects (for example, a Button) to the document. The following code segment adds an InlineUIContainer with ComboBox, RadioButton, and TextBox elements to the document (the result is shown in Figure 35-5) (code file DocumentsDemos/FlowDocumentsDemo/FlowDocument2.xaml):

```
<Paragraph TextAlignment="Center">
  <Span FontSize="36">
    <Italic>cn|elements</Italic>
  </Span>
  <LineBreak />
  <LineBreak />
  <InlineUIContainer>
    <Grid>
      <Grid.RowDefinitions>
        <RowDefinition />
        <RowDefinition />
      </Grid.RowDefinitions>
      <Grid.ColumnDefinitions>
        <ColumnDefinition />
        <ColumnDefinition />
      </Grid.ColumnDefinitions>
      <ComboBox Width="40" Margin="3" Grid.Row="0">
        <ComboBoxItem Content="Filet Mignon" />
        <ComboBoxItem Content="Rib Eye" />
        <ComboBoxItem Content="Sirloin" />
      </ComboBox>
      <StackPanel Grid.Row="0" Grid.RowSpan="2" Grid.Column="1">
        <RadioButton Content="Raw" />
        <RadioButton Content="Medium" />
        <RadioButton Content="Well done" />
      </StackPanel>
      <TextBox Grid.Row="1" Grid.Column="0" Width="140" />
    </Grid>
  </InlineUIContainer>
</Paragraph>
```

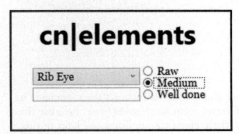

FIGURE 35-5

Block

Block is an abstract base class for block-level elements. Blocks enable grouping elements contained to specific views. Common to all blocks are the properties PreviousBlock, NextBlock, and SiblingBlocks that enable you to navigate from block to block. Setting BreakPageBefore and BreakColumnBefore page and column breaks are done before the block starts. A Block also defines a border with the BorderBrush and BorderThickness properties.

Classes that derive from Block are Paragraph, Section, List, Table, and BlockUIContainer. BlockUIContainer is similar to InlineUIContainer in that you can add elements that derive from UIElement.

Paragraph and Section are simple blocks; Paragraph contains inline elements, and Section is used to group other Block elements. With the Paragraph block you can determine whether a page or column break is allowed within the paragraph or between paragraphs. You can use KeepTogether to disallow breaking within the paragraph; KeepWithNext tries to keep one paragraph and the next together. If a paragraph is broken by a page or column break, MinWidowLines defines the minimum number of lines that are placed after the break; MinOrphanLines defines the minimum number of lines before the break.

The Paragraph block also enables decorating the text within the paragraph with TextDecoration elements. Predefined text decorations are defined by TextDecorations: Baseline, Overline, Strikethrough, and Underline.

The following XAML code shows multiple Paragraph elements. One Paragraph element with a title follows another with the content belonging to this title. These two paragraphs are connected with the attribute KeepWithNext. It's also assured that the paragraph with the content is not broken by setting KeepTogether to True (code file DocumentsDemos/FlowDocumentsDemo/ParagraphDemo.xaml):

```xaml
<FlowDocument xmlns="http://schemas.microsoft.com/winfx/2006/xaml/presentation"
    ColumnWidth="300" FontSize="16" FontFamily="Segoe UI" ColumnRuleWidth="3"
    ColumnRuleBrush="Violet">
    <Paragraph FontSize="36">
        <Run>Lyrics</Run>
    </Paragraph>
    <Paragraph TextIndent="10" FontSize="24" KeepWithNext="True">
        <Bold>
            <Run>Mary had a little lamb</Run>
        </Bold>
    </Paragraph>
    <Paragraph KeepTogether="True">
        <Run>Mary had a little lamb,</Run>
        <LineBreak />
        <Run>little lamb, little lamb,</Run>
        <LineBreak />
        <Run>Mary had a little lamb,</Run>
        <LineBreak />
        <Run>whose fleece was white as snow.</Run>
        <LineBreak />
        <Run>And everywhere that Mary went,</Run>
        <LineBreak />
        <Run>Mary went, Mary went,</Run>
        <LineBreak />
        <Run>and everywhere that Mary went,</Run>
        <LineBreak />
        <Run>the lamb was sure to go.</Run>
    </Paragraph>
    <Paragraph TextIndent="10" FontSize="24" KeepWithNext="True">
        <Bold>
            <Run>Humpty Dumpty</Run>
        </Bold>
    </Paragraph>
    <Paragraph KeepTogether="True">
        <Run>Humpty dumpty sat on a wall</Run>
        <LineBreak />
        <Run>Humpty dumpty had a great fall</Run>
        <LineBreak />
        <Run>All the King's horses</Run>
        <LineBreak />
        <Run>And all the King's men</Run>
        <LineBreak />
        <Run>Couldn't put Humpty together again</Run>
    </Paragraph>
</FlowDocument>
```

The result is shown in Figure 35-6.

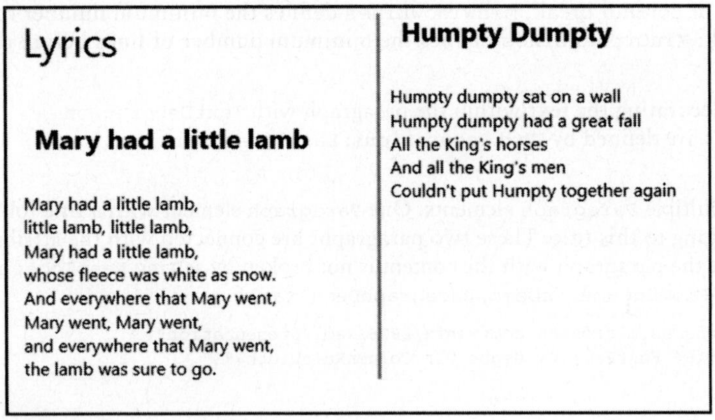

FIGURE 35-6

Lists

The `List` class is used to create textual unordered or ordered lists. `List` defines the bullet style of its items by setting the `MarkerStyle` property. `MarkerStyle` is of type `TextMarkerStyle` and can be a number (`Decimal`), a letter (`LowerLatin` and `UpperLatin`), a roman numeral (`LowerRoman` and `UpperRoman`), or a graphic (`Disc`, `Circle`, `Square`, `Box`). `List` can only contain `ListItem` elements, which in turn can only contain `Block` elements.

Defining the following list with XAML results in the output shown in Figure 35-7 (code file `DocumentsDemos/FlowDocumentsDemo/ListDemo.xaml`):

```
<List MarkerStyle="Square">
  <ListItem>
    <Paragraph>Monday</Paragraph>
  </ListItem>
  <ListItem>
    <Paragraph>Tuesday</Paragraph>
  </ListItem>
  <ListItem>
    <Paragraph>Wednesday</Paragraph>
  </ListItem>
</List>
```

FIGURE 35-7

Tables

The `Table` class is very similar to the `Grid` class that defines rows and columns (see Chapter 34, "Windows Desktop Applications with WPF"). The following example demonstrates creating a `FlowDocument` with a

`Table`. The table is now created programmatically, and the XAML file contains the `FlowDocumentReader` (code file `DocumentsDemos/TableDemo/MainWindow.xaml`):

```
<Window x:Class="TableDemo.MainWindow"
        xmlns="http://schemas.microsoft.com/winfx/2006/xaml/presentation"
        xmlns:x="http://schemas.microsoft.com/winfx/2006/xaml"
        Title="Table Demo" Height="350" Width="525">
  <FlowDocumentReader x:Name="reader" />
</Window>
```

The data that is shown in the table is returned from the property `F1Results` (code file `DocumentsDemos/TableDemo/MainWindow.xaml.cs`):

```
private string[][] F1Results =>
  new string[][]
  {
    new string[] { "1.", "Lewis Hamilton", "384" },
    new string[] { "2.", "Nico Rosberg", "317" },
    new string[] { "3.", "David Riccardio", "238" },
    new string[] { "4.", "Valtteri Botas", "186" },
    new string[] { "5.", "Sebastian Vettel", "167"}
  };
```

To create tables, you can add `TableColumn` objects to the `Columns` property. With `TableColumn` you can specify the width and background.

The `Table` also contains `TableRowGroup` objects. The `TableRowGroup` has a `Rows` property whereby `TableRow` objects can be added. The `TableRow` class defines a `Cells` property that enables adding `TableCell` objects. `TableCell` objects can contain any `Block` element. Here, a `Paragraph` is used that contains the `Inline` element `Run`:

```
var doc = new FlowDocument();
var t1 = new Table();
t1.Columns.Add(new TableColumn
{
  Width = new GridLength(50, GridUnitType.Pixel)
});
t1.Columns.Add(new TableColumn
{
  Width = new GridLength(1, GridUnitType.Auto)
});
t1.Columns.Add(new TableColumn
{
  Width = new GridLength(1, GridUnitType.Auto)
});

var titleRow = new TableRow { Background = Brushes.LightBlue };
var titleCell = new TableCell
{
  ColumnSpan = 3, TextAlignment = TextAlignment.Center
};
titleCell.Blocks.Add(
  new Paragraph(new Run("Formula 1 Championship 2014")
  {
    FontSize=24, FontWeight = FontWeights.Bold
  }));
titleRow.Cells.Add(titleCell);

var headerRow = new TableRow
{
  Background = Brushes.LightGoldenrodYellow
};
headerRow.Cells.Add(
```

```
        new TableCell(new Paragraph(new Run("Pos"))
        {
          FontSize = 14,
          FontWeight=FontWeights.Bold
        }));
    headerRow.Cells.Add(new TableCell(new Paragraph(new Run("Name"))
        {
          FontSize = 14, FontWeight = FontWeights.Bold
        }));
  headerRow.Cells.Add(
    new TableCell(new Paragraph(new Run("Points"))
        {
          FontSize = 14, FontWeight = FontWeights.Bold
        }));
  var rowGroup = new TableRowGroup();
  rowGroup.Rows.Add(titleRow);
  rowGroup.Rows.Add(headerRow);

  List<TableRow> rows = F1Results.Select(row =>
  {
    var tr = new TableRow();
    foreach (var cell in row)
    {
      tr.Cells.Add(new TableCell(new Paragraph(new Run(cell))));
    }
    return tr;
  }).ToList();
  rows.ForEach(r => rowGroup.Rows.Add(r));
  t1.RowGroups.Add(rowGroup);
  doc.Blocks.Add(t1);
  reader.Document = doc;
```

When you run the application, you can see the nicely formatted table as shown in Figure 35-8.

Formula 1 Championship 2014		
Pos	Name	Points
1.	Lewis Hamilton	384
2.	Nico Rosberg	317
3.	David Riccardio	238
4.	Valtteri Botas	186
5.	Sebastian Vettel	167

FIGURE 35-8

Anchor to Blocks

Now that you've learned about the `Inline` and `Block` elements, you can combine the two by using the `Inline` elements of type `AnchoredBlock`. `AnchoredBlock` is an abstract base class with two concrete implementations: `Figure` and `Floater`.

The `Floater` displays its content parallel to the main content with the properties `HorizontalAlignment` and `Width`.

Starting with the earlier example, a new paragraph is added that contains a `Floater`. This `Floater` is aligned to the left and has a width of 120. As shown in Figure 35-9, the next paragraph flows around it (code file `DocumentsDemos/FlowDocumentsDemo/ParagraphKeepTogether.xaml`):

```xml
<Paragraph TextIndent="10" FontSize="24" KeepWithNext="True">
  <Bold>
    <Run>Mary had a little lamb</Run>
  </Bold>
</Paragraph>
<Paragraph>
  <Floater HorizontalAlignment="Left" Width="120">
    <Paragraph Background="LightGray">
      <Run>Sarah Josepha Hale</Run>
    </Paragraph>
  </Floater>
</Paragraph>
<Paragraph KeepTogether="True">
  <Run>Mary had a little lamb</Run>
  <LineBreak />
  <!--...-->
</Paragraph>
```

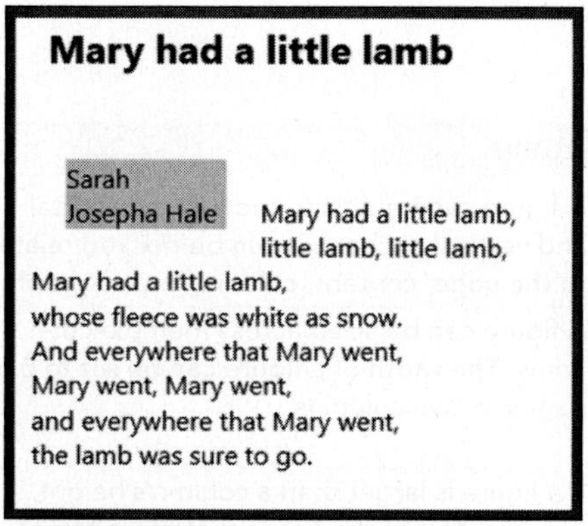

Mary had a little lamb

Sarah Josepha Hale   Mary had a little lamb,
little lamb, little lamb,
Mary had a little lamb,
whose fleece was white as snow.
And everywhere that Mary went,
Mary went, Mary went,
and everywhere that Mary went,
the lamb was sure to go.

FIGURE 35-9

A `Figure` aligns horizontally and vertically and can be anchored to the page, content, a column, or a paragraph. The `Figure` in the following code is anchored to the page center but with a horizontal and vertical offset. The `WrapDirection` is set so that both left and right columns wrap around the figure. Figure 35-10 shows the result of the wrap (code file `DocumentsDemos/FlowDocumentsDemo/FigureAlignment.xaml`):

```xml
<Paragraph>
  <Figure HorizontalAnchor="PageCenter" HorizontalOffset="20"
    VerticalAnchor="PageCenter" VerticalOffset="20" WrapDirection="Both" >
    <Paragraph Background="LightGray" FontSize="24">
      <Run>Lyrics Samples</Run>
    </Paragraph>
  </Figure>
</Paragraph>
```

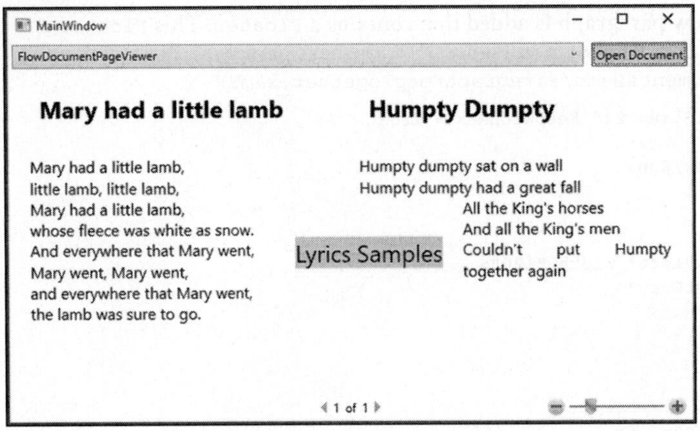

FIGURE 35-10

`Floater` and `Figure` are both used to add content that is not in the main flow. Although these two features seem similar, the characteristics of these elements are quite different. The following table explains the differences between `Floater` and `Figure`.

CHARACTERISTIC	FLOATER	FIGURE
Position	A floater cannot be positioned. It is rendered where space is available.	A figure can be positioned with horizontal and vertical anchors. It can be docked relative to the page, content, column, or paragraph.
Width	A floater can be placed only within one column. If the width is set larger than the column's size, it is ignored.	A figure can be sized across multiple columns. The width of a figure can be set to 0.5 pages or two columns.
Pagination	If a floater is larger than a column's height, the floater breaks and paginates to the next column or page.	If a figure is larger than a column's height, only the part of the figure that fits in the column is rendered; the other content is lost.

FLOW DOCUMENTS

With all the `Inline` and `Block` elements, now you know what should be put into a flow document. The class `FlowDocument` can contain `Block` elements, and the `Block` elements can contain `Block` or `Inline` elements, depending on the type of the `Block`.

A major functionality of the `FlowDocument` class is that it is used to break up the flow into multiple pages. This is done via the `IDocumentPaginatorSource` interface, which is implemented by `FlowDocument`.

Other options with a `FlowDocument` are to set up the default font and foreground and background brushes, and to configure the page and column sizes.

The following XAML code for the `FlowDocument` defines a default font and font size, a column width, and a ruler between columns:

```
<FlowDocument xmlns="http://schemas.microsoft.com/winfx/2006/xaml/presentation"
  ColumnWidth="300" FontSize="16" FontFamily="Segoe UI"
  ColumnRuleWidth="3" ColumnRuleBrush="Violet">
```

Now you just need a way to view the documents. The following list describes several viewers:

➤ `RichTextBox`—A simple viewer that also allows editing (as long as the `IsReadOnly` property is not set to `true`). The `RichTextBox` doesn't display the document with multiple columns but instead in scroll mode. This is similar to the Web layout in Microsoft Word. The scrollbar can be enabled by setting the `HorizontalScrollbarVisibility` to `ScrollbarVisibility.Auto`.

➤ `FlowDocumentScrollViewer`—A reader that is meant only to read but not edit documents. This reader enables zooming into the document. There's also a toolbar with a slider for zooming that can be enabled with the property `IsToolbarEnabled`. Settings such as `CanIncreaseZoom`, `CanDecreaseZoom`, `MinZoom`, and `MaxZoom` enable setting the zoom features.

➤ `FlowDocumentPageViewer`—A viewer that paginates the document. With this viewer you not only have a toolbar to zoom into the document, you can also switch from page to page.

➤ `FlowDocumentReader`—A viewer that combines the functionality of `FlowDocumentScrollViewer` and `FlowDocumentPageViewer`. This viewer supports different viewing modes that can be set from the toolbar or with the property `ViewingMode` that is of type `FlowDocumentReaderViewingMode`. This enumeration has the possible values `Page`, `TwoPage`, and `Scroll`. You can also disable the viewing modes according to your needs.

The sample application to demonstrate flow documents defines several readers such that one reader can be chosen dynamically. Within the `Grid` element you can find the `FlowDocumentReader`, `RichTextBox`, `FlowDocumentScrollViewer`, and `FlowDocumentPageViewer`. With all the readers the `Visibility` property is set to `Collapsed`, so on startup none of the readers appear. The `ComboBox` that is the first child element within the grid enables the user to select the active reader. The `ItemsSource` property of the `ComboBox` is bound to the `Readers` property to display the list of readers. On selection of a reader, the method `OnReaderSelectionChanged` is invoked (code file `DocumentsDemos/FlowDocumentsDemo/MainWindow.xaml`):

```xml
<Grid x:Name="grid1">
  <Grid.RowDefinitions>
    <RowDefinition Height="Auto" />
    <RowDefinition Height="*" />
  </Grid.RowDefinitions>
  <Grid.ColumnDefinitions>
    <ColumnDefinition Width="*" />
    <ColumnDefinition Width="Auto" />
  </Grid.ColumnDefinitions>
  <ComboBox ItemsSource="{Binding Readers}" Grid.Row="0" Grid.Column="0"
    Margin="4" SelectionChanged="OnReaderSelectionChanged"
    SelectedIndex="0">
    <ComboBox.ItemTemplate>
      <DataTemplate>
        <StackPanel>
          <TextBlock Text="{Binding Name}" />
        </StackPanel>
      </DataTemplate>
    </ComboBox.ItemTemplate>
  </ComboBox>
  <Button Grid.Column="1" Margin="4" Padding="3" Click="OnOpenDocument">
    Open Document
  </Button>
  <FlowDocumentReader ViewingMode="TwoPage" Grid.Row="1"
    Visibility="Collapsed" Grid.ColumnSpan="2" />
  <RichTextBox IsDocumentEnabled="True" HorizontalScrollBarVisibility="Auto"
    VerticalScrollBarVisibility="Auto" Visibility="Collapsed"
    Grid.Row="1" Grid.ColumnSpan="2" />
  <FlowDocumentScrollViewer Visibility="Collapsed" Grid.Row="1"
    Grid.ColumnSpan="2" />
  <FlowDocumentPageViewer Visibility="Collapsed" Grid.Row="1"
    Grid.ColumnSpan="2" />
</Grid>
```

The `Readers` property of the `MainWindow` class invokes the `GetReaders` method to return the readers to the `ComboBox` data binding. The `GetReaders` method returns the list assigned to the variable `documentReaders`. In case `documentReaders` was not yet assigned, the `LogicalTreeHelper` class is used to get all the flow document readers within the grid `grid1`. As there is not a base class for a flow document reader nor an interface implemented by all readers, the `LogialTreeHelper` looks for all elements of type `FrameworkElement` that have a property `Document`. The `Document` property is common to all flow document readers. With every reader a new anonymous object is created with the properties `Name` and `Instance`. The `Name` property is used to appear in the `ComboBox` to enable the user to select the active reader, and the `Instance` property holds a reference to the reader to show the reader if it should be active (code file `DocumentsDemos/FlowDocumentsDemo/MainWindow.xaml.cs`):

```
public IEnumerable<object> Readers => GetReaders();

private List<object> _documentReaders = null;
private IEnumerable<object> GetReaders()
{
  return _documentReaders ??
    (
      _documentReaders =
        LogicalTreeHelper.GetChildren(grid1).OfType<FrameworkElement>()
          .Where(el => el.GetType().GetProperties()
          .Where(pi => pi.Name == "Document").Count() > 0)
          .Select(el => new
          {
            Name = el.GetType().Name,
            Instance = el
          }).Cast<object>().ToList());
  }
}
```

> **NOTE** *The coalescing operator (??) used with the* `GetReaders` *method is explained in detail in Chapter 8, "Operators and Casts."*

> **NOTE** *The sample code makes use of the* dynamic *keyword—the variable* `activeDocumentReader` *is declared as* dynamic *type. The* dynamic *keyword is used because the* `SelectedItem` *from the* `ComboBox` *returns either a* `FlowDocumentReader`, *a* `FlowDocumentScrollViewer`, *a* `FlowDocumentPageViewer`, *or a* `RichTextBox`. *All these types are flow document readers that offer a* Document *property of type* `FlowDocument`. *However, there's no common base class or interface defining this property. The* dynamic *keyword allows accessing these different types from the same variable and using the* Document *property. The* dynamic *keyword is explained in detail in Chapter 16, "Reflection, Metadata, and Dynamic Programming."*

When the user selects a flow document reader, the method `OnReaderSelectionChanged` is invoked. The XAML code that references this method was shown earlier. Within this method the previously selected flow document reader is made invisible by setting it to collapsed, and the variable `activeDocumentReader` is set to the selected reader:

```
private void OnReaderSelectionChanged(object sender,
                                      SelectionChangedEventArgs e)
{
  dynamic item = (sender as ComboBox).SelectedItem;
  if (_activedocumentReader != null)
  {
    _activedocumentReader.Visibility = Visibility.Collapsed;
  }
  _activedocumentReader = item.Instance;
}
```

```
private dynamic _activedocumentReader = null;
```

When the user clicks the button to open a document, the method OnOpenDocument is invoked. With this method the XamlReader class is used to load the selected XAML file. If the reader returns a FlowDocument (which is the case when the root element of the XAML is the FlowDocument element), the Document property of the activeDocumentReader is assigned, and the Visibility is set to visible:

```
private void OnOpenDocument(object sender, RoutedEventArgs e)
{
  try
  {
    var dlg = new OpenFileDialog();
    dlg.DefaultExt = "*.xaml";
    dlg.InitialDirectory = Environment.CurrentDirectory;
    if (dlg.ShowDialog() == true)
    {
      using (FileStream xamlFile = File.OpenRead(dlg.FileName))
      {
        var doc = XamlReader.Load(xamlFile) as FlowDocument;
        if (doc != null)
        {
          _activedocumentReader.Document = doc;
          _activedocumentReader.Visibility = Visibility.Visible;
        }
      }
    }
  }
  catch (XamlParseException ex)
  {
    MessageBox.Show($"Check content for a Flow document: {ex.Message}");
  }
}
```

The running application is shown in Figure 35-11. This figure shows a flow document with the FlowDocumentReader in TwoPage mode.

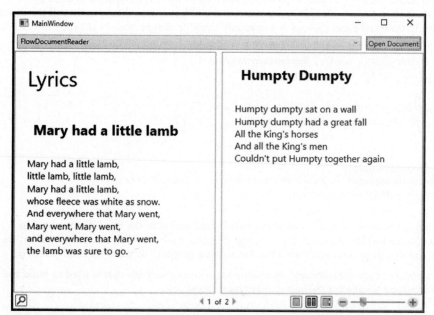

FIGURE 35-11

FIXED DOCUMENTS

Fixed documents always define the same look, the same pagination, and the same fonts—no matter where the document is copied or used. WPF defines the class `FixedDocument` to create fixed documents, and the class `DocumentViewer` to view fixed documents.

This section uses a sample application to create a fixed document programmatically by requesting user input for a menu plan. The data for the menu plan is the content of the fixed document. Figure 35-12 shows the main user interface of this application, where the user can select a day with the `DatePicker` class, enter menus for a week in a `DataGrid`, and click the Create Doc button to create a new `FixedDocument`. This application uses `Page` objects that are navigated within a `NavigationWindow`. Clicking the Create Doc button navigates to a new page that contains the fixed document.

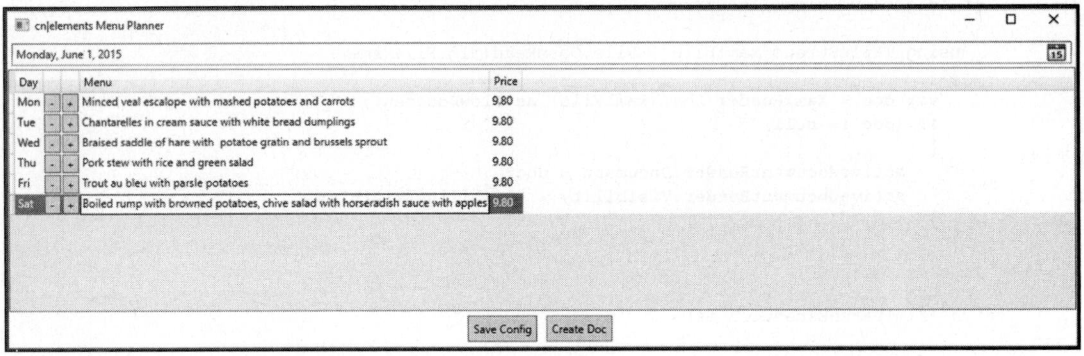

FIGURE 35-12

The event handler for the Create Doc button, `OnCreateDoc`, navigates to a new page. To do this, the handler instantiates the new page: `DocumentPage`. This page includes a handler—`NavigationService_LoadCompleted`—that is assigned to the `LoadCompleted` event of the `NavigationService`. Within this handler the new page can access the content that is passed to the page. Then the navigation is done by invoking the `Navigate` method to page2. The new page receives the object menus that contains all the menu information needed to build the fixed page. `_menus` is a readonly variable of type `ObservableCollection< MenuEntry>` (code file `CreateXps/CreateXps/MenuPlannerPage.xaml.cs`):

```
private void OnCreateDoc(object sender, RoutedEventArgs e)
{
  if (_menus.Count == 0)
  {
    MessageBox.Show("Select a date first", "Menu Planner",
                  MessageBoxButton.OK);
    return;
  }

  var page2 = new DocumentPage();
  NavigationService.LoadCompleted += page2.NavigationService_LoadCompleted;
  NavigationService.Navigate(page2, _menus);
}
```

Within the `DocumentPage`, a `DocumentViewer` is used to provide read access to the fixed document. The fixed document is created in the method `NavigationService_LoadCompleted`. With the event handler, the data that is passed from the first page is received with the `ExtraData` property of `NavigationEventArgs`.

The received `ObservableCollection<MenuEntry>` is assigned to a menus variable that is used to build the fixed page (code file `CreateXps/CreateXps/MenuDocumentPage.xaml.cs`):

```
internal void NavigationService_LoadCompleted(object sender,
  NavigationEventArgs e)
{
  _menus = e.ExtraData as ObservableCollection<MenuEntry>;

  _fixedDocument = new FixedDocument();
  var pageContent1 = new PageContent();
  _fixedDocument.Pages.Add(pageContent1);
  var page1 = new FixedPage();
  pageContent1.Child = page1;
  page1.Children.Add(GetHeaderContent());
  page1.Children.Add(GetLogoContent());
  page1.Children.Add(GetDateContent());
  page1.Children.Add(GetMenuContent());

  viewer.Document = _fixedDocument;

  NavigationService.LoadCompleted -= NavigationService_LoadCompleted;
}
```

Fixed documents are created with the `FixedDocument` class. The `FixedDocument` element only contains `PageContent` elements that are accessible via the `Pages` property. The `PageContent` elements must be added to the document in the order in which they should appear on the page. `PageContent` defines the content of a single page.

`PageContent` has a `Child` property such that a `FixedPage` can be associated with it. To the `FixedPage` you can add elements of type `UIElement` to the `Children` collection. This is where you can add all the elements you've learned about in the last two chapters, including a `TextBlock` element that itself can contain `Inline` and `Block` elements.

In the sample code, the children to the `FixedPage` are created with helper methods `GetHeaderContent`, `GetLogoContent`, `GetDateContent`, and `GetMenuContent`.

The method `GetHeaderContent` creates a `TextBlock` that is returned. The `TextBlock` has the `Inline` element `Bold` added, which in turn has the `Run` element added. The `Run` element then contains the header text for the document. With `FixedPage.SetLeft` and `FixedPage.SetTop` the position of the `TextBox` within the fixed page is defined:

```
private static UIElement GetHeaderContent()
{
  var text1 = new TextBlock
  {
    FontFamily = new FontFamily("Segoe UI"),
    FontSize = 34,
    HorizontalAlignment = HorizontalAlignment.Center
  };
  text1.Inlines.Add(new Bold(new Run("cn|elements")));
  FixedPage.SetLeft(text1, 170);
  FixedPage.SetTop(text1, 40);
  return text1;
}
```

The method `GetLogoContent` adds a logo in the form of an `Ellipse` with a `RadialGradientBrush` to the fixed document:

```
private static UIElement GetLogoContent()
{
  var ellipse = new Ellipse
  {
    Width = 90,
    Height = 40,
    Fill = new RadialGradientBrush(Colors.Yellow, Colors.DarkRed)
```

```
  };
  FixedPage.SetLeft(ellipse, 500);
  FixedPage.SetTop(ellipse, 50);
  return ellipse;
}
```

The method `GetDateContent` accesses the `menus` collection to add a date range to the document:

```
private UIElement GetDateContent()
{
  string dateString = $"{menus[0].Day:d} to {menus[menus.Count - 1].Day:d}";
  var text1 = new TextBlock
  {
    FontSize = 24,
    HorizontalAlignment = HorizontalAlignment.Center
  };
  text1.Inlines.Add(new Bold(new Run(dateString)));
  FixedPage.SetLeft(text1, 130);
  FixedPage.SetTop(text1, 90);
  return text1;
}
```

Finally, the method `GetMenuContent` creates and returns a `Grid` control. This grid contains columns and rows that contain the date, menu, and price information:

```
private UIElement GetMenuContent()
{
  var grid1 = new Grid
  {
    ShowGridLines = true
  };

  grid1.ColumnDefinitions.Add(new ColumnDefinition
  {
    Width= new GridLength(50)
  });
  grid1.ColumnDefinitions.Add(new ColumnDefinition
  {
    Width = new GridLength(300)
  });
  grid1.ColumnDefinitions.Add(new ColumnDefinition
  {
    Width = new GridLength(70)
  });
  for (int i = 0; i < _menus.Count; i++)
  {
    grid1.RowDefinitions.Add(new RowDefinition
    {
        Height = new GridLength(40)
    });
    var t1 = new TextBlock(new Run($"{_menus[i].Day:ddd}"));
    var t2 = new TextBlock(new Run(_menus[i].Menu));
    var t3 = new TextBlock(new Run(_menus[i].Price.ToString()));
    var textBlocks = new TextBlock[] { t1, t2, t3 };

    for (int column = 0; column < textBlocks.Length; column++)
    {
      textBlocks[column].VerticalAlignment = VerticalAlignment.Center;
      textBlocks[column].Margin = new Thickness(5, 2, 5, 2);
      Grid.SetColumn(textBlocks[column], column);
      Grid.SetRow(textBlocks[column], i);
      grid1.Children.Add(textBlocks[column]);
    }
```

```
    }
    FixedPage.SetLeft(grid1, 100);
    FixedPage.SetTop(grid1, 140);
    return grid1;
}
```

Run the application to see the created fixed document shown in Figure 35-13.

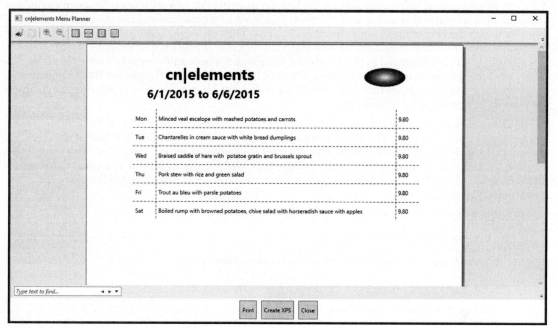

FIGURE 35-13

XPS DOCUMENTS

With Microsoft Word you can save a document as a PDF or an XPS file. XPS is the *XML Paper Specification*, a subset of WPF. Windows includes an XPS reader.

.NET includes classes and interfaces to read and write XPS documents with the namespaces System .Windows.Xps, System.Windows.Xps.Packaging, and System.IO.Packaging.

XPS is packaged in the zip file format, so you can easily analyze an XPS document by renaming a file with an .xps extension to .zip and opening the archive.

An XPS file requires a specific structure in the zipped document that is defined by the XML Paper Specifications (which you can download from http://www.microsoft.com/whdc/xps/xpsspec.mspx). The structure is based on the Open Packaging Convention (OPC) that Word documents (OOXML or Office Open XML) are based on as well. Within such a file you can find different folders for metadata, resources (such as fonts and pictures), and the document itself. Within the document folder of an XPS document is the XAML code representing the XPS subset of XAML.

To create an XPS document, you use the XpsDocument class from the namespace System.Windows.Xps. Packaging. To use this class, you need to reference the assembly ReachFramework as well. With this class you can add a thumbnail (`AddThumbnail`) and fixed document sequences (`AddFixedDocumentSequence`) to the document, as well as digitally sign the document. A fixed document sequence is written by using the interface `IXpsFixedDocumentSequenceWriter`, which in turn uses an `IXpsFixedDocumentWriter` to write the document within the sequence.

If a `FixedDocument` already exists, there's an easier way to write the XPS document. Instead of adding every resource and every document page, you can use the class `XpsDocumentWriter` from the namespace `System.Windows.Xps`. For this class the assembly `System.Printing` must be referenced.

With the following code snippet you can see the handler to create the XPS document. First, a filename for the menu plan is created that uses a week number in addition to the name `menuplan`. The week number is calculated with the help of the `GregorianCalendar` class. Then the `SaveFileDialog` is opened to enable the user to overwrite the created filename and select the directory where the file should be stored. The `SaveFileDialog` class is defined in the namespace `Microsoft.Win32` and wraps the native file dialog. Then a new `XpsDocument` is created whose filename is passed to the constructor. Recall that the XPS file uses a `.zip` format to compress the content. With the `CompressionOption` you can specify whether the compression should be optimized for time or space.

Next, an `XpsDocumentWriter` is created with the help of the static method `XpsDocument.CreateXpsDocumentWriter`. The `Write` method of the `XpsDocumentWriter` is overloaded to accept different content or content parts to write the document. Examples of acceptable options with the `Write` method are `FixedDocumentSequence`, `FixedDocument`, `FixedPage`, `string`, and a `DocumentPaginator`. In the sample code, only the `fixedDocument` that was created earlier is passed (code file CreateXps/CreateXps/MenuDocumentPage.xaml.cs):

```
private void OnCreateXPS(object sender, RoutedEventArgs e)
{
  var c = new GregorianCalendar();
  int weekNumber = c.GetWeekOfYear(_menus[0].Day,
    CalendarWeekRule.FirstFourDayWeek, DayOfWeek.Monday);

  var dlg = new SaveFileDialog
  {
    FileName = $"menuplan{weekNumber}",
    DefaultExt = "xps",
    Filter = "XPS Documents|*.xps|All Files|*.*",
    AddExtension = true
  };
  if (dlg.ShowDialog() == true)
  {
    var doc = new XpsDocument(dlg.FileName, FileAccess.Write,
              CompressionOption.Fast);
    XpsDocumentWriter writer = XpsDocument.CreateXpsDocumentWriter(doc);
    writer.Write(fixedDocument);
    doc.Close();
  }
}
```

By running the application to store the XPS document, you can view the document with an XPS viewer, as shown in Figure 35-14.

To one overload of the `Write` method of the `XpsDocumentWriter` you can also pass a `Visual`, which is the base class of `UIElement`, and thus you can pass any `UIElement` to the writer to create an XPS document easily. This functionality is used in the following printing example.

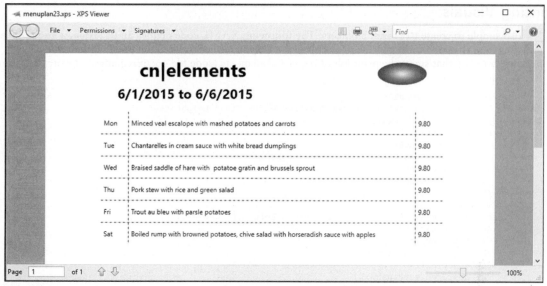

FIGURE 35-14

PRINTING

The simplest way to print a `FixedDocument` that is shown onscreen with the `DocumentViewer` is to invoke the `Print` method of the `DocumentViewer` with which the document is associated. This is all that needs to be done with the menu planner application in an `OnPrint` handler. The `Print` method of the `DocumentViewer` opens the `PrintDialog` and sends the associated `FixedDocument` to the selected printer (code file `CreateXps/CerateXpsDocumentPage.xaml.cs`):

```
private void OnPrint(object sender, RoutedEventArgs e)
{
  viewer.Print();
}
```

Printing with the PrintDialog

If you want more control over the printing process, the `PrintDialog` can be instantiated, and the document printed with the `PrintDocument` method. The `PrintDocument` method requires a `DocumentPaginator` with the first argument. The `FixedDocument` returns a `DocumentPaginator` object with the `DocumentPaginator` property. The second argument defines the string that appears with the current printer and in the printer dialogs for the print job:

```
var dlg = new PrintDialog();
if (dlg.ShowDialog() == true)
{
  dlg.PrintDocument(fixedDocument.DocumentPaginator, "Menu Plan");
}
```

Printing Visuals

It's also simple to create `UIElement` objects. The following XAML code defines an `Ellipse`, a `Rectangle`, and a `Button` that is visually represented with two `Ellipse` elements. With the `Button`, there's a `Click` handler `OnPrint` that starts the print job of the visual elements (code file `DocumentsDemo/PrintingDemo/MainWindow.xaml`):

```xaml
<Canvas x:Name="canvas1">
  <Ellipse Canvas.Left="10" Canvas.Top="20" Width="180" Height="60"
    Stroke="Red" StrokeThickness="3" >
    <Ellipse.Fill>
      <RadialGradientBrush>
        <GradientStop Offset="0" Color="LightBlue" />
        <GradientStop Offset="1" Color="DarkBlue" />
      </RadialGradientBrush>
    </Ellipse.Fill>
  </Ellipse>
  <Rectangle Width="180" Height="90" Canvas.Left="50" Canvas.Top="50">
    <Rectangle.LayoutTransform>
      <RotateTransform Angle="30" />
    </Rectangle.LayoutTransform>
    <Rectangle.Fill>
      <LinearGradientBrush>
        <GradientStop Offset="0" Color="Aquamarine" />
        <GradientStop Offset="1" Color="ForestGreen" />
      </LinearGradientBrush>
    </Rectangle.Fill>
    <Rectangle.Stroke>
      <LinearGradientBrush>
        <GradientStop Offset="0" Color="LawnGreen" />
        <GradientStop Offset="1" Color="SeaGreen" />
      </LinearGradientBrush>
    </Rectangle.Stroke>
  </Rectangle>
  <Button Canvas.Left="90" Canvas.Top="190" Content="Print" Click="OnPrint">
    <Button.Template>
      <ControlTemplate TargetType="Button">
        <Grid>
          <Grid.RowDefinitions>
            <RowDefinition />
            <RowDefinition />
          </Grid.RowDefinitions>
          <Ellipse Grid.Row="0" Grid.RowSpan="2" Width="60"
            Height="40" Fill="Yellow" />
          <Ellipse Grid.Row="0" Width="52" Height="20"
            HorizontalAlignment="Center">
            <Ellipse.Fill>
              <LinearGradientBrush StartPoint="0.5,0" EndPoint="0.5,1">
                <GradientStop Color="White" Offset="0" />
                <GradientStop Color="Transparent" Offset="0.9" />
              </LinearGradientBrush>
            </Ellipse.Fill>
          </Ellipse>
          <ContentPresenter Grid.Row="0" Grid.RowSpan="2"
            HorizontalAlignment="Center"
            VerticalAlignment="Center" />
        </Grid>
      </ControlTemplate>
    </Button.Template>
  </Button>
</Canvas>
```

In the `OnPrint` handler, the print job can be started by invoking the `PrintVisual` method of the `PrintDialog`. `PrintVisual` accepts any object that derives from the base class `Visual` (code file `PrintingDemo/MainWindow.xaml.cs`):

```
private void OnPrint(object sender, RoutedEventArgs e)
{
  var dlg = new PrintDialog();
  if (dlg.ShowDialog() == true)
  {
    dlg.PrintVisual(canvas1, "Print Demo");
  }
}
```

To programmatically print without user intervention, the `PrintDialog` classes from the namespace `System.Printing` can be used to create a print job and adjust print settings. The class `LocalPrintServer` provides information about print queues and returns the default `PrintQueue` with the `DefaultPrintQueue` property. You can configure the print job with a `PrintTicket`. `PrintQueue.DefaultPrintTicket` returns a default `PrintTicket` that is associated with the queue. The `PrintQueue` method `GetPrintCapabilities` returns the capabilities of a printer, and, depending on those, you can configure the `PrintTicket` as shown in the following code segment. After configuration of the print ticket is complete, the static method `PrintQueue.CreateXpsDocumentWriter` returns an `XpsDocumentWriter` object. The `XpsDocumentWriter` class was used previously to create an XPS document. You can also use it to start a print job. The `Write` method of the `XpsDocumentWriter` accepts not only a `Visual` or `FixedDocument` as the first argument but also a `PrintTicket` as the second argument. If a `PrintTicket` is passed with the second argument, the target of the writer is the printer associated with the ticket and thus the writer sends the print job to the printer:

```
var printServer = new LocalPrintServer();
PrintQueue queue = printServer.DefaultPrintQueue;
PrintTicket ticket = queue.DefaultPrintTicket;
PrintCapabilities capabilities = queue.GetPrintCapabilities(ticket);
if (capabilities.DuplexingCapability.Contains(Duplexing.TwoSidedLongEdge))
  ticket.Duplexing = Duplexing.TwoSidedLongEdge;
if (capabilities.InputBinCapability.Contains(InputBin.AutoSelect))
  ticket.InputBin = InputBin.AutoSelect;
if (capabilities.MaxCopyCount > 3)
  ticket.CopyCount = 3;
if (capabilities.PageOrientationCapability.Contains(PageOrientation.Landscape))
  ticket.PageOrientation = PageOrientation.Landscape;
if (capabilities.PagesPerSheetCapability.Contains(2))
  ticket.PagesPerSheet = 2;
if (capabilities.StaplingCapability.Contains(Stapling.StapleBottomLeft))
  ticket.Stapling = Stapling.StapleBottomLeft;
XpsDocumentWriter writer = PrintQueue.CreateXpsDocumentWriter(queue);
writer.Write(canvas1, ticket);
```

SUMMARY

In this chapter you learned how WPF capabilities can be used with documents, and how to create flow documents that adjust automatically depending on the screen sizes and fixed documents that always look the same. You've also seen how to print documents and how to send visual elements to the printer.

The next chapter concludes the client apps programming section of this book with a discussion about deployment.

36

Deploying Windows Apps

WHAT'S IN THIS CHAPTER?

➤ Deployment requirements
➤ Deployment scenarios
➤ Deployment using ClickOnce
➤ Deployment UWP Apps

WROX.COM CODE DOWNLOADS FOR THIS CHAPTER

The wrox.com code downloads for this chapter are found at www.wrox.com/go/professionalcsharp6 on the Download Code tab. The code for this chapter is found in the following examples:

➤ WPFSampleApp
➤ UniversalWinApp

DEPLOYMENT AS PART OF THE APPLICATION LIFE CYCLE

The development process does not end when the source code is compiled and the testing is complete. At that stage, the job of getting the application into the user's hands begins. Whether it's an ASP.NET application, a WPF client application, or a Universal Windows Platform (UWP) app, the software must be deployed to a target environment.

Deployment should be considered very early in the design of the application, as this can influence the technology to be used for the application itself.

The .NET Framework has made deployment much easier than it was in the past. The pains of registering COM components and writing new hives to the registry have been eliminated.

This chapter looks at the options that are available for application deployment, from both a desktop client application (WPF) and UWP apps.

> **NOTE** *Deployment of Web applications is covered in Chapter 45, "Deploying Websites and Services."*

PLANNING FOR DEPLOYMENT

Often, deployment is an afterthought in the development process that can lead to nasty, if not costly, surprises. To avoid grief in deployment scenarios, you should plan the deployment process during the initial design stage. Any special deployment considerations—such as server capacity, desktop security, or the location from which assemblies will be loaded—should be built into the design from the start, resulting in a much smoother deployment process.

Another issue that you should address early in the development process is the environment in which to test the deployment. Whereas unit testing of application code and deployment options can be done on the developer's system, the deployment must be tested in an environment that resembles the target system. This is important to eliminate the dependencies that don't exist on a targeted computer. An example of this might be a third-party library that has been installed on the developer's computer early in the project. The target computer might not have this library on it. It can be easy to forget to include it in the deployment package. Testing on the developer's system would not uncover the error because the library already exists. Documenting dependencies can help to eliminate this potential problem.

Deployment processes can be complex for a large application. Planning for the deployment can save time and effort when the deployment process is actually implemented.

You must choose the proper deployment option with the same care and planning you use for any other aspect of the system you're developing. Choosing the wrong option makes the process of getting the software into the users' hands difficult and frustrating.

Overview of Deployment Options

This section provides an overview of the deployment options that are available to .NET developers. Most of these options are discussed in greater detail later in this chapter:

➤ **xcopy**—The xcopy utility lets you copy an assembly or group of assemblies to an application folder, reducing your development time. Because assemblies are self-discovering (that is, the metadata that describes the assembly is included in the assembly), you do not need to register anything in the registry.

Each assembly keeps track of what other assemblies it requires to execute. By default, the assembly looks in the current application folder for the dependencies. The process of moving (or probing) assemblies to other folders is discussed later in this chapter.

➤ **ClickOnce**—The ClickOnce technology offers a way to build self-updating Windows-based applications. ClickOnce enables an application to be published to a website, a file share, or even a CD. As updates and new builds are made to the application, they can be published to the same location or site by the development team. As the application is used by the end user, it can automatically check the location to see if an update is available. If so, an update is attempted.

➤ **Windows Installer**—There are some restrictions when ClickOnce doesn't work. If the installation requires administrative privileges (for example, for deploying Windows Services), Windows Installer can be the best option.

➤ **UWP apps**—These apps can be deployed from the Windows Store or by using a command-line tool. Creating packages for Windows Store apps is covered later in this chapter.

Deployment Requirements

It is instructive to look at the runtime requirements of a .NET-based application. The CLR has certain requirements on the target platform before any managed application can execute.

The first requirement that must be met is the operating system. Currently, the following operating systems can run .NET 4.6–based applications:

➤ Windows Vista SP2

➤ Windows 7 SP1

➤ Windows 8 (.NET 4.5 is already included)

➤ Windows 8.1 (.NET 4.5.1 is already included)

➤ Windows 10 (.NET 4.6 is already included)

The following server platforms are supported:

➤ Windows Server 2008 SP2

➤ Windows Server 2008 R2 SP1

➤ Windows Server 2012 (.NET 4.5 is already included)

➤ Windows Server 2012 R2 (.NET 4.5.1 is already included)

Windows Store apps that are created with Visual Studio 2012 run on Windows 8 and 8.1. Windows Store apps created with Visual Studio 2013 run on Windows 8.1.

You also must consider hardware requirements when deploying .NET applications. The minimum hardware requirements for both the client and the server are a CPU with 1GHz and 512MB of RAM.

For best performance, increase the amount of RAM—the more RAM the better your .NET application runs. This is especially true for server applications. You can use the Performance Monitor to analyze the RAM usage of your applications.

Deploying the .NET Runtime

When you're using .NET Core with applications, the application includes the runtime. When you're creating apps using the full framework, the .NET runtime needs to be installed on the target system. With Windows 10, .NET 4.6 is already included.

You can download different versions of the .NET runtime from Microsoft MSDN, https://msdn .microsoft.com/library/ee942965.aspx, either Web installer or Offline installer packages. Either you need to offer installation of the runtime with your installation package, or the runtime needs to have been installed before the app is installed.

TRADITIONAL DEPLOYMENT

If deployment is part of an application's original design considerations, deployment can be as simple as copying a set of files to the target computer. This section discusses simple deployment scenarios and different options for deployment.

To see the first deployment option in action, you must have an application to deploy. At first, the ClientWPF solution is used, which requires the library AppSupport.

ClientWPF is a rich client application using WPF. AppSupport is a class library that contains one simple class that returns a string with the current date and time.

The sample applications use AppSupport to fill a label with a string containing the current date. To use the examples, first load and build AppSupport. Then, in the ClientWPF project, set a reference to the newly built AppSupport.dll.

Here is the code for the AppSupport assembly:

```
using System;
namespace AppSupport
{
  public class DateService
  {
    public string GetLongDateInfoString() =>
      $"Today's date is {DateTime.Today:D}";

    public string GetShortDateInfoString() =>
      $"Today's date is {DateTime.Today:d}";
  }
}
```

This simple assembly suffices to demonstrate the deployment options available to you.

xcopy Deployment

xcopy deployment is a term used for the process of copying a set of files to a folder on the target machine and then executing the application on the client. The term comes from the DOS command xcopy.exe. Regardless of the number of assemblies, if the files are copied into the same folder, the application will execute—rendering the task of editing the configuration settings or registry obsolete.

To see how an xcopy deployment works, execute the following steps:

1. Open the ClientWPF solution (ClientWPF.sln) that is part of the sample download file.

2. Change the target to Release and do a full compile.

3. Use the File Explorer to navigate to the project folder \ClientWPF\bin\Release and double-click ClientWPF.exe to run the application.

4. Click the button to see the current date displayed in the two text boxes. This verifies that the application functions properly. Of course, this folder is where Visual Studio placed the output, so you would expect the application to work.

5. Create a new folder and call it ClientWPFTest. Copy just the two assemblies (AppSupport.dll and ClientWPFTest.exe) from the release folder to this new folder and then delete the release folder. Again, double-click the ClientWPF.exe file to verify that it's working.

That's all there is to it; xcopy deployment provides the capability to deploy a fully functional application simply by copying the assemblies to the target machine. Although the example used here is simple, you can use this process for more complex applications. There really is no limit to the size or number of assemblies that can be deployed using this method.

Scenarios in which you might not want to use xcopy deployment are when you need to place assemblies in the global assembly cache (GAC) or add icons to the Start menu. Also, if your application still relies on a COM library of some type, you will not be able to register the COM components easily.

Windows Installer

ClickOnce is Microsoft's preferred technology for installing Windows applications; it is discussed in more depth later in this chapter. However, ClickOnce has some restrictions. ClickOnce installation doesn't require administrator rights and installs applications in a directory where the user has rights. If multiple users are working on one system, the application needs to be installed for all users. Also, it is not possible to install shared COM components and configure them in the registry, install assemblies to the GAC, and register Windows services. All these tasks require administrative privileges.

To do these administrative tasks, you need to create a Windows installer package. Installer packages are MSI files (which can be started from setup.exe) that make use of the Windows Installer technology.

Creating Windows installer packages is not part of Visual Studio 2015, but you can use InstallShield Limited Edition, which is free, with Visual Studio 2015. A project template includes information for the download and registration with Flexera Software.

InstallShield Limited Edition offers a simple wizard to create an installation package based on application information (name, website, version number); installation requirements (supported operating systems and prerequisite software before the installation can start); application files and their shortcuts on the Start menu and the desktop; and settings for the registry. You can optionally prompt the user for a license agreement.

If this is all that you need, and you don't need to add custom dialogs to the installation experience, InstallShield Limited Edition can provide an adequate deployment solution. Otherwise, you need to install another product such as the full version of InstallShield (www.flexerasoftware.com/products/installshield.htm) or the free WiX toolset (http://wix.codeplex.com).

ClickOnce and deployment of UWP apps are discussed in detail in this chapter. Let's start with ClickOnce.

CLICKONCE

ClickOnce is a deployment technology that enables applications to be self-updating. Applications are published to a file share, a website, or media such as a CD. When published, ClickOnce apps can be automatically updated with minimal user input.

ClickOnce also solves the security permission problem. Normally, to install an application the user needs Administrative rights. With ClickOnce, a user without admin rights can install and run the application. However, the application is installed in a user-specific directory. In case multiple users log in to the same system, every user needs to install the application.

ClickOnce Operation

ClickOnce applications have two XML-based manifest files associated with them. One is the application manifest, and the other is the deployment manifest. These two files describe everything that is required to deploy an application.

The *application manifest* contains information about the application such as permissions required, assemblies to include, and other dependencies. The *deployment manifest* contains details about the application's deployment, such as settings and location of the application manifest. The complete schemas for the manifests are in the .NET SDK documentation.

As mentioned earlier, ClickOnce has some limitations, such as assemblies cannot be added to the GAC, and Windows Services cannot be configured in the registry. In such scenarios, Windows Installer is clearly a better choice. You can still use ClickOnce for a large number of applications, however.

Publishing a ClickOnce Application

Because everything that ClickOnce needs to know is contained in the two manifest files, the process of publishing an application for ClickOnce deployment is simply generating the manifests and placing the files in the proper location. The manifest files can be generated in Visual Studio. There is also a command-line tool (mage.exe) and a version with a GUI (mageUI.exe).

You can create the manifest files in Visual Studio 2015 in two ways. At the bottom of the Publish tab on the Project Properties dialog are two buttons: Publish Wizard and Publish Now. The Publish Wizard asks several questions about the deployment of the application and then generates the manifest files and copies all the needed files to the deployment location. The Publish Now button uses the values that have been set in the Publish tab to create the manifest files and copies the files to the deployment location.

To use the command-line tool, mage.exe, the values for the various ClickOnce properties must be passed in. Manifest files can be both created and updated using mage.exe. Typing mage.exe -help at the command prompt gives the syntax for passing in the values required.

The GUI version of mage.exe (mageUI.exe) is similar in appearance to the Publish tab in Visual Studio 2015. You can use the GUI tool to create and update an application and deployment manifest file.

ClickOnce applications appear in the Install/Uninstall Programs control panel applet just like any other installed application. One big difference is that the user is presented with the choice of either uninstalling the application or rolling back to the previous version. ClickOnce keeps the previous version in the ClickOnce application cache.

Let's start with the process of creating a ClickOnce installation. As a prerequisite for this process, you need to have Internet Information Server (IIS) installed on the system, and Visual Studio must be started with elevated privileges. The ClickOnce installation program will be directly published to the local IIS, which requires administrative privileges.

Open the ClientWPF project with Visual Studio, select the Publish tab in the Project properties, and click the Publish Wizard button. The first screen, shown in Figure 36-1, asks for the publish location. Use the local publish\ folder to publish the package to a local folder.

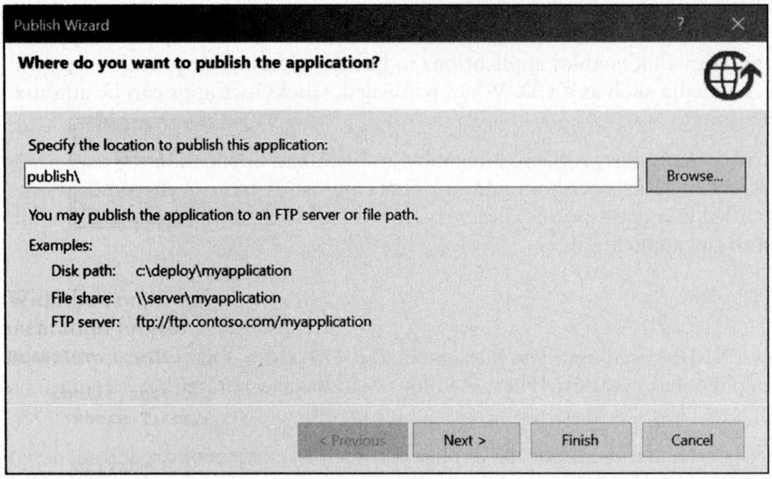

FIGURE 36-1

> **NOTE** *With previous versions of Visual Studio, you could directly install the ClickOnce package from Visual Studio to the local IIS. This is no longer possible with Visual Studio 2015. However, you can create an installation package in a local folder and add it manually to an IIS Website.*

The next screen asks how the users will install the application—from either a website, a file share, or CD-ROM/DVD-ROM (see Figure 36-2). This setting influences how users get updates of the app.

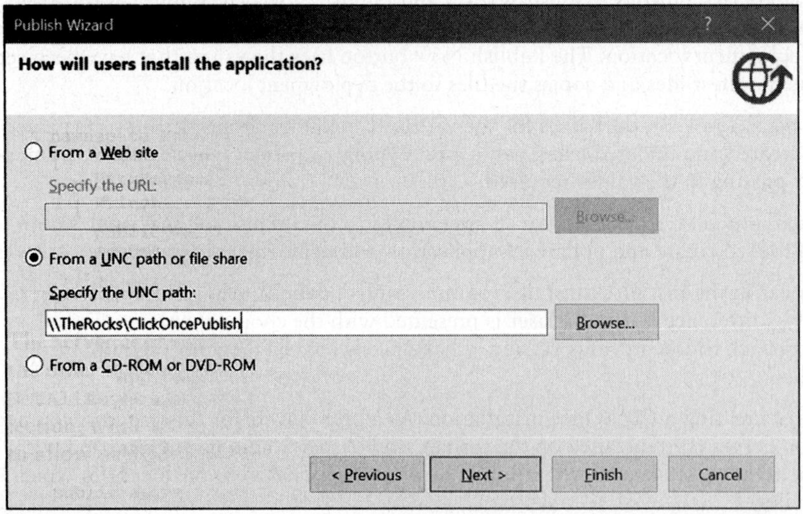

FIGURE 36-2

The third screen provides options for running this application when the client is offline or only when the client system is online (see Figure 36-3). Using the online option, the application runs directly from the network location. Using the offline option, the application is installed locally. Choose the offline option.

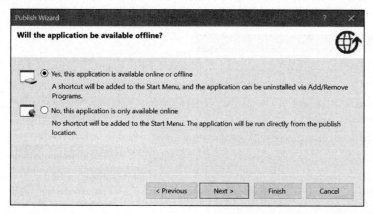

FIGURE 36-3

After the summary screen that follows as the fourth screen, you are ready to publish, and a browser window is opened to install the application. You can find the application files for installation in the folder you selected previously—for example, `publish\`.

Before installing the application using ClickOnce, the next section covers the settings that have been made by the wizard.

ClickOnce Settings

Several properties are available for both manifest files. You can configure many of these properties with the Publish tab (see Figure 36-4) within the Visual Studio project settings. The most important property is the location from which the application should be deployed. I've used a network share.

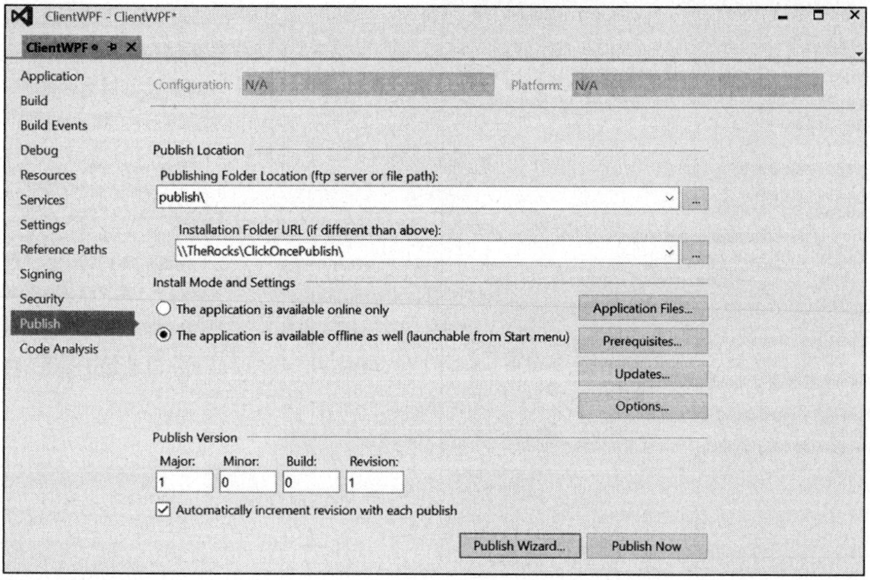

FIGURE 36-4

The Publish tab has an Application Files button that invokes a dialog that lists all assemblies and configuration files required by the application (see Figure 36-5). You can change this configuration; in the list of all files, use the publish status to indicate whether the file should be included with the package. The debug symbols are by default left out. For testing scenarios, you might add these files.

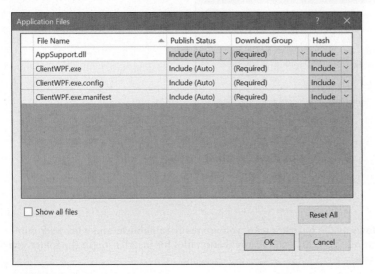

FIGURE 36-5

The Prerequisite button displays a list of common prerequisites that can be installed along with the application. These prerequisites are defined by Microsoft Installer packages and need to be installed before the ClickOnce application can be installed. In Figure 36-6, you can see that .NET Framework 4.6 was detected as a prerequisite and is part of the installation. You have the choice of installing the prerequisites from the same location from which the application is being published or from the vendor's website.

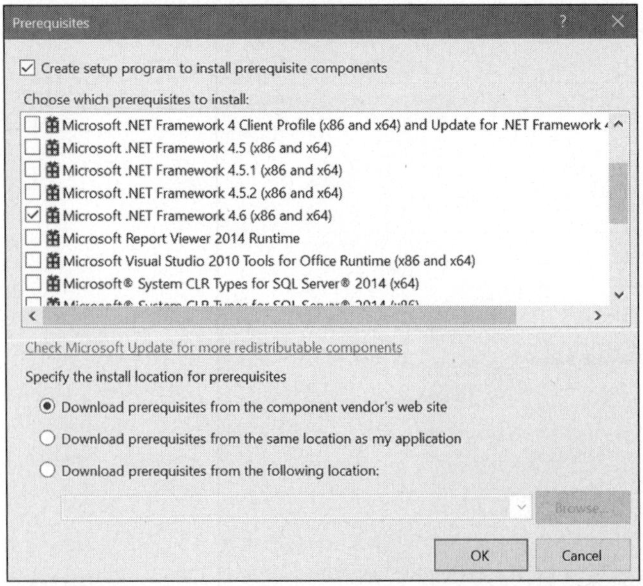

FIGURE 36-6

The Updates button displays a dialog (see Figure 36-7) containing information about how the application should be updated. As new versions of an application are made available, ClickOnce can be used to update the application. Options include checking for updates every time the application starts or checking in the background. If the background option is selected, a specified period of time between checks can be entered. Options for allowing the user to be able to decline or accept the update are available. This can be used to force an update in the background so that users are never aware that the update is occurring. The next time the application is run, the new version is used instead of the older version. A separate location for the update files can be used as well. This way, the original installation package can be located in one location and installed for new users, and all the updates can be staged in another location.

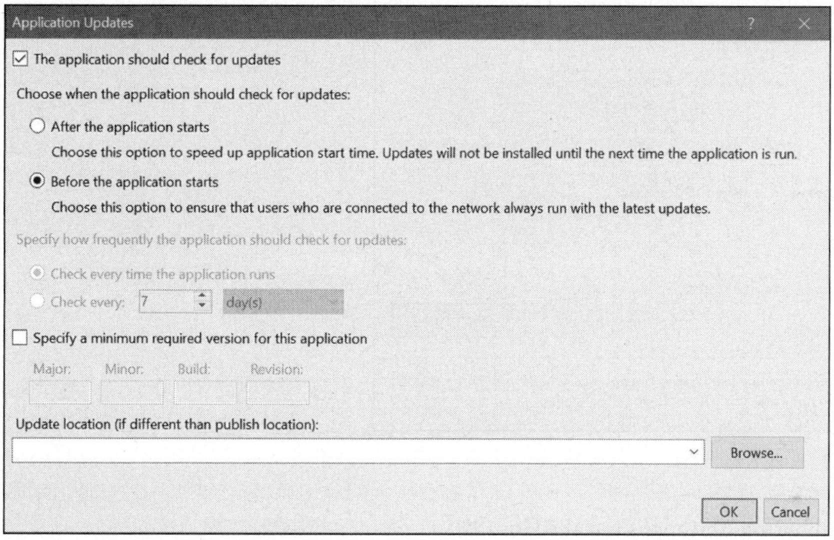

FIGURE 36-7

You can set up the application so that it runs in either online or offline mode. In offline mode the application can be run from the Start menu and acts as if it were installed using the Windows Installer. Online mode means that the application runs only if the installation folder is available.

Application Cache for ClickOnce Files

Applications distributed with ClickOnce are not installed in the `Program Files` folder. Instead, they are placed in an application catch that resides in the `%LocalAppData%\Apps\2.0` folder. Controlling this aspect of the deployment means that multiple versions of an application can reside on the client PC at the same time. If the application is set to run online, every version that the user has accessed is retained. For applications that are set to run locally, the current and previous versions are retained.

This makes it a very simple process to roll back a ClickOnce application to its previous version. If the user selects the Install/Uninstall Programs control panel applet, the dialog presented contains the options to remove the ClickOnce application or roll back to the previous version. An administrator can change the manifest file to point to the previous version. If the administrator does this, the next time the user runs that application, a check is made for an update. Instead of finding new assemblies to deploy, the application restores the previous version without any interaction from the user.

Application Installation

Now let's start the application installation. Copy the files from the `publish` folder to the network share that was specified when you created the package. Then start the `Setup.exe` from the network share. The first dialog shown gives a warning (see Figure 36-8). Because the publisher of the test certificate is not trusted by the system, a red flag is shown. Click the More Information link to get more information about the certificate and see that the application wants full-trust access. If you trust the application, you can click the Install button to install the application. Before adding the ClickOnce package to the production environment, you can buy a trusted certificate to add to the package.

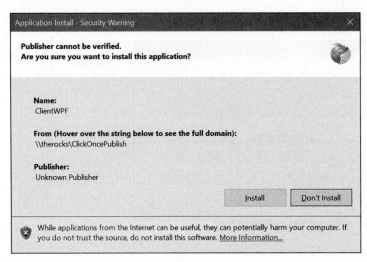

FIGURE 36-8

After you click the Install button, the app is installed locally.

After the installation, you can find the application with the Start menu. In addition, it's listed with Programs and Features in the Control Panel, where you can also uninstall it (see Figure 36-9).

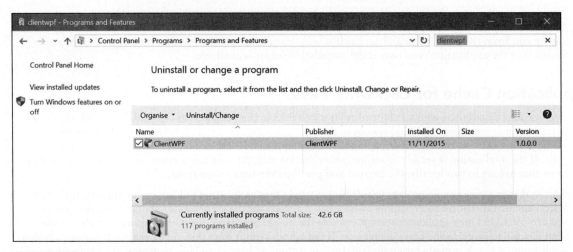

FIGURE 36-9

ClickOnce Deployment API

With the ClickOnce settings you can configure the application to automatically check for updates, as discussed earlier. Often this is not a practical approach. Maybe some super-users should get a new version of the application earlier. If they are happy with the new version, other users should be privileged to receive the update as well. With such a scenario, you can use your own user-management information database, and update the application programmatically.

For programmatic updates, the assembly System.Deployment and classes from the System. Deployment namespace can be used to check application version information and do an update. The following code snippet (code file MainWindow.xaml.cs) contains a click handler for an Update button in the application. It first checks whether the application is a ClickOnce-deployed application by checking the IsNetworkDeployed property from the ApplicationDeployment class. Using the CheckForUpdateAsync method, it determines whether a newer version is available on the server (in the update directory specified by the ClickOnce settings). On receiving the information about the update, the CheckForUpdateCompleted event is fired. With this event handler, the second argument (type CheckForUpdateCompletedEventArgs) contains information on the update, the version number, and whether it is a mandatory update. If an update is available, it is installed automatically by calling the UpdateAsync method (code file ClientWPF/MainWindow.xaml.cs):

```
private void OnUpdate(object sender, RoutedEventArgs e)
{
  if (ApplicationDeployment.IsNetworkDeployed)
  {
    ApplicationDeployment.CurrentDeployment.CheckForUpdateCompleted +=
    (sender1, e1) =>
    {
      if (e1.UpdateAvailable)
      {
        ApplicationDeployment.CurrentDeployment.UpdateCompleted +=
        (sender2, e2) =>
        {
          MessageBox.Show("Update completed");
        };
        ApplicationDeployment.CurrentDeployment.UpdateAsync();
      }
      else
      {
        MessageBox.Show("No update available");
      }
    };
    ApplicationDeployment.CurrentDeployment.CheckForUpdateAsync();
  }
  else
  {
    MessageBox.Show("not a ClickOnce installation");
  }
}
```

By using the Deployment API code, you can manually test for updates directly from the application.

UWP APPS

Installing Windows apps is a completely different story. With traditional .NET applications, copying the executable with the DLLs as shown earlier with xcopy deployment is one way to go. This is not an option with Universal Windows apps.

Universal Windows apps need to be packaged. This enables the app to make the application broadly available in the Windows Store. There's also a different option to deploy Windows apps in an environment without adding it to the Windows Store. This is known as *sideloading*. With all these options it is necessary to create an app package, so let's start with that.

Creating an App Package

A Windows app package is a file with the .appx file extension, which is really just a zip file. This file contains all the XAML files, binaries, pictures, and configurations. You can create a package with either Visual Studio or the command-line utility MakeAppx.exe.

You can create a simple Windows app with the Visual Studio application template Blank App (Universal Windows) that is in the Windows ➪ Universal category. The sample app has the name UniversalWindowsApp.

What's important for the packaging are images in the Assets folder. The files Logo, SmallLogo, and StoreLogo represent logos of the application that should be replaced by custom application logos. The file Package.appxmanifest is an XML file that contains all the definitions needed for the app package. Opening this file from the Solution Explorer invokes the Package Editor, which contains six tabs: Application, Visual Assets, Capabilities, Declarations, Content URIs, and Packaging. The Packaging dialog is shown in Figure 36-10. Here you can configure the package name, the logo for the store, the version number, and the certificate. By default, only a certificate for testing purposes is created. When you associate the app with the store, the certificate is replaced.

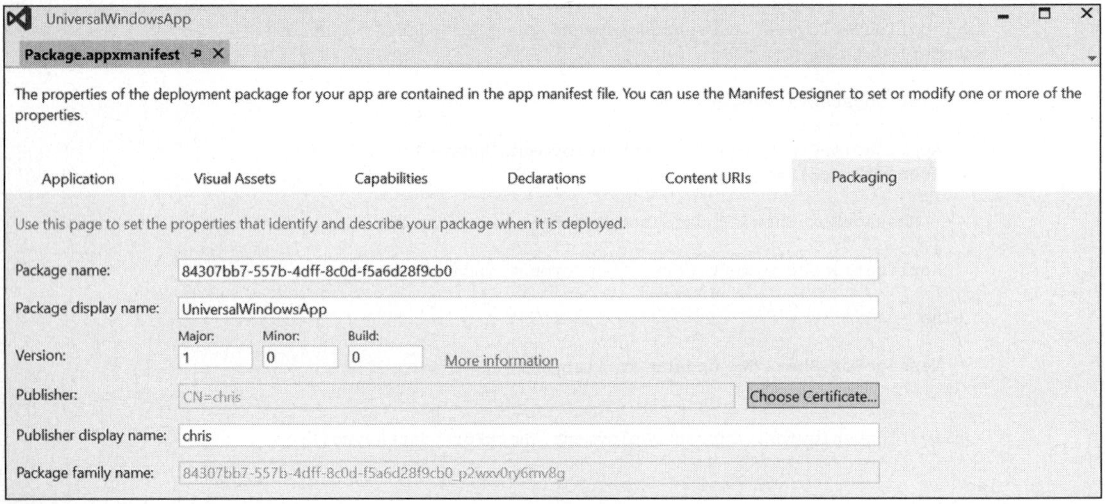

FIGURE 36-10

The Application tab enables configuration of the application name, and a description of the application. With the Visual Assets tab, you can see all the logos—small, square, and wide—that you can associate with the app. Configurable capabilities vary according to the system features and the devices the application is using, for example, the Music Library or the webcam. The user is informed about which capabilities the application is using. If the application does not specify the capabilities it needs, during runtime the application is not allowed to use it. With the Declarations tab, the application can register more features, such as to use it as a share target or to specify whether some functionality should run in the background.

Using Visual Studio, you can create a package by clicking the project in Solution Explorer and select the context menu Store ➪ Create App Packages. The first selection with this Create App Package wizard is to specify whether the application should be uploaded to the Windows Store. If that's not the case, you can use sideloading to deploy the package, as discussed later. In case you didn't register your account with the Windows Store yet, select the sideloading option. In the second dialog of the wizard, select Release instead of Debug Code for the package; you can also select the platforms for which the package should be generated: x86, x64, and ARM CPUs. This is all that's needed to build the package (see Figure 36-11). To view what's in the package, you can rename the .appx file to a .zip file extension and find all the images, metadata, and binaries.

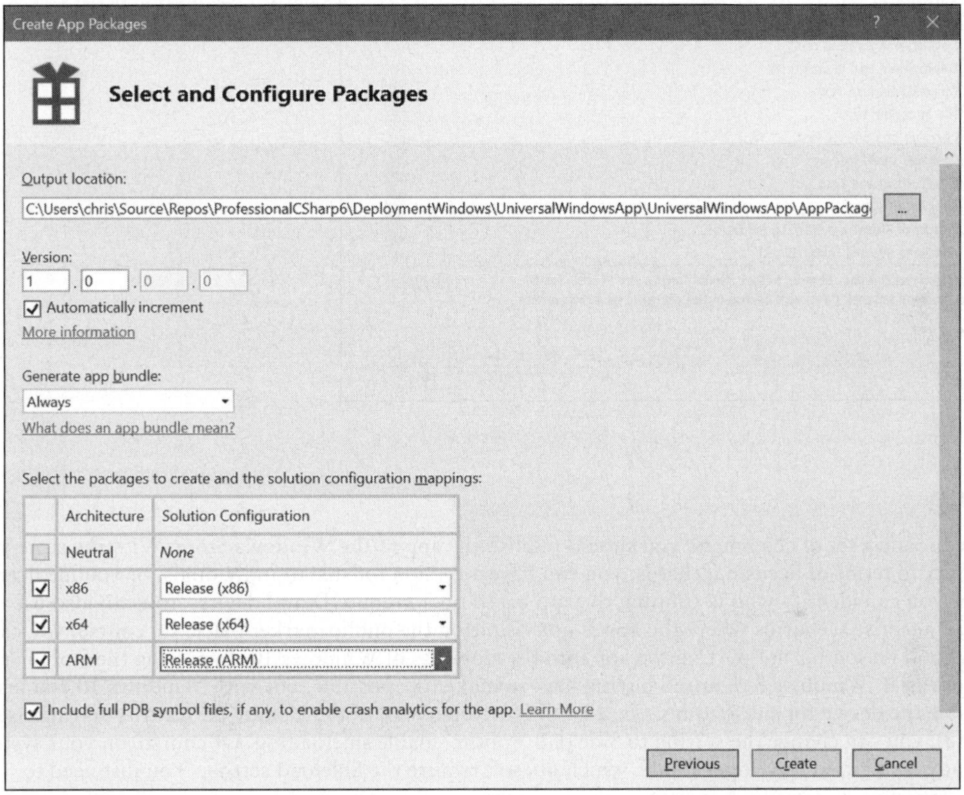

FIGURE 36-11

Windows App Certification Kit

Before submitting an app package to the Windows Store, and also before sideloading it to other devices, you should run the Windows App Certification Kit. This tool is part of the Windows SDK that is installed alongside Visual Studio.

When you deploy your application to the Windows Store, it is necessary for the application to fulfill some requirements. You can check most of the requirements beforehand.

You should give the application some time when you're running this tool. It requires several minutes to test the application and get the results. During this time you shouldn't interact with the tool or your running application. The app is checking to make sure the package is correctly built using release and not debug code, the app does not crash or hang, only supported APIs are called, capabilities are used correctly, cancellation handlers of background tasks are implemented, and more. Just start the tool to see all the tests it runs.

Figure 36-12 shows a dialog for starting the certification kit where you can select what tests to run.

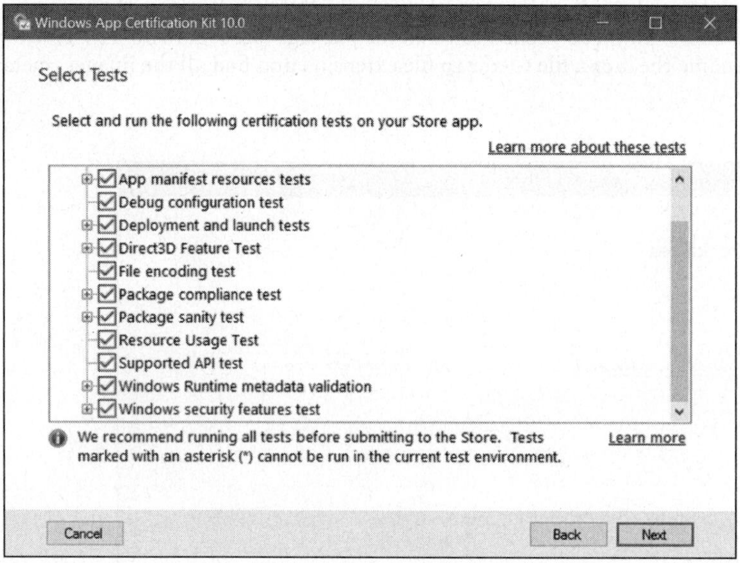

FIGURE 36-12

Sideloading

To have the broadest set of customers, you should publish the app to the Windows Store. With the store you have flexibility in terms of licensing; that is, you can have a version for sale to individuals, or volume licensing whereby you can identify who is running the app based on a unique ID and device. You can also use the store in enterprise scenarios where the app is not visible on the public market place. Of course, you can also have a good reason for not putting the app into the store. As of Windows 10, bypassing the store has become a lot easier. Windows 8 required buying keys to make this possible, but with Windows 10 you just need to enable the device for sideloading. On the For Developers tab of the Update & Security settings (see Figure 36-13), you can change the setting to Sideload Apps to enable sideloading. Of course, on your system you've already configured Developer mode, which doesn't require the Sideload setting. You just need to enable this setting on systems that are not configured with Developer mode.

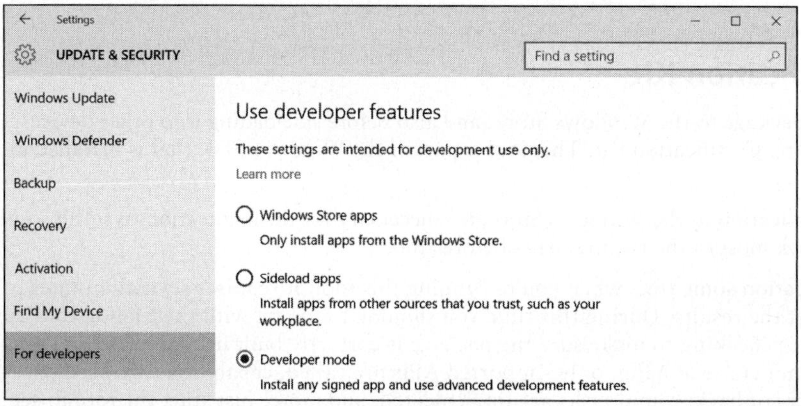

FIGURE 36-13

To install a Windows app with sideloading, you can use `WinAppDeployCmd.exe`. This tool is part of the Windows 10 SDK.

This tool allows you to scan all devices on the network available for installation using

```
WinAppDeployCmd.exe devices
```

To install an app on a device, use the following `install` option:

```
WinAppDeployCmd.exe install -file SampleApp.appx -ip 10.10.0.199 -pin ABC3D5
```

To update an app, you can use the `update` option:

```
WinAppDeployCmd.exe update -file SampleApp.appx -ip 10.10.0.199
```

And to uninstall an app, you use the option `uninstall`:

```
WinAppDeployCmd.exe uninstall -package packagename
```

SUMMARY

Deployment is an important part of the application life cycle that you need to consider from the beginning of the project because the deployment method influences the technology you use. Deploying different application types has been shown in this chapter.

You've seen the deployment of Windows applications using ClickOnce. ClickOnce offers an easy automatic update capability that can also be triggered directly from within the application, as you've seen with the `System.Deployment` API.

You also learned how to deploy UWP apps, which you can publish in the Windows Store, but you can also deploy using command-line tools without using the store.

The next chapter is the first of a group covering services and web applications, starting with ADO.NET to access the database.

PART IV
Web Applications and Services

37

ADO.NET

WHAT'S IN THIS CHAPTER?

- ➤ Connecting to the database
- ➤ Executing commands
- ➤ Calling stored procedures
- ➤ The ADO.NET object model

WROX.COM CODE DOWNLOADS FOR THIS CHAPTER

The wrox.com code downloads for this chapter are found at www.wrox.com/go/
professionalcsharp6 on the Download Code tab. The code for this chapter is
divided into the following major examples:

- ➤ ConnectionSamples
- ➤ CommandSamples
- ➤ AsyncSamples
- ➤ TransactionSamples

ADO.NET OVERVIEW

This chapter discusses how to access a relational database like SQL Server from your C# programs
using ADO.NET. It shows you how to connect to and disconnect from a database, how to use queries,
and how to add and update records. You learn the various command object options and see how commands can be used for each of the options presented by the SQL Server provider classes; how to call
stored procedures with command objects; and how to use transactions.

ADO.NET previously shipped different database providers: a provider for SQL Server and one for
Oracle, using OLEDB and ODBC. The OLEDB technology is discontinued, so this provider shouldn't
be used with new applications. Accessing the Oracle database, Microsoft's provider is discontinued as
well because a provider from Oracle (http://www.oracle.com/technetwork/topics/dotnet/)
better fits the needs. For other data sources (also for Oracle), many third-party providers are available.
Before using the ODBC provider, you should use a provider specific for the data source you access.
The code samples in this chapter are based on SQL Server, but you can easily change it to use different
connection and command objects, such as OracleConnection and OracleCommand when accessing
the Oracle database instead of SqlConnection and SqlCommand.

> **NOTE** *This chapter does not cover the* `DataSet` *to have tables in memory. Datasets enable you to retrieve records from a database and store the content within in-memory data tables with relations. Instead you should use Entity Framework, which is covered in Chapter 38, "Entity Framework Core." Entity Framework enables you to have object relations instead of table-based relations.*

Sample Database

The examples in this chapter use the AdventureWorks2014 database. You can download this database from `https://msftdbprodsamples.codeplex.com/`. With this link you can download a backup of the AdventureWorks2014 database in a zip file. Select the recommended download—`Adventure Works 2014 Full Database Backup.zip`. After unzipping the file, you can restore the database backup using SQL Server Management Studio as shown in Figure 37-1. In case you don't have SQL Server Management Studio on your system, you can download a free version from `http://www.microsoft.com/downloads`.

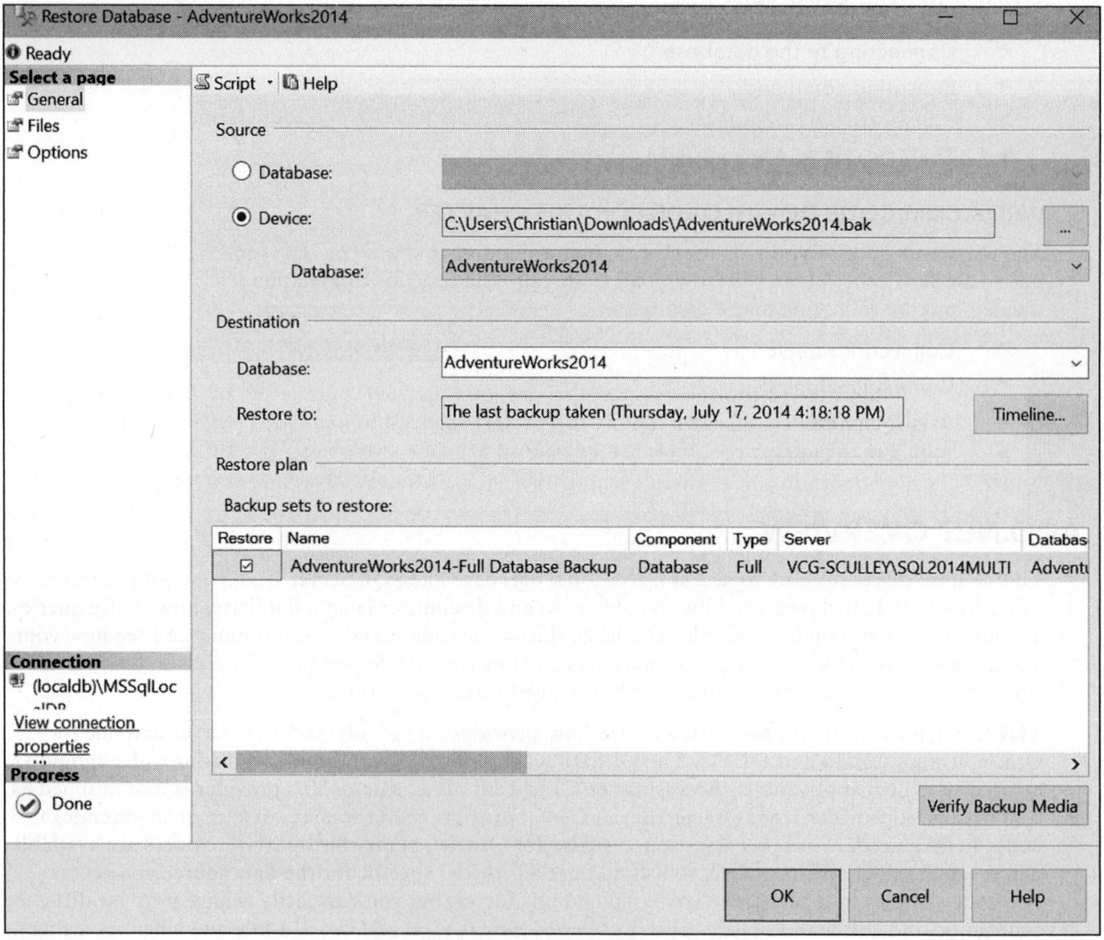

FIGURE 37-1

The SQL server used with this chapter is SQL Server LocalDb. This is a database server that is installed as part of Visual Studio. You can use any other SQL Server edition as well; you just need to change the connection string accordingly.

NuGet Packages and Namespaces

The sample code for all the ADO.NET samples makes use of the following dependencies and namespaces:

Dependencies

NETStandard.Library

Microsoft.Extensions.Configuration

Microsoft.Extensions.Configuration.Json

System.Data.SqlClient

Namespaces

Microsoft.Extensions.Configuration

System

System.Data

System.Data.SqlClient

System.Threading.Tasks

static System.Console

USING DATABASE CONNECTIONS

To access the database, you need to provide connection parameters, such as the machine on which the database is running and possibly your login credentials. You make a connection to SQL Server using the SqlConnection class.

The following code snippet illustrates how to create, open, and close a connection to the AdventureWorks2014 database (code file ConnectionSamples/Program.cs):

```
public static void OpenConnection()
{
  string connectionString = @"server=(localdb)\MSSQLLocalDB;" +
                "integrated security=SSPI;" +
                "database=AdventureWorks2014";
  var connection = new SqlConnection(connectionString);
  connection.Open();

  // Do something useful
  WriteLine("Connection opened");

  connection.Close();
}
```

> **NOTE** *The* SqlConnection *class implements the* IDisposable *interface with the* Dispose *method in addition to the* Close *method. Both do the same, to release the connection. With this, you can use the* using *statement to close the connection.*

In the example connection string, the parameters used are as follows (the parameters are delimited by a semicolon in the connection string):

➤ `server=(localdb)\MSSQLLocalDB`—This denotes the database server to connect to. SQL Server permits a number of separate database server instances to be running on the same machine. Here, you are connecting to the localdb Server and the MSSQLLocalDB SQL Server instance that is created with the installation of SQL Server. If you are using the local installation of SQL Server, change this part to `server=(local)`. Instead of using the keyword `server`, you can use `Data Source` instead. Connecting to SQL Azure, you can set `Data Source=servername.database.windows.net`.

➤ `database=AdventureWorks2014`—This describes the database instance to connect to; each SQL Server process can expose several database instances. Instead of the keyword `database`, you can instead use `Initial Catalog`.

➤ `integrated security=SSPI`—This uses Windows Authentication to connect to the database. In case you are using SQL Azure, you need to set `User Id` and `Password` instead.

> **NOTE** *You can find great information about connection strings with many different databases at* `http://www.connectionstrings.com`.

The `ConnectionSamples` example opens a database connection using the defined connection string and then closes that connection. After you have opened the connection, you can issue commands against the data source; when you are finished, you can close the connection.

Managing Connection Strings

Instead of hard-coding the connection string with the C# code, it is better to read it from a configuration file. With .NET 4.6 and .NET Core 1.0, configuration files can be JSON or XML formats, or read from environmental variables. With the following sample, the connection string is read from a JSON configuration file (code file `ConnectionSamples/config.json`):

```
{
  "Data": {
    "DefaultConnection": {
      "ConnectionString":
        "Server=(localdb)\\MSSQLLocalDB;Database=AdventureWorks2014;
          Trusted_Connection=True;"
    }
  }
}
```

The JSON file can be read using the Configuration API defined in the NuGet package `Microsoft.Framework.Configuration`. To use JSON configuration files, the NuGet package `Microsoft.Framework.Configuration.Json` is added as well. For reading a configuration file, the `ConfigurationBuilder` is created. The `AddJsonFile` extension method adds the JSON file `config.json` to read configuration information from this file—if it is in the same path as the program. To configure a different path, you can invoke the method `SetBasePath`. Invoking the `Build` method of the `ConfigurationBuilder` builds up the configuration from all the added configuration files and returns an object implementing the `IConfiguration` interface. With this, the configuration values can be retrieved, such as the configuration value for `Data:DefaultConnection:ConnectionString` (code file `ConnectionSamples/Program.cs`):

```
public static void ConnectionUsingConfig()
{
  var configurationBuilder =
    new ConfigurationBuilder().AddJsonFile("config.json");
```

```
        IConfiguration config = configurationBuilder.Build();
        string connectionString = config["Data:DefaultConnection:ConnectionString"];
        WriteLine(connectionString);
    }
```

Connection Pools

When two-tier applications were done several years ago it was a good idea to open the connection on application start and close it only when the application was closed. Nowadays, this is not a good idea. The reason for this program architecture was that it takes some time to open a connection. Now, closing a connection doesn't close the connection with the server. Instead, the connection is added to a connection pool. When you open the connection again, it can be taken from the pool, thus it is very fast to open a connection; it only takes time to open the first connection.

Pooling can be configured with several options in the connection string. Setting the option Pooling to false disables the connection pool; by default it's enabled—Pooling = true. Min Pool Size and Max Pool Size enable you to configure the number of connections in the pool. By default, Min Pool Size has a value of 0 and Max Pool Size has a value of 100. Connection Lifetime defines how long a connection should stay inactive in the pool before it is really released.

Connection Information

After creating a connection, you can register event handlers to get some information about the connection. The SqlConnection class defines the InfoMessage and StateChange events. The InfoMessage event is fired every time an information or warning message is returned from SQL Server. The StateChange event is fired when the state of the connection changes—for example, the connection is opened or closed (code file ConnectionSamples/Program.cs):

```
    public static void ConnectionInformation()
    {
      using (var connection = new SqlConnection(GetConnectionString()))
      {
        connection.InfoMessage += (sender, e) =>
        {
          WriteLine($"warning or info {e.Message}");
        };
        connection.StateChange += (sender, e) =>
        {
          WriteLine($"current state: {e.CurrentState}, before: {e.OriginalState}");
        };
        connection.Open();

        WriteLine("connection opened");
        // Do something useful
      }
    }
```

When you run the application, you can see the StateChange event fired and the Open and Closed state:

```
    current state: Open, before: Closed
    connection opened
    current state: Closed, before: Open
```

COMMANDS

The "Using Database Connections" section briefly touched on the idea of issuing commands against a database. A command is, in its simplest form, a string of text containing SQL statements to be issued to the database. A command could also be a stored procedure, shown later in this section.

A command can be constructed by passing the SQL statement as a parameter to the constructor of the `Command` class, as shown in this example (code file `CommandSamples/Program.cs`):

```
public static void CreateCommand()
{
  using (var connection = new SqlConnection(GetConnectionString()))
  {
    string sql = "SELECT BusinessEntityID, FirstName, MiddleName, LastName " +
      "FROM Person.Person";
    var command = new SqlCommand(sql, connection);

    connection.Open();

    // etc.
  }
}
```

A command can also be created by invoking the `CreateCommand` method of the `SqlConnection` and assigning the SQL statement to the `CommandText` property:

```
SqlCommand command = connection.CreateCommand();
command.CommandText = sql;
```

Commands often need parameters. For example, the following SQL statement requires an `EmailPromotion` parameter. Don't be incited to use string concatenation to build up parameters. Instead, always use the parameter features of ADO.NET:

```
string sql = "SELECT BusinessEntityID, FirstName, MiddleName, LastName " +
  "FROM Person.Person WHERE EmailPromotion = @EmailPromotion";
var command = new SqlCommand(sql, connection);
```

When you add the parameter to the `SqlCommand` object, there's a simple way to use the `Parameters` property that returns a `SqlParameterCollection` and the `AddWithValue` method:

```
command.Parameters.AddWithValue("EmailPromotion", 1);
```

A more efficient method that's more programming work is to use overloads of the `Add` method by passing the name and the SQL data type:

```
command.Parameters.Add("EmailPromotion", SqlDbType.Int);
command.Parameters["EmailPromotion"].Value = 1;
```

It's also possible to create a `SqlParameter` object and add this to the `SqlParameterCollection`.

> **NOTE** *Don't be inclined to use string concatenation with SQL parameters. This is often misused for SQL injection attacks. Using* `SqlParameter` *objects inhibits such attacks.*

After you have defined the command, you need to execute it. There are several ways to issue the statement, depending on what, if anything, you expect to be returned from that command. The `SqlCommand` class provides the following `ExecuteXX` methods:

➤ `ExecuteNonQuery`—Executes the command but does not return any output

➤ `ExecuteReader`—Executes the command and returns a typed `IDataReader`

➤ `ExecuteScalar`—Executes the command and returns the value from the first column of the first row of any result set

ExecuteNonQuery

The `ExecuteNonQuery` method is commonly used for UPDATE, INSERT, or DELETE statements, for which the only returned value is the number of records affected. This method can, however, return results if you call a stored procedure that has output parameters. The sample code creates a new record within the `Sales.SalesTerritory` table. This table has a `TerritoryID` as primary key that is an identity column and thus does not need to be supplied creating the record. All the columns of this table don't allow null (see Figure 37-2), but several of them have default values—such as a few sales and cost columns, the `rowguid`, and the `ModifiedDate`. The `rowguid` column is created from the function `newid`, and the `ModifiedDate` column is created from `getdate`. When creating a new row, just the `Name`, the `CountryRegionCode`, and `Group` columns need to be supplied. The method `ExecuteNonQuery` defines the SQL INSERT statement, adds values for the parameters, and invokes the `ExecuteNonQuery` method of the `SqlCommand` class (code file `CommandSamples/Program.cs`):

```
public static void ExecuteNonQuery
{
  try
  {
    using (var connection = new SqlConnection(GetConnectionString()))
    {
      string sql = "INSERT INTO [Sales].[SalesTerritory] " +
        "([Name], [CountryRegionCode], [Group]) " +
        "VALUES (@Name, @CountryRegionCode, @Group)";

      var command = new SqlCommand(sql, connection);
      command.Parameters.AddWithValue("Name", "Austria");
      command.Parameters.AddWithValue("CountryRegionCode", "AT");
      command.Parameters.AddWithValue("Group", "Europe");

      connection.Open();
      int records = command.ExecuteNonQuery();
      WriteLine($"{records} inserted");
    }
  }
  catch (SqlException ex)
  {
    WriteLine(ex.Message);
  }
}
```

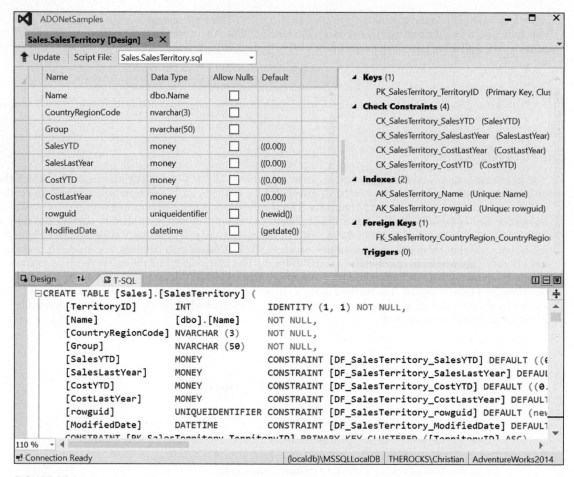

FIGURE 37-2

`ExecuteNonQuery` returns the number of rows affected by the command as an `int`. When you run the method the first time, one record is inserted. When you run the same method a second time, you get an exception because of a unique index conflict. The `Name` has a unique index defined and thus is allowed only once. To run the method a second time, you need to delete the created record first.

ExecuteScalar

On many occasions it is necessary to return a single result from a SQL statement, such as the count of records in a given table or the current date/time on the server. You can use the `ExecuteScalar` method in such situations:

```
public static void ExecuteScalar()
{
  using (var connection = new SqlConnection(GetConnectionString()))
  {
    string sql = "SELECT COUNT(*) FROM Production.Product";
    SqlCommand command = connection.CreateCommand();
    command.CommandText = sql;
    connection.Open();
    object count = command.ExecuteScalar();
```

```
        WriteLine($"counted {count} product records");
    }
  }
```

The method returns an object, which you can cast to the appropriate type if required. If the SQL you are calling returns only one column, it is preferable to use `ExecuteScalar` over any other method of retrieving that column. That also applies to stored procedures that return a single value.

ExecuteReader

The `ExecuteReader` method executes the command and returns a data reader object. The object returned can be used to iterate through the record(s) returned. The `ExecuteReader` sample makes use of an SQL `INNER JOIN` clause that is shown in the following code snippet. This SQL `INNER JOIN` clause is used to get a price history of a single product. The price history is stored in the table `Production.ProductCostHistory`, the name of the product in the table `Production.Product`. With the SQL statement a single parameter is needed for the product identifier (code file `CommandSamples/Program.cs`):

```
private static string GetProductInformationSQL() =>
  "SELECT Prod.ProductID, Prod.Name, Prod.StandardCost, Prod.ListPrice, " +
    "CostHistory.StartDate, CostHistory.EndDate, CostHistory.StandardCost " +
  "FROM Production.ProductCostHistory AS CostHistory  " +
  "INNER JOIN Production.Product AS Prod ON " +
    "CostHistory.ProductId = Prod.ProductId " +
  "WHERE Prod.ProductId = @ProductId";
```

When you invoke the method `ExecuteReader` of the `SqlCommand` object, a `SqlDataReader` is returned. Note that the `SqlDataReader` needs to be disposed after it has been used. Also note that this time the `SqlConnection` object is not explicitly disposed at the end of the method. Passing the parameter `CommandBehavior.CloseConnection` to the `ExecuteReader` method automatically closes the connection on closing of the reader. If you don't supply this setting, you still need to close the connection.

For reading the records from the data reader, the `Read` method is invoked within a `while` loop. The first call to the `Read` method moves the cursor to the first record returned. When `Read` is invoked again, the cursor is positioned to the next record—as long as there's a record available. The `Read` method returns `false` if no record is available at the next position. When accessing the values of the columns, different `GetXXX` methods are invoked, such as `GetInt32`, `GetString`, and `GetDateTime`. These methods are strongly typed as they return the specific type needed, such as `int`, `string`, and `DateTime`. The index passed to these methods corresponds to the columns retrieved with the SQL `SELECT` statement, so the index stays the same even if the database structure changes. With the strongly typed `GetXXX` methods you need to pay attention to values where `null` is returned from the database; here the `GetXXX` method throws an exception. With the data retrieved, only the `CostHistory.EndDate` can be `null`; all other columns can't be null as defined by the database schema. To avoid an exception in this case, the C# conditional statement `? :` is used to check whether the value is null with the `SqlDataReader.IsDbNull` method. In that case, null is assigned to a nullable `DateTime`. Only if the value is not null, the `DateTime` is accessed with the `GetDateTime` method (code file `CommandSamples/Program.cs`):

```
public static void ExecuteReader(int productId)
{
  var connection = new SqlConnection(GetConnectionString());

  string sql = GetProductInformationSQL();
  var command = new SqlCommand(sql, connection);
  var productIdParameter = new SqlParameter("ProductId", SqlDbType.Int);
  productIdParameter.Value = productId;
  command.Parameters.Add(productIdParameter);
  connection.Open();
```

```
using (SqlDataReader reader =
  command.ExecuteReader(CommandBehavior.CloseConnection))
{
  while (reader.Read())
  {
    int id = reader.GetInt32(0);
    string name = reader.GetString(1);
    DateTime from = reader.GetDateTime(4);
    DateTime? to =
      reader.IsDBNull(5) ? (DateTime?)null: reader.GetDateTime(5);
    decimal standardPrice = reader.GetDecimal(6);
    WriteLine($"{id} {name} from: {from:d} to: {to:d}; " +
      $"price: {standardPrice}");
  }
}
```

When you run the application and pass the product ID 717 to the ExecuteReader method, you see this output:

```
717 HL Road Frame–Red, 62 from: 5/31/2011 to: 5/29/2012; price: 747.9682
717 HL Road Frame–Red, 62 from: 5/30/2012 to: 5/29/2013; price: 722.2568
717 HL Road Frame–Red, 62 from: 5/30/2013 to:; price: 868.6342
```

For the possible values for the product ID, check the content of the database.

With the SqlDataReader, instead of using the typed methods GetXXX, you can use the untyped indexer that returns an object. With this, you need to cast to the corresponding type:

```
int id = (int)reader[0];
string name = (string)reader[1];
DateTime from = (DateTime)reader[2];
DateTime? to = (DateTime?)reader[3];
```

The indexer of the SqlDataReader also allows a string to be used instead of the int, passing the column name. This is the slowest method of these different options, but it might fulfill your needs. Compared to the time it costs to make a service call, the additional time needed to access the indexer can be ignored:

```
int id = (int)reader["ProductID"];
string name = (string)reader["Name"];
DateTime from = (DateTime)reader["StartDate"];
DateTime? to = (DateTime?)reader["EndDate"];
```

Calling Stored Procedures

Calling a stored procedure with a command object is just a matter of defining the name of the stored procedure, adding a definition for each parameter of the procedure, and then executing the command with one of the methods presented in the previous section.

The following sample calls the stored procedure uspGetEmployeeManagers to get all the managers of an employee. This stored procedure receives one parameter to return records of all managers using recursive queries:

```
CREATE PROCEDURE [dbo].[uspGetEmployeeManagers]
    @BusinessEntityID [int]
AS
-...
```

To see the implementation of the stored procedure, check the AdventureWorks2014 database.

To invoke the stored procedure, the CommandText of the SqlCommand object is set to the name of the stored procedure, and the CommandType is set to CommandType.StoredProcedure. Other than that, the command is invoked similarly to the way you've seen before. The parameter is created using the CreateParameter method of the SqlCommand object, but you can use other methods to create the parameter used earlier as well. With the parameter, the `SqlDbType`, `ParameterName`, and `Value` properties are filled. Because the stored procedure returns records, it is invoked by calling the method `ExecuteReader` (code file `CommandSamples/Program.cs`):

```
private static void StoredProcedure(int entityId)
{
  using (var connection = new SqlConnection(GetConnectionString()))
  {
    SqlCommand command = connection.CreateCommand();
    command.CommandText = "[dbo].[uspGetEmployeeManagers]";
    command.CommandType = CommandType.StoredProcedure;
    SqlParameter p1 = command.CreateParameter();
    p1.SqlDbType = SqlDbType.Int;
    p1.ParameterName = "@BusinessEntityID";
    p1.Value = entityId;
    command.Parameters.Add(p1);
    connection.Open();
    using (SqlDataReader reader = command.ExecuteReader())
    {
      while (reader.Read())
      {
        int recursionLevel = (int)reader["RecursionLevel"];
        int businessEntityId = (int)reader["BusinessEntityID"];
        string firstName = (string)reader["FirstName"];
        string lastName = (string)reader["LastName"];
        WriteLine($"{recursionLevel} {businessEntityId} " +
          $"{firstName} {lastName}");
      }
    }
  }
}
```

When you run the application and pass the entity ID 251, you get the managers of this employee as shown:

```
0 251 Mikael Sandberg
1 250 Sheela Word
2 249 Wendy Kahn
```

Depending on the return of the stored procedure, you need to invoke the stored procedure with `ExecuteReader`, `ExecuteScalar`, or `ExecuteNonQuery`.

With a stored procedure that contains `Output` parameters, you need to specify the `Direction` property of the `SqlParameter`. By default, the direction is `ParameterDirection.Input`:

```
var pOut = new SqlParameter();
pOut.Direction = ParameterDirection.Output;
```

ASYNCHRONOUS DATA ACCESS

Accessing the database can take some time. Here you shouldn't block the user interface. The ADO.NET classes offer task-based asynchronous programming by offering asynchronous methods in addition to the synchronous ones. The following code snippet is similar to the previous one using the `SqlDataReader`, but it makes use of `Async` method calls. The connection is opened with `SqlConnection.OpenAsync`, the reader is returned from the method `SqlCommand.ExecuteReaderAsync`, and the records are retrieved using `SqlDataReader.ReadAsync`. With all these methods, the calling thread is not blocked but can do other work before getting the result (code file `AsyncSamples/Program.cs`):

```
public static void Main()
{
  ReadAsync(714).Wait();
}
```

```
public static async Task ReadAsync(int productId)
{
  var connection = new SqlConnection(GetConnectionString());

  string sql =
    "SELECT Prod.ProductID, Prod.Name, Prod.StandardCost, Prod.ListPrice, " +
      "CostHistory.StartDate, CostHistory.EndDate, CostHistory.StandardCost " +
    "FROM Production.ProductCostHistory AS CostHistory  " +
    "INNER JOIN Production.Product AS Prod ON " +
      "CostHistory.ProductId = Prod.ProductId " +
    "WHERE Prod.ProductId = @ProductId";

  var command = new SqlCommand(sql, connection);
  var productIdParameter = new SqlParameter("ProductId", SqlDbType.Int);
  productIdParameter.Value = productId;
  command.Parameters.Add(productIdParameter);

  await connection.OpenAsync();

  using (SqlDataReader reader = await command.ExecuteReaderAsync(
    CommandBehavior.CloseConnection))
  {
    while (await reader.ReadAsync())
    {
      int id = reader.GetInt32(0);
      string name = reader.GetString(1);
      DateTime from = reader.GetDateTime(4);
      DateTime? to = reader.IsDBNull(5) ? (DateTime?)null :
        reader.GetDateTime(5);
      decimal standardPrice = reader.GetDecimal(6);
      WriteLine($"{id} {name} from: {from:d} to: {to:d}; " +
        $"price: {standardPrice}");
    }
  }
}
```

Using the asynchronous method calls is not only advantageous with Windows applications but also useful on the server side for making multiple calls simultaneous. The asynchronous methods of the ADO.NET API have overloads to support the CancellationToken for an earlier stop of a long-running method.

> **NOTE** *For more information about asynchronous method calls and the* CancellationToken, *read Chapter 15, "Asynchronous Programming."*

TRANSACTIONS

By default, a single command is running within a transaction. If you need to issue multiple commands, and either all of these or none happen, you can start and commit transactions explicitly.

Transactions are described by the term ACID. ACID is a four-letter acronym for *atomicity, consistency, isolation,* and *durability*:

➤ **Atomicity**—Represents one unit of work. With a transaction, either the complete unit of work succeeds or nothing is changed.

➤ **Consistency**—The state before the transaction was started and after the transaction is completed must be valid. During the transaction, the state may have interim values.

➤ **Isolation**—Transactions that happen concurrently are isolated from the state, which is changed during a transaction. Transaction A cannot see the interim state of transaction B until the transaction is completed.

➤ **Durability**—After a transaction is completed, it must be stored in a durable way. This means that if the power goes down or the server crashes, the state must be recovered at reboot.

> **NOTE** *Transactions and valid state can easily be described as a wedding ceremony. A bridal couple is standing before a transaction coordinator. The transaction coordinator asks the first of the couple: "Do you want to marry this person on your side?" If the first one agrees, the second is asked: "Do you want to marry this person?" If the second one declines, the first receives a rollback. A valid state with this transaction is only that both are married, or none are. If both agree, the transaction is committed and both are in the married state. If one denies, the transaction is aborted and both stay in the unmarried state. An invalid state is that one is married, and the other is not. The transaction guarantees that the result is never in an invalid state.*

With ADO.NET, transactions can be started by invoking the `BeginTransaction` method of the `SqlConnection`. A transaction is always associated with one connection; you can't create transactions over multiple connections. The method `BeginTransaction` returns an `SqlTransaction` that in turn needs to be used with the commands running under the same transaction (code file `TransactionSamples/Program.cs`):

```
public static void TransactionSample()
{
  using (var connection = new SqlConnection(GetConnectionString()))
  {
    await connection.OpenAsync();
    SqlTransaction tx = connection.BeginTransaction();
    // etc.
  }
}
```

> **NOTE** *Indeed, you can create transactions spanning multiple connections. With this, using the Windows operating system, the Distributed Transaction Coordinator is used. You can create distributed transactions using the `TransactionScope` class. However, this class is only part of the full .NET Framework and has not been brought forward to .NET Core; thus it is not part of this book. In case you need to know more about `TransactionScope`, consult a previous edition of the book, such as Professional C# 5 and .NET 4.5.1.*

The code sample creates a record in the `Sales.CreditCard` table. Using the SQL clause `INSERT INTO`, a record is added. The `CreditCard` table defines an auto-increment identifier that is returned with the second SQL statement `SELECT SCOPE_IDENTITY()` that returns the created identifier. After the `SqlCommand` object is instantiated, the connection is assigned by setting the `Connection` property, and the transaction is assigned by setting the `Transaction` property. With ADO.NET transactions, you cannot assign the transaction to a command that uses a different connection. However, you can also create commands with the same connection that are not related to a transaction:

```
public static void TransactionSample()
{
  // etc.
```

```
    try
    {
        string sql = "INSERT INTO Sales.CreditCard " +
            "(CardType, CardNumber, ExpMonth, ExpYear)" +
            "VALUES (@CardType, @CardNumber, @ExpMonth, @ExpYear); " +
          "SELECT SCOPE_IDENTITY()";

        var command = new SqlCommand();
        command.CommandText = sql;
        command.Connection = connection;
        command.Transaction = tx;
    // etc.
    }
```

After defining the parameters and filling the values, the command is executed by invoking the method
ExecuteScalarAsync. This time the ExecuteScalarAsync method is used with the INSERT INTO clause
because the complete SQL statement ends by returning a single result: The created identifier is returned from
SELECT SCOPE_IDENTITY(). In case you set a breakpoint after the WriteLine method and check the result
in the database, you will not see the new record in the database although the created identifier is already
returned. The reason is that the transaction is not yet committed:

```
public static void TransactionSample()
{
    // etc.

        var p1 = new SqlParameter("CardType", SqlDbType.NVarChar, 50);
        var p2 = new SqlParameter("CardNumber", SqlDbType.NVarChar, 25);
        var p3 = new SqlParameter("ExpMonth", SqlDbType.TinyInt);
        var p4 = new SqlParameter("ExpYear", SqlDbType.SmallInt);
        command.Parameters.AddRange(new SqlParameter[] { p1, p2, p3, p4 });

        command.Parameters["CardType"].Value = "MegaWoosh";
        command.Parameters["CardNumber"].Value = "08154711123";
        command.Parameters["ExpMonth"].Value = 4;
        command.Parameters["ExpYear"].Value = 2019;

        object id = await command.ExecuteScalarAsync();
        WriteLine($"record added with id: {id}");

        // etc.
}
```

Now another record can be created within the same transaction. With the sample code, the same command
is used that has the connection and transaction still associated, just the values are changed before invoking
ExecuteScalarAsync again. You could also create a new SqlCommand object that accesses a different table
in the same database. The transaction is committed invoking the Commit method of the SqlTransaction
object. After the commit, you can see the new records in the database:

```
public static void TransactionSample()
{
    // etc.
        command.Parameters["CardType"].Value = "NeverLimits";
        command.Parameters["CardNumber"].Value = "987654321011";
        command.Parameters["ExpMonth"].Value = 12;
        command.Parameters["ExpYear"].Value = 2025;

        id = await command.ExecuteScalarAsync();
        WriteLine($"record added with id: {id}");

        // throw new Exception("abort the transaction");
```

```
            tx.Commit();
        }
        // etc.
    }
```

In case an error occurs, the `Rollback` method makes an undo of all the SQL commands in the same transaction. The state is reset as it was before the transaction was started. You can easily simulate a rollback by uncommenting the exception before the commit:

```
public static void TransactionSample()
{
    // etc.

    catch (Exception ex)
    {
        WriteLine($"error {ex.Message}, rolling back");
        tx.Rollback();
    }
    }
}
```

In case you run the program in debugging mode and have a breakpoint active for too long, the transaction will be aborted because the transaction timeout is reached. Transactions are not meant to have user input while the transaction is active. It's also not useful to increase the transaction timeout for user input, because having a transaction active causes locks within the database. Depending on the records you read and write, either row locks, page locks, or table locks can happen. You can influence the locks and thus performance of the database by setting an isolation level for creating the transaction. However, this also influences the ACID properties of the transaction—for example, not everything is isolated.

The default isolation level that is applied to the transaction is `ReadCommitted`. The following table shows the different options you can set.

ISOLATION LEVEL	DESCRIPTION
ReadUncommitted	Transactions are not isolated from each other. With this level, there is no wait for locked records from other transactions. This way, uncommitted data can be read from other transactions—dirty reads. This level is usually only used for reading records for which it does not matter if you read interim changes, such as reports.
ReadCommitted	Waits for records with a write-lock from other transactions. This way, a dirty read cannot happen. This level sets a read-lock for the current record read and a write-lock for the records being written until the transaction is completed. During the reading of a sequence of records, with every new record that is read, the prior record is unlocked. That's why nonrepeatable reads can happen.
RepeatableRead	Holds the lock for the records read until the transaction is completed. This way, the problem of nonrepeatable reads is avoided. Phantom reads can still occur.
Serializable	Holds a range lock. While the transaction is running, it is not possible to add a new record that belongs to the same range from which the data is being read.
Snapshot	With this level a snapshot is done from the actual data. This level reduces the locks as modified rows are copied. That way, other transactions can still read the old data without needing to wait for releasing of the lock.
Unspecified	Indicates that the provider is using an isolation level that is different from the values defined by the `IsolationLevel` enumeration.
Chaos	This level is similar to `ReadUncommitted`, but in addition to performing the actions of the `ReadUncommitted` value, `Chaos` does not lock updated records.

The following table summarizes the problems that can occur as a result of setting the most commonly used transaction isolation levels.

ISOLATION LEVEL	DIRTY READS	NONREPEATABLE READS	PHANTOM READS
ReadUncommitted	Y	Y	Y
ReadCommitted	N	Y	Y
RepeatableRead	N	N	Y
Serializable	Y	Y	Y

SUMMARY

In this chapter, you've seen the core foundation of ADO.NET. You first looked at the SqlConnection object to open a connection to SQL Server. You've seen how to retrieve the connection string from a configuration file.

This chapter explained how to use connections properly so that they can be closed as early as possible, which preserves valuable resources. All the connection classes implement the IDisposable interface, called when the object is placed within a using statement. If there is one thing you should take away from this chapter, it is the importance of closing database connections as early as possible.

With commands you've seen passing parameters, getting a single return value, and retrieving records using the SqlDataReader. You've also seen how stored procedures can be invoked using the SqlCommand object.

Similar to other parts of the framework where processing can take some time, ADO.NET implements the task-based async pattern that was shown as well. You've also seen how to create and use transactions with ADO.NET.

The next chapter is about the ADO.NET Entity Framework that offers an abstraction to data access by offering a mapping between relations in the database and object hierarchies, and uses ADO.NET classes behind the scenes when you're accessing a relational database.

38

Entity Framework Core

WHAT'S IN THIS CHAPTER?

- ➤ Introducing Entity Framework Core 1.0
- ➤ Using Dependency Injection with Entity Framework
- ➤ Creating a Model with Relations
- ➤ Using Migrations with the .NET CLI Tools and MSBuild
- ➤ Object Tracking
- ➤ Updating Objects and Object Trees
- ➤ Conflict Handling with Updates
- ➤ Using Transactions

WROX.COM CODE DOWNLOADS FOR THIS CHAPTER

The wrox.com code downloads for this chapter are found at www.wrox.com/go/professionalcsharp6 on the Download Code tab. The code for this chapter is divided into the following major examples:

- ➤ Books Sample
- ➤ Books Sample with DI
- ➤ Menus Sample
- ➤ Menus with Data Annotations
- ➤ Conflict Handling Sample
- ➤ Transactions Sample

HISTORY OF ENTITY FRAMEWORK

Entity Framework is a framework offering mapping of entities to relationships. With this, you can create types that map to database tables, create database queries using LINQ, create and update objects, and write them to the database.

After many years of few changes to Entity Framework, the newest version is a complete rewrite. Let's have a look at the history of Entity Framework to see the reasons for the rewrite.

> ➤ **Entity Framework 1**—The first version of Entity Framework was not ready with .NET 3.5, but it was soon available with .NET 3.5 SP1. Another product offering somewhat similar functionality that was already available with .NET 3.5 was LINQ to SQL. Both LINQ to SQL and Entity Framework offered similar features from a wide view. However, LINQ to SQL was simpler to use but was only available for accessing SQL Server. Entity Framework was provider-based and offered access to several different relational databases. It included more features, such as many-to-many mapping without the need for mapping objects, and n-to-n mapping was possible. One disadvantage of Entity Framework was that it required model types to derive from the `EntityObject` base class. Mapping the objects to relations was done using an EDMX file that contains XML. The XML contained is defined by three schemas: the Conceptual Schema Definition (CSD) defines the object types with their properties and associations; the Storage Schema Definition (SSD) defines the database tables, columns, and relations; and the Mapping Schema Language (MSL) defines how the CSD and SSD map to each other.

> ➤ **Entity Framework 4**—Entity Framework 4 was available with .NET 4 and received major improvements, many coming from LINQ to SQL ideas. Because of the big changes, versions 2 and 3 have been skipped. With this edition, *lazy loading* was added to fetch relations on accessing a property. Creating a database was possible after designing a model using *SQL Data Definition Language* (DDL). The two models using Entity Framework were now *Database First* or *Model First*. Possibly the most important feature added was the support for Plain Old CLR Objects (POCO), so it was no longer necessary to derive from the base class `EntityObject`.

With later updates (such as Entity Framework 4.1, 4.2), additional features have been added with NuGet packages. This allowed adding features faster. Entity Framework 4.1 offers the *Code First* model where the EDMX file to define the mappings is no longer used. Instead, all the mapping is defined using C# code—either using attributes or with a fluent API to define the mapping using code.

Entity Framework 4.3 added support for *Migrations*. With this, it is possible to define updates to the database schemas using C# code. The database update can be automatically applied from the application using the database.

> ➤ **Entity Framework 5**—The NuGet package for Entity Framework 5 supported both .NET 4.5 and .NET 4 applications. However, many of the features of Entity Framework 5 have been available with .NET 4.5. Entity Framework was still based on types that are installed on the system with .NET 4.5. New with this release were performance improvements as well as supporting new SQL Server features, such as spatial data types.

> ➤ **Entity Framework 6**—Entity Framework 6 solved some issues with Entity Framework 5, which was partly a part of the framework installed on the system and partly available via NuGet extensions. Now the complete code of Entity Framework has moved to NuGet packages. For not creating conflicts, a new namespace was used. When porting apps to the new version, the namespace had to be changed.

This book covers the newest version of Entity Framework, *Entity Framework Core 1.0*. This version is a complete rewrite and removes old behaviors. This version no longer supports the XML file mapping with CSDL, SSDL, and MSL. Only Code First is supported now—the model that was added with Entity Framework 4.1. Code First doesn't mean that the database can't exist first. You can either create the database first or define the database purely from code; both options are possible.

> **NOTE** *The name* Code First *is somewhat misleading. With Code First, either the code or the database can be created first. Originally with the beta version of Code First, the name was* Code Only. *Because the other model options had* First *in their names, the name Code Only was changed as well.*

The complete rewrite of Entity Framework was also done to not only support relational databases but to also support NoSql databases as well—you just need a provider. Currently, at the time of this writing, provider support is limited, but offers will increase over time.

The new version of Entity Framework is based on .NET Core; thus it is possible to use this framework on Linux and Mac systems as well.

Entity Framework Core 1.0 does not support all the features that were offered by Entity Framework 6. More features will be available over time with newer releases of Entity Framework. You just need to pay attention to what version of Entity Framework you are using. There are many valid reasons to stay with Entity Framework 6, but using ASP.NET Core 1.0 on non-Windows platforms, using Entity Framework with the Universal Windows Platform, and using nonrelational data stores all require the use of Entity Framework Core 1.0.

This chapter introduces you to Entity Framework Core 1.0. It starts with a simple model reading and writing information from SQL Server. Later on, relations are added, and you will be introduced to the change tracker and conflict handling when writing to the database. Creating and modifying database schemas using migrations is another important part of this chapter.

> **NOTE** *This chapter uses the Books database. This database is included with the download of the code samples at* www.wrox.com/go/professionalcsharp6.

INTRODUCING ENTITY FRAMEWORK

The first example uses a single `Book` type and maps this type to the `Books` table in a SQL Server database. You write records to the database and then read, update, and delete them.

With the first example, you create the database first. You can do this with the SQL Server Object Explorer that is part of Visual Studio 2015. Select the database instance (`localdb`) \`MSSQLLocalDB` is installed with Visual Studio), click the Databases node in the tree view, and select Add New Database. The sample database has only a single table named `Books`.

You can create the table `Books` by selecting the Tables node within the Books database and then selecting Add New Table. Using the designer shown in Figure 38-1, or by entering the SQL DDL statement in the T-SQL editor, you can create the table Books. The following code snippet shows the T-SQL code for creating the table. When you click the Update button, you can submit the changes to the database.

```
CREATE TABLE [dbo].[Books]
(
  [BookId] INT NOT NULL PRIMARY KEY IDENTITY,
  [Title] NVARCHAR(50) NOT NULL,
  [Publisher] NVARCHAR(25) NOT NULL
)
```

Creating a Model

The sample application `BookSample` for accessing the `Books` database is a Console Application (Package). This sample makes use of the following dependencies and namespaces:

Dependencies

```
NETStandard.Library

Microsoft.EntityFrameworkCore

Microsoft.EntityFrameworkCore.SqlServer
```

Namespaces

```
Microsoft.EntityFrameworkCore
System.ComponentModel.DataAnnotations.Schema
System
System.Linq
System.Threading.Tasks
static System.Console
```

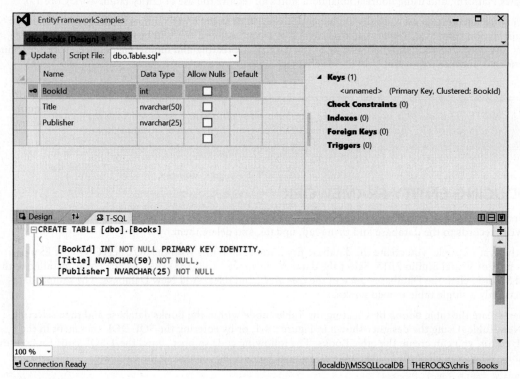

FIGURE 38-1

The class `Book` is a simple entity type that defines three properties. The `BookId` property maps to the primary key of the table, the `Title` property to the `Title` column, and the `Publisher` property to the `Publisher` column. To map the type to the Books table, the `Table` attribute is applied to the type (code file `BooksSample/Book.cs`):

```
[Table("Books")]
public class Book
{
  public int BookId { get; set; }
  public string Title { get; set; }
  public string Publisher { get; set; }
}
```

Creating a Context

The association of the Book table with the database is done creating the BooksContext class. This class derives from the base class DbContext. The BooksContext class defines the Books property that is of type DbSet<Book>. This type allows creating queries and adding Book instances for storing it in the database. To define the connection string, the OnConfiguring method of the DbContext can be overridden. Here, the UseSqlServer extension method maps the context to a SQL Server database (code file BooksSample/BooksContext.cs):

```
public class BooksContext: DbContext
{
  private const string ConnectionString =
    @"server=(localdb)\MSSQLLocalDb;database=Books;trusted_connection=true";

  public DbSet<Book> Books { get; set; }

  protected override void OnConfiguring(DbContextOptionsBuilder optionsBuilder)
  {
    base.OnConfiguring(optionsBuilder);
    optionsBuilder.UseSqlServer(ConnectionString);
  }
}
```

Another option to define the connection string is by using dependency injection, which is shown later in this chapter.

Writing to the Database

The database with the Books table is created; the model and context classes is defined and now you can fill the table with data. The AddBookAsync method is created to add a Book object to the database. First, the BooksContext object is instantiated. With the using statement it is ensured that the database connection is closed. After adding the object to the context using the Add method, the entity is written to the database calling SaveChangesAsync (code file BooksSample/Program.cs):

```
private async Task AddBookAsync(string title, string publisher)
{
  using (var context = new BooksContext())
  {
    var book = new Book
    {
      Title = title,
      Publisher = publisher
    };
    context.Add(book);
    int records = await context.SaveChangesAsync();

    WriteLine($"{records} record added");
  }
  WriteLine();
}
```

For adding a list of books, you can use the AddRange method (code file BooksSample/Program.cs):

```
private async Task AddBooksAsync()
{
  using (var context = new BooksContext())
  {
    var b1 = new Book
    {
      Title = "Professional C# 5 and .NET 4.5.1",
```

```
                    Publisher = "Wrox Press"
                };
                var b2 = new Book
                {
                    Title = "Professional C# 2012 and .NET 4.5",
                    Publisher = "Wrox Press"
                };
                var b3 = new Book
                {
                    Title = "JavaScript for Kids",
                    Publisher = "Wrox Press"
                };
                var b4 = new Book
                {
                    Title = "Web Design with HTML and CSS",
                    Publisher = "For Dummies"
                };
                context.AddRange(b1, b2, b3, b4);
                int records = await context.SaveChangesAsync();

                WriteLine($"{records} records added");
            }
            WriteLine();
        }
```

When you run the application and invoke these methods, you can see the data written to the database using the SQL Server Object Explorer.

Reading from the Database

To read the data from C# code, you just need to invoke the `BooksContext` and access the `Books` property. Accessing this property creates a SQL statement to retrieve all books from the database (code file `BooksSample/Program.cs`):

```
        private void ReadBooks()
        {
            using (var context = new BooksContext())
            {
                var books = context.Books;
                foreach (var b in books)
                {
                    WriteLine($"{b.Title} {b.Publisher}");
                }
            }
            WriteLine();
        }
```

When you open the IntelliTrace Events window during debugging, you can see the SQL statement that is sent to the database (this requires Visual Studio Enterprise edition):

```
SELECT [b].[BookId], [b].[Publisher], [b].[Title]
FROM [Books] AS [b]
```

Entity Framework offers a LINQ provider. With that, you can create LINQ queries to access the database. You can either use the method syntax as shown here:

```
        private void QueryBooks()
        {
            using (var context = new BooksContext())
            {
                var wroxBooks = context.Books.Where(b => b.Publisher == "Wrox Press");
                foreach (var b in wroxBooks)
                {
```

```
        WriteLine($"{b.Title} {b.Publisher}");
      }
    }
    WriteLine();
  }
```

or use the declarative LINQ query syntax:

```
var wroxBooks = from b in context.Books
                where b.Publisher == "Wrox Press"
                select b;
```

With both syntax variants, this SQL statement is sent to the database:

```
SELECT [b].[BookId], [b].[Publisher], [b].[Title]
FROM [Books] AS [b]
WHERE [b].[Publisher] = 'Wrox Press'
```

> **NOTE** *LINQ is discussed in detail in Chapter 13, "Language Integrated Query."*

Updating Records

Updating records can be easily achieved just by changing objects that have been loaded with the context, and invoking SaveChangesAsync (code file BooksSample/Program.cs):

```
private async Task UpdateBookAsync()
{
  using (var context = new BooksContext())
  {
    int records = 0;
    var book = context.Books.Where(b => b.Title == "Professional C# 6")
      .FirstOrDefault();
    if (book != null)
    {
      book.Title = "Professional C# 6 and .NET Core 5";
      records = await context.SaveChangesAsync();
    }
    WriteLine($"{records} record updated");
  }
  WriteLine();
}
```

Deleting Records

Finally, let's clean up the database and delete all records. You do this by retrieving all records and invoking the Remove or RemoveRange method to set the state of the objects in the context to deleted. Invoking the SaveChangesAsync method now deletes the records from the database and invokes SQL Delete statements for every object (code file BooksSample/Program.cs):

```
private async Task DeleteBooksAsync()
{
  using (var context = new BooksContext())
  {
    var books = context.Books;
    context.Books.RemoveRange(books);
    int records = await context.SaveChangesAsync();
    WriteLine($"{records} records deleted");
  }
  WriteLine();
}
```

> **NOTE** *An object-relational mapping tool such as Entity Framework is not useful with all scenarios. Deleting all objects was not done efficiently with the sample code. You can delete all records using a single SQL statement instead of one for every record. How this can be done is explained in Chapter 37, "ADO.NET."*

Now that you've seen how to add, query, update, and delete records, this chapter steps into features behind the scenes and gets into advanced scenarios using Entity Framework.

USING DEPENDENCY INJECTION

Entity Framework Core 1.0 has built-in support for dependency injection. Instead of defining the connection and the use of SQL Server with the DbContext derived class, the connection and SQL Server selection can be injected by using a dependency injection framework.

To see this in action, the previous sample has been modified with the BooksSampleWithDI sample project.

This sample makes use of the following dependencies and namespaces:

Dependencies

> NETStandard.Library
>
> Microsoft.EntityFrameworkCore
>
> Microsoft.EntityFrameworkCore.SqlServer
>
> Microsoft.Framework.DependencyInjection

Namespaces

> Microsoft.EntityFrameworkCore
>
> System.Linq
>
> System.Threading.Tasks
>
> static System.Console

The BooksContext class now looks a lot simpler in just defining the Books property (code file BooksSampleWithDI/BooksContext.cs):

```
public class BooksContext: DbContext
{
  public DbSet<Book> Books { get; set; }
}
```

The BooksService is the new class that makes use of the BooksContext. Here, the BooksContext is injected via constructor injection. The methods AddBooksAsync and ReadBooks are very similar to these methods from the previous sample, but they use the context member of the BooksService class instead of creating a new one (code file BooksSampleWithDI/BooksService.cs):

```
public class BooksService
{
  private readonly BooksContext _booksContext;
  public BooksService(BooksContext context)
  {
    _booksContext = context;
  }

  public async Task AddBooksAsync()
```

```
{
  var b1 = new Book
  {
    Title = "Professional C# 5 and .NET 4.5.1",
    Publisher = "Wrox Press"
  };
  var b2 = new Book
  {
    Title = "Professional C# 2012 and .NET 4.5",
    Publisher = "Wrox Press"
  };
  var b3 = new Book
  {
    Title = "JavaScript for Kids",
    Publisher = "Wrox Press"
  };
  var b4 = new Book
  {
    Title = "Web Design with HTML and CSS",
    Publisher = "For Dummies"
  };
  _booksContext.AddRange(b1, b2, b3, b4);
  int records = await _booksContext.SaveChangesAsync();

  WriteLine($"{records} records added");
}

public void ReadBooks()
{
  var books = _booksContext.Books;
  foreach (var b in books)
  {
    WriteLine($"{b.Title} {b.Publisher}");
  }
  WriteLine();
}
}
```

The container of the dependency injection framework is initialized in the InitializeServices method. Here, a ServiceCollection instance is created, and the BooksService class is added to this collection with a transient lifetime management. With this, the ServiceCollection is instantiated every time this service is requested. For registering Entity Framework and SQL Server, the extension methods AddEntityFramework, AddSqlServer, and AddDbContext are available. The AddDbContext method requires an Action delegate as parameter where a DbContextOptionsBuilder parameter is received. With this options parameter, the context can be configured using the UseSqlServer extension method. This is the similar functionality to register SQL Server with Entity Framework in the previous sample (code file BooksSampleWithDI/Program.cs):

```
private void InitializeServices()
{
  const string ConnectionString =
    @"server=(localdb)\MSSQLLocalDb;database=Books;trusted_connection=true";

  var services = new ServiceCollection();
  services.AddTransient<BooksService>();
  services.AddEntityFramework()
    .AddSqlServer()
    .AddDbContext<BooksContext>(options =>
      options.UseSqlServer(ConnectionString));

  Container = services.BuildServiceProvider();
```

```
    }

    public IServiceProvider Container { get; private set; }
```

The initialization of the services as well as the use of the `BooksService` is done from the `Main` method. The `BooksService` is retrieved invoking the `GetService` method of the `IServiceProvider` (code file `BooksSampleWithDI/Program.cs`):

```
static void Main()
{
  var p = new Program();
  p.InitializeServices();

  var service = p.Container.GetService<BooksService>();
  service.AddBooksAsync().Wait();
  service.ReadBooks();
}
```

When you run the application, you can see that records are added and read from the `Books` database.

> **NOTE** *You can read more information about dependency injection and the* `Microsoft.Framework.DependencyInjection` *package in Chapter 31, "Patterns with XAML Apps," and also see it in action in Chapter 40, "ASP.NET Core," and Chapter 41, "ASP.NET MVC."*

CREATING A MODEL

The first example of this chapter mapped a single table. The second example shows creating a relation between tables. Instead of creating the database with a SQL DDL statement (or by using the designer), in this section C# code is used to create the database.

The sample application `MenusSample` makes use of the following dependencies and namespaces:

Dependencies

```
NETStandard.Library
Microsoft.EntityFrameworkCore
Microsoft.EntityFrameworkCore.SqlServer
```

Namespaces

```
Microsoft.EntityFrameworkCore
Microsoft.EntityFrameworkCore.ChangeTracking
System
System.Collections.Generic
System.ComponentModel.DataAnnotations
System.ComponentModel.DataAnnotations.Schema
System.Linq
System.Threading
System.Threading.Tasks
static System.Console
```

Creating a Relation

Let's start creating a model. The sample project defines a one-to-many relation using the `MenuCard` and `Menu` types. The `MenuCard` contains a list of `Menu` objects. This relation is simply defined by the `Menu` property of type `List<Menu>` (code file `MenusSample/MenuCard.cs`):

```
public class MenuCard
{
  public int MenuCardId { get; set; }
  public string Title { get; set; }
  public List<Menu> Menus { get; } = new List<Menu>();

  public override string ToString() => Title;
}
```

The relation can also be accessed in the other direction; a `Menu` can access the `MenuCard` using the `MenuCard` property. The `MenuCardId` property is specified to define a foreign key relationship (code file `MenusSample/Menu.cs`):

```
public class Menu
{
  public int MenuId { get; set; }
  public string Text { get; set; }
  public decimal Price { get; set; }

  public int MenuCardId { get; set; }
  public MenuCard MenuCard { get; set; }

  public override string ToString() => Text;
}
```

The mapping to the database is done by the `MenusContext` class. This class is defined similarly to the previous context type; it just contains two properties to map the two object types: the properties `Menus` and `MenuCards` (code file `MenusSamples/MenusContext.cs`):

```
public class MenusContext: DbContext
{
  private const string ConnectionString = @"server=(localdb)\MSSQLLocalDb;" +
    "Database=MenuCards;Trusted_Connection=True";

  public DbSet<Menu> Menus { get; set; }
  public DbSet<MenuCard> MenuCards { get; set; }

  protected override void OnConfiguring(DbContextOptionsBuilder optionsBuilder)
  {
    base.OnConfiguring(optionsBuilder);
    optionsBuilder.UseSqlServer(ConnectionString);
  }
}
```

Migrations with .NET CLI

To automatically create the database using C# code, the .NET CLI tools can be extended with the ef tools using the package dotnet-ef. This package contains commands to create C# code for the migration. The commands are made available by installing the dotnet-ef NuGet package. You install it by referencing this package from the tools section in the project configuration file (code file `MenusSample/project.json`):

```
"tools": {
  "dotnet-ef": "1.0.0-*"
}
```

With the `ef` command in place, it offers the commands `database`, `dbcontext`, and `migrations`. The `database` command is used to upgrade the database to a specific migration state. The `dbcontext` command lists all `DbContext` derived types from the project (`dbcontext list`), and it creates context and entity from the database (`dbcontext scaffold`). The `migrations` command allows creating and removing migrations, as well as creating a SQL script to create the database with all the migrations. In case the production database should only be created and modified from the SQL administrator using SQL code, you can hand the generated script over to the SQL administrator.

To create an initial migration to create the database from code, the following command can be invoked from the developer command prompt. This command creates a migration named `InitMenuCards`:

```
>dotnet ef migrations add InitMenuCards
```

The command `migrations add` accesses the `DbContext` derived classes using reflection and in turn the referenced model types. With this information, it creates two classes to create and update the database. With the `Menu`, `MenuCard`, and `MenusContext` classes, two classes are created, the `MenusContextModelSnapshot` and `InitMenuCards`. You can find both types in the `Migrations` folder after the command succeeds.

The `MenusContextModelSnapshot` class contains the current state of the model to build the database:

```
[DbContext(typeof(MenusContext))]
partial class MenusContextModelSnapshot: ModelSnapshot
{
    protected override void BuildModel(ModelBuilder modelBuilder)
    {
        modelBuilder
          .HasAnnotation("ProductVersion", "7.0.0-rc1-16348")
          .HasAnnotation("SqlServer:ValueGenerationStrategy",
            SqlServerValueGenerationStrategy.IdentityColumn);

        modelBuilder.Entity("MenusSample.Menu", b =>
        {
            b.Property<int>("MenuId")
             .ValueGeneratedOnAdd();
            b.Property<int>("MenuCardId");
            b.Property<decimal>("Price");
            b.Property<string>("Text");
            b.HasKey("MenuId");
        });

        modelBuilder.Entity("MenusSample.MenuCard", b =>
        {
            b.Property<int>("MenuCardId")
             .ValueGeneratedOnAdd();

            b.Property<string>("Title");
            b.HasKey("MenuCardId");
        });

        modelBuilder.Entity("MenusSample.Menu", b =>
        {
            b.HasOne("MenusSample.MenuCard")
             .WithMany()
             .HasForeignKey("MenuCardId");
        });
    }
}
```

The `InitMenuCards` class defines `Up` and `Down` methods. The `Up` method lists all the actions that are needed to create the `MenuCard` and `Menu` tables including the primary keys, columns, and the relation. The `Down` method drops the two tables:

```
public partial class InitMenuCards: Migration
{
```

```
protected override void Up(MigrationBuilder migrationBuilder)
{
  migrationBuilder.CreateTable(
    name: "MenuCard",
    columns: table => new
    {
      MenuCardId = table.Column<int>(nullable: false)
        .Annotation("SqlServer:ValueGenerationStrategy",
          SqlServerValueGenerationStrategy.IdentityColumn),
      Title = table.Column<string>(nullable: true)
    },
    constraints: table =>
    {
      table.PrimaryKey("PK_MenuCard", x => x.MenuCardId);
    });

  migrationBuilder.CreateTable(
    name: "Menu",
    columns: table => new
    {
      MenuId = table.Column<int>(nullable: false)
        .Annotation("SqlServer:ValueGenerationStrategy",
          SqlServerValueGenerationStrategy.IdentityColumn),
      MenuCardId = table.Column<int>(nullable: false),
      Price = table.Column<decimal>(nullable: false),
      Text = table.Column<string>(nullable: true)
    },
    constraints: table =>
    {
      table.PrimaryKey("PK_Menu", x => x.MenuId);
      table.ForeignKey(
        name: "FK_Menu_MenuCard_MenuCardId",
        column: x => x.MenuCardId,
        principalTable: "MenuCard",
        principalColumn: "MenuCardId",
        onDelete: ReferentialAction.Cascade);
    });
}

protected override void Down(MigrationBuilder migrationBuilder)
{
  migrationBuilder.DropTable("Menu");
  migrationBuilder.DropTable("MenuCard");
}
}
```

> **NOTE** *With every change you're doing, you can create another migration. The new migration only defines the changes needed to get from the previous version to the new version. In case a customer's database needs to be updated from any earlier version, the necessary migrations are invoked when migrating the database.*
>
> *During the development process, you don't need all the migrations that you might create with the project, as no database with such interim states might exist. In that case you can remove a migration and create a new, larger one.*

Migrations with MSBuild

In case you are using the Entity Framework migrations with MSBuild-based projects instead of DNX, the commands for migration are different. With full framework Console applications, WPF applications, or ASP.NET 4.6 project types, you need to specify migration commands in the NuGet Package Manager Console instead of the Developer Command Prompt. You start the Package Manager Console from Visual Studio via Tools ➪ Library Package Manager ➪ Package Manager Console.

With the Package Manager Console, you can use PowerShell scripts to add and remove migrations. The command

```
> Add-Migration InitMenuCards
```

creates a `Migrations` folder including the migration classes as shown before.

Creating the Database

Now, with the migrations types in place, the database can be created. The `DbContext` derived class `MenusContext` contains a `Database` property that returns a `DatabaseFacade` object. Using the `DatabaseFacade`, you can create and delete databases. The method `EnsureCreated` creates a database if it doesn't exist. If the database already exists, nothing is done. The method `EnsureDeletedAsync` deletes the database. The following code snippet creates the database if it doesn't exist (code file `MenusSample/Program.cs`):

```
private static async Task CreateDatabaseAsync()
{
  using (var context = new MenusContext())
  {
    bool created = await context.Database.EnsureCreatedAsync();

    string createdText = created ? "created": "already exists";
    WriteLine($"database {createdText}");
  }
}
```

> **NOTE** *In case the database exists but has an older schema version, the* `EnsureCreatedAsync` *method doesn't apply schema changes. You can make schema upgrades by invoking the* `Migrate` *method.* `Migrate` *is an extension method to the* `DatabaseFacade` *class that is defined in the* `Microsoft.Data.Entity` *namespace.*

When you run the program, the tables `MenuCard` and `Menu` are created. Based on default conventions, the tables have the same name as the entity types. Another convention is used on creating the primary key: the column `MenuCardId` is defined as primary key because the property name ended with `Id`.

```
CREATE TABLE [dbo].[MenuCard] (
  [MenuCardId] INT            IDENTITY (1, 1) NOT NULL,
  [Title]      NVARCHAR (MAX) NULL,
  CONSTRAINT [PK_MenuCard] PRIMARY KEY CLUSTERED ([MenuCardId] ASC)
);
```

The `Menu` table defines the `MenuCardId` that is a foreign key to the `MenuCard` table. Deleting a `MenuCard` also deletes all associated `Menu` rows because of the `DELETE CASCADE`:

```
CREATE TABLE [dbo].[Menu] (
  [MenuId]     INT            IDENTITY (1, 1) NOT NULL,
  [MenuCardId] INT            NOT NULL,
  [Price]      DECIMAL (18, 2) NOT NULL,
  [Text]       NVARCHAR (MAX)  NULL,
  CONSTRAINT [PK_Menu] PRIMARY KEY CLUSTERED ([MenuId] ASC),
  CONSTRAINT [FK_Menu_MenuCard_MenuCardId] FOREIGN KEY ([MenuCardId])
    REFERENCES [dbo].[MenuCard] ([MenuCardId]) ON DELETE CASCADE
);
```

There are some parts in the creation code that would be useful to change. For example, the size of the Text and Title column could be reduced in size from NVARCHAR(MAX), SQL Server defines a Money type that could be used for the Price column, and the schema name could be changed from dbo. Entity Framework gives you two options to make these changes from code: data annotations and the Fluent API, which are both discussed next.

Data Annotations

One way to influence the generated database is to add data annotations to the entity types. The name of the tables can be changed by using the Table attribute. To change the schema name, the Table attribute defines the Schema property. To specify a different length for a string type, you can apply the MaxLength attribute (code file MenusWithDataAnnotations/MenuCard.cs):

```
[Table("MenuCards", Schema = "mc")]
public class MenuCard
{
  public int MenuCardId { get; set; }
  [MaxLength(120)]
  public string Title { get; set; }
  public List<Menu> Menus { get; set; }
}
```

With the Menu class, the Table and MaxLength attributes are applied as well. To change the SQL type, the Column attribute can be used (code file MenusWithDataAnnotations/Menu.cs):

```
[Table("Menus", Schema = "mc")]
public class Menu
{
  public int MenuId { get; set; }
  [MaxLength(50)]
  public string Text { get; set; }
  [Column(TypeName ="Money")]
  public decimal Price { get; set; }
  public int MenuCardId { get; set; }
  public MenuCard MenuCard { get; set; }
}
```

After applying the migrations and creating the database, you can see the new names of the tables with the schema name, as well as the changed data types on the Title, Text, and Price columns:

```
CREATE TABLE [mc].[MenuCards] (
  [MenuCardId] INT            IDENTITY (1, 1) NOT NULL,
  [Title]      NVARCHAR (120) NULL,
  CONSTRAINT [PK_MenuCard] PRIMARY KEY CLUSTERED ([MenuCardId] ASC)
);

CREATE TABLE [mc].[Menus] (
  [MenuId]     INT           IDENTITY (1, 1) NOT NULL,
  [MenuCardId] INT           NOT NULL,
  [Price]      MONEY         NOT NULL,
  [Text]       NVARCHAR (50) NULL,
  CONSTRAINT [PK_Menu] PRIMARY KEY CLUSTERED ([MenuId] ASC),
  CONSTRAINT [FK_Menu_MenuCard_MenuCardId] FOREIGN KEY ([MenuCardId])
    REFERENCES [mc].[MenuCards] ([MenuCardId]) ON DELETE CASCADE
);
```

Fluent API

Another way to influence the tables created is to use the Fluent API with the OnModelCreating method of the DbContext derived class. Using this has the advantage that you can keep the entity types simple without adding any attributes, and the fluent API also gives you more options than you have with applying attributes.

The following code snippet shows the override of the `OnModelCreating` method of the `BooksContext` class. The `ModelBuilder` class that is received as parameter offers a few methods, and several extension methods are defined. The `HasDefaultSchema` is an extension method that applies a default schema to the model that is now used with all types. The `Entity` method returns an `EntityTypeBuilder` that enables you to customize the entity, such as mapping it to a specific table name and defining keys and indexes (code file `MenusSample/MenusContext.cs`):

```
protected override void OnModelCreating(ModelBuilder modelBuilder)
{
    base.OnModelCreating(modelBuilder);

    modelBuilder.HasDefaultSchema("mc");

    modelBuilder.Entity<MenuCard>()
        .ToTable("MenuCards")
        .HasKey(c => c.MenuCardId);

    // etc.

    modelBuilder.Entity<Menu>()
        .ToTable("Menus")
        .HasKey(m => m.MenuId);

    // etc.
}
```

The `EntityTypeBuilder` defines a `Property` method to configure a property. The `Property` method returns a `PropertyBuilder` that in turn enables you to configure the property with max length values, required settings, and SQL types and to specify whether values should be automatically generated (such as identity columns):

```
protected override void OnModelCreating(ModelBuilder modelBuilder)
{
    // etc.

    modelBuilder.Entity<MenuCard>()
        .Property<int>(c => c.MenuCardId)
        .ValueGeneratedOnAdd();

    modelBuilder.Entity<MenuCard>()
        .Property<string>(c => c.Title)
        .HasMaxLength(50);

    modelBuilder.Entity<Menu>()
        .Property<int>(m => m.MenuId)
        .ValueGeneratedOnAdd();

    modelBuilder.Entity<Menu>()
        .Property<string>(m => m.Text)
        .HasMaxLength(120);

    modelBuilder.Entity<Menu>()
        .Property<decimal>(m => m.Price)
        .HasColumnType("Money");

    // etc.
}
```

To define one-to-many mappings, the `EntityTypeBuilder` defines mapping methods. The method `HasMany` combined with `WithOne` defines a mapping of many menus with one menu card. `HasMany` needs to be chained with `WithOne`. The method `HasOne` needs a chain with `WithMany` or `WithOne`. Chaining `HasOne` with `WithMany` defines a one-to-many relationship; chaining `HasOne` with `WithOne` defines a one-to-one relationship:

```
protected override void OnModelCreating(ModelBuilder modelBuilder)
{
  // etc.

  modelBuilder.Entity<MenuCard>()
    .HasMany(c => c.Menus)
    .WithOne(m => m.MenuCard);
  modelBuilder.Entity<Menu>()
    .HasOne(m => m.MenuCard)
    .WithMany(c => c.Menus)
    .HasForeignKey(m => m.MenuCardId);
}
```

After creating the mapping in the `OnModelCreating` method, you can create migrations as shown before.

Scaffolding a Model from the Database

Instead of creating the database from the model, you can also create the model from the database.

To do this from a SQL Server database you have to add the `EntityFramework.MicrosoftSqlServer.Design` NuGet package in addition to the other packages to a DNX project. Then you can use the following command from the Developer Command Prompt:

```
> dnx ef dbcontext scaffold
"server=(localdb)\MSSQLLocalDb;database=SampleDatabase;
trusted_connection=true" "EntityFramework.MicrosoftSqlServer"
```

The `dbcontext` command enables you to list `DbContext` objects from the project, as well as create `DBContext` objects. The command `scaffold` creates `DbContext`-derived classes as well as model classes. The `dnx ef dbcontext scaffold` needs two required arguments: the connection string to the database and the provider that should be used. With the statement shown earlier, the database `SampleDatabase` was accessed on the SQL `Server (localdb)\MSSQLLocalDb`. The provider used was `EntityFramework.MicrosoftSqlServer`. This NuGet package as well as the NuGet package with the same name and the `Design` postfix need to be added to the project.

After running this command, you can see the `DbContext` derived classes as well as the model types generated. The configuration of the model by default is done using the fluent API. However, you can change that to using the data annotations supplying the `-a` option. You can also influence the generated context class name as well as the output directory. Just check the different available options using the option `-h`.

WORKING WITH OBJECT STATE

After creating the database, you can write to it. In the first sample you've written to a single table. What about writing a relationship?

Adding Objects with Relations

The following code snippet writes a relationship, a `MenuCard` containing `Menu` objects. Here, the `MenuCard` and `Menu` objects are instantiated. The bidirectional associations are assigned. With the Menu, the `MenuCard` property is assigned to the `MenuCard`, and with the `MenuCard`, the `Menus` property is filled with `Menu` objects. The `MenuCard` instance is added to the context invoking the `Add` method of the `MenuCards` property. When you add an object to the context, by default all objects are added to the tree with the state added. Not only the `MenuCard` but also the `Menu objects` are saved. `IncludeDependents` is set. With this option, all the associated Menu objects are added to the context as well. Invoking SaveChanged on the context now creates four records (code file MenusSample/Program.cs):

```
private static async Task AddRecordsAsync()
{
  // etc.
  using (var context = new MenusContext())
  {
    var soupCard = new MenuCard();
    Menu[] soups =
    {
      new Menu
      {
        Text = "Consommé Célestine (with shredded pancake)",
        Price = 4.8m,
        MenuCard = soupCard
      },
      new Menu
      {
        Text = "Baked Potato Soup",
        Price = 4.8m,
        MenuCard = soupCard
      },
      new Menu
      {
        Text = "Cheddar Broccoli Soup",
        Price = 4.8m,
        MenuCard = soupCard
      },
    };

    soupCard.Title = "Soups";
    soupCard.Menus.AddRange(soups);
    context.MenuCards.Add(soupCard);

    ShowState(context);

    int records = await context.SaveChangesAsync();
    WriteLine($"{records} added");

    // etc.
}
```

The method ShowState that is invoked after adding the four objects to the context shows the state of all objects that are associated with the context. The DbContext class has a ChangeTracker associated that can be accessed using the ChangeTracker property. The Entries method of the ChangeTracker returns all the objects the change tracker knows about. With the foreach loop, every object including its state is written to the console (code file MenusSample/Program.cs):

```
public static void ShowState(MenusContext context)
{
  foreach (EntityEntry entry in context.ChangeTracker.Entries())
  {
    WriteLine($"type: {entry.Entity.GetType().Name}, state: {entry.State}," +
      $" {entry.Entity}");
  }
  WriteLine();
}
```

Run the application to see the Added state with these four objects:

```
type: MenuCard, state: Added, Soups
type: Menu, state: Added, Consommé Célestine (with shredded pancake)
```

```
type: Menu, state: Added, Baked Potato Soup
type: Menu, state: Added, Cheddar Broccoli Soup
```

Because of this state, the `SaveChangesAsync` method creates SQL `Insert` statements to write every object to the database.

Object Tracking

You've seen the context knows about added objects. However, the context also needs to know about changes. To know about changes, every object retrieved needs its state in the context. For seeing this in action let's create two different queries that return the same object. The following code snippet defines two different queries where each query returns the same object with the menus as they are stored in the database. Indeed, only one object gets materialized, as with the second query result it is detected that the record returned has the same primary key value as an object already referenced from the context. Verifying whether the references of the variables `m1` and `m2` are the same results in returning the same object (code file `MenusSample/Program.cs`):

```
private static void ObjectTracking()
{
  using (var context = new MenusContext())
  {
    var m1 = (from m in context.Menus
             where m.Text.StartsWith("Con")
             select m).FirstOrDefault();

    var m2 = (from m in context.Menus
             where m.Text.Contains("(")
             select m).FirstOrDefault();

    if (object.ReferenceEquals(m1, m2))
    {
      WriteLine("the same object");
    }
    else
    {
      WriteLine("not the same");
    }

    ShowState(context);
  }
}
```

The first LINQ query results in a SQL `SELECT` statement with a `LIKE` comparison to compare for the string to start with the value `Con`:

```
SELECT TOP(1) [m].[MenuId], [m].[MenuCardId], [m].[Price], [m].[Text]
FROM [mc].[Menus] AS [m]
WHERE [m].[Text] LIKE 'Con' + '%'
```

With the second LINQ query, the database needs to be consulted as well. Here, a `LIKE` comparison is done to compare for a (in the middle of the text:

```
SELECT TOP(1) [m].[MenuId], [m].[MenuCardId], [m].[Price], [m].[Text]
FROM [mc].[Menus] AS [m]
WHERE [m].[Text] LIKE ('%' + '(') + '%'
```

When you run the application, the same object is written to the console, and only one object is kept with the `ChangeTracker`. The state is `Unchanged`:

```
the same object
type: Menu, state: Unchanged, Consommé Célestine (with shredded pancake)
```

To not track the objects running queries from the database, you can invoke the `AsNoTracking` method with the `DbSet`:

```
var m1 = (from m in context.Menus.AsNoTracking()
          where m.Text.StartsWith("Con")
          select m).FirstOrDefault();
```

You can also configure the default tracking behavior of the `ChangeTracker` to `QueryTrackingBehavior.NoTracking`:

```
using (var context = new MenusContext())
{
    context.ChangeTracker.QueryTrackingBehavior =
        QueryTrackingBehavior.NoTracking;
```

With such a configuration, two queries are made to the database, two objects are materialized, and the state information is empty.

> **NOTE** *Using the* `NoTracking` *configuration is useful when the context is used to only read records, but changes are not made. This reduces the overhead of the context as state information is not kept.*

Updating Objects

As objects are tracked, they can be updated easily, as shown in the following code snippet. First, a `Menu` object is retrieved. With this tracked object, the price is modified before the change is written to the database. In between all changes, state information is written to the console (code file `MenusSample/Program.cs`):

```
private static async Task UpdateRecordsAsync()
{
    using (var context = new MenusContext())
    {
        Menu menu = await context.Menus
                              .Skip(1)
                              .FirstOrDefaultAsync();

        ShowState(context);
        menu.Price += 0.2m;
        ShowState(context);

        int records = await context.SaveChangesAsync();
        WriteLine($"{records} updated");
        ShowState(context);
    }
}
```

When you run the application, you can see that the state of the object is `Unchanged` after loading the record, `Modified` after the property value is changed, and `Unchanged` after saving is completed:

```
type: Menu, state: Unchanged, Baked Potato Soup
type: Menu, state: Modified, Baked Potato Soup
1 updated
type: Menu, state: Unchanged, Baked Potato Soup
```

When you access the entries from the change tracker, by default changes are automatically detected. You configure this by setting the `AutoDetectChangesEnabled` property of the `ChangeTracker`. For checking manually to see whether changes have been done, you invoke the method `DetectChanges`. With the invocation of SaveChangesAsync, the state is changed back to Unchanged. You can do this manually by invoking the method AcceptAllChanges.

Updating Untracked Objects

Object contexts are usually very short-lived. Using Entity Framework with ASP.NET MVC, with one HTTP request one object context is created to retrieve objects. When you receive an update from the client, the object must again be created on the server. This object is not associated with the object context. To update it in the database, the object needs to be associated with the data context, and the state changed to create an INSERT, UPDATE, or DELETE statement.

Such a scenario is simulated with the next code snippet. The GetMenuAsync method returns a Menu object that is disconnected from the context; the context is disposed at the end of the method (code file MenusSample/Program.cs):

```
private static async Task<Menu> GetMenuAsync()
{
  using (var context = new MenusContext())
  {
    Menu menu = await context.Menus
                      .Skip(2)
                      .FirstOrDefaultAsync();
    return menu;
  }
}
```

The GetMenuAsync method is invoked by the method ChangeUntrackedAsync. This method changes the Menu object that is not associated with any context. After the change, the Menu object is passed to the method UpdateUntrackedAsync to save it in the database (code file MenusSample/Program.cs):

```
private static async Task ChangeUntrackedAsync()
{
  Menu m = await GetMenuAsync();
  m.Price += 0.7m;
  await UpdateUntrackedAsync(m);
}
```

The method UpdateUntrackedAsync receives the updated object and needs to attach it with the context. One way to attach an object with the context is by invoking the Attach method of the DbSet, and set the state as needed. The Update method does both with one call: attaching the object and setting the state to Modified (code file MenusSample/Program.cs):

```
private static async Task UpdateUntrackedAsync(Menu m)
{
  using (var context = new MenusContext())
  {
    ShowState(context);

    // EntityEntry<Menu> entry = context.Menus.Attach(m);
    // entry.State = EntityState.Modified;

    context.Menus.Update(m);
    ShowState(context);

    await context.SaveChangesAsync();
  }
}
```

When you run the application with the ChangeUntrackedAsync method, you can see that the state is modified. The object was untracked at first, but because the state was explicitly updated, you can see the Modified state:

```
type: Menu, state: Modified, Cheddar Broccoli Soup
```

CONFLICT HANDLING

What if multiple users change the same record and then save the state? Who will win with the changes?

If multiple users accessing the same database work on different records, there's no conflict. All users can save their data without interfering with data edited by other users. If multiple users work on the same record, though, you need to give some thought to conflict resolution. You have different ways to deal with this. The easiest one is that *the last one wins*. The user saving the data last overwrites changes from the user that did the changes previously.

Entity Framework also offers a way for letting the *first one win*. With this option, when saving a record, a verification is needed if the data originally read is still in the database. If this is the case, saving data can continue as no changes occurred between reading and writing. However, if the data changed, a conflict resolution needs to be done.

Let's get into these different options.

The Last One Wins

The default scenario is that the last one saving changes wins. To see multiple accesses to the database, the `BooksSample` application is extended.

For an easy simulation of two users, the method `ConflictHandlingAsync` invokes the method `PrepareUpdateAsync` two times, makes different changes to two `Book` objects that reference the same record, and invokes the `UpdateAsync` method two times. Last, the book ID is passed to the `CheckUpdateAsync` method, which shows the actual state of the book from the database (code file `BooksSample/Program.cs`):

```
public static async Task ConflictHandlingAsync()
{
    // user 1
    Tuple<BooksContext, Book> tuple1 = await PrepareUpdateAsync();
    tuple1.Item2.Title = "updated from user 1";

    // user 2
    Tuple<BooksContext, Book> tuple2 = await PrepareUpdateAsync();
    tuple2.Item2.Title = "updated from user 2";

    // user 1
    await UpdateAsync(tuple1.Item1, tuple1.Item2);
    // user 2
    await UpdateAsync(tuple2.Item1, tuple2.Item2);

    context1.Item1.Dispose();
    context2.Item1.Dispose();

    await CheckUpdateAsync(tuple1.Item2.BookId);
}
```

The `PrepareUpdateAsync` method opens a `BookContext` and returns both the context and the book within a `Tuple` object. Remember, this method is invoked two times, and different `Book` objects associated with different `context` objects are returned (code file `BooksSample/Program.cs`):

```
private static async Task<Tuple<BooksContext, Book>> PrepareUpdateAsync()
{
    var context = new BooksContext();
    Book book = await context.Books
        .Where(b => b.Title == "Conflict Handling")
        .FirstOrDefaultAsync();
    return Tuple.Create(context, book);
}
```

> **NOTE** *Tuples are explained in Chapter 7, "Arrays and Tuples."*

The `UpdateAsync` method receives the opened `BooksContext` with the updated `Book` object to save the book to the database. Remember, this method is invoked two times as well (code file `BooksSample/Program.cs`):

```
private static async Task UpdateAsync(BooksContext context, Book book)
{
  await context.SaveChangesAsync();
  WriteLine($"successfully written to the database: id {book.BookId} " +
    $"with title {book.Title}");
}
```

The `CheckUpdateAsync` method writes the book with the specified `id` to the console (code file `BooksSample/Program.cs`):

```
private static async Task CheckUpdateAsync(int id)
{
  using (var context = new BooksContext())
  {
    Book book = await context.Books
      .Where(b => b.BookId == id)
      .FirstOrDefaultAsync();
    WriteLine($"updated: {book.Title}");
  }
}
```

What happens when you run the application? You see the first update is successful, and so is the second update. When updating a record, it is not verified whether any changes happened after reading the record, which is the case with this sample application. The second update just overwrites the data from the first update, as you can see with the application output:

```
successfully written to the database: id 7038 with title updated from user 1
successfully written to the database: id 7038 with title updated from user 2
updated: updated from user 2
```

The First One Wins

In case you need a different behavior, such as the first user's changes being saved to the record, you need to do some changes. The sample project `ConflictHandlingSample` uses the `Book` and `BookContext` objects like before, but it deals with the first-one-wins scenario.

This sample application makes use of the following dependencies and namespaces:

Dependencies

```
NETStandard.Library
Microsoft.EntityFrameworkCore
Microsoft.EntityFrameworkCore.SqlServer
```

Namespaces

```
Microsoft.EntityFrameworkCore
Microsoft.EntityFrameworkCore.ChangeTracking
System
System.Linq
System.Text
System.Threading.Tasks
static System.Console
```

For conflict resolution, you need to specify the properties that should be verified if any change happened between reading and updating with a *concurrency token*. Based on the property you specify, the SQL UPDATE statement is modified to verify not only for the primary key, but also all properties that are marked with the concurrency token. Adding many concurrency tokens to the entity type creates a huge WHERE clause with the UPDATE statement, which is not very efficient. Instead you can add a property that is updated from SQL Server with every UPDATE statement—and this is what's done with the Book class. The property TimeStamp is defined as timeStamp in SQL Server (code file ConflictHandlingSample/Book.cs):

```
public class Book
{
  public int BookId { get; set; }
  public string Title { get; set; }
  public string Publisher { get; set; }

  public byte[] TimeStamp { get; set; }
}
```

To define the TimeStamp property as a timestamp type in SQL Server, you use the Fluent API. The SQL data type is defined using the HasColumnType method. The method ValueGeneratedOnAddOrUpdate informs the context that with every SQL INSERT or UPDATE statement the TimeStamp property can change, and it needs to be set with the context after these operations. The IsConcurrencyToken method marks this property as required to check whether it didn't change after reading it (code file ConflictHandlingSample/BooksContext.cs):

```
protected override void OnModelCreating(ModelBuilder modelBuilder)
{
    base.OnModelCreating(modelBuilder);
    var book = modelBuilder.Entity<Book>();
    book.HasKey(p => p.BookId);
    book.Property(p => p.Title).HasMaxLength(120).IsRequired();
    book.Property(p => p.Publisher).HasMaxLength(50);
    book.Property(p => p.TimeStamp)
        .HasColumnType("timestamp")
        .ValueGeneratedOnAddOrUpdate()
        .IsConcurrencyToken();
}
```

> **NOTE** *Instead of using the* IsConcurrencyToken *method with the Fluent API, you can also apply the attribute* ConcurrencyCheck *to the property where concurrency should be checked.*

The process of the conflict-handling check is similar to what was done before. Both user 1 and user 2 invoke the PrepareUpdateAsync method, change the book title, and call the UpdateAsync method to make the change in the database (code file ConflictHandlingSample/Program.cs):

```
public static async Task ConflictHandlingAsync()
{
    // user 1
    Tuple<BooksContext, Book> tuple1 = await PrepareUpdateAsync();
    tuple1.Item2.Title = "user 1 wins";

    // user 2
    Tuple<BooksContext, Book> tuple2 = await PrepareUpdateAsync();
    tuple2.Item2.Title = "user 2 wins";

    // user 1
    await UpdateAsync(tuple1.Item1, tuple1.Item2);
    // user 2
```

```
    await UpdateAsync(tuple2.Item1, tuple2.Item2);

    context1.Item1.Dispose();
    context2.Item1.Dispose();

    await CheckUpdateAsync(context1.Item2.BookId);
}
```

The `PrepareUpdateAsync` method is not repeated here, as this method is implemented in the same way as with the previous sample. What's quite different is the `UpdateAsync` method. To see the different timestamps, before and after the update, a custom extension method `StringOutput` for the byte array is implemented that writes the byte array in a readable form to the console. Next, the changes of the `Book` object are shown calling the `ShowChanges` helper method. The `SaveChangesAsync` method is invoked to write all updates to the database. In case the update fails with a `DbUpdateConcurrencyException`, information is written to the console about the failure (code file `ConflictHandlingSample/Program.cs`):

```
private static async Task UpdateAsync(BooksContext context, Book book,
  string user)
{
  try
  {
    WriteLine($"{user}: updating id {book.BookId}, " +
      $"timestamp: {book.TimeStamp.StringOutput()}");
    ShowChanges(book.BookId, context.Entry(book));

    int records = await context.SaveChangesAsync();
    WriteLine($"{user}: updated {book.TimeStamp.StringOutput()}");
    WriteLine($"{user}: {records} record(s) updated while updating " +
      $"{book.Title}");
  }
  catch (DbUpdateConcurrencyException ex)
  {
    WriteLine($"{user}: update failed with {book.Title}");
    WriteLine($"error: {ex.Message}");
    foreach (var entry in ex.Entries)
    {
      Book b = entry.Entity as Book;
      WriteLine($"{b.Title} {b.TimeStamp.StringOutput()}");
      ShowChanges(book.BookId, context.Entry(book));
    }
  }
}
```

With objects that are associated with the context, you can access the original values and the current values with a `PropertyEntry` object. The original values that were retrieved when reading the object from the database can be accessed with the `OriginalValue` property, the current values with the `CurrentValue` property. The `PropertyEntry` object can be accessed with the Property method of an `EntityEntry` as shown in the `ShowChanges` and `ShowChange` methods (code file `ConflictHandlingSample/Program.cs`):

```
private static void ShowChanges(int id, EntityEntry entity)
{
  ShowChange(id, entity.Property("Title"));
  ShowChange(id, entity.Property("Publisher"));
}

private static void ShowChange(int id, PropertyEntry propertyEntry)
{
  WriteLine($"id: {id}, current: {propertyEntry.CurrentValue}, " +
    $"original: {propertyEntry.OriginalValue}, " +
    $"modified: {propertyEntry.IsModified}");
}
```

To convert the byte array of the `TimeStamp` property that is updated from SQL Server for visual output, the extension method `StringOutput` is defined (code file `ConflictHandlingSample/Program.cs`):

```
static class ByteArrayExtension
{
  public static string StringOutput(this byte[] data)
  {
    var sb = new StringBuilder();
    foreach (byte b in data)
    {
      sb.Append($"{b}.");
    }
    return sb.ToString();
  }
}
```

When you run the application, you can see output such as the following. The timestamp values and book IDs differ with every run. The first user updates the book with the original title *sample book* to the new title *user 1 wins*. The `IsModified` property returns `true` for the `Title` property but `false` for the `Publisher` property, as only the title changed. The original timestamp ends with 1.1.209; after the update to the database the timestamp is changed to 1.17.114. In the meantime, user 2 opened the same record; this book still has a timestamp of 1.1.209. User 2 updates this book, but here the update failed because the timestamp of this book does not match the timestamp from the database. Here, a `DbUpdateConcurrencyException` exception is thrown. In the exception handler, the reason of the exception is written to the console as you can see in the program output:

```
user 1: updating id 17, timestamp 0.0.0.0.0.1.1.209.
id: 17, current: user 1 wins, original: sample book, modified: True
id: 17, current: Sample, original: Sample, modified: False
user 1: updated 0.0.0.0.0.1.17.114.
user 1: 1 record(s) updated while updating user 1 wins
user 2: updating id 17, timestamp 0.0.0.0.0.1.1.209.
id: 17, current: user 2 wins, original: sample book, modified: True
id: 17, current: Sample, original: Sample, modified: False
user 2 update failed with user 2 wins
user 2 error: Database operation expected to affect 1 row(s) but actually affected 0 row(s).
Data may have been modified or deleted since entities were loaded.
See http://go.microsoft.com/fwlink/?LinkId=527962 for information on
understanding and handling optimistic concurrency exceptions.
user 2 wins 0.0.0.0.0.1.1.209.
id: 17, current: user 2 wins, original: sample book, modified: True
id: 17, current: Sample, original: Sample, modified: False
updated: user 1 wins
```

When using concurrency tokens and handling the `DbConcurrencyException`, you can deal with concurrency conflicts as needed. You can, for example, automatically resolve concurrency issues. If different properties are changed, you can retrieve the changed record and merge the changes. If the property changed is a number where you do some calculations—for example, a point system—you can increment or decrement the values from both updates and just throw an exception if a limit is reached. You can also ask the user to resolve the concurrency issue by giving the user the information that's currently in the database and ask what changes he or she would like to do. Just don't ask too much from the user. It's likely that the only thing the user wants is to get rid of this rarely shown dialog, which means he or she might click OK or Cancel without reading the content. For rare conflicts, you can also write logs and inform the system administrator that an issue needs to be resolved.

USING TRANSACTIONS

Chapter 37 introduces programming with transactions. With every access of the database using the Entity Framework, a transaction is involved, too. You can use transactions implicitly or create them explicitly with configurations as needed. The sample project used with this section demonstrates transactions in both ways.

Here, the `Menu`, `MenuCard`, and `MenuContext` classes are used as shown earlier with the `MenusSample` project. This sample application makes use of following dependencies and namespaces:

Dependencies

```
NETStandard.Library
Microsoft.EntityFrameworkCore
Microsoft.EntityFrameworkCore.SqlServer
```

Namespaces

```
Microsoft.EntityFrameworkCore
Microsoft.EntityFrameworkCore.Storage
System.Linq
System.Threading
System.Threading.Tasks
static System.Console
```

Using Implicit Transactions

An invocation of the `SaveChangesAsync` method automatically resolves to one transaction. If one part of the changes that need to be done fails—for example, because of a database constraint—all the changes already done are rolled back. This is demonstrated with the following code snippet. Here, the first `Menu` (`m1`) is created with valid data. A reference to an existing `MenuCard` is done by supplying the `MenuCardId`. After the update succeeds, the `MenuCard` property of the `Menu` `m1` is filled automatically. However, the second `Menu` created, `mInvalid`, references an invalid menu card by supplying a `MenuCardId` that is one value higher than the highest ID available in the database. Because of the defined foreign key relation between `MenuCard` and `Menu`, adding this object will fail (code file `TransactionsSample/Program.cs`):

```
private static async Task AddTwoRecordsWithOneTxAsync()
{
  WriteLine(nameof(AddTwoRecordsWithOneTxAsync));
  try
  {
    using (var context = new MenusContext())
    {
      var card = context.MenuCards.First();
      var m1 = new Menu
      {
        MenuCardId = card.MenuCardId,
        Text = "added",
        Price = 99.99m
      };

      int hightestCardId = await context.MenuCards.MaxAsync(c => c.MenuCardId);
      var mInvalid = new Menu
      {
        MenuCardId = ++hightestCardId,
        Text = "invalid",
        Price = 999.99m
      };
      context.Menus.AddRange(m1, mInvalid);

      int records = await context.SaveChangesAsync();
      WriteLine($"{records} records added");
    }
  }
```

```
      catch (DbUpdateException ex)
      {
        WriteLine($"{ex.Message}");
        WriteLine($"{ex?.InnerException.Message}");
      }
      WriteLine();
    }
```

After running the application invoking the method `AddTwoRecordsWithOneTxAsync`, you can verify the content of the database to see that not a single record was added. The exception message as well as the message of the inner exception gives the details:

```
AddTwoRecordsWithOneTxAsync
An error occurred while updating the entries. See the inner exception for details.
The INSERT statement conflicted with the FOREIGN KEY constraint "FK_Menu_MenuCard_MenuCardId".
The conflict occurred in database "MenuCards", table "mc.MenuCards", column 'MenuCardId'.
```

In case writing the first record to the database should be successful even if the second record write fails, you have to invoke the `SaveChangesAsync` method multiple times as shown in the following code snippet. In the method `AddTwoRecordsWithTwoTxAsync`, the first invocation of `SaveChangesAsync` inserts the `m1` Menu object, whereas the second invocation tries to insert the `mInvalid` Menu object (code file `TransactionsSample/Program.cs`):

```
    private static async Task AddTwoRecordsWithTwoTxAsync()
    {
      WriteLine(nameof(AddTwoRecordsWithTwoTxAsync));
      try
      {
        using (var context = new MenusContext())
        {
          var card = context.MenuCards.First();
          var m1 = new Menu
          {
            MenuCardId = card.MenuCardId,
            Text = "added",
            Price = 99.99m
          };
          context.Menus.Add(m1);

          int records = await context.SaveChangesAsync();
          WriteLine($"{records} records added");

          int hightestCardId = await context.MenuCards.MaxAsync(c => c.MenuCardId);
          var mInvalid = new Menu
          {
            MenuCardId = ++hightestCardId,
            Text = "invalid",
            Price = 999.99m
          };
          context.Menus.Add(mInvalid);

          records = await context.SaveChangesAsync();
          WriteLine($"{records} records added");
        }
      }
      catch (DbUpdateException ex)
      {
        WriteLine($"{ex.Message}");
        WriteLine($"{ex?.InnerException.Message}");
      }
      WriteLine();
    }
```

When you run the application, adding the first INSERT statement succeeds, but of course the second one results in a DbUpdateException. You can verify the database to see that one record was added this time:

```
AddTwoRecordsWithTwoTxAsync
1 records added
An error occurred while updating the entries. See the inner exception for details.
The INSERT statement conflicted with the FOREIGN KEY constraint "FK_Menu_MenuCard_MenuCardId".
The conflict occurred in database "MenuCards", table "mc.MenuCards", column 'MenuCardId'.
```

Creating Explicit Transactions

Instead of using implicitly created transactions, you can also create them explicitly. This gives you the advantage of also having the option to roll back in case some of your business logic fails, and you can combine multiple invocations of SaveChangesAsync within one transaction. To start a transaction that is associated with the DbContext derived class, you need to invoke the BeginTransactionAsync method of the DatabaseFacade class that is returned from the Database property. The transaction returned implements the interface IDbContextTransaction. The SQL statements done with the associated DbContext are enlisted with the transaction. To commit or roll back, you have to explicitly invoke the methods Commit or Rollback. In the sample code, Commit is done when the end of the DbContext scope is reached; Rollback is done in cases where an exception occurs (code file TransactionsSample/Program.cs):

```
private static async Task TwoSaveChangesWithOneTxAsync()
{
  WriteLine(nameof(TwoSaveChangesWithOneTxAsync));
  IDbContextTransaction tx = null;
  try
  {
    using (var context = new MenusContext())
    using (tx = await context.Database.BeginTransactionAsync())
    {
      var card = context.MenuCards.First();
      var m1 = new Menu
      {
        MenuCardId = card.MenuCardId,
        Text = "added with explicit tx",
        Price = 99.99m
      };

      context.Menus.Add(m1);
      int records = await context.SaveChangesAsync();
      WriteLine($"{records} records added");

      int hightestCardId = await context.MenuCards.MaxAsync(c => c.MenuCardId);
      var mInvalid = new Menu
      {
        MenuCardId = ++hightestCardId,
        Text = "invalid",
        Price = 999.99m
      };
      context.Menus.Add(mInvalid);

      records = await context.SaveChangesAsync();
      WriteLine($"{records} records added");

      tx.Commit();
    }
  }
  catch (DbUpdateException ex)
  {
    WriteLine($"{ex.Message}");
```

```
        WriteLine($"{ex?.InnerException.Message}");

        WriteLine("rolling back…");
        tx.Rollback();
    }
    WriteLine();
}
```

When you run the application, you can see that no records have been added, although the
SaveChangesAsync method was invoked multiple times. The first return of SaveChangesAsync lists one
record as being added, but this record is removed based on the Rollback later on. Depending on the setting
of the isolation level, the updated record can only be seen before the rollback was done within the transaction, but not outside the transaction.

```
TwoSaveChangesWithOneTxAsync
1 records added
An error occurred while updating the entries. See the inner exception for details.
The INSERT statement conflicted with the FOREIGN KEY constraint "FK_Menu_MenuCard_MenuCardId".
The conflict occurred in database "MenuCards", table "mc.MenuCards", column 'MenuCardId'.
rolling back...
```

> **NOTE** *With the* BeginTransactionAsync *method, you can also supply a value for
> the isolation level to specify the isolation requirements and locks needed in the data-
> base. Isolation levels are discussed in Chapter 37.*

SUMMARY

This chapter introduced you to the features of the Entity Framework Core. You've learned how the object
context keeps knowledge about entities retrieved and updated, and how changes can be written to the
database. You've also seen how migrations can be used to create and change the database schema from C#
code. To define the schema, you've seen how the database mapping can be done using data annotations, and
you've also seen the fluent API that offers more features compared to the annotations.

You've seen possibilities for reacting to conflicts when multiple users work on the same record, as well as
using transactions implicitly or explicitly for more transactional control.

The next chapter shows using Windows Services to create a program that automatically starts with the system. You can make use of Entity Framework within Windows Services.

39

Windows Services

WROX.COM CODE DOWNLOADS FOR THIS CHAPTER

The wrox.com code downloads for this chapter are found at www.wrox.com/go/professionalcsharp6 on the Download Code tab. The code is in the Chapter 39 download and individually named according to the names throughout the chapter.

➤ Quote Server

➤ Quote Client

➤ Quote Service

➤ Service Control

WHAT IS A WINDOWS SERVICE?

Windows Services are programs that can be started automatically at boot time without the need for anyone to log on to the machine. If you need to have programs start up without user interaction or need to run under a different user than the interactive user, which can be a user with more privileges, you can create a Windows Service. Some examples could be a WCF host (if you can't use Internet Information Services (IIS) for some reason), a program that caches data from a network server, or a program that reorganizes local disk data in the background.

This chapter starts with looking at the architecture of Windows Services, creates a Windows Service that hosts a networking server, and gives you information to start, monitor, control, and troubleshoot your Windows Services.

As previously mentioned, Windows Services are applications that can be automatically started when the operating system boots. These applications can run without having an interactive user logged on to the system and can do some processing in the background.

For example, on a Windows Server, system networking services should be accessible from the client without a user logging on to the server; and on the client system, services enable you to do things such as get a new software version online or perform some file cleanup on the local disk.

You can configure a Windows Service to run from a specially configured user account or from the system user account—a user account that has even more privileges than that of the system administrator.

> **NOTE** *Unless otherwise noted, when I refer to a service, I am referring to a Windows Service.*

Here are a few examples of services:

➤ Simple TCP/IP Services is a service program that hosts some small TCP/IP servers: echo, daytime, quote, and others.

➤ World Wide Web Publishing Service is a service of IIS.

➤ Event Log is a service to log messages to the event log system.

➤ Windows Search is a service that creates indexes of data on the disk.

➤ Superfetch is a service that preloads commonly used applications and libraries into memory, thus improving the startup time of these applications.

You can use the Services administration tool, shown in Figure 39-1, to see all the services on a system. You get to the program by entering Services on the Start screen.

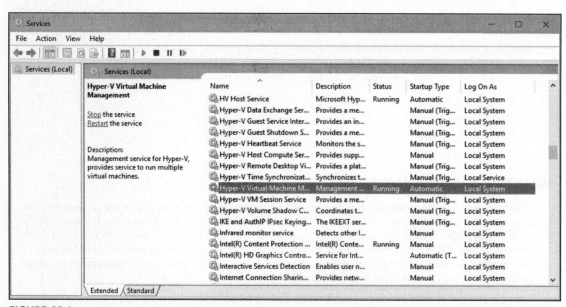

FIGURE 39-1

> **NOTE** *You can't create a Windows Service with .NET Core; you need the .NET Framework. To control services, you can use .NET Core.*

WINDOWS SERVICES ARCHITECTURE

Three program types are necessary to operate a Windows Service:

➤ A service program

➤ A service control program

➤ A service configuration program

The *service program* is the implementation of the service. With a *service control* program, it is possible to send control requests to a service, such as start, stop, pause, and continue. With a *service configuration* program, a service can be installed; it is copied to the file system, and information about the service needs to be written to the registry. This registry information is used by the service control manager (SCM) to start and stop the service. Although .NET components can be installed simply with an xcopy—because they don't need to write information to the registry—installation for services requires registry configuration. You can also use a service configuration program to change the configuration of that service at a later point. These three ingredients of a Windows Service are discussed in the following subsections.

Service Program

In order to put the .NET implementation of a service in perspective, this section takes a brief look at the Windows architecture of services in general, and the inner functionality of a service.

The service program implements the functionality of the service. It needs three parts:

➤ A main function

➤ A service-main function

➤ A handler

Before discussing these parts, however, it would be useful to digress for a moment for a short introduction to the SCM, which plays an important role for services—sending requests to your service to start it and stop it.

Service Control Manager

The SCM is the part of the operating system that communicates with the service. Using a sequence diagram, Figure 39-2 illustrates how this communication works.

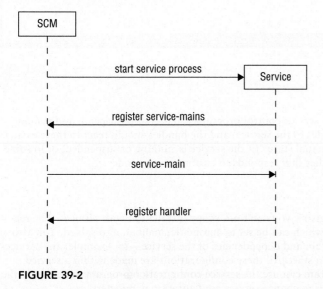

FIGURE 39-2

At boot time, each process for which a service is set to start automatically is started, and so the main function of this process is called. The service is responsible for registering the service-main function for each of its services. The main function is the entry point of the service program, and in this function the entry points for the service-main functions must be registered with the SCM.

Main Function, Service-Main, and Handlers

The main function of the service is the normal entry point of a program, the `Main` method. The main function of the service might register more than one service-main function. The *service-main* function contains the actual functionality of the service, which must register a service-main function for each service it provides. A service program can provide a lot of services in a single program; for example, `<windows>\system32\services.exe` is the service program that includes Alerter, Application Management, Computer Browser, and DHCP Client, among other items.

The SCM calls the service-main function for each service that should be started. One important task of the service-main function is registering a handler with the SCM.

The *handler* function is the third part of a service program. The handler must respond to events from the SCM. Services can be stopped, suspended, and resumed, and the handler must react to these events.

After a handler has been registered with the SCM, the service control program can post requests to the SCM to stop, suspend, and resume the service. The service control program is independent of the SCM and the service itself. The operating system contains many service control programs, such as the Microsoft Management Console (MMC) Services snap-in shown earlier in Figure 39-1. You can also write your own service control program; a good example of this is the SQL Server Configuration Manager shown in Figure 39-3, which runs within MMC.

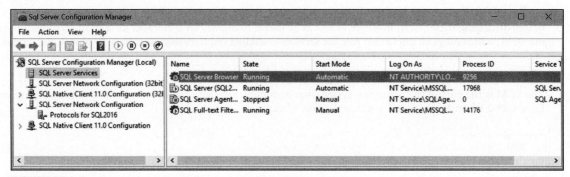

FIGURE 39-3

Service Control Program

As the self-explanatory name suggests, with a service control program you can stop, suspend, and resume the service. To do so, you can send control codes to the service, and the handler should react to these events. It is also possible to ask the service about its actual status (if the service is running or suspended, or in some faulted state) and to implement a custom handler that responds to custom control codes.

Service Configuration Program

Because services must be configured in the registry, you can't use xcopy installation with services. The registry contains the startup type of the service, which can be set to automatic, manual, or disabled. You also need to configure the user of the service program and dependencies of the service—for example, any services that must be started before the current one can start. All these configurations are made within a service configuration program. The installation program can use the service configuration program to configure the service, but this program can also be used later to change service configuration parameters.

Classes for Windows Services

In the .NET Framework, you can find service classes in the `System.ServiceProcess` namespace that implement the three parts of a service:

➤ You must inherit from the `ServiceBase` class to implement a service. The `ServiceBase` class is used to register the service and to answer start and stop requests.

➤ The `ServiceController` class is used to implement a service control program. With this class, you can send requests to services.

➤ The `ServiceProcessInstaller` and `ServiceInstaller` classes are, as their names suggest, classes to install and configure service programs.

Now you are ready to create a new service.

CREATING A WINDOWS SERVICE PROGRAM

The service that you create in this chapter hosts a quote server. With every request that is made from a client, the quote server returns a random quote from a quote file. The first part of the solution uses three assemblies: one for the client and two for the server. Figure 39-4 provides an overview of the solution. The assembly `QuoteServer` holds the actual functionality. The service reads the quote file in a memory cache and answers requests for quotes with the help of a socket server. The `QuoteClient` is a WPF rich–client application. This application creates a client socket to communicate with the `QuoteServer`. The third assembly is the actual service. The `QuoteService` starts and stops the `QuoteServer`; the service controls the server.

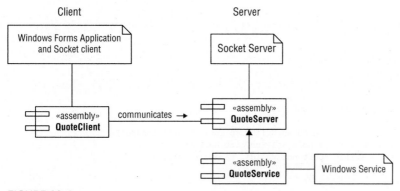

FIGURE 39-4

Before creating the service part of your program, create a simple socket server in an extra C# class library that will be used from your service process. How this can be done is discussed in the following section.

Creating Core Functionality for the Service

You can build any functionality in a Windows Service, such as scanning for files to do a backup or a virus check or starting a WCF server. However, all service programs share some similarities. The program must be able to start (and to return to the caller), stop, and suspend. This section looks at such an implementation using a socket server.

With Windows 10, the Simple TCP/IP Services can be installed as part of the Windows components. Part of the Simple TCP/IP Services is a "quote of the day," or qotd, TCP/IP server. This simple service listens to port 17 and answers every request with a random message from the file `<windows>\system32\drivers\etc\quotes`. With the sample service, a similar server will be built. The sample server returns a Unicode string, in contrast to the qotd server, which returns an ASCII string.

First, create a class library called `QuoteServer` and implement the code for the server. The following walks through the source code of your `QuoteServer` class in the file `QuoteServer.cs`: (code file `QuoteServer/QuoteServer.cs`):

```
using System;
using System.Collections.Generic;
using System.Diagnostics;
using System.IO;
using System.Linq;
using System.Net;
using System.Net.Sockets;
using System.Text;
using System.Threading.Tasks;

namespace Wrox.ProCSharp.WinServices
{
  public class QuoteServer
  {
    private TcpListener _listener;
    private int _port;
    private string _filename;
    private List<string> _quotes;
    private Random _random;
    private Task _listenerTask;
```

The constructor `QuoteServer` is overloaded so that a filename and a port can be passed to the call. The constructor where just the filename is passed uses the default port 7890 for the server. The default constructor defines the default filename for the quotes as `quotes.txt`:

```
    public QuoteServer()
        : this ("quotes.txt")
    {
    }
    public QuoteServer(string filename)
        : this (filename, 7890)
    {
    }
    public QuoteServer(string filename, int port)
    {
      if (filename == null) throw new ArgumentNullException(nameof(filename));
      if (port < IPEndPoint.MinPort || port > IPEndPoint.MaxPort)
        throw new ArgumentException("port not valid", nameof(port));

      _filename = filename;
      _port = port;
    }
```

`ReadQuotes` is a helper method that reads all the quotes from a file that was specified in the constructor. All the quotes are added to the `List<string>` `quotes`. In addition, you are creating an instance of the `Random` class that will be used to return random quotes:

```
    protected void ReadQuotes()
    {
      try
      {
        _quotes = File.ReadAllLines(filename).ToList();
        if (_quotes.Count == 0)
        {
          throw new QuoteException("quotes file is empty");
        }
        _random = new Random();
```

```
    }
    catch (IOException ex)
    {
        throw new QuoteException("I/O Error", ex);
    }
}
```

Another helper method is `GetRandomQuoteOfTheDay`. This method returns a random quote from the quotes collection:

```
protected string GetRandomQuoteOfTheDay()
{
    int index = random.Next(0, _quotes.Count);
    return _quotes[index];
}
```

In the `Start` method, the complete file containing the quotes is read in the `List<string>` quotes by using the helper method `ReadQuotes`. After this, a new thread is started, which immediately calls the `Listener` method—similarly to the `TcpReceive` example in Chapter 25, "Networking."

Here, a task is used because the `Start` method cannot block and wait for a client; it must return immediately to the caller (SCM). The SCM would assume that the start failed if the method didn't return to the caller in a timely fashion (30 seconds). The listener task is a long-running background thread. The application can exit without stopping this thread:

```
public void Start()
{
    ReadQuotes();
    _listenerTask = Task.Factory.StartNew(Listener, TaskCreationOptions.LongRunning);
}
```

The task function `Listener` creates a `TcpListener` instance. The `AcceptSocketAsync` method waits for a client to connect. As soon as a client connects, `AcceptSocketAsync` returns with a socket associated with the client. Next, `GetRandomQuoteOfTheDay` is called to send the returned random quote to the client using `clientSocket.Send`:

```
protected async Task ListenerAsync()
{
    try
    {
        IPAddress ipAddress = IPAddress.Any;
        _listener = new TcpListener(ipAddress, port);
        _listener.Start();
        while (true)
        {
            using (Socket clientSocket = await _listener.AcceptSocketAsync())
            {
                string message = GetRandomQuoteOfTheDay();
                var encoder = new UnicodeEncoding();
                byte[] buffer = encoder.GetBytes(message);
                clientSocket.Send(buffer, buffer.Length, 0);
            }
        }
    }
    catch (SocketException ex)
    {
        Trace.TraceError($"QuoteServer {ex.Message}");
        throw new QuoteException("socket error", ex);
    }
}
```

In addition to the `Start` method, the following methods, `Stop`, `Suspend`, and `Resume`, are needed to control the service:

```
public void Stop() => _listener.Stop();

public void Suspend() => _listener.Stop();

public void Resume() => Start();
```

Another method that will be publicly available is `RefreshQuotes`. If the file containing the quotes changes, the file is reread with this method:

```
public void RefreshQuotes() => ReadQuotes();
    }
}
```

Before you build a service around the server, it is useful to build a test program that creates just an instance of the `QuoteServer` and calls `Start`. This way, you can test the functionality without having to handle service-specific issues. You must start this test server manually, and you can easily walk through the code with a debugger.

The test program is a C# console application, `TestQuoteServer`. You need to reference the assembly of the `QuoteServer` class. After you create an instance of the `QuoteServer`, the `Start` method of the `QuoteServer` instance is called. `Start` returns immediately after creating a thread, so the console application keeps running until `Return` is pressed (code file `TestQuoteServer/Program.cs`):

```
static void Main()
{
    var qs = new QuoteServer("quotes.txt", 4567);
    qs.Start();
    WriteLine("Hit return to exit");
    ReadLine();
    qs.Stop();
}
```

Note that `QuoteServer` will be running on port 4567 on localhost using this program—you have to use these settings in the client later.

QuoteClient Example

The client is a simple WPF Windows application in which you can request quotes from the server. This application uses the `TcpClient` class to connect to the running server and receives the returned message, displaying it in a text box. The user interface contains two controls: a `Button` and a `TextBlock`. Clicking the button requests the quote from the server, and the quote is displayed.

With the `Button` control, the `Click` event is assigned to the method `OnGetQuote`, which requests the quote from the server, and the `IsEnabled` property is bound to the `EnableRequest` method to disable the button while a request is active. With the `TextBlock` control, the `Text` property is bound to the `Quote` property to display the quote that is set (code file `QuoteClientWPF/MainWindow.xaml`):

```
<Button Margin="3" VerticalAlignment="Stretch" Grid.Row="0"
  IsEnabled="{Binding EnableRequest, Mode=OneWay}" Click="OnGetQuote">
  Get Quote</Button>
<TextBlock Margin="6" Grid.Row="1" TextWrapping="Wrap"
  Text="{Binding Quote, Mode=OneWay}" />
```

The class `QuoteInformation` defines the properties `EnableRequest` and `Quote`. These properties are used with data binding to show the values of these properties in the user interface. This class implements the interface `INotifyPropertyChanged` to enable WPF to receive changes in the property values (code file `QuoteClientWPF/QuoteInformation.cs`):

```
using System.Collections.Generic;
using System.ComponentModel;
```

```csharp
using System.Runtime.CompilerServices;

namespace Wrox.ProCSharp.WinServices
{
  public class QuoteInformation: INotifyPropertyChanged
  {
    public QuoteInformation()
    {
      EnableRequest = true;
    }

    private string _quote;
    public string Quote
    {
      get { return _quote; }
      internal set { SetProperty(ref _quote, value); }
    }

    private bool _enableRequest;
    public bool EnableRequest
    {
      get { return _enableRequest; }
      internal set { SetProperty(ref _enableRequest, value); }
    }

    private void SetProperty<T>(ref T field, T value,
                               [CallerMemberName] string propertyName = null)
    {
      if (!EqualityComparer<T>.Default.Equals(field, value))
      {
        field = value;
        PropertyChanged?.Invoke(this, new PropertyChangedEventArgs(propertyName));
      }
    }

    public event PropertyChangedEventHandler PropertyChanged;
  }
}
```

> **NOTE** *Implementation of the interface* `INotifyPropertyChanged` *makes use of the attribute* `CallerMemberNameAttribute`*. This attribute is explained in Chapter 14, "Errors and Exceptions."*

An instance of the class `QuoteInformation` is assigned to the `DataContext` of the Window class `MainWindow` to allow direct data binding to it (code file `QuoteClientWPF/MainWindow.xaml.cs`):

```csharp
using System;
using System.Net.Sockets;
using System.Text;
using System.Windows;
using System.Windows.Input;
namespace Wrox.ProCSharp.WinServices
{
  public partial class MainWindow: Window
  {
    private QuoteInformation _quoteInfo = new QuoteInformation();
    public MainWindow()
```

```
{
  InitializeComponent();
  this.DataContext = _quoteInfo;
}
```

You can configure server and port information to connect to the server from the Settings tab inside the properties of the project (see Figure 39-5). Here, you can define default values for the ServerName and PortNumber settings. With the Scope set to User, the settings can be placed in user-specific configuration files, so every user of the application can have different settings. This Settings feature of Visual Studio also creates a Settings class so that the settings can be read and written with a strongly typed class.

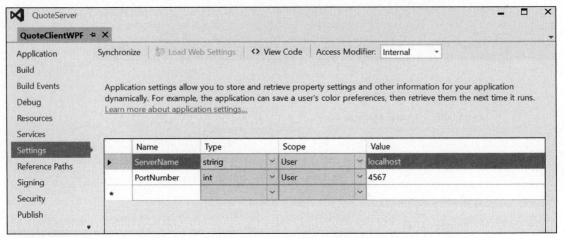

FIGURE 39-5

The major functionality of the client lies in the handler for the Click event of the Get Quote button:

```
protected async void OnGetQuote(object sender, RoutedEventArgs e)
{
  const int bufferSize = 1024;
  Cursor currentCursor = this.Cursor;
  this.Cursor = Cursors.Wait;
  quoteInfo.EnableRequest = false;

  string serverName = Properties.Settings.Default.ServerName;
  int port = Properties.Settings.Default.PortNumber;

  var client = new TcpClient();
  NetworkStream stream = null;
  try
  {
    await client.ConnectAsync(serverName, port);
    stream = client.GetStream();
    byte[] buffer = new byte[bufferSize];
    int received = await stream.ReadAsync(buffer, 0, bufferSize);
    if (received <= 0)
    {
      return;
    }
    quoteInfo.Quote = Encoding.Unicode.GetString(buffer).Trim('\0');
  }
  catch (SocketException ex)
  {
```

```
    MessageBox.Show(ex.Message, "Error Quote of the day",
        MessageBoxButton.OK, MessageBoxImage.Error);
}
finally
{
  stream?.Close();

  if (client.Connected)
  {
    client.Close();
  }
}

this.Cursor = currentCursor;
quoteInfo.EnableRequest = true;
}
```

After starting the test server and this Windows application client, you can test the functionality. Figure 39-6 shows a successful run of this application.

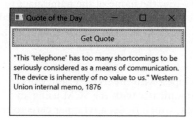

FIGURE 39-6

At this point, you need to implement the service functionality in the server. The program is already running, so now you want to ensure that the server program starts automatically at boot time without anyone logged on to the system. You can do that by creating a service program, which is discussed next.

Windows Service Program

Using the C# Windows Service template from the Add New Project dialog, you can now create a Windows Service program. For the new service, use the name `QuoteService`.

After you click the OK button to create the Windows Service program, the designer surface appears but you can't insert any UI components because the application cannot directly display anything on the screen. The designer surface is used later in this chapter to add components such as installation objects, performance counters, and event logging.

Selecting the properties of this service opens the Properties dialog, where you can configure the following values:

- ➤ `AutoLog`—Specifies that events are automatically written to the event log for starting and stopping the service.
- ➤ `CanPauseAndContinue`, `CanShutdown`, and `CanStop`—Specify pause, continue, shut down, and stop requests.
- ➤ `ServiceName`—The name of the service written to the registry and used to control the service.
- ➤ `CanHandleSessionChangeEvent`—Defines whether the service can handle change events from a terminal server session.
- ➤ `CanHandlePowerEvent`—This is a very useful option for services running on a laptop or mobile devices. If this option is enabled, the service can react to low-power events and change the behavior of

the service accordingly. Examples of power events include battery low, power status change (because of a switch from or to A/C power), and change to suspend.

> **NOTE** *The default service name is* Service1, *regardless of what the project is called. You can install only one* Service1 *service. If you get installation errors during your testing process, you might already have installed a* Service1 *service. Therefore, ensure that you change the name of the service in the Properties dialog to a more suitable name at the beginning of the service's development.*

Changing these properties within the Properties dialog sets the values of your ServiceBase-derived class in the InitializeComponent method. You already know this method from Windows Forms applications. It is used in a similar way with services.

A wizard generates the code but changes the filename to QuoteService.cs, the name of the namespace to Wrox.ProCSharp.WinServices, and the class name to QuoteService. The code of the service is discussed in detail shortly.

The ServiceBase Class

The ServiceBase class is the base class for all Windows Services developed with the .NET Framework. The class QuoteService is derived from ServiceBase; this class communicates with the SCM using an undocumented helper class, System.ServiceProcess.NativeMethods, which is just a wrapper class to the Windows API calls. The NativeMethods class is internal, so it cannot be used in your code.

The sequence diagram in Figure 39-7 shows the interaction of the SCM, the class QuoteService, and the classes from the System.ServiceProcess namespace. You can see the lifelines of objects vertically and the communication going on horizontally. The communication is time-ordered from top to bottom.

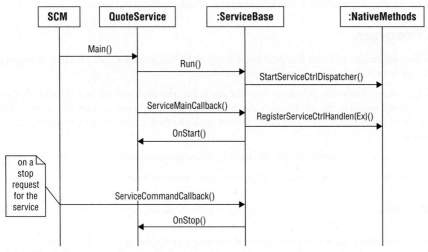

FIGURE 39-7

The SCM starts the process of a service that should be started. At startup, the Main method is called. In the Main method of the sample service, the Run method of the base class ServiceBase is called. Run registers the method `ServiceMainCallback` using `NativeMethods.StartServiceCtrlDispatcher` in the SCM and writes an entry to the event log.

Next, the SCM calls the registered method `ServiceMainCallback` in the service program. `ServiceMainCallback` itself registers the handler in the SCM using `NativeMethods.RegisterServiceCtrlHandler[Ex]` and sets the status of the service in the SCM. Then the `OnStart` method is called. In `OnStart`, you need to implement the startup code. If `OnStart` is successful, the string "Service started successfully" is written to the event log.

The handler is implemented in the `ServiceCommandCallback` method. The SCM calls this method when changes are requested from the service. The `ServiceCommandCallback` method routes the requests further to `OnPause`, `OnContinue`, `OnStop`, `OnCustomCommand`, and `OnPowerEvent`.

Main Function

This section looks into the application template–generated main function of the service process. In the main function, an array of `ServiceBase` classes, `ServicesToRun`, is declared. One instance of the `QuoteService` class is created and passed as the first element to the `ServicesToRun` array. If more than one service should run inside this service process, it is necessary to add more instances of the specific service classes to the array. This array is then passed to the static `Run` method of the `ServiceBase` class. With the `Run` method of `ServiceBase`, you are giving the SCM references to the entry points of your services. The main thread of your service process is now blocked and waits for the service to terminate.

Here is the automatically generated code (code file `QuoteService/Program.cs`):

```
static void Main()
{
    ServiceBase[] servicesToRun = new ServiceBase[]
    {
        new QuoteService()
    };
    ServiceBase.Run(servicesToRun);
}
```

If there is only a single service in the process, the array can be removed; the `Run` method accepts a single object derived from the class `ServiceBase`, so the `Main` method can be reduced to this:

```
ServiceBase.Run(new QuoteService());
```

The service program `Services.exe` includes multiple services. If you have a similar service, where more than one service is running in a single process in which you must initialize some shared state for multiple services, the shared initialization must be done before the `Run` method. With the `Run` method, the main thread is blocked until the service process is stopped, and any subsequent instructions are not reached before the end of the service.

The initialization shouldn't take longer than 30 seconds. If the initialization code were to take longer than this, the SCM would assume that the service startup failed. You need to take into account the slowest machines where this service should run within the 30-second limit. If the initialization takes longer, you could start the initialization in a different thread so that the main thread calls `Run` in time. An event object can then be used to signal that the thread has completed its work.

Service Start

At service start, the `OnStart` method is called. In this method, you can start the previously created socket server. You must reference the `QuoteServer` assembly for the use of the `QuoteService`. The thread calling `OnStart` cannot be blocked; this method must return to the caller, which is the `ServiceMainCallback` method of the `ServiceBase` class. The `ServiceBase` class registers the handler and informs the SCM that the service started successfully after calling `OnStart` (code file `QuoteService/QuoteService.cs`):

```
protected override void OnStart(string[] args)
{
```

```
        _quoteServer = new QuoteServer(Path.Combine(
                        AppDomain.CurrentDomain.BaseDirectory, "quotes.txt"),
                            5678);
        _quoteServer.Start();
    }
```

The _quoteServer variable is declared as a private member in the class:

```
namespace Wrox.ProCSharp.WinServices
{
  public partial class QuoteService: ServiceBase
  {
    private QuoteServer _quoteServer;
```

Handler Methods

When the service is stopped, the OnStop method is called. You should stop the service functionality in this method (code file QuoteService/QuoteService.cs):

```
protected override void OnStop() => _quoteServer.Stop();
```

In addition to OnStart and OnStop, you can override the following handlers in the service class:

➤ OnPause—Called when the service should be paused.

➤ OnContinue—Called when the service should return to normal operation after being paused. To make it possible for the overridden methods OnPause and OnContinue to be called, you must set the CanPauseAndContinue property to true.

➤ OnShutdown—Called when Windows is undergoing system shutdown. Normally, the behavior of this method should be similar to the OnStop implementation; if more time is needed for a shutdown, you can request more. Similarly to OnPause and OnContinue, a property must be set to enable this behavior: CanShutdown must be set to true.

➤ OnPowerEvent—Called when the power status of the system changes. Information about the change of the power status is in the argument of type PowerBroadcastStatus. PowerBroadcastStatus is an enumeration with values such as Battery Low and PowerStatusChange. Here, you will also get information if the system would like to suspend (QuerySuspend), which you can approve or deny. You can read more about power events later in this chapter.

➤ OnCustomCommand—This is a handler that can serve custom commands sent by a service control program. The method signature of OnCustomCommand has an int argument where you retrieve the custom command number. The value can be in the range from 128 to 256; values below 128 are system-reserved values. In your service, you are rereading the quotes file with the custom command 128:

```
protected override void OnPause() => _quoteServer.Suspend();

protected override void OnContinue() => _quoteServer.Resume();

public const int CommandRefresh = 128;
protected override void OnCustomCommand(int command)
{
  switch (command)
  {
    case CommandRefresh:
      quoteServer.RefreshQuotes();
      break;

    default:
      break;
  }
}
```

Threading and Services

As stated earlier in this chapter, the SCM assumes that the service failed if the initialization takes too long. To deal with this, you need to create a thread.

The `OnStart` method in your service class must return in time. If you call a blocking method such as `AcceptSocket` from the `TcpListener` class, you need to start a thread to do so. With a networking server that deals with multiple clients, a thread pool is also very useful. `AcceptSocket` should receive the call and hand the processing off to another thread from the pool. This way, no one waits for the execution of code and the system seems responsive.

Service Installation

Services must be configured in the registry. All services are found in `HKEY_LOCAL_MACHINE\System\ CurrentControlSet\Services`. You can view the registry entries by using `regedit`. Found here are the type of the service, the display name, the path to the executable, the startup configuration, and so on. Figure 39-8 shows the registry configuration of the W3SVC service.

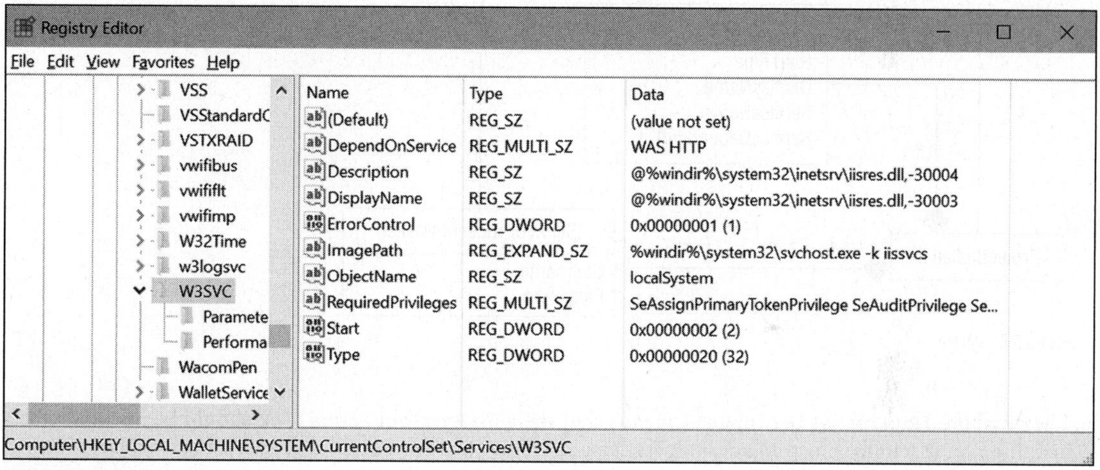

FIGURE 39-8

You can do this configuration by using the installer classes from the `System.ServiceProcess` namespace, as discussed in the following section.

Installation Program

You can add an installation program to the service by switching to the design view with Visual Studio and then selecting the Add Installer option from the context menu . With this option, a new `ProjectInstaller` class is created, along with a `ServiceInstaller` instance and a `ServiceProcessInstaller` instance.

Figure 39-9 shows the class diagram of the installer classes for services.

Keep this diagram in mind as we go through the source code in the file `ProjectInstaller.cs` that was created with the Add Installer option.

The Installer Class

The class `ProjectInstaller` is derived from `System.Configuration.Install.Installer`. This is the base class for all custom installers. With the `Installer` class, it is possible to build transaction-based installations. With a transaction-based installation, you can roll back to the previous state if the installation fails, and any changes made by this installation up to that point will be undone. As shown in Figure 39-9, the `Installer` class has `Install`, `Uninstall`, `Commit`, and `Rollback` methods, and they are called from installation programs.

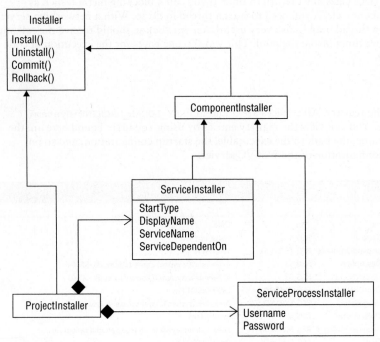

FIGURE 39-9

The attribute `[RunInstaller(true)]` means that the class `ProjectInstaller` should be invoked when installing an assembly. Custom action installers, as well as `installutil.exe` (which is used later in this chapter), check for this attribute.

`InitializeComponent` is called inside the constructor of the `ProjectInstaller` class (code file `QuoteService/ProjectInstaller.cs`):

```
using System.ComponentModel;
using System.Configuration.Install;

namespace Wrox.ProCSharp.WinServices
{
  [RunInstaller(true)]
  public partial class ProjectInstaller: Installer
  {
    public ProjectInstaller()
    {
      InitializeComponent();
    }
  }
}
```

Now let's move to the other installers of the installation program that are invoked by the project installer.

Process Installer and Service Installer

Within the implementation of `InitializeComponent`, instances of the `ServiceProcessInstaller` class and the `ServiceInstaller` class are created. Both of these classes derive from the `ComponentInstaller` class, which itself derives from `Installer`.

Classes derived from `ComponentInstaller` can be used with an installation process. Remember that a service process can include more than one service. The `ServiceProcessInstaller` class is used for the configuration of the process that defines values for all services in this process, and the `ServiceInstaller` class is for the configuration of the service, so one instance of `ServiceInstaller` is required for each service. If three services are inside the process, you need to add three `ServiceInstaller` objects:

```
partial class ProjectInstaller
{
  private System.ComponentModel.IContainer components = null;

  private void InitializeComponent()
  {
    this.serviceProcessInstaller1 =
        new System.ServiceProcess.ServiceProcessInstaller();
    this.serviceInstaller1 =
        new System.ServiceProcess.ServiceInstaller();

    this.serviceProcessInstaller1.Password = null;
    this.serviceProcessInstaller1.Username = null;

    this.serviceInstaller1.ServiceName = "QuoteService";
    this.serviceInstaller1.Description = "Sample Service for Professional C#";
    this.serviceInstaller1.StartType = System.ServiceProcess.ServiceStartMode.Manual;

    this.Installers.AddRange(
      new System.Configuration.Install.Installer[]
          {this.serviceProcessInstaller1,
            this.serviceInstaller1});
  }

  private System.ServiceProcess.ServiceProcessInstaller
      serviceProcessInstaller1;
  private System.ServiceProcess.ServiceInstaller serviceInstaller1;

}
```

The class `ServiceProcessInstaller` installs an executable that contains a class that derives from the base class `ServiceBase`. `ServiceProcessInstaller` has properties for the complete service process. The following table describes the properties shared by all the services inside the process.

PROPERTY	DESCRIPTION
Username, Password	Indicates the user account under which the service runs if the `Account` property is set to `ServiceAccount.User`.
Account	With this property, you can specify the account type of the service.
HelpText	A read-only property that returns the help text for setting the username and password.

The process that is used to run the service can be specified with the `Account` property of the `ServiceProcessInstaller` class using the `ServiceAccount` enumeration. The following table describes the different values of the `Account` property.

VALUE	DESCRIPTION
LocalSystem	Setting this value specifies that the service uses a highly privileged user account on the local system, and acts as the computer on the network.
NetworkService	Similarly to LocalSystem, this value specifies that the computer's credentials are passed to remote servers; but unlike LocalSystem, such a service acts as a nonprivileged user on the local system. As the name implies, this account should be used only for services that need resources from the network.
LocalService	This account type presents anonymous credentials to any remote server and has the same privileges locally as NetworkService.
User	Setting the Account property to ServiceAccount.User means that you can define the account that should be used from the service.

ServiceInstaller is the class needed for every service; it has the following properties for each service inside a process: StartType, DisplayName, ServiceName, and ServicesDependentOn, as described in the following table.

PROPERTY	DESCRIPTION
StartType	The StartType property indicates whether the service is manually or automatically started. Possible values are ServiceStartMode.Automatic, ServiceStartMode.Manual, and ServiceStartMode.Disabled. With the last one, the service cannot be started. This option is useful for services that shouldn't be started on a system. You might want to set the option to Disabled if, for example, a required hardware controller is not available.
DelayedAutoStart	This property is ignored if the StartType is not set to Automatic. Here, you can specify that the service should not be started immediately when the system boots but afterward.
DisplayName	DisplayName is the friendly name of the service that is displayed to the user. This name is also used by management tools that control and monitor the service.
ServiceName	ServiceName is the name of the service. This value must be identical to the ServiceName property of the ServiceBase class in the service program. This name associates the configuration of the ServiceInstaller to the required service program.
ServicesDependentOn	Specifies an array of services that must be started before this service can be started. When the service is started, all these dependent services are started automatically, and then your service will start.

> **NOTE** *If you change the name of the service in the* ServiceBase-*derived class, be sure to also change the* ServiceName *property in the* ServiceInstaller *object!*

> **NOTE** *In the testing phases, set* StartType *to* Manual. *This way, if you can't stop the service (for example, when it has a bug), you still have the possibility to reboot the system; but if you have* StartType *set to* Automatic, *the service would be started automatically with the reboot! You can change this configuration later when you are sure that it works.*

The ServiceInstallerDialog Class

Another installer class in the `System.ServiceProcess.Design` namespace is `ServiceInstallerDialog`. This class can be used if you want the system administrator to enter the account that the service should use by assigning the username and password during the installation.

If you set the `Account` property of the class `ServiceProcessInstaller` to `ServiceAccount.User` and the `Username` and `Password` properties to `null`, you see the Set Service Login dialog at installation time (see Figure 39-10). You can also cancel the installation at this point.

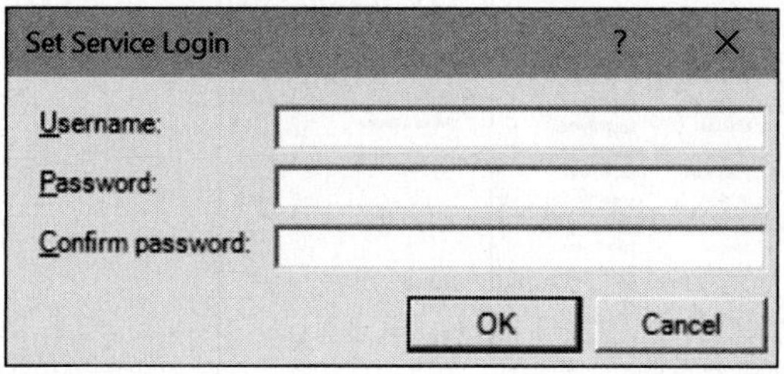

FIGURE 39-10

installutil

After adding the installer classes to the project, you can use the `installutil.exe` utility to install and uninstall the service. You can use this utility to install any assembly that has an `Installer` class. The `installutil.exe` utility calls the method `Install` of the class that derives from the `Installer` class for installation, and `Uninstall` for the uninstallation.

The command-line inputs for the installation and uninstallation of our example service are as follows:

```
installutil quoteservice.exe
installutil /u quoteservice.exe
```

> **NOTE** *If the installation fails, be sure to check the installation log files,* `InstallUtil.InstallLog` *and* `<servicename>.InstallLog`. *Often, you can find very useful information, such as "The specified service already exists."*

After the service has been successfully installed, you can start the service manually from the Services MMC (see the next section for details), and then you can start the client application.

MONITORING AND CONTROLLING WINDOWS SERVICES

To monitor and control Windows Services, you can use the Services MMC snap-in that is part of the Computer Management administration tool. Every Windows system also has a command-line utility, `net.exe`, which enables you to control services. Another Windows command-line utility is `sc.exe`. This utility has much more functionality than `net.exe`. You can also control services directly from the Visual Studio Server Explorer. In this section, you also create a small Windows application that makes use of the `System.ServiceProcess.ServiceController` class to monitor and control services.

MMC Snap-in

Using the Services snap-in to the MMC, you can view the status of all services (see Figure 39-11). It is also possible to send control requests to services to stop, enable, or disable them, as well as to change their configuration. The Services snap-in is a service control program as well as a service configuration program.

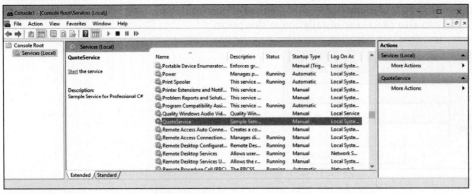

FIGURE 39-11

Double-click QuoteService to get the Properties dialog shown in Figure 39-12. From here you can view the service name, the description, the path to the executable, the startup type, and the status. The service is currently started. The account for the service process can be changed by selecting the Log On tab in this dialog.

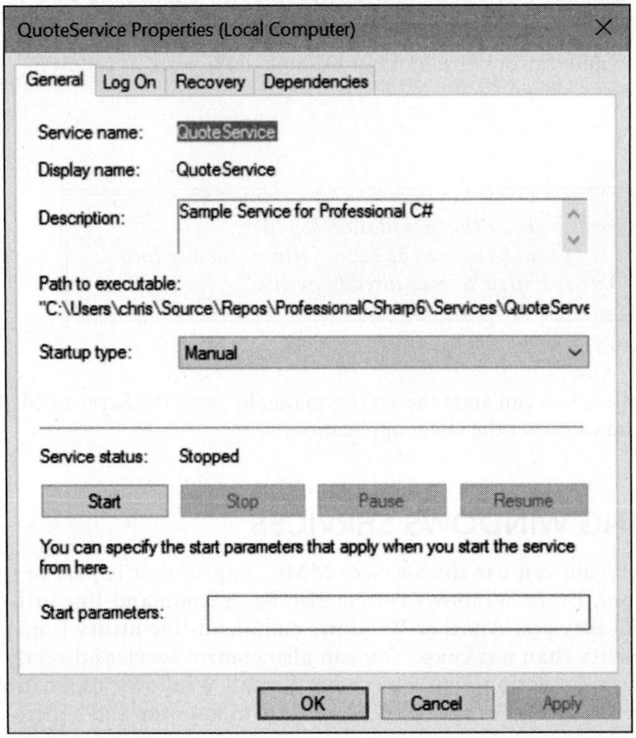

FIGURE 39-12

net.exe Utility

The Services snap-in is easy to use, but system administrators cannot automate it because it is not usable within an administrative script. To control services with a tool that can be automated with a script, you can use the command-line utility net.exe. The net start command shows all running services, net start servicename starts a service, and net stop servicename sends a stop request to the service. It is also possible to pause and continue a service with net pause and net continue (if the service allows it, of course).

sc.exe Utility

Another little-known utility delivered as part of the operating system is sc.exe. This is a great tool for working with services. You can do much more with sc.exe than with the net.exe utility. With sc.exe, you can check the actual status of a service, or configure, remove, and add services. This tool also facilitates the uninstallation of the service if it fails to function correctly.

Visual Studio Server Explorer

To monitor services using the Server Explorer within Visual Studio, select Servers from the tree view, and then select your computer, then the Services element. You can see the status of all services as shown in Figure 39-13. By selecting a service, you can see the properties of the service.

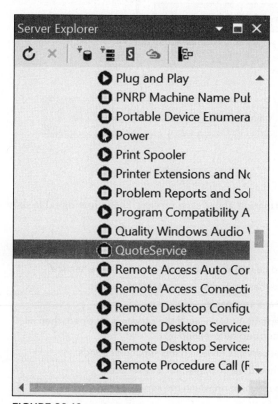

FIGURE 39-13

Writing a Custom Service Controller

In this section, you create a small WPF application that uses the `ServiceController` class to monitor and control Windows Services.

Create a WPF application with a user interface as shown in Figure 39-14. The main window of this application has a list box to display all services; four text boxes to show the display name, status, type, and name of the service; and six buttons. Four buttons are used to send control events, one button is used for a refresh of the list, and one button is used to exit the application.

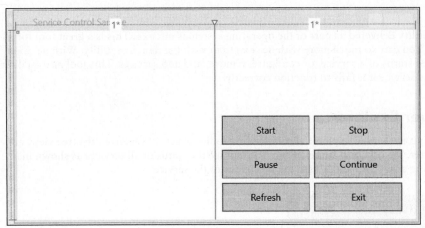

FIGURE 39-14

> **NOTE** *You can read more about WPF and XAML in Chapters 29 through 35.*

Monitoring the Service

With the `ServiceController` class, you can get information about each service. The following table shows the properties of the `ServiceController` class:

PROPERTY	DESCRIPTION
CanPauseAndContinue	Returns `true` if pause and continue requests can be sent to the service.
CanShutdown	Returns `true` if the service has a handler for a system shutdown.
CanStop	Returns `true` if the service is stoppable.
DependentServices	Returns a collection of dependent services. If the service is stopped, then all dependent services are stopped beforehand.
ServicesDependentOn	Returns a collection of the services on which this service depends.
DisplayName	Specifies the name that should be displayed for this service.
MachineName	Specifies the name of the machine on which the service runs.
ServiceName	Specifies the name of the service.

PROPERTY	DESCRIPTION
ServiceType	Specifies the type of the service. The service can be run inside a shared process, whereby more than one service uses the same process (Win32ShareProcess), or run in such a way that there is just one service in a process (Win32OwnProcess). If the service can interact with the desktop, the type is InteractiveProcess.
Status	Specifies the service's status, which can be running, stopped, paused, or in some intermediate mode such as start pending, stop pending, and so on. The status values are defined in the enumeration ServiceControllerStatus.

In the sample application, the properties DisplayName, ServiceName, ServiceType, and Status are used to display the service information. CanPauseAndContinue and CanStop are used to enable or disable the Pause, Continue, and Stop buttons.

To get all the needed information for the user interface, the class ServiceControllerInfo is created. This class can be used for data binding and offers status information, the name of the service, the service type, and information about which buttons to control the service should be enabled or disabled.

> **NOTE** *Because the class* System.ServiceProcess.ServiceController *is used, you must reference the assembly* System.ServiceProcess.

ServiceControllerInfo contains an embedded ServiceController that is set with the constructor of the ServiceControllerInfo class. There is also a read-only property Controller to access the embedded ServiceController (code file ServiceControlWPF/ServiceControllerInfo.cs):

```
public class ServiceControllerInfo
{
  public ServiceControllerInfo(ServiceController controller)
  {
    Controller = controller;
  }

  public ServiceController Controller { get; }
  // etc.
}
```

To display current information about the service, the ServiceControllerInfo class has the read-only properties DisplayName, ServiceName, ServiceTypeName, and ServiceStatusName. The implementation of the properties DisplayName and ServiceName just accesses the properties of those names of the underlying ServiceController class. With the implementation of the properties ServiceTypeName and ServiceStatusName, more work is needed—the status and type of the service cannot be returned that easily because a string should be displayed instead of a number, which is what the ServiceController class returns. The property ServiceTypeName returns a string that represents the type of the service. The ServiceType you get from the property ServiceController.ServiceType represents a set of flags that can be combined by using the bitwise OR operator. The InteractiveProcess bit can be set together with Win32OwnProcess and Win32ShareProcess. Therefore, the first check determines whether the InteractiveProcess bit is set before continuing to check for the other values. With services, the string returned will be `"Win32 Service Process"` or `"Win32 Shared Process"` (code file `ServiceControlWPF/ServiceControllerInfo.cs`):

```csharp
public class ServiceControllerInfo
{
    // etc.
    public string ServiceTypeName
    {
        get
        {
            ServiceType type = controller.ServiceType;
            string serviceTypeName = "";
            if ((type & ServiceType.InteractiveProcess) != 0)
            {
                serviceTypeName = "Interactive ";
                type -= ServiceType.InteractiveProcess;
            }
            switch (type)
            {
                case ServiceType.Adapter:
                    serviceTypeName += "Adapter";
                    break;
                case ServiceType.FileSystemDriver:
                case ServiceType.KernelDriver:
                case ServiceType.RecognizerDriver:
                    serviceTypeName += "Driver";
                    break;
                case ServiceType.Win32OwnProcess:
                    serviceTypeName += "Win32 Service Process";
                    break;
                case ServiceType.Win32ShareProcess:
                    serviceTypeName += "Win32 Shared Process";
                    break;
                default:
                    serviceTypeName += "unknown type " + type.ToString();
                    break;
            }
            return serviceTypeName;
        }
    }

    public string ServiceStatusName
    {
        get
        {
            switch (Controller.Status)
            {
                case ServiceControllerStatus.ContinuePending:
                    return "Continue Pending";
                case ServiceControllerStatus.Paused:
                    return "Paused";
                case ServiceControllerStatus.PausePending:
                    return "Pause Pending";
                case ServiceControllerStatus.StartPending:
                    return "Start Pending";
                case ServiceControllerStatus.Running:
                    return "Running";
                case ServiceControllerStatus.Stopped:
                    return "Stopped";
                case ServiceControllerStatus.StopPending:
                    return "Stop Pending";
                default:
```

```
            return "Unknown status";
        }
      }
    }

    public string DisplayName => Controller.DisplayName;

    public string ServiceName => Controller.ServiceName;

    // etc.
  }
```

The `ServiceControllerInfo` class has some other properties to enable the Start, Stop, Pause, and Continue buttons: `EnableStart`, `EnableStop`, `EnablePause`, and `EnableContinue`. These properties return a Boolean value according to the current status of the service (code file `ServiceControlWPF/ServiceControllerInfo.cs`):

```
public class ServiceControllerInfo
{
  // etc.

  public bool EnableStart => Controller.Status == ServiceControllerStatus.Stopped;

  public bool EnableStop => Controller.Status == ServiceControllerStatus.Running;

  public bool EnablePause =>
    Controller.Status == ServiceControllerStatus.Running &&
        Controller.CanPauseAndContinue;

  public bool EnableContinue => Controller.Status == ServiceControllerStatus.Paused;
}
```

In the `ServiceControlWindow` class, the method `RefreshServiceList` gets all the services using `ServiceController.GetServices` for display in the list box. The `GetServices` method returns an array of `ServiceController` instances representing all Windows Services installed on the operating system. The `ServiceController` class also has the static method `GetDevices` that returns a `ServiceController` array representing all device drivers. The returned array is sorted with the help of the extension method `OrderBy`. The sort is done by the `DisplayName` as defined with the lambda expression that is passed to the `OrderBy` method. Using `Select`, the `ServiceController` instances are converted to the type `ServiceControllerInfo`. In the following code, a lambda expression is passed that invokes the `ServiceControllerInfo` constructor for every `ServiceController` object. Last, the result is assigned to the `DataContext` property of the window for data binding (code file `ServiceControlWPF/MainWindow.xaml.cs`):

```
protected void RefreshServiceList()
{
  this.DataContext = ServiceController.GetServices().
    OrderBy(sc => sc.DisplayName).
    Select(sc => new ServiceControllerInfo(sc));
}
```

The method `RefreshServiceList`, to get all the services in the list box, is called within the constructor of the class `ServiceControlWindow`. The constructor also defines the event handler for the `Click` event of the buttons:

```
public ServiceControlWindow()
{
  InitializeComponent();

  RefreshServiceList();
}
```

Now, you can define the XAML code to bind the information to the controls. First, a `DataTemplate` is defined for the information that is shown inside the `ListBox`. The `ListBox` contains a `Label` in which the `Content` is bound to the `DisplayName` property of the data source. As you bind an array of `ServiceControllerInfo` objects, the property `DisplayName` is defined with the `ServiceControllerInfo` class (code file `ServiceControlWPF/MainWindow.xaml`):

```
<Window.Resources>
  <DataTemplate x:Key="listTemplate">
    <Label Content="{Binding DisplayName}"/>
  </DataTemplate>
</Window.Resources>
```

The `ListBox` that is placed in the left side of the window sets the `ItemsSource` property to `{Binding}`. This way, the data that is shown in the list is received from the `DataContext` property that was set in the `RefreshServiceList` method. The `ItemTemplate` property references the resource `listTemplate` that is defined with the `DataTemplate` shown earlier. The property `IsSynchronizedWithCurrentItem` is set to `True` so that the `TextBox` and `Button` controls inside the same window are bound to the current item selected with the `ListBox`:

```
<ListBox Grid.Row="0" Grid.Column="0" HorizontalAlignment="Left"
  Name="listBoxServices" VerticalAlignment="Top"
  ItemsSource="{Binding}"
  ItemTemplate="{StaticResource listTemplate}"
  IsSynchronizedWithCurrentItem="True">
</ListBox>
```

To differentiate the `Button` controls to start/stop/pause/continue the service, the following enumeration is defined (code file `ServiceControlWPF/ButtonState.cs`):

```
public enum ButtonState
{
  Start,
  Stop,
  Pause,
  Continue
}
```

With the `TextBlock` controls, the `Text` property is bound to the corresponding property of the `ServiceControllerInfo` instance. Whether the `Button` controls are enabled or disabled is also defined from the data binding by binding the `IsEnabled` property to the corresponding properties of the `ServiceControllerInfo` instance that return a Boolean value. The `Tag` property of the buttons is assigned to a value of the `ButtonState` enumeration defined earlier to differentiate the button within the same handler method `OnServiceCommand` (code file `ServiceControlWPF/MainWindow.xaml`):

```
<TextBlock Grid.Row="0" Grid.ColumnSpan="2"
  Text="{Binding /DisplayName, Mode=OneTime}" />
<TextBlock Grid.Row="1" Grid.ColumnSpan="2"
  Text="{Binding /ServiceStatusName, Mode=OneTime}" />
<TextBlock Grid.Row="2" Grid.ColumnSpan="2"
  Text="{Binding /ServiceTypeName, Mode=OneTime}" />
<TextBlock Grid.Row="3" Grid.ColumnSpan="2"
  Text="{Binding /ServiceName, Mode=OneTime}" />
<Button Grid.Row="4" Grid.Column="0" Content="Start"
  IsEnabled="{Binding /EnableStart, Mode=OneTime}"
  Tag="{x:Static local:ButtonState.Start}"
  Click="OnServiceCommand" />
<Button Grid.Row="4" Grid.Column="1" Name="buttonStop" Content="Stop"
  IsEnabled="{Binding /EnableStop, Mode=OneTime}"
  Tag="{x:Static local:ButtonState.Stop}"
  Click="OnServiceCommand" />
<Button Grid.Row="5" Grid.Column="0" Name="buttonPause" Content="Pause"
```

```
      IsEnabled="{Binding /EnablePause, Mode=OneTime}"
      Tag="{x:Static local:ButtonState.Pause}"
      Click="OnServiceCommand" />
  <Button Grid.Row="5" Grid.Column="1" Name="buttonContinue"
      Content="Continue"
      IsEnabled="{Binding /EnableContinue,
      Tag="{x:Static local:ButtonState.Continue}"
      Mode=OneTime}" Click="OnServiceCommand" />
  <Button Grid.Row="6" Grid.Column="0" Name="buttonRefresh"
      Content="Refresh"
      Click="OnRefresh" />
  <Button Grid.Row="6" Grid.Column="1" Name="buttonExit"
      Content="Exit" Click="OnExit" />
```

Controlling the Service

With the `ServiceController` class, you can also send control requests to the service. The following table describes the methods that can be applied.

METHOD	DESCRIPTION
Start	Tells the SCM that the service should be started. In the example service program, OnStart is called.
Stop	Calls OnStop in the example service program with the help of the SCM if the property CanStop is true in the service class.
Pause	Calls OnPause if the property CanPauseAndContinue is true.
Continue	Calls OnContinue if the property CanPauseAndContinue is true.
ExecuteCommand	Enables sending a custom command to the service.

The following code controls the services. Because the code for starting, stopping, suspending, and pausing is similar, only one handler is used for the four buttons (code file `ServiceControlWPF/MainWindow.xaml.cs`):

```
protected void OnServiceCommand(object sender, RoutedEventArgs e)
{
  Cursor oldCursor = this.Cursor;
  try
  {
    this.Cursor = Cursors.Wait;
    ButtonState currentButtonState = (ButtonState)(sender as Button).Tag;
    var si = listBoxServices.SelectedItem as ServiceControllerInfo;
    if (currentButtonState == ButtonState.Start)
    {
      si.Controller.Start();
      si.Controller.WaitForStatus(ServiceControllerStatus.Running,
        TimeSpan.FromSeconds(10));
    }
    else if (currentButtonState == ButtonState.Stop)
    {
      si.Controller.Stop();
      si.Controller.WaitForStatus(ServiceControllerStatus.Stopped,
      TimeSpan.FromSeconds(10));
    }
    else if (currentButtonState == ButtonState.Pause)
    {
      si.Controller.Pause();
      si.Controller.WaitForStatus(ServiceControllerStatus.Paused,
        TimeSpan.FromSeconds(10));
    }
    else if (currentButtonState == ButtonState.Continue)
```

```
          {
            si.Controller.Continue();
            si.Controller.WaitForStatus(ServiceControllerStatus.Running,
              TimeSpan.FromSeconds(10));
          }
          int index = listBoxServices.SelectedIndex;
          RefreshServiceList();
          listBoxServices.SelectedIndex = index;
        }
        catch (System.ServiceProcess.TimeoutException ex)
        {
          MessageBox.Show(ex.Message, "Timout Service Controller",
            MessageBoxButton.OK, MessageBoxImage.Error);
        }
        catch (InvalidOperationException ex)
        {
          MessageBox.Show(String.Format("{0} {1}", ex.Message,
            ex.InnerException != null ? ex.InnerException.Message :
              String.Empty), MessageBoxButton.OK, MessageBoxImage.Error);
        }
        finally
        {
          this.Cursor = oldCursor;
        }
      }

      protected void OnExit(object sender, RoutedEventArgs e) =>
        Application.Current.Shutdown();

      protected void OnRefresh_Click(object sender, RoutedEventArgs e) =>
        RefreshServiceList();
```

Because the action of controlling the services can take some time, the cursor is switched to the wait cursor in the first statement. Then a `ServiceController` method is called depending on the pressed button. With the `WaitForStatus` method, you are waiting to confirm that the service changes the status to the requested value, but the wait maximum is only 10 seconds. After that, the information in the `ListBox` is refreshed, and the selected index is set to the same value as it was before. The new status of this service is then displayed.

Because the application requires administrative privileges, just as most services require that for starting and stopping, an application manifest with the `requestedExecutionLevel` set to `requireAdministrator` is added to the project (application manifest file `ServiceControlWPF/app.manifest`):

```xml
<?xml version="1.0" encoding="utf-8"?>
<asmv1:assembly manifestVersion="1.0"
    xmlns="urn:schemas-microsoft-com:asm.v1"
    xmlns:asmv1="urn:schemas-microsoft-com:asm.v1"
    xmlns:asmv2="urn:schemas-microsoft-com:asm.v2"
    xmlns:xsi="http://www.w3.org/2001/XMLSchema-instance">
  <assemblyIdentity version="1.0.0.0" name="MyApplication.app"/>
  <trustInfo xmlns="urn:schemas-microsoft-com:asm.v2">
    <security>
      <requestedPrivileges xmlns="urn:schemas-microsoft-com:asm.v3">
        <requestedExecutionLevel level="requireAdministrator"
            uiAccess="false" />
      </requestedPrivileges>
    </security>
  </trustInfo>
</asmv1:assembly>
```

Figure 39-15 shows the completed, running application.

FIGURE 39-15

TROUBLESHOOTING AND EVENT LOGGING

Troubleshooting services is different from troubleshooting other types of applications. This section touches on some service issues, problems specific to interactive services, and event logging.

The best way to start building a service is to create an assembly with the functionality you want and a test client, before the service is actually created. Here, you can do normal debugging and error handling. As soon as the application is running, you can build a service by using this assembly. Of course, there might still be problems with the service:

➤ Don't display errors in a message box from the service (except for interactive services that are running on the client system). Instead, use the event logging service to write errors to the event log. Of course, in the client application that uses the service, you can display a message box to inform the user about errors.

➤ The service cannot be started from within a debugger, but a debugger can be attached to the running service process. Open the solution with the source code of the service and set breakpoints. From the Visual Studio Debug menu, select Processes and attach the running process of the service.

➤ Performance Monitor can be used to monitor the activity of services, and you can add your own performance objects to the service. This can add some useful information for debugging. For example, with the Quote service, you could set up an object to provide the total number of quotes returned, the time it takes to initialize, and so on.

Services can report errors and other information by adding events to the event log. A service class derived from `ServiceBase` automatically logs events when the `AutoLog` property is set to `true`. The `ServiceBase` class checks this property and writes a log entry at start, stop, pause, and continue requests.

Figure 39-16 shows an example of a log entry from a service.

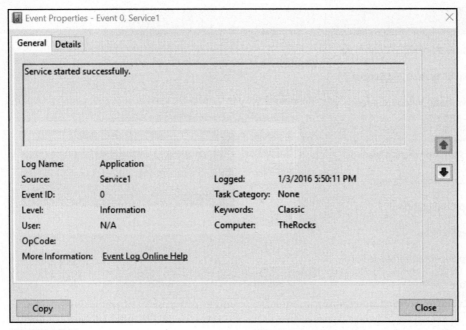

FIGURE 39-16

> **NOTE** *You can read more about event logging and how to write custom events in Chapter 20, "Diagnostics and Application Insights."*

SUMMARY

In this chapter, you have seen the architecture of Windows Services and how you can create them with the .NET Framework. Applications can start automatically at boot time with Windows Services, and you can use a privileged system account as the user of the service. Windows Services are built from a main function, a service-main function, and a handler; and you looked at other relevant programs in regard to Windows Services, such as a service control program and a service installation program.

The .NET Framework has great support for Windows Services. All the plumbing code that is necessary for building, controlling, and installing services is built into the .NET Framework classes in the `System .ServiceProcess` namespace. By deriving a class from `ServiceBase`, you can override methods that are invoked when the service is paused, resumed, or stopped. For installation of services, the classes `ServiceProcessInstaller` and `ServiceInstaller` deal with all registry configurations needed for services. You can also control and monitor services by using `ServiceController`.

In the next chapter you can read about ASP.NET Core 1.0, a technology that makes use of a web server that itself is typically running within a Windows Service (if the server is used on the Windows operating system).

40

ASP.NET Core

WROX.COM CODE DOWNLOADS FOR THIS CHAPTER

The wrox.com code downloads for this chapter are found at http://www.wrox.com/go/
professionalcsharp6 on the Download Code tab. The code for this chapter contains this example
project: WebSampleApp.

ASP.NET CORE 1.0

After 15 years of ASP.NET, ASP.NET Core 1.0 is a complete rewrite of ASP.NET. It features modular
programming, is fully open sourced, is lightweight for best use on the cloud, and is available to non-
Microsoft platforms.

A full rewrite of ASP.NET gives a lot of advantages, but this also means reworking existing web applications based on older versions of ASP.NET. Is it necessary to rewrite existing web applications to
ASP.NET Core 1.0? Let's try to answer this question.

ASP.NET Web Forms is no longer part of ASP.NET Core 1.0. However, having web applications
that include this technology does not mean you have to rewrite them. It's still possible to maintain
legacy applications written with ASP.NET Web Forms with the full framework. ASP.NET Web
Forms even received some enhancements with the newest version ASP.NET 4.6, such as asynchronous model binding.

ASP.NET MVC is still part of ASP.NET Core 1.0. Because ASP.NET MVC 6 has been completely rewritten, you need to make some changes to web applications written with ASP.NET MVC 5 or older versions to bring them to the new application stack.

Converting ASP.NET Web Forms to ASP.NET MVC might be a lot of work. ASP.NET Web Forms abstracts HTML and JavaScript from the developer. Using ASP.NET Web Forms, it's not necessary to know HTML and JavaScript. Instead you use server-side controls with C# code. The server-side controls themselves return HTML and JavaScript. This programming model is similar to the old Windows Forms programming model. With ASP.NET MVC, developers need to know HTML and JavaScript. ASP.NET MVC is based on the *Model-View-Controller* (MVC) pattern, which makes unit testing easy. Because ASP.NET Web Forms and ASP.NET MVC are based on very different architecture patterns, it can be a huge undertaking to migrate ASP.NET Web Forms applications to ASP.NET MVC. Before taking on this task, you should create a checklist of the advantages and the disadvantages of keeping the old technology with your solution and compare this with the advantages and disadvantages of going to the new technology. You will still be able to work with ASP.NET Web Forms for many years to come.

> **NOTE** *My website at* http://www.cninnoation.com *was originally created with ASP.NET Web Forms. I've converted this website with an early version of ASP.NET MVC to this new technology stack. Because my original site already made use of a lot of separate components to abstract the database and service code, it was not really a huge undertaking and was done very fast. I was able to use the database and service code directly from ASP.NET MVC. On the other hand, if I had used Web Forms controls to access the database instead of using my own controls, it would have been a lot more work.*

> **NOTE** *This book does not cover the legacy technology ASP.NET Web Forms. ASP.NET MVC 5 is also not covered. This book has a focus on new technologies; consequently with regard to web applications, the material is based on ASP.NET 5 and ASP.NET MVC 6. These technologies should be used for new web applications. In case you need to maintain older applications, you should read older editions of this book, such as Professional C# 5.0 and .NET 4.5.1, which covers ASP.NET 4.5, ASP.NET Web Forms 4.5, and ASP.NET MVC 5.*

This chapter covers the foundation of ASP.NET Core 1.0, and Chapter 41 explains using ASP.NET MVC 6, a framework that is built on top of ASP.NET Core 1.0.

WEB TECHNOLOGIES

Before getting into the foundations of ASP.NET later in this chapter, this section describes core web technologies that are important to know when creating web applications: HTML, CSS, JavaScript, and jQuery.

HTML

HTML is the markup language that is interpreted by web browsers. It defines elements to display various headings, tables, lists, and input elements such as text and combo boxes.

HTML5 has been a W3C recommendation since October 2014 (http://w3.org/TR/html5), and it is already offered by all the major browsers. With the features of HTML5, several browser add-ins (such as Flash and Silverlight) are not required anymore because the things the add-ins do can now be done directly with HTML and JavaScript. Of course, you might still need Flash and Silverlight because not all websites have moved to the new technologies or your users might still be using older browser versions that don't support HTML5.

HTML5 adds new semantic elements that search engines are better able to use for analyzing the site. A `canvas` element enables the dynamic use of 2D shapes and images, and `video` and `audio` elements make the `object` element obsolete. With recent additions to the media source (`http://w3c.github.io/media-source`), adaptive streaming is also offered by HTML; previously this had been an advantage of Silverlight.

HTML5 also defines APIs for drag-and-drop, storage, web sockets, and much more.

CSS

Whereas HTML defines the content of web pages, CSS defines the look. In the earlier days of HTML, for example, the list item tag `<li>` defined whether list elements should be displayed with a circle, a disc, or a square. Nowadays such information is completely removed from HTML and is instead put into a cascading style sheet (CSS).

With CSS styles, you can use flexible selectors to select HTML elements, and you can define styles for these elements. You can select an element via its ID or its name, and you can define CSS classes that can be referenced from within the HTML code. With newer versions of CSS, you can define quite complex rules for selecting specific HTML elements.

As of Visual Studio 2015, the web project templates make use of Twitter Bootstrap. This is a collection of CSS and HTML conventions, and you can easily adapt different looks and download ready-to-use templates. Visit `www.getbootstrap.com` for documentation and basic templates.

JavaScript and TypeScript

Not all platforms and browsers can use .NET code, but nearly every browser understands *JavaScript*. One common misconception about JavaScript is that it has something to do with Java. In fact, only the name is similar because Netscape (the originator of JavaScript) made an agreement with Sun (Sun invented Java) to be allowed to use Java in the name. Nowadays, both of these companies no longer exist. Sun was bought by Oracle, and now Oracle holds the trademark for Java.

Both Java and JavaScript (and C#) have the same roots—the C programming language. JavaScript is a functional programming language that is not object-oriented, although object-oriented capabilities have been added to it.

JavaScript enables accessing the *document object model* (DOM) from the HTML page, which makes it possible to change elements dynamically on the client.

ECMAScript is the standard that defines the current and upcoming features of the JavaScript language. Because other companies are not allowed to use the term Java with their language implementations, the standard has the name ECMAScript. Microsoft's implementation of JavaScript had the name JScript. Check `http://www.ecmascript.org` for the current state and future changes of the JavaScript language.

Even though many browsers don't support the newest ECMAScript version, you can still write ECMAScript 5 code. Instead of writing JavaScript code, you can use *TypeScript*. The TypeScript syntax is based on ECMAScript, but it has some enhancements, such as strongly typed code and annotations. You'll find many similarities between C# and TypeScript. Because the TypeScript compiler compiles to JavaScript, TypeScript can be used in every place where JavaScript is needed. For more information on TypeScript, check `http://www.typescriptlang.org`.

Scripting Libraries

Beside the JavaScript programming language, you also need scripting libraries to make life easier.

➤ jQuery (`http://www.jquery.org`) is a library that abstracts browser differences when accessing DOM elements and reacting to events.

> ➤ Angular (http://angularjs.org) is a library based on the MVC pattern for simplifying development and testing with single-page web applications. (Unlike ASP.NET MVC, Angular offers the MVC pattern with client-side code.)

The ASP.NET web project template includes jQuery libraries and Bootstrap. Visual Studio 2015 supports IntelliSense and debugging JavaScript code.

> **NOTE** *Styling web applications and writing JavaScript code is not covered in this book. You can read more about HTML and styles in* HTML and CSS: Design and Build Websites *by John Ducket (Wiley, 2011); and get up to speed with* Professional JavaScript for Web Developers *by Nicholas C. Zakas (Wrox, 2012).*

ASP.NET WEB PROJECT

Start by creating an empty ASP.NET Core 1.0 Web Application named WebSampleApp (see Figure 40-1). You start with an empty template and add features as you make your way through this chapter.

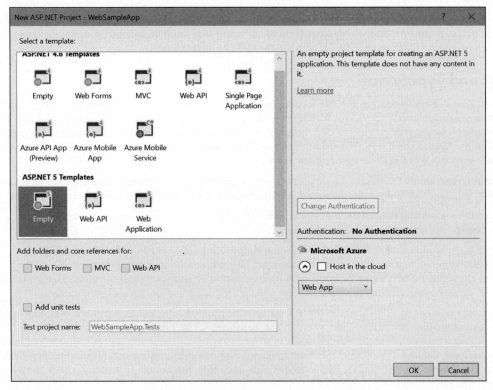

FIGURE 40-1

> **NOTE** *With the sample code download of this chapter, you need to uncomment specific code blocks in the* Startup *class to activate the features discussed. You can also create the project from scratch. There's not too much code to write to see all the functionality in action.*

After you've created the project, you see a solution and a project file named `WebSampleApp`, which includes a few files and folders (see Figure 40-2).

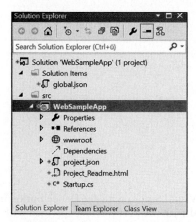

FIGURE 40-2

The solution includes the `global.json` configuration file. This file lists the directories of the solution. You can see this with the values of the `projects` key in the following code snippet. The `src` directory contains all the projects of the solution with the source code. The `test` directory is for defining the unit tests, although they don't exist yet. The `sdk` setting defines the version number of the SDK used (code file `global.json`).

```
{
    "projects": [ "src", "test" ],
    "sdk": {
        "version": "1.0.0-0"
    }
}
```

Within the project structure, when you open the file `Project_Readme.html` with a browser, you see some overall information about ASP.NET Core 1.0. You can see a `References` folder within the project folder. This contains all the referenced NuGet packages. With an empty ASP.NET Web Application project, the only packages referenced are `Microsoft.AspNetCore.IISPlatformHandler` and `Microsoft.AspNetCore.Server.Kestrel`.

`IISPlatformHandler` contains a Module for IIS that maps the IIS infrastructure to ASP.NET Core 1.0. `Kestrel` is a new web server for ASP.NET Core 1.0 that you can also use on the Linux platform.

You can also find the references for the NuGet packages within the `project.json` file. (In the following code snippet, they are in the `dependencies` section.) The `frameworks` section lists the supported .NET frameworks, such as `net452` (.NET 4.5.2) and `netstandard1.0` (.NET Core 1.0). You can remove the one you don't need for hosting. The `exclude` section lists the files and directories that should not be used for compiling the application. The `publishExclude` section lists the files and folders that should not be published (code file `WebSampleApp/project.json`):

```
{
    "version": "1.0.0-*",
    "compilationOptions": {
        "emitEntryPoint": true
    },

    "dependencies": {
        "NETStandard.Library": "1.0.0-*",
        "Microsoft.AspNetCore.IISPlatformHandler": "1.0.0-*",
        "Microsoft.AspNetCore.Server.Kestrel": "1.0.0-*"
    },
```

```
"frameworks": {
  "net452": { },
  "netstandard1.0": {
    "dependencies": {
      "NETStandard.Library": "1.0.0-*"
    }
  }
},
"content": [ "hosting.json" ]
"exclude": [
  "wwwroot",
  "node_modules"
],
"publishExclude": [
  "**.user",
  "**.vspscc"
]
}
```

You can configure the web server that is used while developing with Visual Studio with the Debug option in Project settings (see Figure 40-3). By default, IIS Express is configured with the port number specified with the Debug settings. IIS Express derives from Internet Information Server (IIS) and offers all the core features of IIS. This makes it easy to develop the web application in practically the same environment where the application will be hosted later (if IIS is used for hosting).

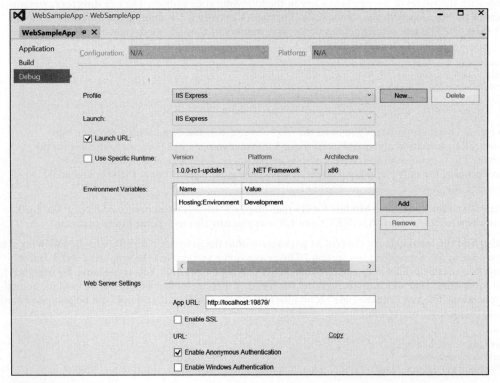

FIGURE 40-3

To run the application with the Kestrel server, you can select the web profile with the Debug Project settings. The options that are available with the list in the Profile options are the commands listed in `project.json`.

The settings that you change with the Visual Studio project settings influence the configuration of the `launchSettings.json` file. With this file you can define some additional configurations such as command line arguments (code file `WebSampleApp/Properties/launchsettings.json`):

```json
{
  "iisSettings": {
    "windowsAuthentication": false,
    "anonymousAuthentication": true,
    "iisExpress": {
      "applicationUrl": "http://localhost:19879/",
      "sslPort": 0
    }
  },
  "profiles": {
    "IIS Express": {
      "commandName": "IISExpress",
      "launchBrowser": true,
      "environmentVariables": {
        "Hosting:Environment": "Development"
      }
    },
    "web": {
      "commandName": "web",
      "launchBrowser": true,
      "launchUrl": "http://localhost:5000/",
      "commandLineArgs": "Environment=Development",
      "environmentVariables": {
        "Hosting:Environment": "Development"
      }
    }
  }
}
```

The `Dependencies` folder in the project structure in Solution Explorer shows the dependencies on the JavaScript libraries. When you create an empty project, this folder is empty. You add dependencies later in this chapter in the section "Adding Static Content."

The `wwwroot` folder is the folder for static files that need to be published to the server. Currently, this folder is empty, but as you work through this chapter you add HTML and CSS files and JavaScript libraries.

A C# source file—`Startup.cs`—is included with an empty project as well. This file is discussed next.

During the creation of the project, these dependencies and namespaces are needed:

Dependencies

```
Microsoft.AspNetCore.Http.Abstractions

Microsoft.AspNetCore.IISPlatformHandler

Microsoft.AspNetCore.Server.Kestrel

Microsoft.AspNetCore.StaticFiles

Microsoft.AspNetCore.Session

Microsoft.Extensions.Configuration

Microsoft.Extensions.Configuration.UserSecrets

Microsoft.Extensions.Logging

Microsoft.Extensions.Logging.Console

Microsoft.Extensions.Logging.Debug

Microsoft.Extensions.PlatformAbstractions

Newtonsoft.Json
```

```
System.Globalization
System.Text.Encodings.Web
System.Runtime
```

Namespaces

```
Microsoft.AspNetCore.Builder;
Microsoft.AspNetCore.Hosting;
Microsoft.AspNetCore.Http;
Microsoft.Extensions.Configuration
Microsoft.Extensions.DependencyInjection
Microsoft.Extensions.Logging
Microsoft.Extensions.PlatformAbstractions
Newtonsoft.Json
System
System.Globalization
System.Linq
System.Text
System.Text.Encodings.Web
System.Threading.Tasks
```

STARTUP

It's time to start to get some functionality out of the web application. To get information about the client and return a response, you need to write a response to the HttpContext.

The empty ASP.NET web application template creates a Startup class that contains the following code (code file WebSampleApp/Startup.cs):

```
using Microsoft.AspNetCore.Builder;
using Microsoft.AspNetCore.Hosting;
using Microsoft.AspNetCore.Http;
using Microsoft.Extensions.DependencyInjection;
// etc.

namespace WebSampleApp
{
  public class Startup
  {
    public void ConfigureServices(IServiceCollection services)
    {
    }

    public void Configure(IApplicationBuilder app, ILoggerFactory loggerFactory)
    {
      app.UseIISPlatformHandler();
      // etc.

      app.Run(async (context) =>
      {
        await context.Response.WriteAsync("Hello World!");
      });
```

```
        }

        public static void Main(string[] args)
        {
          var host = new WebHostBuilder()
            .UseDefaultConfiguration(args)
            .UseStartup<Startup>()
            .Build();
          host.Run();
        }
      }
    }
```

The entry point for the web application is the `Main` method. With the `emitEntryPoint` configuration you've seen earlier in the `project.json` configuration file you can define if a `Main` method should be used. You also defined the `Main` method with .NET Core console applications created in this book. Only libraries don't need a `Main` method.

With the default implementation as it is generated from the Visual Studio template, the web application is configured with the help of a `WebHostBuilder` instance. Using the `WebHostBuilder`, the method `UseDefaultConfiguration` is invoked. This method receives the command-line arguments and creates a configuration that includes the optional hosting file (`hosting.json`), adds environmental variables, and adds the command-line arguments to the configuration. The method `UseStartup` defines to use the `Startup` class, which in turn invokes the methods `ConfigureServices` and `Configure`. The last method invoked with the `WebApplicationBuilder` is the `Build` method, which returns an object implementing the interface `IWebApplication`. With the returned application object, the `Run` method is invoked, which starts the hosting engine; now the server is listening and waiting for requests.

The `hosting.json` file is used to configure the server (code file `WebSampleApp/hosting.json`):

```
    {
      "server": "Microsoft.AspNetCore.Server.Kestrel",
      "server.urls": "http://localhost:5000"
    }
```

Because the `Startup` class is passed to the `UseStartup` method with a generic template parameter, in turn the methods `ConfigureServices` and `Configure` are invoked.

The `Configure` method receives an internal application builder type via dependency injection that implements the interface `IApplicationBuilder`. This interface is used to define services used by the application. Calling the `Use` method of this interface, you can build the HTTP request pipeline to define what should be done in answer to a request. The `Run` method is an extension method for the interface `IApplicationBuilder`; it invokes the `Use` method. This method is implemented via the `RunExtensions` extension class in the assembly `Microsoft.AspNetCore.Http.Abstractions` and the namespace `Microsoft.AspNetCore.Builder`.

The parameter of the `Run` method is a delegate of type `RequestDelegate`. This type receives an `HttpContext` as a parameter, and it returns a `Task`. With the `HttpContext` (the `context` variable in the code snippet), you have access to the request information from the browser (HTTP headers, cookies, and form data) and can send a response. The code snippet returns a simple string—Hello, World!—to the client, as shown in Figure 40-4.

FIGURE 40-4

> **NOTE** *If you're using Microsoft Edge for testing the web application, you need to enable localhost. Type **about:flags** in the URL box, and enable the Allow Localhost Loopback option (see Figure 40-5). Instead of using the built-in user interface of Microsoft Edge to set this option, you can also use a command line option: the utility* `CheckNetIsolation`. *The command* `CheckNetIsolation LoopbackExempt -a -n=Microsoft.MicrosoftEdge_8wekyb3d8bbwe` *enables localhost similarly to using the more friendly user interface for Microsoft Edge. The utility* `CheckNetIsolation` *is useful if you want to configure other Windows apps to allow localhost.*

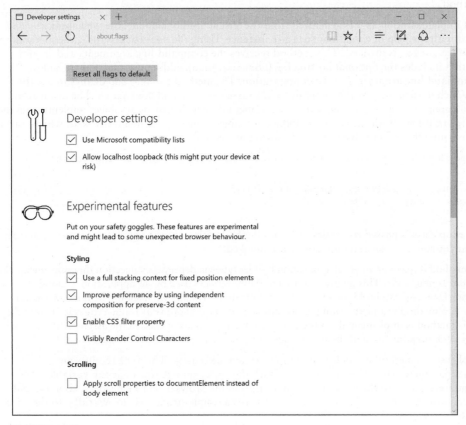

FIGURE 40-5

Adding logging information to your web application is really useful to get more information about what's going on. For this, the `Configure` method of the `Startup` class receives an `ILoggerFactory` object. With this interface you can add logger providers using the `AddProvider` method, and you create a logger implementing the `ILogger` interface with the `CreateLogger` method. The `AddConsole` and `AddDebug` methods shown in the following code snippet are extension methods to add different providers. The `AddConsole` method adds a provider to write log information to the console, the `AddDebug` method adds a provider to write log information to the debugger. Using both of these methods without passing argument values, a default is used to configure log messages. The default specifies to write log messages of type information and higher. You can use different overloads to specify other filters for logging, or you can use configuration files to configure logging (code file `WebSampleApp/Startup.cs`):

```
public void Configure(IApplicationBuilder app, ILoggerFactory loggerFactory)
{
  // etc.
  loggerFactory.AddConsole();
  loggerFactory.AddDebug();

  // etc.
}
```

With the `ILogger` interface you can write custom log information using the `Log` method.

ADDING STATIC CONTENT

Usually you don't want to just send simple strings to the client. By default, simple HTML files and other static content can't be sent. ASP.NET 5 reduces the overhead as much as possible. Even static files are not returned from the server if you do not enable them.

To enable static files served from the web server, you can add the extension method `UseStaticFiles` (and comment the previously created `Run` method):

```
public void Configure(IApplicationBuilder app, ILoggerFactory loggerFactory)
{
  app.UseiISPlatformHandler();
  app.UseStaticFiles();

  //etc.
}
```

As soon as you add this code line with the same capitalization to the `Configure` method, the smart tag from the editor offers adding the NuGet package `Microsoft.AspNet.StaticFiles`. Select this, and the NuGet package is downloaded and listed in `project.json`:

```
"dependencies": {
  "Microsoft.AspNetCore.IISPlatformHandler": "1.0.0-*",
  "Microsoft.AspNetCore.Server.Kestrel": "1.0.0-*",
  "Microsoft.AspNetCore.StaticFiles": "1.0.0-*"
},
```

The folder where you add static files is the `wwwroot` folder within the project. You can configure the name of the folder in the `project.json` file with the `webroot` setting. If no folder is configured, it's `wwwroot`. With the configuration and the NuGet package added, you can add an HTML file to the `wwwroot` folder (code file `WebSampleApp/wwwroot/Hello.html`), as shown here:

```
<!DOCTYPE html>
<html>
<head>
  <meta charset="utf-8" />
  <title></title>
</head>
<body>
  <h1>Hello, ASP.NET with Static Files</h1>
</body>
</html>
```

Now you make a request to the HTML file from the browser after starting the server—for example, `http://localhost:5000/Hello.html`. Depending on the configuration you are using, the port number might differ for your project.

> **NOTE** *When creating web applications with ASP.NET MVC, you also need to know HTML, CSS, JavaScript, and some JavaScript libraries. As this book's focus is C# and .NET, the content for these topics is kept to a minimum. I just cover the most important tasks you need to know with ASP.NET MVC and Visual Studio.*

Using a JavaScript Package Manager: npm

With web applications, you typically need some JavaScript libraries. Before Visual Studio 2015, JavaScript libraries were available as NuGet packages—similarly to how .NET assemblies are available as NuGet packages. Because the communities around script libraries typically don't use the NuGet server, they also don't create NuGet packages. Extra work was required from Microsoft or Microsoft-friendly communities to create NuGet packages for JavaScript libraries. Instead of using NuGet, communities around JavaScript use servers with functionality similar to NuGet.

The Node Package Manager (*npm*) is a package manager for JavaScript libraries. Originally coming from Node.Js (a JavaScript library for server-side development), npm is strong with server-side scripts. However, more and more client-side scripting libraries are available with npm as well.

Using Visual Studio 2015, you can add npm to the project by adding the *NPM Configuration File* from the item templates. When you add the item template, the package.json file is added to the project:

```
{
    "version": "1.0.0",
    "name": "ASP.NET",
    "private": "true",
    "devDependencies": {
    }
}
```

With the file open within Visual Studio, you can see the npm logo in the editor, as shown in Figure 40-6.

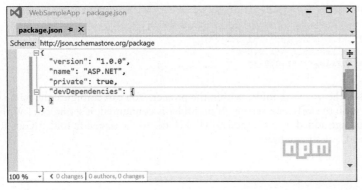

FIGURE 40-6

> **NOTE** *The* package.json *file is visible in the Solution Explorer only if you click the button Show All Files.*

If you start adding JavaScript libraries to the `devDependencies` section of this file, the npm server is contacted as you type to allow completing the JavaScript library, and to show available version numbers. When you select the version number in the editor, you also get the offer for a ^ and ~ prefix. Without the prefix, exactly the version of the library with the exact name you typed is retrieved from the server. With the ^ prefix, the latest library with the same major version number is retrieved; with the ~ prefix, the latest library with the same minor version number is retrieved.

The following `package.json` file references a few gulp libraries and the rimraf library. As you save the `package.json` file, the npm packages are loaded from the server. In the Solution Explorer you can see the npm-loaded libraries in the Dependencies section. The Dependencies section has an npm child node where all the libraries loaded are shown.

```json
{
    "version": "1.0.0",
    "name": "ASP.NET",
    "private": "true",
    "devDependencies": {
        "gulp": "3.9.0",
        "gulp-concat": "2.6.0",
        "gulp-cssmin": "0.1.7",
        "gulp-uglify": "1.2.0",
        "rimraf": "2.4.2"
    }
}
```

What are these JavaScript libraries referenced good for? *gulp* is a build system that is discussed in the next section. *gulp-concat* concatenates JavaScript files; *gulp-cssmin* minifies CSS files; *gulp-uglify* minifies JavaScript files; and *rimraf* allows you to delete files in a hierarchy. Minification removes all unnecessary characters.

After the packages are added, you can easily update or uninstall the package using the npm node within the Dependencies section in Solution Explorer.

Building with Gulp

Gulp is a build system for JavaScript. Whereas npm can be compared to NuGet, gulp can be compared to .NET Development Utility (DNU). JavaScript code is interpreted; why do you need a build system with JavaScript? There are a lot of things to do with HTML, CSS, and JavaScript before putting these files on the server. With a build system, you can convert Syntactically Awesome Stylesheets (SASS) files (CSS with scripting features) to CSS, you can minify and compress files, you can start unit tests for scripts, and you can analyze JavaScript code (for example, with JSHint)—there are a lot useful tasks you can do.

After adding gulp with npm, a *Gulp Configuration File* can be added using a Visual Studio item template. This template creates the following gulp file (code file `MVCSampleApp/gulpfile.js`):

```javascript
/*
This file is the main entry point for defining Gulp tasks and using Gulp plugins.
Click here to learn more. http://go.microsoft.com/fwlink/?LinkId=518007
*/

var gulp = require('gulp');

gulp.task('default', function () {
    // place code for your default task here
});
```

The editor with the gulp logo is shown in Figure 40-7.

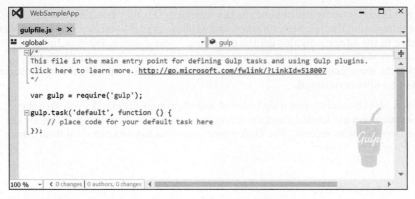

FIGURE 40-7

Now let's add some tasks to the gulp file. The first lines define required libraries for this file and assign variables to the scripts. Here, the libraries that have been added with npm are in use. The `gulp.task` function creates gulp tasks that you can start using the Visual Studio Task Runner Explorer:

```
"use strict";
var gulp = require("gulp"),
    rimraf = require("rimraf"),
    concat = require("gulp-concat"),
    cssmin = require("gulp-cssmin"),
    uglify = require("gulp-uglify")

var paths = {
    webroot: "./wwwroot/"
};

paths.js = paths.webroot + "js/**/*.js";
paths.minJs = paths.webroot + "js/**/*.min.js";
paths.css = paths.webroot + "css/**/*.css";
paths.minCss = paths.webroot + "css/**/*.min.css";
paths.concatJsDest = paths.webroot + "js/site.min.js";
paths.concatCssDest = paths.webroot + "css/site.min.css";

gulp.task("clean:js", function (cb) {
    rimraf(paths.concatJsDest, cb);
});

gulp.task("clean:css", function (cb) {
    rimraf(paths.concatCssDest, cb);
});

gulp.task("clean", ["clean:js", "clean:css"]);

gulp.task("min:js", function () {
    gulp.src([paths.js, "!" + paths.minJs], { base: "." })
        .pipe(concat(paths.concatJsDest))
        .pipe(uglify())
        .pipe(gulp.dest("."));
});

gulp.task("min:css", function () {
    gulp.src([paths.css, "!" + paths.minCss])
        .pipe(concat(paths.concatCssDest))
        .pipe(cssmin())
```

```
            .pipe(gulp.dest("."));
});

gulp.task("min", ["min:js", "min:css"]);
```

Visual Studio 2015 offers a Task Runner Explorer (see Figure 40-8) for gulp files. Double-click on a task to start it. You can also map the gulp tasks to Visual Studio commands. This way gulp tasks are started automatically when a project is opened, before or after the build, or when the Clean menu entry is selected within the Build menu.

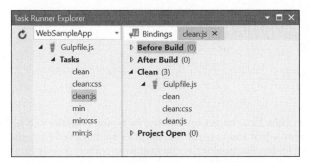

FIGURE 40-8

> **NOTE** *Another JavaScript build system supported by Visual Studio is Grunt. The focus in Grunt is building via configuration, whereas the focus in Gulp is on building via JavaScript code.*

Using Client-Side Libraries with Bower

Most client-side JavaScript libraries are available via *Bower.* Bower is a package manager like npm. Whereas the npm project started with JavaScript libraries for server-side code (although many client-side scripting libraries are also available with npm), Bower offers thousands of JavaScript client libraries.

Bower can be added to an ASP.NET web project by using the item template *Bower Configuration File.* This template adds the file bower.json as shown here:

```
{
  "name": "ASP.NET",
  "private": true,
  "dependencies": {
  }
}
```

Adding Bower to the project also adds the .bowerrc file that configures Bower. By default, when you use the directory setting, the script files (as well as CSS and HTML files that come with the scripting libraries) are copied to the wwwroot/lib directory:

```
{
  "directory": "wwwroot/lib"
}
```

> **NOTE** *Similar to NPM, you need to click the Show All Files button in the Solution Explorer to see the bower-related files.*

Visual Studio 2015 has special support for Bower. Figure 40-9 shows the Bower logo in the editor.

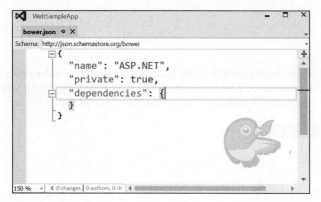

FIGURE 40-9

If you start adding scripting libraries to the `bower.json` file, you get IntelliSense by typing both the name of the library and the version number. Similarly to npm, when you save the file, libraries are retrieved from the server and can be found within the `Dependencies` folder. Because of the configuration within `.bowerrc`, the files from the scripting libraries are copied to the `wwwroot/lib` folder (code file `MVCSampleApp/.bowerrc`):

```
{
  "name": "ASP.NET",
  "private": true,
  "dependencies": {
    "bootstrap": "3.3.5",
    "jquery": "2.1.4",
    "jquery-validation": "1.14.0",
    "jquery-validation-unobtrusive": "3.2.5"
  }
}
```

Management of Bower packages is also available with the Manage Bower Packages tool that you can access by clicking the application context menu Manage Bower Packages. This tool is very similar to the NuGet Package Manager; it just makes it easy to manage Bower packages (see Figure 40-10).

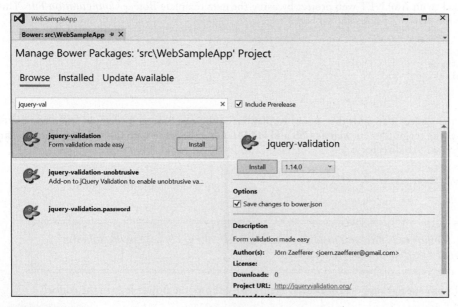

FIGURE 40-10

Now that the infrastructure is in place, it's time to get into the HTTP request and response.

REQUEST AND RESPONSE

With the HTTP protocol, the client makes a request to the server. This request is answered with a response.

The request consists of a header and, in many cases, body information to the server. The server uses the body information to define different results based on the needs of the client. Let's have a look at what information can be read from the client.

To return an HTML-formatted output to the client, the GetDiv method creates a div element that contains span elements with the passed arguments key and value (code file WebSampleApp/ RequestAndResponseSample.cs):

```
public static string GetDiv(string key, string value) =>
  $"<div><span>{key}:</span> <span>{value}</span></div>";
```

Because such HTML div and span tags are needed to surround strings in following examples, extension methods are created to cover this functionality (code file WebSampleApp/HtmlExtensions.cs):

```
public static class HtmlExtensions
{
  public static string Div(this string value) =>
    $"<div>{value}</div>";

  public static string Span(this string value) =>
    $"<span>{value}</span>";
}
```

The method GetRequestInformation uses an HttpRequest object to access Scheme, Host, Path, QueryString, Method, and Protocol properties (code file WebSampleApp/RequestAndResponseSample.cs):

```
public static string GetRequestInformation(HttpRequest request)
{
  var sb = new StringBuilder();
  sb.Append(GetDiv("scheme", request.Scheme));
  sb.Append(GetDiv("host", request.Host.HasValue ? request.Host.Value :
    "no host"));
  sb.Append(GetDiv("path", request.Path));
  sb.Append(GetDiv("query string", request.QueryString.HasValue ?
    request.QueryString.Value : "no query string"));

  sb.Append(GetDiv("method", request.Method));
  sb.Append(GetDiv("protocol", request.Protocol));

  return sb.ToString();
}
```

The Configure method of the Startup class is changed to invoke the GetRequestInformation method and pass the HttpRequest via the Request property of the HttpContext. The result is written to the Response object (code file WebSampleApp/Startup.cs):

```
app.Run(async (context) =>
{
  await context.Response.WriteAsync(
    RequestAndResponseSample.GetRequestInformation(context.Request));
});
```

Starting the program from Visual Studio results in the following information:

```
scheme:http
host:localhost:5000
path: /
query string: no query string
method: GET
protocol: HTTP/1.1
```

Adding a path, such as `http://localhost:5000/Index`, to the request results in the path value set:

```
scheme:http
host:localhost:5000
path: /Index
query string: no query string
method: GET
protocol: HTTP/1.1
```

When you add a query string, such as `http://localhost:5000/Add?x=3&y=5`, the query string accessing the property `QueryString` shows up:

```
query string: ?x=3&y=5
```

In the next code snippet you use the `Path` property of the `HttpRequest` to create a lightweight custom routing. Depending on the path that is set by the client, different methods are invoked (code file `WebSampleApp/Startup.cs`):

```
app.Run(async (context) =>
{
  string result = string.Empty;
  switch (context.Request.Path.Value.ToLower())
  {
    case "/header":
      result = RequestAndResponseSample.GetHeaderInformation(context.Request);
      break;
    case "/add":
      result = RequestAndResponseSample.QueryString(context.Request);
      break;
    case "/content":
      result = RequestAndResponseSample.Content(context.Request);
      break;
    case "/encoded":
      result = RequestAndResponseSample.ContentEncoded(context.Request);
      break;
    case "/form":
      result = RequestAndResponseSample.GetForm(context.Request);
      break;
    case "/writecookie":
      result = RequestAndResponseSample.WriteCookie(context.Response);
      break;
    case "/readcookie":
      result = RequestAndResponseSample.ReadCookie(context.Request);
      break;
    case "/json":
      result = RequestAndResponseSample.GetJson(context.Response);
      break;
    default:
      result = RequestAndResponseSample.GetRequestInformation(context.Request);
      break;
  }
  await context.Response.WriteAsync(result);
});
```

The following sections implement the different methods to show request headers, query strings, and more.

Request Headers

Let's have a look at what information the client sends within the HTTP header. To access the HTTP header information, the `HttpRequest` object defines the Headers property. This is of type `IHeaderDictionary`, and it contains a dictionary with the name of the header and a string array for the values. Using this information, the `GetDiv` method created earlier is used to write `div` elements for the client (code file `WebSampleApp/RequestAndResponseSample.cs`):

```
public static string GetHeaderInformation(HttpRequest request)
{
  var sb = new StringBuilder();

  IHeaderDictionary headers = request.Headers;
  foreach (var header in request.Headers)
  {
    sb.Append(GetDiv(header.Key, string.Join("; ", header.Value)));
  }
  return sb.ToString();
}
```

The results you see depend on the browser you're using. Let's compare a few of them. The following is from Internet Explorer 11 on a Windows 10 touch device:

```
Connection: Keep-Alive
Accept: text/html,application/xhtml+xml,image/jxr,*.*
Accept-Encoding: gzip, deflate
Accept-Language: en-Us,en;q=0.8,de-AT;q=0.6,de-DE;q=0.4,de;q=0.2
Host: localhost:5000
User-Agent: Mozilla/5.0 (Windows NT 10.0; WOW64; Trident/7.0; Touch; rv:11.0)
like Gecko
```

Google Chrome version 47.0 shows this information, including version numbers from AppleWebKit, Chrome, and Safari:

```
Connection: keep-alive
Accept: text/html,application/xhtml,application/xml;q=0.9,image/webp,*.*;q=0.8
Accept-Encoding: gzip, deflate, sdch
Accept-Language: en-Us;en;q=0.8
Host: localhost:5000
User-Agent: Mozilla/5.0 (Windows NT 10.0; WOW64) AppleWebKit/537.36
(KHTML, like Gecko) Chrome 47.0.2526.80 Safari/537.36
```

And Microsoft Edge comes with this information, including version numbers from AppleWebKit, Chrome, Safari, and Edge:

```
Connection: Keep-Alive
Accept: text/html,application/xhtml+xml,image/jxr,*.*
Accept-Encoding: gzip, deflate
Accept-Language: en-Us,en;q=0.8,de-AT;q=0.6,de-DE;q=0.4,de;q=0.2
Host: localhost:5000
User-Agent: Mozilla/5.0 (Windows NT 10.0; Win64; x64) AppleWebKit/537.36
(KHTML,
```

What can you get out of this header information?

The `Connection` header was an enhancement of the HTTP 1.1 protocol. With this header the client can request to keep connections open. Usually with HTML, the client makes multiple requests, e.g. to get the images, CSS, and JavaScript files. The server might honor the request, or it might ignore the request in case the load is too high and it's better to close the connection.

The `Accept` header defines the mime formats the browser accepts. The list is in order by the preferred formats. Depending on this information, you might decide to return data with different formats based on the client's needs. IE prefers HTML followed by XHTML and JXR. Google Chrome has a different list. It prefers these formats: HTML, XHTML, XML, and WEBP. With some of this information, a quantifier is also defined. The browsers used for the output all have `*.*` at the end of this list to accept all data returned.

The `Accept-Language` header information shows the languages the user has configured. Using this information, you can return localized information. Localization is discussed in Chapter 28, "Localization."

> **NOTE** *In ancient times, the server kept long lists of browser capabilities. These lists have been used to know what feature is available with which browser. To identify a browser, the agent string from the browser was used to map the capabilities. Over time, browsers lied by giving wrong information, or they even allowed the user to configure the browser name that should be used so that they could get some more features (because browser lists often were not updated on the server). In the past, Internet Explorer (IE) often required different programming than all the other browsers. Microsoft Edge is very different from IE and has more features in common with other vendors' browsers. That's why Microsoft Edge shows Mozilla, AppleWebKit, Chrome, Safari, and Edge in the* `User-Agent` *string. It's best not to use this* `User-Agent` *string at all for getting a list of features available. Instead, check for specific features you need programmatically.*

The header information that you've seen so far that was sent with the browser is what is sent for very simple sites. Usually, there will be more detail, such as cookies, authentication information, and also custom information. To see all the information that is sent to and from a server, including the header information, you can use the browser's developer tools and start a Network session; you'll see not only all the requests that are sent to the server but also header, body, parameters, cookies, and timing information as shown in Figure 40-11.

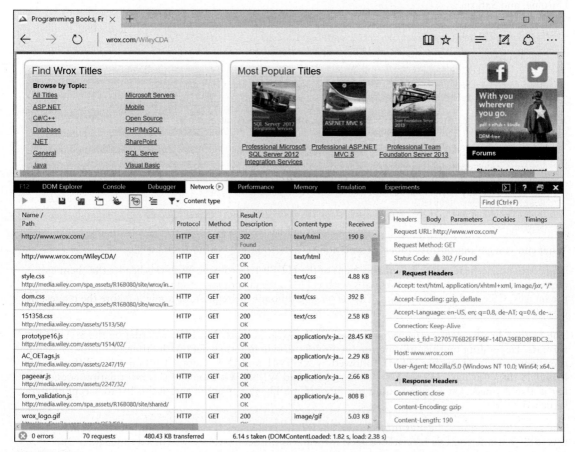

FIGURE 40-11

Query String

You can use the `Add` method to analyze the query string. This method requires x and y parameters, makes an addition if these parameters are numbers, and returns the calculation within a `div` tag. The method `GetRequestInformation` shown in the previous section demonstrated how to access the complete query string using the `QueryString` property of the `HttpRequest` object. To access the parts of the query string, you can use the `Query` property. The following code snippet accesses the values of x and y by using the `Get` method. This method returns null if the corresponding key is not found in the query string (code file `WebSampleApp/RequestAndResponseSample.cs`):

```
public static string QueryString(HttpRequest request)
{
  var sb = new StringBuilder();
  string xtext = request.Query["x"];
  string ytext = request.Query["y"];
  if (xtext == null ⊠ ytext == null)
  {
    return "x and y must be set";
  }
  int x, y;
  if (!int.TryParse(xtext, out x))
  {
    return $"Error parsing {xtext}";
  }
  if (!int.TryParse(ytext, out y))
  {
    return $"Error parsing {ytext}";
  }
  return $"{x} + {y} = {x + y}".Div();
}
```

The `IQueryCollection` returned from the `Query` string also enables you to access all the keys using the `Keys` property, and it offers a `ContainsKey` method to check whether a specified key is available.

Using the URL `http://localhost:5000/add?x=39&y=3` shows this result in the browser:

```
39 + 3 = 42
```

Encoding

Returning data that has been entered by a user can be dangerous. Let's do this with the `Content` method. The following method directly returns the data that is passed with the query data string (code file `WebSampleApp/RequestAndResponseSample.cs`):

```
public static string Content(HttpRequest request) =>
  request.Query["data"];
```

Invoking this method using the URL `http://localhost:5000/content?data=sample`, just the string sample is returned. Using the same method, users can also pass HTML content such as `http://localhost:5000/content?data=<h1>Heading 1</h1>` What's the result of this? Figure 40-12 shows that the h1 element is interpreted by the browser, and the text is shown with the heading format. There are cases where you want to allow this—for example, when users (maybe not anonymous users) are writing articles for a site.

FIGURE 40-12

Without checking the user input, it is also possible for the users to pass JavaScript such as `http://localhost:5000/content?data=<script>alert("hacker");</script>`. You can use the JavaScript alert function to make a message box pop up. It's similarly easy to redirect the user to a different site. When this user input is stored in the site, one user can enter such a script, and all other users who open this page are redirected accordingly.

Returning user-entered data should always be encoded. Let's have a look at how the result looks with and without encoding. You can do HTML encoding using the `HtmlEncoder` class as shown in the following code snippet (code file `WebSampleApp/RequestResponseSample.cs`):

```
public static string ContentEncoded(HttpRequest request) =>
  HtmlEncoder.Default.Encode(request.Query["data"]);
```

> **NOTE** *Using the* `HtmlEncoder` *requires the NuGet package* `System.Text.Encodings.Web`.

When the application is run, the same JavaScript code with encoding is passed using `http://localhost:5000/encoded?data=<script>alert("hacker");</script>`, and the client just sees the JavaScript code in the browser; it is not interpreted (see Figure 40-13).

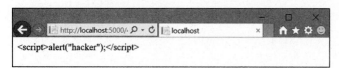

```
<script>alert("hacker");</script>
```

FIGURE 40-13

The encoded string that is sent looks like the following example—with the character reference less-than sign (<), greater-than sign (>), and quotation mark ("):

```
<script>alert("hacker");</script>
```

Form Data

Instead of passing data from the user to the server with a query string, you can use the form HTML element. This example uses an HTTP POST request instead of GET. With a POST request the user data are passed with the body of the request instead of within the query string.

Using form data is defined with two requests. First, the form is sent to the client with a GET request and then the user fills in the form and submits the data with a POST request. The method that is invoked passing the `/form` path in turn invokes the `GetForm` or `ShowForm` method, depending on the HTTP method type (code file `WebSampleApp/RequestResponseSample.cs`):

```
public static string GetForm(HttpRequest request)
{
  string result = string.Empty;
  switch (request.Method)
  {
    case "GET":
      result = GetForm();
      break;
    case "POST":
      result = ShowForm(request);
      break;
    default:
```

```
        break;
    }
    return result;
}
```

The form is created with an input element named `text1` and a Submit button. Clicking the Submit button invokes the form's `action` method with an HTTP method as defined with the `method` argument:

```
private static string GetForm() =>
    "<form method=\"post\" action=\"form\">" +
      "<input type=\"text\" name=\"text1\" />" +
      "<input type=\"submit\" value=\"Submit\" />" +
    "</form>";
```

For reading the form data, the `HttpRequest` class defines a `Form` property. This property returns an `IFormCollection` object that contains all the data from the form that is sent to the server:

```
private static string ShowForm(HttpRequest request)
{
    var sb = new StringBuilder();
    if (request.HasFormContentType)
    {
        IFormCollection coll = request.Form;
        foreach (var key in coll.Keys)
        {
            sb.Append(GetDiv(key, HtmlEncoder.Default.Encode(coll[key])));
        }
        return sb.ToString();
    }
    else return "no form".Div();
}
```

Using the `/form` link, the form is received with the GET request (see Figure 40-14). When you click the Submit button, the form is sent with the POST request, and you can see the `text1` key of the form data (see Figure 40-15).

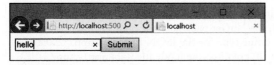

FIGURE 40-14

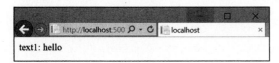

FIGURE 40-15

Cookies

To remember user data between multiple requests, you can use cookies. Adding a cookie to the `HttpResponse` object sends the cookie within the HTTP header from the server to the client. By default, a cookie is temporary (not stored on the client), and the browser sends it back to the server if the URL is the same domain where the cookie was coming from. You can set the Path to restrict when the browser returns the cookie. In this case, the cookie is only returned when it comes from the same domain and the path `/cookies` is used. When you set the `Expires` property, the cookie is a persistent cookie and thus is stored on the client. When the expiration time passes, the cookie will be removed. However, there's no guarantee that the cookie isn't removed earlier (code file `WebSampleApp/RequestResponseSample.cs`):

```
public static string WriteCookie(HttpResponse response)
{
  response.Cookies.Append("color", "red",
    new CookieOptions
    {
      Path = "/cookies",
      Expires = DateTime.Now.AddDays(1)
    });
  return "cookie written".Div();
}
```

The cookie can be read again by reading the `HttpRequest` object. The `Cookies` property contains all the cookies that are returned by the browser:

```
public static string ReadCookie(HttpRequest request)
{
  var sb = new StringBuilder();
  IRequestCookieCollection cookies = request.Cookies;
  foreach (var key in cookies.Keys)
  {
    sb.Append(GetDiv(key, cookies[key]));
  }
  return sb.ToString();
}
```

For testing cookies, you can also use the browser's developer tools. The tools show all the information about the cookies that are sent and received.

Sending JSON

The server returns more than HTML code; it also returns many different kind of data formats, such as CSS files, images, and videos. The client knows what kind of data it receives with the help of a mime type in the response header.

The method `GetJson` creates a JSON string from an anonymous object with `Title`, `Publisher`, and `Author` properties. To serialize this object with JSON, the NuGet package `NewtonSoft.Json` is added, and the namespace `NewtonSoft.Json` imported. The mime type for the JSON format is `application/json`. This is set via the `ContentType` property of the `HttpResponse` (code file `WebSampleApp/RequestResponseSample.cs`):

```
public static string GetJson(HttpResponse response)
{
  var b = new
  {
    Title = "Professional C# 6",
    Publisher = "Wrox Press",
    Author = "Christian Nagel"
  };

  string json = JsonConvert.SerializeObject(b);
  response.ContentType = "application/json";
  return json;
}
```

> **NOTE** *To use the JsonConvert class, the NuGet package Newtonsoft.Json needs to be added.*

This is the data returned to the client.

```
{"Title":"Professional C# 6","Publisher":"Wrox Press",
 "Author":"Christian Nagel"}
```

> **NOTE** *Sending and receiving JSON is covered in Chapter 42, "ASP.NET Web API."*

DEPENDENCY INJECTION

Dependency injection is deeply integrated within ASP.NET Core. This design pattern gives loose coupling as a service is used only with an interface. The concrete type that implements the interface is injected. With the ASP.NET built-in dependency injection mechanism, injection happens via constructors that have arguments of the injected interface type.

Dependency injection separates the service contract and the service implementation. The service can be used without knowing the concrete implementation—just a contract is needed. This allows replacing the service (e.g. logging) in a single place for all using the service.

Let's have a more detailed look at dependency injection by creating a custom service.

Defining a Service

First, a contract for a sample service is declared. Defining a contract via an interface enables you to separate the service implementation from its use—for example, to use a different implementation for unit testing (code file `WebSampleApp/Services/ISampleService.cs`):

```
public interface ISampleService
{
  IEnumerable<string> GetSampleStrings();
}
```

You implement the interface `ISampleService` with the class `DefaultSampleService` (code file `WebSampleApp/Services/DefaultSampleService.cs`):

```
public class DefaultSampleService : ISampleService
{
  private List<string> _strings = new List<string> { "one", "two", "three" };
  public IEnumerable<string> GetSampleStrings() => _strings;
}
```

Registering the Service

Using the `AddTransient` method (which is an extension method for `IServiceCollection` defined in the assembly `Microsoft.Extensions.DependencyInjection.Abstractions` in the namespace `Microsoft.Extensions.DependencyInjection`), the type `DefaultSampleService` is mapped to `ISampleService`. When you use the `ISampleService` interface, the `DefaultSampleService` type is instantiated (code file `WebSampleApp/Startup.cs`):

```
public void ConfigureServices(IServiceCollection services)
{
  services.AddTransient<ISampleService, DefaultSampleService>();
  // etc.
}
```

The built-in dependency injection service defines several lifetime options. Using the `AddTransient` method, the service is newly instantiated every time the service is injected.

Using the `AddSingleton` method, the service is instantiated only once. Every injection makes use of the same instance:

```
services.AddSingleton<ISampleService, DefaultSampleService>();
```

The `AddInstance` method requires you to instantiate a service and pass the instance to this method. This way you're defining the lifetime of the service:

```
var sampleService = new DefaultSampleService();
services.AddInstance<ISampleService>(sampleService);
```

With the fourth option, the lifetime of the service is based on the current context. With ASP.NET MVC, the current context is based on the HTTP request. As long as actions for the same request are invoked, the same instance is used with different injections. With a new request, a new instance is created. For defining a context-based lifetime, the `AddScoped` method maps the service contract to the service:

```
services.AddScoped<ISampleService>();
```

Injecting the Service

After the service is registered, you can inject it. A controller type named `HomeController` is created in the directory `Controllers`. The built-in dependency injection framework makes use of constructor injection; thus a constructor is defined that receives an `ISampleService` interface. The method `Index` receives an `HttpContext` and can use this to read request information, and it returns a HTTP status value. Within the implementation, the `ISampleService` is used to get the strings from the service. The controller adds some HTML elements to put the strings in a list (code file `WebSampleApp/Controllers/HomeController.cs`):

```
public class HomeController
{
  private readonly ISampleService _service;
  public HomeController(ISampleService service)
  {
    _service = service;
  }

  public async Task<int> Index(HttpContext context)
  {
    var sb = new StringBuilder();
    sb.Append("<ul>");
    sb.Append(string.Join("", _service.GetSampleStrings().Select(
        s => $"<li>{s}</li>").ToArray()));
    sb.Append("</ul>");
    await context.Response.WriteAsync(sb.ToString());
    return 200;
  }
}
```

> **NOTE** *This sample controller directly returns HTML code. It's better to separate the functionality from the user interface and to create the HTML code from a different class—a view. For this separation it's best to use a framework: ASP.NET MVC. This framework is explained in Chapter 41.*

Calling the Controller

To instantiate the controller via dependency injection, the `HomeController` class is registered with the `IServiceCollection` services. This time you do not use an interface; thus you need only the concrete implementation of the service type with the `AddTransient` method call (code file `WebSampleApp/Startup.cs`):

```
public void ConfigureServices(IServiceCollection services)
{
  services.AddTransient<ISampleService, DefaultSampleService>();
  services.AddTransient<HomeController>();
  // etc.
}
```

The `Configure` method that contains the route information is now changed to check for the `/home` path. If this expression returns `true`, the `HomeController` is instantiated via dependency injection by calling the `GetService` method on the registered application services. The `IApplicationBuilder` interface defines an `ApplicationServices` property that returns an object implementing `IServiceProvider`. Here, you can access all the services that have been registered. Using this controller, the `Index` method is invoked by passing the `HttpContext`. The status code is written to the response object:

```
public void Configure(IApplicationBuilder app, ILoggerFactory loggerFactory)
{
  app.Run(async (context) =>
  {
    // etc.
    if (context.Request.Path.Value.ToLower() == "/home")
    {
      HomeController controller =
        app.ApplicationServices.GetService<HomeController>();
      int statusCode = await controller.Index(context);
      context.Response.StatusCode = statusCode;
      return;
    }
  });
  // etc.
}
```

Figure 40-16 shows the output of the unordered list when you run the application with a URL to the home address.

FIGURE 40-16

ROUTING USING MAP

With the previous code snippet, the `HomeController` class was invoked when the path of the URL equals `/home`. You didn't pay attention to query strings or subfolders. Of course, you could do this by checking only a subset of the string. However, there's a much better way. ASP.NET supports subapplications with an extension of the `IApplicationBuilder`: the `Map` method.

The following code snippet defines a map to the `/home2` path and runs the `Invoke` method of the `HomeController` (code file `WebSampleApp/Startup.cs`):

```
public void Configure(IApplicationBuilder app, ILoggerFactory loggerFactory)
{
  // etc.
  app.Map("/home2", homeApp =>
  {
```

```
    homeApp.Run(async context =>
    {
      HomeController controller =
        app.ApplicationServices.GetService<HomeController>();
      int statusCode = await controller.Index(context);
      context.Response.StatusCode = statusCode;
    });
  });

  // etc.
}
```

Instead of using the `Map` method, you can also use `MapWhen`. With the following code snippet, the map managed by `MapWhen` applies when the path starts with `/configuration`. The remaining path is written to the variable remaining and can be used to differ with the method invocations:

```
PathString remaining;
app.MapWhen(context =>
  context.Request.Path.StartsWithSegments("/configuration", out remaining),
    configApp =>
    {
      configApp.Run(async context =>
      {
        // etc.
      }
    });
```

Instead of just using the path, you can also access any other information of the `HttpContext`, such as the host information of the client (`context.Request.Host`) or authenticated users (`context.User.Identity.IsAuthenticated`).

USING MIDDLEWARE

ASP.NET Core makes it easy to create modules that are invoked before the controller is invoked. This can be used to add header information, verify tokens, build a cache, create log traces, and so on. One middleware module is chained after the other until all connected middleware types have been invoked.

You can create a middleware class by using the Visual Studio item template Middleware Class. With this middleware type, you create a constructor that receives a reference to the next middleware type. `RequestDelegate` is a delegate that receives an `HttpContext` as parameter and returns a `Task`. This is exactly the signature of the `Invoke` method. Within this method, you have access to request and response information. The type `HeaderMiddleware` adds a sample header to the response of the `HttpContext`. As the last action, the `Invoke` method invokes the next middleware module (code file `WebSampleApp/Middleware/HeaderMiddleware.cs`):

```
public class HeaderMiddleware
{
  private readonly RequestDelegate _next;

  public HeaderMiddleware(RequestDelegate next)
  {
    _next = next;
  }

  public Task Invoke(HttpContext httpContext)
  {
    httpContext.Response.Headers.Add("sampleheader",
      new string[] { "addheadermiddleware"});
    return _next(httpContext);
  }
}
```

For making it easy to configure the middleware type, the extension method `UseHeaderMiddleware` extends the interface `IApplicationBuilder` where the method `UseMiddleware` is called:

```
public static class HeaderMiddlewareExtensions
{
  public static IApplicationBuilder UseHeaderMiddleware(
    this IApplicationBuilder builder) =>
      builder.UseMiddleware<HeaderMiddleware>();
}
```

Another middleware type is `Heading1Middleware`. This type is similar to the previous middleware type; it just writes heading 1 to the response (code file `WebSampleApp/Middleware/Heading1Middleware.cs`):

```
public class Heading1Middleware
{
  private readonly RequestDelegate _next;

  public Heading1Middleware(RequestDelegate next)
  {
    _next = next;
  }

  public async Task Invoke(HttpContext httpContext)
  {
    await httpContext.Response.WriteAsync("<h1>From Middleware</h1>");
    await _next(httpContext);
  }
}

public static class Heading1MiddlewareExtensions
{
  public static IApplicationBuilder UseHeading1Middleware(
    this IApplicationBuilder builder) =>
      builder.UseMiddleware<Heading1Middleware>();
}
```

Now it's the job of the `Startup` class and the `Configure` method to configure all the middleware types. The extension methods are already prepared for invocation (code file `WebSampleApp/Startup.cs`):

```
public void Configure(IApplicationBuilder app, ILoggerFactory loggerFactory)
{
  // etc.

  app.UseHeaderMiddleware();
  app.UseHeading1Middleware();

  // etc.
}
```

When you run the application, you see the header returned to the client (using the browser's developer tools), and the heading shows up in every page, no matter which of the previously created links you use (see Figure 40-17).

FIGURE 40-17

SESSION STATE

A service that is implemented using middleware is *session state*. Session state enables temporarily remembering data from the client on the server. Session state itself is implemented as middleware.

Session state is initiated when a user first requests a page from a server. While the user keeps opening pages on the server, the session continues until a timeout (typically 10 minutes) occurs. To keep state on the server while the user navigates to a new page, state can be written to a session. When a timeout is reached, the session data is removed.

To identify a session, on the first request a temporary cookie with a session identifier is created. This cookie is returned from the client with every request to the server until the browser is closed, and then the cookie is deleted. Session identifiers can also be sent in the URL string as an alternative to using cookies.

On the server side, session information can be stored in memory. In a web farm, session state that is stored in memory doesn't propagate between different systems. With a sticky session configuration, the user always returns to the same physical server. Using sticky sessions, it doesn't matter that the same state is not available on other systems (with the exception when one server fails). Without sticky sessions, and to also deal with failing servers, options exist to store session state within distributed memory of a SQL server database. Storing session state in distributed memory also helps with process recycling of the server process; recycling kills session state also if you're using just a single server process.

For using session state with ASP.NET, you need to add the NuGet package `Microsoft.AspNet.Session`. This package gives the `AddSession` extension method that can be called within the `ConfigureServices` method in the `Startup` class. The parameter enables you to configure the idle timeout and the cookie options. The cookie is used to identify the session. The session also makes use of a service that implements the interface `IDistributedCache`. A simple implementation is the cache for in-process session state. The method `AddCaching` adds the following cache service (code file `WebSampleApp/Startup.cs`):

```
public void ConfigureServices(IServiceCollection services)
{
  services.AddTransient<ISampleService, DefaultSampleService>();
  services.AddTransient<HomeController>();
  services.AddCaching();
  services.AddSession(options =>
    options.IdleTimeout = TimeSpan.FromMinutes(10));
}
```

> **NOTE** *Other implementations of* `IDistributedCache` *are* `RedisCache` *and* `SqlServerCache` *in the NuGet packages* `Microsoft.Extensions.Caching.Redis` *and* `Microsoft.Extensions.Caching.SqlServer`.

For using the session, you need to configure the session by calling the `UseSession` extension method. You need to invoke this method before any response is written to the response—such as is done with the `UseHeaderMiddleware` and `UseHeading1Middleware`—thus `UseSession` is called before the other methods. The code that uses session information is mapped to the /session path (code file `WebSampleApp/Startup.cs`):

```
public void Configure(IApplicationBuilder app, ILoggerFactory loggerFactory)
{
  // etc.
  app.UseSession();
  app.UseHeaderMiddleware();
  app.UseHeading1Middleware();

  app.Map("/session", sessionApp =>
  {
```

```
      sessionApp.Run(async context =>
      {
        await SessionSample.SessionAsync(context);
      });
    });
    // etc.
}
```

You can write session state using `Setxxx` methods, such as `SetString` and `SetInt32`. These methods are defined with the `ISession` interface that is returned from the `Session` property of the `HttpContext`. Session data is retrieved using `Getxxx` methods (code file `WebSampleApp/SessionSample.cs`):

```
public static class SessionSample
{
  private const string SessionVisits = nameof(SessionVisits);
  private const string SessionTimeCreated = nameof(SessionTimeCreated);

  public static async Task SessionAsync(HttpContext context)
  {
    int visits = context.Session.GetInt32(SessionVisits) ?? 0;
    string timeCreated = context.Session.GetString(SessionTimeCreated) ??
      string.Empty;
    if (string.IsNullOrEmpty(timeCreated))
    {
      timeCreated = DateTime.Now.ToString("t", CultureInfo.InvariantCulture);
      context.Session.SetString(SessionTimeCreated, timeCreated);
    }
    DateTime timeCreated2 = DateTime.Parse(timeCreated);
    context.Session.SetInt32(SessionVisits, ++visits);
    await context.Response.WriteAsync(
      $"Number of visits within this session: {visits} " +
      $"that was created at {timeCreated2:T}; " +
      $"current time: {DateTime.Now:T}");
  }
}
```

> **NOTE** *The sample code uses an invariant culture to store the time when the session was created. The time shown to the user is using a specific culture. It's a good practice to use invariant cultures storing culture-specific data on the server. Information about invariant cultures and how to set cultures is explained in Chapter 28, "Localization."*

CONFIGURING ASP.NET

With web applications, it's necessary to store configuration information that can be changed by system administrators—for example, connection strings. In the next chapter you create a data-driven application where a connection string is needed.

Configuration of ASP.NET Core 1.0 is no longer based on the XML configuration files `web.config` and `machine.config` as was the case with previous versions of ASP.NET. With the old configuration file, assembly references and assembly redirects were mixed with database connection strings and application settings. This is no longer the case. You've seen the `project.json` file to define assembly references. Connection strings and application settings are not defined there. Application settings are typically stored within `appsettings.json`, but the configuration is a lot more flexible and you can choose to make your configuration with several JSON or XML files and with environment variables.

A default ASP.NET configuration file—`appsettings.json`—is added from the item template ASP.
NET Configuration File. The item template automatically creates the `DefaultConnection` setting; the
`AppSettings` have been added later on (code file `WebSampleApp/appsettings.json`):

```
{
  "AppSettings": {
    "SiteName": "Professional C# Sample"
  },
  "Data": {
    "DefaultConnection": {
      "ConnectionString":
"Server=(localdb)\\MSSQLLocalDB;Database=_CHANGE_ME;Trusted_Connection=True;"
    }
  }
}
```

You need to configure the configuration file that's used. You do this in the constructor of the Startup class.
The ConfigurationBuilder class is used to build the configuration from configuration files. There can be
more than one configuration file.

The sample code adds `appsettings.json` to the `ConfigurationBuilder` using the extension
method `AddJsonFile`. After the setup of the configuration is done, the configuration files are read
using the Build method. The returned `IConfigurationRoot` result is assigned to the read-only
property `Configuration`, which makes it easy to read configuration information later on (code file
WebSampleApp/Startup.cs):

```
public Startup(IHostingEnvironment env)
{
  var builder = new ConfigurationBuilder()
    .AddJsonFile("appsettings.json");

  // etc.
  Configuration = builder.Build();
}

public IConfigurationRoot Configuration { get; }
// etc.
```

You can use the methods `AddXmlFile` to add an XML configuration file, `AddEnvironmentVariables`
to add environment variables, and `AddCommandLine` to add command line arguments to the
configuration.

For the configuration files, by default the current directory of the web application is used. In
case you need to change the directory, you can invoke the method `SetBasePath` before invoking the method `AddJsonFile`. To retrieve the directory of the web application, you can inject the
`IApplicationEnvironment` interface in the constructor and use the `ApplicationBasePath` property.

Reading the Configuration

The different configuration values are read by mapping the /configuration/appsettings, /configura-
tion/database, and /configuration/secret links (code file WebSampleApp/Startup.cs):

```
PathString remaining;
app.MapWhen(context =>
  context.Request.Path.StartsWithSegments("/configuration", out remaining),
    configApp =>
    {
      configApp.Run(async context =>
```

```
      {
        if (remaining.StartsWithSegments("/appsettings"))
        {
          await ConfigSample.AppSettings(context, Configuration);
        }
        else if (remaining.StartsWithSegments("/database"))
        {
          await ConfigSample.ReadDatabaseConnection(context, Configuration);
        }
        else if (remaining.StartsWithSegments("/secret"))
        {
          await ConfigSample.UserSecret(context, Configuration);
        }
      });
    });
```

The configuration can now be read by using the indexer of the `IConfigurationRoot` object. You can access the hierarchical elements of the JSON tree by using a colon (code file `WebSampleApp/ConfigSample.cs`):

```
public static async Task AppSettings(HttpContext context,
  IConfigurationRoot config)
{
  string settings = config["AppSettings:SiteName"];
  await context.Response.WriteAsync(settings.Div());
}
```

This is similar to accessing the database connection string:

```
public static async Task ReadDatabaseConnection(HttpContext context,
  IConfigurationRoot config)
{
  string connectionString = config["Data:DefaultConnection:ConnectionString"];
  await context.Response.WriteAsync(connectionString.Div());
}
```

Running the web application accessing the corresponding `/configuration` URLs returns the values from the configuration file.

Different Configurations Based on the Environment

When running your web application with different environments—for example, during development, testing, and production—you might also use a staging server because it's likely you are using some different configurations. You don't want to add test data to the production database.

ASP.NET 4 created transformations for XML files to define the differences from one configuration to the other. This can be done in a simpler way with ASP.NET Core 1.0. For the configuration values that should be different, you can use different configuration files.

The following code snippet adds the JSON configuration files with the environment name—for example, `appsettings.development.json` or `appsettings.production.json` (code file `WebSampleApp/Startup.cs`):

```
var builder = new ConfigurationBuilder()
  .AddJsonFile("appsettings.json")
  .AddJsonFile($"appsettings.{env.EnvironmentName}.json", optional: true);
```

You can configure the environment by setting an environmental variable or application arguments in the project properties as shown in Figure 40-18.

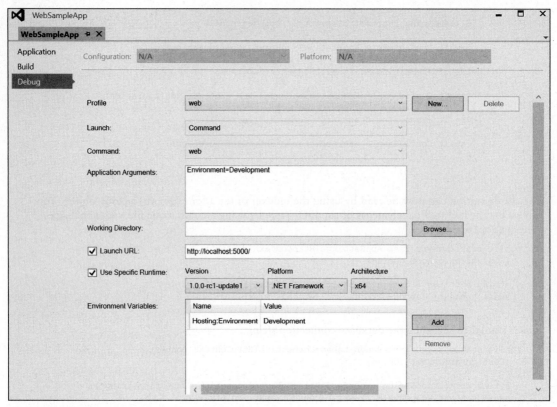

FIGURE 40-18

To verify the hosting environment programmatically, extension methods are defined for the `IHostingEnvironment`, such as `IsDevelopment`, `IsStaging`, and `IsProduction`. To test for any environmental name, you can pass a verification string to `IsEnvironment`:

```
if (env.IsDevelopment())
{
    // etc.
}
```

User Secrets

Having the connection string in the configuration file is not a big problem as long as Windows authentication is used. When you store username and password with the connection string, adding the connection string to a configuration file and storing the configuration file along with the source code repository can be a big issue. Having a public repository and storing Amazon keys with the configuration can lead to losing thousands of dollars very quickly. Hackers' background jobs comb through public GitHub repositories to find Amazon keys to hijack accounts and create virtual machines for making Bitcoins. You can read `http://readwrite.com/2014/04/15/amazon-web-services-hack-bitcoin-miners-github` to find out more about this situation.

ASP.NET Core 1.0 has some mitigations around this: user secrets. With user secrets, configuration is not stored in a configuration file of the project; it's stored in a configuration file associated with your account.

With the installation of Visual Studio, the SecretManager is already installed on your system. On other systems, you need to install the NuGet package `Microsoft.Extensions.SecretManager`.

After the SecretManager is installed and secrets are defined with the application, you can use the command-line tool `user-secret` to set, remove, and list user secrets from the application.

Secrets are stored in this user-specific location:

```
%AppData%\Microsoft\UserSecrets
```

An easy way to manage user secrets is from the Solution Explorer in Visual Studio. Select the project node and open the context menu to select Manage User Secrets. When you select this the first time in the project, it adds a secret identifier to `project.json` (code file `WebSampleApp/project.json`):

```
"userSecretsId": "aspnet5-WebSampleApp-20151215011720"
```

This identifier represents the same subdirectory you will find in the user-specific `UserSecrets` folder. The Manage User Secrets command also opens the file `secrets.json`, where you can add JSON configuration information:

```
{
    "secret1":  "this is a user secret"
}
```

The user secrets are now added only if the hosting environment is `Development` (code file `WebSampleApp/Startup.cs`):

```
if (env.IsDevelopment())
{
   builder.AddUserSecrets();
}
```

This way your secrets are not stored in the code repository, and they can be stolen only by hacking your system.

SUMMARY

In this chapter, you explored the foundation of ASP.NET and web applications. You've seen tools such as npm, Gulp, and Bower, and how they are integrated with Visual Studio. The chapter discussed dealing with requests from the client and answering with a response. You've seen the foundation of ASP.NET with dependency injection and services, and you've seen a concrete implementation using dependency injection such as session state. You've also seen how configuration information can be stored in different ways, such as JSON configuration for different environments such as development and production, and how to store secrets such as keys to cloud services.

The next chapter shows how ASP.NET MVC 6, which uses the foundation discussed in this chapter, can be used to create web applications.

41

ASP.NET MVC

WHAT'S IN THIS CHAPTER?

➤ Features of ASP.NET MVC 6
➤ Routing
➤ Creating Controllers
➤ Creating Views
➤ Validating User Inputs
➤ Using Filters
➤ Working with HTML and Tag Helpers
➤ Creating Data-Driven Web Applications
➤ Implementing Authentication and Authorization

WROX.COM CODE DOWNLOADS FOR THIS CHAPTER

The wrox.com code downloads for this chapter are found at http://www.wrox.com/go/professionalcsharp6 on the Download Code tab. The code for this chapter is divided into the following major examples:

➤ MVC Sample App
➤ Menu Planner

SETTING UP SERVICES FOR ASP.NET MVC 6

Chapter 40, "ASP.NET Core," showed you the foundation of ASP.NET MVC: ASP.NET Core 1.0 Chapter 40 shows you middleware and how dependency injection works with ASP.NET. This chapter makes use of dependency injection by injecting ASP.NET MVC services.

ASP.NET MVC is based on the MVC (Model-View-Controller) pattern. As shown in Figure 41-1, this standard pattern (a pattern documented in *Design Patterns: Elements of Reusable Object-Oriented Software* book by the Gang of Four [Addison-Wesley Professional, 1994]) defines a model that implements data entities and data access, a view that represents the information shown to the user, and a controller that makes use of the model and sends data to the view. The controller receives a request from the browser and returns a response. To build the response, the controller can make use of a model to provide some data, and a view to define the HTML that is returned.

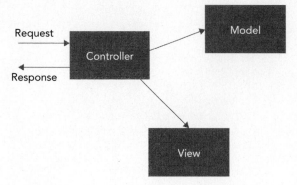

FIGURE 41-1

With ASP.NET MVC, the controller and model are typically created with C# and .NET code that is run server-side. The view is HTML code with JavaScript and just a little C# code for accessing server-side information.

The big advantage of this separation in the MVC pattern is that you can use unit tests to easily test the functionality. The controller just contains methods with parameters and return values that can be covered easily with unit tests.

Let's start setting up services for ASP.NET MVC 6. With ASP.NET Core 1.0 dependency injection is deeply integrated as you've seen in Chapter 40. You can create an ASP.NET MVC 6 project selecting the ASP.NET Core 1.0 Template Web Application. This template already includes NuGet packages required with ASP.NET MVC 6, and a directory structure that helps with organizing the application. However, here we'll start with the Empty template (similar to Chapter 40), so you can see what's all needed to build up an ASP.NET MVC 6 project, without the extra stuff you might not need with your project.

The first project created is named `MVCSampleApp`. To use ASP.NET MVC with the web application `MVCSampleApp`, you need to add the NuGet package `Microsoft.AspNet.Mvc`. With the package in place, you add the MVC services by invoking the extension method `AddMvc` within the `ConfigureServices` method (code file `MVCSampleApp/Startup.cs`):

```
using Microsoft.AspNetCore.Builder;
using Microsoft.AspNetCore.Hosting;
using Microsoft.AspNetCore.Http;
using Microsoft.Extensions.Configuration;
using Microsoft.Extensions.DependencyInjection;
// etc.

namespace MVCSampleApp
{
  public class Startup
  {
    // etc.

    public void ConfigureServices(IServiceCollection services)
    {
      services.AddMvc();
      // etc.

    }
    // etc.
    public static void Main(string[] args)
    {
      var host = new WebHostBuilder()
```

```
            .UseDefaultConfiguration(args)
            .UseStartup<Startup>()
            .Build();
        host.Run();
    }
  }
}
```

The `AddMvc` extension method adds and configures several ASP.NET MVC core services, such as configuration features (`IConfigureOptions` with `MvcOptions` and `RouteOptions`); controller factories and controller activators (`IControllerFactory`, `IControllerActivator`); action method selectors, invocators, and constraint providers (`IActionSelector`, `IActionInvokerFactory`, `IActionConstraintProvider`); argument binders and model validators (`IControllerActionArgumentBinder`, `IObjectModelValidator`); and filter providers (`IFilterProvider`).

In addition to the core services it adds, the `AddMvc` method adds ASP.NET MVC services to support authorization, CORS, data annotations, views, the Razor view engine, and more.

DEFINING ROUTES

Chapter 40 explains how the `Map` extension method of the `IApplicationBuilder` defines a simple route. This chapter shows how the ASP.NET MVC routes are based on this mapping to offer a flexible routing mechanism for mapping URLs to controllers and action methods.

The controller is selected based on a route. A simple way to create the default route is to invoke the method `UseMvcWithDefaultRoute` in the `Startup` class (code file `MVCSampleApp/Startup.cs`):

```
public void Configure(IApplicationBuilder app)
{
  // etc.
  app.UseIISPlatformHandler();

  app.UseStaticFiles();
  app.UseMvcWithDefaultRoute();
  // etc.
}
```

> **NOTE** *The extension method* `UseStaticFiles` *is discussed in Chapter 40. This method requires adding the* `Microsoft.AspNet.StaticFiles` *NuGet package.*

With this default route, the name of the controller type (without the `Controller` suffix) and the method name make up the route, such as `http://server[:port]/controller/action`. You can also use an optional parameter named `id`, like so: `http://server[:port]/controller/action/id`. The default name of the controller is `Home`; the default name of the action method is `Index`.

The following code snippet shows another way to specify the same default route. The `UseMvc` method can receive a parameter of type `Action<IRouteBuilder>`. This `IRouteBuilder` interface contains a list of routes that are mapped. You define routes using the `MapRoute` extension method:

```
app.UseMvc(routes =< with => routes.MapRoute(
    name: "default",
    template: "{controller}/{action}/{id?}",
    defaults: new {controller = "Home", action = "Index"}
  ));
```

This route definition is the same as the default one. The `template` parameter defines the URL; the `?` with the `id` defines that this parameter is optional; the `defaults` parameter defines the default values for the `controller` and `action` part of the URL.

Let's have a look at this URL:

```
http://localhost:[port]/UseAService/GetSampleStrings
```

With this URL, `UseAService` maps to the name of the controller, because the `Controller` suffix is automatically added; the type name is `UseAServiceController`; and `GetSampleStrings` is the action, which represents a method in the `UseAServiceController` type.

Adding Routes

There are several reasons to add or change routes. For example, you can modify routes to use actions with the link, to define `Home` as the default controller, to add entries to the link, or to use multiple parameters.

You can define a route where the user can use links—such as `http://<server>/About` to address the `About` action method in the `Home` controller without passing a controller name—as shown in the following snippet. Notice that the controller name is left out from the URL. The `controller` keyword is mandatory with the route, but you can supply it with the defaults:

```
app.UseMvc(routes => routes.MapRoute(
    name: "default",
    template: "{action}/{id?}",
    defaults: new {controller = "Home", action = "Index"}
));
```

Another scenario for changing the route is shown in the following code snippet. In this snippet, you are adding the variable `language` to the route. This variable is set to the section within the URL that follows the server name and is placed before the controller—for example, `http://server/en/Home/About`. You can use this to specify a language:

```
app.UseMvc(routes => routes.MapRoute(
    name: "default",
    template: "{controller}/{action}/{id?}",
    defaults: new {controller = "Home", action = "Index"}
).MapRoute(
    name: "language",
    template: "{language}/{controller}/{action}/{id?}",
    defaults: new {controller = "Home", action = "Index"}
);
```

If one route matches and the controller and action method are found, the route is taken; otherwise the next route is selected until one route matches.

Using Route Constraints

When you map the route, you can specify constraints. This way, URLs other than those defined by the constraint are not possible. The following constraint defines that the `language` parameter can be only `en` or `de` by using the regular expression `(en)|(de)`. URLs such as `http://<server>/en/Home/About` or `http://<server>/de/Home/About` are valid:

```
app.UseMvc(routes => routes.MapRoute(
    name: "language",
    template: "{language}/{controller}/{action}/{id?}",
    defaults: new {controller = "Home", action = "Index"},
    constraints: new {language = @"(en)|(de)"}
));
```

If a link should enable only numbers (for example, to access products with a product number), the regular expression \d+ matches any number of numerical digits, but it must match at least one:

```
app.UseMvc(routes => routes.MapRoute(
  name: "products",
  template: "{controller}/{action}/{productId?}",
  defaults: new {controller = "Home", action = "Index"},
  constraints: new {productId = @"\d+"}
));
```

Now you've seen how routing specifies the controller that is used and the action of the controller. The next section, "Creating Controllers," covers the details of controllers.

CREATING CONTROLLERS

A *controller* reacts to requests from the user and sends a response. As described in this section, a view is not required.

There are some conventions for using ASP.NET MVC. Conventions are preferred over configuration. With controllers you'll also see some conventions. You can find controllers in the directory Controllers, and the name of the controller class must be suffixed with the name Controller.

Before creating the first controller, create the Controllers directory. Then you can create a controller by selecting this directory in Solution Explorer, select Add ⇨ New Item from the context menu, and select the MVC Controller Class item template. The HomeController is created for the route that is specified.

The generated code contains a HomeController class that derives from the base class Controller. This class also contains an Index method that corresponds to the Index action. When you request an action as defined by the route, a method within the controller is invoked (code file MVCSampleApp/Controllers/HomeController.cs):

```
public class HomeController : Controller
{
  public IActionResult Index() => View();
}
```

Understanding Action Methods

A controller contains action methods. A simple action method is the Hello method from the following code snippet (code file MVCSampleApp/Controllers/HomeController.cs):

```
public string Hello() => "Hello, ASP.NET MVC 6";
```

You can invoke the Hello action in the Home controller with the link http://localhost:5000/Home/Hello. Of course, the port number depends on your settings, and you can configure it with the web properties in the project settings. When you open this link from the browser, the controller returns just the string Hello, ASP.NET MVC 6; no HTML—just a string. The browser displays the string.

An action can return anything—for example, the bytes of an image, a video, XML or JSON data, or, of course, HTML. Views are of great help for returning HTML.

Using Parameters

You can declare action methods with parameters, as in the following code snippet (code file MVCSampleApp/Controllers/HomeController.cs):

```
public string Greeting(string name) =>
  HtmlEncoder.Default.Encode($"Hello, {name}");
```

> **NOTE** *The* `HtmlEncoder` *requires the NuGet package* `System.Text.Encodings.Web.`

With this declaration, the `Greeting` action method can be invoked to request this URL to pass a value with the `name` parameter in the URL: `http://localhost:18770/Home/Greeting?name=Stephanie`.

To use links that can be better remembered, you can use route information to specify the parameters. The `Greeting2` action method specifies the parameter named `id`.

```
public string Greeting2(string id) =>
   HtmlEncoder.Default.Encode($"Hello, {id}");
```

This matches the default route `{controller}/{action}/{id?}` where `id` is specified as an optional parameter. Now you can use this link, and the `id` parameter contains the string `Matthias`: `http://localhost:5000/Home/Greeting2/Matthias`.

You can also declare action methods with any number of parameters. For example, you can add the `Add` action method to the Home controller with two parameters, like so:

```
public int Add(int x, int y) => x + y;
```

You can invoke this action with the URL `http://localhost:18770/Home/Add?x=4&y=5` to fill the x and y parameters.

With multiple parameters, you can also define a route to pass the values with a different link. The following code snippet shows an additional route defined in the route table to specify multiple parameters that fill the variables x and y (code file `MVCSampleApp/Startup.cs`):

```
app.UseMvc(routes =< routes.MapRoute(
   name: "default",
   template: "{controller}/{action}/{id?}",
   defaults: new {controller = "Home", action = "Index"}
).MapRoute(
   name: "multipleparameters",
   template: "{controller}/{action}/{x}/{y}",
   defaults: new {controller = "Home", action = "Add"},
   constraints: new {x = @"\d", y = @"\d"}
));
```

Now you can invoke the same action as before using this URL: `http://localhost:18770/Home/Add/7/2`.

> **NOTE** *Later in this chapter, in the section "Passing Data to Views," you see how parameters of custom types can be used and how data from the client can map to properties.*

Returning Data

So far, you have returned only string values from the controller. Usually, an object implementing the interface `IActionResult` is returned.

Following are several examples with the `ResultController` class. The first code snippet uses the `ContentResult` class to return simple text content. Instead of creating an instance of the `ContentResult` class and returning the instance, you can use methods from the base class `Controller` to return `ActionResults`. In the following example, the method `Content` is used to return text content. The `Content` method enables specifying the content, the MIME type, and encoding (code file `MVCSampleApp/Controllers/ResultController.cs`):

```
public IActionResult ContentDemo() =>
   Content("Hello World", "text/plain");
```

To return JSON-formatted data, you can use the `Json` method. The following sample code creates a `Menu` object:

```
public IActionResult JsonDemo()
{
  var m = new Menu
  {
    Id = 3,
    Text = "Grilled sausage with sauerkraut and potatoes",
    Price = 12.90,
    Date = new DateTime(2016, 3, 31),
    Category = "Main"
  };
  return Json(m);
}
```

The `Menu` class is defined within the `Models` directory and defines a simple POCO class with a few properties (code file `MVCSampleApp/Models/Menu.cs`):

```
public class Menu
{
  public int Id {get; set;}
  public string Text {get; set;}
  public double Price {get; set;}
  public DateTime Date {get; set;}
  public string Category {get; set;}
}
```

The client sees this JSON data in the response body. JSON data can easily be consumed as a JavaScript object:

```
{"Id":3,"Text":"Grilled sausage with sauerkraut and potatoes",
 "Price":12.9,"Date":"2016-03-31T00:00:00","Category":"Main"}
```

Using the `Redirect` method of the `Controller` class, the client receives an HTTP redirect request. After receiving the redirect request, the browser requests the link it received. The `Redirect` method returns a `RedirectResult` (code file `MVCSampleApp/Controllers/ResultController.cs`):

```
public IActionResult RedirectDemo() => Redirect("http://www.cninnovation.com");
```

You can also build a redirect request to the client by specifying a redirect to another controller and action. `RedirectToRoute` returns a `RedirectToRouteResult` that enables specifying route names, controllers, actions, and parameters. This builds a link that is returned to the client with an HTTP redirect request:

```
public IActionResult RedirectRouteDemo() =>
  RedirectToRoute(new {controller = "Home", action="Hello"});
```

The `File` method of the `Controller` base class defines different overloads that return different types. This method can return `FileContentResult`, `FileStreamResult`, and `VirtualFileResult`. The different return types depend on the parameters used—for example, a string for a `VirtualFileResult`, a `Stream` for a `FileStreamResult`, and a `byte` array for a `FileContentResult`.

The next code snippet returns an image. Create an Images folder and add a JPG file. For the next code snippet to work, create an `Images` folder in the `wwwroot` directory and add the file `Matthias.jpg`. The sample code returns a `VirtualFileResult` that specifies a filename with the first parameter. The second parameter specifies the `contentType` argument with the MIME type `image/jpeg`:

```
public IActionResult FileDemo() =>
  File("~/images/Matthias.jpg", "image/jpeg");
```

The next section shows how to return different `ViewResult` variants.

Working with the Controller Base Class and POCO Controllers

So far, all the controllers created have been derived from the base class `Controller`. ASP.NET MVC 6 also supports controllers—known as known as POCO (Plain Old CLR Objects) controllers—that do not derive from this base class. This way you can use your own base class to define your own type hierarchy with controllers.

What do you get out of the `Controller` base class? With this base class, the controller can directly access properties of the base class. The following table describes these properties and their functionality.

PROPERTY	DESCRIPTION
ActionContext	This property wraps some other properties. Here you can get information about the action descriptor, which contains the name of the action, controller, filters, and method information; the `HttpContext`, which is directly accessible from the `Context` property; the state of the model that is directly accessible from the `ModelState` property, and route information that is directly accessible from the `RouteData` property.
Context	This property returns the `HttpContext`. With this context you can access the `ServiceProvider` to access services registered with dependency injection (`ApplicationServices` property), authentication and user information, request and response information that is also directly accessible from the `Request` and `Response` properties, and web sockets (if they are in use).
BindingContext	With this property you can access the binder that binds the received data to the parameters of the action method. Binding request information to custom types is discussed later in this chapter in the section "Submitting Data from the Client."
MetadataProvider	You use a binder to bind parameters. The binder can make use of metadata that is associated with the model. Using the `MetadataProvider` property, you can access information about what providers are configured to deal with metadata information.
ModelState	The `ModelState` property lets you know whether model binding was successful or had errors. In case of errors, you can read the information about what properties resulted in errors.
Request	With this property you can access all information about the HTTP request: header and body information, the query string, form data, and cookies. The header information contains a `User-Agent` string that gives information about the browser and client platform.
Response	This property holds information that is returned to the client. Here, you can send cookies, change header information, and write directly to the body. Earlier in this chapter, in the section Startup, you've seen how a simple string can be returned to the client by using the `Response` property.
Resolver	The `Resolver` property returns the `ServiceProvider` where you can access the services that are registered for dependency injection.
RouteData	The `RouteData` property gives information about the complete route table that is registered in the startup code.
ViewBag ViewData	You use these properties to send information to the view. This is explained later in the section "Passing Data to Views."
TempData	This property is written to the user state that is shared between multiple requests (whereas data written to `ViewBag` and `ViewData` can be written to share information between views and controllers within a single request). By default, `TempData` writes information to the session state.
User	The `User` property returns information, including identity and claims, about an authenticated user.

A POCO controller doesn't have the `Controller` base class, but it's still important to access such information. The following code snippet defines a POCO controller that derives from the object base class (you can use your own custom type as a base class). To create an `ActionContext` with the POCO class, you can create a property of this type. The `POCOController` class uses `ActionContext` as the name of this property, similar to the way the `Controller` class does. However, just having a property doesn't set it automatically. You need to apply the `ActionContext` attribute. Using this attribute injects the actual `ActionContext`. The `Context` property directly accesses the `HttpContext` property from the `ActionContext`. The `Context` property is used from the `UserAgentInfo` action method to access and return the `User-Agent` header information from the request (code file `MVCSampleApp/Controllers/POCOController.cs`):

```
public class POCOController
{
  public string Index() =>
    "this is a POCO controller";

  [ActionContext]
  public ActionContext ActionContext {get; set;}
  public HttpContext Context => ActionContext.HttpContext;
  public ModelStateDictionary ModelState => ActionContext.ModelState;

  public string UserAgentInfo()
  {
    if (Context.Request.Headers.ContainsKey("User-Agent"))
    {
     return Context.Request.Headers["User-Agent"];
    }
    return "No user-agent information";
  }
}
```

CREATING VIEWS

The HTML code that is returned to the client is best specified with a view. For the samples in this section, the `ViewsDemoController` is created. The views are all defined within the `Views` folder. The views for the `ViewsDemo` controller need a `ViewsDemo` subdirectory. This is a convention for the views (code file `MVCSampleApp/Controllers/ViewsDemoController.cs`):

```
public ActionResult Index() => View();
```

> **NOTE** *Another place where views are searched is the* `Shared` *directory. You can put views that should be used by multiple controllers (and special partial views used by multiple views) into the* `Shared` *directory.*

After creating the `ViewsDemo` directory within the `Views` directory, the view can be created using Add ➪ New Item and selecting the MVC View Page item template. Because the action method has the name `Index`, the view file is named `Index.cshtml`.

The action method `Index` uses the `View` method without parameters, and thus the view engine searches for a view file with the same name as the action name in the `ViewsDemo` directory. The `View` method used in the controller has overloads that enable passing a different view name. In that case, the view engine looks for a view with the name passed to the `View` method.

A view contains HTML code mixed with a little server-side code, as shown in the following snippet (code file `MVCSampleApp/Views/ViewsDemo/Index.cshtml`):

```
@{
  Layout = null;
}
<!DOCTYPE html>
<html>
<head>
  <meta charset="utf-8" />
  <meta name="viewport" content="width=device-width, initial-scale=1.0" />
  <title>Index</title>
</head>
<body>
  <div>
  </div>
</body>
</html>
```

Server-side code is written using the @ sign, which starts the Razor syntax, which is discussed later in this chapter. Before getting into the details of the Razor syntax, the next section shows how to pass data from a controller to a view.

Passing Data to Views

The controller and view run in the same process. The view is directly created from within the controller. This makes it easy to pass data from the controller to the view. To pass data, you can use a `ViewDataDictionary`. This dictionary stores keys as strings and enables object values. You can use the `ViewDataDictionary` with the `ViewData` property of the `Controller` class—for example, you can pass a string to the dictionary where the key value `MyData` is used: `ViewData["MyData"] = "Hello"`. An easier syntax uses the `ViewBag` property. `ViewBag` is a dynamic type that enables assigning any property name to pass data to the view (code file `MVCSampleApp/Controllers/SubmitDataController.cs`):

```
public IActionResult PassingData()
{
  ViewBag.MyData = "Hello from the controller";
  return View();
}
```

> **NOTE** *Using dynamic types has the advantage that there is no direct dependency from the view to the controller. Dynamic types are explained in detail in Chapter 16, "Reflection, Metadata, and Dynamic Programming."*

From within the view, you can access the data passed from the controller in a similar way as in the controller. The base class of the view (`WebViewPage`) defines a `ViewBag` property (code file `MVCSampleApp/Views/ViewsDemo/PassingData.cshtml`):

```
<div>
  <div>@ViewBag.MyData</div>
</div>
```

Understanding Razor Syntax

As discussed earlier when you were introduced to views, the view contains both HTML and server-side code. With ASP.NET MVC you can use Razor syntax to write C# code in the view. Razor uses the @ character as a transition character. Starting with @, C# code begins.

With Razor you need to differentiate statements that return a value and methods that don't. A value that is returned can be used directly. For example, `ViewBag.MyData` returns a string. The string is put directly between the HTML div tags as shown here:

```
<div>@ViewBag.MyData</div>
```

When you're invoking methods that return void, or specifying some other statements that don't return a value, you need a Razor code block. The following code block defines a string variable:

```
@{
    string name = "Angela";
}
```

You can now use the variable with the simple syntax; you just use the transition character @ to access the variable:

```
<div>@name</div>
```

With the Razor syntax, the engine automatically detects the end of the C# code when it finds an HTML element. There are some cases in which the end of the C# code cannot be detected automatically. You can resolve this by using parentheses as shown in the following example to mark a variable, and then the normal text continues:

```
<div>@(name), Stephanie</div>
```

Another way to start a Razor code block is with the `foreach` statement:

```
@foreach(var item in list)
{
    <li>The item name is @item.</li>
}
```

> **NOTE** *Usually text content is automatically detected with Razor—for example, Razor detects an opening angle bracket or parentheses with a variable. There are a few cases in which this does not work. Here, you can explicitly use @: to define the start of text.*

Creating Strongly Typed Views

Passing data to views, you've seen the `ViewBag` in action. There's another way to pass data to a view—pass a *model* to the view. Using models allows you to create *strongly typed views*.

The `ViewsDemoController` is now extended with the action method `PassingAModel`. The following example creates a new list of `Menu` items, and this list is passed as the model to the `View` method of the `Controller` base class (code file `MVCSampleApp/Controllers/ViewsDemoController.cs`):

```
public IActionResult PassingAModel()
{
    var menus = new List<Menu>
    {
        new Menu
        {
            Id=1,
            Text="Schweinsbraten mit Knödel und Sauerkraut",
            Price=6.9,
            Category="Main"
        },
        new Menu
        {
```

```
          Id=2,
          Text="Erdäpfelgulasch mit Tofu und Gebäck",
          Price=6.9,
          Category="Vegetarian"
      },
      new Menu
      {
          Id=3,
          Text="Tiroler Bauerngröst'l mit Spiegelei und Krautsalat",
          Price=6.9,
          Category="Main"
      }
  };
  return View(menus);
}
```

When model information is passed from the action method to the view, you can create a strongly typed view. A strongly typed view is declared using the model keyword. The type of the model passed to the view must match the declaration of the model directive. In the following code snippet, the strongly typed view declares the type IEnumerable<Menu>, which matches the model type. Because the Menu class is defined within the namespace MVCSampleApp.Models, this namespace is opened with the using keyword.

The base class of the view that is created from the .cshtml file derives from the base class RazorPage. With a model in place, the base class is of type RazorPage<TModel>; with the following code snippet the base class is RazorPage<IEnumerable<Menu>>. This generic parameter in turn defines a Model property of type IEnumerable<Menu>. With the code snippet, the Model property of the base class is used to iterate through the Menu items with @foreach and displays a list item for every menu (code file MVCSampleApp/ViewsDemo/PassingAModel.cshtml):

```
@using MVCSampleApp.Models
@model IEnumerable<Menu>
@{
  Layout = null;
}

<!DOCTYPE html>
<html>
<head>
    <meta name="viewport" content="width=device-width" />
    <title>PassingAModel</title>
</head>
<body>
    <div>
      <ul>
        @foreach (var item in Model)
        {
          <li>@item.Text</li>
        }
      </ul>
    </div>
</body>
</html>
```

You can pass any object as the model—whatever you need with the view. For example, when you're editing a single Menu object, you'd use a model of type Menu. When you're showing or editing a list, you can use IEnumerable<Menu>.

When you run the application showing the defined view, you see a list of menus in the browser, as shown in Figure 41-2.

FIGURE 41-2

Defining the Layout

Usually many pages of web applications share some of the same content—for example, copyright information, a logo, and a main navigation structure. Until now, all your views have contained complete HTML content, but there's an easier way to managed the shared content. This is where layout pages come into play.

To define a layout, you set the `Layout` property of the view. For defining default properties for all views, you can create a view start page. You need to put this file into the `Views` folder, and you can create it using the item template MVC View Start Page. This creates the file `_ViewStart.cshtml` (code file `MVCSampleApp/Views/_ViewStart.cshtml`):

```
@{
    Layout = "_Layout";
}
```

For all views that don't need a layout, you can set the `Layout` property to `null`:

```
@{
    Layout = null;
}
```

Using a Default Layout Page

You can create the default layout page using the item template MVC View Layout Page. You can create this page in the `Shared` folder so that it is available for all views from different controllers. The item template MVC View Layout Page creates the following code:

```
<!DOCTYPE html>
<html>
<head>
    <meta name="viewport" content="width=device-width" />
    <title>@ViewBag.Title</title>
</head>
<body>
    <div>
        @RenderBody()
    </div>
</body>
</html>
```

The layout page contains the HTML content that is common to all pages (for example, header, footer, and navigation) that use this layout page. You've already seen how views and controllers can communicate with the `ViewBag`. The same mechanism can be used with the layout page. You can define the value for `ViewBag.Title` within a content page; from the layout page, it is shown in the preceding code snippet within the HTML `title` element. The `RenderBody` method of the base class `RazorPage` renders the content of the content page and thus defines the position in which the content should be placed.

With the following code snippet, the generated layout page is updated to reference a style sheet and to add header, footer, and navigation sections to every page. `environment`, `asp-controller`, and `asp-action` are Tag Helpers that create HTML elements. Tag Helpers are discussed later in this chapter in the "Helpers" section (code file `MVCSampleApp/Views/Shared/_Layout.cshtml`):

```
<!DOCTYPE html>
<html>
<head>
    <meta charset="utf-8" />
    <meta name="viewport" content="width=device-width, initial-scale=1.0" />
    <environment names="Development">
        <link rel="stylesheet" href="~/css/site.css" />
    </environment>
    <environment names="Staging,Production">
        <link rel="stylesheet" href="~/css/site.min.css"
            asp-append-version="true" />
```

```
      </environment>
      <title>@ViewBag.Title - My ASP.NET Application</title>
  </head>
  <body>
      <div class="container">
        <header>
          <h1>ASP.NET MVC Sample App</h1>
        </header>
        <nav>
          <ul>
            <li><a asp-controller="ViewsDemo" asp-action="LayoutSample">
              Layout Sample</a></li>
            <li><a asp-controller="ViewsDemo" asp-action="LayoutUsingSections">
              Layout Using Sections</a></li>
          </ul>
        </nav>
        <div>
          @RenderBody()
        </div>
        <hr />
        <footer>
          <p>
            <div>Sample Code for Professional C#</div>
            © @DateTime.Now.Year - My ASP.NET Application
          </p>
        </footer>
    </div>
  </body>
</html>
```

A view is created for the action `LayoutSample` (code file `MVCSampleApp/Views/ViewsDemo/`
`LayoutSample.cshtml`). This view doesn't set the `Layout` property and thus uses the default layout. The
following code snippet sets `ViewBag.Title`, which is used within the HTML `title` element in the layout:

```
@{
    ViewBag.Title = "Layout Sample";
}
<h2>LayoutSample</h2>
<p>
    This content is merged with the layout page
</p>
```

When you run the application now, the content from the layout and the view is merged, as shown in Figure 41-3.

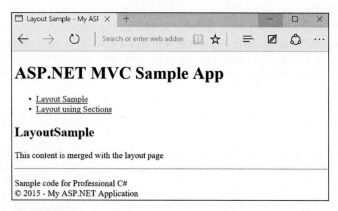

FIGURE 41-3

Using Sections

Rendering the body and using the `ViewBag` is not the only way to exchange data between the layout and the view. With section areas you can define where the named content should be placed within a view. The following code snippet makes use of a section named `PageNavigation`. Such sections are required by default, and loading the view fails if the section is not defined. When the `required` parameter is set to `false`, the section becomes optional (code file `MVCSampleApp/Views/Shared/_Layout.cshtml`):

```
<!-- etc. -->
<div>
  @RenderSection("PageNavigation", required: false)
</div>
<div>
  @RenderBody()
</div>
<!-- etc. -->
```

Within the view page, the `section` keyword defines the section. The position where the section is placed is completely independent from the other content. The view doesn't define the position within the page; this is defined by the layout (code file `MVCSampleApp/Views/ViewsDemo/LayoutUsingSections.cshtml`):

```
@{
    ViewBag.Title = "Layout Using Sections";
}
<h2>Layout Using Sections</h2>
Main content here
@section PageNavigation
{
  <div>Navigation defined from the view</div>
  <ul>
    <li>Nav1</li>
    <li>Nav2</li>
  </ul>
}
```

When you run the application, the content from the view and the layout are merged according to the positions defined by the layout, as shown in Figure 41-4.

FIGURE 41-4

> **NOTE** *Sections aren't used only to place some content within the body of an HTML page; they are also useful for allowing the view to place something in the head—for example, metadata from the page.*

Defining Content with Partial Views

Whereas layouts give an overall definition for multiple pages from the web application, you can use partial views to define content within views. A partial view doesn't have a layout.

Other than that, partial views are similar to normal views. Partial views use the same base class as normal views, and they have a model.

Following is an example of partial views. Here you start with a model that contains properties for independent collections, events, and menus as defined by the class `EventsAndMenusContext` (code file `MVCSampleApp/Models/EventsAndMenusContext.cs`):

```
public class EventsAndMenusContext
{
    private IEnumerable<Event> events = null;
    public IEnumerable<Event> Events
    {
      get
      {
        return events ?? (events = new List<Event>()
          {
            new Event
            {
              Id=1,
              Text="Formula 1 G.P. Australia, Melbourne",
              Day=new DateTime(2016, 4, 3)
            },
            new Event
            {
              Id=2,
              Text="Formula 1 G.P. China, Shanghai",
              Day = new DateTime(2016, 4, 10)
            },
            new Event
            {
              Id=3,
              Text="Formula 1 G.P. Bahrain, Sakhir",
              Day = new DateTime(2016, 4, 24)
            },
            new Event
            {
              Id=4,
              Text="Formula 1 G.P. Russia, Socchi",
              Day = new DateTime(2016, 5, 1)
            }
          });
      }
    }

    private List<Menu> menus = null;
    public IEnumerable<Menu> Menus
    {
      get
      {
        return menus ?? (menus = new List<Menu>()
          {
            new Menu
            {
              Id=1,
              Text="Baby Back Barbecue Ribs",
              Price=16.9,
              Category="Main"
```

```
        },
        new Menu
        {
          Id=2,
          Text="Chicken and Brown Rice Piaf",
          Price=12.9,
          Category="Main"
        },
        new Menu
        {
          Id=3,
          Text="Chicken Miso Soup with Shiitake Mushrooms",
          Price=6.9,
          Category="Soup"
        }
      });
    }
  }
}
```

The context class is registered with the dependency injection startup code to have the type injected with the controller constructor (code file MVCSampleApp/Startup.cs):

```
public void ConfigureServices(IServiceCollection services)
{
services.AddMvc();
services.AddScoped<EventsAndMenusContext>();
}
```

This model will now be used with partial view samples in the following sections, a partial view that is loaded from server-side code, as well as a view that is requested using JavaScript code on the client.

Using Partial Views from Server-Side Code

In the ViewsDemoController class, the constructor is modified to inject the EventsAndMenusContext type (code file MVCSampleApp/Controllers/ViewsDemoController.cs):

```
public class ViewsDemoController : Controller
{
  private EventsAndMenusContext _context;
  public ViewsDemoController(EventsAndMenusContext context)
  {
    _context = context;
  }
  // etc.
```

The action method UseAPartialView1 passes an instance of EventsAndMenus to the view (code file MVCSampleApp/Controllers/ViewsDemoController.cs):

```
public IActionResult UseAPartialView1() => View(_context);
```

The view page is defined to use the model of type EventsAndMenusContext. You can show a partial view by using the HTML Helper method Html.PartialAsync. This method returns a Task<HtmlString>. With the sample code that follows, the string is written as content of the div element using the Razor syntax. The first parameter of the PartialAsync method accepts the name of the partial view. With the second parameter, the PartialAsync method enables passing a model. If no model is passed, the partial view has access to the same model as the view. Here, the view uses the model of type EventsAndMenusContext, and the partial view just uses a part of it with the type IEnumerable<Event> (code file MVCSampleApp/Views/ViewsDemo/UseAPartialView1.cshtml):

```
@model MVCSampleApp.Models.EventsAndMenusContext
@{
```

```
    ViewBag.Title = "Use a Partial View";
    ViewBag.EventsTitle = "Live Events";
}
<h2>Use a Partial View</h2>
<div>this is the main view</div>
<div>
  @await Html.PartialAsync("ShowEvents", Model.Events)
</div>
```

Instead of using an async method, you can use the synchronous variant `Html.Partial`. This is an extension method that returns an `HtmlString`.

Another way to render a partial view within the view is to use the HTML Helper method `Html.RenderPartialAsync`, which is defined to return a `Task`. This method directly writes the partial view content to the response stream. This way, you can use `RenderPartialAsync` within a Razor code block.

You create the partial view similar to the way you create a normal view. You have access to the model and also to the dictionary that is accessed by using the `ViewBag` property. A partial view receives a copy of the dictionary to receive the same dictionary data that can be used (code file MVCSampleApp/Views/ViewsDemo/ShowEvents.cshtml):

```
@using MVCSampleApp.Models
@model IEnumerable<Event>
<h2>
  @ViewBag.EventsTitle
</h2>
<table>
  @foreach (var item in Model)
  {
    <tr>
      <td>@item.Day.ToShortDateString()</td>
      <td>@item.Text</td>
    </tr>
  }
</table>
```

When you run the application, the view, partial view, and layout are rendered, as shown in Figure 41-5.

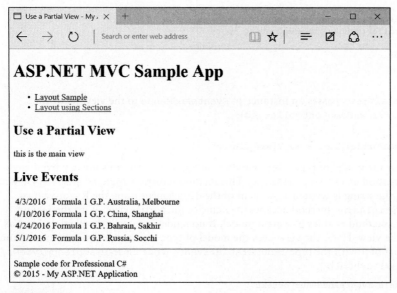

FIGURE 41-5

Returning Partial Views from the Controller

So far the partial view has been loaded directly without the interaction with a controller, but you can also use controllers to return a partial view.

In the following code snippet, two action methods are defined within the class `ViewsDemoController`. The first action method `UsePartialView2` returns a normal view; the second action method `ShowEvents` returns a partial view using the base class method `PartialView`. The partial view `ShowEvents` was already created and used previously, and it is used here. With the method `PartialView` a model containing the event list is passed to the partial view (code file `MVCSampleApp/Controllers/ViewDemoController.cs`):

```
public ActionResult UseAPartialView2() => View();

public ActionResult ShowEvents()
{
  ViewBag.EventsTitle = "Live Events";
  return PartialView(_context.Events);
}
```

When the partial view is offered from the controller, the partial view can be called directly from client-side code. The following code snippet makes use of jQuery: An event handler is linked to the `click` event of a button. Inside the event handler, a GET request is made to the server with the jQuery `load` function to request `/ViewsDemo/ShowEvents`. This request returns a partial view, and the result from the partial view is placed within the `div` element named `events` (code file `MVCSampleApp/Views/ViewsDemo/UseAPartialView2.cshtml`):

```
@model MVCSampleApp.Models.EventsAndMenusContext
@{
  ViewBag.Title = "Use a Partial View";
}
<script src="~/lib/jquery/dist/jquery.js"></script>
<script>
  $(function () {
    $("#getEvents").click(function () {
      $("#events").load("/ViewsDemo/ShowEvents");
    });
  });
</script>
<h2>Use a Partial View</h2>
<div>this is the main view</div>
<button id="FileName_getEvents">Get Events</button>
<div id="FileName_events">
</div>
```

Working with View Components

ASP.NET MVC 6 offers a new alternative to partial views: *view components*. View components are very similar to partial views; the main difference is that view components are not related to a controller. This makes it easy to use them with multiple controllers. Examples of where view components are really useful are dynamic navigation of menus, a login panel, or sidebar content in a blog. These scenarios are useful independent of a single controller.

Like controllers and views, view components have two parts. With view components the controller functionality is taken over by a class that derives from `ViewComponent` (or a POCO class with the attribute `ViewComponent`). The user interface is defined similarly to a view, but the method to invoke the view component is different.

The following code snippet defines a view component that derives from the base class `ViewComponent`. This class makes use of the `EventsAndMenusContext` type that was earlier registered in the `Startup` class to be available with dependency injection. This works similarly to the controllers with constructor injection. The

InvokeAsync method is defined to be called from the view that shows the view component. This method can have any number and type of parameters, as the method defined by the IViewComponentHelper interface defines a flexible number of parameters using the params keyword. Instead of using an async method implementation, you can synchronously implement this method returning IViewComponentResult instead of Task<IViewComponentResult>. However, typically the async variant is the best to use—for example, for accessing a database. The view component needs to be stored in a ViewComponents directory. This directory itself can be placed anywhere within the project (code file MVCSampleApp/ViewComponents/EventListViewComponent.cs):

```
public class EventListViewComponent : ViewComponent
{
  private readonly EventsAndMenusContext _context;
  public EventListViewComponent(EventsAndMenusContext context)
  {
    _context = context;
  }

  public Task<IViewComponentResult> InvokeAsync(DateTime from, DateTime to)
  {
    return Task.FromResult<IViewComponentResult>(
      View(EventsByDateRange(from, to)));
  }

  private IEnumerable<Event> EventsByDateRange(DateTime from, DateTime to)
  {
    return _context.Events.Where(e => e.Day >= from && e.Day <= to);
  }
}
```

The user interface for the view component is defined within the following code snippet. The view for the view component can be created with the item template MVC View Page; it uses the same Razor syntax. Specifically, it must be put into the Components/[viewcomponent] folder—for example, Components/EventList. For the view component to be available with all the controls, you need to create the Components folder in the Shared folder for the views. When you're using a view component only from one specific controller, you can put it into the views controller folder instead. What's different with this view, though, is that it needs to be named default.cshtml. You can create other view names as well; you need to specify these views using a parameter for the View method returned from the InvokeAsync method (code file MVCSampleApp/Views/Shared/Components/EventList/default.cshtml):

```
@using MVCSampleApp.Models;
@model IEnumerable<Event>

<h3>Formula 1 Calendar</h3>
<ul>
  @foreach (var ev in Model)
  {
    <li><div>@ev.Day.ToString("D")</div><div>@ev.Text</div></li>
  }
</ul>
```

Now as the view component is completed, you can show it by invoking the InvokeAsync method. Component is a dynamically created property of the view that returns an object implementing IViewComponentHelper. IViewComponentHelper allows you to invoke synchronous or asynchronous methods such as Invoke, InvokeAsync, RenderInvoke, and RenderInvokeAsync. Of course you can only invoke these methods that are implemented by the view component, and only use the parameters accordingly (code file MVCSampleApp/Views/ViewsDemo/UseViewComponent.cshtml):

```
@{
  ViewBag.Title = "View Components Sample";
}
```

```
<h2>@ViewBag.Title</h2>
<p>
  @await Component.InvokeAsync("EventList", new DateTime(2016, 4, 10),
    new DateTime(2016, 4, 24))
</p>
```

Running the application, you can see the view component rendered as shown in Figure 41-6.

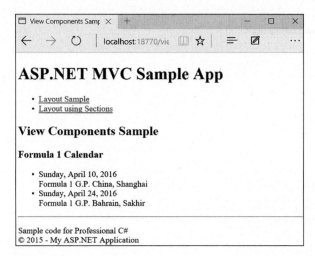

FIGURE 41-6

Using Dependency Injection in Views

In case a service is needed directly from within a view, you can inject it using the `inject` keyword:

```
@using MVCSampleApp.Services
@inject ISampleService sampleService
<p>
    @string.Join("*", sampleService.GetSampleStrings())
</p>
```

When you do this, it's a good idea to register services using the `AddScoped` method. As previously mentioned, registering a service that way means it's only instantiated once for one HTTP request. Using `AddScoped`, injecting the same service within a controller and the view, it is only instantiated once for a request.

Importing Namespaces with Multiple Views

All the previous samples for views have used the `using` keyword to open all the namespaces needed. Instead of opening the namespaces with every view, you can use the Visual Studio item template MVC View Imports Page to create a file (`_ViewImports.cshtml`) that defines all using declarations (code file `MVCSampleApp/Views/_ViewImports.cshtml`):

```
@using MVCSampleApp.Models
@using MVCSampleApp.Services
```

With this file in place, there's no need to add all the `using` keywords to all the views.

SUBMITTING DATA FROM THE CLIENT

Until now you used only HTTP GET requests from the client to retrieve HTML code from the server. What about sending form data from the client?

To submit form data, you create the view `CreateMenu` for the controller `SubmitData`. This view contains an HTML form element that defines what data should be sent to the server. The form method is declared as an HTTP POST request. The `input` elements that define the input fields all have names that correspond to the properties of the `Menu` type (code file `MVCSampleApp/Views/SubmitData/CreateMenu.cshtml`):

```
@{
  ViewBag.Title = "Create Menu";
}
<h2>Create Menu</h2>
<form action="/SubmitData/CreateMenu" method="post">
<fieldset>
  <legend>Menu</legend>
  <div>Id:</div>
  <input name="id" />
  <div>Text:</div>
  <input name="text" />
  <div>Price:</div>
  <input name="price" />
  <div>Category:</div>
  <input name="category" />
  <div></div>
  <button type="submit">Submit</button>
</fieldset>
</form>
```

Figure 41-7 shows the opened page within the browser.

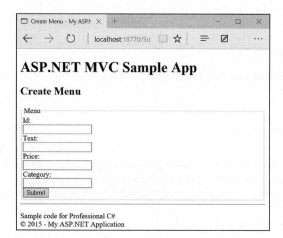

FIGURE 41-7

Within the `SubmitData` controller, two `CreateMenu` action methods are created: one for an HTTP GET request and another for an HTTP POST request. Because C# has different methods with the same name, it's required that the parameter numbers or types are different. Of course, this requirement is the same with action methods. Action methods also need to differ with the HTTP request method. By default, the request method is GET; when you apply the attribute `HttpPost`, the request method is POST. For reading HTTP POST data, you could use information from the `Request` object . However, it's much simpler to define the `CreateMenu` method with parameters. The parameters are matched with the name of the form fields (code file `MVCSampleApp/Controllers/SubmitDataController.cs`):

```
public IActionResult Index() => View();

public IActionResult CreateMenu() => View();
```

```
[HttpPost]
public IActionResult CreateMenu(int id, string text, double price,
    string category)
{
  var m = new Menu { Id = id, Text = text, Price = price };
  ViewBag.Info =
    $"menu created: {m.Text}, Price: {m.Price}, category: {m.Category}";
  return View("Index");
}
```

To display the result, just the value of the `ViewBag.Info` is shown (code file `MVCSampleApp/Views/SubmitData/Index.cshtml`):

```
@ViewBag.Info
```

Model Binder

Instead of using multiple parameters with the action method, you can also use a type that contains properties that match the incoming field names (code file `MVCSampleApp/Controllers/SubmitDataController.cs`):

```
[HttpPost]
public IActionResult CreateMenu2(Menu m)
{
  ViewBag.Info =
    $"menu created: {m.Text}, Price: {m.Price}, category: {m.Category}";
  return View("Index");
}
```

When the user submits the data with the form, a `CreateMenu` method is invoked that shows the `Index` view with the submitted menu data, as shown in Figure 41-8.

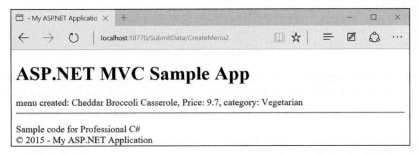

FIGURE 41-8

A model binder is responsible for transferring the data from the HTTP POST request. A model binder implements the interface `IModelBinder`. By default the `FormCollectionModelBinder` class is used to bind the input fields to the model. This binder supports primitive types, model classes (such as the `Menu` type), and collections implementing `ICollection<T>`, `IList<T>`, and `IDictionary<TKey, TValue>`.

In case not all the properties of the parameter type should be filled from the model binder, you can use the `Bind` attribute. With this attribute you can specify a list of property names that should be included with the binding.

You can also pass the input data to the model using an action method without parameters, as demonstrated by the next code snippet. Here, a new instance of the `Menu` class is created, and this instance is passed to the `TryUpdateModelAsync` method of the `Controller` base class. `TryUpdateModelAsync` returns false if the updated model is not in a valid state after the update:

```
[HttpPost]
public async Task<IActionResult> CreateMenu3Result()
{
  var m = new Menu();
  bool updated = await TryUpdateModelAsync<Menu>(m);
  if (updated)
  {
    ViewBag.Info =
      $"menu created: {m.Text}, Price: {m.Price}, category: {m.Category}";
    return View("Index");
  }
  else
  {
    return View("Error");
  }
}
```

Annotations and Validation

You can add some annotations to the model type; the annotations are used when updating the data for validation. The namespace System.ComponentModel.DataAnnotations contains attribute types that can be used to specify some information for data on the client and can be used for validation.

The Menu type is changed with these added attributes (code file MVCSampleApp/Models/Menu.cs):

```
public class Menu
{
  public int Id { get; set; }
  [Required, StringLength(50)]
  public string Text { get; set; }
  [Display(Name="Price"), DisplayFormat(DataFormatString="{0:C}")]
  public double Price { get; set; }
  [DataType(DataType.Date)]
  public DateTime Date { get; set; }
  [StringLength(10)]
  public string Category { get; set; }
}
```

Possible attribute types you can use for validation are CompareAttribute to compare different properties, CreditCardAttribute to verify a valid credit card number, EmailAddressAttribute to verify an e-mail address, EnumDataTypeAttribute to compare the input to enumeration values, and PhoneAttribute to verify a phone number.

You can also use other attributes to get values for display and error messages—for example, DataTypeAttribute and DisplayFormatAttribute.

To use the validation attributes, you can verify the state of the model using ModelState.IsValid within an action method as shown here (code file MVCSampleApp/Controllers/SubmitDataController.cs):

```
[HttpPost]
public IActionResult CreateMenu4(Menu m)
{
  if (ModelState.IsValid)
  {
    ViewBag.Info =
      $"menu created: {m.Text}, Price: {m.Price}, category: {m.Category}";
  }
  else
  {
    ViewBag.Info = "not valid";
  }
  return View("Index");
}
```

If you use tool-generated model classes, you might think it's hard to add attributes to properties. As the tool-generated classes are defined as partial classes, you can extend the class by adding properties and methods, by implementing additional interfaces, and by implementing partial methods that are used by the tool-generated classes. You cannot add attributes to existing properties and methods if you can't change the source code of the type, but there's help for such scenarios! Assume the `Menu` class is a tool-generated partial class. Then a new class with a different name (for example, `MenuMetadata`) can define the same properties as the entity class and add the annotations, as shown here:

```
public class MenuMetadata
{
  public int Id { get; set; }
  [Required, StringLength(25)]
  public string Text { get; set; }
  [Display(Name="Price"), DisplayFormat(DataFormatString="{0:C}")]
  public double Price { get; set; }
  [DataType(DataType.Date)]
  public DateTime Date { get; set; }
  [StringLength(10)]
  public string Category { get; set; }
}
```

The `MenuMetadata` class must be linked to the `Menu` class. With tool-generated partial classes, you can create another partial type in the same namespace to add the `MetadataType` attribute to the type definition that creates the connection:

```
[MetadataType(typeof(MenuMetadata))]
public partial class Menu
{
}
```

HTML Helper methods can also make use of annotations to add information to the client.

WORKING WITH HTML HELPERS

HTML Helpers are helpers that create HTML code. You can use them directly within the view using Razor syntax.

`Html` is a property of the view base class `RazorPage` and is of type `IHtmlHelper`. HTML Helper methods are implemented as extension methods to extend the `IHtmlHelper` interface.

The class `InputExtensions` defines HTML Helper methods to create check boxes, password controls, radio buttons, and text box controls. The `Action` and `RenderAction` helpers are defined by the class `ChildActionExtensions`. Helper methods for display are defined by the class `DisplayExtensions`. Helper methods for HTML forms are defined by the class `FormExtensions`.

The following sections get into some examples using HTML Helpers.

Using Simple Helpers

The following code snippet uses the HTML Helper methods `BeginForm`, `Label`, and `CheckBox`. `BeginForm` starts a form element. There's also an `EndForm` for ending the form element. The sample makes use of the `IDisposable` interface implemented by the `MvcForm` returned from the `BeginForm` method. On disposing of the `MvcForm`, `EndForm` is invoked. This way the `BeginForm` method can be surrounded by a `using` statement to end the form at the closing curly brackets. The method `DisplayName` directly returns the content from the argument; the method `CheckBox` is an `input` element with the `type` attribute set to `checkbox` (code file `MVCSampleApp/Views/HelperMethods/SimpleHelper.cshtml`):

```
@using (Html.BeginForm()) {
  @Html.DisplayName("Check this (or not)")
  @Html.CheckBox("check1")
}
```

The resulting HTML code is shown in the next code snippet. The CheckBox method creates two input elements with the same name; one is set to hidden. There's a good reason for this behavior: If a check box has a value of false, the browser does not pass this information to the server with the forms content. Only check box values of selected check boxes are passed to the server. This HTML characteristic creates a problem with automatic binding to the parameters of action methods. A simple solution is performed by the CheckBox helper method. This method creates a hidden input element with the same name that is set to false. If the check box is not selected, the hidden input element is passed to the server, and the false value can be bound. If the check box is selected, two input elements with the same name are sent to the server. The first input element is set to true; the second one is set to false. With automatic binding, only the first input element is selected to bind:

```
<form action="/HelperMethods/SimpleHelper" method="post">
  Check this (or not)
  <input id="FileName_check1" name="check1" type="checkbox" value="true" />
  <input name="check1" type="hidden" value="false" />
</form>
```

Using Model Data

You can use helper methods with model data. This example creates a Menu object. This type was declared earlier in this chapter within the Models directory and passes a sample menu as a model to the view (code file MVCSampleApp/Controllers/HTMLHelpersController.cs):

```
public IActionResult HelperWithMenu() => View(GetSampleMenu());

private Menu GetSampleMenu() =>
  new Menu
  {
    Id = 1,
    Text = "Schweinsbraten mit Knödel und Sauerkraut",
    Price = 6.9,
    Date = new DateTime(2016, 10, 5),
    Category = "Main"
  };
```

The view has the model defined to be of type Menu. The DisplayName HTML Helper returns the text from the parameter, as shown with the previous sample. The Display method uses an expression as the parameter where a property name can be passed in the string format. This way this property tries to find a property with this name and accesses the property accessor to return the value of the property (code file MVCSampleApp/Views/HTMLHelpers/HelperWithMenu.cshtml):

```
@model MVCSampleApp.Models.Menu
@{
    ViewBag.Title = "HelperWithMenu";
}
<h2>Helper with Menu</h2>
@Html.DisplayName("Text:")
@Html.Display("Text")
<br />
@Html.DisplayName("Category:")
@Html.Display("Category")
```

With the resulting HTML code, you can see this as output from calling the DisplayName and Display methods:

```
Text:
Schweinsbraten mit Kn&#246;del und Sauerkraut
<br />
Category:
Main
```

NOTE *Helper methods also offer strongly typed variants to access members of the model. See the "Using Strongly Typed Helpers" section for more information.*

Defining HTML Attributes

Most HTML Helper methods have overloads in which you can pass any HTML attributes. For example, the following TextBox method creates an input element of type text. The first parameter defines the name; the second parameter defines the value that is set with the text box. The third parameter of the TextBox method is of type object that enables passing an anonymous type where every property is changed to an attribute of the HTML element. Here, the result of the input element has the required attribute set to required, the maxlength attribute to 15, and the class attribute to CSSDemo. Because class is a C# keyword, it cannot be directly set as a property. Instead it is prefixed with @ to generate the class attribute for CSS styling:

```
@Html.TextBox("text1", "input text here",
    new { required="required", maxlength=15, @class="CSSDemo" });
```

The resulting HTML output is shown here:

```
<input class="Test" id="FileName_text1" maxlength="15" name="text1" required="required"
    type="text" value="input text here" />
```

Creating Lists

For displaying lists, helper methods such as DropDownList and ListBox exist. These methods create the HTML select element.

Within the controller, first a dictionary is created that contains keys and values. The dictionary is then converted to a list of SelectListItem with the custom extension method ToSelectListItems. The DropDownList and ListBox methods make use of SelectListItem collections (code file MVCSampleApp/Controllers/HTMLHelpersController.cs):

```
public IActionResult HelperList()
{
    var cars = new Dictionary<int, string>();
    cars.Add(1, "Red Bull Racing");
    cars.Add(2, "McLaren");
    cars.Add(3, "Mercedes");
    cars.Add(4, "Ferrari");
    return View(cars.ToSelectListItems(4));
}
```

The custom extension method ToSelectListItems is defined within the class SelectListItemsExtensions that extends IDictionary<int, string>, the type from the cars collection. Within the implementation, a new SelectListItem object is returned for every item in the dictionary (code file MVCSampleApp/Extensions/SelectListItemsExtensions.cs):

```
public static class SelectListItemsExtensions
{
    public static IEnumerable<SelectListItem> ToSelectListItems(
        this IDictionary<int, string> dict, int selectedId)
    {
        return dict.Select(item =>
            new SelectListItem
            {
                Selected = item.Key == selectedId,
                Text = item.Value,
                Value = item.Key.ToString()
            });
```

```
        }
    }
```

With the view, the helper method `DropDownList` directly accesses the Model that is returned from the controller (code file `MVCSampleApp/Views/HTMLHelpers/HelperList.cshtml`):

```
@{
    ViewBag.Title = "Helper List";
}
@model IEnumerable<SelectListItem>
<h2>Helper2</h2>
@Html.DropDownList("carslist", Model)
```

The resulting HTML creates a `select` element with `option` child elements as created from the `SelectListItem` and defines the selected item as returned from the controller:

```
<select id="FileName_carslist" name="carslist">
  <option value="1">Red Bull Racing</option>
  <option value="2">McLaren</option>
  <option value="3">Mercedes</option>
  <option selected="selected" value="4">Ferrari</option>
</select>
```

Using Strongly Typed Helpers

The HTML Helper methods offer strongly typed methods to access the model passed from the controller. These methods are all suffixed with the name `For`. For example, instead of the `TextBox` method, here the `TextBoxFor` method can be used.

The next sample again makes use of a controller that returns a single entity (code file `MVCSampleApp/Controllers/HTMLHelpersController.cs`):

```
public IActionResult StronglyTypedMenu() => View(GetSampleMenu());
```

The view uses the `Menu` type as a model; thus the methods `DisplayNameFor` and `DisplayFor` can directly access the `Menu` properties. By default, `DisplayNameFor` returns the name of the property (in this example, it's the `Text` property), and `DisplayFor` returns the value of the property (code file `MVCSampleApp/Views/HTMLHelpers/StronglyTypedMenu.cshtml`):

```
@model MVCSampleApp.Models.Menu
@Html.DisplayNameFor(m => m.Text)
<br />
@Html.DisplayFor(m => m.Text)
```

Similarly, you can use `Html.TextBoxFor(m => m.Text)`, which returns an input element that enables setting the `Text` property of the model. This method also makes use of the annotations added to the `Text` property of the `Menu` type. The `Text` property has the `Required` and `MaxStringLength` attributes added, which is why the `data-val-length`, `data-val-length-max`, and `data-val-required` attributes are returned from the `TextBoxFor` method:

```
<input data-val="true"
  data-val-length="The field Text must be a string with a maximum length of 50."
  data-val-length-max="50"
  data-val-required="The Text field is required."
  id="FileName_Text" name="Text"
  type="text"
  value="Schweinsbraten mit Knödel und Sauerkraut" />
```

Working with Editor Extensions

Instead of using at least one helper method for every property, helper methods from the class `EditorExtensions` offer an editor for all the properties of a type.

Using the same `Menu` model as before, with the method `Html.EditorFor(m => m)` the complete user interface (UI) for editing the menu is built. The result from this method invocation is shown in Figure 41-9.

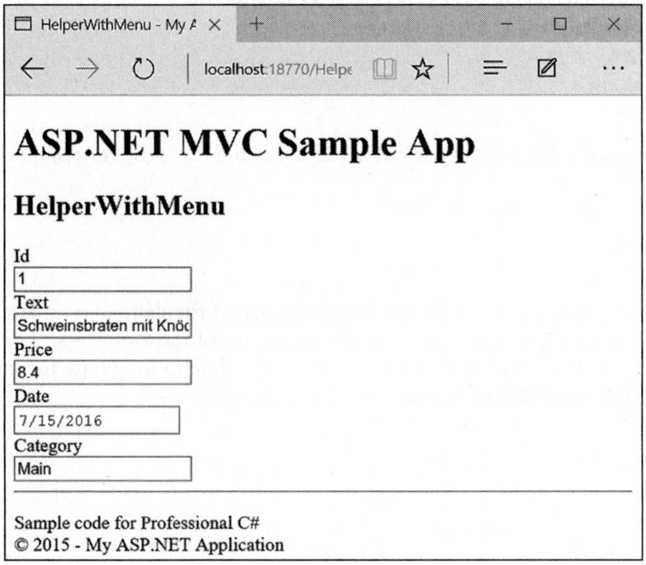

FIGURE 41-9

Instead of using `Html.EditorFor(m => m)`, you can use `Html.EditorForModel`. The method `EditorForModel` makes use of the model of the view without the need to specify it explicitly. `EditorFor` has more flexibility in using other data sources (for example, properties offered by the model), and `EditorForModel` needs fewer parameters to add.

Implementing Templates

A great way to extend the outcome from HTML Helpers is by using templates. A *template* is a simple view used—either implicitly or explicitly—by the HTML Helper methods. Templates are stored within special folders. Display templates are stored within the `DisplayTemplates` folder that is in the view folder (for example, `Views/HelperMethods`) or in a shared folder (`Shared/DisplayTemplates`). The shared folder is used by all views; the specific view folder is used only by views within this folder. Editor templates are stored in the folder `EditorTemplates`.

Now have a look at an example. With the `Menu` type, the `Date` property has the annotation `DataType` with a value of `DataType.Date`. When you specify this attribute, the `DateTime` type by default does not show as date and time; it shows only with the short date format (code file `MVCSampleApp/Models/Menu.cs`):

```
public class Menu
{
  public int Id { get; set; }
  [Required, StringLength(50)]
  public string Text { get; set; }
  [Display(Name="Price"), DisplayFormat(DataFormatString="{0:c}")]
  public double Price { get; set; }
  [DataType(DataType.Date)]
  public DateTime Date { get; set; }
  [StringLength(10)]
```

```
    public string Category { get; set; }
}
```

Now the template for the date is created. With this template, the `Model` is returned using a long date string format `D`, which is embedded within a `div` tag that has the CSS class `markRed` (code file `MVCSampleApp/Views/HTMLHelpers/DisplayTemplates/Date.cshtml`):

```
<div class="markRed">
  @string.Format("{0:D}", Model)
</div>
```

The `markRed` CSS class is defined within the style sheet to set the color red (code file `MVCSampleApp/wwwroot/styles/Site.css`):

```
.markRed {
  color: #f00;
}
```

Now a display HTML Helper such as `DisplayForModel` can be used to make use of the defined template. The model is of type `Menu`, so the `DisplayForModel` method displays all properties of the `Menu` type. For the `Date` it finds the template `Date.cshtml`, so this template is used to display the date in long date format with the CSS style (code file `MVCSampleApp/Views/HTMLHelpers/Display.cshtml`):

```
@model MVCSampleApp.Models.Menu
@{
    ViewBag.Title = "Display";
}
<h2>@ViewBag.Title</h2>
@Html.DisplayForModel()
```

If a single type should have different presentations in the same view, you can use other names for the template file. Then you can use the attribute `UIHint` to specify the template name, or you can specify the template with the template parameter of the helper method.

GETTING TO KNOW TAG HELPERS

ASP.NET MVC 6 offers a new technology that can be used instead of HTML Helpers: *Tag Helpers*. With Tag Helpers you don't write C# code mixed with HTML; instead you use HTML attributes and elements that are resolved on the server. Nowadays many JavaScript libraries extend HTML with their own attributes (such as Angular), so it's very convenient to be able to do use custom HTML attributes with server-side technology. Many of the ASP.NET MVC Tag Helpers have the prefix `asp-`, so you can easily see what's resolved on the server. These attributes are not sent to the client but instead are resolved on the server to generate HTML code.

Activating Tag Helpers

To use the ASP.NET MVC Tag Helpers, you need to activate the tags by calling `addTagHelper`. The first parameter defines the types to use (a `*` opens all Tag Helpers of the assembly); the second parameter defines the assembly of the Tag Helpers. With `removeTagHelper`, the Tag Helpers are deactivated again. Deactivating Tag Helpers might be important—for example, to not get into naming conflicts with scripting libraries. You're most likely not getting into a conflict using the built-in Tag Helpers with the `asp-` prefix, but conflicts can easily happen with other Tag Helpers that can have the same names as other Tag Helpers or HTML attributes used with scripting libraries.

To have the Tag Helpers available with all views, add the `addTagHelper` statement to the shared file `_ViewImports.cshtml` (code file `MVCSampleApp/Views/_ViewImports.cshtml`):

```
@addTagHelper *, Microsoft.AspNet.Mvc.TagHelpers
```

Using Anchor Tag Helpers

Let's start with Tag Helpers that extend the anchor a element. The sample controller for the Tag Helpers is `TagHelpersController`. The `Index` action method returns a view for showing the anchor Tag Helpers (code file `MVCSampleApp/Controllers/TagHelpersController.cs`):

```
public class TagHelpersController : Controller
{
  public IActionResult Index() => View();

  // etc.
}
```

The anchor Tag Helper defines the `asp-controller` and `asp-action` attributes. With these, the controller and action methods are used to build up the URL for the anchor element. With the second and third examples, the controller is not needed because it's the same controller the view is coming from (code file `MVCSampleApp/Views/TagHelpers/Index.cshtml`):

```
<a asp-controller="Home" asp-action="Index">Home</a>
<br />
<a asp-action="LabelHelper">Label Tag Helper</a>
<br />
<a asp-action="InputTypeHelper">Input Type Tag Helper</a>
```

The following snippet shows the resulting HTML code. The `asp-controller` and `asp-action` attributes generate an `href` attribute for the a element. With the first sample to access the `Index` action method in the `Home` controller, as both are defaults as defined by the route, an `href` to / is all that's needed in the result. When you specify the `asp-action` `LabelHelper`, the `href` directs to `/TagHelpers/LabelHelper`, the action method `LabelHelper` in the current controller:

```
<a href="/">Home</a>
<br />
<a href="/TagHelpers/LabelHelper">Label Tag Helper</a>
<br />
<a href="/TagHelpers/InputTypeHelper">Input Type Tag Helper</a>
```

Using Label Tag Helpers

In the following code snippet, which demonstrates the features of the label Tag Helper, the action method `LabelHelper` passes a `Menu` object to the view (code file `MVCSampleApp/Controllers/TagHelpersController.cs`):

```
public IActionResult LabelHelper() => View(GetSampleMenu());

private Menu GetSampleMenu() =>
  new Menu
  {
    Id = 1,
    Text = "Schweinsbraten mit Knödel und Sauerkraut",
    Price = 6.9,
    Date = new DateTime(2016, 10, 5),
    Category = "Main"
  };
}
```

The `Menu` class has some data annotations applied to influence the outcome of the Tag Helpers. Have a look at the `Display` attribute for the `Text` property. It sets the `Name` property of the `Display` attribute to `"Menu"` (code file `MVCSampleApp/Models/Menu.cs`):

```
public class Menu
{
  public int Id { get; set; }
```

```
    [Required, StringLength(50)]
    [Display(Name = "Menu")]
    public string Text { get; set; }

    [Display(Name = "Price"), DisplayFormat(DataFormatString = "{0:C}")]
    public double Price { get; set; }

    [DataType(DataType.Date)]
    public DateTime Date { get; set; }

    [StringLength(10)]
    public string Category { get; set; }
}
```

The view makes use of `asp-for` attributes applied to `label` controls. The value that is used for this attribute is a property of the model of the view. With Visual Studio 2015, you can use IntelliSense for accessing the `Text`, `Price`, and `Date` properties (code file `MVCSampleApp/Views/TagHelpers/LabelHelper.cshtml`):

```
@model MVCSampleApp.Models.Menu
@{
    ViewBag.Title = "Label Tag Helper";
}
<h2>@ViewBag.Title</h2>

<label asp-for="Text"></label>
<br/>
<label asp-for="Price"></label>
<br />
<label asp-for="Date"></label>
```

With the generated HTML code, you can see the `for` attribute, which references elements with the same name as the property names and the content that is either the name of the property or the value of the `Display` attribute. You can use this attribute also to localize values:

```
<label for="Text">Menu</label>
<br/>
<label for="Price">Price</label>
<br />
<label for="Date">Date</label>
```

Using Input Tag Helpers

An HTML `label` typically is associated with an `input` element. The following code snippet gives you a look at what's generated using `input` elements with Tag Helpers:

```
<label asp-for="Text"></label>
<input asp-for="Text"/>
<br/>
<label asp-for="Price"></label>
<input asp-for="Price" />
<br />
<label asp-for="Date"></label>
<input asp-for="Date" />
```

Checking the result of the generated HTML code reveals that the `input` type Tag Helpers create a `type` attribute depending on the type of the property, and they also apply the `DateType` attribute. The property `Price` is of type `double`, which results in a number input type. Because the `Date` property has the `DataType` with a value of `DataType.Date` applied, the input type is a date. In addition to that you can see `data-val-length`, `data-val-length-max`, and `data-val-required` attributes that are created because of annotations:

```
<label for="Text">Menu</label>
<input type="text" data-val="true"
    data-val-length=
        "The field Menu must be a string with a maximum length of 50."
```

```
    data-val-length-max="50"
    data-val-required="The Menu field is required."
    id="FileName_Text" name="Text"
    value="Schweinsbraten mit Knödel und Sauerkraut" />
<br/>
<label for="Price">Price</label>
<input type="number" data-val="true"
    data-val-required="The Price field is required."
    id="FileName_Price" name="Price" value="6.9" />
<br />
<label for="Date">Date</label>
<input type="date" data-val="true"
    data-val-required="The Date field is required."
    id="FileName_Date" name="Date" value="10/5/2016" />
```

Modern browsers have a special look for HTML 5 input controls such as date control. The input date control of Microsoft Edge is shown in Figure 41-10.

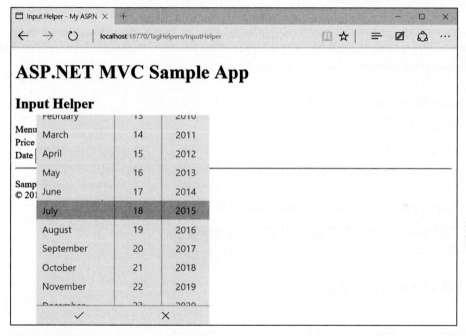

FIGURE 41-10

Using a Form with Validation

For sending data to the server, the input fields need to be surrounded by a form. A Tag Helper for the form defines the action attribute by using asp-method and asp-controller. With input controls, you've seen that validation information is defined by these controls. The validation errors need to be displayed. For display, the validation message Tag Helper extends the span element with asp-validation-for (code file MVCSampleApp/Views/TagHelpers/FormHelper.cs):

```
<form method="post" asp-method="FormHelper">
  <input asp-for="Id" hidden="hidden" />
  <hr />
  <label asp-for="Text"></label>
  <div>
    <input asp-for="Text" />
    <span asp-validation-for="Text"></span>
  </div>
```

```
<br />
<label asp-for="Price"></label>
<div>
  <input asp-for="Price" />
  <span asp-validation-for="Price"></span>
</div>
<br />
<label asp-for="Date"></label>
<div>
  <input asp-for="Date" />
  <span asp-validation-for="Date"></span>
</div>
<label asp-for="Category"></label>
<div>
  <input asp-for="Category" />
  <span asp-validation-for="Category"></span>
</div>
<input type="submit" value="Submit" />
</form>
```

The controller verifies whether the receive data is correct by checking the `ModelState`. In case it's not correct, the same view is displayed again (code file `MVCSampleApp/Controllers/TagHelpersController.cs`):

```
public IActionResult FormHelper() => View(GetSampleMenu());

[HttpPost]
public IActionResult FormHelper(Menu m)
{
  if (!ModelState.IsValid)
  {
    return View(m);
  }
  return View("ValidationHelperResult", m);
}
```

When you run the application, you can see error information like that shown in Figure 41-11.

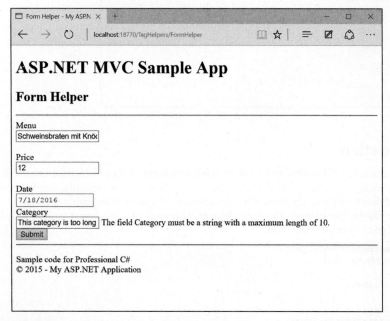

FIGURE 41-11

Creating Custom Tag Helpers

Aside from using the predefined Tag Helpers, you can create a custom Tag Helper. The sample custom Tag Helper you build in this section extends the HTML table element to show a row for every item in a list and a column for every property.

The controller implements the method `CustomHelper` to return a list of `Menu` objects (code file `MVCSampleApp/Controllers/TagHelpersController.cs`):

```csharp
public IActionResult CustomHelper() => View(GetSampleMenus());

private IList<Menu> GetSampleMenus() =>
  new List<Menu>()
  {
    new Menu
    {
      Id = 1,
      Text = "Schweinsbraten mit Knödel und Sauerkraut",
      Price = 8.5,
      Date = new DateTime(2016, 10, 5),
      Category = "Main"
    },
    new Menu
    {
      Id = 2,
      Text = "Erdäpfelgulasch mit Tofu und Gebäck",
      Price = 8.5,
      Date = new DateTime(2016, 10, 6),
      Category = "Vegetarian"
    },
    new Menu
    {
      Id = 3,
      Text = "Tiroler Bauerngröst'l mit Spiegelei und Krautsalat",
      Price = 8.5,
      Date = new DateTime(2016, 10, 7),
      Category = "Vegetarian"
    }
  };
```

Now step into the Tag Helper. The custom implementation needs these namespaces:

```csharp
using Microsoft.AspNet.Mvc.Rendering;
using Microsoft.AspNet.Razor.Runtime.TagHelpers;
using System.Collections.Generic;
using System.Linq;
using System.Reflection;
```

A custom Tag Helper derives from the base class `TagHelper`. The attribute `TargetElement` defines what HTML elements are extended by the Tag Helper. This Tag Helper extends the `table` element; thus the string `"table"` is passed to the constructor of the element. With the property `Attributes`, you can define a list of attributes that are assigned to the HTML element that are used by the Tag Helper. This Tag Helper makes use of the `items` attribute. You can use the Tag Helper with this syntax: `<table items="Model"></table>`, where `Model` needs to be a list that can be iterated. In case you're creating a Tag Helper that should be used with multiple HTML elements, you just need to apply the attribute `TargetElement` multiple times. To automatically assign the value of the `items` attribute to the `Items` property, the attribute `HtmlAttributeName` is assigned to this property (code file `MVCSampleApp/Extensions/TableTagHelper.cs`):

```csharp
[TargetElement("table", Attributes = ItemsAttributeName)]
public class TableTagHelper : TagHelper
{
  private const string ItemsAttributeName = "items";

  [HtmlAttributeName(ItemsAttributeName)]
```

```
    public IEnumerable<object> Items { get; set; }

    // etc.
  }
```

The heart of the Tag Helper is in the method `Process`. This method needs to create HTML code that is returned from the helper. With the parameters of the `Process` method you receive a `TagHelperContext` This context contains both the attributes of the HTML element where the Tag Helper is applied and all child elements. With the table element, rows and columns could already have been defined, and you could merge the result with the existing content. In the sample, this is ignored, and just the attributes are taken to put them in the result. The result needs to be written to the second parameter: the `TagHelperOutput` object. For creating HTML code, the `TagBuilder` type is used. The `TagBuilder` helps create HTML elements with attributes, and it deals with closing of elements. To add attributes to the `TagBuilder`, you use the method `MergeAttributes`. This method requires a dictionary of all attribute names and their values. This dictionary is created by using the LINQ extension method `ToDictionary`. With the `Where` method, all of the existing attributes—with the exception of the items attribute—of the table element are taken. The `items` attribute is used for defining items with the Tag Helper but is not needed later on by the client:

```
public override void Process(TagHelperContext context, TagHelperOutput output)
{
  TagBuilder table = new TagBuilder("table");
  table.GenerateId(context.UniqueId, "id");
  var attributes = context.AllAttributes
    .Where(a => a.Name != ItemsAttributeName).ToDictionary(a => a.Name);
  table.MergeAttributes(attributes);
  // etc.
}
```

> **NOTE** *In case you need to invoke asynchronous methods within the Tag Helper implementation, you can override the* `ProcessAsync` *method instead of the* `Process` *method.*

> **NOTE** *LINQ is explained in Chapter 13, "Language Integrated Query."*

Next create the first row in the table. This row contains a `tr` element as a child of the `table` element, and it contains `td` elements for every property. To get all the property names, you invoke the `First` method to retrieve the first object of the collection. You access the properties of this instance using reflection, invoking the `GetProperties` method on the `Type` object, and writing the name of the property to the inner text of the `th` HTML element:

```
    // etc.
    var tr = new TagBuilder("tr");
    var heading = Items.First();
    PropertyInfo[] properties = heading.GetType().GetProperties();
    foreach (var prop in properties)
    {
      var th = new TagBuilder("th");
      th.InnerHtml.Append(prop.Name);
      th.InnerHtml.AppendHtml(th);
    }
    table.InnerHtml.AppendHtml(tr);
    // etc.
```

> **NOTE** *Reflection is explained in Chapter 16.*

The final part of the `Process` method iterates through all items of the collection and creates more rows (`tr`) for every item. With every property, a `td` element is added, and the value of the property is written as inner text. Last, the inner HTML code of the created `table` element is written to the output:

```
foreach (var item in Items)
{
  tr = new TagBuilder("tr");
  foreach (var prop in properties)
  {
    var td = new TagBuilder("td");
    td.InnerHtml.Append(prop.GetValue(item).ToString());
    td.InnerHtml.AppendHtml(td);
  }
  table.InnerHtml.AppendHtml(tr);
}
output.Content.Append(table.InnerHtml);
```

After you've created the Tag Helper, creating the view becomes very simple. After you've defined the model, you reference the Tag Helper with `addTagHelper` passing the assembly name. The Tag Helper itself is instantiated when you define an HTML `table` with the attribute `items` (code file `MVCSampleApp/Views/TagHelpers/CustomHelper.cshtml`):

```
@model IEnumerable<Menu>
@addTagHelper "*, MVCSampleApp"

<table items="Model" class="sample"></table>
```

When you run the application, the table you see should look like the one shown in Figure 41-12. After you've created the Tag Helper, it is really easy to use. All the formatting that is defined using CSS still applies as all the attributes of the defined HTML table are still in the resulting HTML output.

FIGURE 41-12

IMPLEMENTING ACTION FILTERS

ASP.NET MVC is extensible in many areas. For example, you can implement a controller factory to search and instantiate a controller (interface `IControllerFactory`). Controllers implement the `IController` interface. Finding action methods in a controller is resolved by using the `IActionInvoker` interface. You can use attribute classes derived from `ActionMethodSelectorAttribute` to define the HTTP methods allowed. The model binder that maps the HTTP request to parameters can be customized by implementing the `IModelBinder` interface. The section "Model Binder" uses the `FormCollectionModelBinder` type. You can use different view engines that implement the interface `IViewEngine`. This chapter uses the Razor view engine. You can also customize by using HTML Helpers, Tag Helpers, and action filters. Most of the extension points are out of the scope of this book, but action filters are likely ones that you will implement or use, and thus these are covered here.

Action filters are called before and after an action is executed. They are assigned to controllers or action methods of controllers using attributes. Action filters are implemented by creating a class that derives from the base class `ActionFilterAttribute`. With this class, the base class members `OnActionExecuting`, `OnActionExecuted`, `OnResultExecuting`, and `OnResultExecuted` can be overridden. `OnActionExecuting` is called before the action method is invoked, and `OnActionExecuted` is called when the action method is completed. After that, before the result is returned, the method `OnResultExecuting` is invoked, and finally `OnResultExecuted` is invoked.

Within these methods, you can access the `Request` object to retrieve information of the caller. Using the `Request` object you can decide some actions depending on the browser, you can access routing information, you can change the view result dynamically, and so on. The code snippet accesses the variable language from routing information. To add this variable to the route, you can change the route as described earlier in this chapter in the section "Defining Routes." By adding a `language` variable with the route information, you can access the value supplied with the URL using `RouteData.Values` as shown in the following code snippet. You can use the retrieved value to change the culture for the user:

```
public class LanguageAttribute : ActionFilterAttribute
{
  private string _language = null;
  public override void OnActionExecuting(ActionExecutingContext filterContext)
  {
    _language = filterContext.RouteData.Values["language"] == null ?
      null : filterContext.RouteData.Values["language"].ToString();
    //…
  }
  public override void OnResultExecuting(ResultExecutingContext filterContext)
  {
  }
}
```

> **NOTE** *Globalization and localization, setting cultures, and other regional specifics are explained in Chapter 28, "Localization."*

With the created action filter attribute class, you can apply the attribute to a controller as shown in the following code snippet. Using the attribute with the class, the members of the attribute class are invoked with every action method. Instead, you can also apply the attribute to an action method, so the members are invoked only when the action method is called:

```
[Language]
public class HomeController : Controller
{
```

The `ActionFilterAttribute` implements several interfaces: `IActionFilter`, `IAsyncActionFilter`, `IResultFilter`, `IAsyncResultFilter`, `IFilter`, and `IOrderedFilter`.

ASP.NET MVC includes some predefined action filters, such as a filter to require HTTPS, authorize callers, handle errors, or cache data.

Using the attribute `Authorize` is covered later in this chapter in the section "Authentication and Authorization."

CREATING A DATA-DRIVEN APPLICATION

Now that you've read about all the foundations of ASP.NET MVC, it's time to look into a data-driven application that uses the ADO.NET Entity Framework. Here you can see features offered by ASP.NET MVC in combination with data access.

> **NOTE** *The ADO.NET Entity Framework is covered in detail in Chapter 38, "Entity Framework Core."*

The sample application `MenuPlanner` is used to maintain restaurant menu entries in a database. Only an authenticated account may perform maintenance of the database entries. Browsing menus should be possible for non-authenticated users.

This project is started by using the ASP.NET Core 1.0 Web Application template. For the authentication, you use the default selection of Individual User Accounts. This project template adds several folders for ASP.NET MVC and controllers, including a `HomeController` and `AccountController`. It also adds several script libraries.

Defining a Model

Start by defining a model within the `Models` directory. You create the model using the ADO.NET Entity Framework. The `MenuCard` type defines some properties and a relation to a list of menus (code file `MenuPlanner/Models/MenuCard.cs`):

```
public class MenuCard
{
  public int Id { get; set; }
  [MaxLength(50)]
  public string Name { get; set; }
  public bool Active { get; set; }
  public int Order { get; set; }
  public virtual List<Menu> Menus { get; set; }
}
```

The menu types that are referenced from the `MenuCard` are defined by the `Menu` class (code file `MenuPlanner/Models/Menu.cs`):

```
public class Menu
{
  public int Id { get; set; }
  public string Text { get; set; }
  public decimal Price { get; set; }
  public bool Active { get; set; }
  public int Order { get; set; }
  public string Type { get; set; }
  public DateTime Day { get; set; }
  public int MenuCardId { get; set; }
  public virtual MenuCard MenuCard { get; set; }
}
```

The connection to the database, and the sets of both `Menu` and `MenuCard` types, are managed by `MenuCardsContext`. Using `ModelBuilder`, the context specifies that the `Text` property of the `Menu` type may not be null, and it has a maximum length of 50 (code file `MenuPlanner/Models/MenuCardsContext.cs`):

```
public class MenuCardsContext : DbContext
{
  public DbSet<Menu> Menus { get; set; }
  public DbSet<MenuCard> MenuCards { get; set; }
```

```
      protected override void OnModelCreating(ModelBuilder modelBuilder)
      {
        modelBuilder.Entity<Menu>().Property(p => p.Text)
          .HasMaxLength(50).IsRequired();
        base.OnModelCreating(modelBuilder);
      }
    }
```

The startup code for the web application defines `MenuCardsContext` to be used as data context, and reads the connection string from the configuration file (code file `MenuPlanner/Startup.cs`):

```
    public IConfiguration Configuration { get; set; }

    public void ConfigureServices(IServiceCollection services)
    {
      // Add Entity Framework services to the services container.
      services.AddEntityFramework()
              .AddSqlServer()
              .AddDbContext<ApplicationDbContext>(options =>
                  options.UseSqlServer(
                    Configuration["Data:DefaultConnection:ConnectionString"]))
              .AddDbContext<MenuCardsContext>(options =>
                  options.UseSqlServer(
                    Configuration["Data:MenuCardConnection:ConnectionString"]));

      // etc.
    }
```

With the configuration file, the `MenuCardConnection` connection string is added. This connection string references the SQL instance that comes with Visual Studio 2015. Of course, you can change this and also add a connection string to SQL Azure (code file `MenuPlanner/appsettings.json`):

```
    {
      "Data": {
        "DefaultConnection": {
          "ConnectionString": "Server=(localdb)\\mssqllocaldb;
            Database=aspnet5-MenuPlanner-4d3d9092-b53f-4162-8627-f360ef6b2aa8;
            Trusted_Connection=True;MultipleActiveResultSets=true"
        },
        "MenuCardConnection": {
          "ConnectionString": "Server=(localdb)\\mssqllocaldb;Database=MenuCards;
            Trusted_Connection=True;MultipleActiveResultSets=true"
        }
      },
      // etc.
    }
```

Creating a Database

You can use Entity Framework commands to create the code to create the database. With a command-line prompt, you use the .NET Core Command Line (CLI) and the `ef` command to create code to create the database automatically. Using the command prompt, you must set the current folder to the directory where the `project.json` file is located:

```
    >dotnet ef migrations add InitMenuCards --context MenuCardsContext
```

> **NOTE** *The dotnet tools are discussed in Chapter 1, ".NET Application Architectures", and Chapter 17, "Visual Studio 2015."*

Because multiple data contexts (the `MenuCardsContext` and the `ApplicationDbContext`) are defined with the project, you need to specify the data context with the `--context` option. The `ef` command creates a `Migrations` folder within the project structure and the `InitMenuCards` class with an `Up` method to create the database tables, and the `Down` method to delete the changes again (code file MenuPlanner/Migrations/[date]InitMenuCards.cs):

```
public partial class InitMenuCards : Migration
{
  public override void Up(MigrationBuilder migrationBuilder)
  {
    migrationBuilder.CreateTable(
      name: "MenuCard",
      columns: table => new
      {
        Id = table.Column<int>(nullable: false)
          .Annotation("SqlServer:ValueGenerationStrategy",
            SqlServerValueGenerationStrategy.IdentityColumn),
        Active = table.Column<bool>(nullable: false),
        Name = table.Column<string>(nullable: true),
        Order = table.Column<int>(nullable: false)
      },
      constraints: table =>
      {
        table.PrimaryKey("PK_MenuCard", x => x.Id);
      });
    migrationBuilder.CreateTable(
      name: "Menu",
      columns: table => new
      {
        Id = table.Column<int>(nullable: false)
          .Annotation("SqlServer:ValueGenerationStrategy",
            SqlServerValueGenerationStrategy.IdentityColumn),
        Active = table.Column<bool>(nullable: false),
        Day = table.Column<DateTime>(nullable: false),
        MenuCardId = table.Column<int>(nullable: false),
        Order = table.Column<int>(nullable: false),
        Price = table.Column<decimal>(nullable: false),
        Text = table.Column<string>(nullable: false),
        Type = table.Column<string>(nullable: true)
      },
      constraints: table =>
      {
        table.PrimaryKey("PK_Menu", x => x.Id);
        table.ForeignKey(
          name: "FK_Menu_MenuCard_MenuCardId",
          column: x => x.MenuCardId,
          principalTable: "MenuCard",
          principalColumn: "Id",
          onDelete: RefeerentialAction.Cascade);
      });
  }
  public override void Down(MigrationBuilder migration)
  {
    migration.DropTable("Menu");
    migration.DropTable("MenuCard");
  }
}
```

Now you just need some code to start the migration process, filling the database with initial sample data. The `MenuCardDatabaseInitializer` applies the migration process by invoking the extension method `MigrateAsync` on the `DatabaseFacade` object that is returned from the `Database` property. This in turn checks whether the database associated with the connection string already has the same version as the database specified with the migrations. If it doesn't have the same version, required Up methods are invoked to get to the same version. In addition to that, a few MenuCard objects are created to have them stored in the database (code file MenuPlanner/Models/MenuCardDatabaseInitializer.cs):

```
using Microsoft.EntityFrameworkCore;
using System.Linq;
using System.Threading.Tasks;

namespace MenuPlanner.Models
{
  public class MenuCardDatabaseInitializer
  {
    private static bool _databaseChecked = false;

    public MenuCardDatabaseInitializer(MenuCardsContext context)
    {
      _context = context;
    }
    private MenuCardsContext _context;

    public async Task CreateAndSeedDatabaseAsync()
    {
      if (!_databaseChecked)
      {
        _databaseChecked = true;

        await _context.Database.MigrateAsync();

        if (_context.MenuCards.Count() == 0)
        {
          _context.MenuCards.Add(
            new MenuCard { Name = "Breakfast", Active = true, Order = 1 });
          _context.MenuCards.Add(
            new MenuCard { Name = "Vegetarian", Active = true, Order = 2 });
          _context.MenuCards.Add(
            new MenuCard { Name = "Steaks", Active = true, Order = 3 });
        }

        await _context.SaveChangesAsync();
      }
    }
  }
}
```

With the database and model in place, you can create a service.

Creating a Service

Before creating the service, you create the interface IMenuCardsService that defines all the methods that are needed by the service (code file MenuPlanner/Services/IMenuCardsService.cs):

```
using MenuPlanner.Models;
using System.Collections.Generic;
using System.Threading.Tasks;

namespace MenuPlanner.Services
{
  public interface IMenuCardsService
  {
    Task AddMenuAsync(Menu menu);
    Task DeleteMenuAsync(int id);
```

```
        Task<Menu> GetMenuByIdAsync(int id);
        Task<IEnumerable<Menu>> GetMenusAsync();
        Task<IEnumerable<MenuCard>> GetMenuCardsAsync();
        Task UpdateMenuAsync(Menu menu);
    }
}
```

The service class `MenuCardsService` implements the methods to return menus and menu cards, and it creates, updates, and deletes menus (code file `MenuPlanner/Services/MenuCardsService.cs`):

```
using MenuPlanner.Models;
using Microsoft.EntityFrameworkCore;
using System.Collections.Generic;
using System.Linq;
using System.Threading.Tasks;

namespace MenuPlanner.Services
{
  public class MenuCardsService : IMenuCardsService
  {
    private MenuCardsContext _menuCardsContext;
    public MenuCardsService(MenuCardsContext menuCardsContext)
    {
      _menuCardsContext = menuCardsContext;
    }

    public async Task<IEnumerable<Menu>> GetMenusAsync()
    {
      await EnsureDatabaseCreated();

      var menus = _menuCardsContext.Menus.Include(m => m.MenuCard);
      return await menus.ToArrayAsync();
    }

    public async Task<IEnumerable<MenuCard>> GetMenuCardsAsync()
    {
      await EnsureDatabaseCreated();

      var menuCards = _menuCardsContext.MenuCards;
      return await menuCards.ToArrayAsync();
    }

    public async Task<Menu> GetMenuByIdAsync(int id)
    {
      return await _menuCardsContext.Menus.SingleOrDefaultAsync(
        m => m.Id == id);
    }

    public async Task AddMenuAsync(Menu menu)
    {
      _menuCardsContext.Menus.Add(menu);
      await _menuCardsContext.SaveChangesAsync();
    }

    public async Task UpdateMenuAsync(Menu menu)
    {
      _menuCardsContext.Entry(menu).State = EntityState.Modified;
      await _menuCardsContext.SaveChangesAsync();
    }

    public async Task DeleteMenuAsync(int id)
    {
      Menu menu = _menuCardsContext.Menus.Single(m => m.Id == id);
```

```
        _menuCardsContext.Menus.Remove(menu);
        await _menuCardsContext.SaveChangesAsync();
    }

    private async Task EnsureDatabaseCreated()
    {
        var init = new MenuCardDatabaseInitializer(_menuCardsContext);
        await init.CreateAndSeedDatabaseAsync();
    }
  }
}
```

To have the service available via dependency injection, the service is registered in the service collection using the `AddScoped` method (code file `MenuPlanner/Startup.cs`):

```
public void ConfigureServices(IServiceCollection services)
{
    // etc.
    services.AddScoped<IMenuCardsService, MenuCardsService>();
    // etc.
}
```

Creating a Controller

ASP.NET MVC offers scaffolding to create controllers for directly accessing the database. You can do this by selecting the Controllers folder in Solution Explorer, and from the context menu select Add ⇨ Controller. The Add Scaffold dialog opens. From the Add Scaffold dialog, you can select MVC 6 Controller views, using Entity Framework. Clicking the Add button opens the Add Controller dialog shown in Figure 41-13. With this dialog, you can select the Menu model class and the Entity Framework data context `MenuCardsContext`, configure to generate views, and give the controller a name. Create the controller with the views to look at the generated code including the views.

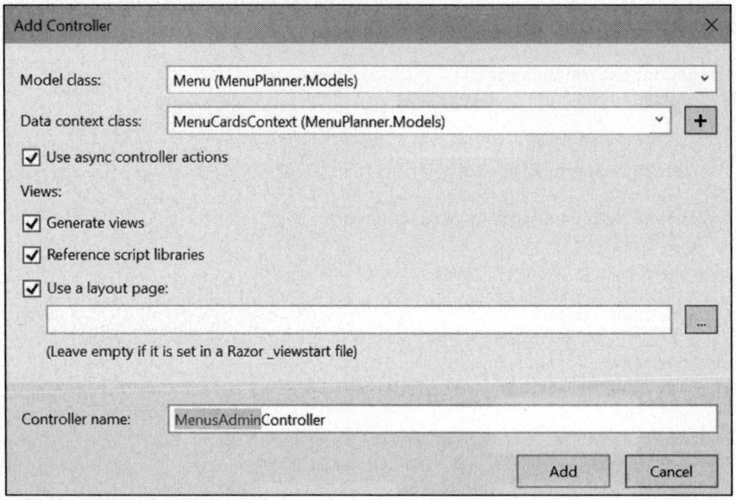

FIGURE 41-13

The book sample doesn't use the data context directly from the controller but puts a service in between. Doing it this way offers more flexibility. You can use the service from different controllers and also use the service from a service such as ASP.NET Web API.

NOTE *ASP.NET Web API is discussed in Chapter 42.*

With the following sample code, the ASP.NET MVC controller injects the menu card service via constructor injection (code file `MenuPlanner/Controllers/MenuAdminController.cs`):

```
public class MenuAdminController : Controller
{
  private readonly IMenuCardsService _service;
  public MenuAdminController(IMenuCardsService service)
  {
    _service = service;
  }
  // etc.
}
```

The `Index` method is the default method that is invoked when only the controller is referenced with the URL without passing an action method. Here, all `Menu` items from the database are created and passed to the `Index` view. The `Details` method returns the `Details` view passing the menu found from the service. Pay attention to the error handling. When no ID is passed to the `Details` method, an HTTP Bad Request (400 error response) is returned using the `HttpBadRequest` method from the base class. When the menu ID is not found in the database, an HTTP Not Found (404 error response) is returned via the `HttpNotFound` method:

```
public async Task<IActionResult> Index()
{
  return View(await _service.GetMenusAsync());
}

public async Task<IActionResult> Details(int? id = 0)
{
  if (id == null)
  {
    return HttpBadRequest();
  }
  Menu menu = await _service.GetMenuByIdAsync(id.Value);
  if (menu == null)
  {
    return HttpNotFound();
  }
  return View(menu);
}
```

When the user creates a new menu, the first `Create` method is invoked after an HTTP GET request from the client. With this method, `ViewBag` information is passed to the view. This `ViewBag` contains information about the menu cards in a `SelectList`. The `SelectList` allows the user to select an item. Because the `MenuCard` collection is passed to the `SelectList`, the user can select a menu card with the newly created menu.

```
public async Task<IActionResult> Create()
{
  IEnumerable<MenuCard> cards = await _service.GetMenuCardsAsync();
  ViewBag.MenuCardId = new SelectList(cards, "Id", "Name");
  return View();
}
```

NOTE *To use the* `SelectList` *type, you must add the NuGet package* `Microsoft.AspNet.Mvc.ViewFeatures` *to the project.*

After the user fills out the form and submits the form with the new menu to the server, the second `Create` method is invoked from an HTTP POST request. This method uses model binding to pass the form data to the `Menu` object and adds the `Menu` object to the data context to write the newly created menu to the database:

```
[HttpPost]
[ValidateAntiForgeryToken]
public async Task<ActionResult> Create(
  [Bind("Id","MenuCardId", "Text", "Price", "Active", "Order", "Type", "Day")]
  Menu menu)
{
  if (ModelState.IsValid)
  {
    await _service.AddMenuAsync(menu);
    return RedirectToAction("Index");
  }

  IEnumerable<MenuCard> cards = await _service.GetMenuCardsAsync();
  ViewBag.MenuCards = new SelectList(cards, "Id", "Name");
  return View(menu);
}
```

To edit a menu card, two action methods named `Edit` are defined—one for a GET request, and one for a POST request. The first `Edit` method returns a single menu item; the second one invokes the `UpdateMenuAsync` method of the service after the model binding is done successfully:

```
public async Task<IActionResult> Edit(int? id)
{
  if (id == null)
  {
    return HttpBadRequest();
  }

  Menu menu = await _service.GetMenuByIdAsync(id.Value);
  if (menu == null)
  {
    return HttpNotFound();
  }

  IEnumerable<MenuCard> cards = await _service.GetMenuCardsAsync();
  ViewBag.MenuCards = new SelectList(cards, "Id", "Name", menu.MenuCardId);
  return View(menu);
}

[HttpPost]
[ValidateAntiForgeryToken]
public async Task<IActionResult> Edit(
    [Bind("Id", "MenuCardId", "Text", "Price", "Order", "Type", "Day")]
    Menu menu)
{
  if (ModelState.IsValid)
  {
    await _service.UpdateMenuAsync(menu);
    return RedirectToAction("Index");
  }

  IEnumerable<MenuCard> cards = await _service.GetMenuCardsAsync();
  ViewBag.MenuCards = new SelectList(cards, "Id", "Name", menu.MenuCardId);
  return View(menu);
}
```

The last part of the implementation of the controller includes the `Delete` methods. Because both methods have the same parameter—which is not possible with C#—the second method has the name

`DeleteConfirmed`. However, the second method can be accessed from the same URL Link as the first `Delete` method, but the second method is accessed with HTTP POST instead of GET using the `ActionName` attribute. This method invokes the `DeleteMenuAsync` method of the service:

```
public async Task<IActionResult> Delete(int? id)
{
  if (id == null)
  {
    return HttpBadRequest();
  }
  Menu menu = await _service.GetMenuByIdAsync(id.Value);
  if (menu == null)
  {
    return HttpNotFound();
  }
  return View(menu);
}

[HttpPost, ActionName("Delete")]
[ValidateAntiForgeryToken]
public async Task<IActionResult> DeleteConfirmed(int id)
{
  Menu menu = await _service.GetMenuByIdAsync(id);
  await _service.DeleteMenuAsync(menu.Id);
  return RedirectToAction("Index");
}
```

Creating Views

Now it's time to create views. The views are created within the folder `Views/MenuAdmin`. You can create the view by selecting the `MenuAdmin` folder in Solution Explorer and select Add ⇨ View from the context menu. This opens the Add View dialog as shown in Figure 41-14. With this dialog you can choose List, Details, Create, Edit, Delete templates, which arrange HTML elements accordingly. The Model class you select with this dialog defines the model that the view is based on.

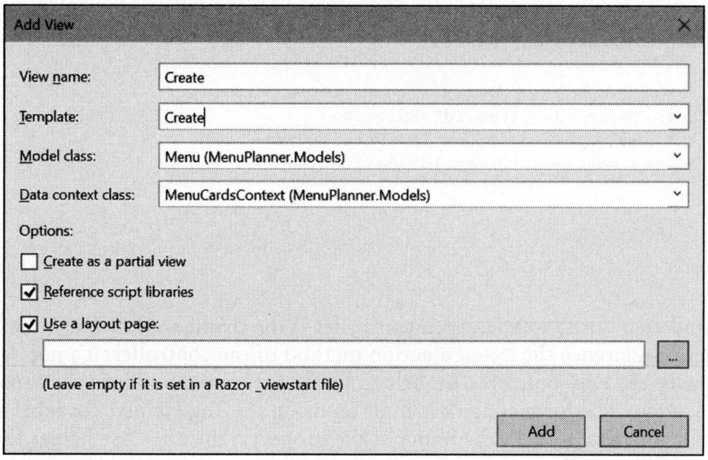

FIGURE 41-14

The `Index` view, which defines an HTML table, has a `Menu` collection as its model. For the header elements of the table, the HTML element label with a Tag Helper `asp-for` is used to access property names for display. For displaying the items, the menu collection is iterated using `@foreach`, and every property value is accessed with a Tag Helper for the input element. A Tag Helper for the anchor element creates links for the Edit, Details, and Delete pages (code file MenuPlanner/Views/MenuAdmin/Index.cshtml):

```
@model IList<MenuPlanner.Models.Menu>
@{
    ViewBag.Title = "Index";
}
<h2>@ViewBag.Title</h2>
<p>
    <a asp-action="Create">Create New</a>
</p>
@if (Model.Count() > 0)
{
  <table>
    <tr>
      <th>
        <label asp-for="@Model[0].MenuCard.Item"></label>
      </th>
      <th>
        <label asp-for="@Model[0].Text"></label>
      </th>
      <th>
        <label asp-for="Model[0].Day"></label>
      </th>
    </tr>
    @foreach (var item in Model)
    {
      <tr>
        <td>
          <input asp-for="@item.MenuCard.Name" readonly="readonly"
            disabled="disabled" />
        </td>
        <td>
          <input asp-for="@item.Text" readonly="readonly"
            disabled="disabled" />
        </td>
        <td>
          <input asp-for="@item.Day" asp-format="{0:yyyy-MM-dd}"
            readonly="readonly" disabled="disabled" />
        </td>
        <td>
          <a asp-action="Edit" asp-route-id="@item.Id">Edit</a>
          <a asp-action="Details" asp-route-id="@item.Id">Details</a>
          <a asp-action="Delete" asp-route-id="@item.Id">Delete</a>
        </td>
      </tr>
    }
  </table>
}
```

In the MenuPlanner project, the second view for the MenuAdmin controller is the Create view. The HTML form uses the asp-action Tag Helper to reference the Create action method of the controller. It's not necessary to reference the controller with the asp-controller helper, as the action method is in the same controller where the view was coming from. The form content is built up using the Tag Helpers for label and input elements. The asp-for helper for the label returns the name of the property; the asp-for helper for the input element returns the value (code file MenuPlanner/Views/MenuAdmin/Create.cshtml):

```
@model MenuPlanner.Models.Menu
@{
  ViewBag.Title = "Create";
}

<h2>@ViewBag.Title</h2>
```

```
<form asp-action="Create" method="post">
  <div class="form-horizontal">
    <h4>Menu</h4>
    <hr />
    <div asp-validation-summary="ValidationSummary.All" style="color:blue"
      id="FileName_validation_day" class="form-group">
      <span style="color:red">Some error occurred</span>
    </div>

    <div class="form-group">
      <label asp-for="@Model.MenuCardId" class="control-label col-md2"></label>
      <div class="col-md-10">
        <select asp-for="@(Model.MenuCardId)"
          asp-items="@((IEnumerable<SelectListItem>)ViewBag.MenuCards)"
          size="2" class="form-control">
          <option value="" selected="selected">Select a menu card</option>
        </select>
      </div>
    </div>
    <div class="form-group">
      <label asp-for="Text" class="control-label col-md-2"></label>
      <div class="col-md-10">
        <input asp-for="Text" />
      </div>
    </div>
    <div class="form-group">
      <label asp-for="Price" class="control-label col-md-2"></label>
      <div class="col-md-10">
        <input asp-for="Price" />
        <span asp-validation-for="Price">Price of the menu</span>
      </div>
    </div>
    <div class="form-group">
      <label asp-for="Day" class="control-label col-md-2"></label>
      <div class="col-md-10">
        <input asp-for="Day" />
        <span asp-validation-for="Day">Date of the menu</span>
      </div>
    </div>
    <div class="form-group">
      <div class="col-md-offset-2 col-md-10">
        <input type="submit" value="Create" class="btn btn-default" />
      </div>
    </div>
  </div>
</form>
<a asp-action="Index">Back</a>
```

The other views are created similarly to the views shown here, so they are not covered in this book. Just get the views from the downloadable code.

You can now use the application to add and edit menus to existing menu cards.

IMPLEMENTING AUTHENTICATION AND AUTHORIZATION

Authentication and authorization are important aspects of web applications. If a website or parts of it should not be public, users must be authorized. For authentication of users, different options are available when creating an ASP.NET Web Application (see Figure 41-15): No Authentication, Individual User Accounts, and Work and School Accounts. The Windows Authentication selection is not available for ASP. NET Core 5.

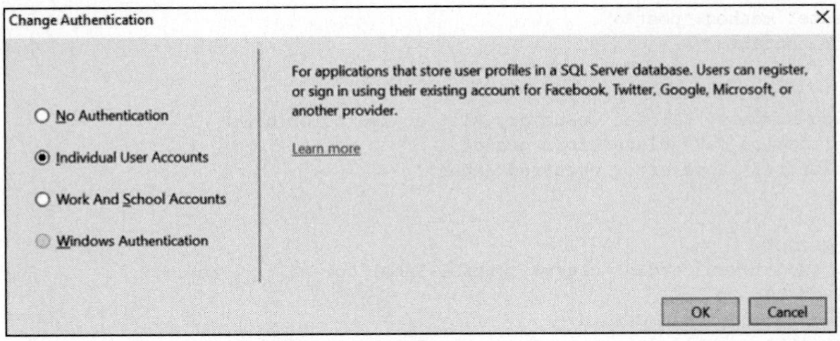

FIGURE 41-15

With Work and School Accounts, you can select an Active Directory from the cloud to do the authentication.

Using Individual User Accounts, you can store user profiles within an SQL Server database. Users can register and log in, and they also can use existing accounts from Facebook, Twitter, Google, or Microsoft.

Storing and Retrieving User Information

For user management, user information needs to be added to a store. The type `IdentityUser` (namespace `Microsoft.AspNet.Identity.EntityFramework`) defines a name and lists roles, logins, and claims. The Visual Studio template that you've used to create the `MenuPlanner` application created some noticeable code to save the user: the class `ApplicationUser` that is part of the project derives from the base class `IdentityUser` (namespace `Microsoft.AspNet.Identity.EntityFramework`). The `ApplicationUser` is empty by default, but you can add information you need from the user, and the information will be stored in the database (code file `MenuPlanner/Models/IdentityModels.cs`):

```
public class ApplicationUser : IdentityUser
{
}
```

The connection to the database is made via the `IdentityDbContext<TUser>` type. This is a generic class that derives from `DbContext` and thus makes use of the Entity Framework. The `IdentityDbContext<TUser>` type defines properties `Roles` and `Users` of type `IDbSet<TEntity>`. The `IDbSet<TEntity>` type defines the mapping to the database tables. For convenience, the `ApplicationDbContext` is created to define the `ApplicationUser` type as the generic type for the `IdentityDbContext` class:

```
public class ApplicationDbContext : IdentityDbContext<ApplicationUser>
{
  protected override void OnModelCreating(ModelBuilder builder)
  {
    base.OnModelCreating(builder);
  }
}
```

Starting Up the Identity System

The connection to the database is registered with the dependency injection service collection in the startup code. Similar to the `MenuCardsContext` that you created earlier, the `ApplicationDbContext` is configured to use SQL Server with a connection string from the `config` file. The identity service itself is registered using the extension method `AddIdentity`. The `AddIdentity` method maps the type of the user and role classes that are used by the identity service. The class `ApplicationUser` is the previously mentioned class that derives from `IdentityUser`; `IdentityRole` is a string-based role class that derives from `IdentityRole<string>`. An overloaded method of the `AddIdentity` method allows you to configure the identity system with two-factor authentication; e-mail token providers; user options, such as requiring unique e-mails; or a regular expression that requires a username to match. `AddIdentity` returns an `IdentityBuilder` that allows additional configurations for the identity system, such as the entity framework context that is used (`AddEntityFrameworkStores`), and the token providers (`AddDefaultTokenProviders`). Other providers that can be added are for errors, password validators, role managers, user managers, and user validators (code file `MenuPlanner/Startup.cs`):

```
public void ConfigureServices(IServiceCollection services)
{
  services.AddEntityFramework()
    .AddSqlServer()
    .AddDbContext<ApplicationDbContext>(options =>
      options.UseSqlServer(
        Configuration["Data:DefaultConnection:ConnectionString"]))
    .AddDbContext<MenuCardsContext>(options =>
      options.UseSqlServer(
        Configuration["Data:MenuCardConnection:ConnectionString"]));

  services.AddIdentity<ApplicationUser, IdentityRole>()
    .AddEntityFrameworkStores<ApplicationDbContext>()
    .AddDefaultTokenProviders();

  services.Configure<FacebookAuthenticationOptions>(options =>
  {
    options.AppId = Configuration["Authentication:Facebook:AppId"];
    options.AppSecret = Configuration["Authentication:Facebook:AppSecret"];
  });

  services.Configure<MicrosoftAccountAuthenticationOptions>(options =>
  {
    options.ClientId =
      Configuration["Authentication:MicrosoftAccount:ClientId"];
    options.ClientSecret =
      Configuration["Authentication:MicrosoftAccount:ClientSecret"];
  });

  // etc.
}
```

Performing User Registration

Now let's step into the generated code for registering and logging in the user. The heart of the functionality is within the `AccountController` class. The controller class has the `Authorize` attribute applied, which restricts all action methods to authenticated users. The constructor receives a user manager, sign-in manager, and database context via dependency injection. E-mail and SMS sender are used for two-factor authentication. In case you don't implement the empty `AuthMessageSender` class that is part of the generated code, you can remove the injection for `IEmailSender` and `ISmsSender` (code file `MenuPlanner/Controllers/AccountController.cs`):

```
[Authorize]
public class AccountController : Controller
{
  private readonly UserManager<ApplicationUser> _userManager;
  private readonly SignInManager<ApplicationUser> _signInManager;
  private readonly IEmailSender _emailSender;
  private readonly ISmsSender _smsSender;
  private readonly ApplicationDbContext _applicationDbContext;
  private static bool _databaseChecked;
```

```
    public AccountController(
      UserManager<ApplicationUser> userManager,
      SignInManager<ApplicationUser> signInManager,
      IEmailSender emailSender,
      ISmsSender smsSender,
      ApplicationDbContext applicationDbContext)
    {
      _userManager = userManager;
      _signInManager = signInManager;
      _emailSender = emailSender;
      _smsSender = smsSender;
      _applicationDbContext = applicationDbContext;
    }
```

To register a user, you define `RegisterViewModel`. This model defines what data the user needs to enter on registration. From the generated code, this model only requires e-mail, password, and confirmation password (which must be the same as the password). In case you would like to get more information from the user, you can add properties as needed (code file MenuPlanner/Models/AccountViewModels.cs):

```
    public class RegisterViewModel
    {
      [Required]
      [EmailAddress]
      [Display(Name = "Email")]
      public string Email { get; set; }

      [Required]
      [StringLength(100, ErrorMessage =
        "The {0} must be at least {2} characters long.", MinimumLength = 6)]
      [DataType(DataType.Password)]
      [Display(Name = "Password")]
      public string Password { get; set; }

      [DataType(DataType.Password)]
      [Display(Name = "Confirm password")]
      [Compare("Password", ErrorMessage =
        "The password and confirmation password do not match.")]
      public string ConfirmPassword { get; set; }
    }
```

User registration must be possible for non-authenticated users. That's why the `AllowAnonymous` attribute is applied to the `Register` methods of the `AccountController`. This overrules the `Authorize` attribute for these methods. The HTTP POST variant of the Register method receives the `RegisterViewModel` object and writes an `ApplicationUser` to the database by calling the method `_userManager.CreateAsync`. After the user is created successfully, sign-in is done via `_signInManager.SignInAsync` (code file MenuPlanner/Controllers/AccountController.cs):

```
    [HttpGet]
    [AllowAnonymous]
    public IActionResult Register()
    {
      return View();
    }

    [HttpPost]
    [AllowAnonymous]
    [ValidateAntiForgeryToken]
    public async Task<IActionResult> Register(RegisterViewModel model)
    {
      EnsureDatabaseCreated(_applicationDbContext);
      if (ModelState.IsValid)
      {
```

```
        var user = new ApplicationUser
        {
          UserName = model.Email,
          Email = model.Email
        };
        var result = await _userManager.CreateAsync(user, model.Password);
        if (result.Succeeded)
        {
          await _signInManager.SignInAsync(user, isPersistent: false);
          return RedirectToAction(nameof(HomeController.Index), "Home");
        }
        AddErrors(result);
      }

      // If we got this far, something failed, redisplay form
      return View(model);
    }
```

Now the view (code file `MenuPlanner/Views/Account/Register.cshtml`) just needs information from the user. Figure 41-16 shows the dialog that asks the user for information.

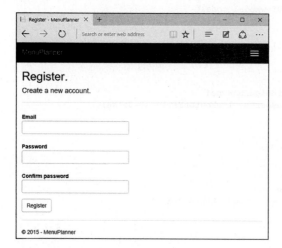

FIGURE 41-16

Setting Up User Login

When the user registers, a login occurs directly after the successful registration is completed. The `LoginViewModel` model defines `UserName`, `Password`, and `RememberMe` properties—all the information the user is asked with the login. This model has some annotations used with HTML Helpers (code file `MenuPlanner/Models/AccountViewModels.cs`):

```
public class LoginViewModel
{
  [Required]
  [EmailAddress]
  public string Email { get; set; }

  [Required]
  [DataType(DataType.Password)]
  public string Password { get; set; }

  [Display(Name = "Remember me?")]
```

```
    public bool RememberMe { get; set; }
}
```

To log in a user that is already registered, you need to call the `Login` method of the `AccountController`. After the user enters login information, the sign-in manager is used to validate login information with `PasswordSignInAsync`. If login is successful, the user is redirected to the original requested page. If login fails, the same view is returned to give the user one more option to enter the username and password correctly (code file `MenuPlanner/Controllers/AccountController.cs`):

```csharp
[HttpGet]
[AllowAnonymous]
public IActionResult Login(string returnUrl = null)
{
  ViewData["ReturnUrl"] = returnUrl;
  return View();
}

[HttpPost]
[AllowAnonymous]
[ValidateAntiForgeryToken]
public async Task<IActionResult> Login(LoginViewModel model,
  string returnUrl = null)
{
  EnsureDatabaseCreated(_applicationDbContext);
  ViewData["ReturnUrl"] = returnUrl;
  if (ModelState.IsValid)
  {
    var result = await _signInManager.PasswordSignInAsync(
      model.Email, model.Password, model.RememberMe, lockoutOnFailure: false);
    if (result.Succeeded)
    {
      return RedirectToLocal(returnUrl);
    }
    if (result.RequiresTwoFactor)
    {
      return RedirectToAction(nameof(SendCode),
        new { ReturnUrl = returnUrl, RememberMe = model.RememberMe });
    }
    if (result.IsLockedOut)
    {
      return View("Lockout");
    }
    else
    {
      ModelState.AddModelError(string.Empty, "Invalid login attempt.");
      return View(model);
    }
  }
  return View(model);
}
```

Authenticating Users

With the authentication infrastructure in place, it's easy to require user authentication by annotating the controller or action methods with the `Authorize` attribute. Applying this attribute to the class requires the role for every action method of the class. If there are different authorization requirements on different action methods, the `Authorize` attribute can also be applied to the action methods. With this attribute, it is verified if the caller is already authorized (by checking the authorization cookie). If the caller is not yet authorized, a 401 HTTP status code is returned with a redirect to the login action.

Applying the attribute `Authorize` without setting parameters requires users to be authenticated. To have more control you can define that only specific user roles are allowed to access the action methods by assigning roles to the `Roles` property as shown in the following code snippet:

```
[Authorize(Roles="Menu Admins")]
public class MenuAdminController : Controller
{
```

You can also access user information by using the `User` property of the `Controller` base class, which allows a more dynamic approval or deny of the user. For example, depending on parameter values passed, different roles are required.

> **NOTE** *You can read more information about user authentication and other information about security in Chapter 24, "Security."*

SUMMARY

In this chapter, you explored the latest web technology to make use of the ASP.NET MVC 6 framework. You saw how this provides a robust structure for you to work with, which is ideal for large-scale applications that require proper unit testing. You saw how easy it is to provide advanced capabilities with minimum effort, and how the logical structure and separation of functionality that this framework provides makes code easy to understand and easy to maintain.

The next chapter continues with ASP.NET Core but discusses communication with services in the form of the ASP.NET Web API.

42

ASP.NET Web API

WHAT'S IN THIS CHAPTER?

➤ Overview of the ASP.NET Web API
➤ Creating Web API controllers
➤ Using repositories with dependency injection
➤ Creating .NET clients calling REST APIs
➤ Using Entity Framework from services
➤ Creating Metadata using Swagger
➤ Using OData

WROX.COM CODE DOWNLOADS FOR THIS CHAPTER

The wrox.com code downloads for this chapter are found at www.wrox.com/go/
professionalcsharp6 on the Download Code tab. The code for this chapter is divided into the
following major examples:

➤ Book Service Sample
➤ Book Service Async Sample
➤ Book Service Client App
➤ Metadata Samples

OVERVIEW

When Windows Communication Foundation (WCF) was announced with .NET 3.0, it was *the* technology for communication and replaced several other technologies in the .NET stack (a few mentioned here are .NET Remoting and ASP.NET Web Services). The goal was to have one communication technology that is very flexible and fulfills all needs. However, WCF was initially based on SOAP (Simple Object Access Protocol). Nowadays we have many scenarios where the powerful SOAP enhancements are not needed. For simpler scenarios such as HTTP requests returning JSON, WCF is too complex. That's why another technology was introduced in 2012: ASP.NET Web API. With the release of ASP.NET MVC 6 and Visual Studio 2015, the third major version of ASP.NET Web API was released. ASP.NET MVC and ASP.NET Web API previously had different types and configurations (the previous versions were ASP.NET MVC 5 and ASP.NET Web API 2), but ASP.NET Web API is now part of ASP.NET MVC 6.

ASP.NET Web API offers a simple communication technology based on Representational State Transfer (REST). REST is an architecture style based on some constraints. Let's compare a service that is based on the REST architectural style with a service that makes use of SOAP to see these constraints.

Both REST services and services making use of the SOAP protocol make use of a client-server technology. SOAP services can be stateful or stateless; REST services are always stateless. SOAP defines its own message format with a header and body to select a method of the service. With REST, HTTP verbs such as GET, POST, PUT, and DELETE are used. GET is used to retrieve resources, POST to add new resources, PUT to update resources, and DELETE to delete resources.

This chapter takes you through a journey covering various important aspects of ASP.NET Web API—creating a service, using different routing methods, creating a client, using OData, securing the service, and using custom hosts.

> **NOTE** *SOAP and WCF are covered in Chapter 44, "Windows Communication Foundation."*

CREATING SERVICES

Let's start with creating a service. Using the new .NET Core framework, you need to start with an ASP.NET web application and select the ASP.NET Core 1.0 Template Web API (see Figure 42-1). This template adds folders and references needed with ASP.NET Web API. You can also use the template Web Application in case you need both web pages and services.

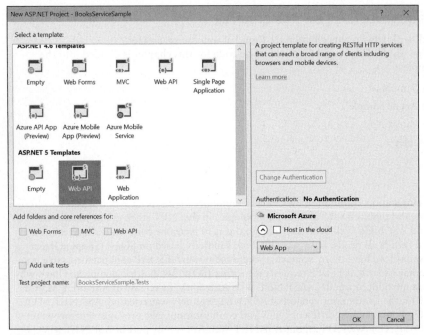

FIGURE 42-1

> **NOTE** *ASP.NET MVC is discussed in Chapter 41, "ASP.NET MVC," the core tech-nology that is the foundation of ASP.NET MVC in Chapter 40, "ASP.NET Core."*

The directory structure that is created with this template contains folders that are needed for creating the services. The Controllers directory contains the Web API controllers. You've seen such controllers already in Chapter 41, and indeed, ASP.NET Web API and ASP.NET MVC make use of the same infrastructure. This was not the case with previous versions.

The Models directory is for the data model. You can add your entity types to this directory, as well as repositories that return model types.

The service that is created returns a list of book chapters and allows adding and deleting chapters dynamically. The sample project that offers this service has the name BookServiceSample.

Defining a Model

First you need a type that represents the data to return and change. The class defined in the Models directory has the name BookChapter and includes simple properties to represent a chapter (code file BookServiceSample/Models/BookChapter.cs):

```
public class BookChapter
{
  public Guid Id { get; set; }
  public int Number { get; set; }
  public string Title { get; set; }
  public int Pages { get; set; }
}
```

Creating a Repository

Next, you create a repository. The methods offered by the repository are defined with the inter-face IBookChapterRepository—methods to retrieve, add, and update book chapters (code file BookServiceSample/Models/IBookChaptersRepository.cs):

```
public interface IBookChaptersRepository
{
  void Init();
  void Add(BookChapter bookChapter);
  IEnumerable<BookChapter> GetAll();
  BookChapter Find(Guid id);
  BookChapter Remove(Guid id);
  void Update(BookChapter bookChapter);
}
```

The implementation of the repository is defined by the class SampleBookChaptersRepository. The book chapters are kept in a collection class. Because multiple tasks from different client requests can access the collection concurrently, the type ConcurrentList is used for the book chapters. This class is thread safe. The Add, Remove, and Update methods make use of the collection to add, remove, and update book chapters (code file BookServiceSample/Models/SampleBookChapterRepository.cs):

```
public class SampleBookChaptersRepository: IBookChapterRepository
{
  private readonly ConcurrentDictionary<Guid, BookChapter> _chapters =
    new ConcurrentDictionary<Guid, BookChapter>();

  public void Init()
```

```
{
  Add(new BookChapter
  {
    Number = 1,
    Title = "Application Architectures",
    Pages = 35
  });
  Add(new BookChapter
  {
    Number = 2,
    Title = "Core C#",
    Pages = 42
  });
  // more chapters
}

public void Add(BookChapter chapter)
{
  chapter.Id = Guid.NewGuid();
  _chapters[chapter.Id] = chapter;
}

public BookChapter Find(Guid id)
{
  BookChapter chapter;
  _chapters.TryGetValue(id, out chapter);
  return chapter;
}

public IEnumerable<BookChapter> GetAll() => _chapters.Values;

public BookChapter Remove(Guid id)
{
  BookChapter removed;
  _chapters.TryRemove(id, out removed);
  return removed;
}

public void Update(BookChapter chapter)
{
  _chapters[chapter.Id] = chapter;
}
}
```

> **NOTE** *With the sample code, the* Remove *method makes sure that the* BookChapter *passed with the* id *parameter is not in the dictionary. If the dictionary already does not contain the book chapter, that's okay.*
>
> *An alternative implementation of the* Remove *method can throw an exception if the book chapter passed cannot be found.*

> **NOTE** *Concurrent collections are discussed in Chapter 12, "Special Collections."*

With the startup, the SampleBookChapterRepository is registered with the AddSingleton method of the dependency injection container to create just one instance for all clients requesting the service. In this code snippet, an overloaded method of `AddSingleton` is used that allows passing a previously created instance, which allows initializing the instance by invoking the `Init` method (code file `BookServiceSample/Startup.cs`):

```
public void ConfigureServices(IServiceCollection services)
{
  services.AddMvc();
  IBookChaptersRepository repos = new SampleBookChaptersRepository();
  repos.Init();
  services.AddSingleton<IBookChaptersRepository>(repos);

  // etc.
}
```

Creating a Controller

The ASP.NET Web API controller uses the repository. The controller can be created from the Solution Explorer context menu Add New Item ⇨ Web API Controller Class. The controller class to manage book chapters is named `BookChaptersController`. This class derives from the base class `Controller`. The route to the controller is defined with the `Route` attribute. The route starts with `api` followed by the name of the controller—which is the name of the controller class without the `Controller` postfix. The constructor of the `BooksChapterController` requires an object implementing the interface `IBookChapterRepository`. This object is injected via dependency injection (code file `BookServiceSample/Controllers/BookChaptersController.cs`):

```
[Route("api/[controller]")]
public class BookChaptersController: Controller
{
  private readonly IBookChapterRepository _repository;
  public BookChaptersController(IBookChapterRepository bookChapterRepository)
  {
    _repository = bookChapterRepository;
  }
}
```

The `Get` method that is created from the template is renamed and modified to return the complete collection of type `IEnumerable<BookChapter>`:

```
// GET api/bookchapters
[HttpGet]
public IEnumerable<BookChapter> GetBookChapters() => _repository.GetAll();
```

The `Get` method with a parameter is renamed to `GetBookChapterById` and filters the dictionary of the repository with the `Find` method. The parameter of the filter, `id`, is retrieved from the URL. The repository's `Find` method returns null if the chapter was not found. In this case, `NotFound` is returned. `NotFound` returns a 404 (not found) response. When the object is found, it is returned creating a new `ObjectResult`: The `ObjectResult` returns a status code 200 with the book chapter in the body:

```
// GET api/bookchapters/guid
[HttpGet("{id}", Name=nameof(GetBookChapterById))]
public IActionResult GetBookChapterById(Guid id)
{
  BookChapter chapter = _repository.Find(id);
  if (chapter == null)
  {
    return NotFound();
  }
  else
  {
    return new ObjectResult(chapter);
  }
}
```

> **NOTE** *Read Chapter 41 for information on defining routes.*

On adding a new book chapter, the method `PostBookChapter` is added. This method receives a `BookChapter` as part of the HTTP body that is assigned to the method parameter after deserialization. In case the parameter chapter is null, an `BadRequest` (HTTP error 400) is returned. Adding the `BookChapter`, this method returns `CreatedAtRoute`. `CreatedAtRoute` returns the HTTP status 201 (Created) with the object serialized. The returned header information contains a link to the resource—that is, a link to the `GetBookChapterById` with the `id` set to the identifier of the newly created object:

```
// POST api/bookchapters
[HttpPost]
public IActionResult PostBookChapter([FromBody]BookChapter chapter)
{
  if (chapter == null)
  {
    return BadRequest();
  }
  _repository.Add(chapter);
  return CreatedAtRoute(nameof(GetBookChapterById), new { id = chapter.Id },
    chapter);
}
```

Updating items is based on the HTTP PUT request. The `PutBookChapter` method updates an existing item from the collection. In case the object is not yet in the collection, `NotFound` is returned. If the object is found, it is updated, and a success result 204—no content with an empty body—is returned:

```
// PUT api/bookchapters/guid
[HttpPut("{id}")]
public IActionResult PutBookChapter(Guid id, [FromBody]BookChapter chapter)
{
  if (chapter == null || id != chapter.Id)
  {
    return BadRequest();
  }
  if (_repository.Find(id) == null)
  {
    return NotFound();
  }
  _repository.Update(chapter);
  return new NoContentResult();
}
```

With the HTTP DELETE request, book chapters are simply removed from the dictionary:

```
// DELETE api/bookchapters/5
[HttpDelete("{id}")]
public void Delete(Guid id)
{
  _repository.Remove(id);
}
```

With this controller in place, it is already possible to do first tests from the browser. Opening the link `http://localhost:5000/api/BookChapters` returns JSON.

Port 5000 is the default port number when using the Kestrel web server. You can select this server in the Debug section of the project properties (see Figure 42-2) by choosing the Web profile.

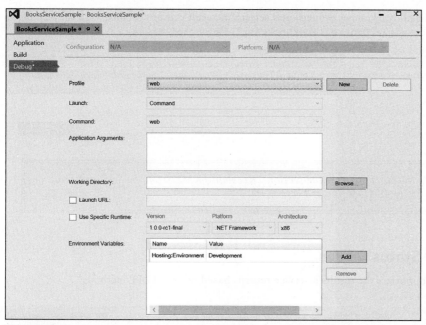

FIGURE 42-2

When you open this link in a browser, a JSON array is returned as shown:

```
[{"Id":"2d0c7eac-cb37-409f-b8da-c8ca497423a2",
  "Number":6,"Title":"Generics","Pages":22},
 {"Id":"d62e1182-3254-4504-a56b-f0441ee1ce8e",
  "Number":1,"Title":"Application Architectures","Pages":35},
 {"Id":"cb624eed-7e6c-40c6-88f2-28cf03eb652e",
  "Number":4,"Title":"Inheritance","Pages":18},
 {"Id":"6e6d48b5-fa04-43b5-b5f5-acd11b72c821",
  "Number":3,"Title":"Objects and Types","Pages":30},
 {"Id":"55c1ea93-2c0d-4071-8cee-cc172b3746b5",
  "Number":2,"Title":"Core C#","Pages":42},
 {"Id":"5c391b33-76f3-4e12-8989-3a8fbc621e96",
  "Number":5,"Title":"Managed and Unmanaged Resources","Pages":20}]
```

Changing the Response Format

ASP.NET Web API 2 returned JSON or XML, depending on the requested format by the client. With ASP.
NET MVC 6, when returning an `ObjectResult`, by default JSON is returned. In case you need to return
XML as well, you can add the NuGet package `Microsoft.AspNet.Mvc.Formatters.Xml` and add a call
to `AddXmlSerializerFormatters` to the `Startup` class. `AddXmlSerializerFormatters` is an extension
method for the `IMvcBuilder` interface and can be added using fluent API to the `AddMvc` method (code file
`BooksServiceSample/Startup.cs`):

```csharp
public void ConfigureServices(IServiceCollection services)
{
    services.AddMvc().AddXmlSerializerFormatters();

    IBookChaptersRepository repos = new SampleBookChaptersRepository();
    repos.Init();
    services.AddSingleton<IBookChaptersRepository>(repos);
}
```

With the controllers, the allowed content type(s) and selectable result can be specified with the `Produces` attribute (`BooksServiceSample/Controllers/BookChaptersController.cs`):

```
[Produces("application/json", "application/xml")]
[Route("api/[controller]")]
public class BookChaptersController: Controller
{
  // etc.
}
```

> **NOTE** *Later in this chapter, in the section "Receiving XML from the Service," you see how to receive XML-formatted responses.*

REST Results and Status Codes

The following table summarizes the results a service returns based on the HTTP methods:

HTTP METHOD	DESCRIPTION	REQUEST BODY	RESPONSE BODY
GET	Returns a resource	Empty	The resource
POST	Adds a resource	The resource to add	The resource
PUT	Updates a resource	The resource to update	None
DELETE	Deletes a resource	Empty	Empty

The following table shows important HTTP status codes as well as the `Controller` method with the instantiated object that returns the status code. To return any HTTP status code, you can return an `HttpStatusCodeResult` object that can be initialized with the status code you need:

HTTP STATUS CODE	CONTROLLER METHOD	TYPE
200 OK	Ok	OkResult
201 Created	CreatedAtRoute	CreatedAtRouteResult
204 No Content	NoContent	NoContentResult
400 Bad Request	BadRequest	BadRequestResult
401 Unauthorized	Unauthorized	UnauthorizedResult
404 Not Found	NotFound	NotFoundResult
Any status code		StatusCodeResult

All success status codes start with 2; error status codes start with 4. You can find a list of status codes in RFC 2616: `http://www.w3.org/Protocols/rfc2616/rfc2616-sec10.html`

CREATING AN ASYNC SERVICE

The previous sample code made use of a synchronous repository. Using Entity Framework Core with your repository, you can use either synchronous or asynchronous methods. Entity Framework supports both. However, many technologies, for example calling other services with the `HttpClient` class, offer only asynchronous methods. This can lead to an asynchronous repository as shown in the project `BooksServiceAsyncSample`.

With the asynchronous project, the `IBookChaptersRepository` has been changed to an asynchronous version. This interface is defined to use it with repositories accessing asynchronous methods, such as network or database clients. All the methods return a `Task` (code file `BooksServiceAsyncSample/Models/IBookChaptersRepository.cs`):

```
public interface IBookChaptersRepository
{
  Task InitAsync();
  Task AddAsync(BookChapter chapter);
  Task<BookChapter> RemoveAsync(Guid id);
  Task<IEnumerable<BookChapter>> GetAllAsync();
  Task<BookChapter> FindAsync(Guid id);
  Task UpdateAsync(BookChapter chapter);
}
```

The class `SampleBookChaptersRepository` implements the asynchronous methods. When reading and writing from the dictionary, asynchronous functionality is not needed, so the `Task` to return is created using the `FromResult` method (code file `BooksServiceAsyncSample/Models/SampleBookChaptersRepository.cs`):

```
public class SampleBookChaptersRepository: IBookChaptersRepository
{
  private readonly ConcurrentDictionary<string, BookChapter> _chapters =
    new ConcurrentDictionary<string, BookChapter>();

  public async Task InitAsync()
  {
    await AddAsync(new BookChapter
    {
      Number = 1,
      Title = "Application Architectures",
      Pages = 35
    });
    //... more book chapters
  }

  public Task AddAsync(BookChapter chapter)
  {
    chapter.Id = Guid.NewGuid();
    _chapters[chapter.Id] = chapter;
    return Task.FromResult<object>(null);
  }

  public Task<BookChapter> RemoveAsync(Guid id)
  {
    BookChapter removed;
    _chapters.TryRemove(id, out removed);
    return Task.FromResult(removed);
  }

  public Task<IEnumerable<BookChapter>> GetAllAsync() =>
    Task.FromResult<IEnumerable<BookChapter>>(_chapters.Values);

  public Task<BookChapter> FindAsync(Guid id)
  {
    BookChapter chapter;
    _chapters.TryGetValue(id, out chapter);
    return Task.FromResult(chapter);
  }
```

```
public Task UpdateAsync(BookChapter chapter)
{
  _chapters[chapter.Id] = chapter;
  return Task.FromResult<object>(null);
}
}
```

The API controller `BookChaptersController` just needs a few changes to be implemented as asynchronous. The controller methods return a `Task` as well. With this it is easy to invoke the asynchronous methods of the repository (code file `BooksServiceAsyncSample/Controllers/BookChaptersController.cs`):

```
[Produces("application/json", "application/xml")]
[Route("api/[controller]")]
public class BookChaptersController: Controller
{
  private readonly IBookChaptersRepository _repository;
  public BookChaptersController(IBookChaptersRepository repository)
  {
    _repository = repository;
  }

  // GET: api/bookchapters
  [HttpGet()]
  public Task<IEnumerable<BookChapter>> GetBookChaptersAsync() =>
    _repository.GetAllAsync();

  // GET api/bookchapters/guid
  [HttpGet("{id}", Name = nameof(GetBookChapterByIdAsync))]
  public async Task<IActionResult> GetBookChapterByIdAsync(Guid id)
  {
    BookChapter chapter = await _repository.FindAsync(id);
    if (chapter == null)
    {
      return NotFound();
    }
    else
    {
      return new ObjectResult(chapter);
    }
  }

  // POST api/bookchapters
  [HttpPost]
  public async Task<IActionResult> PostBookChapterAsync(
    [FromBody]BookChapter chapter)
  {
    if (chapter == null)
    {
      return BadRequest();
    }
    await _repository.AddAsync(chapter);
    return CreatedAtRoute(nameof(GetBookChapterByIdAsync),
      new { id = chapter.Id }, chapter);
  }

  // PUT api/bookchapters/guid
  [HttpPut("{id}")]
  public async Task<IActionResult> PutBookChapterAsync(
    string id, [FromBody]BookChapter chapter)
  {
    if (chapter == null || id != chapter.Id)
```

```
    {
      return BadRequest();
    }
    if (await _repository.FindAsync(id) == null)
    {
      return NotFound();
    }

    await _repository.UpdateAsync(chapter);
    return new NoContentResult();
  }

  // DELETE api/bookchapters/guid
  [HttpDelete("{id}")]
  public async Task DeleteAsync(Guid id)
  {
    await _repository.RemoveAsync(id);
  }
}
```

For the client, it doesn't matter if the controller is implemented as synchronous or asynchronous. The client creates the same HTTP requests for both kinds.

CREATING A .NET CLIENT

Using the browser to call the service is a simple way to handle testing. The clients more typically make use of JavaScript—this is where JSON shines—and .NET clients. In this book, a Console Application (Package) project is created to call the service.

The sample code for BookServiceClientApp makes use of the following dependencies and namespaces:

Dependencies

```
NETStandard.Library
Newtonsoft.Json
System.Net.Http
System.Xml.XDocument
```

Namespaces

```
Newtonsoft.Json
System
System.Collections.Generic
System.Linq
System.Linq.Xml
System.Net.Http
System.Net.Http.Headers
System.Text
System.Threading.Tasks
static System.Console
```

Sending GET Requests

For sending HTTP requests, you use the HttpClient class. This class is introduced in Chapter 25, "Networking." In this chapter, this class is used to send different kinds of HTTP requests. To use the

HttpClient class, you need to add the NuGet package System.Net.Http and open the namespace System .Net.Http. To convert JSON data to a .NET type, the NuGet package Newtonsoft.Json is added.

> **NOTE** *JSON serialization and using Json.NET is discussed in Chapter 27, "XML and JSON."*

With the sample project, the generic class HttpClientHelper is created to have just one implementation for different data types. The constructor expects a base address of the service (code file BookServiceClientApp/HttpClientHelper.cs):

```
public abstract class HttpClientHelper<T>
  where T: class
{
  private Uri _baseAddress;

  public HttpClientHelper(string baseAddress)
  {
    if (baseAddress == null)
      throw new ArgumentNullException(nameof(baseAddress));
    _baseAddress = new Uri(baseAddress);
  }
  // etc.
}
```

The method GetInternalAsync makes a GET request to receive a list of items. This method invokes the GetAsync method of the HttpClient to send a GET request. The HttpResponseMessage contains the information received. The status code of the response is written to the console to show the result. In case the server returns an error, the GetAsync method doesn't throw an exception. An exception is thrown from the method EnsureSuccessStatusCode that is invoked with the HttpResponseMessage instance that is returned. This method throws an exception in case the HTTP status code is of an error type. The body of the response contains the JSON data returned. This JSON information is read as string and returned (code file BookServiceClientApp/HttpClientHelper.cs):

```
private async Task<string> GetInternalAsync(string requestUri)
{
  using (var client = new HttpClient())
  {
    client.BaseAddress = _baseAddress;
    HttpResponseMessage resp = await client.GetAsync(requestUri);
    WriteLine($"status from GET {resp.StatusCode}");
    resp.EnsureSuccessStatusCode();
    return await resp.Content.ReadAsStringAsync();
  }
}
```

The server controller defines two methods with GET requests: one method that returns all chapters and the other one returns just a single chapter but requires the chapter's identifier with the URI. The method GetAllAsync invokes the GetInternalAsync method to convert the returned JSON information to a collection, while the method GetAsync converts the result to a single item. These methods are declared virtual to allow overriding them from a derived class (code file BookServiceClientApp/HttpClientHelper.cs):

```
public async virtual Task<T> GetAllAsync(string requestUri)
{
  string json = await GetInternalAsync(requestUri);
  return JsonConvert.DeserializeObject<IEnumerable<T>>(json);
}
```

```
public async virtual Task<T> GetAsync(string requestUri)
{
  string json = await GetInternalAsync(requestUri);
  return JsonConvert.DeserializeObject<T>(json);
}
```

Instead of using the generic `HttpClientHelper` class from the client code, a specialization is done with the `BookChapterClient` class. This class derives from `HttpClientHelper` passing a `BookChapter` for the generic parameter. This class also overrides the `GetAllAsync` method from the base class to have the returned chapters sorted by the chapter number (code file BookServiceClientApp/BookChapterClient.cs):

```
public class BookChapterClient: HttpClientHelper<BookChapter>
{
  public BookChapterClient(string baseAddress)
    : base(baseAddress) { }

  public override async Task<IEnumerable<BookChapter>> GetAllAsync(
    string requestUri)
  {
    IEnumerable<BookChapter> chapters = await base.GetAllAsync(requestUri);
    return chapters.OrderBy(c => c.Number);
  }
}
```

The `BookChapter` class contains the properties that are received with the JSON content (code file BookServiceClientApp/BookChapter.cs):

```
public class BookChapter
{
  public Guid Id { get; set; }
  public int Number { get; set; }
  public string Title { get; set; }
  public int Pages { get; set; }
}
```

The `Main` method of the client application invokes the different methods to show GET, POST, PUT, and DELETE requests (code file BookServiceClientApp/Program.cs):

```
static void Main()
{
  WriteLine("Client app, wait for service");
  ReadLine();
  ReadChaptersAsync().Wait();
  ReadChapterAsync().Wait();
  ReadNotExistingChapterAsync().Wait();
  ReadXmlAsync().Wait();
  AddChapterAsync().Wait();
  UpdateChapterAsync().Wait();
  RemoveChapterAsync().Wait();
  ReadLine();
}
```

The method `ReadChaptersAsync` invokes the `GetAllAsync` method from the `BookChapterClient` to retrieve all chapters and shows the titles of the chapters on the console (code file BookServiceClientApp/Program.cs):

```
private static async Task ReadChaptersAsync()
{
  WriteLine(nameof(ReadChaptersAsync));
  var client = new BookChapterClient(Addresses.BaseAddress);
  IEnumerable<BookChapter> chapters =
```

```
    await client.GetAllAsync(Addresses.BooksApi);

  foreach (BookChapter chapter in chapters)
  {
    WriteLine(chapter.Title);
  }
  WriteLine();
}
```

When you run the application (starting both the service and the client app), the ReadChaptersAsync method shows the OK status code and the titles from the chapters:

```
ReadChaptersAsync
status from GET OK
Application Architectures
Core C#
Objects and Types
Inheritance
Managed and Unmanaged Resources
Generics
```

The method ReadChapterAsync shows the GET request to retrieve a single chapter. With this, the identifier of a chapter is added to the URI string (code file BookServiceClientApp/Program.cs):

```
private static async Task ReadChapterAsync()
{
  WriteLine(nameof(ReadChapterAsync));
  var client = new BookChapterClient(Addresses.BaseAddress);
  var chapters = await client.GetAllAsync(Addresses.BooksApi);
  Guid id = chapters.First().Id;
  BookChapter chapter = await client.GetAsync(Addresses.BooksApi + id);
  WriteLine($"{chapter.Number} {chapter.Title}");
  WriteLine();
}
```

The result of the ReadChapterAsync method is shown here. It shows the OK status two times because the first time this method retrieves all the chapters before sending a request for a single chapter:

```
ReadChapterAsync
status from GET OK
status from GET OK
1 Application Architectures
```

What if a GET request is sent with a nonexistent chapter identifier? How to deal with this is shown in the method ReadNotExistingChapterAsync. Calling the GetAsync method is similar to the previous code snippet, but an identifier that does not exist is added to the URI. Remember from the implementation of the HttpClientHelper class, the GetAsync method of the HttpClient class does not throw an exception. However, the EnsureSuccessStatusCode does. This exception is caught with a catch to the HttpRequestException type. Here, an exception filter is also used to only handle exception code 404 (not found) (code file BookServiceClientApp/Program.cs):

```
private static async Task ReadNotExistingChapterAsync()
{
  WriteLine(nameof(ReadNotExistingChapterAsync));
  string requestedIdentifier = Guid.NewGuid().ToString();
  try
  {
    var client = new BookChapterClient(Addresses.BaseAddress);
    BookChapter chapter = await client.GetAsync(
      Addresses.BooksApi + requestedIdentifier.ToString());
    WriteLine($"{chapter.Number} {chapter.Title}");
  }
  catch (HttpRequestException ex) when (ex.Message.Contains("404"))
```

```
  {
    WriteLine($"book chapter with the identifier {requestedIdentifier} " +
      "not found");
  }
  WriteLine();
}
```

> **NOTE** *Handling exceptions and using exception filters is discussed in Chapter 14,*
> *"Errors and Exceptions."*

The result of the method shows the `NotFound` result from the service:

```
ReadNotExistingChapterAsync
status from GET NotFound
book chapter with the identifier d38ea0c5-64c9-4251-90f1-e21c07d6937a not found
```

Receiving XML from the Service

In the section "Changing the Response Format," the XML format was added to the service. With a service that is enabled to return XML beside JSON, XML content can be explicitly requested by adding the accept header value to accept application/xml content.

How this can be done is shown in the following code snippet. Here, the `MediaTypeWithQualityHeaderValue` specifying `application/xml` is added to the `Accept` headers collection. Then, the result is parsed as XML using the `XElement` class (code file `BookServiceClientApp/BookChapterClient.cs`):

```
public async Task<XElement> GetAllXmlAsync(string requestUri)
{
  using (var client = new HttpClient())
  {
    client.BaseAddress = _baseAddress;
    client.DefaultRequestHeaders.Accept.Add(
      new MediaTypeWithQualityHeaderValue("application/xml"));
    HttpResponseMessage resp = await client.GetAsync(requestUri);
    WriteLine($"status from GET {resp.StatusCode}");
    resp.EnsureSuccessStatusCode();
    string xml = await resp.Content.ReadAsStringAsync();
    XElement chapters = XElement.Parse(xml);
    return chapters;
  }
}
```

> **NOTE** *The* `XElement` *class and XML serialization are discussed in Chapter 27.*

From the Program class, the `GetAllXmlAsync` method is invoked to directly write the XML result to the console (code file `BookServiceClientApp/Program.cs`):

```
private static async Task ReadXmlAsync()
{
  WriteLine(nameof(ReadXmlAsync));
```

```
    var client = new BookChapterClient(Addresses.BaseAddress);
    XElement chapters = await client.GetAllXmlAsync(Addresses.BooksApi);
    WriteLine(chapters);
    WriteLine();
}
```

When you run this method, you can see that now XML is returned from the service:

```
ReadXmlAsync
status from GET OK
<ArrayOfBookChapter xmlns:xsi="http://www.w3.org/2001/XMLSchema-instance"
  xmlns:xsd="http://www.w3.org/2001/XMLSchema">
  <BookChapter>
    <Id>1439c261-2722-4e73-a328-010e82866511</Id>
    <Number>4</Number>
    <Title>Inheritance</Title>
    <Pages>18</Pages>
  </BookChapter>
  <BookChapter>
    <Id>d1a53440-94f2-404c-b2e5-7ce29ad91ef6</Id>
    <Number>3</Number>
    <Title>Objects and Types</Title>
    <Pages>30</Pages>
  </BookChapter>
  <BookChapter>
    <Id>ce1a5203-5b77-43e9-b6a2-62b6a18fac44</Id>
    <Number>38</Number>
    <Title>Windows Store Apps</Title>
    <Pages>45</Pages>
  </BookChapter>
  <!--... more chapters ...-->
```

Sending POST Requests

Let's send new objects to the service using the HTTP POST request. The HTTP POST request works similarly to the GET request. This request creates a new object server side. The `PostAsync` method of the `HttpClient` class requires the object that is added with the second parameter. You use Json.NET's `JsonConvert` class to serialize the object to JSON. With a successful return, the `Headers.Location` property contains a link where the object can be retrieved again from the service. The response also contains a body with the object returned. When the object changed from the service, the `Id` property was filled in the service code on creating the object. This new information is returned by the `PostAsync` method after deserialization of the JSON code (code file `BookServiceClientApp/HttpClientHelper.cs`):

```
public async Task<T> PostAsync(string uri, T item)
{
  using (var client = new HttpClient())
  {
    client.BaseAddress = _baseAddress;
    string json = JsonConvert.SerializeObject(item);
    HttpContent content = new StringContent(json, Encoding.UTF8,
      "application/json");
    HttpResponseMessage resp = await client.PostAsync(uri, content);
    WriteLine($"status from POST {resp.StatusCode}");
    resp.EnsureSuccessStatusCode();
    WriteLine($"added resource at {resp.Headers.Location}");

    json = await resp.Content.ReadAsStringAsync();
    return JsonConvert.DeserializeObject<T>(json);
  }
}
```

With the `Program` class, you can see the chapter that is added to the service. After invoking the `PostAsync` method of the `BookChapterClient`, the returned `Chapter` contains the new identifier (code file `BookServiceClientApp/Program.cs`):

```
private static async Task AddChapterAsync()
{
  WriteLine(nameof(AddChapterAsync));
  var client = new BookChapterClient(Addresses.BaseAddress);
  BookChapter chapter = new BookChapter
  {
    Number = 42,
    Title = "ASP.NET Web API",
    Pages = 35
  };
  chapter = await client.PostAsync(Addresses.BooksApi, chapter);
  WriteLine($"added chapter {chapter.Title} with id {chapter.Id}");
  WriteLine();
}
```

The result of the `AddChapterAsync` method shows a successful run to create the object:

```
AddChapterAsync
status from POST Created
added resource at http://localhost:5000/api/BookChapters/0e99217d-8769-46cd-93a4-2cf615cda5ae
added chapter ASP.NET Web API with id 0e99217d-8769-46cd-93a4-2cf615cda5ae
```

Sending PUT Requests

The HTTP PUT request—used for updating a record—is sent with the help of the `HttpClient` method `PutAsync`. `PutAsync` requires the updated content with the second parameter, and the URL to the service including the identifier in the first (code file `BookServiceClientApp/HttpClientHelper.cs`):

```
public async Task PutAsync(string uri, T item)
{
  using (var client = new HttpClient())
  {
    client.BaseAddress = _baseAddress;
    string json = JsonConvert.SerializeObject(item);
    HttpContent content = new StringContent(json, Encoding.UTF8,
      "application/json");
    HttpResponseMessage resp = await client.PutAsync(uri, content);
    WriteLine($"status from PUT {resp.StatusCode}");
    resp.EnsureSuccessStatusCode();
  }
}
```

In the `Program` class, the chapter Windows Store Apps is updated to a different chapter number and the title Windows Apps (code file `BookServiceClientApp/Program.cs`):

```
private static async Task UpdateChapterAsync()
{
  WriteLine(nameof(UpdateChapterAsync));
  var client = new BookChapterClient(Addresses.BaseAddress);
  var chapters = await client.GetAllAsync(Addresses.BooksApi);
  var chapter = chapters.SingleOrDefault(c => c.Title == "Windows Store Apps");
  if (chapter != null)
  {
    chapter.Number = 32;
    chapter.Title = "Windows Apps";
    await client.PutAsync(Addresses.BooksApi + chapter.Id, chapter);
    WriteLine($"updated chapter {chapter.Title}");
  }
```

```
      WriteLine();
  }
```

The console output of the UpdateChapterAsync method shows an HTTP NoContent result and the updated chapter title:

```
UpdateChapterAsync
status from GET OK
status from PUT NoContent
updated chapter Windows Apps
```

Sending DELETE Requests

The last request shown with the sample client is the HTTP DELETE request. After invoking GetAsync, PostAsync, and PutAsync of the HttpClient class, it should be obvious that the format is DeleteAsync. What's shown in this code snippet is that the DeleteAsync method just needs a URI parameter to identify the object to delete (code file BookServiceClientApp/HttpClientHelper.cs):

```
public async Task DeleteAsync(string uri)
{
  using (var client = new HttpClient())
  {
    client.BaseAddress = _baseAddress;
    HttpResponseMessage resp = await client.DeleteAsync(uri);
    WriteLine($"status from DELETE {resp.StatusCode}");
    resp.EnsureSuccessStatusCode();
  }
}
```

The Program class defines the RemoveChapterAsync method (code file BookServiceClientApp/Program.cs):

```
private static async Task RemoveChapterAsync()
{
  WriteLine(nameof(RemoveChapterAsync));
  var client = new BookChapterClient(Addresses.BaseAddress);
  var chapters = await client.GetAllAsync(Addresses.BooksApi);
  var chapter = chapters.SingleOrDefault(c => c.Title == "ASP.NET Web Forms");
  if (chapter != null)
  {
    await client.DeleteAsync(Addresses.BooksApi + chapter.Id);
    WriteLine($"removed chapter {chapter.Title}");
  }
  WriteLine();
}
```

When you run the application, the RemoveChapterAsync method first shows the status of the HTTP GET method as a GET request is done first to retrieve all chapters, and then the successful DELETE request on deleting the ASP.NET Web Forms chapter:

```
RemoveChapterAsync
status from GET OK
status from DELETE OK
removed chapter ASP.NET Web Forms
```

WRITING TO THE DATABASE

Chapter 38, "Entity Framework Core," introduced you to mapping objects to relations with the Entity Framework. An ASP.NET Web API controller can easily use a DbContext. In the sample app, you don't need to change the controller at all; you just need to create and register a different repository for using the Entity Framework. All the steps needed are described in this section.

Defining the Database

Let's start defining the database. For using Entity Framework with SQL Server, the NuGet packages `EntityFramework.Core` and `EntityFramework.MicrosoftSqlServer` need to be added to the service project. To create the database from code, the NuGet package `EntityFramework.Commands` is added as well.

The `BookChapter` class was already defined earlier. This class stays unchanged for filling instances from the database. Mapping to properties is defined in the `BooksContext` class. With this class, the `OnModelCreating` method is overridden to map the `BookChapter` type to the `Chapters` table and to define a unique identifier for the `Id` column with a default unique identifier created from the database. The `Title` column is restricted to a maximum of 120 characters (code file `BookServiceAsyncSample/Models/BooksContext.cs`):

```
public class BooksContext: DbContext
{
  public DbSet<BookChapter> Chapters { get; set; }

  protected override void OnModelCreating(ModelBuilder modelBuilder)
  {
    base.OnModelCreating(modelBuilder);
    EntityTypeBuilder<BookChapter> chapter = modelBuilder
      .Entity<BookChapter>();
    chapter.ToTable("Chapters").HasKey(p => p.Id);
    chapter.Property<Guid>(p => p.Id)
      .HasColumnType("UniqueIdentifier")
      .HasDefaultValueSql("newid()");
    chapter.Property<string>(p => p.Title)
      .HasMaxLength(120);
  }
}
```

To allow creation of the database using .NET CLI tools, the `ef` command is defined in the `project.json` configuration file to map it to the `EntityFrameworkCore.Commands` (code file `BookServiceAsyncSample/project.json`):

```
"tools": {
  "dotnet-ef": "1.0.*"
},
```

With the dependency injection container, Entity Framework and SQL Server need to be added to invoke the extension methods `AddEntityFramework` and `AddSqlServer`. The just-created `BooksContext` needs to be registered as well. The `BooksContext` is added with the method `AddDbContext`. With the options of this method, the connection string is passed (code file `BookServiceAsyncSample/Startup.cs`):

```
public async void ConfigureServices(IServiceCollection services)
{
  services.AddMvc().AddXmlSerializerFormatters();

  // etc.

  services.AddEntityFramework()
    .AddSqlServer()
    .AddDbContext<BooksContext>(options =>
      options.UseSqlServer(
        Configuration["Data:BookConnection:ConnectionString"]));

  // etc.
}
```

The connection string itself is defined with the application settings (code file `BookServiceAsyncSample/appsettings.json`):

```
"Data": {
  "BookConnection": {
    "ConnectionString":
      "Server=(localdb)\\mssqllocaldb;Database=BooksSampleDB;
      Trusted_Connection=True;MultipleActiveResultSets=true"
  }
},
```

With this in place, it's now possible to create migrations and the database. To add code-based migrations to the project, you can start this `dnx` command from a Developer Command Prompt where you change the current directory to the directory of the project—the directory where the `project.json` file is placed. This statement uses the `ef` command that is defined in the `project.json` file to invoke migrations and add the `InitBooks` migration to the project. After a successful run of this command, you can see a `Migrations` folder in the project with classes to create the database:

```
>dotnet ef migrations add InitBooks
```

The following command creates the database based on the connection string defined with the startup code:

```
>dotnet ef database update
```

Creating the Repository

For using the `BooksContext`, you need to create a repository implementing the interface `IBookChaptersRepository`. The class `BookChaptersRepository` makes use of the `BooksContext` instead of using an in-memory dictionary as was done with the `SampleBookChaptersRepository` (code file `BookServiceAsyncSample/Models/BookChaptersRepository.cs`):

```csharp
public class BookChaptersRepository: IBookChaptersRepository, IDisposable
{
  private BooksContext _booksContext;

  public BookChaptersRepository(BooksContext booksContext)
  {
    _booksContext = booksContext;
  }

  public void Dispose()
  {
    _booksContext?.Dispose();
  }

  public async Task AddAsync(BookChapter chapter)
  {
    _booksContext.Chapters.Add(chapter);
    await _booksContext.SaveChangesAsync();
  }

  public Task<BookChapter> FindAsync(Guid id) =>
    _booksContext.Chapters.SingleOrDefaultAsync(c => c.Id == id);

  public async Task<IEnumerable<BookChapter>> GetAllAsync() =>
    await _booksContext.Chapters.ToListAsync();

  public Task InitAsync() => Task.FromResult<object>(null);

  public async Task<BookChapter> RemoveAsync(Guid id)
```

```
    {
        BookChapter chapter = await _booksContext.Chapters
            .SingleOrDefaultAsync(c => c.Id == id);
        if (chapter == null) return null;

        _booksContext.Chapters.Remove(chapter);
        await _booksContext.SaveChangesAsync();
        return chapter;
    }

    public async Task UpdateAsync(BookChapter chapter)
    {
        _booksContext.Chapters.Update(chapter);
        await _booksContext.SaveChangesAsync();
    }
}
```

If you are wondering about the use of the context, read Chapter 38, which covers more information about the Entity Framework Core.

To use this repository, you have to remove the `SampleBookChaptersRepository` from the registration in the container (or comment it out), and add the `BookChaptersRepository` to let the dependency injection container create an instance of this class when asked for the interface `IBookChapterRepository` (code file `BookServiceAsyncSample/Startup.cs`):

```
public async void ConfigureServices(IServiceCollection services)
{
    services.AddMvc().AddXmlSerializerFormatters();
    // comment the following three lines to use the DookChaptersRepository
    //IBookChaptersRepository repos = new SampleBookChaptersRepository();
    //services.AddSingleton<IBookChaptersRepository>(repos);
    //await repos.InitAsync();

    services.AddEntityFramework()
        .AddSqlServer()
        .AddDbContext<BooksContext>(options => options.UseSqlServer(
            Configuration["Data:BookConnection:ConnectionString"]));

    services.AddSingleton<IBookChaptersRepository, BookChaptersRepository>();
}
```

Now—without changing the controller or the client—you can run the service and client again. Depending on the data you enter initially in the database, you see results for the GET/POST/PUT/DELETE requests.

CREATING METADATA

Creating metadata for a service allows getting a description on the service, and also allows you to create the client by using this metadata. With web services using SOAP, metadata have been around since the early days of SOAP—with the Web Services Description Language (WSDL). WSDL is explained in detail in Chapter 44. Nowadays, metadata for REST services is here as well. Currently it's not a standard as with WSDL, but the most popular framework for describing APIs is Swagger (http://www.swagger.io). As of January 2016, the Swagger specification has been renamed to OpenAPI, and a standard is in the works (http://www.openapis.org).

To add Swagger or OpenAPI to an ASP.NET Web API service, you can use Swashbuckle. The NuGet package `Swashbuckle.SwaggerGen` contains code to generate swagger, the package `Swashbuckle.SwaggerUi` to offer a dynamically created user interface. Both packages will be used to extend the `BooksServiceSample` project.

After you add the NuGet packages, you need to add Swagger to the service collection. `AddSwaggerGen` is an extension method to add swagger services to the collection. To configure Swagger, you invoke the methods `ConfigureSwaggerDocument` and `ConfigureSwaggerSchema`. `ConfigureSwaggerDocument` configures the title, description, and the API version. `ConfigureSwaggerSchema` defines how the generated JSON schema should look. The sample code is configured that obsolete properties are not shown, and enum values should be shown as strings (code file `BooksServiceSample/Startup.cs`):

```csharp
public void ConfigureServices(IServiceCollection services)
{
  // Add framework services.
  services.AddMvc();

  IBookChaptersRepository repos = new SampleBookChaptersRepository();
  repos.Init();
  services.AddSingleton<IBookChaptersRepository>(repos);

  services.AddSwaggerGen();
  services.ConfigureSwaggerDocument(options =>
  {
    options.SingleApiVersion(new Info
    {
      Version = "v1",
      Title = "Book Chapters",
      Description = "A sample for Professional C# 6"
    });
    options.IgnoreObsoleteActions = true;
  });

  services.ConfigureSwaggerSchema(options =>
  {
    options.DescribeAllEnumsAsStrings = true;
    options.IgnoreObsoleteProperties = true;
  }
}
```

What's left is the Swagger configuration in the `Configure` method of the `Startup` class. The extension method `UseSwaggerGen` specifies that a JSON schema file should be generated. The default URL that you can configure with `UseSwaggerGen` is `/swagger/{version}/swagger.json`. With the document configured in the previous code snippet, the URL is `/swagger/v1/swagger.json`. The method `UseSwaggerUi` defines the URL for the Swagger user interface. Using the method without arguments, the URL is `swagger/ui`, but of course you can change this URL by using a different overload of the `UseSwaggerUi` method:

```csharp
public void Configure(IApplicationBuilder app, IHostingEnvironment env,
  ILoggerFactory loggerFactory)
{
  loggerFactory.AddConsole(Configuration.GetSection("Logging"));
  loggerFactory.AddDebug();

  app.UseIISPlatformHandler();
  app.UseStaticFiles();
  app.UseMvc();

  app.UseSwaggerGen();
  app.UseSwaggerUi();
}
```

When you run the application with Swagger configured, you can see nice information about the APIs offered by the service. Figure 42-3 shows the APIs offered by the `BooksServiceSample`, the template generated by `Values` service, and the `BooksService` sample. You can also see the title and description as configured with the Swagger document.

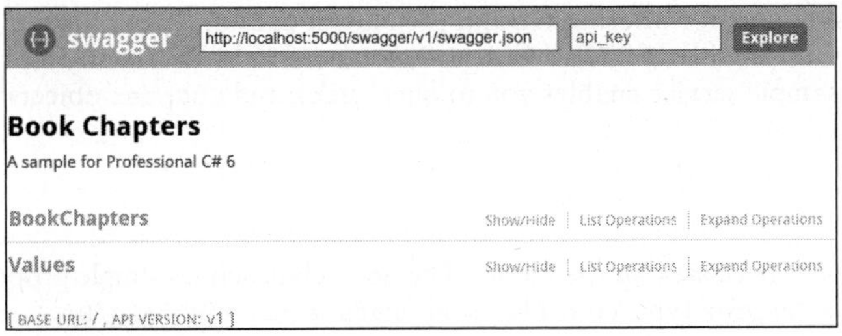

FIGURE 42-3

Figure 42-4 shows the details of the `BookChapters` service. You can see details of every API including the model, and also test the API calls.

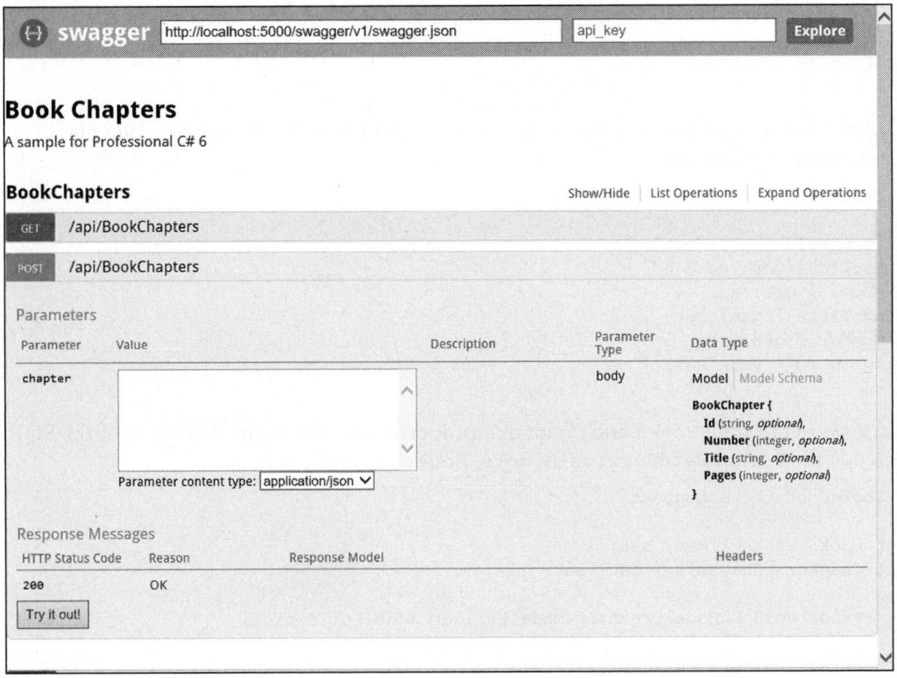

FIGURE 42-4

CREATING AND USING ODATA SERVICES

The ASP.NET Web API offers direct support for the Open Data Protocol (OData). OData offers CRUD access to a data source via the HTTP protocol. Sending a GET request retrieves a collection of entity data; a POST request creates a new entity; a PUT request updates existing entities; and a DELETE request removes an entity. In this chapter you've already seen the HTTP methods mapped to action methods in the controller. OData is built on JSON and AtomPub (an XML format) for the data serialization. You've seen direct support of JSON and XML with the ASP.NET Web API as well. What OData offers more of is that every resource can be accessed with simple URI queries. For having a look into that, and how this is solved with ASP.NET Web API, let's get into a sample and start with a database.

With the service application `BooksODataService`, for offering OData, the NuGet package `Microsoft.AspNet.OData` needs to be added. To use OData with ASP.NET Core 1.0, you need at least version 6 of the `Microsoft.AspNet.OData` package. The sample service enables you to query `Book` and `Chapter` objects and the relation between.

Creating a Data Model

The sample service defines the `Book` and `Chapter` classes for the model. The `Book` class defines simple properties and a one-to-many relationship with the `Chapter` type (code file `BooksODataService/Models/Book.cs`):

```
public class Book
{
  public Book()
  {
    Chapters = new List<Book>();
  }

  public int BookId { get; set; }
  public string Isbn { get; set; }
  public string Title { get; set; }
  public List<Chapter> Chapters { get; }
}
```

The `Chapter` class defines simple properties and a many-to-one relation to the `Book` type (code file `BooksODataService/Models/Book.cs`):

```
public class Chapter
{
  public int ChapterId { get; set; }
  public int BookId { get; set; }
  public Book Book { get; set; }
  public string Title { get; set; }
  public int Number { get; set; }
  public string Intro { get; set; }
}
```

The `BooksContext` class defines the `Books` and `Chapters` properties as well as the definition of the SQL database relations (code file `BooksODataService/Models/BooksContext.cs`):

```
public class BooksContext: DbContext
{
  public DbSet<Book> Books { get; set; }
  public DbSet<Chapter> Chapters { get; set; }

  protected override void OnModelCreating(ModelBuilder modelBuilder)
  {
    base.OnModelCreating(modelBuilder);
    EntityTypeBuilder<Book> bookBuilder = modelBuilder.Entity<Book>();
    bookBuilder.HasMany(b => b.Chapters)
      .WithOne(c => c.Book)
      .HasForeignKey(c => c.BookId);
    bookBuilder.Property<string>(b => b.Title)
      .HasMaxLength(120)
      .IsRequired();
    bookBuilder.Property<string>(b => b.Isbn)
      .HasMaxLength(20)
      .IsRequired(false);

    EntityTypeBuilder<Chapter> chapterBuilder = modelBuilder.Entity<Chapter>();
    chapterBuilder.Property<string>(c => c.Title)
      .HasMaxLength(120);
  }
}
```

Creating a Service

With ASP.NET Core 5, you can easily add OData Services. You don't need to make many changes to a controller. Of course, you need to add OData to the dependency injection container (code file `BooksODataService/Startup.cs`):

```
public void ConfigureServices(IServiceCollection services)
{
  services.AddMvc();

  services.AddEntityFramework()
   .AddSqlServer()
   .AddDbContext<BooksContext>(options => options.UseSqlServer(
     Configuration["Data:BookConnection:ConnectionString"]));
  services.AddOData();
}
```

The `BooksController` class just needs the `EnableQuery` attribute applied. This makes it an OData controller. You can use OData queries to access the controller. The `Route` attribute applied to the `BooksController` class defines an `odata` prefix for the route. This is just a convention, and you can change the route as you like (code file `BooksODataService/Controllers/BooksController.cs`):

```
[EnableQuery]
[Route("odata/[controller]")]
public class BooksController: Controller
{
  private readonly BooksContext _booksContext;

  public BooksController(BooksContext booksContext)
  {
    _booksContext = booksContext;
  }

  [HttpGet]
  public IEnumerable<Book> GetBooks() =>
    _booksContext.Books.Include(b => b.Chapters).ToList();


  // GET api/values/5
  [HttpGet("{id}")]
  public Book GetBook(int id) =>
    _booksContext.Books.SingleOrDefault(b => b.BookId == id);

  // etc.
}
```

Other than the change with the `EnableQuery` attribute, no other special actions are needed for the controller.

OData Query

Now it's an easy task to get all the books from the database using this URL (the port number might differ on your system):

```
http://localhost:50000/odata/Books
```

For getting just a single book, the identifier of the book can be passed with the URL. This request calls the `GetBook` action method passing the key that returns a single result:

```
http://localhost:50000/odata/Books(9)
```

Each book has multiple results. With a URL query it's also possible to get all the chapter results of one book:

```
http://localhost:50000/odata/Books(9)/Chapters
```

OData offers more query options that are supported by ASP.NET Web API. The OData specification allows passing parameters to the server for paging, filtering, and sorting. Let's get into these.

To return only a limited number of entities to the client, the client can limit the count using the `$top` parameter. This also allows paging by using `$skip`; for example, you can skip 3 and take 3:

```
http://localhost:50000/odata/Books?$top=3&$skip=3
```

With `$skip` and `$top` options, the client decides the number of entities to retrieve. In case you want to restrict what the client can request—for example, having millions of records that should never be requested with one call—you can limit this by configuring the `EnableQuery` attribute. Setting the `PageSize` to 10 only returns 10 entities at max:

```
[EnableQuery(PageSize=10)]
```

There are many more named parameters for the `Queryable` attribute to restrict the query—for example, the maximum skip and top values, the maximum expansion depth, and restrictions for sorting.

To filter the requests based on properties of the `Book` type, the `$filter` option can be applied to properties of the `Book`. To filter only the books that are from the publisher Wrox Press, you can use the `eq` operator (equals) with `$filter`:

```
http://localhost:50000/odata/Books?$filter=Publisher eq 'Wrox Press'
```

You can use `lt` (less than) and `gt` (greater than) logical operators with `$filter` as well. This request returns only chapters with more than 40 pages:

```
http://localhost:50000/odata/Chapters?$filter=Pages gt 40
```

To request a sorted result, the `$orderby` option defines the sorting order. Adding the `desc` keyword makes the sorting in descending order:

```
http://localhost:50000/odata/Book(9)/Chapters?$orderby=Pages%20desc
```

You can easily make all these requests to the service by using the `HttpClient` class. However, there are other options as well, such as by using a WCF Data Services created proxy.

> **NOTE** *With the service, you can also restrict the query options by setting the* `AllowedQueryOptions` *of the* `EnableQuery` *attribute. You can also restrict logical and arithmetic operators with the properties* `AllowedLogicalOperators` *and* `AllowedArithmeticOperators`.

SUMMARY

This chapter described the features of the ASP.NET Web API that is now part of ASP.NET MVC. This technology offers an easy way to create services that can be called from any client—be it JavaScript or a .NET client—with the help of the `HttpClient` class. Either JSON or XML can be returned.

Dependency injection was already used in several chapters of this book, particularly in Chapter 31, "Patterns with XAML Apps." In this chapter you've seen how easy it is to replace a memory-based repository using a dictionary with a repository by making use of the Entity Framework.

This chapter also introduced you to OData with which it's easy to reference data in a tree using resource identifiers.

The next chapter continues with web technologies and gives information on publish and subscribe technologies such as WebHooks and SignalR.

43

WebHooks and SignalR

WHAT'S IN THIS CHAPTER?

➤ Overview of SignalR

➤ Creating a SignalR hub

➤ Creating a SignalR client with HTML and JavaScript

➤ Creating a SignalR .NET client

➤ Using groups with SignalR

➤ Overview of WebHooks

➤ Creating WebHook receivers for GitHub and Dropbox

WROX.COM CODE DOWNLOADS FOR THIS CHAPTER

The wrox.com code downloads for this chapter are found at www.wrox.com/go/professionalcsharp6 on the Download Code tab. The code for this chapter is divided into the following major examples:

➤ Chat Server using SignalR

➤ WPF Chat Client using SignalR

➤ SaaS WebHooks Receiver Sample

OVERVIEW

With .NET you can use events to get notifications. You can register an event handler method with an event, also known as subscribing to events, and as soon as the event is fired from another place, your method gets invoked. Events cannot be used with web applications.

Previous chapters have covered a lot about web applications and web services. What was common with these applications and services is that the request was always started from the client application. The client makes an HTTP request and receives a response.

What if the server has some news to tell? There's nothing like events that you can subscribe to, or are there? With the web technologies you've seen so far, this can be resolved by the client polling for new information. The client has to make a request to the server to ask whether new information is available. Depending on the request interval defined, this way of communication results in either a high load of requests on the network that just result in "no new information is available," or the client misses actual information and when asking for new information receives information that is already old.

If the client is itself a web application, the direction of the communication can be turned around, and the server can send messages to the client. This is how WebHooks work.

With clients behind a firewall, using the HTTP protocol there's no way for the server to initiate a connection to the client. The connection always needs to be started from the client side. Because HTTP connections are stateless, and clients often can't connect to ports other than port 80, WebSockets can help. WebSockets are initiated with an HTTP request, but they're upgraded to a WebSocket connection where the connection stays open. Using the WebSockets protocol, the server can send information to the client over the open connection as soon as the server has new information.

> **NOTE** *Using WebSockets from lower-level API calls is discussed in Chapter 25, "Networking."*

SignalR is an ASP.NET web technology that offers an easy abstraction over WebSockets. Using SignalR is a lot easier than programming using the sockets interface. Also, if the client does not support the WebSocket API, SignalR automatically switches to a polling mechanism without you having to change the program.

> **NOTE** *At the time of this writing, SignalR for ASP.NET Core 1.0 is not yet available. That's why this chapter shows using SignalR 2 using ASP.NET 4.6 and ASP.NET Web API 2. Check* http://www.github.com/ProfessionalCSharp *for additional samples with SignalR 3 for ASP.NET Core 1.0 as SignalR 3 becomes available.*

WebHooks is a technology that is offered by many SaaS (Software as a Service) providers. You can register with such a provider, provide a public Web API to the service provider, and this way the service provider can call back as soon as new information is available.

This chapter covers both SignalR and WebHooks. As these technologies complement each other, they can also be used in combination.

ARCHITECTURE OF SIGNALR

SignalR consists of multiple NuGet packages that can be used on the server and the client side.

NUGET PACKAGE	DESCRIPTION
`Microsoft.AspNet.SignalR`	This package references other packages for the server-side implementation.
`Microsoft.AspNet.SignalR.Core`	This is the core package for SignalR. This package contains the Hub class
`Microsoft.AspNet.SignalR.SystemWeb`	This NuGet package contains extensions for ASP.NET 4.x to define the routes.
`Microsoft.AspNet.SignalR.JavaScript`	This NuGet package contains JavaScript libraries for SignalR clients.
`Microsoft.AspNet.SignalR.Client`	This NuGet package contains types for .NET clients. A `HubProxy` is used to connect to a `Hub`.

With SignalR, the server defines a hub where clients connect to (see Figure 43-1). The hub keeps a connection to every client. Using the hub, you can send a message to every client connected. You can either send messages to all clients, or select specific clients or groups of clients to send messages to.

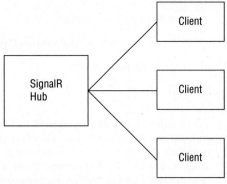

A SIMPLE CHAT USING SIGNALR

The first SignalR sample application is a chat application, which is easy to create with SignalR. With this application, multiple clients can be started to communicate with each other via the SignalR hub. When one of the client applications sends a message, all the connected clients receive this message in turn.

FIGURE 43-1

The server application is written with ASP.NET 4.6, one of the clients is created with HTML and JavaScript, and the other client application is a .NET application using WPF for the user interface.

Creating a Hub

As previously mentioned, ASP.NET Core is not supported with SignalR—at least at the time of this writing. That's why you start creating a hub with a new ASP.NET Web Application, select the Empty ASP.NET 4.6 template, and name it ChatServer. After creating the project, add a new item and select SignalR Hub class (see Figure 43-2). Adding this item also adds the NuGet packages that are needed server side.

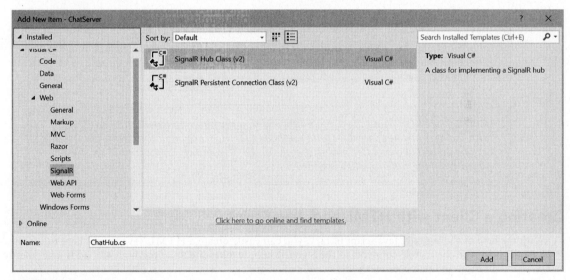

FIGURE 43-2

To define the URL for SignalR, you can create an OWIN Startup class (using the OWIN Startup Class item template) and add the invocation to MapSignalR to the Configuration method. The MapSignalR method defines the signalR URI as a path for requests to the SignalR hubs (code file ChatServer/Startup.cs):

```
using Microsoft.Owin;
using Owin;

[assembly: OwinStartup(typeof(ChatServer.Startup))]

namespace ChatServer
```

```
{
  public class Startup
  {
    public void Configuration(IAppBuilder app)
    {
      app.MapSignalR();
    }
  }
}
```

The main functionality of SignalR is defined with the hub. The hub is indirectly invoked by the clients, and in turn the clients are called. The class `ChatHub` derives from the base class `Hub` to get the needed hub functionality. The method `Send` is defined to be invoked by the client applications sending a message to the other clients. You can use any method name with any number of parameters. The client code just needs to match the method name as well as the parameters. To send a message to the clients, the `Clients` property of the `Hub` class is used. The `Clients` property returns an `IHubCallerConnectContext<dynamic>` that allows sending messages to specific clients or to all connected clients. The sample code invokes the `BroadcastMessage` with all connected clients using the `All` property. The `All` property (with the `Hub` class as the base class) returns a `dynamic` object. This way you can invoke any method name you like with any number of parameters; the client code just needs to match this (code file `ChatServer/ChatHub.cs`):

```
public class ChatHub: Hub
{
  public void Send(string name, string message)
  {
    Clients.All.BroadcastMessage(name, message);
  }
}
```

> **NOTE** *The* dynamic *type is explained in Chapter 16, "Reflection, Metadata, and Dynamic Programming."*

> **NOTE** *Instead of using the* dynamic *type within the hub implementation, you can also define your own interface with methods that are invoked in the client. How this can be done is shown later in this chapter in the "Grouping Connections" sections, when grouping functionality is added.*

Creating a Client with HTML and JavaScript

With the help of the SignalR JavaScript library, you can easily create a HTML/JavaScript client to use the SignalR hub. The client code connects to the SignalR hub, invokes the `Send` method, and adds a handler to receive the `BroadcastMessage` method.

For the user interface, two simple input elements are defined to allow entering the name and the message to send, a button to call the `Send` method, and an unordered list where all the messages received are shown (code file `ChatServer/ChatWindow.html`):

```
Enter your name <input type="text" id="name" />
<br />
Message <input type="text" id="message" />
<button type="button" id="sendmessage">Send</button>
<br />
<ul id="messages">
</ul>
```

The scripts that need to be included are shown in the following code snippet. The versions might differ with your implementation. jquery.signalR defines the client side functionality for the SignalR implementation. The hub proxy is used to make the call to the SignalR server. The reference to the script signalr/hubs contain automatically generated scripting code that creates hub proxies that matches the custom code from the hub code (code file ChatServer/ChatWindow.html):

```
<script src="Scripts/jquery-1.11.3.js"></script>
<script src="Scripts/jquery.signalR-2.2.0.js"></script>
<script src="signalr/hubs"></script>
```

After including the script files, custom script code can be created to make the call to the hub, and to receive the broadcasts. In the following code snippet, $.connection.chatHub returns a hub proxy to invoke the methods of the ChatHub class in turn. chat is a variable defined to in turn use this variable instead of accessing $.connection.chatHub. Assigning a function to chat.client.broadcastMessage defines the function that is invoked when the BroadcastMessage is called by the server-side hub code. As the BroadcastMessage method passes two string parameters for the name and the message, the declared function matches the same parameters. The parameter values are added to the unordered list item within a list item element. After defining the implementation of the broadcastMessage call, you make a connection to the server by starting the connection with $.connection.hub.start(). As soon as the start of the connection is completed, the function assigned to the done function is invoked. Here, the click handler to the sendmessage button is defined. When you clicking this button, a message to the server is sent using chat.server.send, passing two string values (code file ChatServer/ChatWindow.html):

```
<script>
  $(function () {
    var chat = $.connection.chatHub;

    chat.client.broadcastMessage = function (name, message) {
      var encodedName = $('<div />').text(name).html();
      var encodedMessage = $('<div />').text(message).html();
      $('#messages').append('<li>' + encodedName + ':     ' +
        encodedMessage + '</li>');
    };

    $.connection.hub.start().done(function () {
      $('#sendmessage').click(function () {
        chat.server.send($('#name').val(), $('#message').val());
        $('#message').val('');
        $('#message').focus();
      });
    });
  });
</script>
```

When you run the application, you can open multiple browser windows—even using different browsers—you can enter names and messages for a chat (see Figure 43-3).

FIGURE 43-3

When you use the Internet Explorer Developer Tools (press F12 while Internet Explorer is open) you can use Network Monitoring to see the upgrade from the HTTP protocol to the WebSocket protocol, as shown in Figure 43-4.

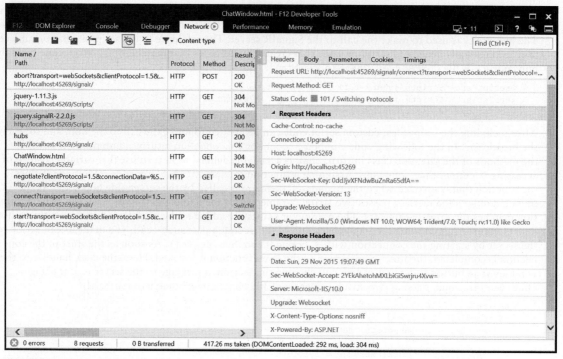

FIGURE 43-4

Creating SignalR .NET Clients

The sample .NET client application to use the SignalR server is a WPF application. The functionality is similar to the HTML/JavaScript application shown earlier. This application makes use of these NuGet packages and namespaces:

NuGet Packages

```
Microsoft.AspNet.SignalR.Client

Microsoft.Extensions.DependencyInjection

Newtonsoft.Json
```

Namespaces

```
Microsoft.AspNet.SignalR.Client

Microsoft.Extensions.DependencyInjection

System

System.Collections.ObjectModel

System.Net.Http

System.Windows
```

The user interface of the WPF application defines two `TextBox`, two `Button`, and one `ListBox` element to enter the name and message, to connect to the service hub, and to show a list of received messages (code file `WPFChatClient/MainWindow.xaml`):

```xml
<TextBlock Text="Name" />
<TextBox Text="{Binding ViewModel.Name, Mode=TwoWay}" />
<Button Content="Connect" Command="{Binding ViewModel.ConnectCommand}" />
```

```xml
<TextBlock Text="Message" />
<TextBox Text="{Binding ViewModel.Message, Mode=TwoWay}" />
<Button Content="Send" Command="{Binding ViewModel.SendCommand, Mode=OneTime}" />
<ListBox ItemsSource="{Binding ViewModel.Messages, Mode=OneWay}" />
```

In the startup code of the application, the dependency injection container is defined, and services as well as view models are registered (code file WPFChatClient/App.xaml.cs):

```csharp
public partial class App: Application
{
  protected override void OnStartup(StartupEventArgs e)
  {
    base.OnStartup(e);
    IServiceCollection services = new ServiceCollection();
    services.AddTransient<ChatViewModel>();
    services.AddTransient<GroupChatViewModel>();
    services.AddSingleton<IMessagingService, MessagingService>();

    Container = services.BuildServiceProvider();
  }

  public IServiceProvider Container { get; private set; }
}
```

Within the code-behind file of the view, the ChatViewModel is assigned to the ViewModel property using the dependency injection container (code file WPFChatClient/MainWindow.xaml.cs):

```csharp
public partial class MainWindow: Window
{
  public MainWindow()
  {
    InitializeComponent();
    this.DataContext = this;
  }

  public ChatViewModel ViewModel { get; } =
    (App.Current as App).Container.GetService<ChatViewModel>();
}
```

> **NOTE** *WPF is covered in detail in Chapter 34, "Windows Desktop Applications with WPF." The Model-View-ViewModel (MVVM) pattern is explained in Chapter 31, "Patterns with XAML Apps."*

The hub-specific code is implemented in the class ChatViewModel. First, have a look at the bound properties and commands. The property Name is bound to enter the chat name, the Message property to enter the message. The ConnectCommand property maps to the OnConnect method to initiate the connection to the server; the SendCommand property maps to the OnSendMessage method to send a chat message (code file WPFChatClient/ViewModels/ChatViewModel.cs):

```csharp
public sealed class ChatViewModel: IDisposable
{
  private const string ServerURI = "http://localhost:45269/signalr";
  private readonly IMessagingService _messagingService;
  public ChatViewModel(IMessagingService messagingService)
  {
    _messagingService = messagingService;

    ConnectCommand = new DelegateCommand(OnConnect);
    SendCommand = new DelegateCommand(OnSendMessage);
  }
```

```
public string Name { get; set; }
public string Message { get; set; }

public ObservableCollection<string> Messages { get; } =
  new ObservableCollection<string>();

public DelegateCommand SendCommand { get; }

public DelegateCommand ConnectCommand { get; }

// etc.
}
```

The `OnConnect` method initiates the connection to the server. First, a new `HubConnection` object passing the URL to the server is created. With the `HubConnection`, the proxy can be created using `CreateHubProxy`, passing the name of the hub. Using the proxy, methods of the service can be called. To register with messages that are returned from the server, the `On` method is invoked. The first parameter passed to the `On` method defines the method name that is called by the server; the second parameter defines a delegate to the method that is invoked. The method `OnMessageReceived` has the parameters specified with the generic parameter arguments of the `On` method: two strings. To finally initiate the connection, the `Start` method on the `HubConnection` instance is invoked (code file `WPFChatClient/ViewModels/ChatViewModel.cs`):

```
private HubConnection _hubConnection;
private IHubProxy _hubProxy;

public async void OnConnect()
{
  CloseConnection();
  _hubConnection = new HubConnection(ServerURI);
  _hubConnection.Closed += HubConnectionClosed;
  _hubProxy = _hubConnection.CreateHubProxy("ChatHub");
  _hubProxy.On<string, string>("BroadcastMessage", OnMessageReceived);

  try
  {
    await _hubConnection.Start();
  }
  catch (HttpRequestException ex)
  {
    _messagingService.ShowMessage(ex.Message);
  }
  _messagingService.ShowMessage("client connected");
}
```

Sending messages to SignalR requires only calls to the `Invoke` method of the `IHubProxy`. The first parameter is the name of the method that should be invoked by the server; the following parameters are the parameters of the method on the server (code file `WPFChatClient/ViewModels/ChatViewModel.cs`):

```
public void OnSendMessage()
{
  _hubProxy.Invoke("Send", Name, Message);
}
```

When receiving a message, the `OnMessageReceived` method is invoked. Because this method is invoked from a background thread, you need to switch back to the UI thread that updates bound properties and collections (code file `WPFChatClient/ViewModels/ChatViewModel.cs`):

```
public void OnMessageReceived(string name, string message)
{
  App.Current.Dispatcher.Invoke(() =>
  {
    Messages.Add($"{name}: {message}");
  });
}
```

When you run the application, you can receive and send messages from the WPF client as shown in Figure 43-5. You can also open the web page simultaneously and communicate between them.

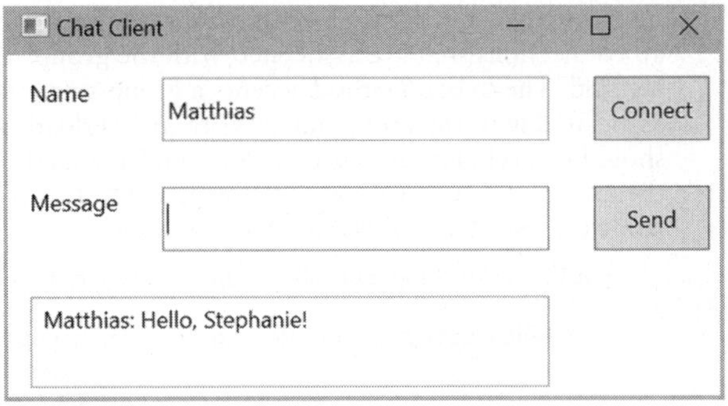

GROUPING CONNECTIONS

Usually you don't want to communicate among all clients, but you instead want to communicate among a group of clients. There's support out of the box for such a scenario with SignalR.

In this section, you add another chat hub with grouping functionality and also have a look at other options that are possible using SignalR hubs. The WPF client application is extended to enter groups and send a message to a selected group.

FIGURE 43-5

Extending the Hub with Groups

To support a group chat, you create the class `GroupChatHub`. With the previous hub, you saw how to use the `dynamic` keyword to define the message that is sent to the clients. Instead of using the `dynamic` type, you can also create a custom interface as shown in the following code snippet. This interface is used as a generic parameter with the base class `Hub` (code file `ChatServer/GroupChatHub.cs`):

```
public interface IGroupClient
{
  void MessageToGroup(string groupName, string name, string message);
}

public class GroupChatHub: Hub<IGroupClient>
{
  // etc.
}
```

`AddGroup` and `LeaveGroup` are methods defined to be called by the client. Registering the group, the client sends a group name with the `AddGroup` method. The `Hub` class defines a `Groups` property where connections to groups can be registered. The `Groups` property of the `Hub` class returns `IGroupManager`. This interface defines two methods: `Add` and `Remove`. Both of these methods need a group name and a connection identifier to add or remove the specified connection to the group. The connection identifier is a unique identifier associated with a client connection. The client connection identifier—as well as other information about the client—can be accessed with the `Context` property of the `Hub` class. The following code snippet invokes the `Add` method of the `IGroupManager` to register a group with the connection, and the `Remove` method to unregister a group (code file `ChatServer/GroupChatHub.cs`):

```
public Task AddGroup(string groupName) =>
  Groups.Add(Context.ConnectionId, groupName);

public Task LeaveGroup(string groupName) =>
  Groups.Remove(Context.ConnectionId, groupName);
```

> **NOTE** *The* `Context` *property of the* `Hub` *class returns an object of type* `HubCallerContext`. *With this class, you can not only access the connection identifier associated with the connection, but you can access other information about the client, such as the header, query string, and cookie information from the HTTP request and also information about the user. This information can be used for user authentication.*

Invoking the Send method—this time with three parameters including the group—sends information to all connections that are associated with the group. The Clients property is now used to invoke the Group method. The Group method accepts a group string to send the MessageToGroup message to all connections associated with the group name. With an overload of the Group method you can add connection IDs that should be excluded. Because the Hub implements the interface IGroupClient, the Groups method returns the IGroupClient. This way, the MessageToGroup method can be invoked using compile-time support (code file ChatServer/GroupChatHub.cs):

```
public void Send(string group, string name, string message)
{
    Clients.Group(group).MessageToGroup(group, name, message);
}
```

Several other extension methods are defined to send information to a list of client connections. You've seen the Group method to send messages to a group of connections that's specified by a group name. With this method, you can exclude client connections. For example, the client who sent the message might not need to receive it. The Groups method accepts a list of group names where a message should be sent to. You've already seen the All property to send a message to all connected clients. Methods to exclude sending the message to the caller are OthersInGroup and OthersInGroups. These methods send a message to one specific group excluding the caller, or a message to a list of groups excluding the caller.

You can also send messages to a customized group that's not based on the built-in grouping functionality. Here, it helps to override the methods OnConnected, OnDisconnected, and OnReconnected. The OnConnected method is invoked every time a client connects; the OnDisconnected method is invoked when a client disconnects. Within these methods, you can access the Context property of the Hub class to access client information as well as the client-associated connection ID. Here, you can write the connection information to a shared state to have your server scalable using multiple instances, accessing the same shared state. You can also select clients based on your own business logic, or implement priorities when sending messages to privilege specific clients.

```
public override Task OnConnected()
{
    return base.OnConnected();
}

public override Task OnDisconnected(bool stopCalled)
{
    return base.OnDisconnected(stopCalled);
}
```

Extending the WPF Client with Groups

After having the grouping functionality with the hub ready, you can extend the WPF client application. For the grouping features, another XAML page associated with the GroupChatViewModel class is defined.

The GroupChatViewModel class defines some more properties and commands compared to the ChatViewModel defined earlier. The NewGroup property defines the group the user registers to. The SelectedGroup property defines the group that is used with the continued communication, such as sending a message to the group or leaving the group. The SelectedGroup property needs change notification to update the user interface on changing this property; that's why the INotifyPropertyChanged interface is implemented with the GroupChatViewModel class, and the set accessor of the property SelectedGroup fires a notification. Commands to join and leave the group are defined as well: the EnterGroupCommand and LeaveGroupCommand properties (code file WPFChatClient/ViewModels/GroupChatViewModel.cs):

```
public sealed class GroupChatViewModel: IDisposable, INotifyPropertyChanged
{
    private readonly IMessagingService _messagingService;
    public GroupChatViewModel(IMessagingService messagingService)
    {
        _messagingService = messagingService;
```

```
      ConnectCommand = new DelegateCommand(OnConnect);
      SendCommand = new DelegateCommand(OnSendMessage);
      EnterGroupCommand = new DelegateCommand(OnEnterGroup);
      LeaveGroupCommand = new DelegateCommand(OnLeaveGroup);
    }

    private const string ServerURI = "http://localhost:45269/signalr";

    public event PropertyChangedEventHandler PropertyChanged;

    public string Name { get; set; }
    public string Message { get; set; }
    public string NewGroup { get; set; }

    private string _selectedGroup;
    public string SelectedGroup
    {
      get { return _selectedGroup; }
      set
      {
        _selectedGroup = value;
        PropertyChanged?.Invoke(this, new PropertyChangedEventArgs(
          nameof(SelectedGroup)));
      }
    }

    public ObservableCollection<string> Messages { get; } =
      new ObservableCollection<string>();
    public ObservableCollection<string> Groups { get; } =
      new ObservableCollection<string>();

    public DelegateCommand SendCommand { get; }
    public DelegateCommand ConnectCommand { get; }
    public DelegateCommand EnterGroupCommand { get; }
    public DelegateCommand LeaveGroupCommand { get; }
    // etc.
  }
```

The handler methods for the `EnterGroupCommand` and `LeaveGroupCommand` commands are shown in the following code snippet. Here, the `AddGroup` and `RemoveGroup` methods are called within the group hub (code file `WPFChatClient/ViewModels/GroupChatViewModel.cs`):

```
public async void OnEnterGroup()
{
  try
  {
    await _hubProxy.Invoke("AddGroup", NewGroup);
    Groups.Add(NewGroup);
    SelectedGroup = NewGroup;
  }
  catch (Exception ex)
  {
    _messagingService.ShowMessage(ex.Message);
  }
}

public async void OnLeaveGroup()
{
  try
  {
    await _hubProxy.Invoke("RemoveGroup", SelectedGroup);
    Groups.Remove(SelectedGroup);
  }
```

```
    catch (Exception ex)
    {
      _messagingService.ShowMessage(ex.Message);
    }
  }
}
```

Sending and receiving the messages is very similar to the previous sample, with the difference that the group information is added now (code file `WPFChatClient/ViewModels/GroupChatViewModel.cs`):

```
public async void OnSendMessage()
{
  try
  {
    await _hubProxy.Invoke("Send", SelectedGroup, Name, Message);
  }
  catch (Exception ex)
  {
    _messagingService.ShowMessage(ex.Message);
  }
}

public void OnMessageReceived(string group, string name, string message)
{
  App.Current.Dispatcher.Invoke(() =>
  {
    Messages.Add($"{group}-{name}: {message}");
  });
}
```

When you run the application, you can send messages for all groups that have been joined and see received messages for all registered groups, as shown in Figure 43-6.

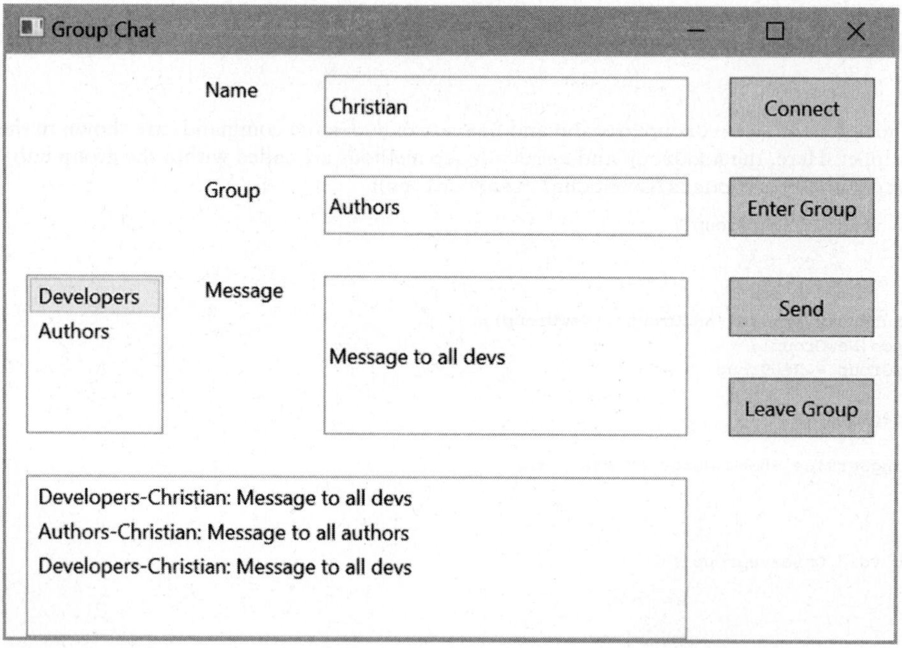

FIGURE 43-6

ARCHITECTURE OF WEBHOOKS

WebHooks offer publish/subscribe functionality with web applications. That's the only similarity between WebHooks and SignalR. Otherwise, WebHooks and SignalR are very different and can take advantage of each other. Before discussing how they can be used together, let's get into an overview of WebHooks.

With WebHooks, an SaaS (Software as a Service) service can call into your website. You just need to register your site with the SaaS service. The SaaS service than calls your website (see Figure 43-7). In your website, the *receiver controller* receives all messages from WebHooks senders and forwards it to the corresponding receiver. The *receiver* verifies security to check whether the message is from the registered sender, and then it forwards the message to the handler. The *handler* contains your custom code to process the request.

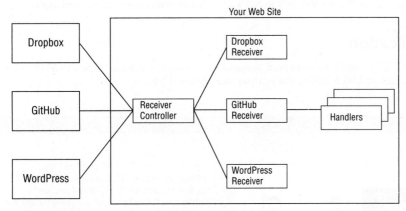

FIGURE 43-7

Contrary to the SignalR technology, the sender and receiver are not always connected. The receiver just offers a service API that is invoked by the sender when needed. The receiver needs to be available on a public Internet address.

The beauty of WebHooks is the ease of use on the receiver side and the support it receives from many SaaS providers, such as Dropbox, GitHub, WordPress, PayPal, Slack, SalesForce, and others. More new providers are coming every week.

Creating a sender is not as easy as creating a receiver, but there's also great support with an ASP.NET Framework. A sender needs a registration option for WebHook receivers, which is typically done using a Web UI. Of course you can also create a Web API instead to register programmatically. With the registration, the sender receives a secret from the receiver together with the URL it needs to call into. This secret is verified by the receiver to only allow senders with this secret. As events occur with the sender, the sender fires a WebHook, which in reality involves invoking a web service of the receiver and passing (mostly) JSON information.

Microsoft's ASP.NET NuGet packages for WebHooks make it easy to implement receivers for different services by abstracting the differences. It's also easy to create the ASP.NET Web API service that verifies the secrets sent by the senders and forward the calls to custom handlers.

To see the ease of use and the beauty of WebHooks, a sample application is shown to create Dropbox and GitHub receivers. When creating multiple receivers you see what's different between the providers and what functionality is offered by the NuGet packages. You can create a receiver to other SaaS providers in a similar manner.

CREATING DROPBOX AND GITHUB RECEIVERS

To create and run the Dropbox and GitHub receiver example, you need both a GitHub and a Dropbox account. With GitHub you need admin access to a repository. Of course, for learning WebHooks, it's fine to use just one of these technologies. What's needed with all the receivers, no matter what service you use, is for you to have a way to make your website publicly available—for example, by publishing to Microsoft Azure.

Dropbox (`http://www.dropbox.com`) offers a file store in the cloud. You can save your files and directories and also share them with others. With WebHooks you can receive information about changes in your Dropbox storage—for example, you can be notified when files are added, modified, and deleted.

GitHub (`http://www.github.com`) offers source code repositories. .NET Core and ASP.NET Core 1.0 are available in public repositories on GitHub, and so is the source code for this book (`http://www.github.com/ProfessionalCSharp/ProfessionalCSharp6`). With the GitHub WebHook you can receive information about push events or about all changes to the repository, such as forks, updates to Wiki pages, issues, and more.

Creating a Web Application

Start by creating an ASP.NET Web Application named `SaasWebHooksReceiverSample`. Select MVC with the ASP.NET 4.6 Templates and add Web API to the options (see Figure 43-8).

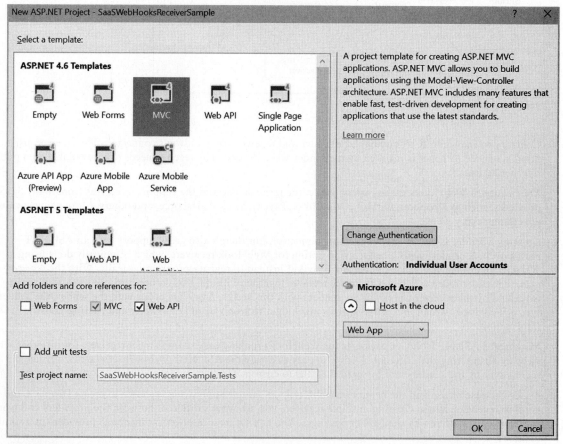

FIGURE 43-8

Next, add the NuGet packages `Microsoft.AspNet.WebHooks.Receivers.Dropbox` and `Microsoft.AspNet.WebHooks.Receivers.GitHub`. These are the NuGet packages that support receiving messages from Dropbox and GitHub. With the NuGet package manager you'll find many more NuGet packages that support other SaaS services.

Configuring WebHooks for Dropbox and GitHub

You can initialize WebHooks for Dropbox by invoking the extension method `InitializeReceiveDropboxWebHooks` and initialize WebHooks for GitHub by invoking the extension method `InitializeReceiveGitHubWebHooks`. You invoke these methods with `HttpConfiguration` in the startup code (code file SaaSWebHooksReceiverSample/App_Start/WebApiConfig.cs):

```csharp
using System.Web.Http;

namespace SaaSWebHooksReceiverSample
{
  public static class WebApiConfig
  {
    public static void Register(HttpConfiguration config)
    {
      config.MapHttpAttributeRoutes();

      config.Routes.MapHttpRoute(
        name: "DefaultApi",
        routeTemplate: "api/{controller}/{id}",
        defaults: new { id = RouteParameter.Optional }
      );

      config.InitializeReceiveDropboxWebHooks();
      config.InitializeReceiveGitHubWebHooks();
    }
  }
}
```

To only allow messages from the defined SaaS services, secrets are used. You can configure these secrets with the application settings. The key for the settings is predefined from the code in the NuGet packages. For Dropbox, the key `MS_WebHookReceiverSecret_Dropbox` is used, with GitHub `MS_WebHookReceiverSecret_GitHub`. Such a secret needs to be at least 15 characters long.

In case you would like to use different Dropbox accounts or different GitHub repositories, you can use different secrets to define multiple secrets with identifiers, as shown in the following code snippet (code file SaaSWebHooksReceiverSample/Web.config):

```xml
<appSettings>
  <add key="webpages:Version" value="3.0.0.0" />
  <add key="webpages:Enabled" value="false" />
  <add key="ClientValidationEnabled" value="true" />
  <add key="UnobtrusiveJavaScriptEnabled" value="true" />
  <add key="MS_WebHookReceiverSecret_Dropbox"
    value="1234512345123451234567890067890,
    dp1=98765432100098765432100098988" />
  <add key="MS_WebHookReceiverSecret_Github"
    value="12345678901234567890123456789000,
    gh1=9876543210987654321O, gh2=8765432109876543210" />
</appSettings>
```

Implementing the Handler

The functionality of the WebHook is implemented in the `WebHookHandler`. What can be done in this handler? You can write the information to a database, to a file, to invoke other services, and so on. Just be aware that the implementation shouldn't take too long—just a few seconds. In cases where the implementation takes too long, the sender might resend the request. For longer activities, it's best to write the information to a queue and work through the queue after the method is finished—for example, by using a background process.

For the sample application receiving an event, a message is written into the Microsoft Azure Storage queue. For using this queuing system you need to create a Storage account at http://portal.azure.com. With the sample application, the Storage account is named professionalcsharp. For using Microsoft Azure Storage, you can add the NuGet package WindowsAzure.Storage to the project.

After creating the Azure Storage account, open the portal and copy the account name and primary access key, and add this information to the configuration file (code file SaaSWebHooksSampleReceiver/web.config):

```
<add key="StorageConnectionString"
  value="DefaultEndpointsProtocol=https;
    AccountName=add your account name;AccountKey=add your account key==" />
```

To send a message to the queue, you create the QueueManager. In the constructor, you create a CloudStorageAccount object by reading the configuration files from the configuration file. The CloudStorageAccount allows accessing the different Azure Storage facilities such as queue, table, and blob storage. The method CreateCloudQueueClient returns a CloudQueueClient that allows creating queues and writing messages to queues. If the queue does not yet exist, it is created by CreateIfNotExists. The AddMessage of the queue writes a message (code file SaaSWebHooksSampleReceiver/WebHookHandlers/QueueManager.cs):

```
public class QueueManager
{
    private CloudStorageAccount _storageAccount;

    public QueueManager()
    {
        _storageAccount = CloudStorageAccount.Parse(
          ConfigurationManager.AppSettings["StorageConnectionString"]);
    }

    public void WriteToQueueStorage(string queueName, string actions,
      string json)
    {
        CloudQueueClient client = _storageAccount.CreateCloudQueueClient();

        CloudQueue queue = client.GetQueueReference(queueName);
        queue.CreateIfNotExists();
        var message = new CloudQueueMessage(actions + "--" + json);
        queue.AddMessage(message);
    }
}
```

Next, let's get into the most important part of the WebHook implementation: the custom handlers for the Dropbox and GitHub events. A WebHook handler derives from the base class WebHookHandler and overrides the abstract method ExecuteAsync from the base class. With this method, you receive the receiver and the context from the WebHook. The receiver contains the information about the SaaS service—for example, github and dropbox with the sample code. After the responsible receiver received the event, all the handlers are invoked one after the other. If every handler is used for a different service, it's best to check the receiver first and compare it to the corresponding service before executing the code. With the sample code, both handlers invoke the same functionality with the only difference being different queue names. Here, just one handler would suffice. However, because you usually have different implementations based on the SaaS service, two handlers have been implemented in the sample code where each checks for the receiver name. With the WebHookHandlerContext you can access a collection of actions, which is a list of reasons why the WebHook was fired, information about the request from the caller, and the JSON object that was sent from the service. The actions and the JSON object are written to the Azure Storage queue (code file `SaaSWebHooksSampleReceiver/WebHookHandlers/GithubWebHookHandler.cs`):

```
public class GithubWebHookHandler: WebHookHandler
{
  public override Task ExecuteAsync(string receiver,
    WebHookHandlerContext context)
  {
    if ("GitHub".Equals(receiver, StringComparison.CurrentCultureIgnoreCase))
    {
      QueueManager queue = null;
      try
      {
        queue = new QueueManager();
        string actions = string.Join(", ", context.Actions);
        JObject incoming = context.GetDataOrDefault<JObject>();

        queue.WriteToQueueStorage("githubqueue", actions, incoming.ToString());
      }
      catch (Exception ex)
      {
        queue?.WriteToQueueStorage("githubqueue", "error", ex.Message);
      }
    }
    return Task.FromResult<object>(null);
  }
}
```

With the implementation in a production scenario you can already read information from the JSON object and react accordingly. However, remember that you should do the work within the handler within a few seconds. Otherwise the service can resend the WebHook. This behavior is different based on the providers.

With the handlers implemented, you can build the project and publish the application to Microsoft Azure. You can publish directly from the Solution Explorer in Visual Studio. Select the project, choose the Publish context menu, and select a Microsoft Azure App Service target.

> **NOTE** *Publishing your website to Microsoft Azure is explained in Chapter 45, "Deploying Websites and Services."*

After publishing you can configure Dropbox and GitHub. For these configurations, the site already needs to be publicly available.

Configuring the Application with Dropbox and GitHub

To enable WebHooks with Dropbox, you need to create an app in the Dropbox App Console at `https://www.dropbox.com/developers/apps`, as shown in Figure 43-9.

To receive WebHooks from Dropbox, you need to register the public URI of your website. When you host the site with Microsoft Azure, the host name is `<hostname>.azurewebsites.net`. The service of the receiver listens at `/api/webhooks/incoming/provider`—for example, with Dropbox at `https://professionalcsharp.azurewebsites.net/api/webhooks/incoming/dropbox`. In case you registered more than one secret, other than the URIs of the other secrets, add the secret key to the URI, such as `/api/webhooks/incoming/dropbox/dp1`.

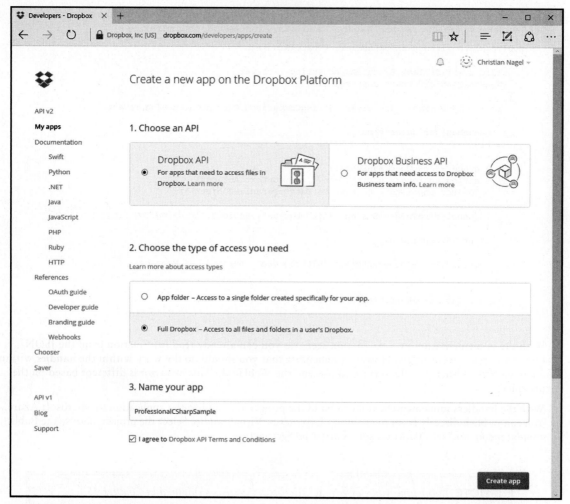

FIGURE 43-9

Dropbox verifies a valid URI by sending a challenge that must be returned. You can try that out with your receiver that is configured for Dropbox to access the URI `hostname/api/webhooks/incoming/dropbox/?challenge=12345`, which should return the string `12345`.

To enable WebHooks with GitHub, open the Settings of a GitHub repository (see Figure 43-10). There you need to add a payload link, which is `http://<hostname>/api/webhooks/incoming/github` with this project. Also, don't forget to add the secret, which must be the same as defined in the configuration file. With the GitHub configuration, you can select either `application/json` or Form-based `application/x-www-form-urlencoded` content from GitHub. With the events, you can select to receive just push events, all events, or select individual events.

> **NOTE** *If you use an ASP.NET Web App, you can use a Wizard to enable WebHooks with GitHub.*

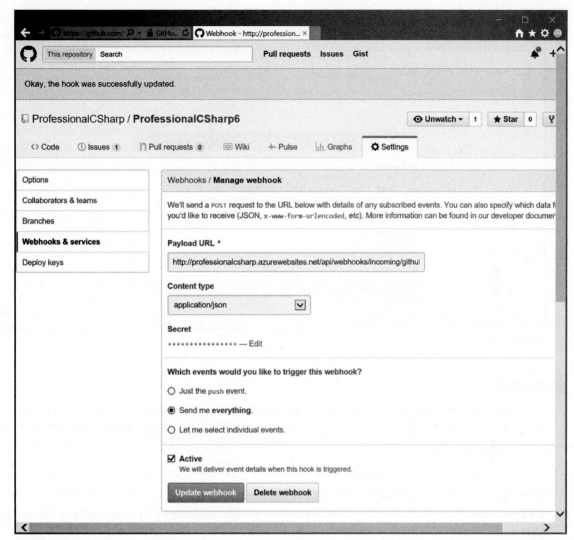

FIGURE 43-10

Running the Application

With the configured public web application, as you make changes to your Dropbox folder or changes in your GitHub repository, you will find new messages arriving in the Microsoft Azure Storage queue. From within Visual Studio, you can directly access the queue using the *Cloud Explorer*. Selecting your storage account within the Storage Accounts tree entry, you can see the Queues entry that shows all the generated queues. When you open the queue, you can see messages like the one shown in Figure 43-11.

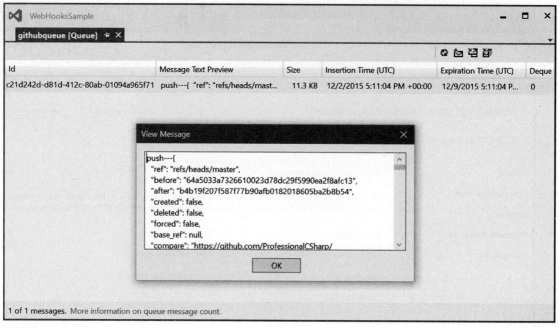

FIGURE 43-11

SUMMARY

This chapter described publish/subscribe mechanisms with web applications. With SignalR there's an easy way to make use of the WebSocket technology that keeps a network connection open to allow passing information from the server to the client. SignalR also works with older clients in that as a fallback polling is used if WebSockets is not available.

You've seen how to create SignalR hubs and communicate both from a JavaScript as well as a .NET client.

With SignalR's support of groups, you've seen how the server can send information to a group of clients.

With the sample code you've seen how to chat between multiple clients using SignalR. Similarly, you can use SignalR with many other scenarios—for example, if you have some information from devices that call Web APIs with the server, you can inform connected clients with this information.

In the coverage of WebHooks you've seen another technology based on a publish/subscribe mechanism. WebHooks is unlike SignalR in that it can be used only with receivers available with public Internet addresses because the senders (typically SaaS services) publish information by calling web services. With the features of WebHooks, you've seen that many SaaS services provide WebHooks, and it's easy to create receivers that receive information from these services.

To get WebHooks forwarded to clients that are behind the firewall, you can combine WebHooks with SignalR. You just need to pass on WebHook information to connected SignalR clients.

The next chapter gives you information about Windows Communication Foundation (WCF), a mature technology that is based on SOAP and offers advanced features for communication.

44

Windows Communication Foundation

WHAT'S IN THIS CHAPTER?

- ➤ WCF overview
- ➤ Creating a simple service and client
- ➤ Defining service, operation, data, and message contracts
- ➤ Implementing a service
- ➤ Using binding for communication
- ➤ Creating different hosts for services
- ➤ Creating clients with a service reference and programmatically
- ➤ Using duplex communication
- ➤ Using routing

WROX.COM CODE DOWNLOADS FOR THIS CHAPTER

You can find the wrox.com code downloads for this chapter at www.wrox.com/go/professionalcsharp6 on the Download Code tab. The code for this chapter is divided into the following major examples:

- ➤ Simple service and client
- ➤ WebSockets
- ➤ Duplex communication
- ➤ Routing

WCF OVERVIEW

Chapter 42 covered ASP.NET Web API, a communication technology based on Representational State Transfer (REST). The big and older brother for communication between client and server is Windows Communication Foundation (WCF). This technology was originally invented with .NET 3.0 to replace different technologies, such as .NET Remoting for fast communication between .NET applications and ASP.NET Web Services and Web Services Enhancements (WSE) for platform-independent communication. Nowadays, WCF is much more complex compared to ASP.NET Web API, but it also offers some more features, such as reliability, transactions, and web services security. In case you don't need any of these advance communication features, ASP.NET Web API might be the better choice. WCF is important for these additional features and to support legacy applications.

The major namespace covered in this chapter is `System.ServiceModel`.

> **NOTE** *Although most chapters in this book are based on the new .NET Framework stack—.NET Core 1.0—this chapter requires the full framework. The client-side part of WCF is available with .NET Core, but the server side requires the full .NET Framework. With these samples, .NET 4.6 is used. Where possible, I make use of .NET Core. The libraries used for defining the contracts and doing data access are built using .NET Core.*

You can get the following from WCF:

➤ **Hosting for components and services**—Just as you can use custom hosts with .NET Remoting and Web Service Enhancements (WSE), you can host a WCF service in the ASP.NET runtime, a Windows service, a COM+ process, or a WPF application for peer-to-peer computing.

➤ **Declarative behavior**—Instead of the requirement to derive from a base class (this requirement exists with .NET Remoting and Enterprise Services), attributes can be used to define the services. This is similar to web services developed with ASP.NET.

➤ **Communication channels**—Although .NET Remoting is flexible for changing the communication channel, WCF is a good alternative because it offers the same flexibility. WCF offers multiple channels to communicate using HTTP, TCP, or an IPC channel. Custom channels using different transport protocols can be created as well.

➤ **Security infrastructure**—For implementing platform-independent web services, you must use a standardized security environment. The proposed standards are implemented with WSE 3.0, and this continues with WCF.

➤ **Extensibility**—.NET Remoting has a rich extensibility story. It is not only possible to create custom channels, formatters, and proxies but also to inject functionality inside the message flow on the client and on the server. WCF offers similar extensibilities; however, here the extensions are created by using SOAP headers.

The final goal is to send and receive messages between a client and a service across processes or different systems, across a local network, or across the Internet. This should be done, if required, in a platform-independent way and as fast as possible. From a distant view, the service offers an endpoint that is described by a contract, a binding, and an address. The contract defines the operations offered by the service; binding gives information about the protocol and encoding; and the address is the location of the service. The client needs a compatible endpoint to access the service.

Figure 44-1 shows the components that participate with a WCF communication.

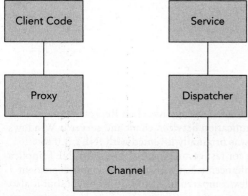

FIGURE 44-1

The client invokes a method on the proxy. The proxy offers methods as defined by the service but converts the method call to a message and transfers the message to the channel. The channel has a client-side part and a server-side part that communicate across a networking protocol. From the channel, the message is passed to the dispatcher, which converts the message to a method call invoked with the service.

WCF supports several communication protocols. For platform-independent communication, web services standards are supported. For communication between .NET applications, faster communication protocols with less overhead can be used.

Chapter 42 describes communication across HTTP using REST programming style passing objects in a JavaScript Object Notation (JSON) format, and a description of the service API with Swagger. With WCF, some other technologies are important: SOAP, a platform-independent protocol that is the foundation of several web service specifications to support security, transactions, and reliability, and the Web Services Description Language (WSDL) that offers metadata to describe the service.

SOAP

For platform-independent communication, you can use the SOAP protocol; it is directly supported from WCF. SOAP originally was shorthand for Simple Object Access Protocol, but since SOAP 1.2 this is no longer the case. SOAP no longer is an object access protocol because instead messages are sent that can be defined by an XML schema. Now it's not an acronym anymore; SOAP is just SOAP.

A service receives a SOAP message from a client and returns a SOAP response message. A SOAP message consists of an envelope, which contains a header and a body:

```
<s:Envelope xmlns:s="http://schemas.xmlsoap.org/soap/envelope/">
  <s:Header>
  </s:Header>
  <s:Body>
    <ReserveRoom xmlns="http://www.cninnovation.com/RoomReservation/2015">
      <roomReservation xmlns:a=
        "http://schemas.datacontract.org/2004/07/Wrox.ProCSharp.WCF.Contracts"
        xmlns:i="http://www.w3.org/2001/XMLSchema-instance">
        <a:Contact>UEFA</a:Contact>
        <a:EndTime>2015-07-28T22:00:00</a:EndTime>
        <a:Id>0</a:Id>
        <a:RoomName>Athens</a:RoomName>
        <a:StartTime>2015-07-28T20:00:00</a:StartTime>
        <a:Text>Panathinaikos-Club Brugge</a:Text>
      </roomReservation>
    </ReserveRoom>
  </s:Body>
</s:Envelope>
```

The header is optional and can contain information about addressing, security, and transactions. The body contains the message data.

WSDL

A Web Services Description Language (WSDL) document describes the operations and messages of the service. WSDL defines metadata of the service that can be used to create a proxy for the client application.

The WSDL contains this information:

➤ **Types** for the messages described using an XML schema.

➤ **Messages** sent to and from the service. Parts of the messages are the types defined with an XML schema.

➤ **Port types** map to service contracts and list operations defined with the service contract. Operations contain messages; for example, an input and an output message as used with a request and response sequence.

➤ **Binding** information that contains the operations listed with the port types and that defines the SOAP variant used.

➤ **Service** information that maps port types to endpoint addresses.

> **NOTE** *With WCF, WSDL information is offered by Metadata Exchange (MEX) endpoints.*

CREATING A SIMPLE SERVICE AND CLIENT

Before going into the details of WCF, start with a simple service. The service is used to reserve meeting rooms.

For a backing store of room reservations, a simple SQL Server database with the table `RoomReservations` is used. The database is created with the sample application using Entity Framework Migrations.

Following are the next steps to create a service and a client:

1. Create service and data contracts.
2. Create a library to access the database using the Entity Framework Core.
3. Implement the service.
4. Use the WCF Service Host and WCF Test Client.
5. Create a custom service host.
6. Create a client application using metadata.
7. Create a client application using shared contracts.
8. Configure diagnostics.

Defining Service and Data Contracts

To start, create a new solution with the name `RoomReservation`. Add a new project of type Class Library to the solution, and name the project `RoomReservationContracts`.

The sample code for the `RoomReservationContracts` library makes use of the following dependencies and namespaces:

Dependencies

```
System.ComponentModel.DataAnnotations
System.Runtime.Serialization
System.ServiceModel
```

Namespaces

```
System
System.Collections.Generic
System.ComponentModel
System.ComponentModel.DataAnnotations
System.Runtime.CompilerServices
System.Runtime.Serialization
System.ServiceModel
```

Create a new class named `RoomReservation`. This class contains the properties `Id`, `RoomName`, `StartTime`, `EndTime`, `Contact`, and `Text` to define the data needed in the database and sent across the network. For sending the data across a WCF service, the class is annotated with the `DataContract` and the `DataMember` attributes. The attributes `StringLength` from the namespace `System.ComponentModel.DataAnnotations` can not only be used with validation on user input but they can also define column schemas on creating the database table (code file RoomReservation/RoomReservationContracts/RoomReservation.cs):

```
using System;
using System.Collections.Generic;
using System.ComponentModel;
using System.ComponentModel.DataAnnotations;
using System.Runtime.CompilerServices;
using System.Runtime.Serialization;

namespace Wrox.ProCSharp.WCF.Contracts
{
  [DataContract]
  public class RoomReservation : INotifyPropertyChanged
  {
    private int _id;

    [DataMember]
    public int Id
    {
      get { return _id; }
      set { SetProperty(ref _id, value); }
    }

    private string _roomName;

    [DataMember]
    [StringLength(30)]
    public string RoomName
    {
      get { return _roomName; }
      set { SetProperty(ref _roomName, value); }
    }

    private DateTime _startTime;

    [DataMember]
    public DateTime StartTime
    {
      get { return _startTime; }
      set { SetProperty(ref _startTime, value); }
    }

    private DateTime _endTime;

    [DataMember]
    public DateTime EndTime
    {
      get { return _endTime; }
      set { SetProperty(ref _endTime, value); }
    }

    private string _contact;

    [DataMember]
    [StringLength(30)]
    public string Contact
    {
```

```
      get { return _contact; }
      set { SetProperty(ref _contact, value); }
    }

    private string _text;

    [DataMember]
    [StringLength(50)]
    public string Text
    {
      get { return _text; }
      set { SetProperty(ref _text, value); }
    }

    protected virtual void OnNotifyPropertyChanged(string propertyName)
    {
      PropertyChanged?.Invoke(this,
        new PropertyChangedEventArgs(propertyName));
    }

    protected virtual void SetProperty<T>(ref T item, T value,
      [CallerMemberName] string propertyName = null)
    {
      if (!EqualityComparer<T>.Default.Equals(item, value))
      {
        item = value;
        OnNotifyPropertyChanged(propertyName);
      }
    }

    public event PropertyChangedEventHandler PropertyChanged;
  }
}
```

Next, create the service contract. The operations offered by the service can be defined by an interface. The interface `IRoomService` defines the methods `ReserveRoom` and `GetRoomReservations`. The service contract is defined with the attribute `ServiceContract`. The operations defined by the service have the attribute `OperationContract` applied (code file RoomReservation/RoomReservationContracts/IRoomService.cs).

```
using System;
using System.ServiceModel;

namespace Wrox.ProCSharp.WCF.Contracts
{
  [ServiceContract(
    Namespace="http://www.cninnovation.com/RoomReservation/2016")]
  public interface IRoomService
  {
    [OperationContract]
    bool ReserveRoom(RoomReservation roomReservation);

    [OperationContract]
    RoomReservation[] GetRoomReservations(DateTime fromTime, DateTime toTime);
  }
}
```

Data Access

Next, create a library used to access, read, and write reservations to the database named `RoomReservationData` with Entity Framework 6.1. The class to define the entities was already defined with the `RoomReservationContracts` assembly, so this assembly needs to be referenced. Also the `Microsoft.EntityFrameworkCore` as well as `Microsoft.EntityFrameworkCore.SqlServer` NuGet packages are required.

The sample code for all the `RoomReservationData` library makes use of the following dependencies and namespaces:

Dependencies

```
Microsoft.EntityFrameworkCore
Microsoft.EntityFrameworkCore.Commands
Microsoft.EntityFrameworkCore.SqlServer
```

Namespaces

```
Microsoft.EntityFrameworkCore
System
System.Linq
Wrox.ProCSharp.WCF.Contracts
```

Now the `RoomReservationContext` class can be created. This class derives from the base class `DbContext` to act as a context for the ADO.NET Entity Framework and defines a property named `RoomReservations` to return a `DbSet<RoomReservation>` (code file `RoomReservation/RoomReservationData/RoomReservationContext.cs`):

```
using Microsoft.EntityFrameworkCore;
using Wrox.ProCSharp.WCF.Contracts;

namespace Wrox.ProCSharp.WCF.Data
{
  public class RoomReservationContext : DbContext
  {
    protected void override OnConfiguring(
      DbContextOptionsBuilder optionsBuilder)
    {
      optionsBuilder.UseSqlServer(@"server=(localdb)\mssqllocaldb;" +
        @"Database=RoomReservation;trusted_connection=true");
    }

    public DbSet<RoomReservation> RoomReservations { get; set; }
  }
}
```

Entity Framework defines the `OnConfiguring` method with the `DbContext` where the data context can be configured. The `UseSqlServer` extension method (that is defined within the `EntityFramework.MicrosoftSqlServer` NuGet package) allows setting the connection string to the database.

The commands to create the database depend on whether you created a .NET 4.6 class library or a .NET Core class library. With a .NET 4.6 class library, you can create the database using the NuGet Package Manager Console and apply the following commands. With the `Add-Migration` command, a `Migrations` folder is created in the project with code to create the table `RoomReservation`. The `Update-Database` command applies the migration and creates the database.

```
> Add-Migration InitRoomReservation
> Update-Database
```

Functionality that will be used by the service implementation is defined with the `RoomReservationRepository` class. The method `ReserveRoom` writes a new record to the database, and

the method `GetReservations` returns a collection of `RoomReservation` for a specified time span (code file
`RoomReservation/RoomReservationData/RoomReservationRepository.cs`):

```
using System;
using System.Linq;
using Wrox.ProCSharp.WCF.Contracts;

namespace Wrox.ProCSharp.WCF.Data
{
  public class RoomReservationRepository
  {
    public void ReserveRoom(RoomReservation roomReservation)
    {
      using (var data = new RoomReservationContext())
      {
        data.RoomReservations.Add(roomReservation);
        data.SaveChanges();
      }
    }

    public RoomReservation[] GetReservations(DateTime fromTime,
      DateTime toTime)
    {
      using (var data = new RoomReservationContext())
      {
        return (from r in data.RoomReservations
                where r.StartTime > fromTime && r.EndTime < toTime
                select r).ToArray();
      }
    }
  }
}
```

> **NOTE** *Chapter 38, "Entity Framework Core," gives you the details of the ADO
> .NET Entity Framework, including configuring migrations with .NET Core
> projects.*

Service Implementation

Now you can step into the implementation of the service. Create a WCF service library named
`RoomReservationService`. By default, this library type contains both the service contract and the service
implementation. If the client application just uses metadata information to create a proxy for accessing the
service, this model is okay to work with. However, if the client might use the contract types directly, it is a
better idea to put the contracts in a separate assembly as it was done here. With the first client that is done,
a proxy is created from metadata. Later you can see how to create a client to share the contract assembly.
Splitting the contracts and implementation is a good preparation for this.

The service class `RoomReservationService` implements the interface `IRoomService`. The service is
implemented just by invoking the appropriate methods of the `RoomReservationData` class (code file
`RoomReservation/RoomReservationService/RoomReservationService.cs`):

```
using System;
using System.ServiceModel;
using Wrox.ProCSharp.WCF.Contracts;
using Wrox.ProCSharp.WCF.Data;

namespace Wrox.ProCSharp.WCF.Service
```

```
      {
        [ServiceBehavior(InstanceContextMode = InstanceContextMode.PerCall)]
        public class RoomReservationService : IRoomService
        {
          public bool ReserveRoom(RoomReservation roomReservation)
          {
            var data = new RoomReservationRepository();
            data.ReserveRoom(roomReservation);
            return true;
          }

          public RoomReservation[] GetRoomReservations(DateTime fromTime,
              DateTime toTime)
          {
            var data = new RoomReservationRepository();
            return data.GetReservations(fromTime, toTime);
          }
        }
      }
```

Figure 44-2 shows the assemblies created so far and their dependencies. The RoomReservationContracts assembly is used by both RoomReservationData and RoomReservationService.

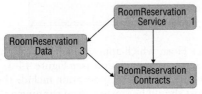

FIGURE 44-2

WCF Service Host and WCF Test Client

The WCF Service Library project template creates an application configuration file named App.config that you need to adapt to the new class and interface names. The service element references the service type RoomReservationService, including the namespace; the contract interface needs to be defined with the endpoint element (configuration file RoomReservation/RoomReservationService/app.config):

```xml
<?xml version="1.0" encoding="utf-8" ?>
<configuration>
  <system.web>
    <compilation debug="true" />
  </system.web>
  <system.serviceModel>
    <services>
      <service name="Wrox.ProCSharp.WCF.Service.RoomService">
        <endpoint address="" binding="basicHttpBinding"
            contract="Wrox.ProCSharp.WCF.Service.IRoomService">
          <identity>
            <dns value="localhost" />
          </identity>
        </endpoint>
        <endpoint address="mex" binding="mexHttpBinding"
            contract="IMetadataExchange" />
        <host>
          <baseAddresses>
            <add baseAddress=
"http://localhost:8733/Design_Time_Addresses/RoomReservationService/Service1/"
```

```
                  />
              </baseAddresses>
            </host>
          </service>
        </services>
        <behaviors>
          <serviceBehaviors>
            <behavior>
              <serviceMetadata httpGetEnabled="True" httpsGetEnabled="True"/>
              <serviceDebug includeExceptionDetailInFaults="False" />
            </behavior>
          </serviceBehaviors>
        </behaviors>
      </system.serviceModel>
    </configuration>
```

> **NOTE** *The service address* `http://localhost:8733/Design_Time_Addresses`
> *has an access control list (ACL) associated with it that enables the interactive user*
> *to create a listener port. By default, a nonadministrative user is not allowed to*
> *open ports in listening mode. You can view the ACLs with the command-line util-*
> *ity* `netsh http show urlacl` *and add new entries with* `netsh http add urlacl`
> `url=http://+:8080/MyURI user=someUser listen=yes`

Starting this library from Visual Studio 2015 starts the WCF Service Host, which appears as an icon in the notification area of the taskbar. Clicking this icon opens the WCF Service Host window (see Figure 44-3), where you can see the status of the service. The project properties of a WCF library application include the tab WCF options, where you can select whether the WCF service host should be started when running a project from the same solution. By default, this option is turned on. Also, with the Debug configuration of the project properties, you can find the command-line argument `/client: "WcfTestClient.exe"` defined. With this option, the WCF Service host starts the WCF Test Client (see Figure 44-4), which you can use to test the application. When you double-click an operation, input fields appear on the right side of the application that you can fill to send data to the service. When you click the XML tab, you can see the SOAP messages that have been sent and received.

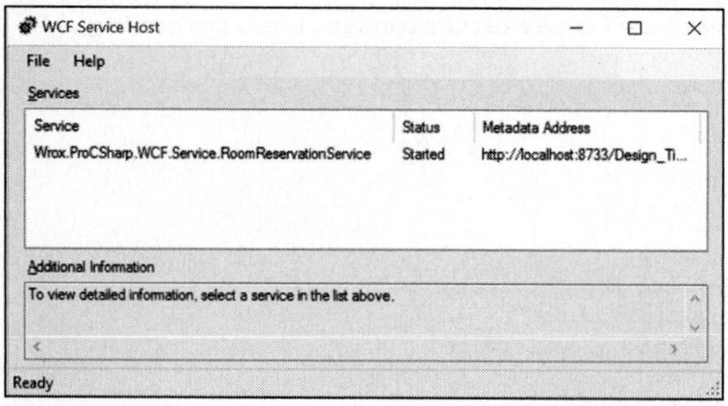

FIGURE 44-3

Custom Service Host

WCF enables services to run in any host. You can create a Windows Presentation Foundation (WPF) application for peer-to-peer services. Or you can create a Windows service or host the service with Windows

Activation Services (WAS) or Internet Information Services (IIS). A console application is also good to demonstrate a simple custom host.

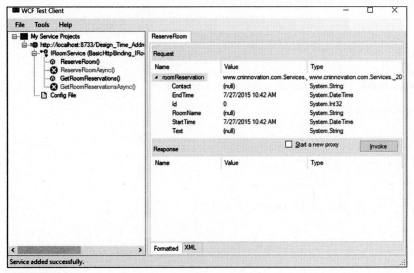

FIGURE 44-4

With the service host, you must reference the library `RoomReservationService` in addition to the assembly `System.ServiceModel`. The service is started by instantiating and opening an object of type `ServiceHost`. This class is defined in the namespace `System.ServiceModel`. The `RoomReservationService` class that implements the service is defined in the constructor. Invoking the `Open` method starts the listener channel of the service—the service is ready to listen for requests. The `Close` method stops the channel. The code snippet also adds a behavior of type `ServiceMetadataBehavior`. This behavior is added to allow creating a client application by using WSDL (code file RoomReservation/RoomReservationHost/Program.cs):

```
using System;
using System.ServiceModel;
using System.ServiceModel.Description;
using Wrox.ProCSharp.WCF.Service;
using static System.Console;

namespace Wrox.ProCSharp.WCF.Host
{
  class Program
  {
    internal static ServiceHost s_ServiceHost = null;

    internal static void StartService()
    {
      try
      {
        s_ServiceHost = new ServiceHost(typeof(RoomReservationService),
          new Uri("http://localhost:9000/RoomReservation"));
        s_ServiceHost.Description.Behaviors.Add(
          new ServiceMetadataBehavior
          {
            HttpGetEnabled = true
          });
        myServiceHost.Open();
      }
```

```
            catch (AddressAccessDeniedException)
            {
                WriteLine("either start Visual Studio in elevated admin " +
                    "mode or register the listener port with netsh.exe");
            }
        }

        internal static void StopService()
        {
            if (s_ServiceHost != null &&
                s_ServiceHost.State       == CommunicationState.Opened)
            {
                s_ServiceHost.Close();
            }
        }

        static void Main()
        {
            StartService();

            WriteLine("Server is running. Press return to exit");
            ReadLine();

            StopService();
        }
    }
}
```

For the WCF configuration, you can copy the application configuration file created with the service library to the host application. You can edit this configuration file with the WCF Service Configuration Editor (see Figure 44-5).

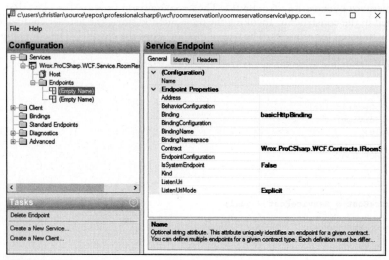

FIGURE 44-5

Instead of using the configuration file, you can configure everything programmatically and also use several defaults. The sample code for the host application doesn't need any configuration file. The second parameter of the `ServiceHost` constructor defines a base address for the service. With the protocol of this base address, a default binding is defined. The default for the HTTP is the `BasicHttpBinding`.

Using the custom service host, you can deselect the WCF option to start the WCF Service Host in the project settings of the WCF library.

WCF Client

For the client, WCF is flexible in what application type can be used. The client can be a simple console application. However, for reserving rooms, you create a simple WPF application with controls, as shown in Figure 44-6.

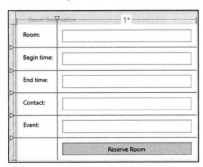

FIGURE 44-6

Because the service host is configured with the `ServiceMetadataBehavior`, it offers a MEX endpoint. After the service host is started, you can add a service reference from Visual Studio. After you add the service reference, the dialog shown in Figure 44-7 pops up. Enter the link to the service metadata with the URL `http://localhost:9000/RoomReservation?wsdl`, and set the namespace name to `RoomReservationService`. This defines the namespace of the generated proxy class.

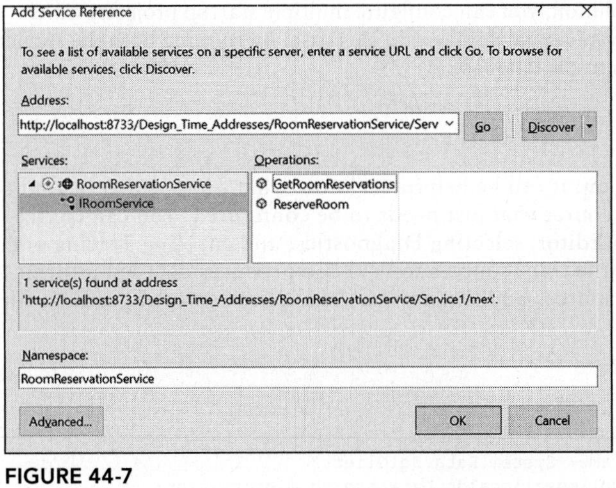

FIGURE 44-7

Adding a service reference adds references to the assemblies `System.Runtime.Serialization` and `System.ServiceModel`, and it also adds a configuration file containing the binding information and the endpoint address to the service.

From the data contract, the class `RoomReservation` is generated as a partial class. This class contains all `[DataMember]` elements of the contract. The class `RoomServiceClient` is the proxy for the client that contains methods that are defined by the operation contracts. Using this client, you can send a room reservation to the running service.

In the code file `RoomReservation/RoomReservationClient/MainWindow.xaml.cs`, the `OnReserveRoom` method is invoked with the `Click` event of the button. The `ReserveRoomAsync` is invoked with the service proxy. The `reservation` variable receives the data from the UI via data binding.

```
public partial class MainWindow : Window
{
  private RoomReservation _reservation;

  public MainWindow()
  {
    InitializeComponent();
     reservation = new RoomReservation
    {
      StartTime = DateTime.Now,
      EndTime = DateTime.Now.AddHours(1)
    };
    this.DataContext = _reservation;
  }

  private async void OnReserveRoom(object sender, RoutedEventArgs e)
  {
    var client = new RoomServiceClient();
    bool reserved = await client.ReserveRoomAsync(reservation);
    client.Close();
    if (reserved)
    {
      MessageBox.Show("reservation ok");
    }
  }
}
```

With the settings of the `RoomReservation` solution, you can configure multiple startup projects, which should be `RoomReservationClient` and `RoomReservationHost` in this case. By running both the service and the client, you can add room reservations to the database.

Diagnostics

When running a client and service application, it can be helpful to know what's happening behind the scenes. For this, WCF makes use of a trace source that just needs to be configured. You can configure tracing using the Service Configuration Editor, selecting Diagnostics, and enabling Tracing and Message Logging. Setting the trace level of the trace sources to `Verbose` produces detailed information. This configuration change adds trace sources and listeners to the application configuration file as shown here:

```
<?xml version="1.0" encoding="utf-8" ?>
<configuration>
  <connectionStrings>
    <add
      name="RoomReservation" providerName="System.Data.SqlClient"
      connectionString="Server=(localdb)\mssqllocaldb;Database=RoomReservation;
      Trusted_Connection=true;MultipleActiveResultSets=True" />
  </connectionStrings>

  <system.diagnostics>
    <sources>
      <source name="System.ServiceModel.MessageLogging"
```

```
              switchValue="Verbose,ActivityTracing">
          <listeners>
            <add type="System.Diagnostics.DefaultTraceListener" name="Default">
              <filter type="" />
            </add>
            <add name="ServiceModelMessageLoggingListener">
              <filter type="" />
            </add>
          </listeners>
        </source>
        <source propagateActivity="true" name="System.ServiceModel"
            switchValue="Warning,ActivityTracing">
          <listeners>
            <add type="System.Diagnostics.DefaultTraceListener" name="Default">
              <filter type="" />
            </add>
            <add name="ServiceModelTraceListener">
              <filter type="" />
            </add>
          </listeners>
        </source>
      </sources>
      <sharedListeners>
        <add initializeData=
          "c:\logs\wcf\roomreservation\roomreservationhost\app_messages.svclog"
          type="System.Diagnostics.XmlWriterTraceListener, System,
          Version=4.0.0.0, Culture=neutral, PublicKeyToken=b77a5c561934e089"
          name="ServiceModelMessageLoggingListener"
          traceOutputOptions="DateTime, Timestamp, ProcessId, ThreadId">
          <filter type="" />
        </add>
        <add initializeData=
          "c:\logs\wcf\roomreservation\roomreservationhost\app_tracelog.svclog"
          type="System.Diagnostics.XmlWriterTraceListener, System,
          Version=4.0.0.0, Culture=neutral, PublicKeyToken=b77a5c561934e089"
          name="ServiceModelTraceListener"
          traceOutputOptions="DateTime, Timestamp, ProcessId, ThreadId">
          <filter type="" />
        </add>
      </sharedListeners>
    </system.diagnostics>
    <startup>
      <supportedRuntime version="v4.0" sku=".NETFramework,Version=v4.6" />
    </startup>
    <system.serviceModel>
      <diagnostics>
        <messageLogging logEntireMessage="true" logMalformedMessages="true"
          logMessagesAtTransportLevel="true" />
        <endToEndTracing propagateActivity="true" activityTracing="true"
          messageFlowTracing="true" />
      </diagnostics>
    </system.serviceModel>
  </configuration>
```

> **NOTE** *The implementation of the WCF classes uses the trace sources named* System.ServiceModel *and* System.ServiceModel.MessageLogging *for writing trace messages. You can read more about tracing and configuring trace sources and listeners in Chapter 20, "Diagnostics and Application Insights."*

When you start the application, the trace files soon get large with verbose trace settings. To analyze the information from the XML log file, the .NET SDK includes the Service Trace Viewer tool, `svctraceviewer.exe`. Figure 44-8 shows the client application with some data entered, and Figure 44-9 shows the view from the `svctraceviewer.exe` after selecting the trace and message log files. The `BasicHttpBinding` is light with the messages sent across. If you change the configuration to use the `WsHttpBinding`, you see many messages related to security. Depending on your security needs, you can choose other configuration options.

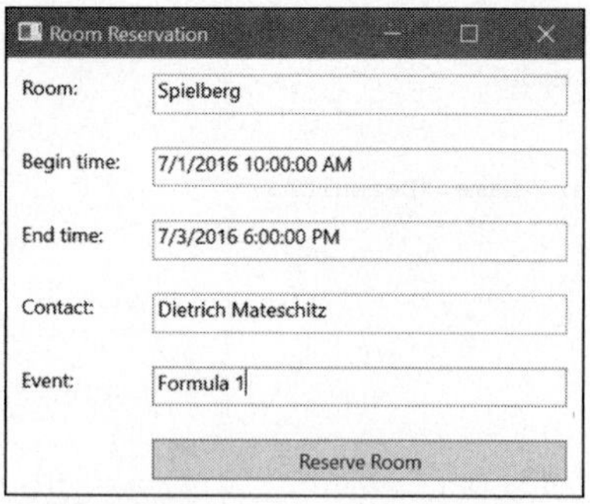

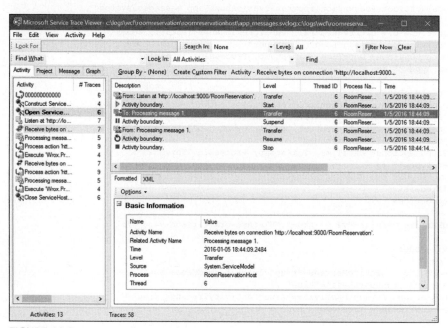

FIGURE 44-8

FIGURE 44-9

The following sections discuss the details and different options of WCF.

Sharing Contract Assemblies with the Client

With the previous WPF client application, a proxy class was created using the metadata, adding a service reference with Visual Studio. You can also create a client by using the shared contract assembly as is shown now. Using the contract interface, the `ChannelFactory<TChannel>` class is used to instantiate the channel to connect to the service.

The constructor of the class `ChannelFactory<TChannel>` accepts the binding configuration and endpoint address. The binding must be compatible with the binding defined with the service host, and the address defined with the `EndpointAddress` class references the URI of the running service. The `CreateChannel` method creates a channel to connect to the service. Then you can invoke methods of the service (code file `RoomReservation/RoomReservationClientSharedAssembly/MainWindow.xaml.cs`):

```csharp
using System;
using System.ServiceModel;
using System.Windows;
using Wrox.ProCSharp.WCF.Contracts;

namespace RoomReservationClientSharedAssembly
{
  public partial class MainWindow : Window
  {
    private RoomReservation _roomReservation;

    public MainWindow()
    {
      InitializeComponent();
      _roomReservation = new RoomReservation
      {
        StartTime = DateTime.Now,
        EndTime = DateTime.Now.AddHours(1)
      };
      this.DataContext = _roomReservation;
    }

    private void OnReserveRoom(object sender, RoutedEventArgs e)
    {
      var binding = new BasicHttpBinding();
      var address = new EndpointAddress(
        "http://localhost:9000/RoomReservation");
      var factory = new ChannelFactory<IRoomService>(binding, address);
      IRoomService channel = factory.CreateChannel();
      if (channel.ReserveRoom(_roomReservation))
      {
        MessageBox.Show("success");
      }
    }
  }
}
```

CONTRACTS

A contract defines what functionality a service offers and what functionality can be used by the client. The contract can be completely independent of the implementation of the service.

The contracts defined by WCF can be grouped into four different contract types: Data, Service, Message, and Fault. The contracts can be specified by using .NET attributes:

➤ **Data contract**—The data contract defines the data received by and returned from the service. The classes used for sending and receiving messages have data contract attributes associated with them.

➤ **Service contract**—The service contract is used to define the WSDL that describes the service. This contract is defined with interfaces or classes.

➤ **Operation contract**—The operation contract defines the operation of the service and is defined within the service contract.

➤ **Message contract**—If you need complete control over the SOAP message, a message contract can specify what data should go into the SOAP header and what belongs in the SOAP body.

➤ **Fault contract**—The fault contract defines the error messages that are sent to the client.

The following sections explore these contract types further and discuss versioning issues that you should think about when defining the contracts.

Data Contract

With the data contract, CLR types are mapped to XML schemas. The data contract is different from other .NET serialization mechanisms: with runtime serialization, all fields are serialized (including private fields); with XML serialization, only the public fields and properties are serialized. The data contract requires explicit marking of the fields that should be serialized with the `DataMember` attribute. This attribute can be used regardless of whether the field is private or public, or if it is applied to a property.

```
[DataContract(Namespace="http://www.cninnovation.com/Services/2016")]
public class RoomReservation
{
  [DataMember] public string Room { get; set; }
  [DataMember] public DateTime StartTime { get; set; }
  [DataMember] public DateTime EndTime { get; set; }
  [DataMember] public string Contact { get; set; }
  [DataMember] public string Text { get; set; }
}
```

To be platform-independent and provide the option to change data with new versions without breaking older clients and services, using data contracts is the best way to define which data should be sent. However, you can also use XML serialization and runtime serialization. XML serialization is the mechanism used by ASP.NET web services; .NET Remoting uses runtime serialization.

With the attribute `DataMember`, you can specify the properties described in the following table.

DATAMEMBER PROPERTY	DESCRIPTION
Name	By default, the serialized element has the same name as the field or property where the `[DataMember]` attribute is applied. You can change the name with the `Name` property.
Order	The `Order` property defines the serialization order of the data members.
IsRequired	With the `IsRequired` property, you can specify that the element must be received with serialization. This property can be used for versioning. If you add members to an existing contract, the contract is not broken because, by default, the fields are optional (`IsRequired=false`). You can break an existing contract by setting `IsRequired` to true.
EmitDefaultValue	The property `EmitDefaultValue` defines whether the member should be serialized if it has the default value. If `EmitDefaultValue` is set to true, the member is not serialized if it has the default value for the type.

Versioning

When you create a new version of a data contract, pay attention to what kind of change it is and act accordingly if old and new clients and old and new services should be supported simultaneously.

When defining a contract, you should add XML namespace information with the `Namespace` property of the `DataContractAttribute`. This namespace should be changed if a new version of the data contract is created that breaks compatibility. If just optional members are added, the contract is not broken—this is a compatible change. Old clients can still send a message to the new service because the additional data is not needed. New clients can send messages to an old service because the old service just ignores the additional data.

Removing fields or adding required fields breaks the contract. Here, you should also change the XML namespace. The name of the namespace can include the year and the month—for example, `http://`

`www.cninnovation.com/Services/2016/08`. Every time a breaking change is done, the namespace is changed—for example, by changing the year and month to the actual value.

Service and Operation Contracts

The service contract defines the operations the service can perform. You use the attribute `ServiceContract` with interfaces or classes to define a service contract. The methods that are offered by the service have the attribute `OperationContract` applied, as you can see with the interface `IRoomService`:

```
[ServiceContract]
public interface IRoomService
{
    [OperationContract]
    bool ReserveRoom(RoomReservation roomReservation);
}
```

The possible properties that you can set with the `ServiceContract` attribute are described in the following table.

SERVICECONTRACT PROPERTY	DESCRIPTION
`ConfigurationName`	This property defines the name of the service configuration in a configuration file.
`CallbackContract`	When the service is used for duplex messaging, the property `CallbackContract` defines the contract that is implemented in the client.
`Name`	The `Name` property defines the name for the `<portType>` element in the WSDL.
`Namespace`	The `Namespace` property defines the XML namespace for the `<portType>` element in the WSDL.
`SessionMode`	With the `SessionMode` property, you can define whether sessions are required for calling operations of this contract. The possible values `Allowed`, `NotAllowed`, and `Required` are defined with the `SessionMode` enumeration.
`ProtectionLevel`	The `ProtectionLevel` property defines whether the binding must support protecting the communication. Possible values defined by the `ProtectionLevel` enumeration are `None`, `Sign`, and `EncryptAndSign`.

With the `OperationContract`, you can specify properties, as shown in the following table.

OPERATIONCONTRACT PROPERTY	DESCRIPTION
`Action`	WCF uses the `Action` of the SOAP request to map it to the appropriate method. The default value for the `Action` is a combination of the contract XML namespace, the name of the contract, and the name of the operation. If the message is a response message, `Response` is added to the `Action` string. You can override the `Action` value by specifying the `Action` property. If you assign the value "*", the service operation handles all messages.
`ReplyAction`	Whereas `Action` sets the `Action` name of the incoming SOAP request, `ReplyAction` sets the `Action` name of the reply message.
`AsyncPattern`	If the operation is implemented by using an asynchronous pattern, set the `AsyncPattern` property to true. The async pattern is discussed in Chapter 15, "Asynchronous Programming."
`IsInitiating IsTerminating`	If the contract consists of a sequence of operations, the initiating operation should have the `IsInitiating` property assigned to it; the last operation of the sequence needs the `IsTerminating` property assigned. The initiating operation starts a new session; the server closes the session with the terminating operation.

OPERATIONCONTRACT PROPERTY	DESCRIPTION
IsOneWay	With the IsOneWay property set, the client does not wait for a reply message. Callers of a one-way operation have no direct way to detect a failure after sending the request message.
Name	The default name of the operation is the name of the method the operation contract is assigned to. You can change the name of the operation by applying the Name property.
ProtectionLevel	With the ProtectionLevel property, you define whether the message should be signed or encrypted and signed.

With the service contract, you can also define the requirements that the service has from the transport with the attribute [DeliveryRequirements]. The property RequireOrderedDelivery defines that the messages sent must arrive in the same order. With the property QueuedDeliveryRequirements, you can define that the message should be sent in a disconnected mode, for example, by using Message Queuing.

Message Contract

A message contract is used if complete control over the SOAP message is needed. With the message contract, you can specify what part of the message should go into the SOAP header and what belongs in the SOAP body. The following example shows a message contract for the class ProcessPersonRequestMessage. The message contract is specified with the attribute MessageContract. The header and body of the SOAP message are specified with the attributes MessageHeader and MessageBodyMember. By specifying the Position property, you can define the element order within the body. You can also specify the protection level for header and body fields.

```
[MessageContract]
public class ProcessPersonRequestMessage
{
  [MessageHeader]
  public int employeeId;

  [MessageBodyMember(Position=0)]
  public Person person;
}
```

The class ProcessPersonRequestMessage is used with the service contract defined with the interface IProcessPerson:

```
[ServiceContract]
public interface IProcessPerson
{
  [OperationContract]
  public PersonResponseMessage ProcessPerson(
    ProcessPersonRequestMessage message);
}
```

Another contract that is important for WCF services is the fault contract. This contract is discussed in the next section.

Fault Contract

By default, the detailed exception information that occurs in the service is not returned to the client application. The reason for this behavior is security. You wouldn't want to give detailed exception information to a third party by using your service. Instead, the exception should be logged on the service (which you can do with tracing and event logging), and an error with useful information should be returned to the caller.

You can return SOAP faults by throwing a `FaultException`. Throwing a `FaultException` creates an untyped SOAP fault. The preferred way to return errors is to generate a strongly typed SOAP fault.

The information that should be passed with a strongly typed SOAP fault is defined with a data contract, as shown with the `RoomReservationFault` class (code file `RoomReservation/RoomReservationContracts/RoomReservationFault.cs`):

```
[DataContract]
public class RoomReservationFault
{
  [DataMember]
  public string Message { get; set; }
}
```

The type of the SOAP fault must be defined by using the `FaultContractAttribute` with the operation contract:

```
[FaultContract(typeof(RoomReservationFault))]
[OperationContract]
bool ReserveRoom(RoomReservation roomReservation);
```

With the implementation, a `FaultException<TDetail>` is thrown. With the constructor, you can assign a new `TDetail` object, which is a `StateFault` in the example. In addition, error information within a `FaultReason` can be assigned to the constructor. `FaultReason` supports error information in multiple languages.

```
FaultReasonText[] text = new FaultReasonText[2];
text[0] = new FaultReasonText("Sample Error", new CultureInfo("en"));
text[1] = new FaultReasonText("Beispiel Fehler", new CultureInfo("de"));
FaultReason reason = new FaultReason(text);

throw new FaultException<RoomReservationFault>(
  new RoomReservationFault() { Message = m }, reason);
```

With the client application, exceptions of type `FaultException<RoomReservationFault>` can be caught. The reason for the exception is defined by the `Message` property; the `RoomReservationFault` is accessed with the `Detail` property:

```
try
{
  // etc.
}
catch (FaultException<RoomReservationFault> ex)
{
  WriteLine(ex.Message);
  StateFault detail = ex.Detail;
  WriteLine(detail.Message);
}
```

In addition to catching the strongly typed SOAP faults, the client application can also catch exceptions of the base class of `FaultException<Detail>`: `FaultException` and `CommunicationException`. By catching `CommunicationException`, you can also catch other exceptions related to the WCF communication.

> **NOTE** *During development you can return exceptions to the client. To enable exceptions propagated, you need to configure a service behavior configuration with the* `serviceDebug` *element. The* `serviceDebug` *element has the attribute* `IncludeExceptionDetailInFaults` *that can be set to true to return exception information.*

SERVICE BEHAVIORS

The implementation of the service can be marked with the attribute `ServiceBehavior`, as shown with the class `RoomReservationService`:

```
[ServiceBehavior]
public class RoomReservationService: IRoomService
{
    public bool ReserveRoom(RoomReservation roomReservation)
    {
        // implementation
    }
}
```

The attribute `ServiceBehavior` is used to describe behavior as is offered by WCF services to intercept the code for required functionality, as shown in the following table.

SERVICEBEHAVIOR PROPERTY	DESCRIPTION
`TransactionAutoCompleteOnSessionClose`	When the current session is finished without error, the transaction is automatically committed. This is similar to the `AutoComplete` attribute used with Enterprise Services.
`TransactionIsolationLevel`	To define the isolation level of the transaction within the service, the property `TransactionIsolationLevel` can be set to one value of the `IsolationLevel` enumeration.
`ReleaseServiceInstanceOn TransactionComplete`	When the transaction finishes, the instance of the service recycles.
`AutomaticSessionShutdown`	If the session should not be closed when the client closes the connection, you can set the property `AutomaticSessionShutdown` to `false`. By default, the session is closed.
`InstanceContextMode`	With the property `InstanceContextMode`, you can define whether stateful or stateless objects should be used. The default setting is `InstanceContextMode.PerCall` to create a new object with every method call. Other possible settings are `PerSession` and `Single`. With both of these settings, stateful objects are used. However, with `PerSession` a new object is created for every client. `Single` enables the same object to be shared with multiple clients.
`ConcurrencyMode`	Because stateful objects can be used by multiple clients (or multiple threads of a single client), you must pay attention to concurrency issues with such object types. If the property `ConcurrencyMode` is set to `Multiple`, multiple threads can access the object, and you must deal with synchronization. If you set the option to `Single`, only one thread accesses the object at a time. Here, you don't have to do synchronization; however, scalability problems can occur with a higher number of clients. The value `Reentrant` means that only a thread coming back from a callout might access the object. For stateless objects, this setting has no meaning because new objects are instantiated with every method call and thus no state is shared.

SERVICEBEHAVIOR PROPERTY	DESCRIPTION
UseSynchronizationContext	With user interface code, members of controls can be invoked only from the creator thread. If the service is hosted in a Windows application, and the service methods invoke control members, set the `UseSynchronizationContext` to `true`. This way, the service runs in a thread defined by the `SynchronizationContext`.
IncludeExceptionDetailInFaults	With .NET, errors show up as exceptions. SOAP defines that a SOAP fault is returned to the client in case the server has a problem. For security reasons, it's not a good idea to return details of server-side exceptions to the client. Thus, by default, exceptions are converted to unknown faults. To return specific faults, throw an exception of type `FaultException`. For debugging purposes, it can be helpful to return the real exception information. This is the case when changing the setting of `IncludeExceptionDetailIn Faults` to true. Here a `FaultException<TDetail>` is thrown where the original exception contains the detail information.
MaxItemsInObjectGraph	With the property `MaxItemsInObjectGraph`, you can limit the number of objects that are serialized. The default limitation might be too low if you serialize a tree of objects.
ValidateMustUnderstand	The property `ValidateMustUnderstand` set to true means that the SOAP headers must be understood (which is the default).

To demonstrate a service behavior, the interface `IStateService` defines a service contract with two operations to set and get state. With a stateful service contract, a session is needed. That's why the `SessionMode` property of the service contract is set to `SessionMode.Required`. The service contract also defines methods to initiate and close the session by applying the `IsInitiating` and `IsTerminating` properties to the operation contract:

```
[ServiceContract(SessionMode=SessionMode.Required)]
public interface IStateService
{
  [OperationContract(IsInitiating=true)]
  void Init(int i);

  [OperationContract]
  void SetState(int i);

  [OperationContract]
  int GetState();

  [OperationContract(IsTerminating=true)]
  void Close();
}
```

The service contract is implemented by the class `StateService`. The service implementation defines the `InstanceContextMode.PerSession` to keep state with the instance:

```
[ServiceBehavior(InstanceContextMode=InstanceContextMode.PerSession)]
public class StateService: IStateService
```

```
{
  int _i = 0;

  public void Init(int i)
  {
    _i = i;
  }

  public void SetState(int i)
  {
    _i = i;
  }

  public int GetState()
  {
    return _i;
  }

  public void Close()
  {
  }
}
```

Now the binding to the address and protocol must be defined. Here, the basicHttpBinding is assigned to the endpoint of the service:

```
<?xml version="1.0" encoding="utf-8" ?>
<configuration>
  <system.serviceModel>
    <services>
      <service behaviorConfiguration="StateServiceSample.Service1Behavior"
        name="Wrox.ProCSharp.WCF.StateService">
        <endpoint address="" binding="basicHttpBinding"
            bindingConfiguration=""
            contract="Wrox.ProCSharp.WCF.IStateService">
        </endpoint>
        <endpoint address="mex" binding="mexHttpBinding"
            contract="IMetadataExchange" />
        <host>
          <baseAddresses>
            <add baseAddress="http://localhost:8731/Design_Time_Addresses/
                              StateServiceSample/Service1/" />
          </baseAddresses>
        </host>
      </service>
    </services>
    <behaviors>
      <serviceBehaviors>
        <behavior name="StateServiceSample.Service1Behavior">
          <serviceMetadata httpGetEnabled="True"/>
          <serviceDebug includeExceptionDetailInFaults="False" />
        </behavior>
      </serviceBehaviors>
    </behaviors>
  </system.serviceModel>
</configuration>
```

If you start the service host with the defined configuration, an exception of type InvalidOperationException is thrown. The error message with the exception gives this error message: Contract Requires Session, but Binding 'BasicHttpBinding' Doesn't Support It or Isn't Configured Properly to Support It.

Not all bindings support all services. Because the service contract requires a session with the attribute [Serv iceContract(SessionMode=SessionMode.Required)], the host fails because the configured binding does not support sessions.

As soon as you change the configuration to a binding that supports sessions (for example, the wsHttpBind-ing), the server starts successfully:

```
<endpoint address="" binding="wsHttpBinding"
  bindingConfiguration=""
  contract="Wrox.ProCSharp.WCF.IStateService">
</endpoint>
```

With the implementation of the service, you can apply the properties in the following table to the service methods, with the attribute OperationBehavior.

OPERATIONBEHAVIOR PROPERTY	DESCRIPTION
AutoDisposeParameters	By default, all disposable parameters are automatically disposed. If the parameters should not be disposed, you can set the property AutoDisposeParameters to false. Then the sender is responsible for disposing the parameters.
Impersonation	With the Impersonation property, the caller can be impersonated, and the method runs with the identity of the caller.
ReleaseInstanceMode	The InstanceContextMode defines the lifetime of the object instance with the service behavior setting. With the operation behavior setting, you can override the setting based on the operation. The ReleaseInstanceMode defines an instance release mode with the enumeration ReleaseInstanceMode. The value None uses the instance context mode setting. With the values BeforeCall, AfterCall, and BeforeAndAfterCall, you can define recycle times with the operation.
TransactionScopeRequired	With the property TransactionScopeRequired, you can specify whether a transaction is required with the operation. If a transaction is required and the caller already flows a transaction, the same transaction is used. If the caller doesn't flow a transaction, a new transaction is created.
TransactionAutoComplete	The TransactionAutoComplete property specifies whether the transaction should complete automatically. If the TransactionAutoComplete property is set to true, the transaction is aborted if an exception is thrown. The transaction is committed if it is the root transaction and no exception is thrown.

BINDING

A binding describes how a service wants to communicate. With binding, you can specify the following features:

- ➤ Transport protocol
- ➤ Security
- ➤ Encoding format
- ➤ Transaction flow
- ➤ Reliability
- ➤ Shape change
- ➤ Transport upgrade

Standard Bindings

A binding is composed of multiple binding elements that describe all binding requirements. You can create a custom binding or use one of the predefined bindings that are shown in the following table.

STANDARD BINDING	DESCRIPTION
BasicHttpBinding	BasicHttpBinding is the binding for the broadest interoperability, the first-generation web services. Transport protocols used are HTTP or HTTPS; security is available only from the transport protocol.
WSHttpBinding	WSHttpBinding is the binding for the next-generation web services, platforms that implement SOAP extensions for security, reliability, and transactions. The transports used are HTTP or HTTPS; for security the WS-Security specification is implemented; transactions are supported, as has been described, with the WS-Coordination, WS-AtomicTransaction, and WS-BusinessActivity specifications; reliable messaging is supported with an implementation of WS-ReliableMessaging. WS-Profile also supports Message Transmission Optimization Protocol (MTOM) encoding for sending attachments. You can find specifications for the WS-* standards at http://www.oasis-open.org.
WS2007HttpBinding	WS2007HttpBinding derives from the base class WSHttpBinding and supports security, reliability, and transaction specifications defined by Organization for the Advancement of Structured Information Standards (OASIS). This class offers newer SOAP standards.
WSHttpContextBinding	WSHttpContextBinding derives from the base class WSHttpBinding and adds support for a context without using cookies. This binding adds a ContextBindingElement to exchange context information. The context binding element was needed with Windows Workflow Foundation (WF) 3.0.
WebHttpBinding	This binding is used for services that are exposed through HTTP requests instead of SOAP requests. This is useful for scripting clients—for example, ASP.NET AJAX.
WSFederationHttpBinding	WSFederationHttpBinding is a secure and interoperable binding that supports sharing identities across multiple systems for authentication and authorization.
WSDualHttpBinding	The binding WSDualHttpBinding, in contrast to WSHttpBinding, supports duplex messaging.
NetTcpBinding	All standard bindings prefixed with the name Net use a binary encoding used for communication between .NET applications. This encoding is faster than the text encoding with WSxxx bindings. The binding NetTcpBinding uses the TCP/IP protocol.
NetTcpContextBinding	Similar to WSHttpContextBinding, NetTcpContextBinding adds a ContextBindingElement to exchange context with the SOAP header.
NetHttpBinding	This is a new binding since .NET 4.5 to support the Web Socket transport protocol.
NetPeerTcpBinding	NetPeerTcpBinding provides a binding for peer-to-peer communication.
NetNamedPipeBinding	NetNamedPipeBinding is optimized for communication between different processes on the same system.
NetMsmqBinding	The binding NetMsmqBinding brings queued communication to WCF. Here, the messages are sent to the message queue.

STANDARD BINDING	DESCRIPTION
MsmqIntegrationBinding	MsmqIntegrationBinding is the binding for existing applications that uses message queuing. In contrast, the binding NetMsmqBinding requires WCF applications on both the client and server.
CustomBinding	With a CustomBinding the transport protocol and security requirements can be completely customized.

Features of Standard Bindings

Depending on the binding, different features are supported. The bindings starting with WS are platform-independent, supporting web services specifications. Bindings that start with the name Net use binary formatting for high-performance communication between .NET applications. Other features are support of sessions, reliable sessions, transactions, and duplex communication; the following table lists the bindings supporting these features.

FEATURE	BINDING
Sessions	WSHttpBinding, WSDualHttpBinding, WsFederationHttpBinding, NetTcpBinding, NetNamedPipeBinding
Reliable Sessions	WSHttpBinding, WSDualHttpBinding, WsFederationHttpBinding, NetTcpBinding
Transactions	WSHttpBinding, WSDualHttpBinding, WSFederationHttpBinding, NetTcpBinding, NetNamedPipeBinding, NetMsmqBinding, MsmqIntegrationBinding
Duplex Communication	WsDualHttpBinding, NetTcpBinding, NetNamedPipeBinding, NetPeerTcpBinding

Along with defining the binding, the service must define an endpoint. The endpoint is dependent on the contract, the address of the service, and the binding. In the following code sample, a ServiceHost object is instantiated, and the address http://localhost:8080/RoomReservation, a WsHttpBinding instance, and the contract are added to an endpoint of the service:

```
static ServiceHost s_host;

static void StartService()
{
  var baseAddress = new Uri("http://localhost:8080/RoomReservation");
  s_host = new ServiceHost(typeof(RoomReservationService));

  var binding1 = new WSHttpBinding();
  s_host.AddServiceEndpoint(typeof(IRoomService), binding1, baseAddress);
  s_host.Open();
}
```

In addition to defining the binding programmatically, you can define it with the application configuration file. The configuration for WCF is placed inside the element <system.serviceModel>. The <service> element defines the services offered. Similarly, as you've seen in the code, the service needs an endpoint, and the endpoint contains address, binding, and contract information. The default binding configuration of wsHttpBinding is modified with the bindingConfiguration XML attribute that references the binding configuration wsHttpBinding. This is the binding configuration you can find inside the <bindings> section, which is used to change the wsHttpBinding configuration to enable reliableSession.

```
<?xml version="1.0" encoding="utf-8" ?>
<configuration>
  <system.serviceModel>
    <services>
```

```
                <service name="Wrox.ProCSharp.WCF.RoomReservationService">
                  <endpoint address=" http://localhost:8080/RoomReservation"
                      contract="Wrox.ProCSharp.WCF.IRoomService"
                      binding="wsHttpBinding" bindingConfiguration="wsHttpBinding" />
                </service>
            </services>
            <bindings>
              <wsHttpBinding>
                <binding name="wsHttpBinding">
                  <reliableSession enabled="true" />
                </binding>
              </wsHttpBinding>
            </bindings>
          </system.serviceModel>
        </configuration>
```

Web Sockets

Web Sockets is a new communication protocol based on TCP. The HTTP protocol is stateless. With HTTP the server can close the connection every time it answers the request. If a client wants to receive ongoing information from the server, this always had some issues with the HTTP protocol.

Because the HTTP connection is kept, one way to deal with this would be to have a service running on the client, and the server connects to the client and sends responses. If a firewall is between the client and the server, this usually doesn't work because the firewall blocks incoming requests.

Another way to deal with this is to use another protocol than the HTTP protocol. The connection can stay alive. The issue with other protocols is that the port needs to be opened with the firewall. Firewalls are always an issue, but they are needed to keep the bad folks out.

The way such a scenario was usually done is by instantiating the request every time from the client. The client polls the server to ask if there's something new. This works but has the disadvantage that either the client asks too many times for news when there is none and thus increases the network traffic, or the client does get old information.

A new solution for this scenario is the Web Sockets protocol. This protocol is defined by the World Wide Web Consortium (W3C, http://www.w3.org/TR/websockets) and starts with an HTTP request. Starting with an HTTP request from the client, the firewall usually allows the request. The client starts with a GET request with `Upgrade: websocket Connection: Upgrade` in the HTTP header, along with the WebSocket version and security information. If the server supports the WebSocket protocol, the server answers with an upgrade and switches from HTTP to the WebSocket protocol.

With WCF, the two bindings new since .NET 4.5 support the WebSocket protocol: `netHttpBinding` and `netHttpsBinding`.

Now get into a sample to make use of the WebSocket protocol. Start with an empty web application used to host the service.

The default binding for the HTTP protocol is the `basicHttpBinding`. This can be changed to define the `protocolMapping` to specify the `netHttpBinding` as shown. This way it's not necessary to configure the service element to match the contract, binding, and address to an endpoint. With the configuration, `serviceMetadata` is enabled to allow the client to reference the service with the Add Service Reference dialog (configuration file `WebSocketsSample/WebSocketsSample/Web.config`).

```
          <configuration>
            <!-- etc. -->
            <system.serviceModel>
              <protocolMapping>
                <remove scheme="http" />
                <add scheme="http" binding="netHttpBinding" />
                <remove scheme="https" />
```

```
            <add scheme="https" binding="netHttpsBinding" />
          </protocolMapping>
          <behaviors>
            <serviceBehaviors>
              <behavior name="">
                <serviceMetadata httpGetEnabled="true" httpsGetEnabled="true" />
                <serviceDebug includeExceptionDetailInFaults="false" />
              </behavior>
            </serviceBehaviors>
          </behaviors>
          <serviceHostingEnvironment aspNetCompatibilityEnabled="true"
              multipleSiteBindingsEnabled="true" />
        </system.serviceModel>
      </configuration>
```

The service contract is defined by the interfaces `IDemoServices` and `IDemoCallback`. `IDemoService` is the service interface that defines the method `StartSendingMessages`. The client invokes the method `StartSendingMessages` to start the process that the service can return messages to the client. The client therefore needs to implement the interface `IDemoCallback`. This interface is invoked by the server and implemented by the client.

The methods of the interfaces are defined to return Task. With this the service can easily make use of asynchronous features, but this doesn't go through to the contract. Defining the methods asynchronously is independent of the WSDL generated (code file `WebSocketsSample/WebSocketsSample/IDemoService.cs`):

```
using System.ServiceModel;
using System.Threading.Tasks;

namespace WebSocketsSample
{
  [ServiceContract]
  public interface IDemoCallback
  {
    [OperationContract(IsOneWay = true)]
    Task SendMessage(string message);
  }
  [ServiceContract(CallbackContract = typeof(IDemoCallback))]
  public interface IDemoService
  {
    [OperationContract]
    void StartSendingMessages();
  }
}
```

The implementation of the service is done in the `DemoService` class. Within `StartSendingMessages`, the callback interface to go back to the client is retrieved with `OperationContext.Current.GetCallbackChannel`. When the client invokes the method, it returns immediately as soon as the first time the `SendMessage` method is invoked. The thread is not blocked until the `SendMessage` method completes. With `await`, a thread just comes back to the `StartSendingMessages` when the `SendMessage` is completed. Then a delay of 1 second occurs before the client receives another message. In case the communication channel is closed the `while` loop exits (code file `WebSocketsSample/WebSocketsSample/DemoService.svc.cs`:

```
using System.ServiceModel;
using System.ServiceModel.Channels;
using System.Threading.Tasks;

namespace WebSocketsSample
{
  public class DemoService : IDemoService
  {
    public async Task StartSendingMessages()
    {
```

```
                IDemoCallback callback =
                  OperationContext.Current.GetCallbackChannel<IDemoCallback>();

                int loop = 0;
                while ((callback as IChannel).State == CommunicationState.Opened)
                {
                  await callback.SendMessage($"Hello from the server {loop++}");
                  await Task.Delay(1000);
                }
              }
            }
          }
```

The client application is created as a console application. Because metadata is available with the service, adding a service reference creates a proxy class that can be used to call the service and also to implement the callback interface. Adding the service reference not only creates the proxy class, but also adds the netHttpBinding to the configuration file (configuration file WebSocketsSample/ClientApp/App.config):

```xml
<?xml version="1.0" encoding="utf-8" ?>
<configuration>
  <startup>
    <supportedRuntime version="v4.0" sku=".NETFramework,Version=v4.6" />
  </startup>
  <system.serviceModel>
    <bindings>
      <netHttpBinding>
        <binding name="NetHttpBinding_IDemoService">
          <webSocketSettings transportUsage="Always" />
        </binding>
      </netHttpBinding>
    </bindings>
    <client>
      <endpoint address="ws://localhost:20839/DemoService.svc"
        binding="netHttpBinding"
        bindingConfiguration="NetHttpBinding_IDemoService"
        contract="DemoService.IDemoService"
        name="NetHttpBinding_IDemoService" />
    </client>
  </system.serviceModel>
</configuration>
```

The implementation of the callback interface just writes a message to the console with the information received from the service. To start all the processing, a DemoServiceClient instance is created that receives an InstanceContext object. The InstanceContext object contains an instance to the CallbackHandler, a reference retrieved by the service to go back to the client (code file WebSocketsSample/ClientApp/Program.cs):

```csharp
using System;
using System.ServiceModel;
using ClientApp.DemoService;
using static System.Console;

namespace ClientApp
{
  class Program
  {
    private class CallbackHandler : IDemoServiceCallback
    {
      public void SendMessage(string message)
      {
        WriteLine($"message from the server {message}");
      }
```

```
      }

      static void Main()
      {
        WriteLine("client… wait for the server");
        ReadLine();
        StartSendRequest();
        WriteLine("next return to exit");
        ReadLine();
      }

      static async void StartSendRequest()
      {
        var callbackInstance = new InstanceContext(new CallbackHandler());
        var client = new DemoServiceClient(callbackInstance);
        await client.StartSendingMessagesAsync();
      }
    }
  }
```

When you run the application, the client requests the messages from the service, and the service responds independent of the client:

```
client… wait for the server
next return to exit
message from the server Hello from the server 0
message from the server Hello from the server 1
message from the server Hello from the server 2
message from the server Hello from the server 3
message from the server Hello from the server 4
Press any key to continue . . .
```

HOSTING

WCF is flexible when you are choosing a host to run the service. The host can be a Windows service, WAS or IIS, a Windows application, or just a simple console application. When creating a custom host with Windows Forms or WPF, you can easily create a peer-to-peer solution.

Custom Hosting

Start with a custom host. The sample code shows hosting of a service within a console application; however, in other custom host types, such as Windows services or Windows applications, you can program the service in the same way.

In the Main method, a ServiceHost instance is created. After the ServiceHost instance is created, the application configuration file is read to define the bindings. You can also define the bindings programmatically, as shown earlier. Next, the Open method of the ServiceHost class is invoked, so the service accepts client calls. With a console application, you need to be careful not to close the main thread until the service should be closed. Here, the user is asked to press Return to exit the service. When the user does this, the Close method is called to actually end the service:

```
using System;
using System.ServiceModel;
using static System.Console;

class Program
{
  static void Main()
  {
    using (var serviceHost = new ServiceHost())
```

```
      {
        serviceHost.Open();

        WriteLine("The service started. Press return to exit");
        ReadLine();

        serviceHost.Close();
      }
    }
  }
```

To abort the service host, you can invoke the `Abort` method of the `ServiceHost` class. To get the current state of the service, the `State` property returns a value defined by the `CommunicationState` enumeration. Possible values are `Created`, `Opening`, `Opened`, `Closing`, `Closed`, and `Faulted`.

> **NOTE** *If you start the service from within a Windows Forms or WPF application and the service code invokes methods of Windows controls, you must be sure that only the control's creator thread is allowed to access the methods and properties of the control. With WCF, this behavior can be achieved easily by setting the* `UseSynchronizatonContext` *property of the attribute* `[ServiceBehavior]`.

WAS Hosting

With Windows Activation Services (WAS) hosting, you get the features from the WAS worker process such as automatic activation of the service, health monitoring, and process recycling.

To use WAS hosting, you just need to create a website and a `.svc` file with the `ServiceHost` declaration that includes the language and the name of the service class. The code shown here is using the class `Service1`. In addition, you must specify the file that contains the service class. This class is implemented in the same way that you saw earlier when defining a WCF service library.

```
<%@ServiceHost language="C#" Service="Service1" CodeBehind="Service1.svc.cs" %>
```

If you use a WCF service library that should be available from WAS hosting, you can create a `.svc` file that just contains a reference to the class:

```
<%@ ServiceHost Service="Wrox.ProCSharp.WCF.Services.RoomReservationService" %>
```

> **NOTE** *Using IIS with WAS doesn't restrict you to the HTTP protocol. With WAS you can use .NET TCP and Message Queue bindings. In the intranet, this is a useful scenario.*

Preconfigured Host Classes

To reduce the configuration necessities, WCF also offers some hosting classes with preconfigured bindings. One example is located in the assembly `System.ServiceModel.Web` in the namespace `System.ServiceModel.Web` with the class `WebServiceHost`. This class creates a default endpoint for HTTP and HTTPS base addresses if a default endpoint is not configured with the `WebHttpBinding`. Also, this class adds the `WebHttpBehavior` if another behavior is not defined. With this behavior, simple HTTP `GET` and `POST`, `PUT`, and `DELETE` (with the `WebInvoke` attribute) operations can be done without additional setup (code file `RoomReservation/RoomReservationWebHost/Program.cs`).

```csharp
using System;
using System.ServiceModel;
using System.ServiceModel.Web;
using Wrox.ProCSharp.WCF.Service;
using static System.Console;

namespace RoomReservationWebHost
{
  class Program
  {
    static void Main()
    {
      var baseAddress = new Uri("http://localhost:8000/RoomReservation");
      var host = new WebServiceHost(typeof(RoomReservationService),
        baseAddress);
      host.Open();

      WriteLine("service running");
      WriteLine("Press return to exit…");
      ReadLine();

      if (host.State == CommunicationState.Opened)
      {
        host.Close();
      }
    }
  }
}
```

To use a simple HTTP GET request to receive the reservations, the method `GetRoomReservation` needs a `WebGet` attribute to map the method parameters to the input from the GET request. In the following code, a `UriTemplate` is defined that requires `Reservations` to be added to the base address followed by `From` and `To` parameters. The `From` and `To` parameters in turn are mapped to the `fromTime` and `toTime` variables (code file RoomReservationService/RoomReservationService.cs).

```csharp
[WebGet(UriTemplate="Reservations?From={fromTime}&To={toTime}")]
public RoomReservation[] GetRoomReservations(DateTime fromTime,
  DateTime toTime)
{
  var data = new RoomReservationData();
  return data.GetReservations(fromTime, toTime);
}
```

Now the service can be invoked with a simple request as shown. All the reservations for the specified time frame are returned.

```
http://localhost:8000/RoomReservation/Reservations?From=2012/1/1&To=2012/8/1
```

> `System.Data.Services.DataServiceHost` *is another class with preconfigured features. This class derives itself from* `WebServiceHost`.

CLIENTS

A client application needs a proxy to access a service. There are three ways to create a proxy for the client:

➤ **Visual Studio Add Service Reference**—This utility creates a proxy class from the metadata of the service.

➤ **ServiceModel Metadata Utility tool (Svcutil.exe)**—You can create a proxy class with the `Svcutil` utility. This utility reads metadata from the service to create the proxy class.

➤ **ChannelFactory class**—This class is used by the proxy generated from Svcutil; however, it can also be used to create a proxy programmatically.

Using Metadata

Adding a service reference from Visual Studio requires accessing a WSDL document. The WSDL document is created by an MEX endpoint that needs to be configured with the service. With the following configuration, the endpoint with the relative address mex uses the mexHttpBinding and implements the contract IMetadataExchange. To access the metadata with an HTTP GET request, the behaviorConfiguration MexServiceBehavior is configured.

```xml
<?xml version="1.0" encoding="utf-8" ?>
<configuration>
  <system.serviceModel>
    <services>
      <service behaviorConfiguration=" MexServiceBehavior "
        name="Wrox.ProCSharp.WCF.RoomReservationService">
        <endpoint address="Test" binding="wsHttpBinding"
          contract="Wrox.ProCSharp.WCF.IRoomService" />
        <endpoint address="mex" binding="mexHttpBinding"
          contract="IMetadataExchange" />
        <host>
          <baseAddresses>
            <add baseAddress=
      "http://localhost:8733/Design_Time_Addresses/RoomReservationService/" />
          <baseAddresses>
        </host>
      </service>
    </services>
    <behaviors>
      <serviceBehaviors>
        <behavior name="MexServiceBehavior">
          <! - To avoid disclosing metadata information,
          set the value below to false and remove the metadata endpoint above
          before deployment - >
          <serviceMetadata httpGetEnabled="True"/>
        </behavior>
      </serviceBehaviors>
    </behaviors>
  </system.serviceModel>
</configuration>
```

Similar to the Add service reference from Visual Studio, the Svcutil utility needs metadata to create the proxy class. The Svcutil utility can create a proxy from the MEX metadata endpoint, the metadata of the assembly, or WSDL and XSD documentation:

```
svcutil http://localhost:8080/RoomReservation?wsdl /language:C# /out:proxy.cs
svcutil CourseRegistration.dll
svcutil CourseRegistration.wsdl CourseRegistration.xsd
```

After the proxy class is generated, it just needs to be instantiated from the client code, the methods need to be called, and finally the Close method must be invoked:

```
var client = new RoomServiceClient();
client.RegisterForCourse(roomReservation);
client.Close();
```

Sharing Types

The generated proxy class derives from the base class ClientBase<TChannel> that wraps the ChannelFactory<TChannel> class. Instead of using a generated proxy class, you can use the

`ChannelFactory<TChannel>` class directly. The constructor requires the binding and endpoint address; next, you can create the channel and invoke methods as defined by the service contract. Finally, the factory must be closed:

```
var binding = new WsHttpBinding();
var address = new EndpointAddress("http://localhost:8080/RoomService");

var factory = new ChannelFactory<IStateService>(binding, address);

IRoomService channel = factory.CreateChannel();
channel.ReserveRoom(roomReservation);

// etc.
factory.Close();
```

The `ChannelFactory<TChannel>` class has several properties and methods, as shown in the following table.

CHANNELFACTORY MEMBERS	DESCRIPTION
`Credentials`	`Credentials` is a read-only property to access the `ClientCredentials` object assigned to the channel for authentication with the service. The credentials can be set with the endpoint.
`Endpoint`	`Endpoint` is a read-only property to access the `ServiceEndpoint` associated with the channel. The endpoint can be assigned in the constructor.
`State`	The `State` property is of type `CommunicationState` to return the current state of the channel. `CommunicationState` is an enumeration with the values `Created`, `Opening`, `Opened`, `Closing`, `Closed`, and `Faulted`.
`Open`	The `Open` method is used to open the channel.
`Close`	The `Close` method closes the channel.
`OpeningOpenedClosingClosedFaulted`	You can assign event handlers to get informed about state changes of the channel. Events are fired before and after the channel is opened, before and after the channel is closed, and in case of a fault.

DUPLEX COMMUNICATION

The next sample application shows how a duplex communication can be done between the client and the service. The client starts the connection to the service. After the client connects to the service, the service can call back into the client. Duplex communication was shown earlier with the WebSocket protocol as well. Instead of using the WebSocket protocol (which has been supported since Windows 8 and Windows Server 2012), duplex communication can also be done with the `WsHttpBinding` and the `NetTcpBinding` as shown here.

Contract for Duplex Communication

For duplex communication, a contract must be specified that is implemented in the client. Here the contract for the client is defined by the interface `IMyMessageCallback`. The method implemented by the client is `OnCallback`. The operation has the operation contract setting `IsOneWay=true` applied. This way, the service doesn't wait until the method is successfully invoked on the client. By default, the service instance can be invoked from only one thread. (See the `ConcurrencyMode` property of the service behavior, which is, by default, set to `ConcurrencyMode.Single`.)

If the service implementation now does a callback to the client and waits to get an answer from the client, the thread getting the reply from the client must wait until it gets a lock to the service object. Because the service object is already locked by the request to the client, a deadlock occurs. WCF detects the deadlock and throws an exception. To avoid this situation, you can change the `ConcurrencyMode` property to the value `Multiple` or `Reentrant`. With the setting `Multiple`, multiple threads can access the instance concurrently. Here, you must implement locking on your own. With the setting `Reentrant`, the service instance stays single-threaded but enables answers from callback requests to reenter the context. Instead of changing the concurrency mode, you can specify the `IsOneWay` property with the operation contract. This way, the caller does not wait for a reply. Of course, this setting is possible only if return values are not expected.

The contract of the service is defined by the interface `IMyMessage`. The callback contract is mapped to the service contract with the `CallbackContract` property of the service contract definition (code file `DuplexCommunication/MessageService/IMyMessage.cs`):

```
public interface IMyMessageCallback
{
  [OperationContract(IsOneWay=true)]
  void OnCallback(string message);
}

[ServiceContract(CallbackContract=typeof(IMyMessageCallback))]
public interface IMyMessage
{
  [OperationContract]
  void MessageToServer(string message);
}
```

Service for Duplex Communication

The class `MessageService` implements the service contract `IMyMessage`. The service writes the message from the client to the console. To access the callback contract, you can use the `OperationContext` class. `OperationContext.Current` returns the `OperationContext` associated with the current request from the client. With the `OperationContext`, you can access session information, message headers and properties, and, in the case of a duplex communication, the callback channel. The generic method `GetCallbackChannel` returns the channel to the client instance. This channel can then be used to send a message to the client by invoking the method `OnCallback`, which is defined with the callback interface `IMyMessageCallback`. To demonstrate that it is also possible to use the callback channel from the service independently of the completion of the method, a new thread that receives the callback channel is created. The new thread sends messages to the client by using the callback channel (code file `DuplexCommunication/MessageService/MessageService.cs`).

```
public class MessageService: IMyMessage
{
  public void MessageToServer(string message)
  {
    WriteLine($"message from the client: {message}");
    IMyMessageCallback callback =
        OperationContext.Current.GetCallbackChannel<IMyMessageCallback>();

    callback.OnCallback("message from the server");

    Task.Run(() => TaskCallback(callback));
  }

  private async void TaskCallback(object callback)
  {
    IMyMessageCallback messageCallback = callback as IMyMessageCallback;
    for (int i = 0; i < 10; i++)
    {
```

```
      messageCallback.OnCallback(#$"message {i}");
      await Task.Delay(1000);
    }
  }
}
```

Hosting the service is the same as it was with the previous samples, so it is not shown here. However, for duplex communication, you must configure a binding that supports a duplex channel. One of the bindings supporting a duplex channel is `wsDualHttpBinding`, which is configured in the application's configuration file (configuration file `DuplexCommunication/DuplexHost/app.config`):

```xml
<?xml version="1.0" encoding="utf-8" ?>
<configuration>
  <system.serviceModel>
    <services>
      <service name="Wrox.ProCSharp.WCF.MessageService">
        <endpoint address="" binding="wsDualHttpBinding"
          contract="Wrox.ProCSharp.WCF.IMyMessage" />
        <host>
          <baseAddresses>
            <add baseAddress=
  "http://localhost:8733/Design_Time_Addresses/MessageService/Service1" />
          </baseAddresses>
        </host>
      </service>
    </services>
  </system.serviceModel>
</configuration>
```

Client Application for Duplex Communication

With the client application, the callback contract must be implemented as shown here with the class `ClientCallback` that implements the interface `IMyMessageCallback` (code file `DuplexCommunication/MessageClient/Program.cs`):

```csharp
class ClientCallback: IMyMessageCallback
{
  public void OnCallback(string message)
  {
    WriteLine($"message from the server: {message}");
  }
}
```

With a duplex channel, you cannot use the `ChannelFactory` to initiate the connection to the service as was done previously. To create a duplex channel, you can use the `DuplexChannelFactory` class. This class has a constructor with one more parameter in addition to the binding and address configuration. This parameter specifies an `InstanceContext` that wraps one instance of the `ClientCallback` class. When passing this instance to the factory, the service can invoke the object across the channel. The client just needs to keep the connection open. If the connection is closed, the service cannot send messages across it.

```csharp
private async static void DuplexSample()
{
  var binding = new WSDualHttpBinding();
  var address = new EndpointAddress("http://localhost:8733/Service1");

  var clientCallback = new ClientCallback();
  var context = new InstanceContext(clientCallback);

  var factory = new DuplexChannelFactory<IMyMessage>(context, binding,
    address);
```

```
        IMyMessage messageChannel = factory.CreateChannel();

        await Task.Run(() => messageChannel.MessageToServer("From the client"));
    }
```

Duplex communication is achieved by starting the service host and the client application.

ROUTING

Using the SOAP protocol has some advantages to HTTP GET requests with REST. One of the advanced features that can be done with SOAP is routing. With routing, the client does not directly address the service, but a router in between that forwards the request.

There are different scenarios to use this feature. One is for failover (see Figure 44-10). If the service cannot be reached or returns in an error, the router calls the service on a different host. This is abstracted from the client; the client just receives a result.

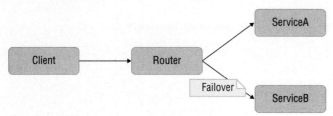

FIGURE 44-10

Routing can also be used to change the communication protocol (see Figure 44-11). The client can use the HTTP protocol to call a request and sends this to the router. The router acts as a client with the net.tcp protocol and calls a service forwarding the message.

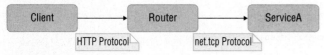

FIGURE 44-11

Using routing for scalability is another scenario (see Figure 44-12). Depending on a field of the message header or also information from the message content, the router can decide to forward a request to one or the other server. Requests from customers that start with the letter A–F go to the first server, G–N to the second one, and O–Z to the third.

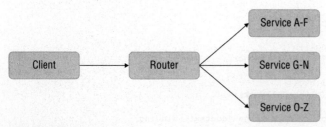

FIGURE 44-12

Sample Routing Application

With the routing sample application, a simple service contract is defined where the caller can invoke the `GetData` operation from the `IDemoService` interface (code file `RoutingSample/DemoService/IDemoService.cs`):

```
using System.ServiceModel;
namespace Wrox.ProCSharp.WCF
{
  [ServiceContract(Namespace="http://www.cninnovation.com/Services/2016")]
  public interface IDemoService
  {
    [OperationContract]
    string GetData(string value);
  }
}
```

The implementation of the service just returns a message with the `GetData` method. The message contains the information received along a server-side string that is initialized from the host. This way you can see the host that returned the call to the client (code file `RoutingSample/DemoService/DemoService.cs`):

```
using System;
using static System.Console;

namespace Wrox.ProCSharp.WCF
{
  public class DemoService : IDemoService
  {
    public static string Server { get; set; }

    public string GetData(string value)
    {
      string message = $"Message from {Server}, You entered: {value}";
      WriteLine(message);
      return message;
    }
  }
}
```

Two sample hosts just create a `ServiceHost` instance and open it to start the listener. Each of the hosts defined assigns a different value to the `Server` property of the `DemoService`.

Routing Interfaces

For routing, WCF defines the interfaces `ISimplexDataGramRouter`, `ISimplexSessionRouter`, `IRequestReplyRouter`, and `IDuplexSessionRouter`. Depending on the service contract, you can use different interfaces. You can use `ISimplexDataGramRouter` with operations that have the `OperationContract` with `IsOneWay` settings. With `ISimplexDatagramRouter`, sessions are optional. You can use `ISimplexSessionRouter` for one-way messages like `ISimlexDatagramRouter`, but here sessions are mandatory. You use `IRequestReplyRouter` for the most common scenario: messages with request and response. With duplex communications (for example, with the `WsDualHttpBinding` used earlier), you use the interface `IDuplexSessionRouter`.

Depending on the message pattern used, a custom router needs to implement the corresponding router interface.

WCF Routing Service

Instead of creating a custom router, you can use the `RoutingService` from the namespace `System.ServiceModel.Routing`. This class implements all the routing interfaces, and thus you use it with all the message patterns. It can be hosted just like any other service. In the StartService method, a new ServiceHost is instantiated by passing the RoutingService type. This is just like the other hosts you've seen before (code file RoutingSample/Router/Program.cs):

```
using System;
using System.ServiceModel;
using System.ServiceModel.Routing;
using static System.Console;

namespace Router
{
  class Program
  {
    internal static ServiceHost s_routerHost = null;

    static void Main()
    {
      StartService();
      WriteLine("Router is running. Press return to exit");
      ReadLine();
      StopService();
    }

    internal static void StartService()
    {
      try
      {
        _routerHost = new ServiceHost(typeof(RoutingService));
        _routerHost.Faulted += myServiceHost_Faulted;
        _routerHost.Open();
      }
      catch (AddressAccessDeniedException)
      {
        WriteLine("either start Visual Studio in elevated admin " +
          "mode or register the listener port with netsh.exe");
      }
    }

    static void myServiceHost_Faulted(object sender, EventArgs e)
    {
      WriteLine("router faulted");
    }

    internal static void StopService()
    {
      if (_routerHost != null &&
          _routerHost.State == CommunicationState.Opened)
      {
        _routerHost.Close();
      }
    }
  }
}
```

Using a Router for Failover

More interesting than the hosting code is the configuration of the router. The router acts as a server to the client application and as a client to the service. So both parts need to be configured. The configuration as shown here offers the wsHttpBinding as a server part and uses the wsHttpBinding as a client to connect to the service. The service endpoint needs to specify the contract that is used with the endpoint. With the request-reply operations offered by the service, the contract is defined by the `IRequestReplyRouter` interface (configuration file `Router/App.config`):

```
<system.serviceModel>
  <services>
    <service behaviorConfiguration="routingData"
      name="System.ServiceModel.Routing.RoutingService">
      <endpoint address="" binding="wsHttpBinding"
        name="reqReplyEndpoint"
        contract="System.ServiceModel.Routing.IRequestReplyRouter" />
      <endpoint address="mex" binding="mexHttpBinding"
        contract="IMetadataExchange" />
      <host>
        <baseAddresses>
          <add baseAddress="http://localhost:8000/RoutingDemo/router" />
        </baseAddresses>
      </host>
    </service>
  </services>
  <!-- etc. -->
```

The client part of the router defines two endpoints for services. For testing the routing service, you can use one system. Of course, usually the hosts run on a different system. The contract can be set to * to allow all contracts to pass through to the services covered by these endpoints.

```
<system.serviceModel>
  <!-- etc. -->
  <client>
    <endpoint address="http://localhost:9001/RoutingDemo/HostA"
      binding="wsHttpBinding" contract="*" name="RoutingDemoService1" />
    <endpoint address="http://localhost:9001/RoutingDemo/HostB"
      binding="wsHttpBinding" contract="*" name="RoutingDemoService2" />
  </client>
  <!-- etc. -->
```

The `behavior` configuration for the service becomes important for routing. The `behavior` configuration named `routingData` is referenced with the service configuration you've seen earlier. For routing, the routing element must be set with the behavior, and here a routing table is referenced using the attribute `filterTableName`.

```
<system.serviceModel>
  <!-- etc. -->
  <behaviors>
    <serviceBehaviors>
      <behavior name="routingData">
        <serviceMetadata httpGetEnabled="True"/>
        <routing filterTableName="routingTable1" />
        <serviceDebug includeExceptionDetailInFaults="true"/>
      </behavior>
    </serviceBehaviors>
  </behaviors>
  <!-- etc. -->
```

The filter table named `routingTable1` contains a filter with the `filterType` `MatchAll`. This filter matches with every request. Now every request from the client is routed to the endpoint name `RoutingDemoService1`. If this service fails and cannot be reached, the backup list takes importance. The backup list named `failOver1` defines the second endpoint used in case the first one fails.

```
<system.serviceModel>
  <!-- etc. -->
  <routing>
    <filters>
      <filter name="MatchAllFilter1" filterType="MatchAll" />
```

```
      </filters>
      <filterTables>
        <filterTable name="routingTable1">
          <add filterName="MatchAllFilter1" endpointName="RoutingDemoService1"
            backupList="failOver1" />
        </filterTable>
      </filterTables>
      <backupLists>
        <backupList name="failOver1">
          <add endpointName="RoutingDemoService2"/>
        </backupList>
      </backupLists>
    </routing>
```

With the routing server and routing configuration in place, you can start the client that makes a call to a service via the router. If everything is fine, the client gets an answer from the service running in host 1. If you stop host 1, and another request from the client, host 2 takes responsibility and returns an answer.

Bridging for Protocol Changes

If the router should act to change the protocol, you can configure the host to use the netTcpBinding instead of the wsHttpBinding. With the router, the client configuration needs to be changed to reference the other endpoint.

```
<endpoint address="net.tcp://localhost:9010/RoutingDemo/HostA"
  binding="netTcpBinding" contract="*" name="RoutingDemoService1" />
```

That's all that needs to be done to change the scenario.

Filter Types

With the sample application, a match-all filter has been used. WCF offers more filter types.

FILTER TYPE	DESCRIPTION
Action	The Action filter enables filtering depending on the action of the message. See the Action property of the OperationContract.
Address	The Address filter enables filtering on the address that is in the To field of the SOAP header.
AddressPrefix	The AddressPrefix filter does not match on the complete address but on the best prefix match of the address.
MatchAll	The MatchAll filter is a filter that matches every request.
XPath	With the XPath message filter, an XPath expression can be defined to filter on the message header. You can add information to the SOAP header with a message contract.
Custom	If you need to route depending on the content of the message, a Custom filter type is required. With a custom filter type, you need to create a class that derives from the base class MessageFilter. Initialization of the filter is done with a constructor that takes a string parameter. This string can be passed from the configuration initialization.

If multiple filters apply to a request, priorities can be used with filters. However, it's best to avoid priorities as this decreases performance.

SUMMARY

In this chapter, you learned how to use Windows Communication Foundation for communication between a client and a server. WCF can be used in a platform-independent way to communicate with other platforms, but it can also take advantage of specific Windows features.

WCF has a heavy focus on contracts to make it easier to isolate developing clients and services, and to support platform independence. It defines three different contract types: service contracts, data contracts, and message contracts. You can use several attributes to define the behavior of the service and its operations.

You saw how to create clients from the metadata offered by the service and also by using the .NET interface contract. You learned the features of different binding options. WCF offers not only bindings for platform independence, but also bindings for fast communication between .NET applications. You've seen how to create custom hosts and also make use of the WAS host. You saw how duplex communication is achieved by defining a callback interface, applying a service contract, and implementing a callback contract in the client application.

45

Deploying Websites and Services

WHAT'S IN THIS CHAPTER?

➤ Deployment preparations

➤ Deployment to Internet Information Server

➤ Deployment to Microsoft Azure

➤ Deployment using Docker

WROX.COM CODE DOWNLOADS FOR THIS CHAPTER

The wrox.com code downloads for this chapter are found at www.wrox.com/go/
professionalcsharp6 on the Download Code tab. The code for this chapter is found in the
following examples:

➤ WebDotnetFramework

➤ WebDotnetCore

DEPLOYING WEB APPLICATIONS

ASP.NET web applications traditionally have been deployed on Internet Information Server (IIS).
Also, it was important to have on the server the same version of the .NET Framework as was used
during development. Using .NET Core, this is no longer the case. .NET Core not only runs on
Windows, but also on Linux. Also, the runtime that is needed with the application is delivered as a
part of the application. These changes give you more deployment options to run your application.

This chapter shows different options for deploying web applications. One, of course, is to deploy the
application on a local Internet Information Server. It's also easy to deploy to Microsoft Azure. Using
Microsoft Azure, you can easily scale applications, and you don't need to buy all the systems you
probably need up front. You also add additional systems as needed and only buy for the time you need
these systems.

This chapter shows you how to create a Docker image with Visual Studio. Docker allows you to prepare the infrastructure you need for your application. You can directly use these Docker images on
the target systems, and all the infrastructure is in place.

> **NOTE** *This book doesn't cover all the different configuration options for IIS and Microsoft Azure and what can be done with Docker. Consult other books to get more detail. This chapter just gives you the most important information about these topics that you need to know as a developer.*

PREPARING FOR DEPLOYMENT

What needs to be deployed with web applications? Static files as HTML, CSS, JavaScript, and image files, the binary compiled image from the C# source files, and the database. Configuration files are needed as well. Configuration files contain application settings, including connection strings to connect to the database. Most likely, the application settings differ between testing and production environments. You probably have a staging environment as well so you can do some final tests before moving to production. You need to change the configuration between the different environments as well.

To deploy sample applications, you create two applications: one application using the .NET Framework 4.6 and the other application with ASP.NET Core 1.0 using .NET Core. Both applications use a database that's accessed using the Entity Framework Core.

> **NOTE** *Read Chapter 38 for more information about the Entity Framework Core.*

Creating an ASP.NET 4.6 Web Application

Create the first application named `WebDotnetFramework` with the Visual Studio project template ASP.NET Web Application. Select the ASP.NET 4.6 template MVC and select the Authentication Individual User Accounts (see Figure 45-1).

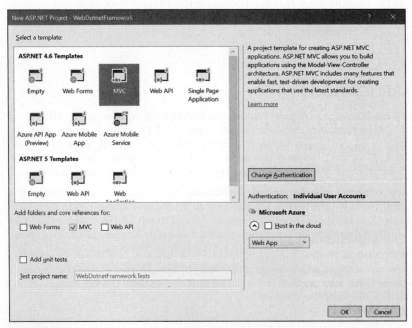

FIGURE 45-1

When you run this application, a few screens are available, and you can register a new user (see Figure 45-2). This registration creates a database on the SQL LocalDB instance that is installed with Visual Studio.

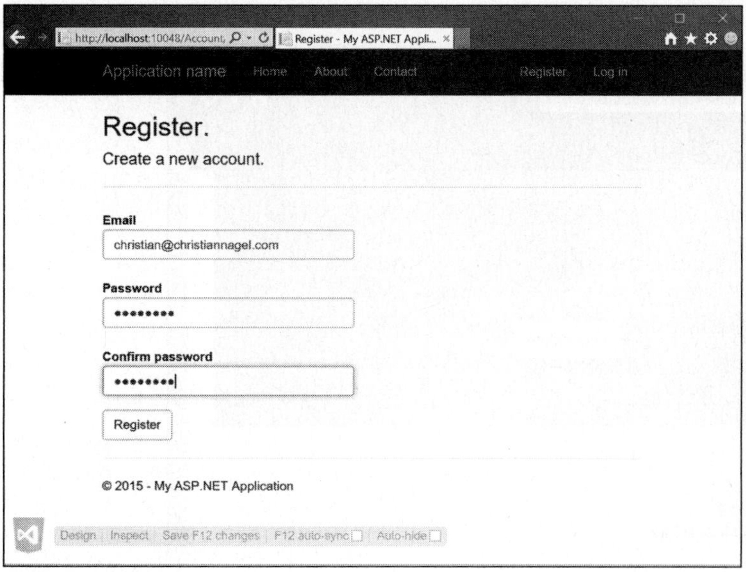

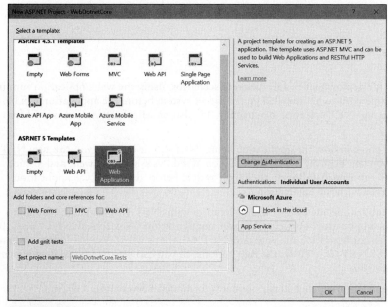

FIGURE 45-2

Creating an ASP.NET Core 1.0 Web Application

Create the second application named `WebDotnetCore` again using the Visual Studio project template ASP. NET Web Application, but now select the ASP.NET Core 1.0 template Web Application, again using Authentication with Individual User Accounts (see Figure 45-3).

FIGURE 45-3

Running this application results in the screen shown in Figure 45-4. Again, a LocalDB database is created on registering a user.

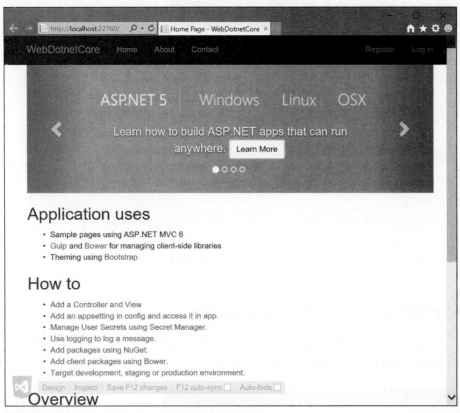

FIGURE 45-4

Having both these applications for deployment fulfills different scenarios: using the web application running .NET 4.6 requires the .NET Framework to be installed on the target system before the application can be deployed. You need a system having .NET 4.6 available; usually IIS (also on Microsoft Azure) is used for deployment.

With ASP.NET Core 1.0, either you can host the application using .NET 4.5 or later, or you can use .NET Core 1.0. Using .NET 5 Core, you can host the application on non-Windows systems as well, and it's not required that you have the .NET runtime installed on the target system before deploying the application. The .NET runtime can be delivered with the application.

Using ASP.NET Core 1.0, you can still decide to host the application with .NET 4.6, which has similarities to the deployment of the first application. However, the web configuration file with ASP.NET Core 1.0 looks very different from the Web configuration file with ASP.NET 4.6; that's why I decided for this chapter to give you ASP.NET 4.6 and ASP.NET Core 1.0 as the two options, so you can see the typical deployment needs you have with your application.

Let's start deploying the web application on your local Internet Information Server (IIS).

Configuration Files with ASP.NET 4.6

One important part of the web application is the configuration file. With ASP.NET 4.6, the configuration file (`Web.config`) is in an XML format and contains application settings, database connections strings, ASP.NET configurations such as authentication and authorization, session state, and more, as well as assembly redirection configuration.

In terms of deployment, you have to consider different versions of this file. For example, if you are using a different database for the web application that is running on the local system, there's a special testing database for the staging server, and of course there's a live database for the production server. The connection string is different for these servers. Also, the debug configuration differs. If you create separate `Web.config` files for these scenarios and then add a new configuration value to the local `Web.config` file, it would be easy to overlook changing the other configuration files.

Visual Studio offers a special feature to deal with that. You can create one configuration file and define how the file should be transformed to the staging and deployment servers. By default, with an ASP.NET web project, in the Solution Explorer you can see a `Web.config` file alongside `Web.Debug.config` and `Web.Release.config`. These two later files contain only transformations. You can also add other configuration files—for example, for a staging server. You do this by selecting the solution in Solution Explorer, opening the Configuration Manager, and adding a new configuration (for example, a Staging configuration as shown in Figure 45-5). As soon as a new configuration is available, you can select the `Web.config` file and choose the Add Config Transform option from the context menu. This then adds a config transformation file with the name of the configuration—for example, `Web.Staging.config`.

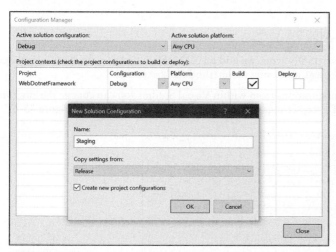

FIGURE 45-5

The content of the transformation configuration files just defines transformations from the original configuration file. For example, the compilation element below `system.web` is changed to remove the `debug` attribute as follows:

```
<system.web>
    <compilation xdt:Transform="RemoveAttributes(debug)" />
```

Configuration Files with ASP.NET Core 1.0

Configuration files with ASP.NET Core 1.0 are very different from the previous ASP.NET versions. By default, JSON configuration files are used, but you can use other file formats, such as XML files, as well.

project.json is the configuration file for the project that contains dependencies to NuGet packages, application metadata, and supported .NET Framework versions. Contrary to the previous ASP.NET versions, this information is separated from the application settings and connection strings.

You can add all the different application configuration files in the constructor of the Startup class. The default code generated adds the appsettings.json file with the extension method AddJsonFile, and environment variables with the extension method AddEnvironmentVariables. The Build method of the ConfigurationBuilder creates an IConfigurationRoot that can be used to access the settings in the configuration files. With ASP.NET 4.6, you've seen transformation to create different configurations for different environments. This is handled differently with ASP.NET Core 1.0. Here, a JSON file with an environmental name in the filename is used to define the settings that differ (code file WebCoreFramework/Startup.cs):

```
public Startup(IHostingEnvironment env)
{
  var builder = new ConfigurationBuilder()
    .AddJsonFile("appsettings.json")
    .AddJsonFile($"appsettings.{env.EnvironmentName}.json",
      optional: true);

  if (env.IsDevelopment())
  {
    builder.AddUserSecrets();
  }

  builder.AddEnvironmentVariables();
  Configuration = builder.Build();
}

public IConfigurationRoot Configuration { get; set; }
```

In case you prefer XML configurations over JSON, you can add an XML file by adding the NuGet package Microsoft.Extensions.Configuration.Xml and using the method AddXmlFile.

For testing the different environmental configurations from within Visual Studio, you can change the environmental variable EnvironmentName in the Debug settings of the Project Properties, as shown in Figure 45-6.

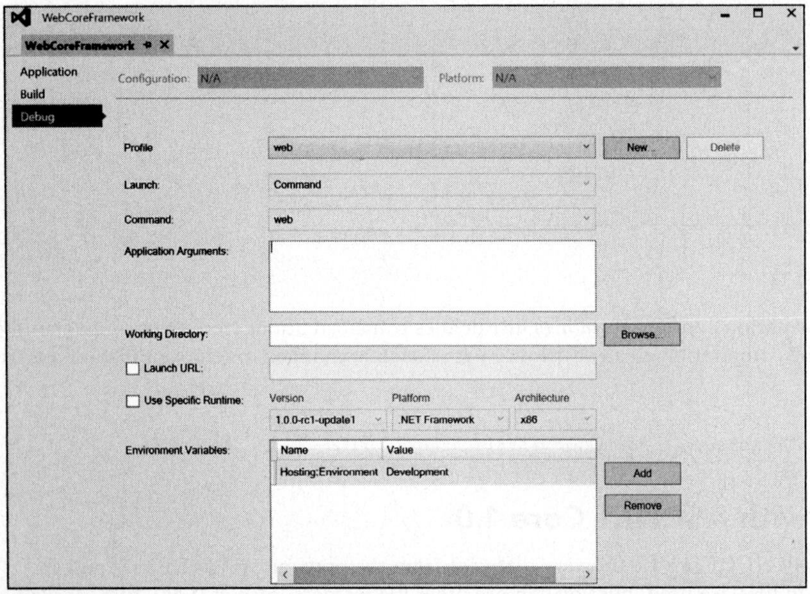

FIGURE 45-6

> **NOTE** *Within the development environment, you add user secrets with the* `AddUserSecrets` *method. Secret configuration, such as keys for a cloud service, had better not be configured within the source code that is checked in with a source code repository. User secrets store such information elsewhere for the current user. This functionality is shown in Chapter 40, "ASP.NET Core."*

DEPLOYING TO INTERNET INFORMATION SERVER

Let's start with deployment to IIS. Before deploying the web application to IIS, you need to make sure that Internet Information Services is available on your system. You can install IIS with the Windows Features (select Programs and Features, and use the Turn Windows Features On or Off link) as shown in Figure 45-7. At least you need these options:

- .NET Extensibility 4.6
- ASP.NET 4.6
- Default Document
- Static Content
- IIS Management Console
- IIS Management Scripts and Tools
- IIS Management Service

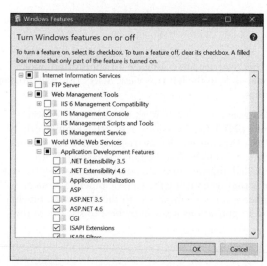

FIGURE 45-7

Depending on your security and other requirements, you might need other options as well.

Preparing a Web Application Using IIS Manager

After you start the IIS Manager, you can prepare the server for installing the web application. Figure 45-8 shows the IIS Manager started on a Windows 10 system.

FIGURE 45-8

Creating an Application Pool

The web application needs a process to run within. For this, you need to configure an application pool. Within the IIS Manager, you can see the Application Pools node in the left tree view. Select this node to configure existing application pools, as well as create new ones.

Figure 45-9 shows creating a new application pool named ProCSharpPool. With the Add Application Pool dialog you can select the version of the .NET runtime (.NET CLR version). For .NET Framework 4.6 and other 4.x versions you need to select .NET CLR 4.0 for the runtime. Be aware that .NET Framework versions after 4.0 updated the 4.0 runtime, so these updates need to be installed on the system. With Windows 10 and Windows Server 2016, .NET 4.6 is installed anyway. With this dialog you can also select the Managed Pipeline Mode. All you need to know here is that when using the Classic pipeline mode, native handlers and modules are running within the application pool, whereas with the Integrated pipeline mode .NET modules and handlers are used. So with newer applications it's usually best to stick with the Integrated pipeline mode.

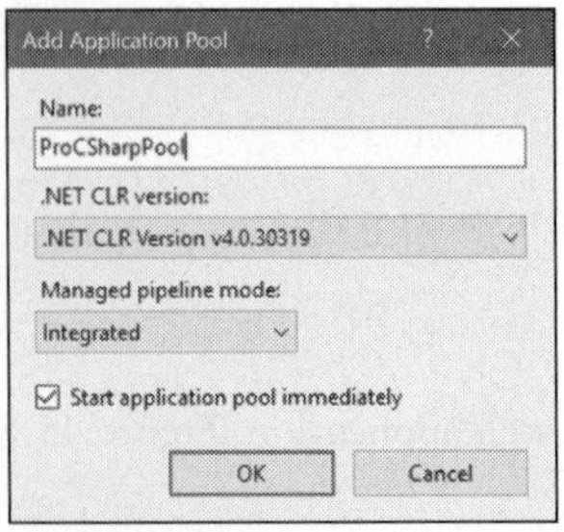

FIGURE 45-9

After creating the application pool, you can configure a lot more options in the Advanced Settings (see Figure 45-10). Here you can configure the number of CPU cores to use, the user identity of the process, health monitoring, a Web Garden (multiple number of processes to be used), and more.

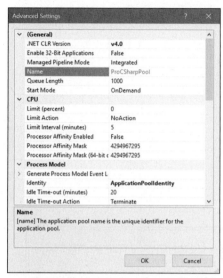

FIGURE 45-10

Creating a Website

After defining a pool, you can create a website. The default website listens to port 80 for all IP addresses of the system. You can either use this existing website or configure a new one. Figure 45-11 configures a new website that uses the `ProCSharpPool` application pool, is defined within the physical path `c:\inetpub\ProCSharpWebRoot`, and listens to port 8080. With multiple websites, you need to either use different port numbers, have multiple IP addresses configured on the system where different websites are accessible through different addresses, or use different hostnames. With different hostnames, the client needs to send the hostname requested within the HTTP header. This way IIS can decide which website the request should be forwarded to.

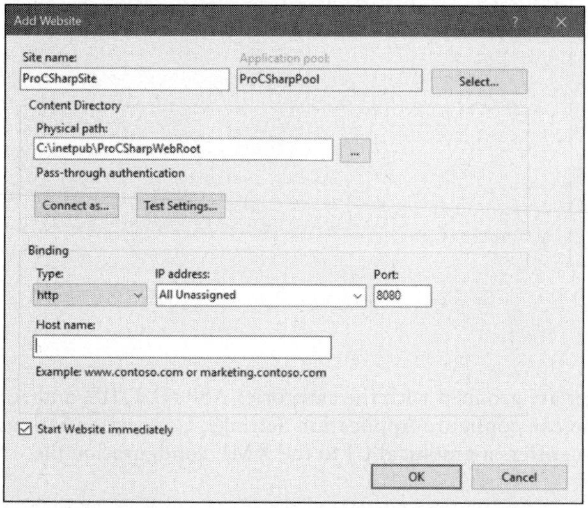

FIGURE 45-11

Later you can modify bindings to the IP address, port number, and hostname by clicking the Edit button in the Site Binding dialog (see Figure 45-12). You can also define other protocols such as net.tcp or net.http that can be used to host a Windows Communication Foundation (WCF) application. For this to be available, you need to install optional Windows features: WCF Services are available with the .NET Framework 4.6 Advanced Services in the Turn Windows Features On or Off management tool.

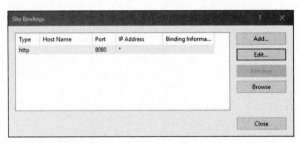

FIGURE 45-12

> **NOTE** *Read Chapter 44, "Windows Communication Foundation," for more information about WCF.*

Creating an Application

Next, you can create an application. Figure 45-13 shows creating an application named ProCSharpApp within the site ProCSharpSite running within the application pool ProCSharpPool.

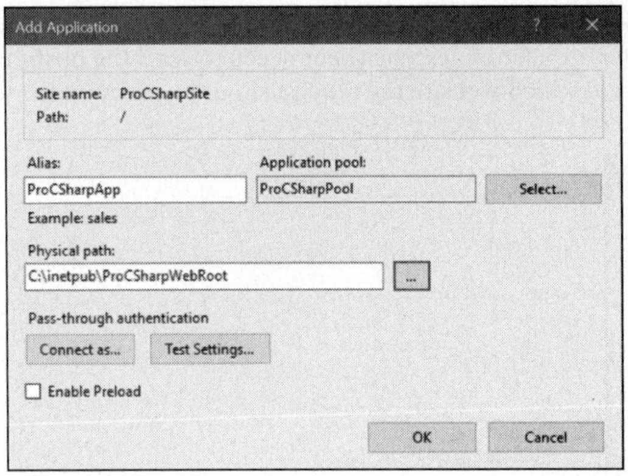

FIGURE 45-13

The configurations available with the IIS Manager are grouped with the categories ASP.NET, IIS, and Management settings (see Figure 45-14). Here you can configure Application Settings, Connection Strings, Session State, and more. Mainly this configuration offers a graphical UI to the XML configuration file web.config.

FIGURE 45-14

Web Deploying to IIS

When you have an application prepared in the IIS Manager, you can directly deploy the web application from within Visual Studio to IIS. Before doing this, create a new empty database with IIS named `ProCSharpWebDeploy1` on the server `(localdb)\MSSQLLocalDB`. You can do this from within Visual Studio in the SQL Server Object Explorer. Select SQL Server, Databases, and Add New Database.

With the configuration file `Web.Staging.config`, add the connection string to the new SQL Server database instance and add the transformation as shown to change the connection string defined by `Web.config` (code file `WebDotnetFramework/Web.Staging.config`):

```
<connectionStrings>
  <add name="DefaultConnection"
    connectionString="Data Source=(localdb)\MSSQLLocalDB;
    Initial Catalog=WebDeploy1;Integrated Security=True;
    Connect Timeout=30;Encrypt=False;
    TrustServerCertificate=False;ApplicationIntent=ReadWrite;
    MultiSubnetFailover=False"
    providerName="System.Data.SqlClient"
    xdt:Transform="SetAttributes" xdt:Locator="Match(name)" />
</connectionStrings>
```

For deploying the database directly with the deployment, you can configure the Package/Publish SQL configuration with the Project Properties (see Figure 45-15). Here you can import the connection string from the `web.config` file. You can also add custom SQL scripts with the deployment and either deploy only the database schema or also copy the data as well.

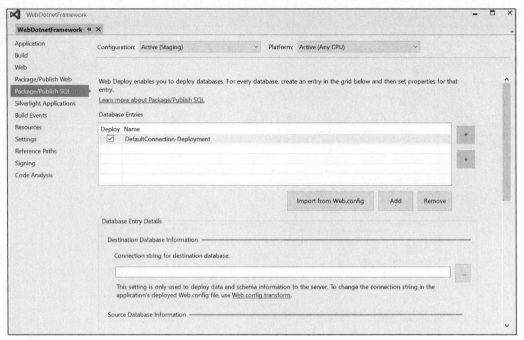

FIGURE 45-15

To deploy directly to the local IIS, Visual Studio needs to be started in elevated mode (Run as Administrator).

After you open the project `WebDotnetFramework` that you created earlier, in the Solution Explorer select the project and open the application context menu Publish. With the opened Publish Web dialog (see Figure 45-16) you need to select Custom as the publish target. Name the profile `PublishToIIS`, as this is what you do next.

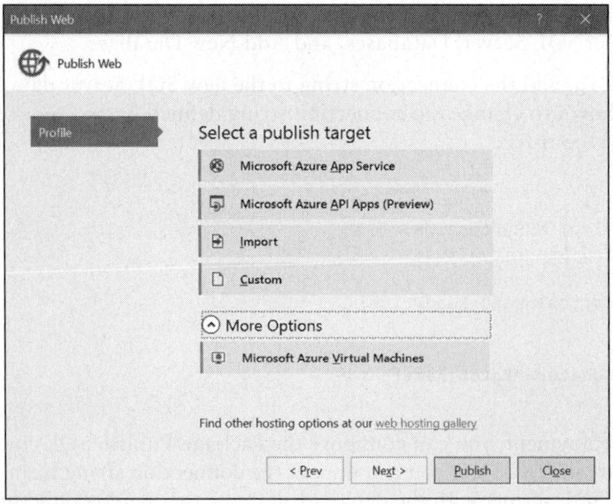

FIGURE 45-16

With the Connection configuration, select Web Deploy in the Publish Method drop-down menu. Define the server, the site name, and the destination URL to publish to the local IIS (see Figure 45-17).

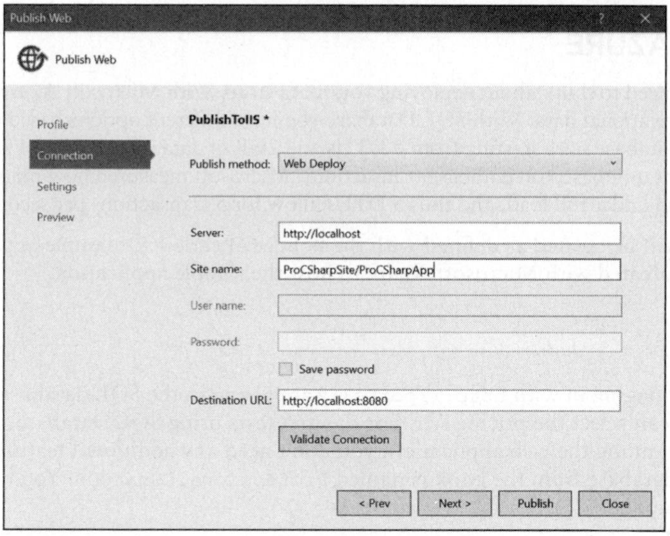

FIGURE 45-17

With the Settings tab (see Figure 45-18) you configure file publish options. Here, you can select the configuration to choose the corresponding web configuration file. You can precompile the source files during publishing. This way you don't need to deliver the C# source files with the package. Also, you can exclude files from the App_Data folder. This folder can be used for file uploading and a local database. In case you have only test data in this folder, you can safely exclude this folder from the package. Also, you can select the database connection string with the Package/Publish SQL configuration.

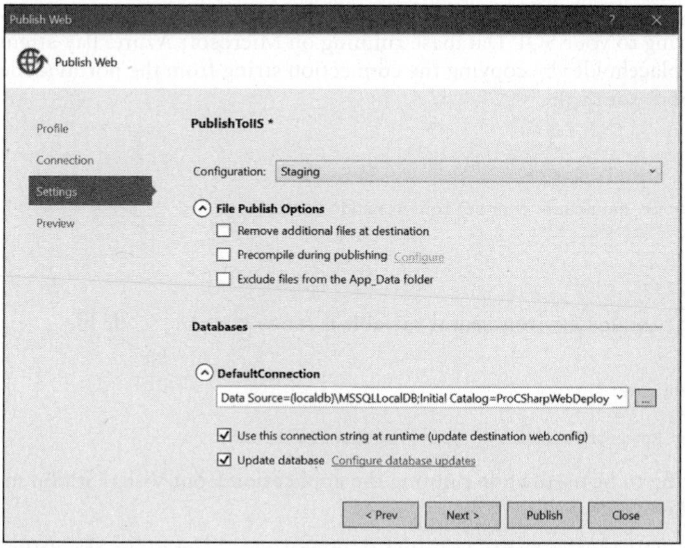

FIGURE 45-18

When you publish successfully, you will find the files copied to the previously configured application within IIS, and the browser opened to the home page.

DEPLOYING TO MICROSOFT AZURE

When deploying to Microsoft Azure, you need to think about deploying your data store. With Microsoft Azure, SQL Database is a good option to deploy relational data. With SQL Database you have different options based on Database Transaction Units (DTUs) and database sizes starting from 5 DTUs and 2GB of data up to 1750 DTUs and 1 TB of data. A DTU is a measurement unit based on database transactions. Microsoft measured how many transactions could be completed per second under full load, and thus 5 DTUs allow for 5 transactions per second.

After creating the database, the tables will be created as defined with the `WebCoreFramework` sample application. Then, a web application will be created with Microsoft Azure to host the sample application.

Creating a SQL Database

You can create a new SQL Database by logging in with `http://portal.azure.com` in the SQL databases section. When creating a database, you can select the pricing tier. For the first tests using SQL Database, select the cheapest edition—Basic. For running the web application, you don't need any additional features. You can change it later as needed. The database from the book is named `ProfessionalCSharpDB`. You need to use a different name as this name is unique.

To directly access the database from Visual Studio, you need to change the firewall setting of the SQL server and allow your local IP address to access the server. Your local IP address is shown with the Firewall settings.

Testing the Local Website with SQL Azure

Before deploying the website to Microsoft Azure, try to change the database connection string to use the SQL Database on Microsoft Azure and test the website locally.

First, you need to get the connections string to the Azure Database. Find your connection string in the Azure Portal by selecting the SQL Database. The connection string is accessible from the Essentials configuration.

With Visual Studio, open the `WebCoreFramework` project and add a new JSON file named `appsettings.staging.json`. Add the connection string to your SQL Database running on Microsoft Azure. Pay attention to adding the password that just has a placeholder by copying the connection string from the portal (code file `WebDotnetCore/appsettings.json.config`):

```
{
  "Data": {
    "DefaultConnection": {
      "ConnectionString": "add your database connection string"
    }
  }
}
```

This file is loaded when the `Host:Environment` environmental variable is set to `Staging` (code file `WebDotnetCore/Startup.cs`):

```
var builder = new ConfigurationBuilder()
  .AddJsonFile("appsettings.json")
  .AddJsonFile($"appsettings.{env.EnvironmentName}.json", optional: true);
```

Remember, you can configure this setting to be used while running the application from Visual Studio in the Project>Debug properties (see Figure 45-6).

To add the tables to the SQL Database, you can use Entity Framework migrations. Migrations are configured for the Entity Framework model with the `ApplicationDbContext`.

When you run the application locally, the database tables are created because the Migrations folder exists to contain information about the needed tables and schemas, as well as the invocation of `Database.Migrate` in the Startup code (code file `WebCoreFramework/Startup.cs`):

```
try
{
  using (var serviceScope = app.ApplicationServices
    .GetRequiredService<IServiceScopeFactory>().CreateScope())
  {
    serviceScope.ServiceProvider
      .GetService<ApplicationDbContext>()
      .Database.Migrate();
  }
}
catch { }
```

To manually handle the migration and create the initial tables, you can start the Developer Command Prompt, change the current directory to the directory where the `project.json` file of the project is stored, and set the environmental variable to use the correct configuration file for the connect string:

```
>set Hosting:Environment-staging
```

You also start the web server with the command

```
>dotnet run
```

and start the migration with the `database` command:

```
>dotnet ef database update
```

The website now runs locally with the SQL Database in the cloud. It's time to move the website to Microsoft Azure.

Deploying to a Microsoft Azure Web App

Using the Azure Portal, you can create an Azure web app where the website can be hosted. From the Solution Explorer in Visual Studio, you can select the Publish Web context menu. Microsoft Azure App Service is one of the available options. Using this option, you can deploy the website to Microsoft Azure.

After selecting Microsoft Azure App Service, you can log in to Microsoft Azure and select one of your web apps. You can also create a new web app directly from this dialog.

After deployment is completed, you can use the website from the cloud.

DEPLOYING TO DOCKER

Another option for publishing is Docker. Docker offers a new concept for deployment. Instead of installing all requirements and preparing the correct configuration on the target system before installing the web application, you can supply a complete Docker image that contains everything needed.

Would it not be possible to do the same using a virtual machine image and load this on a Hyper-V server? The problem with virtual machine images is that they are huge, containing the complete operating system and every tool needed. Of course, you can use virtual machine images with Microsoft Azure. Prepare an image, and install the web application after installing the web server infrastructure.

This is very different from Docker. Docker is built up using an onion-like system. A layer is built up above another layer. Every layer just contains the differences from the other layer. You can use one already-prepared system that includes the requirements from the operating system, add another layer for the web server, and then add one or more layers for the website you want to deploy. These images are small as only changes are recorded.

If you add the Visual Studio Extension Tools for Docker, you can see another option with the Publish menu: to deploy a Docker image. This deployment is available for Windows Server 2016 as well as different Linux variants. Just select the image you like and deploy your website. Of course, when you're running on Linux, only .NET Core is available.

SUMMARY

How you deploy web applications has undergone big changes in the last years. Creating installer packages is rarely used nowadays. Instead, you can directly publish from Visual Studio.

You've seen how to publish to an Internet Information Server that can be hosted on premise (a custom-managed IIS), as well as how to publish to a server on Microsoft Azure. Using Microsoft Azure, a lot of work managing the infrastructure can be avoided.

You've also read about an introduction to Docker, another deployment option that allows creating small prepared images where everything needed for the one running the application is prepared to run.

INDEX

INDEX

P

Connect with Wrox.

Participate
Take an active role online by participating in our P2P forums @ p2p.wrox.com

Wrox Blox
Download short informational pieces and code to keep you up to date and out of trouble

Join the Community
Sign up for our free monthly newsletter at newsletter.wrox.com

Wrox.com
Browse the vast selection of Wrox titles, e-books, and blogs and find exactly what you need

User Group Program
Become a member and take advantage of all the benefits

Wrox on **twitter**
Follow @wrox on Twitter and be in the know on the latest news in the world of Wrox

Wrox on **facebook**.
Join the Wrox Facebook page at facebook.com/wroxpress and get updates on new books and publications as well as upcoming programmer conferences and user group events

Contact Us.
We love feedback! Have a book idea? Need community support?
Let us know by emailing wrox-partnerwithus@wrox.com